The Scrapbook History
of Pro Football

1893-1977

The Scrapbook History of Pro Football

BY

Richard M. Cohen, Jordan A. Deutsch,
Roland T. Johnson and David S. Neft

BOBBS-MERRILL

Indianapolis/New York

Published by The Bobbs-Merrill Company, Inc.
Indianapolis/New York

Manufactured in the United States of America

Second printing

Library of Congress Cataloging in Publication Data
Main entry under title:

Cohen, Richard M.
   The scrapbook history of pro football

   1. Football—History—Miscellanea.   2. Football—Biography
—Miscellanea.   I. Title.
GV950.N43   796.33′2′09   76-11613
ISBN 0-672-52029-X

ACKNOWLEDGMENTS

The authors would like to express their deep appreciation to the following individuals, institutions, libraries, and newspapers who were so cooperative in extending their time and facilities during the preparation of this book:

        Mark Swayne, *Visual and Technical Coordinator*
        Nancy McCormack, *Technical Consultant*
        Bill Loughman, *Research Advisor*

Baseball Hall of Fame:
        Jack Redding, *Librarian*
        Cliff Kachline, *Historian*

Pro Football Hall of Fame:
        Jim Campbell, *Historian*

M-K Super Pictures, Inc.

Microfilm Corporation of America:
        Dick Schmidt
        Pat Hochstetler

Hartford Public Library, Reference and General Reading Department:
        Josephine Sale, *Head*
        Martha Nolan, *Assistant Head*
        Dorothy Brickett, Ann Casey, Rosalie Fawcett, Carol Fitting, Shirley Kiefer, Fernando Labault, Beverly Loughlin, Betty Mullendore, Gene Seymour, *Research Assistants*

Library of Congress Annex, Serial Division:
        Katherine Gould, *Assistant Head, Reference Section*
        Paul Boswell, Henry Brzezanski, Porter Humphrey, William Laing, Anne Lewis, Susan Miller, Jean Sansobrino, Joan Sullivan, *Reference Librarians*
        Norman Chase, William Moten, *Deck Attendants*

        The staff of the newspaper collection of the New York Public Library Annex

        The staff of the newspaper division of the Danbury Public Library

The authors would also like to thank those newspapers who were good enough to allow the use of their material even though it could not be incorporated in this edition:

        Atlanta Constitution, Cleveland Press, Columbus Dispatch, Houston Chronicle, Indianapolis News, Indianapolis Star, Milwaukee Sentinel, Minneapolis Tribune, Philadelphia Bulletin, Rochester Democrat & Chronicle, San Diego Union, San Francisco Chronicle, St. Louis Globe Democrat, St. Louis Post-Dispatch.

Design and production:
        Helen Barrow, Libra Graphics, Inc. and Roxana Laughlin

The authors' wives:
        Thea Deutsch, Nancy Cohen, Judy Johnson, Naomi Neft—a special thanks for their faith and cooperation throughout the project.

All comments and inquiries on this book should be sent to:
        SPORTS PRODUCTS, INC.
        415 Main Street
        Ridgefield, CT 06877

Foreword

I doubt if there was, or ever will be, a kid in the United States who didn't, or doesn't, keep a scrapbook. Sure, many of them never got pasted-up, nor the clippings trimmed down, but almost all of us at one time or another ripped, clipped or tore things out of newspapers and/or magazines.

Maybe it was only the *Collier's* All-American team of 1926 with Hal Broda, Herb Joesting and Benny Friedman, or the high school All-American team of 1954 from *Scholastic* magazine with Tom Vershinski, Nick Pietrosante and Tom Secules, or the International News Service All-NFL team of 1947 with Len Younce, Al Wistert and Steve Van Buren. Whether it was a single item, a handful of articles or something as detailed as the zealously-kept multiple volumes of men like Vic Frolund, Jim Stewart and Erwin Hess, all of us had the early makings of a scrapbook.

For me, it was the late 1940s. We had just moved from Atco, New Jersey (population: 1,347) to Selinsgrove, Pennsylvania (population: 4,368) and to help ease the pangs of leaving all my fifth-grade friends Mom and Dad subscribed to the *Philadelphia Bulletin,* the paper we read in Jersey. I read and re-read those sports pages. After several repeats I still couldn't bear to throw them away. Clipping those old accounts and saving them was the only answer.

Writers such as Dick Cresap and Ed Pollock were informing their readership of the great Eagle team Greasy Neale was putting together. The prose of these sportswriters made names like Van Buren, Thompson, Muha, Craft, Sears, Kish and McHugh come to life.

Aiding the written word were those now camp publicity shots of Van Buren stiff-arming an imaginary tackle on his way to an 80-yard touchdown run, ball always in his right arm because an injury to his left elbow prevented him from "toting the pigskin" any other way, knees pumping like the proverbial pistons as he stomped over a phantom defender; Tommy Thompson, sighting through his one good eye a streaking Pete Pihos and "letting it fly"; Al Wistert, "determination written all over his face, clearing the way"; Alex Wojciechowicz posed over the ball in that exaggerated straddle-legged stance of his.

As the season progressed, the publicity stills gave way to actual game action photos, complete with dotted lines showing the flight of the ball, arrows pointing to the "prolate spheroid," and neat little boxes with players' names hovering just over the heads of the players in order to allow a young reader to determine Clyde "Smackover" Scott from Elroy "Crazylegs" Hirsch.

Dad did considerable traveling in those days, and thoughtfully brought or sent home sports pages from such far-away newspapers as the *St. Louis Post-Dispatch,* the *Detroit Free Press,* the *Boston Globe* and the *Cleveland Plain Dealer.*

What a special treat it was to receive a *San Francisco Examiner.* A certain mystique always surrounded the 49ers for me. Here was this great and colorful team...names like Bruno Banducci, Frankie Albert, Norm Standlee, Visco Grgich, Alyn Beals and Johnny Strzykalski...and hardly any way for an Eastener to learn about them. Monday's *Bulletin* went to press, at least the up-state edition, too early to have much about a West Coast game, and by Tuesday, Sunday's game was stale. So, about all a would-be 49ers' fan had to go on was a one-line score.

The same enthusiasm greeted the *Los Angeles Times.* Bob Waterfield, Norm Van Brocklin, Tom Fears, Dick Huffman, Fred Naumetz, "Crazylegs" Hirsch, "Vitamin" Smith, "Deacon Dan" Towler, "Tank" Younger et al. Names only, until those sports pages gave them life.

These write-ups and pictures were kept almost religiously. Helping to amplify them were a set of 1948 Bowman gum cards, which could be lined-up by teams in a loosely-constructed T-formation. It was almost as good as television . . . something which wouldn't come to the mountains of Central Pennsylvania until the cable of the mid-1950s.

No magazine was safe from my pair of rounded-point scissors . . . *Collier's, Saturday Evening Post, Life, Look* and the football annuals, Street & Smith, *Football Illustrated,* Stanley Woodward's *Football* and *Pro Football Illustrated.* Being a picture freak, I cut up the mags with little or no regard for the written word once it had been read, re-read a few times and digested. This disregard would later be regretted deeply and often. More than a few agonizing minutes were spent when page 21 had a picture of Johnny Lujack and page 22 featured Buddy Young. Whom to choose?

Too bad a fifty-cent-a-week allowance couldn't handle two of everything. Then these gut-twisting decisions wouldn't have to be made. True, the magazines only cost 25¢, but then there would be nothing left to go to the Stanley and see Bob Waterfield, Sammy Baugh, Sid Luckman and "Indian Jack" Jacobs in *Triple Threat.* "The ticket lady," (no one really ever bothered to call her Miss Bowersox) wasn't going to buy my age at 11 and 11/12ths too much longer, and this would mean that the cost of a ticket would soar from 12¢ to 30¢, the cost of an adult admission.

While I never really got around to making up a pro football scrapbook, I did keep all those pictures and clippings. It was almost an overwhelming experience recently to re-locate an old Gimbel's suit box in my parents' attic which contained all those thought-to-be-lost treasures.

Talk about nostalgia. How about Lou Rymkus, Lin Houston, Hardy Brown, Billy Stone, Chick Jagade, John Martinkovic, John Wozniak, Dick Barwegan, Sisto Averno, Chet Mutryn, Verl Lillywhite, Lynn Chandnois, Toy Ledbetter and Roy Barni?

No matter who we are or to what degree we got into collecting, we owe a real debt of gratitude to the authors of this book. They've tied together what we never got around to, outgrew, lost, gave away, or worse yet, simply threw away. Now in a concise and attractive way, *The Scrapbook History of Pro Football* covers our era of pro football and more.

It begins with the redoubtable Pudge Heffelfinger taking a $500 cash payment for a game in 1892 and goes right up to today. Along the way, you'll get acquainted, or reacquainted, with the men, the times, the games and the events which make pro football the most vibrant game in America today.

As you browse through the pages, more than once you'll lean back, close your eyes and picture yourself in Section 4 of the East Stands at old Shibe Park in Philadelphia or Section MM at Kezar Stadium in San Francisco and remember "that play when Bosh Pritchard/Hugh McElhenny ran through the entire Giant/Ram team for that 78-yarder."

Jim Campbell, *Librarian/Researcher*
PRO FOOTBALL HALL OF FAME

FIRST FOOTBALL GAME

Courtesy
Pro Football Hall of Fame

AMERICA'S FIRST PRO FOOTBALL TEAM, 1893, GREENSBURG, PENNA. Lawson Fiscus, second top row, right, Princeton Tigers' greatest halfback, 1891-1892, Turned Pro for Greensburg, 1893--Compliments of Vernon C. Berry, Pro Football Historian, Jeannette, Penna., had second Pro team, 1894.

THE MAN WHO STARTED PRO FOOTBALL. Newspaper publisher David J. Berry put pro football on the map in the United States as far back as 1894. He started the legendary Greensburg group, also the great Latrobe teams and later was in charge of the Pittsburgh Pros. Berry began as a player-coach but in a Varsity-Yanigan game his jaw was broken and he turned to the managing end of the sport. Harry Ryan, a big name in Latrobe football circles, served as advisor to Berry until 1902 when he went to Philadelphia. While in the City of Brotherly Love Ryan guided teams against the Pittsburgh Pros, then directed by his former partner.

1894

THE ASSOCIATION GAME.

Some Points About How It Will be Played in the New Professional League.

New York, Oct. 15.—Something of a novelty for New York in the way of foot ball is on the list for this season. It will be furnished by the American League of Professional Foot Ball Clubs, which began a series of contests early in October. The game will not be that of the American universities and colleges, which is so well known to the New York public, but the old-time game of so-called Association foot ball, which is the popular variety of the game in England.

The scheme for the organization of the league originated some time ago, and now all the arrangements have practically been completed. The league will consist of six clubs—one each in this city, Brooklyn, Boston, Philadelphia, Baltimore and Washington.

Each club will play a series of five games with every other club in the league, and a pennant will be awarded to the winner at the end of the season, following the example of the base ball league. The games in this city and in Brooklyn are to be played at the Polo Grounds and at Eastern Park respectively.

1893

WARD ON FOOT BALL.

The New York Captain Does Not Consider the Game Available For Professional Purposes.

New York, Oct. 25.—The remarkable growth of foot ball during the last few years is responsible for the suggestion that a professional foot ball league be organized. John M. Ward, the manager of the New York Base Ball Club, was an interested spectator at Manhattan Field on Saturday, and after the game a reporter asked him what he thought about a professional league of foot ball players. Said he:

"A professional foot ball league may eventually come, but many obstacles lie in its path before such a scheme can gain the confidence and popularity of the public. There are plenty of men who could play foot ball professionally, and play it well, but there are comparatively few who would do it. There is a certain romantic halo hovering over the college foot ball player which you could not get around a man who played the game for a salary. If professionals, particularly in a game against a college team, should use the same tactics used at Manhattan Field on Saturday, the professionals would be called loafers and blackguards. There would be a vast difference slugging professionally and as an amateur.

"I do not think that foot ball, as at present played, could be made popular from a professional standpoint. The game is so complicated that, while college men understand the technicalities and beauties, the general public does not. At present there is too much massing forces and the forming of human pyramids for the game to be wholly satisfactory, from a spectator's standpoint.

"In my trip around the world in 1889, with the All-America and Chicago teams, I was a close observer of all outdoor games in the various countries where we visited. Foot ball, as played in the different countries attracted me particularly, and the game, to my mind to be successful professionally in this country, would be the one played by the Australians. In the antipodes they play a game similar, in many respects, to the Gaelic or Association game. There is more free kicking and open play, and I think that that sort of a game would eventually become popular here."

1894

Foot Ball Game
SCORE CARD.
—
Pittsburg Athletic Club,
—VS.—
OAKMONT,
P. A. C. PARK,
Saturday, Nov. 3d.

Smith & McKee, Printers, 155 Frankstown Ave.

1894

THAT PROFESSIONAL LEAGUE.

Doubts as to Its Success Entertained at Washington.

Washington, Oct. 15.—Washington people who are partial to outdoor sports are wondering if the new Professional Foot Ball League will prove a success. The game is probably the most exciting sport of its kind which has ever been devised for the entertainment of any people, and with even fair weather conditions and careful management for a time should prove a paying investment for those who have put their dollars into the business. It is rather unfortunate that the game could not be started under more favorable auspices in certain respects. The excitement attending the close finish of the National League championship season served to turn attention away from the new game and kept several of the managers of teams so closely occupied that matters of much importance were neglected, and the interests of the new League have suffered in consequence. Now, however, the managers who have charge of the six foot ball teams in the League are devoting their attention to the business exclusively, and matters may take on a boom. If they are successful enough to work up a reasonable degree of interest in the sport in this preliminary season much better things may be looked for in the hereafter. It has become generally understood that the promoters of the Foot Ball League are content to lose money this fall in order to educate prospective regular patrons into an understanding of the various features which are the enjoyable portion of the sport.

When that is accomplished they propose to play the game at night by the aid of electric lights. Their idea is to string enough powerful electric lights over the playing grounds in the several cities to make every play in the gridiron plainly discernible to the spectators. Then a schedule will be arranged to play games at least two nights in each week in the six cities during the summer. It is argued that such an arrangement at a time when the theatres are closed would draw large crowds, and there is considerable reason in the argument. If the people take kindly to the game now, the permanency of the sport is assured, and next summer will see strengthened teams, and features added which will add materially to the excitement of the contests.

AN EARLY UNIFORM

1895

1894

A STRAIGHT TIP.

The Professionals Need to Mend Their Manners and Speech.

The managers of the professional foot ball games in this city, says the New York Sun, will find it necessary to call their players to pretty sharp account, as far as their talk is concerned, if they expect ladies and people of refinement to visit the Polo Grounds. In the game between the New York and Brooklyn clubs the other day there was an amount of profanity, obscenity and general abuse utterly unprecedented in the history of first-class sport in this city. There were very few ladies present, it is true, but those who were there and attempted to follow the game had their ears assailed with such talk that it is not likely that any of them will visit the grounds again. The effort of the foot ball managers is attracting a great deal of attention, for it is still an open question whether professional foot ball can succeed professional base ball in public favor. The game under the Association rules was apparently new to most of the spectators, and they found some difficulty in following it at first. Undoubtedly most of them looked for a game such as the college clubs put up. The new game is exciting, despite the fact that the men are not allowed to use their hands, but the first duty of the managers is to make it possible for ladies and schoolboys to follow the sport without being shocked by hearing the sort of epithets which have thus far characterized the players.

AS WAS EXPECTED.

The American League of Professionals Forced to Give it up.

A meeting of the American Association of Professional Football Clubs was held in New York last Thursday. All clubs were represented. After a full discussion it was deemed for the best interest of all club members that the season be brought to a close on October 20. The late period at which the Association got under way, on account of the prolongation of the base ball season, and the difficulty of avoiding conflict with the regular college foot ball games proved a serious obstacle to carrying out a schedule of games, but the Association feels that with the experience it has gained it will be in good condition to reorganize in the opening of 1895. The Association will, during the winter, arrange to formulate a new association on somewhat different lines, ready for spring work.

Following is the valedictory of the secretary, Mr. George Stackhouse, who backed the New York Club and became tired so very soon:

"After a full discussion of the situation and receiving reports from the various clubs it was deemed for the best interest of all club members that the season be brought to a close October 20. It was determined that all clubs should pay salaries in full up to November 1, 1894."

A prominent member of the Association says the failure to make a success of the enterprise was largely due to the fact that the members had failed to take the advice of persons who could have aided them, and since the opening of the season over $2000 had been lost. The clubs interested were: New York, Boston, Baltimore, Washington, Philadelphia and Brooklyn. It is pretty safe betting that this League will not be revived for some years, at least not by those who have just had their fingers burned.

Dec. 1 1895

GREAT JOY IN LATROBE.

ITS FOOTBALL TEAM MAKES THE PROUD GREENSBURG ELEVEN BITE THE DUST.

SCORE, FOUR TO NOTHING.

Welsh Carries the Ball Over the Line, and Men Hug Each Other.

'TWAS A FAMOUS VICTORY.

Latrobe yesterday was in a tumult of excitement. Men who had not been on speaking terms for years met, shook hands and joined in yells and screams that scandalised the straight-laced people of the community. But when the latter discovered the cause of the jollification they also fell into line and went to bed with enlarged heads and husky voices. It was a great day for Latrobe, for its football team had beaten the famous Greensburg aggregation. It was a grand battle, and the best team won. For two 25-minute halves the teams wrestled on the gridiron like giants. In the first half not a score was made. The second half was, if possible, fought more fiercely than the first. After 15 minutes of hard play the spectators were electrified by seeing Welsh cantering around Greensburg right end, closely hugged by Howard. For 30 yards Welsh ran with the Greensburg men trying to get at him, but they did not succeed in catching him until he was over the line for the only touchdown of the game. The Latrobe people, with open mouths, silently watched Welsh as he sped along, and Howard as he kept the opposing players off. But when the line was crossed the people simply went crazy. They hugged and kissed each other, and some really cried in their joy. All united in a shout such as has never been heard in that quiet place before. The game was a clean one in spite of the fierce struggle, no slugging being indulged in. After Latrobe made the touchdown, Boyer, Latrobe's quarterback, was accidentally hit by somebody and had to leave the field. Dovey taking his place. Boyer was the only player not on the regular team. Rode, the regular quarterback, was crippled and could not play. The Greensburg team was the same that lined up against P. A. C., except Robinson at half back. Atherton at half back and Copeland and Wyant in the line. Blank, a W. and J. man, was in the line for Greensburg. Howard, Welsh and Boyer played a splendid game, and much of the credit of the victory is due to their grand work. Line-up:

Latrobe—4.		Greensburg A. C.—0.
Jacoby	Left end	Irwin
Ryan (capt.)	Left tackle	Theurer
Shumacher	Left guard	Blank
Flickinger	Center	Shearer
Scott	Right guard	Thomas
Faxman	Right tackle	Coulter
McDyne	Right end	T. Donohue
Boyer	Quarterback	Laird
Welsh	Left half	Fiscus
Howard	Right half	J. Donohue
Abbaticchio	Fullback	Mechling

Touchdowns—Welsh, 1. Referee—J. M. Howard, Latrobe. Umpire—C. W. Sutton, Indiana.

Nov. 3 **1895**

The Canton Eleven Defeats the West End Team in a Good Game.

Many Brilliant Plays Were Made Which Were Greatly Appreciated by the Crowd—A Full Description of One of the Best Games Ever Played in Canton —Notes of Interest.

The game Saturday afternoon between the Canton and West End teams resulted in a victory for the former in a hard fought contest. The game was the first participated in by either eleven this year and both teams being anxious for the victory the playing was quite rough at times.

The West Ends won the toss and took the ball, Canton taking the north goal. Atkins kicked off, Bald securing the ball and made a fine run 30 yards, the Canton backs then bucked the line for 25 yards more. Cantons lost the ball on a fumble, the West Ends securing it and making 30 yards on the play. The West end boys forced the ball to Cantons 25 yard line, Cantons then braced up and West Ends were forced to punt. Here they sprung a surprise on their opponents. Atkins played close to the line but instead of bucking the line made a beautiful drop kick, kicking a goal from the field, scoring 5 points. The Cantons were taken completely by surprise as they were playing low for Atkins to buck their line.

The teams again lined up for the kick off. Johnson kicked the ball well into W. E.'s territory, Stokey securing it, but was downed in his tracks. The W. E.'s sent Hallam and Stokey around the ends for good gains until they were in the center of field. The Cantons line played good, tackling by Bald, Johnson and Herbst secured the ball for Cantons on downs.

The teams scrimmaged fiercely, Johnson bucked the line for several good gains. The ball was next passed to Piero who broke through and made a run of 35 yards within two yards of the W. Ends goal. The ball was then shoved over the W. Ends line for a touchdown. John failed at goal.

The teams lined up for a kick off. Atkins kicked out of bounds on the second trial. He again made a failure. The ball was then given the Cantons. Kaufman kicked off the W. Ends making a poor return of the ball. The teams lined up. The W. Ends could make no gains and the ball went to the Canton team on downs. Time was called with the ball with W. End's territory.

In the second half Pumphrey replaced Pfouts at left guard and Lynn was put on at right end in place of Bald. Johnson kicked off and the W. Ends could not advance the ball five yards and Canton took it. By good line play and end runs they gained rapidly. Piero secured the ball and went through right end for a 15 yard gain. The The ball was within six inches of the W. Ends goal. Canton then massed for a center buck and the ball was pushed over with ease. Johnson failed at goal.

Both teams lined up for the kick off. Johnson secured the ball and by good interference by Locke, Piero, Herbst and Kagle made 25 yards. By good runs by Piero and Kagle and bucking the line the ball was rapidly advanced into W. End territory. The ball was fumbled and the W. Ends secured it but could make no gains as Canton's line was invincible and Atkins was forced to punt. Carkness was now rapidly coming on and Herbst had a chance to secure the ball but could scarcely see it and Lyttle fell on it. W. Ends soon lost it again and Piero now made the star run of the game. Securing the ball he whirled rapidly and ran around right end making a run of 70 yards for a touchdown. Johnson failed at goal owing to darkness.

One of the features of the game was Kagle's superb tackle of Cunningham when the auburn haired captain tried to get around left end tackling his man low he carried him back for a seven yard loss

The game was an interesting one and from the start both teams were on their mettle. Considerable trouble was experienced in keeping the crord off the field, and it should not be allowed in games to follow: The line-up was as follows:

CANTONS		WEST ENDS
Mayforth	left end	H. Hallam
Herbst	left tackle	Parrott
Pfonts } Pumphrey }	left guard	Gauchet
Eitner	center	Quinlan
Beenout	right guard	Turnbull
Locke	right tackle	Lyttle
Bald } Lynn }	right end	Cunningham Capt.
Kagle	left half	J. Hallam
Piero	right half	Stokey
Kaufman	quarter back	Jahn
Johuson, Capt.	full back	Atkins

Referee Kirby, Umpire Rowlen, Lineman C. Pumphrey.

Punts.

The Canton team has some splendid materially and with more team work will make a strong eleven. The boys will meet some fast teams in the near future. Oscar Pfouts is manager and Lennie Anderson secretary and treasurer.

The Canton's have secured Eitner, of last year's team for Canton, and are to be congratulated in getting this fine player.

The West End boys have a good team in the field this year, much stronger than last year.

The Canton's have secured quarters for practice, and will try hard to have a winning team this year.

Eitner and Quinlan had quite an argument at center, but the Canton center outplayed his man at all points.

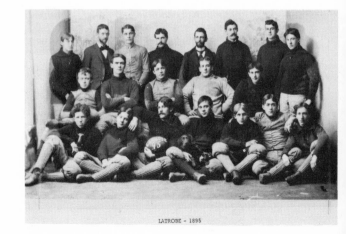

LATROBE - 1895

Nov. 28 **1897**

RED-HOT FOOTBALL WHILE IT LASTED.

GREENSBURG DEFEATS LATROBE IN A CONTEST OF TWO SHORT HALVES.

WRANGLE ABOUT A RINGER.

It Delays the Bitter Battle Until Darkness Nearly Sets In.

LATROBE LADIES ARE LOYAL.

Yesterday's game at Latrobe between the Latrobe and Greensburg football teams was the most unsatisfactory of the big contests of the season. It was advertised to begin at 3 o'clock, but it was 20 minutes after 4 before the ball was set in motion. Three thousand people gathered in the grounds and sat in the dampness alternately yelling to keep up their enthusiasm and stamping to keep the blood warm in their veins, while the two teams stood in the middle of the field doing nothing but jawing at each other. The whole trouble was caused by the fact that Greensburg had Core, the W. & J. guard, in their line. According to an agreement between the two teams neither side was entitled to play any man yesterday who was not either in the game last Saturday or among the subs. Latrobe claimed that Core, although on the side lines on Saturday, was not in uniform, and therefore could not be classed among the subs. Greensburg claimed that it had a right to use him, as he was designated a sub by wearing a Greensburg sweater on that day. Latrobe insisted that a sweater was not a uniform, and strenuously opposed the enrollment of the W. & J. guard. Latrobe did not object to Crookston or Flowers, both of whom were in the line-up, as they were in uniform on the side lines in Saturday's game. But the line was strictly drawn on Core. Latrobe agreed to leave the matter for decision in the hands of two Pittsburg gentlemen, but Greensburg declined to submit. Bluffs good and hard were hurled to and fro, and finally the Greensburg bucks boarded their bus and drove out of the grounds. The Latrobe players a moment later crawled into their conveyance and also drove out of the grounds. On the outside the teams met again and another wordy warfare ensued. Both sides, however, were not so strong in the bluffing business, and the upshot was that the wagons returned to the grounds, where they were received with a mixture of hoots and cheers. Core was sent to the side lines, and as the sun began to sink in the western skies the game commenced.

That there is a bitter feeling between the hamlets of Greensburg and Latrobe was evident to anybody who was in Latrobe yesterday. The feeling was without a good-natured coating, and was shared by people of all conditions and sexes. The female population of Latrobe was particularly loyal. Not a female in the burg could be seen who did not wear the colors of the football team. It is said that not an inch of either blue or red ribbon could be secured in Latrobe for love or money after noon yesterday. Large and noisy delegations of Greensburgers invaded the powerful village, but at every twist and turn loyal female Latrobists glanced disdainfully at the shouting marchers, and some even grew livid with rage. This was the case among old and young. An old lady turned her back after spitting at a Greensburg crowd and then defiantly waved a yard or more of red and blue ribbon. It would be supposed that the defeat of the pets would have stunned the loyal female population. Not so. After the game, although not being altogether successful in hiding their disappointment, the ladies began cheering for W. & J. whenever the colors of Greensburg met their gaze. "It took two teams to beat us" shouted a lovely beauty as she jumped the fence for a short cut to town, and all Latrobe took up the cry.

It was getting dark when the two teams met for battle. On account of the late time it was agreed to play two 20-minute halves. The contest began with Sterrett, of Greensburg kicking off to Latrobe's 25-yard line. Abbaticchio snatched up the ball and ran 17 yards before he was planted in the soft sod. Fitch went through Greensburg's line for two yards, and Gass made one yard around Greensburg's left end. Abbaticchio could not gain, as the ball went to Greensburg on downs on Latrobe's 45-yard line. Sterrett hit the line with a mighty shock, but could not move it, the Latrobe adherents going wild. Big MacKenzie was now given the ball and made five yards. The Greensburg shouters now broke loose. They had barely stopped shouting when Barclay dashed around Greensburg's left end for 10 yards, placing the ball on Latrobe's 30-yard line. This gave the Greensburgers a good chance to renew their cheers. Robinson gained one yard, and two more shoves took the ball to Latrobe's 23-yard line. Latrobe was making a desperate chance and fought bitterly for every inch of ground. Barclay raised another great shout by cutting around left end for eight yards, taking the ball to Latrobe's 15-yard line. The contest now grew desperate. Robinson looked sad when he was stopped for no gain. Cherry, with set teeth, dashed five yards, and was rewarded with a salvo of cheers. McFarland cut the line for five more yards and the ball was now five yards from goal. It looked like a touchdown for Greensburg, and every Latrobe adherent held his breath. Dunsmore plunged for three yards, getting the ball two yards from goal. McFarland dove into Latrobe's forces and advanced the ball two feet from the goal line. The Latrobe boys stuck to their posts, though their eyes threatened to pop out of their heads. The Greensburg players now bunched for consultation, and then there was a great crash. Slowly the heaving bunch of players swayed to and fro, then fell in a heap. The ball was still two feet from goal and next to Latrobe on downs. A shout that went rattling and roaring along all sides of the gridiron told that Latrobe was still in the fight.

Abbaticchio at once punted and drove the ball to his own 33-yard line, when Barclay fell on it. A high pass to Flower sent the ball five yards back, then Barclay dropped on it and saved it for his side. Red-headed Crookston skirted Latrobe's left end for three yards, when he was most forcibly sat down upon. Sterrett saved the ball by diving for five yards, putting the ball on Latrobe's 30-yard line. Joe Donohue tried to advance the ball, but was thrown back for a loss of five yards. Joe remained on the ground for quite a while. Incidentally it may be mentioned that this was the first, last and only time that a player remained on the ground, though one of the hottest battles on record. Barclay tried to make up Joe's loss, but was pinned, after gaining only one yard. Sterrett was compelled to kick. He sent the ball to Latrobe's five-yard line, where Abbaticchio waited on it. He dug his heels into the ground, but just as he was about to fasten his hands on the ball Crookston ran into him, toppled him over six different ways, the ball darting to one side, then Thomas fell on it five yards from Latrobe's goal. Up jumped the handsome Italian, claimed foul interference, as he had heeled for a fair catch. Although all the Latrobe players and half the spectators joined in the appeal, the umpire would not allow the claim and the ball was in possession of Greensburg. A loud, savage, exultant shout showed that the umpire's decision was a popular one among Greensburgers. Barclay hit Latrobe's line like a pile-driver, but could not move it. Sterrett tried it and gained two feet. Then McFarland sank into the heaving, quivering mass, which trembled like a huge jelly cake, and then collapsed suddenly. When the pile dissolved McFarland was seen over the line with the ball buried under him. It was a touchdown, and the Greensburg rooters went wild. Joe Donohue kicked goal. Score: Greensburg 6, Latrobe 0.

Abbaticchio kicked off to Greensburg's 40-yard line and a Latrobe man secured the ball. Now the Latrobes began a fierce warfare. Gass went around left end for two yards, and Fitch raised a commotion by breaking through and running eight yards before he was caught on Greensburg's 30-yard line on the extreme upper end of the gridiron. A mighty cheer shook the air when at the next play Fitch was seen to round Greensburg's left end, get clear of all the players and deposit the ball behind the line between the goal posts. But the ball was taken back to the 25-yard line, where Fitch had run out bounds. Fitch tried again, but could not gain an inch. Again he hit the line, and this time gained five yards. Then Latrobe got five yards for offside play. Gass advanced it three yards, getting the ball 12 yards from goal. Fitch went through for four yards, and the ball was now eight yards from goal. Fitch made another dive, but was hurled back for a loss of three yards. Trenchard tried his hand, but could not gain a foot. Fitch cut through the center on a fake kick, but lost the ball on downs on Greensburg's eight-yard line. This was the nearest the Latrobes came to the goal line in the entire game. Barclay failed to gain, and Robinson was thrown back to the six-yard line, when the first half ended.

There was no change in the line-up of either side. It was getting dusk, and therefore the decision was reached to play only a 15-minute half.

Abbaticchio kicked off to Greensburg's 20-yard line, and Sterrett made a splendid run, bringing the ball back 25 yards. Barclay gained five yards, and Robinson five more, placing the ball on the center line. MacKensie now began his famous walking act. He carried the ball five yards. Again he walked, this time getting seven yards. Donohue darted for three yards, placing the ball on Latrobe's 40-yard line. Barclay gained two yards, and then the Greensburg bunch was hurled back five yards. The collisions were simply awful, but the players on both sides were there to stay. Not a man fell by the wayside. Crookston, red hair and all, now made the air shiver with cheers as he skirted Latrobe's left end for 20 yards, placing the ball 23 yards from goal, where he was heavily thrown by Trenchard. Barclay failed to move the line, and Sterrett could gain only two yards. Barclay gained one yard, and then lost the ball on downs on Latrobe's 20-yard line. A fight occurred here on the side lines, but it was speedily checked by a slim policeman with a fat mace.

Fitch, Gass and Abbaticchio advanced the ball seven yards, which gave Latrobe a right to keep it. Okeson went around Greensburg's left end for three yards, and Fitch and Barclay took it five yards. Gass ran out of bounds skirting Greensburg's left end, but advanced the ball five yards, depositing it on Latrobe's 40-yard line. The Latrobe players on the next play got twisted in their signals. Trenchard ran toward Greensburg's right end with hands outstretched, as if he expected the ball, but no ball came his way. He looked disgusted as he saw all the players falling on one place. When the players got up the ball was in possession of Greensburg. Latrobe had seen the ball for the last time, and it was on their 40-yard line. Dunsmore cut the line for seven yards, and Sterrett for three. Donohue took it three yards nearer goal, and Sterrett placed it on Latrobe's 25-yard line. Robinson came limping out of the bunch, but he didn't limp long. McFarland rushed for two yards, and Robinson shot through for three more, getting the ball 20 yards from the line. Sterrett carried it two yards further, and Crookston added another two yards, when the whistle blew the end of the game, with the ball on Latrobe's 16-yard line. At once there was a rush by the players of both sides for possession of the ball. They jerked each other hither and thither, and the spectators ran to the scene. Soon there was a howling mob on the gridiron, and half of them did not know what they were howling about. Robinson had tucked the ball under his arm, and began to walk away with it. Some of the Latrobe players objected, but they were soon shown the flaw in their claim, shook hands all around and parted, just as the lean policeman and the fat mace were about to get in their work. Then the loyal female population sang their death song and shouted derisively for W. & J. The line-up:

Latrobe—0.		Greensburg—6.
Okeson	Left end	Crookston
White	Left tackle	Dunsmore
S. Johnson	Left guard	MacKenzie
Hammer	Center	Thomas
Krebbs	Right guard	Fightner
Ryan	Right tackle	McFarland
Trenchard	Right end	Donohue
Brallier	Quarterback	Flowers
Gass	Left half	Barclay
Fitch	Right half	Robinson
Abbaticchio	Fullback	Sterrett

Touchdown — McFarland. Goal from touchdown—Donohue. Referee—Mr. Rhenn. Umpire—Mr. Harrold. Linesmen—Messrs. Sadler and Howard. Timekeeper—Will H. Hastings. Time—20 and 15-minute halves.

There is some talk of having a third meeting, the game to take place at Exposition park. Latrobe is willing, but Greensburg is non-committal.

BARNEY DREYFUSS' CHAMPS OF 1898. In 1898 the Pittsburgh Pros, owned and managed by the late Barney Dreyfuss and W. C. Temple, won the pro league championship. The members of that squad are exhibited here with photos of Temple, left, and Dreyfuss in the oval insets. Players' contracts that season ranged up to $800 and the entire squad enjoyed a prosperous campaign. Pittsburgh won the title with Greensburg and Latrobe finishing in the runner-up spots.

Shown last in the middle row is Walter Okeson, who coached the celebrated 1897 squad at Latrobe. Dr. Roller of Penn is shown third from left in the last row. At his left is John Gammons of touchdown-making fame during the Spanish-American war period. Lawler, Weinstein, Poe, Overfield, Hall, Jackson, Gelbert, Wallace, Stewart and Brooke were other members of the 1898 championship team. This team also won the first all-star game in pro football in that war year at Pittsburgh's Exposition Park.

Nov. 23 1902

PHILLIES WIN FROM PIRATES

Defeat the Pittsburg A. C. Team in a Hard Game, 11 to 0

TWO BRIGHT STARS

Washburn and Barrett Electrify the Spectators With Some Hair-Raising Runs

In a game full of brilliant runs, the All-Philadelphia Professional football team yesterday vanquished their rivals from Pittsburg by a score of 11 to 0.

In view of the previous game, wh n the Philadelphias lost in Pittsburg, there was much speculation on this contest. Pittsburg, having lost to the Athletics in a close game were determined to take revenge on the Phillies. Kennedy's men were not a bit dismayed over the fact that they had lost in the game to Pittsburg over a month ago. Neither did the knowledge of extra re-enforcements by Manager Berry dampen their confidence. It was all the greater credit to their playing an' Kennedy's coaching that they won by such an excellent score.

The game was delayed over the inability of the captains to choose a satisfactory referee. Finally Dr. McCloskey, the old Penn centre, was chosen to assist Stauffer, who had been agreed upon as umpire.

Captain Kennedy won the toss and chose the goal near the grandstand, with a fair wind upon his back.

Captain Richardson elected to have the ball kicked off to him.

Pittsburg were only able to gain a few yards and punted. The Phillies ran the ball back for ten yards, and then, after vainly trying to puncture the Pittsburg centre, Roller was called upon to punt.

It was evident that both teams had a good defense and neither could hope to steadily advance the ball.

Soon after the start Pittsburg secured the ball by a fumble on the Phillies' 25-yard line, and by steady line plunges carried it to the Phillies' 10-yard line. The home team then took a splendid brace and secured the pigskin on downs.

The Pittsburg team seemed to lose heart over this failure to gain and were never dangerous thereafter.

The half ended with the ball in midfield and the honors even.

While the teams were resting the critics were commenting on the lack of ginger each team displayed while running the ball.

Each had a magnificent defense, which was aggressive and frequently nailed the runner for a loss; this is all the more remarkable when one considers that neither team ever practices a defensive game.

When the second half started it was easily seen that Kennedy must have given his team a lecture, for they awoke from their trance and played fast football. The interference moved quickly and compactly.

The bright, particular stars were Washburn and Barrett. Time and again these two players got away for hair-raising runs of 25 yards and 30 yards.

They were greatly aided by fine interference made by their guards and full-back. It was unfortunate that Poe was held on one of these runs by one of the guards, for the umpire had his eyes open and Barrett lost the result of his good effort. Nor were the honors all on the Phillies' side, for Richardson, of the Pittsburg team, made several beautiful dodging runs for substantial gains. The first score came after two good sprints by Washburn, followed by good line plunging by Scholl until the ball was on the Pittsburg's one-yard line; another effort found it one foot short, then Roller was intrusted with the spheroid and made the first score. He added another point by kicking a goal.

An exchange of punts followed, in which Roller greatly outkicked Richardson. Kennedy decided to try for another score and called repeatedly on Roller, Barrett and Washburn.

The little half-back from Bucknell finally got a going and dodging through a broken field scored five points more. The punt out was successful, but the goal failed. Sherlock was brought into the game and Richardson went to half-back, from where he made some pretty runs.

The whistle sounded with the ball in Pittsburg's possession on the Phillies' 35-yard line.

The work of Kirkoff was conspicuous, his line breaking being all that one could wish. Schrontz and Ellis were the two other Pittsburg players who deserve commendation.

Randolph and Ryan were the stars in defensive work for the Phillies. It was a great game, and reflects much credit upon Kennedy's coaching. The line-up:

Phillies.	Positions.	Pittsburg.
Stehle	Right end	Poe
Ryan	Right tackle	Lang, Winstein
Teas	Right guard	Lawler
Bachman	Centre	Shiring
Randolph	Left guard	Kirkoff
Scholl	Left tackle	McSully
Gelbert	Left end	Schrontz
Kennedy, Capt.	Quarter-back	Richardson, Capt.
Washburn	Right half-back	Crol us
Barrett	Left half-back	McChesney, Miller
Roller	Full-back	Ellis

Umpire—N. P. Stauffer, U. of Pa. Referee—E. McCloskey, U. of Pa. Timekeepers—Zimmerman and Eagan. Linesmen—McCarthy and Welts. Time of halves—30 and 25 minutes. Touchdowns—Roller, Barrett. Goal from touchdown—Roller. Disqualified—Lang. Substitutions—Miller for McChesney, Wintsein for Lang.

Nov. 28 1902

NO SCORE BY EITHER SIDE.

PITTSBURG AND ATHLETICS MEET IN ONE OF THE BEST CONTESTS EVER SEEN.

GAMMONS AND DAVIDSON.

They Play the Star Roles for Their Respective Teams in the Muddy Field.

The football game at the Coliseum yesterday afternoon between the Pittsburg and Athletic team for the professional championship was one of the best ever seen in this locality. It was a case of giants meeting giants, with neither side having an advantage. The game ended in a score of 0 to 0. The game did not begin until some time after 3 o'clock. The cause of the delay was the fact that the manager of the Athletics would not allow his men to go upon the field until he had the guarntee of $2,000 in his hands in cool cash. Dave Berry, manager of the Pittsburg team, was in a quandary. The first $2,000 taken in was attached for ground rent, and enough cash to satisfy the Athletic management was not in sight. It was then that W. E. Corey, of Homestead, stepped into the track. Mr. Corey was one of the backers of the great Homestead team of 1900 and 1901, and is a true sportsman. He stood good for the guarantee, and Connie Mack, who is at the head of the Athletic team, at once ordered his men to go upon the field. The spectators, numbering between 3,500 and 4,000, had become impatient, and displayed their feeling by stamping vigorously and yelling loudly. When the Athletic players tumbled upon the field they were greeted with a tremendous salvo. Very little time was lost and the game was soon in full swing.

The backs of the Athletics were extremely active. Davidson, Cure and Steinberg often cut through the Pittsburg line for gains. But when the ball came too near Pittsburg's goal, which was the case in the second half, the Stars checked the advance of the Athletics effectively. In fact, the tackling on both sides was good, everyone taking a hand in the business.

The Athletics four times tried for goals from the field and each time it proved a failure. Each attempt was made from a place kick. Cure using his foot, which had been previously carefully cleaned of all mud. The last time he tried it the Athletics had the ball on Pittsburg's 32-yard line with about 55 seconds to play. The ball lit into a mud puddle on the 5-yard line. Grammors fell on it, but the pigskin shot from under him and Sweet got it. It was a dangerous predicament for the Stars. For the first time in the game their goal was threatened. The spectators held their breath in spite of the fact that only a few seconds remained to play. Cure hit the Star line a tremendous whack and took the ball to the 3-yard line. It was an awful clash. Then the referee's whistle sounded the end of the game. The Lord only knows what would have happened had there been even a half minute more to play.

The muddy condition of the grounds marred an otherwise splendid contest. But the result satisfied the spectators that the teams are evenly matched. Not a better contest was ever played in Pittsburg. It will no doubt gratify the spectators to learn that the teams will meet again to-morrow to have it out. The Athletics claim the professional championship, having won two games and lost only one. They insist that the result of the game to-morrow will not offset their standing should it go against them. But the contest will decide which is the better eleven. It is probable that no more evenly matched football teams ever went on the gridiron. Line-up:

PITTSBURG—0.		ATHLETICS—0.
Schrontz	Left end	Baeder
McNulty	Left tackle	Pierce
Kirkhoff	Left guard	McFarland
Shiring	Center	Sweet
Lawler	Right guard	Kingdon
Lang	Right tackle	Wallace
Poe	Right end	Merriman
Richardson	Quarterback	Hewitt
Gammons	Left half	Steinberg
McChesney	Right half	Cure
Crolius	Fullback	Davidson

Referee—Dr. Farrar. Umpire—R. W. Hochenber'y. Time—30 and 25-minute halves. Substitutions—Crolius for McChesney, Ellis for Crolius.

1905

CARLISLE INDIANS
VS:
CANTON
AT—
CANTON
WEDNESDAY NOVEMBER 22nd
GAME CALLED 2:30 P. M. SHARP.
Special Street Car and Suburban Service.

Statistics of Canton-Carlisle Game.

	Canton. 1	2	Total.	Carlisle. 1	2	Total.
Yards advanced through line.	37 1-2	25	62 1-2	12	8	20
Yards advanced around ends.	28	15	43	5	3	8
Yards punts carried back.....	33	17	50	50	48	98
Yards kick-offs carried back..	29	0	29	0	30	30
Total yards carried	127 1-2	47	184 1-2	67	49	156
Number of punts	6	8	14	2	6	8
Yards punted	215	240	455	60	200	260
Number of kick-offs...........	1	1	2	1	0	1
Ball lost on downs	1	0	1	0	0	0
Ball lost on fumbles	1	0	1	1	2	3
Forced to punt...............	6	3	9	4	3	7
Penalties	1	1	2	1	0	1
Yards inflicted	5	15	20	5	0	5
Yards lost	3	0	3	3	2 1-2	5 1-2

1905

STATISTICS OF CANTON-MASSILLON GAME.

	CANTON. 1	2	Total.	MASSILLON. 1	2	Total.
Yards advanced through line......	21	18	39	42	120	162
Yards advanced around end.......	29	3	32	49	4	53
Kick-offs carried back...........	15	0	15	12	25	37
Punts carried back.............	20	5	25	70	10	80
Total yards carried.............	85	26	111	173	159	332
Punts	300	95	395	135	85	220
Number of punts..................	6	3	9	3	2	5
Kick-offs......................	75	90	165	45	45	90
Ball lost on downs...............	0	0	0	2	0	2
Ball lost on fumbles.............	3	0	3	3	0	3
Yards lost....................	5	1	4	4	1	5
Forced to punt.................	3	0	0	20	15	35
Penalties.....................	0	0	0	20	15	35

STARS NO MATCH FOR TEAM WORK

Massillon Tigers Triumphed Over Canton's Famous Aggregation.

A REMARKABLE CONTEST

Never Before Did So Many Heroes of the Gridiron Take Part in a Professional Game—Salmon the Man Who Brought Victory to the Tigers—Heston a Disappointment.

STAFF SPECIAL.

MASSILLON, O., Nov. 30.—In a smashing battle in which two teams composed of a selection of the star players of the east and west pitted against each other, the professional club championship of Ohio was defended successfully by the Massillon Tigers this afternoon, when they defeated the Canton Giants by the score of 14 to 4.

In one way it was the most remarkable game probably ever witnessed in the middle west , and in all probability it will be some years when two teams face each other whose line ups embrace such a collection of heroes of the gridiron game. With such renowned players as Heston of Michigan, Smith of U. of P. Reynolds, the star back, who was barred from playing with Pennsylvania; Farabaugh of Lehigh, Grover and James of Michigan, Drake of Cornell, Salmon of Notre Dame, Wallace of U. of P., beside Dr. Rayl, Ernest, Cure, Kauffman, Hall, Kirchoff, Riley, Moran, McFarland and Hayden, who have already been made famous on previous contests. However, this game has proven conclusively that no matter how many star players a team may bring together at the eleventh hour, the brawn, with fewer stars, but who have been drilled together and have the team work, which is the sole secret of success in football, is the one to win.

Canton's re-enforcements arrived at headquarters on Monday and had but three days in which to become acquainted with each other and the lack of familiarity and team work proved the undoing of the Giants today. On the other hand, Massillon imported but two stars and their team play and staying qualities wore the wearers of the red and white eleven down so completely that in the middle of the second half when Rayl left the game the Cantonites were so groggy that Massillon swept them off their feet.

Fumbling must also be considered as it was a direct result from one of these misplays by Willie Heston that gave Massillon the opportunity of scoring the first touchdown.

Scarcely in any part of the universe are two towns closely situated where more rivalry exists than between Canton and "Tigertown." Apparently every person who has been interviewed by the census writer at each town believes body and soul in the rugby game and to say that they are ardent advocates of the pigskin game does not explain the enthusiasm which was manifested in these rival towns today.

Influential businessmen had previously donated and solicited enough finances to put a team on the field. Funds were not withheld one particle and the one thought was to secure the better eleven. All fall there has been quantities of gossip about this game and the betting during the last few days has been heavy. Wagers, one of $5,000 and another of $4,000, were among those placed at Massillon, but wagers of $100 and $200 were as frequent as flies in summer. Canton placed implicit confidence in the new players she had signed and plunged heavily. This morning Canton was draped in red and white, the colors of the team, and crowds started for Massillon, with pockets bulging with coin, as early as 9:30.

Line up:

Massillon—14.	Position.	Canton—4.
Schrontz	Left end	Graver
McNulty	Left tackle	Ernst (c) Rayl and
Kerchoff	Left guard	Ozersky
Shirring	Center	Kauffman
McFarland, Scholl	Turner and
and Haag	Right guard	Hall
Lang	Right tackle	Wallace
McChesney	Right end	Farabaugh
Hayden	Quarterback	James T. Nesser and
Riley	Left halfback	Heston Drake and
		Reynolds and
Moran	Right halfback	Murphy Smith and
Salmon	Fullback	Cure

Touchdowns—Salmon 2. Goals from placement—Salmon. Drop kick—Reynolds. Referees—Gaston of O. and J.; Poe of Princeton. Head linesman—Gessler of W. and J. Linesmen—Lind of Mount Union and Batzley. Head timekeeper—O. U. Walker of Alliance. Timers—Luther Day of Canton and Burt Coleman of Massillon.

HESTON ON HAND FOR BIG GAME

Famous Michigan Star Will Surely Take Part in Canton-Massillon Contest.

Massillon Has Also Landed a Few Famous Gridiron Celebrities.

SPECIAL TO THE PLAIN DEALER.

CANTON, O., Nov. 28.—As Thanksgiving day approaches the Canton and Massillon teams are putting on their finishing touches for the professional championship of the state. With the Canton team in training at Congress lake and the Massillon Tigers going through the system on a farm the public is barred from their quarters and know little of the details. The field at Massillon is covered with hay and special efforts will be made to keep it dry for the event. Canton's team represents a pick of college stars, as recommended by "Hurry Up" Yost of Michigan and the players are signed by Manager Will Day of this city, who formerly played with the Michigan eleven.

Heston of Michigan and Turner of Dartmouth, the newest members of the Canton team, arrived in the city tonight and secured rooms. The following is the official line up as announced by the management of the local athletic club last night:

Left end, Graver of Michigan; left tackle, Ernst of LaFayette; left guard, Rayl of Cleveland; center, Kaufman of Case; right guard, Hall of Princeton and Michigan; quarterback, Wallace of Pennsylvania; right end, Turner of Michigan; quarterback, James of Michigan; halfbacks, Heston of Michigan and Reynolds of Pennsylvania; fullback, Smith of Pennsylvania and Cure of Lafayette. Subs, ends, Sutter of W. and J.; Volk of Akron and Shields of Canton; tackle, Bedur of Akron; guard, Heimberger of W. and J.; center, Allardice of Canton; quarterback, Jackson of O. S. U.; halfbacks, Pearson of Cornell, Murphy of W. and J., Streibinger and Hardy of Hiram; fullback, Ozersky.

Nov. 14　1906

The Canton Bulldog and the Massillon Tiger Will Soon be Face to Face

—Courtesy of the Cleveland News.

1906

MONEY OFFER FOR TIGERS?

In Signed Statement Management of Massillon Team Accuses Gamblers and Explains Why Walter East Was Fired From Tiger Team

MASSILLON, O., Nov. 26.—In a written statement, issued today and signed by Manager E. J. Stewart of the Tiger football team and H. A. Croxton, one of the team's backers, the charge is made that an attempt was made to bribe some of the Tiger players this season. The statement in part says:

"With the conclusion of the series of games between Canton and Massillon, for the world's championship football honors, the time has now arrived to make clear some peculiar and unpleasant conditions which have surrounded the Tigers' coach and management during the entire season.

"Many Massillon fans were surprised at the discharge of Walter R. East, who, during the early season, played right end on the Tiger team, inasmuch as East had shown wonderful abilities in this position.

"The reasons for East's discharge by the Tiger management were not made public at the time. It was suspected by a few that he had been a traitor to the team, and the reason was that he had offered by the management, for the reason that it would have done irreparable damage to professional football in this vicinity, and the management and coach firmly believed that the Tigers could win the game at Canton, notwithstanding the handicap of being unable to use old signals, plays and styles of play which had been practiced all season.

"For this reason the explanation was not offered. Now the time has arrived for an exposure of one of the greatest plots which has ever been attempted along these lines in Ohio.

"East was the man who attempted to engineer the deal, with Coach Bloody Wallace of the Canton team as an accomplice, and they were backed by a crowd of gamblers who agreed to furnish $50,000 to be used for betting purposes and all expenses incurred and $5,000 in cash to the Tigers' coach and management.

"East and Wallace and their accomplices figured on the old adage that 'every man has his price,' but they made the mistake of their sporting lives when they figured that the Massillon team, coach and management could be bought. Their scheme was that Canton was to win the first game, Massillon win the second game and a third game should be played in Cleveland, and this game to be played on its merits. East represented that one year ago he 'framed' a date deal whereby Western University of Pennsylvania lost to State college by the score of 6 to 0, that no suspicion was attached to him and that it would be just as easy to 'fix' the Canton-Massillon series.

"He also claimed that the Akron Baseball club of which he was manager during the past season finished in second place instead of first place because there was more money in it for him, and again no suspicion was entertained as to crookedness.

"The proof of the reliability of this article in the nature of the signed papers can be found in the safe of the Massillon Iron & Steel plant, and Mr. Croxton, whose services have so materially assisted the Tiger team this fall, will be pleased to exhibit them to any and all who care to see them.

"The above is given upon our authority, with all the proofs in our possession.

(Signed)　"E. J STEWART,
"H. A. CROXTON."

MASSILLON TIGERS**1906 AGATHON FIELD

Top row left to right: Elmer Vogt, Harry Anderson
Emery Powell, Orrie Ames, Mel Trotter, Tim Nolan
Leavitt Shertzer, Herman L. Vogt-Coach
2nd row: Bob Featheringham, Bordner, Albert Bonk
John Fisher, Miller, Getz, Mully Miller

1913

Sporting Life

JAMES THORPE

1914

SPECIAL TO THE PLAIN DEALER.

AKRON, O., Oct. 4.—Peggy Parratt's state professional champions were defeated today by the Columbus Pan Handles, 26 to 0. The Pan Handles came to Akron with the six famous Nesser brothers in the line-up, who, aided and abetted by two dashing halfbacks in Ruh and Smoot, proved too much for the Akron Indians.

Reprinted from
The Cleveland Plain Dealer

1914

AKRON INDIANS BEAT CANTON FOOTBALLERS

Parratt's Warriors Win by Using Powerful Attack.

CANTON, O., Nov. 26.—Peggy Parratt's Akron team was an easy winner in today's game with Canton, taking the contest 21 to 0. These teams met earlier in the month Canton winning 7 to 0.

Canton lacked a powerful attack, and was never able to gain consistently against Akron. The locals presented a patched up team, several men having left the line-up after the death of Center Harry Turner, who was fatally hurt in the first game with Akron.

Akron gained on straight football and at the open game, and piled up a considerable advantage through the punting of Davidson. The line-up:

Canton—0.	Position.	Akron—21.
H. Dagenhart	L. E.	Rockne
Speck	L. T.	Edwards
W. Dagenhart	L. G.	Goebel
Schlott	C.	Waldsmith
Snyder	R. G.	Olson
Erbe	R. T.	Powell
A. Nesser	R. G.	Davidson
Hamilton	Q.	Parratt
Ruh	L. H.	F. Nesser
McDonald	R. H.	Kagy
Peters	F.	Collins

Substitutes—Davidson for Rockne, Rockne for Kagy, Wetz for F. Nesser, Davidson for Parratt, Axtell for Davidson, Parratt for Davidson, T. Nesser for Erbe, Zimmerman for McDonald, Zettler for Ruh, Zimmerman for A. Nesser, DeDonald for Zimmerman.

Touchdowns—F. Nesser, Parratt, Collins. Goals from touchdown—Davidson 3. Referee Blythe of Mount Union. Umpire—Riley. Head linesman—Scherry of Ohio State.

Reprinted from
The Cleveland Plain Dealer

1915

Detroit Defeats Canton.

DETROIT, Oct. 24.—The Detroit Heralds defeated the crack Canton football team here today by a score of 9 to 3. Line-up:

Canton—3.	Position.	Heralds—9.
Axtell	L. E.	D. Shields
Edwards	L. T.	G. Shields
Dagenhart	L. G.	Mitchell
Schultz	C.	Stewart
Waldsmith	R. G.	Newashe
Powell	R. T.	Schlee
Gardner	R. E.	Glockson
Hamilton	Q.	Latham
Iddings	L. H.	Kelly
Julian	R. H.	Wilson
Peters	F.	Dunne

Touchdown—D. Shields. Goals from dropkick—D. Shields, Hamilton.

Referee—Lane, Michigan. Umpire—Blyle, Mount Union. Head Linesman—Patterson, Washington and Jefferson. Time of quarters—12m.

Reprinted from
The Cleveland Plain Dealer

1915

MASSILLON BEATS CANTON BULLDOGS IN FAST CONTEST

Dorias, Former Notre Dame Quarter, Makes Three Drop Kick Field Goals.

Thorpe, Indian Athlete Who Played With Giants, Stars for Canton.

SPECIAL TO THE PLAIN DEALER.

MASSILLON, O., Nov. 14.—The Massillon Tigers, seeking the state professional football championship of the state, today defeated the Canton Bulldogs 16 to 0. More than 5,000 fans witnessed the contest.

Dorias starred for Massillon, kicking three goals from drop kicks, while Jim Thorpe, Indian athlete, who played with the New York Nationals, did the best work for Canton.

Tigers—16.	Position.	Canton—0.
White	L. E.	Axtell
Jones	L. T.	Edwards
Cole	L. G.	Schlott
Lee	C.	Schultz
Portmann	R. G.	Powell
Campbell	R. T.	Waldsmith
Finnegan	R. E.	Gardner
Dorias	Q.	Hamilton
Fleming	L. H.	Wagner
Maurle	R. H.	Juliar
Hogan	F.	Peters

Substitutions—Massillon, Kagy for Finnegan, Burns for Kagy, Kagy for Fleming, Fleming for Kagy, Kagy for Burns, Collins for Hogan; Canton, Drumm for Schlott, Speck for Powell, Wagner for Gardner, Fischer for Wagner, Julian for Peters, Thorpe for Julian, Peters for Thorpe, Thorpe for Peters.

Touchdown—Hogan. Goal after touchdown—Fleming. Goals from drop kick—Dorias 3.

Referee—Conner of Bates. Umpire—Durfee of Williams. Head linesman—East of Massillon. Time of quarters—15m.

Reprinted from
The Cleveland Plain Dealer

1915

COLUMBUS PAN HANDLES PLAY PATRICIANS TIE

Battle Evenly in Scoreless Contest at Youngstown.

YOUNGSTOWN, O., Nov. 21.—In one of the greatest football games ever seen in this city the Patricians and Pan Handles of Columbus battled through sixty minutes of play here today without either being able to score. Columbus had the ball on the Patricians' two-yard line twice and again on the three-yard line, but the locals held for downs.

The nearest the Patricians came to scoring was when Ashbaugh's two boots from the forty-five and thirty-five-yard lines, respectively, fell short by narrow margins.

The sensational playing of Verdernach, former Carlisle Indian star, was the greatest exhibition of the grid game ever seen here.

Patricians—0.	Position.	Pan Handles—0.
Verdernack	L. E.	F. Nesser
Steel	L. T.	Jones
Yeckel	L. G.	P. Kuehner
Cavanaugh	C.	Dunn
Tobin	R. G.	Brigaam
Benson	R. T.	A. Nesser
Ashbaugh	R. E.	Ted Nesser
Thomas	Q.	Pickeret
Getz	L. H.	Shoots
Eberhart	R. H.	Ruh
McLaughrey	F.	Frank Nesser

Substitutions—Pan Handles, R. Kuehner for Ruh; Patricians, Richards for Yeckel, Loos for Cavanaugh, Wilkoff for Tobin, Steyers and Duval for Benson, Edwards for Thomas, Gillespie and Thomas for Eberhart.

Referee—Reach, Umpire—Stowe. Head linesman—Flad. Timers—Vericee and Flynn. Time of quarters—15m.

Reprinted from
The Cleveland Plain Dealer

1915

FOOTBALL TOLL SIXTEEN FOR 1915 CAMPAIGN

This is One Less Than Lost Life Last Year.

CHICAGO, Nov. 27.—(Leased Wire.)—Football claimed sixteen lives during the 1915 season, which came to a close today. Last year the toll was one less.

Not a single death was recorded in any game in which the players were known to be trained physically as well as mentally for the severe test.

In most cases those who lost their lives were members of high school, semi-pro and prairie elevens where there is little or no system of physical training.

In the year's toll, four players were 15 years old or under, one being only 11 years old. Four of them were only 17 years old while the others ranged to 21 years. Only three had college affiliations and in one of these cases it was said that an unnecessary tackle killed the player.

Reprinted from
The Cleveland Plain Dealer

1915

THORPE'S TOE GIVES CANTON PROS VICTORY

CANTON, O., Nov. 28.—Jim Thorpe's toe gave the Canton Bulldogs a victory over the Massillon Tigers today when the two greatest aggregations of ex-college football stars ever gathered on professional teams in Ohio played their second game.

Thorpe in the first period drop kicked the ball from the forty-five-yard line for three points. In the third quarter, after Massillon had held Canton without an inch gain on three downs, Thorpe made a place kick from the thirty-eight-yard line. That was all the scoring done.

Near the finish Massillon was in scoring distance. On the fourth down Dorias made a forward pass to Rockne inside the twenty-yard limit. Rockne ran into the crowd on the side line, and when the players were pulled from him it was found that Smith, colored Michigan Aggie man, who played with Canton, had the ball back of his own goal. Rockne had fumbled. Referee Connor allowed a touchback, and a lengthy argument ensued in the fast nearing darkness.

Canton—6.	Position.	Massillon—0.
Wagner	L. E.	Rockne
Abel	L. T.	Jones
Edwards	L. G.	Cole
Waldsmith	C.	Hayes
Davis	R. G.	Portman
Smith	R. T.	Day
Gardner	R. E.	Cherry
Lambert	Q.	Dorias
Fisher	L. H.	Kagy
Thorpe	R. H.	Fleming
Julian	F.	Hanley

Substitutions—Schultz for Waldsmith, Whitacre for Lambert, Specht for Edwards, Baxter for Kagy.

Referee—Connor, of Bates. Umpire—Cosgrove of Cornell. Head linesman—Jones of Ohio State. Time of periods—15m.

Reprinted from
The Cleveland Plain Dealer

THE DAYTON TRIANGLES
1916

Top: A. O. Davison (Secr.-Treas.)
Top Row: Dellinger (T), Stoecklein (G), Murray (G), Partlow (HB), Palmer (E), Clark (G)
Middle Row: Fenner (E), Cutler (T), Mahrt (QB), Sacksteder (HB), Zimmerman (FB), Reese (C), Talbot (Coach)
Bottom Row: Dungan (E), Zile (E), Decker (FB)

**FOOT BALL
EXCURSION
TO
TOLEDO**

Sunday Oct. 22, 1916

VIA

ANN ARBOR RAILROAD

TOLEDO MAROONS

OHIO CHAMPIONS 1915

VS

MASSILLON TIGERS

World's Champions

AT

ARMORY PARK

TWO MINUTES WALK FROM ANN ARBOR DEPOT

75c —— ADMISSION —— 75c

The Toledo Maroons were the 1915 Champions of Ohio and are one of the fastest teams in the country. A thrilling game is assured.

1916

He Warbled; Cost $2,500

It cost one Massillon rooter, a well known Massillon man, just $2,500 to open his mouth at the Courtland shortly after the lunch hour Sunday.

This ill-advised Tiger fan declared in the lobby that the Bulldogs would have no chance against the orange and black. Jim Thorpe overheard the remark and asked the boastful Massillonian whether he cared to stand back of it. The Tigerite did, but was somewhat taken back when the famous Indian wrote out a check for $2,500 and asked that it be covered. The Massillon man stood by his guns. Now he's wiser and Thorpe richer by $2,500.

Massillon had plenty of money to stake on the outcome of the game, while many of the Canton bugs were rather shy. They evidently feared the hoodoo which Massillon has been in former years. Now that the jinx has been chased the wagering in years to come is likely to be more lively.

1916

THE SIX NESSER BROTHERS

Columbus vs. Cleveland

1916

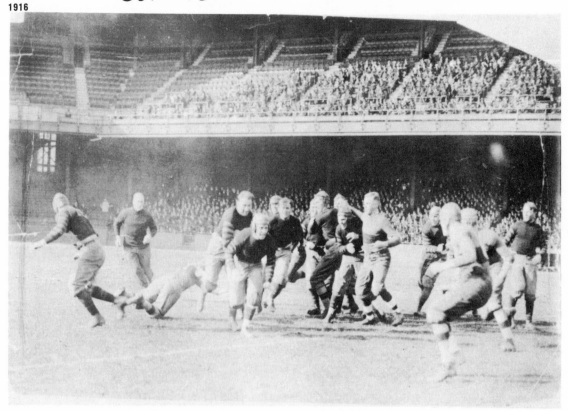

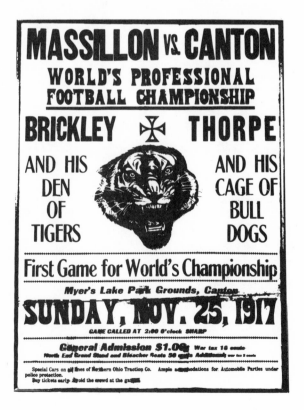

Courtesy
Pro Football Hall of Fame

FRANK HIED   A. F. RANNEY

AKRON PROFESSIONAL FOOTBALL TEAM

LEAGUE PARK

OFFICE
21 N. SUMMIT STREET
BELL MAIN 1766

CARROLL AND BEAVER STREETS
AKRON, OHIO

E. W. TOBIN, Coach
C. COPLEY, Captain

MINUTES OF MEETING — SEPTEMBER 17th-1920.

Meeting called to order at 8:15 P.M., by Chairman, Mr. Hay. Teams represented were, Canton Bulldogs, Cleveland Indians, Dayton Triangles, Akron Professionals, Massillon Tigers, Rochester, N.Y., Rock Island, Ill., Muncie, Ind., Staley A.C. Decatur, Ill., Racine Cardinals, Wisconsin, and Hammond, Ind.

Minutes of previous meeting were given in a resume by the Chairman.

Old Business.

Massillon withdrew from professional football for the season of 1920.

New Business.

It was moved and seconded that a permanent organization be formed to be known as American Professional Football Association. Motion carried.

Moved and seconded that officers be now elected, consisting of President, Vice President, Secretary and Treasurer. Carried.

Mr. Jim Thorpe was unanimously elected President, Mr. Stan Cofall, Vice President, and Mr. A. F. Ranney, Secretary and Treasurer.

Moved and seconded that a fee of $100.00 be charged for membership in the Association. Carried.

Moved and seconded that the president appoint a committee to work in conjunction with a lawyer to draft a Constitution, bylaws and rules for the Association. Carried.

Mr. Thorpe appointed Mr. A. A. Young of Hammond, Chairman, and Messrs. Cofall, Flannigan and Storch associates.

Moved and seconded that all Clubs mail to the Secretary by Jan y 1, 1921, a list of all players used by them this season, the Secretary to furnish all Clubs with duplicate copy of same, so that each Club would have first choice in services for 1921 of his team of this season. Carried.

Moved and seconded that all members have printed upon their stationery, "Member of American Professional Football Association". Carried.

Mr. Marshall of the Brunswick-Balke Collender Company, Tire Division, presented a silver loving cup to be given the team, awarded the championship by the Association. Any team winning the cup three times should be adjudged the owner.

It was moved and seconded that a vote of thanks be extended by the Secretary to Mr. Marshall.

The meeting was adjourned.

Next meeting to be called by the President some time in January 1921.

A F Ranney

Thorpe Heads Gridmen.

CANTON, Ohio, Setember 20.—Jim Thorpe, famous Indian foot ball player and coach of the Canton Bulldogs, a local professional team, has been chosen head of the American Professional Foot Ball Association.

Representatives of eleven cities unanimously voted Thorpe to the presidency, with Stanley Cofall of Cleveland as vice president and Art Tanney of Akron, secretary and treasurer.

A decision was reached to refrain from luring players out of college for the professional game.

Oct. 11

GRID PROS SCRAP TO 0-0 DRAW AS 10,000 LOOK ON

Twenty-six college alumni, representing two professional football teams, scuffled to a draw, 0 to 0, before 10,000 gridiron fans yesterday at Cub park. But the opinions of the critical rooters gave a shade decision to the Racine Cardinals, piloted by Paddy Driscoll, over their opponents, George Falcon's Chicago Tigers.

CHICAGO TIGERS [0]		R. CARDINALS [0]	
R. E.	Knopp	LaRose	L. E.
R. T.	Bennett	Brennan	L. T.
R. G.	Keefe	Chappell	L. G.
J.	Des Jardien	Whalen	C.
L. G.	Volz	Voight Clark	R. G.
L. T.	Matthews	Gillies	R. T.
L. E.	Meagher	O'Connor	
Q. B.	Ghee	Florence	R. E.
R. H. B.	Malone	Driscoll	Q. B.
L. H. B.	Barrett	Hallstrom	L. H. B.
F. B.	G. Falcon	Curran	R. H. B.
	Eiseler	McInery	F. B.

Referee—Thomas, Illinois. Umpire—Moore, Boston. Field Judge—Cermak, Illinois. Head Linesman—Wyatt, Missouri.

Reprinted from
Chicago Daily Tribune

1920 DECATUR STALEYS SQUAD PICTURE — Forerunners of the Chicago Bears Football Club

Dec. 6

STALEYS CRUSH CARDINALS, 10-0, IN TITULAR TILT

Although their superiority was apparent at most stages, the powerful Staleys of Decatur, Ill., had to toil strenuously to whip the Chicago Cardinals yesterday at Cub park in a game on which the midwest "pro" honors hinged. The downstaters wound up with a 10 to 0 advantage, but with a little less stubborn resistance on the part of the Cardinals and a little more accuracy in the toe of "Dutch" Sternaman the victors would have amassed twice as many points.

BOB KOEHLER.
[TRIBUNE Photo.]

11,000 View Struggle.

Fully 11,000, the largest crowd in the history of local pro football, viewed the game. Most of the rooters came with hopes of seeing the Cardinals repeat their 7 to 6 victory of last Sunday over the Decatur team. The locals had only one chance to do business, however. That was in the second period when the Cardinals passed and drove to the Staleys' seven yard mark, only to lose the ball when Sachs failed to connect with a pass.

The Staleys scored their only touchdown early in the second period. They marched from midfield on a series of open and close plays until they were only a couple of yards from the goal. Bob Koehler then ripped through center for the points, and Sternaman kicked goal.

Sternaman's Kicks Wild.

Five attempts at goal kicks were made by Sternaman, and four were missed, even though he went to the trouble to encase his foot in a dry shoe prior to each attempt. The first attempt in the opening period resulted in a huge loss because of a bad pass. In the third period the Staleys recovered a Cardinal fumble and then advanced to the Cards' 40 yard line, where Sternaman made another try. The ball went wide of the posts. The other attempts were in the fourth period, one going over. Lineup:

Staleys [10]		Cardinals [0]
R. E.	Halas	Sachs, LaRoss.. L. E.
R. T.	Blacklock	Gillies .... L. T.
R. G.	Jones	Zola .... L. G.
C.	Trafton	Clark .... C.
L. G.	May	Chapel .... R. G.
L. T.	Ingwerson	Carey, Brennan R. T.
L. E.	Chamberlain	Florence .... R. E.
Q. B.	Pearce	Driscoll .... Q. B.
R. H.	Lanum	Curran, Hallstrom L. H.
	Conzelman	
L. H.	Sternaman	McInerney ...... R. H.
F. B.	Koehler	Charpier, Egan.. F. B.

Touchdown—Koehler. Goal from touchdown—Sternaman. Goal from field—Sternaman.

Dec. 5

10,000 N. Y. FANS SEE BUFFALO NIP CANTON PROS., 7-3

New York, Dec. 4.—In the first professional football game played in this city in many years, the Buffalo All-Americans defeated the Canton Bull dogs, 7 to 3, at the Polo grounds this afternoon. The teams were so well matched that consistent gains were out of the question. The game drew a crowd of 10,000.

Jim Thorpe, former Carlisle Indian school star, kicked a field goal from placement for Canton in the third period, following the recovery of a Buffalo fumble, and a few minutes later "Swede" Youngstrom, one of the greatest linesmen ever developed at Dartmouth, picked up a blocked punt from the toe of Thorpe and ran over the line for Buffalo's touchdown, from which Weldon kicked goal. Lineup:

Buffalo [7].		Canton [3].
L. E...	Shelton, Cornell	Higgins, Pa. St. R. E.
L. T...	Thornhill, Pitt	Henry, W. & J... R. T.
L. G...	Brace, Brown	Speck, Canton... R. G.
C......	Wray, Penn	Feeney, N. Dame... C.
R. G...	Youngstrom, Dartmouth	O'Connor, Georgetown .... L. G.
R. T...	Little, Penn	Buck, Wiscon... L. T.
R. E...	Miller, Penn	Lowe, Fordham. L. E.
Q. B...	Hughitt, Mich.	Griggs, Dallas... Q. B.
L. B...	Weldon, Lafayette	Thorpe, Carlisle. R. B.
R. B......	Anderson, Colgate	Calac, Carlisle... L. B.
F. B.	Pat Smith Mich	Guyon, Carlisle.. F. B.

Touchdown—Youngstrom. Goal from touchdown—Weldon. Field goal—Thorpe [place]. Referee—R. W. Maxwell, Swarthmore. Umpire—C. McCarthy, Germantown academy. Head linesman—Carson, Penn State.

Reprinted from
Chicago Daily Tribune

Reprinted from
Chicago Daily Tribune

The American Professional Football Association
UNIFORM PLAYER'S CONTRACT

The .... Buffalo Football Club, Inc. .... here in called the Club, and .... Oscar Anderson .... of .... Erie, Pa. .... herein called the Player.

The Club is a member of The American Professional Football Association. As such, and jointly with the other members of the Association, it is obligated to insure to the public wholesome and high-class professional football by defining the relations between Club and Player, and between Club and Club.

In view of the facts above recited the parties agree as follows:

1. The Club will pay the Player a salary for his skilled services during the playing season of 1921., at the rate of $........ ...... per game.

2. The salary above provided for shall be paid by the Club as follows:

After each game

3. The Player agrees that during said season he will faithfully serve the Club, and pledges himself to the American public to conform to high standards of fair play and good sportsmanship.

4. The Player will not play football during 192.. otherwise than for the Club, except in case the Club shall have released said Player, and said release has been approved by the officials of The American Professional Football Association.

5. The Player accepts as part of this contract such reasonable regulations as the Club may announce from time to time.

6. This contract may be terminated at any time by the Club upon six (6) days' written notice to the Player.

7. The Player submits himself to the discipline of The American Professional Football Association and agrees to accept its decisions pursuant to its Constitution and By-Laws.

8. Any time prior to August 1st, 192.. , by written notice to the Player, the Club may renew this contract for the term of that year, except that the salary rate shall be such as the parties may then agree upon, or, in default of agreement, such as the Club may fix.

9. In default of agreement, the Player will accept the salary rate thus fixed or else will not play during said year otherwise than for the Club, unless the Club shall release the Player.

10. The reservation of the Club of the valuable right to fix the salary rate for the succeeding year, and the promise of the Player not to play during said year otherwise than with the Club, have been taken into consideration in determining the salary specified herein and the undertaking by the Club to pay said salary is the consideration for both the reservation and the promise.

11. In case of dispute between the Player and the Club the same shall be referred to the officials of The American Professional Football Association, and their decision shall be accepted by all parties as final.

Signed this 25th .... day of August .... A. D. 1921 .....

Witnesses:

Florence S. McHail

Edward Grille

Buffalo Football Club, Inc.

By .... Coach

O C Anderson

Duplicate Copy to be held by Player.

Sept. 26

AKRON PROS OPEN GRID YEAR WITH 14 TO 0 WIN OVER PANHANDLES TEAM

Akron Team Shows Up Well, But Lacking Practice—New Men Make Impression—Pollard Is Star

THE AKRON PROS, world's championship professional football team, won its first game of the 1921 season at League park Sunday, defeating the Columbus Panhandles 14 to 0.

Weather conditions were right for the game and close to 2,000 people took advantage of the opportunity to see the football champions in their opening game.

Though fairly evenly played the game was almost entirely devoid of thrills. Fritz Pollard's spectacular play and the scoring of the two touchdowns gave the fans their few opportunities to cheer.

Pollard lived up to the nice things said about him during the last week. Squirming and twisting away from would be tacklers, he made several sensational sprints that won him cheers.

The game as a whole, seemed a matter of condition. With only a week's practice tucked under their belts, the Akron players suffered a hard ordeal, playing through the long periods. Columbus on the other hand, had been practicing for a month and their players weathered the long periods in better style.

Reprinted from
The Akron Beacon Journal

Aug. 28

ENROLLS THREE TO MEMBERSHIP IN GRID LEAGUE

At a meeting of the American Professional Football association held at the Hotel La Salle yesterday Green Bay, Minneapolis Marines, and Evansville were admitted to membership.

The schedule of games will be ready for publication early next month. Any club guilty of tampering with college players will be expelled. University authorities will be notified whenever a college player makes a request to play on any eleven in the organization.

President Joseph F. Carr of Columbus, O., presided, and the following cities were represented: Rochester, Buffalo, Canton, Akron, Cleveland, Toledo, Dayton, Fort Wayne, Decatur, Rock Island, Louisville, Chicago, Cincinnti, Detroit, Evansville, Minneapolis, and Green Bay.

Reprinted from
Chicago Daily Tribune

CANTON HELD TO TIE BY HAMMOND

Professional Football Teams Score Touchdown Each in Close Game.

(Plain Dealer Special)

CANTON, O., Oct. 9.—Canton and the Hammond, (Ind.) eleven fought to a tie in their professional football game here this afternoon, the final count being 7 to 7. It was a thrilling engagement, with Canton playing uphill most of the time. Hammond's touchdown was the result of misunderstood signals. Canton had the ball at midfield in the second quarter when a pass from center was not covered by any of the backs. End Hanke, ex-Minnesota university captain, picked up the pigskin and ran thirty-five yards for the first score, not a Bulldog being close enough to make a tackle. Canton tied the score in the third period, and the credit went to Halfback Way of Penn State.

Catching a forward pass from Griggs of Texas, Way netted thirty-seven yards and a touchdown. Feeney's goal knotted the score. Ex-collegians of note were in the line-up for each team.

Canton played better defensive ball than Hammond, but the visitors were able to make three first downs in the fourth period due to aerial maneuvers. Capt. Risely of Hammond failed a placement kick from the thirty-two-yard line in the third period, and Halfback Jones of Hammond failed to drop kick from the forty-five-yard line in the fourth period, while Feeney of Canton with fifty seconds of play remaining was not able to place kick from Hammond's twenty-five-yard line.

Canton—7.	Position.	Hammond—7.
Steel	L. E.	Williams
West	L. T.	Risely
Kellison	L. G.	Green
Feeney	C.	Depler
Osborne	R. G.	Olta
Henry	R. T.	Tallant
Higgins	R. E.	Hanke
Kempton	Q.	Hess
Robb	L. H.	Derr
Griggs	R. H.	Knohs
Smith	F.	King

Canton .... 0 0 7 0—7
Hammond .... 0 7 0 0—7

Touchdowns—Hanke, Way. Goals from touchdowns—Feeney, Risely. Field goals—Failed, Feeney, Risely, Jones.

Substitutions—Canton: Carroll for Steele, Way for Robb, Slackford for Smith. Hammond: Hartung for Green, Mathys for Hess, Jones for Derr, Falcon for King, King for Knohs, Knohs for Hanke.

Referee—Durfee (Williams). Umpire—Wyman (Case). Head linesman—O'Brien (Mount Union). Time of periods—12m.

Reprinted from
The Cleveland Plain Dealer

AKRON ELEVEN BEATS CHICAGO

Pollard Stars in 23 to 0 Win Over Cardinals.

(Plain Dealer Special)

CHICAGO, Oct. 9.—Akron, recognized as one of the strongest professional football teams in the country, started on its way for the championship by defeating the Chicago Cardinals, managed by Chris O'Brien, at Normal park today, 23 to 0.

The game was featured by the sterling playing of Fritz Pollard, former star of Brown university. The slippery colored halfback started the scoring in the opening period by tearing off one of his characteristic fifty-yard runs. During the course of his dash, he pivoted out of the grasp of several Cardinal players, sidestepped others and planted the oval squarely between the posts.

Akron—23.	Position.	Cardinals—0.
Bierce	R. E.	Sachs
Copley	R. T.	Rydzewski
Nesser	R. G.	Brennan
Bailey	C.	Knight
Tobin	L. G.	Zola
Johnson	L. T.	Gilles
Flowers	L. E.	O'Connor
Sheeks	Q.	Driscoll
Pollard	R. H.	Barry
King	L. H.	Hallstrom
Kramer	F.	Kochler

Touchdowns—Pollard 2, King. Goals from touchdowns—King 2. Goals from field—Sheeks.

Reprinted from
The Cleveland Plain Dealer

GREEN BAY PACKERS BEAT HAMMOND, 14-7

GREEN BAY, Wis., Nov. 13.—Getting the jump on their opponents in the first quarter the Green Bay Packers defeated the Hammond Professionals today, 14 to 7. A blizzard which swept the field during the closing periods spoiled the Packers' aerial attack.

Lineup:

PACKERS (14).		HAMMOND (7).
Demoe	L.E.	Williams
Coughlin	L.T	Risley
Smith	L.G	Hart
Murray	C.	Depler
Wilson	R.G.	Ortiz
Buck	R.T.	Tallant
Hayes	R.E.	Hanke
Lambeau	Q.B.	Mathys
Barry	L.B.	Hess
Malone	R.H.	Dorr
Schmael	F.B.	Gillo

Reprinted from
The Chicago Herald Examiner

Nov. 14

STALEYS DEFEAT ISLANDERS, 3-0

Rock Island's powerful eleven lost its second game of the season to the Staleys yesterday afternoon at Cub Park, 3 to 0. "Dutch" Sternaman, former Illinois star halfback, booted a field goal from placement during the second quarter. The Sternaman family is in the field goal limelight the last few days, "Dutch's" brother, the little Illinois quarterback, hoisting two drop kicks over against the Maroons at Urbana Saturday.

This victory, which made six straight for the Staleys, was gained after the fiercest play of the season. The field was slippery and heavy from recent snowstorms, and line plunging featured. The Staleys used their heavy backfield men owing to the conditions, Bolan, ex-Purdue, being at fullback most of the afternoon and Lanum, former Illinois, at halfback alongside of Sternaman. Pete Stinchcomb was in only a brief time, Pard Pearce covering the quarterback job.

Visitors Fight Hard.

The Independents put up a splendid fight, with Conzelman, ex-Great Lake star, and Johnson, formerly of the Municipal Pier eleven, leading in the attacks. Conzelman was in nearly every play.

Rock Island had the ball frequently in the Staley territory, but the local line would stiffen when threatened seriously. A penalty in the last few moments was costly to the Independents. They had the ball on the Staley 15-yard line when a substitute guard, coming in for Rock Island, made the mistake of talking to his mates before a play was run off. This cost the Independents 15 yards in a penalty. After a couple of tries at the forward pass Rock Island fumbled on the 18-yard line, and the whistle blew shortly afterward.

Sternaman changed his shoes on the field to kick a goal. He missed one from the 23-yard line. But, after Rock Island fumbled and lost the ball on the first play at the 20-yard line, Sternaman tried again from almost the same spot, and it went over for the only score of the game.

Ball Hard to Handle.

Ken Huffine, Staley star fullback, had his wind knocked out early in the battle, and Bolan, another ex-Purdue man, substituted for him.

The ball was slippery and soggy, being hard to handle. As a result there were several fumbles, and the punts didn't carry far. Pearce gave a fine exhibition of handling punts, grabbing one that was going over his head.

Several hundred fans from Rock Island accompanied the Independents and there was a lot of cheering.

Lineup:

STALEYS (3).		ROCK ISLAND (0).
Chamberlain	L. E.	Wenig
Scott	L. T.	Travis
Taylor	L. G.	Lyle
Trafton	C.	Karps
Smith	R. G.	Keefe
Blacklock	R. T.	Hoaly
Halas	R. E.	Smith
Pearce	Q. B.	Conzelman
Sternaman	L. H	Novak
Lanum	R. H.	Brigeford
Huffine	F. B	Gavin

Goal from placement—Sternaman.

Reprinted from
The Chicago Herald Examiner

Nov. 21

Staleys Win! Stinchcomb Scoring Touchdown

PETE STINCHCOMB treated the rooters at the Cub park yesterday afternoon to some of the thrillers that made him an all-American halfback with Ohio State. The former Buckeye got two of the touchdowns in the 22-to-7 triumph the Staleys registered over the Cleveland Tigers, one of them being featured by an eighty-yard run.

Because of the heavy and slippery field it was difficult for the backs to get away on many long runs, but this didn't seem to affect Stinchcomb. He was easily the feature of the day. His first touchdown came early in the second period. The Tigers had kicked across the Staley goal line and, on the first play from the 20-yard line, Stinchcomb started a wide end run, broke away from a sea of tacklers and went the 80 yards with several Tigers in full pursuit.

During the third quarter, after a series of gains, a forward pass, Huffine to Sternaman, was good for 20 yards, putting the ball on Cleveland's 10-yard line. A spread play was called for and Stinchcomb raced across the line. He was tackled as he dove across, fumbled the ball, but Pearce fell on it for the touchdown. Shortly afterward Cleveland got busy, a forward pass, Guyon to Calac, carrying the pigskin to Staley's 3-yard line. Calac then plunged over for the touchdown.

In the fourth quarter Sternaman booted a place kick from the field from the 35-yard line and shortly afterward Stinchcomb made the last touchdown of the game on a short end run. Lineup:

STALEYS.		CLEVELAND.
Chamberlain	L.E.	Corcoran
Scott	L.T.	O'Connor
Taylor	L.G.	Pearlman
Trafton	C.	Tandy
Smith	R.G.	Murphy
Blacklock	R.T.	Lowe
Halas	R.E.	Baujaum
Pearce	Q.B.	Brower
Sternaman	L.H.	Haas
Stinchcomb	R.H.	Guyon
Huffine	F.B.	Calac

Referee — Cahn, Chicago. Umpire — Thomas, Purdue. Head linesman—Whitlock, Chicago. Touchdowns—Stinchcomb (2), Pearce, Calac. Field goal—Sternaman. Goals after touchdowns—Guyon, Sternaman.

Reprinted from
The Chicago Herald Examiner

Dec. 12

STALEYS SPLASH WAY TO 10 TO 0 VICTORY

STERNAMAN AND CHAMBERLIN ARE DECATUR STARS

GUY CHAMBERLIN

PLAYING in a rainstorm and on a sea of mud, the Staleys made good as national pro champions by blanking the powerful Canton Bulldogs, 10 to 0, yesterday afternoon at the Cub Park. Up to this battle the Bulldogs had been beaten only once all season and had held the Buffalo All-Americans to a tie. A fair-sized crowd braved the weather. Twice before this Fall Canton had been unable to play here because of the mud, once with the Staleys and once with the Cardinals.

Fast play was impossible, the players sliding and wallowing almost ankle deep in the mud. After three or four plays the numbers on the backs of the men were obliterated, and it was almost impossible to tell friend from foe.

In spite of this there was little time taken out for injuries. Big Trafton, the Staley's great center, was hurt before the teams lined up, diving at the Bulldog who had received the initial kickoff, and being forced to leave the game. As a result the battle between him and Feeney, the Canton center, both old Notre Dame stars, failed to materialize.

No Score Till Late.

Both of the Staley scores came in the last half. "Dutch" Sternaman booting the wet pigskin across the bar on a place kick and Chamberlin receiving a forward pass from Harley while standing behind the Canton goal line.

It was a battle of great lines, with plunges featuring. End runs were nigh an impossibility, as the fleet backs, like "Pete" Stinchcomb,

"Chick" Harley and "Pie" Way, three All-American halfbacks, couldn't get footing. The best sprint of the afternoon was "Chick" Harley's run of eight yards when he started the play at the opening of the third quarter. Stinchcomb worked the first half and Harley the second. They did all the punting for the Staleys, and both were in rare form considering the water-soaked ball.

"Dutch" Misses Kick.

Neither side could do much in the first half. Once "Pete" Henry fumbled a bad pass on a punt, and the Staleys got possession of it. This happened on the Bulldogs' 30-yard line, and "Dutch" Sternaman tried for a place kick, but missed.

In the second quarter "Pie" Way replaced Smith of Centre at left half and did some brilliant work from then on. Towards the end of this period Stinchcomb punted to the Canton 4-yard line, where the ball was fumbled and George Halas recovered it. The Bulldog line showed its caliber here by throwing back three assaults. A forward pass failed just before the half ended.

The Staleys worked the ball down the field after the kickoff in the third quarter, Harley's run and a short forward pass, with some short plunges off tackle and through the line, placing it on the Canton 20-yard line. It was here that Sternaman changed his shoes and booted the goal for 3 points from the 25-yard line.

Harley Tosses One.

A little later the Staleys gained possession of the ball at the Canton 12-yard line. The quarter ended here, but when the fourth was started Harley tossed one for twelve yards to End Chamberlin for a touchdown. Sternaman kicked the goal, making the score: Staleys, 10; Canton, 0.

The lineup:

STALEYS (10).		CANTON (0.)
Chamberlin	L.E.	Steele
Scott	L.T.	Speck
Taylor	L.G.	Griffith
Trafton	C.	Feeney
Smith	R.G.	Osburn
Blacklock	R.T.	Henry
Halas	R.E.	Blackford
Pearce	Q.B.	Robb
Sternaman	L.H.	Smith
Stinchcomb	R.H.	Griggs
Huffine	F.B.	Falcon

Substitutions—Mintun for Trafton, Harley for Stinchcomb, Bolan for Huffine, Way for Smith. Touchdown—Chamberlin. Goal after touchdown—Sternaman. Field goal—Sternaman. Referee—Lambert, Oberlin. Umpire—Thomas, Purdue. Head linesman—Whitlock, Chicago.

Reprinted from
The Chicago Herald Examiner.

Dec. 19

STALEYS-CARDS FAIL TO SCORE

CHICAGO'S pro football title remains undecided as a result of yesterday's 0 to 0 game between the national champion Staleys and the Cardinals at the Cub Park. Several thousand shivering rooters braved the cold to see one of the hardest fought battles of the season. Fast play was difficult, as the field was covered with a layer of snow and the footing underneath was treacherous.

Three times the Cardinals failed at a field goal and the Staleys, within easy striking distance, lost the ball on downs when a forward pass was incomplete. These were the only scoring possibilities during the afternoon.

During a good share of the time the Cardinals kept the ball in the Staley territory, due largely to Paddy Driscoll's superb play. The Staleys had much of their strength out of the game, Center Trafton being forced to sit on the side line due to an injury in the Canton battle. Fullback Huffine didn't play and Dutch Sternaman was unable to make many of his slashing runs because of a limp.

There was a lot of excellent work in the rival lines. Buckeye, the Cardinal right guard, loomed up brilliantly, as did also the two visiting ends, Sachs and O'Connor. McMahon, the great Harvard quarterback, carried the ball several times on a fake play, hitting the line with much power.

Backfield Handicapped.

Chick Harley and Pete Stinchcomb, the Ohio All-American halfbacks, were unable to get going for any big distances, being handicapped by the field. They tore off a few short gains and Harley did some nice punting.

Toward the end of the battle the Cardinals opened up an overhead game and had fair success, three straight forward passes gaining a total of thirty yards. Sachs and O'Connor were on the receiving end.

After the ball had been worked back and forth during the first quarter the Cards finally reached the Staley 30-yard line, where McMahon's try at a place kick was blocked. In the second quarter a Staley fumble at their own 20-yard line gave the ball to the Cards. The latter lost it a couple of plays later on a fumble. After an exchange of punts and still another kick Paddy Driscoll essayed a drop kick from the Staley 35-yard line at a difficult angle and missed. A forward pass, Driscoll to Steger, advanced the ball to the Staley 25-yard line a few minutes later, and McMahon tried a place kick, which went astray.

Staleys' Big Chance.

A fumble at the Cardinal 20-yard line in the third quarter gave the Staleys their chance. Harley and Stinchcomb got away with a short forward pass, but the opportunity to score vanished when an incomplete pass lost them the ball on downs.

Several forward passes, added to some plunges, carried the ball down to the Staley 30-yard line in the fourth quarter, where another try at a field goal failed.

The lineup:

STALEYS		CARDINALS
Chamberlin	L.E.	Sachs
Scott	L.T.	Ietilke
Taylor	L.G.	Voght
Mintun	C.	Rydzewski
Smith	R.G.	Buckeye
Blacklock	R.T.	McInerney
Halas	R.E.	O'Connor
Pearce	Q.B.	McMahon
Stern'n, Stinch b	L.H.	Driscoll
Harley	R.H.	Steger
Bolan	F.B.	Koehler

Referee—Cahn, Chicago. Umpire—Moore, Boston Tech. Head linesman—Whitlock, Chicago.

Reprinted from
The Chicago Herald Examiner

1921

	W	L	T	Pct.
Chi. Bears*	10	1	1	.909
Buffalo	9	1	2	.900
Akron	7	2	1	.778
Green Bay	6	2	2	.750
Canton	4	3	3	.571
Dayton	4	3	1	.571
Rock Island	5	4	1	.556
Chi. Cardinals	2	3	2	.400
Cleveland	2	6	0	.250
Rochester	2	6	0	.250
Detroit	1	7	1	.125
Columbus	0	6	0	.000
Cincinnati	0	8	0	.000

*Staleys

PRO GRIDDERS TO SHUN COLLEGIANS

National Football Association to Punish Clubs Tampering With Students.

(Plain Dealer Special)

CANTON, O., Jan. 28.—The college football player whose student days are not ended, is not wanted by moguls of professional teams, who met here in annual session tonight and changed the name of the organization from the National Professional Football Association to the National Football Association.

Drastic legislation was penned by franchise holders and one franchise held by Green Bay, Wis., was canceled following apologies by representatives of that town for violating the rule, prohibiting the playing of collegians, while still enrolled as students. Green Bay was the only team that abused the rule in 1921. The new rule covering collegians binds the professional teams to post $1,000 which reverts to the league treasury if a violation is proved. The offending team's franchise automatically is forfeited. Teams were pledged not to negotiate with players during their college year.

Philadelphia is the new unit of the association. At the next meeting in May, action will be announced on applications for franchises from Racine, Wis.; Milwaukee, Duluth, Toledo and Sioux City, all being represented here.

The following cities are enrolled for the 1922 campaign: Chicago (two teams), Buffalo, Philadelphia, Rochester, Washington, New York, Canton, Akron, Dayton, Columbus, Cleveland, Cincinnati, Toledo, Muncie, Louisville, Evansville, Detroit, Minneapolis, Rock Island and Decatur.

Joseph F. Carr of Columbus was re-elected president with James Dunn of Minneapolis, vice president, and Carl Storck of Dayton, secretary and treasurer. President Carr was empowered to name officials for games. Carr also will map out 1922 schedules.

Reprinted from
The Cleveland Plain Dealer

Nov. 13

Thorpe Scores; Still Wonder

Chicago—Post-graduate football fans at the Cub park Sunday were treated to an unexpected thrill when Jim Thorpe played the greater part of the second half for his Oorang Indians and scored a touchdown on the Chicago Bears. Although the Indians were finally beaten, 33 to 6, they looked like a real football eleven when Indian Jim was in.

Four former Carlisle captains were in the lineup during the rainy afternoon—Thorpe, Joe Guyon, Center Busch and Pete Calac. And their trainer, John Morrison, was the first of the Carlisle captains.

Rarely has the presence of one player made so great a difference as when Thorpe went in. It seemed as if his team improved fully 50 per cent. Their defense stiffened and they started carrying the ball down the field. Thorpe took it many times himself, and showed he can forward pass.

A picturesque element was inserted in the battle when Thorpe crossed the Bear line in the final quarter, carrying the ball 10 yards in three wallops in spite of the fiercest efforts to check him. Six Dakota braves, garbed in war bonnets and paint, who had put on some dances before the pastime, ran on the field and gloatingly went through an original snake dance.

The Bears started as if they were going to roll up an enormous score. The Indians fumbled the initial kickoff, and the ball was recovered by the Bears at the Oorang 40-yard line. Several line plays followed. Dutch Sternaman crashed 18 yards off tackle, and Joe Sternaman finally broke through the line for a touchdown. Dutch Sternaman kicked goal for the extra point. The Bears continued the fierce attack until the third quarter.

Reprinted from
The Milwaukee Journal

Nov. 13

Many Stars on Thorpe's Team

Two of the heaviest and fastest half backs in the post graduate football league are Joe Guyon and Attache of the Oorang Indians, who clash with the Milwaukee Badgers at the Athletic park Sunday. Guyon, former Georgia Tech star, weighs 190 pounds and Attache is five pounds lighter. Guyon had the advantage of playing in the east and came to Walter Camp's attention, receiving high honors on the all-American while with the Golden Tornadoes. Attache went to the little known Sherman Indian school of Riverside, Calif., but he was so great a halfback that he was picked out on the all-Pacific coast eleven. Jim Thorpe, former Carlisle all-around wonder in Athletics has passed his active playing life in football, but he has coached the Oorangs in many of the tricks that made him famous. There is a second edition of Thorpe on the eleven in the person of Long Time Sleep, the 195-pound right tackle from the Flathead tribe of Montana. Long Time Sleep doesn't live up to his name, being one of the greatest all-around athletes living. Not only did he show proficiency in football both at Carlisle and Haskell, but he is a noted baseball, la crosse and hockey player and boxer. His English name is Nicholas Lassley and during the war he served overseas with an Indian detachment.

Reprinted from
The Milwaukee Journal

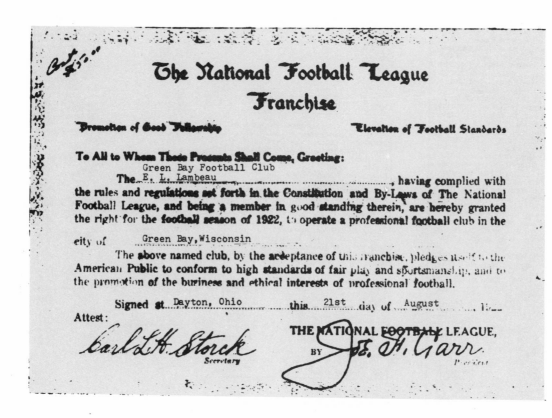

The National Football League
Franchise

Promotion of Good Fellowship   Elevation of Football Standards

To All to Whom These Presents Shall Come, Greeting:

The Green Bay Football Club
E. L. Lambeau _____, having complied with the rules and regulations set forth in the Constitution and By-Laws of The National Football League, and being a member in good standing therein, are hereby granted the right for the football season of 1922, to operate a professional football club in the

city of Green Bay, Wisconsin

The above named club, by the acceptance of this franchise, pledges itself to the American Public to conform to high standards of fair play and sportsmanship, and to the promotion of the business and ethical interests of professional football.

Signed at Dayton, Ohio _____ this 21st day of August ____

Attest:

Carl L. H. Storck
Secretary

THE NATIONAL FOOTBALL LEAGUE,
BY Jos. F. Carr
President

2,000 NOBLE FANS WATCH CARDS WIN

BY LAMBERT G. SULLIVAN.

PADDY DRISCOLL

WHILE the boys were in the dressing room last night digging the mud out of their eyes and ears with shoe horns, Paddy Driscoll remarked to Bob Koehler:

"We certainly must like this game to play a day like this."

"Yeh," replied Bob. "But how about those guys who sat up in the grandstand all afternoon?"

Which summarizes perfectly yesterday's 7 to 0 victory won by the Chicago Cardinals over the Akron Indians at Comiskey Park. When you see a vaudeville act in which the trained seals play on the mouth organ, you don't exclaim over the beauty of the music but you do marvel that it is music at all. Just so, yesterday, after watching the Cardinal-Indian game, you didn't marvel over the quality of football but that it was played at all.

Cold in Grand Stand.

But you marvelled more than anything else that 2,000 hardy sportsmen could congeal through two hours in the grandstand, which was wet as a widow's tears and cold as a landlord's heart.

Ordinarily, when writing a football story, it is customary to pick out the heroes of the day. But inasmuch as Chris O'Brien neglected to give us a list of persons who sat in the grand stand, this story will have to content itself with anonimity in heroes.

Just let it go as the "Noble 2,000."

Driscoll Spears Pass.

Paddy Driscoll's good right ear was responsible for the only score of the game. Along toward the end of the second quarter, A. McMahon, standing on his 40-yard line, shot out a forward pass. Two Indians were standing where the ball was about to drop when suddenly out of nowhere Driscoll appeared, and, leaping high, he speared the ball.

With a clear field in front of him Paddy started for the goal, but Jean, a tackle for the Indians, proved even fleeter of foot than the nimble Paddy. Hot after Driscoll, he was close enough at the 10-yard line to essay a flying tackle.

Straight and true, he flashed into the flying Paddy. The two went up into the air; Paddy came down on his ear on the 5-yard line and triumphantly slid and slithered through the foot-deep mud to and across the goal line for the only score of the day.

It was a bit hard on Paddy's ear, but it was a noble victory, nevertheless.

CARDINALS (7).		AKRON (0)
Egan	L. E.	Daum
Rundquist	L. T.	Spiers
Zola	L. G.	Jean
McInerney	R. G.	Flowers
Buckeye	C.	Nesser
Gilles	R. T.	Jolley
Anderson	R. E.	Corcoran
A. McMahon	Q. B.	Sheeks
Driscoll	L. H.	Kramer
Bryan	R. H.	Mills
Koehler	F. B.	King

Score by periods:

Cardinals	0	0	7	0—7
Akron	0	0	0	0—0

Touchdowns—Driscoll. Point after touchdown—Drop kick by Driscoll. Substitutes—Cards, Sachs for Egan, Brennan for Zola, Leonard for Gilles; Akron, Neale for Spiers, Steele for Sheeks. Referee—Starkey. Umpire—Holway. Head linesman—Mallory.

Nov. 27

Green Bay Is Victor, 13 to 0

Green Bay — Milwaukee's highly touted Badger professional football team went down in decisive defeat here Sunday before the Green Bay Blues, by a score of 13 to 0.

The local team showed its superiority at practically all stages of the game. In the fourth quarter alone was Milwaukee able to make consistent gains and their rush in this period ended when a Badger forward pass was intercepted near the 25-yard line.

Green Bay's first touchdown came as the direct result of a succession of clever forward passes, the last of which, a toss from Lambeau to Mathys, netted 40 yards and placed the ball on Milwaukee's 4-yard line. Lambeau smashed his way through on the first play and kicked the goal.

Milwaukee punt was blocked early in the fourth period in the shadow of the visitors' goal posts and on the second play Lambeau went over for a touchdown, subsequently missing the goal.

The superior play of the Green Bay line, Cub Buck's great punting and the Bays' wonderful passing, were accountable for Milwaukee's defeat.

The teams lined up as follows:

GREEN BAY [13]		MILWAUKEE [0]
Hayes	L. E.	Lallon
Buck	L. T.	Webb
Woodin	L. G.	Tomlin
Niemann	C.	Pierrotti
Lyle	R. G.	Duffy
Earps	R. T.	Alexander
Howard	R. E.	Robeson
Mathys	Q.	Conzelman
Usher	L. H.	Purdy
Lambeau	R. H.	Green
Mills	F.	Doane

Referee—Cahn, Chicago. Umpire—Sylvester, Appleton. Head linesman—Poettger, Kenosha. Linesman—Bernhardt, Green Bay, and Mooney, Milwaukee. Timers—Abrams, Green Bay, and M. McGuirk, Milwaukee. Time of period—13 minutes. Substitutions—Milwaukee: Collins for Fallon; Green Bay: Wheeler for Hayes, Hayes for Howard, Nadolny for Woodin, Gardner for Lyle, Lauer for Mathys.

Score by periods:

Green Bay	0	7	0	6—13
Milwaukee	0	0	0	0—0

Touchdowns—Lambeau, 2; goal kicks after touchdown, Lambeau, 1.

Dec. 11

Chicago—If there was any question about the post-graduate football championship of Chicago the Cardinals settled it Sunday at White Sox park, walloping the Chicago Bears, 9 to 0. Paddy Driscoll, star of the Cards, kicked three goals from the field.

Whenever the Bears got their powerful attack started it seemed as if somebody would fumble and then Paddy Driscoll would punt the ball out of danger. Paddy was very much in evidence, making a field goal in each of the first three quarters.

The stars of the battle, outside of Driscoll, were Healey, the Bears' Dartmouth lineman, and E. Anderson, the Notre Dame end of the Cards.

The lineup:

BEARS		CARDINALS (9)
Halas, Englund	R. E.	E. Anderson
Blacklock	R. T.	Rundquist
La Fleur	R. G.	Buckeye
Larson	C.	McInerney
Healey	L. G.	Brennan
Scott	L. T.	Gilles
Garvey	L. E.	Egan
Pearce	Q.	A. McMahon
J. Sternaman, Walquist	R. H.	Mohardt
Stinchcomb, E. Sternaman	L. H.	Driscoll
Lanum, Bolan	F.	Koehler

Goals from field—Driscoll, 3. Referee—Cahn (Chicago). Umpire—Kagy (Western Reserve). Head linesman—Eckstrom (Dartmouth).

CANTON WINS OVER TOLEDO; CLAIMS TITLE

Bulldogs Slash Way to 18 to 0 Victory in Pro Grid Game at Toledo.

GUY CHAMBERLIN

TOLEDO, Dec. 10.—The Canton Bulldogs claimed the national professional football championship of the United States here this afternoon when they closed the national professional football league season by defeating the fast Toledo Maroon eleven, 18 to 0. The Canton Bulldogs finished their season with a 1,000 percentage, winning all their games but two, the Toledo Maroons and the Dayton Triangles both playing tie games with Canton. The Bulldogs completely outclassed the Maroons in today's clash, although the Toledo eleven was made up entirely of former college stars.

The Maroons never had a look in, only three times making first down. Chamberlain, Henry and Sacksteder starred for Canton, while the Steen Brothers, Tanner and Horning, put up a clever defensive game for the Maroons.

Henry's wonderful kicking was one of the features of the game. Twice he drop kicked goals, once from the 45-yard line in the first quarter and again from the 40-yard line in the final quarter. In the second period Canton made a touchdown on a long, beautiful executed forward pass, Smythe to Chamberlain followed by a line buckle by Elliott.

Canton made another touchdown in the fourth quarter on a long forward pass, Sacksteder to Chamberlain, Chamberlain going over for the touchdown. Lineup:

TOLEDO (0).		CANTON (18)
King	L. E.	Chamberlin
Kelly	R. T.	Henry
R. Stein	L. G.	Osborne
Conrad	C.	Speck
H. Stein	R. G.	Taylor
Horning	R. T.	Lyman
Kendrick	R. E.	Carroll
Simpson	Q. B.	Roberts
Roberts	L. H.	Griggs
Phelan	R. H.	McQuade
Falcon	F. B.	Elliott

Touchdowns — Chamberlain, Elliott. Goal from drop kick—Henry (2). Referee—Lambert. Umpire—Pfeffer. Head linesman—Schults. Substitutions—Tanner for Falcon. Stacksteder for Gregg.

World's Champions

CANTON BULLDOGS

1922

LONG PASSES WIN GAME FOR CANTON

Hammond Unable to Register First Down Against Bulldogs.

(Plain Dealer Special)

CANTON, O., Sept. 30.—The Canton Bulldogs, national professional champions, defeated Hammond, Ind., 17-0, here today, in the opening league game of the season. The stout line of the locals was too much for the visitors, who failed to register a first down during the entire game. In forward passing they were as unsuccessful.

Wilbur Henry, roly-poly tackle from W. and J., starred again for the local team. Time and again he halted the Hammond players without a gain or threw them for losses while on the offense he made holes for the backfield in addition to making substantial gains by carrying the ball himself. He scored the first Canton points by drop-kicking from the thirty-seven-yard line.

Close second to Henry was Louie Smith, Centre college graduate, who was responsible for Canton's touchdowns. He threw a pass of twenty-six yards to Griggs to score the first touchdown in the third period and in the fourth period passes of thirty and twenty-eight yards, the latter to Carroll, accounted for the other markers.

Comstock, Conover and Roderick also played stellar games. "Inky" Williams was the big noise for Hammond. He was the only visitor who could halt the Cantonians. Hammond showed a fairly stout line, and only nine first downs were made by the Bulldogs, four of these through forward passes.

Canton—17.	Position.	Hammond—0.
Chamberlain	L. E.	Williams
Lyman	L. T.	Tallant
Comstock	L. G.	Seibert
Conover	C.	Olts
Speck	R. G.	Berry
Henry	R. T.	Usher
Carroll	R. E.	Hanke
Roberts	Q.	Pollard
Robb	L. H.	Hess
Roderick	R. H.	Ditweiler
Elliott	F.	Knopp

Substitutions—Canton: L. Smith for Robb, Osborne for Speck, Jones for Elliott, Griggs for Roderick, R. Smith for Osborne, Griggs for Carroll, Roderick for Griggs, Elliott for Jones. Hammond: Sullivan for Hess, Gearing for Ditweiler, Larson for Gearing, Lovaczy for Usher, Gearing for Larson, Ditweiler for Gearing, Hess for Ditweiler, Larson for Hess.
Touchdowns—Carroll, Griggs. Points from touchdowns—Henry (drop kicks) 2. Drop kick—Henry, 37-yard line.
Referee—Durfee (Williams.) Umpire—Bletzer (Mount Union). Head linesman—Wad (Carnegie).

Reprinted from
The Cleveland Plain Dealer

CANTON BULLDOGS WALLOP TRIANGLES

Defeat Dayton Eleven, 30 to 0, in Third Successive Victory of Season.

CANTON, O., Oct. 14.—The Canton Bulldogs successfully defended the national pro football championship 30 to 0 here this afternoon against the Dayton Triangles. It was the third straight victory for Canton, which team has not yet been scored upon.

Sensational open field running by Robb and Griggs and Henry's dropkicking featured for Canton. Henry registered twelve of Canton's points, dropkicking from field three times and adding the extra points from touchdowns the same number of times.

Canton—30.	Position.	Dayton—0.
Chamberlain	L. E.	Thiele
Lyman	L. T.	Hathaway
Comstock	L. G.	Dellinger
Conover	C.	A. Kinderdine
Williams	R. G.	Berns
Henry (W. & J.)	R. T.	Sauers
Mullin	R. E.	Reese
Robb	Q.	Abbott
Smith	L. H.	Bacon
Roderick	R. H.	Partlow
Elliott	F.	Huffine
Canton		3 10 3 14—30

Substitutions—Canton: Griggs for Roderick, Roberts for Robb, Jones for Elliott, Speck for Williams, Carroll for Mullin. Dayton: Fenner for Thiele, Beasley for Dellinger, B. Kinderdine for Huffine, Thiele for Fenner.
Touchdowns—Griggs 2, Elliott. Points from touchdown—Henry (drop kicks) 3. Drop kicks—Henry 3 (38-yard line, 35-yard line, 45-yard line).
Referee—Otis. Umpire—Bletzer (Mount Union). Head linesman—Wade (Carnegie). Timekeeper—McGregor (Mount Union). Time of periods—15m.

Reprinted from
The Cleveland Plain Dealer

Oct. 29

Aerial Attack Beats Packers

Green Bay—Outclassing the Packers at their own game, forward passing, the Racine Legion uncorked a superb overhead attack and defeated the Packers, 24 to 3, in a pro-league game here Sunday before a big crowd. It was the worst defeat ever suffered by the Green Bay team.

The Legion was first to score. Hank Gillo getting a field goal toward the close of the opening quarter. Late in the second period, Barr passed to Romney, who ran for a touchdown.

Early in the second half, Halladay grabbed a snappy toss from Barr and another touchdown resulted. Then Cub Buck kicked a field goal for the Packers. In the fourth period, Elliott was on the receiving end of a touchdown throw from Barr.

The Packers died with their boots on and several times they held for downs on their three yard line. Barr, Elliott and Halladay played brilliantly for Racine.

The Legion's win over the Packers puts Racine on the top of the heap in the race for the state pro title, which is now held by the Green Bay team.

Lineup:

GREEN BAY		RACINE
Gray	L. E.	Meyers
Buck	L. T.	Braman
Woodin	L. G.	Gorman
Niemann	C.	Mintun
Gardner	R. G.	Tong
Earps	R. T.	Smith
Wheeler	R. E.	Hallac
Mathys	Q. B.	Ba
Basing	L. H.	Ellio
Lambeau	R. H.	Romne
Gavin	F. B.	Gill

Referee, Whyte, Milwaukee; umpire, White, Green Bay; head linesman, Coffeen, Beloit.
Touchdowns—Elliott, Romney, Halladay. Goals after touchdowns—Gillo, 3. Field goals—Gillo, Buck.

Reprinted from
The Milwaukee Journal

Oct. 1

Badgers Beat Thorpe Eleven

Playing the best brand of professional football seen here in years, the newly organized Milwaukee Badgers Sunday defeated Jim Thorpe's Indians, 13 to 2. The Indians' lone score resulted from a safety made on a Badger fumble.

Jimmy Conzelman, quarter and captain of the Badgers, showed great form in both open and field running, passing and generalship. Milwaukee has a well-balanced team. With a line that averages around the 210-pound mark and a backfield of merit, Sunday's opener was a sign that the Badgers will be strong contenders for professional honors this season.

Doane, Mooney and Erickson, in their respective backfield positions, gave fans their money's worth when they tore through the redmen's line and raced round their ends and for long gains. Doane played in exceptional form for this early in the season.

Milwaukee scored its first touchdown when Winkleman, end, intercepted one of Thorpe's forward passes and raced 35 yards through a broken field to a score. Conzelman kicked goal. The second score resulted from a series of line plunges that took Conzelman over for a touchdown.

In the last half Thorpe brought spectators to their feet with the greatest kick ever seen on a Milwaukee gridiron. Jim, punting from the Indian goal line, sent the sphere hurtling 75 yards through the air. Calac, hefty Indian back, tore away to several good gains and showed himself a good man on defense.

A crowd of 4,000 witnessed the game. Next Sunday the Badgers play the strong Columbus Tigers.

MILWAUKEE (13)		OORANGS (2)
R.E.	Winkleman	Woodchuck L.E.
R.T.	Vassau	Big Bear L.T.
R.G.	Underwood	Lone Wolf L.G.
C.	Larsen	Long Time Sleep. C.
L.G.	Nadolney	Buffalo R.G.
L.T.	Blailock	Little Twig R.T.
L.E.	Sachs	Calac R.E.
Q.	Conzelman	Red Fox Q.
R.H.	Erickson	Thorpe L.H.
L.H.	Mooney	Tomahawk R.H.
F.	Doane	Eagle Feather F.

Touchdowns—Conzelman, Winkleman. Safety—Conzelman. Goal from touchdown—Conzelman.

Reprinted from
The Milwaukee Journal

1923

	W	L	T	Pct.
Canton	11	0	1	1.000
Chi. Bears	9	2	1	.818
Green Bay	7	2	1	.778
Milwaukee	7	2	3	.778
Cleveland	3	1	3	.750
Chi. Cardinals	8	4	0	.667
Duluth	4	3	0	.571
Buffalo	5	4	3	.556
Columbus	5	4	1	.556
Racine	4	4	2	.500
Toledo	2	3	2	.400
Rock Island	2	3	3	.400
Minneapolis	2	5	2	.286
St. Louis	1	4	2	.200
Hammond	1	5	1	.167
Dayton	1	6	1	.143
Akron	1	6	0	.143
Marion	1	10	0	.091
Rochester	0	2	0	.000
Louisville	0	3	0	.000

Sept. 22

Packers Defeat Chicago Bears

BY SPECIAL CORRESPONDENT OF THE JOURNAL
Green Bay—The Green Bay Packers defeated the Chicago Bears here Sunday, 5 to 0, in a bitterly-contested football argument before a capacity crowd. Hanny was dumped behind his own goal line for a safety in the second quarter, while Cub Buck booted a placement between the uprights for the Packers in the fourth period.

The lineup:

PACKERS		BEARS
Milton	L. E.	Hanny
Buck	L. T.	Scott
Woodin	L. G.	Anderson
Earps	C.	Trafton
Cadner	R. G.	Lafour
Rosatti	R. T.	Blacklock
Voss	R. E.	Halas
Mathys	Q.	J. Sternaman
Basing	L. H.	E. Sternaman
Lambeau	R. H.	Walquist
Hendrix	F.	Knopp

Substitutions—Packers: Lewellen for Basing; O'Donnell for Milton; Cassing for Lewellen; Bears, England for Hanny; Healy for Scott; O'Connell for Trafton; Hurst for Lafour; Mullen for Halas; Bryan for J. Sternaman; Hendrick for E. Sternaman; Greenwood for Walquist; Bolan for Knopp.

Sept. 29

Racine Scores Win in Opener

BY SPECIAL CORRESPONDENT OF THE JOURNAL
Racine—The National League Football association season was officially ushered in here Sunday with the Racine Legion winning from Hammond, 10 to 0.

While the game lacked many of the thrills so common on the grid, it suggested that the local eleven will be a factor to be considered in the pro title chase this fall. The Racine line was especially impressive, Hammond's three downs all being made on passes. The Legionaires made their downs six times.

"Death" Halliday scored a touchdown in the first quarter on a pass from Elliott and "Shorty" Barr drop kicked in the closing period.

"Rowdy" Elliott led the Racine attack, with "Chuck" Palmer and Milton Romney, while the defensive play of Halliday, "Kibo" Krumm and Don Murray stood forth. "Inky" Williams' receiving of passes featured Hammond's play.

Sept. 29

Rock Island Holds Bears to 0-0 Tie

Rock Island, Ill.—With Jim Thorpe, world famous Indian athlete, starring in the backfield, the Rock Island Independents held the Chicago Bears to a scoreless tie here Sunday. The Bears kept Rock Island on the defensive the entire first half and threatened to score several times, but lost the ball on downs.

Joe Sternaman missed a try for a field goal by a few inches in the second period. In the second half the Independents came back strong and with consistent line plunges by Thorpe advanced the ball to the 20-yard mark, where the Bears' defense tightened. Punts were regularly exchanged thereafter, with neither side having a distinct advantag.

Sept. 29

Driscoll Beats Badgers, 17-7

BY SPECIAL CORRESPONDENT OF THE JOURNAL
Chicago—The Milwaukee Badgers dropped their first game of the season here Sunday, losing to the Chicago Cardinals, 17 to 7. Paddy Driscoll was the shining light for the victors, scoring 11 points and paving the way to the others.

The teams battled on even terms until one minute before the first half ended. Driscoll then booted a place kick between the uprights from the 52-yard line.

The Badgers took a new lease on life in the third period and scored a touchdown when Conzelman shot a pass to Erickson and the latter, twisting through a broken field, ran 45 yards for a touchdown.

The break came after the next play. After the Badgers kicked off, Driscoll punted, the ball touched Conzelman and Hanke fell on it, over the goal line, for a touchdown.

Desperate, the Badgers opened up with passes in the last period and one of them fell into the arms of King, Cardinal half, who carried it to the Badgers' 3-yard line before being downed. Two line tries failed but a third, with Driscoll carrying the ball, gained the touchdown.

Oct. 27

Chicago Cards Lose

BY SPECIAL CORRESPONDENT OF THE JOURNAL
Chicago—Hammond, Ind., Sunday afternoon defeated the Chicago Cardinals in a professional league game, 6 to 3. This put the Cardinals out of the race for first place.

Butler, the negro star from Dubuque, was the best player on the field. He was the only one that made consistent gains. Driscoll was stopped dead and failed to gain more than a yard during the whole game.

Oct. 6

PRO GRIDDERS USHER IN SEASON WITH HOT GAME AT DUNN FIELD

Joe Sternaman of Chicago Team Features With Long Runs and Two Touchdowns but All-'round Strength of Clevelanders Prevails.

BY HARRY G. McDAVITT.

THE Cleveland Bulldogs, sole possessors of the world professional football championship, made a spectacular debut before their new home following yesterday afternoon at Dunn Field by defeating the very flashy and unusually powerful Chicago Bears, 16 to 14. †

Cleve. B.—16.	Position.	Chic. B.—14.
Chamberlain	L. E.	Hanny
Lyman	L. T.	Healey
R. Comstock	L. G.	Anderson
Osborne	C.	Trafton
R. Smith	R. G.	McMillan
Muirhead	R. T.	Blacklock
Bierce	R. E.	Halas
Roberts	Q.	J. Sternaman
Workman	L. H.	E. Sternaman
Noble	R. H.	Walquist
Elliott	F.	Knop

Chicago Bears	7	0	7	0—14
Cleveland Bulldogs	3	0	13	0—16

Substitutions—Cleveland: B. Jones for Elliott, Honaker for Chamberlain, Elliott for Workman, Chamberlain for Bierce, O. Smith for Muirhead, Muirhead for Lyman, Workman for Noble, Lyman for Muirhead, Work for Lyman, Wolf for Elliott. Chicago: Mullen for Halas, Scott for Healey, Bryan for S. Sternaman, Kendrick for Walquist, Johnson for Knop, Walquist for Kendrick, Healey for Scott, Knop for Johnson, Halas for Mullen, E. Sternaman for Bryan.

Scoring—First period: Drop kick—Elliott (Cleveland). Touchdown—Joe Sternaman (Chicago). Goal following touchdown (drop kick)—Joe Sternaman (Chicago). Third period: Touchdown—B. Jones (Cleveland). Goal following touchdown (drop kick)—O. Smith (Cleveland). Touchdown—O. Smith (Cleveland). Goal from touchdown missed (drop kick)—Elliott (Cleveland). Fourth period: Touchdown—Joe Sternaman (Chicago). Goal following touchdown (drop kick)—Joe Sternaman (Chicago).

Referee—Dr. F. A. Lambert (O. S. U.) Umpire—Raymond Eichenlaub (Notre Dame). Head linesman—Maj. J. B. Eckstrom (Dartmouth). Field judge—J. L. Pratt.

Time of periods—15m.

AKRON IS BEATEN BY CARDINALS

Paddy Driscoll Boots Two From Field.

CHICAGO, Nov. 16.—Scoring a touchdown and two field goals, the Chicago Cardinals won from Akron today, 13 to 0, in a national pro football battle. Two thousand fans saw the game.

Driscoll tried a field goal from the twenty-yard line in the first period but the ball went wide. In the second and fourth quarters, however, he met with success in his efforts, scoring twice by that method. Akron failed in its attempts to use the aerial method.

Nov. 3

Dunn, Conzelman Star

Chicago — Dunn and Conzelman starred for the visitors as the Milwaukee Badgers downed the Chicago Cardinals, 17 to 8, in a national professional league football game here Sunday afternoon.

Paddy Driscoll was the individual star of the Chicago team. Conzelman, running 95 yards to the Cardinals two-yard line, paved the way for the visitors' first touchdown.

The Cardinals scored a touchdown late in the second quarter on short passes and runs by Driscoll.

A long pass from Dunn to Conzelman placed the ball on the 5-yard line in the third quarter and Dunn took it over. He then kicked goal.

Dunn electrified the stands later by returning one of Driscoll's punts 55 yards before being forced out of bounds.

MILWAUKEE		CHICAGO
Neary	L. E.	McNulty
Widerquist	L. T.	McInerney
Jean	L. G.	Brennan
Larson	C.	Hartong
McGinnis	R. G.	Buckeye
Weller	R. T.	Gillies
Swanson	R. E.	Anderson
Dunn	Q.	Driscoll
Conzelman	L. H.	McErwin
Winkleman	R. H.	Hurlburt
Doane	F.	Koehler

Substitutions: Milwaukee—Mooney for Doane. Chicago—McMahon for Hartong; Clark for Buckeye; Feitz for McMahon; Smith for Driscoll. Touchdowns—Doane, Koehler, Dunn. Points after touchdowns—Dunn, 2. Field goal—Winkleman. Officials—Referee, Roblee; umpire, Engel; head linesman, Holloway.

Packer Pass Beats Racine in Last Period

BY SPECIAL CORRESPONDENT OF THE JOURNAL

Green Bay—A sensational catch of a forward pass by Tillie Voss, after he had been knocked to the ground behind the Racine goal line, enabled the Green Bay Packers to defeat the local Legion eleven, 6 to 3, here Sunday in a thrilling game before a huge crowd.

The touchdown came on the opening play in the fourth quarter. Capt. Lambeau, standing on the 45-yard line, zipped the pigskin to Voss, who collided with Giaver. Tillie went down on his knees, but lunged forward and grabbed the oval, just inches off the ground. Buck missed the goal.

A fumble during the first scrimmage of the game gave Racine the ball on the Packers' 25-yard line and Gillo lost little time in kicking a field goal.

"Cub" Buck's splendid punting featured, he averaged 60 yards.

The lineup:

GREEN BAY		RACINE
Murray-Duford	L. E.	Bramm
Buck	L. T.	Murray
Woodin	L. G.	Bentzin
Earps	C.	Minten
Gardner	R. G.	King
Rosatti	R. T.	Smith
Voss	R. E.	Halliday
Mathys	Q.	Romney
Basing	L. H.	Giaver
Lambeau	R. H.	Elliott-Mohardt
Hendrian	F.	Gillo-Barr

Rock Island Ties Bears

Chicago—Rock Island and the Chicago Bears battled to a 3 to 3 tie here Sunday afternoon in a national professional football league game. Armstrong scored a field goal for the visitors in the second quarter while Joe Sternaman tied the score early in the fourth quarter with a 35-yard kick.

Nov. 24

10,000 Witness Bears in Victory; Referee Banishes Two for Slugging

BY SPECIAL CORRESPONDENT OF THE JOURNAL

Chicago—Joe Sternaman again assumed the hero role for the Chicago Bears here Sunday afternoon, making a 29-yard drop kick that gave the local eleven a 3 to 0 victory over the Green Bay, Wis., Packers in a national pro league football game.

Sternaman's kick came early in the third quarter, after Blacklock, the stellar Bear tackle, recovered Mathys' fumble on Green Bay's 28-yard line. After three plays failed to gain, Sternaman made his kick.

The contest kept the crowd of 10,000 on its toes throughout.

Fumbles and intercepted passes gave the game an uncertainty and it was not until the last few minutes that the result was certain. The game ended with the ball on the Packers' five-yard line, after Kendrick had snared one of Lambeau's heaves.

The Green Bay eleven had only one chance to score. Early in the second quarter, Joe Sternaman dropped a punt and Earps recovered it on the Bears' 18-yard line. The local forward wall held and Buck's placement kick went wild of the goal.

Hanny and Voss were banished from the game by Referee St. Johns after they had started slugging each other.

The lineup:

CHICAGO		GREEN BAY
Hanny	L. E.	O'Donnell
Healey	L. T.	Buck
Lafleur	L. G.	Wooden
Trafton	C.	Earps
McMillen	R. G.	Gardner
Blacklock	R. T.	Rosatti
Mullen	R. E.	Voss
Bryan	Q.	Marthys
Sternaman	L. H.	Lambeau
Kendrick	R. H.	Llewellen
Lanum	F.	Hendrian

Field goal—Joe Sternaman.
Substitutions—Chicago: Joe Sternaman for Bryan, Halas for Mullen, Knop for Lanum, Anderson for Lafleur, Scott for Hanny, Mullen for Scott. Green Bay: Murray for Voss, Basing for Llewellen.

FINAL STANDINGS

Cleveland	7	1	1	.875
Chi. Bears	6	1	4	.857
Frankford	11	2	1	.846
Duluth	5	1	0	.833
Rock Island	6	2	2	.750
Green Bay	8	4	0	.667
Buffalo	6	4	0	.600
Racine	4	3	3	.571
Chi. Cardinals	5	4	1	.556
Columbus	4	4	0	.500
Hammond	2	2	1	.500
Milwaukee	5	8	0	.385
Dayton	2	7	0	.222
Kansas City	2	7	0	.222
Akron	1	6	0	.143
Kenosha	0	5	1	.000
Minneapolis	0	6	0	.000
Rochester	0	7	0	.000

Dec. 8

Chicago Bears Win for Lead

BY SPECIAL CORRESPONDENT OF THE JOURNAL

Chicago—The Chicago Bears steam rollered their way into first place in the National Professional Football league Sunday, by beating the Cleveland Bull Dogs, 23 to 0.

At no time did Cleveland threaten to score. Dutch Sternaman ran 20 yards for the second touchdown. Joe Sternaman made a 30-yard run that paved the way for his field goal.

The lineup:

CHICAGO		CLEVELAND
Hanny	L. E.	Chamberlain
Healy	L. T.	Lyman
Anderson	L. G.	Edwards
Trafton	C.	Osborne
McMillen	R. G.	J. Jones
Blacklock	R. T.	Comstock
Halas	R. E.	Work
J. Sternaman	Q.	Roberts
Ed Sternaman	L. H.	Workman
Walquist	R. H.	B. Jones

Dec. 15

Thorpe Team Defeats Bears

SPECIAL CORRESPONDENT OF THE JOURNAL

Chicago — Jim Thorpe's Rock Islanders won the third game of their series with the Chicago Bears here Sunday, 7 to 6. Twice before this season the teams have tied.

In this game the Indians took an immediate advantage over the champions of the National Professional league and were in the lead throughout. Joe Sternaman made the touchdown for the Chicagoans just two minutes before the end of the game by a sensational plunge and run. But then he failed to make the kick from the 15-yard line and the Islanders won.

The lineup:

ROCK ISLAND		CHICAGO BEARS
Little Twig	L. E.	Mullen
A. Scott	L. T.	Joe Scott
Wiederquist	L. G.	La Fleur
Kolls	C.	Trafton
Thompson	R. G.	McMillen
Slater	R. T.	Blacklock
Swanson	R. E.	Halas
Ursila	Q.	Bryan
Guyon	L. H. B.	Lanum
Bradshaw	R. H. B.	Kendrick
Gavin	F. B.	White

Substitutions — Rock Island, Phelan for Gavin; Bears, Knop for White; E. Sternaman for Lanum; J. Sternaman for Kendick; Walquist for Bryan; Healy for Blacklock; Anderson for La Fleur.
Touchdowns—Swanson, J. Sternaman. Point after Touchdown—Ursella.

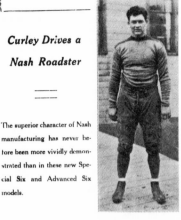
FOUR NEW CLUBS IN PRO LEAGUE

N. Y., Providence, Detroit and Pottsville Taken.

CHICAGO, Aug. 1—(AP)—Four
new clubs were admitted to membership in the national professional
foot ball league at the annual meeting of club members here today, increasing the membership to twenty
clubs.

The new clubs are Providence, R.
I., Pottsville, Pa., New York and
Detroit. Canton, O., was reinstated
after a year's lapse.

The fall schedule will be adopted
tomorrow.

Rock Island in Romp.

ROCK ISLAND, Ill., Nov. 22.—The Rock
Island Independents ran roughshod over the
Milwaukee Badgers in the second half of a
National Professional league football game here
today to annihilate the Wisconsin eleven by a
40 to 7 score.

Rock Island—40. Position. Milwaukee—7.
Littlewig .... L. E. .... Neary
Weiderquist .... L. T. ...... Donnagan
Thompson .... L. G. .... Nadolny
Declerk .... C. .... Traynor
Burton .... R. G. ...... Rydzwsky
Slater .... R. T. .... Brumm
Roemer .... R. E. .... Roester
Armstrong .... Q. .... Mason
Lamb .... L. H. .... Blood
McCarthy .... R. H. .... Bryan
Novak .... F. .... Delaporta
Substitutions Rock Island: Kolls for Little-
twig, Urzella for Novak. Milwaukee: Favey for
Nadolny.
Touchdowns McCarthy, Armstrong 2, Lamb
3, Neary. Points after touchdowns—Lamb 2,
Urzella 2.
Referee Cahn (Chicago). Umpire—Moore
(Kentucky). Head linesman—Morris (Rock
Island). Time of quarters—15m.

Oct. 18

BEHMAN'S PLACEMENT WINS FOR JACKETS

Majestic Boot From 40-Yard Mark Snatches Victory From Bob Folwell's All-American Aggregation; Final Score 5 to 3

EMBOSSED in rich scarlet and blue
hues as befits an all-American
eleven, the New York Giants held
no terrors for the Frankford team as
the Yellowjackets assumed a victorious
pose, 5 to 3, yesterday in a National
League clash at Frankford avenue and
Devereux streets.

Fifteen thousand swept into the
Yellowjackets Stadium to see gay
Chamberlain's eleven vanquish the
haughty Knickerbockers form neath
the shade of Coogan's Bluff for their
sweetest conquest of the year.

That a well-drilled eleven in which
individual performance is sacrificed on
the altar of team play can beat a team
composed of stars was decisively
proven by the lads from up "L" way
yesterday.

The Yellowjackets held the ball in
the invaders' territory throughout most
of the game and only the stubborn
and adamantine defense presented by
Coach Bob Folwell's team, when
Frankford held the ball within scoring
radius prevented several Yellowjackets'
pointers.

Frankford scored a safety in the first
period only to have the lead snatched
from the Hornets by a drop-kick from
the talented boot of Matt Brennan
standing on the 15-yard line in the second period.

Behman's Toe Wins Game

In the clever and deadly toe of Captain Rus Behman victory lurked for the
Yellowjackets. After he and Welch had
fooaled several attempts to score via
the field goal and placement route, Rus
dropped back on his forty-yard mark
in the third period once again to attempt a placement boot. The leather
came back in a beautiful spiral to Les
Haws, former Dartmouth scintillant
from Springsteen, once a Lehigh gallant.

Haws dropped the ball to earth and
Behman calmly, with nonchalance befitting a youngster kicking a pigskin
against his back fence, swung his boot.
The leather rose sure and true and flied
to the goal posts. It wavered slightly
just as the bar was reached, clearing
the wood by the margin of a few inches.

Everybody realized that that dropkick had snatched victory from the very
jaws of defeat, that a certain New York
victory had been transmuted by Behman's magic alchemy into a Hornet
triumph.

The ranks of the Yellowjackets
which were beginning to filter into the
game, the latter being out on his
feet, having given forth his last ounce
of energy now braced and the Giants
never again really threatened.

In the desperate fury once frenzied
might of a last minute try for victory,
New York carried the ball from midfield to Frankford's twenty-yard line
on a continued and uninterrupted drive
for a touchdown, a score that meant
the game.

Springsteen Blocks Punt

On the third down with six yards to
go, Johnny McBride, who once upon
a time strove for the glory of Syracuse University, retreated as if he was
going to try a forward. Dick Alexander, Gotham centre and erstwhile
Yellowjacket, went back a miserable
toss and McBride was knocked for a
loss of 19 yards. Thorpe, the famous
feet, having given forth his last ounce
have his punt blocked by Springsteen
with a Frankford recovery.

The last hope of New York had gone
a glimmering, cascading to the limbo
of blasted hopes, and never-to-be-re-
alized dreams.

Numbering in their galaxy a half-
dozen or so All-Americans, New York
was never able to penetrate the fierce
defense of the Yellow Jackets for any
sort of consistent gain.

Jim Thorpe, the Carlisle Redskin,
who seemed to have seen his best days,
did most of the punting for New York
and right good job he made of it. Millstead, of Yale, a member of Walter
Camp's last All-American team, shone
resplendent for the Giants, but
such former greats as Bomer, the Vanderbilt end, Heine Benkert, of Rutgers,
and Brute Carney, Navy player, were
only ordinary performers.

Homan Shines For Jackets

On the other hand the unsung and
unheralded Babe Homan, of Lehigh,
who played a bang of a game in the
first half before he was replaced by
Haws, as George Sullivan went to halfback, brought the crowd to its feet several times in acclaim of his sterling
broken field performance.

Tex Hamer, former Penn captain,
was the same reliable player all afternoon, sharing the laurels with Welsh,
the big guard.

In the first period in an effort to
score Fitzke tried a drop kick from his
45-yard line. It went wide of the posts
Shortly afterward when the Hornets
again had the ball in scoring range,
the Idaho battering ram missed another drop. Kicking was more the
vogue and Welsh missed a placement
from his 55-yard line.

Late in the first period Guy Chamberlain blocked Thorpe's punt from his
10-yard line and fell on it behind the
line for what seemed to be a touchdown. But before the game both teams
had decided to count pigskins which
touched the bleacher fence in close
proximity to the goal posts, either a
touchback or a grounded forward. In
this instance it was a touchback and
the Yellowjackets reaped only two
points instead of six.

At the start of the second half, Sullivan took the ball from midfield to his
30-yard line through right tackle.
Welsh now tried a drop kick from his
45-yard line. It went astray, but shortly afterward Behman came through
with his kick that won the game.

The Lineup

Frankford	Positions	New York Giants
Chamberlain	Left end	Nash
Behman	Left tackle	Milstead
Hoffman	Left guard	Carney
Springsteen	center	Alexander
Welsh	Right guard	Williams
Marms	Right tackle	Bedner
R. Crowther	Right end	Bomer
Homan	Quarterback	Hendrian
Haws	Left half-back	Thorp
Fitzke	Right half-back	Benkert
Hamer	Full-back	McBride

Referee—Powell, Buffalo. Umpire—Winters,
Philadelphia. Head Linesman—Newell, Penn.

Frankford	2	0	3	0	—5
New York Giants	0	3	0	0	—3

Drop kick—Behman, New York. Placement
—Behman, Yellowjackets. Touchback—Cham-
berlain. Substitutions—Brennan for Hendrian,
Hendrian for Brennan, Parnell for Millstead.
Carton for Chamberlain, Sullivan for Haws,
Haws for Homan. Time of periods—Fifteen
minutes.

$30,500 IS RED'S FOR FIRST GAME

Grange Disregards Advice of "Dad" and Zuppke Not to be Grid "Pro."

Signs With Chicago Bears for Six Dates, One on Thanks Day.

CHICAGO, Nov. 22.—(AP)—Harold (Red) Grange today plunged into the business of capitalizing his gridiron fame by signing to play professional football, against the wishes of his father as well as George Huff, director of athletics of the University of Illinois, Coach Robert Zuppke and others who had hoped he would accept other offers held out to him.

The famous redhead contracted with the Chicago Bears to play his first game with them in the Chicago National League park Thanksgiving day, against Chicago Cardinals.

Grange also signed Charles C. Pyle, a Champaign (Ill.) theatrical man, as his manager.

Investigated Offers.

Grange said that Pyle had merely acted as his good friend and advisor for the last few weeks and had spent his own funds investigating the countless offers made the football player.

Pyle's contract with Grange is for two years. While neither would discuss the terms, it was said that Pyle would receive 25 per cent. of Grange's earnings on the professional gridiron, in motion pictures and other ventures.

The twenty-two-year-old star said he had decided to play professional football, instead of accepting other alluring offers because he had no training or experience that would have enabled him to accept the others.

CANTON ELEVEN COPS 6-0 GAME

Robb Runs Thirty Yards Against Columbus.

(Plain Dealer Special)

CANTON, O., Nov. 22.—The Canton Bulldogs defeated the Columbus representatives of the National Professional football league, 6 to 0, in a game here this afternoon. Canton scored in the first quarter after a series of bucks brought the ball to the Columbus forty-yard line. On the next play Hogan passed over the center of the line to Robb, who ran thirty yards for the touchdown.

Columbus showed a great defensive team and had a fine running attack. They threatened in the second half when a Canton fumble was recovered on the Canton five-yard line. Four plays failed to make the required distance to the goal line.

The punting and passing of Hogan was a feature of the game.

Canton—6.	Position.	Columbus—0.
Culver	L. E.	Rub
Lyman	L. T.	Ellis
Flattery	L. G.	Duvall
McRoberts	C.	Nemecek
Comstock	R. G.	Muhlbarger
Kyle	R. T.	Petcoff
Carroll	R. E.	Davis
Hogan	Q.	Rapp
Jones	L. H.	Tynes
Robb	R. H.	Lynch
Calac	F.	Nesser

Canton .... 6 0 0 0—6

Substitutions: Columbus: Ruhleder for Nesser, Albanese for Lynch.

Touchdown Robb.

Referee Lambert (Ohio State). Umpire Keagy (Reserve). Time of quarters—12m.

Reprinted from
The Cleveland Plain Dealer

RED OUT; $18,000 RETURNED TO FANS

Bears Suffer Humiliating Defeat of 21 to 0 at Detroit.

DETROIT, Dec. 12.—(AP)—A Grangeless Chicago Bears team was defeated 21 to 0 by the Detroit Panthers before a paid attendance of 4,111 today.

Announcement that Grange would not play was made late yesterday, with the statement that ticket purchasers would be refunded their money if they so desired. The refund, it was stated tonight, was approximately $18,000.

The victory gave the Panthers third place in the National Football league standings.

The score by periods:

Panthers	7	0	7	7—21
Bears	0	0	0	0—0

RED & CO. ATTRACT 36,000 AT PHILLY

Mohardt and Healy are Chicago Stars; "No. 77" Fails in Attempted Long Gallops.

SHIBE PARK, PHILADELPHIA, Dec. 5.—Red Grange and his supporting cast of football minstrels, the Bears, continued their triumphant tour by crushing the Philadelphia Yellow Jackets, 14 to 7, in a fiercely contested battle here today. 36,000 fans sat through a rain to see Red do his stuff in the mud.

Grange scored both of his team's touchdowns but he did not get away for any of his long gallops. He smashed through center from the one-yard line for both touchdowns, the first on the second play of the second period and the second late in the final quarter. Joe Sternaman kicked both goals.

Philadelphia's only touchdown came in the third period on a long pass from Stockton to Jones. It was a twenty-yard shot from the Yellow Jacket fifty-two-yard line. Jones found himself in a clear field after he received the pass and ran the remaining thirty-two yards to the goal line without being touched.

Johnny Mohardt, former Notre Dame star, and Ed Healy, the big Dartmouth tackle, were the individual stars for the Bears. Mohardt was the Bears' most reliable ground gainer and Healy played a marvelous defensive game. Time and again he broke through and spilled the Philadelphia backs for loss. He also blocked a punt and knocked down several attempted passes. He was down the field on every punt and tackled Homan, the Philly quarterback, so fiercely that he was forced to leave the game.

Scalpers Tossed for Loss.

The crowd was slow in arriving and a goodly number of those present effected the yellow collegiate slickers. The well known scalpers were thrown for a total loss by the rain. They offered grand stand tickets, choice ones too, for $1 and were glad to accept 50 cents.

Two bands paraded the field before the start of the game and a tottering Civil War veteran, in full uniform, and carrying Old Glory headed the parade.

The Yellow Jackets were late in arriving and Grange and Britton posed for photographers while waiting for their opponents.

RED, RED, RED!

Chicago.	Position.	Frankford.
Hanny	L. E.	Chamberlin
Healy	L. T.	Lyman
Fleckenstein	L. G.	Hoffman
Trafton	C.	Springsteen
McMillen	R. G.	Spagna
Murry	R. T.	Lowe
Halas	R. E.	Crowther
J. Sternaman	Q.	Homan
Grange	L. H.	Hamer
E. Sternaman	R. H.	Sullivan
Walquist	F.	Stockton

Chicago ..... 0 7 0 7—14
Frankford ... 0 0 7 0— 7

Touchdowns—Grange 2, Jones. Points after touchdowns—J. Sternaman 2, Hamer.

Substitutions—Chicago, Knop for E. Sternaman, Mohardt for Walquist Anderson for Fleckenstein, Bryan for Grange, Scott for Healy, Crawford for McMillen, Britton for Mohardt, Grange for Bryan, Henly for Scott, McMillen for Crawford, J. Sternaman for Britton; Frankford, Jones for Sullivan, Smythe for Homan.

Policy of The Green Bay Football Corporation

MEMBER OF THE NATIONAL FOOTBALL LEAGUE

The policy of the GREEN BAY FOOTBALL CORPORATION, is to promote clean, healthful sport; to maintain for the City of Green Bay a football team that will be a leader in this great American out-door sport. This team is composed of former College stars and will have the leading football teams of the country as opponents. Our City will gain added publicity in supporting games that will attract nation-wide attention and be recognized as a promoter of clean sports and recreation. Financial gain derived from the season's playing is donated to the American Legion.

70,000 SEE RED, RECORD N. Y. GATE

Grange Shows Appreciation by Scoring Touchdown; Bears Win, 19-7.

BY DAMON RUNYON.

NEW YORK, Dec. 6.—I here preach from the old familiar text, "it pays to advertise."

There gathered at the Polo Grounds in Harlem this afternoon the largest crowd that ever witnessed a football game on the island of Manhattan, drawn by the publicity that has been given one individual—Red Harold Grange, late of the University of Illinois.

Seventy thousand, men, women and children were in the stands, blocking the aisles and runways. Twenty thousand more were perched on Coogan's bluffs and the roofs of apartment houses overlooking the baseball home of McGraw's club, content with just an occasional glimpse of the whirling mass of players on the field far below and wondering which was Red Grange.

It is said he took down in the neighborhood of $25,000 for his end today and the total gate must have gone well over $100,000. That is what the profession terms "heavyweight money."

No Big Feats Early.

Grange played through the first period and part of the second without performing any astonishing feats. Then he took a rest. As the final period started and Red was still absent the huge crowd that had gathered on a peaceful Sunday to see him and no one else, set up a concerted chant "we want Grange!"

They gave the ball to Grange again and he just failed of first down on New York's one-yard line. The ball went to the big town footballers and they wiggled out of immediate danger, but a moment later McBride tried a forward pass to Bomar.

The muddy lean-flanked figure of Red Grange came from nowhere. He reached up and grabbed the ball in the air, whirled and sprinted across the New York goal line for a touchdown. No New York was close to him as he loped along, his knees lifting high with every stride and his hips swaying.

Friedman Bunch There.

A number of young men appeared on the field wearing red and blue feathers in their hats (the colors of Mr. Gibson's territory of Coogan's Bluffs). They seemed greatly interested in Mr. Benny Friedman, the Michigan quarterback, who strolled about the field between the halves. Big Bill Edwards, president of Mr. Enright's police college, was on hand with some of his undergraduates and many other famous collegians were scattered about the premises.

Chicago—19.	Position.	New York—7.
Hanny	L. E.	Jappe
Healy	L. T.	Millstead
Anderson	L. G.	Carney
Trafton	C.	Alexander
McMillan	R. G.	Williams
Murry	R. T.	Farnall
Halas	R. E.	Bomar
J. Sternaman	Q.	Pain
Grange	L. H.	Haines
Walquist	R. H.	Benkert
K. Sternaman	F.	McBride

Chicago	12	0	0	7—19
New York	0	7	0	0— 7

Substitutions—Chicago: Knop for K. Sternaman, Mohardt for Walquist, Smith for Trafton, Trafton for Smith, Scott for Healy, K. Sternaman for Knop, Knop for J. Sternaman, Ryan for Grange, Grange for Ryan, Britton for Mohardt. New York: White for Benkert, Temlin for Williams, Williams for Farnall, Reynolds for Jappe, Rooney for Haynes, Wallbridge for Alexander.

Touchdowns—J. Sternaman 2, Grange, White. Points after touchdowns—J. Sternaman (drop kick), McBride (placement).

Referee—William S. Crowell (Swarthmore). Umpire—Tom Thorpe (Columbia). Head linesman—Jack Rearden (New Hampshire State). Field judge—William Hollenback (Pennsylvania). Time of periods—15m.

Reprinted from
The Cleveland Plain Dealer

NEVERS DOES "GRANGE" AND SIGNS TO PLAY PRO GAME FOR $50,000

Stanford University, Cal., Dec. 12.—(Associated Press.)—The lure of professional football has claimed another college gridiron star—Ernie Nevers, captain of the 1925 Stanford football team and probably the greatest fullback to wear a cardinal jersey since the university's founding in 1892.

In announcing today that he had come to terms with a group of Jacksonville, Fla., capitalists to lead a team representing that city, Nevers said the venture stood to net him a sum totaling more than $50,000.

BULLDOGS DOWN JACKETS, 3 TO 0

Doc Elliott's Ten-Yard Drop Kick Decides Close Battle of Pro Teams.

PHILADELPHIA, Pa., Dec. 12.—The Cleveland Bulldogs squeezed out a victory over the Frankford Yellow Jackets in the final game of the local National league football season here this afternoon by the score of 3 to 0.

The winning points came in the final minutes of the second quarter on a drop kick by "Doc" Elliott from the ten-yard line after two line plunges failed. The final period, like the first, was fiercely contested, with Frankford holding the edge in the running attack, but unable to muster a scoring punch.

The game was featured by two nice runs by Two-Bits Homan, the 138-pound quarterback of the Yellow Jackets. Once Homan got loose for thirty yards and another time achieved fifteen yards before being dropped. Hamer also carried the ball well for Frankford. Wolfe was the outstanding ground gainer of the first half for the invaders.

Reprinted from
The Cleveland Plain Dealer

Pottsville
MAROONS

1925

World Champions

Dec. 13

POTTSVILLE MAROONS LOSE LEAGUE FRANCHISE; CALLED "OUTLAWS" FOR GAME HERE

SOME important results of Pottsville's pro grid champions of 1925, meeting with the Four Horsemen yesterday afternoon at Shibe Park are that they have forfeited their franchise in the National League of Professional Football Players, have been outlawed from the league and been deprived of their title, according to disclosures made public yesterday by the president of the league.

The Steam Rollers of Providence, Rhode Island, were slated to lock horns with Dr. Streigel's eleven today, but the league prexy announced that the game will not be played, since the ville is outlawed and if the Steam Rollers played the game they too would be deprived of their standing. By playing the Four Horsemen, according to Joe Carr, the league head, Pottsville infringed on the Frankford Yellowjackets' territorial rights and automatically became outlawed from the league.

Dr. Streigel, the well-known Pottsville physician and owner of the Maroons, who triumphed 9 to 7 over the famous South Bend Collegians, claims that he had a verbal permission from the secretary of the league to play the game. This was when he had been approached by Frank Schumann, the Philadelphia promoter to meet the Four Horsemen, and was before Pottsville had won the league title by defeating the Chicago Cardinals for titular honors in the post season tilt waged out in the Windy City recently.

At this opportune juncture the league secretary pulled a Cozy Dolan and proceeded to forget all about the verbal permission he had given Dr. Streigel over the long distance telephone. That eminent allopath then received word from Joe Carr that the game could not be played.

"Do you have written permission?" queried the esteemed Mr. Carr, of Streigel. The upshot of the whole matter was that Streigle informed the league head that he was going on with the game regardless and did so.

Reports emanating from Providence yesterday were to the effect that the Yellowjackets of Frankford, bruised from their 3 to 0 defeat at the hands of the Cleveland eleven, and not the Pottsville Maroons, would meet the Steam Rollers today. The rules of the league provide that for special and post season games within the radius of 20 miles, the team within that range has first call.

Reprinted from
The Philadelphia Inquirer

GRANGE MUST REST FOR ENTIRE WEEK

"Red's" Left Arm Placed in Splints; Thousands of Detroit Fans Disappointed

DETROIT, Mich., Dec. 12.

ANOTHER myth has been punctured. Phantoms are not invulnerable. Harold "Red" Grange, the phantom of the gridiron, is down for the count. He could not play this afternoon with the Chicago Bears against the Detroit Panthers at Navin Field. Neither can he play tomorrow in Chicago. He must rest for a week with his left limb in splints, and it all started from a little bruise.

Grange's team, the Chicago Bears, were beaten by the Detroit eleven, the final score being 21 to 0. Hadden went over for a pair of touchdowns, while Gonzelman also scored.

Grange and his cavalcade descended upon Detroit Friday evening, but it was far from the group of merrymakers. Five games in six days had taxed the strength of nearly every man on the squad and their one desire was to find a place of rest and stay there. Grange looked weary and drawn. Deep lines in his face showed that the strain to which he had been subjected had made its impression.

At Navin Field a steady stream of ticket holders were at hand this morning to get their money back. Officials in charge estimated that half the 8000 tickets sold during the week would be returned because the iceman could not play this afternoon. The management had announced Friday that it would redeem tickets up to 2.30 P. M., today.

Although he admitted he was dog-tired, "Red" was willing to play. He said he would gladly start against the Panthers if a doctor would sanction it. Dr. George I. Waldbott was called to Grange's room in Webster Hall, and after a thorough examination of his left arm not only ordered him to stay out of the game today and tomorrow, but placed the arm in splints. Dr. Waldbott said the muscles of the left arm were seriously inflamed and he believed the arteries also were inflamed. This is a dangerous condition, as blood clots may form, and if one of these should reach the heart or brain death would result, the physician said.

Grange did not accept the doctor's orders gracefully. He said he wanted to play, and didn't want to carry his arm in splints for a week. "It all started from a small bruise in that St. Louis game on December 2," said Grange. "It did not look serious and wasn't painful, so I had it rubbed and used hot applications.

"In Washington it was bruised again, and in the Boston game it gave me a lot of pain. I'd be all right now if I had not played that game in Pittsburgh. I went in hoping I could protect myself, but the first time I was hit hard the pain came back, and at the end of the first quarter I couldn't raise my arm. I'm sorry I can't play in Detroit, for I'd like to go good here."

The injured arm is swollen to almost twice its normal size, the swelling extending from the wrist almost to the shoulder. Grange, however, took much comfort in the fact that the swelling had reduced slightly since Thursday night.

C. C. Pyle, Grange's manager, is the man on whose head the Bears are heaping all their abuse. He is the man who scheduled them for five games in six days. Their one complaint is that a man who didn't know anything about football was allowed to make the schedule. Pyle isn't with the team. He has left for California. Frank Z. Zambreno is his representative, while Grange has "Dinty" Moore and "Doc" Cooley to direct his affairs.

Although Grange is getting the lion's share of the gate receipts, he is well liked by the members of the Bears' squad. Every man denied rumors that there was any jealousy or ill feeling toward "Red." He was a good player and a fine companion, according to his teammates, and they all wished him well in all of his many financial ventures. Grange himself denied he was tired of professional football and wanted to quit.

Detroit.	Positions	Chicago Bears.
Holtman	Left end	Hanny
Sonnenberg	Left tackle	Healy
McNamara	Left guard	Fleckenstein
E. Vick	Centre	Trafton
Hogan	Right guard	Anderson
Mills	Right tackle	Murray
Voss	Right end	Halas
R. Vick	Quarter-back	J. Sternaman
Conzelman	Left half-back	E. Sternaman
Hadden	Right half-back	Bryan
Doane	Full-back	Knop

Detroit .... 7 0 14 0—21
Chicago .... 0 0 0 0— 0

Touchdowns—Hadden 2, Conzelman. Points after touchdown—Sonnenberg 3. Referee—Ritter. Umpire—White. Head linesman—Edwards. Substitutions—Britton for Knop, Blackblock for Murry, Marion for Doane, Fleischman for McNamara, Crook for Vick.

Reprinted from
The Philadelphia Inquirer

HARRY STUHLDREHER CALLED AN OUTLAW

National League Claims He Violated Rule by Playing With Blues.

POTTSVILLE TEAM IS ALSO "IN BAD"

Chicago Cardinals Involved in Dispute Over Championship.

Chicago, Dec. 13 — (Associated Press.)—The squabble between the Chicago Cardinals and the Pottsville, Pa. Maroons, for the championship of the National Professional Football League may end with the outlawing of the Pottsville team, giving the Cardinals a clear title, Joseph Carr, president of the league, indicated today.

With both teams claiming the title before yesterday's games, a new situation developed. The Cardinals beat Hammond, Ind. Pros. 13 to 0, and Pottsville trimmed a team headed by the "four horsemen" of Notre Dame at Philadelphia, 9 to 7.

President Carr said the Pottsville team in playing the "four horsemen" violated the rules and may lose its franchise. The game in Philadelphia, he said, was played in the territory of the Frankford Yellowjackets which has the Philadelphia territory and therefore the game has been ruled an outlaw contest.

Stuhldreher on Pan.

Also Harry Stuhldreher, one of the Four Horsemen has been ruled a professional outlaw because at the beginning of the season he signed to play with the Providence, R. I. Steam Rollers of the National League, but jumped the contract and played with an independent team at Hartford, Conn., in playing against him, the entire Pottsville team has laid itself liable to being outlawed.

As the league standing now is, the Cardinals have won eleven games, lost two and played one tie. Pottsville has won ten games, lost two. Cardinal officials said they were claiming the title but that the entire matter would have to be threshed out at the league meeting in January.

REDLESS BEARS BEATEN, 8 TO 0

18,000 See N. Y. Giants in Victory.

CUBS PARK, CHICAGO, Dec. 13. —The New York Giants defeated the Grangeless Bears 9 to 0, in a national professional football league game here today. The bruised and battered Bears showed something less than half their normal efficiency.

Jack McBride's forty-yard goal from placement in the first quarter, and Phil White's touchdown later in the fourth quarter, represented the margin in the Giants' victory.

Eighteen thousand fans witnessed the combat. Several thousand people who had made reservations for the game demanded and received back their money, when it was learned that Grange would not play.

Giants—9.	Position.	Bears—0.
Zappe	L. E.	Hanny
Milstead	L. T.	Healy
Carney	L. G.	Fleckenstein
Alexander	C.	Anderson
Tomlin	R. G.	McMillan
Parnell	R. T.	Murry
Bomar	R. E.	Halas
Haines	Q.	J. Sternaman
Benkert	L. H.	Bryan
McBride	R. H.	Walquist
P. White	F.	Knop

Substitutions—Bears: Trafton for Anderson, White for Knop, E. Sternaman for Walquist, Mullen for Halas, Walquist for White, Britton for E. Sternaman, Anderson for Trafton. Touchdown—P. White. Goal from field—Mc-Bride.

Referee—Cahn. Umpire—Ritter. Head linesman—Edwards.

Reprinted from
The Cleveland Plain Dealer

GRANGE TO REST UNTIL CHRISTMAS

Will Not Appear at Dunn Field Against Bulldogs, as Scheduled.

DANVILLE, Ill., Dec. 15.—(AP)— Harold (Red) Grange shoved his left arm and shoulder beneath an X-ray here today for examination by Dr. E. B. Cooley. Later, upon treatment, Grange was greatly pleased, saying it was the first time since his injury at Pittsburgh that he was able to straighten the injured member which has since caused his absence from a number of pro-football games.

"X-ray examination of Grange's left arm at a local hospital verified former diagnoses, showing ruptured muscles and a slight hemorrhage," said Dr. Coolley.

Ordered to Remain Idle.

"I examined Red's arm Sunday at Chicago and instructed him to cancel all playing engagements at least until Christmas, and he has done so," resumed the surgeon. "He will be able to resume playing by that time in my opinion."

George (Polly) Parratt, manager of the Cleveland Bulldogs, the team which the Chicago Bears and Grange were scheduled to play here on Saturday, was not in Cleveland last night. Consequently, it could not be learned if he had received word of the cancellation of Saturday's scheduled contest.

NEVERS INJURED IN AUTO-ACCIDENT

Cut About Face and Head by Flying Glass; Coming East.

SAN MATEO, Dec. 19.—(AP)— Ernie Nevers, captain of the 1925 Stanford university football eleven, who recently turned professional on a fat offer from an eleven in Florida, was cut about the face and head by flying glass when an automobile in which he was riding collided with another near here today. He received emergency treatment at a hospital here and left soon afterward.

Nevers was on his way to the Stanford campus to pack his belongings preparatory to starting east when the car in which he was riding collided with another. Nevers declared he was not badly hurt. After treatment he continued to the campus to pack his bags.

GRANGE, BEARS OPEN 2D TOUR

Red's Absence for Week Costs $75,000.

CHICAGO, Dec. 20.—Harold (Red) Grange, the most talked about football player in America, and the Bears, strengthened and rested, will leave Chicago's wintry atmosphere behind them Monday when they begin their second tour for touchdowns and gold which will carry them to Florida, Louisiana, Texas and California.

Grange has fully recovered from the injury to his left arm, which prevented him from playing for more than a week and which cost him and his managers in the neighborhood of $75,000. Red says he is ready to resume his now famous business of manufacturing touchdowns in his own inimitable way. Which, of course, remains to be seen.

Reprinted from
The Cleveland Plain Dealer

RED TOO FAST FOR TAMPA COP

Grange Caught Speeding on Highway.

TAMPA, Fla., Dec. 31.—(AP)— Harold (Red) Grange proved too swift for local highways this afternoon and was arrested for breaking the speed laws. A traffic officer pulled up in front of Grange's car going sixty-five miles per hour and stopped the star's car.

Grange was released after posting bond of $25.

With Grange in the car were Jim Barnes, British golf champion; Miss Helen Wainwright, Olympic swimming champion, and Johnny Farrel, golf professional from New York.

RED GETS STADIUM; PASS NEW GRID BAN

Grange Leases Yankee Field Pending Franchise From League; College Players Hit by Edict.

NEW YORK, Feb. 6.—Red Grange, former Illinois All American football star, has secured a five-year lease on the Yankee stadium for professional football, Ed Barrow, business manager of the Yankees, confirmed today.

Barrow, who had just returned from Chicago, where he is said to have closed the contract with Grange, said that the arrangements would give Grange all the Sunday and holiday dates from Oct. 15 to Dec. 31.

The Saturday dates, he said, had been reserved by the Yankee owners for college football games.

The lease includes a clause calling for a five-year renewal option, Grange asserted.

* * * *

DETROIT, Feb. 6.—(AP)—Collegiate gridiron stars are barred hereafter from participating in professional football games until after their class has been graduated, under a rule adopted today by representatives of the twenty clubs of the national football league, in semi-annual session here.

The action, which was unanimous, was a direct result of the appearance as a professional of Harold (Red) Grange last fall immediately after his college football career was ended.

Grange, who is attending the meeting with C. C. Pyle, his manager, applied for a franchise in the league. The franchise, he said, would be located in New York.

It was apparent that reefs are ahead of Grange's plans to put another professional football team in New York. Before he can obtain a franchise the New York Giants, who hold the only franchise in New York city at present, must give their consent. There were indications tonight that this consent may be withheld.

In urging Grange's request for a place in the league, Pyle pointed out that the largest crowd that ever witnessed a professional football game—about 63,000—turned out to see Grange in New York.

There are five other applicants for franchises in the circuit—St. Louis, Racine, Boston, Baltimore and Newark. Action on these applications will be made Sunday.

Reprinted from
The Cleveland Plain Dealer

GRANGE DENIED GRID FRANCHISE

Red Phantom and Manager Threaten "Revolution" in Pro Football Ranks.

DETROIT, Feb. 7.—(AP)—A revolution in the ranks of professional football was threatened tonight after Red Grange was denied a franchise in the National Professional Football league.

Through C. C. Pyle, his manager, Grange announced that if the National league did not change its mind about issuing a franchise to operate a club in the New York Yankees stadium, Pyle would immediately start plans to form an opposition circuit, possibly taking in some of the clubs now holding franchises in the National league.

CLEVELAND'S OUT OF GRID LEAGUE

Quits Pro Footfall Circuit at Philly; Trio of New Teams Enter.

PHILADELPHIA, July 11.—(AP)—A number of changes in the membership of the National Football league, adoption of a playing schedule for next fall and approval of the new forward pass rule, featured the closing session today of the league's annual meeting. A franchise was granted Los Angeles, Cal., which with Brooklyn, N. Y., and Hartford, Conn., granted franchises yesterday, brings three new teams into the league.

The Pottsville, Pa., and Racine, Wis., clubs were reinstated, while Cleveland, Minneapolis and New Britain, Conn., withdrew from membership.

Dr. J. K. Striegel, head of the Pottsville club, was fined $2,500 for playing the Four Horsemen of Notre Dame in Philadelphia last fall while Frankford, territorial franchise holder, was playing a league game here. The playing of this game led to the dropping of Pottsville from the league after the team had won the 1925 championship.

The league will open its season on Sept. 19 and close Dec. 7. In the opening games Akron will meet the Frankford Yellowjackets at Philadelphia; Columbus will play at Canton, Chicago Bears at Green Bay, Brooklyn at Providence, Hammond at Racine and Detroit at Milwaukee.

The relation of the league toward college football was the subject of extended discussion and in order that a clearer understanding may be had with the colleges, a committee was appointed to confer in New York tomorrow with Brig. Gen. Palmer A. Pierce, president of the Intercollegiate Athletic Union.

Joseph H. Carr, president of the league, made a strong plea for strict adherence to the rule recently passed that no college player could be signed until he has been graduated. He announced that many former college stars had been signed by league members, but that their identity would not be revealed for the present.

The only player of prominence whose name was made public, was Ernie Nevers, all American fullback of California. He will have charge of the Duluth club which will be known as the "Nevers Eskimos."

Mr. Carr said the Los Angeles club was backed by moving picture interests of the Pacific coast and would be composed of leading college players. Most of its early contests will be played away from home. At the close of the regular playing season, a number of the foremost clubs of the east and middle west will go to the coast for a series of games.

Sept. 7

Grange's Film Proves Big Hit on Broadway

New York—Some time back propagandists were announcing that Red Grange, the "galloping ghost" of the University of Illinois football team, was "a bust" in the movies, heading back to Wheaton and his ice trade, and done with the show world for all time.

Grange's first motion picture, "One Minute to Play," opened at the Colony theater on Broadway Sunday night, with the football star making a personal appearance at each showing, and from present indications—it is turning thousands away and selling six weeks ahead—may enjoy a run comparable with those of the bigger film production of the past. New York reviewers are agreed that Grange's film play ranks with the best of all time and some even go so far as to predict Red will prove the natural successor to Rudolph Valentino.

Already the film debut of the great Illini star has inspired several praising editorials in New York dailies and one, the Daily News, with the largest newspaper circulation in America, devotes its entire editorial space to an editorial entitled "Red and Rudy," which says, in part:

"If the girls liked Valentino, the boys, we think, are going to like Red Grange. His first is a dandy film. . . .

"And how they get the football into the picture! Never has a football game been done so well on the screen. . . .

"There's a sweet love story in 'One Minute to Play,' but no whinnying and whickering and convulsive nostrils. It may be too wholesome for Broadway—we hope not—but we predict this one will go like a house afire in the wide open spaces."

Reprinted from
The Milwaukee Journal

No. 3. E. C. "DUTCH" STERNAMAN, Illinois

"Dutch" Sternaman, one of the team's coaches, has the unique distinction of always having played at left halfback. From the days of 1911-12-13-14, when he trotted out on the gridiron of the Springfield, Ill., high school, to his present activities on the Bears, he has continuously held down that job. From 1916 to 1919 "Dutch" played on the Illinois U varsity, with the exception of the year of 1918 when he was at Camp Funston, coaching the army eleven there. Sternaman has been a member of the Bears since the organization of the team, and has won a name for himself as a field goal kicker.

No. 7. GEORGE HALAS, Illinois

George Halas, right end and one of the coaches of the team, is a Chicago boy, and graduated in 1913 from Crane Tech, where he starred four years at tackle and halfback. Transferring his allegiance to Illinois, he played at end on Bob Zuppke's eleven in 1915, 1916 and 1917. When the famous Great Lakes team traveled from coast to coast in 1918, beating some of the greatest teams in the country, Halas played end and was one of the coaches of the Great Lakes eleven. Halas has been with the Bears since the team was organized, and has an enviable record at end. He made the trip with the Bears through the South and West in 1925-1926.

AKRON LOSES PRO GRID OPENER, 7-0

Buffalo Scores in Second Period to Annex Close Tussle.

BUFFALO, N. Y., Sept. 26.—Buffalo Rangers defeated Akron in the opening of the national pro football league season here today, 7 to 0.

Buffalo scored its lone touchdown in the second quarter when Cramer and Pollard interfered with Mule Wilson, who was endeavoring to spear Kendrick's pass on the two-yard line. Wilson missed the peg but Buffalo won the ball through this interference and on the next play Kendrick hit the right side of the Akron line for two yards and the touchdown. Wilson kicked the goal for extra point from placement.

Akron threatened in the final period when Pollard twice heaved successful forward passes, once to Daum and again to Newman. This gained the visitors twenty yards but they were halted on Buffalo's thirty-two-yard line. Akron made first down only twice, once on Pollard's passes in that final period and once in the opening quarter on a penalty.

Buffalo made its yardage six times, thrice on rushes, twice on forwards and once on penalty.

The visitors found the Buffalo line too stalwart to cope with. Time and again rushes off right and left side were stalled.

Pollard played brilliantly, hitting the Bison line like a locomotive, but he was all alone in his efforts.

Buffalo—7.	Position.	Akron—0.
Guffey	L. E.	Daum
McGilbra	L. T.	Casey
Swarzer	L. G.	Seidelson
Kirk	C.	Barry
Irvin	R. G.	Nesser
Wilcox	R. T.	Robleder
Feist	R. E.	Bissell
Kendrick	Q.	Pollard
Wilson	L. H.	Griggs
Hopson	R. H.	Newman
Paxton	F.	Cramer
Buffalo		0 7 0 0—7

Substitutions—Buffalo: Narran for Wilson, Vaughan for Narran. Akron: Mills for Pollard, Wendler for Griggs, Ursulla for Wendler, Pollard for Mills.

Touchdown—Kendrick. Point after touchdown—Wilson. Placement—Wilson.

Referee—Paul Fitting (Erie). Umpire—George O'Brien (Lockport). Head linesman—Tom Timlin.

RED GRANGE'S ELEVEN LOSES TO PANTHERS

Cleveland Pro Grid Team Surprises by Whipping Famed New York Outfit, 10 to 0.

RECORD THRONG TURNS OUT FOR FIRST GAME

22,000 Fans See Phantom Fail to Dazzle New Local Squad.

BY RUSSELL M. NEEDHAM.

Harold Edmund Grange, the distinguished pigskin purveyor and ice peddler, went back to New York last night completely stopped and soundly thrashed after opening his 1926 gridiron offensive here for more and greener bank notes.

The largest crowd ever to watch a football game in Cleveland, estimated at 22,000, saw the Cleveland Panthers down Grange's Yankees, 10 to 0, at the new Luna Park bowl.

The ghostly galloper turned out one piece of master craftsmanship. That was a twenty-one-yard return of a punt late in the second quarter. He grabbed the ball and darted for the nearest sideline, as is his habit, side stepping and straight arming profusely as he went. He was finally forced out of bounds when Dick Wolfe tripped him with a shoe string tackle and Red Roberts and Cookie Cunningham bounced him out of bounds.

The flaming youth of Wheaton wasn't so much from scrimmage. Once he dashed off tackle for nine yards and another time he ran the same direction for twelve. A third time he had a nice ten-yard game before him, but spoiled it by fumbling.

Red took care of a seat on the bench during most of the second half, when the Yankees made their only threat, a dash that netted three of their four first downs and carried the ball to the Panther three-yard line, where Cleveland held for downs.

The Yankees, aside from Grange, were nothing at all to get enthused about.

Grange Scores Twice As Yankees Trounce Rock Island Eleven

(Special to The Courant.)
Rock Island, Ill., Oct. 3.

The New York Yankees pro grid team defeated the Rock Island Independents 26 to 9 before 5,000 on a field of mud today. Fry intercepted a pass on his own 18 yard line in the first period and ran 82 yards behind a wedge of interference for the first touchdown.

New York took the ball on Rock Island's 20-yard line early in the second period and Grange scored after receiving a 15 yard pass from Pease.

In the third period Grange went around end for 20 yards and a touchdown after a 25 yard penalty inflicted on Rock Island and placed the Yankees within scoring distance. In the last few minutes of play Goebel recovered a fumble on Rock Island's 5 yard line. Hubert smashed over.

Reprinted from
The Hartford Courant

OFFICIAL PROGRAM 1926

CHICAGO BEARS
vs
AKRON INDIANS
SUNDAY, OCTOBER 31, 2:15 P. M.

CHICAGO BEARS FOOTBALL CLUB INC.
CUBS PARK
Price 10 Cents

Fritz Pollard and Jim Thorpe Shine In Scoreless Tie

(Special to The Courant.)
Akron, Oct. 10.

Akron Indians and Canton Bulldogs played to a scoreless tie in a National League game here today in which Fritz Pollard and Jim Thorpe, veteran All-American stars, vied with each other for honors. Ralph Chase, 1925 All-American tackle from Pittsburgh University, made his professional debut with Akron. Line play of both teams was outstanding.

Reprinted from
The Hartford Courant

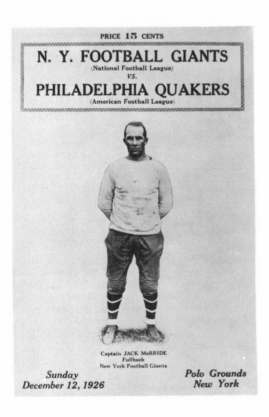

PRICE 15 CENTS

N. Y. FOOTBALL GIANTS
(National Football League)
vs.
PHILADELPHIA QUAKERS
(American Football League)

Captain JACK McBRIDE
Fullback
New York Football Giants

Sunday
December 12, 1926

Polo Grounds
New York

Frankford Pro Eleven Wins National Title

Philadelphia, Dec. 18 (AP).—The Frankford Yellow Jackets, of this city, today won the National League professional football championship by holding the Pottsville (Pa.) team to a tie, neither team scoring. The game was played in extremely cold weather, but 7,000 persons were out to see the contest.

The weather was too cold for good football and both teams resorted to much punting. Had Frankford lost today the Chicago Bears would have had a chance to capture the title by winning their game tomorrow with the Green Bay Packers.

	W	L	T	Pct.
Frankford	14	1	1	.933
Chi. Bears	12	1	3	.923
Pottsville	10	2	1	.833
Kansas City	8	3	1	.727
Green Bay	7	3	3	.700
Los Angeles	6	3	1	.667
N.Y. Giants	8	4	1	.667
Duluth	6	5	2	.545
Buffalo	4	4	2	.500
Chi. Cardinals	5	6	1	.455
Providence	5	7	0	.417
Detroit	4	6	2	.400
Hartford	3	7	0	.300
Brooklyn	3	8	0	.273
Milwaukee	2	7	0	.222
Akron	1	4	3	.200
Dayton	1	4	1	.200
Racine	1	4	0	.200
Columbus	1	6	0	.143
Canton	1	9	3	.100
Hammond	0	4	0	.000
Louisville	0	4	0	.000

Grange Hurt in Pro Game

Chicago — (P) — Red Grange, two years ago the "galloping ghost" of the Western conference, was recovering Monday from the most serious injury of his dozen years of football, a pulled tendon in the calf of his right leg. In the last few minutes of play Sunday, while the Chicago Bears were defeating Grange's New York Yankees, 12-0, Trafton of the Bears collided with Grange with such force that Grange hit the ground stunned. He was carried off the field.

It was feared Grange's knee had been dislocated, but an examination showed only the pulled tendon, which Grange hoped would heal in time for him to continue the Yankees' schedule in the National Football league.

"It was one of the cleanest football games I ever played in," said Grange, while a trainer steamed and rubbed his injured leg.

News of the League

President Joe F. Carr of the National league thinks this is going to be pro football's banner year. Reports from around the circuit show a much increased interest in the postgraduate game, according to the league proxy.

There will be twelve spokes in the National loop this season. The circuit is made up of N. Y. Yanks and Giants, Chicago Bears and Cards, Providence, Pottsville, Cleveland, Buffalo, Yellow Jackets, Dayton, Duluth and Green Bay.

Cleveland is building its hopes around Benny Friedman the Michigan all-American footballer. Owner Brandt is going the limit to place a winner on the field and he has rounded up a number of collegiate luminaries.

The Red Grange-Pyle combination will play their home games at the Yank stadium in New York. Grange's troopers are to travel during the first half of the season and won't be seen on Broadway until early in November.

Jerry Corcoran, who ran the Columbus club in the National loop for a number of years, is the "father" of an Ohio State pro league. Short railroad jumps between the eight cities will tend to cut down the traveling overhead.

Ernie Nevers is feeling fit again and will be ready to step into his full-back job when the whistle blows for the Duluth Eskimos. The former Golden West star was operated on for appendicitis in August. He has recovered rapidly.

"Sneeze" Achiu has signed his contract to perform with the Dayton Triangles. Achiu is the Chinese football wonder who played stellar ball for Dayton university. He is also credited with being a 10-second dash artist.

Johnny Bryan is running an independent club in Milwaukee this year but he has booked a number of games with league teams. Bryan's outfit is being backed by the Eagles. A week from Sunday, Milwaukee plays against Duluth.

Oct. 3

Benny Friedman and Giant Pros Stage Scoreless Tie

Benny's Forward Pass Plays Bring First Downs, But No Touchdowns in Opener Here.

BY AL SOMMER.

After four scoreless quarters by the New York Giants and Benny Friedman's Cleveland Bulldogs, in the National league's 1927 inaugural at Luna Park stadium yesterday, nearly 3,000 customers were willing to attest that goose-eggs on the scoreboard do not make for spectacular football.

Too much of the defensive game kept long runs scarce and allowed the grass around the goal posts to go unmolested from football cleats.

Benny Friedman's professional bow before the home folks was not made with the football finesse that marked him as Michigan's All-American. Just as beauty cannot be a foil for beauty, Benny found his pigskin craft matched with defensive cunning to equal it.

Field Goal Try Is Blocked.

Twice he passed in the second quarter with much of the old deadly aim and the Bulldogs made their greatest threat of the game by recording three of their four first downs, all of which were made by passing. One to Bloodgood netted twenty yards and another to Randels brought fifteen. Catching one of Feather's tosses for twenty, Benny was leading the way to the goal, only to be held on the next three downs. On the fourth, a dropkick was blocked by the Giants, Rehnquist recovering just in time to hear the whistle at the half.

Twice were the distinguished digits of Fat Henry's largest toe called upon to dropkick, from the twenty and thirty-seven-yard lines as a phase of the Giant attack, but the famous W. and J. heavyweight

missed both of 'em. McBride, once a famous Syracuse back, elected the placement three times only to have his boot go askew.

On first downs, the Bulldogs were outplayed two to one. The punting was about ever although Doug Wycoff, of Georgia Tech fame, got the best boot of the day, a seventy-yard spiral that backed the Bulldogs far into their own territory.

Tim Mara, famous New York sportsman and owner of the New York Giants eleven, was in the stands watching his high-priced performers and probably thinking of the thoughts of Col. Jacob Ruppert when his $70,000 bambino Ruth is at bat. So was Joe Carr, president of the National Pro league.

Another famous spectator at the professional pastiming was Bo McMillan, he of the Praying Colonels when the couple hundred Centre students decided to play the collegiate game one fall not so long ago.

Bulldogs—0.	Position.	Giants—0.
Cunningham	L. E.	Stahlman
Cobb	L. T.	(c) S. Owen
Rehnquist	L. G.	Alexander
Smith	C.	Biggs
McGee	R. G.	Nesser
W. Owen	R. T.	Henry
Munn	R. E.	Hubbard
Perry	Q.	Imlay
Thomas	L. H.	Haines
Friedman	R. H.	Wycoff
Feather	F.	McBride

Substitutions—Cleveland: Bloodgood, q.; Weberg, f.; Howard, rg.; Dewitz, lh.; Simmons, lh.; Bagby, f.; Krysl, rt.; Randels, le. New York: Wilson, rh.; Guyon, rs.; Jappe, le.; Murtagh, c.; Stahlman, le.; Biggs, c.; Marker, re.; Wycoff, rh.; White, rh.; Haggerty, f.

Referee—T. Hughitt. Umpire—Powell. Head linesman—Fitting.

Reprinted from
The Cleveland Plain Dealer

Nov. 14

Chicago Bears Win Over Pottsville, 30-12

Chicago—(AP)—The Chicago Bears resumed their interrupted string of football victories in the National Football league by outplaying Pottsville 30-12 Sunday. Paddy Driscoll, the Bears' star, rested up in the first period, which ended scoreless, and then went in to drive the Bears through the Pottsville line for repeated long gains. The Bears made two safeties before they got their first touchdown. Sternaman's passes to White and Senn accounted for two touchdowns for the Chicagoans. Driscoll kicked two of the Bears' four tries at goal, while Pottsville missed both chances.

BULLDOGS LOSE TO JACKETS, 22 TO 0

Create Surprise in League With Slashing Attack Over Benny.

PHILADELPHIA, Nov. 12.—The remodeled edition of the Philadelphia Yellow Jackets created a real sensation in the Frankford Stadium this afternoon, when they romped away to a clear victory over the Cleveland Bulldogs in a National League game, triumphing by the margin 22 to 0. The same elevens play a return game in Cleveland Sunday.

The Yellow Jackets took advantage of the breaks, and with a series of stellar performances by Ken Mercer and Charley Rogers, as well as an invincible aerial attack, marched through to a top-heavy score. Odds on the game were 2 to 1 in favor of Cleveland when the game started and the locals had only a remote outside chance.

Cleveland was led by Benny Friedman, former Michigan All-American and heralded as one of the greatest Middle Western college quarterbacks of all time. Friedman started to show his stuff in the early stages of the game, but later he pulled two costly fumbles. Benny saw service in only part of the game.

For Philadelphia, Kassel, a second string end, created a stir when he received one of Friedman's fumbles in the final period and dashed almost the whole length of the field for a touchdown. Ken Mercer twice kicked from placement for six points.

Frankf'd—22.	Position.	Cleveland—0.
J. Weir	L. E.	Munn
Ed Weir	L. T.	Cobb
Comstock	L. G.	Rehnquist
Maxwell	C.	Smith
Connaughton	R. G.	Howard
Behman	R. T.	Owen
Kassel	R. E.	Bacchus
Rogers	Q.	Friedman
Mercer	L. H.	Thomas
Ford	R. H.	Wibers
Wilcox	F.	Feather

Philadelphia .... 0 15 0 7—22

Substitutions—Philadelphia: Fitzgibbons for Ford, Youngstrom for Behman, Kostos for J. Weir, Homan for Rogers. Filak for Connaughton. Cleveland: Dewitz for Thomas, Krysl for Owen, Thomas for Dewetz. Bloodgood for Friedman. Touchdowns—Rogers, Kassel. Points after touchdowns—Mercer 2 (placement). Field goals—Mercer 2 (placement). Safety —Thomas.

Referee — Thomas Hughitt (Buffalo). Umpire — Crowley (Washington). Head linesman—Purnell (Frankford). Time of periods—15m.

Reprinted from
The Cleveland Plain Dealer

FRIEDMAN'S TEAM IN 26-0 WIN OVER CANTON BULLDOGS

Benny Simply Forward Passes Cleveland to Victory in Game Termed "Title Tilt."

CANTON, O., Dec. 4.—The Cleveland Bulldogs made merry at expense of the Canton Bulldogs here this afternoon, rolling up a 26 to 0 victory, in a game which was termed for the professional championship of the state.

All the points were made in the first half and all were directly brought about by Benny Friedman. Four times he tossed passes to teammates and on the other occasion he broke through the Canton line and ran 36 yards for a touchdown. He kicked goal on two attempts.

Friedman left the game at the end of the first half and did not return. Throughout the second session it was an open battle with the local eleven several times carrying the ball deep into Cleveland's territory, but never managing to take it across.

While he was in the game Friedman tossed ten passes, eight being completed for a total gain of 238 yards.

The first touchdown came in the early part of the second period, when Friedman tossed a 12-yard pass to Thomas, who ran the remaining 40 yards. Friedman missed goal.

In the second quarter Bacchus galloped 19 yards after receiving a 20-yard pass from Friedman. Friedman kicked goal. The next two came in rapid succession, Friedman racing 36 yards for the first after 18 and 25-yard passes had put the ball in scoring position. The final one came when Friedman passed to Bacchus who ran for a touchdown, a total of 65 yards. Friedman kicked goal after the second.

It was announced before the game that "Hall" Broda, All-American end, from Brown, had been released from the Cleveland team.

Clevela'd—26.	Position.	Canton—0.
Munn	L. E.	Daum
Cobb	L. T.	Caldwell
Caywood	L. G.	Gibson
Rohnquist	C.	Barry
Howard	R. G.	Flattery
Owens	R. T.	Nichols
Bacchus	R. E.	Bissell
Friedman	Q.	Robb
Thomas	L. H.	Griggs
Simmons	R. H.	Roderick
Wiberg	F.	Calac

Cleveland ..... 6 20 0 0—26

Substitutions—Cleveland: Blockgood for Friedman, Randel for Munn, Krysl for Owens. Canton: Marker for Griggs, Casmer for Roderick.

Touchdowns—Thomas, Bacchus 2, Friedman. Points after touchdown—Friedman 2.

Referee—Durfee. Umpire—Karsh. Head linesman—Watts.

ALL GIANT WINS ARE BY SHUTOUTS. GIANTS OUTSCORE OPPOSITION 213 TO 20.

GRANGE JEERED IN GOTHAM TILT

Red, Playing With Yanks, Razzed As Giants Take 14-0 Decision.

New York, Dec. 4 (Special).—Red Grange, the hero of many a hard-fought football game and the idol of a nation, realized today as he lined up behind the retreating Yankees on the snowy, wind-swept field at the Polo Grounds, that fame is futile and the wages thereof is the razzberry.

Even though Grange played every minute of the game against the Giants and did his best with a bad leg, it was not he who was cheered by the crowd of approximately 8,000 persons who braved a snowstorm and the bitter cold wind to see for themselves whether the Yankees could beat the Giants.

Handed Bronx Cheer.

It was Hinkey Haines and Jack McBride whose names were shouted out into the storm and borne upward by the wind. All Grange got was the Bronx cheer, a prolonged boo, which must have fallen strangely on the ears of one who has known nothing but the approving roars of many a multitude.

It was Haines who was applauded vociferously in the first period. Haines, the former Penn State star, twisted himself loose from two tacklers on his own 20-yard line and dodged past the entire Yankee team to run 80 yards to a touchdown.

Then McBride brought the crowd to its feet in the third quarter by plowing through the Yankee line like a steam shovel in the course of a general push that started from the Yankees' 45-yard line and ended when McBride, with only a yard to go, went over for the second touchdown. McBride made extra points for both scores from placement. So, the Giants defeated the Yankees the first game they have played for the championship of the city by a score of 14 to 0. At the same time the Giants retained their grip on the leadership of the National Football League.

Use Straight Football.

In this game between the two local professional teams, each with its quota of former college stars, the Giants made 11 first downs to the Yankees' nine. Most of the Giants' yardage was made by straight, old-fashioned football. They tried nine forward passes. Only one was completed, a short one from McBride to Corgan in the third period while the Giants were moving toward their second touchdown.

The Yankees had better luck with their passing game. They tried 19 passes and completed six of them. All told, 10 passes were intercepted—five by the Giants and five by the Yankees. The Giants had three of their passes grounded and the Yankees had eight.

It was their inability to complete their passes at critical moments that cost the Yankees the game. They had the ball on the Giants' 30-yard line in the first period when Hagerty intercepted a pass. They were on the Giants' 25-yard line in the fourth period and later on the 15-yard line. McBride intercepted a pass from the 25-yard line and White took the ball away from the Yankees after they had recovered a fumble and were on the 15-yard mark.

	W	L	T	Pct.
N.Y. Giants	11	1	1	.917
Green Bay	7	2	1	.778
Chi. Bears	9	3	2	.750
Cleveland	8	4	1	.667
Providence	8	5	1	.615
N.Y. Yankees	7	8	1	.467
Frankford	6	9	3	.400
Pottsville	5	8	0	.385
Chi. Cardinals	3	7	1	.300
Dayton	1	6	1	.143
Duluth	1	8	0	.111
Buffalo	0	5	0	.000

Nov. 12

New Yorkers Flash Threat in Last Minute, but Bays Block Drop Kick

Green Bay 0. New York Yankees 0.
Frankford 24. Pottsville 0.
Chicago Bears 27. Dayton 0.
New York Giants 19, Detroit 19.

THE STANDINGS

	Won	Tied	Lost	Pct.
Frankford	7	1	1	.875
Providence	5	0	1	.833
Green Bay	4	2	2	.667
New York Giants	4	2	2	.667
Chicago Bears	4	1	2	.667
Detroit	3	1	2	.600
Chicago Cardinals	1	0	2	.333
Pottsville	1	1	5	.167
New York Yankees	1	1	6	.167
Dayton	0	0	6	.000

BY OLIVER E. KUECHLE
OF THE JOURNAL STAFF

Green Bay, Wis.—Neither the Packers nor the Yankees had a scoring punch in their National league football game before 6,000 fans here Sunday and it ended in a scoreless tie. The game was fought almost entirely between New York's 20-yard line and midfield, except for the last two minutes, when a long pass, Kelly to Gibby Welch, gave the Yankees first down on Green Bay's 12-yard line. They couldn't advance any farther, however, and on the fourth down the Blues blocked Grube's drop kick.

This was New York's only real threat of the game. Unable to do anything against the powerful Green Bay line the Yanks went into the air a lot, even deep in their own territory, and though they completed a fair percentage of these shots they never had possession of the ball beyond midfield until the last few minutes, as mentioned above.

Bays Miss Big Chance

Green Bay, too, got inside the 20-yard line only once. In the third quarter Lewellen and O'Boyle carried the ball to the 18-yard line. The line opened dandy holes for them and they drove through at top speed. Further attempts to advance went for naught, however, and on fourth down O'Boyle's place kick sailed wide.

The Packers clearly had the edge in running plays, but their vaunted passing attack went haywire. They completed only five out of 24 heaves.

That probably tells better than anything else why the big Blue team, one of the leaders in the league and favorites to win this game, got no better than a tie.

Punting Is Excellent

Lewellen again sent soaring punts down the field that helped keep the play in enemy territory or around midfield. Several of them he placed exceptionally well, the ball rolling out of bounds inside the 10-yard line. Flaherty, former Gonzaga star, did the booting for the Yanks and he, too, made a man's job of it most of the time. One or two of his kicks were bad, but the rest of them sailed as he intended them to. He had the help of an exceptionally fast end, Grube, who covered punts like a hawk and as often as not nailed the receiver in his tracks.

It was a rough game and the officials had to warn the players several times to stay within sportsmanlike limits.

GREEN BAY		NEW YORK
Dilweg	L. E.	Grube
Perry	L. T.	Gallagher
Minick	L. G.	L. McLean
Earp	C.	MacArthur
Jones	R. G.	Hogue
Ashmore	R. T.	Michaelske
O'Donnel	R. E.	Flaherty
Dunn	Q.	Welch
Lewellen	L. H.	Salemni
Kotal	R. H.	Smith
O'Boyle	F.	Pritchard

Substitutions—Packers, Nash for O'Donnell, Cahoon for Perry, Perry for Ashmore, Baker for O'Boyle. Marks for Dunn, Lambeau for Lewellen: New York Yankees, Kelly for Salemni. Molenda for Pritchard, Rausch for MacArthur. Referee. Lawrie (Chicago); umpire, Christensen (Menominee); head linesman, Johnson (Chicago).

Bears Beat Dayton

Chicago—(P)—Flashing a brilliant passing attack the Chicago Bears trounced the Dayton Triangles 27 to 0, in a National Professional league football game at Wrigley field Sunday.

The first touchdown came in the first period when Walquist drove over from the five-yard line. In the second period Senn passed 30 yards to Wallace and then hurled to Sturtridge for 20 yards and a third touchdown.

After scoring another touchdown by a 20-yard pass from Joe Sternaman to Senn, the Bears sent in their reserves. Paddy Driscoll kicked two goals for extra points after touchdown and Sturnaman booted the third

Dec. 10

Packer Pass Defeats Bears in Final Game

10,000 Fans Attend the Last Pro Tilt of the Season at Chicago; Touchdown at Finish

Pro Grid Standings

	W	L	T	Pct.
Providence	8	2	1	.888
Detroit	7	1	2	.778
Frankford (Phils)	10	2	3	.769
Chicago Bears	7	1	4	.636
Green Bay	6	3	4	.600
New York Giants	4	2	6	.400
New York Yankees	3	1	8	.273
Pottsville	2	0	8	.200
Chicago Cardinals	1	0	5	.167
Dayton	0	0	7	.000

BY SPECIAL CORRESPONDENT OF THE JOURNAL

Chicago—A sensational catch of a forward pass by Dick O'Donnell in the last two minutes of play gave the Green Bay Packers a 6-0 victory over the Chicago Bears at Cubs park Sunday before a crowd of 10,000. The game, which brought the pro football season here to a close, was filled with thrills. Each team had several chances to score, but always the defense tightened to avert the danger.

The Bears' best opportunity came in the first quarter, when Driscoll garnered a long pass from Walquist and galloped to the 12-yard line. The Packers held tight and Driscoll was forced to try a drop kick, which went wide. Shortly before the end of the game the Packers rushed the ball deep into Bear territory, where the Bears held and Molenda's placement try failed. Driscoll punted and Dunn returned 10 yards to the Bear 48-yard mark.

Molenda failed on a line smash and then Dunn dropped back and threw a long pass almost as the Bear line was upon him. O'Donnell made a sensational catch and ran 15 yards for the score. The touchdown threw 700 Green Bay fans into hysterics of joy. In the two remaining minutes the Bears tried a vain passing attack which ended when Dunn intercepted a pass and averted further danger.

PACKERS		BEARS
Dilweg	L. E.	Voss
Perry	L. T.	Lyman
Minick	L. G.	Buckler
Earp	C.	Fleckenstein
Jones	R. G.	McMillen
Ashmore	R. T.	Evans
Nash	R. E.	Carlson
Dunn	Q.	Sternman
Lewellen	L. H.	Driscoll
Kotal	R. H.	Senn
Molenda	F.	White
Packers		0 0 0 6
Bears		0 0 0 0

Substitutions—Packers: Darling for Earp, O'Donnell for Nash. Cahoon for Perry. Bears: Walquist for Senn, Senn for Driscoll, Driscoll for Senn. Wallace for Carlson, Sturtridge for Walquist. Touchdowns—O'Donnell.

Dec. 3

Driscoll Stars as Bears Win

Chicago—(AP)—With Paddy Driscoll playing the leading role with his long dashes, passes and kicks, the Chicago Bears overwhelmed the Frankford Yellowjackets of Philadelphia, 28 to 6, at their National Professional league football game at Wrigley field Sunday.

The Yellowjackets outplayed the Bears in the first period when they scored their only touchdown, but thereafter it was all Bears. After failing to make a first down in the initial period, the Bears came back with 20 points in the second quarter. A pass, Driscoll to Sturtridge, netted ** yards and the first touchdown. The second was made after Driscoll slashed 48 yards to the two-yard line from where White plunged over. Driscoll scored the other two touchdowns on passes and end runs. He also drop kicked for all extra points.

Wally Diehl, fullback for the Frankford Yellowjackets football team, suffered a fractured skull in Sunday's game. Diehl was injured in the second period when he was tackled while carrying the ball. He was taken to the American hospital and was reported resting fairly comfortably Sunday night.

Packers Tied at Providence

Pro Grid Standings

	W	L	T	Pct.
Providence	8	2	1	.239
Frankford (Philadelphia)	9	2	3	.750
Detroit	6	1	2	.750
Chicago Bears	7	1	3	.700
Green Bay	5	3	4	.556
New York Giants	4	2	5	.444
New York Yankees	3	1	7	.300
Pottsville	2	0	8	.200
Chicago Cardinals	1	0	5	.167
Dayton	0	0	7	.000

BY SPECIAL CORRESPONDENT OF THE JOURNAL.

Providence, R. I.—Playing one of their best games of the season the Green Bay Packers battled the Providence Steamrollers to a 7-7 tie here Sunday before a crowd of 9,000.

The Steamrollers, 1928 pennant winners, have a powerful machine which includes a couple of wrestlers, Sonnenberg and Spellman, but the Bays more than held their own.

Right from the opening whistle the Bays cut loose with a high powered attack which soon had the crowd groaning "Hold 'em Rollers—hold 'em." After one march down the field Providence found itself and did some ground gaining, with Wildcat Wilson running from a kick formation.

Break Costs Score

It was a seesaw battle up until the middle of the second quarter when the Packers unleashed several forward passes and got a bad break. With the goal line only two feet away Marks plunged over but Sonnenberg hit him like an elephant and the ball slipped out of his grasp. There was a wild scramble and when the referee pulled the players apart Smith had the ball and it went for a touchback.

Early in the third quarter the Packers chalked up their touchdown. Three passes put the ball on the 20-yard line for a first down. Two line plunges hit a stone wall and then Lewellen passed to Marks, who juggled the ball but stumbled across the line with it for a touchdown. O'Boyle kicked the goal.

The touchdown seemed to steam up the rollers and after receiving the next kickoff crashed their way down the field which terminated in a touchdown when Oden outran O'Boyle and grabbed a pass for a score.

Count Is Tied

Sonnenberg added the goal kick, knotting the count at 7 all.

Once after this the Rollers threatened, but Sonnenberg's attempted place kick was blocked by O'Boyle, who picked up the oval and traveled to mid-field before he was caught from behind by Oden.

The lineup:

PROVIDENCE		GREEN BAY
Hanney	L. E	Dilweg
Sonnenberg	L. T	Cahoon
Rhenquist	L. G	Bowdoin
C. Smith	C	Earpes
Fleischman	R. G	Woodin
Jackson	R. T	Perry
Spellman	R. E	O'Donnell
Oden	Q	Lewellen
Wilson	L. H	Marks
J. Cronin	R. H	Kotal
Haddon	F	Webber

Touchdowns—Marks, Oden. Points after touchdowns—O'Boyle (placement), Sonnenberg (placement). Substitutions—Providence: A. Wilson for Fleischman, O. Smith for Jackson, B. Cronin for Spellman, Simmons for J. Cronin; Green Bay: Darling for Earpes, Minick for Bowdoin, Hearnden for Marks, O'Boyle for Webber.

Driscoll Wants to Quit as Winner

Chicago—(AP)—Paddy Driscoll, who has been playing football and playing it well for almost 20 years, wants to quit the game, but he wants to quit as a winner.

Sunday Paddy, who is well up in his thirties, announced he had donned the moleskins as a player for the last time when he trotted on the field to help the Chicago Bears fight their old professional enemies, the Green Bay Packers. But the Packers won, 6 to 0. So Paddy changed his mind.

"Don't know whether I'll quit or not," he said. "I believe I'll play until I can quit as a winner."

One of the greatest triple threat men ever to prance upon a gridiron, Driscoll has been an outstanding star since his days at Northwestern university back in 1916. In 1918 he was the outstanding player on the famous Great Lakes eleven, the first team ever awarded a national championship by sports writers and critics. Since that time he has been playing professional football. Despite his age he is fast and often gets away for long dashes, outfooting football stars many years his junior. Drop kicking is his forte.

1928

	W	L	T	Pct.
Providence	8	1	2	.889
Frankford	11	3	2	.786
Detroit	7	2	1	.778
Green Bay	6	4	3	.600
Chi. Bears	7	5	1	.583
N.Y. Giants	4	7	2	.364
N.Y. Yankees	4	8	1	.333
Pottsville	2	8	0	.200
Chi. Cardinals	1	5	0	.167
Dayton	0	7	0	.000

Sept. 16

Packers Beat Portsmouth

SPECIAL CORRESPONDENT OF THE JOURNAL.

Green Bay, Wis.—The Green Bay Packers opened the professional football season by defeating Portsmouth, Ohio, 14-0, in a clean cut contest here Sunday. The Packers were celebrating their eleventh anniversary as a professional football club and the attendance broke all records for an opening game. Some 5,000 were present.

Lewellen, Brown county's district attorney and veteran Packer halfback, scored the first touchdown in the second quarter. The score came after Brumbaugh, former Florida halfback with Portsmouth, picked up a long punt back on his own goal line and attempted to run with it. He was downed on his four-yard line. Armil punted out of bounds on the 10-yard line and a few seconds later Lewellen crashed over for the counter. Bo Molenda made the extra point from placement.

In the final period the Packers again got a break when Armil, Portsmouth quarterback, fumbled a bad pass from center. The Packers recovered on Portsmouth's six-yard line and Lidberg, Packer fullback, crashed over the line. Blood dropkicked for the extra point.

Portsmouth was never dangerous but the Ohioans fought doggedly from the first to the last whistle. Led by Chuck Bennett, former Indian halfback, and Father Lumpkin of Georgia Tech fame, the visitors presented a strong battle front but Lewellen's educated toe, coupled with some brilliant line work by Michalske and Kern, gave the Packers a commanding edge.

The lineup:

PACKERS		PORTSMOUTH
Dilweg	L. E.	Webber
Cahoon	L. T.	Jolley
Michalske	L. G.	Ongley
Darling	C.	Randolph
Bowdoin	R. G.	McClure
Perry	R. T.	Harris
O'Connell	R. E.	Joseph
Dunn	Q.	Armil
Blood	L. H.	Bennett
Baker	R. H.	Fyock
Lidberg	F.	Lumpkin
Packers	0 7 0 7—14	
Portsmouth	0 0 0 0— 0	

Substitutions—P a c k e r s, Lewellen for Blood, Kotal for Baker, Molenda for Lidberg, Earpe for Daling, Kern for Cahoon, Young for Bowdoin, Woodin for Michalske, McCrary for Molenda, Ashmore for Perry, Lidberg for McCrary, Darling for Earpe, Baker for Kotal, Lewellen for Dunn, Blood for Baker, Michalske for Woodin, Zuidmulder for Blood, Evans for Lewellen, Laabs for Baker; Portsmouth, Magliceau for Jolley, Brumbaugh for Fyock, Witt for Bennett, Jolley for Magliceau, Fyock for Brumbaugh, Bennett for Witt, Mayer for Joseph, McClure for Meyers, Deweez for Ongley, Meyers for McClure, Magliceau for Bennett, Witt for Armil, Machieu for Lumpkin, Brumbaugh for Fyock. Touchdowns — Lewellen, Lidberg. Points after touchdowns—Molenda, Blood. Officials—Referee, Doyle (Menominee); umpire. Iverson (Sheboygan); head linesman, Downer (Milwaukee).

Reprinted from
The Milwaukee Journal

Nov. 25

Magnificent Defense Against Forward Passes Brings Victory

Green Bay Plays Like a College Team: Winners Alert

BY A. D. GANNON
Special to the Milwaukee Journal

NEW YORK—The Green Bay Packers crushed the aspirations of the New York Giants and Benny Friedman to the national professional football championship Sunday afternoon at the Polo Grounds 20 to 6.

It was one of the Packers' most decisively delivered wallopings of the season and made their ninth straight victory this year. Also it was the Giants' first defeat in nine games. More than 25,000 saw the game.

A varied assault, alertness and a magnificent defense against Friedman's remarkable passing game contributed to the victory. Almost equally remarkable was the completeness of the Packer's repertoire of tactics with Verne Lewellen outkicking his opponents and passing as skillfully, if not more so, than Friedman, with the almost horizontal shattering plunging of Bo Molenda, the uncanny pass snatching of McCrary and Dilweg and the ground gaining tricks of Blood.

Reprinted from
The Milwaukee Journal

GREEN BAY		GIANTS
Dilweg	LE	Flaherty
Kern	LT	S. Owen
Michalske	LG	Ashburn
Earpe	C	Westopal
Bowdoin	RG	Caywood
Hubbard	RT	W. Owen
Nash	RE	Munn
McCrary	Q	Friedman
Blood	LR	Plansky
Lewellen	RH	Sedbrooke
Molenda	F	Feather
Green Bay	7 0 0 13—20	
Giants	0 0 6 0— 6	

Touchdowns: McCrary, Plansky, Molenda, Blood. Points after touchdowns Molenda 2.

Substitutions: Green Bay Minick for Bowdoin. Giants Howard for S. Owen, Murtagh for Westopal, McMullen for Ashburn, Moran for Sedbrooke, Hagerty for Plansky, Meilzinar for S. Owen. Campbell for Munn, S. Owen for Meilzinar, Plansky for Hagerty, Munn for Campbell, Meilzinar for McMullen, Campbell for Flaherty, Hagerty for Moran, Ashburn for W. Owen, Howard for S. Owen, Snyder for Hagerty.

Referee: T. Hughitt (Buffalo) umpire F. Hoban (Baltimore), linesman Powell (Philadelphia), field judge, John Hennessy (Brooklyn).

80-Yard March in Last Quarter Causes Collapse of Losers

Nov. 25

Nevers Is Star; Cards Win, 19-0

Chicago—(*P*)—Ernie Nevers threw passes, ran and smashed the line to score three touchdowns and give the Chicago Cardinals a 19 to 0 victory over the Dayton Triangles in a National Professional football game at Comiskey park Sunday.

Nevers scored through tackle for the first Card touchdown in the first period and he went through the line for the second one after intercepting a Dayton pass in the second session. He shoved over for the final Cardinal touchdown in the third period after a march which started when Kassel recovered a Triangle fumble.

First for Bisons

Chicago—(*P*)—The Buffalo Bisons of the National Professional Football league, won their first game of the season Sunday, trouncing the Chicago Bears, 19 to 7. Chuck Weimer, left halfback for the Bisons, broke a 7-7 tie in the last period by place kicking two goals from the field and later bucked over for the Bison's second touchdown.

Get Your Tickets Early

Every seat in the park will be reserved for next Sunday's game with the Chicago Bears but there will be no increase in prices. An extra 1000 seats will be set up to handle what promises to be the largest crowd that ever witnessed a football game in Green Bay. There will be standing room for 1,500 while the seating capacity of the park will house nearly 9,000.

Annual Excursion of Yellow Jackets to New York This Sunday

World's Champion Bugle Corps of Frankford Legion Post and Yellow Jacket's Band to Accompany Rooters on Special Train to View Battle with New York Giants at Polo Grounds

BUGLE CORPS TO GIVE EXHIBITION DRILL

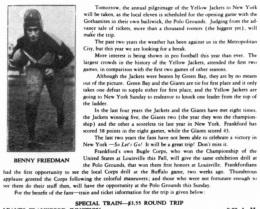

BENNY FRIEDMAN

Tomorrow, the annual pilgrimage of the Yellow Jackets to New York will be taken, as the local eleven is scheduled for the opening game with the Gothamites in their own bailiwick, the Polo Grounds. Judging from the advance sale of tickets, more than a thousand rooters (the biggest yet), will make the trip.

The past two years the weather has been against us in the Metropolitan City, but this year we are looking for a break.

More interest is being shown in pro football this year than ever. The largest crowds in the history of the Yellow Jackets, attended the first two games, in comparison with the first two games of other seasons.

Although the Jackets were beaten by Green Bay, they are by no means out of the picture. Green Bay and the Giants are tie for first place and it only takes one defeat to topple either for first place, and the Yellow Jackets are going to New York Sunday to endeavor to knock one leader from the ladder.

In the last four years the Jackets and the Giants have met eight times, the Jackets winning five, the Giants two (the year they won the championship) and the other a scoreless tie last year in New York. Frankford has scored 38 points in the eight games, while the Giants scored 43.

The last two years the fans have not been able to celebrate a victory in New York —So Let's Go! It will be a great trip! Don't miss it.

Frankford's own Bugle Corps, who won the Championship of the United States at Louisville this Fall, will give the same exhibition drill at the Polo Grounds, that won them first honors at Louisville. Frankfordians had the first opportunity to see the local Corps drill at the Buffalo game, two weeks ago. Thunderous applause greeted the Corps following the colorful maneuvers; and those who were not fortunate enough to see them do their stuff then, will have the opportunity at the Polo Grounds this Sunday.

For the benefit of the fans—train and ticket information for the trip is given below:

SPECIAL TRAIN—$3.55 ROUND TRIP

LEAVES FRANKFORD JUNCTION	. . . .	9:00 A. M.
" FRANKFORD	. . . .	9:02 A. M.
" WISSINOMING	. . . .	9:05 A. M.
" TACONY	. . . .	9:08 A. M.

RETURNING

LEAVES NEW YORK (Penna. Station) . . . . 9:05 P. M.

Tickets for special train and game on sale at the official ticket office of the Frankford Athletic Association (2d floor) Lawson Building, Paul Street and Frankford Avenue.

FOX MOVIETONE TO TAKE MOVIES

Word has been received from Dr. March, of the New York Giants, that the Fox Motion Picture Corporation and Fox Movietone News will take motion pictures of the Champion Bugle Corps, Yellow Jackets' Band and crowd for National distribution at the New York game at the Polo Grounds. He also advises that ex-Governor Al Smith will attend the game with a party of two hundred newsboys from Lower New York.

LET'S GO!!!

Dec. 9

Green Bay in Final Victory Over Bears

Wisconsin Team First to Complete Season Undefeated

Pro Grid Standings

Club—	Won	Lost	Tied	Pct.
Green Bay	12	0	1	1.000
New York	12	1	1	.923
Frankford	9	4	5	.692
Chicago Cards	6	6	1	.500
Boston	4	4	0	.500
Stapleton	3	4	3	.429
Orange	3	4	4	.429
Providence	4	6	2	.400
Chicago Bears	4	8	2	.333
Buffalo	1	7	1	.125
Minneapolis	1	9	0	.100
Dayton	0	6	0	.000

SUNDAY'S RESULTS

Green Bay 25, Chicago Bears 0.
Cardinals 26, Orange 6.
New York 31, Frankford 0.
New York 12, Frankford 0 (played Saturday).

BEARS		PACKERS
Johnson	L. E.	Dilweg
Nelson	L. T.	Kern
Carlson	L. G.	Michaleske
Pearson	C.	Earpe
Kopcha	R. G.	Bowdoin
Murry	R. T.	Hubbard
Fleckenstein	R. E.	O'Donnell
Driscoll	Q.	Dunn
Grange	L. H.	Lewellen
Walquist	R. H.	Kotal
Holmer	F.	Lidberg

Touchdowns—Lidberg, Lewellen, Kotal 1 Point after touchdown—Dunn (placement). Substitutions—Bears: Sternaman for Driscoll, Garland Grange for Fleckenstein, Poliski for Kopcha, Senn for Walquist, Elness for Grange. Packers: Nash for O'Donnell, Perry for Hubbard, Woodin for Bowdoin, Darling for Earpe, O'Donnell for Dilweg, McCrary for Lidberg. Officials—Referee, Durfee (Columbus); umpire, Karsh (Columbus); head linesman, Olson (Gary).

Reprinted from
The Milwaukee Journal

Dec. 11

Mob Packers at Green Bay

20,000 Out to Welcome Football Champions Home

BY STAFF CORRESPONDENT OF THE JOURNAL

Green Bay, Wis.—Nearly 20,000 citizens of this city worked themselves into a veritable frenzy Monday night welcoming home the victorious champions of professional football, the Green Bay Packers.

Green Bay actually surprised itself and an astonished squad of grid heroes. As the train, with the special coach bearing the team, moved cautiously into the city, a mighty din of whistles, automobile horns and voices from thousands of throats rose in the night air.

The first blast of the train whistle, several blocks from the station, was the signal for the loosing of the emotions of thousands.

Rush Upon Tracks

The milling throng that blocked every street to traffic for blocks about the depot surged upon the tracks at the risk of their lives for their first glimpse of the victors.

It was necessary to bring the train to a complete stop as it approached the depot and husky policemen fought with crowds to clear the way. Passengers in the first few cars were startled out of their magazines and wondered what it was all about.

As the special car moved slowly into the depot, the strains of "Hail, Hail, the Gang's All Here" carried the city's first greeting.

The team expected a welcome but nothing like that. The police, augmented by a company of home guards, made futile attempts to control the crowds.

Helpless Against Mob

It was 15 minutes before the players wormed their way through the shouting and enthusiastic crowd to the waiting busses, where even the reception committee stood helpless against the mob.

After the players, with their wives and sweethearts, who boarded the train either at Chicago or De Pere, were bundled aboard the busses, a parade through the city was begun.

It moved through the west side, then crossed the river, wended its way through the business district on the east side and stopped at the city hall, where Mayor John Diener pronounced the official welcome. The procession was headed by the American Legion band.

During the parade shouting throngs lined every street. The crowds after compelled the busses to come to a complete stop.

Reprinted from
The Milwaukee Journal

Nov. 17

Bays Play Worst Game of Season

Nevers and Rose Star as Chicago Eleven Upsets All the Dope

BY OLIVER E. KUECHLE
OF THE JOURNAL STAFF

CHICAGO, Ill.—Its a long, long winning streak that doesn't end up somewhere. Ask the Green Bay Packers today. They know. On top of the football world with 22 straight victories since 1928, not counting the tie with Philadelphia last year, they lost to the Chicago Cardinals before 12,000 pop eyed, almost unbelieving fans at Comiskey park here Sunday afternoon, 13 to 6.

Amazing as this was, one of the major upsets in the National league this fall, even more so was the way they lost. They were no more the great team that played such perfect football in beating the Bears a week ago than Comiskey park is Wrigley field. They were a second rate team at best, almost a sloppy rate second team in spots, foozling their passes or dropping them, fumbling, having a punt blocked, muffing their signals. As something indicative of their entire play, for instance, they gained only 59 yards from scrimmage all afternoon against a club they themselves had pushed up and down the field in a previous meeting in September.

Let Down

A let down after their bruising battle with the Bears a week ago undoubtedly explains it. The men were dead, without physical zip or mental pepper, and their mechanical football alone was no weapon at all.

All this, of course, does not take anything away from the Cardinals. Ernie Nevers men played hard, smart ball and clearly deserved to win, perhaps even by more than they did, since they had the ball on Green Bay's one-yard line when the game ended. It does tell, however, what sort of club they beat.

All was not gloom in the Green Bay camp Sunday night, however, as you might expect after a catastrophe like this. The while the Cardinals dealt so rudely with the champions the Bears beat the Giants in New York, 12 to 0, and as a result the leaders kept their relative positions, the Packers in first place with a standing of 8-1-.889 and the Giants in second place with a standing of 10-2-.834. They will meet at the Polo Grounds Sunday and as likely as not they will settle the 1930 race then and there.

The line-ups:

PACKERS		CARDINALS
Haycraft	L. E.	Kennedy
Hubbard	L. T.	Tinsley
Michaleske	L. G.	Kiessling
Darling	C.	Randolph
Franta	R. G.	Blumer
Perry	R. T.	Slater
O'Donnell	R. E.	Kassell
Lewellen	Q.	Baker
Pape	L. H.	Bolden
Englemann	R. H.	Rose
Lidberg	F.	Nevers
Packers		0 6 0 0— 6
Cardinals		0 6 0 7—13

Substitutions— Packers: Molenda for Lidberg. Dilweg for Haycraft. Blood for Pape. Dunn for Englemann. Earpe for Darling. Zuver for Franta. Nash for O'Donnell. Kern for Hubbard. Hubbard for Perry. Cardinals: Boyd for Belden. Gordon for Tonsley.

News of the League

John Depler's Brooklyn aggregation gave a good account of itself in Chicago by battling the Bears to a no-score tie. The Bruins threatened in the final minutes but Brooklyn held tight for downs on its 4-yard stripe.

The Green Bay Packers celebrated the raising of the 1929 championship pennant by administering a 14 to 0 defeat to the Chicago Cardinals. Dilweg and Lewellen, two of the Packers' All-Americans, made the touchdowns.

Wally Diehl, Frankford's steller fullback, is assisting Bull Behman in the Yellow Jackets coaching this season. Diehl will have charge of the backfield candidates while Behman will pay special attention to the forwards.

Jack McBride, a veteran of professional football, is making the grade with Brooklyn. The former Syracuse all-American fullback is bucking the line just as he did in his "rah rah" days at the Salt City institution.

Business is booming in a professional way at Green Bay. Some 2,500 additional seats have been constructed at the Packer Stadium, yet the management is looking for sell-outs at the Bear, New York and Frankford games.

George Trafton, veteran Bear center, is working his head off to win a regular post again this fall. The former Notre Dame center reported in good condition and it looks as if his comeback may be crowned with success.

Packers Raise Pro Grid Flag, Then Crush Cardinals, 14-0

Green Bay, Wis., Sept. 21.—[Special.]—The Green Bay Packers celebrated the raising of the 1929 National Professional football league pennant by defeating the Chicago Cardinals, 14 to 0, in the opening game of the league season here today before a crowd of 8,000.

The first quarter was scoreless with the Cardinals gaining some ground and holding their own. At the close of the first period, Johnny Blood replaced Engelmann at half back for the Packers, and swept around the Cardinal ends for long gains or broke through the line

The Cardinals couldn't get their passing attack organized, and every attempt to gain by this means was smothered. Late in the first quarter Molenda intercepted a Cardinal pass. Blood swept right end for 30 yards, placing the ball on the Cardinal 42 yard line. Lewellen got through tackle for 20 yards, and Blood and Molenda drove the ball to the 12 yard line as the quarter ended.

Pass Brings Touchdown.

When the second period started, Dunn picked up two yards for a first down, and Lewellen broke through for a touchdown. Dunn's kick from placement was good and the score was Packers, 7; Cardinals, 0.

At the opening of the third period Arnold Herber, Green Bay quarter back, passed 20 yards to Dilweg, who ran 20 yards for the second touchdown. Molenda kicked the goal from placement.

The Cardinals fought desperately in the final period, but Nevers was smothered when he attempted to launch the Cardinals' passing game. Later in the period he, was penalized 15 yards for grounding the ball when tackled in an attempt to pass far back of his line.

Belden, Bogss and McDonnell, Kassell, Kiesling and Slater turned in a good day's work for the Cards, but they were never able to threaten the Packers' goal.

Lewellen's punting gave the Pack-

On the Run

PACKERS [14].		CARDINALS [0].
Radick	L. E.	Kassell
Hubbard	L. T.	Slater
Michalske	L. G.	Bloomer
Darling	C.	Erickson
Bowdoin	R. G.	Kiesling
Sleight	R. T.	Williams
Nash	R. E.	Keneally
Herber	Q. B.	Baker
Lewellen	L. H.	Belden
Englemann	R. H.	McDonald
Molenda	F. B.	Flenniken

Touchdowns—Lewellen, Dilweg.

Points after touchdowns—Dunn, Molenda.

Substitutions—Packers: Dilweg for Radick; Blood for Engleman; Dunn for Herber; Perry for Hubbard; Earpe for Darling; Hanny for Sleight; Fitzgibbon for Lewellen; Woodin for Bowdoin; Bloodgood for Herber; McCrary for Molenda; Earpe for Hubbard; Zuver for Darling; Radick for Nash; Zuidmulder for Fitz Gibbons. Cardinals: Nevers for Flenniken; Gordon for Williams; Rooney for McDonald; Vessor for Kassell; Diehl for Bloomer; Failing for Keisling; Weaver for Kiesling; Randolph for Erickson; Pappio for Nevers; Gordon for Slater; Nevers for Rose; Belden for Pappio; Gordon for Tinsley.

Referee—Hall [Minneapolis]. Umpire—Keefe [Milwaukee]. Headlinesman—Iverson [Sheboygan].

ers an advantage in the first half of the game. Belden, Boyd, and Nevers punted for the Cardinals.

Next Sunday the Packers will meet the Chicago Bears here.

STAPLETON, 12; NEWARK, 6.

Stapleton, N. Y., Sept. 21.—(AP)—The Stapleton team of the National Professional Football league defeated Newark today, 12 to 6.

Ken Strong scored for the Stapes in the first period of an off thrust and Johnny Buckley added a second touchdown on a pass from Wykoff in the second period. Newark was held scoreless until the final quarter when Smith passed to Teddy Andonlewicz over the goal line. All tries for extra points were blocked.

Lest You Forget!

True Sport—Charity and Community Spirit—Slogan of F. A. A.

The management of the F. A. A. takes this opportunity to inform its patrons that the association is purely a community organization, and all profits derived from the games, etc., are donated to charity. Ever since the association was organized its policy has been to donate to local charity, and to this end the officers, directors and members of the F. A. A. give their untiring services and at the same time endeavor to give Frankford and the Greater Northeast a winning football team that will bring prestige to our town. Just keep these two facts in mind and remember when you attend the games you are not only supporting the team but giving to charity as well.

F. A. A. MANAGEMENT.

BEARS HELD TO SCORELESS TIE BY BROOKLYN PROS

Chicagoans Halted One Step from Goal.

No Decision

BEARS [0].		BROOKLYN [0].
Johnsos	L. E.	Stramiello
Nagurski	L. T.	Jolly
Schuette	L. G.	Garvey
Pearson	C.	Schieb
Frump	R. G.	Gillison
Murry	R. T.	Worden
G. Grange	R. E.	Plank
Sternaman	Q. B.	Yablok
H. Grange	L. H.	Hagberg
Nesbitt	R. H.	Thomas
Lintzenich	F. B.	McBride

Substitutions—Brooklyn: Cuneo for Worden, Lett for Jolly, Schubra for Hagberg, Weimer for Schubra, Greenberg for McBride. Bears: Trafton for Pearson, Carlson for Schuette, McMullen for Frump, Senn for Nesbitt, Walquist for Senn, Holmer for H. Grange, Steinbach for Murry, Lyman for Steinbach, Drury for Johnsos, Pauly for Nagurski, Nagurski for Lintzenich, Brumbaugh for Sternaman, Fleckenstein for G. Grange.

Referee—James Durfee, Columbus, O. Umpire—Carl Olson, Gary, Ind. Head linesman—L. F. Scott, Milwaukee, Wis.

BY WILFRID SMITH.

Chicago's Bears failed in their drive for a last minute victory by a step in the opening professional football game yesterday at Mills stadium against Brooklyn. While the Bears missed scoring by this narrowest of margins, the Brooklyn attack was equally impotent. Ten thousand opening day fans watched the elevens struggle up and down the dusty gridiron to a scoreless tie.

Sept. 22

The Chicago drive in the closing minutes deserved success. For a time it seemed the Bears could not be denied, as they ran and passed 75 yards to place the ball four yards from the Brooklyn goal with a first down. But Carl Brumbaugh, late of Florida university, who had replaced Joie Sternaman at quarter back, sent four plays at the center of the Brooklyn line, which massed to meet the plunges and halted the final effort a step from the goal line.

Both Make 15 First Downs.

Brooklyn took the ball, but after one play time was called.

While the Bears' goal line failure climaxed an afternoon of futility, both teams showed a surprising offense for an early season game. Each eleven counted 15 first downs, the Bears penetrating Brooklyn's defense on two other occasions while the Dodgers twice smashed toward victory. Once in the first quarter the Bear forwards broke through to smother the attack and again the fourth quarter Bronko Nagurski recovered a fumble to call a halt.

Coach Ralph Jones of the Bears used 23 players and they demonstrated the value of their three weeks of seasoning. Brooklyn, coached by John Depler, veteran pro star, also was well conditioned. The easterners had an advantage in that yesterday's contest was their second. They came to Chicago from the training camp at Magnetic Springs, O.

Recruits Make Good.

In addition to Bronko Nagurski, who served a spell in the line before returning at full back, the Bears' recruits fulfilled predictions. Joe Lintzenich, St. Louis university full back; Frank Pauly, tackle; Lyle Drury, a teammate of Lintzenich, and Dick Nesbitt, star of last year's Drake university eleven, gave excellent performances. Nesbitt was forced from the game in the second quarter when he fell as he was tackled and split the muscles on his left shoulder. He will be out of the game for several weeks.

Lintzenich furnished the Bears with some long distance kicking which they have needed for several seasons. One of his efforts traveled more than 70 yards.

Dec. 1

Grange Is Star; Savoldi Plays

Chicago, Ill.—(AP)—Red Grange had another one of his galloping days Sunday and the Chicago Bears defeated the Portsmouth Spartans, 14 to 6, in a National league football game. Fourteen thousand spectators saw the contest played in the mud.

Grange did not get away for any long runs, but he gained every time he started, scored a touchdown, tossed a pass to Luke Johnsos for the other and intercepted two Spartan passes.

The Bears scored in each of the first two periods, and the Spartans got their touchdown in the second, with Bill Glassgow carrying it over after he, with Mayes McLain and Chuck Bennett, had staged a 59-yard drive.

In spite of the $1,000 fine assessed against them for signing and using Joe Savoldi, the Bears employed the jumping Italian Sunday. He carried the ball six times for 31 yards.

Cagle Fails To Get Loose In Pro Debut As Giants Triumph

New York, Nov. 23—The New York Giants took the leadership in the National Football League today, defeating the Green Bay Packers, 13 to 6, before a crowd of 45,000 at the Polo Grounds. Each team has lost two games, but the Giants have won two more than the Packers.

Chris Cagle, former Army star, made his professional debut, but failed to get away for any long runs. He was injured in the first period, but came back midway in the third session and finished the game.

The Giants counted first in the second quarter, Badgro taking the ball over on a long pass from Friedman. Moran got away for an 84-yard dash early in the third period, carrying the ball to the one-yard line, from where Friedman plunged over, after the Packers had held for three downs, for the second touchdown.

Although set back frequently by penalties, the Packers scored late in the third quarter. Lewellen circled end for the last five yards after two passes had carried the champions from midfield. A pass near the end of the game put the Packers down on the five-yard marker again, but the Giants' line held.

Dec. 14

FRIEDMAN'S 2 TOUCHDOWNS CLINCH GAME

Crowd Braves Icy Weather, Contributes $150,000 to Charity to See Notre Dame Greats.

Rockne Stars Lose.

All-Stars.	Pos.	N. Y. Giants.
C. Collins	L.E.	Badgro (Southern Cal.)
Joe Bach	L.T.	W. Owen (Phillips U.)
H. Anderson	L.G.	Caywood (St. John's)
Adam Walsh	C.	Murtagh (Georgetown)
Noble Kizer	R.G.	Comstock (Georgetown)
Rip Miller	R.T.	Grant (N. Y. U.)
Ed Hunsinger	R.E.	Campbell (Emporia T.)
H. Stuhldreher	Q.	Friedman (Michigan)
Don Miller	L.H.	Sedbrook (Phillips U.)
Jim Crowley	R.H.	Wiberg (Neb. Wes.)
Elmer Layden	F.	Feather (Kan. Aggies)

Notre Dame All-Stars 0   0   0   0— 0
New York Giants... 2 13   7   0—22

Touchdowns — Friedman 2. Campbell. Points after touchdowns—Friedman (place kick). Moran (place kick). Safety—Stuhldreher.

Dec. 15

Dunn's Throw to Englemann Brings Score

Portsmouth Crosses Line in Second Quarter but Lewis Misses Try for Point

BY OLIVER E. KUECHLE
OF THE JOURNAL STAFF

PORTSMOUTH, Ohio — You folks up in Green Bay get out the red light, kill the fatted goose and split up that $5,000 players' purse, because the wars are over and the mighty Packers once more sit on top of the National league throne.

Holding the Portsmouth Spartans to a 6-6 tie here Sunday afternoon in one of the rip snorting classics of the football season, the Packers cinched their second straight National championship. They went into the game with a percentage standing of .769 against New York's .765 and by virtue of the tie they came out of it the same way. It was the first time in the history of the league that a winner has repeated.

Team Worn to Frazzle

Happy, of course, over the tie and the championship it gave them the Packers shuffled off the field in the dusk here Sunday worn to a frazzle by the terrific fight they had to put up just to hold their own. Those Spartans who carried Portsmouth's purple into the battle Sunday were as tough as any club the Packers have had to face this season. They didn't have much of a pass attack themselves, or much of a defense against passes for which the Packers today chorus thanks, but they smashed out yards on the ground as few other clubs in the National league ever have against the champions.

Even the mighty Bears, with such sledgehammers as Nagurski and Nes-

The Figures

First Downs—Green Bay 11, Portsmouth 9.
Passes Attempted—Green Bay 19, Portsmouth 8.
Passes Completed—Green Bay 9, Portsmouth 2.
Passes Incomplete—Green Bay 8, Portsmouth 4.
Passes Intercepted—Green Bay 2, Portsmouth 2.
Gains on Passes—Green Bay 113 yards, Portsmouth 45 yards.
Penalties—Green Bay 30 yards, Portsmouth 10 yards.
Yards From Scrimmage—Green Bay 109, Portsmouth 201.
Yards Lost From Scrimmage—Green Bay 19, Portsmouth 22.
Average Punts—Green Bay 44 yards, Portsmouth 39 yards.
Yards Returning Punts—Green Bay 10, Portsmouth 45.
Fumbles—Green Bay 4, Portsmouth 3.

bitt, never did more through Green Bay's line than Portsmouth with Chuck Bennett, Father Lumpkin, Mayes McLain and Tiny Lewis.

Penalties Halt Rally

The Packers came back in the closing minutes, after Blood had intercepted a pass in mid-field and got down to Portsmouth's 35-yard line but two 15-yard penalties in succession took all the wind out of their sails. What was the difference, however, a tie was as good as a victory, and the championship once more belongs to that hotbed of football—Green Bay.

The line-ups:

GREEN BAY		PORTSMOUTH
Dilweg	L. E.	Braidwood
Hubbard	L. T.	Douds
Bowden	L. G.	Roberts
Darling	R. G.	Smith
Michalske	C.	Graham
Kern	R. T.	Lyons
Nash	R. E.	Josephs
Dunn	Q.	Peters
Lewellen	L. H.	Lumpkin
Englemann	R. H.	Bennett
Molenda	F.	Lewis

Green Bay .... 6 0 0 0— 6
Portsmouth ... 0 0 6 0— 6

Substitutions—Green Bay: Sleight for Hubbard. Earpe for Darling. Blood for Englemann. McCrary for Lewellen. Woodin for Bowdoin. Portsmouth: Wesley for Smith. Roberts for Meyers. Schleusner for Douds. Kahl for Peters. Fleckenstein for Josephs. McLain for Lumpkin. Kahl for Bennett. Braidwood for Josephs. Officials—Referee. James Durfee; umpire. Robert Karch, head linesman, Al Dudley.

CLEVELAND IS GRANTED PRO GRID FRANCHISE

Former Brooklyn Pilot to Be Associated With Local Backer to Put Club in 1931 Campaign.

(Plain Dealer Special)

CHICAGO, July 12.—Cleveland was granted a franchise in the National Professional Football League here today in the second and final day's meeting of league officials. The organization of Cleveland gives the pro league a ten-club circuit for the 1931 season.

The franchise was awarded to Jerry Corcoran, former manager of the Brooklyn club in the league. Corcoran will be associated with a Cleveland man in the financing of the team, according to Joseph Carr of Columbus, O., who was re-elected president and secretary today.

Who his associate will be Corcoran did not divulge, but he is expected to be Samuel H. Deutsch, prominent Cleveland sportsman, who has backed several professional clubs in that city in the past. Several other Cleveland men are said to be seeking an interest in the team.

Seeks New Stadium.

Deutsch has been negotiating for the use of Cleveland's new municipal Stadium as a site for the team's home games.

Applications of Milwaukee, Wis., and Cincinnati, O., for franchises this fall were passed on to the executive committee, which will not act on them until next year. Both cities may be taken into the league in 1932.

The 1931 schedule opens Sept. 13, with Brooklyn at Portsmouth, O., and will conclude Dec. 13, when the Green Bay Packers play the Chicago Bears at Wrigley Field. The tentative schedule drawn today is subject to revision.

* * *

Reprinted from
The Cleveland Plain Dealer

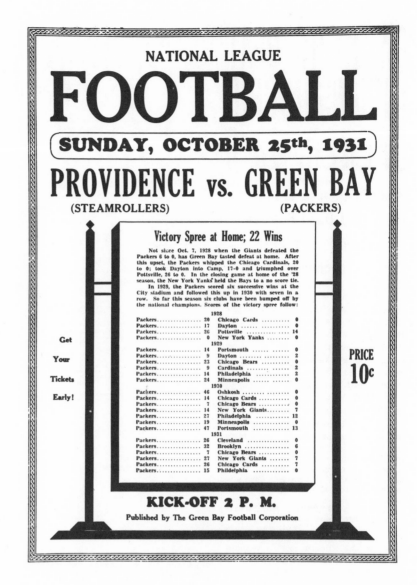

Nevers Runs Wild to Subdue Packers, 21-13

CHICAGO, Nov. 15.—(AP)—Ernie Nevers led the Chicago Cardinals to a 21 to 13 triumph over the league-leading Green Bay Packers, in a National Football League game today at Wrigley Field.

It was the first time in ten years a Chicago Cardinal eleven has been able to defeat a Green Bay team, and also the first defeat for the Packers in ten starts this year. The Cardinal-Packer rivalry started in 1921, and sixteen games have now been played.

Nevers gave one of his greatest exhibitions in lifting the Cards to victory over the great team from the north. In the first period he tossed a 15-yard pass to Bill Glasgow for a touchdown and place kicked for the extra point. Early in the second session Tom Nash, Packer end, blocked one of Nevers punts and fell on it for a score but Red Dunn failed to add the point.

With Nevers slashing through the Packer line the Cards took the ball to the Packer 5-yard mark from where Beldin plunged over and the former Stanford ace again place kicked for the point. Rogge, Cardinal end, intercepted a Packer pass in the final period and galloped 43 yards to the 10-yard line, and after the Green Bay line had driven the Cardinals back, Nevers faded to the 32 yard line and passed to Les Malloy who received the ball on the 4-yard line and stepped over.

Nevers once again place kicked for the point. A series of Packer passes took the ball into scoring territory just before the game ended, and Bruder rammed over for another Packer score. Dunn made the point.

* * *

PACKERS BEAT INDIANS IN GRID OPENER, 26-0

Mishel's Passes and Kriss' 50-Yard Dash Feature; Wilson Races 39 for Touchdown.

(Plain Dealer Special)

GREEN BAY, Wis., Sept. 13.—The Cleveland Indians opened their National Professional Football League schedule against the title holding Green Bay Packers here this afternoon and lost, 26 to 0.

About half of the game was played in a drizzle, which held the crowd at City Stadium down to 6,000.

Cleveland threatened to score on but one occasion, when an attack was hurled back four yards from the Green Bay line. Late in the fourth period Kriss executed a 50-yard dash, but the champions halted the advance 30 yards short of scoring territory.

Frank (Moon) Baker, Northwestern's All-American end, scored the first touchdown by capturing Mule Wilson's pass and scampering a few steps to the Indian goal. Woodin made the extra point attempt.

Mishel Hurls Passes.

Cleveland pushed right back, with Mishel tossing pass after pass. He finally slammed one at Hurley, elongated end, who was dropped by Gantenbein near the Green Bay goal. Novotny added a few more yards on a double pass play, but the Packer wall braced and Green Bay punted out of danger.

Saunders, Southern California flash, and Hank Bruder, Northwestern ace, entered the game at the start of the second period and raced to a touchdown. On a fake pass to Bruder, Saunders scampered 25 yards. Bruder gained seven more and Saunders clicked on a left end run, sweeping 38 yards for the score. Groves missed the kick.

A long pass from Herber to Johnny Blood in the third period pushed the ball two and a half yards from the goal and McCrary smacked the line for the third touchdown. Woodin missed the goal.

Dec. 7

PACKERS UPSET IN FINAL BATTLE BUT WIN CHAMPIONSHIP

Bears Score Early and Gain 7-6 Verdict In Hard-Fought Game.

Pass to Litzenich and Place Kick Gives Bruins Winning Margin Before 18,000.

NO DISGRACE

PACKERS		BEARS
	L. E.	
Dilweg		Johnsos
	L. T.	
Stahlman		Tackwell
	L. G.	
Michaleske		Carlson
	C.	
Barragar		Pearson
	R. G.	
Comstock		McMullen
	R. T.	
Sleight		Burdick
	R. E.	
Nash		Drury
	Q.	
Fitzgibbons		Brumbaugh
	L. H.	
Lewellen		Red Grange
	R. H.	
Blood		Litzenich
	F.	
Molenda		Franklin

Score by Quarters
Packers .... 0 6 0 0—6
Bears .... 7 0 0 0—7

Scoring
Touchdowns: Packers—Blood. Bears—Litzenich. Point after touchdown—Tackwell.

Substitutions
Packers—Dunn for Fitzgibbons, Englemann for Blood, Saunders for Molenda, Bruder for Lewellen, Don Carlos for Barragar, Earpe for Don Carlos, Grove for Dunn, Hubbard for Stahlmann, Gantenbein for Nash.
Bears—Buckler for Burdick, Murry for McMullen, Joesting for Franklin, Walquist for Brumbaugh, Nesbit for Litzenich, Trafton for Pearson, Garland Grange for Drury.
Officials: Referee—Durfee. Umpire—Kitter. Field judge—Elliott. Head linesman—Laurie.

NATIONAL LEAGUE

	W.	L.	T.	Pct.
Green Bay	12	2	0	.857
Portsmouth	11	3	0	.786
Chicago Bears	8	4	0	.667
Chicago Cards	5	4	0	.556
New York	6	6	1	.500
Providence	4	4	3	.500
Stapleton	4	6	1	.500
Cleveland	2	8	0	.200
Brooklyn	2	12	0	.143
Philadelphia	1	6	1	.143

After Bo Molenda intercepted Workman's pass late in the fourth quarter, Mule Wilson slipped around his left end for 39 yards and a touchdown. Dunn's placement for the extra point was effective.

G. Bay—26.	Position.	Cleveland—0.
Baker	L. E.	Lamme
Jannisen	L. T.	Ridler
Woodin	L. G.	Gregory
Don Carlos	C.	Pritchfield
Bowdoin	R. G.	Hudson
Perry	R. T.	Jolley
Gantenbein	R. E.	Braidwood
Fitzgibbon	Q.	Mishel
Wilson	L. H.	Novotny
Davenport	R. H.	Clark
McCrary	F.	Cornsweet

Packers .... 7 6 6 7—26

Substitutions — Packers: Grove, q.; Herber, q.; Engleman, lh.; Michalske, rg.; Saunders, f.; Dilweg, le.; Bruder, rh.; Sleight, rt.; Grove, q.; Comstock, lg.; Stahlman, lt.; Earpe, c.; Johnson, f.; Saunders, f.; Dun, q.; Bruder, q.; Molenda, f. Cleveland: Ridler, lt.; Kriss, rh.; Wilson, c.; Vokety, f.; Hurley, le.; Jessen, rt.; Nesser, lt.; Cullen, lt.; Braidwood, le.; Munday, lg.; Workman, q.

Touchdowns—Baker, McCrary, Saunders, Wilson. Points after touchdown—Dunn, Woodin.

Referee—Hughitt (Michigan). Umpire—Erdlitz (Oshkosh). Head linesman—Scott (Marquette).

ALL-PRO TEAMS

The Teams

FIRST ELEVEN

L. E.—Dilweg, Green Bay.
L. T.—Hubbard, Green Bay.
L. G.—Michaleske, Green Bay.
C.—McNally, Chicago Cards.
R. G.—Gibson, New York.
R. T.—Christensen, Portsmouth.
R. E.—Badgro, New York.
Q. B.—Clark, Portsmouth.
L. H. B.—Grange, Chicago Bears.
R. H. B.—Blood, Green Bay.
F. B.—Nevers, Chicago Cards.

SECOND ELEVEN

L. E.—Johnson, Chicago Bears.
L. T.—Douds, Portsmouth.
L. G.—Kiesling, Chicago Cards.
C.—Hein, New York.
R. G.—Graham, Providence.
R. T.—Stahlman, Green Bay.
R. E.—McKalip, Portsmouth.
Q. B.—Dunn, Green Bay.
L. H. B.—Strong, Stapleton.
R. H. B.—Presnell, Portsmouth.
F. B.—Molenda, Green Bay.

THIRD ELEVEN

L. E.—Flaherty, New York.
L. T.—Gordon, Brooklyn.
L. G.—Carlson, Chicago Bears.
C.—Barragar, Green Bay.
R. G.—Bodenger, Portsmouth.
R. T.—W. Owen, New York.
R. E.—Rose, Providence.
Q. B.—Friedman, New York.
L. H. B.—Nesbit, Chicago Bears.
R. H. B.—Lumpkin, Portsmouth.
F. B.—Joesting, Chicago Bears.

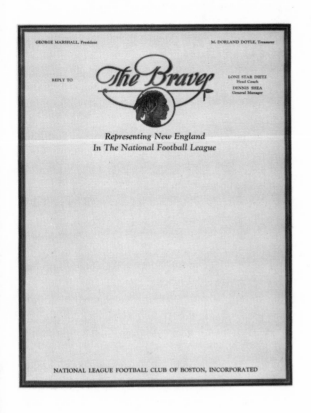

NESSER STILL PLAYING

SPARTANS OPEN

With 33-To-0 Win

Over Grand Rapids's Independent Eleven—New Men Share In Portsmouth Victory.

SPECIAL DISPATCH TO THE ENQUIRER.

Portsmouth, Ohio, September 18— A shirt-sleeved, straw-hatted crowd saw the Portsmouth Spartans crush the Grand Rapids, Mich., Independent Professional football team today 33 to 0. It was the season's pro-league opener here.

In their victory march, the Spartans used every style offensive and to perfection, end runs, passes and close formation, line crushing rolled up eight first downs, while the Grand Rapids made but one, Portsmouth tried eight passes, completing four for gains of 96 yards.

Gustowsky, of Oklahoma, a full back, led the array of new Spartans, ripping the line for consistent gains. Griffen, a former Spartan, came out of a year's retirement to play a bang-up game at center.

Members of last year's Spartans showed to advantage in the contest, Half Backs Alford, Presnell and Lumpkin cinched positions this year.

Al Nesser, of Columbus, Ohio, 47 year-old gridder, did fine work for Grand Rapids, at an end.

Reprinted from
The Cincinnati Enquirer

Oct. 3

BRAVES LOSE IN SLASHING GAME

Pro Football Has Fancy Start in Boston---Brooklyn Dazzles in Hard, Rugged Clash, 14-0

BY J. W. MOONEY

A crowd of about 6000, anxious to get a peek at this new pro grid game in Boston, watched Bennie Friedman's Brooklyn Dodgers beat the Boston Braves, 14 to 0, on two beautiful forward passes yesterday afternoon at Braves Field.

Most of the fans, used to college and high school games around Boston, were expected to be critical of the professional venture, and they expected to see somewhat of a different brand of the game as the propaganda had been, that once out of college the stars lost the old spark for the game and played it more on their feet than otherwise.

HARD, RUGGED CLASH

But in that hard, rugged clash yesterday the players were strewn all over the place. They all had to be big tough and rugged to take it. College halfbacks looking on must have realized that they wouldn't get places against that crowd of giants.

Often it is discussed at length when two college stars are to oppose each other. The individual battle is looked for on such an occasion. In yesterday's game they were all stars fighting it out with just as much of a will to win as they ever did in their lives. It wasn't just an afternoon of play for them. They had to make good to hold their jobs.

After the game we happened to make the remark to Coach Lud Wray of the Braves that the boys really looked as though they were out there trying to make their letters. It is hard to tell what the coach expects, but he came back with the retort that some of his crowd were making their letters, letters telling them that they can take the train back home.

Brooklyn's attack clicked and functioned better than the Braves'. The Dodgers had backs who were more artful in their flight. At times they really made the Braves look bad on tackling. Jack Thomason, former Georgia Tech star, gave a great exhibition of running in punts. True he didn't make so much yardage for his work was no snap, but he certainly could wiggle out of the tight places.

Bennie Friedman, Michigan's great forward passer, threw passes like a catcher throws a baseball down to second. They were deadly and accurate and he had a fine receiver in Jack Grossman, the 200-pound back from Rutgers. And Friedman showed himself as a clever sideline stepper when he faded back for a fake forward and then raced like sixty for 25 yards down a crooked path evading or shoving off tacklers with a straight arm that carried him right up to the two-yard line.

And right there the Braves, who won many followers, put up a goal line defence that was a knockout. Three times the great Grossman lunged for a space to squeeze through. The second time he moved up to within a foot of the line. The third time Jim Musick smacked him prettily for a loss. In desperation Friedman had to resort to the air once more and his swell pass shot at an angle across the scrimmage line and to the front corner of the end zone where Grossman snatched it in before it could be batted down by two Braves, close to the play.

Reprinted from **The Boston Post**, with permission of **The Boston Globe**

Dec. 5

Packer Eleven Plays Ragged Ball in Losing Crucial Tilt of Campaign

Outcome Assures Spartans of at Least a Tie for the Championship; Ohio Team's Passing Attack and Dutch Clark's Great Kicking Are Features; Crowd of 12,000 Sees Hostilities

BY OLIVER E. KUECHLE
OF THE JOURNAL STAFF

PORTSMOUTH, Ohio—"What a bunch of bums," a funny, red nosed gentleman near the press box yelled.

"Yah, cheese champs," another countered, holding his nose between his fingers in a most peculiar way.

"How'd you birds ever get a rep," a third shouted.

As you undoubtedly know by this time, our mighty Packers, three times national professional league football champions, took it smack on the chin from Portsmouth's Spartans here Sunday afternoon. The score was 19 to 0, and if the truth about the game, and those nasty digs from up in the stands must be told, our heroes did have the faint odor of limburger about them all afternoon. It certainly wasn't heliotrope.

The Packers have seldom played such stupid ball as they did in having themselves kicked out of the championship campaign here Sunday. On the fag end of a hard trip, which probably explains everything, they went all to pieces at once. They were no more the league leaders who had won 10 games, lost one and tied one than white is black, and the pity of it is that more than 12,000 fans, drawn here from all over Ohio by the magnet of a great team's reputation, had to see them at their worst.

You can figure out yourself how badly they fared by looking over a few of the details. You know the Packers, but not this team of Sunday that completed only one out of 17 forward passes, averaged only 23 yards on 11 punts, permitted the other fellows to complete five out of nine passes and tried to buck center for more than two yards on fourth down deep in their own territory. They were not the Packers you know.

Spartans Look Good

On the other mitt, the Spartans looked like world beaters, which is usually the way in contests like this. They had all the dash and verve of a first class college team at homecoming, and all the polish that, usually, only the Packers have at their best. They were like kids at a carnival of clowns after the game, throwing their headgears into the air and jumping after them, while the dippy home crowd swarmed out in a near riot to reach them and carry them off.

It was a costly game for the Packers to lose. It not only knocked them out of a chance for their fourth straight championship, as related before, but it spoiled all their plans for a barnstorming trip of six games in California and Hawaii this winter. They had to win or tie here Sunday and then do the same with the Bears in the season's finale at Chicago next Sunday to take the trip west. They had to be champions.

The Spartans, as a result of the victory, assured themselves of at least a tie for the championship, depending on what the Bears do with the Packers. If the Bears win they will tie Portsmouth for first place and the two of them will probably meet in a play-off Dec. 18. If the Bears get no better than a tie with Green Bay, however, or lose, Portsmouth will have an undisputed title.

GREEN BAY		PORTSMOUTH
Barrager	C	Randolph
Michalske	L G	Bodenger
Zeller	R G	Emerson
Hubbard	R T	Davis
Stahlman	L T	Christiansen
Gantenbein	R E	Ebding
Rose	L E	McKalip
Grove	Q	Clark
Bruder	L H	Lumpkin
Engelman	R H	Presnell
Hinkle	F	Gutowsky

Substitutions: Blood for Grove, Herber for Bruder, Bruder for Engelman, Dilweg for Rose, Bultman for Barrager, Lewellen for Bruder, Comstock for Zeller. Officials: Referee, Maurice Meyer (Cleveland); umpire, Herbert Dell (Columbus); head linesman Ray Brinson (Cincinnati).

A Few More 'Ifs'

Except for the game between Green Bay and the Chicago Bears at Cubs' park Sunday, the National football race is over. The one game that remains still has an important bearing on the championship, however. To the Bears it means a share of the championship with Portsmouth, or else . . . Here are the "ifs" involved in this last game.

If the Bears beat the Packers the final standings of the three leaders will be as follows:

Portsmouth	6	1	4	.857
Chicago	6	1	6	.857
Green Bay	10	3	1	.769

If the Bears tie the Packers the teams will wind up this way:

Portsmouth	6	1	4	.857
Chicago	5	1	7	.833
Green Bay	10	2	2	.833

And if the Packers beat the Bears, here is how they will finish:

Portsmouth	6	1	4	.857
Green Bay	11	2	1	.846
Chicago	5	2	6	.714

Dec. 5

Bears Defeat Giants, 6 to 0

Pass to Johnsos Scores Lone Touchdown Early in Game

BY LEASED WIRE TO THE JOURNAL

Chicago, Ill.—The Chicago Bears defeated the New York Football Giants, 6 to 0, Sunday at Wrigley field by a sudden attack shortly after the opening kick off.

Three plays resulted in a touchdown and then, although outplayed to the end of the game, the Bears managed to spoil all of the New York threats to tie the score.

Although the first three plays by the Bears decided the game the six point lead was in continual dispute in the second half. During the final

Pro Standing

	W	L	T	Pct.
Portsmouth	6	1	4	.857
Chicago Bears	5	1	6	.833
Green Bay	10	2	1	.833
Boston	4	4	2	.500
New York	4	6	2	.400
Brooklyn	3	9	0	.250
Chicago Cardinals	2	6	2	.250
Stapleton	2	7	3	.222

SUNDAY'S RESULTS
Portsmouth 19, Green Bay 0.
Chicago Bears 6, New York 0.
Boston 7, Brooklyn 0.

NEXT SUNDAY'S GAME
Green Bay vs. Chicago Bears at Chicago.

30 minutes the Giants camped on the Bears' goal line, threatening to tie the score six times. But the Bears' secondary, when it was crowded back to the goal, slapped down the Giants' passes.

Shortly after the opening kick off Red Grange stepped down the center to take Molesworth's pass to the 29 yard line, a gain of 18 yards. On the next play Johnsos scored, running 15 yards after taking Molesworth's toss. Tiny Engebretsen's placekick was partly blocked and failed to add the extra point.

Dec. 12

GREEN BAY DEFEATED BY CHICAGO, 9 TO 0

Bears Stage Rally in Fourth Period, Win

Teams Engage In Great Fight for Honors On Snow-covered Field.

FINAL PACKER GAME

Field Goal by Engebretsen and Long Run by Nagurski Give Bears Tie for Title.

NATIONAL LEAGUE

	W.	T.	L.	Pct.
Portsmouth	6	4	1	.857
Chicago Bears	6	6	1	.857
Green Bay	10	1	3	.767
Boston	4	2	4	.500
New York	4	2	6	.400
Brooklyn	3	0	9	.250
Chicago Cardinals	2	2	6	.250
Stapleton	2	3	7	.222

BY ARTHUR W. BYSTROM

CHICAGO—Chicago's Bears and the Porthmouth Spartans are co-champions of the National professional football league today— and Green Bay's eleven trails the pair.

The final chapter in the Packer's 1932 demise was written here Sunday afternoon when the Chicago eleven battled the three times Wisconsin title holders into submission by a score of 9 to 0.

Reprinted from
The Green Bay Press Gazette

PACKERS AND BEARS LEAD ALL-PRO ELEVEN

Each Places Three Men on Team Picked for Associated Press by League's Coaches.

COLUMBUS, Ohio, Dec. 17 (P).—Green Bay, Chicago Bears and Portsmouth, the three leading teams in the National Football League, grabbed the lion's share of places on the all-professional eleven selected for The Associated Press by seven of the eight coaches in the league.

On the first team three places each went to Green Bay and the Bears. The selections:

FIRST TEAM.

Player.	Team.	Pos.	College Attended.
Flaherty, New York	L.E.	Gonzaga
Hubbard, Green Bay	L.T.	Geneva
Carlson, Chic. Bears	L.G.	Oregon State
Barrager, Green Bay	C.	So. California
Kiesling, Chic. Cards	R.G.	St. Thomas
Edwards, Boston	R.T.	Wash. State
Johnsos, Chic. Bears	R.E.	Northwestern
Clark, Portsmouth	Q.B.	Col. College
Herber, Green Bay	L.H.	St. Regis
Lumpkin, Portsmouth	R.H.	Georgia Tech
Nagurski, Chic. Bears	F.B.	Minnesota

SECOND TEAM.

Dilweg, Green Bay	L.E.	Marquette
Christensen, P'm'th	L.T.	Oregon U.
Hurley, Boston	L.G.	Wash. State
Hein, New York	C.	Wash. State
Bodenger, Portsmouth	R.G.	Tulane
Williams, Chic. Cards	R.T.	Tex. Christian
Hewitt, Chic. Bears	R.E.	Michigan
Molesw'th, Chi. Bears	Q.B.	Monmouth
Grange, Chic. Bears	L.H.	Illinois
Grossman, Brooklyn	R.H.	Rutgers
Hinkle, Green Bay	F.B.	Bucknell

Lineup:

Chicago Bears		Portsmouth Spartans
Johnson	le	McKalip
Buckler	lt	Davis
Carlson	lg	Rodenger
Miller	c	Randolph
Kopcha	rg	Emerson
Burdick	rt	Christensen
Hewitt	re	Ebding
Molesworth	qb	Gutowsky
Grange	lhb	Presnell
Nesbitt	rhb	Cavosie
Nagurski	fb	Lumpkin

Officials: Referee, Bob Cahn, New York; umpire, G. A. Brown, Indiana; head linesman, Meyer Morris, Rock Island.

Champions Rally In Final Quarter To Down Spartans

Bronko Nagurski Passes to Red Grange Behind Goal Line For Only Touchdown

Fumble Pass Brings Safety

Both Teams Threaten Several Times Before Bruins Finally Pierce Defense—12,000 Attend

Chicago Stadium, Chicago, Ill., Dec. 18.—(AP.)—The Chicago Bears won the national professional football championship tonight in an indoor game, defeating Portsmouth's Spartans, 9 to 0. Twelve thousand fans saw the game.

Both teams made a scoring threat in the first period, but failed to register. The Spartans, with Cavosie, right half, and Presnell ripping through the Bears' line, advanced the ball to the eleven yard mark, but missed scoring when Gutowsky attempted to pass to Lumpkin behind the goal. The Bears battered their way to Portsmouth's 10 yard with Grange, Nagurski and Nesbitt carrying the attack. Grange was knocked out and left the game after making a 15 yard slash through the Spartan line. He was replaced by Corbett at left half.

In the closing minutes of the second period, Johnny Cavosie, the Spartans right half, intercepted a pass and charged to the Bears six yard after a dash of ten yards. Presnell banged center for a yard and then Gutowsky clipped off another yard. In another smash, Gutowsky battered his way two and a half yards from the Bears goal, but the Chicagoans defense stiffened and the Spartans lost the ball.

The third period was largely a punting duel between Cavosie and Nesbitt. George Corbett, who went into the game as a substitute for Grange, provided stirring runs for the Bears, but did not get within scoring distance. Presnell of the Spartans gave the crowd a scare when he fumbled but recovered after scrambling a couple of yards to regain possession of the ball.

The Bears broke the deadlock in the fourth period when Nesbitt intercepted Lumpkin's pass and ran 10 yards to the Spartans' 13 yard line. Nagurski sliced the line for five yards. Then he shot a five yard pass to "Red" Grange, who had just returned to the game. Grange caught it back of the goal line. The pigskin barely cleared the heads of the players. Engebretsen place-kicked for the extra point, making the score 7 to 0.

The Spartans fell victim to a blunder that cost them a safety just before the game ended. Wilson, attempting to pass, fumbled a bad pass from center and the ball went behind the goal line with Wilson going back after it to register the safety.

Dec. 13

Pro Football League Will Change System of Rating Teams in 1933

BY OLIVER E. KUECHLE

In any system of figuring, except the percentage system which ignores tie games, the Green Bay Packers, with their 10 victories, three defeats and one tie, would be champions of the National league today. As it is, because ties do not enter into the reckonings which the league uses, the Packers are in third place while the Chicago Bears, with six victories, one defeat and six ties, and the Portsmouth Spartans, with six victories, one defeat and four ties, jointly roost in first place.

Something will be done about tie games at the annual meeting of the league in June. Not only do the Packers, who suffered most under the percentage system this season, want a change, but the Bears and Spartans, both of whom share in the championship today because of it, want one, too. The eastern clubs feel the same way, and out of the June powwow will undoubtedly come a solution.

Several different systems have already been suggested. Under each one, if used today, the Packers would be champions. There is the system which the hockey leagues use. A victory counts two points, a tie one point and a defeat nothing. The team with the highest point total wins. If it had

been used this season, the clubs would have finished this way:

	W	L	T	Pts.
Green Bay	10	3	1	21
Bears	6	1	6	18
Portsmouth	6	1	4	16

There is the system under which a tie game counts a victory and a defeat both. In that system of figuring the teams would have finished like this:

	W	L	Pct.
Green Bay	11	4	.733
Portsmouth	10	5	.667
Bears	12	7	.632

A plan almost similar provides that a tie game counts half a victory and half a defeat. This year it would have left the clubs stand as follows:

	W	L	Pct.
Green Bay	10.5	3.5	.750
Portsmouth	8	3	.727
Bears	9	4	.692

Another suggestion has been made that in the event of a tie game, first one team and then the other take the ball on the 10-yard line and keep it until it is carried across the goal. The team requiring the least number of downs would win the game.

Which ever plan the league adopts doesn't make a great deal of difference. It is the important thing that something be done. It will be.

Meanwhile, the Packers have packed away their white flannels, Johnny Blood has bought himself a ukulele, and the club has left Green Bay on the first lap of its journey to Hawaii. The boys will sail from Los Angeles Friday night, and a week from Sunday, Christmas day, will play the University of Hawaii at Honolulu in the first of two exhibition games. A week later they will meet an all-star island eleven. The second game, the day after New Year's eve, ought to be a dandy.

How the University of Hawaii can retain its amateur rating after playing the Packers is something of a mystery around here. Lambeau doesn't understand it either. The promoters, however, who have deposited $10,000 in a Honolulu bank for Green Bay's expenses, claim they have obtained permission "from the A. A. U." Just what jurisdiction the A. A. U. has over college sports on the island nobody here knows. The arrangement must be far different from what it is in this country, where the A. A. U. and colleges like each other about as well as two strange bulldogs. All of it is beyond Lambeau, except that 10 grand. With that in the bank, whether the Packers play the University of Hawaii or the Waiki-Waiki Fireflys doesn't make any difference.

Reprinted from
The Milwaukee Journal

Pro Gridders Adopt Split Schedule; Packers Open With Boston Sept. 17

Chicago, Ill. – (AP) – The National football league, grown up to a 10-club circuit, will decide its championship by a play-off next season.

At the annual meeting here Saturday and Sunday applications by Philadelphia, Pittsburgh and Cincinnati interests were granted, while the Staten Island club was permitted to withdraw for one year. The latter organization, however, must return to activity by 1934 or forfeit its franchise.

The league will be divided into two sections, with Pittsburgh, Philadelphia, New York, Brooklyn and Boston in the eastern end, and Green Bay, the two Chicago clubs – Bears and Cardinals, Portsmouth, Ohio, and Cincinnati in the west. They will play the usual intersectional schedule, but the leaders of the two divisions will meet for the title.

The Philadelphia team will be coached by Lud Wray, former Pennsylvania star and coach, while Jap Dowds, formerly of Washington and Jefferson, will direct Pittsburgh. Bill Jolley, who coached Cleveland in 1930, will handle Cincinnati.

The schedule, not yet complete, will open with the Chicago Cardinals at Pittsburgh Wednesday, Sept. 13. Philadelphia and Pittsburgh will play on weekday nights until the Pennsylvania blue laws are changed to permit Sunday games. Green Bay will open on Sept. 17 against Boston and the champion Chicago Bears will get into action at Green Bay a week later.

Joe E. Carr of Columbus, Ohio, was re-elected president and secretary and Carl Strock of Detroit was again elected vice president and treasurer.

Seek To Speed Up Game —Put Posts On Goal Line

Pittsburgh, Feb. 26.—(AP)—Rule changes designed to pep up the game were made today by the National Professional Football League.

Club owners made the forward pass legal from any point behind the line of scrimmage and moved the goal posts up to the goal line in an effort to increase thrills and reduce the number of tie games.

Joe F. Carr, president of the league, predicted these changes will make the game more spectacular and put the "foot" back in football by encouraging kicking.

The owners agreed that steps should be taken to balance the offense and defense to make the game more exciting for the spectator.

The collegiate "five yard rule," making it permissible to move the ball in ten yards whenever it is in play within five yards from the sidelines, also was approved.

After lengthy discussion, the 25-yard penalty for clipping was retained. The college penalty recently was lowered from 25 to 15 yards.

Carr said the clipping rule is enforced rigidly in "pro" football, regardless of the heavy penalty, and the owners agreed the game would not be benefited by lowering it.

The college fumble rule, prohibiting defensive men from running with recovered fumbles, was retained.

Applications for membership were received from Philadelphia, Pittsburgh, Cincinnati and Cleveland. The Pennsylvania bids were made contingent upon repeal of the state's Sunday "blue laws."

Under the league's constitution, the circuit may have as many as 12 clubs. The directors will act on the applications later.

The circuit now has eight teams—Boston, Brooklyn, New York, Staten Island, Chicago Bears, Chicago Cardinals, Green Bay Packers and Portsmouth.

Oct. 19

BATTLES RUSHES FOR 215 YARDS

REDSKINS SHADE N. Y. GIANTS, 21-20

Newman Reels Off 85 Dazzling Yards----Battles, Weller Brilliant In Great Offensive Grid War

BY JACK BARNWELL

A thundering barrage of bombshells shattered the serenity of the Sabbath at Fenway Park yesterday afternoon, and after four blasting periods the raging Redskins tomahawked the burly Giants of New York by the score of 21 to 20, in as bristling a battle as has ever been staged on the soil of Boston.

Square shouldered and steel spined lines crashed, hinge hipped backs dashed and flashed, forwards and laterals crackled in the air, and 18,000 astounded lovers of football were thrilled by an All-America display of gridiron pyrotechnics as they never have been before.

Spirited Crowd Roots for Redskin Eleven

The spirit of the crowd was as surprising as some of the great runs pulled off on the Fenway Park gridiron yesterday. The fans warmed right up to the Redskins, and they gave Battles a cheer that came right from the heart. It was a partisan crowd all through the game, and though they cheered Newman's great runs and passes, they doubly cheered the deeds of the Redskins.

Oct. 23

REDSKINS CRUSH CARDINALS, 10-0

Battle Tallies Touchdown While Musick Place Kicks Goal---Two Chased---Lillard Stopped Cold

BY JACK BARNWELL

The whip-tongue of the fiery-eyed Indian that has lashed the Redskins for seven straight days produced the desired effect midst the landscape of Fenway Park, yesterday afternoon, when the enraged warriors of Lone Star Dietz tore into the argumentative and calloused Chicago Cardinals, made Joe Lillard, the "midnight express" from Caponeville, look like the Toonerville trolley and whaled out a 10 to 0 victory.

STOP LILLARD

The ebony-hued tornado, who has sliced lines and swept ends in destructive fashion all through his career, was never handcuffed as he was by the Redskins. They kept their sharp eyes trained on him all through the skirmish and so disgusted was the dusky gentleman at his repeated failures to break loose, the train home didn't pull out of town soon enough last night.

The deception of the Notre Dame system that swept Holy Cross to triumph over Harvard on the day before was like the attack of North Overshoe so far as the Redskins were concerned. They had blood in their eyes and fight in their hearts and upset almost everything that was hurled at them. The line was sturdy from stem to stern and fellows like Jack Riley, Turk Edwards and Jim Kamp are to be thanked for stopping Mr. Lillard particularly. When they crashed him they planted him in the sod with a thud. They rushed his passes and punts and pulled his flying pins from under him so often he didn't know whether he was playing football or looking for a divorce in Reno. It's a safe bet he's black and blue this morning.

Offence Clicks

On the other hand their own spinners, reverses and passes clicked in spectacular fashion and often enough to assure them of victory. They ripped out plenty of ground throughout the four chapters but only once were they able to invade the Chicago citadel for six points. On another occasion their dazzling offence swept them into position for a placement boot that accounted for three of their total points. Sweet Musick was sweeter than ever yesterday afternoon. He crashed and smashed the Cardinal frontier so often that count was lost. Whenever a yard or two was needed the former Trojan would stiffen his neck, bend low and plow ahead for four, six or more yards. Not once did he fail to deliver when called to.

OVER 55,000 FANS HAVE SEEN REDSKINS

Professional football is a success in Boston judging by the crowd that has been patronizing the Redskins' battles at Fenway Park, Sunday afternoons. More than 55,000 fans have attended the three games to date. The opener with the Giants drew over 17,000. The second game with the Portsmouth Spartans was attended by 21,000 and around 18,-000 saw yesterday's battle with the Chicago Cardinals.

Second Big Period

e second stanza was the productive for the Redskins. Therein they scored all of their 10 points. Shortly after it opened Musick, while standing on the midfield bias, whipped a long forward down the field. Gip Battles, fleet footed Redskin back, was tearing away in the direction of the Cardinals' goal and when he was crossing the 25-yard mark he threw his long arms into the air and snared the ball. The leaping clutch was as beautiful as Jean Harlow and Battles wiggled onward to the imaginary 18-yard stripe before he was brought to earth by Lillard.

A touchdown was in their nostrils. The line of gold pants dug in their cleats and opened up holes for Musick big enough to send the whole Redskin band through. After a five-yard penalty was inflicted on the visitors Musick hacked out six yards on two smashes, the second of which gave Boston's happy warriors a first down with only seven more to go.

Battles Scored

The deceptive double reverse with Battles spinning on the end of it and sweeping around left end enabled Gip to wheel to the two-yard mark where he was knocked to his knees by big Tim Moynihan, Notre Dame's old All-America centre. As Battles rose to his feet two more Cards smacked him, but he wriggled himself loose and spun over the goal line for the touchdown. The post point was pumped into the score from the toe of Musick via placement.

Very few minutes elapsed before Musick brought music out of the Redskin band again when he toed three more points into the total from the 15-yard line on a placement that was as clear and straight as any ever kicked.

Reprinted from **The Boston Post**, with permission of **The Boston Globe**

The summary:

REDSKINS	CARDINALS
Frankian, le	re, Nesbit
Edwards, lt	rt, Gordon
Kamp, lg	rg, Bergerson
Crow, c	c, Yarr
McMurdo, rg	lg, Handler
Riley, rt	lt, Williams
Collins, re	le, Creighton
LaPresta, qb	qb, Malloy
Battles, lhb	rhb, Lillard
Pinckert, rhb	lhb, Tipton
Musick, fb	fb, Hinchman

Score by periods:
Redskins .... 0 10 0 0—10

Touchdown—Battles. Point after touchdown—Musick. Goal from field—Musick (placement).

Substitutions — Redskins: le, Hokuf; lt, Kamp; lg, Hurley; c, Johnson; rg, Waters, Cherne; rt, McMurdo; qb, Ansit, Weller; lhb, Horstmann; fb Hohner. Cardinals; lg, Naugler, Kiesling, Auer; lt, Tinsley; qb, Rogge; rhb, Hanson, Moe; lhb, Koken, Lainbart, Nesbit; fb, Hinchman.

Officials — Referee: Halloran; umpire, Rooney; head linesman, Mooney; field judge, Pierotti. Time—Four 15m. periods.

;IANTS DEFEAT BRAVES BEFORE ,ARGE CROWD

;avanaugh Day Observed And $15,000 Given To Widow.

:LOSE GAME STAGED

By The Associated Press

NEW YORK, Nov. 13—Football ne professional kind, paid its debt unday to the late Maj. Frank Cavnaugh, war hero and college coach, s the New York Giants beat the Boston Red Skins, 7 to 0, before a rowd of 30,000 at the Polo Grounds the first memorial game of its ind ever played.

The Giants won in the second uarter when Harry Newman, once Iichigan's great passer, opened up ith a flock of aerials and for the nly time in the afternoon found is targets. He heaved one of 19 ards to Ray Flaherty after Ken trong opened the scoring drive rom his own 43 with a 10-yard urst through tackle. He ran 10 nore himself, then faded back from he Boston 15 and whipped a line ass into the end zone.

Cliff Battles, Boston back, nocked the ball down, but as it as falling big "Boz" Molenda eized it, and sank down over the oal line with the only touchdown f the game.

Impressive tribute was paid to he memory of Cavanaugh, former oach of Dartmouth, Holy Cross nd Fordham, who died a few nonths ago from complications reulting from shell wounds suffered n France.

The "day" had been planned for avanaugh long before he died as tribute to the man who developed ordham's greatest elevens. He urned over the reins at the end f last year's campaign to Jimmy rowley when his sight had failed lmost to total blindness.

He left no estate for his widow nd seven minor children. So proessional football, with which he as never connected, donated 40 er cent of Sunday's receipts to the amily of the "iron major." It was stimated Mrs. Cavanaugh would eceive a sum in excess of $15,000.

oston	Pos.	New York
rankian	LE	Badgro
dwards	LT	Morgan
amp	LG	Gibson
row	C	Hein
lacMurde	RG	Reese
iley	RT	Irwin
ollins	RE	Flaherty
psit	QB	Newman
attles	LH	Strong
inckert	RH	Burnett
'usick	FB	Molenda

ew York Giants .... 0 7 0 0—7
oston Redskins .... 0 0 0 0—0

Giants scoring: Touchdown—Molen-a. Point after touchdown—Strong. iant substitutions—End, Campbell; ackles, Grant, Owen; guard, Satentein; fullback, Krause. Boston substiutions—End, Hokuf; guards, Cherne, Vaters; center, Johnson; halfback, 'ampiglio; fullback, Horstman. Offiials—Referee, Tom Thorp; umpire, W. 3. Elcock; head linesman, Tom Mc-'abe; field judge, William Halleran.

National League Team.

The Champion Chicago Bears and the New York Giants, Eastern division leaders who lost to the Bears in the title play-off, dominate the all-league team selected by votes of the National Football League coaches, it was announced yesterday through The Associated Press.

The Bears and the Giants each placed three players on the first team. New York also came through with four second-team representatives to the Bears' three. Other clubs represented on the first all-league team are the Green Bay Packers, the Brooklyn Dodgers, the Boston Redskins and Portsmouth Spartans.

Bill Hewitt, former Michigan end now playing with the Bears, was the only player to poll a perfect vote under the system of allowing five votes for a first choice and three for a second-team selection.

The teams, with the votes for each player, follow:

FIRST TEAM.

Player.	Team.	Pos.	Votes.
Hewitt	Bears	End	50
Hubbard	Green Bay	Tackle	28
Hickman	Brooklyn	Guard	24
Hein	New York	Centre	2[illegible]
Kopcha	Bears	Guard	24
Edwards	Boston	Tackle	26
Badgro	New York	End	33
Newman	New York	Quarterback	32
Presnell	Portsmouth	Halfback	26
Battles	Boston	Halfback	35
Nagurski	Bears	Fullback	38

SECOND TEAM.

Flaherty	New York	End	14
Grant	New York	Tackle	24
Carlson	Bears	Guard	21
Miller	Bears	Centre	27
Gibson	New York	Guard	23
Musso	Bears	Tackle	24
Ebding	Portsmouth	End	11
Friedman	Brooklyn	Quarterback	14
Strong	New York	Halfback	24
Hansen	Philadelphia	Halfback	16
Musick	Boston	Fullback	23

Other players named in the voting were:

ENDS—Campbell, New York, 10; Hokuf, Boston, 5; Carter, Philadelphia, 5; Riblett, Brooklyn, 5; Nash, Brooklyn, 3; Mooney, Cincinnati, 3; Kenneally, Philadelphia, 3.

TACKLES—Christensen, Portsmouth, 13; Gordon, Cardinals, 11; Lyman, Bears, 9; Munday, Cincinnati, 5; Riley, Boston, 5; Morgan, New York, 3; Turnbow, Philadelphia, 3; Burdick, Cincinnati, 3; Lubratovich, Brooklyn, 3; Owen, New York, 3.

GUARDS — Emerson, Portsmouth, 13; Michalske, Green Bay, 10; Hurley, Boston, 9; Jones, New York, 8; Bodenger, Portsmouth, 5; Hubbard, Green Bay, 8; Zyntell, Philadelphia, 5; Macmurdo, Boston, 8; Lee, Cincinnati, 3.

CENTRES—McNally, Cardinals, 11; Morrison, Brooklyn, 8; Eiler, Pittsburgh, 5.

QUARTERBACKS—Molesworth, Bears, 9; Herber, Green Bay, 3.

HALFBACKS — Hinkle, Green Bay, 11; Richards, New York, 6; Kelly, Brooklyn, 8; Monnett, Green Bay, 8; Schaake, Portsmouth, 5; Herber, Green Bay, 5; Lefebvre, Cincinnati, 3; Pinckert, Boston, 3; Caddell, Portsmouth, 8; Lillard, Cardinals, 3; Gutowsky, Portsmouth, 3.

FULLBACKS—Hinkle, Green Bay, 13; Corzine, Cincinnati, 5.

BEARS BEAT GIANTS FOR TITLE, 23-21

Forward-Lateral, Nagurski to Hewitt to Karr, Brings the Deciding Touchdown.

AIR DUEL THRILLS 30,000

Manders Aids Victors With 3 Field Goals—Newman Completes 12 Passes.

STATISTICS OF THE GAME.

	Bears.	Giants.
First downs	13	13
Yards gained rushing	165	80
Forward passes	16	19
Forwards completed	7	13
Yards gained, forwards	141	201
Forwards intercepted by	1	1
Yards gained, laterals	19	0
Number of punts	10	14
Distance of punts, yards	420	440
Runback of punts, yards	58	59
Penalties	7	3
Yards lost, penalties	35	15

By The Associated Press.

CHICAGO, Dec. 17.—In a sensational forward passing battle the Chicago Bears won the national professional football championship today by beating the New York Giants, 23 to 21. The game was witnessed by 30,000.

The Bears, trailing by 21 to 16, seized victory out of the air in the dramatic closing minutes of the game. Billy Karr, right end, who learned his football at West Virginia, plucked a long lateral pass and, eluding two Giant tacklers who chased him desperately, galloped 25 yards for the deciding score.

The game was a thrilling combat of forward passing skill, desperate line plunging and gridiron strategy that kept the chilled spectators on their feet in constant excitement.

The lead changed hands six times during the furious sixty minutes of play, with first the Bears holding command and then the Giants taking it away from them.

An Offensive Battle.

The struggle was a revelation to college coaches who advocate no changes in the rules. It was strictly an offensive battle and the professional rule of allowing passes to be thrown from any point behind the line of scrimmage was responsible for most of the thrills.

The Bears' attack was led by Bronko Nagurski, former University of Minnesota plunging fullback, who individually gained 65 yards in fourteen attempts and started the forward-lateral pass that was responsible for the winning touchdown.

A notable performance was turned in also by Jack Manders. The former Gopher kicked three goals from placement, one for 40 yards in four attempts and added a goal after touchdown for a total of ten points.

Newman Passing Star.

Harry Newman, Michigan's all-American quarterback in 1932, was the outstanding star in the Giants' attack. He tossed seventeen passes, completing twelve for a total of 201 yards.

Hailed as the greatest offensive teams in professional football, the rivals did not waste any time in proving it, although the gridiron was slippery, particularly the grassy spots, because of mist and fog that hung over the field as the game started.

Molesworth quick-kicked over Newman's head and gave the Bears their first scoring chance. Strong returned the punt to the Giants' 42-yard line. There Nagurski plucked a pass out of the air and raced to the Giants' 26-yard line. Ronzani slashed right tackle, going to the 15-yard line.

Three plays netted only eight yards, but the ball was placed in a spot for Manders to place kick from the 16-yard line. The ball sailed squarely between the goal posts.

Giants' Defense Tightens.

In the second period, Ronzani tossed a pass to Molesworth, netting the Bears 17 yards and placing the ball on the Giants' 29-yard line. The New York team's defenses tightened, but Manders, called upon for the second time to place kick, booted the oval between the goal posts on a 40-yard effort.

The Giants, stirred to desperation, came back with a touchdown, with Badgro taking Newman's pass and running 29 yards to score. Richards paved the way for the touchdown with a 30-yard drive off left tackle to the Bears' 39-yard line. Strong added the extra tally on a placement kick.

The Bears missed another scoring opportunity just before the half ended, when Grange got away on a 17-yard gallop around left end, going to the Giants' 9-yard line. There Manders attempted another field goal, but this time he failed.

With both teams fighting desperately and using all the strategy at their command, things began to happen in the third period. No sooner did the Bears get the ball than they went right down the field.

Kicks Another Field Goal.

Ronzani gained 15 yards on one play, and a pass, Molesworth to Brumbaugh, brought the ball to Giants' 13-yard line. Once more the Giants' defense stiffened, but Manders again dropped back to the 19-yard line to score with another field goal that gave the Bears a 9-to-7 margin.

The lead did not last long, however, as the Giants, in a sensational display of passing, with Newman heaving the ball to Burnett, Richards and Krause, drove straight down the field for 61 yards and a touchdown, Krause going over. Strong kicked the point.

That score was accomplished in only eight plays. The last pass Newman threw to Krause was caught as the latter was chased out of bounds on the 1-yard line. He went over two plays later.

Then the Bears took a turn at scoring with amazing speed, and in six plays chalked up a touchdown.

A pass, Corbett to Brumbaugh, that gained 67 yards, provided the spark. It brought the ball to the Giants' 8-yard line, with Nagurski, after two plays, tossing a pass over the goal line to Karr. Manders added the extra point, and the Bears went into the lead again, 16 to 14.

The Giants, however, struck back on the kickoff. They took the ball on the 26-yard line, and with a passing attack carried to the 8-yard line. There Newman wound up the spectacular display by tossing a pass to Strong in the end zone for a touchdown. Again Strong added the extra point, and the Giants led, 21 to 16.

Resume Overhead Attack.

Then came the thrilling climax. The Bears, apparently beaten, took to the air. The first pass, Molesworth to Brumbaugh, brought the ball to the 32-yard line. The next one, hurled from the line of scrimmage, Nagurski to Hewitt, was followed by a long lateral to Karr.

Karr caught it out in the open and started for the Giants' goal. Ken Strong and another Giant tore after him, but Ronzani, formerly of Marquette University, knocked Strong out of the way and Karr raced across the goal with the winning point.

The line-up:

CHI. BEARS (23).		N. Y. GIANTS (21).
Hewitt	L.E.	Badgro
Lyman	L.T.	Grant
Carlson	L.G.	Gibson
Miller	C.	Hein
Kopcha	R.G.	Jones
Musso	R.T.	Owen
Karr	R.E.	Flaherty
Brumbaugh	Q.B.	Newman
Molesworth	R.H.	Strong
Ronzani	R.H.	Burnett
Nagurski	F.B.	Molenda

SCORE BY PERIODS.

Chicago Bears	3	3	10	7—23
New York Giants	0	7	7	7—21

Touchdowns — Badgro, Krause, Strong, Karr 2. Field goals—Manders 3 (placements). Points after touchdown Brumbaugh, Manders, Strong 3 (placements).

Substitutions—New York Giants: backs, Richards, Krause; tackle, Irwin; quarter, Clancy; end, Campbell. Chicago Bears: backs, Manders, Grange, Corbett, Sisk; centre, Pearson; tackle, Richards; guard, Stahlman.

Referee—Tommy Hughitt, Buffalo. Umpire—Bobby Cahn, Chicago. Field judge—Roert Karch, Columbia. Linesman—Dan Tehan, Cincinnati.

Sept. 1

Chicago Bears Held to Scoreless Tie by All-Stars

Laws of Iowa Gets 62 Yards in Nine Plays

Collection of College Men Hold Edge Over Pro Rivals Through Most of Much Ballyhooed Tilt

BY OLIVER E. KUECHLE
OF THE JOURNAL STAFF

Chicago, Ill. — Chicago's Bears, champions of the National Professional Football league last season, and by virtue of this supposedly the greatest football team in the land, had little more than a growl in their game with the college all-stars before 80,000 fans here Friday night, and if you really want to know the truth it wasn't much of a growl at that. The game ended in a scoreless tie.

Maybe because some of them still looked as though they had spent the summer eating corn and pork, or maybe because they couldn't get as steamed up over this whole affair as their frisky rivals just out of school, but the Bears found themselves outplayed most of the way. It wasn't a great difference, but it was still enough to leave little doubt of where the edge belonged—and after all, they were the Bears.

A Defensive Game

As you might expect from two teams with only two weeks of practise behind them, they played better ball on defense than on offense, and offered little at any time in the way of real scoring threats. In this again, however, the stars had an edge. At various times, they reached Chicago's 14-yard line, 27-yard line and 25-yard line. Once here, however, they promptly fumbled. To top it off, Bill Smith of Washington twice tried place kicks from outside the 20 that failed, although one of them, with Pardonner holding the ball, just missed the upright by a foot.

Against this, the Bears, their vaunted running game completely chilled and held to some 51 yards 'for the evening, submitted little more. They reached the nine-yard line, the 20 and 24 at different times, but then accommodatingly proceeded to fumble themselves. With passes, they did their heaviest damage although they completed only three.

There will always be fumbling in these early games, but here, as you may guess, there was more than usual. It was probably due to the smaller ball which made its first appearance of the season, rather than to exceptional butter fingers. What the college teams will do in their early games will be interesting to watch. There is little doubt the new ball is harder to handle.

Sept. 24

Lions Beat Giants

Detroit, Mich.—The Detroit Lions made their debut in the National Professional Football league Sunday an auspicious one by defeating the New York Giants, 9-0.

In the second quarter Dutch Clark made a dropkick from the 11-yard line and later Roy (Father) Lumpkin scored a touchdown on an intercepted pass.

Clark was one of the outstanding ball carriers on the field and his dropkick in the second quarter was perfectly placed. With only a minute to play, Lumpkin, former Georgia Tech star, intercepted Danowski's pass and ran 45 yards for the touchdown.

Reprinted from
The Milwaukee Journal

GRID AND IRON, DETROIT LIONS MASCOTS

Oct. 8

Lions Have Edge Most of the Way

Gutowsky Holds Ball for Former Nebraska Star on Kick

BY OLIVER E. KUECHLE
OF THE JOURNAL STAFF

Green Bay, Wis. A sensational 54-yard place kick by Glenn Presnell, one of the "great" of "greats" at the University of Nebraska seven, eight years ago, gave the Detroit Lions a well deserved 3 to 0 victory over the Packers here Sunday afternoon. It was the first time this line-up, which until this year played under Portsmouth's purple, ever beat the Bays on this lot.

You read about kicks like Presnell's but maybe only once in a lifetime see one. It was perfect. With Gutowsky holding the ball on Detroit's 46-yard line in the second quarter, Presnell stepped into it, whipped it in a high parabola down the field, and while the crowd let out a yip of amazement, watched it sail smack between the uprights. It couldn't have been neater. With the perfect direction it had, and the height, it would have been good at 64 yards or more. And that was the ball game.

Reprinted from
The Milwaukee Journal

DETROIT RUSHES FOR 426 YARDS

Nov. 4

Pirates First to Score on Lions; Lose, 40-7

Detroit, Mich. - (AP) - Stung by the first score made against them in eight straight games, the Detroit Lions Sunday routed the Pittsburgh Pirates, 40 to 7, in a National Professional Football league game. It was Detroit's eighth victory in as many starts.

A 22-yard pass to Skladany from Vaughan gave the Pirates the first score of the game and the only one made against Detroit this season, marring the Lions' great defensive record. Skladany, former all-American from Pittsburgh, made a great catch and raced 40 yrads to score.

That was the only time Pittsburgh had the ball in Detroit territory. Pittsburgh made only four first downs during the entire game to 12 for Detroit. Skladany starred for the invaders, playing a great defensive game.

Ernie Caddel, former Stanford star, had a field day, his great speed enabling him to score three touchdowns. Frank Christensen, Clark and Ebding scored the others, with Clark place kicking one extra point and drop kicking two others, and Presnell, who relieved Clark, converting another point.

PHILADELPHIA EAGLES WIN.

Set League Scoring Record, Routing Cincinnati, 64 to 0.

PHILADELPHIA, Nov. 6 (AP).— The Philadelphia Eagles galloped through the mud in Temple Stadium to a new National Football League scoring record today with a 64-to-0 triumph over the Cincinnati Reds.

Swede Hanson, former Temple star, and Carter, right end, were the leading scorers, registering three touchdowns apiece. Matesic, former Pitt ace; Ed Storm, former Santa Clara star; Ellstrom and Red Kirkman each scored once.

The line-up:

PHILAD'PHIA (64).		CINCINNATI (0).
Kenneally	L.E.	Mooney
Cuba	L.T.	Elser
Willson	L.G.	Caywood
Lipski	C.	Mullineaux
Kresky	R.G.	Lee
MacMurdo	R.T.	Munday
Carter	R.E.	Tackwell
Kirkman	Q.B.	A. Clark
Ellstrom	L.H.	Saumer
Matesic	R.H.	Pope
Storm	F.B.	Corzine

SCORE BY PERIODS.

Philadelphia ......26 6 12 20—64
Cincinnati ....0 0 0 0— 0

Touchdowns—Carter 3, Hanson 3, Storm, Ellstrom, Matesic, Kirkman. Points after touchdowns—Weiner 3 (placements), Matesic (placement).

Substitutes—Philadelphia: Hanson, Lackman, Weiner, Pilconis, Zizak, Gonya, Kajek. Cincinnati: Bushby, Lewis, Corzine, Maples, Lay, Howell, Aspatore.

Referee—R. B. Kinney. Umpire—C. G. McLee. Linesman—Walter Males. Field Judge—Howard Carroll.

Nov. 12

Gunners Make Debut With a 6-0 Victory

St. Louis, Mo. - (AP) - The St. Louis Gunners made their debut in the National Professional Football league Sunday by whipping the Pittsburgh Pirates, 6-0, before 13,678 fans. Bill Senn and Gene Alford each kicked a field goal in the second period to account for the scoring. Early in the period Senn, former Knox college player, drop kicked from the 35. Alford tried a place kick a few minutes later and missed, but his second attempt, from the 12, sailed between the uprights.

The Standings

WESTERN DIVISION	W	L	T
Chicago Bears	10	0	0
Detroit	10	0	0
Green Bay	5	5	0
Chicago Cardinals	4	5	0
St. Louis	1	9	0

EASTERN DIVISION	W	L	T
New York	6	4	0
Boston	5	5	0
Brooklyn	4	4	0
Philadelphia	2	7	0
Pittsburgh	2	10	0

Nov. 30

90 YARD RUN BY GRIFFITH WINS FOR CARDINALS

Return of Kickoff Beats Green Bay, 6-0.

One Up on Packers

GREEN BAY [0].		CARDINALS [6].
Rose	L. E.	Creighton
Perry	L. T.	Field
Michalske	L. G.	Volok
Buffman	C.	Hughes
Jones	R. G.	Mehringer
Schwammel	R. T.	Gordon
Norgard	R. E.	Duggins
Goldenberg	Q. B.	Greene
Monnett	L. H.	Cook
Grove	R. H.	Griffith
Hinkle	F. B.	Mikulak

Touchdown—Griffith.

Substitutions: Green Bay—Laws for Grove, Bruder for Goldenberg, Jorgenson for Perry, Engebretsen for Perry, Peterson for Norgard, Perry for Michalske, Norgard for Peterson, Dilweg for Rose.

Cardinals—Tipton for Mehringer, Sarboe for Greene, Cuppoletti for Field, McNally for Hughes, Russell for Griffith, Mehringer for Gordon, Isaacson for Volok, Smith for Creighton, Neuman for Duggins, Horstmann for Mikulak, Gordon for Isaacson, Handler for Cuppoletti.

BY GEORGE STRICKLER.

Homer Griffith streaked 90 yards through mud and water with the opening kickoff at Wrigley field yesterday to give the Cardinals a 6 to 0 victory over the Green Bay Packers before the smallest crowd of the National Professional league season in Chicago. Only 3,500 saw the game, which closed the Cardinals' league schedule and gave them a two to one advantage over the Packers in the season series. It was the Cardinals' fifth victory, against six defeats.

Griffith also ran the Packers into defeat at Milwaukee eleven days ago when he picked his way 55 yards through the same sort of sloppy footing to break a scoreless tie.

End Leaves Opening.

Al Norgard, Packer right end, a former Stanford player, opened the way for Griffith's dash yesterday when he disregarded one of the cardinal principles of end play by cutting in toward midfield as he went down on Clark Hinkle's kickoff. He lost himself in a pack of Cardinals and was cut down, leaving his side of the gridiron unprotected. Griffith reversed to the left to swing down the unguarded lane, side stepped Hinkle at the 50 yard line and headed for the goal line.

Bob Monnett, fleet Packer half back, caught Griffith at the 10 yard line and threw him with a headlock, but Griffith bounded off the ground and continued to the goal. Cook's attempt for the extra point was wide.

Reprinted from
The Chicago Tribune

Dec. 3

Bears Defeat Lions for Thirteenth Straight Win

Nov. 30

CHICAGO RALLY OVERCOMES 16-7 DETROIT LEAD

Manders Kicks Two Field Goals.

Pro Champs Again Topple Detroit, 10 to 7

Nagurski Scores Chicago Touchdown; Manders Adds a Field Goal From 30-Yard Line

Final Standings

NATIONAL LEAGUE
Western Division

	W	l.	T
Bears	13	0	0
Detroit	10	3	0
Green Bay	7	6	0
Cardinals	5	6	0
St. Louis	1	10	0

Eastern Division

New York	8	5	0
Boston	6	6	0
Brooklyn	4	7	0
Philadelphia	4	7	0
Pittsburgh	2	10	0

Won't Be Beaten

BEARS [19]		DETROIT [16].
Hewitt	L.E.	Mitchell
Lyman	L.T.	Johnson
Kiesling	L.G.	Knox
Kawal	C.	Bernard
Carlson	R.G.	Emerson
Musso	R.T.	G. Christiansen
Karr	R.E.	Schneller
Brumbaugh	Q.B.	Clark
Molesworth	L.H.	Lumpkin
Ronzani	R.H.	Caddel
Nagurski	F.B.	Gutowsky

Touchdowns—Gutowsky [2], Ronzani, Hewitt.

Points after touchdowns—Clark [drop kick]; Manders [place kick].

Field goals—Presnell, Manders, 2 [all place kicks].

Substitutions: Detroit—McKalip for Mitchell; Richards for Johnson; Bodenger for Knox; Mupke for Bodenger; Emerick for G. Christiansen; Ebding for Schneller; Minchman for Lumpkin; Rowe for Hinchman; Presnell for Caddel.

Bears—Rosequist for Lyman; Pearson for Kiesling; Zeller for Pearson; Miller for Kawal; Buss for Musso; Johnsos for Karr; Corbett for Molesworth; Grange for Corbett; Manders for Ronzani; Nisk for Manders; Manders for Nagurski.

Referee—Bobby Cahn [Chicago]. Umpire—Meyer Morris [Ohio Wesleyan]. Field judge—Gunnar Elliott [Notre Dame]. Head linesman—J. J. Ritter [Purdue].

Coaches— Potsy Clark [Detroit]; George Halas [Chicago Bears].

BY WILFRID SMITH.
[Chicago Tribune Press Service.]

Detroit, Mich., Nov. 29.—Chicago's Bears will not be whipped. Chicago knows this and Detroit had its lesson today.

Detroit's Lions, bitter rivals of the Bears for the western championship of the national professional league, were defeated at the University of Detroit stadium by these fighting Bears, 19 to 16. By their victory—their twelfth consecutive triumph of the present campaign in which they are defending their national title—the Bears now will face the winners of the eastern section of the league for the championship.

Twenty-six thousand, a crowd of roaring, partisan fans which jammed the stadium until hundreds crouched along the white chalk lines of the end zones, saw the Lions dash to the first touchdown of the game. Then, these Lions, a fast, shifty, inspired team, smashed through the Bears' defenses to lead at the intermission, 16 to 7.

Dec. 11

Pro Club Owners Change Five Grid Rules

Bears Rally Once More.

No team in three years has scored such an advantage over the Bears in 30 minutes of play. It seemed that the champions, long famous for their tremendous finishes, were destined to lose. Despite their touchdown in the first half, which, at the time had tied the score at 7-7, the Bears had not shown the driving power expected. Handicapped by the loss of the fleet Beattie Feathers, leading ground gainer of the league, and the hard charging Joe Kopcha, a valiant guard, the Bears' attack had lacked precision and their defense had yielded to Detroit's battering.

But once more the champions rallied. From the opening kickoff of the second half, they followed every play as eagerly as hounds follow a scent; seized every opportunity, and from them Jack Manders kicked two field goals. The Bears trailed, 16 to 13.

Pass to Hewitt Scores.

Once more the Bears capitalized on alertness. Joe Zeller intercepted a pass and raced to the Detroit 4 yard line. Twice Nagurski smashed into the line until the ball rested one yard short of the goal. A third time big Bronko received the pass from center but this time he stopped at the line and lobbed the ball to Bill Hewitt in the end zone for the touchdown. It didn't matter that Nagurski's try for the point was blocked, for Chicago led, 19 to 16.

Six minutes remained. As the hand of the mammoth wooden clock slowly paced the flying seconds, the Lions flashed a last, desperate bid for victory. From their own 20 yard line the Lions smashed and passed for five consecutive first downs. Nearer and nearer they plunged toward victory until again a vast wave of sound reverberated from stand to stand.

But in the last minute, the Bears summoned new strength to check the drive. They wrested the ball 14 yards short of the goal. And as Detroit's last play, a forward pass, fell incomplete in the end zone, the Lions saw their championship hopes vanish in the gray haze of the November afternoon.

Penalties Will Be Made From Point of Play

Adopt Pass Changes; Ball Out of Bounds Is Now to Be Brought in 15 Yards; Waiver Rule Accepted

FROM THE JOURNAL'S NEW YORK BUREAU

New York, N. Y.—Club owners of the National Professional Football league, meeting here Monday, made five changes in the rules, all designed to equalize offense and defense, open up the game and make it more interesting and understandable to the spectators. The changes were:

All penalties will be inflicted from the point where the ball was put in play and not from the point where the foul occurred.

A pass thrown beyond the line of scrimmage intended as a lateral but going forward shall be declared downed at the point of throwing.

The ball when fumbled is free except when kicked or thrown.

A fourth-down pass or a second pass into the end zone goes back to the point where the ball was put in play, except when the ball was put in play inside the 20-yard line.

A ball out of bounds shall be brought in 15 yards.

Waiver Rule Effected

In addition, the league adopted a waiver rule similar to that in effect in major league baseball, providing that no player may be sold or traded after the sixth league game unless waivers have been obtained from the other clubs.

Giants Go Mad to Sink Bears, 30-13

New York in Amazing Comeback, Wins in Last Half Over Chicago to Capture Pro Grid Title

POLO GROUNDS, NEW YORK, Dec. 9 (AP)—As amazing a comeback as any kind of football—college or professional — ever has seen, rocketed the New York Giants into the professional championship today, conquerors of the Chicago Bears, 30 to 13, in a ball game that was more like a fantastic dream.

STRONG AT HIS GREATEST

Trailing 13 to 3 when the second half opened, Ken Strong, an astounding football player today, led a fourth quarter attack that scored four touchdowns on the team they called the greatest finisher in football.

Strong himself scored twice, once on a brilliant 42-yard slash through the Bears' left tackle, again on an 8-yard dash through the same spot, while Ike Frankian, former St. Mary's hero, tallied once on a forward pass and Ed Danowski, last year's Fordham quarterback, completed the uprising with a 9-yard burst through the Bears' left side.

Crowd of 46,000 Goes Wild

Strong also kicked two points after touchdown and in the first quarter booted a 38-yard field goal, winding up his day with a total of 17 points.

A crowd of 46,000, shivering in the clear cold of the season's climax here, went absolutely mad with excitement as the Giants smashed the reign of the Bears, undefeated all season. Twice the Bears beat the Giants in this season's regular campaign, after whipping them 23 to 21 last year for the league title. The Bears hadn't been beaten up to today since the Giants did it 3 to 0 in the 1933 season.

Bears Pile Up Early Lead

The Bears started out today as though repeating their previous triumphs was just a matter of course. The Giants' opening march in the first quarter, a surge of 55 yards, wound up with Strong dropping back to the Bears' 38-yard line to boot a placement for the first three points. Then the Bears took over the ball game.

With Keith Molesworth and the big nag, Broncho Nagurski, splitting the Giant line despite the glazed and slippery footing, the Bears took the lead in the second quarter when a 50-yard march ended with Nagurski going over from the two-yard line. Then another Bear drive wilted on the 10-yard line, Jack Manders, place-kicking specialist from Minnesota, added an 18-yard field goal to the point he kicked after Nagurski's touchdown.

The Bears led 10 to 3, and stretched it to 13 to 3, as Manders, one of the deadliest place kickers in the game, took advantage of Strong's fumble to boot another field goal from the 23-yard line for the only scoring in the third quarter. The Giants appeared to be thoroughly licked.

But the Giants still had to loose their passing attack and it thoroughly dumb-

founded the secondary defence of the Bears. The drive Strong started near the end of the third period with a 25-yard runback of a kick to his own 30, wound up in the first New York touchdown, as Danowski passed to Ray Flaherty, one end, then to Dale Burnett, halfback, then to Flaherty, then to Strong and finally to Ike Frankian, the other end, for the score.

Giants March to Victory

The Giants pressed forward mercilessly. After an exchange of kicks, Strong burst through the left side of the Bears' line and raced 42 yards for the second New York touchdown, putting his team ahead, 17 to 13, as he placidly kicked the goal.

An intercepted pass just short of midfield set the Giants going again, and they ripped the Bears' line until Strong went through the same left side hole for eight yards and another touchdown. With only a minute to play, big Bo Molenda, Giants' fullback, snared another pass, brought it back 15 yards to the Bears' 21, and inaugurated another putsch that wound up with Danowski ripping inside the weak Bear left tackle for the final touchdown.

The paid attendance was officially listed at 35,059 and the net receipts were $64,504. After deductions for taxes, etc., the net pool of $58,503.60 was divided as follows: Players' pool, $26,911.40; league's share, $5850.36; each club's share, $8775.40. Each member of the winning team received $621 as his share of the pool, while $114 each went to the defeated Bears.

The lineups:

GIANTS	BEARS
Frankian, le	le. Hewitt
Morgan, lt	lt. Lyman
Gibson, lg	lg. Carlson
Heir, c	c. Kawal
Jones, rg	rg. Pearson
Irvin, rt	rt. Musso
Flaherty, re	re. Karr
Danowski, qb	qb. Brumbaugh
Burnett, lhb	lhb. Ronzani
Strong, rhb	rhb. Molesworth
Molenda, fb	fb. Nagurski

Score by periods:
Giants 3   0   0 27—30
Bears .... 0 10   3   0—13

Giants scoring: Touchdowns—Strong 2, Frankian, Danowski. Field goal—Strong. Points after touchdowns—Strong 2, Molenda (all placements).
Bears scoring: Touchdown—Nazurski. Field goals—Manders 2. Point after touchdown—Manders (all placements).
Giants substitutions—Tackles, Owne. Grant; backs, Richards, McBride.
Bears substitutions — End, Johnson; tackle, Buss; backs, Sisk, Manders and Masterson.
Officials—Referee, Bob Cahn, Chicago; umpire, Bill Lowe, Dartmouth; head linesman, George Byrara, Notre Dame; field judge, Myer, Ohio Wesleyan.

GIANT BALL CARRIERS DON BASKETBALL SHOES IN LAST HALF OF TILT

NEW YORK—Some sports performers have been accused of having brains in their feet, but it remained for Steve Owen, coach of the New York Giants' pro football team, at the suggestion of Ray Flaherty, end and captain, to put the idea more or less into practice.

The result was that today the Giants are the professional football champions of the world. And Flaherty is pro football's new, big "brain."

After the Chicago Bears had made the Giants look rather foolish in the first half, which ended with the Bears leading 10-3, Flaherty decided the Giants' feet weren't "thinking" properly.

It was so cold the players' cleats wouldn't sink into the frozen turf. The result was that at times the players appeared to be skating rather than hitting the line or skirting ends.

Between the halves Owen ordered ends and backfield men to take off their football shoes and don the regulation rubber-soled basketball shoes, which was done.

Reprinted from
The Green Bay Press Gazette

LEAGUE MAY PAY BACK SALARY TO ST. LOUIS ELEVEN

Columbus, O., Dec. 20.—(AP)—Players on the St. Louis Gunners, National Professional league football team, will be paid their back salaries even if the league has to dig into its own treasury for the funds, Joe F. Carr, president of the organization, said today.

The St. Louis club, transferred from Cincinnati in midseason, finished the year in a financial muddle, with the result that the players have not been paid for a couple of weeks.

President Carr said he did not think the league would be compelled to pay the salaries, since arrangements are being made in St. Louis to meet the situation through a new financial set-up which may involve a change in ownership.

Sept. 16

Don Hutson's Debut

Cards Defeat Packers, 7 to 6, in Pro Opener

Chicago Upsets Crippled Green Bay Team but Wins Only by Margin of Pardonner's Kick

BY OLIVER E. KUECHLE
OF THE JOURNAL STAFF

Green Bay, Wis. — Outplayed almost all the way, the Packers bowed to the Cards in the first start of the National league race here Sunday afternoon, 7-6.

A point after touchdown by Paul Pardonner, late of Purdue and one of the Big Ten's finest kicking specialists in recent years, decided the game and hung a crepe on what up to Sunday here had been high hopes for a championship year.

It's always tough to lose by one point, and in a way this was too, although the scoreboard in this case doesn't begin to tell how completely the invaders, with a hard, fast charging line, well along for this time of the campaign, and a diamond studded set of backs, led by Nichelini, Russell, Petersen and Mukulak, dominated the play. It looked like a lesson in football at times for the boys.

The line-ups:

CARDINALS		GREEN BAY
Smith	L. E.	Gantenbein
Fields	L. T.	Smith
Cuppoletti	L. G.	Evans
Hughes	C.	Butler
Tipton	R. G.	Engebretsen
Gordon	R. T.	Schwammel
Neumann	R.E.	Rose
Pardonner	Q.	Schneidman
Russell	L. H.	Monnett
Cook	R. H.	Laws
Mikalak	F.	Johnston

Packers ....0 6 0 0—6
Cardinals ....7 0 0 0—7

Substitutes—Packers: Hubbard, Goldenberg, Bruder, O'Connor, Kiesling, Blood, Svendsen, Siebold, Perry, Hutson, McDonald, Tennor, Herber. Cardinals: Nichelini, Sarboe, Blazine, Peterson, Isaacson, Deskin, Creighton, Volak, Dowell, Mehringer, Pangle, Hansen. Officials—Cahn, referee; Elliott, umpire; Keefe, head linesman; W. Wyman, field judge. Scoring touchdowns—Smith, Johnston. Point after touchdown—Pardonner.

Reprinted from
The Milwaukee Journal

Sept. 22

Giants Beat Pirates, 42-7

Pro League Champs Open Season Before Record Crowd of 24,000

BY LEASED WIRE TO THE JOURNAL

Pittsburgh, Pa. — The New York Giants made a good start in defense of their National Football league championship Sunday, defeating the Pittsburgh Pirates, 42 to 7, before 24,000 spectators, the largest crowd ever to witness a pro game in this city.

Scoring in every period except the third, the Giants won handily, gaining two for one against the eleven which defeated Philadelphia in its opener a week ago.

Dale Burnett was the only Giant double scorer, tallying twice on passes from Ed Danowski. The other Giants to count were Kink Richards, who was the outstanding ball carrier; Bo Molenda, Stu Clancy and Tony Sarausky.

Reprinted from
The Milwaukee Journal

New York Football Giants

DINNER
One Dollar and Fifty Cents

Puree of Tomato Soup, Croutons   Consomme
—
Broiled Tenderloin Steak, Fresh Mushroom Sauce

Chateau Potatoes   New Stringless Beans
—
Assorted Bread
—
Lettuce and Beet Salad, French Dressing,
Chopped Eggs
—
Mince Pie, Hot or Cold

Ice Cream   Chilled Grapefruit
—
Tea   ·Coffee   Milk

December 1, 1935

PENNSYLVANIA RAILROAD

Nov. 4

Fists Fly in Pro Game at Fenway

Redskins Lose, 7-6, to Philadelphia As Battle Rages During a Wild Third Period

BY JACK BARNWELL

While rival combatants tatooed jaws with haymakers in a game that called for cast iron limbs and concrete chins as well as cleats and helmets, Philadelphia's Eagles toed the Redskins out of victory yesterday afternoon at Fenway Park, when the citizens of Quietville dropped an aerial bomb at the start of the second period and converted the post point to win, 7 to 6.

FEELING HIGH

From kickoff to curfew feeling ran beyond degrees on the thermometer. Beneath various pileups knuckles kissed jaws rather frequently but not until the third period did the boys toe off. In the open for the entertainment of onlookers. Suddenly in that session everyone started swinging at everything and anything within reach of a healthy right hook. Substitutes rushed from rival benches. Spectators poured on the field from the sidelines and a pair of police officers waltzed to the scene of action.

After a few eyes were decorated, cooler heads called their logic into play and a peace pact was drawn up for the running off of the next play. All who didn't belong withdrew to their proper precincts while the game went on per schedule. No boxing matches followed within public view but for the balance of the game it was still a very aggressive affray.

Early Scoring

All the scoring had taken place prior to this pugilistic outburst. The Redskins, although deprived of the services of Cliff Battles, who is nursing a wounded shoulder, drew first blood while the final seconds of the opening chapter were ticking off the clock.

Peculiarly it took the absence of Battles to have Shepherd's light reach the height of fulmination. The youthful product of Western Maryland hit his professional peak yesterday, and it is kind of hard to believe he is going to Detroit. All through the ball game he stood out like a blonde in a brunette chorus line.

It was Shepherd who personally accounted for the Redskin points. He tacked a 54-yard scamper on to the end of a wild 54-yard journey and crossed into the promised land without a hand touching his garments.

Philadelphia had carried the fight to the Caseys right from the start. The Boston boys had their backs to the wall when all of a sudden Shepherd went haywire.

Reprinted from **The Boston Post**,
with permission of **The Boston Globe**

Dec. 16

Detroit Lions Defeat New York for Pro Football Crown,

GIANTS DEFEAT PIRATES, 13-0, IN FINAL GAME

Push Over Touchdown, Kick 2 Field Goals as 8000 Brave Rain.

By Associated Press

NEW YORK, Dec. 8.—The New York Giants rang down the curtain on the national pro football league season today by scuttling the Pittsburgh Pirates, 13 to 0, at the Polo Grounds. Rain kept the attendance to about 8000.

The Giants scored a touchdown and two field goals and missed a second touchdown by less than a yard. The Pirates didn't threaten once.

Second Stringers Score.

Coach Steve Owens started his second team but replaced it with the varsity to protect a three-point lead, the colt rang up in the first period. Leland Shaffer speared a Pirate heave on Pittsburgh's 40 and the Giants marched down to the 28-yard line from which point Harry Newman delivered a field goal.

In the second, Ed Danowski fired a short overhead pass to Tod Goodwin, who stepped 55 yards for a touchdown. Ken Strong concerted.

Strong Kicks Field Goal.

The Giants scored their last three points when Strong kicked a field goal from the Pirate 44-yard stripe with less than a minute to play.

But for Strong's toe, the Giants would have been stopped cold in the second half. Once they marched from their own 49-yard line to the Pirate one, but the Pittsburgh line braced and took the ball on downs. Another drive carried them from their 48 to the Pirate 12, but it bogged down when Kink Richards lost 12 yards on two plays and the visitors took over.

The Giants made 16 first downs to Pittsburgh's 4.

Lineups and summary:

```
..ew York.    Positions.    Pittsburgh.
Singer..........Left end..........Vidoni
Quatse.........Left tackle........Bray
Kaplan.........Left guard.........Rado
Del Isola......Center.............Ciccone
Jones..........Right guard........Hoel
Irvin..........Right tackle.......Niccolai
Mitchell.......Right end..........Smith
Newman.........Quarterback........Turley
Shaffer........Left halfback......Gildea
Sarausky.......Right halfback.....Strutt
Krause.........Fullback...........Wetzel
Pittsburgh ............ 0  0  0  0— 0
New York .............. 3  7  0  3—13
```

Touchdown, Goodwin (sub for Mitchell). Point after touchdown, Strong (sub for Krause). Field Goals, Newman, Strong. Substitutions—Pittsburgh: Sortet, Smith, Oleniczak, Hayduk, Skoronski, Levey, Heller, Casper, Zanienelli, Sebastian; New York: Goodwin, Franklin, Grant, Morgan, Hein, Richards, Danowski, Molenda, Corzine, Strong. Referee. Tom Thorpe. Umpire, B. A. Savage. Head linesman, John Reardon. Field Judge, G. Gammell.

Final Standings of Clubs.

EASTERN DIVISION.

	W.	L.	T.	PC.	For.	Agst.
New York	9	3	0	.750	180	
Brooklyn	5	6	1	.455	90	141
Pittsburgh	4	8	0	.333	100	209
Boston	2	8	1	.200	65	123
Philadelphia	2	9	0	.182	60	179

WESTERN DIVISION.

	W.	L.	T.	PC.	For.	Agst.
Detroit	7	3	2	.700	191	111
Green Bay	8	4	0	.667	181	96
Chicago Bears	6	4	2	.600	192	106
Chicago Cards	6	4	2	.600	99	97

New Champs Display Power, Scoring Punch

Make First Touchdown Six Plays After Kick-Off; Clark Runs 40 Yards for Second Marker

BY SPECIAL CORRESPONDENT OF THE JOURNAL

Detroit, Mich.—The Detroit Lions were crowned as champions of the National Professional Football league here Sunday when they defeated the New York Giants, 26-7, in a sectional play-off for the champoinship.

Playing on a field made soggy by four days' rain and in a snowstorm, the Lions demonstrated superiority over the Giants in all departments except punting, where Frank Christensen averaged 39 yards to 43 for Ken Strong and Ed Danowski.

Detroit Gains Heavily

Detroit surprised the Giants with the viciousness of its attack early in the game and gained a working margin six plays after the opening kick-off when Gutowski plunged over for a touchdown.

Strong kicked off to Caddel and he ran the ball back to Detroit's 38. Caddel made four yards around left end, failed on a forward pass and then shot one to Frank Christensen, who went to the Giants' 32-yard line. Gutowski completed a beautiful forward to Klemicki, who was downed on the eight-yard line. Presnell hit center for three yards and Gutowski lugged the ball over.

Giant Pass Intercepted

With a little over a minute to go in the first period Frank Christensen snagged Danowski's forward pass on the Detroit 27-yard line and ran to the Giants' 45 before he was stopped. Clark and Caddel made five yards and then Clark, taking the ball on the 40-yard line, reversed the field and ran the rest of the way to a touchdown.

Neither team was able to count in the second period although the Giants once had the ball on the Detroit four-yard line where they were repulsed.

The Giants scored their touchdown after five minutes of play in the third period. With the ball on Detroit's 41-yard line, Danowski passed to Ken Strong. Gutowski leaped for the ball, barely touched it and deflected it to Strong who ran unmolested to the goal. Strong kicked goal.

Danowski's Kick Blocked

The fourth period saw Detroit sew up the game by scoring with less than two minutes to go. Danowski tried a quick kick and it was blocked by Klewicki with Frank Christensen recovering on the Giants' 26-yard line. Parker, Caddel and Clark combined to carry the ball to the Giants' two-yard line. With the New York secondary massed behind center Caddel skirted wide around left end to score and Clark kicked the extra point.

```
DETROIT          NEW YORK
Klewicki .....L. E.........Franklan
Johnson ......L. T.........Morgan
Monahan ......L. G.........Jones
Randolph .....C...........Hein
Emerson ......R. G.........Owen
G.Christensen R. T.........Grant
Schneller ....R. E.........Goodwin
Presnell .....Q...........Danowski
F.Christensen R. H.........Strong
Caddel .......L. H.........Richards
Gutowski .....F............Corzine
Detroit........13  0  0  13—26
New York.......  0  0  7   0— 7
```

Substitutes—Detroit: Morse, Clark, Shepperd, Knox, Ward, Hupke, Parker, Vaughan, Kaska, Stacy. New York: Singer, Bellinger, Del Isola, Mitchell, Newman, Shaffer, Irwin, Krause, Kaplain. Touchdowns — Gutowski, Clark, Caddel, Parker, Strong. Points after touchdown — Presnell (place kick), Clark (place kick). Strong (place kick). Officials —Referee, Hughitt (Michigan); umpire, Cahn (Chicago); field judge, Meyer (Ohio Wesleyan); head linesman, Robb (Pittsburgh).

Dec. 20

Clark Leads Pro Scorers

Star of Detroit Champs Piles Up 65 Points; Hutson Runner-Up

FROM THE JOURNAL'S NEW YORK BUREAU

New York, N. Y.—Scoring honors in the National Football league were captured by Earl (Dutch) Clark of the champion Detroit Lions, according to the official statistics released Thursday.

Clark rolled up 65 points on six touchdowns, 16 points after touchdown and one field goal. His total gave him a substantial lead over Don Hutson, Alabama recruit of the Green Bay Packers, who finished second with 43 points. Hutson, an end, led the league in touchdowns scored, and added one extra point.

Although he was kept on the sidelines with injuries much of the season, Dale Burnett of New York, with six touchdowns for 36 points, finished in a triple deadlock for third place with Ernie Caddel of the Lions and Bill Karr, Chicago Bears, pass receiving specialist.

Feb. 10

Chicago Bears Granted Option on Jay Berwanger

Philadelphia, Pa. *(AP)* The Chicago Bears of the National Professional Football league have obtained the right to sign Jay Berwanger, the one man team of the University of Chicago last fall, if and when he turns pro, it was learned Sunday night. An authoritative source disclosed this information as the National league wound up its annual two-day meeting.

First choice on Berwanger fell to the Philadelphia Eagles under the league ruling favoring last place teams in selection of incoming collegiate talent. But the Eagles signed away their right to get Berwanger because they feared they could not meet his reported demand for $1,000 a game for turning pro.

Eagles to Get Tackle

In return, the Eagles will get an unidentified tackle from the Bears.

The league adopted a plan Sunday to equalize strength among the nine clubs by giving the weaker elevens first call on the services of prospective newcomers from colleges.

At the same time, the league received from Los Angeles an application for a franchise there, and decided to permit a club to operate on the Pacific coast on a probationary basis during the coming year.

Use "Draft" System

In its new plan for selection of college prospects, the league ruled that hereafter, at the end of the regulation season, club owners will submit the names of eight college prospects. The 72 names will be listed, and the tail-end club of the league will have first call on any one of the candidates.

Under this system, the last place club will have first chance to establish negotiations with upcoming players without interference from other teams. This selection will be followed by each club having a choice in the reverse order of the standing of the clubs at the close of the season.

Bell to Control Eagles

PHILADELPHIA, April 28 *(AP)*.— Bert Bell, president of the Philadelphia Eagles Football Club, assumed full control of the club at a stockholders meeting today and announced he will coach the National League team next season. Bell, former University of Pennsylvania player and coach, succeeds Lud Wray, who has been in charge of the professional team since it was organized.

GRID PROS HELD TO TIE RESULT

Detroit Football Eleven Forced To Rally Against College All-Stars

Chicago Game Draws Crowd Of 76,361—Charity Fund Is $130,146

ALL-STARS, 7; DETROIT, 7

[By the Associated Press]

Chicago, Sept. 2—In a last-minute drive the Detroit Lions, champions of professional football, rallied to battle one of the greatest groups of college all-stars ever assembled to a 7-to-7 tie on Soldier Field tonight.

The game was witnessed by 76,361 spectators, with the gate receipts at $130,146.

The Lions, offering nothing spectacular in the way of offense excepting Earl (Dutch) Clark's gallop of 32 yards in the first period, seized advantage of a break that enabled them to get into scoring position.

Clark Leads Attack

Returning to the game for the final period, Clark, the former Colorado College All-American, inspired his players in a furious assault. He ripped off nine yards in three smashes and then the Lions punted to the All-Stars 28-yard line. On the next play Alphonse (Tuffy) Leemans, of George Washington University, who had played a smashing running game, was hit hard and fumbled on the All-Stars' 28. Tom Hupke, Lions' guard, pounced on the ball.

The Lions' drive for a touchdown was then started. Ernie Caddel, Lions' halfback who played the entire game, ripped through for 12 yards for a first down on the 17-yard line. Clark then took the ball in two drives, adding eight.

While the All-Stars were apparently expecting Clark to take the ball on the next play, Caddel took the ball on a reverse and ran around his left end, almost untouched, and sprawled across the goal line for the touchdown after an eight-yard sprint. Clark drop-kicked perfectly for the point and the count was deadlocked as it remained.

Sept. 13

Smukler Helps Defeat Giants

Pop Warner's Fullback Sensational in Debut With Philadelphia

Philadelphia, Pa. *(AP)* Hank Reese's field goal with four minutes to play gave the Philadelphia Eagles a 10 to 7 victory over the champion New York Giants in the opener of the National Professional Football league Sunday.

Nearly 30,000 saw Reese, former Temple university player, drop back from his center position twice successively to boot goals from placement on the 13-yard line. The first was nullified when the Eagles were ruled offside.

Dave Smukler, another former Temple athlete, made his professional debut with the outstanding individual performance of the day. Smukler shot a 19-yard pass to Manske, who lateraled it to Carter on the Giants' 20 in the first period. Carter then squirmed past several tacklers to the goal line. Smukler added the extra point from placement.

Smukler tossed a 43-yard aerial to Manske to start the winning drive. The Giants stiffened on the three-yard marker and Reese made his boot.

The Giants scored early in the fourth quarter after a 54-yard drive which ended with Ed Danowski tossing a 10-yard pass to Burnett. Manton kicked the extra point.

Sept. 14

Packer Fan Dies of Heart Attack; One Hurt in Fall

BY SPECIAL CORRESPONDENT OF THE JOURNAL

Green Bay, Wis.—William Hurth, 58, Black Creek, died of a heart attack, and Robert Denis, 21, Green Bay, suffered a broken back during Sunday's football game here between the Green Bay Packers and the Chicago Cardinals. Hurth, seated in the stands, collapsed during an exciting play. Denis fell from a tree outside the stadium from which he had been watching the contest. His condition is critical.

Reprinted from
The Milwaukee Journal

Field Judge Attacked Following Ruling Which Gave Giants 21-17 Win

New York, Oct. 25 (AP)—The New York Giants defeated the Philadelphia Eagles, 21 to 17, today in a National League football game and immediately after the final whistle, Field Judge George Vergara was attacked by two Philadelphia players for ruling interference on a Giant pass which led to the winning touchdown.

Trailing, 14 to 17, and with less than three minutes left, Ed Danowski passed to Winnie Anderson. The ball was yards ahead of the intended receiver, but Vergara charged Swede Hanson with interference on the 15-yard line. The Eagles protested in vain. Two plays later Danowski passed to Kink Richards, who was hauled down on the 3, and on the next thrust Richards crossed the line.

Tillie Manton converted from placement.

After the game several thousand of the 15,000 spectators swarmed on the field and the Eagle players surrounded Vergara. George Mulligan and Joe Pivaronik, Eagles' reserve end and guard who did not play, charged into Vergara, but no harm was done as Referee Tom Thorpe intervened quickly. Vergara came out of the melee with his bow tie askew and a torn shirt.

Turk Edwards Stars As Redskins Scalp Giants Team, 14-0

Hub Team's Giant Tackle Blocks Kicks and Recovers Fumbles in Outstanding Performance

Battles Scores On 74-Yard Run

Bay Staters Will Play Green Bay Packers Next Sunday For League Championship

New York, Dec. 6.—(AP.)—Behind their chieftain bold, 260 pound Turk Edwards, the Boston Redskins sunk the New York Giants, 14 to 0, and won the Eastern Championship of the National Football League today in a game played through mud and rain at the Polo Grounds before a crowd of 17,000 spectators.

Boston's touchdowns were scored by Don Irwin in the second period and Cliff Battles in the third, the latter on 74-yard return of a punt, but it was the ponderous Edwards who blocked kicks, recovered fumbles, took falls out of ball-carriers and generally made life miserable for the Giants.

As the result of their smashing triumph over the Giants, rulers of the East for the past four years, the Redskins will play Greenbay Packers, western title holders, for the league championship next Sunday. The game will be played either in Boston or New York.

Packers Win Pro Championship

Dec. 14

Green Bay Scores Sudden Touchdown to Start Each Half; Redskins March 78 Yards for Lone Tally

BY OLIVER E. KUECHLE
OF THE JOURNAL STAFF

New York, N. Y. Green Bay's mighty, dazzling, air minded Packers mounted the throne of professional football at the Polo Grounds Sunday afternoon with a smashing 21 to 6 victory over the Boston Redskins.

It was a battle between champions of the western and eastern divisions of the league and paid off not only in that intangible thing called the "title" but also in a crack at the college all-stars in Chicago next September, and that means money.

With irresistible fury and a spectacular pass attack engineered by Arnie Herber the Packers literally overwhelmed their rivals from the city of beans and culture.

Half Ends, 7-6

Through most of the first half, which ended 7 to 6, it was very much a ball game, the kind everybody around here predicted it would be, but it was little more than a rout the second half. The deadly arrows with which these men of Lambeau almost literally shot their way into the western division championship also rained their death all over the field here and Boston couldn't do anything about it. Bedraggled and disorganized, the Redskins dragged themselves off the field at the finish, a thoroughly chastened ball club.

Despite the fact the game was played on neutral grounds, it attracted a paid attendance of 29,545 and a gate of $33,741. In rough estimates, each of the winning Packers, who voted to split their end into 30 shares, will receive about $250 for their day's work and each of the Redskins about $180. A perfect day for football, after almost a week of rain, helped bring out the crowd. The field, although it dried out under Sunday morning's sun, was heavy.

Herber hurled his arrows all over

Herber's Darts Turn Bruising Tilt Into Rout

the field, tossing 23 of them in the course of the afternoon, and while he completed only nine, which is only an ordinary average for him, he and his receivers made the nine pay. The first touchdown was directly a result of a 40-yard pass, Herber to Hutson; the second was also directly the result of a pass, Herber to Gantenbein, and the third was scored after a series of passes had helped swing the play deep into Boston territory. Hutson scored the first touchdown, Gantenbein the second and Monnett the third.

The Statistics

	Boston	Green Bay
First downs	8	7
Yards gained rushing	53	87
Yards gained forward passes	91	153
Yards gained lateral passes	—14	0
Total yards gained	130	230
Number of passes	27	23
Passes completed	7	9
Passes intercepted by	2	1
Lateral passes	3	0
Laterals completed	2	0
Number of punts	10	7
Distance of punts	343	246
Average distance of punts	31	35
Run back of punts, yards	43	15
Number of penalties	3	3
Yards lost, penalties	25	15
Fumbles	5	2
Own fumbles recovered	3	1

GREEN BAY		BOSTON
Gantenbein	L E	Millner
E Smith	L T	Edwards
Engebretsen	L G	Olsson
Svendsen	C	Bausch
Evans	R G	Karcher
Gordon	R T	Barber
Hutson	R E	Malone
Bruder	Q	R Smith
Sauer	L H	Battles
Herber	R H	Justice
Hinkle	F	Irwin

Green Bay Packers ..... 7 0 7 7—21
Boston Redskins ..... 0 6 0 0— 6

Substitutes—Green Bay: Clemens, Kiesling, Schwammel, Miller, Schneidman, Paulekas, Laws, Seibold, Goldenberg, Blood, Scherer, Butler, Johnson. Boston: Temple, Pinckert, Weisenbaugh, O'Brien, McChesney, Sinko, Rentner, Tosi, Siemering, Carroll, E. Smith, Busich.

Officials: Referee, W. G. Crowell (Swarthmore); umpire, Bob Cahn (Chicago); head linesman, M. J. Meyer (Cincinnati); field judge, William Halloran (Providence).

Reprinted from
The Milwaukee Journal

Dodgers Win by 100-0 From St. Louis Eleven

WICHITA, Kan., Dec. 13 (AP).—Scoring at the rate of almost two points a minute, the Brooklyn Dodgers of the National Football League defeated the St. Louis Terriers, 100 to 0, in an exhibition professional game today before an estimated crowd of 4,000 persons. The Dodgers gained 300 yards on forward passes and 274 by rushing.

CLEVELAND ELEVEN IS IN PRO LEAGUE

Back in National Football Circuit for First Time Since 1934 Season

FIVE CLUBS IN EACH GROUP

Schedules of Teams Cut From 12 to 11 Games—Carr Again Elected President

By The Associated Press.

CHICAGO, Feb. 12.—The National Football League became a ten-club circuit again today for the first time since 1934 when Cleveland was taken back into the fold.

Club owners, sitting in the first session of their annual two-day meeting, voted Cleveland a franchise after hearing assurances of financial stability from Homer Marshman, president of the Cleveland club, which operated in the American League last year. The admission of Cleveland, which will play in the Western section, will balance the league, with five teams operating in each division.

The magnates also voted to trim the schedule for each team from twelve games to eleven. This was done, President Joe E. Carr said, to close the regular season a week earlier in an effort to assure better weather for the championship playoff battle between the Eastern and Western division leaders.

DODGERS GET PARKER

Duke All-America Halfback to Join Club for Remainder of Season

NORFOLK, Va., Nov. 2 (AP).—Clarence (Ace) Parker, Duke's all-America halfback last year, said today he had agreed to play the remainder of the football season with the Brooklyn Dodgers of the National League.

The Brooklyn management advised Parker that it would send a plane to Norfolk tomorrow for him.

Parker is owned by the Philadelphia Athletics of the American Baseball League, whose manager, Connie Mack, consented to his football contract.

Sept. 2

Sam Baugh's Pass, Stalwart Defense Give Stars 6-0 Victory Over Packers

* * *

The Washington football Redskins should credit Branch Rickey with an assistant. . . . Sammy Baugh, the passing fool from Texas Christian, signed with the Redskins. . . . Later he signed to play baseball with the Cards. . . . Later contract stipulated there would be no football. . . . Poor Sammy was in a strut trying to make up his mind. . . . Along came Dickey. . . . "We want no contract breakers," he told Baugh. . . . "You report to Washington." . . . Sammy did—by air. . . . Incidentally, he has one of the best contracts in the league—two seasons at 7,500 potatoes a year.

* * *

Sept. 12

Detroit Lions Defeat Rams

Victors Build Up a 21 to 0 Lead in First Half; Score on Foe's Mistakes

Cleveland, Ohio (AP)—The Detroit Lions crushed the Cleveland Rams, 28 to 0, in a National league professional football game here Friday night.

One of Detroit's scores was made on a bad pass from center that rolled over the Cleveland goal line, and another on a blocked pass which Tom Hupke recovered and raced 43 yards for a touchdown.

Detroit led, 21 to 0, at the half. Ernie Caddell, former Stanford star, accounted for the final score early in the third period on a 27-yard run.

Harry Ebding, Lion end, scored after picking up a Ram fumble in the second period and Hupke's touchdown run after he intercepted a Ram forward came in the same quarter. Monahan added both points.

Pros Stopped on Goal Line; Drives Falter

Drake of Purdue Brilliant on Pass Defense: Herber Goes Out With Injured Arm in Third Period

The Statistics

	All-stars	Green Bay
First downs	8	18
Yards gained by rushing (net)	65	126
Forward passes attempted	13	40
Forward passes completed	7	18
Yards gained by forward passes	115	202
Yards lost, attempted forward passes	19	9
Forward passes intercepted by	3	0
Yards gained, run back of intercepted passes	47	0
Punting average (from scrimmage)	39.1	39
*Total yards, kicks returned	54	35
Opponents' fumbles recovered	0	0
Yards lost by penalties	45	10

*Includes punts and kickoffs.

ALL-STARS		GREEN BAY
Tinsley (L.S.U.)	L. E.	Hutson
Widseth (Minn.)	L. T.	E. Smith
Starcevich (Wash.)	L. G.	Engebretson
E. Svendsen (Minn.)	C.	G. Svendsen
Reid (N.W.)	R. G.	Evans
Daniell (Pitts.)	R. T.	Gordon
Wendt (Ohio State)	R. E.	Gantenbein
Huffman (Ind.)	Q.	Bruder
Larue (Pitts.)	L. H.	Miller
Drake (Purdue)	R. H.	Herber
Francis (Neb.)	F.	Hinkle

All-stars—L. E., Antil (Minn.), Galetka (Miss. State); L. T., Dennerlein (St. Mary's), Steinkemper (Notre Dame); L. G., Lautar (Notre Dame), Glassford (Pittsburgh); C., Basrak (Duquesne), Wiatrik (Washington); R. G., Bassi (Santa Clara), Smith (Ohio State); R. T., Bjork (Oregon), Henrion (Carnegie Tech), Kopczak (Notre Dame); R. E., Stromberg (Army); Q. B., Wilkinson (Minn.); L. H., Baugh (Texas Christian), Agett (Michigan State), Wilke (Notre Dame); R. H., Cardwell (Nebraska), Haine (Washington State); F. B., Jankowski (Wisconsin), Toth (N. W.), Danbom (Notre Dame).

Packers—L. E., Becker; L. T., Siebold; L. G., Michalski, Lettlow; C., Lester; R. G., Goldenberg, Schammel; R. T., Butler; R. E., Scherer; Q. B., Schneideman; L. H., Sauer, Monnett; R. H., Laws; F. B., Johnson.

Sept. 16

Redskins Top Giants, 13 to 3

Riley Smith, Sam Baugh Lead Washington Pro '11' to Victory

Washington, D. C. (AP)—Riley Smith booted two field goals and raced 60 yards for a touchdown Thursday night to score all of Washington's points as the Redskins made their National Pro Football league debut here with a 13 to 3 triumph over the New York Giants. Nearly 24,500 fans saw the game.

Sam Baugh, the Texas Christian slinging star, playing his first pro game, overshadowed the Giants famed tosser, Ed Danowski.

With Don Irwin leading the charge, the Redskins moved 70 yards in the first quarter and Smith place-kicked a field goal from the 19-yard line. Twice in the second period the Redskins stopped the Giants just short of touchdowns, once on the 12-yard line and again on the one-foot line. Manton missed a field goal try from the 30 but place-kicked from the 14-yard line to tie the score.

Baugh turned loose his passing act in the fourth period but the Giants stopped the Redskins short of a touchdown and Riley booted a field goal from the 18-yard line. Shortly afterward, Smith intercepted a pass from Jim Neill and romped 60 yards for the touchdown. Smith booted the extra point.

Washington Redskins

TAKE EASTERN DIVISION CROWN

58,285 Fans See Cliff Battles Lead Scalping Of Gothamites

Worst Defeat Handed Losers Since They Entered Pro League

REDSKINS, 49; GIANTS, 14

[By the Associated Press]

New York, Dec. 5—The Washington Redskins unleashed blinding power, overland and in the air, today to whip the New York Giants, 49 to 14, and win the Eastern division championship of the National Professional Football League.

A crowd of 58,285 jammed the Polo Grounds to capacity. It was rewarded with a game that exceeded a movie scenario writer's fondest dreams. Led by Cliff Battles, former West Virginia Wesleyan star; Sammy Baugh and the mammoth Turk Edwards, the invaders riddled the Maramen's defense with a varied and brilliant offense and, except for a spurt in the third period, bottled up the New York attack.

The crowd, which included 7,000 Washington rooters, was the largest to watch a professional football game in New York since Red Grange's debut at the Yankee Stadium, 13 years ago to the day.

Chicago Bears' Eleven Tops Cardinals, 42-28

Chicago, Dec. 5 (AP)—The Chicago Bears, previously having clinched the Western division title, finished their regular National Pro Football League schedule today by romping over their home-town rivals, the Cardinals, 42 to 28, in a game which had to be called in the final minutes because of darkness.

The game, which established a scoring record for the season, was played before 7,313 fans who lit bonfires in the wind-swept stands. During the darkness of the fourth period several players became engaged in a heated argument which ended with several being escorted off the field.

The Bears, in winning their ninth game of the season against one defeat and one tie, spotted the cards two touchdowns in the first period and then roared back with 13 points in the second and a 27 point blast in the third.

The Bears and Washington Redskins, who won the East title today by defeating New York's Giants, meet next Sunday at Wrigley Field for the National League championship.

44,977 SEE PACKERS UPSET BEARS, 24-14

Chicago Throng Sets Record as Home Team Gets First Defeat but Keeps Lead

GREEN BAY PASSES DECIDE

Hutson's 78-Yard Gain Opens Scoring and He Nabs Aerial to Set Up Field Goal

By The Associated Press.

CHICAGO, Nov. 7.—Green Bay's champion Packers struck a lusty blow in defense of their National Football League laurels today by a spectacular triumph over the Chicago Bears, 24 to 14, before a record throng of 44,977 at Wrigley Field.

The setback failed to shake the Bears from the top of the Western division, but it was their first reverse of the season in seven starts, and the manner in which it was achieved gave ample evidence that the big team from the little Wisconsin town was in full stride. The triumph was Green Bay's sixth against two defeats.

A Thrilling Struggle

The outcome of the battle, a thriller that had the biggest crowd in the history of Chicago professional football on its feet from the second period on, left the Bears with a record of five victories, one defeat and a tie. The previous record attendance was 34,530, set when the Bears defeated Detroit's Lions two weeks ago.

Green Bay's great aerial combination of Arnie Herber and Don Hutson started a 17-point raid in the second period, from which the Bears never quite recovered. Herber passed from deep in his own territory to Hutson, who snatched a 38-yard shot and ran 40 more to score.

A few minutes later a 33-yard Herber-to-Hutson pass took the ball to the Bear 23 and set up a 29-yard field goal by Ernie Smith for another 3 points. Just before the end of the half, Eddie Jankowski grabbed a pass from Ray Buivid as it slipped from Ray Nolting's fingers and ran 23 to tally.

Dec. 12

Baugh's Great Passing Defeats Bears, 28 to 21

Redskins Win National Title

Slinging Sam Completes 15 of 28 Tosses, Three for Touchdowns and One for Scoring Position

By OLIVER E. KUECHLE
Of The Journal Staff

Chicago, Ill. — The million dollar arm that whipped the Packers in the all-star game and that whipped just about everything else it was called upon to go against this fall, lashed out again in the championship play-off between Washington and Chicago here Sunday afternoon and whipped the Bears, 28 to 21.

The million dollar arm, if you haven't guessed, is Sammy Baugh's, of course, and the whole story of the battle Sunday, on which hung the professional championship of the year, is the story of what that amazing arm did.

Completes 15 Passes

Four times Washington crossed the Bears' goal and four times Baugh and his remarkable arm, for which Owner George Marshall of the Redskins pays a measly $7,500 a season, did almost all the damage. On three of the touchdowns, Baugh figured directly, pitching to Millner twice and Justice once for scores, and on the fourth, he hurled the ball into position on Chicago's 10-yard line, from where Cliff Battles finally scored on a run. All told, he completed 15 out of 29 and gained some 335 yards through the air. It was easily one of the greatest passing performances in the history of the game.

But while Baugh stole the show and alone accounted for the difference between victory and defeat, this was more than a one-man team.

The Statistics

	Wash'gton	Bears
First downs	15	11
Yards gained rushing	76	110
Forward passes attempted	11	25
Forward passes completed	24	8
Gains on passes	388	208
Loss on passes	40	24
Passes intercepted by	3	3
Interceptions run back	27	40
Punting average	30	47
All kicks returned	36	68
Opponents' fumbles recov.	1	3
Yards penalized	5	15

Reprinted from
The Milwaukee Journal

Dec. 12

Whizzer Goes to Pittsburgh

Drawing Changed to Benefit Weaker Clubs; Farm System, Play-off Series Favored by Owners

Chicago, Ill. (AP)—Pittsburgh's Pirates of the National Professional Football league were awarded the right to negotiate with Whizzer White, Colorado's sensational all-American halfback, Saturday at the annual draft meeting of the league.

The names of 113 players were posted for draft, some of whom may decide not to prolong their football careers in the interest of financial gains. Conspicuously missing was Yale's all-American Clint Frank, who had stated he would not play professional football.

Draft Is Changed

Each second division club was permitted to draft five players for each three taken by the first division clubs. Heretofore, each club has drafted one man at a time, starting with the lowest club and picking in reverse order again and again.

Favor Play-off Series

The magnates also favored a play-off system in which the teams finishing first in each division would meet the second-place team in the other section, with the winners meeting for the championship.

A recommendation was made to increase the player limit of each club from 25 to 30 players beginning with the first game of the season. The owners also increased the league "take" for each game from one-half of 1%, the increased revenue to be used to pay officials. Heretofore the home club has paid the officials.

The players were given the right to appeal to the president of the league in the question of contract and salary disputes. Heretofore they had no such recourse.

The complete draft list:

Tempting Offer to Hold Game for League Title in South Received by Carr

COLUMBUS, Ohio, Dec. 23 (AP).—President Joe F. Carr of the National Football League said today the circuit's 1938 play-off game may be staged at Miami, Fla., instead of on a frozen Northern gridiron.

Damon Runyon, sports writer, news columnist and author, made the offer on behalf of "wealthy sports interests in Miami," Carr said.

Western Division

Cleveland—Corbett Davis, Indiana, back; Benton, Arkansas, end; Routt, Texas A. and M., guard; Markov, Washington, tackle; Franco, Fordham, tackle; Hamilton, Arkansas, end; Chesbro, Colgate, tackle; Mayberry, Florida, back; Ream, Ohio State, end; Maras, Duquesne, tackle; Hoptowit, Washington State, guard; Spaddaccini, Minnesota, back.

Chicago Cardinals—Robbins, Arkansas, back; Popovich, Montana, back; Patrick, Pittsburgh, fullback; Herwig, California, center; Barbartsky, Fordham, tackle; Brunansky, Duke, tackle; Cherry, Hardin-Simmons, back; Lavington, Colorado, end; Daugherty, Santa Clara, center; Sloan, Arkansas, back; Kinderdine, Indiana, end; Mautner, Holy Cross, center.

Detroit—Wojiecieuchowicz, Fordham, center; Smith, Oklahoma, end; Bershak, North Carolina, end; Schleckman, Utah, tackle; Szakash, Montana, back; Nardi, Ohio State, back; Sirtosky, Indiana, guard; Wolfe, Ohio State, center; Douglass, Kansas, back; Frank, Yale, back.

Green Bay—Cecil Isbell, Purdue, back; Schreyer, Purdue, tackle; Sweeney, Notre Dame, end; Uram, Minnesota, back; Kovatch, Northwestern, end; Ragazzo, Western Reserve, tackle; Howell, Nebraska, back; Barnhart, Greeley State, guard; Tinsley, Georgia, guard; Falkenstein, St. Mary's, back.

Chicago Bears—Gray, Oregon State, back; Famiglietti, Boston U. back; Zarnas, Ohio State, guard; Masterson, Miami, end; Ramsey, Oregon State, guard; Sims, Georgia Tech, back; Schwarz, San Francisco, tackle; Weger, Butler, tackle; Mickovsky, Case, back; Dreher, Denver, end.

Eastern Division

Philadelphia — McDonald, Ohio State, back; Riffle, Albright, back; Bukant, Washington (Mo.), back; Meek California, back; Shirey, Nebraska, tackle; Ramsay, Texas Tech, end; Lannon, Iowa, end; Woltman, Purdue, tackle; Kolberg, Oregon State, back; Kriel, Baylor, tackle; Hinkle, Vanderbilt, center; Micheloson, Pittsburgh, back.

Brooklyn—Brumbaugh, Duquesne, back; Kilgrow, Alabama, back; Kinnard, Miss., tackle; Moore, Colorado, center; Merlin, Vanderbilt, guard; Schwartz, California, end; Monsky, Alabama, guard; Noyes, Montana, tackle; Stringham, Brigham Young, back; Sivell, Auburn, guard; Druze, Fordham, end; Mark, North Carolina State, center.

Pittsburgh—White, Colorado, back; Fulcheck, Indiana, back; Wolfe, Texas, back; Matisi, Pittsburgh, tackle; Midler, Minnesota, tackle; Platukis, Duquesne, end; King, Minnesota, end; Burnette, North Carolina, back; McDonough, Utah, end; McCarty, Notre Dame, center; Krause, Baldwin-Wallace, tackle; Koharich, Notre Dame, guard.

New York—Karamatic, Gonzaga, back; Vanzo, Northwestern, back; Konneman, Georgia Tech, back; Souchak, Pittsburgh, end; Noah, West Virginia, back; Doyle, Nebraska, tackle; Grimstead, Washington State, tackle; Oldershaw, Santa Barbara, guard; Hackney, Duke (no position indicated); Melnus, Villanova, tackle.

Washington—Farkas, Detroit, back; Chapman, California, back; Price, Mississippi State, center; Dohrmann, Nebraska, end; Young, Texas A. and M., tackle; Hartman, Georgia, back; Parks, Oklahoma, center; Abbitt, Elon, back; Johnson, Washington, end; Bartos, North Carolina, tackle.

PRO GRID FINALLY ENTICES WHIZZER

Accepts Pirates' $15,000 Offer, Delays Entrance at Oxford U.

By the Associated Press.

PITTSBURGH, August 1.—Coach Johnny Blood of the Pittsburgh pro football Pirates said today Byron "Whizzer" White, Colorado's all-America quarterback, had accepted an offer of $15,000 to play the 1938 season with the Pirates.

Blood said White told him in a telephone conversation he had arranged to delay until January his entrance at Oxford University, England, where he was awarded a Rhodes scholarship.

White agreed, the Pirate mentor said, to report at Loretto, Pa., the Pirates' training camp, on August 10, four days after the opening of the team's practice sessions. Blood added that the contract would be signed at that time.

White's decision to play followed an interchange of telegrams over the week end, in which Whizzer disclosed for the first time he was reconsidering the offer. A few weeks ago, he said he definitely had abandoned any idea of playing.

White asked permission to play with the College All-Stars at Chicago next month, but Blood said it was not granted.

April 11

Five New Rules

Five new rules were written into the pro code. The changes follow:

On kick-offs out of bounds, the ball shall be placed in play on the receiving team's 45 yard line, instead of the 35 yard stripe. Committee members expressed the opinion the rule would stop deliberate attempts to kick out the ball.

Any two players who have been withdrawn from the game during the fourth period may return to the game once. The rule was intended to prevent an injured player from staying in the contest because a substitute was forbidden to re-enter the game.

All penalties inflicted upon the defensive team within the 10 yard line shall be one-half the distance to the goal line. Previously the rule applied only to off-side penalties.

The referee may penalize defensive teams 15 yards for deliberate roughing of a forward passer after the ball has left his hands. The change was made, the committee said, because of the pummeling Sammy Baugh, Arnold Herber and other topnotch passers received.

A forward pass incomplete in the end zone shall be ruled a touchback only on the fourth down. If the complete pass on fourth down originated outside the 20 yard line the defensive team shall be given the ball at the point at which the play originated.

Sept. 1

Pros Beaten in Aerial Duel

Baugh Always a Threat but It's Purdue Back Who Steals the Show Before Crowd of 74,250

By OLIVER E. KUECHLE
Of The Journal Staff

Chicago, Ill. Once again a team that lived by the pass has died by the pass.

Washington's Redskins, champions of the pro league, and with Slingin' Sammy Baugh, the "passingest" team in football, bowed in the annual all-star football game here Wednesday night because they faced a bunch of college boys who, for the evening at least, passed just a little better than they. The score was 28 to 16.

Really, it was one boy who passed them to death—Cecil Isbell of Purdue. Almost single handed, with an amazing display of "high, hard fast ones," he escorted Bo McMillin's "pore little college boys" to their victory—the most interesting, the most convincing and the most thrilling by far in the five year history of the series. The college boys have now won two and the pros one. Two games have ended in ties.

Without Isbell, McMillin's "pore li'l college boys," as he himself dubbed them, were almost well named. They had no other offensive gesture that was worth a hoot. They gained something like 23 yards rushing all night. But with Isbell—well, with Isbell they couldn't be stopped.

Keep Pros at Bay

Isbell's passing was directly responsible for one touchdown and indirectly responsible for only one other, but aside from this it was the big factor in keeping the pros in general at bay. He flipped them here and he flipped them there, and the pros just didn't know what to do about it. All told, he completed 7 out of 13, pitched two others which receivers had smack in their hands but dropped, and came consistently close to the receiver on every other one.

WASHINGTON		ALL STARS
Millner	L. E.	Schwartz
Edwards	L. T.	Shirey
Olsson	L. G.	Routt
Carroll	C.	Wolf
Karcher	R. G.	Monsky
Barber	R. T.	Markov
Malone	R. E.	Sweeney
Smith	Q.	Puplis
Baugh	L. H.	Uram
Pinckert	R. H.	Isbell
Krause	F.	Patrick

All-Stars	3	0	12	13—28
Redskins	7	3	0	6—16

Substitutes — All Stars: Ends, Kovatch (Northwestern), P. Smith (Oklahoma), Benton (Arkansas), Wolfe (Texas), Birr (Indiana), Zachary (Purdue), Gustitus (St. Ambrose); tackles, Kinard (Mississippi), Kevorkian (Harvard), Barbartsky (Fordham), Ryba (Alabama), Dixon (Boston college); guards, Zaras (Ohio State), Ruetz (Notre Dame), Hoptowit (Washington), Calvano (Northwestern), Kuharitch (Notre Dame); centers, McCarty (Notre Dame), Dougherty (Santa Clara), Wegner (Northwestern), Nebel (Xavier), Gallagher (Yale); backs, McDonald (Ohio State), Vanzo (Northwestern), Coffis (Stanford), Rohm (Louisiana State), J. White (Princeton), Gmitro (Minnesota), Hackney (Duke), B. White (Colorado), Heap (Northwestern), Kilgrow (Alabama), Popovich (Montana), Spadaccini (Minnesota), Calhoun (Loyola at New Orleans), Davis (Indiana). Washington—Ends, McChesney, Moore; tackles, Wilkin, Bond; guards, Young, Kahn; center, Parks; backs, Tuckey, Justice, Karamatic.

Reprinted from
The Milwaukee Journal

Aug. 7

Grant of Grid Fame Killed by Lightning

Dedham, Mass. - (AP) - Lightning on a golf course Saturday killed Leonard T. Grant, 32, of Dedham, former captain of the New York university football squad and now an assistant coach for the New York Giants, professional football team.

Grant was playing golf at the Norfolk club with Roger Shine, Calvin Tucker and James McCartney. The foursome was on the fourth fairway when a thunderstorm broke.

"You're not going to quit, are you?" demanded Grant.

Before his companions could answer, lightning struck Grant.

Three physicians who were playing near by hurried to the scene. They found his pulse throbbing weakly, but he died while they were attempting resuscitation.

Grant was a tackle at New York university from 1927 through 1929, and captain in 1929. During the years he played, NYU lost only five games and became famous nationally for the first time.

After graduation in 1930 Grant joined the New York Giants professional football team. He played with the Giants until three years ago when he became an assistant coach.

Sept. 10

Lions Beat Pittsburgh in Grid Opener, 16-7

White Scores Pirate Points

Detroit Counts Field Goal and 2 Touchdowns During Opening Half Attack; Caddell, Cardwell Star

Detroit Mich.-(AP)-Scoring all of their points in the first half, the Detroit Lions conquered the Pittsburgh Pirates, 16 to 7, Friday night in the opening game of the National Professional Football league season.

Byron (Whizzer) White, former Colorado university star who signed for a reported salary of $15,000, registered Pittsburgh's only touchdown on a plunge from the two yard line late in the final period. Earl (Dutch) Clark, Detroit quarterback and coach, remained on the sidelines because of an ankle injury.

Even if His Team Lost, Whizzer Still Is Worth $15,000

Detroit, Mich.-(AP)-Despite the fact that his debut as a paid football player was for a losing cause, everyone connected with the Pittsburgh Pirates from Owner Art Rooney down to the waterboy was confident Saturday that a brilliant future awaits Byron (Whizzer) White in the National Professional league.

White, most publicized college player of 1937, made his bow Friday night as the Detroit Lions conquered the Pirates, 16 to 7, in the first game of the professional season.

"I think he is worth every cent of the $15,000 I am paying him," said Rooney after the game. "I am sold on him."

DETROIT LIONS 1938
5042 Cass Ave. Telephone Temple 1-5432

Enclosed please find remittance for $_____ for _____

Season Tickets, Tax and Postage.

☐ Box Seats   (Indicate by X desired price   ☐ Upper Deck
☐ Grandstand Seats   and Upper or Lower Deck)   ☐ Lower Deck

Print _____
        Last Name   First Name   Middle Name

Print _____
        Number and Street   City   State

Phone _____

		Boxes (Tax inc.)	Grandstand (Tax inc.)
WASHINGTON REDSKINS	OCTOBER 16th, 2:00 P. M.	$ 3.30	$ 2.20
CHICAGO CARDINALS	OCTOBER 23rd, 2:00 P. M.	3.30	2.20
CLEVELAND RAMS	NOVEMBER 6th, 2:00 P. M.	3.30	2.20
GREEN BAY PACKERS	NOVEMBER 13th, 2:00 P. M.	3.30	2.20
CHICAGO BEARS	NOVEMBER 24th, 11:00 A. M.	3.30	3.30
PHILADELPHIA EAGLES	DECEMBER 4th, 2:00 P. M.	3.30	2.20
	TOTAL at Full Price	$19.80	$14.30
(over)	SEASON TICKET PRICE	$16.00	$11.50

Nov. 14

Packers Crush Detroit to Clinch Western Title

Settle Issue in First Half

Uram's 70 Yard Gallop High Spot of 28 to 7 Victory Before Record Breaking Crowd of 45,000

Journal Special Correspondence
Detroit, Mich.—A crowd of 45,000, the largest ever to attend a football game in Detroit, Sunday saw the Green Bay Packers trounce the Lions by a 28 to 7 score and clinch a tie for the western division title in the National Professional Football league.

With only one game, with the New York Giants, remaining on their regular schedule, the Packers are established as western champions. They have lost one less game than Detroit and have won three more. The championship will mean a play-off with the eastern leader, either Washington or the Giants, for the league title.

Pro Standings

EASTERN DIVISION

	W	L	T	Pct.	Pts.	OP
New York	6	2	0	.750	136	69
Washington	5	2	2	.714	133	118
Brooklyn	4	3	2	.571	118	130
Philadelphia	3	6	0	.333	119	150
Pittsburgh	2	6	0	.250	65	127

WESTERN DIVISION

	W	L	T	Pct.	Pts.	OP
Green Bay	8	2	0	.800	220	103
Detroit	5	3	0	.625	91	77
Chicago Bears	5	4	0	.556	163	128
Cleveland	3	6	0	.333	101	177
Chicago Cards	1	8	0	.111	77	144

GREEN BAY		DETROIT
Hutson	L. E.	Patt
Seibold	L. T.	Johnson
Letlow	L. G.	Graham
Mullenaux	C.	Wojciechowicz
Goldenberg	R. G.	Radovich
Lee	R. T.	Christensen
Gantenbein	R. E.	Moscrip
Schneidman	Q.	Huffman
Isbell	L. H.	McDonald
Laws	R. H.	Cardwell
Hinkle	F.	Gutowsky

Green Bay	0	14	7	7—28
Detroit	0	0	7	0— 7

Touchdowns—Hinkle (2), Isbell, Uram, Shepherd. Points after touchdowns—Engebretsen (2), Hinkle, Hutson, Shepherd. Officials—Referee, W. Cochrane (Kalamazoo college); umpire, M. J. Myer (Ohio Wesleyan); field judge, Carl Brubaker (Ohio State); linesman, George M. Brown (Ohio university).

Substitutions—Green Bay: Backs, Herber, Paul Miller, Uram, Jankowski; ends, Scherer, C. Mullenaux, Becker; tackles, Butler, Ray; guard, Engebretsen; center, Lester. Detroit: Backs, Shepherd, Ryan, Clark, Vanzo, Cadell; ends, Klewicki, Morse, Moscrip; tackles, Reynolds, Rogers, Matisi; guards, Feldhaus, Wagner; center, Stokes.

Reprinted from
The Milwaukee Journal

Dec. 8

1938 Pro Draft List

Green Bay Packers –Buhler, Minnesota, back; Brock, Nebraska, center; Hovlund, Wisconsin, guard; Craig, South Carolina, end; Tweddell, Minnesota, tackle; Kell, Notre Dame, tackle; Hall, Texas Christian, back; Gavre, Wisconsin, back; Sprague, Southern Methodist, end; Kaplanoff, Ohio State, tackle (transferred to Brooklyn); Elmer, Minnesota, center; Badgett, Georgia, tackle; Greenfield, Arizona, center; Bellin, Wisconsin, back; Yerby, Oregon, end; Balazs, Iowa, back; Brennan, Michigan, guard; Schultz, Minnesota, tackle; Hofer, Notre Dame, back; Gunther, Santa Clara, back.

New York Giants–Neilson, Arizona, back; Chickerneo, Pittsburgh, back; Willis, Clemson, back; Ginney, Santa Clara, guard; Woodell, Arkansas, center; Zagar, Stanford, tackle; Mills, Nebraska, tackle; Roberts, Depaul, tackle; Miller, Washington, back; Schroeder, Texas A. and M., end; Aills, Centenary, back; Watson, North Carolina, back; Dugan, Oklahoma, tackle; Panish, Bradley, back; Sanders, Southern Methodist, tackle; Dolman, California, end; Paulman, Stanford, back; Smith, Tulane, center; Tonelli, Notre Dame, back; Rhodes, Texas, guard.

Brooklyn Dodgers–McLeod, Dartmouth, back; Haak, Indiana, tackle; Young, Oklahoma, end; Bottari, California, back; Kinnis, Missouri, center; Janiak, Ohio U, back; Schoenbaum, Ohio State, tackle; Hill, Duke, center; Kline, Texas Christian, guard; Bradley, Mississippi, back; Lenc, Augustana, end; Heikkinen, Michigan, guard; Gembis, Wayne, back; Carnelly, Carnegie Tech, back; Trunzo, Wake Forest, guard; Gross, Bradley, guard; Siegal, Columbia, end; Morin, Iowa State, tackle; Anderson, Kansas, guard; Popp, Toledo, end.

Chicago Bears–Osmanski, Holy Cross, fullback; Wysocki, Villanova, end; Delaney, Holy Cross, tackle; Beinor, Notre Dame, tackle (transferred to Brooklyn); Heilman, Iowa State, end; Dannies, Pittsburgh, center; Bray, Kalamazoo Teachers, guard; Wood, Tennessee, back; Braga, San Francisco, back; Roise, Idaho, back; Bock, Iowa State, guard; Stolfa, Luther, back; Voigts, Northwestern, tackle; Armstrong, Tarkio, tackle; Masters, Newberry, end; Sherman, Chicago, back; Simonich, Notre Dame, back; Vogeler, Oklahoma Aggies, center; Forte, Montana, tackle; Kiseater, Iowa State, halfback.

Detroit Lions — Pingel, Michigan State, back; Weiss, Wisconsin, back; Maronic, North Carolina, tackle; Wenlick, Oregon State, end; Tully, East Texas Teachers, back; Trzuskowski, Idaho, tackle; Callihan, Nebraska, back; George, Southern California, tackle; Calvelli, Stanford, center; Coughlan, Santa Clara, guard; Hutchins, Iowa State, guard; Means, Washington, guard; Hodge, East Texas Teachers, end; Lazetich, Montana, back; Neihaus, Dayton, tackle; Niemantz, New Mexico, back; Tonelli, Southern California, guard; McDonald, Illinois, center; Waters, Brigham Young, end; Howe, Xavier, tackle.

Washington Redskins–Hale, Texas Christian, tackle; Holm, Alabama, back; Todd, Texas A. and M., back; Anderson, California, back; Lumpkin, Georgia, center; Russell, Auburn, tackle; Moore, Minnesota, back; Johnson, Washington, back; German, Centre, back; O'Mara, Duke, back; Slavinski, Washington, guard; Hoffmann, Southern California, back; Tipton, Duke, back; Farmain, Washington State, tackle; Shugart, Iowa State, tackle; Morgan, Southern California, back; Smith, St. Benedict's, tackle; Kooh, Centre, tackle; Kubic, Villanova, back; Kruber, Washington, back.

Chicago Cardinals–Aldrich, Texas Christian, center; Goldberg, Pittsburgh, back; Wolff, Santa Clara, tackle; Stebbins, Pittsburgh, back; Daddio, Pittsburgh, end; G. Faust, Minnesota, back; Dwyer, New Mexico, back; Hinkebein, Kentucky, center; Brown, Notre Dame, end; Crowder, Oklahoma, back; Wyatt, Tennessee, end; Thomas, Oklahoma, guard; Sabodis, Citadel, center; Miatovitch, San Francisco, tackle; Clarke, Santa Clara, guard; Goins, Clemson, end; Elkins, Marshall, back; Huffman, Marshall, end; Kochel, Fordham, guard; Rice, San Francisco, tackle.

Pittsburgh Pirates–Luckman, Columbia, back (transferred to Chicago Bears); Manders, Drake, back (transferred to Brooklyn); Patterson, Baylor, back; McCullough, Oklahoma, back; Wheeler, North Dakota State, back; Boyd, Baylor, end; Palumbo, Detroit, back; Nelson, Michigan State, end; Petro, Pittsburgh, guard; Lee, Carnegie Tech, back; Tomasetti, Bucknell, back; Cochrane, St. Louis U, back; Hoffman, Pittsburgh, end; Clary, South Carolina, back; Tosi, Niagara, guard; Lezouski, Pittsburgh, guard; Longhi, Notre Dame, center; Shirk, Kansas, end; Peters, Washington, end; Sheldrake, Washington, end.

Cleveland Rams–Hall, Mississippi, back; Smith, Southwestern, back; Tarbox, Texas Tech, back; Garard, St. Mary's, tackle; Gatto, Louisiana State, tackle; McGerry, Utah, tackle; Dowd, St. Mary's, center; Brunner, Tulane, back; Bostwick, Alabama, guard; Petrick, Indiana, end; Roth, Cornell, guard; Adams, Ohio U, tackle; Hitt, Mississippi college, end; Ryland, UCLA, center; Friend, Louisiana State, tackle; Reupke, Iowa State, back; Parry, St. Mary's, back; Atty, West Virginia, guard; Lane, Bucknell, back; Graham, Indiana, back.

Philadelphia Eagles — O'Brien, Texas Christian, back; Newton, Washington, back; Mihal, Purdue, tackle; Dewell, Southern Methodist, end; Costan, Texas A. and M., center; Schuehle, Rice, back; Ippolitto, Purdue, back; Sommers, La Salle, tackle; Britt, Texas A. and M., end; McKeever, Cornell, tackle; Humphrey, Purdue, center; Kraynick, North Carolina, back; White, Texas Christian, tackle; Alexis, Ohio State, tackle; Watkins, West Texas Teachers, back; Hall, Brown, back; Riddle, South Dakota State, end; Gainor, North Dakota, end; White, Tulsa, back; Gormley, Louisiana State, center.

Reprinted from
The Milwaukee Journal

Dec. 9

Agents Discover Giant Office Selling Ducats to Sunday's Game Above Face Value

From The Journal's N. Y. Bureau

New York, N. Y.—Federal agents invaded the offices of Tim Mara's New York football Giants Thursday, paid $2 above face value for several tickets to Sunday's Packer-Giant championship game at the Polo Grounds, and then arrested Tim's niece, Helen Mara, 29, for failure to stamp the amount received on the back of the ducats for revenue tax purposes.

"I've been framed," protested Mara, who accompanied his niece and a clerk, Charles Chaplin, 21, to United States Commissioner Garrett W. Cotter's office. "There isn't any truth in all these complaints."

The niece was released in her uncle's custody and Chaplin gave $250 bail.

The arrests recalled several accusations concerning Sunday's game between the Giants and the Green Bay Packers for the pro football championship of the world.

Tickets have been difficult to obtain from the beginning for the event, which 50,000 to 60,000 are expected to pay $100,000 for the privilege of witnessing—without counting the profits of speculators.

According to Assistant United States Attorney Jesse Moss, ticket brokers themselves were forced to pay a $2 bonus on each ticket at the offices of the Giants. The government agents said they paid $6.80 for $4.40 tickets and an average increase of $2 on cheaper admissions.

Mara's niece was in charge of the office. Tim, veteran sports promoter, is head of the organization.

In addition to the Giants, Mara's interests include large bookmaking activities. He was a fight promoter in the days of Tex Rickard.

Mara said he had known Chaplin since he was a small boy. The 21 year old student works in Mara's office to help pay for his schooling.

"I am convinced," said Mara, "that his terrible crime is nothing worse than an error in making change."

Reprinted from
The Milwaukee Journal

Dec. 12

Giants' Early Attack Defeats Green Bay for Title, 23 to 17

Blocked Kicks Give 9-0 Lead

Packers Move Out in Front as Second Half Starts; Freak Decision Stalls Late March

By PAT GANNON
Of The Journal Staff

New York, N. Y. — In a roaring football game in which men limped off the field in twos and threes, the New York Giants Sunday defeated the Green Bay Packers, 23 to 17, for the National Professional Football league championship.

The Packers sorely missed Don Hutson, their great pass catcher. He played a few minutes in the second period, then limped off with his bad knee damaged again. He came back on the field with Herber in the final minute for a last desperate pass attempt, which failed.

Record Crowd Attends

Green Bay stormed up the field time and again in the last quarter, but never could go the route. An odd twist practically broke the Packers' hearts near the end and perhaps saved the game for the Giants. Her-

The Statistics

	New York	Packers
First downs	15	14
Yards, net rushing	113	164
Yards on passes	99	214
Total yards gained	212	378
Forward passes tried	18	19
Passes completed	8	8
Passes intercepted by	1	1
Laterals attempted	1	1
Laterals completed	1	1
Average distance of punts	42	39
Yards run back	42	14
Fumbles	1	2
Opponents fumbles recov.	2	0
Yards penalized	10	20

ber completed a pass to Gantenbein from his own 44 to the Giants' 40, but the officials ruled that Gantenbein was an ineligible receiver and gave the ball to the Giants on the Packers' 44.

Pro Pay-Off

From The Journal's N. Y. Bureau

New York, N. Y. The figures on the Giants-Packers championship game follow:

Attendance	48,120
*Net receipts	$68,331.80
Giants' share	17,151.40
Individual player's share	504.45
Packers' share	11,234.23
Individual player's share	368.84
Washington (second in eastern division)	2,938.56
Detroit (second in western division)	2,838.56

*Federal taxes deducted.

Battling in the east-west play-off before a crowd of 48,120 at the Polo Grounds, the Packers lost the game after a valiant fight. They were knocked off their pins in the first quarter, but recovered and came back to take the lead in the second half before finally conceding defeat.

The largest crowd ever to see a play-off game paid a total of $68,-331.80.

The Giants won the ball game by astute play, two blocked kicks being turned into a touchdown and a field goal early in the game, putting the Packers down, 9 to 0, before they were well steamed up. The Green Bay team, with amazing fortitude, came back, however, to take the lead in the second half.

Important Money Involved

Loss of the game not only cost the Packers the long end of the gate, but also a junket to the Pacific coast to play against a team of All-Stars Jan. 15.

It also means loss of a chance to participate in the all-star game next fall—a pot that runs from $20,000 to $30,000.

The line-ups:

NEW YORK		GREEN BAY
Poole	L. E.	Becker
Widseth	L. T.	Seibold
Dell Isola	L. G.	Letlow
Hein	C.	Lee Mulleneaux
Tuttle	R. G.	Goldenberg
Parry	R. T.	Lee
Howell	R. E.	Gantenbein
Danowski	Q.	Schneidman
Soar	L. H.	Isbell
Cuff	R. H.	Laws
Shaffer	F.	Hinkle
Green Bay	0 14 3 0—17	
Giants	9 7 7 0—23	

Substitutions—Giants, Leemans, Lunday, Haden, Barnum, Karris, Gildea, Burnett, Barnard, Falaschi, Gelatka, Johnson, Mellus, Galazin, Cope, Hanken, Cole. Green Bay: Paul Miller, Bruder, Hutson, Jankowski, Uram, Carl Mulleneaux, Engebretsen, Butler, Scherer, Herber, Ray, Svendsen, Monnett, Johnston. Officials — Referee, Bobby Cahn (Chicago); umpire, Tom Thorp (Columbia); head linesman, Larry Conover (Penn State); field judge, J. L. Meyer (Ohio Wesleyan). Touchdowns — Green Bay, C. Mulleneaux, Hinkle. New York, Leemans, Barnard, Soar. Point after touchdown—Green Bay, Engebretsen 2. New York, Cuff 2. Field Goals—Green Bay, Engebretsen. New York, Cuff.

Reprinted from
The Milwaukee Journal

Dec. 14

Hinkle, Hutson, Letlow Choices of Coaches; Name Hein for Sixth Straight Time

New York, N. Y.–(AP)–Three members of the New York Giants, National Professional Football league champions, and three members of the Green Bay Packers, the runners-up, Tuesday were named to the 1938 all-league team selected by the circuit's 10 coaches.

The Giants, who whipped the Packers, 23-17, in Sunday's title match, are represented by Halfback Ed Danowski, the league's top passer; Center Mel Hein, named to the team for the sixth straight year, and Tackle Ed Widseth. Fullback Clarke Hinkle, the season's leading scorer; Don Hutson, star pass catching end, and Russ Letlow, guard, won places for Green Bay.

In addition to Hinkle, who was honored with a first team berth for the third year in a row, and Hein, there were two other holdovers from the 1937 eleven—Tackle Joe Stydahar of the Chicago Bears and Gaynell Tinsley, Chicago Cardinal end. The other nominees were Danny Fortmann of the Bears, guard; Ace Parker of the Brooklyn Dodgers, quarterback, and Lloyd Cardwell, Detroit Lions' halfback.

Widseth led in the voting with 46 points to 45 for Hinkle, 43 for Hein and 41 for Hutson. Danowski, in addition to his 25 points for halfback, placed second in the quarterback race with 16.

March 23

O'Brien Signs With Eagles

TCU Star Will Get About $10,000 and a Cut of Gate Receipts

Fort Worth, Tex. - (AP) - Davey O'Brien, who shook his head for months at tempting offers to play professional football, capitulated Wednesday for a salary said to be among the highest in the pro ranks.

The Texas Christian university's All-American quarterback insisted for months that he'd rather hunt oil than touchdowns but, in the face of the Philadelphia

Davey O'Brien

Eagles' bid, he decided that his career as a geologist could wait.

Bert Bell, owner of the Eagles, did not disclose the salary, but it was said to be around $10,000, with a cut of the gate receipts.

Joe Carr Dies

Joe Carr, Columbus, Ohio, president of the National Professional Football league and promotion director for the minor leagues of baseball, died Saturday at Columbus.

LUCKMAN IS SIGNED FOR PRO FOOTBALL

Ex-Columbia Star Agrees to Bears' Two-Year Contract After Repeated Refusals

ATTRACTIVE TERMS GIVEN

Chicago Team Owner, Declining to Reveal Sum, Says It Is High for First-Year Man

CHICAGO, July 24 (AP).—The money lure of professional football became too great today for Sid Luckman, Columbia University triple-threat star of last season. Luckman, 194-pound back, signed a two-year contract with the Chicago Bears of the National League.

Luckman had said repeatedly he would pass up the pro game to help his brother run a trucking business in New York. But after signing today he said he would retain an interest in the concern and work there during the off-season.

The Bear recruit completed sixty-six passes in 132 attempts for 866 yards in 1938. He gained 4.6 yards per try in ninety-two times and did most of the team's punting.

In accordance with his policy, George Halas, owner of the Bears, declined to divulge contract terms, but said Luckman "got one of the most attractive contracts we have ever offered a freshman player."

He added Luckman would alternate at quarterback and left halfback, the same as the veteran Bernie Masterson.

Oct. 28

Green Bay Runs Up 21 to 0 Score in Three Quarters and Needs It in Fourth as Chicago Passes Connect

By OLIVER E. KUECHLE

In a wild offensive spree in which some 740 yards were rolled up and seven touchdowns scored, Green Bay defeated the Chicago Cardinals for the second time this season here Sunday afternoon, 27-20.

A record breaking crowd of 18,965 paid, largest by 3,000 ever to see the Packers play here, sat in on the show and left the field at dusk with goose pimples still scampering up and down their spines.

Packers Start Fast

Through the first three quarters it looked as though the Packers might win under wraps. They built up a 21-0 lead and apparently had the game well in hand. In their premature moment of triumph, however, they suddenly found themselves lost in a deluge of passes again as against Cleveland a week ago and without anything that resembled a pass defense, without an "umbrella," they almost blew the game.

The Cardinals quickly rushed three touchdowns home in the fourth quarter, all on passes, while the Packers, rather luckily, sandwiched their fourth one, and winning one, in between.

As against Cleveland a week ago, the Packers all but collapsed every time the Cardinals went into the air. They ran in circles frantically looking for the flying ball, and they seldom found it until some red shirt had his arms around it. Something, it is very clear, must be done on pass defense, if they hope to continue in the fight.

Look Good Offensively

On their own account, however, they looked much more like a ball club than ever before this season. Hutson scored the first touchdown on a great 80 yard run after taking a short pass from Herber, Hinkle accounted for the second on a short dig from the one yard line, Andy Uram hung up the third on a sensational 95 yard run from scrimmage and Hutson accounted for the fourth on a short pass over the line from Herber.

Against this, Smith scored two touchdowns for the Cardinals and Goldberg one. Goldberg's touchdown was scored with less than a minute and a half left.

Reprinted from
The Milwaukee Journal

Oct. 16

Redskins Crush Pirates, 44-14, Again Breaking Scoring Record

Eclipse Mark of 41 Points Set in Previous Game on Home Gridiron—Filchock's Pass to Farkas Gains 99 Yards for Tally

Ball Tops an Upright

Ruled 'Not Enough;' Means Title

NEW YORK, Dec. 4.—(AP)—Beyond any possible doubt, Bill Halloran, of Providence, R. I., today is foot ball's most discussed official here in the East.

Halloran called "no good" an attempted field goal by the Washington Redskins Sunday in the dying seconds of their Eastern professional championship foot ball game with the New York Giants—and thereby cost the Redskins an estimated $1.000 apiece and started the fans fighting.

It was a decision that might have made a Solomon wince. The ball, kicked by Beau Russell, former Auburn tackle, went sailing over one of the uprights in the dreary gloom of the Polo Grounds. That would have given Washington a 10-9 victory.

But Halloran, former Brown star, wig-wagged his hands. The ball had gone over one of the uprights, but that wasn't enough. New league rules say the ball must be wholly "within the plane" of the uprights—not partially.

Halloran thought the kick was more out than in. One friend quoted him as saying. "It was just like an umpire calling a ball or a strike, it was that close."

There was instant reaction to the split-second decision. The Redskins, having lost the game, 9-7, were not pleased. The Giants, having won their second straight Eastern Division title, thought Halloran's eyesight superb.

Russell said his kick "was close and could have been called either way."

Said Coach Ray Flaherty of the Redskins: "If that guy has got a conscience, he'll never have another good night's sleep as long as he lives."

Spokesmen of the National League Service Bureau, trying to smooth things over, stated they considered Halloran "one of the finest officials in the country."

Halloran, after making his report to the National League officials, quietly left town. Before he went he said he "didn't think Ed. Justice, Washington player, tried to hit me."

Halloran was alone in that thought, for everybody else in the park thought so—and that was enough of an excuse for many of the 60,000 present to start trading punches with neighbors. The extra curricular feuding lasted a half hour after the game.

Grid Marks Smashed By Pro Stars

Only One Record Stands as Play for Pay Players Run Wild to Establish New Standards

New York, Dec. 4.—(AP.)—They completely re-wrote the National Football League's record book this year.

In an unprecedented sweep, fourteen records were broken and one tied in the 19th year of the play for pay sport. Every offensive record, with one exception, was wiped off the books as the Chicago Bears, the Cleveland Rams, the Washington Redskins, the Philadelphia Eagles, the New York Giants and the Detroit Lions all participated in the record wrecking orgy.

The Chicago Bears cracked six of the marks as their fine quartet of Sid Luckman, Billy Patterson, Bob MacLeod and Bill Osmanski gave them a fresh and freshman impetus that could not be denied.

The Bears accounted for four records in ground gaining and two in scoring by running up 298 points and 3988 yards against opponents.

Washington and Green Bay also exceeded the former 11-game marks in these departments of play. The antics of those three clubs largely was responsible for the new league scoring high of 1692 points—208 more than were chalked up last year.

New Passing Marks.

Four new passing records were written into the books, and they, in turn, led to a fifth mark—a new high in efficiency for the league. Cleveland with 127 completions in 253 tosses for 50.1 per cent broke the former mark for 250 or more passes thrown. The Rams also broke the old completion total by 13.

Washington eclipsed the league efficiency mark by over nine per cent by completing 117 out of 201 passes for 58.2 per cent. Detroit and Philadelphia each completed 21 passes in one game, three more than the old mark. A total of 951 completions out of 2238 brought the league efficiency mark to 42.4 per cent—or two per cent better than ever before.

New York, with 14 field goals, reached a new high in that department and helped elevate the league total to 55. Both are new records. Detroit tied another field goal mark with four successful placements in one game.

The only record to stand against this avalanche was the 2885 yards made rushing by the Detroit Lions in their 1936 campaign.

EASTERN DIVISION	W	L	T	Pct.	Pts.	OP
N.Y. Giants	9	1	1	.900	168	85
Washington	8	2	1	.800	242	94
Brooklyn	4	6	1	.400	108	219
Philadelphia	1	9	1	.100	105	200
Pittsburgh	1	9	1	.100	114	216

NFL championship: Green Bay 27, New York 0

WESTERN DIVISION	W	L	T	Pct.	Pts.	OP
Green Bay	9	2	0	.818	233	153
Chi. Bears	8	3	0	.727	298	157
Detroit	6	5	0	.545	145	150
Clev. Rams	5	5	1	.500	195	164
Chi. Cardinals	1	10	0	.091	84	254

Green Bay Packers Swamp Giants, 27-0, To Take Pro Football Title

N. Y. DEFENSE FAILS IN GAME

Arnold Herber's Passes Bring First Score For Victors

Great Line Play Stops Eastern Squad In Air And On Ground

[By the Associated Press]

Milwaukee, Dec. 10.—The Green Bay Packers, cutting loose with a devastating running and aerial attack, crushed the New York Giants today, 27 to 0, in the national professional football championship before 32,000 wind-chilled spectators.

The sellout crowd which jammed into Fair Park for the annual title playoff game saw the Western Division champions move to the front with a first-period touchdown and hold a wide advantage in all departments of play.

The Giants, who had won the Eastern Division title with a great exhibition of defensive football during the regular National League season, cracked wide open at the seams and never were in the ball game after the first few minutes.

Strong Wind Helps

A strong wind aided the Packers in their first touchdown march, but later in the game they outclassed the defending champions regardless of whether the wind was with or against them.

It was Green Bay's fifth national championship, two more than any other team ever has won.

Midway of the first period the Packers began rolling from New York's 40-yard line, after getting the ball there on a short punt.

Arnold Herber tossed two passes for yards and aided Cecil Isbell in driving to the 7-yard line.

Then Don Hutson, Green Bay's great pass-catching end, drifted wide to the left and two Giants dashed to cover him. Herber fired a bullet pass over center to Milt Gantenbein, who caught the ball in the end zone. Paul Engebretsen placekicked the point.

Attack Stalls

The Giants advanced to Green Bay's 35 early in the first period, but there the attack stalled. Ward Cuff tried a field goal from the 42-yard line, but it was low and wide. In the second period the Giants twice got within field-goal distance, but neither try was good.

Len Barnum tried one from his own 47-yard line and later Cuff tried another from the Green Bay 41 and missed by inches.

In this period the Giants had the wind at their backs, but Green Bay's inspired line play left them equally helpless on the ground and in the air.

Joe Laws started the second Packer scoring drive when he returned a punt 30 yards to his own 45. Isbell and Clark Hinkle drove to the New Yorkers' 23 in seven plays. Stopped cold at this point, Engebretsen went into the game and split the uprights with a field goal from the 29-yard marker.

Shortly afterward, Milt Gantenbein plucked one of Ed Danowski's passes out of the air and returned four yards to New York's 33. Laws failed to gain and Hinkle drove through the line to the 31.

Perfect Pass Play

Then Isbell, on a perfectly executed play, tossed a high, lazy pass to Laws, who took the ball on the six-yard line and romped across untouched.

The husky Giants were mystified completely by the play, no one being near enough to Laws even to make a serious effort to reach the receiver.

Engebretsen again added the point from placement.

Punts 58 Yards

Late in this period the New Yorkers got their first real scoring chance after Tuffy Leemans had punted 58 yards over the goal line. Green Bay was penalized 15 yards for holding, and then punted. John Dell Isola partially blocked the kick and the New Yorkers gained possession on the Packers' 16.

But Charles Brock, in the alert fashion which characterized Packer play all the way, intercepted Danowski's pass on the 10 and returned three yards to his own 13. Then the Packers punted out to safety.

A 30-yard pass from Herber to Harry Jacunski set up the Packers' second field goal, advancing the ball to the Giants' 25. Andy Uram picked up two yards, but Herber lost four and then fumbled. Carl Mulleneaux recovered on the 32-yard line. Ernie Smith dropped back to the 42 and booted the 3-pointer, giving the Packers a 20-0 margin.

The Giants, now desperate, again tried passing from deep in their own territory.

Bud Svendsen intercepted an aerial on the 30 and returned to the Giants' 15. Uram hit center for three, then Jacunski on an end-around rammed the ball to the 1-yard line in two tries. On the next play Jankowski cracked guard for a touchdown. Ernie Smith placekicked the point.

New York's only sustained drive came in the waning minutes against Green Bay reserves. Eddie Miller and Hank Soar moved the ball from their own 47 to the 14-yard line with passes and runs, then Miller passed flat to Leland Shaffer, who battered his way to the 3-yard line on the last play of the game.

New York Giants		Green Bay Packers
Poole	L.E.	Hutson
Cope	L.T.	Ray
Dell Isola	L.G.	Letlow
Hein	C.	Svendsen
Tuttle	R.G.	Goldenberg
Mellus	R.T.	Lee
Howell	R.E.	Gantenbein
Danowski	Q.B.	Craig
Richards	L.H.	Isbell
Cuff	R.H.	Laws
Falaschi	F.B.	Hinkle

Score by periods:

New York	0	0	0	0—0
Green Bay	7	0	10	10—27

Green Bay scoring Touchdowns—Gantenbein, Laws, Jankowski (sub for Hinkle). Points from try after Touchdown—Engebretsen (sub for Letlow) (2, placekicks). Smith (sub for Ray) (placekick). Goals from field—Engebretsen (placement). Smith (placement).

Substitutions—New York, ends. Walls. Kline. Gelatka; tackles. Parry. Widseth; guards. Oldershaw. Cole; center. Lunday; Backs. Shaffer. Leemans. Burnett. Barnum. Owen. Soar. Miller. Green Bay, ends. Jacunski. Mulleneaux. Moore. tackles. Smith. Kell. Schultz. guards. Engebretsen. Tinsley. Zarnas. centers. Brock. Greenfield; Backs. Herber. Uram. Jankowski. Bruder. Balazs. Lawrence. Weisgerber.

Pro Grid Champions Get $703.97 Apiece

Milwaukee. Dec. 10 (P)—The national professional football championship game netted each member of the winning Green Bay Packers' squad $703.97. Members of the losing New York Giants' squad received $455.57.

The payoff classic netted a gate of $75,918.50. Of this amount $23,231.08 went to the Packers and $15,487.37 to the Giants.

This year's title game netted about $7,000 more than last year's championship battle between the same two teams in New York. Official attendance was 32,279.

Bell to Retire as Coach

PHILADELPHIA. Dec. 14 (P)—Bert Bell, owner-coach of the Philadelphia Eagles, professional football team, said tonight he will retire as coach and devote all his time to the front office details as soon as Heinie Miller, his new coach, "learns the ropes" in National League football.

Pro Football League Approves Detroit Sale

New York, Feb. 2—(AP.) — The executive committee of the National Professional Football League today ratified the purchase of the Detroit Lions franchise by Fred L. Mandel, Jr., of Chicago and his associates, Tony Owens of Chicago and Charles Chaplin of New York.

Mandel bought the club for the reported sum of $225,000 from George A. Richards last month.

Mandel had already named George Clark as the Lions' coach and announced that William A. Alfs, vice-president under Richards, would be president of the club.

Bid Will Be Considered If Another Club Applies

Need Western Team to Match Up With Boston If Divisions Are to Be Even; Cost of Franchises Boosted to $50,000

New York, April 13.—(AP.)—The National Football League turned down a Boston application for a franchise today, then boosted the cost of new franchises from $10,000 to $50,000 and increased its player limit for each club at the second session of its annual meeting today.

The application of William A. Shea for a franchise for a new Boston club was returned. President Carl Storck explained, because the league had no western club to match a new eastern member. It was decided to continue the present ten-club setup, with five teams in each division, for the 1940 season.

Will Be Considered.

In returning the application, Storck informed Shea that if at any time a situation develops where there is a western team to pair up with a new eastern member, his application will be carefully considered. Boston formerly operated a National League club which was shifted to Washington.

The new price for franchises applies only to those granted by the league to new members. The price for the transfer of an operating franchise to a new owner would be based entirely upon its market value.

The raising of the player limit from 27 to 33 players was the only other important business transacted.

THE NATIONAL FOOTBALL LEAGUE
UNIFORM PLAYER'S CONTRACT

The PRO FOOTBALL, INC. herein called the Club,

and A. GLENN EDWARDS, of WASHINGTON, D.C.

herein called the Player.

The Club is a member of The National Football League. As such, and jointly with the other members of the League, it is obligated to insure to the public wholesome and high-class professional football by defining the relations between Club and Player, and between Club and Club.

In view of the facts above recited the parties agree as follows:

1. The Club will pay the Player a salary for his skilled services during the playing season of 19 40, at the rate of $3,000.00 per season dollars for each regularly scheduled League game played. For all other games the Player shall be paid such salary as shall be agreed upon between the Player and the Club. As to games scheduled but not played, the Player shall receive no compensation from the Club other than actual expenses.

Plus transportation to and from training camp. If team wins championship player agrees to participate in one exhibition game as per the terms of this contract. Player is not to receive compensation for exhibition games other than herein stipulated.

2. The salary above provided for shall be paid by the Club as follows: Seventy-five per cent (75%) after each game and the remaining twenty-five per cent (25%) at the close of the season or upon release of the Player by the Club.

3. The Player agrees that during said season he will faithfully serve the Club, and pledges himself to the American public to conform to high standards of fair play and good sportsmanship.

4. The Player will not play football during 19 40 otherwise than for the Club, except in case the Club shall have released said Player, and said release has been approved by the officials of The National Football League.

5. The Player will not participate in an exhibition game after the completion of the schedule of the Club and prior to August 1 of the following season, without permission of the President of the League.

6. The Player accepts as part of this contract such reasonable regulations as the Club may announce from time to time.

7. This contract may be terminated at any time by the club giving notice in writing to the player within forty-eight (48) hours after the day of the last game in which he is to participate with his club.

8. The Player submits himself to the discipline of The National Football League and agrees to accept its decisions pursuant to its Constitution and By-Laws.

9. Any time prior to August 1st, 19 41, by written notice to the Player, the Club may renew this contract for the term of that year, except that the salary rate shall be such as the parties may then agree upon, or in default of agreement, such as the Club may fix.

10. The Player may be fined or suspended for violation of this contract, but in all cases the Player shall have the right of appeal to the President of The National Football League.

11. In default of agreement, the Player will accept the salary rate thus fixed or else will not play during said year otherwise than for the Club, unless the Club shall release the Player.

12. The reservation of the Club of the valuable right to fix the salary rate for the succeeding year, and the promise of the Player not to play during said year otherwise than with the Club, have been taken into consideration in determining the salary specified herein and the undertaking by the Club to pay said salary is the consideration for both the reservation and the promise.

13. In case of dispute between the Player and the Club the same shall be referred to the President of The National Football League, and his decision shall be accepted by all parties as final.

14. Verbal contracts between Club and Player will not be considered by this League, in the event of a dispute.

Signed this 5th day of MARCH A.D. 19 40.

Witnesses:

PRO FOOTBALL, INC.

By George Marshall

A. Glen Edwards (Player)

Original copy to be held by Club Management

Eagles' Davey O'Brien To Join FBI At Close of Grid Season

Washington, Nov. 17.—(AP.)—Davey O'Brien, former all-America quarterback and now star of the Philadelphia Eagles professional football team, will join the Federal Bureau of Investigation as a special agent at the close of the football season, it was learned today.

O'Brien applied for appointment to J. Edgar Hoover's staff early last summer and recently passed the preliminary investigations and examination with what a FBI official described as "flying colors." O'Brien, who has been getting $10,000 a season with the Eagles, will receive $3200 as a FBI agent.

Now 23 years old, O'Brien majored in geology while at Texas Christian University, where he was graduated in 1939.

He was approved as an agent under "special qualifications" since he is neither a lawyer nor an expert accountant, the two requirements under which most agents are accepted.

When the football season ends, O'Brien will report to the FBI training barracks at the Quantico, Va., Marine Headquarters for seven weeks of intensive study and training. Some of the nation's most highly qualified men in a dozen fields will teach him such courses as jiu-jitsu, handling of firearms and the law of evidence.

MEL HEIN—HIS DAY
N. Y. Giants vs. Brooklyn Dodgers

CAPTAIN MEL HEIN
The Giants' All-Time Center

POLO GROUNDS   **Sunday, Dec. 1, 1940**

HAIL TO THE REDSKINS!!

Wotcha waitin' for? Start singin'

HAIL TO THE REDSKINS, Hail Vic-to-ry.

Braves on the war-path, Fight for old D. C.

Scalp 'em, swamp 'em. We will take 'em big score.

Read 'em, weep 'em. Touch-down we want heap more.

Fight on. Fight on 'till you have won.

Sons of Wash-ing-ton (Rah! Rah! Rah!)

HAIL TO THE REDSKINS, Hail Vic-to-ry.

Braves on the war-path, Fight for old D. C.

Eagles Catch 33 O'Brien Aerials But Drop Game to Redskins, 13-6

Washington Players Join 25,838 in Ovation for Record Breaker in His Farewell— Baugh's 85-Yard Punt Sets Mark

By The Associated Press.

WASHINGTON, Dec. 1—The Redskins today won the Eastern division championship of the National Football League, beating Philadelphia, 13 to 6, but the magnificent performance of little Davey O'Brien of the Eagles stole the show. As he bowed out of football, O'Brien set a world record of thirty-three completed passes in one game.

Playing 59 minutes and 43 seconds, the former Texas Christian University back threw completed passes with an ease that made the Redskins look ridiculous. The previous mark of twenty-three completed passes was set this season by Sammy Baugh of Washington.

As Davey left the field the crowd of 25,838 rose and filled Griffith Stadium with a deafening roar. The Washington players joined in the ovation. O'Brien plans to go to work for the Federal Bureau of Investigation within a few days.

By beating O'Brien's Eagles, the Redskins earned the right to play the Chicago Bears here next Sunday for the professional championship.

More Laurels for Baugh

While O'Brien was breaking the record, two other players set new marks. Don Looney, the Eagles' great end, caught fourteen passes to break the old mark of eight for one game. Baugh, who earlier this season set a mark for yardage gained on completions, turned in the best punt in the history of the pro game, 85 yards from scrimmage, to better Parker Hall's record of 80.

As O'Brien filled the air with passes his running almost went unnoticed. Time and again when he found his ends and backs covered he charged with the ball. Twisting and turning his 151 pounds between the Redskin forwards, some of whom weigh over 230, Davey gained three first downs rushing.

Adding to the brilliance of O'Brien's passing was the fact that none of his sixty heaves was intercepted. His total gain through the air was 316 yards, also a new mark.

The Redskins scored their touchdowns in the second and third periods, the first on Wilbur Moore's 27-yard run on a reverse to his left and the second on Dick Todd's

The Statistics

	Wash.	Phila.
First downs	12	19
Yards gained rushing	220	16
Forward passes	9	60
Forwards completed	5	33
Yards gained, forwards	36	316
Forwards intercepted by	0	2
*Av. dist. of punts, yards	54	45
‡Run-back of kicks, yards	89	45
Rival fumbles recovered	1	1
Yards lost, penalties	15	10

*From line of scrimmage.
‡Includes punts and kick-offs.

plunge from the 4-yard stripe. Sandy Sanford missed the first extra point but Bob Masterson booted the next.

Murray's Kick Blocked

The Eagles got their touchdown in the final period, O'Brien passing to Frank Emmons after Baugh's record punt had set the Eagles back on their 2-yard line. Davey shattered the Redskins' defense, passing the Eagles straight down the field to the touchdown, breaking and setting new records on his way. His final pass went 13 yards to Emmons. Masterson blocked Fran Murray's kick for the extra point.

As the fourth period neared its end O'Brien launched a drive from his 31 to the Washington 22. Mixed with his passing were Davey's two fine runs.

The line-up:

WASHINGTON (13)		PHILADELPHIA (6)
Masterson	L.E.	Looney
Wilkin	L.T.	Somers
Farman	L.G.	Schultz
Titchenal	C.	Cherundolo
Slivinski	R.G.	Bassi
Barber	R.T.	Ragazzo
Malone	R.E.	Wendlick
Krause	Q.B.	O'Brien
Baugh	L.H.	Riffle
Justice	R.H.	Kolberg
Johnston	F.B.	Emmons

SCORE BY PERIODS

Washington ....0 6 7 0—13
Philadelphia ....0 0 0 6— 6

Touchdowns—Moore, Todd, Emmons. Point after touchdown—Masterson (placement).

SUBSTITUTES

Washington—Ends: McChesney, Sanford. Tackle: Russell. Guards: Stralka, Shugart. Centers: Carroll, Andrako. Backs: Pinckert, Morgan, Seymour, Zimmerman, Filchock, Moore, Todd, Meade.

Philadelphia—End: Ramsey. Tackle: Woltman, Thompson, Schmitt. Backs: Murray, Hackney, Arnold, Bukant.

Referee—William H. Friesell, Princeton. Umpire—E. A. Geiges, Temple. Linesman—Larry Conover, Penn State. Field judge—E. E. Miller, Penn State.

Chicago Bears Draft Harmon, But Tommy Says He Won't Play

400 College Seniors Selected By Professional Football Teams In Annual Drawing

[By the Associated Press]

Washington, Dec. 10—As if they weren't already a pretty fair ball club, the World Champion Chicago Bears won first call today on the football services of Tommy Harmon, Michigan's All-America halfback, if Tommy changes his mind and decides to play football for money next year.

Harmon's name was the first drawn in the annual draft of the National Professional Football League. Actually he was selected by the Philadelphia Eagles, under a rule which permits the league's last-place team to make the first draw, but through a previous agreement the Eagles yielded first choice to the Bears.

Bears Pro Champions

The Bears won the pro championship last Sunday when they crushed the Washington Redskins, 73 to 0.

When Tommy, in New York, was informed that he was the No. 1 choice, he said again that he was not interested in pro football. He previously has expressed a preference for radio work. Today's draw, he said, did not influence his decision not to play.

The names of Harmon and 400-add other college seniors whose services are sought by the ten professional teams were placed side by side on a group of blackboards. From this list the team owners, crowded with their coaches in a smoke-filled hotel room, made their selections.

Cardinals Get Second Pick

The Chicago Cardinals, given second choice, drew Jarrin' John Kimbrough, of Texas A. M., another highly prized All-America. Other first choices:

Pittsburgh Steelers—Norman Standlee, Stanford fullback, who also was transferred to the Bears under a pre-season trade agreement.

Cleveland Rams—Rudy Mucha, University of Washington center.

Detroit Lions—Jim Thomason, Texas A. & M. back.

New York Giants—George Franck, Minnesota back.

Green Bay Packers—George Paskvan, Wisconsin fullback.

Brooklyn Dodgers—(Picking in their own right)—Don Scott, Ohio State quarterback.

Washington Redskins — Forest Eva-

shevski, Michigan blocking back, who cleared the way for many of Harmon's touchdown sprints.

Negotiations Forbidden

While nothing prevents Harmon from refusing to be drafted, the league's rules prohibit any team except the one that drafted him from negotiating for his services for the 1941 season.

A new rule is expected to prevent future agreements such as those which enabled Owner George Halas of the Bears to acquire bargaining rights on three of the first ten players drafted.

The Chicago owner expressed hope that he could persuade Harmon to sign a contract. The Michigan star was chosen the outstanding sports figure of 1940 in an Associated Press poll.

To strengthen further his powerful Bears, Halas also drafted Hugh Gallarneau, Stanford back, and Charles O'Rourke, highly regarded back from Boston College.

Fast-running and blocking backs were in demand by most of the other teams during the first five rounds of the drawing.

Among the players selected by the Pittsburgh Steelers was Jim Ringgold, Wake Forest back from Baltimore.

Pittsburgh Pro Team Purchased By Group Headed By Thompson

Washington, Dec. 9 (P)—Sale of the franchise of the Pittsburgh Steelers to a syndicate headed by Alexis Thompson, New York drug products manufacturer, was approved tonight by the National Professional Football League.

At the same time the league approved the purchase of a half interest in the Philadelphia Eagles by Arthur J. Rooney, owner of the Steelers. Bert Bell, president of the Eagles, will continue to head the Philadelphia club. Financial considerations of both deals were not disclosed.

Chicago Crushes Washington By 73-0 Count To Take Pro Football Title

BEAR GRIDDERS AMASS 11 TOUCHDOWNS TO BREAK LEAGUE SCORING RECORD

Westerners Also Set New Mark In Rolling Up 492 Yards Against Hapless Redskin Eleven To Complete Smashing Debacle

By JESSE A. LINTHICUM

Washington, Dec. 8 — Unleashing astonishing power on the ground and an uncanny aerial offense and defense, the Chicago Bears swamped the Washington Redskins this afternoon, to win the professional football championship by a score of 73 to 0.

It was a Redskin massacre that should call for an investigation by the Commissioner in charge of Indian Affairs.

The Bears, winner in the western section of the National League, were r:dhot this afternoon and as they clicked with the precision of a well-oiled machine they found opposing them a jittery outfit that made costly mistakes when scoring opportunities arose.

New Records Set

Washington had many scoring chances as the statistics will show. The Redskins made 18 first downs against 17 for the Bears, but the long scoring runs of the Chicago team are not counted as first downs, according to the rules.

The superiority of the victors is shown in the yardage gained. The Bears gained a total of 492 yards, 372 by rushing.

The size of the score and the yardage gained by the Bears constitute new records in professional football. The previous high score of 64 points was made in a game won by Philadelphia from Cincinnati six years ago.

Chicago struck with cyclonic force right from the start and the Bears rolled on and on, scoring touchdowns in every period and sending the Washington fans, who were pent up to a highly enthusiastic state at game time, to the depths of despair.

Before many of the fans had been seated the Bears tallied their first touchdown and at the end of the initial period were out in front to the tune of 21 to 0.

Visitors Slight Favorite

The Redskins held the Westerners to one touchdown in the second, but the Bears, intent on rolling up the count as they smarted under a 7-to-3 defeat administered by Washington three weeks ago, added 26 points in the third and 19 in the final quarter.

The visiting team was a slight favorite, odds of 7 to 5 having been quoted on the contest, but the size of the score made the game the . big upset of the professional season. An 11-touchdown margin simply was incredible.

After the first quarter the Redskin slaughter was inevitable, and when the half closed with the Bears leading, 28 to 0, Chicago fans moved around the crowd offering to wager 15 to 1 on their team. And those odds appeared at the time to be justified. The Redskins were just that futile.

Sid Luckman, former Columbia star, was the sparkplug of the Bears in the early stages of the game, but Chicago's victory was not a one-man achievement. The Bears used practically every one on the squad, and one set of backs was almost as powerful as the others. Clark was the only player to score more than one touchdown. He made two.

The Redskins, famed for their forward passing attack, found the Bears intercepting tosses and turning them into touchdowns all afternoon.

Reprinted from
The Baltimore Sun

The lineups:

Chicago Bears		Wash. Redskins
Nowaskey	L E	Masterson
George Wash.		Miami
Stydahar	L T	Wilkin
West Virginia		St. Mary's
Portmann	L G	Farman
Colgate		Wash. State
Turner	C	Tichenal
Hardin-Simmons		San Jose State
Musso	R G	Slivinski
Millikin (Ill.)		Washington
Artoe	R T	Barber
California		San Francisco
Wilson	R E	Malone
Northwestern		Texas Aggies
Luckman	Q B	Krause
Columbia		Gonzaga
Nolting	L H	Baugh
Cincinnati		Texas Christian
McAfee	R H	Justice
Duke		Gonzaga
Osmanski	F B	Johnston
Holy Cross		Washington

Score by periods:

Chicago Bears ... 21 7 26 19—73
Washington .... 0 0 0 0— 0

Touchdowns Osmanski. Luckman, Maniaci (sub for Osmanski). Kavanaugh (sub for Wilson). Pool (sub for Wilson). Nolting. McAfee. Turner. Clark (2). (sub for Nolting). Famiglietti (sub for McAfee). Points from try after touchdown—Snyder (sub for Nolting. 2). Manders (sub for McAfee). Martinovich (sub for Musso). Plasman (sub for Nowaskey). Stydahar (all placekicks). Maniaci (sub for Osmanski). forward pass

Chicago Substitutions Ends — Siegel. Columbia: Manske. Northwestern: Plasman, Vanderbilt: Kavanaugh. Louisiana State. Pool. Stanford Tackles—Mihal. Purdue. Kolman. Temple: Torrance. Louisiana State. Guards—Martinovich. College of Pacific: Forte. Montana: Baisi. West Virginia. Centers—Bausch. Kansas: Chesney. DePaul. Backs—Famiglietti. Boston University: Clark. West Virginia Manders. Minnesota. Maniaci. Fordham. Snyder. Ohio U.: Sherman. Chicago. Masterson. Nebraska: Swisher. Northwestern. McClean. Stanselm's.

Washington Substitutions: Ends —McChesney. U C L A. Sanford. Alabama. Millner. Notre Dame. Tackles. Fisher. Southern California: Russell. Auburn. Guards—Stralka. Georgetown. Shugart. Iowa State. Centers—Carroll. Nevada. Parks. Oklahoma. Andrako. Ohio State. Backs—Pinckert. Southern California. Morgan. Southern California. Seymour. Oklahoma. Zimmerman. San Jose State. Filchock. Indiana. Moore. Minnesota. Todd. Texas Aggies Hare. Gonzaga. Hoffman. Southern California Farkas. Detroit. Meade. Maryland.

Comment On The Redskin Rout

[*Special Dispatch to The Sun*]

Washington, Dec. 8—Two very pertinent sports questions rise out of the Massacre of Griffith Stadium, in which the Chicago Bears annihilated the Redskins today.

How could a football team as powerful as the Redskins appeared to be in the season just past collapse so completely?

Why was Sammy Baugh lifted from the starting lineup and kept out as much as he was?

Beat Bears Earlier

Just three weeks ago these same Redskins beat the Bears, 7-3. It is true that the Bears were the recipients of a lot of bad breaks in that game, but at no time did they show any degree of superiority over the Redskins which would indicate any score such as yesterday's.

Bernie Harter, sports editor of the Washington *Herald* and a former college football star, when asked for his opinion, said:

"It is just one of those football oddities that can't be readily explained. I talked to Ray Flaherty, Redskin coach, after the game, asking whether the team was stale. He said he did not think so, but did say that after the Brooklyn game he was never able to get the boys back to their early season offensive sharpness.

Missed Pass Hurt

Harter continued: "Pro coaches such as Curly Lambeau, Steve Owen, Jimmy Conzelman and Jock Sutherland seemed to think that when Charley Malone missed Baugh's long pass right after the Bears' first score the Redskins seemed to break. If this pass had been completed it was a sure touchdown and, with the score even, the game would have developed into a dog-fight.

"They went on to say that right after this the Bears got several more easy touchdowns and this had a tendency to make the Redskins press, and therefore their offense and defense started to backfire.

"The team never quit, but under continued bad breaks they went to pieces. Several of the linemen, Wee Willie Wilkin, in particular, played their best ball of the season.

Not "Marked Men"

"As to the Baugh incident, when the team was fighting from behind, the use of Filchock and Zimmerman was probably due to the fact that they are not "marked men," as is Baugh. Both, however, are polished passers as well as being threats in other ways. Flaherty probably thought that either one would have a better chance of

starting a rally that would bring recovery than Baugh.

In so far as the size of the score is concerned George Marshall, Washington owner, told George Halas, coach-owner of the Bears, that had the Chicagoans been able to run up a 100-to-0 score it would have been all right. This is professional football and the only way to keep it honest is score as often as you can."

Marshall "Mortified"

Marshall went on to say, "We had the greatest crowd in Washington's history and we played our poorest game. I am mortified to think what we did to that crowd, which came all hopped up and ready to cheer itself hoarse. We couldn't even make a game of it. That was what hurt.

"We were awful and you don't need to ask me if we are going to clean house. Some of these boys are going to be embarrassed when the time comes to make contracts for next year. We can remedy a bad ball club, but it's going to be hard to make up to that crowd for what we did to them Incidentally, I guess nobody ever saw a better football team than the Bears."

Flaherty didn't have much to say. There was not much he could say.

Shirley Povich of the Washington *Post* said: "The Bears are what happened to the Redskins. For yesterday they were the perfect football team. Everything they did was right and after the first touchdown everything the Redskins did was wrong."

Redskins Demoralized

Povich went on to sum it up substantially as did Harter. Two quick touchdowns and Malone's miss on what would have been the tying marker completely demoralized the Redskins.

Dutch Bergman, head football coach at Catholic University and one of the veteran coaches of the country, summed it up in the *Herald* as follows: "The greatest exhibition of offensive football I have ever seen. The Bears did everything perfectly."

Merrell Whittlesey, who covered the Washington dressing room for the *Post*, had this statement from Sammy Baugh: "The most humiliating thing I ever had happen to me in a football game."

In The Dressing Room

From the Bears' dressing room came a story by Eddie Gilmore, of the Associated Press, that may be part of the explanation of why the victors kept the pressure on full force during the whole game.

"I know now what the Washington Redskins were up against—I just fought my way out of the Chicago

Bears' dressing room." he wrote. "They weren't sore at me, either.

"It was quite a scene. Thirty-three mastodons charging around a room 24 feet square, waving their huge arms and yelling like a pack of Tarzans wired for amplification.

"Something happened to the showers to add to the confusion. Steam filled the place, and every time you took a faint step a huge Bear — sometimes wrapped in a towel and more often not—smacked into you.

"I lost my hat and George Musso (weight 275 pounds) stepped on it with a big wet foot.

"Bull Dog Turner (weight 235 and still growing) rushed in from behind.

"Joe Maniaci, who weighs only 218, let me off light. He hit me, but only with a wet towel.

"It was all accidental, of course.

"Whacky with joy, the Bears piled into the dressing room and pandemonium broke loose.

"They lifted George Halas, their coach, onto their shoulders. . . . They pounded Hunk Anderson, the line coach, on the back until he begged them to let him up. . . . Modestly, Halas took their applause.

"It was just one of those days," he said. "Everything we did, we did right. Everything they did, they did wrong. Of course, they helped beat themselves. Things like passing from their own 10-yard line, I mean."

"From the heights of the steamy room, Musso, the man-mountain guard, boomed down that the Redskins just happened to be the object of revenge.

"Remember," he shouted, "they beat us for the championship in 1937. They also beat us here three weeks ago. We were just fired up and we went out there to kick the pants off them."

The whole thing sums up to Bob Zuppke's famous statement, "A football takes a funny bounce." And seemingly so did the Redskins.

Biff Jones Sees Bears Use "T" Formation

Washington. Dec. 8 (P)—Major Biff Jones, head coach of Nebraska's Rose Bowl-bound Cornhuskers, saw anything but a pleasant sight today as he watched the Chicago Bears wallop the Washington Redskins, 73-0, today in the National Professional League play-off.

Biff and his assistant, Glenn Presnell, were on hand to pick up some information on the Bears' "T" formation offensive because Stanford, the Huskers' bowl rival, also uses that brand of attack.

What they saw was the Bears scoring 11 touchdowns against a big professional club that was supposed to know all about defense for the "T" formation.

April 3

Thompson Will Take Pittsburgh Pros To Philly in Big Deal

Eagles Exchange Sites With Iron Men In Gridiron Swap to Be Ratified At League Meeting Friday

Another shift in the professional football situation in Pittsburgh developed last night with official word that Art Rooney and Bert Bell, co-owners of the Philadelphia Eagles, will bring that team here, and Alexis Thompson, who purchased the Pittsburgh team from Rooney, will move his club to Philadelphia.

Rooney was in Chicago yesterday to attend a league meeting to be held Friday, at which time the proposed shift will be ratified.

While the move had been contemplated for several weeks, observers agreed it was one of the most unusual swaps in sports history.

"In other words," said a statement issued by Bell to the Associated Press on the eve of the league's annual meeting in Chicago, "this puts Thompson in Philadelphia as the owner of the Philadelphia franchise and Rooney and Bell in Pittsburgh as owners of the Pittsburgh franchise."

Art Rooney

The statement said the deal was consummated "by mutual agreement," both parties feeling that they benefited. Observers also said Thompson, who lives in New York, had long wished to transfer operations closer to his home.

Players in Shift

The shift of the Rooney-Bell team from Philadelphia to Pittsburgh means the return here of such players as Brumbaugh, Noppenberg, Klick and Pirro, backs; George Platukis, Walt Kichefski and Lumb, ends; Ted Doyle and Clark Goff, tackles, and Carl Nery and Jack Sanders, guards. These players were sent to Philadelphia when Thompson purchased the Pittsburgh team and Rooney bought into the Philadelphia franchise.

The team coming here will also have Don Looney, Joe Wendlick, ends; Somers and Thompson, guards; Schultz and Bassi, guards; Cherundolo and Harper, centers; Hackney, Emmons, Kolberg, Newton, Murray and Jones, backs.

The Pittsburgh team that will go to Philadelphia takes in: Ends Sortet, Boyd, Foodenberg, Campbell, Pavkov, Perko, Grabinski, Sullivan, Maras, Patterson, Condit, Tomasetti, Johnstown, Bruder, McDonough and Thompson. These players were on the local club when Thompson bought the franchise and in addition Thompson obtained from Philadelphia Ramsey, Carter, Ragazzo, Woltman, Ted Schmitt, Watkins and Bukant.

Rooney Wanted to Stay Home

The deal was put through because Rooney wanted to keep identified in his hometown with a professional team, rather than own part interest in the Philadelphia Eagles, and because Thompson finds Philadelphia more to his liking as a base because he works out of New York City.

What financial arrangements were made to make the big switch was not disclosed in the reports available last night.

The new team to come here has drafted the following players: Arthur Jones, Richmond back; Marion Pugh, Texas A and M back; Al Ghesquiere, Detroit back; Royal Kahler, Nebraska tackle; Howard Hickey, Arkansas end; Mush Battista, Florida guard; Pete Rogers, Texas Teachers back; Don Williams, Texas tackle; Marshall Seinstrom, Oregon back; John Patrick, Penn State back; Joe Hogue, Colgate back; Wesley Dodson, Mississippi back; Alex Luchachick, Boston College end; William Conatser, Texas A and M back; Joe McFadden, Georgetown back; John Shouk, West Virginia end; L. B. Russell, Hardin-Simmons back; Mike Frenella, Akron tackle.

Reprinted from
The Pittsburgh Post-Gazette

LAYDEN GAINS WIDE POWERS

Pro Commissioner May Impose Fines Up To $25,000

Grid Meeting Ends In Harmony; Each Team Faces 11 Games

[By the Associated Press]

Chicago, April 6—The most important meeting in the 21-year history of the National Football League ended today on a harmonious note with newly inducted Commissioner Elmer Layden in control of the organization for the next five years.

The powers delegated to the former Notre Dame athletic director and coach are fully as sweeping, if not more so, than the authority held by Kenesaw M. Landis, ruler of baseball.

Layden, who signed the five-year contract last night, presided at today's rules and schedule meeting. The 11-game schedule for each team was completed except for a few probable changes, but will not be released for several weeks.

The new constitution of the league rules that Layden shall have final authority on all squabbles between players and clubs, levy and collect fines, govern conduct of club owners and all their employes in any activity connected with the sport, and have complete control of the league finances.

Maximum Fine $25,000

A maximum misconduct fine of $25,000 was set with Layden having complete authority to determine the amount.

Layden will open league headquarters in Chicago immediately and the New York office will be closed.

The league made eleven alterations in its playing code today, the major changes dealing with the illegal shift and fouls committed on kicking plays. The revisions were announced by Layden.

The major changes:

1. The penalty for a foul during a kickoff or a kick from scrimmage shall be enforced from the scrimmage line previous to the play unless (in case of a punt) it is fair catch interference.

2. The penalty for an illegal pause after a shift is reduced from 15 to 5 yards.

Change Rules On Kicks

3. Touching of a kicked ball beyond the scrimmage line before it has been touched by the receiving team is no longer considered a foul. If the ball is recovered by the kicking team it is awarded to the receivers at the spot of recovery unless it has been touched by the receivers. Any kick from scrimmage which crossed the receivers' goal line after touching a player of either team shall be a touchback. Previously, a ball touched by the receiving team and recovered over the goal line by the kicking team was a touchdown.

Other changes were of a minor nature, owners and coaches expressing themselves as well satisfied in general with the pro rules as they now stand. The minor alterations included:

The penalty for a disqualifying foul was reduced from half the distance to the goal line to 15 yards; double fouls after the ball is dead in the field of play will be disregarded except when one or both are of a disqualifying nature; penalty for a foul by the opponents of the scoring team shall be enforced on the kickoff; a forward pass now may be batted in any direction, irrespective of the act being made to prevent an opponent from catching the ball.

LAYDEN SIGNS PACT TO HEAD PRO GRID LOOP

Elmer Accepts Five-Year Contract As Club Owners Meet

[By the Associated Press]

Chicago, April 5—Elmer Layden became the National Pro-Football League's first commissioner-president today.

The former Notre Dame gridiron coach, chosen by club owners to rule the circuit as commissioner and also fill the presidential post which Carl Storck resigned yesterday, signed a five-year contract calling for an annual salary of $20,000.

Layden took more than three hours to study the new league constitution before formally accepting the post. In fact, his deliberation had the owners slightly anxious as they awaited his decision.

"I merely wanted to be sure that this constitution was all right," Layden said. "After all, its something I'll have to work with for five years."

No Statements

While there was no statement from Layden or the owners as to what Layden's powers will be, it was known that he will be the No. 1 administrative figure in the circuit. One of his first jobs will be the drafting of the 1941 schedule, a problem expected to keep the league club owners in session through tomorrow.

"I'll visit every league city and study the complete picture before deciding what our future course will be," Layden said. "Even though our game is the fastest growing sport we know there still is room for improvement."

Aldo Donelli Named To Coach Pittsburgh Pros

Head Man at Duquesne Will Also Handle Steelers, Succeeding Bell

Pittsburgh, Sept. 25.—(AP.)—Aldo (Buff) Donelli, one of the most successful young gridiron mentors in college circles, undertook today the precedent-shattering job of coaching the Pittsburgh professional Steelers while continuing as head man at Duquesne University.

Under this arrangement, Donelli will put the football business on a two-shift-a-day basis, devoting his morning trick to the pro gridders and turning to his collegiate chore in the afternoon.

With the Steelers he will try to develop a consistent winner—something six coaching predecessors in nine seasons have failed to do.

The job of toting water on both shoulders arose for Donelli when Bert Bell, co-owner of the National Professional League team, resigned as coach and chose Donelli as successor with the approval of Art Rooney, Bell's partner.

Both Donelli and Bell said that Buff's dual role has the permission of the Rev. Raymond D. Kirk, president of Duquesne University.

"It means that I have been permitted to help out the Steelers," explained the likeable Buff who won fame as an international soccer player long before he was heard of as an expert in the American type of football.

Donelli took over at Duquesne two years ago and piloted the collegiate gridders through two successful years, winning 17 games, losing one with one tied and adding another victory in the opening game of the current season. His collegiate contract still has a full year to run after this year.

The Duquesne-Steeler mentor refused to say at this time whether he intended to sever his connections with either the university or the pros at the end of the 1941 season.

Donelli long has been regarded as a natural for professional team coaching because his system features a tricky, well-concealed attack which could be adapted readily to the pros wide-open style of play.

Bell ended a 21-year career as collegiate and professional coach yesterday to devote his time to the business interests of the Steelers. He said he quit for the best interests of the pro club which had lost the first two games of the season under his leadership.

Bert Bell Develops Deceptive Flanker Attack for Steelers

By The Associated Press

Hershey, Pa., Aug. 12.

BERT BELL, rotund co-owner coach of the Pittsburgh Steelers, is flirting with the idea of using a flanker in his backfield this season to give more punch and deception to the offensive.

Many football teams have plays calling for a flanker—one of the most common being to send an end to the sidelines—but Bell doesn't believe it has been used generally in pro circles as a permanent backfield formation.

The way he sizes it up, a wingback playing anywhere from five to ten yards off to the right and a yard and a half behind the scrimmage line "is in a position to do any one of four things as a blocker, and go anywhere as a receiver."

"The flanker," he explained, "can be used to block out an end, tackle, strong backer-up, or the weak backer-up. He can also swerve down the field for passes. This gives him a lot of mobility and at the same time keeps the other team guessing.

"It requires a shifty, fast man for the spot and Francis Maher, rookie from Toledo University, and the veteran Jay Arnold both looked good at the job in the first intersquad game recently," Bell said.

He added that plans now call for the flanker formation to be used permanently throughout the season, which will mean that referees will have a job on their hands.

Pro rules allow such a flanker to be in motion before the ball is snapped, providing, however, that he is stepping away from the line of scrimmage at the exact time the pigskin leaves the center's hands.

Final Returns in the Nation-Wide Poll to Select College All-American Team of 1941 Follow:

★

ENDS

Rankin, Purdue	1,297,308
Rucinski, Indiana	1,241,763
McGee, Regis	834,514
Severin, North Carolina	752,892
Elrod, Mississippi State	728,458
Frutig, Michigan	691,397
Vosberg, Marquette	664,514
Graff, Stanford	659,076
Pettit, Iowa	603,841
Carlson, Jamestown, N. D.	439,905
McCoy, Emporia	398,116
Bodney, Tulane	296,428
Schultz, Centre	234,773
Johnson, Minnesota	224,372
Philip, Wisconsin	219,883
O'Brien, Notre Dame	204,596
Lorenz, Wisconsin	161,338
Thuerk, St. Joseph's, Ind.	123,192
Gerhardt, Missouri Val.	119,284
Prochaska, Neb.	94,076
MacDowell, Washington	87,397
Goodreault, Boston Coll.	86,113
Harris, Indiana	85,279
Smith, Northwestern	84,992
Britt, Arkansas	56,098
Kelley, Cornell	33,483
Krueger, So. California	31,764
Eggers, Valparaiso	30,375
Darnell, Duke	17,286

TACKLES

Drahos, Cornell	961,474
Pannell, Texas Aggies	875,263
Uremovich, Indiana	817,882
Ruffa, Duke	724,316
Hartman, Rice	683,094
Routt, Texas Aggies	667,255
Shires, Tennessee	659,193
Foran, St. Benedict's	623,487
Pavelec, Detroit	611,648
Enich, Iowa	609,176
Tripson, Miss. State	501,196
Williams, William Jewell	406,253
Gallagher, Notre Dame	332,574
Neff, Purdue	152,844
Tornow, Wisconsin	147,392
Riggs, Illinois	130,208
Sturgeon, N. Dak. State	91,403
Behm, Nebraska	74,107
Kahler, Nebraska	66,352
Aarts, Northwestern	62,084

GUARDS

Lio, Georgetown	1,284,078
O'Boyle, Tulane	1,052,754
Lokanc, Northwestern	984,216
Suffridge, Tennessee	961,517

McMahon, Rockhurst	947,286
Kerasiotis, St. Ambrose	732,112
Bucchianeri, Indiana	724,493
Allson, Nebraska	651,984
Asa, Bradley Tech	592,276
Sohn, So. California	581,637
Kinard, Mississippi	408,319
Kelly, Notre Dame	276,522
Kemnitz, Marquette	232,419
Kuusisto, Minnesota	229,183
Sukup, Michigan	178,612
Genoar, Loras	137,254
Embick, Wisconsin	134,228
Brovarney, Detroit	128,654
Gage, Wisconsin	124,107
Cemore, Creighton	112,493
Bernhardt, Illinois	106,116
Hutton, Charleston Tea.	99,642
Kerr, Boston college	86,258
Fritz, Michigan	84,793
Gubanich, Notre Dame	73,042
Schwass, Ripon	66,388
Luebcke, Iowa	65,207
Gile, Wisconsin	64,773
Robnett, Texas Aggies	36,219
McIntyre, Columbia	35,874

CENTERS

Mucha, Washington	1,256,184
Hall, Warrensburg (Mo.)	1,197,418
Osterman, Notre Dame	953,276
Gladchuk, Boston college	931,558
Hiemenz, Northwestern	784,902
Nelson, Baylor	651,738
Whitlow, Rice	642,522
Apolskis, Marquette	473,106
Bjorklund, Minnesota	317,442
Briggs, Marquette	274,531
Buck, Colgate	69,284
Burruss, Nebraska	61,362
Andruska, Iowa	52,118
Axton, Purdue	23,054

QUARTER BACKS

Evashevski, Michigan	1,357,674
Paffrath, Minnesota	1,348,263
Schulte, Rockhurst	1,224,054
Christman, Missouri	996,127
Hayes, Notre Dame	981,433
Pugh, Texas Aggies	962,329
Matuszczak, Cornell	952,046
Milliner, Manchester, Ind.	878,284
Olson, Bradley	569,172
Petsch, Nebraska	62,096
Stasica, Colorado	54,287
Toczylowski, Boston coll.	35,116
Scott, Ohio State	34,874
Phillips, Marquette	29,562

Ehni, Illinois	29,433

FULL BACKS

Paskvan, Wisconsin	914,327
Piepul, Notre Dame	832,114
Kimbrough, Texas Aggies	814,932
Standlee, Stanford	742,554
McKeever, St. Benedict's	734,097
Kracum, Pittsburgh	592,443
Morrow, Ill. Wesleyan	547,102
Davis, Duke	531,384
Peoples, So. Californ'a	527,293
Murphy, Iowa	433,116
Jefferson, Miss. State	398,394
Gloden, Tulane	259,472
Trebbin, St. Olaf	59,763
Peterson, Illinois	55,227
Marefos, St. Mary's (Cal.)	21,542

HALF BACKS

Harmon, Michigan	1,421,586
Franck, Minnesota	1,259,214
Gallarneau, Stanford	993,057
McGannon, Notre Dame	972,103
Jensen, Rockhurst	964,364
Hahnenstein, Northwestern	959,032
Saggau, Notre Dame	948,752
McAdams, Washington	926,844
O'Rourke, Boston coll.	917,259
Rohrig, Nebraska	886,163
Eshmont, Fordham	852,978
Banta, So. California	841,463
Allerdice, Princeton	837,254
Mallouf, So. Methodist	784,116
Robinson, U. C. L. A.	763,254
Thomason, Texas Aggies	741,972
Jones, Richmond	726,484
Reagan, Pennsylvania	607,217
Byelene, Purdue	532,528
Larson, Culver-Stockton	491,833
Armstrong Miss. college	482,704
Luther, Nebraska	248,112
Black, Louisiana	239,056
Knolla, Creighton	208,493
Canadeo, Gonzaga	191,862
Soper, Northwestern	141,738
Suddarth, Charleston T.	134,982
Tennant, Wisconsin	132,519
Foxx, Tennessee	118,426
Ghesquiere, Detroit	107,903
Hopp, Nebraska	98,256
Elting, Illinois	74,597
Raiter, Carleton	71,425
Montgomery, Boston col.	68,217
Kromer, Michigan	43,118
Goodnight, Hardin-Simm.	37,084
Gallagher, Iowa	36,852
Osmanski, Holy Cross	31,419

Hinkle Sets Record

Clark Hinkle, with 37 yards to his credit Sunday, took the lead among the National league's all-time ground gainers with 3,504 yards. Ace Gutowsky of Detroit, who has quit football, held the old mark of 3,478. Hinkle needed 11 yards Sunday to pass him.

Grid Dodgers Defeat Eagles By 24-13 Score

Philadelphia. Sept. 27 (P)—The more experienced Brooklyn Dodgers had their hands full tonight against the Philadelphia Eagles, but chalked up their second straight victory in the National Professional Football League, 24 to 13, before 16,341 fans at Shibe Park. Referee "Red" Friesell suffered a broken leg when he was accidentally hit by a Brooklyn player in the first quarter.

Friesell, who lives in Pittsburgh, wore a gray shirt that somewhat resembled the uniforms worn by the Eagles.

He was taken to the Temple University Hospital and was reported to be resting comfortably.

Eagles' Coach Protests Brooklyn Grid Victory

Philadelphia, Sept. 29 (AP)—The Philadelphia Eagles of the National Professional Football League today protested Brooklyn's 24-to-13 victory here Saturday night.

In a letter to League Commissioner Elmer Layden, the Eagles coach, Earle (Greasy) Neale asked that the game be declared "no contest" and replayed.

Neale specifically protested the calling of 45 yards in penalties that set up Brooklyn's second touchdown in the first quarter. Motion pictures, Neale said, showed Bob Krieger, Eagles end, was clipped from the rear by Merlyn Condit, Brooklyn halfback. The penalty was called, but the 15 yards was paced off against the Eagles instead of Brooklyn. Neale then rushed onto the field and another 15 yards was added for unsportsmanlike conduct.

Meantime Referee Red Friesell, whose leg was broken in the first quarter, was reported resting comfortably at Temple Hospital.

Donelli May Withdraw Resignation

Commissioner Layden Forces Coach's Hand But Weather May Unravel Knotty Situation

Pittsburgh, Nov. 6.—(AP.)—Aldo (Buff) Donelli, who quit today as football coach of the pro Pittsburgh Steelers to "keep a promise" to his former college squad at Duquesne University, disclosed tonight he may return to the pro job within 48 hours "due to the weather."

It seems a snowstorm blowing in from the west may prevent the diminutive coach from flying to San Francisco to attend the Duquesne-St. Mary's contest on Sunday.

Donelli said that on resigning as coach of the undefeated and untied Dukes to take the pro job five weeks ago, he promised the Duquesne squad he would be on the bench for all its games.

Vetoed Desire.

Elmer Layden, commissioner of the National Pro League, and incidentally a former Duquesne coach, vetoed Donelli's desire to coach both the college and pro teams and flatly informed Buff this week he would have to quit the Steelers if he went to San Francisco and left the Steelers in charge of an assistant.

Layden has taken the position Donelli's conduct would tend to make his pro coaching job look like a part-time one.

"In event I can't make the trip West, I may go back to the Steelers and lead them Sunday in Philadelphia," said Donelli.

Art Rooney, president of the Steelers, nodded his approval of the statement, although adding:

"I don't know yet what Bert Bell will say about it."

Bell is co-owner of the club. He resigned as coach when Donelli was hired.

Donelli directed the Steelers' practice today and said he would do the same tomorrow. He planned to leave Friday on at 6 p. m. (EST) plane for the west, weather permitting.

Dukes Unbeaten.

Duquesne has been undefeated in 11 straight games over a two-year span while the Steelers have failed to win a game this year, dropping five straight under Donelli.

But this contrast in records had nothing to do with Donelli leaving the pro ranks. Art Rooney had confidence in Buff and intended to charge off this year to experience.

Rooney said Walt Kiesling, assistant coach, would head the Steelers the remainder of the year. Kiesling was head coach last year, relinquishing the job to co-owner Bell, Donelli's predecessor.

BEARS WHIP LIONS, 24-7

CHAMPIONS SET 4 MORE RECORDS IN 8TH VICTORY

Jefferson Runs 101 Yards for Detroit.

Record Breakers

CHICAGO [24].		DETROIT [7].
Plasman	L.E.	Andersen
Kolman	L.T.	Pavelec
Fortmann	L.G.	Lio
Turner	C.	Logan
Bray	R.G.	Batinski
Artoe	R.T.	Furst
Siegal	R.E.	Szakash
Luckman	Q.B.	Callihan
Nolting	L.H.	Jefferson
Gallarneau	R.H.	Tomasetti
Osmanski	F.B.	Belichick

Chicago Bears ....7 7 7 3—24
Detroit ....0 0 7 0— 7

Touchdowns—Gallarneau, Standlee, McAfee, Jefferson.

Points after touchdowns—Snyder [3], Lio. Field goal—Maniaci.

Substitutions: Bears—Ends, Nowaskey, Snyder, Pool, Wilson, Kavanaugh; tackles, Federovitch, Stydahar; guards, Baisi, Forte, Musso; center, Matuza; backs, Clark, Snyder, McAfee, Standlee, Swisher, McLean, Famiglietti, Maniaci, Bussey.

Detroit—Ends, Fiske, Britt; tackles, Tripson, Crabtree, Uremovich; guard, Mattiford; backs, White, Booth, Matthews, Moore, Piepul, Noppenberg.

Referee — Ronald Gibbs. Umpire—John Schommer. Field Judge—Chuck Sweeney. Head linesman—Joe Lipp.

BY EDWARD PRELL.
[Chicago Tribune Press Service.]
Detroit, Mich., Nov. 23.—During the process of a methodical 24 to 7 victory over the Detroit Lions in Briggs stadium this afternoon, the Chicago Bears broke four more National Football league records, making six in all for the season.

But all these heroics before 28,657 partially frozen spectators only kept the champions the same distance away—no more, no less—from Green Bay's Packers, who also had quite a day in Pittsburgh. It increased the suspicion, too, that these old rivals will have to meet after the season's end—on Dec. 14—to determine the western division honors.

Break Three of Their Own Marks.

The Bears owned three of the four marks which they cracked today. They raised their total scoring for the season to 313 points, breaking their old one of 298 for 11 league games, set in 1938. Their total also surpasses the 308 in 17 games made by the New York Giants in 1927. Today's three touchdowns made it 44 for the season, two more than the Bears' mark set in 1939. Record No. 4 was in the matter of first downs, the Bears making 25 to pass their mark of 24 set against Cleveland in Wrigley field on Nov. 9. Earlier in the season the Bears had set new standards in total yards gained and yards gained by passing in a single game.

Detroit's touchdown, scored after the Bears had taken a 21 to 0 lead in the third quarter, was close to being a record maker, too. It was a 101 yard kickoff return by Billy Jefferson, freshman half back from Mississippi State. The record for returning kickoffs is 102 yards, made by Doug Russell of the Cardinals against Cincinnati in 1934.

Reprinted from
The Chicago Tribune

HUTSON CRACKS SCORING MARK

Takes Three Touchdown Tosses From Isbell, Converts Twice

Washington Bows After Leading 17 To 0 At Half Time

GREEN BAY, 22; REDSKINS, 17

[By the Associated Press]

Washington, Nov. 30—The Green Bay Packers struck through the air for three touchdowns in the second half to trounce Washington, 22 to 17, today as Don Hutson, the old Alabama flash, shattered three National Pro Football League scoring records.

Trailing by 17 points at the half, the Packers swept the Redskins off their feet in the third and fourth periods, with Cecil Isbell, the veteran from Purdue, filling the air with passes which Hutson snared time and again with almost uncanny skill.

A crowd of 35,594, largest of the year in the Capital, saw the game which gave the Packers a record of 10 victories in 11 games this season and a share in the Western Division championship of the league.

Hutson Scores 95 Points

Hutson scored three touchdowns and kicked two conversions to run his season total to 95 points, bettering the old record of 79 established several years back by automatic Jack Manders, of the Chicago Bears.

Hutson stretched his lifetime scoring mark to 395 points in seven seasons of pro football, cracking Manders' record of 385. Hutson's three touchdowns gave him 12 for the year, or one better than the season mark Washington's Andy Farkas set up in 1939.

Another record went into the discard when Isbell completed 14 passes, most of them to Hutson, for 167 yards, sending his 1941 aerial yardage to 1,488. Washington's Sammy Baugh, who also played a whale of a ball game today, set the old mark of 1,367 yards last year.

White's Farewell

Plays Brilliantly In Leading Detroit Lions to 21-3 Victory Over Chicago Cardinals

DETROIT, Nov. 30 (AP)—Bryon (Whizzer) White bade farewell to professional football today by leading the Detroit Lions to a 21 to 3 National League victory over the Chicago Cardinals before 17,051 spectators. White, soon to join the Nation's armed forces, returned an intercepted pass 51 yards for one touchdown and passed for another.

The 24-years-old former Colorado All-America halfback and Rhodes scholar galloped for his touchdown in the first period on a picture play and shot a 23-yard pass to Bill Fisk in the end zone for Detroit's final score in the third period. In between, guard Augie Lio also contributed a touchdown, taking a lateral pass from tackle Phil Uremovich for the score after a Cardinal fumble. Lio placekicked three extra points.

The Cardinals, who dominated the statistics with 13 first downs to nine and had an edge in yards by rushing and passing, evaded a shutout on Bill Daddio's placement kick from behind the 17 yard line in the first period. In the closing minutes the Cards marched to the three but lost the ball.

Owner's Birthday

The victory, coming as a personal gift to owner Fred L. Mandel, Jr., on his 33d birthday, assured the Lions of at least a tie for third place in the Western Division and undisputed possession if the Cardinals lose to the Chicago Bears next week.

At the outset it appeared that the Whizzer might be headed for a displeasing final to his brilliant football career. He fumbled the second time he carried the ball and the Cardinals recovered on Detroit's 25 for an early scoring opportunity.

John Martin crossed the goal line after taking a pass but the play was called back and Chicago penalized. The Lions still were fighting off the attacking Cards when White speared John Clement's pass and twisted his way down the sidelines behind a thin wall of interference. At the 25 he shook himself loose from the last defender and sprinted across the goal.

Daddio's kick came in the last minute of the period after the Cardinals got the ball on Detroit's 31 on an exchange of fumbles.

Another White Run

White got away for another long run in the second period when he took a punt over his shoulder at the goal line, whirled and ran 64 yards. Four times the Lions were halted inside the 20 yard line in this period but maintained their 7 to 3 lead to the intermission.

The Cardinals marched 48 yards to open the second half before the attack stalled and Daddio's kick from behind Detroit's 18 was wide. The Whizzer's 57-yard punt pushed the threatening Chicagoan back, and then the Lions turned a fumble and a pass interception into touchdowns three minutes apart.

Uremovich, former Indiana star whom the Lions picked up from the Philadelphia Eagles, grabbed Clement's fumble and ran 25 yards to the five where he lateralled to Lio for the score. Guard John Wiethe's interception of Clement's pass paved the way for White's touchdown toss to Fisk.

After Chicago's belated march was halted near the goal, White returned to the game in the last 10 seconds and completed a pass from the end zone for a first down. The crowd gave him a mighty ovation. Summary:

DETROIT	CHICAGO
Anderson, le	re, Ivy
Tripson, lt	rt, Babartsky
Lio, lg	rg, Huffman
Nelson, c	c, Apolskis
Batinski, rg	lg, Kuharich
Crabtree, rt	lt, Davis
Szakash, re	le, Dewell
Callihan, qb	qb, Vanzo
White, lhb	rhb, Martin
Booth, rhb	lhb, Clement
Belichick, fb	fb, Goldberg

	1	2	3	4	
Detroit	7	0	14	0	—21
Cardinals	3	0	0	0	—3

Cardinals scoring: field goal, Daddio (for Dewell) (place-kick).

Detroit scoring: touchdowns, White, Lio, Fisk (for Szakash); points after touchdown, Lio 3 (place-kicks).

Substitutions: Cardinals—ends, Daddio, Evans; tackles, Baker, Busler; guards, Murphy, Lokanc, Popovich; center, Chiatek; backs, Parker, Johnson, McCullough, Morrow, Hall, Mallouf.

Detroit—end, Fisk, tackles, Uremovich, Furst, Pavelec; guards, Radovich, Wiethe; center, Moore; backs, Mathews, Tomasetti, Hopp, Parsons,

Dec. 22

Bill Dudley of Virginia Is Picked by Steelers

Chicago, Ill.—The first choice of each team in the annual National Pro Football league draft follows:

Pittsburgh—Bill Dudley of Virginia.

Bears—Frankie Albert of Stanford.

Green Bay—Urban Odsen of Minnesota.

Philadelphia—Pete Kmetovic of Stanford.

Washington—Bill De Correvont of Northwestern.

Detroit—Bob Westfall of Michigan.

Cardinals—Steve Lach of Duke.

Cleveland—Jack Wilson of Baylor.

Brooklyn—Bob Robertson of Southern California.

New York—Merle Hapes of Mississippi.

Eastern Division	W	L	T	Pct.	Pts.	OP
New York	8	3	0	.727	238	114
Brooklyn	7	4	0	.636	158	127
Washington	6	5	0	.545	176	174
Philadelphia	2	8	1	.200	119	218
Pittsburgh	1	9	1	.100	103	276

Western Division	W	L	T	Pct.	Pts.	OP
*Chi Bears	10	1	0	.909	396	147
Green Bay	10	1	0	.909	258	120
Detroit	4	6	1	.400	121	195
Chi Cards	3	7	1	.300	127	197
Clev. Rams	2	9	0	.182	116	244

*—Bears defeated Green Bay, 33-14, in Divisional Playoff

Gain Right To Play New York Giants For Pro Football Title

Bears-Packers Game Statistics

Chicago, Dec. 14.—(AP)— Statistics of the Chicago Bears-Green Bay Packers football game.

	Packers	Bears
First downs	12	14
Yds. gained by rushing (net)	35	267
Forward passes attempted	28	14
Forward passes completed	11	5
Yds. gained by forward passes	222	48
Yds. lost, attempted passes	54	15
Forward passes intercepted by	0	2
Yds. gained, runback of int. passes	0	19
Punting avg. (from scrimmage)	28.5	37.8
(x) total yds. kicks returned	155	124
Opponents fumbles recovered	3	2
Yd. lost by penalties	46	128

(x) includes punts and kickoffs.

Chicago, Dec. 14.—(AP)—The Chicago Bears scored 24 points in a wild second period today to defeat the Green Bay Packers 33 to 14 and win the Western Division playoff in the National Professional Football League.

The Bears also won the right to meet the New York Giants here next Sunday for the league championship.

With 43,425 spectators sitting in bright sunshine and the temperature at 16 degrees, the Bears tore the turf of Wrigley Field in that second stanza for three touchdowns, three conversion points and a field goal, gaining a 30-7 half time lead.

Packers Grab Lead

The Packers made a terrific battle of it for the opening period, scoring the first touchdown after one minute 56 seconds to take a 7-0 lead. The Bears scored on Hugh Gallarneau's 81-yard punt return for a touchdown just before the period ended.

Bob Snyder's 23-yard field goal, which opened the second period, put the Chicagoans ahead, 9-7, and from then on it was strictly the Bears.

Bruins Break Loose After Green Bay Takes Lead in First Two Minutes

Fumbles Figure In First Scores

Chicago Never Behind After Snyder Boots Field Goal to Open Second Quarter

The Packers got a mere 35 yards by rushing compared to 267 for Chicago. But their passing game, despite a sharp Bear defense around end Don Hutson, amassed 222 yards to 48 for Chicago.

Lineups:

GREEN BAY		CHICAGO BEARS
Hutson	le	Plasman
Ray	lt	Kolman
McLaughlin	lg	Fortmann
Svendsen	c	Turner
Goldenberg	rg	Bray
Schultz	rt	Artoe
Riddick	re	Siegal
Craig	qb	Luckman
Isbell	lh	Nolting
Rohrig	rh	Gallarneau
Hinkle	fb	Standlee

Score by periods:
Green Bay .... 7 0 7 0—14
Chicago Bears .... 6 24 0 3—33

Green Bay scoring: Touchdowns, Hinkle, Van Avery (for Isbell). Points after touchdowns, Hutson 2 (placement).
Chicago Bears scoring: Touchdowns, Gallarneau, Standlee 2, Swisher (for Nolting) Points after touchdowns, Stydahar 3 (for Kolman), Field goals, Snyder 2 (for Luckman) (placements).
Substitutions: Green Bay—Ends, Mulleneaux, Jacunski, Frutig, Urban, William Johnson; tackles, Lee, Pannell; guards, Kuusisto, Tinsley, Howard Johnson; center, Brock, Greenfield; backs, Van Every, Uram, Jankowski, Buhler, Paskvan, Canadeo, Laws.
Bears—Ends, Nowaskey, Wilson, Kavanaugh, Pool; tackles, Stydahar, Federovitch, Mihal; guards, Forte, Musso, Lahar; center, Matuza, Hughes; backs, McLean, Snyder, McAfee, Swisher, Osmanski, Maniaci.

STILL THE CHAMPIONS

GIANTS (9).	Pos.	BEARS (37).
Jim Poole	L. E.	Dick Plasman
John Mellus	L. T.	Ed Kolman
Kayo Lunday	L. G.	Danny Fortmann
Mel Hein	C.	Clyde Turner
Len Younce	R. G.	Ray Bray
Bill Edwards	R. T.	Lee Artoe
Jim Howell	R. E.	John Siegal
Nello Falaschi	Q. B.	Sid Luckman
George Franck	L. H.	Ray Nolting
Ward Cuff	R. H.	Hugh Gallarneau
Tuffy Leemans	F. B.	Norman Standlee

Score by periods:
New York .... 6 3 0 0— 9
Chicago .... 3 6 14 14—37

Scoring: Giants—touchdowns, Franck. Field goal, Cuff (placement). Bears—touchdowns, Standlee, 2; McAfee (sub for Gallarneau); Kavanaugh (sub for Plasman).
Points after, Snyder (sub for Luckman), Artoe, Maniaci (sub for Standlee)—(placements) McLean (sub for Nolting—(drop kick).
Field goals—Snyder, 3 (placements).
Substitutions: Giants—ends, Horne, Walls, Lummus; tackles, Blazine, Cope; guards, Sohn, Oldershaw, Tuttle; center, Gladchuk; backs, Yeager, Soar, Principe, Eakin, Eshmont, McLain, Shaffer, Marefos.
Bears—Ends, Kavanaugh, Pool, Nowaskey, Wilson; tackles, Stydahar, Federovich, Mihal; guards, Forte, Musso, Baisi, Lahar; center, Matuza, Hughes; backs, Snyder, McAfee, Osmanski, McLean, Swisher, Maniaci, Famiglietti, Clark, Bussey.
Officials—Referee, Emil Heintz; umpire, John Schommer; field judge, Charles Sweeney; head linesman, Charles Berry.

Second Half Surge Of Power Results In Triumph By 37 To 9

Giants and Bears Game Statistics

Chicago, Dec. 21.—(AP)—Statistics of the Chicago Bears-New York football game.

	N.Y.	Chi.
First downs	8	20
Yards gained by rushing (net)	80	207
Forward passes attempted	15	19
Forward passes completed	3	11
Yards gained by forward passes	73	182
Yards lost by attempted forward passes	5	12
Forward passes intercepted by	0	3
Yards gained, runback of of int. passes	0	19
Punting average (from scrimmage)	37.7	53.5
xTotal yards, kicks returned	124	36
Opponents' fumbles recovered	1	2
Yards lost by penalties	31	65

x Includes punts and kickoffs.

Chicago, Dec. 21.—(AP)—Held on even terms for more than a half, the Chicago Bears won their second National Professional Football League championship today by defeating the New York Giants 37 to 9 with a surge of power in the last two periods.

It was the first time in the history of the league that the defending champion ever had repeated. The Bears did it with a pair of touchdowns in the third period and another pair in the last.

The Bears, champions of the western division of the league, tore loose when the score was tied at 9 to 9 only because Bob Snyder had booted home three field goals to match the touchdown and field goal the Giants had amassed.

A skimpy crowd of 13,500—smallest of the season in Wrigley Field—saw the contest. The gate, smaller than that netted when these two teams met here in a pre-season exhibition game, cut heavily into the participating players' pool.

The final statistics showed the Bears piling up 182 yards by passing, and 207 yards by plunging, most of it by George McAfee and Norman Standlee. Compared with this, New York gained only 73 yards by passing and 80 by rushing. The Bears also led in first downs, 20 to 8.

Exceed Giant Total.

McAfee gained 81 yards and Standlee 89, each exceeding the total rushing yardage of the entire New York team. Sid Luckman's accurate forward passes paved the way for two Chicago touchdowns, including the one that broke the 9-9 deadlock and ended all effective New York resistance.

Throughout the first half and for 7 minutes of the third period the Giants played a bangup defensive game and kept the Bears well away from the goal line.

The Bears led at the start, 3-0, on the first of Bob Snyder's three field goals—tying the record for three-pointers in title play set by Jack Manders of the Bears in the 1933 finals. The Giants came back for a touchdown on two terrific passes by Tuffy Leemans to lead at the end of the first quarter, 6-3.

Leemans heaved his first aerial 23 yards to Ward Cuff, who made a sensational catch on the Bears' 36. Tuffy ran four yards, then threw to George Franck. With End Jim Poole throwing a powerful block to remove the Bear safety man, Franck raced over the goal line.

Western Champs Repeat For First Time in League History Before Skimpy Crowd

New York Team Strong For Half

Standlee and McAfee Spearheads of Crushing Attack; Bob Snyder Boots Three Field Goals

Call On Snyder.

The Bears, on Luckman's passes, moved to the New York 32 as the first period ended. Blocked by stout defensive play, the Chicagoans again called on Snyder who made good from the 39 to tie the score.

The Giants subsequently were forced to punt and booted the ball to their 47. Running plays by McAfee and Bill Osmanski gained to the 29, but again the Giants held, and Snyder kicked field goal No. 3. That put the Chicagoans ahead, 9-6, the score at half time.

The Giants still had a piece to say, particularly Franck who turned in a 34 yard run to open the third period and put the ball on the Bears' 46. Cuff and Leemans picked up 10 yards and the Bears backed away five on an offside penalty. Leemans passed 20 yards to Cuff on the five, but the Bears got tough and held, so Cuff kicked a field goal from the 16. That deadlocked the count, 9-9.

The Bears launched a touchdown drive after the kickoff. Standlee ran from his own 30 to the 40, and then to the 43. Luckman passed to Dick Plasman on the New York 34 and then to Johnny Siegal on the eight, the end making a great diving catch. Standlee charged four yards, Hugh Gallarneau one and Standlee plowed three yards for the touchdown. Snyder converted.

Standlee Tallies.

Danny Fortmann soon intercepted one of Leemans' passes on the Chicago 32. McAfee, Standlee and Ray McLean went to the goal line in seven plays, Standlee scoring and Joe Maniaci kicking the point. The Bears led, 23-9, as the third period ended.

Another pass interception—this one by Center Bulldog Turner—gave the ball to the Bears on their 46 as the final period got under way. Standlee and McAfee went 15 yards and Luckman passed to the charging Standlee who ran to the Giants' 23. The Bears were set back on a holding penalty and then Luckman's long pass to McLean was ruled complete on the five-yard line on Chet Gladchuk's interference.

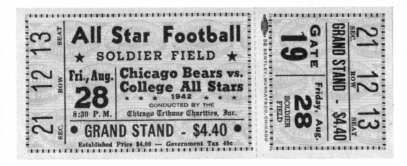

t. 28

iants Beat Redskins Without First Down

Long Pass and 70 Yard Run With Interception Win, 14-7; Redskins Make 14 First Downs

Washington, D. C.-(AP)-The Washington Redskins ran up 14 first owns and held the New York iants to none here Sunday, but the inal score of their National Football league game was New York 14, Washington 7.

On the Giants' very first play, Tuffy Leemans passed from midfield to nd Will Walls on the 20 and Walls an the rest of the way. Cuff converted.

The Redskins tied the score in the econd quarter. After Dick Todd nd Sam Baugh had run the ball rom the Giants' 45 to the 32, Baugh assed to Justice on the 17, Seymour it the line for six, Baugh passed o Kovatch on the five, Seymour ugged to the two and then plunged ver. Masterson added the point.

Dick Poillon's long punts kept the iants back on their heels after hat until late in the third period. The Redskins hammered at the goal ine repeatedly but could not score. Then O'Neale Adams, Giant end, ntercepted Poillon's pass, intended or Masterson, and ran 70 yards for he winning touchdown. Cuff kicked gain.

	New York	Wash.
irst downs (net)	0	14
ards gained rushed	1	120
orward passes attempted....	1	25
orward passes completed....	1	12
ards by forward passing	50	113
assesc intercepted by	2	0
ntercepted passes run back..	70	0
unting average	39	38
ards all kicks returned	14	48
pponents' fumbles recovered	1	0
ards lost by penalties	42	35

ec. 7

Giant-Dodger Football Auctioned for $150,000

New York, N. Y. – (AP) – A total of $419,275 in United States war bonds was pledged Sunday in the auction etween halves for the football used by the New York Giants and the Brooklyn Dodgers in their pro game. It went to a spectator who bid $150,-000.

Dec. 7

Isbell, Hutson Hog Records

Packers Surpass Two Team Marks as Play Ends for Season

New York, N. Y.-(AP)-Several new records were on the books Sunday after the National Football league closed its regular season with three games which had no bearing on the final standings.

Most of the record performances were turned in by Cecil Isbell and Don Hutson of the Green Bay Packers. Hutson kicked three extra points Sunday for a total of 33 this season, breaking the league mark of 31 set in 1934 by Jack Manders of the Bears. He added a field goal which boosted his own scoring mark to 138 points for the season. A week ago he increased his record for passes caught to 74.

Davey O'Brien's passing records, set while with Philadelphia, were shattered. Isbell ended the season with 24 touchdown passes (a record), scoring by this means in 23 straight games to break his own mark of 15 last year; made 145 completions (O'Brien had 124); gained 2,001 yards to snap his own record of 1,479 set last fall.

Bud Schwenk, the Cardinal rookie who broke O'Brien's collegiate records at Washington university, St. Louis, shelved another held by the Texas mite as a pro. Schwenk threw 295 passes. O'Brien's record was 277.

Nov. 23

Don Hutson Sets Eight Records in Game With Giants

From The Journal's N. Y. Bureau

New York, N. Y.—Whenever Don Hutson sets a record he does it in wholesale lots. he set eight marks and equaled another when the Packers and Giants played their 21-21 tie at the Polo Grounds Sunday. Furthermore, he drew to within two extra points of Jack Manders' seemingly unbreakable mark of 31 conversions in a season.

Here are the records he set when he caught 14 passes for 134 yards, scored two touchdowns and kicked three extra points against the Giants:

71 passes caught for the season to eclipse the figure of 58 he had jointly held with Don Looney of the Philadelphia Eagles.

1,166 yards gained on receptions for the season, surpassing his own 1,032.

16 touchdown passes received for the season. eliminating his own record of 14.

125 points for the season, bettering his own total of 110.

14 passes caught in one game to equal Looney's record.

71 touchdown passes caught in his pro career.

5,470 yards gained on passes caught in his pro career.

511 points scored in his pro career.

73 touchdowns scored in his pro career.

Reprinted from
The Milwaukee Journal

Dec. 7

StubbornCards Lose to Bears

Chicago, Ill.—(P)—The Chicago Cardinals bowed to the invincible Bears Sunday, 21-7, but the glory went to the Cardinals. The Bears went into the game with the avowed intention of breaking their own National league scoring record and of hanging up the best defensive record since 1927. The stubborn Cardinals thwarted both efforts. The game ended the league schedule for both teams, but the Bears will meet the Redskins at Washington, D. C., next Sunday in the annual east-west playoff for the title.

Coach Jimmy Conzelman's boys yielded only three touchdowns to the team which had averaged 35.5 points in the preceding 10 games, so the Bears, with 376 points for the season, fell 20 points short of the record. On top of this, the Cardinals cashed in their only opportunity in the fourth quarter.

Charley O'Rourke of the Bears, back on his own 10 yard line to kick, bobbled the pass and was hemmed in. He threw the ball away and Champ Seibold, former Green Bay Packer, caught it and ran four yards for a touchdown. Ivy added the extra point.

The Bears scored in the first quarter when Johnny Martin of the Cardinals fumbled a low pass from center on his own 23. Hugh Gallarneau recovered and was downed on the seven but rammed over on the next play.

The other two Bear tallies were made in the third quarter. The Cards had moved to the Bears' 33. Martin took a short pass from Bud Schwenk, bobbled it and Dan Fortmann snatched the ball and ran 69 yards. The Bears went 70 yards in five plays the next time they got the ball, with Gallarneau scoring on a 37 yard pass from Sid Luckman.

The statistics:

	Bears	Cards
First downs	12	5
Yards gained rushing	204	-17
Forward passes attempted	13	27
Forward passes completed	3	10
Yards gained passing	61	73
Passes intercepted by	3	2
Yards interceptions run back	9	41
Punting average	37.5	37
Yards all kicks returned	78	113
Opponents' fumbles recovered	1	1
Yards lost by penalties	119	21

Score by quarters:

Bears	7	0	14	0—21
Cardinals	0	0	0	7— 7

Bears scoring—Touchdowns: Gallaneau 2, Fortmann. Points after touchdown: Maznicki 3 (placements). Cardinals scoring—Touchdown: Seibold. Point after touchdown: Ivy (placement).

Staunch Line Play Checks Chicago In Grid Loop Playoff

Baugh and Farkas Lead Washington Attack After Bears Score First on Fumble

Washington, Dec. 13.—(AP.)—As a fitting climax of this daffiest gridiron season in years, the Washington Redskins won professional football's world series today, ending the two-year reign of the fearful Chicago Bears with a 14-6 conquest for the most amazing upset of the campaign.

Against the same club that mopped them up over this same Griffith Stadium gridiron by 73 points just two years ago, the Redskins came back to take sweet revenge not only by trampling the big bad Bears but actually outplaying them from start to finish.

Before a sell-out crowd of 36,006 strictly partisan fans the Redskin line, which was torn apart and chopped up in the 1940 debacle, threw monkey wrenches into the mighty model "T" machine from Chicago that had rolled over its last 24 opponents in a row. All the Bears' pet plays, particularly the quick opening line smashes for which they are famous, were wrecked throughout the afternoon.

Standout Surprise.

With the line operating as this Washington front wall never had functioned before, the Redskins rolled to triumph on Sammy Baugh's solid pitching arm and the ball-carrying antics of Anvil Andy Farkas, the ex-Detroit University flier. This astonishing triumph over a club that hadn't been beaten since mid-season of 1941, that went into today's game so lop-sided a betting favorite that bookmakers were offering 20 points against Washington's chances, was easily the standout surprise of a gridiron year that was full of them. It surpasses even the Holy Cross conquest of Boston College and Auburn's magic against Georgia.

And the fans who filled this American League baseball park and contributed to a record National League playoff gate of $113,260.40 realized it. At the finish, thousands poured onto the field, tore down the goal posts, crowded around the players with roaring cheers and formed a milling mass in the center of the field for 15 minutes, yelling and dancing.

CHICAGO		WASHINGTON
Nowaskey	le	Masterson
Kolman	lt	Wilken
Fortmann	lg	Farman
Turner	c	Aldrich
Bray	rg	Silvinski
Artoe	rt	Young
Wilson	re	Cifers
Luckman	qb	R. Hare
Nolting	lh	Baugh
Gallarneau	rh	Justice
Famiglietti	fb	Farkas

Chicago	0	6	0	0— 6
Washington	0	7	7	0—14

Chicago scoring: Touchdown. Artoe. Washington scoring: Touchdowns. Moore (for Justice), Farkas; points after touchdown. Masterson 2 (placekicks).

Substitutions: Chicago: Ends Siegel. Pool; tackles Stydahar, Hoptowit; guards Drulis. Akin, Musso; center Mattuza; backs, O'Rourke. Clark. Maznicki, McLean, Osmanski. Petty. Washington: Ends, none; tackles. Beinor, Davis; guards Stralka. Shugart; center, none; backs, C. Hare. Moore. Todd. Seymour.

SEEKS SPORTS PLACE IN WAR

Marshall Suggests Government Clarify Position Regarding Athletes

Magnate Says Civilian Program Should Be Abolished If Unnecessary

[By the Associated Press]

Washington, Dec. 16 - George P. Marshall, owner of the world champion Washington Redskins, said today the United States should follow the example of other warring nations by assigning spectator sports a definite place in the war program.

Marshall told reporters the Government should either recognize the value of spectator sports as a morale builder or abolish them altogether. As things now stand, he said, sport programs must operate on a day-to-day basis because of a lack of directives from the Government.

Seeks Clear Ruling

"If sports aren't important to civilian morale, they should be stopped or put on a plane the Government thinks is necessary during wartime." Marshall said, adding that although the army and navy had set up athletic programs for servicemen no sports plan has been outlined for civilians.

The Redskin owner estimated that 2,000 athletes could supply the football and baseball needs of the country. He urged that servicemen be relieved of military duties for participation in civilian sports during specific periods of each year.

Grid Draft Delayed

Marshall emphasized that he was not recommending that men be relieved of duty if actively engaged on a foreign fighting front.

The football magnate commented that lack of sports direction from the Government prompted the National Football League to postpone its annual draft of collegians two days ago.

Pro Standings

WESTERN DIVISION (FINAL)

	W	L	T	Pct.
Chicago Bears	11	0	0	1.000
Green Bay	8	2	1	.800
Cleveland	5	6	0	.454
Chicago Cards	3	8	0	.272
Detroit	0	11	0	.000

EASTERN DIVISION

	W	L	T	Pct.
Washington	10	1	0	.909
Pittsburgh	7	4	0	.637
New York	5	5	1	.500
Brooklyn	3	8	0	.272
Philadelphia	2	9	0	.182

April 7

Rams Withdraw

CLEVELAND KEEPS TITLE TO PLAYERS

Gridders Will Revert to Loop Until War Ends; Nine Clubs Vote to Play

By John Dietrich

Cleveland is definitely out of the National Football League for the duration of the war.

That the Cleveland Rams will not be playing here next fall was announced yesterday in Chicago, where the other nine club owners of the professional circuit granted Cleveland's petition to suspend operations until the war is over.

The request was based on the explanation that the two owners of the Cleveland club, Dan Reeves of New York and Fred Levy, jr., of Louisville, are both officers in the army air force, and have no time to devote to operation of the franchise. Reeves is a lieutenant and Levy a major.

The petition was presented by Charles (Chili) Walsch, recently appointed the new coach of the Rams, and Percy Cowan, Chicago investment broker who handles business affairs of Levy and Reeves.

War Clause in Contract

Walsh, who was named the Rams' coach after the recent resignation of Earl (Dutch) Clark, now finds himself a coach without a team. However, Walsh said that his contract included a "war clause" covering the possibility that the Rams' franchise might be suspended.

Cowan and Walsh said nothing of shifting the Cleveland franchise to some other city, which is a hopeful sign for the revival of professional football here after the war.

Of the 10 teams in the National League, Cleveland was the only one to withdraw. Owners of the other nine clubs pledged that they would continue to operate.

Cleveland's players will revert to the league, to be distributed among the remaining clubs and thus alleviate some of the league's manpower shortage. Cleveland will retain title to these players, for use when the Rams re-enter competition.

Walsh estimated that 14 to 18 Cleveland players would be available for the pool. Three of them are believed to be Halfback Dante Magnani, Tackle Chet Adams and Guard Riley Matheson, named on the second all-league team last year. Parker Hall, the team's ace halfback, has gone into the navy, and Fullback Gaylon Smith announced recently that he had retired from the game.

Reprinted from
The Cleveland Plain Dealer

Ted Collins Awarded Franchise For Boston In National Grid Loop

Chicago, June 20 (AP)—Ted Collins, manager of Singer Kate Smith, was awarded a franchise for Boston, Mass., today by the National Football League, to become operative in the 1944 season. Collins will become a voting member at the first draft meeting after the 1943 season, the owners decided.

The petitions of Movie Actor Don Ameche for a franchise in Los Angeles and of Sports Promoter Charley Murray for Buffalo, N. Y., received favorable attention from the league but were tabled until the December meeting. Ameche previously had sought rights for a club in Buffalo but switched today to Los Angeles.

Collins was represented by his attorney, William A. Shea, of New York, and Ameche by his close friend, Arch Ward, sports editor of the Chicago Tribune. Murray spoke for himself.

The makeup of the league for the 1943 season was assured at eight clubs. Seven of last year's members voted yesterday to continue and the Philadelphia and Pittsburgh clubs were merged as an eighth team.

Sept. 21

Team's TD's Equal
Whole Total of 1942

By SAM GREENE

On his way to the locker room at Briggs Stadium after the Detroit Lions had opened the National Foot Ball League season with a 35-to-17 victory over the Chicago Cardinals, Fred Mandel was accosted by a jubilant stranger.

"You got a great ball club," the stranger said.

"I wouldn't say it's a great club," Mandel replied, "but it's a great improvement."

The owner of the Lions knew that success over the undermanned Cardinals, probably the weakest team in the professional circuit, was a notable achievement only in its relation to the famine of last fall. He knew that Hunk Anderson had sat unworried in the press box as he scouted the Lions for the Chicago Bears. He had seen no look of anxiety on the face of Red Smith,

assistant coach of the Green Bay Packers, as he appraised the new Detroit team.

Mandel realized that an accurate assay of the Lions must make due allowance for the quality of the opposition. On that basis, conquest of the Cardinals called for restraint in enthusiasm though it did justify the boast of "great" improvement." Last year the Lions couldn't lick any kind of opposition. In winning yesterday, they scored their first victory since Nov. 30, 1941, when another Cardinal team was the victim, 21 to 3.

The "great improvement" is traceable principally to a new two-man coaching staff—Gus Dorais and Joe Bach. They are responsible for a changed attitude among the Lions and for a type of offense that stresses the gambling spirit. In the light of Sunday's developments, it is tenable to believe that the Lions will be spectacular and defiant even in the defeats that inevitably will come.

Reprinted from
The Detroit News

Packers Top Lions With Air Offense

Hutson Accounts for 12 Points as Green Bay Wins 27-6; Detroit Passes Boomerang

STATISTICS.	Green Bay	Detroit
First downs	41	9
Yards gained rushing (net)	114	44
Forward passes attempted	39	29
Forward passes completed	21	12
Yards by forward passing	326	118
Forward passes intercepted by	9	1
Yards gained runback of int. passes	137	24
Punting aver. (from scrimmage)	35	43
Total yards, all kicks returned	68	81
Opponent fumbles recovered	1	3
Yards lost by penalties	50	26

Detroit, Oct. 24.—(AP.) — Ageless Don Hutson scored 12 points today as the Green Bay Packers rebounding from a crushing defeat to Washington, whipped the Detroit Lions 27 to 6 in a National Football League game before 41,463 spectators. Hutson scored one touchdown, set up another and booted three extra points and a 13-yard field goal.

With Tony Canadeo, their league leading ground gainer, stopped cold, the Packers turned to the air with devastating results. Rookie Irving Comp personally connected on 14 or 18 tosses for 201 yards, and the Packers totaled 21 completions for 326 yards through the air.

Passing Backfires.

Conversely, the Detroit passing game backfired as the Packers turned nine interceptions, a league record, into scoring opportunities.

Luckman Tosses Seven Touchdown Passes
Sets New Scoring, Yardage Marks For National Grid Loop

Throws Gain 453 Yards, Beating Isbell's Record By 80; Conversion Record Made

STATISTICS.	Bears	Giants
First downs	23	7
Yards gained rushing (net)	194	93
Forward passes attempted	38	26
Forward passes completed	22	7
Yards gained forward passes	508	73
Forward passes intercepted by	1	2
Yards gained run-back of int. passes	5	12
Average distance of punts	39	46
xTotal yards kicks returned	266	113
Opponent's fumbles recovered	1	0
Yards loss by penalties	80	44

x—Includes return of kickoffs and unsuccessful place kicks.

New York, Nov. 14.—(AP.)—Sid Luckman put on the greatest air raid in National Football League history today, pitching seven touchdown passes and heaving for a total of 453 yards altogether as he piloted the bone-crushing Chicago Bears to a 56 to 7 triumph over the New York Giants.

One of the largest New York crowds ever to see a pro game—56,591—saw Sid take his airplane ride up and down the polo grounds gridiron on his way to his rewriting job on the record books.

His seven scoring aerials for one game wiped out the old mark of six set up by Sammy Baugh of Washington only two weeks ago and his 453-yards overhead advance smashed the existing previous high of 333 which Cecil Isbell posted for Green Bay on November 1, 1942.

Sets New Conversion Mark.

And just by way of icing on the cake, Sid's understudy, Bob Snyder, came in after each Bear touchdown to boot the extra point. He shot a total of eight through the goal posts to shatter the previous record of seven set by Riley Smith for Washington against the Giants five years back.

It was by all odds the greatest display of aerial fireworks ever seen

Andy Farkas Makes Three Touchdowns

Sammy Baugh Completes 16 Passes For 199 Yards Before 42,800 at Polo Grounds

STATISTICS.	R.	G.
First downs	13	8
Net yards gained rushing	83	57
Forward passes attempted	22	20
Forward passes completed	17	4
Yards gained forward passes	213	57
Passes intercepted	2	3
Yards runback of intercepted passes	66	5
Average distance of punts	44	36
xTotal yards kicks returned	100	121
Opponents fumbles recovered	0	1
Yards lost by penalties	83	35

x—Includes punts and kickoffs.

Polo Grounds, New York, Dec. 19.—(AP.) — Slingin' Sammy Baugh and Anvil Andy Farkas, a one-two punch with a tremendous kick, carried the Washington Redskins to the eastern championship of the National Professional football league today with a 28 to 0 triumph over the New York Giants.

Beaten by the New Yorkers the last two Sundays thus throwing the Eastern division race into a deadlock, Washington pulled together today and with Anvil Andy scoring three touchdowns and Slingin' Sammy pitching for 16 completed passes and 199 yards, they never gave the Giants a chance.

A crowd of 42,800 at the Polo Grounds watched the league's defending champions grab this divisional playoff and qualify to take on the bone-crushing Chicago Bears in Chicago next Sunday in the intersectional finals.

A Baugh Production.

Without taking a thing away from Farkas' fearful line-blasting that gave the 'Skins a reasonable facsimile of the running attack they needed so woefully the last two losing weeks, this was strictly a Baugh production today, and Slingin' Sammy played the role right up to the muzzle.

In addition to his usual one-man air-raid, the one-time Texas Christian twirler got off a pair of quick-kicks for 44 and 67 yards, respectively, and intercepted two enemy heaves. He ran one back 44 yards to the Giant six and one of his own pass completions was a touchdown toss—an 11 yarder to Ted Lapka late in the game for the final Redskin marker.

Except for this flip the Redskins did all their bell-ringing through the line. Anvil Andy blasted over twice in the second period on a pair of two-yard bucks and added another in the final chapter on a half-yard explosion. He scored each of his tallies on the same smash—simply by blowing a hole through the Giants' left guard.

Sid Luckman Stars As Bears Rout Redskins, 41-21

Hurls Five Scoring Passes In Football Finale For Duration

Victorious Bears Receive $1135.81

Chicago, Dec. 26.—(AP.) Winning pro football's championship today was worth $1135.81 to each Chicago Bear cut in on a full share.

A record gross gate of $120,- 500.05 and a record "divisible net" of $93,113.63 plus $5000 from radio rights left $37,- 036.98 for the Bears to split. The Redskins drew down $24,- 724.65 or $754.60 for each full share.

The Green Bay and New York clubs, second-place finishers in the western and eastern divisions, respectively, took $3,433.98 each to divide among their players.

Sets Championship Playoff Record, Beating Baugh's Old Mark By Two; 34,320 Attend

STATISTICS.

	W.	C.
First downs	11	12
Yds. gain. by rush. (net)	45	168
Forw'd pass. attempted	22	27
Forw'd pass. completed	10	14
Yds. gain. forw'd passes	182	276
Forw'd pass int. by	0	4
Yds. gain. runback of int. passes	0	68
Punt. ave. (from scrim.)	48.4	32
Tot. yds. all kicks ret.	204	87
Opp fumbles recovered	0	0
Yds. lost by penalties	20	81

Bears Chase Foes' Owner From Bench

Marshall Discovered Sitting With Chicago Players in Final Minute of First Half

Chicago, Dec. 26.—(AP.)—There were cheers—loud, raucous, merry—in the Chicago Bears' dressing room after their 41-21 victory today over the Washington Redskins for the National Football League championship, but there were angry remarks, too, by the bear bosses who suddenly discovered in the tense moments at the end of the first half that George Marshall, Redskins' owner, was sitting on their bench.

While the newly-crowned champions posed for photographs and slapped Bronko Nagurski, Sid Luckman and Harry Clark on their bare backs for their great play, acting general manager Ralph Brizzolara charged Marshall had "snuck up on the Bears' bench just as the first half was in its final minute."

Beat a Hasty Retreat.

The only intimation the crowd of 34,320 had that something was wrong was when Brizzolara leaped to his feet and screamed at the raccoon skin coated Marshall who started beating a rapid retreat. Brizzolara sent Jack Goldie, assistant trainer, after the Washington magnate and Goldie called police, who escorted Marshall under the stands.

Marshall shortly returned to his box seat where he proclaimed: "You can say for me that Brizzolara is not a gentleman. And I'll never speak to him again."

Brizzolara fumed. "That's the lowest way there can be of trying to win a game, to sneak down to our bench, apparently to steal the instructions we're giving our players. Yes, we threw him out—not invited him out."

Marshall protested he had merely come down to the Bears' bench to visit, and said he thought the half would end by the time he got there. He insisted his arrival there while play was still going on was merely a case of poor timing on his part and no effort to eavesdrop.

Of all the Bears, the merchant-marine-bound Luckman took the longest to remove his suit because of the press of well-wishers.

Aimed For Good Farewell.

Sure, Sid realized he was setting a new all-time record when he threw five touchdown passes. "I knew it was my last game for a while and I really wanted to make it a good one. Say, how many yards did I make running, 64? Boy, I was watching those Redskins and when they thought I was going to pass and didn't chase me, I lit out on 'em."

Nagurski, who ended a five-year retirement to play one more year at the age of 35 "because George Halas wanted me to," said this was his last game. "After all," he grinned, "I can't go on taking care of Halas all my life."

Halas, a lieutenant commander in the Navy and on leave from his job as owner-coach of the Bears, grinned right back. "Sure the Bronk will play again," Halas said. "We're counting on him for next year."

Co-coach Hunk Anderson beamed happily. "That line of ours really rose up to the occasion. Better than they did in the Green Bay game. After that four weeks' layoff we weren't gun shy and went to work. The Bronk had spark for them and they really blocked for him."

Chicago, Dec. 26. — (AP.) — Sid Luckman, making his last fling in football before reporting to active duty in the Merchant Marine, kept his passing arm as busy as the second hand on a watch today as he rifled five touchdown passes to give the Chicago Bears a 41-21 victory over the Washington Redskins and the national pro championship before a crowd of 34,320.

In regaining the title from Washington, the Bears spotted their rivals seven points at the outset of the second period then exploded for two touchdowns in each of the last three quarters.

Sammy Baugh, the Redskins' National Football League passing champion for 1943, was roughed up considerably in the first quarter and a half and finally was removed for observation in the dressing room after receiving a vicious crack on the head. He returned in the second half and twirled a 17-yard touchdown pass to Andy Farkas in the third period and a 25-yard scoring toss to Joe Aguirre in the fourth chapter.

Sets Playoff Record.

Luckman's five scoring aerials set a national championship playoff record which Baugh had held since 1937 when his three touchdown pitches beat the Bears. This was the fourth title match between the two teams since then, and the scorecard now stands with each club winning twice.

Dante Magnani and Harry Clark each tallied twice for the Bears after grabbing Sid's passes, and by the fourth period the game was so safely tucked away that the Bears' great quarterback did a bit of clowning by aiming at old Bronko Nagurski. The Nag, who did his full share of ripping up the Washington forwards, nabbed the pass for a nine-yard gain.

In all, Luckman hit on 14 of 26 aerials for a gain of 276 yards. Baugh made good on 7 out of 11 for 106 yards and his teammate, George Cafego, connected on 3 out of 11 for 76. The Bears outrushed Washington 168 yards to 45 and gained 276 yards by the air to 182.

Washington set up the game's first score late in the first period when Cafego's 21-yard pass to Aguirre was ruled complete after interference to move the Redskins to the Bears three. In the first two seconds of the second quarter, Farkas rammed over.

Luckman then went to work, spearing Ray McLean for 29 yards. Then on a screen play, he hit Clark who scooted 31 yards behind three blockers to score with Ray Hare dangling from his waist. The play capped a 67-yard parade.

Luckman Does Some Carrying.

The Bears ate up 70 yards in eight plays to tally again, Luckman running 24 yards then 15 more on a quarterback sneak to give Nagurski a chance to slam through tackle from the three.

In the third quarter, Bears pushed their lead to 27-7, after Luckman intercepted two passes to accelerate the touchdown thrusts.

A flat pass to Nagnani was good for a 36-yard payoff, and a screen play sent Magnani off on a 64-yard jog for another marker.

Luckman's 29-yard toss to Jim Benton topped a 56-yard drive at the start of the fourth period. The Bears kept possession of the ball with an onside kickoff, getting it on their 47 after Washington had touched it. From there Luckman's aerial attack wiped out a 15-yard holding penalty and gave him his chance to hit Clark for 18 yards and another score.

Bob Snyder added all but one of the Bears' extra points by placekicks.

WASHINGTON		BEARS
Masterson	le	Benton
Rymkus	lt	Sigillo
Shugart	lg	Fortmann
Smith	c	Turner
Slivinski	rg	Musso
Pasqua	rt	Hoptowit
Aguirre	re	Wilson
Hare	qb	Snyder
Cafego	lh	Clark
Seno	rh	Magnani
Farkas	fb	Masters

Washington .... 0 7 7 7—21
Bears .... 0 14 13 14—41

Washington scoring: Touchdowns—Farkas 2. Aguirre. Points after touchdown—Masterson 2 (placekicks), Aguirre (placekick).

Bears scoring: Touchdowns—Clark 2, Nagurski (for Masters), Magnani 2, Benton. Points after touchdown—Snyder 5 (placekicks).

Substitutions: Washington — Ends, Piasecky, Lapka; tackles, Wilkin; guards, Zeno, Fiorentino, Leon; centers—Hayden; backs—Baugh, Seymour, Moore, Gibson, Akins, Setasica.

Bears—Ends, Pool, Berry; tackles—Steinkemper, Babartsky, Mundee; guards—Ippolito, Logan; centers—Matuza; backs—McLean, Luckman, Famiglietti, Nagurski, McEnulty, Nolting, Vodicka.

Pro Football Opens Doors To Collegians

Club Owners Wipe Out Restrictions Hampering Efforts To Replenish Depleted Rosters

Philadelphia, April 19.—(AP.)—
—The National Football League tackled the manpower problem today and wiped out most of the restrictions that would have hampered the professional clubs in their efforts to replenish depleted rosters through tonight's draft of college players.

Opening their three-day spring meeting, the club owners devoted about nine hours to discussing an eligibility rule that would permit a wide choice of players without encroaching upon the rights of colleges, and came up with a resolution that says in effect that they may sign any athlete who isn't actually playing college football.

League Permission.

They agreed that any player whose class has graduated from college is eligible to play pro football and that players who have left school or whose colleges have discontinued football also may be signed for the coming season with the permission of the league office. Graduation will be regarded as taking place four years after matriculation in any college, including junior colleges, regardless of whether the player still is eligible for intercollegiate competition.

This resolution was adopted as an emergency measure, replacing for this year the pro-college code adopted in 1926 which virtually forbids the signing of any player whose three-year term of college eligibility has not been used up, without permission of the college authorities.

The Boston Yankees were awarded first pick in the league's draft of college players and the new league member chose Angelo Bertelli, last year's Notre Dame backfield star.

First round drawings were:
Chicago Cardinals, Pat Harder of Wisconsin; Brooklyn Dodgers, Creighton Miller of Notre Dame; Detroit Lions, Otto Graham of Northwestern; Philadelphia Eagles, Steve Van Buren of Louisiana State; New York Giants, Billy Hillenbrand of Indiana; Green Bay Packers, Mervin Pregulman of Michigan; Washington Redskins, Mike Micka of Colgate; Chicago Bears, Ray Evans of Kansas; Pittsburgh Steelers, John Podesto of St. Mary's (Calif.) and college of the Pacific; Cleveland Rams, Tony Butkovich of Illinois and Purdue.

National Football Loop Prohibits Frays After Championship Decided

Philadelphia, April 21—(AP.)—
The national football league prohibited all post-season games after the championship is decided and placed restrictions on player trades today.

Continuance of pre-season all-star games was approved, however, at the league's spring meeting.

New by-laws approved included these restrictions:

1. No player shall be permitted to participate in games after his team's schedule is finished without permission of commissioner Elmer Layden. Such permission would extend for one game only and not more than two men may play on any one team.

2. A player involved in a trade or sale may not be traded or sold again after the receiving team has played three games, unless waivers are obtained.

The league's spring meeting was recessed tonight after work was started on a schedule calling for participation of 11 teams in the fall campaign.

After several hours of work it appeared likely that the owners had dropped discussion of team mergers or other methods of avoiding complexities due to an odd number of teams.

This apparently assured full operation by the Boston Yankees, the lone addition to league membership this year.

Aug. 14

'Beefy' Bears Must Reduce

Fines Are Threatened

Collegeville, Ind.-(AP)-The Chicago Bears, preparing for their meeting with the College All-Stars at Evanston, Ill., Aug. 30, have decided to do something about their "beef trust" —a dozen portly gentlemen many pounds over their best playing weight.

Unless the corpulent 12 shorten their reaches at the training table and lose weight fast, they will be fined $50 each.

Tackle Al Babartsky, former Fordham star, has to cut down from 240 to 225. Others who will have to go on a restricted diet include Bulldog Turner, 258; Gary Famiglietti, 249; Jame Sweeney, 259; Ed Simonich, 237; Doug Mc Enulty, 237; Dom Sigillo, 235; Fred Mundee, 227; Elmo Kelly, 225; Jimmy Fordham, 225; Paul Podmajesky, 224, and Pete Gudauskas, 225.

The Bears have not progressed beyond the tackling dummy stage in their contact work, postponing scrimmages until the rookie studded squad masters T formation blueprints.

SAYS REDSKIN IS SUSPENDED

Marshall Cites McAdams For Signing With Seattle

San Diego, Cal., Aug. 9 (AP)—
The Pacific Coast's private professional football war, started when the American League was formed this year in opposition to the Pacific Coast circuit, now threatens to become nationwide.

A bombshell was tossed into the situation today when George P. Marshall, owner of the Washington Redskins, informed the American League that Dean McAdams, former University of Washington star, stands suspended for five years, under the by-laws of the National League in which the Redskins operate, for signing with the Seattle Bombers, a member of the new league on the Pacific Coast.

Traded For Masterson

According to Marshall, McAdams is the property of the Redskins, having been traded recently by the Brooklyn Dodgers for End Bob Masterson of the Washington team.

Other statements and counter-statements flew thick and fast.

McAdams, the center of the controversy, was quoted from Seattle as saying he has no commitments with the Redskins and told Marshall he did not expect to return east this fall and added: "I'm not jumping any contract with the Redskins.

Never Had Contract

"I never had any signed contract. I understand other National League players will play Pacific Coast football this fall."

Hardly had McAdams' statement hit the wires when Jerry Giesler, famed criminal attorney, of Los Angeles and president of the American League, let out this blast:

"I am not cognizant of any contract irregularity concerning McAdams. We are going to do what's right, but at the same time we are not going to be intimidated. Ours is a policy of fair play and cooperation with all other leagues in the best interest of sports. This is no time, in my opinion, for intersports fights."

Sept. 3

Millionaires Organize New Pro Grid League

'All-America Conference' Will Operate in Key Cities Starting Next Season

Chicago, Ill.-(AP)-Organization of the All-America Football conference, a new coast to coast professional football league, sponsored by "men of millionaire incomes," was announced here Saturday. A spokesman said the new league would begin operations next year.

An eight club league is a certainty and a 10 club league is a probability. Seven franchises have already been awarded as follows: Chicago, John L. Keeshin, president of a trucking concern; New York, Mrs. Lou Gehrig, widow of the famous Yankee baseball player, and Ray J. Ryan, oil company president; Baltimore, Commander Gene Tunney, former heavyweight boxing champion; Buffalo, James Breuil and Will Bennett, oil company executives, and Sam Cordavano, construction company head; Cleveland, Arthur McBride, taxicab company owner; Los Angeles, Actor Don Ameche and Christy Walsh, former newspaper syndicate director; and San Francisco, Anthony J. Morabito and Allan E. Sorrell, co-owners of a lumber terminal concern, and Ernest J. Turre, construction company manager at Phoenix, Ariz.

In addition, the spokesman said, prominent businessmen in Detroit, Philadelphia and Boston have sought franchises for their cities. Organization of the league was started several months ago and was completed during the last two days at a meeting of club owners here.

The owners adopted two resolutions which, according to a statement, "are certain to help shape the success of the conference" and avoid talent raids on the long established National Professional Football league. They were:

1. No club will be allowed to employ a coach or player who is under contract to any team in the National Football league.

2. No player will be admitted into the organization who has college football eligibility remaining.

Pointing out that the wealthy owners of the new league "are prepared to engage in a battle of dollars" with the National league, if necessary, the spokesman said the restriction on talent raids would avoid such conflict.

The second resolution, he asserted, was intended to protect college football since many undergraduate players whose careers were interrupted by war might prefer grabbing "quick money" in football to returning to their studies after the war.

Nov. 6

Rookie Sparks Eagles Victory

Defeat Brooklyn, 21-7

Brooklyn, N. Y.-(AP)-Steve Van Buren, star rookie from Louisiana State, sparked the Philadelphia Eagles to a 21-7 triumph over the winless Brooklyn Tigers before 15,289 at Ebbets field Sunday in a National Football league game. Van Buren scored two of the Eagles' three touchdowns. The first was made in the opening period when he reversed his field and sprinted 44 yards. A few minutes later he scored again on a 71 yard run.

All through the game Van Buren was a threat with his speed around the ends and on kick returns.

The Eagles, tied with the Washington Redskins for the eastern division lead, struck for their third touchdown in the second period on a pass and run play that went 54 yards. Roy Zimmerman passed 33 yards to Mel Bleeker, who then galloped 21 yards.

The Tigers, playing their first game under the coaching of Ed Kubale and Frank Bridges, dominated play in the second half, although the Eagles threatened just before the gun on another run by Van Buren.

The Tiger tally came in the third on a 59 yard play on which Cecil Johnson tossed 29 yards to Andy Kowalski, who went the remaining 30 yards.

	Phil.	Bkln.
First downs	4	6
Yards gained rushing (net)....	203	14
Forward passes attempted.....	9	27
Forward passes completed......	2	7
Yards by forward passes	60	106
Forward passes intercepted by..	5	2
Yards gained runback intercepted passes	55	0
Punting average (from scrimmage)	38	53
Total yards all kicks returned...	54	159
Opponents' fumbles recovered...	0	4
Yards lost by penalties.........	90	70

Score by periods:

Philadelphia	14	7	0	0—21
Brooklyn	0	0	7	0— 7

Scoring—Philadelphia: Touchdowns, Van Buren 2, Bleeker; points after touchdowns, Zimmerman 3 (placements). Brooklyn: Touchdown, Kowalski, point after touchdown, Kinard (placement).

Sept. 8

Packers Defeat Tigers; Penalties Set Record

Brock and Hutson Tally for Green Bay and Pug Manders for Brooklyn in 14-7 Battle

By OLIVER E. KUECHLE

The Packers and officials both came through at state fair park Sunday afternoon as the National league football season opened before a small and sweltering crowd of 12,994.

The Packers came through by staggering home with a one touchdown victory over the Brooklyn Tigers, 14-7, in a brawling sort of game, and the officials by calling 30 penalties, most of them against Brooklyn, for a new league record in total yards and number both.

Staggered is the right word to describe the victory. Maybe it was the heat or the constant and no doubt justified interference of the officials or the fact that this was an opening game. Whatever it was, though, the Packers, so highly touted in

The Statistics

	Green Bay	Brooklyn
First downs	15	16
Total yardage	218	258
Yards rushing	102	138
Yards passing	116	120
Passes attempted	22	27
Passes completed	8	10
Passes intercepted	3	3
Fumbles	0	2
Penalty yardage	9 for 84	21 for 165
Average distance punts.	37.4	37.5
Yards kick-off returned.	39	0

early season speculation, hardly looked the part of first rate contenders as they sputtered around with just enough good football to finish in front.

Reprinted from
The Milwaukee Journal

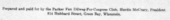

Football Commissioner Post Goes To Crowley

Chicago, Nov. 21 (AP)—Lieut. Com. James (Sleepy Jim) Crowley today accepted a contract to serve as commissioner of the All-America Conference, new professional football league expected to begin operations next year.

Crowley, left halfback of the famous Four Horsemen of Notre Dame University two decades ago, now is athletic officer and football coach at Sampson Naval Training Center, Sampson, N. Y. He recently returned from 16 months' of service with the navy in the Pacific.

Terms of the contract were not made public, but it was understood the league had offered him a five-year contract at $25,000 a year. He will take over his duties as soon as the war ends and he is discharged by the navy.

Nov. 26

Chicago Bears Bounce Eagles From Lead, 28-7

Defeat Drops Philly Pros to Third Place in Eastern Section of League; Penalty Record Set

Philadelphia, Pa.-(AP)-The Chicago Bears, deposed as champions of the National Football league, took a hand in settling the muddled eastern division race here by handing the Philadelphia Eagles their first defeat, 28-7, before a crowd of 34,000 at Shibe park. The Eagles slid to third place behind the Washington Redskins and the New York Giants, who are now tied for the lead.

Never beaten by the Eagles, the Bears scored twice in the first period, once in the second and once in the last, despite losses of 170 yards through penalties, many for delaying the game. The losses set a league record, eclipsing the Dodgers' 165 yard total run up in a game against the Green Bay Packers earlier this season.

The statistics and scoring:

	Bears	Eagles
First downs	9	1
Yards rushing	91	2
Passes attempted	20	26
Passes completed	5	9
Yards passes	85	94
Passes intercepted by	5	2
Punting average	41.6	43.6
Yards all kicks returned	72	162
Opponents' fumbles recovered	1	0
Yards penalties	170	15
Eagles	0 0 0 7— 7
Bears	14 7 0 7—28

Bears scoring—Touchdowns: Margarita, Fordham, Smeja, Famiglietti. Extra points: Gudauskas 4 (placement). Eagles scoring—Touchdown: Miller. Extra point: Zimmerman.

Dec. 17

Packers Defeat Giants, 14 to 7; Win National Pro Grid Crown

Ted Fritsch Scores Both Green Bay Markers, One on a Buck, Other on Nifty Pass

By OLIVER E. KUECHLE
Of The Journal Staff

New York, N. Y.—The Christmas goose hangs high in Green Bay today.

Coming up with one of their best games of the fall, a complete reversal of their showing on this same field a month ago, the mighty men of the north, the Packers, beat New York in the championship play-offs of the National Football league before a near capacity crowd of 46,016 at the Polo Grounds Sunday afternoon, 14-7.

The goose hangs high today, indeed. A month ago, in losing to these same Giants, 24-0, the Packers looked like something the cat dragged in. They lacked poise and fire and execution. They lacked almost everything in fact—except 11 men on the field. Sunday, with the blue chips down, they looked like champions. In reversal they had everything — most of all 11 men, no matter what the combination, with an eager desire to play hard, rocking football. They took a 14-0 lead in the second quarter with well conceived football, and then with alert defensive play, protected their lead against New York's countercharge in the second half.

Fritsch Scores Twice

It was just as tough a game as the score suggests. For a few minutes in the second quarter, it looked as though the Packers might make it a mild rout. Once under way, after an uneventful first quarter, they scored twice easily, but that was only for a few minutes. The Giants still had ideas of their own, and in the second half, it was a rocking, socking football game which delighted the huge crowd right down to the gun.

The irrepressible Ted Fritsch, one of those who showed the biggest reversal over his performance a month ago, scored both of Green Bay's touchdowns. On the first, he bucked over from the two yard line on fourth down after a drive of 48 yards. On the second, he caught a pass in the flat from Irv Comp and dashed 27 yards across the goal after a drive of 63 yards. Hutson, whose faking on Fritsch's second touchdown sucked the Giants completely out of position, added both of the extra points.

Ward Cuff, the old Marquette star who came up with one of the best all-around games of his career, scored New York's touchdown, bucking over from the one on the first play of the fourth quarter after a succession of Arnie Herber's passes had carried the Giants into this position from midfield. The reliable Ken Strong, in his fourteenth year with New York, booted the extra point.

The Statistics

	Giants	Packers
First downs rushing	5	9
First downs passing	4	2
First downs penalty	1	0
Total first downs	10	11
Yards gained rushing	70	162
Yards gained passing	117	73
Total yards gained	187	235
Passes attempted	22	11
Passes completed	8	3
Passes intercepted	3	4
Punts number	10	11
Punting average	41	37
Yards punts returned	32	89
Yards kick-offs returned	75	12
Yards penalized	30	45
Fumbles	1	2
Opp. fumbles recovered	0	0

The game broke all play-off records financially. It attracted a gross gate of $146,205.15, a net gate, after taxes, of $121,703, and it provided a players' pool of $81,466.51 of which the Packers' as champions, will split $41,896.64. The Giants received $27,-931.91 and the second place clubs in each division of the league, the Bears, Lions and Eagles, $11,637.96.

The line-ups:

Green Bay Packers		New York Giants
Hutson	L. E.	O. Adams
Ray	L. T.	Cope
Kuusisto	L. G.	Younce
C. Brock	C.	Help
Goldenberg	R. G.	Sivell
Bereziey	R. T.	Carroll
Jacunski	R. E.	Liebel
Craig		Calligaro
Comp	L. H.	Herber
Laws	R. H.	Cuff
Fritsch	F.	Livingston

Green Bay Packers ...... 0 14 0 0—14
New York Giants .... 0 0 0 7— 7

Green Bay scoring—Touchdowns: Fritsch 2. Extra points: Hutson 2 (placements). New York scoring—Touchdown: Cuff. Extra point: Strong (placement). Substitutions—New York: End, Weiss; tackle, Blozis; guards, Avedisian, Umont; backs, Petrilas, Paschal, Sulaitis, Barker, Strong. Green Bay: End, Wheba; tackles, Croft, Schwemmel; guards, Tinsley, Sorenson; backs, L. Brock, Perkins, Duhart.

Reprinted from
The Milwaukee Journal

Dec. 18

New Pro League Has Novel Plan of Selecting Players

Akron, Ohio-(AP)-Representatives of the newly organized United States Football league, which plans to operate franchises in six cities next year, met here Sunday and discussed an entirely new method of selecting players.

League President Harold (Red) Grange said players who would play on league teams would be distributed from a players' pool selected by a league scouting organization.

"We propose to establish a central scouting system and the scouts will select players and distribute them to the various teams in the league with the main thought of keeping an even balance of power among the teams," Grange explained. "Under this revolutionary plan of signing players the league has abandoned the draft system, which has worked to a disadvantage in pro football."

PAUL BROWN SIGNS TO COACH PRO TEAM

Gets Five-Year Contract With Cleveland of All-America Football Conference

ALSO IS GENERAL MANAGER

Great Lakes Mentor to Start New Duties After Release From Navy Service

CHICAGO, Feb. 8 (AP)—Lieut. Paul Brown, football coach at Great Lakes Naval Training Center and former Ohio State University mentor, today signed a five-year contract as head coach and general manager of the Cleveland professional team in the new All-America Conference.

The 36-year-old Brown, whose 1942 Ohio State team won the mythical national championship, thus will not return to Ohio State, from which he had leave of absence.

Arthur McBride, Cleveland taxicab magnate who owns the All-America franchise in that city, did not disclose terms of the contract, but asserted it was the best ever given to a football coach. From another source, however, it was reported Brown's annual salary would exceed $15,000. McBride also disclosed that his team would use Municipal Stadium, which seats 83,000.

Brown, replaced at Ohio State last season by Carroll Widdoes, his former assistant, who directed the Buckeyes to the Western Conference championship, followed Lieut. Comdr. Jack Meagher of the Iowa Seahawks and Buck Shaw of Santa Clara in signing coaching contracts in the proposed league. Meagher, former Auburn mentor, was signed by Miami and Shaw by San Francisco.

Efforts Made To Put Tigers Into Stadium

Tim Mara Announces Deal Off; League Limits Entries

New York, April 9.—(AP.)—The proposed Brooklyn Tigers-Boston Yanks merger was declared off today as the National Football League went into the fourth day of its annual meeting. Whether this declaration was final remained to be seen, however, as Brooklyn and the New York Giants continued to maneuver for a favorable position on the plan to move the Tigers into Yankee stadium.

While the league as a whole concerned itself with constitutional changes and plans for taking care of returning service men, representatives of the three clubs involved engaged in private conferences. Finally Tom Gallery, general manager of the Dodgers, emerged to remark, "we've withdrawn from the merger." He offered no explanation.

The league, however, took another step toward the 12-club circuit that was believed to be one stipulation under which the Giants might permit the Tigers to use the Bronx ball park. This was a constitutional change, effective in 1946, permitting no fewer than ten clubs nor more than twelve to make up the circuit. This ruled out any idea of expanding to 16 clubs and also gave the league control over mergers and suspensions.

Player Limit Set.

After voting to keep the player limit at 28 men, the club owners decided that each club may take on five discharged service men in addition to these 28 men after the club's first game of 1945 provided that the men were on the club's active list at the time of their induction and that they were placed or placed on inactive military status after the club's first game of 1945. Boston, a new club last year, was excepted from the first proviso. No club, however, can use more than 28 players in one game.

Two experimental rule changes, each for one year, were adopted at a night meeting. They provide for the ball to be put into play 20 yards from the sidelines, instead of the present 15, after an out-of-bounds play; and that a substitution can be made while time is in provided the player withdrawn gets off the field before the ball is snapped. If the ball is snapped before the player is off the field, the club making the substitution has its choice of taking a five-yard penalty or having a timeout charged against it.

Several other changes were adopted. They prohibit blocking with swinging elbows or forearm; if an opponent is struck with such a block above the shoulder, the offending player is to be banished from the game and a 15-yard penalty inflicted; if the blow is below the shoulder it will be regarded as unnecessary roughness and a 15-yard penalty inflicted; permit the ball on the try for extra point to be put in play on the two-yard line, as at present, or anywhere back of that line; and prohibited use of rubber tees for kickoffs.

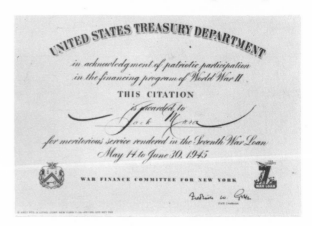

Green Bay Crushes Detroit, 57-21, As Hutson Makes 4 Touchdowns

MILWAUKEE, Oct. 7 (AP)—Green Bay's Packers, led once again by brilliant Don Hutson, packed a 41-point aerial scoring orgy into the second quarter today, then rolled on to a 57 to 21 triumph over Detroit for their second straight victory in defense of their national football league championship.

A near-capacity attendance of 23,500 fans watched with amazement as the Packers, outplayed by a mild margin through a scoreless first period and into the second, bounded to the front as Irv Comp and Don McKay passed for five touchdowns, four of them to Hutson, and intercepted a Detroit heave for another. Don also converted on seven tries.

Hutson placed-kicked five extra points to collect some kind of a record total for one quarter, of 29 points. Comp tossed three of the touchdown shots, one of them to Clyde Goodnight, Hutson's left end understudy. Ted Fritsch rounded out the wild scoring by intercepting one of cotton price's tosses and galloping 69 yards over the goal line.

Hutson Kick Blocked

The Lions achieved the distinction of blocking one of Hutson's tries for the extra point.

The Packers picked up the rest of their points on a safety in the third quarter when Goodnight threw Dave Ryan behind the Lion goal line as the Detroit back attempted to run back a punt; a 50-yard touchdown pass from Lou Brock to Comp in the same session, and another touchdown in the final quarter when center Charlie Brock intercepted Ryan's pass and ran 34 yards over the goal line.

The Lion scoring was done by Chuck Fenenbock on an 8-yard dash in the second quarter, Bob Westfall's 7-yard drive in the third and a 62-yard aerial from Ryan to Johnny Greene late in the final period. Bill Callihan kicked the extra point.

The Lions started things in the fantastic second quarter, but they were only the party of the second part from there on as the Packers gave their breath-taking demonstration of aerial artistry.

A short kick by Roy McKay gave Detroit the ball on the Packer 29 near the end of the opening session. Chuck Fenenbock passed 16 yards to Jack Matheson, then ran the ball to the 8. On the first play of the second quarter, Fenenbock raced over and Bill Callihan place-kicked for the other point.

Statistics of the Game

	G.B.	Detroit
First downs	7	15
Yds gained, rush'g (net)	53	137
Forward passes	17	34
Forwards completed	8	13
Yards gained, forwards	242	244
Forwards intercepted by	6	1
Run-back of intercepted passes, yards	137	3
*Av. dist. of punts, yds.	29	23½
Run-back of all kicks, yds.	60	148
Opponents' fumbles recovered	1	0
Yards lost, penalties	65	79

*From line of scrimmage.

Goodnight Snares Toss

Then it started. On the first play after the kick-off, McKay whipped one to Hutson which covered 56 yards for a score, the slender Packer end grabbing the ball on the Detroit 38 and flitting away from the Lion defenders.

A few minutes later Ryan kicked out on the Detroit 41, and Irv Comp fired another beauty to Clyde Goodnight for the second touchdown. The next time the Packers got the ball, Comp flipped one to Hutson for six yards and on the next play McKay tossed another shot to the Packer star who again raced away from the bewildered Lions.

Ben Starret intercepted a pass from Cotton Price and returned it 39 yards to the Detroit 17, and the Packers went through the Comp-to-Hutson maneuver for another score on the following play. Ted Fritsch interrupted Hutson's string by intercepting another Price pass and galloped 69 yards for a touchdown. Comp and Hutson finished the exhibition with a six-yard touchdown pass.

The line-up:

GREEN BAY (57)		DETROIT (21)
Goodnight	L.E.	Greene
Croft	L.T.	Kostiuk
Kuusisto	L.G.	Batinski
C. Brock	C.	Wojciechowicz
Timley	R.G.	Kaporch
Lipscomb	R.T.	Sigillo
Mason	R.E.	Matheson
Craig	Q.H.	Callihan
McKay	L.H.	Price
L. Brock	R.H.	Van Tone
Fritsch	F.B.	Nelson

SCORE BY PERIODS

Green Bay .... 0 41 9 7—57
Detroit .... 0 7 7 7—21

Touchdowns—Fenenbock (for Price), Westfall (for Nelson), Greene, Hutson 4 (for Goodnight, Fritsch, Comp, C. Brock. Safety—Ryan (tackled by Goodnight). Points after touchdown—Hutson 7, Callihan 3 (placements).

SUBSTITUTES

Detroit—End: Robertson. Tackles: Lindon, Mesak, Szczymanski. Center: Williams. Backs: Farkas, Westfall, Fenenbock, Dehane, Krol, Snadden, Trebotich, Hackney. Green Bay—Ends: Hutson, Luhn, Urban, Keuper, Frutig, Mulleneaux. Tackles: Neal, McPherson, Ray. Guards: Crimmons, Sorenson, Tollefson, Buchaner. Backs: Laws, Starrett, Comp, Perkins.

FOOTBALL BROADCASTING IS A TRICKY BUSINESS

Because it's one of the toughest, most exciting and noisiest games in the world, it takes a keen mind and a real love of the sport to give a colorful and vivid word picture of gridiron action. And what's more important to air audiences is the accuracy in statistics and good judgment of distances. That's what makes football sportscasting such a tricky business, explains Red Barber, ace sportscaster, who handles the microphone assignment for the WHN (1050 KC) exclusive Sunday afternoon broadcasts of the New York Giants Pro Football games.

Barber, and Connie Desmond who collaborates on the broadcasts of the games, have notched more than 10,000 sportscasting hours in their 30 cumulative years in the business. Red started his career while matriculating at Florida University. He was studying for a teacher's degree, working his way through the University, when the college radio station sent him an emergency call to read a professor's lecture on "Certain Aspects of Bovine Obstetrics." When he finished, the program director asked young Barber how much he'd want to apply all his talents to announcing. Red asked $50 a month for a part-time job and was accepted. On vacations from his job, Barber toured the country auditioning at larger stations, and was finally called by Powell Crosley, baseball and radio magnate, to describe the Cincinnati Reds' games. He stayed for five years, then left to come to Dodger-land, even though it meant a decrease in salary. The rest is broadcasting history.

While Barber is known as America's No. 1 baseball broadcaster, he doesn't have to take a back-seat to anyone when it comes to football. He's been touring the nation's gridirons for more than a decade, broadcasting the best college games of the week, and was hired four years ago for the more difficult pro football assignments as the voice of the New York Football Giants.

Sportscaster Connie Desmond can claim 14 years behind the microphone. The trade mark "Red Barber and Connie Desmond" is a brand name which in its four years of operations has become recognized as insurance of top notch sportscasting down kilocycle lane. And it is no wonder the duo can count 30 years of sportscasting to their credit between them.

Desmond has been describing both football and baseball games since his entry into the radio industry back in 1931. A native of Toledo, Connie did the mike jobs on American Association and Big Ten Football games until he was brought to New York to do the major league games, in 1942. The following year was the first time that Con-

Walter (Red) Barber, above, looks like he's dressed for a visit to the North Pole. However, it's only the famed redhead's working clothes for his Sunday afternoon Radio assignments broadcasting the New York Football Giants' National League's championship games at the Polo Grounds to his tremendous air-wave fan following. Barber is one of the nation's top Radio sports broadcasters. He has long handled the Football Giants' games for Station WHN.

nie was paired with Red to do the games on WHN, New York. It was what is known in the trade as a "Happy Marriage," a combination of talents which assured good sports listening from opening minute to the final play.

Wherever the Giants play, WHN is there. This will be the seventh consecutive year that WHN has brought its listeners along the Eastern seacoast, the exclusive play-by-play description of each N. Y. Giants' game. Up until three years ago when Red and Connie accepted the air assignment, Bert Lee and Dick Fishell did the broadcasts. Bert Lee, with the assistance of Ward Wilson, now conducts the very popular WHN football program, "Take A Tip From Me," immediately before each game. After the game, the pair go on the air with "Sports Extra."

Bert Lee and Ward Wilson are also teamed each season to broadcast the New York Rangers' hockey games from Madison Square Garden. Sportsman Lee also conducts such programs as "Today's Baseball," "Warm-Up Time" and "Sports Final" throughout the year.

This quartet of sportscasters—Barber, Desmond, Lee and Wilson—combine to make Sunday afternoons one of the most enjoyable for radio sports fans.

Rams Beat Lions, 28-21; Win Western Pro Title

Detroit, Nov. 22 (AP)—The Cleveland Rams helped themselves to their first Western Division championship of the National Football League today by trimming the Detroit Lions, 28-21, before a crowd of 40,000 fans.

Sharpshooter Bob Waterfield, former U.C.L.A. star, fired two touchdown passes as he and Jim Benton put on one of the slickest forward-passing exhibitions seen in Briggs Stadium. Waterfield also ran for a touchdown.

The Ram ace completed 12 of 21 throws of 329 yards, getting into position to make it more than a mile in total yardage for the season. His completions today, including ten to Benton for 303 yards, gave him a season's total of 1,449 yards.

NEW PENALTY RECORD
GREEN BAY CHECKS BOSTON TEAM, 38-14

Yanks Suffer First Defeat of Season—Hutson's 17 Points Pace Packers' Attack

STATISTICS OF THE GAME

	Green Bay	Yanks
First downs	16	12
Yards gained, rushing	253	59
Forward passes	21	24
Forwards completed	7	11
Yards gained, forwards	179	183
Forwards intercepted by	0	3
*Av. dist. of punts, yds.	52.3	44.7
Yards lost, penalties	179	110
*From line of scrimmage.		

MILWAUKEE, Oct. 21 (AP)—The champion Green Bay Packers got back on the victory road today by dealing the Yanks of Boston their first beating of the National Football League season, 38 to 14.

Van Buren Breaks Hutson's 'TD' Record

Philadelphia, Pa.—Led by S t e v e Van Buren, who scored three touchdowns, the Philadelphia Eagles trounced the Boston Yankees here Sunday afternoon, 35-7.

It was a futile bid by the Eagles to crawl back into the championship picture in the east, the Washington Redskins cinching the eastern title by beating the Giants, but it was a great day personally for Van Buren. His three touchdowns gave him a total of 18 for the season — a new league record. Don Hutson of the Green Bay Packers set the old record with 17 in 1942.

The 200 pound halfback from the Bayou country, was the center of attraction from start to finish. The 27,905 fans who gathered in Shibe park for the closing day were ready to see a record established—and they saw it.

Van Buren did all his scoring in the last half, his first touchdown was hung up on a 29 yard sprint after he had taken a lateral from Al Sherman. Van Buren tied Hutson's record with only four minutes of play left. He bulled across from the seven yard line, carrying two men with him. The climactic tally was scored with one minute to go and was a driving line smash from eight yards out. He added to his glory by booting extra points after his last two touchdowns.

Thus he ran up a season's total of 110 points, 13 better than Hutson's 97. Van Buren also locked away the ground gaining championship of the season.

The three touchdowns and two extra points also gave him a season's total of 110 with which he also passed Hutson as the season's scoring champion. With 847 yards, he also won the season's ground gaining title.

	Boston	Philadelphia
First downs	8	18
Yards gained rushing	98	227
Forward passes attempted	16	25
Forward passes completed	4	13
Yards by forward passing	33	139
Forward passes intercepted by	2	4
Punting average	25.4	35.8
Yards lost by penalties	25	95

Reprinted from
The Milwaukee Journal

Cards Overcome Aerial Thrusts By Luckman to Down Bears, 16-7

Rock Chicago Rivals Back on Fast Running Attack, With Cantor Supplying Spark, to Snap Losing String at 29 Games

CHICAGO, Oct. 14 (AP)—The Cardinals, sparked by Leo Cantor, former New York Giant player, fought back in the second and third quarters today for two touchdowns to defeat the Bears and the vaunted aerial attack of Sid Luckman, 16—7. The victory was the first for the Cardinals in almost three years, and ended a string of twenty-nine consecutive losses.

Statistics of the Game

	Cards.	Bears.
First downs	17	8
Yards gained, rushing	241	17
Forward passes	11	30
Forwards completed	3	17
Yards gained, forwards	86	196
Forwards, intercepted by	1	1
*Av. dist. of punts, yds.	37.2	41.8
Run-back of punts, yds.	43	67
Fumbles recovered	1	0
Yards lost, penalties	32	42
*From line of scrimmage.		

Dan Topping Fires Guns Opening Football War

Brooklyn Owner Says Dispute With Tim Mara Prompted Break With National League

New York, N. Y. (AP) It was war to the hilt Thursday between the National Football league and the new All-America Professional conference which plans to start operating next fall.

Dan Topping brought matters to a head Wednesday when he bolted the National league for the new organization. This gained for the new group the use of the Yankee stadium and its coveted seating capacity of 80,000.

Move Beneficial to Sport

Topping, owner of the Brooklyn franchise in the National league which this year was merged with Boston, and part owner of the New York Yankees, declared he had made the break because Tim Mara, owner of the New York football Giants, declined to agree on playing dates.

"An agreement has been reached with the All-America conference for a franchise at Yankee stadium," Topping said. "It is, in our opinion, a move that should be beneficial not only to professional football in general but to New York and Brooklyn. Ray Flaherty, our coach, has spent the last three months since his discharge from the navy lining up additional talent to round out our roster. Many former Brooklyn players have returned from the services and hope to have them all back before the opening of the season.

Mara Is Surprised

Topping said his team would be known as the New York Football Yankees. It is the ninth club in the conference that already has awarded franchises to Brooklyn, Buffalo, Chicago, Baltimore, Cleveland, Los Angeles, Miami and San Francisco. Jim Crowley, commissioner of the conference, said that a tenth franchise would be awarded soon.

Mara declared he was "surprised, but not shocked" at Topping's move. "We have been doing business here at the Polo grounds for at least 21 years while teams in the Yankee stadium have come and gone," he said. Elmer Layden, commissioner of the National circuit which last spring had granted Topping permission to switch his Brooklyn franchise to the stadium, subject to Mara's approval, reserved comment until he heard officially from Topping.

RAMS CAPTURE PRO GRID TITLE

Beat Redskins, 15-14, With Aid Of Freak Safety

Cleveland, Dec. 16 (AP)—The Cleveland Rams won the National Professional Football League championship today by nosing out the Washington Redskins, 15 to 14, on the strength of two touchdown passes by Bob Waterfield and a freak first-period safety. Freezing weather held the crowd to 32,178 fans.

The freak came up in the early minutes of a bitter battle played on a field that was a reasonable facsimile of a hockey rink. And for all the rest of the game meant to the final result, the boys might just as well have gone home right there, for they fought it out even up the rest of the way.

Waterfield Stars

Bob Waterfield threw two touchdown passes and the Redskins had to play all but a few moments without the great Baugh. Frank Filchock filled in admirably with a pair of scoring pitches of his own.

This thirteenth annual playoff was settled almost before anyone in the crowd realized it.

After holding for downs on their own 5, the Redskins took over. Baugh dropped back into the end zone in kick formation, but instead tried a daring pass to Wayne Millner, racing over on the right flat.

Goes For Safety

The ball was at the height of its trajectory—when it hit squarely against the goal post and bounced back into the end zone. Slingin' Sammy fell on it, but it went for an automatic safety and the two points that meant the game.

It wasn't long afterward that Sammy was hit—and hard—and apparently injured. For the rest of the day he played only briefly and not until the second half did he complete his one and only pass of the game for a one-yard gain.

Meantime, Waterfield celebrated the signing of his new three-year Cleveland contract by completing 14 of 27 pitches for a grand total of 172 yards and both the home club's scores.

Jim Benton Scores

One of these was to his pet battery mate, Jim Benton from Arkansas, covering 38 yards. The other went to Jim Gillette, 185-pound line bucker, and was good for 45 yards.

Gillette was easily the outstanding ball toter on the field. He carried the ball seventeen times and picked up 101 yards, which was more than three times as much as the entire Redskin team gained on the ground through the day.

With Riley Matheson, all-league lineman, leading the way, the Ram forwards held the Washingtons to a not-so-grand total of 32 yards gain on the ground—exactly 10 more than the all-time playoff low of 22.

Redskins Take 7-2 Lead

Midway in the second period the Rams' freak safety didn't look as if it would count for much, for the Redskins pushed a score across to take the lead. Ki Aldrich, the Washington center, who was the standout lineman of the game, set this up by intercepting one of Waterfield's passes and putting it down on the Washington 48.

A roughing penalty against the Rams and two line bucks moved Washington to Cleveland 40. On the next play, Steve Bagarus got behind Waterfield, took Filchock's long pitch on the Ram 12, and waltzed across. Joe Aguirre added the point, although late in the game he missed two tough field-goal tries.

Rams Go Ahead, 9-7

The Rams came right back to regain the lead before the half, however, and this time they went in front to stay. Taking a kick on their own 30, they went all the way, with Gillette banging away for 24 yards in two tries, Waterfield hurling to Benton on the Redskin 38 and then heaving the payoff pitch to Big Jim, who took it on the 13 and ran it over.

Here the Rams got their second break. Waterfield's extra point try was partially blocked and caromed into the air. It bounced against the cross bar of the goal posts, and went over instead of falling back.

The Rams sewed it up by taking the opening kickoff in the second half and driving 81 yards. Line plays moved them to the 32 and a Waterfield-Benton pass advanced to the 40. Gillette swept his own left end three times to go to the Redskin 38.

Gillette Scores For Rams

Then after a penalty had pushed the Rams back to the 45, Waterfield cut loose at his high hard one. Gillette picked it out from among three Washington defenders on the 9 and scored it. Waterfield's kick was wide.

The Redskins came back to earn their final marker. De Fruiter, a 190-pound Nebraskan, went 15 yards to the Washington 45 after the Redskins received a kick on their own 30, and Filchock went to work from there.

He fired a short one to Bagarus who scampered all the way to the Ram six. Filchock was thrown for a loss on the 17, but shovel-passed to Sal Rosato who went to the 9 and then heaved to Oklahoma Bob Seymour, waiting all alone in the end zone.

Washington		Cleveland
Aguirre	L E	Konetsky
Davis	L T	Schultz
Stralka	L G	Matheson
Aldrich	C	Scarry
Whited	R G	Lazetich
Unverer	R T	Bouley
Furley	R E	Pritko
Baugh	Q B	Waterfield
Bagarus	L H	Gehrke
Condit	R H	Gillette
Akins	F B	Greenwood

Score by quarters:
Washington .... 0 7 7 0—14
Cleveland ..... 2 7 6 0—15

Washington Touchdowns—Bagarus, Seymour (sub for Bagarus). Points after touchdown—Aguirre (2). Safety—Automatic. Cleveland Touchdowns—Benton (sub for Konetsky), Gillette. Point after touchdown—Waterfield.

Washington Substitutes—Ends, Millner, Piasecky. Tackles, Audet, Sharp, Korniszewski. Guards, Lolotai, Sharp. Center, Demao. Backs, Filchock, Seymour, Todd, De Fruiter, De Correvont, Rosato, Hare.

Cleveland Substitutes—Ends, Benton, Hickey, Hamilton. Tackle, Eason. Guards, Lear, Mergenthal. Center, Harding. Backs, Nemeth, Reisz, West, Kich.

Statistics

Cleveland		Washington
14	First downs	8
180	Yards rushing	32
192	Yards passing	179
27	Forwards attempted	39
14	Forwards completed	16
2	Passes intercepted	3
35	Yards interceptions returned	11
38	Average distance punts	39
104	Yards kicks returned	144
0	Opponents' fumbles recovered	1
60	Yards lost, penalties	38

Halas Seeks Fewer Subs In Pro Loop

Owner of Bears Chief Foe of Free Substitute Rule Now Employed

Chicago, Jan. 5.—(AP.)— The National Football League, proponent of the free substitution rule that has been gaining favor the past two years with collegiate code makers, will discuss the possibility of tossing that legislation out the window at its annual meeting opening Wednesday in New York.

Chief foe of the rule that allows substitutions, even of entire teams, at any time without penalty, will be George S. Halas, owner-coach of the Chicago Bears who recently was discharged as a commander after four years in the Navy.

Halas's suggestion will be but one of ten changes in the NFL code to be considered at the meeting.

The free substitution rule came into the game as a wartime measure, due in part to somewhat lowered quality of material, especially among the reserves. Because of the rule, most coaches had

LAYDEN QUITS PRO GRID JOB

Bell To Succeed Him As Head Of National League

New York, Jan. 11 (AP)—Elmer Layden, president of the National Football League, resigned tonight and will be succeeded by Bert Bell, president of the Pittsburgh Steelers.

Layden made his resignation effective tonight although his five-year contract was not due to expire until April 1.

Layden has been offered an advisory post with the league at a salary of $20,000 a year for an indefinite period, but the former Notre Dame star has not yet decided if he will accept.

Bell, who has been associated with the National League for thirteen years, must dispose of his holding in the Steelers before taking up his post as president and commissioner. Bell will receive $20,000 a year.

NEW DRAFT PLAN FOR ALL-AMERICA

Football League Will Pick Only Those College Men Who Want to Join Pros

By The Associated Press.

CHICAGO, Jan. 5—Coaches of the newly organized All-America Conference today proposed a "secret" draft of college football stars and at the same time criticized player-selection methods of the long-established, rival National Football League.

Mal Stevens, former Yale and New York University coach and now mentor of the All-America Brooklyn entry, said at a news conference at the new league's organizational meeting that the circuit would pick college seniors on a limited basis.

"The National League puts college seniors on the block like pieces of property with 500 or more names listed for hire," asserted Stevens. "That practice has irked college athletic directors and coaches."

Asks for a List

Stevens, speaking on behalf of the other league coaches, said the All-America had written to the National Collegiate Coaches Association, asking for a list of college players known to be interested in continuing football as professionals.

The plan of the All-America will be to approach interested players only after their coaches have given a go-ahead.

"There's no sense in publicizing a list of players who have no intention of entering the professional field," Stevens continued. "The National League has conducted this draft system mainly to advance its own game by flaunting names of college stars before the public eye."

The coaches also criticized the National Football League's free substitution rule, just as owner-coach George Halas of the Chicago Bears has proposed its elimination.

The All-America which ostensibly will adopt the National League rule book, in substance, said it would follow the collegiate rule on substitutions.

3 PRO ELEVENS SEEK LOS ANGELES FIELD

Coliseum Weighs for 2 Weeks Bids by Rams, All-America and Coast League Clubs

LOS ANGELES, Jan. 15 (AP)—After hearing spokesmen for three professional football teams, the commissioner of Los Angeles' Memorial Coliseum today took under advisement for two weeks all requests for gridiron dates next fall.

Applications, which the Coliseum will study before its next meeting Jan. 29, came from the recently transferred Los Angeles Rams of the National League, the local All-America conference franchise, the Hollywood Bears' Pacific Coast League entry—and the two traditional college users, Southern California and U. C. L. A.

Ace Parker Joins New Pro-Grid Loop

New York, Jan. 20 (AP)—Clarence (Ace) Parker, veteran halfback who won the National Football League's most valuable player award in 1940, has signed a contract with the New York Yankees of the All-America Conference, the Yankee office announced today.

Parker, who played pro football five years before the war, returned to the gridiron last season after 43 months in the Navy and was a member of the National League club operated jointly by Boston and Brooklyn. Dan Topping, owner of the Brooklyn franchise, recently shifted it to the All-America circuit.

A 1936 all-American selection at Duke, Parker has been offered the managership of Portsmouth (Va.) baseball club in the Piedmont League this year, but told the Yankees he would turn it down because the football squad will begin training in August, long before the baseball season closes.

However, the 32-year-old athlete plans to play in the Portsmouth infield until time to report to Coach Ray Flaherty of the Yankees.

National League Warns Gridder

New York, Jan. 15 (AP)—A final warning to "contract-jumping" players—aimed particularly at those who have "jumped" to the young All-America Conference—was sounded today by the National League and virtually all the rest of the country's professional football moguls.

To make sure there can be no loopholes, the National League magnates reviewed and reaffirmed their law which automatically bars any "jumping" player for five years. Immediately, an official of the Pacific Coast League said the rule would be recognized and followed by the three loops which joined the National last week in the newly organized "National Association of Professional Football Leagues." These are, in addition to the Coast Circuit, the Dixie League and American Association.

Nearing the end of their longest and probably most important annual meeting, the National League moguls threw this one more pitch in their out-and-out war with the All-America, and then turned to unsnarling their schedule for 1946

Bertelli Restrained From Playing

Yanks Welcome Court Action; Sign Governelli for 4 Years at $10,000

Paul Brown Lauds Fullback; Ted Fritsch Leaves for Home

By John Dietrich

BOWLING GREEN, O., Aug. 8—The Cleveland Browns of the All-America Conference revealed today that they have added a second great Negro football player for a tryout in professional ranks.

The newcomer is Marion Motley, giant fullback who lives in Canton and was a star with Coach Paul Brown's Great Lakes Naval Training Station team.

Motley, who weighs around 225 pounds, made a surprise entrance here this afternoon, and immediately was given a uniform and went through the Browns' workout on the Bowling Green University field.

"He could play a game tomorrow," said Brown after the squad had left the field. "We have the same plays, same formations, same signals we used at Great Lakes."

Ten days ago, Coach Brown popped his first surprise when Bill Willis, former all-American tackle from Ohio State, came here for a tryout. Willis, playing at guard, has been a sensation in practice.

Reprinted from
The Cleveland Plain Dealer

CLEVELAND ELEVEN WILL KEEP ADAMS

Court Upholds Tackle's Right to Play for Browns Instead of Los Angeles Rams

CLEVELAND, Aug. 29 (AP)—The legal right of tackle Chet Adams to play professional football with the All-American Conference's Cleveland Browns was upheld in Federal Court late today when Judge Emerich B. Freed denied an injunction sought by the champion Los Angeles Rams of the National Football League.

The Rams contended Adams had broken a contract signed with the Cleveland Rams before the team was moved to the West Coast. Judge Freed ruled the Cleveland Rams had ceased to exist as of the date of the transfer of their franchise to Los Angeles and that Adams' obligations under the contract became impossible of performance.

The 235-pound lineman, who played four seasons with the Cleveland Rams and one with the Green Bay Packers before entering the Army, is scheduled to play his first game with the Browns against the Brooklyn Dodgers in an exhibition at the Akron Rubber Bowl tomorrow night.

Adams was a Cleveland high school and Ohio University football star before signing with the Rams in 1939. He contended he wanted to finish his football days in Cleveland as his home town and the city of his employment off the gridiron.

RECORD 60,135 SEE BROWN SQUAD WIN

Cleveland All-America Eleven Beats Miami Seahawks, 44-0, as Groza Stars

CLEVELAND, Sept. 6 (AP)—Before the largest crowd ever to see a regularly-scheduled professional football game—60,135 paid—the Cleveland Browns launched the All-America Football Conference campaign tonight by smothering an offensively impotent Miami Seahawk club, 44 to 0.

The previous regular season record crowd was reported at the 57,000 mark, attracted by New York and Washington in the National Football League at the Polo Grounds several years ago.

Highlight of the contest as the kicking of Lou Groza, six-foot three-inch, 225-pound tackle from Martins Ferry, O., who booted five points after touchdown and three field goals for 14 points.

The line-up:

CLEVELAND (44)		MIAMI (0)
Speedie	L. E.	Ulrich
Daniel	L. T.	Olenski
Saban	L. G.	Taylor
Scarry	C. C.	Witlow
Groza	R. G.	Jungmichel
Adams	R. T.	Ellenson
Coppage	R. E.	Scott
Lewis	Q. B.	Tarrant
E. Jones	L. H.	Nelson
Greenwood	R. H.	Erdlitz
Fekete	F. B.	D. Jones

SCORE BY PERIODS

Cleveland .... 10 17 0 17—44
Miami .... 0 0 0 0—0

Touchdowns—Cleveland: Speedie, Lavelli (sub for Coppage), Colella (sub for E. Jones), Greenwood, Terrell (sub for Greenwood). Points after touchdown—Cleveland: Groza 5. Field Goals—Cleveland: Groza 3.

Officials—Hughitt, umpire; Slutz, referee; Gordon, head linesman; Gross, Young, judges.

FORTY-NINERS BOW TO N. Y. SQUAD, 21-7

Yankees of All-America Loop Win San Francisco Opener as Parker, Sanders Excel

SAN FRANCISCO, Sept. 8 (AP)—Combining crushing ground power with a clever passing attack, the New York Yankees defeated the San Francisco Forty-niners, 21 to 7, today in the new All-America Conference's official football season inaugural in Kezar Stadium before an estimated crowd of 35,000 fans.

FIELD GOALS HELP EAGLES BEAT RAMS

Zimmerman Boots Two, Lio One in 25-14 Victory as 30,500 Watch at Los Angeles

STATISTICS OF THE GAME

	Eagles.	Rams.
First downs	14	13
Yards gained, rushing	179	160
Forward passes	21	36
Forwards completed	11	11
Yards gained, forwards	175	118
Forwards intercepted by	4	0
*Av. dist. of punts, yds.	34.8	35.3
Run-back of punts, yds.	192	126
Opponent fumbles recov.	1	2
Yards lost, penalties	40	46

*From point where ball was kicked.

LOS ANGELES, Sept. 29 (AP)—A hard driving Philadelphia Eagles team today pounded and kicked a 25-14 victory over the champion Los Angeles Rams in the first National Football League game played in the West.

Some 30,500 fans braved a sweltering and occasionally sprinkling day to see the visitors repeat their last year's defeat of the former Cleveland team.

Owner of Rockets Sues George Halas

Chicago, Oct. 1.—(AP.)—Owner John L. Keeshin of the Chicago Rockets said today he had filed a $250,000 libel suit against Owner-Coach George Halas and the Chicago Bears as result of comment allegedly made by Halas regarding Keeshin's effort to sign Bears quarterback Sid Luckman as Rocket coach.

Keeshin said statements given to the press and radio by Halas yesterday were derrogatory.

Halas later said in a statement "I have been advised that the suit has been filed, but I haven't seen a copy of the complaint and I have referred the matter to my attorneys."

Meanwhile, Luckman announced he would "stick with Halas" in preference to a reported three to five year coaching contract with the Rockets at $25,000 annually.

PLAYERS RETAINED AS ROCKET COACHES

Wilkin, Dove and Mathews to Direct Chicago Pro Eleven for Rest of Season

CHICAGO, Oct. 2 (P)—John L. Keeshin, president of the Chicago Rockets, said today his All-America Football Conference club would be coached for the remainder of the season by the three players who took over the reins last week when Richard E. (Dick) Hanley and the Rockets parted company.

Keeshin's decision followed a 29-1 vote by members of the squad in favor of keeping the three player-coaches, rather than hiring a new head coach. The three are Wee Willie Wilkin, Bob Dove and New Mathews.

Keeshin, who yesterday filed a $250,000 libel suit against George Halas, owner-coach of the Chicago Bears of the National League, asserted he was "standing behind" his unique coaching triumvirate. "The trio will handle all coaching affairs for the balance of the Rockets' season," he said.

The suit against Halas was based on the latter's alleged remarks concerning Keeshin's effort to sign Sid Luckman, Bear quarterback, as Rocket coach.

Keeshin said he had talked to Luckman about taking over the job left vacant by Hanley last Wednesday just before a game here with Buffalo. Keeshin announced Hanley's resignation at that time, but Hanley told reporters he had been fired.

Keeshin said Chuck Palmer, coach at Chicago's Fenger High School, would serve as adviser to the player-coaches.

Record Pro Football Crowd of 71,134

BROWNS OUTPLAY DONS' SQUAD, 31-14

Cleveland Gains Seventh in Row in All-America Loop by Second-Half Surge

2 LONG RUNS BY MOTLEY

He Goes 49 and 68 Yards for Touchdowns—Groza Boots Field Goal From the 48

STATISTICS OF THE GAME

	Cleve.	Dons.
First downs	10	21
Yards gained rushing	224	274
Forwards attempted	10	20
Forwards completed	4	10
Yards gained, forwards	129	121
Forwards intercepted by	1	0
*Punting average	36	43.5
Run-back of kicks, yds.	54	143
Rival fumbles recovered	2	2
Yards lost, penalties	35	20

*From line of scrimmage.

CLEVELAND, Oct. 20 (P)—The unbeaten Cleveland Browns spotted Los Angeles a first period touchdown and then roared back to defeat the Dons, 31 to 14, in the stadium today before 71,134 fans, the largest crowd in professional football history. It was Cleveland's seventh straight victory and Los Angeles' second loss in the All-America Football Conference.

Cleveland Holds Statistical Edge In Pro Circuit

New York, Dec. 18.—(AP.)—Cleveland holds the statistical edge over the New York Yankees, going into Sunday's All-America Football Conference playoff game, by dominating the league in team offense and defense.

Paul Brown's Western Division champions scored more points than any team in the circuit, 423, and allowed fewer enemy scores, 137. The Yanks held the opposition to a total of 2620 yards in 14 games, best in the league, but the Cleveland team topped most of the other important departments of play.

The Browns made the most yards, 4244, to Los Angeles' 4142 and uncorked the best aerial offense with gains of 2266 to Brooklyn's 2258 yards. The San Francisco 49ers led in rushing yardage with 2175 to Buffalo's 2046 although the Bisons' average of 4.08 yards per rush was tops.

In dominating the final team statistics, Cleveland scored most touchdowns, 55, led in touchdowns by rushing, 33, and by passing, 22. They also added most extra points, 52, and most field goals, 13.

Despite their sweep of scoring honors, the Browns were fifth in first downs, a department topped by Los Angeles.

Three clubs finished above .500 in pass competitions, Los Angeles making connections with 54.3 per cent of its forwards.

Chicago Bears Win National League Grid Title

'BIG BETTOR' HELD UNDER $25,000 BAIL

Charged With Offering $2,500 Bribes To Two Giant Players

New York, Dec. 15 (AP)—With one man under $25,000 bail on a charge of bribing an athlete, New York police tonight pressed their investigation of an unsuccessful attempt to fix the National Football League's title game, in which the Chicago Bears downed the New York Giants, 24-14.

The probe, first of its kind here since the Brooklyn basketball scandal two years ago, was announced by Mayor William O'Dwyer, law-enforcement officials and league heads just a few hours before the two professional teams lined up at the Polo Grounds this afternoon.

Alvin J. Paris, a self-styled "big bettor" on athletic contests, was arraigned on a bribery charge, accused of having offered Merle Hapes and Frank Filchock, Giant backfield men, $2,500 each to agree not to play their best in the championship contest.

Police Exonerate Players

Police exonerated both players but Hapes was kept out of the game at the order of Bert Bell, commissioner of the league. Filchock, the key man in the Giants' backfield, played virtually all the game.

Bell announced that Hapes's $1,295.57 cut in the losers' $51,-823.19 player pool was being held up pending further hearing.

"It doesn't in any way mean that Hapes is guilty," Bell emphasized. "I feel it is only the proper procedure due to the circumstances."

The commissioner also emphasized that Filchock was completely exonerated.

"He is absolutely in the clear," Bell said.

LAST-QUARTER RALLY DECIDES

Luckman's Touchdown, Field Goal Break 14-14 Tie

New York, Dec. 15 (AP)—The Chicago Bears won the National Football League championship today by pushing over ten points in the fourth quarter to whip the New York Giants, 24 to 14, at the Polo Grounds.

For three periods, the game but out-weighed New Yorkers, fought Chicago on even terms, but the pressure of numbers told, and the Bears chalked up ten points in the final quarter to pull out a 24-to-14 victory and parade to their fifth championship in the fourteen years of the annual East-West classic.

Twice before the sectional play-off was first put into the books the Bears also brought home the loop crown to give them the all-time high of seven.

Records Are Broken

This one was one of the biggest, fanciest title games of them all, with records falling during the cold wintry afternoon of football. Financially, it was a huge success, with the greatest play-off crowd in history, 58,346 customers jamming the stands and ringing a louder tune on the cash registers than ever before for a gross gate of $282,955.25.

From this, each victorious Bear collected a new record winning players' share of $1,975.82, and each defeated Giant had a new high of $1,295.57 in take-home pay for a loser.

And on the gridiron, marks were shattered, with Sid Luckman eclipsing Sammy Baugh's playoff passing yardage record and, by tossing for one of the Bear touchdowns, breaking a tie between himself and the Redskin star for scoring through the air.

Passes To Kavanaugh

His touchdown toss was for 21 yards to Ken Kavanaugh, the long wingman from Louisiana State, early in the first quarter, marking the seventh time he had pitched for a tally in his playoff career.

That started the Bears on the way, and they made it 14-0 on a 39-yard gallop with an intercepted pass by Dante Magnani, the scatback from St. Mary's of California, just before the opening quarter closed.

But the Giants came back to score a touchdown in the first chapter on a 38-yard heave from Frank Filchock, the ex-Indiana passer who approached the "great" class today, to Hank Leibel. They tied it up in the third period when Filchock threw another point-making aerial to Steve Filipowicz, and for a while it seemed as if they might do the impossible and overturn the ten-point favorites.

Giants Suffer Setbacks

There was no doubt they reached their top height for the season as they fought and battled to come through despite injuries and a heavy blow when Merle Hapes was declared ineligible in the pre-dawn hours pending investigation of alleged bribery attempts to throw the championship tussle.

Things got even worse, for before the battle was half over, their kicking mainstay and best runner, Frank Reagan, ex-Penn player, was taken out with a broken nose, and George Franc, the 190-pound linebacker from Minnesota, was sidelined with a shoulder injury.

But in spite of their fierce fight, they just didn't have enough left when the Bears turned on the pressure.

Luckman Scores

Early in the fourth quarter, Luckman scored on a 19-yard quarterback sneak to top off a 70-yard drive. Then Frank Maznicki, the expert kicker from Boston College, booted a 26-yard field goal in the fading minutes and put the decision beyond hope for the Giants.

"Only Thing Against Hapes"

"The only thing we have against Hapes," Bell declared, "is that he did not bring the story directly to Steve Owen or any of the Giant officials."

Filchock, who played a tremendous game for the Giants, said flatly in the dressing room after the contest, "I don't know a thing about it."

Both the police and league officials said the investigation would continue "to see if it will lead anywhere else or if anyone else is involved" in what appeared to be the biggest scandal in the sports world since the infamous Black Sox World Series of 1919.

George Monoghan, assistant district attorney, said that Paris, 28-year-old officer of a novelty company, had signed a statement in which he said he had offered Hapes and Filchock $2,500 in cash for each, plus a $1,000 bet for each of them on the Bears to win if the two Giant players would "lay down" in the game with Chicago.

$20,000 Bet Reported

Both players refused, Monoghan said, but Paris "called his associates and said he could do business with the pair" and the associates then bet $20,000 on the Bears to win by ten points.

[Editor's Note—The Bears won by ten points.]

Cleveland Beats New York, 14-9

GRAHAM STARS FOR WINNERS

41,181 See Browns Subdue Yankees In Pro Game

Cleveland, Dec. 22 (AP)—Otto Graham, playing his first year of professional football, brought his Cleveland mates the championship of the young All-America Football Conference today by guiding them to a 14-to-9 victory over the New York Yankees in a snow-flecked playoff game.

It was Graham, a college star at Northwestern, who pitched for 50 of the 69 yards the Browns traveled in the second period for their first touchdown and it was the same dark-haired athlete who flung a 16-yard aerial to Dante Lavelli for the second touchdown, with only four minutes to go in the final quarter.

And then when the New Yorkers, who had been out in front by 9 to 7, came driving back, it was Graham who intercepted an Ace Parker pass to halt the frantic drive. Graham jumped between a pair of New Yorkers with such fury, he lost a part of his shirt—but he came up with the ball.

41,181 Fans Attend

Being without a part of a shirt wasn't the correct thing for this playoff game that lured 41,181 fans to snow-covered Municipal Stadium. The 5-inch fall of Friday and Saturday night was heaped on the sidelines and a fine sifting of snow drifted down all during the fray.

The gridiron itself had been protected before game time by a tarpaulin, but the frozen condition of the turf hampered play. The temperature, however, stayed near the freezing point, in contrast to the "refrigeration bowl" of last year when the Cleveland Rams defeated the Washington Redskins, 15 to 14, in two-below weather for the National League title.

The victory, Cleveland's third over New York this year, thus meant the title of the first All-America Conference season went to a collection of professional youngsters, coached by Paul Brown, who was coaching the Massillon (Ohio) High School six years ago.

16 Passes Click

Graham threw 27 passes during the title contest and 16 of them found their targets for 213 yards. One of the tosses was intercepted.

Not only did he do all the Browns' passing, but his play-calling on the ice-crested field brought raves from other league coaches who watched from the shelter of the press box.

ALL-AMERICA LOOP AWARDS FRANCHISE TO BALTIMORE CLUB

Group Headed by Rodenberg Acquires Pro Football Rights Relinquished by Miami

FLORIDA PLAYERS IN DEAL

25 Drafted College Stars Also Involved—Dan Topping and MacPhail Among Backers

By The Associated Press.

BALTIMORE, Dec. 28—The All-America Professional Football Conference announced today a delayed Christmas present for Baltimore—a franchise in the new one-year-old league, supplanting the defunct Miami Seahawks.

The announcement was made at a news conference attended by James Crowley, All-America commissioner, and Robert D. Rodenberg of Washington, who was awarded the franchise at a figure of "around $100,000."

Baltimore made a strong bid for the franchise at the All-America meeting in Cleveland on Dec. 20, and although the decision was deferred, Crowley disclosed today that club owners had adopted unanimously a resolution favoring Baltimore.

Final decision was made, Crowley said, at a meeting in New York on Dec. 26.

Rodenberg and his associates, from Washington, have agreed to post a $250,000 guarantee at the annual conference meeting in New York on Jan. 27, and Crowley said "I understand the funds already have been subscribed to."

The Baltimore club will drop the name "Seahawks," Rodenberg said, and residents of the city will be asked to submit a name in a contest to be conducted soon.

Rodenberg said Baltimore had been awarded contractual rights to players on the Miami roster, and disclosed that the recent league draft in Cleveland had made twenty-five college players eligible to Baltimore.

Although they must bid against opposition from the National Football League, Rodenberg said that two of them were All-America selections this year, Guard Weldon Humble of Rice and End Elmer Madar of Michigan.

Two Backs Drafted

Also drafted were two backs, Ernie Case of U. C. L. A., All-America second team selection, and Arnold Tucker of Army, third All-America team choice. In addition there was Hubert Bechtol of Texas, 1944-1945 All-America End.

Crowley said that Miami had first call on the services of Charles Trippi, All-America back from Georgia this year, but that the league decided to permit the New York Yankees to take Trippi in a trade with Baltimore for three players. This was done to permit the Yankees to bid for Trippi's services as a baseball player as well.

Crowley said Dan Topping, Yankee football owner and part owner of the Yankee baseball club, would be joined by Del Webb and Larry MacPhail of the baseball Yankees in backing the football team.

Rodenberg said his associates were J. C. Herbert Bryant, Alexandria, Va., business man and former University of Virginia football player; Karl Corby, Washington realtor; his brother, William R. Rodenberg, Washington attorney, and Mrs. Agnes Shevlin, Washington furniture store executive.

Rodenberg announced the names of the college players drafted at the recent Cleveland meeting, including three All-America selections, to which he would have access.

In addition to Humble, Rice guard; Madar, Michigan end, and Bechtol, the others are:

BACKS—Arnold Tucker, Army; Ernie Case, U. C. L. A.; Leo Daniels, Texas A. and M.; Jim Canady, Texas; Gerald Doherty, Delaware; Rudolph Mobley, Hardin-Simmons; Tommy Mont, Maryland; Tex Reilly, Colorado; Vic Schwall, Northwestern; John Sims, Tulane; Howard Turner, North Carolina State.

ENDS—Bill Baumgartner, Minnesota; Franklin Hubbell, Tennessee; John North, Vanderbilt.

TACKLES—Russ Deal, Indiana; Jim Kekeris, Missouri; Jim Landrigan, Holy Cross; Don Malmberg, U. C. L. A.; Tony Stalloni, Delaware.

GUARDS—Harold Brown, Indiana; Gaston Burgeois, Tulane; Gene Lamoure, Fresno State; B. Vanderclute, Wesleyan.

CENTER—James Brieske, Michigan.

RECEIVE FULL PRO GAME CUT

Filchock And Hapes Paid Losers' Share Of Pool

New York, Jan. 10 (AP)—Frank Filchock and Merle Hapes, who were offered bribes to throw last month's National Football League championship, were paid their $1.295.57 shares from the player's pool, it was learned today, although Hapes was barred from the game and authorities knew before the kickoff that Filchock had been approached.

Filchock's cut in the players' pool was paid to him shortly after the December 15 game. Hapes' slice of the playoff pie, it was learned, was sent to him only yesterday, after both players had been questioned by National League Commissioner Bert Bell.

At the time the case broke—early on the morning of the game—Bell issued a statement that Hapes' share would be held up pending further investigation.

Reached at his office later, Bell explained "there is nothing in the National League constitution" by which the money could have been withheld from the ex-Mississippi Back. He pointed out that the Giant players, in their regular prechampionship game meeting, "voted full shares" to both Hapes and Filchock, and that therefore, under league rules, they had to be paid.

Trippe Receives Offer Of $60,000

New York, Jan. 11 (AP)—Charley Trippi, Georgia's All-America halfback, arrived here today and found an offer of $60,000 awaiting him to play football for the next four years for the New York Yankees of the All-America Conference.

Trippi went immediately into a huddle with Owner Dan Topping and Coach Ray Flaherty of the Football Yankees and Larry MacPhaoil, president of the baseball Yankees, who are trying to land him for both clubs.

Whether they reached an agreement was not made known immediately. Trippi is one of the most sought-after athletes in collegiate ranks today because of his ability on both the gridiron and the baseball diamond.

The Georgia ace told newsmen that Charles Bidwell, owner of the Chicago Cardinals in the National Football League, had agreed to match Topping's offer of a four-year contract at $15,000 a year, plus a bonus.

He also has been offered $30,000 to sign a baseball contract with the Boston Red Sox, Trippi disclosed.

BELL GRANTED GRID POWERS

National Pro League Moves To Crush Attempted Fixes

Chicago, Jan. 23 (AP)—The National Football League today gave Commissioner Bert Bell dictatorial power designed to crush attempted fixing of its games, including life banishment of implicated players.

The ten-member league also studied a membership bid by the San Francisco Clippers, of the Pacific Coast Football League, a minor league affiliate in the same town in which the All-America Conference has a major league entry.

League officials, opening a three-day session, unanimously amended its constitution to give Commissioner Bell virtually the same blanket authority regarding gambling that professional baseball extended the late Kenesaw Mountain Landis after the "Black Sox" scandal of 1919.

May Banish Offenders

Spurred by the attempted "fix" by a New York gambler of its title playoff between the New York Giants and the Chicago Bears last month, the National circuit empowered Bell not only to banish or otherwise punish any of its personnel involved in a fix or attempted fix, but also to bar from league parks any person deemed "detrimental to the best interests of the National Football League and/or professional football."

The latter was aimed at known gamblers or other "easy money" gentry who customarily frequent pro football games. Presumably a list of such persons would be given special police details for ejection at each park.

Judge Landis often buttonholed police at baseball games during his regime as commissioner and pointed out certain characters he wanted tossed out of the park for gambling.

Code Not Retroactive

The revised code is not retroactive and will not affect the case of Backs Frank Filchock and Merle Hapes, of the Giants, who were offered bribes in the playoff game.

However, the two players are suspended indefinitely and Bell can end their National League careers by failing to approve their contracts in final settlement of the case, which still is being investigated by the New York district attorney.

Under the amended constitution, any player, official or employé who has knowledge of a bribe offer or who receives "an offer directly or indirectly, by insinuation or by implication to control or fix, or accepts or bets anything of value on a professional football game in any manner whatsoever," must report the instance to his club officials or the commissioner.

Fine Also Applicable

Failure to do so will be punishable by suspension for life, indefinitely or a specified time, and/or a fine up to $2,000, cancellation of contract, and/or sale of stock or any interests whatsoever of the guilty party be it "member club, club officer, league officer, director, player, coach, official or employé."

The commissioner's decision in such cases will be final and without appeal.

The bid for a San Francisco franchise was presented by Frank Ciraolo, owner of the San Francisco Clippers, and J. Rufus Klawans, commissioner of the Pacific Coast League.

SEARCH IS ON FOR 3D 'FIXER'

Believed To Be Key Figure In Football Bet Case

New York, Jan. 28 (AP)—David (Pete) Krakauer, said by the district attorney's office to have handled $70,000 in bets in a day, was sought tonight in a nation-wide hunt on charges of being a key figure in the professional football title game bribery case.

A district attorney spokesman identified Krakauer, 44-year-old ex-convict, as the third man indicted yesterday by a grand jury on the word of Alvin J. Paris, who was convicted January 8 of offering bribes in an attempt to fix the December 15 contest.

The police alarm, flashed at the request of Frank S. Hogan, district attorney, identified Krakauer as a "known gambler" who "may frequent race tracks and seashore resorts."

Disappeared From Hospital

Krakauer was questioned at a Bronx hospital last month in the football investigation, but he disappeared from there. He was being treated for a cardiac ailment.

The two others indicted—Harvey Stemmer and Jerome Zarowitz—pleaded innocent at their arraignment today. Zarowitz was held in $10,000 bail. Stemmer already is serving a penitentiary term for attempted bribery of Brooklyn College basketball players in 1945.

Zarowitz, 32, was said by police to have been a clerk in the Elizabeth (N.J.) office of a gambling ring, for which Paris was front man.

The trio were indicted on two bribery counts and one conspiracy count each in the football-fix scheme.

Tell Of Bribe Offers

Frank Filchock and Merle Hapes, New York Giants' backfield stars, testified at Paris's trial they were offered bribes of $2,500 each and a $1,000 bet on the Chicago Bears, plus off-season jobs supposed to bring them $15,000. The Bears won the National League championship game, 24 to 14.

Police said that tapped conversations on Paris's telephone line disclosed that Stemmer participated in the scheme through telephone calls made from Bellevue Hospital where he was assigned as a trusty from Ricker's Island Penitentiary.

Hogan's office steadily pushed its investigation today into attempts of gamblers to penetrate boxing and professional football in New York, questioning numerous Broadway habitués, sports figures and gamblers.

"Jacobs Beach" Is Rocked

Meanwhile, denizens of "Jacobs Beach," headquarters of the New York fistic fraternity at Madison Square Garden, were rocked by the revelation that a $100,000 bribe had been offered hard-punching Rocky Graziano to throw a fight.

JUDGE DECRIES SPORTS BRIBES

Alvin Paris Scheduled To Be Sentenced Monday

New York, April 2 (AP)—General Sessions Judge Saul S. Streit handed out prison terms today to three men convicted of trying to fix a professional football title game after declaring they "attempted to destroy the faith and confidence of the public in American sport."

Sentences of five to ten years were given David Krakauer and Harvey Stemmer while Jerome Zarowitz received an indeterminate sentence with a maximum of three years.

The three were convicted March 9, largely on the testimony of Alvin J. Paris, of scheming with Paris to offer bribes to two New York Giants backfield stars to lay down in their December 15 National League championship contest with the Chicago Bears.

Paris Convicted In January

Paris, dapper 28-year-old playboy, had been convicted on similar charges in January, but sentence was deferred until after the trial of his accomplices. He is scheduled to be sentenced next Monday.

After asserting "Americans are a sports-loving people" and pointing out that 12,000,000 persons attended college grid games last year as well as many additional millions at professional contests, Judge Streit said:

"Athletes become models for millions of youngsters throughout the nation.

"The public, youth and adult as well, has faith in its athletes, and anyone who tampers with this faith and corrupts an athlete or a sport, injures the confidence of millions of people who believe they are witnessing contests played in the American tradition of honesty and fair play."

Was Serving Prison Term

Stemmer, 37, was serving a prison sentence for attempted bribery of Brooklyn College basketball players at the time of the football fix plot. Testimony at the trial indicated he left the prison on several occasions and made numerous phone calls to Paris. He completed the basketball sentence last Friday.

Judge Streit sentenced Stemmer to two consecutive terms of two and a half to five years each on two bribery convictions in the football case, and suspended sentence on a conspiracy count.

Krakauer, 42, who has a record of six previous convictions and once was described by the district attorney's office as a gambler, handling $70,000 in bets in a day, was given a five to ten year term on a bribery count and a suspended sentence on a conspiracy count.

Zarowitz, 33, who had testified he was a clerk in an Elizabeth (N.J.) bookmaking establishment run by Paris's stepfather, Eddie Ginsberg, was convicted only on a conspiracy count.

Grid Loop Rules On Eligibility

Pittsburgh, July 20 (AP)—The National Football League today adopted a rule prohibiting the signing of players who retain intercollegiate eligibility beyond the time their classes normally would have graduated.

The ruling bans signing of college stars for the professional league who register for classes after an absence—such as war service—and thus retain eligibility beyond their normal graduation year.

The ruling was not retroactive. Previously, the league's bidding for players was limited to men whose original classes had graduated or who had received a diploma in an accelerated course.

Players signed under the old ruling will remain under contract under today's broadened rule.

League Commissioner Bert Bell announced the new ruling was part of the circuit's "avowed desire to cooperate with the colleges and prevent 'raiding.' "

Asked whether the rival All-America conference would be requested to draft a similar rule, Bell said:

"We tend strictly to our own business."

Filchock And Hapes Suspended Indefinitely In Pro Grid 'Fix'

Philadelphia, April 3 (AP)—Merle Hapes and Frank Filchock, New York Giants' backfield players who became entangled in gamblers' attempts to fix the National Football League's championship game last December 15, today were suspended indefinitely in the latest chapter of the biggest sport scandal since the 1919 World Series.

League Commissioner Bert Bell announced that he had found the two "guilty of actions deterimental to the welfare of the National League and of professional football," adding:

"This suspension prevents the employment of Hapes or Filchock by any club in the National Football League as player, coach or in any capacity whatsoever."

3 New Yorkers Sentenced

The commissioner's ruling all but wrote finis to the playing days of Hapes, who once roamed the backfield at the University of Mississippi, and Filchock, pro star since leaving Indiana University campus.

The decision came just 24 hours after three New York men had been sentenced for attempting to bribe the players to throw the game. David K. Krakauer, Harvey Stemmer and Jerome Zarowitz were given prison sentences while a fourth man, Alvin Paris, will be sentenced Monday.

Testimony at the trial of the four showed that neither Hapes nor Filchock accepted the offered bribe. Both were placed on the league's suspended list originally on January 8, the day Paris was convicted in New York on charges of trying to fix the game between the Giants and Chicago Bears.

Neither Player Accepted

Hapes, however, was not permitted to play in the game, won by the Bears, 24-10. The former Mississippi star admitted to Mayor William O'Dwyer of New York a few hours before the game that he received the offer. Filchock, a great passer playing with the Giants for the first season after understudying Sammy Baugh at Washington, denied he had been approached.

During the Paris trial, however, Filchock admitted he had not told the New York Mayor the truth. Paris testified that he made an offer of $2,500 in cash and a $1,000 bet to Hapes a week before the game. Two days later, he said he made the same offer to the ex-Indiana player.

Paris also testified that neither player accepted. During the week before the title game, he said he attempted to change their minds, but the day before the fray became convinced they would not accept the offers.

Hapes Comments On Ruling

Bell, while declining to comment on his ruling, pointed out that he gave the two players the limit—except for a possible fine—under the rules in effect at the time of the bribe attempt.

He added, however, that had the code adopted at the league's January meeting been in force, he would have had the power to bar both for life.

Hapes, who recently accepted a coaching position at the Bryan Consolidated School near Jackson, Miss., said that he felt Commissioner Bell's action "was a little bit stiff."

"It's a bunch of baloney about hurting the league," he added. "All that they got against us is just not reporting the attempt. I didn't think we did anything to hurt the league.

"But I'm through with professional football, anyway."

Filchock, who lives in Washington, was not immediately available for comment.

Charles Bidwell Dies In Chicago Hospital

Chicago, April 19 (AP)—Charles W. Bidwill, owner of the Chicago Cardinals professional football team, died today of pneumonia in St. George's Hospital.

The 51-year-old lawyer and sportsman died at 8.40 A.M., after lapsing into a coma several days ago. He was placed in an oxygen tent shortly after he was stricken with pneumonia last Tuesday.

Besides owning the Cardinals, Bidwill was president of the National Jockey Club which operates the Sportsmen's Park race track in Suburban Cicero, and was also managing director of the Hawthorne race track, also in Cicero.

The
PHILADELPHIA EAGLES
NATIONAL FOOTBALL LEAGUE
1947 SEASON TICKET

EST. PRICE $21.53
FED. TAX 4.31
CITY AMUSE. TAX 2.16   TOTAL $28.00

THIS PRICE INCLUDES TICKETS FOR
7 GAMES (FIRST GAME AT MUNICIPAL STADIUM)
SHIBE PARK Lehigh Ave. at 21st St.

EAST STAND

Sec.

Row

Seat

BROWNS OPEN A.-A.PLAY,30-14, OVER BUFFALO

Good Start

CLEVELAND [30]		BUFFALO [14]
Speedie	L.E.	Gibson
Blandin	L.T.	Duggan
Ulinski	L.G.	Lahar
Scarry	C.	Corley
Willis	R.G.	Pirro
Simonetti	R.T.	Doherty
Lavelli	R.E.	Coppage
Graham	Q.B.	Ratterman
Jones	L.E.	Bykovich
Colella	R.H.	Koch
Motley	F.B.	Tomasetti

Buffalo	0	0	14	0—14
Cleveland	13	14	0	3—30

Touchdowns—Cleveland: Jones, Motley [2], Lavelli; Buffalo: Tomasetti, Coppage. Points after touchdowns—Cleveland: Groza [3]; Buffalo: Juzwik [2]. Field goal—Cleveland: Groza.

[Chicago Tribune Press Service]

Cleveland, Sept. 6—The Cleveland Browns are off and running again. Last night they struck for 27 quick points, then allowed the Buffalo Bills to get out of the gridiron doghouse long enough to score a couple of touchdowns. A crowd of 63,263 watched the 1946 champions in their rather easily attained 30 to 14 triumph.

There might have been more of Ohio's football minded fans in the Municipal stadium except for a rainstorm which hit the city and environs just before the dinner hour. But the turnout scored a slight decision over that at the opening All-America conference game here last year when 60,133 watched the Browns rout Miami, 44 to 0.

Among interested spectators at the contest was the entire coaching staff of the National league Chicago Bears. George Halas, Luke Johnsos, Paddy Driscoll, and Gene Ronzani, in nearby Akron for Sunday's exhibition with the Boston Yanks, came over from that city to have a look. Apparently they saw plenty.

Otto Graham's sharp passing, long runs by Edgar [Special Delivery] Jones and Ermal Allen, rookie from Kentucky, put the Bills back on their heels when they yielded two touchdowns in each of the first two periods. Buffalo, which had upset the New York Yankees last week, oddly enough owed its brief prosperity this evening to a powerful running game which netted two scores in the third period.

George Ratterman, the Bills' gifted young quarter back, did not get adequate protection and three of his passes were intercepted in the scond quarter, one of them resulting in a touchdown. Chet Mutryn, a former Brownie, was the most effective runner for the outclassed Bills.

Ratterman completed only three out of 16 passes, while Graham had a .500 rating with 12 good ones in 25 pitches.

Reprinted from
The Chicago Tribune

Sept. 8

HILLENBRAND LEADS ATTACK

Local Pros Score On First And Second Half Kickoffs

By ROBERT ELMER

Two runs of 95 and 57 yards each by Billy Hillenbrand led the Colts to a 16-7 victory over the Brooklyn Dodgers in Baltimore's All-America Professional Football Conference opener yesterday in the Stadium.

Scoring both touchdowns on the first and second-half kickoffs and adding a clinching field goal in the final period, the Colts got off to a most auspicious start, and the crowd of 27,418, which suffered through intermittent rain and sunshine, went home elated over the surprising result.

Having lost two exhibition games, and being a new team, the Colts were the decided underdog. But, after being outplayed in the first thirty minutes, they rallied sharply in the final half to win.

Teams Put On Fine Show

Despite the poor football weather, which is believed to have cut the crowd, the two teams put on a fine show, and very few spectators left the premises before the final gun.

The rain and muddy field hampered Brooklyn's principal attacking weapon—the passing of Glenn Dobbs—but it was the strong second half rally by the Colts which proved too much for the visitors.

Trailing 7-6 at half time, the Colts promptly touched off a demonstration among their many rooters, when Hillenbrand took Brooklyn's kickoff on his own five-yard line and raced 95 yards for a touchdown.

Nemeth Kicks Extra Point

The former Indiana star received Phil Martinowich's kickoff on his own five, about a like distance from the west side line. Picking up steam, he moved swiftly over the soft turf, but appeared to be a dead duck as a convoy of Brooklyn defenders closed in on the 35.

However, the elusive halfback managed to wriggle his way clear, and with the help of a key block by Johnny Mellus went the rest of the way unmolested. Nemeth came off the bench to placekick the extra point and give the Colts a 13-7 lead.

Reprinted from The Baltimore Sun

Stadium Lineup

Colts		Brooklyn
Brchtol	L.E.	McCarthy
Mellus	L.T.	Ruby
French	L.G.	Bernhardt
Phillips	C.	Gibson
Lio	R.G.	Buffington
Pernich	R.T.	Williams
Sigurdson	R.E.	Nelson
Schwenk	Q.B.	McDonald
Hillenbrand	L.H.	Harris
Terrell	R.H.	Gafford
Castiglia	F.B.	Colmer

Score by quarters:

Colts	6	0	7	3—16
Brooklyn	7	0	0	0—7

Touchdowns—Colts: Castiglia, Hillenbrand; Brooklyn: Dobbs. Points after touchdowns—Nemeth, Martinowich. Field Goal—Case. Substitutions: ends, Getchell, Davis, Meyers, Baumgartner; tackles, Klug, Kasap, Hekkers, Landrigan; gu rds, Higgins, Marine, Yokas, Zorich; centers, Kodba, Handley, Nolander; backs, Galvin, Mobley, Dudish, Mertes, Nemeth, Vardian, Cure, Wright, Case. Brooklyn: ends, Patanelli, Scruggs, Hein; tackles, Wetz, Daukas, Huneke, Meiszkowski; guards, W. Jones, Jeffers, A. Harris; centers, Gustafson, Warrington; backs, Tackett, Dub Jones, Akins, Perina, Tevis, Dobbs, Nygren. Time of periods—15 minutes.

Statistics

Colts		Dodgers
9	First downs	8
5	Rushing	7
4	Passing	1
0	Penalty	0
59	Net yards rushing	89
111	Net yards forwards	19
170	Net yards rushing and passing	112
19	Forwards attempted	11
11	Forwards completed	3
0	Intercepted by	2
0	Yards interceptions return	27
13	Yards lost attempting to pass	0
3	Punts, number	6
34.3	Punts, average*	45
3	Returned by	2
0	Blocked by	0
226	Yards kicks returned	58
92	Punts returned	19
134	Kickoffs returned	79
0	Field goal attempts returned	0
3	Fumbles	8
3	Ball lost	4
1	Penalties	2
5	Yards lost on penalties	13
16	Final score	7
2	Touchdowns	1
1	Conversions	1
1	Goals from field	0
0	Safeties	0

*From point of kick.

Filchock's Grid Playing Causes Stir In Canada

Hamilton. Ont., Sept. 13 (AP)—Frank Filchock, husky back who has been bounced out of pro football in both the United States and Canada, played in the Hamilton-Ottawa game today and immediately touched off another incident.

Filchock was barred from United States play because he failed to report a bribe attempt last December while a member of the New York Giants. Recently the Big Four League of Canada, of which both Ottawa and Hamilton are members, also barred him.

Eddie Langs, president of the Hamilton team, said only that "of course, Frank will play for us." Eddie Emerson, head of the Ottawa team, said he felt his club had won the game by forfeit the moment Filchock stepped on the field.

League President Doug Chilman said he was trying to arrange a league meeting for next week to iron out the matter but that Ottawa refused to attend.

Because of the pregame publicity regarding the case, more than 12,000 spectators watched today's game.

Pro Football Star Killed in Crash

Chicago, Oct. 24. (AP.) Jefferson Davis Burkett, 26, Chicago Cardinals punting star, was aboard a United Airlines DC-6 plane which crashed today at Bryce Canyon, Utah, the airlines said.

Burkett underwent an appendectomy last Saturday and was unable to return to Chicago with his professional football team Monday after its game last Sunday with the Los Angeles Rams.

Burkett, former three-sport athlete at Louisiana State University, prior to missing Sunday's game against Los Angeles, led the National Football League in punting with an average of 47.4 yards on 11 kicks. It was his first professional season.

Dec. 10

BUD SCHWENK TAKES HONORS

Colts' Quarterback Led In Pass Completions

By STUART B. McIVER

Bud Schwenk, Colts' quarterback, threw more passes and completed more than any other player in the All-America Conference during the past season, final statistics for 1947 revealed.

Schwenk completed five more passes than did Otto Graham, quarterback for the Cleveland Browns, but Graham had a higher percentage of completions.

Graham will appear in a playoff game against the New York Yankees Sunday for the conference championship. He will probably surpass Schwenk's completion total in that game—but Bud will still hold the mark for regular season play.

Schwenk, who last year was Graham's understudy at Cleveland, threw 327 passes and completed 168 for 2,236 yards. Thirteen of his passes were completed for touchdowns. His completion and attempt totals set new records not only for the conference but for all pro football.

Graham's 163 completions out of 269 attempts gave him a total of 2,753 yards—tops for the circuit—and his 25 touchdown passes also were the most any player tossed.

Reprinted from
The Baltimore Sun

Spec Sanders, of the Yankees led the conference in rushing, total offense and in scoring. Sanders rushed 1,432 yards and passed for 1,442 more for a total of 2,874 yards, 49 more than Graham amassed. Schwenk was third in total offense with 2,294.

Sanders scored 19 touchdowns for 114 points. The top scorer for the Colts was Billy Hillenbrand who had 12 touchdowns good for 60 points.

Mac Speedie and Dante Davell Cleveland ends, finished one-two in pass receiving. Speedie caught 6 passes for 1,146 yards and Lavel caught 49 for 799 yards.

Lamar Davis caught more passes than any other Colts—46 for 51 yards — but Hillenbrand gained more yardage by pass receiving 702.

The best punting average was compiled by Mickey Colmer, Brooklyn, who averaged 44.7 yards for 56 kicks. John Galvin, of the Colts, kicked 66 times for an average of 36 yards.

Hillenbrand was third in punt returns and fourth in kickoff returns. Glenn Dobbs, of Los Angeles, returned 19 punts 215 yards for the best record, while Hillenbrand ran back 13 for 201 yards.

Chet Mutryn, of Buffalo, returned 21 kickoffs 691 yards. Hillenbrand's total was 466 yards for 18 returns.

The Colts also permitted the longest pass interception return and the longest field goal to be scored against them. At Chicago Bill Bass of the Rockets ran one of Schwenk's passes back 82 yards and at the Stadium here, Ben Agajanian kicked a 53-yard field goal for the Dons.

CHRISTMAN STARS IN 30-21 TRIUMPH

His Passes Beat Bears and Give Chicago Cards Their First Title in Division

48,632 WATCH STRUGGLE

Victors Hold Command After Dimancheff Goes 50 Yards to Score in First Period

STATISTICS OF THE GAME

	Cards.	Bears.
First downs	10	20
Yards gained, rushing	82	155
Forward passes	22	38
Forwards completed	10	16
Yards gained, forwards	247	352
Forwards intercepted by	4	1
*Av. dist. of punts, yds.	35.9	39
†Run-back of kicks, yds.	61	114
Rival fumbles recovered	2	1
Yards lost, penalties	70	102

*From line of scrimmage.
†Includes punts and kick-offs.

CHICAGO, Dec. 14 (AP)—The inspired Chicago Cardinals scored on an 80-yard touchdown play the first time they got the ball today to touch off a drive that carried them to a 30-21 triumph over the Chicago Bears and to their first Western Division pennant in the history of the National Football League.

The Bears' great quarterback, Sid Luckman, was constantly rushed off his feet by the aggressive Cardinals and as a result Luckman had one of his poorest days of the season. Thus the Redbirds, for the first time in pro football history, captured their third consecutive triumph over their Chicago city rivals.

The victory, gained before a record football crowd of 48,632 for Wrigley Field, also marked the first time since 1922 that the Southsiders had beaten the Bears twice in a single season, having trounced them, 31—7, in October.

The Cardinals nipped the Bears, 35-28, in the final pro game in Chicago last season with the club's owner Charlie Bidwill cheering them on. Bidwill then set out to make a championship outfit for 1947, signing Charlie Trippi for $100,000. Shortly after building the structure for a strong title contender, Bidwill died.

Mrs. Bidwill Sees Victory

His dreams were realized today. His widow, who has seen the Cards win nine while dropping three games this season, and his two sons, Bill and Charles Jr., yelled themselves hoarse. Bill was on the sidelines with the club throughout the contest.

On Dec. 28 here in Comiskey Park, the Cardinals will play next Sunday's winner of the Philadelphia Eagles-Pittsburgh Steelers game for the national crown. The Eagles tied the Steelers by beating the Green Bay Packers, 28—14, today, forcing a play-off for Eastern honors.

The line-up:

CARDINALS (30)		BEARS (21)
Dewell	L.E.	Kavanaugh
Bulger	L.T.	Davis
Arms	L.G.	Drulis
Banonis	C.	Turner
Apolskis	R.G.	Bray
Mauldin	R.T.	Stickel
Kutner	R.E.	Keane
Christman	Q.B.	Luckman
Trippi	L.H.	Kindt
Goldberg	R.H.	Gallarneau
Harder	F.B.	J. Osmanski

SCORE BY PERIODS

Cardinals	14	13	0	3—30
Bears	7	0	0	14—21

Touchdowns—Dimancheff, Kavanaugh, Angsman 2, Keane, Sacrinty, Kutner. Points after touchdown—Harder 3, McLean 3 (placements). Field goal—Harder (placement).

SUBSTITUTES

Cardinals—Ends: Ivy, Doolan, Parker. Tackles: Zimny, Spot. Coomer, Plasman. Guards: Andros, Nichols. Centers: Blackburn, Campbell. Backs: Angsman, Mallouf, Cochran, Schwall, DeCorrevont, Rankin, Dimancheff. Bears—Ends: Jarmoluk, Cifers, Smith. Sprinkle. Tackles: Kolman, Ecker, Hartman. Guards: Milner, Preston. Centers: Clarkson. Garrett. Backs: Fenimore, Farris, Gulyanics. Holovak, McAfee, McLean, Minini, Mullins. W. Osmanski, Reader, Sacrinty.

103

Van Buren Gets 3 Touchdowns As Philadelphia Scores, 28-14

Eagles Trip Packers and Deadlock Steelers for Eastern Laurels—Ace Back Sets a New Ground-Gaining Record for League

PHILADELPHIA, Dec. 14 (AP)—Steve Van Buren scored three touchdowns and set a new National Football League ground-gaining record today to lead the Philadelphia Eagles to a 28-to-14 victory over the Green Bay Packers and tie for the Eastern division title with the Pittsburgh Steelers.

The Eagles and Steelers will meet in Pittsburgh next Sunday to determine the Eastern representative in the league championship play off at Chicago against the Cardinals on Dec. 28.

Van Buren plunged one yard in the first period; two yards in the second quarter and galloped 38 yards through a demoralized Packer defense in the third session he gained a total of 96 yards to eclipse the rushing efforts of Beattie Feathers for the Chicago Bears in 1934. Feathers gained 1,004 yards on 117 carries, while Van Buren netted 1,008 yards in 217 attempts.

Statistics of the Game

	Phila.	Gr. Bay
First downs	17	17
Yards gained, rushing	178	167
Forward passes	19	39
Forwards completed	12	16
Yards gained, forwards	220	220
Forwards intercepted by	6	1
*Av. dist. of punts, yds.	47	31.2
‡Run-back of kicks, yds.	68	109
Rival fumbles recovered	0	1
Yards lost, penalties	120	67

*From line of scrimmage.
‡Includes punts and kick-offs.

AAFC CLUB ATTENDANCE RECORD

Club	Date	Opponent	Attendance
Baltimore	9/28/47	New York	51,583*
Brooklyn	9/12/47	Cleveland	18,876
Buffalo	11/ 2/47	Cleveland	43,167*
Chicago	9/13/46	Cleveland	51,962
Cleveland	10/ 5/47	New York	80,067*
Los Angeles	9/12/47	New York	82,675†
New York	11/23/47	Cleveland	70,060*
San Francisco	10/26/47	Cleveland	54,523*

* City professional record
† All-time professional record

Cleveland Beats New York, 14-3

OTTO GRAHAM PACES ATTACK

Back Leads Browns To Second Straight Crown

New York, Dec. 14 (AP)—Otto Graham passed and directed the Cleveland Browns to a second straight All-America Conference title today in a 14-to-3 triumph over the New York Yankees.

The same two teams tangled a year ago at Cleveland, in the first championship playoff, and the Browns won that one, 14 to 9. Although this was the sixth time the two elevens have met, the Yankees played as if this was their first encounter with Graham.

The Northwestern alumnus scored the first Brown marker on a quarterback sneak and set up the second with his passing. Thus for the third straight year a Cleveland eleven is champion of a major pro loop. Prior to the Brown triumph of a year ago, the erstwhile Rams had mastered all foes in the National League.

61,879 View Game

It was Graham, completing 14 passes out of 21 attempts for 112 yards, who denied the Yankees the right to place the All-America grid crown beside the World Series trophies won in baseball earlier this fall. And for the second year he kept Ray Flaherty, Yankee coach, from becoming the only mentor to have had championships in both the National and the All-America.

A thermometer that hovered near the freezing mark kept the crowd down to 61,879, of whom 60,103 paid.

But the cold and the frozen field didn't handicap Graham or his Cleveland mates although the Yankees skidded about as if they were trying out for the United States Olympic hockey squad.

Graham Warms Up

Graham did make some concession to the cold. When he wasn't in the fray, he was on the sidelines and tossing to a teammate much as a baseball pitcher would.

The first period was virtually over when the Browns began a 67-yard march that was climaxed by Graham sneaking over from the 1. Marion Motley, the 232-pound Cleveland fullback made 52 yards of this distance in one blast down the middle.

Graham's tosses to Edgar Jones and Lewis Mayne were the vital factors in the second Cleveland touchdown, which the former registered from the four on a perfect handoff from the quarterback in the third period.

Johnson Boots Field Goal

It wasn't until after the second quarter was under way that the Yankees made the first of their three appearances on the Brown side of the midfield stripe. And the experience exhilarated them to such an extent that they banged all the way to the six, primarily on the running of Spec Sanders and Buddy Young. When the attack bogged there, Harvey Johnson came in and split the uprights for a field goal.

Two fumbles by Young and numerous spills by Yankee ball carriers on the frozen field probably hurt their attack. But it is also true that Cleveland lost at least two touchdowns by the breaks. The most spectacular was the one nullified when Jones stepped outside the end zone to snag a Graham pass.

The customers contributed a gross gate of $209,820.50 of which the players in today's contest will split $78,472.92. Each Brown player will receive $1,191.99 and each Yankee will get $794.66.

Statistics

Cleveland		New York
15	First downs	13
172	Yards gained rushing (net)	123
21	Forward passes attempted	18
14	Forward passes completed	7
112	Yards by forward passes	89
1	Forward passes intercepted by	0
13	Yards gained runback inter. passes	0
45	Punting average (from scrimmage)	36
53	Total yards all kicks returned	97
2	Opponent fumbles recovered	1
45	Yards lost by penalties	20

Cleveland		New York
Young	L.E	Russell
Groza	L.T	Kinard
Ulinski	L.G	Bentz
Saban	C	Sossamon
Willis	R.G	Barwegan
Adams	R.T	N. Johnson
Yonakor	R.E	Alford
Graham	Q.B	Cheatham
Lewis	L.H	Sanders
Colella	R.H	Sweiger
Motley	F.B	Young

Score by periods:

Cleveland ..... 7 0 7 0—14
New York ..... 0 3 0 0— 3

Cleveland—Scoring: Touchdowns, Graham, Jones (for Colella), point after touchdown, Groza (placekick), Saban (placekick).
New York—Scoring: Field goal, H. Johnson (for Cheatham).

EAGLES DEFEAT STEELERS, 21-0

Capture Eastern Division Grid Title; Thompson Stars

Pittsburgh, Dec. 21 (AP)—The Philadelphia Eagles won the National Football League's Eastern Division title by walloping the Pittsburgh Steelers, 21-0, today, and a brilliant performance by Quarterback Tommy Thompson made their playoff victory appear ridiculously simple.

The Eagles' clear-cut triumph put them into the league championship finals against the Chicago Cardinals in Chicago next Sunday.

Thompson unveiled what was probably his greatest game in six years as a professional by completing 11 of 17 passes for 131 yards, including the first two Philadelphia touchdowns.

Van Buren Scores

Thompson guaranteed Eagle Coach Earle Neale a pleasant Christmas with 13:19 of the first period gone by hitting Halfback Steve Van Buren with a spot pass in the flat. Van Buren took the ball on the Steeler 15 and galloped unmolested for the touchdown.

End Pete Pihos set up this score by blocking Bib Cifers' punt, giving the Eagles possession on the Pittsburgh 14 where the ball rolled out of bounds. Thompson's touchdown pass came on third down after two line plays ended in a net loss of one yard.

Thompson was on the scoring target again in 6.32 of the second quarter with a toss to End Jack Ferrante. The Eagle end made the catch on the Steeler 20 and ran for the touchdown. This score climaxed a 69-yard drive, set in motion by an eight-yard Thompson pass to Russ Craft which gained 15 more as the Steelers were penalized for roughness on the play.

Pritchard Goes 79 Yards

Bosh Pritchard quenched whatever hopes the partisan crowd may have had by scooping in a Cifers punt on his own 21 in the third period and running 79 yards for a touchdown. Pritchard made the catch midway between the sidelines, darted to his right and was put into the clear by a beautiful block by Ben Kish. He had a green-shirted escort the remainder of the way.

The Steelers were virtually helpless until the third period when a drive from their own 34 carried to the Philadelphia nine where it ended one yard short of a first down. The closest Pittsburgh came in the first half was the Philadelphia 45, their only penetration of Eagle territory in that time.

First-Division Title

Thompson's field generalship was well-nigh flawless. He used Van Buren, Joe Muha and Pritchard to flay the Steelers between the tackles and, when Pittsburgh attempted to close up, Tommy turned on his aerial offensive, which made Pittsburgh almost helpless.

The Eagles had a scoring chance the first time they laid hands on the ball in the first period, driving from their 37 to the Pittsburgh 20 before the bid fizzled on a fourth-down incompletion of a fake field-goal attempt, in which Al Sherman flipped the ball.

The blocked punt by Pihos put the Eagles on the road to victory a minute later.

By winning, the Eagles gained their first Eastern Division title, defeating a team which was also in a playoff for the first time. The Eagles and Steelers were forced into a divisional playoff when each ended the regular season with eight wins and four losses.

FOUR PRO RECORDS FALL IN FOOTBALL

Bears Set Marks for Yardage and First Downs—Baugh, Luckman Top Performers

PHILADELPHIA, Dec. 8 (AP)—Four old National Football League records lay smashed today and two others, already broken this season, reached new highs.

The Chicago Bears, though outpassed to a 17-14 defeat by a fighting Los Angeles Rams eleven yesterday, managed to exceed two of their proudest offensive marks—most first downs in a season (set in 1946) and most yards gained (established 1941).

Slingin' Sammy Baugh, the Washington Redskins' master of the forward pass, broke a five-year-old league standard for the most passes attempted in one season. And the Bears' Sid Luckman, who enjoys nearly as great success with the aerial heave as Sammy and who stayed a step behind Baugh, also by breaking the most-passes mark, established a record he'll probably do little boasting about — getting more passes intercepted than anyone else.

Added 27 to the Record

The Bears racked up 27 first downs yesterday for an eleven-game total of 239—113 rushing, 110 passing, 16 on penalties and 24 touchdowns from scrimmage. The old mark was 214 in a dozen games last year.

The National loop statistician reported the Chicagoans — they battle the rival Windy City Cardinals for the Western Division crown next Sunday— have amassed 4,551 yards from scrimmage this season. This is 286 better than the '41 record. The new yardage total adds up this way: 1,804 by rushing, 2,746 by passing and exactly 36 inches on a lateral.

Baugh has tossed 313 passes in eleven games this season, completing 185 for a near 60 per cent average. Luckman has heaved 299 aerials, hitting the target successfully on 166 occasions, in also surpassing the mark of 295 passes thrown by the Cardinals' Wilson Schwenk in 1942. Schwenk, incidentally, only completed 126—a below par 45 per cent.

But Schwenk's loss was also his gain, figuratively speaking, anyway. Luckman sometimes has had little—luck, that is. Twenty-eight of his passes this season have been intercepted, surpassing Schwenk's "wrong-catch-pass" mark written into the record books in '42.

More Yardage Piled On

The Texas Christian University alumnus—that's Baugh—and the ex-Columbia University star that's Luckman—continued to pile on yardage to their new total-gained-by-passing mark. Baugh now has 2,595, Luckman 2,505. A week ago, both smashed the record of 2,194 yards set in 1943 by Lickman (that's right).

The most punts in a season standard also has been surpassed. The Boston Yanks' Howard Maley last week broke the record of 64 set by Roy McKay of the Green Bay Packers in 1946. Maley now has one game left. Robert Ciphers of the Pittsburgh Steelers surpassed the mark yesterday. He's kicked 68.

Steve Van Buren, the Philadelphia Eagles' star halfback and the league's leading ground-gainer, inched closer to a new loop rushing record. He's now bucked the line 194 times for 912 yards—and has one game left to crack the 13-year-old standard of 1,004 yards set by the Bears' Beattie Feathers.

Neale Blames Footing For Eagles' Loss

Jim Conzelman Claims Cardinals Out-Tricked Philadelphia Eleven

Chicago, Dec. 28.—(AP.)—While the Chicago Cardinals hilariously celebrated their first National Football League truimph since 1925, the crestfallen Philadelphia Eagles bitterly bemoaned their 28-21 "tennis shoe" defeat on cement-like Comiskey Park gridiron today.

Coach Jimmy Conzelman pranced around the Cardinals' dressing room after the game that capped the longest season in NFL history and hugged every player, particularly Charley Trippi and Elmer Angsman, whose pair of sensational long runs each produced all four Cardinal touchdowns.

In the Eagles' dressing room, Coach Earle (Greasy) Neale snorted: "we did everything but beat them."

Neale had a bone to pick with officials who called the Eagles after the first five minutes for "illegal equipment"—sharply honed cleats on regular football shoes.

The Cardinals trotted onto the field in "sneakers," while the Eagles tried to play with regular football shoes, but switched to gym shoes when the officials objected to their irregular shoe cleats.

As for the bolt-out-of-the-blue touchdown runs by Trippi, covering 44 yards on a scamper from scrimmage and a 75 yard punt return, and by Angsman on two 70-yard explosions from scrimmage, Neale blamed everything on the field footing.

"We had our defensive men all set, but they just couldn't recover on the slippery field when Angsman and Trippi set sail," explained Neale.

"It won't show in the final score, but at the start of the game we were penalized five yards for illegal equipment when we could have made a first down, and that cost us plenty," added the Eagle skipper.

Conzelman credited Trippi's 44-yard touchdown run and the two 70 yard scampers by Angsman to surprise attacks on Philadelphia's eight-man defensive line. "They were delayed smashes that caught Philadelphia entirely off guard and left their secondary badly faked out of position," said Conzelman.

The silver-maned Cardinal coach pointed out that it was the second National Football League title he had won. "Don't forget I coached Providence, R. I., to the league title in 1928," asserted Conzelman.

Almost every Cardinal player except battered Fullback Pat Harder joined in the post-game celebration marked by picture-snapping and back-slapping. Harder, who sustained a whooping black eye, needed physician's care.

Conzelman said he had not mentioned the late Charley Bidwill, Cardinal club owner, nor Halfback Jeff Burkett, who was killed in a plane crash, in his pre-game pep-talk. "These boys were plenty grim without trying to inject a maudlin note," Conzelman said.

Mrs. Violet Bidwill, the former club owner's widow, broke into tears after the game.

"It's just too bad that Charles couldn't have seen this," she sobbed.

Statistics

Philadelphia		Pittsburgh
17	First Downs	7
124	Net Yards Gained Rushing	102
18	Forward Passes Attempted	18
11	Forward Passes Completed	4
131	Yards Forward Passing	52
0	Forwards Intercepted By	0
36	Yards Gained Runback Inter'c'tions	0
127	Punting Average	40
2	Total Yards, All Kicks Returned	65
49	Opponents' Fumbles Recovered	2
	Yards Lost By Penalties	65

PHILADELPHIA		PITTSBURGH
Ferrante	L. E.	Mehelich
McDowell	L. T.	Wiley
Patton	L. G.	Moore
Wojciechowicz	C.	Cherundolo
Kilroy	R. G.	Mastrangelo
Wistert	R. T.	Wydo
Pihos	R. E.	Davis
Prescott	Q. B.	Seabright
Steele	L. H.	Slater
Craft	R. H.	Cifers
Muha	F. B.	Compagno

Score by periods:

Philadelphia	7	7	7	0	—21
Pittsburgh	0	0	0	0	— 0

Philadelphia Scoring: Touchdowns—Van Buren (for Steele), Ferrante, Pritchard (for Craft). Points after touchdown—Patton, 3 (placements).

Senior Loop Continues To Ignore All-America

New York, Jan. 17 (AP)—Continuing its aloof policy of ignoring the rival All-America Conference, the National Football League today turned down a chance to get together with the younger circuit when it rejected a proposal for a common draft without resorting to a vote.

The decision left the two leagues as far apart as ever and apparently killed any possible chance of a professional world championship game in 1948, a hope expressed by Admiral Jonas Ingram, commissioner of the All-America loop.

Rounding out a three-way annual conclave, the National League also tabled San Francisco's application for a franchise for one year, adopted seven rules recommended by the rules committee, and threw the unfinished job of completing its playing schedule into the hands of Commissioner Bert Bell.

Yanks, Bears In Deal

In addition, a couple of owners found time to engineer a deal, with the Boston Yanks trading their draft rights to George Connor, Notre Dame's star tackle, to the Chicago Bears for Mike Jarmoluk, 255-pound end and tackle, who formerly starred for Temple University.

The Yanks had acquired the draft rights to Connor in the mid-season deal that sent Paul Governali to the New York Giants. Jarmoluk came to the Bears two years ago in a trade with the Detroit Lions.

The league took but five minutes to dispose of the common draft motion, which was introduced by Al Ennis, general manager of the Philadelphia Eagles. The motion originally was made by Alexis Thompson, wealthy young owner of the Eagles. Thompson did not attend the meetings, passing them up for a trip to Switzerland with the United States Olympic bobsled team.

No Second To Motion

"We did not need to vote on the matter," Bell advised newspapermen, "since the motion did not receive a second. According to the rules of parliamentary procedure, a motion must have a second before it can be discussed. An exception was made in this case, since we wanted to give the proposer a chance to give his views."

Ennis, who argued that a common draft would save owners of both leagues "considerable sums of money," said he was not surprised when he received no backing.

"I knew that we stood all alone, and I was not surprised at the result," he said. "All I did was follow instructions."

LAYNE SIGNS WITH BEARS

Turns Down More Money From Colts For Chicago Bid

Austin, Texas, Feb. 28 (AP)—Bobby Layne, the University of Texas' passer, said today he had signed a three-year contract with the Chicago Bears, of the National Football League, thus turning down a $77,000 bid from the Baltimore Colts, of the All-America Conference, that would have paid him more money.

He declared he did it because the Bears have a better team.

And he also revealed that he had passed up a bonus for signing because he wanted to play college baseball this spring.

Lost $20,000 In Deal

It is estimated that the move cost Bobby about $20,000—$10,000 in the bonus and $10,000 in the contract.

University of Texas athletic officials have informed Layne that he can sign a pro contract and remain eligible so long as he does not accept any money until after he leaves school. At Dallas, James H. Stewart, executive secretary of the Southwest Conference, said he would not choose to give an opinion on this point "until I study the rule further." He also said he would not give a ruling unless it was requested.

The amount the great Texas quarterback will receive from the Bears was not revealed, but it was reliably reported that it would be $10,000 less than the contract dangled before him by Baltimore for a three-year stint at a price the Colts management said was "more money than any college football player ever has been offered."

"Money's Not Everything"

"Money's not everything," said Bobby, "You've got to take other things into consideration. I think the Bears are a better club. They will be a better team to play for because they are well-established. You know you're going to be with good players always. You can always be sure of it."

Cecil Isbell, coach of Baltimore, yesterday revealed that the Colts had offered Layne a $10,000 bonus for signing, $20,000 for the first year, $22,000 for the second and $25,000 for the third. George Halas, owner-coach of the Bears, in announcing at Phoenix, Ariz., today that Layne had signed a three-year contract, said the money involved was not as much as Baltimore had offered.

Layne, 21 years old in December, is considered the most gifted quarterback ever produced in the southwest and is rated as probably its greatest passer.

SUTHERLAND DIES AFTER OPERATION

Brain Surgery Fails To Save Noted Football Coach

Pittsburgh, April 11 (AP)—Jock Sutherland, one of the nation's leading college and professional football coaches, died early today after an operation for a malignant brain tumor.

The 59-year-old coach of the Pittsburgh Steelers of the National Football League—Dr. John Bain Sutherland—succumbed at 4.15 A.M. Death came four hours after he had undergone the second of two emergency brain operations.

Sutherland was found wandering near his mired auto on a country road near Bandana, Ky., last Wednesday. At that time he was able to tell his name but was otherwise incoherent. He was treated at a Cairo (Ill.) hospital for possible mental exhaustion.

Two Four-Hour Operations

He was flown to Pittsburgh Friday night. The brain condition was discovered yesterday and an immediate four-hour exploratory operation performed. Doctors then discovered the tumor.

Another four-hour surgery was performed last night, but physicians said they were unable to do anything because the tumor was of a malignant nature.

Sutherland left Pittsburgh three weeks ago on a combined vacation and scouting trip for the Steelers. As usual, he traveled alone.

He is known to have visited Wallace Wade at Duke University, Durham, N.C., and to have been in New Orleans. His movements from the time he left New Orleans until he was found are a mystery.

Gilmer's Stand on All-Star Game Upheld by Football Commissioner

Bell Holds Ex-Alabama Ace Within Rights in Refusing to Play Unless Fully Insured —Rejects Ward's Request to Bar Star

PHILADELPHIA, Aug. 26 (AP)—The National Football League ruled today a rookie player need not jeopardize his future by playing in a college all-star charity game without "full" contract protection.

In a precedent-making decision, Commissioner Bert Bell upheld the right of passing star Harry Gilmer to stay out of the All-Star Chicago-Cardinals game held Aug. 20 under the sponsorship of Chicago Tribune Charities, Inc.

Tribune Charities had demanded that Gilmer be barred under a contract rule from playing non-championship games with the Washington Redskins.

Bell rejected the Tribune request. He said his "first interest" is to protect the players and the public.

The Commissioner, restating the case, said Gilmer had agreed to play for the All-Stars on condition he receive $150 plus full insurance coverage of his Redskins' contract.

The Tribune "refused to insure him, as he requested," Bell declared, adding:

Calls Demands Fair

"Gilmer's demand for full protection against loss under his contract * * * was, in my opinion, both reasonable and fair."

At Chicago, Arch Ward, sports editor of the Chicago newspaper and vice president of Tribune Charities, said:

"His (Bell's) arguments are absolutely ridiculous and the whole matter is in the hands of the Tribune law department."

In a statement, Ward said all other All-Star players had been insured against injury to the amount of $8,000. Ward said he had declined to insure Gilmer against injury for the full amount of his contract, reported to be $80,000.

CARDS' ACE TACKLE DIES AFTER GAME

Mauldin Is Victim of Acute Heart Attack—Texan Had Played With Longhorns

CHICAGO, Sept. 25 (AP)—A heart attack caused the death of Stanley Mauldin, star tackle for the Chicago Cardinals, in the team's dressing room two hours after the Cardinals had defeated the Philadelphia Eagles, 21 to 14, in a rugged opening game at Comiskey Park last night.

Mauldin, 27, father of a 5-year-old son, collapsed after taking a shower, sank into a coma and died without regaining consciousness despite efforts of specialists to revive him.

Coroner A. L. Brodie said an autopsy indicated that Mauldin died of "an acute heart attack." Dr. A. C. Webb, a coroner's physician, who performed the examination with Dr. Sidney Portis, a heart specialist as observer, reported he found no evidence of a brain injury or any other injury severe enough to cause death.

Mauldin's death was the second tragic blow that struck the Cardinals, champions of the National Football League, in less than a year. Last Oct. 24 Halfback Jefferson Burkett, formerly of Louisiana State, was killed in a plane crash at Bryce Canyon, Utah, with forty-two persons aboard. Burkett was returning from Los Angeles to Chicago after an emergency appendectomy. His teammates had returned earlier after suffering their first defeat of the 1947 season.

Complained of Headache

Mauldin, who played only part of last night's game, appeared normal when he left the field for the dressing room. However, he complained of a headache previous to the game and said he received a severe kick in the head during the contest. After his shower, Mauldin was offered a cigarette, but declined it and while talking with Line Coach Phil Handler started to collapse.

"Coach, I feel a little dizzy," Mauldin complained.

Handler caught the dying player in his arms and, with the help of others, carried him to a rubbing table, which he never left.

Two physicians and a fire department inhalator squad worked for more than an hour trying to revive Mauldin. His wife, Helen, Coach Jimmy Conzelman of the Cardinals and players kept the vigil, while several hundred fans awaited anxiously outside the dressing room.

Mauldin, a 6 foot 2 inch Texan, formerly was a star with the Texas Longhorns. He was born at Amarillo, Tex., Dec. 27, 1920. A hard but clean player, Mauldin had the admiration of not only his Cardinal teammates, but his opponents as well. He never had to be warned by officials for unsportsmanlike playing.

ALBERT AGAIN PACES ATTACK FOR LEADERS

Directs Coast Eleven To Eighth Straight League Victory

New York, Oct. 17 (AP)—The San Francisco Forty-Niners defeated the New York Yankees, 21 to 7, today in an All-American Conference football game as Quarterback Frankie Albert, of the Coast eleven, bewildered his opponents with a clever display of ball-handling and passing.

It was the eighth straight league triumph for the Californians, who share the top in the western half of the loop with Cleveland, also unbeaten.

Albert wasn't the entire show as the two teams battled on virtually even terms, but it was his heady play that held the Forty-Niners together despite a vicious New York line that threw San Francisco backs for loss after loss.

CAPACITIES OF AAFC PARKS

Club	Park	Normal	*Overflow
Baltimore	Municipal Stadium	58,000	60,000
Brooklyn	Ebbets Field	34,000	37,000
Buffalo	Civic Stadium	36,426	43,167
Chicago	Soldier Field	59,178	75,000
Cleveland	Municipal Stadium	77,707	85,000
Los Angeles	Memorial Coliseum	105,000	106,500
New York	Yankee Stadium	72,980	75,000
San Francisco	Kezar Stadium	59,636	59,636

* Includes standing room and/or temporary seats

Redskins Routed By Eagles, 45-0

Washington, Oct. 17 (AP)—The Philadelphia Eagles overwhelmed the Washington Redskins, 45 to 0, in a National League football game today at Griffith Stadium.

While Steve Van Buren was busy scoring three touchdowns, the Redskins were so bottled up that not until a couple of minutes before the game ended did they get into scoring territory.

The first four times the Eagles got the ball they held on to it until they scored. They took the opening kickoff and drove 80-yards on seven plays. Tommy Thompson passing to Pete Pihos for 19 yards and the score. Again in the first quarter they marched 78 yards on 14 plays. This time Thompson tossed a lateral to Van Buren, who hustled around his left end for the six points.

In the second period, the Eagles' Cliff Patton booted a 23-yard field goal. Then they marched 67 yards in 14 plays, and Van Buren went over from the three.

In the third period, Bosh Pritchard went 32 yards for the score. Van Buren was back for the next touchdown, from seven yards out, while Ernie Steele ran over from the four for the final touchdown, in the last quarter.

Chicago Cardinals Rout N.Y. Giants, 63-35

New York, Oct 17 (AP)—With Ray Mallouf pitching four touchdown passes, the Chicago Cardinals flattened the New York Giants, 63 to 35, at the Polo Grounds today.

Two new National Football League records were set during the game.

The Cards' victory produced the highest scoring game in the circuit's history—98 points. The previous high for points was 87 set when Philadelphia beat Washington, 45-42, on September 28, 1947.

Pat Harder established a new mark for converting points after touchdown. He kicked nine to beat the old record of eight set by Bob Snyder, of the Chicago Bears, against the Giants in 1943.

Chicago Bears Trounce Detroit Lions By 28-0

Chicago, Oct. 17 (AP)—The undefeated Chicago Bears scored a 28 to 0 triumph over the Detroit Lions for their fourth straight National Football League decision today.

A weather-chilled throng watched the National loop's only unbeaten club punch across a touchdown in each of the first two quarters and then get across two more in the final period.

The Lions, suffering their fourth straight league loss, made their deepest penetration into Bear territory in the third period, reaching Chicago's 19 yard stripe.

The Bears gave their two rookie quarterbacks, Johnny Lujack and Bobby Layne, a chance to show their stuff, but it was the old T-master, Sid Luckman who put the game under control.

Luckman, who pitched only six passes and completed four, really settled the issue in the first period when he fired a 6-yard payoff toss to End Ken Kavanaugh. That touchdown capped an 88-yard Bear march which got its most impetus from a 49-yard pass from Luckman to Don Kindt.

Kindt scampered 66 yards for the Bears' second touchdown in the second period.

The Bears chalked up touchdown No. 3 at the outset of the fourth quarter on a 2-yard plunge by George Gulyanics after a 37-yard drive.

The final score came with eight seconds left on a 1-yard smash by Joe Osmanski. Lujack converted after all four Bear touchdowns.

BROWNS BEAT FORTY-NINERS

Take Western Division Lead With 14-To-7 Triumph

ALL-AMERICA

Cleveland, Nov. 14 (AP)—Cleveland's Browns, two-time champions of the All-America Football Conference, took undisputed possession of the league's western division lead today as they handed San Francisco its first loss in 11 starts, 14 to 7.

It was the tenth victory of the year for the unbeaten Browns, and the rugged game was played before 82,769 fans, largest crowd ever to see a professional league contest.

The Browns got a break, and their first touchdown, in the first 45 seconds as Halfback Forrest Hall fumbled the opening kickoff and Capt. Lou Saban, of the Browns, recovered on the Forty-Niners 14.

Redskins Down Yanks, 59-21, As Baugh Stars

NATIONAL LEAGUE

Washington, Oct. 31 (AP)—Sammy Baugh threw four touchdown passes, and picked up a total of 446 yards with his tosses, as the Washington Redskins downed the Boston Yanks today, 59 to 21, in a National League football game.

The Redskins pass master completed 17 of his 24 tosses.

Baugh's magnificent passing broke the National Football League record, set by Sid Luckman, of the Chicago Bears. Luckman picked up 433 yards passing against the New York Giants in 1943.

Passes To Todd

There was no stopping Slingin' Sam today. Here's the way those touchdown passes came:

1. To Halfback Dick Todd, who was in the clear and ran so fast no one even bothered to follow him. The distance: 78 yards.
2. To Joe Tereshinski, 214-pound end, who also got in the clear. Distance: 74 yards.
3. To Hal Crisler, skinny end, a 49-yard touchdown gallop this time.
4. To Todd again, this one for 38 yards.

Playing second fiddle to Baugh was Dan Sandifer, rookie Redskin back, who intercepted four of Roy Zimmerman's Boston passes and ran two of them back for touchdowns.

Runs 50 Yards

He made a great run each time, as he artfully dodged his way for 35 and 50-yard touchdowns.

Baugh's passing also set up another touchdown and a field goal. One of his tosses, to Tom Farmer, was good for 48 yards. When a holding penalty set the Redskins back, Dick Poillon booted a 43-yard field goal.

On the touchdown, Baugh's passes carried Washington to the one, and Poillon smacked it over to become high point man for the day. His eight points after touchdown helped give him a total of 17.

Halfback Howard Hartley, with a 26-yard around end dash, got the other six pointer.

The Yankees managed to match the Redskins for one period.

The first quarter ended at 14 to 14, with Bill Paschal scoring both touchdowns. One was a line plunge, the other a 23-yard pass from Roy Zimmerman. The Yanks picked up another touchdown in the third quarter, with a 12-yard toss, Zimmerman to Joe Golding.

The 59 points were the most ever made by a Redskin team. Their best previous total was 49, against the New York Giants in 1937.

[Picture on page 16.]

Statistics

Boston		Washington
22	First downs	20
109	Net yards gained rushing	109
40	Forward passes attempted	34
19	Forward passes completed	22
224	Yards forward passing	501
1	Forwards intercepted by	6
10	Yards gained runback interceptions	134
47	Punting average	49
233	Total yards, all kicks returned	155
4	Opponent fumbles recovered	2
10	Yards lost by penalties	75

Lineups

BOSTON

Left End—Tyree.
Left Tackles—Jarmouluh, Nolan.
Left Guards—Barzilauskas, McClure.
Centers—Dommanovich, Gadwin, Marichia.
Right Guards—Botinski, Sabasteanski, Batinski.
Right Tackles—Vogelaar, Dairs, Roman.
Right Ends—Scollard, Heywood.
Quarterbacks—Nelson, Zimmerman.
Left Halfs—Chipley, Paschal, Slosburg.
Right Halfs—Golding, Seno, Ryan.
Fullbacks—Hazelhurst, Mikka, Romboli, Nuehlheuser.

WASHINGTON

Left Ends—McKee, Taylor.
Left Tackles—Sanchez, Koniszewski, Edwards.
Left Guards—Katrishen, Steber.
Center—Ehrhardt.
Right Guards—Boensch, Butkar, Gray.
Right Tackles—Adams, Roussos.
Right Ends—Tereshinski, Crisler, Turley.
Quarterbacks—Poillon, Mont, Baugh.
Left Halfs—Sandifer, Livingston.
Right Halfs—Farmer, Todd, Hartley, Madarik.
Fullbacks—Quirk, Hollar, Castiglia.

Boston	14	0	7	0—21
Redskins	14	14	10	21—59

Boston scoring: Touchdowns—Paschal, 2; Golding. Points after touchdown, Zimmerman, 3. (Placements). Washington scoring: Touchdowns—Todd, 2; Sandifer, 2; Tereshinski, Crisler, Poillon, Hartley. Points after touchdowns, Poillon, 8. (Placements). Field goal, Poillon—(placement).

Graham Tallies

Otto Graham, former Northwestern All-American, missed on a pass, but on the second play scampered around end for the score after faking another aerial.

The Westerners came back with an 82-yard march for their score in the same session, Fullback Joe Perry hitting center for a yard to climax the drive which consumed 18 plays and featured John Strzykalski's 24-yard jaunt around right-end and a 14-yard pass by Frankie Albert.

The Browns put the game on ice as they went 84 yards in 11 plays after the second-half kickoff, with Edgar Jones skirting end for the counter. Lou Groza, the Browns' placekicker who missed two attempted field goals from around midfield, made good on both extra-point tries.

Completes Three Passes

In the second scoring series Graham uncorked three completed passes in four attempts, hitting Bob Cowan for 13 and 28 yards, and Ara Parseghian for 15. Graham connected on 12 of 26 passes for 147 yards, while left-handed Albert tried 15, completing 6 for 32 yards.

Just after their second touchdown the Browns rolled back to the Forty-Niner 18-yard line, but Verl Lillywhite intercepted a pass in the end zone to end the splurge.

PLAYER DRAFTS ALREADY HELD

AP Learns Pro Football Loops Had Secret Meetings

New York, Nov. 30 (AP)—From various sources the Associated Press learned today that both the All-America Conference and the National Football League have held secret draft meetings in hopes of out-smarting each other in the race for the top players of 1948.

The All-America Conference meeting was held in Chicago in mid-summer while the National League meeting was in Pittsburgh three weeks ago, with selection of playoff sites as the announced purpose of the meeting.

Overlooked Stan Heath

So thoroughly did the conference scouts have the collegiate talent throughout the country nailed down that only Stan Heath, of Nevada, who came from nowhere to be one of the country's best passers, was overlooked.

Since then the New York Yankees have taken it upon themselves to sign Heath. He was drafted by Green Bay in the secret National League session.

The Philadelphia Eagles drew the draft rights to Charles Bednarik, of Pennsylvania, in a bonus draft of the National League. He was picked by Brooklyn in the conference.

Voyles To See Bednarik

Carl Voyles, coach and general manager of the Dodgers, said today he had approached Bednarik and would see him again next week but added that the 1947 All-America center had not been signed.

It is the high bidding between the rival leagues for the drafted players that has brought much woe to both circuits.

Ted Collins, owner of the Boston Yanks of the N.F.L., recently said he had lost $720,000 in four years, partly due to the high salaries and bonuses that must be paid to lure players.

Accepts Highest Offer

Lex Thompson, of the Philadelphia Eagles, toyed with the idea of a peace meeting recently in which a common draft would be instituted. Under that plan a player would be drafted by only one club. As it is now he is drafted by two rivals and customarily accepts the highest offers.

A year ago the National League reportedly had an early draft meeting and beat the All-America scouts to most of the players. This year, apparently, the younger circuit got started first.

Lists Formal Meetings

Each circuit has a formal draft meeting scheduled for later this month, coinciding with their title games.

Heath, originally overlooked by the conference, visited his parents in Milwaukee during the Thanksgiving holiday and today the Milwaukee Journal carried a story in which it reported he had been offered $40,000 for two seasons to join the Yankees.

Kusserow To Dodgers

Some of the top stars reportedly drafted by the All-America clubs are: Lou Kusserow, Columbia, by the Dodgers; Frank Tripucka, Notre Dame quarterback, and Abe Gibson, of Purdue, by Buffalo; Alex Sarkisian, Northwestern center, by Cleveland; John Rauch, star passer at Georgia, and Pete Elliott, of Michigan, by the Yankees, and Guard Bill Fischer and Halfback Terry Brennan, of Notre Dame, by the Chicago Rockets.

FORTY-NINERS WIN BY 38-21

Albert Paces Victors' Attack Against Los Angeles

ALL-AMERICA

Los Angeles, Dec. 5 (AP)—Frankie Albert and the San Francisco Forty-Niners whipped the Los Angeles Dons, 38 to 21 here today.

In so doing, wrote some new records into the professional football book in the windup of the All-America Conference campaign.

Coliseum official attendance figures show the Dons played to 286,317 fans in seven home games this season, compared with 300,924 for seven games last year.

Passes Score

Fireball Frankie sent the Forty-Niners into a three-touchdown lead in the first quarter and they were never seriously threatened from then on.

Albert threw three touchdown passes, the longest good for 59 yards to Halfback Johnny Strzykalski, and ran his total scoring strikes for the season to 29. This eclipsed the pro football record established several seasons ago by Sid Luckman, of the Chicago Bears, who completed 28.

Beals Betters Record

Albert's right end, Alyn Beals, caught two of the touchdown throws, one good for 35, and ran his season's total to 14, bettering his 1947 A.A.F.C. record of 10 and his record of scoring in each game to 31, also a league record.

Dobbs attempted 55 more passes and completed 27 for 405 yards. He gained 26 yards running and captured the league's total offense record for the season with 2,942 yards.

Dobbs Breaks Own Mark

San Francisco walked off with most of the record performances for the season. Included were: Yards rushing—3,663 (old record, 2,930, New York Yankees, 1947); Total offensive yards—5,767 (old record 5,547 Cleveland); Touchdowns—69 (old 56, Cleveland).

Dobbs had a 49.1 average in punting, breaking his old record of 47.8 in 1946 when he was with Brooklyn. He completed 185 passes out of 369 attempts, bettering the 168 out of 327 completed by Bud Schwenk.

Statistics

San Francisco		Los Angeles
17	First downs	22
369	Net yards gained rushing	46
12	Forward passes attempted	56
6	Forward passes completed	27
121	Yards forward passing	405
7	Forwards intercepted by	0
35	Yds. gained runback interceptions	0
44	Punting average	49
68	Total yds. all kicks returned	170
1	Opponent fumbles recovered	2
112	Yards lost by penalties	54

TWENTY FIGURES MADE

Colts Gain Most Ground By Air, 2,899 Yards

New York, Dec. 6 (AP) — Twenty new single-season team records and eight all-time major league marks were written into the All-America Football Conference books during the '48 season.

Figures announced today show that the San Francisco Forty-Niners moved to a new Major League record of 3,663 yards by rushing and to 152 first downs lugging the ball. Their great overall attack yielded 495 points, including 69 touchdowns and 64 points after touchdown—new all-time marks.

Total Offense Mark

The Forty-Niners total gain of 5,767 yards also established a new offensive high. Buffalo set a new league record by getting off 899 rushing and passing plays.

San Francisco ran 603 ground plays, a new league record, averaged a record 6.07 yards a clip, and made 39 touchdowns by rushing. They also scored 30 touchdowns by passing, another conference mark.

Dobbs Aids Punt Record

Los Angeles weighed in with a new all-time team punting average of 47.2 yards, thanks mainly to Glenn Dobbs's individual average of 49.1.

The unbeaten Cleveland Browns set two new conference marks, 243 first downs and 104 of them by passing, and had a record low of 11 fumbles lost.

Brooklyn's 410 pass attempts was a new league high, and Los Angeles had the most completions in the circuit's three-year history—195. Buffalo averaged 16.9 yards on 33 punt returns, shading the previous record.

Los Angeles with 405 yards and Brooklyn with 387 both broke the former single game passing record. Brooklyn won the pass defense championship, yielding 1,985 yards during the season to Cleveland's 2,097. Baltimore gained the most ground through the air, 2,899 yards.

Cardinals Win Western Title By Defeating Bears, 24 To 21

NATIONAL LEAGUE

Chicago, Dec. 12 (AP)—The Chicago Cardinals rallied in the last quarter to score two touchdowns in six minutes and defeat the Chicago Bears, 24 to 21, today to win the western division title of the National Football League.

It was the Cardinals' No. 2 quarterback, Ray Mallouf, who was the hero. Inserted after Paul Christman's passes failed to click, Mallouf ushered the defending national league champions on an 85 yard scoring drive which consumed only two minutes to shave the Bears lead to 21 to 17.

Intercepts Lujack's Pass

The Bears no sooner had taken the ensuing kickoff than Johnny Lujack's pass was intercepted by Center Vince Banonis on the Bear 42 and returned to the 18. As the record Wrigley Field crowd went wild, Mallouf tossed six yards to Charlie Trippi. Then Elmer Angsman bolted the remaining 12 off tackle to score.

Pat Harder added his third successive conversion. Running his string for the season to 53, and the Cardinals were ahead 24 to 21.

The victory sends the Cardinals against the Eagles Eastern Division champions at Philadelphia next Sunday for the National League crown.

Lujack's only pass interception of the day—by Banonis—set up the Cardinals' clinching tally in the fourth quarter. Otherwise the Bears' star rookie, who played all but ten minutes of the entire contest, was perfection-plus.

Statistics

Cardinals		Bears
20	First downs	20
172	Net yards gained rushing	156
21	Forward passes attempted	30
8	Forward passes completed	19
119	Yards forward passing	300
3	Forwards intercepted by	1
40	Yards gained runback intercep.	6
35.7	Punting average	47.2
38	Total yards, all kicks returned	147
2	Opponents fumbles recovered	0
24	Yards lost by penalties	81

Completes 15 Passes

He fired 24 passes, completed 15 for 237 yards and two touchdowns. His 43-yard aerial play to Don Kindt set up the third Bear touchdown on the first play of the final period.

The Bears dominated the first half with a display of great line action. They held the Cardinals to a total offense gain of 64 yards while they themselves were piling up 240 and a 14-to-3 halftime lead.

Gain 291 Yards

The second half punch of the Cardinals gave the South Siders a net gain for the game of 291 yards —172 by rushing and 119 by passing—to the Bears 156-300 for 456.

The Bears scored in the opening five minutes on a 78-yard drive. featuring Lujack's 25-yard toss to Ken Kavanaugh and nine to Jim Keane. Johnny climaxed it with a 15-yard scoring pitch to Kavanaugh. Then he booted the first of his three extra points.

Lujack completed the first six passes he hurled.

Dewell Recovers Fumble

Bill Dewell recovered J. R. Boone's fumble at midfield and Christman's 21-yard toss was ruled complete on interference. This set up a 34-yard field goal by Harder which eventually became the difference in the score,

Buffalo Bills Rally To Win Playoff, 28-17

Overtake Baltimore In Final Minutes to Cop Division Crown

Baltimore, Dec. 12. — (AP.)— The Buffalo Bills, in a breathless burst of power, scored two touchdowns in the last three minutes of play today to defeat the Baltimore Colts, 28 to 17, in a playoff for the All America Conference Eastern Division football championship.

At the end of the game, bitterly disappointed Baltimore fans surged onto the field and began pummeling Linesman Fay Vincent and Referee Sam Giangreco who had nullified several long Baltimore gains with penalties. But police rescued the officials and dispersed the crowd.

The Buffalo victory today, reversing the Baltimore win last week which finished the two teams in a tie for the division lead and caused the playoff, matched the Bills against the unbeaten Cleveland Browns, Western Division champs, for the league title. The two teams play next Sunday at Cleveland.

Sideline Judge Thomas Whalen also was attacked and suffered a black eye. The other two were unhurt.

There were less than three minutes left and Baltimore led, 17-14, when Buffalo's George Ratterman, a deadly passer under any conditions, whipped a 10-yard aerial to Al Baldwin, who basketed the ball on the Baltimore 15 and raced the rest of the way for a touchdown. That put Buffalo ahead 21-17 after the conversion.

Hirsch Intercepts Pass.

Then, with the clock running out, Buffalo added the clincher. Ed Hirsch intercepted Y. A. Tittle's pass on the Baltimore 20 and ran it back for another Bill touchdown.

Baltimore jumped to a 3-0 lead in the first period on Rex Grossman's 16-yard field goal, then fell behind 7-3 when the Bills tallied in the second.

It was a five-yard jump pass from Ratterman to O'Connor which put the Bills in front of the opening play of the second period after they had recovered a fumble at midfield to launch their drive.

But came the third period, and Baltimore, a rags-to-riches team which was built up on league handouts after finishing in the cellar last year, made its bid for the championship, scoring two touchdowns and two conversions to surge ahead.

Baltimore's first drive in the period began when Billy Hillenbrand took the kickoff in the end zone and ran it out to his 29 yard line. Two Tittle passes to End Windell Williams moved the Colts to the Bills' 44. Hillenbrand added three and Stormy Pfohl gained five yards more.

An interference penalty on a pass gave Baltimore the ball on the Bills 20. Two Baltimore fumbles by Lu Gambino and Hillenbrand were recovered by the Colts and Tittle passed to Lamar Davis for a first down on the Bills 11. Pfohl made a first down on the nine yard line. On the next play, Mertes shot around left end to score standing up. Grossman kicked the extra point and Baltimore led 10-7.

Mertes Goes Over.

Buffalo couldn't gain after the kick-off and the Colts began an 88-yard march from their own 12 for another touchdown. With Hillenbrand, Mertes and Pfohl grinding out the yardage, the Colts moved downfield in short jumps to the Bills 47-yard line. Tittle's pass to Mertes and alternating line bucks by Mertes and Pfohl moved the Colts to the four. Pfohl picked up a yard and Mertes added two more to put the ball on the one. He went over on the next play. Grossman converted to give the Colts a 17-7 lead.

The Bills didn't give up, however. They cut loose with a three-touchdown barrage in the last period for victory.

Taking over on their own 20, the Bills scored in five plays. Ratterman passed from his own 34 yard line to Gompers on the Colts 40. Gompers raced all the way from there for the Buffalo touchdown, cutting the Colt lead to 17-14 after Armstrong kicked the extra point.

Then came the scoring drive that brought a Buffalo victory. Ratterman began it with a 15 yard pass to O'Connor on the Bills 40. Another pass to Chick Maggioli was good to the Colts 44. Two Tomasetti bucks moved the ball down to the 25 when Ratterman whipped his winning pass to Baldwin. Armstrong kicked the extra point.

Then Hirsch intercepted Tittle's pass for the clincher.

Statistically the game was all Baltimore's. They ground out 24 first downs for a new conference record in one game to Buffalo's 11, piled up a total offense of 394 yards to Buffalo's 297 and dominated both the rushing and passing departments.

EAGLES DEFEAT CARDS, 7-0, IN NATIONAL LEAGUE

National

Philadelphia, Dec. 19 (AP)—The Philadelphia Eagles performed like a set of animated snow plows today to whip the Chicago Cardinals, 7 to 0, in the National Football League's "world's championship" playoff game in a driving snowstorm.

Playing under miserable weather conditions on a field that was inches deep in snow before the finish, the Eagles found their footing in the final quarter to push over the only touchdown of the game.

Big Steve Van Buren, who learned his football under sunny Louisiana skies, made that one score on a 5-yard smash through tackle just as the final quarter started and Cliff Patton converted to complete the scoring job.

Eagles Earn Victory

But the Eagles had the better of the strenuous tussle all the way and earned their victory through hard, bruising line play and brilliant running by Van Buren, Bosh Pritchard and Tommy Thompson. They were only two yards away from another score when the game ended.

The weather, surprisingly, did not keep the fans away. Virtually all of the 37,000 seats in Shibe Park were sold in advance and 28,864 die-hard fans actually turned up and sat through the proceedings. They did it the hard way, too, for the wet snow disrupted surface transportation, forcing many of them to walk long distances to reach the park, where several thousands sat in uncovered stands.

East's First Win Since '42

The Eagles' victory brought the National League title to an Eastern division team for the first time since 1942, when the Washington Redskins turned back the Chicago Bears. It also was the first league championship for the Eagles, who lost to the Cardinals, 28 to 21, in last year's playoff at Chicago.

Their predecessors, the Frankford Yellow Jackets—a Philadelphia club—won the championship in 1926 before the playoffs were instituted.

Breaks Decide Game

The result was something in the nature of an upset, as the defending champions had been installed as 3½ point favorites and they still were given a one-point edge in the betting this morning when the weather made it obvious that the breaks would decide the contest.

And that's exactly what happened. Time after time Philadelphia got the breaks, recovering fumbles and intercepting passes. It was a fumble just before the end of the fourth Quarter that set up the lone touchdown.

Cardinals Fumble

The Cards, shoved back into their own territory by Joe Muha's booming punts when the Eagles had the advantage of the wind, had just taken the ball on the 19-yard line. Quarterback Ray Mallouf got into a mixup and there was a fumble on the first play. Frank Kilroy, veteran Philadelphia guard, fell on the ball on the 17. Coach Jimmy Conzelman later explained, "It was nobody's fault, just a mixup on the handoff."

Pritchard slashed through to the eleven as the quarter ended and on the first two plays of the last period Muha and Thompson picked up six yards more. Then Van Buren, who was virtually unstoppable in spite of the soft, slippery footing, took a hand-off from Thompson, went through a big hole between guard and tackle and raced over the goal line.

Cliff Patton Converts

The Eagles dropped to their knees and scraped the snow away from a patch of dirt for the conversion attempt and Patton booted the ball truly between the uprights.

Earlier in the game Patton had missed two fields goals attempts—one from 12 yards out and one from 39 yards. Later he tried a 30-yard placement which also failed.

Besides getting the breaks, the Eagles earned their victory fairly, as the statistics show. They made 17 first downs to Chicago's seven, gained 225 yards by rushing and seven more on two completed passes. The Cardinals gained only 96 yards on the ground and completed three passes for 35 yards.

Snow Covers Field

These figures were very respectable considering the weather condition. The field was covered by about four inches of heavy snow when attendants started to remove the tarpaulins and the start of the game was delayed a half hour before the canvas could be taken off.

Statistics

Chicago		Philadelphia
7	First downs	16
96	Yards gained rushing (net)	225
35	Yards gained passing	7
11	Forward passes attempted	12
3	Passes completed	2
2	Passes intercepted by	1
20	Yards interceptions returned by	0
17.4	Average distance of punts	32
62	Yards all kicks returned	29
1	Opponent's fumbles recovered	2
33	Yards in penalties	17

Lineups

CHICAGO
Left Ends—Cochran, Kutner, Ravensberg.
Left Tackles—Timmr, Coomer.
Left Guards—Ramsey, Colhouer, Nichols.
Centers—Banonis, Blackburn.
Right Guards—Andros, Apolskis.
Right Tackles—Bulger, Saol, Loepfe.
Right Ends—Claff, Dewell, Goldman.
Quarterbacks—Davis, Mallouf, Boswell.
Left Halfbacks — Trippi, DiMancheff.
Right Halfbacks—Angsman, Goldberg.
Fullbacks—Harder, Yablonski.

PHILADELPHIA
Left Ends—Greene, Ferrante, Humbert.
Left Tackles—MacDowell, Sears, Douglas.
Left Guards—Maronic, Patton, O'Connell.
Centers—Lindskog, Wojciechowicz.
Right Guards—Kilroy, Barnes, Magee.
Right Tackles—Wistert, Savitsky.
Right Ends—Armstrong, Thos.
Quarterback—Thompson.
Left Halfbacks—Steele, Van Buren.
Right Halfbacks—Craft, Pritchard.
Fullbacks—Muha, Myers.

Score by quarters:
Chicago .... 0 0 0 0—0
Philadelphia ... 0 0 0 7—7
Philadelphia scoring: Touchdown—Van Buren. Point after touchdown—Patton (placement)

Warring Pro Football Factions Meeting Today for Peace Talks

All-America and National League Owners to Hold Parley in Philadelphia—Draft Action Is Put Off by Both Loops

PHILADELPHIA, Dec. 19 (AP)—Commissioner Bert Bell of the National Football League announced tonight that he and a National League owners' committee would meet here tomorrow with All-America Conference officials to discuss the professional football situation.

Bell's formal announcement, given out after a closed meeting of owners in their hotel headquarters here, said:

"A committee from the All-America Conference is coming to Philadelphia tomorrow to meet with the commissioner and representatives of the National Football League.

"The NFL draft meeting scheduled to start tomorrow morning has been postponed until afternoon, evening or possibly Tuesday."

Bell, whose attitude for the past three years has been to ignore completely the existence of the A.A.C., made his announcement after being informed the All-America group was on the way to Philadelphia.

Tim Mara of the New York Giants, discussing the latest developments, said, "I will have to wait and see what the other league has to offer before I can really comment on the matter.

"After all, since they are coming here I assume they do have something to offer."

Balked in efforts to fly here by the driving snow storm that forced cancellation of all flights from Cleveland to Philadelphia, the AAC owners disclosed in Cleveland they were traveling by train and would arrive early tomorrow morning.

Jonas Ingram, AAC commissioner, announced that his loop's committee was composed of Ben F. Lindheimer of the Los Angeles Dons; Dan Topping of the New York Yankees; Arthur (Mickey) McBride of the Cleveland Browns; James Breuil of the Buffalo Bills, and Tony Morabito of the San Francisco Forty-niners.

The first definite step in forty-eight hours of rumors that the two leagues were going to bury the hatchet came from Cleveland when Ingram disclosed his league had postponed its draft meeting until Tuesday and would confer with NFL.

The meeting of the two leagues had been indicated earlier in the week by remarks made by Alexis Thompson, owner of the National League Philadelphia Eagles, and George Halas, coach and owner of the National League Chicago Bears. Both Thompson and Halas called for a "sensible solution" to the pro football war.

All of the league owners were polled last night by The Associated Press on their feelings about a solution to the football cold war that has skyrocketed player salaries and other expenses and driven several franchises in both leagues into the red. While none would come right out and call for a conference of the two groups, enough hedged to make peace talks appear inevitable.

Motley Paces Browns To 49-To-7 Victory Over Bills In All-America Conference

All-America

Cleveland, Dec. 19 (AP)—Fullback Marion Motley scored three touchdowns today to lead the Cleveland Browns to a 49-to-7 victory over the Buffalo Bills and give the Browns their third straight All-America Football Conference championship.

The unbeaten Browns made a rout of the championship playoff game in the snow-decked Lakeside Stadium. Only 22,981 fans, the smallest crowd of the season, watched in the 33-degree temperature.

Snow Falls Before Game

Snow fell most of the morning then subsided at noon. It began again late in the second quarter and continued intermittently throughout the remainder of the game.

But it didn't bother the Browns. They triumphed with ease to become the first pro team ever to play an entire season without being beaten or tied and first ever to win three titles in a row.

It was the fourth straight year that a Cleveland eleven had competed in a football title playoff game, all resulting in victories. In 1945 the Cleveland Rams, now the Los Angeles Rams, of the National League, defeated Washington.

Graham Leads Attack

During most of the past three seasons, in which Coach Paul Brown's clubs have won 41, lost three and tied one, the attack has been spearheaded by Otto Graham, the all-pro quarterback who handles the T-formation.

He did his usual good job again against the Bills but it was Motley who made the title game a rout.

The 238-pound fullback romped 29 yards for the first of his three touchdowns. It came late in the third period. He went 31 yards for the next one but had to go only five yards for his final which he set up with a 24-yard drive to the Bills' 10-yard line.

Lead, 14-0, At Half

The Browns had built up a 14-to-0 advantage at the half, while the Bills had manufactured only four first downs. George Ratterman, Bills' passing star, was held to a total yardage of minus one in the first half.

The Browns scored in the first period when Tommy James intercepted a Ratterman pass on the midfield stripe and lugged it back 30 yards. Seven plays later Edgar Jones went over from the three. Lou Groza followed with the first of his seven conversions.

Young Recovers Fumble

The count moved to 14 to 0 when George Young scooped up Rex Bumgardner's fumble and ran 18 yards to a score.

Jones also got the first Brown touchdown after the rest, James again intercepting a Ratterman pass to get the Cleveland team in action. James grabbed the ball on the Bills' 23 and carried it to the 21. Two plays took it to the nine and then Graham flipped to Jones for the tally.

The last Brown marker came in the waning seconds after Motley's three in a row, as spectators lined the playing field and pelted snow balls at the players. Center Lou Saban intercepted Jim Still's pass on the Bill 39 and raced into the end zone.

George Ratterman Hurt

Buffalo crossed midfield only four times and only twice under its own power. The Bills registered their lone score in the third when Still took over the passing job from Ratterman who was injured. They moved 52 yards on three of Still's passes that were caught by Bumgardner, William O'Connor and Alton Baldwin.

During the second period Buffalo drove to the Browns' 6 before being halted.

Carries 14 Times

Motley carried the ball 14 times for 133 yards—more than twice the ground gained by the entire Buffalo team. Graham tossed 24 times and completed 11 for 118 yards.

Ratterman and Still each pitched 18 times for the Bills with the former completing only 5 and Still 6. Between the two they picked up 104 yards.

In first downs. Cleveland led by only 15 to 12, each getting 2 on penalties.

Statistics

	Buffalo		Cleveland
First downs	12		15
Net yards gained rushing	63		218
Forward passes attempted	36		26
Forward passes completed	11		11
Yards forward passing	104		118
Forwards intercepted by	1		5
Yards gained runback of interceptions	2		80
Punting average	42		33
Total yards all kicks returned	51		107
Opponent's fumbles recovered	1		3
Yards lost by penalties	27		90

Lineups

CLEVELAND
Left Ends—Speedie. Young. Gil'om.
Left Tackles—Groza. Adams. Pucci.
Left Guards—Ulinski. Humble. Agase.
Centers—Gatski. Saban. Maceau.
Right Guards—Gaudio. Willis. Houston.
Right Tackles—Rymkus. Grigg. Simonetti.
Right Ends—Lavelli. Yonaker. Kosikowski.
Quarterbacks—Graham. Lewis. Terlep.
Left Halfbacks—Edgar Jones. Coletta. Boedeker. Sensanbaugher.
Right Halfbacks—Dub Jones. James. Paraseghian. Cowan.
Fullbacks—Motley. Adamle. Cline.

BUFFALO
Left Ends—Baldwin. Massa. Balatti.
Left Tackles—Armstrong. Kissell.
Left Guards—Lahar. King. Scott.
Centers—Statuto. Hirsch. Prewitt. Baldwin.
Right Guards—Pirro. Wyhonic.
Right Tackles—Kerns. Carpenter. Whalen.
Right Ends—O'Connor. Klaiday. Gibson.
Quarterbacks—Ratterman. Still.
Left Halfbacks—Mutryn. Schneider. Wizbicki.
Right Halfbacks—Bumgardner. Maggioli.
Fullbacks—Tomasetti. Kulbitski. Schuette.

Score by periods:

Cleveland	7	7	14	21	—49
Buffalo	0	0	7	0	—7

Cleveland scoring: Touchdowns—Edgar Jones (2). Young. Motley (3). Saban Points after touchdowns—Groza (7) (placements)
Buffalo scoring: Touchdown—Baldwin Point after touchdown—Armstrong (placement.

Eagles Sold To Syndicate By Thompson

James Clark to Head Philadelphia Group Of New Owners

Philadelphia, Jan. 15.—(AP.)—A syndicate of 100 Philadelphia business men bought the Philadelphia Eagles for $250,000 today to "bring local football back to the community."

The National Football League champions have been owned for eight years by Alexis Thompson, New York millionaire. Thompson said he sold the Philadelphia Franchise because he found it a losing proposition even with a title winning team.

The new owners, headed by James P. Clark, former Democratic city chairman, said, "civic pride and interest in the community have been the factors chiefly motivating the purchase.

"None of the club's new officers will receive any salary," said Clark, adding, "we want this great Philadelphia sports enterprise to maintain its success and acquire the character of a true city project."

Rumor AAC Talking With George Halas

Ben Lindheimer Hints Door Is Not Closed to Peace With Rivals

Chicago, Jan. 20.—(AP.)—Representatives of the All-America Conference reportedly met with Owner Coach George Halas of the rival National Football League tonight, preliminary to executive sessions held by both leagues.

A rumor that an inter-league huddle was held at Halas' office could not be confirmed, but both leagues were an hour late in starting separate executive meetings.

Late arrivals at the Stevens Hotel where the All-America session were Benjamin Lindheimer, chairman of the AAC executive committee, Dan Topping of the New York Yankees and Arthur McBride of the Cleveland Browns.

Lindheimer previously had announced that an All-America session tonight would result in a statement of definite operational plans for the 1949 season. He had strongly indicated that the conference would continue as an eight-club league.

Lindheimer previously had announced that an All-America session tonight would result in a statement of definite operational plans for the 1949 season. He had strongly indicated that the conference would continue as an eight-club league.

Lindheimer, however, did not discount the possibility of further peace conferences with the National League, also gathered here for a business session.

The National League today cleaned up most of its business except schedule making and the owners apparently were twiddling their thumbs awaiting a peace approach by the AAC.

However, Topping declared: "We are getting further away from peace all the time."

Lindheimer declined to comment on strong reports that he would sell his Los Angeles Dons interest and purchase the Chicago Rockets, perhaps the weakest club in the All-America eight-club line-up.

Lindheimer very broadly hinted that the door was not completely slammed on some sort of peace with the National Football League.

National Loop Gives Bell 10-Year Pact, Cuts Limit On Players

Chicago, Jan. 20.—(AP.)—The National Football League, apparently looking ahead to a secure future, today gave Commissioner Bert Bell a 10-year contract, guaranteed visiting teams a $20,000 take and cut player limits in a minor economy move.

Bell, with three years to serve on a contract signed in 1947, will draw a salary of approximately $30,000 on his new 10-year pact.

Clubs traveling on the road in 1949 will receive a minimum of $20,000 when they play—an increase of $5000.

The guarantee is made to offset the "gate" percentage should it fall below $20,000. Visiting teams receive 40 per cent of the gross. At some parks last year the take barely covered expenses although a $15,000 guarantee was assured. One exception was teams playing against the Chicago Bears in Wrigley Field where the "gate" percentage was well above the guarantee—ranging from $35,000 to $40,000.

The All America Conference has a guarantee of $15,000 and percentage is based on 32 per cent of the net.

The club player limit was reduced from 35 to 32, a saving of approximately $20,000 per team.

Commissioner Bell said the $20,000 would be the equivalent of the added money that would be taken in if attendance increased and the games began drawing a $100,000 gate, the league's goal.

The NFL voted to test the free substitution rule for 1949, allowing subs to enter the game at any time rather than during a "time out" and when the ball is exchanged.

The optional use of plastic, rather than all-leather, helmets was okayed. Player benches also may be on the same side of the field instead of opposite sides. This was agreed to offset beefs that in some fields the separation of opposing player benches detracted from the view of paying customers.

The NFL continued its business meeting without discussing 1949 schedules. This was significant because the All America Conference has yet to determine next season's operations, whether with a full eight team complement or a reduced alignment. There still was a possibility of the NFL taking in two AAC members which would mean a new mapping of schedules.

Feb. 1

BROWN SIGNS NEW 5-YEAR CONTRACT

Reprinted from
The Cleveland Plain Dealer

GRID COACH
AGREES TO
EXTENSION

WILL OPERATE WITH 7 TEAMS NEXT SEASON

Chicago Rockets Given $300,000 Financial Boost By League

Chicago, Jan. 21 (AP)—The All-America Football Conference today changed from an eight to seven-club league, merging the New York and Brooklyn entries in a surprise renewal of its grim box office war with the National Football League.

Almost simultaneously, the National loop adjourned its annual meeting, which was held in a hotel across the street from the All-America headquarters. The National League leaders apparently were stunned and perhaps chagrined by the A.A.C.'s announcement it had drawn a fresh battle for a fourth season renewal of their costly feud.

"United And Happy Front"

Instead of collapsing, or merging with the National League as freely predicted during the sessions of the two leagues, the All-America announced after a four-day executive huddle that it would present a "united and happy front" against the 30-year-old National League.

Besides consolidating the Dodgers and Yankees for a 1949 stand at Yankee Stadium, the All-America also gave its Chicago Rockets—the league's weakest sister—a $300,-000 financial shot in the arm.

Rockets To Be Strengthened

Under new ownership, the Rockets will get player strength from the merged Brooklyn club and, according to the All-America's plans for a "new look," will be a fitting rival of the National League's Cardinals and Bears in the battle for Chicago fan patronage.

The National League's only action today was granting a New York franchise to the former Boston Yanks, who will play at the Polo Grounds, sharing dates with the New York football giants.

Strader To Coach Yanks

Thus, the All-America apparently had strengthened its position on the pivotal New York front, having only one entry — the combined Dodger-Yankee club—to compete against the Giants and Boston Yanks.

Owner Dan Topping, of the New York Yankees, and Branch Rickey, of the Brooklyn Dodgers, disclosed jointly that Red Strader, coach of the Yankees, would be head coach of the Dodger-Yankee combination and Carl Voyles, the head Brooklyn coach, would become Strader's assistant.

Rickey, Topping Partners

Under the new setup, Rickey will be a partner of Topping's and the Yankee Stadium will be leased to their club. Topping is co-owner of the New York baseball Yankees, who operate Yankee Stadium.

The Chicago Rockets now have "$300,000 on the line" for the 1949 season, according to Ben F. Lindheimer, chairman of the A.A.C. executive committee and owner of the Los Angeles Dons. Lindheimer, widely described as an "angel" of the Rockets in previous seasons, denied that he would have any interest in the refinanced Chicago entry. He said the new ownership setup would be announced in a week.

To Decide Schedule Later

The National League adjourned without any announcement of its 1949 schedule, but Commissioner Bell said the individual clubs would be mailed copies of the proposed schedule and would release their own slates.

The All-America Conference continued its schedule, but Lindheimer said the meeting was devoted mainly to details of the revised line-up and that a schedule on a home-and-home basis for each club probably would be developed at a later meeting.

Bell Says "Good Luck"

The All-America's statement of continuance plans with a seven-club league was accepted spiritedly by the National League, which fully had expected a collapse of the rival circuit.

Declared Bert Bell, commissioner of the National League:

"I have nothing to say except 'good luck.'"

Bell, who yesterday was handed a new ten-year contract by his league, said he had heard of no official "peace" gestures between the two leagues.

Halas Skeptical Of Success

However, Owner-Coach George Halas, of the Chicago Bears, heading a group of National Leaguers, conferred with Arthur McBride, owner of the A.A.C.'s Cleveland Browns in the wee hours this morning.

At that session the National League related an offer it previously had made in a "peace" conference at Philadelphia last month: to accept the San Francisco Forty-Niners and Cleveland for a 12-club single league.

Today, Halas declared that as a seven-club league, the A.A.C. would have little chance for success.

Rockets Change Name; Obtain 26 New Players

Chicago Team Now Hornets

Brooklyn Club Transfers Athletes After Merger With Yanks

Chicago, Ill. -(AP)- The Chicago Rockets of the All-America Football conference had a new name and a new owner Wednesday, along with a flock of new players and some fresh money to carry them into the 1949 professional campaign.

The new name is the Hornets. The new owner is James C. Thompson, 52, owner of the Chicago Opera building, who has backed the club with $300,000. The club obtained 26 players from the Brooklyn Dodgers, who merged with the New York Yankees. The list of players follows:

Backs—Bob Chappuis, Bob Hoernschemeyer, Jim Smith, Walt McDonald, Carl Allen, Hardy Brown, Jim Camp, Nick Forkovitch, Hugo Marcolini and Lee Tevis.

Ends — Henry Folberg, Dan Edwards, Saxon Judd, Max Morris, Edwin Scruggs and Harry Burrus.

Tackles—Ralph Sazio, John Clowes, Garland Williams.

Guards—Herbert St. John, Robert Leonetti, Harry Buffington and Amos Harris.

Centers—George Strohmeyer, Caleb Warrington and Edsel Gustafson.

In addition, the Hornets obtained halfback Bob Sweiger from the New York Yankees and rights to tackle Graham Armstrong of Buffalo and tackles Pete Berezney and Lee Artoe of the Baltimore Colts.

Meanwhile, a few old Rocket skeletons were jiggling in the All-America closet.

Dick Hanley, who coached the Chicago club in 1946, filed suit Wednesday in superior court for $38,750 in back pay. Commissioner O. O. Kessing, who attended the Hornet coming out party, said Hanley presumably would have to settle with John Keeshin, the first of four different Chicago club owners.

Seven Dodger Players Are Kept by Yankees

New York, N. Y.—The New York Yankees of the All-America Football conference, who merged forces with the Brooklyn Dodgers Tuesday, have retained seven players from the latter club. The others have been sent to the Chicago Hornets.

Players retained by the Yankees are tackle Martin Ruby, fullbacks Lou Kusserow, Ray Ramsey and Mickey Colmer, guard John Wozniak, halfback Roy (Monk) Gafford and end Scott Beasley.

There were reports Wednesday that the Yankees would get George Ratterman, Buffalo Bills passing ace, in a deal.

In the National league the transplanted Boston Yankees, who share the Polo Grounds with the New York Giants, have changed their name to the New York Bulldogs to avoid confusion with the All-America Yankees.

Bulldogs Obtain Bobby Layne From Bears In Trade

New York, June 13. The professional football "war" sizzled like the weather today with the announcement that the Chicago Bears were sending Bobby Layne, T-formation quarterback, to their National League brothers, the New York Bulldogs, for a bundle of cash and two players.

Ted Collins, owner of the Bulldogs, who are moving into the Polo Grounds next fall from Boston to seek a share of the Metropolitan football gravy, fearlessly pronounced the deal "the biggest in the history of the National League."

Layne, who led the University of Texas Longhorns to two Southwest Conference titles and was an all-conference selection for four years from '44 through '47, joined the Chicago club last season but was used sparingly because of injuries.

His transfer to the Bulldogs means that Collins has landed the outstanding passer he has been seeking with which to battle the combined Brooklyn-New York club of the All-America Conference for the favor of local fans next autumn. The two teams from the rival leagues will be in direct and bitter competition for patronage on several Sundays.

The NFL New York Giants, who permitted Collins to bring his team into the Polo Grounds, don't have many scheduled collisions with the All-America club.

ROOKIE QUARTERBACK

GEORGE BLANDA

Promising rookie signal caller, who has been the Bears' pre-season sensation. Blanda will appear against the Los Angeles Rams, October 9th. Hails from the University of Kentucky 6:1½ and weighs 195 pounds.

Van Buren Sets Record as Eagles Rally to Down Lion Eleven, 22-14

DETROIT, Oct. 3 (AP)—Halfback Steve Van Buren of the Philadelphia Eagles set a new National Football League lifetime ground gaining record tonight as he smashed over for two fourth-period touchdowns to give the Eagles a 22-24 victory over the Detroit Lions.

Van Buren piled up 135 yards in 33 tries to run his total to 3,951 yards for his league career. The former Louisiana State University star, now in his sixth year as a pro, eclipsed the record of 3,860 yards set by Clarke Hinkle of the Green Bay Packers in ten years as a pro.

Statistics of the Game

	Eagles	Lions
First downs	25	13
Yards gained, rushing	236	102
Forward passes	26	22
Forwards completed	19	7
Yards gained, forwards	101	69
Passes intercepted by	2	2
*Av. dist. of punts, yds.	39	36
Fumbles	2	1
Rival fumbles recovered	1	2
Yards lost, penalties	68	90

*From line of scrimmage.

Oct. 9

49ers Wallop Browns; Dons Beat Buffalo Bills

Frankie Albert Sparks Frisco to 56-28 Win; Los Angeles Humbles Foe, 42-28

By the Associated Press

San Francisco's rugged Forty-niners smashed the defending champion Cleveland Browns Sunday, 56-28, to take command of the All-America Football conference.

Playing before 59,770 home town fans, the Forty-niners scored in every period to hand the Browns their first defeat in 30 starts. Frankie Albert, Frisco's southpaw slinger, highlighted the thrill a minute contest by firing five touchdown passes.

The Forty-niners bolted to a lightning 21-0 edge on two Albert fireballs and a one foot buck by little John Strzkalski.

Led by quarterback Otto Graham, who pitched three touchdowns in the first half, Cleveland cut the deficit slightly but trailed at half time, 35-21.

In the second half Albert took control again, pitching 24 yards to Eddie Carr, giving the 49ers a 42-21 edge. Joe Perry and Carr added two additional tallies in the final quarter to complete the route.

Cleveland's last defeat, nearly two years ago in November, 1947, was inflicted by the Los Angeles Dons, 13-10.

In another contest the Los Angeles Dons beat the Buffalo Bills, 42-28, before a Los Angeles crowd of 16,757. The game was a passing duel between the Dons' Glenn Dobbs and the Bills' George Ratterman.

Ratterman collected 305 yards through the air, good for a pair of touchdowns. Dobbs, meanwhile, amassed 283 yards passing and 48 more running.

CLEVELAND-SAN FRANCISCO

	Cleveland	San Francisco
First downs	10	17
Yards gained rushing (net)	86	258
Forward passes attempted	26	31
Forward passes completed	13	18
Yards by forward passes	281	249
Forward passes intercepted by	4	3
Yards gained, runback of intercepted passes	27	23
Punting average (from scrimmage)	30.05	43.4
Total yards all kicks returned	155	203
Opponents' fumbles recovered	3	0
Yards lost by penalties	50	35
Cleveland	7 14 0 7—28	
San Francisco	21 14 7 14—56	

Scoring summary:
Cleveland Touchdowns—Speedie 2, Lavelli, Motley. Points after touchdowns—Groza 4 (place kicks).
San Francisco touchdowns—Strzykalski 2, Perry 2, Beals, Susoeff, Carr 2. Points after touchdowns—Vetrano 8 (place kicks).

BUFFALO-LOS ANGELES DONS

	Buffalo	Los Angeles
First downs	19	19
Net yards gained rushing	187	187
Forward passes attempted	35	27
Forward passes completed	18	18
Yards forward passing	319	283
Forwards intercepted by	0	3
Yards gained runback interceptions	0	13
Punting average	37	39
Total yards all kicks returned	113	133
Opponent fumbles recovered	2	3
Yards lost by penalties	57	90
Buffalo	7 14 7 0—28	
Los Angeles	0 21 14 7—42	

Buffalo Scoring—Touchdowns: Cline, Mutryn, A. Baldwin, Lukens. Points after touchdowns—Adams 4.
Los Angeles Scoring — Touchdowns: Dobbs, Grimes 2, Wilkins, Rodgers, Wimberly. Points after touchdowns—Nelson 6.

Bears Turn Back Lions by 28-7; Lujack Shows Way With Passes

Ex-Notre Dame Star's Tosses Good for Two Touchdowns in Snowstorm at Detroit— Smith Runs 102 Yards for Losers

DETROIT, Nov. 24 (AP)—The Chicago Bears had a comparatively easy time today rolling to a 28-7 decision over the Detroit Lions before 24,385 chilled fans, who braved a snowstorm to see the National Football League game.

Detroit's sole consolation was a sensational 102-yard run by Bob Smith, who intercepted a Sid Luckman pass in the Detroit end zone and went all the way for a touchdown.

It set a league record for return of an intercepted pass. The old mark of 100 yards was held by Vern Huffman of Detroit and set in 1937 against Brooklyn.

Statistics of the Game

	Bears.	Detroit.
First downs	18	9
Yards gained, rushing	144	40
Forward passes	24	25
Forwards completed	16	8
Yards gained, forwards	192	70
Forwards intercepted by	4	1
*Av. dist. of punts, yds.	42	39
Runback of kicks, yds.	84	159
Rival fumbles recovered	1	1
Yards lost, penalties	77	32

*From line of scrimmage.

Bears Down Cardinals, 52 to 21, As Lujack Passes for Six Scores

Quarterback Connects on 24 of 40 Aerials for 468-Yard Gain, New League Record —Kavanaugh, Hoffman Tally Twice

CHICAGO, Dec. 11 (AP)—Playing his finest game in two years as a Chicago Bear quarterback, Johnny Lujack passes and set a National Football League record with an aerial gain of 468 yards as his team routed the Chicago Cardinals, 52—21.

A Wrigley Field throng of 50,101 sat through a drizzle to watch the crosstown rivals battle in their fifty-seventh meeting on a slippery, muddy gridiron. It was the Bears' thirty-eighth victory in pro football's oldest rivalry and their ninth in twelve league starts this season.

Today's score also was the most decisive since the Northsiders hoisted a 53-7 verdict over the Cards in 1941.

Baugh's Record Smashed

Lujack's fancy aerial work bested by 22 yards the record gain of 446 registered by Washington's Sammy Baugh against Boston on Oct. 31, 1948. Lujack completed twenty-four out of forty tosses and connected for four touchdowns in the first half to give the Bears an overwhelming 31-7 edge.

The former Notre Dame star, who is on the Bear payroll for about $20,000 per season, missed by only one touchdown pitch of matching the league mark set by the Bears' Sid Luckman against the New York Giants in 1943.

As it was, Johnny nearly had three more pay-off pitches to his credit. In the first quarter, he hit Julie Rykovich for 12 yards only to have the receiver fumble on the 1-yard line. Ken Kavanaugh was brought down from behind on the Cardinal 2 after taking a 10-yard pass in the third. And in the fourth, Kavanaugh also was caught on the Card 12 after a 58-yard toss from Lujack.

Blanda Kicks Field Goal

The Bears clinched the game with two touchdowns in the first five minutes on Lujack's 52-yard toss to George McAfee and one for 17 yards to Kavanaugh.

In the second, Lujack connected with Kavanaugh for 37 and a third counter then hit Jackrabbit Boone

Statistics of the Game

	Bears.	Cards.
First downs	24	17
Yards gained, rushing	128	48
Forward passes	42	31
Forwards completed	24	19
Yards gained, forwards	468	280
*Av. dist. of punts, yds.	43.6	44.7
‡Runback of kicks, yds	161	131
Rival fumbles recovered	2	1
Yards lost, penalties	102	50

*From line of scrimmage.
‡Includes punts and kick-offs.

for 18 and a fourth. George Blanda added a 25-yard field goal in the final minute of the second period.

The Bears struck mainly on the ground for an 80-yard touchdown parade at the outset of the third. George Gulyanics went over from the 2.

In the finale, Lujack's aerials paid off for 6 yards to John Hoffman and 65 to Hoffman. Lujack converted after each score.

The Cardinals, gaining 280 yards by passing, counted on Paul Christman's 3-yard flip to Charlie Trippi in the first, his 49-yard connection with Mal Kutner in the third, and his 19-yard completion to Trippi in the fourth.

Pat Harder converted, raising his scoring tally to 102 points for the season.

The line-up:

CHICAGO BEARS (52)
Left Ends—Kavanaugh, Milner, Dugger.
Left Tackles—Connor, Davis, Bauman.
Left Guards—Drulis, Preston, Flanagan.
Centers—Turner, Clarkson, Szymanski.
Right Guards—Bray, Serini.
Right Tackles—Stenn, Stickel.
Right Ends—Keane, Sprinkle.
Quarterbacks—Lujack, Blanda.
Left Halfbacks—Gulyanics, Boone, Dreyer, Magnani.
Right Halfbacks—Rykovich, McAfee, Perina, Decorrevont.
Fullbacks—Hoffman, Klndt, Cody.

CHICAGO CARDINALS (21)
Left Ends—Ravensberg, Dewell, Wham, Dove.
Left Tackles—Fischer, Goldsberry.
Left Guards—Petrovich, Coemer.
Centers—Blackburn, Banonis, Campbell.
Right Guards—Ramsey, Apolskis, Nichols.
Right Tackles—Andros, Zimny.
Right Ends—Kutner, Cain.
Quarterbacks—Christman, Hardy, Nussbaumer.
Left Halfbacks—Trippi, Davis, Cochran.
Right Halfbacks—Angsman, Self, Schwall.
Fullbacks—Harder, Clatt, Dimancheff, Yablonski.

SCORE BY PERIODS
Chicago Bears .... 14 17 7 14—52
Chicago Cardinals .... 7 0 7 7—21
Touchdowns—McAfee, Trippi 2, Kutner, Kavanaugh 2, Boone, Gulyanics, Hoffman 2. Field goal—Blanda. Points after touchdown—Lujack 7, Harder 3.

BEARS TURN BACK STEELERS BY 30-21

Fight Off Pittsburgh Rally in Last Period as Gage Dashes 97 Yards to Pace Losers

STATISTICS OF THE GAME

	Bears.	St'lers.
First downs	19	14
Yards gained, rushing	154	140
Forward passes	30	22
Forwards completed	13	10
Yards gained, forwards	201	207
Forwards intercepted by	4	2
*Av. dist. of punts, yds.	42.4	45.7
‡Run-back of kicks, yds.	113	80
Rival fumbles recovered	2	1
Yards lost, penalties	66	23

*From line of scrimmage.
‡Includes punts and kick-offs.

CHICAGO Dec. 4 (AP)—The Chicago Bears beat off a last period Pittsburgh rally—which was paced by Rookie Bobby Gage's record-tying 97-yard touchdown run—to whip the Steelers, 30—21, in a National Football League thriller today.

A chilled Wrigley Field crowd of 36,071 was stunned by Pittsburgh's comeback, touched off by the former Clemson Comet's sprint, the longest run from scrimmage of the season, topping the 82-yard scoring spurt by the Chicago Cardinals' Elmer Angsman against Detroit Oct. 23. It matched the league record set by Andy Uram of Green Bay against the Cardinals in 1939.

Pittsburgh also established a team record for itself. It was the first time the Steelers had scored more than one touchdown against the Bears since the two clubs began battling in 1934.

Fans Clamor For Pro Grid Title Game

Most of Owners Also Approve; Bell Calls Plan Unconstitutional

Philadelphia, Dec. 10.—(AP.)—The fans want it, most of the club owners want it, but there will be no world championship professional football game in 1949.

That's what Bert Bell, pro football czar said today.

The reason: "It's unconstitutional."

While the peace pipes were still being puffed at the end of the bitter four-year pro football war, the clamor arose for a championship game between the titleholders of the National Football League and All-America Conference.

On December 19, the day after the NFL championship game, the circuits merge into the National-American Football League and all the bars to contests between teams in rival leagues will be lowered.

But there won't be any this year, Bell said.

The commissioner said "the season will be over and the NFL constitution forbids post-season games. The constitution can't be changed until the first meeting of the new league January 19."

Pro Football Warfare Ends As Rival Loops Join Hands

Three All-America Conference Elevens Merge With 10 National League Clubs to Form National-American Football League

Philadelphia, Dec. 9.—(AP.)—Professional football's four-year war was settled across a conference table today. The All America Conference merged into the National Football League. Thus ended one of the most costly wars in the history of athletics. Losses to club owners soared to upwards of two million dollars in the protracted battle for players and attendance. The new league is to be called the National-American Football League, the NAF. It is to be made up of 13 teams: The complete 10-club NFL and three from the fledgling AAC.

Nobody said so at the hastily summoned press conference at which the report was flashed, but the merger unquestionably is a victory for the older NFL, which fought for four years to drive the AAC out of business.

Bert Bell, the chubby, affable Philadelphia Main Liner, remains at the helm of the new loop as commissioner. He signed for a new 10-year pact at an undisclosed salary. Bell had been commissioner of the NFL.

O. O. Kessing, commissioner of the AAC, resigns at the close of the current season. He tendered his resignation some weeks ago.

Under the new setup, Emil R. Fischer of the Green Bay Packers will become president of the National Division and Daniel Sherby of the Cleveland Browns head of the American Division.

Stoneham Starts Move.

If there is one man responsible for the merger, it is Horace Stoneham, ruddy-faced owner of the New York baseball Giants.

Stoneham is owner of the Polo Grounds, where two New York NFL teams played in 1949 and lost a considerable amount of money.

Bell and J. Arthur Friedlund, representing the AAC, told newsmen that Stoneham started the merger move by summoning Bell and Friedlund to New York last Friday.

They talked for a while there and then came to Philadelphia two days ago. Round-the-clock conferences came to an end shortly after noon today and the two men, tired but jubilant, summoned reporters to break the news.

Bell, unshaved but beaming, joined with the dapper Friedlund to announce the new league was conceived 'not only in the interest of the public but also to assure the permanency of professional football."

These are the 13 teams in the NAF:

From the NFL: Philadelphia, New York Giants, New York Bulldogs, Washington, Pittsburgh, Chicago Bears, Chicago Cardinals, Detroit, Green Bay and Los Angeles.

From the AAC: San Francisco 49ers, Cleveland Browns, Baltimore Colts.

The league is to be split into the National and American divisions with the winners of the divisions meeting in a world football championship. Makeup of the divisions has not yet been determined.

The new league comes into being on December 19, the day after the NFL championship game.

Bell said there definitely would not be a post season game this season between the winners of the two leagues.

"The constitution of the National League forbids post season games," said Bell "and by agreement the new organization has adopted the constitution of the NFL."

Collins Buys Yankees.

The complication in the merger is what will happen to the players on the three AAC teams liquidated in the move and to the college players already drafted by clubs in the two circuits for the 1950 season.

The AAC and NFL draft meetings were canceled.

All of these players will be tossed into a giant pool when the NAF gets together at its first meeting, tentatively arranged for January.

It will take approval of 11 of the 13 teams for any player to be assigned to a new club.

Bell said that the only players who will not be affected by the formation of the new league are the 32 players on each of the rosters of the 13 teams in the new league.

The two New York teams are special cases, however. Dan Topping's New York Yankees of the AAC was purchased outright by Ted Collins, owner of the New York Bulldogs. Collins acquired the right to deal with all but six of the players on the Yankees.

Those six go to the New York Giants. The names of the six players were not disclosed.

In addition to the Yankees, the Buffalo Bills, Los Angeles Dons and Chicago Hornets of the AAC are going out of business. The Hornets are to be broken up completely, while the Dons merge with Los Angeles Rams and the Bills with the Cleveland Browns.

James Breuil, owner of the Buffalo club of the AAC, has acquired what Bell and Friedlund said was "a substantial interest" in the Browns and has exclusive rights of that club to present exhibition games at Buffalo.

Connie Mack Had Team.

Professional football was born in 1895 in a game at Latrobe, Pa. Connie Mack, owner-manager of the Philadelphia Athletics, organized a team in 1902.

The National Football League was organized in 1921 although it wasn't known by that name until a year later. Its first name was the American Professional Football Association. The league was reorganized in 1927 and six years later the circuit was broken up into Eastern and Western divisions with the winners playing for the world championship.

In 1946, however, eight teams got together and organized themselves as the All America Conference.

It was at that point that the war started.

Salaries of players soared into astronomical figures as teams from the two leagues fought a battle of dollars for their services. Competition between the leagues and owners' costs rose sharply but there was no comparable rise in receipts.

Thompson Quit Fight.

Some club owners, notably Alexis Thompson, millionaire head of the Philadelphia Eagles of the NFL, quit the fight, saying it was costing too much. Other owners grumbled.

Last winter it appeared as if the two leagues would get together. Representatives met for three days at Philadelphia, but they couldn't agree on a merger plan.

Hints of a peace between the loops were dropped sporadically ever since then, but it wasn't until Stoneham got Bell and Friedlund together that something concrete was done.

Friedlund is general counsel and secretary of the baseball New York Yankees and the football Yankees. He and Bell and George Weiss, vice-president and general manager of the baseball Yankees, conferred briefly in New York at Stoneham's invitation before the confab moved here and Weiss dropped out.

The merger plan had been a closely-guarded secret. It came with an unexpected suddenness.

"We do things in a hurry when we do them," Bell remarked.

"Especially when there's a lot of money involved," someone suggested.

Chortled Bell: "You're darned right."

ROWNS WIN 4TH STRAIGHT CHAMPIONSHIP

dgar And Dub Jones Star In All-America Pro Football Victory

Cleveland, Dec. 11 (AP)—Cleveland's Browns won the All-America Conference football championship for the fourth straight year today, defeating the San Francisco Forty-Niners, 21 to 7, in the final playoff game.

Thus the Browns completed their four-year domination of the All-America loop, which has merged with the older National League, effective after next week.

Each Tallies Once

It marked the first time a professional team had won its league championship for four straight years—and the Browns did it in impressive style on a muddy, slippery field.

This game was "for the boys"—the players getting 70 per cent of the gate—and the Jones boys, Edgar and Dub, put the big share on ice for the Cleveland club. Each scored a touchdown.

Edgar Jones, playing one of his finest games, scored the first touchdown for the Browns in seven minutes and 20 seconds of the first period. He climaxed a 56-yard seven-play drive with a two-yard plunge into the end zone.

Motley Races 63 Yards

The second Cleveland tally came on the most spectacular scoring play of the game—a 63-yard sprint off tackle by big Marion Motley. The huge Negro cracked through the line on a trap play, was deep in the San Francisco backfield before anyone saw him, and he was going away as he crossed the goal line.

That run put the Browns ahead, 14 to 0, and the Forty-Niners struck right back for their only marker.

The Forty-Niners, winging along on the fine passing arm of Frankie Albert, rolled 74 yards to their one score in the first 14 seconds of the final period. Albert connected with his end, Paul Salata, on a 24-yard toss for the touchdown on fourth down.

Vetrano Doesn't Miss

That set the stage for Joe Vetrano, San Francisco's place-kick expert, to boot his one hundred and seventh consecutive point after touchdown and a record of having scored in all the 56 games played by the Forty-Niners.

With Cleveland ahead by only 14 to 7 now, Dub Jones, from Tulane, clinched the victory with a 4-yard touchdown plunge in the final session. The marker coming on the eleventh play after the Browns started marching 69 yards away.

The contest, before 22,550 fans, was a rugged one all the way with much of the play on the ground. It was the cleanest of the season, despite players being unrecognizable because of the mud after the first few minutes.

Only One 5-Yard Penalty

Not one penalty was called on the Forty-Niners, and only one offside on the Browns, making a five-yard penalty total for the contest. Neither team picked up an opposing fumble and no passes were intercepted, although the Browns threw 17, and the losers hit the airways 25 times.

The Browns had the better of both ground-gaining departments, outgaining the Forty-Niners, 217 to 122 yards, on the ground, and 128 to 108 in the air.

Sam Cathcart, former Santa Barbara State back who ate up 116 yards on the ground in the losers' previous appearance here, was held to 11 yards in nine attempts today.

Albert Losers' Star

Motley, aided by his great scoring run, was the big gainer with 75 yards in eight attempts for the Browns. Edgar Jones made 63 in 16 jaunts, and Otto Graham, the Cleveland pass-master, sneaked nine times for 62.

Albert was the big threat for the Californians, picking up 41 yards in five runs, most of them coming after he was apparently trapped on pass attempts. Fullback Joe Perry was next with 36 yards in a half dozens tries.

VAN BUREN IS STAR WITH 196 YARDS GAINED

Pihos And Skladany Score On Forward Pass And Blocked Kick

NATIONAL LEAGUE

Los Angeles, Dec. 18 (AP)—The Philadelphia Eagles defeated the Los Angeles Rams today, 14 to 0, to win the National Football League championship for the second straight year.

The Eagles, masters in every department of play, scored one touchdown in the second quarter on the pasing of Tommy Thompson, and added another in the third on a blocked punt.

Biggest disappointment was the weather and the crowd.

It rained all night preceding the game—Los Angeles' first view of a major league title show; it rained during most of the game and reduced the contest to a rather sluggish exhibition.

Battle In Mud

The owners and the players wanted to postpone the game until Christmas Day, and so did thousands of protesting Los Angeles fans. But Commissioner Bert Bell, in Philadelphia, forced the contest—the seventeenth National League title playoff—to go on.

As a result of the weather, only 22,245 fans braved the pelting rain to see the battle of the mud. Paid attendance was 27,980 for seats sold in advance, and 70,000 and more were expected had the skies been clear.

Van Buren Breaks Records

The Rams' passing attack, Los Angeles' major weapon, was completely nullified by the mud and the charging, ever-aggressive Philadelphia linemen. The Rams only gained 98 yards overhead—completing a mere 10 of the 27 passes Waterfield and his understudy, Norman Van Brocklin, attempted.

The real hero of the game, although he never scored, was Steve Van Buren. He wrote two new records into the National Football League books.

The onetime Louisiana State star gained a net 196 yards in 31 trips with the ball, breaking the record for one title game set at 159 yards by Elmer Angsman for the Chicago Cardinals in whipping Philadelphia in the 1947 playoff. Angsman carried the ball only ten times.

Tops Nagurski's Mark

Van Buren also erased a record held by the great Bronko Nagurski, who amassed 214 yards in 57 carries in four title games for the Chicago Bears. Van Buren, on 75 carries in three games, now has 320 yards rushing.

Twice Van Buren uncorked crushing gains that set up scoring opportunities. One went for 49 yards deep into Ram territory, but the chance was lost when Jim Parmer fumbled on the Ram seven. Another 23-yard explosion went for naught when one of Thompson's passes was intercepted.

The big Eagle line refused to back down in the sloppy going, and wound up handing the Rams the dubious distinction of gaining less on the ground than any club in the history of the National League playoff.

The Rams managed to gain only 21 yards rushing, one less than the previous low mark of 22 registered by the Washington Redskins the year the Chicago Bears walloped them, 73 to 0, in 1940.

Once the Rams got to the Eagle 25, again to the 37. That was the

Buffalo Bid Turned Down By Grid Loop

Rams Lead Opposition To Fourteenth Eleven For Combined Circuit

Philadelphia, Jan. 20.—(AP.)—Buffalo and Houston lost their uphill battles for National-American Football League franchises today. NAFL owners voted against admitting a fourteenth member.

Oakland, Calif., also was rejected on the same ballot but that city's chances admittedly were forlorn. Commissioner Bert Bell said "practically the whole discussion was on Buffalo."

"Nobody was opposed to Buffalo," said Bell, "providing a satisfactory schedule could be worked out."

Dan Reeves, president of the Los Angeles Rams who voted against the applicants, summed up the opposition standpoint.

"We were afraid to vote them in," said Reeves, "until we saw how the schedule would be affected by them. We have nothing against Buffalo. In fact we were very much impressed by their efforts."

Bell, refusing to announce the total of the voice vote, said "quite a few were in favor and quite a few against." The measure required a unanimous vote to pass.

Doak Walker Acquired By Detroit Club

Southern Methodist Ace Signs With Pro Eleven At Estimated $38,000

Detroit, Feb. 25.—(AP.)—The Detroit Lions announced today the signing of Doak Walker, Southern Methodist's heralded halfback, for a three-year contract totalling an estimated $38,000.

(In Dallas, Walker said at a press conference that he had received a bonus of a "couple of cleats and shoelaces."

(He would not say how much he would receive in salary and bonus, but one reliable source said it was more than an estimate of $38,000 announced in Detroit and probably was "around $60,000.")

All America gave the Lions two of the most celebrated college football players of the 1949 season. Next year Walker will team with Notre Dame's Leon Hart, who recently signed with the Lions for approximately the same terms.

Coach Bo Mc Millin hailed the acquisition of Walker with delight.

"He was great in college," he said of the four-sport star, "and now with his lot cast to one sport, he'll be greater still."

Walker said, "I've had my eye on professional football for some time. A few years will give me the necessary experience I want to enter college coaching."

"I'm certainly happy to be with Detroit," Walker said. It had been easy to negotiate with Mc Millin, he added, because of McMillin's close friendship with Matty Bell, coach at Southern Methodist. Bell was Bo's high school teammate at North Fort Worth, Tex., and later at Centre College.

The 23-years-old Walker weighs 173 pounds and stands five feet 11 inches. He played a total of 35 games in college including the 1948 and 1949 Cotton Bowl games. He gained 2076 yards in 501 plays for better than four yards a try, completed 138 passes in 239 attempts for 1786 yards and caught 29 passes for 479 yards. He had a four-year punting average of 39.6 yards a try. His total points scored in four years were 303.

The Doaker was a versatile athlete. Besides winning four letters in football, he picked up three in baseball and one in basketball. He also was good in track, swimming and tennis.

Walker has recovered fully from an injury and illness that kept him out of play for part of the 1949 college schedule, Mc Millin reported.

In Dallas, Tex., it was announced Walker will be married March 17 to Miss Norma Peterson of Dallas, his college sweetheart.

Curly Lambeau Quits to Coach the Cardinals

LEADER OF PACKERS ENDS 31-YEAR REIGN

Lambeau Resigns Because of Differences Over Policy. Goes to Chicago Cards

SIGNS TWO-YEAR CONTRACT

To Be Vice President as Well as Coach—Green Bay Has No Successor in View Now

CHICAGO, Feb. 1 (P)—Earl L. (Curly) Lambeau, dean of professional football coaches with thirty-one years as leader of the Green Bay Packers, today became head mentor of the Chicago Cardinals.

Lambeau, 51 years old, accepted a two-year contract as Cardinal field head and vice president after resigning at Green Bay to "restore the harmony so necessary if the Packers are to keep their place in major league football."

Lambeau becomes the fourteenth Cardinal coach since the club was organized in 1921, succeeding Raymond (Buddy) Parker, who resigned last December. Lambeau's salary was not disclosed, but he will run the Cardinal club.

Interested in Isbell

At a press conference, Lambeau said he was interested in signing Cecil Isbell, former coach of the Baltimore Colts, who starred as a passer for him at Green Bay. He also said he planned to continue the T-formation, which the Cardinals used successfully last season.

"I am confident I can do a better coaching job for the Cardinals than I did at Green Bay," he added.

Lambeau organized the Packers in 1919, a year before Owner-Coach George Halas of the Chicago Bears founded the Decatur, Ill. Staleys, forerunners of the Bears. Both were iron men of the National Football League, now the National-American League.

Now they resume their long rivalry on the field on a cross-town basis. That would help the turnstiles at Comiskey Park and Wrigley Field, where the Cards and Bears respectively operate.

The Cardinals caught Lambeau on the recoil after front-office bickering at Green Bay. His letter of resignation today, addressed to Emil R. Fischer, Packer president, clearly indicated that he was quitting instead of playing second fiddle at Green Bay.

The letter conceded that Packer policy changes the past several years, with which Lambeau disagreed, "brought about a dangerous disunity of purpose within the corporation, one which in my opinion threatens the existence of the club. No organization can survive divided against itself."

Field is "Wide Open"

At his winter home in Miami Beach, Fla., Fischer said Lambeau's resignation "was not entirely unexpected."

"We wish Curly all the success in the world in his new job and feel that his move is in the best interests of both Curly and the Packers," Fischer added.

"Fans can expect immediate action on the matter of choosing a new coach. I might add that the field is wide open."

Last season, the Packers won only two of twelve games and, after the third game, Lambeau turned over the coaching to his three aides, Tom Stidham, Bob Snyder and Charles Brock.

Lambeau's lifetime record with the Packers includes six National League titles, seven divisional championships and one first-place tie. In all, his Packers won 236 games, lost 111 and tied twenty-three in league competition.

Green Bay's best season was in 1929, when the Packers won thirteen and tied one in fourteen starts, scoring 212 points and yielding only 24.

The success of the Packers in Green Bay, a northern Wisconsin community of 46,000, was one of the wonders of professional football. Much of it came from canny direction of Lambeau, one of the game's leading forward pass stylists.

National Football League Keeps Name, Designates 2 'Conferences'

Combination Title Assumed After 'Merger' With All-America Is Dropped—Group Winners to Meet for Championship

PHILADELPHIA, March 3 (AP)— In a roundabout way, the National Football League admitted today that it didn't merge with the All-America Conference. Instead, it merely gobbled up the A. A. C.

Commissioner Bert Bell didn't put it that way in announcing that professional football would operate next season as the National Football League and not the National-American Football League.

But the implication was clear. He said 1950 marks the thirty-first continuous year of the N. F. L.

Last December, Bell, in announcing the "merger," described the National-American as a "new league." It expired today without one football game having been played.

Bell said the decision to stick by the old name was made upon advice of counsel and unanimous consent of the thirteen club owners.

In 1950 the league will have thirteen instead of ten teams and a new designation for its two branches.

Ten Teams Last Year

Last year there were five teams each in the league's divisions, labeled "Eastern" and "Western."

In 1950 the divisions become "conferences," to be known as the National and American.

This step obviously is aimed at putting pro football on the same basis as major league baseball with two leagues and a world series of football.

The conferences are made up this way:

American — Chicago Cardinals, Cleveland Browns, New York Giants, Philadelphia Eagles, Pittsburgh Steelers and Washington Redskins.

National—Baltimore Colts, Chicago Bears, Detroit Lions, Green Bay Packers, Los Angeles Rams, New York Bulldogs and San Francisco 49ers.

The three teams which played last year in the All-America Conference are Cleveland, Baltimore and San Francisco.

Schedule Is Explained

The schedule will be played in this manner:

The six teams in the American Conference and six of those in the National—Baltimore is the exception—will play twelve games. Each team will play home-and-home games with the other five clubs in its conference, one with a "traditional rival" and one against Baltimore.

The Colts are the league's "swing" team, playing each of the other twelve clubs once during the season.

The winners in the two conferences will meet in a championship game at the end of the regular season.

Each conference will have its own president, with Dan Sherby of Cleveland head of the American Conference and Emil R. Fisher of Green Bay president of the National.

April 9

Layne Landed with No Cash

Straight Deal Made With Ted Collins

By WATSON SPOELSTRA

Bo McMillin swung an astonishing deal Saturday when he acquired Quarterback Bobby Layne from the New York Yanks in exchange for Fullback Camp Wilson.

"It was a straight trade, with not a nickel in cash thrown in," declared the Detroit Lion general manager and coach.

Detroit thus obtained one of the National Football League's best T-formation quarterbacks for a 27-year-old fullback who rode the bench most of last season.

HIGH SALARIED MAN

If the dollar sign is considered, the transaction is easier to understand. Layne, 23-year-old Texan, is in the top pay brackets. He drew $20,000 last year although this obviously will be

Bobby Layne   Camp Wilson

scaled down in the general cuts that have followed the pro football merger.

Besides, Owner Ted Collins of the Yanks has another high-salaried quarterback, George Ratterman. This smooth-passing former Notre Dame field general jumped the Buffalo Bills of the All-America Conference before the merger went through. He is now Collins' No. 1 man.

Wilson was paid $9,500 last season by the Lions.

McMillin said he expected to sign Layne without trouble. There were reports that he talked to Layne in a recent visit to Texas.

PRAISED BY HALAS

Layne, whose arm carried University of Texas to high national ranking, joined the Chicago Bears two years ago. At that time Owner George Halas called him the best long-range quarterback prospect in the game but Halas had two other exceptional men, Sid Luckman and Johnny Lujack.

When Collins moved his Boston franchise into New York last year, he desperately needed a "name" quarterback.

Halas finally agreed to part with Layne but Collins paid the top price. The Bears still are collecting on it in extra draft choices.

For the Yanks, Layne finished sixth in league passing last fall. He completed 155 of 299 passes for 1,796 yards. He ranked well ahead of the three Detroit passers—Fred Enke, Frank Tripucka and Clyde LeForce.

Wilson was Detroit's leading ground gainer three years in a row but last fall his production fell off. He was a holdout and camp reports put him in McMillin's doghouse. He carried the ball 68 times for 222 yards, ranking far down in the league.

Layne weighs 198 and stands 6 feet 1.

Layne's shift to the Lions reunites him with Doak Walker. They were high school teammates in Dallas, Tex. As rivals in college, Layne led Texas to a conference title with a 12-7 triumph over Walker's SMU team in 1945. In 1947, it was Walker's passing and kicking that gave SMU the crown with a 14-13 victory over Layne and Texas.

Reprinted from
The Detroit News

BELL ENDS BAN ON FILCHOCK

Former N.F.L. Gridder Declared Free Agent

Philadelphia, July 13 (AP)—Bert Bell, National Football League Commissioner, today ended the indefinite suspension of Frank Filchock, New York Giants' star, barred from the league three years ago after he was offered a bribe.

Filchock and a teammate, Merle Hapes, were suspended after a hearing before Bell in 1947. They admitted that they received and rejected a bribe offer and did not report it to their club or the league.

Three men were convicted and sentenced to jail for offering money to Filchock and Hapes to "fix" the N.F.L. championship game between the Giants and the Chicago Bears.

Neither Accused

Neither Filchock nor Hapes was accused of accepting any money. Bell said he lifted the suspension on Filchock after a thorough investigation showed the 33-year-old backfield star "has at all times conducted himself in a manner reflecting the highest standards of sportsmanship."

Filchock has been playing with the Montreal professional football club in Canada. Bell said Filchock "has made a real contribution to the promotion and development of clean sports in Canada."

No action was taken today on Hapes. Bell said he had just received an application from Hapes seeking lifting of the suspension and had not had time to study it.

Free To Negotiate

Filchock may now negotiate as a free agent with any N.F.L. club for a job as player or coach.

Despite the fact Filchock now is eligible to return to the N.F.L., Coach Lew Hayman of the Montreal Alouettes said Frank would return next fall to the Canadian Big Four League.

"We definitely want to make this clear," Hayman said, adding:

"We're very happy. Commissioner Bell's decision clears a cloud that has been hanging over Frank for some time, and which should have been cleared long ago."

Plan No Offer

Jack Mara, owner of the Giants, who no longer have rights to Filchock's services, said he was "glad to hear that Frank has been reinstated, that his name has been cleared."

"We do not plan to make him an offer because we are stressing youth," Mara said. "But he certainly would be a handy man for some club."

Filchock, a star at Indiana University, played with the Washington Redskins from 1938 through 1945 and with the Giants for the 1946 season.

Won Passing Title

In 1944 he won the league passing championship, shading his illustrious Washington teammate, Sammy Baugh. Filchock completed 84 of 147 passes for 1,139 yards while Baugh succeeded on 82 of 146 tosses for 849 yards.

Lifting of the suspension followed a hearing during which Filchock and Leo Dandurand, president of the Montreal club, presented testimonials from clergymen, business men and sportsmen lauding Filchock's conduct.

New York's Mayor William O'Dwyer and assistant district attorney George Monaghan also urged lifting of the suspension.

The bribe offer was made shortly before the 1948 championship game. Hapes was barred from the game but Filchock played and the Bears won, 24 to 14.

The suspension order was issued April 3, 1947.

GRAHAM PITCHES THREE TOUCHDOWN PASSES AND SCORES ON SNEAK PLAY

71,237 Watch Opening Game Of Professional Grid League

Philadelphia, Sept. 16 (AP)—The Cleveland Browns defeated the Philadelphia Eagles, 35 to 10, in the opening game of the National Football League at Municipal Stadium tonight.

Otto Graham, Brown quarterback, paced the victors with three touchdown passes and scored once himself as 71,237 fans looked on.

The game marked the official marriage of the defunct All-America Conference with the National League which now is known as the National Football League.

Game Roughly Played

Four years of bitter athletic civil war and $8,000,000 of money was spent before this game could take place. And so keen was the interest that a huge crowd sat under the stars in ideal weather for the contest.

Officially, there is peace between the two factions in professional football's new combine. But there was none on the field between their respective champions.

In the very first quarter, John McGee, of the Eagles, was sent to the showers for playing too rough. Penalties were numerous the remainder of the way but the lads kept their tempers in check.

Hits With 21 Passes

Much of this heated feeling among the players was generated by the past records of the two clubs. The Browns won the title in the All-America Conference all four years of its life.

The Eagles have won the National League title the past two years.

Of the Browns first four touchdowns, Graham passed for three and scored the fourth himself. He handed off to Rex Bumgardner for the fifth just seconds before the final gun.

In all, the Northwestern alumnus threw 38 passes and 21 reached their targets. The flips added 346 yards to the Browns total yardage.

Scott Hurt In Game

While Graham monopolized all the honors on the field his expected rival for the headlines, Steve Van Buren, did not play. Van Buren, N.F.L. ground-gaining record holder, has been out for a month with an injured toe.

Clyde Scott, former Navy and Arkansas star, who also was an Olympic hurdler, was lost to the Eagles in the first half after putting most of the zip in the Philadelphians machine in the early moments

The Browns also were hurt by an injury, Lou Groza going out in the opening minutes and forcing 280-pound Forrest Griggs to take over the point-kicking after touchdowns and on the field-goal attempts.

There never was much question as to the final outcome after the first 10 minutes of the first quarter when Graham began finding the mark. He flipped to Dub Jones for the first marker on a 59-yard play. That, with Grigg's conversion, made the score 7 to 3.

Pro Statistics And Lineups

Statistics

Cleveland		Philadelphia
23	First downs	24
141	Rushing yardage	148
346	Passing yardage	118
38	Passes attempted	37
21	Passes completed	11
3	Passes intercepted	2
5	Punts	6
39.8	Punting average	40.3
2	Fumbles lost	2
98	Yards penalized	45

Lineups

EAGLES
Left Ends—Ferrante, Green, Hix
Left Tackles—Sears, Barnes, Wistert
Left Guards—Patton, Magee
Centers—Bednarik, Lindskog, Wojciechowicz
Right Guards—Maronic, Giannelli, Barnes
Right Tackles—Kilroy, MacDowell, Jarmoluk, Stickel
Right Ends—Pihos, Armstrong, Willey
Quarterbacks—Thompson, Mackrides, Reagan
Left Halfbacks—Scott, Craft
Right Halfbacks—Zeigler, Parmer, Sutton, McHugh
Fullbacks—Myers, Muha, Willey

BROWNS
Left Ends—Speedie, Martin, Young, Gillom
Left Tackles—Groza, Palmer, Kissel
Left Guards—Gibron, Humble, Agase
Centers—Gatski, Thompson, Herring
Right Guards—Houston, Willis
Right Tackles—Rymkus, Grigg, Sandusky
Right Ends—Lavelli, Ford
Quarterbacks—Graham, Gorgal, Lewis
Left Halfbacks—Bumgardner, Lahr, Carpenter
Right Halfbacks—Jones, James, Phelps
Fullbacks—Motley, Adamle, Cole

| Cleveland | 7 | 7 | 7 | 14—35 |
| Philadelphia | 3 | 0 | 0 | 7—10 |

Cleveland scoring: Touchdowns—Speedie, 2; Lavelli, Graham, Bumgardner. Points after touchdown—Grigg, 5 (placement).
Philadelphia scoring: Touchdowns—Pihos. Point after touchdown—Patton (placement). Field goal: Patton.

Eagles Run Wild To Trounce Cards By Score Of 45-7

Chicago, Sept. 24.—(AP)—The Philadelphia Eagles converted three intercepted passes and two recovered fumbles into touchdowns today to romp over the bewildered and inept Chicago Cardinals 45-7 in a National Football League game.

The Cards, making their season start in the American Conference of the league, misfired so badly at times that they drew boos from the Comiskey Park crowd of 24,914.

Card quarterback Jim Hardy was the goat of the game. In 39 passes he completed only 12 and had eight filched, one shy of a league record. Russ Craft intercepted four of them and Joe Sutton three. Five of the Eagles' six touchdowns were touched off by stolen Hardy passes or Hardy fumbles.

The Eagles, who lost their opener a week ago 35-10 to the Cleveland Browns, scored 10 points in the first quarter and blew the game wide open with 21 in the second for a 31-0 halftime lead. They tallied twice in the third. The finale was scoreless.

A recovered Hardy fumble also set up an eventual 27-yard field goal by Cliff Patton who also booted six extra points.

The Eagles ground out 200 yards rushing in the first half whole holding the Cards to 27 and wound up with a 331 total to 110.

Frank Tripucka, Hardy's understudy, was inserted midway in the last period. He was in for only three plays before being helped off the field with an ankle injury. The Eagles' great runner, Steve Van Buren, was sidelined in the opening quarter with a torn rib cartilage.

The Cards' only spurt of the contest was in the third when Hardy passed 51 yards to Mal Kutner and then 34 more for a touchdown to rookie Francis Polsfoot of Washington State.

The Eagles scored only one tuchdown without capitalizing on Cardinal errors. That was in the second period after stopping a 62-yard Chicago drive on their one foot line. Jim Parmer and freshman Toy Ledbetter of Oklahoma Aggies alternated in the ground in a 94-yard march entirely on the ground with the former capping it from the six.

Here is how the other touchdowns came:

Sutton stole Hardy's pass to ignite a 60-yard push led by Van Buren's running and Thompson's passing. Thompson tossed seven yards to Pete Pihos for the pay-off.

Craft's filch of Hardy's toss set up Thompson's 12-yard touchdown pitch to Neill Armstrong.

Less than two minutes later Jay MacDowell recovered Hardy's fumble on the Cardinal 15 and Jim Parmer finally drilled over from the 2.

Vic Sears captured Hardy's fumble on the Chicago 27 and Thompson passed 12 yards to Pihos who lateraled to Jack Ferrante for the marker.

Sutton ran back Hardy's pass 32 yards then lateraled to Frank Reagan who scampered 46 more to score.

Eagles
Left ends—Ferrante, Green.
Left tackles—Sears, Stickel.
Left guards—Patton, Barnes, Magee.
Centers—Bednarik, Lindskog, Wojciechowicz.
Right guards—Maronic, Giannelli.
Right tackles—Kilroy, Jarmoluk, MacDowell, Wistert.
Right ends—Nihos, Hix, Armstrong.
Right tackles—Kilroy, Jarmoluk, MacDowell, Wistert.
Right ends—Nihos, Hix, Armstrong, Willey.
Quarterbacks—Thompson, Mackrides.
Left halfs—Parmer, Ledbetter, Van Buren.
Right halfs—Ziegler, McHugh, Craft, Sutton, Reagan.
Fullbacks—Myers, Muha.

Cardinals
Left ends—Polsfoot, Shaw, Dove.
Left tackles—Fischer, Hock, Lipinski.
Left guards—Andros, Petrovich, Bagdon.
Centers—Blackburn, Banonis.
Right guards—G. Ramsey, Apolskis, K. Ramsey.
Right tackes—Jennings, Goldsberry.
Right ends—Kutner, Wham, Hennesey.
Quarterbacks—Hardy, Tripucka.
Left halfs—Trippi, R. Ramsey, Davis, Gehrke.
Right halfs—Angles, Paul, Schwall, Nussbaumer.
Fullbacks—Harder, Yablonski, Cowhig, Svoboda.

| Eagles | 10 | 21 | 14 | 0—45 |
| Cardinals | 0 | 0 | 7 | 0—7 |

Eagles scoring: Touchdowns, Pihos, Armstrong, Parmer 2, Ferrante, Reagan; points after touchdown, Patton 6; field goal, Patton.
Cardinals scoring: Touchdown, Polsfoot; point after touchdown, Harder.

STATISTICS

	Eagles	Cardinals
First down	26	12
Rushing Yardage	331	110
Passing yardage	154	193
Passes attempted	27	42
Passes completed	10	12
Passes intercepted	8	3
Punts	1	3
Punting average	37.7	43.3
Fumbles lost	1	4
Yards penalized	89	25

RAMS OVERWHELM BALTIMORE, 70-27

Clip Point, Conversion Marks and Tie Touchdown Record in Los Angeles Contest

STATISTICS OF THE GAME

	Rams.	Colts.
First downs	28	25
Yds. gained, rushing	188	143
Forward passes	25	39
Forwards completed	17	16
Yds. gained, forwards	359	299
Passes intercepted by	3	4
Punts	3	5
*Av. dist. of punts, yds.	45.6	39.2
Fumbles lost	1	1
Yards lost, penalties	162	85

*From line of scrimmage

LOS ANGELES, Oct. 22 (AP)—The Los Angeles Rams set two new professional football records and tied two more today in drubbing the victoryless Baltimore Colts, 70 to 27.

The Rams' point total is the highest on record for a single team in league play. The Chicago Cardinals held the previous mark, 65 points, against the New York Bulldogs in 1949.

The Rams made 10 points after touchdown. The Cardinals kicked nine against the New York Giants in 1948.

Bob Waterfield kicked nine of those points today. This ties Pat Harder's record in that same Cardinal-Giants game of 1948.

The total number of touchdowns by a single team—ten—ties the mark the Philadelphia Eagles set against Cincinnati in 1934.

The grand total of fourteen

The Line-Up

LOS ANGELES (70)

Left Ends—Fears, Brink.
Left Tackles—Huffman, Champagne.
Left Guards—Finlay, Vasicek, Lazetich.
Centers—Statuto, Naumetz, Paul
Right Guards—Stephenson, Thompson, West.
Right Tackles—Reinhard, Bouley.
Right Ends—Hirsch, Zilly, Boyd, Smith.
Quarterbacks—Van Brocklin, Waterfield.
Left Halfbacks—Davis, Williams, Sims.
Right Halfbacks—Barry, V. T. Smith, Kalmanir, Lewis
Fullbacks—Hoerner, Towler, Younger, Pasqua-riello.

BALTIMORE (27)

Left Ends—Fletcher, Owens, Crisler.
Left Tackles—Murray, Blandin, Cole.
Left Guards—Schweder, King.
Centers—Williams, Grossman.
Right Guards—Cooper, Averno.
Right Tackles—French, Donovan
Right Ends—Crisler, North, Oristaglio.
Quarterbacks—Burk, Tittle.
Left Halfbacks—Mutryn, Zalejski, Rich.
Right Halfbacks—Stone, Collins, Mazzanti, Maggioli
Fullbacks—Buksar, Kissell, Campbell, Spavital.

SCORE BY PERIODS

Los Angeles ....21 14 14 21—70
Baltimore ....13 0 7 7—27
Touchdowns — Hirsch, Smith 2, Hoerner, Towler, Waterfield, Boyd 2, Fears, Pasquariello, Stone, Burk, Mutryn 2. Points after touchdown—Waterfield 9, Hirsch, Grossman 3.

touchdowns in the game fell one short of the total compiled by the Cardinals and the Giants in 1948.

The defeat was the eighteenth straight for luckless Baltimore in a string that ranges back more than a year through exhibitions and the Colts' play in the defunct All-America Conference.

Filchock Is Given Chance By Baltimore

Banned Football Star Returns to Pro Loop In Surprising Move

Baltimore, Nov. 8.—(AP)—The Baltimore Colts today gave Frank Filchock his chance to come back to the National Football League from which he'd been banned four years because of a bribe offer.

"It's mighty good to be back," said the 33-years-old backfield player who spent the last four seasons playing for the Montreal Alouettes in the Canadian League.

In Montreal, however, Leo Dandurand, president of the Alouettes, said Filchock's service with the U. S. team would be only part time.

"Filchock belongs to the Alouettes, lives in Canada the year around and has signed only to play three games with the Colts," Dandurand said.

The Alouettes executive said Filchock "definitely" would be back next year for the Canadian football season, which ends several weeks before the U. S. loop.

Abe Watner, Colt president, said he gave Filchock a contract promarily "to give Frank another chance to play in this country."

RAMS' AIR ASSAULT DOWNS LIONS, 65-24

Van Brocklin Tosses for Five Touchdowns—Triplett Runs 97 Yards for Detroit

LOS ANGELES, Oct. 29 (AP)—The Los Angeles Rams overwhelmed the Detroit Lions with devastating aerial blasts and rocked them into a 65-24 defeat today in a National Football League contest before 27,475.

Nine times the Rams scorched the scoreboard with touchdowns, plus a field goal. Six of the touchdowns came via the air—five of the strikes hurled by Norm Van Brocklin for 43, 42, 30, 31 and 13 yards.

The Rams' big splurge came in the third quarter when they crossed the goal line six times for 41 points. Coach Joe Stydahar ordered the aerial game grounded at this point. That ended the scoring for Los Angeles.

Detroit, in taking its worst licking in its series with the Rams, was hampered by the absence of two stars. Halfback Doak Walker was used only as a kicking specialist and in the first quarter sent Detroit into a temporary 3 point lead with a 47-yard field goal. He also converted after Detroit's three touchdowns. Left end Cloyce Fox, ace pass receiver, was unable to play at all.

Detroit's Wally Triplett uncorked four amazing kick-off returns, traveling ninety-seven yards for a touchdown, seventy-four on another that set up the field goal, and runs of eighty-one and forty-two yards on the others.

Waterfield, the Rams' alternate quarterback, completed another touchdown pass for sixty-seven yards, kicked a thirty-yard field goal and converted seven times.

Detroit's substitute quarterback, Fred Enke, connected with two scoring throws in the last half.

Of the three Los Angeles touchdowns scored on the ground, one came on the spectacular ninety-three yard return of a kick-off by V. T. Smith.

The line-up:

LOS ANGELES RAMS (65)

Left Ends—Fears, Brink, Smyth.
Left Tackles—Huffman, Champagne.
Left Guards—Finlay, Vasicek, Paul.
Centers—Statuto, Naumetz.
Right Guards—Stephenson, West, Thompson, Lazetich.
Right Tackles—Reinhard, Bouley.
Right Ends—Hirsch, Zilly, Boyd, Keane.
Quarterback—Van Brocklin, Waterfield.
Left Halfbacks—Davis, Williams, Sims.
Right Halfbacks—Barry, Smith, Kalamanir, Lewis.
Fullbacks—Hoerner, Towler, Younger.

DETROIT LIONS (24)

Left Ends—Greene, Rifenburg, Hafen.
Left Tackle—Bulger, McGraw, Prehlik.
Left Guards—Creekmur, Sobolecki, Flanagan.
Center.—Watson, Simmons, Lininger.
Right Guards—Brown, Bingaman.
Right Tackles—Jaszewski, Cifelli.
Right End—Hart, Cain.
Quarterbacks—Layne, Enke.
Left Halfbacks—Pearson, Walker, Doll, Triplett, Self.
Right Halfbacks—Cline, Magnani, Smith, Krall.
Fullbacks—Panelli, Schroll.

SCORE BY PERIODS

Los Angeles Rams ....7 17 41 0—65
Detroit Lions ....3 7 7 7—24
Touchdowns—Fears 2, Triplett, Greene 2, Van Brocklin, Smith 2, Hirsch, Davis, Towler, Boyd. Field goals—Walker, Waterfield. Points after touchdown:—Waterfield 7, Walker 3, Hirsch.

GIANTS RUSH FOR 423 YARDS

Giants Rally To Overcome Colts, 55-20

New Yorkers Switch To T-Formation For Smashing Victory

Baltimore, Nov. 19.— (AP) — Switching to the T and exploding like TNT after trailing 20-7 at halftime, the New York Giants pulverized the Baltimore Colts 55-20 today.

Quarterback Travis Tidwell directed the Giants to their second highest scoring total in history after quarterback Chuck Conerly got nowhere with the A single wing formation of attack. The Giants' biggest point output was 56 points against the Philadelphia Eagles in 1933.

Tidwell and the T formation came in for the Giants midway in the second period with the score 13-0 against them. After the rampaging Colts added another score to the delirious delight of 14,573 fans in Memorial Stadium, the former Auburn quarterback got the New Yorkers straightened out and headed for their seventh win against two losses in the National Football League.

Personally, he threw two touchdown passes to end Bob McChesney and went over the goal once himself. Eddie Price, the pride of Tulane, bucked for two scores and the others were credited to Jim Ostendarp, a Baltimorean, Randall Clay and Bob Jackson.

They Never Stopped

Price and pitchouts from Tidwell started taking Baltimore apart two minutes before the end of the half and they never stopped. A 38-yard Price gambol set up the first score and his 62-yard ramble preceded the next.

When it wasn't Price, Gene Roberts was romping through the Colt line while Tidwell kept the Giants moving in the air. The Giants rolled 424 yards on the ground.

The Colts started galloping on the fourth play of the game when they scored on a 79-yard play in which halfback Jim Spavitau ran 19 yards and lateraled to center Joel Williams who went the rest of the way.

They stormed to the one-foot line only to fumble and picked up two more touchdowns on passes by Y. A. Tittle to Billy Stone and Hal Crisler. At that stage, a stunning upset loomed for the Colts who have won only once this season.

But things changed fast and furiously once Coach Steve Owens junked the single wing attack which never got inside the Colt 40. Besides piling up seven touchdowns, the Giants never let the Colts beyond midfield until the last minute in the second half.

Score by periods:
New York ....0 7 21 27—55
Baltimore ....6 11 0 0—20
New York scoring: Touchdowns—Price 2, McChesney 2, Tidwell, Ostendarp, Clay, Jackson. Conversions—Poole 7.
Baltimore scoring: Touchdowns—Stone, Williams, Crisler. Conversions—Kissell 2.

RAMS OVERWHELM GREEN BAY BY 51-14

LOS ANGELES, Dec. 3 (AP)—The Los Angeles Rams struck the Green Bay Packers numb with a record-breaking 51-14 victory today and assured themselves of at least a tie with the Chicago Bears for the National Conference title in the National Football League.

The Rams heard the news of the Chicago Cardinals' 20-10 triumph over the Bears just before taking the field before 39,323 fans here. So the Rams proceeded to blast the Packers into submission.

The Rams will play the Bears here Dec. 17 if the Bears defeat Detroit next week. Today's game ended the regular season for Los Angeles.

Quarterback Norm Van Brocklin threw three touchdown strikes; his alternate, Bob Waterfield, rang up two more, and the other two tallies came on ground plays. Glenn Davis tallied twice.

The Rams rolled up 351 yards via the air and 199 on the ground for a total of 550. They held Green Bay to 139 yards rushing and 109 passing.

The season records established with today's game are as follows:

	Rams	Old Mark
Scoring	466	396, Bears, 1947
Touchdowns	64	56, Bears, 1941
Passing yardage	3,709	3,336, Redskins, 1947
Total yardage	5,420	5,053, Bears, 1947
First downs	275	253, Bears, 1947
Passes attempted	453	418, Redskins, 1947
Passes completed	253	231, Redskins, 1947
Touchdown passes	31	29, Redskins, 1947
Conversions	59	55, Cardinals, 1948
Yds. via interceptns.	512	456, Lions, 1950

INDIVIDUAL RECORDS

Passes received, game—18 by Tom Fears (old mark of 14 held by four others).

Passes received, season—84 by Fears (old mark of 77 set by Fears, 1949).

Conversions, season—54 by Bob Waterfield (old mark of 53 set by Pat Harder Chicago Cardinals, 1948).

Conversions player's career—230 by Waterfield (old mark held by Don Hutson of Green Bay).

SCORE BY PERIODS

Los Angeles .... 0 16 21 14—51
Green Bay .... 0 7 0 7—14

Touchdowns—Los Angeles: Davis 2, Fears 2, Hirsch, Smith, Younger. Green Bay: Mann, Cook. Points after touchdown—Los Angeles: Waterfield 6, Hirsch. Green Bay: Fritsch, Tonnemaker. Safety—Reinhard on blocked punt.

GROZA'S 2 FIELD GOALS PUT CLEVELAND ELEVEN INTO CHAMPIONSHIP GAME

Bob Waterfield's Passes Pace Los Angeles To Triumph In National Division Playoff Game On Coast

The Cleveland Browns defeated the New York Giants, 8 to 3, yesterday in Cleveland to win the playoff for the American Conference title in the National Football League, while the Los Angeles Rams won from the Chicago Bears, 24 to 7, in their National Conference playoff.

The two winners will meet next Sunday at Cleveland for the league championship.

Los Angeles

Los Angeles, Dec. 17 (AP)—The Los Angeles Rams defeated the Chicago Bears today, 24 to 14, to move into the National Football League's championship game next week.

A near free-for-all battle halted the game in the waning seconds, and it was several minutes before the field was cleared.

Playing perhaps the greatest game of his life before 83,501 fans. Quarterback Bob Waterfield struck the Bears three times through the air for touchdowns. On the receiving end was the Ram's record breaking end. Tom Fears.

Cleveland

Cleveland, Dec. 17 (AP)—Lou Groza booted the Cleveland Browns into the American division championship with two field goals today defeating the New York Giants 8 to 3 in the national professional football playoff.

The victory first over New York in three attempts this year by the four-time All-America Conference champions, catapults the Browns into the league championship game here next Sunday.

Although Groza's two placekicks in two attempts provided the victory margin, the Browns defensive team gained much of the credit for the conquest through a great goal line stand midway in the final period before a crowd of 33,054

Storybook Finish Provided By Groza

'Toe' Kicks 16-Yard Goal In Closing 20 Seconds Of Battle

By JIM SCHLEMMER

Cleveland Browns, the team they said would be lucky to win one game in their first season in the "big league," won one Sunday which made them champions of the National Football League and of all the professional football world.

It was their 12th win in 14 games of the regular season and the championship playoffs; their 17th in 19 games, counting the pre-season exhibition.

No other club in the league had a record even closely comparable except the New York Giants, whom the Browns defeated last Sunday to get into yesterday's title fracas with the Los Angeles Rams.

The Browns, in defeating the Rams, 30-28, on Lou Groza's field goal from 16 yards out in the final 20 seconds of a thriller-diller, became champions for their fifth straight year. They are only five years old.

* * *

Four of these seasons, in the now defunct All-American Conference, the Browns were sneered at by the staid old National Leaguers and pooh-poohed for their claim of being the "greatest team in football."

The sneering and pooh-poohing remained this season, even though the Browns had been taken into the National League. But no longer can there be any doubt as to their right to be known as football's greatest team.

The only team the Browns did not beat this season was the New York Yankees .....The only team the Browns did not play.

While the Browns are sitting down to a Christmas dinner befitting the champions that they are, most of the others in the league will find themselves eating crow....... and humble pie.

* * *

HAPPIEST OF all the Browns is Paul Brown himself.

Staggered when the Rams scored on an 82-yard touchdown pass on the first offensive play of the game........

Set back on his heels later when the Browns failed on a conversion effort which would have tied the score at 14-14 ......

Stunned in the third quarter when Marion Motley fumbled and the Rams recovered for a touchdown which put them 28-20 ahead.....

Shocked in the fourth quarter when Otto Graham, who shared hero honors with Groza, had the misfortune to fumble and lose the ball to the Rams on their 22-yard line just when it looked like the Browns had momentum up for a winning touchdown drive ...

Brown went into the nearest stage to berserk when Groza's field goal went sailing over the bar and between the uprights for the points that meant victory .....

Just 20 seconds from the end of a gruelling season that had its be-

Statistics

	L. Angeles	Cleveland
First downs	22	22
Rushing yardage	106	111
Passing yardage	312	298
Passes attempted	32	33
Passes completed	18	22
Passes intercepted by	1	5
Punts	4	5
Punting average	50.76	38.6
Fumbles lost	0	3
Yards penalized	48	25

ginning way back there at Bowling Green in mid-July .....When it was much warmer than it was yesterday.

* * *

FOR THAT field goal, which by the way was Groza's 16th of the season and marked the fourth game he had won for the Browns by the field goal route, made Paul Brown unique among coaches.

Brown has now completed a grand slam in football coaching he has a championship team at Severn Prep, where he began his fabulous career.

He had numerous state championship teams at Massillon High .... He had a national championship team at Ohio State, a winning team at Great Lakes during the war; four championship teams in the All-America Conference and now the championship of the National Football League without any possible further dispute to his greatness.

* * *

TITLE CONTEST WORTH $1,116

Each Cleveland Brown Given Amount For Beating Rams

Cleveland, Dec. 25 (AP)—Each of the Cleveland Browns tucked $1,116.16 into his Christmas stocking today—a Christmas present for defeating the Los Angeles Rams yesterday in the star-spangled National Football League championship game.

In a startling finish so unbelievable you'd laugh at it if you saw it in a movie, the Browns came from a point behind to triumph by 30 to 28 in the last 20 seconds on Lou Groza's 16-yard field goal.

Waterfield Vs. Graham

It was a record-setting duel and a pitcher's battle, with Bob Waterfield, of the Rams and Otto Graham, of the Browns, doing the pitching.

Waterfield, off and running with an 82-yard scoring pass to Glenn Davis on the opening play from scrimmage, completed 18 of 31 passes for 312 yards and a single touchdown. But Graham connected on 22 of 33 aerials for 298 yards and 4 touchdowns.

It was Groza's unerring toe which provided the payoff, however, for the second straight week. Last Sunday he booted a pair of three-pointers to vanquish the New York Giants 8 to 3 in the American Division playoff.

Misses Field Goal

Waterfield muffed his chance to wrap up the victory when he missed a field goal from 15 yards out in the fading minutes of the second period.

The Browns, four-time champions of the now defunct All-American Conference, thus brought to Cleveland the city's sixth straight pro title. The Rams won the National

League crown here in 1945 before shifting to Los Angeles, and the Browns were never headed in their four years in the All-America.

Coach Paul E. Brown of the victors extended his phenomenal record in pro ball, winning 12 of 14 championship games this year in addition to victories in five exhibitions. His only losses were a pair to the New York Giants, the victims in last week's division playoff.

Browns' Record

In five years of professional ball, not counting exhibitions, the Browns have won 64, lost 6 and tied 3 games.

Yesterday's nip-and-tuck classic, played in 29-degree temperature and in a 28-mile wind, was tagged by Commissioner Bert Bell as "the greatest football game I've ever seen."

After Waterfield's sensational pass to Davis on the first play, the Browns countered with a 31-yard Graham to Bub Jones pass to tie the count. Fullback Dick Hoerner put the Rams back in front with a 4-yard plunge to end the first period scoring.

The Rams were blanked in the second, but Graham's 35-yard pass to Dante Lavelli pulled Cleveland up to a 13-to-14 deficit at the half—the extra point being muffed because of a poor pass from center.

Rams Come Back

A 39-yard Graham to Lavelli pass put the Browns ahead 20 to 14 early in the third session, but the Rams came back with a 71-yard march to send Hoerner over from the 1-yard line. The Rams then made it 27 to 20 as End Larry Brink picked up a fumble on the Brown 6 and ambled over for another score.

The Browns moved right in at the start of the final quarter with a 65-yard march climaxed by Graham's 14-yard scoring toss to Rex Bumgardner.

EVERYBODY LOOKS—IT'S THE TITLE

This unusual picture shows all 22 players taking time out from their blocks to study the cross bars in the final 20 seconds of the Browns-Rams game. Of course it's news to Browns' fans that Lou Groza's boot went over the bars successfully to give the Browns the title, 30-28. Even the umpire's curiosity got the best of him. He took a peek, too.

Graham Sets Pace In 28-27 Gridiron Win

American Conference All-Stars Prevail in Los Angeles Contest

Los Angeles, Jan. 14. — (AP) — Quarterback Otto Graham, scoring two big touchdowns, led his American Conference teammates to a bruising 28-27 triumph over the National Conference today in the pro-bowl postseason football game before 53,676 fans in Memorial Coliseum.

The Cleveland Browns field general, overshadowed in the aerial department for most of the game by brilliant Bob Waterfield of the Los Angeles Rams, his foe in the recent National Football League championship battle, took to the ground in the third period and scored twice to bring victory to the American All-Stars.

The lineups:

NATIONAL CONFERENCE

Left end — Fears (Rams), Box (Lions), Brink (Rams).
Left tackle—Davis (Rams), Huffman (Rams).
Left guard—Barwegan (Bears), Grigich (49ers).
Center—Ecklund (N. Y. Yanks), Turner (Bears), Neal (Packers).
Right guard — Greekmur (Lions), Bray (Bears).
Right tackle—McGraw (Lions), Nomellini (49ers), Connor (Bears).
Right end—Edwards (Yanks), Sprinkle (Bears).
Quarterback — Waterfield (Rams), Van Brocklin (Rams), LuJack (Bears), Albert (49ers).
Left half—Davis (Rams), Walker (Lions), Doll (Lions).
Right half—Grimes (Packers), Stryzalski (49ers), Sanders (NY Yanks), Lewis (Rams).
Fullback—Hoerner (Rams), Toth (NY Yanks), Standlee (49ers).
AMERICAN CONFERENCE
Left end—Speedie (Browns), Green (Eagles), Plhos (Eagles).
Left tackle—Groza (Browns), Weinmeister (Giants).
Left guard—Humble (Browns), Fischer (Cards).
Center—Walsh (Steelers), Bednarik (Eagles), Cannady (Giants).
Right guard — Willis (Browns), Barnes (Eagles).
Right tackle—Wistert (Eagles), Derogatis (Giants), Lipscomb (Redskins).
Right end—Shaw (Cards), Dove (Cards).
Quarterback — Graham (Browns), Hardy (Cards), Gilmer (Redskins).
Left half—Robert (Giants), Geri (Steelers), Schnellbacher (Giants).
Right half—Angsman (Cards), Dudley (Redskins), Tunnell (Giants).
Fullback—Motley (Browns), Barder (Cards), Adamle (Browns), Shipkey (Steelers).

Score by quarters:
Americans   7 7 14 0—28
Nationals   7 13 7 0—27
American scoring: Touchdowns—Dudley, Shaw, Graham 2. Conversions—Groza 2, Harder.
National scoring: Touchdowns—Edwards, Fears 2. Conversions—Waterfield 3. Field goals—Waterfield 2.

STATISTICS

	A	N
First downs	17	18
Rushing yardage	23	24
Passing yardage	252	294
Passes attempted	35	44
Passes completed	19	21
Passes intercepted	3	0
Punts	6	7
Punting average	39.6	40.3
Fumbles lost	2	1
Yards penalized	51	27

Colts Quit Pro Football After Loss Of $760,000

New York Giants Get Top Bonus Pick at Annual Draft Meeting and Grab Kyle Rote; Chicago Bears Select Bob Williams

Chicago, Jan. 18.—(AP)—The Baltimore Colts — an artistic and financial flop — quit the National Football League today just before the loop's annual draft handed Southern Methodist's great Kyle Rote to the New York Giants as top bonus pick. The Chicago Bears did perhaps the most effective mopping up in the draft a few hours after Owner Abraham Watner of the Colts failed in a quest for veteran player help from each of the other clubs and surrendered the Baltimore franchise. That left the league with 12 clubs.

The Bears parlayed two draft claims from previous player deals into these acquisitions:

Notre Dame Quarterback Bob Williams, who was picked as No. 1 in the regular draft by defunct Baltimore in behalf of the Bears. Had the Colts stayed in the league and been able to retain Williams, a Baltimore boy, it might have been a big lift at the gate for the Colts.

Fleet Halfback Billy Stone of the Colts was first round choice of the New York Yanks, who also owed the Colts a player.

The Colts' 28 active players were tossed into the hopper of 1950 collegiate seniors up for the 1951 pro draft.

$760,000 Loss

Big news of the opening session of the league's four-day annual session was the folding of the Colts, who dropped $760,000 in four years of professional football.

Watner, a dignified, quiet-spoken Baltimore cemetery owner, obviously made the other 12 club owners breath easier when he threw in the sponge in a surprise executive session which lasted an hour and a half.

This session delayed opening of the draft until mid-afternoon, some four hours after it was originally scheduled.

Results of the first three draft rounds:

BONUS SELECTION
New York Giants—Kyle Rote, back, Southern Methodist.

FIRST-ROUND SELECTIONS
Chicago Bears—Bob Williams, back, Notre Dame; Billy Stone, back. Baltimore Colts; Gene Schroeder, end, Virginia.
San Francisco—Y. A. Tittle, back, Baltimore Colts.
Washington— Leon Heath, back, Oklahoma.
Green Bay—Bob Gain, tackle, Kentucky.
Chicago Cardinals—Jerry Groom, center, Notre Dame.
Philadelphia—Ebert Van Buren, back, Louisiana State.
Detroit Lions—Chet Mutryn, Baltimore Colts.
Pittsburgh—Clarence Avinger, back, Alabama.
Los Angeles—Bud McFadin, guard, Texas.
New York Giants—Jim Spavital, back, Baltimore Colts.
Cleveland—Ken Konz, back, Louisiana State.

SECOND-ROUND SELECTIONS
Washington—Eddie Salem, back, Alabama.
Green Bay—Rip Collins, back, Baltimore.
San Francisco—Pete Schabarum, back, California.
Chicago Cardinals—Don Joyce, tackle, Tulane.
Detroit—Dick Stanfel, guard, University of San Francisco.
Pittsburgh—Chuck Ortmann, back, Michigan.
Philadelphia—Traded to Washington Jim Stanton, tackle, Wake Forest.
New York Yanks—Ken Jackson, tackle, Texas.
Chicago Bears—Bill George, tackle, Wake Forest.
Los Angeles—Herb Rich, back, Baltimore.
New York Giants—Ray Krouse, tackle, Maryland.
Cleveland—Bucky Curtis, end, Vanderbilt.

THIRD-ROUND SELECTIONS
Green Bay—Fred Cone, back, Clemson.
San Francisco — Bill Mixon, back, Georgia.
Washington—Walter Yowarsky, tackle, Kentucky.
Chicago Cardinals—Don Stonesifer, end, Northwestern.
Pittsburgh—George Sulima, end, Boston University.
Philadelphia—Al Bruno, end, Kentucky.
Detroit—Dorne Dibble, end, Michigan State.
New York Yanks—Mike McCormack, tackle, Kansas.
Los Angeles—Charles Toogood, tackle, Nebraska.
Chicago Bears—Whizzer White, back, Arizona State.
New York Giants—Everett Grandelius, back, Michigan State.
Cleveland—Jerome Helluin, tackle, Tulane.

Filchock Given Boot By Montreal Eleven

Montreal, Jan. 20. — (AP) — The Montreal Standard said today Frank Filchock, 34-year-old quarterback with the Montreal Alouettes for two seasons, has been told he does not figure in the team's plans for 1951 and can make a deal for himself elsewhere.

The Standard says Coach Lew Hayman, attending a Big Four Football League meeting in Toronto, confirmed Filchock's status.

Sports Editor Larry O'Brien wrote that he talked with Filchock by telephone at the quarterback's home in Silver Spring, Md., and Frank admitted he was trying to get his release to take an offer as playing coach made him by "another Canadian city."

Browns' Graham Signed At Highest Pro Salary

By The Associated Press

CLEVELAND, April 27—Quarterback Otto Graham, passing ace of the Cleveland Browns, signed for another two years today with the professional football champions.

Salary terms were not disclosed, but Coach Paul Brown indicated Graham would be the highest paid player in the game.

Graham, now 29, will be playing his sixth season with the Browns. In the past five seasons he has completed 729 passes in 1,314 attempts for 10 touchdowns and 12,028 yards. That gives him an average aerial gain per season of 2,406 yards.

YANK ELEVEN WARNS RATTERMAN OF SUIT

MONTREAL, July 3 (/P)—George Ratterman, star quarterback of the New York Football Yanks, was threatened today with court action for signing to play with the Montreal Alouettes of the Canadian Big Four Football Union.

The former Notre Dame star, who played with the Buffalo Bisons of the defunct All-America Conference, signed a Montreal contract yesterday.

"If he is jumping the team to play in Canada, I shall start legal action immediately to force him to fulfill his contractual obligation," said Ted Collins, the Yanks' owner, at his summer home in Lake Placid, N. Y.

Ratterman, at a press conference, said he felt legally free to play in Canada.

"I feel I am a free agent," Ratterman said, "my lawyer has confirmed that I am not legally bound to the New York Yanks."

Collins claimed Ratterman was bound by a three-year contract which expires next year.

Ratterman's version was: "Collins had me sign a one-year contract. * * * I'm not jumping the National League but am coming to Canada and the Alouettes because here I believe I will have more business opportunities."

Ratterman, a native of Cincinnati, lives in Englewood, N. J., with his wife and two children.

RAMS WIN HUFFMAN CASE

Court Puts Permanent Ban on Football Star Shifting

CHARLESTON, W. Va., July 1 (/P)—The first court test of a National Football League player contract resulted today in a clear-cut victory for club owners.

Judge Julian F. Bouchelle of the Kanawha County Circuit Court, made permanent an order restraining Tackle Dick Huffman of Charleston from playing with any team other than the Los Angeles Rams, with whom he has starred for four seasons.

The decision, which is almost certain to be appealed, upheld the validity of a Ram contract with Huffman which expired May 1, but which granted the club a further option, which it exercised, on the tackle's services until May 1, 1952.

The Huffman case developed after he signed, on May 26, to play with the Winnipeg, Canada, Bombers in 1951-52. He had argued that his Ram contract was unfair to him, and that he had signed no agreement for this year.

COURT ORDER BARS RATTERMAN SHIFT

Yank Eleven Gets Temporary Injunction to Keep Star From Canadian League

By The Associated Press.

Two more National Football League clubs appealed to the courts yesterday to keep star players from "jumping" to the Canadian Big Four Union.

In Houston the Chicago Cardinals asked the court to prevent Bill Blackburn, a center, from playing with Calgary.

Judge Alfred E. Stein issued a court order in Newark Superior Court, directing George Ratterman, New York Yanks' passing ace, to show cause why he should not be restrained from playing with any team except the Yanks. Ratterman announced Monday he had signed to play with the Montreal Alouettes.

The order on Ratterman is returnable next Tuesday. The New York team has a three-year-contract with the former Notre Dame player, owner Ted Collins declared. Montreal said Ratterman was signed as a free agent.

District Judge W. P. Hamblen issued a temporary restraining order in the case of Blackburn, former Rice Institute star. District Judge Dan Jackson will rule today whether Blackburn will be forbidden from playing with Calgary.

On Monday, at Charleston, W. Va., Tackle Dick Huffman of the Los Angeles Rams said his contract was unfair and obligated him to play with one club the rest of his professional career. The Rams obtained a temporary injunction in Kanawha County Circuit Court, Charleston, restraining Huffman, former Tennessee tackle, from playing with the Winnipeg Blue Bombers.

Huffman failed to show up in his home town, but attorneys said final court action was expected in two weeks. John Morrison, Rams' attorney, said the club had the right to exercise an option on Huffman for 1951 by May 1, and did so.

RAMS EASILY BEAT YANKS BY 54 TO 14

Van Brocklin Passes for 554 Yards, New League Record— Tosses for Five Touchdowns

LOS ANGELES, Sept. 28 (/P)—Quarterback Norman Van Brocklin set a new National Football League passing record tonight as he pitched the Los Angeles Rams to a 54-14 victory over the New York Yanks.

A crowd of 30,315 cheered the ex-Oregon star as he exceeded the record for passing yardage set in 1949 by Johnny Lujack of the Chicago Bears, finally racking up an unprecedented 554 yards. Lujack's mark was 468.

Van Brocklin's strong right arm carried almost the entire offensive load. The top Ram quarterback, Bob Waterfield, was benched by injuries. So was Halfback Glenn Davis but the Rams' offense seemed to suffer little.

Van Brocklin threw five touchdown passes, four of them to Elroy (Crazylegs) Hirsch.

The Yanks never could put together a consistent offensive drive.

Their two touchdowns came on a 79-yard punt return by Buddy Young and a 30-yard gallop by Art Tait when he intercepted a Van Brocklin pitchout.

Van Brocklin hit Hirsch from 46 yards out, again from 47. Vitamin T. Smith snared another throw for 67 yards. Van Brocklin himself scored once from the one-foot line to cap a 97-yard drive. Dick Hoerner bulled his way for 22, carrying two men with him to complete the Rams' first-half scoring.

The Ram offense slowed to a walk early in the second half but Van Brocklin finally nailed Hirsch for a touchdown toss good for 26 yards. In the fourth period, as a Ram drive showed signs of bogging down on the one, Van Brocklin sent the rest of the team pounding into center, then dropped back to fire one at Hirsch, yards from the nearest New Yorker. Hirsch scored easily.

Van Brocklin almost made it six touchdown passes in the closing moments but Tommy Kalmanir was pulled down a yard short and Dan Towler punched it across.

The Rams set a league record when they piled up 735 total yards, topping the old mark of 682 set by the Chicago Bears in 1943. Their 34 first downs beat by two their own record. It was held jointly with the Chicago Cardinals.

SCORE BY PERIODS

Rams	21	13	7	13—54
Yanks	0	7	0	7—14

Jones Sprints to Six Touchdowns, Equals Mark as Browns Win, 42-21

CLEVELAND, Nov. 25 (AP)—Dub Jones, a lanky right halfback, tied the National Football League's scoring record today by sprinting for six touchdowns as the Cleveland Browns walloped the Chicago Bears, 42 to 21.

It was the eighth straight triumph for the champion Browns, who lost their opener to San Francisco.

The loss dropped the Bears into a tie for second in the pro league's National Division. Cleveland retained its hold on first place in the American Division.

Jones, who caught passes from Otto Graham for two of the touchdowns and ran for the other four, matched the mark set in 1929 by Ernie Nevers. Nevers scored his touchdowns for the Chicago Cardinals against the Bears. The most scored since then in a single game by one man were Bob Shaw's five for the Cardinals against Baltimore in 1950.

Fourth Year of Pro Ball

The last five times Jones—who weighs 205 pounds and stands 6 feet 4 inches and is in his fourth year of pro football—got his hands on the ball he scored touchdowns. In all, he ran 116 yards in nine attempts.

After a scoreless first period, the Browns went 34 yards in twelve plays for their first touchdown, Jones hitting off left guard for the last two. In the second quarter, the Browns went 61 yards in six plays for another tally. Jones grabbed a pass from Graham for the last 34 yards of that march.

In the third period, Jones ended a 69-yard, five-play touchdown march by sprinting left end for 11 yards.

Chicago scored its first touchdown shortly after that, going 60 yards in six plays, the last three on a run by George Gulyanics.

But on the first play after the touchdown, Jones went around left end again, cut back toward his right and ran 27 for another Brown touchdown. Ken Carpenter's 48-yard kick-off return and a 15-yard penalty set that one up.

Carpenter, Jones Click

Carpenter, in the fourth period, ran from his own 27 to the Chicago 43 and on the next play Jones snaked around right end and ran over the goal again. Jones' last touchdown was on a 43-yard pass play from Graham.

With the score hopelessly against them, the Bears then scored their last two six-pointers. Ed Sprinkle grabbed a fumble by Graham and went 64 yards for one. The other came on a 19-yard pass from Bob Williams to Chuck Hunsinger on the last play of the game.

A total of 37 penalties for 374 yards were called by the busy officials. The Browns were set back 21 times with 209 yards, eclipsing a record set by Green Bay in 1945 of 17 penalties costing 184 yards. The Bears, who got nine first downs on Brown penalties lost 165 yards on 16 calls.

Once, a 94-yard run to the end zone by Don Shula, who intercepted a Chicago pass, was called back for a roughing the passer penalty, which gave the Bears a first down on the Cleveland nine.

It was the first time that the Bears had ever played the Browns in a National Football League game Cleveland had won two previous exhibitions.

The line-up:

CLEVELAND BROWNS (42)
Left Ends—Speedie, Young, Gillom.
Left Tackles—Groza, Kissell, Palmer.
Left Guards—Gibron, Thompson, Agase.
Centers—Gatski Herring.
Right Guards—Houston, Gaudio, Willis.
Right Tackles—Sandusky, Grigg, Rymkus.
Right Ends—Lavelli, Ford, Oristaglio.
Quarterbacks—Graham, Lewis, Shula.
Left Halfbacks—Carpenter, Lahr, Baumgardner.
Right Halfbacks—Jones, James, Taseff.
Fullbacks—Motley, Adamle, Cole, Jagade.

CHICAGO BEARS (21)
Left Ends—Hoffman, Wightkin.
Left Tackles—Connor, Davis, Cowan.
Left Guards—Barwegen, Dempsey.
Centers—Turner, Moser, Clarkson.
Right Guards—Serini, Stautberg.
Right Tackles—Stenn, Bray, Hansen.
Right Ends—Keane, Schroeder, Sprinkle.
Quarterbacks—Romanik, Lujack, Williams.
Left Halfbacks—Gulyanics, Hunsinger, White, Boone, Kindt.
Right Halfbacks—Tykovich, Stone, Rowland.
Fullbacks—Dottley, Blanda, Morrison.

SCORE BY PERIODS
Browns ....0 14 14 14—42
Bears ....0 0 7 14—21
Touchdowns—Browns: Jones 6. Points after touchdowns—Groza 6. Touchdowns—Bears: Gulyanics, Sprinkle, Hunsinger. Points after touchdowns—Blanda 2, White.

Statistics of the Game

	Cleve.	Bears
First downs	22	22
Rushing yardage	273	74
Passing yardage	277	182
Passes attempted	19	41
Passes completed	12	15
Passes intercepted by	2	1
Number of punts	3	7
Punting average, yds.	38	39½
Fumbles lost	3	0
Yards penalized	209	165

WATERFIELD STAR OF 42-14 TRIUMPH

His 5 Scoring Passes Against Packers Pace Rams to 3d Group Title in Row

WILLIAMS RUNS 99 YARDS

Los Angeles Plays Browns on Coast for National League Crown Next Sunday

STATISTICS OF THE GAME

	L.A.	G.B.
First downs	18	20
Rushing yardage	151	45
Passing yardage	256	379
Passes attempted	27	56
Passes completed	15	27
Passes intercepted by	2	2
Number of punts	6	4
Punting average, yds.	44.3	43.5
Fumbles lost	1	3
Yards penalized	59	74

LOS ANGELES, Dec. 16 (AP)—The Los Angeles Rams, with an unblushing bow to the San Francisco Forty-Niners, marched into their third straight conference title today and the right to battle the Cleveland Browns for the National Football League championship here next Sunday.

In a wild climax to the 1951 regular season, the Rams climbed into the title picture by thrashing the Green Bay Packers, 42—14, while up north San Francisco was knocking the Detroit Lions out of the championship.

It is no figure of speech to say that the Rams played with an eye on the Packers and both ears tuned in for developments at San Francisco.

No less excited was the crowd of 23,698, which kept rapt attention on the Bay City battle by portable radios and reports relayed from the press box high atop the Coliseum.

Mighty Shout Goes Up

A mighty shout went up when word arrived that the Forty-Niners, trailing by 3 points, had a first down on the Lion 2. Players on the Ram bench leaped to their feet, and the men on the field drew a 5-yard penalty for delaying the game as they joined in the excitement. Coach Joe Stydahar clasped his hands, almost in prayer, and the immediate issue with the Packers was pushed far into the background.

The biggest roar developed when the final score from up north was shouted over the loudspeakers. There was a big laugh a moment later when Field Announcer Frank Bull declared that the Rams had the ball on the Forty-Niners' 22-yard line.

All this far overshadowed the fact that Capt. Bob Waterfield pitched five touchdown passes, three to his star right end, Elroy Hirsch, the longest for 73 yards. The other Ram score was on a brilliant run by Safety Man Jerry Williams—99 yards after taking a field goal try by the Packers' Fred Cone.

Hirsch's three touchdown passes raised his season total to seventeen and tied the league record established in 1942 by Don Hutson of Green Bay.

14-14 Tie at Half

The stubborn Packers held the vaunted Rams to a 14-14 tie at the half.

The clash with Cleveland will be the Rams' third successive try for the championship. Philadelphia beat them here in the mud in 1949 and Cleveland nipped them in the snow on the edge of Lake Erie last Christmas.

Los Angeles held the National Conference lead until Detroit beat the Rams last week.

Waterfield's passing brilliance accounted for touchdowns for Hirsch of 73, 37 and 19 yards; to Dick Hoerner for 15, and to Left End Tom Fears for 39.

The Packers scored their two touchdowns on throws by Quarterback Tobin Rote, who hit Billy Grimes for a 33-yarder and Carlton Elliott for 14. They made it a battle for two periods, but wilted under the battering runs of the Rams' bull elephant backfield, notably Hoerner and Deacon Dan Towler, and Waterfield's superb artistry.

The unpredictable Rams were mobbed by admirers as they left the field. Few bothered to recall that they had never beaten Paul Brown's Browns and that early this fall the Clevelanders had downed them by a 38-23 score.

Finishes Tenth Season

Tony Canadeo, oldest member of the Green Bay team in point of service, said he was playing his last game.

Canadeo, 31, finished his tenth season in the National Football League. A six-foot, 190-pound halfback, he was once known as they "gray ghost of Gonzaga."

The old man of the Packers showed that he was still spry, however, as he cavorted against the Rams, taking one pass for a 46-yard gain.

He became today the second man in league history to pass the 4,000-yard rushing mark. The first was Steve Van Buren of the Philadelphia Eagles.

SCORE BY PERIODS
Los Angeles ....14 0 14 14—42
Green Bay ....7 7 0 0—14
Touchdowns—Green Bay: Grimes, Elliott. Los Angeles: Hoerner, Hirsch 3, Fears, Williams. Points after touchdown—Green Bay: Cone 2. Los Angeles: Waterfield 6.

LOS ANGELES WINS ON LATE PASS, 24-17

Van Brocklin-to-Fears Aerial, Gaining 73 Yards, Finishes Browns' 5-Year Reign

11-GAME STREAK HALTED

Graham's Fumble Aids Rams— Groza 52-Yard Field Goal Sets Play-Off Record

STATISTICS OF THE GAME

	L.A.	Cleve.
First downs	20	22
Rushing yardage	81	92
Passing yardage	253	280
Passes attempted	30	41
Passes completed	13	19
Passes intercepted by	2	3
Number of punts	5	4
Punting average, yds.	43.4	37
Fumbles lost	1	1
Yards penalized	25	41

LOS ANGELES, Dec. 23 (AP)— Los Angeles' spectacular Rams, with a tie-breaking 73-yard pass play in the final quarter, captured the National League championship today from the Cleveland Browns in a battle that ended the visitors' five-year rule in professional football. The score was 24—17.

Left End Tommy Fears of the Rams, racing down the field, gathered in a tremendous pass thrown by Norman Van Brocklin, the Rams' alternate quarterback, and tore on to complete the day's longest play that sent the Rams off the field with their first championship since the club moved here from Cleveland in 1946.

That throw ended the Browns' domination of the old National League and marked their first defeat in a title game in a string stretching back to 1946, when they became the rulers of the now-defunct All-America Conference.

It culminated a series of breaks, thrills and spills which left the record-breaking crowd of 59,475 limp with excitement and must have provided an equal thrill to the millions of television followers across the nation.

First Victory in 4 Tries

It also marked the first victory in four tries for Los Angeles over the precision-built machine from Cleveland, and the first time the Ram coach, Joe Stydahar, out-foxed Paul Brown, the talented young master from Massilon, Ohio, in five coaching duels, including last year's pro bowl.

Once again the Rams were not without a nod from Lady Luck.

A fumble by Cleveland's quarterback wizard, Otto Graham, when 240-pound defensive end Larry Brink hit him on a pass attempt was picked up by End Andy Robustelli in the third quarter and turned into a touchdown that put the Rams ahead, 14—10.

That break and the Van Brocklin-Fears touchdown pass play erased a brilliant performance by Graham and a 52-yard field goal by Lou (The Toe) Groza that set a new record for the play-off.

The pay-off was a personal triumph for the Rams' No. 1 quarterback and captain, Bob Waterfield, who had led the club to its only other N. F. L. title in 1945.

The Rams scored first on a 55-yard drive in the second period that ended with Fullback Dick Hoerner crashing over from the 1-yard mark.

Groza's marvelous place-kick put the Browns on the scoreboard and then Cleveland struck quickly for a touchdown to take a 10-7 lead at half-time. The combination of Brink and Robustelli took advantage of the Graham fumble to put the Rams in front, 14—10, in the third quarter. Early in the fourth Waterfield's 17-yard field goal made it 17—10.

Graham Sparks Drive

Graham gathered his forces together for an explosive punch that netted 70 yards in ten plays, Automatic Otto contributing a 34-yard run down the sideline. Ken Carpenter went over right tackle for a yard, and when Groza added the point, the game was tied at 17—17 and the fray headed into its final eight minutes.

The Browns never stopped threatening, and it appeared they might duplicate their victory in the final twenty-eight seconds of the championship game with the Rams in Cleveland last December — a 30-28 decision, accomplished on a Groza field goal.

The Rams were not to be denied this time before the largest crowd ever to see an N. F. L. title contest. The old record was 58,346 in the Polo Grounds between the New York Giants and the Chicago Bears in 1946.

Twice the Rams missed, or the Browns stopped, scoring chances. Fears caught an arching pass and fought his way to a 48-yard gain to the Brown 1. Soon afterward Marvin Johnson intercepted a Graham pass and ran it back 35 to the Brown 1.

Altogether, the Rams had seven cracks at the Cleveland line, failed to cross the goal and on the second try had to settle for Waterfield's field goal.

Cleveland had its heartbreaks, too. The Browns took the opening kick-off and marched from their 23 to the Rams' 16. The drive stalled and Groza stepped back for a field goal from the 23. There was a groan from the outnumbered Brown supporters when it sailed to the left for a miss.

In the third period, with the Rams leading, 14—10, Graham fired a strike to Mac Speedie, who was in the clear and ran to a touchdown, but the play was called back because a Browns' lineman was detected holding.

Cleveland's first score was a study in Graham perfection. He hit Speedie for 14, Marion Motley for 23, and Dub Jones for the final 17 of a swift 54-yard scoring sequence.

Waterfield guided the Rams on their first scoring series, passing for 18, to Vitamin T. Smith, for 15 to Hoerner and barging deep into the Browns' territory. Pass interference was called on Cleveland's Tommy Thompson on the 12 and the Rams hammered across, with Dan Towler making a big 6 to reach the 1. Hoerner went over from there.

Fears last year's all-pro end who was on the injured list much of the season, climbed back to renown with his performance. Tommy earned 146 yards in four catches, including the winning touchdown. He overshadowed Elroy Hirsch, this year's league leader who had 56 yards in four receptions.

The Groza field goal eclipsed the old title-game distance of 42 yards, held jointly by Ward Cuff of the Giants and Ernie Smith of Green Bay. Cuff set his against Green Bay in 1938 and Smith tied it against the Giants the next year.

Local fans, who had seen the Rams win eight games and lose four in the regular season and were well aware that Cleveland had lost just one game and had won eleven straight going into the match, mobbed the Rams as the gun sounded.

Even Stydahar—275 pounds or more—was lifted bodily and carried off the field in triumph.

The Rams collected $2,108.44 apiece and each Cleveland player got $1,483.12 as the players' pool totaled $156,551.42 from a paid attendance of 57,540. It is based on 70 per cent of the net receipts. Gross receipts, including $75,000 for television and radio rights, were $325,970.

The gross and the players' share topped the previous high for the title game, set in 1946 between the Bears and Giants at the Polo Grounds. Gross receipts in that contest, for which no video or radio rights were sold, were $282,955.25. The winning Bears got $1,975,82 and the Giants $1,295,57.

AMERICAN CONFERENCE	W	L	T	Pct.	Pts.	Op
Cleveland	11	1	0	.917	331	152
N.Y. Giants	9	2	1	.818	254	161
Washington	5	7	0	.417	183	296
Pittsburgh	4	7	1	.364	183	235
Philadelphia	4	8	0	.333	234	264
Chi. Cardinals	3	9	0	.250	210	287

NATIONAL CONFERENCE	W	L	T	Pct.	Pts.	Op
Los Angeles	8	4	0	.667	392	261
Detroit	7	4	1	.636	336	259
San Francisco	7	4	1	.636	255	205
Chi. Bears	7	5	0	.583	286	282
Green Bay	3	9	0	.250	254	375
N.Y. Yanks	1	9	2	.100	241	382

The line-up:

LOS ANGELES RAMS (24)
Left Ends—Fears, Brink, Hecker, Keane.
Left Tackles—Simensen, Winkler.
Left Guards—McLaughlin, Paul, Reid.
Centers—McLaughlin, Paul, Reid.
Right Guards—Lange, Thompson, Collier.
Right Tackles—Dahms, Toogood, Halliday.
Right Ends—Hirsch, Robustelli, Boyd.
Quarterbacks—Waterfield, Van Brocklin.
Left Halfbacks — Towler, Davis, Williams, Johnson.
Right Halfbacks—Younger, Smith, Kalmanir, Lewis, Rich.
Fullback—Hoerner.

CLEVELAND BROWNS (17)
Left Ends—Speedie, Young, Gillom.
Left Tackles—Groza, Kissell, Palmer.
Left Guards—Gibron, Thompson, Agase.
Centers—Gatski, Herring.
Right Guards—Gaudio, Willis, Houston.
Right Tackles—Rymkus, Sandusky, Grigg.
Right Ends—Lavelli, Ford, Oristaglio.
Quarterbacks—Graham, Lewis, Shula.
Left Halfbacks—Carpenter, Lahr, Baumgardner.
Right Halfbacks—Jones, James, Taseff.
Fullbacks—Motley, Adamle, Cole, Jagade.

SCORE BY PERIODS

Los Angeles Rams ....0 7 7 10—24
Cleveland Browns ....0 10 0 7—17

Touchdowns—Hoerner, Towler, Fears, Jones, Carpenter. Points after touchdowns—Waterfield 3, Groza 2. Field goals—Waterfield, Groza.

Browns' Play-Off Record

ALL-AMERICA CONFERENCE

1946—Cleveland 14, New York Yankees 9.

1947—Cleveland 14, New York Yankees 3.

1948—Cleveland 49, Buffalo Bills 7.

1949—Cleveland 21, San Francisco 49ers 7.

NATIONAL LEAGUE

1950—Cleveland 30, Los Angeles Rams 28.

1951—Los Angeles Rams 24, Cleveland 17.

Pro Grid Group Rejects Plan Of Eliminating Extra Point

New York. Jan. 16 (AP)—The National Football League rules committee. in effect. tonight rejected proposals for elimination of the point after touchdown and for a sudden-death playoff of tie games.

The committee voted. 7 to 5, in favor of eliminating the extra point and making each touchdown count seven points, but a 10-2 vote is necessary for passage.

Commissioner Bert Bell, who recommended both changes, said the proposed rules would still be brought up at Friday's business meeting but. "in my mind I don't think they can pass."

The committee, a recommending body. voted. 9 to 3. for sudden death. This means another vote would have to be obtained for passage.

Those opposing sudden death were the Chicago Bears, New York Giants and Pittsburgh.

The five clubs which lined up against elimination of the extra point were Los Angeles, Detroit, Cleveland, Pittsburgh and New York Giants.

The rules group did recommend by an 11-to-1 vote. with Washington opposing, that all players in the league be numbered uniformly according to positions.

Under this plan centers would wear numbers in the 50s, guards in the 60's, tackles in the 70's. fullbacks in the 30's and quarterbacks in the 'teens.

This would not apply to such established stars such as Sammy Baugh, who has No. 33; Bob Watterfield, No. 7; Otto Graham, No. 60, and others.

WADE PICKED AS TOP CHOICE

Vanderbilt Back First Player Chosen In N.F.L. Draft

New York, Jan. 17 (AP)—The top prize of the 1951 college football crop—Vanderbilt's Bill Wade—fell to the champion Los Angeles Rams today in a National League draft that saw a marked trend away from single-wing talent.

The Rams won the coveted "bonus" pick in a blind draw with six other clubs and immediately put the finger on the 6-foot-2, 202-pound T-quarterback from Nashville, Tenn., rated by the pros as the outstanding prospect for the money game.

Wade, a brilliant long passer, hard runner and big enough to play defense, probably won't be available for two years since he is committed under a V-5 program to two years of naval duty. However, the Rams, with two fine quarterbacks in Bob Waterfield and Norm Van Brocklin, figure they can wait.

Pair Of Ends

After harnessing Wade, the Rams proceeded to pick up a pair of All America ends — Bob Carey, of Michigan State, and Dewey McConnell, of Wyoming, in the regular draft, a drawn-out, all-day affair.

Only the San Francisco Fortyniners, who plucked three All-America stars in the first five ballots, apparently fared as well in cushioning their squad for the future. The Forty-niners picked up Hugh McElhenny, Washington's plowing fullback; Pat O'Donohue, Wisconsin end, and Bob Toneff, Notre Dame tackle.

Single-wing tailbacks went begging in the draw. Princeton's Dick Kazmaier, the most decorated college player of the 1951 season, wasn't picked until the fifteenth round. when the Chicago Bears took him.

The name of Hank Lauricella, All-America wheelhorse of Tennessee's national champions, didn't fall until the seventeenth round. He was the two hundred and first player chosen and was picked by the Detroit Lions.

Kazmaier Not Interested

Kazmaier has insisted he is not interested in pro football and Lauricella is headed for military service.

Want Home Grown Talent With Doak Walker 'Must'

Reported to Have Made $250,000 Bid to Detroit For Former Southern Methodist Star; League Gives Collins $100,000 and Takes Over Obligations

NEW YORK, Jan. 20—(AP)—The Dallas Rangers began a move to give their National Football League team a sharp Texas flavor today with a $250,000 bid for Detroit's Doak Walker. The New York Yanks' controversial, red-ink franchise was shifted to the Texas city late last night in a triple-pass maneuver that sheared Radio Producer Ted Collins of his professional football interests. Bert Bell, NFL commissioner, said papers and a check for $300,000 are in the mail from the Dallas purchaser, textile tycoon Giles Miller, and the deal should be completed by the middle of next week.

Already, however, the new owners apparently are busy trying to round up home-grown talent.

Walker Becomes 'Must'

Walker, a Dallas boy who was a three-time All-America halfback at Southern Methodist University, became No. 1 on their "must have" list. He is the gridiron idol of the Lone Star State.

Nick Kerbawy, general manager of the Detroit club, said he had received telephone calls from Dallas papers today asking the prospects of luring Walker away from the Lions.

Kerbawy said he gave the Texans no hope. Walker, he added firmly, is not for sale.

"The calls were not from Miller," the Detroit executive said, "but they were from persons who seemed to have a voice in the venture.

"They asked would we be willing to take $250,000 for Walker, payable $25,000 a year for ten years. I told them no. But they gave every indication they're not giving up."

Walker's crowd appeal is credited with helping double the seating capacity of the Cotton Bowl (now 75,349) where the pro games will be played.

By odd coincidence, Walker originally was drafted by the yanks but later was traded to the Lions for Johnny Rauch.

The Washington Redskins also girded for offers from the new Dallas owners. particularly for Baylor's All-America Quarterback Larry Isbell and Smu's Center Dick Hightower, both plucked in the recent draft.

Might Trade Isbell

"I don't know whether we'd take George Ratterman for Isbell but we might," said Redskins' owner George Marshall.

Another rumor sweeping the convention headquarters of the league was that the Texans also may try to grab the Redskins' Sammy Baugh as coach. Most of the club directors and coaches, however, gave little credence to this.

Sept. 29

Texans Dropped by Giants, 24 to 6, in Pro Loop Debut

By CHARLES BURTON

The New York Giants, American Conference title favorites, initiated Dallas into the National Football League Sunday with a 24-to-6 victory in the Cotton Bowl.

Gov. Allen Shivers and approximately 17,499 other fans saw the Texans score first, but the Giants most often as big league football came into the Southwest for the first time.

Gala opening-day ceremonies marked the contest, with Shivers telling the throng that it was a pleasure to welcome "this new era in sports in Texas." And, said the Governor, Texas owes Giles Miller,

Reprinted from
The Dallas Morning Times

INCOMPLETE BUT LOOK CLOSE

THIS PASS PLAY, caught by Cameraman Nick Dudar during Browns-Redskins pro game in Cleveland, was ruled incomplete but note (arrow) how a Brownie defender has grabbed the wrist of Hugh Taylor, Redskin end.

Reprinted from
The Cleveland Plain Dealer

BIG DEFICIT FORCES CLUB FROM TEXAS

Dallas Expected to Complete Schedule on Road Under Operation of N. F. L.

DALLAS, Nov. 12 (P)—The Dallas franchise in professional football folded today after incurring losses that reached nearly a quarter of a million dollars, with the season a little more than half finished.

Giles Miller, president of the Texans, a club that came to Dallas last winter as the first major league professional football franchise in the state, announced that it would be turned back to the National Football League. It thus will become a "road club" operated by the league and apparently will play no more games in Dallas.

Miller explained that the club did not have sufficient funds to meet its obligations, adding, "for that matter, unless additional funds were made available immediately this club could not play its next game." Miller showed reporters a telegram he said he was sending to the league commissioner, Bert Bell, turning the club back to the league.

Bell Calls Hearing

Miller and other club officials tonight received a telegram from Bell saying that notice is "hereby given" of a hearing to determine the disposition of the Dallas team, including its franchise, player contracts and all other matters relating to its operation at the league offices in Philadelphia on Friday.

Bell said that all persons having or claiming any interest in the team would be heard.

John Coyle, one of five trustees representing the sixteen stockholders, said that sufficient financial backing had been obtained to operate the club on a long-range basis but that "interim financing" could not be obtained for several reasons. These included legal technicalities that prevented the franchise being sold at this time. Some forty bondholders have, in effect, a mortgage on the club.

Coyle said it was planned to bid for the club in December and perhaps buy it back. "We feel that we can make a go of it if we have the proper chance," he said.

Seven Straight Losses

Miller said Bell had assured him that the league would make necessary arrangements for the club to finish its schedule. Thus the Texans, when they leave Friday with Coach Jim Phelan for Detroit to play their next game, will be bidding Dallas goodbye.

The Texans have lost seven straight games and in their home appearance drew only about 13,000 fans a game. It takes about 24,000 a game to pay expenses.

The franchise, held last year by the New York Yanks, was bought by Miller for $100,000. The lease on Yankee Stadium for eight years at $25,000 a year also was assumed by Dallas but none of this will be paid, Coyle said.

Coyle said that when Dallas bought the club, there apparently was great interest in pro football here and that the territory with a potential of 1,000,000 appeared to assure at least 25,000 per game.

Dallas still has home games with the Chicago Bears and Detroit Lions and away games with Detroit, Green Bay and the Philadelphia Eagles.

Bell said in Philadelphia that the league was not going to operate Dallas for the profit of the present owners. He indicated that if the Dallas franchise and player contracts were turned back to the league for operation, the N. F. L. would reap any profits or foot any loss.

Sammy Baugh Ends Pro Career Sitting On Redskins' Bench

Washington. Dec. 14 (AP)—Sammy Baugh, who smashed 16 records during his 16 years in pro football, wound up his fabulous playing career today sitting on the bench watching his Washington Redskin teammates pull out a last second 27-to-21 victory over the Philadelphia Eagles.

Baugh's farewell to the National Professional Football League was overshadowed by the thrilling Redskin comeback which blasted the Eagles' hopes for a championship.

Ruined Finale

Fate even conspired to rob the 38-year-old Texan of a last-minute dramatic appearance in the game. Redskin coach Curley Lambeau had planned to put Baugh into the contest for a final series of plays which would officially end his playing days.

Baugh started in the game, but was in only three plays while the Redskins were on the offensive. He never had any chance to display his pass throwing ability.

But, the hepped-up. Redskin didn't score their winning touchdown until there were but 18 seconds left to play. Even then, it was quarterback Eddy Lebaron, who has replaced Baugh as regular quarter-back, who plunged across for the winning touchdown.

Fans Remember

As the final gun sounded, hundreds of fans showed they remembered the lean Texan who has been Mr. Football in Washington ever since he joined the Redskins fresh from Texas Christian University in 1937.

About 500 autograph-seeking fans surrounded Baugh at the 40 yard line and kept him signing programs for nearly an hour after the game ended.

Photographers, caught in the Melee, climbed up on the shoulders of obliging fans to record Sammy's farewell signing performance.

Perspiration dripping down his nose, Baugh trooped into the steamy Redskin dressing room afterward, escorted by nearly a dozen photographers anxious to picture his goodbye to his coach, teammates and friends.

Baugh posed repeatedly, either in Indian headdress, or in the act of storing away his famous number 33 jersey for the last time in between handshakes and continued requests for his autograph.

Nice Ending

"It was sure nice to knock them off," Baugh said to little Lebaron.

To reporters, he vowed that he would do it all over again if he were starting out fresh from T.C.U. to make a living.

"Pro football has been good to me," he said nodding his head vigorously.

The usually taciturn Texan pulled on his pointed black leather cowboy boots and his soft brown

SAMMY BAUGH

cowboy Stetson just before leaving.

A reporter friend jokingly asked if he planned "to lay around" on his Texas ranch during the next few weeks.

"Lay around. hell," Baugh answered with a smile. "You don't lay around on a ranch. I've got a lot of feeding to do for my cattle."

Shrewd Business Man

Baugh, a shrewd business man as well as quarterback, has invested his savings in a ranch at Rotan. Texas, where he has 300 head of cattle.

Accompanied by another Redskin. Baugh arranged to start driving his station wagon to Texas for a reunion with his wife and four sons. Shortly before Baugh left, Joe Tereshniski handed Sammy the football used in today's game as a farewell memento.

As he was ready to walk out of the dressing room for the last time. Baugh disclosed he probably would accept a job as assistant coach at Hardin Simmons College in West Texas.

"It's close by and I can drive home every night to the family," he said.

Sammy edged to the door, stopped for a final look at the nearly deserted dressing room and then with a half smile walked off into the night, a gift ham instead of a football cradled in his right arm.

Sam Baugh holds these 16 National Football League records:
Most passes completed. 1,709.
Most passes completed one season. 1947—210.
Most passes attempted. 3,016.
Most passes attempted one season. 1947—354.
Most passes intercepted. 206.
Most yards gained passing—22,085.
Most yards gained passing one season. 1947—2,938.
Most touchdown passes. 187.
Best passing efficiency (500 or more attempts)—56.6 per cent.
Best passing efficiency one season. 1945—70.3 per cent.
Most passes one game—14. (held with two others).
Best punting average one season. 1942—48.7 yards on 30 punts.
Most years as active player in national football league. 16.
CHAMPIONSHIP GAME RECORDS
Longest punt. 85 yards.
Most years participated. 5.
Most yards gained passing one game. 335.

LOS ANGELES HALTS STEELERS, 28 TO 14

Van Brocklin Leads Rams to Conference Tie as 71,130 Look On in Coliseum

STATISTICS OF THE GAME

	L. A.	Pitts.
First downs	27	18
Rushing yardage	158	109
Passing yardage	358	282
Passes attempted	43	48
Passes completed	24	23
Passes intercepted by.	3	4
Number of punts	5	5
Punting average, yds.	42.2	47.0
Fumbles lost	1	2
Yards penalized	45	25

LOS ANGELES, Dec. 14 (AP) — Propelled by the brilliant three-touchdown passing of Norman Van Brocklin, the Los Angeles Rams defeated the Pittsburgh Steelers, 28 to 14, today and climbed into a tie with Detroit for the National Conference title in the National Football League.

Honors for Waterfield

The day marked the farewell for Quarterback Bob Waterfield, and he was duly honored. But it was his alternate, the Flying Dutchman from Oregon, and his bevy of pass-catchers, plus a fighting Ram defense that stopped the Steeler running attack cold and sent the tremendous crowd home happy.

Van Brocklin decorated the scoreboard with two 6-point throws to left end Tom Fears, tosses that flew only 5 and 10 yards, but his masterpiece was one that went for 65 yards to Elroy (Crazy Legs) Hirsch.

Rounding out the Ram scoring was a touchdown by Dick (Night Train) Lane, who took one of his three interceptions of the day back 42 yards to put the Rams in front, 14—0, in the second period.

Lane's three interceptions brought his season's total to 14 for a new league record, previously held by Dan Sandifer of Washington and Spec Sanders of the old New York Yankees.

Harder Sparks Playoff Triumph

DETROIT (AP)—Pat Harder scored 19 points to boost his Detroit Lions to the National Conference championship of the National Football League here Sunday.

The Lions turned back a last-period thrust and whipped the defending pro champ Los Angeles Rams 31-21 in muddy, fog-wrapped Briggs Stadium before 47,645 fans.

The victory put the Lions in the NFL title championship game next Sunday at Cleveland against the American Conference champion Cleveland Browns.

Harder, an ineffective runner but a great blocker all season, scored on 12 and 4-yard plunges, kicked

ROARING ON

RAMS 21
LEFT ENDS: Fears, Carey, Brink
LEFT TACKLES: Simensen, Teeuws, Winkler.
LEFT GUARDS: Daugherty, Thompson, McFadin.
CENTERS: McLaughlin, Paul.
RIGHT GUARDS: Lange, Putnam, West.
RIGHT TACKLES: Dahms, Toogood, Casner.
RIGHT ENDS: Hirsch, Hecker, Robustelli.
QUARTERBACKS: Van Brocklin, Waterfield.
LEFT HALFBACKS: Towler, Quinlan, Williams.
RIGHT HALFBACKS: Smith, Bariy, Rich, Dwyer, Lewis.
FULLBACKS: Younger, Myers.
LIONS 31
LEFT ENDS: Box, Swiackl, Earon.
LEFT TACKLES: Creekmur, Miller, McGraw
LEFT GUARDS: Martin, Campbell, Flanagan.
CENTERS: Banonis, Torgeson.
RIGHT GUARDS: Stanfel, Bingaman.
RIGHT TACKLES: Cifelli, Prchlik.
RIGHT ENDS: Hart, Doran.
QUARTERBACKS: Layne, Hardy, Dublinski, Doll.
LEFT HALFBACKS: Walker, David, Hill
RIGHT HALFBACKS: Bailey, Hoernschemeyer, Christiansen, Smith, Lary.
FULLBACKS: Harder, Cline.
SCORING
Lions 7   7   10   7—31
Rams 0   7   0   14—21
TOUCHDOWNS—Lions: Harder 2, Hart. Hoernschemeyer. Rams: Fears, Towler, Smith
EXTRA POINTS—Lions: Harder 4. Rams Waterfield 3.
FIELD GOAL—Lions: Harder.

Pro Football Title
LAYNE, WALKER SCORE
TOUCHDOWNS FOR LIONS

Gillom's 22-Yard Punt Gives Detroiters Early Advantage; Coach Brown Attributes Loss On Gridiron To 'Little Things'

Cleveland, Dec. 28 (AP)—The younger Detroit Lions smashed through a veteran Cleveland Browns team today for two touchdowns and a field goal to win 17-7 and cop their first professional championship in 17 years.

The alert Lions capitalized on the breaks and led all the way in what was essentially a defensive battle. A crowd of 50,934 watched in a temperature of about 30 degrees.

Longest Run

The longest and most spectacular run of the day was a dash by Detroit halfback Doak Walker for 67 yards and a touchdown in the third quarter. Walker shot through the left side of the line, cut back to the right and picked his way through the entire secondary. It was his first touchdown this season.

Walker had missed seven games because of a pulled leg muscle, but he scored 11 touchdowns in his first year of pro football and six last year.

The break that led to the Lion's first score was a poor punt by Horace Gillom, the league's leading kicker. It wobbled out of bounds at midfield, only 22 yards from the line of scrimmage. That was just before the end of the first quarter.

Layne Hits Box

In the last two plays of the quarter, Bobby Layne hit Cloyce Box in the clear with a 10-yarder, then bootlegged around left end on the next play for 13 more. Fullback Pat Harder fought through the center to within inches of a first down on the Browns' 17 and Walker picked up those inches.

Layne shot a low pass to Bill Swiacki for 14 yards and the Lions were on the Browns' 2. Walker gained 5 to offset a 5-yard penalty and on second down Layne shouldered through the middle for the touchdown.

The Browns' lone touchdown followed by only four minutes Walker's spectacular dash in the third quarter. Their drive carried 78 yards in ten plays, slowed by a 15-yard shoving penalty. Graham who had gained only 9 yards in ten pass attempts during the first half, began to click. He hit End Dante Lavelli for 9 and 11, Pete Brewster for 22 and Ray Renfro for 8 and carried for 12 himself during the drive.

Jagade Scores

Harry Jagade went over from the seven with Tackle Thurman McGraw and Safety Man Don Doll hanging on. Lou Groza booted the extra point.

The Browns made another threat in the fourth quarter, driving from their own 17 to the Lions' 21. Big Marion Motley sparked this drive by carrying a pitchout 42 yards to the Lions' five. He stepped out of bounds just before he fell and slid against the goal line flag.

The drive sputtered when Linebacker Dick Flanagan knocked down a fourth-down Graham pass.

Another break for the Lions occurred midway in the last period, when Halfback Ken Carpenter fumbled Bob Smith's punt and Lion End Jim Martin recovered on the Browns' 24. A personal foul set the Lions back 15 yards but they cashed in for three points when Harder booted a field goal on fourth down with the ball on the 29.

Browns' Final Threat

Before the game was over, the Browns marched 77 yards to the Lions' 8 in a final ill-starred threat. The big gain was a 31-yard Graham pass to Brewster, who couldn't outrun Jack Christiansen and was hauled down on the 8.

Graham then tossed three incomplete passes and the Browns drew a 5-yard penalty for too much time in the huddle. On his last chance, Graham hit Brewster in the end zone with a pass that appeared to be worth six points, but the officials held that an ineligible receiver, Renfro, had tipped the ball.

Although Graham completed 20 out-of-34 passes for 191 yards, he was at his top form only in flashes, many of his passes at crucial points were far off the mark. His performance today gave him a National Football League championship-game record for the most passes attempted, and most completed.

He now has 61 completions in 107 attempts in three title games. Bob Waterfield of the Los Angeles Rams held the old record of 95 tries and 46 completions in four games.

End Lavelli also set a mark by running his total of championship game passes caught to 19 in three games. He caught four to surpass the mark of 16 catches in four title games by Wayne Milliner, of Boston and Washington.

The Browns' aerial attack, their chief weapon, was greatly weakened because End MacSpeedie and Halfback Dub Jones both sat out the whole game. They twisted knees two weeks ago when the Browns lost to the Giants in New York.

Jones and Speedie had accounted for 105 of the Browns' 184 good passes and 1,562 of the 2,839 yards the Brownies gained by air this season.

On the ground, where the Browns outgained the Lions 229 yards to 199, Jagade, a sophomore pro from Indiana, led all the backs on the field with 104 in 15 tries.

Walker made 97 in 10 carries with the bulk of the Detroit ground gained. Motley, at 32, the oldest man on the field, came out with the best average per thrust. In six attempts he ran 74 yards.

The nationally televised and broadcast game netted gross receipts of $314,318 that meant record shares for the players participating. Each Detroit player got $2,274.77 while the Browns drew shares of $1,712.49 each.

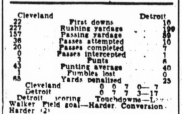

Statistics

Cleveland		Detroit
22	First downs	10
227	Rushing yardage	199
157	Passing yardage	89
36	Passes attempted	10
20	Passes completed	7
0	Passes intercepted	1
3	Punts	8
43	Punting average	40
1	Fumbles lost	0
65	Yards penalized	25

Cleveland	0	0	7	0—7
Detroit	0	7	7	3—17

Detroit scoring   Touchdowns—Layne, Walker   Field goal—Harder.   Conversion Harder (2).

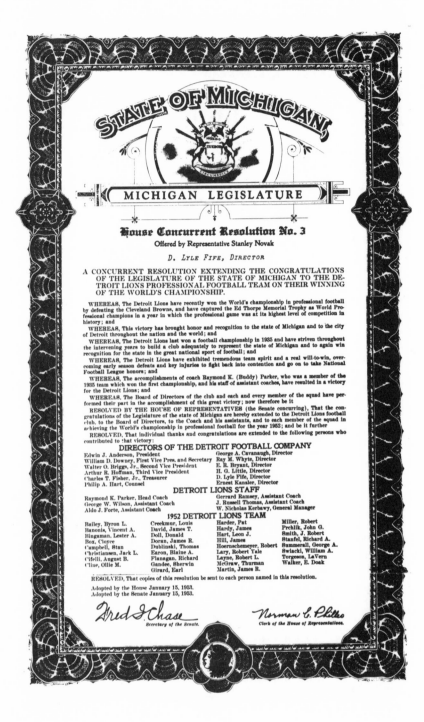

STATE OF MICHIGAN

MICHIGAN LEGISLATURE

House Concurrent Resolution No. 3

Offered by Representative Stanley Novak

D. LYLE FIFE, DIRECTOR

A CONCURRENT RESOLUTION EXTENDING THE CONGRATULATIONS OF THE LEGISLATURE OF THE STATE OF MICHIGAN TO THE DETROIT LIONS PROFESSIONAL FOOTBALL TEAM ON THEIR WINNING OF THE WORLD'S CHAMPIONSHIP.

WHEREAS, The Detroit Lions have recently won the World's championship in professional football by defeating the Cleveland Browns, and have captured the Ed Thorpe Memorial Trophy as World Professional champions in a year in which the professional game was at its highest level of competition in history; and

WHEREAS, This victory has brought honor and recognition to the state of Michigan and to the city of Detroit throughout the nation and the world; and

WHEREAS, The Detroit Lions last won a football championship in 1935 and have striven throughout the intervening years to build a club adequately to represent the state of Michigan and to again win recognition for the state in the great national sport of football; and

WHEREAS, The Detroit Lions have exhibited tremendous team spirit and a real will-to-win, overcoming early season defeats and key injuries to fight back into contention and go on to take National Football League honors; and

WHEREAS, The accomplishments of coach Raymond K. (Buddy) Parker, who was a member of the 1935 team which won the first championship, and his staff of assistant coaches, have resulted in a victory for the Detroit Lions; and

WHEREAS, The Board of Directors of the club and each and every member of the squad have performed their part in the accomplishment of this great victory; now therefore be it

RESOLVED BY THE HOUSE OF REPRESENTATIVES (the Senate concurring), That the congratulations of the Legislature of the state of Michigan are hereby extended to the Detroit Lions football club, to the Board of Directors, to the Coach and his assistants, and to each member of the squad in achieving the World's championship in professional football for the year 1952; and be it further

RESOLVED, That individual thanks and congratulations are extended to the following persons who contributed to that victory:

DIRECTORS OF THE DETROIT FOOTBALL COMPANY

Edwin J. Anderson, President	George A. Cavanaugh, Director
William D. Downey, First Vice Pres. and Secretary	Ray M. Whyte, Director
Walter O. Briggs, Jr., Second Vice President	E. R. Bryant, Director
Arthur R. Hoffman, Third Vice President	H. G. Little, Director
Charles T. Fisher, Jr., Treasurer	D. Lyle Fife, Director
Philip A. Hart, Counsel	Ernest Kanzler, Director

DETROIT LIONS STAFF

Raymond K. Parker, Head Coach	Gerrard Ramsey, Assistant Coach
George W. Wilson, Assistant Coach	J. Russell Thomas, Assistant Coach
Aldo J. Forte, Assistant Coach	W. Nicholas Kerbawy, General Manager

1952 DETROIT LIONS TEAM

Bailey, Byron L.	Creekmur, Louis	Harder, Pat	Miller, Robert
Banonis, Vincent A.	David, James T.	Hardy, James	Prchlik, John G.
Bingaman, Lester A.	Doll, Donald	Hart, Leon J.	Smith, J. Robert
Box, Cloyce	Doran, James R.	Hill, James	Stanfel, Richard A.
Campbell, Stan	Dublinski, Thomas	Hoernschemeyer, Robert	Summerall, George A.
Christiansen, Jack L.	Earon, Blaine A.	Lary, Robert Yale	Swiacki, William A.
Cifelli, August B.	Flanagan, Richard	Layne, Robert L.	Torgeson, LaVern
Cline, Ollie M.	Gandee, Sherwin	McGraw, Thurman	Walker, E. Doak
	Girard, Earl	Martin, James R.	

RESOLVED, That copies of this resolution be sent to each person named in this resolution.

Adopted by the House January 15, 1953.
Adopted by the Senate January 15, 1953.

Fred I. Chase
Secretary of the Senate.

Norman E. Philbo
Clerk of the House of Representatives.

FIRST ROUND

First-round draft choices follow.

Baltimore—Billy Vessels, Oklahoma halfback. Washington, Scarbath; Chicago Cards, John Olszewski, fullback, California; Pittsburg, Ted Marchibroda, quarterback, Detroit; Chicago Bears, William Anderson, halfback, Compton (Cal.) Junior College; Green Bay, Al Carmichael, halfback, Southern California; New York, Bobby Marlow, halfback, Alabama; Philadelphia, draft choice traded to Los Angeles Rams, who picked Donn Moomaw, linebacker, U.C.L.A.; San Francisco, Tom Stolhandske, end, Texas; Cleveland, Doug Atkins, tackle, Tennessee; Los Angeles, Ed Barker, end, Washington State; Detroit, Harley Sewell, guard, Texas.

FOOTBALL OWNERS NAMED

Baltimore Group of 5 Officially Gets Pro Franchise

BALTIMORE, Jan. 11 (AP)—A group of five Baltimoreans, including a former Penn football player, Carroll Rosenbloom, tonight officially received a National Football League franchise.

The announcement climaxed a two-year struggle to regain the berth surrendered to the league two years ago by Abe Watner, then president of the Baltimore Colts.

William Macmillan, counsel for the old Colt board of directors and one of the leaders in the comeback drive, said: "The ownership of the Baltimore team has been determined and agreed upon."

Besides Rosenbloom, the new owners include Thomas Mullan, William F. Hilgenberg, one of the old directors; Zanvyl Krieger, another former director, and Bruce Livie, racing stable owner who conducted the recent sale of season tickets to clinch the deal.

Dick Hoerner May Snag Colt-Lion Grid Deal

Dallas, Jan. 22 (AP)—A $500 bonus which Fullback Dick Hoerner claims is due him from the defunct Dallas Texans may throw a wrench into the first deal consummated by the Baltimore Colts, the team which replaced Dallas in the National Pro Football League.

Baltimore swapped Hoerner, an all-pro fullback when he played for the Los Angeles Rams, to the Detroit Lions for Quarterback Tom Dublinski.

Hoerner told the Dallas *Morning News* after the trade was announced that he legally considered himself a free agent and not bound by any deals involving him by the Baltimore Club.

"I have a letter in my possession signed by Coach Jim Phelan of the Texans, in which I was promised a $500 bonus if I played in eight of 12 games scheduled by the Texans," Hoerner said. "I kept my end of the deal by appearing in ten games. I am still waiting to collect the bonus."

He said that he had been informed that the Texans's failure to pay the bonus automatically made him a free agent.

Hoerner, now working for a radio station here, said he doubted if he would join Detroit even if that club offered to settle the bonus. He said he liked his job here.

In Philadelphia, N.F.L. Commissioner Bert Bell said that Hoerner had been paid everything that was coming to him under his regular contract, but that, if he had any other agreements, Bell would be glad to see them. Bell said he would give Hoerner a hearing on the matter.

Jim Thorpe, Great Athlete, Dies At 64 In Los Angeles

LOS ANGELES, March 28 (AP) — Jim Thorpe, one of the nation's great all-around athletes of a bygone era, died today of a heart attack. Thorpe, 64, suffered the attack in his trailer at suburban Lomita. A fire department rescue squad futilely attempted to revive him.

Thorpe, the famed Carlisle Indian, was an almost legendary figure in the sports world. In the early years of this century he distinguished himself as a great football player.

And in the 1912 Olympic Games at Stockholm, he won fame as the greatest all-round track and field performer of his day. He won both the decathlon and pentathlon.

Eating Meal

Thorpe was eating a meal in his trailer with his wife Patricia when he collapsed.

Her screams brought a neighbor, Colby Bradshaw, running. He administered artificial respiration until a fire department rescue squad arrived.

Firemen said that for a moment during artificial respiration, Thorpe regained consciousness and seemed to recognize his wife, then slipped away.

He was pronounced dead by Dr. Rachel E. Jenkins of an emergency hospital, who had administered adrenalin directly into the heart in an effort to save Thorpe.

Three years ago in an Associated Press poll, sportswriters voted Thorpe as the greatest male athlete in the first half of this century. He was far ahead of Babe Ruth, the runner-up for the honor.

Underwent Surgery

After making Walter Camp's All-American team for two years as a sensational runner, kicker and passer at Carlisle (Pa.) Indian Institute, in 1911 and 1912, he played professional football and baseball for 16 years. For six years he was in the big leagues with the New York Giants.

But in the autumn of his life he met economic reverses. In 1951 it was revealed that he was flat broke and a charity case in a Philadelphia hospital. He had undergone surgery there for removal of a lip cancer.

Various movements were started to aid him. Baseball raised a substantial sum. A group of sportsmen and businessmen organized the Fair Play for Thorpe committee.

His fabulous career was depicted in a movie, "Jim Thorpe, All-American."

Thorpe recently was associated in operation of a restaurant in Wilmington, Calif., not far from his trailer home.

Frequent Speaker

He realized funds from the movie of his life and was a frequent speaker. The demand for his appearances indicated the old Carlisle Indian still retained his popularity among sports fans.

He was seriously ill last summer while in Henderson, Nev., but showed the old stamina to recover.

Big Jim, who stood 6 feet 1 inch and weighed 185 pounds in his prime, was born in a one-room log cabin near Shawnee, Okla., May 28, 1888, one of twin boys. His twin brother died at the age of 8.

Jim's mother gave him the Indian tribal name of Wa-tho-huck, meaning Bright Path. Thorpe's mother was an Indian, his father part Indian. His paternal grandfather was an Irishman who took as his bride a granddaughter of the famous Sac and Fox warrior, Chief Black Hawk.

Nobody knows how many sports Big Jim could have excelled in. He wasn't too strong on the rigors of training, relying on his great natural co-ordination and speed.

Ahead Of Grange

He first gained prominence in sports at Carlisle Institute under Coach Glenn (Pop) Warner. He started playing football in 1907. The next year he kicked three field goals to beat Penn State, 12-5, and squirmed 60 yards to tie Pennsylvania, 6-6. He played left half.

He dropped out of school for two years. But Warner coaxed him back and he achieved his greatest gridiron stardom in 1911-12.

Modern sports experts have picked him as the football player of the Century, ranking him ahead of Red Grange. He and Grange were almost unanimous choices for the halfback posts on an all-time All-America football team.

In the 1912 Olympics, with almost no specialized training, he set point totals in the decathlon and pentathlon which stood for 20 years.

He won every pentathlon event except the javelin throw. He was outstanding in running, high jumping, pole vaulting and in the weight events.

Greatest In World

King Gustav V of Sweden told him: "Sir, you are the greatest athlete in the world."

He returned home a hero. A year later he was saddened when it was revealed that in 1910 he had played baseball for pay with the Rocky Mount club in the Eastern Carolina League. His salary was $60 a month. This branded him a professional.

He was stripped of his medals and his marks were removed from the record books. Years later a congressional subcommittee decided to see what could be done to have his trophies returned to him, but nothing came of it.

After he finished school, several major league clubs bid for his services. The New York Giants reportedly paid him $5,000 to sign. He wasn't happy with the New York club and was moved to Boston, where he batted .327 in 60 games. He remained in the National League for six years, playing 77 games for Cincinnati in 1917.

Later he did well in the minors, winding up his baseball career in 1928 with Akron. He was 40 then. Between baseball seasons he played pro football.

In 1913 Jim married Iva Miller, who got herself enrolled at Carlisle on the pretense she was part Indian. She presented him with three daughters, Gail, Charlotte and Grace and one son, who died in infancy.

They were divorced 10 years later and in 1926 Jim married Frieda Kirkpatrick. They had four sons—Phil, William, Richard and Jack. They were divorced in 1943 and two years later the Great Indian athlete married Patricia Askew, whom he had met 30 years earlier while playing professional football.

BELL ECONOMY BID FAILS

Commissioner's Move to Reduce Player Limit to 30 Loses

PHILADELPHIA, Jan. 23 (AP)—The National Football League's club owners beat down Commissioner Bert Bell's pet economy move tonight and decided to retain the present player limit of 33 active men on each squad.

Bell had proposed a reduction of the list to 30 men, with the elimination of the "injured reserve" list. But that motion failed to muster the required number of votes and so did several compromise proposals.

Earlier the owners passed on an amendment ruling a player no longer could jump to a Canadian team, then jump right back again.

Hereafter, a player who reports and plays in Canada first must be cleared of contract-jumping at a hearing. Then he must sign and report to his United States club before the first game of the season in order to be eligible to play that season.

Another constitutional change provides that if a member of a championship team is sold, traded or claimed on waivers prior to the All-Star game the following year, he must be paid half his game salary.

COLT 56-YARD BOOT CHECKS BEARS, 13-9

Rechichar Sets League Record on First Pro Field-Goal Try —Scores Touchdown

STATISTICS OF THE GAME

	Colts	Bears
First downs	9	20
Rushing yardage	90	147
Passing yardage	74	225
Passes attempted	20	34
Passes completed	12	19
Passes intercepted by	4	1
Number of punts	9	5
Punting average, yds.	34	36
Fumbles lost	2	4
Yards penalized	51	57

BALTIMORE, Sept. 27 (AP)—Bert Rechichar's first field-goal attempt in professional football was good today for a National Football League record of 56 yards and was the winning margin in the Baltimore Colts' 13—9 victory over the Chicago Bears.

The former Tennessee player sent 23,715 fans into delirium by also running back an intercepted pass 35 yards for a touchdown. Buck McPhail, who had done all the field-goal kicking for the Colts during six exhibition games, booted a dividend 3-pointer in the fourth period.

Billy Stone, who had been with the Colts before they quit professional football after 1950, scored for the Bears on a 24-yard run in the first quarter.

Rechichar matched that touchdown midway in the second period and then put the Colts in front with his record-breaking boot on the last play of the half.

McPhail earlier had missed a field-goal try from the 45, and the fans were puzzled when Rechichar lined up to try from 10 yards farther back, since his ability to kick had been unknown. The ball sailed through the uprights to beat by two yards the former league record set by Glenn Presnell of Detroit against Green Bay on Oct. 7, 1934.

The Baltimore fans, hungry after two seasons without pro football, were nervous early in the last quarter when Quarterback Fred Enke was tackled behind his goal by Bob Hensley for a Chicago safety to make the score 10—9.

But Oklahoma's McPhail, another rookie, stretched the advantage with his field goal from the 12.

SCORE BY PERIODS

```
Baltimore Colts ............ 0  10  0  3—13
Chicago Bears .............. 7   0  0  2— 9
```

Baltimore scoring—Touchdown: Rechichar. Point after touchdown: McPhail. Field goals: Rechichar, McPhail. Chicago scoring—Touchdown: Stone. Point after touchdown: Blanda. Safety: Hensley (Enke).

Eagles Trounce Giants By 30-7

Philadelphia, Nov. 8 (AP)—The Philadelphia Eagles walloped the New York Giants, 30-7, today in a National Football League game that was slow moving at the start but wound up in a flurry of touchdowns, flying fists, snowballs and a spectacular exhibition of passing by the Eagles' Bobby Thomason.

Thomason, the N.F.L.'s second best passer before today, pitched four touchdown passes and gained 437 yards with his pin-point aerials. His overall performance was the fourth best in league history.

He completed 22 of 44 passes during the cold afternoon and faultlessly directed the Philadelphia club to its fourth straight victory and a solid hold on second place in the Eastern division.

Only Norman Van Brocklin's 554 yards in 1951, John Lujack's 468 in 1949 and Sammy Baugh's 446 in 1948 surpassed Thomason's passing effort.

Stangely enough, Thomason, now in his fouth year as a pro, was a bench warmer until the fourth game of this season and was called upon then only in desperation.

Statistics

Giants		Eagles
10	First downs	21
64	Rushing yardage	54
28	Passing yardage	460
27	Passes attempted	43
10	Passes completed	24
1	Passes intercepted	2
10	Punts	5
40.5	Punting average	33
1	Fumbles lost	1
24	Yards penalized	123

93,751 Watch Los Angeles Eleven Take Thriller From Detroit, 37-24

Rams Rally From a 10-Point Deficit to Topple Lions, Gain Undisputed Division Lead

LOS ANGELES, Nov. 1 (AP)—The Los Angeles Rams spotted the Detroit Lions a 10-point lead, caught and passed them in the third period and went on to whip them, 37—24, today in a game marked by spectacular long-scoring plays. A crowd of 93,751 watched.

The victory gave the Rams the undisputed lead of the Western Conference of the National Football League. They now have a season record of five triumphs and one loss. Detroit now has a 4-2 record.

The Rams cracked the backs of the Lions and took the lead midway in the third quarter when Don Paul, linebacker, intercepted a Bobby Layne pass, dashed 15 yards, lateraled to Woodley Lewis, who sped 45 down the sideline. The touchdown put Los Angeles in front for the first time by a 23-17 margin.

The Rams increased the lead on another pass interception. Jack Dwyer took the ball 31 yards, and Quarterback Norman Van Brocklin and Halfback V. T. Smith got together on a pass for the final touchdown on a play covering 54 yards.

Some Sensational Plays

The crowd, largest ever to see a regular season professional football game, was treated to a sensational variety of plays. The previous top attendance at a pro game was 85,425 when the Rams and Chicago Bears played here in 1949.

Halfback Jack Christiansen started the excitement when he intercepted a Van Brocklin pass and raced down the sidelines 92 yards. Coupled with Doak Walker's previous 38-yard field goal, the run gave Detroit its first quarter margin of 10—0.

Before the fireworks were over, Detroit Halfback Jug Girard made an 85-yard kick-off run that set up a touchdown and Los Angeles' Skeet Quinlan flew 74 yards from scrimmage for another 6-pointer.

Detroit held a 17-9 lead at the half, but was shut out in the sec-

Statistics of the Game

	Rams	Lions
First downs	14	19
Rushing yardage	222	129
Passing yardage	170	116
Passes attempted	22	31
Passes completed	12	12
Passes intercepted by	4	3
Punts	3	5
Punting average, yds.	42.6	42.4
Fumbles lost	1	0
Yards penalized	25	45

ond half until the final minute. Then the Lions went 63 yards in eight plays, with Bob Hoernschemeyer scoring from the one.

Christiansen's electrifying burst came when the Rams were on the Detroit 15 and threatening to score. Quinlan put the Rams back into the game with a five-yard dash that capped a 58-yard march. The try for extra point was missed.

The Rams crept up 10—9 when Ben Agajanian booted an 18-yard field goal. But Girard's 85-yard dash put Detroit on the Ram 1 and it took three plays and a final three-yard pass from Layne to Leon Hart to increase the Detroit margin to 17—9.

Three in Third Quarter

The Rams belted the Lions for three touchdowns in the third quarter starting off with Quinlan's 74-yarder.

Things began to get hot in the final minutes. Defensive Halfback Jim David was banished from the game for taking a poke at End Bob Boyd. He missed the punch.

A moment later Detroit was penalized 15 yards for some sort of disturbance from the bench. During the squabble Sherwin Gandee was spotted tossing a cup of water from the sidelines into Ram End Larry Brink's face.

SCORE BY PERIODS

```
Los Angeles Rams .......... 0   9  21  7—
Detroit Lions ............ 10   7   0  7—
```

Los Angeles Rams scoring — Touchdowns: Quinlan 2, Lewis, Dwyer, Smith. Conversions: Agajanian 4. Field goal: Agajanian. Detroit Lions scoring—Touchdowns: Christiansen, Hart, Hoernschemeyer. Conversions: Walker 3. Field goal: Walker.

Video Ruling Is Pleasing To Bert Bell

PHILADELPHIA, Nov. 12 (AP) — The National Football League's right to "blackout" telecasting of league games which might compete with home games was upheld today in a ruling by the U. S. District Court.

NFL Commissioner Bert Bell promptly said the league won "its most important point" in the government's anti-trust suit attacking the league's controls over television and radio broadcasts.

But the league lost three other points. Outlawed by Judge Allan K. Grim were the league's:

. Restrictions on telecasts of games to league cities when the home team is playing out of town.

. Restrictions on radio broadcasts of league games.

. Rule that Commissioner Bell could veto radio and television broadcasting contracts to enforce radio and television restrictions.

Appeal to Lawyers

Bell, after reading the decision in the two-year-old case, said "football won the most important part of its case." He said he would need time to study "the restrictions which the order of the court will impose upon the league" but the court "has understood the vital need of professional football today, namely, the protection of our home gate if we are to continue our existence."

Any appeal, Bell said, "is up to our lawyers."

What all the legal terminology means is this: for example, the league can prohibit the telecasting of the game between Cleveland and San Francisco into Philadelphia Sunday when the Philadelphia Eagles are at home against Baltimore.

When the Eagles play in New York, however, the league cannot prohibit the telecasting of a game, for instance, between the Detroit Lions and the Los Angeles Rams.

The NFL constitution now prevent radio broadcasts of other games within the home area of a league team when that team is either playing at home or televising or broadcasting there a home. But Judge Grim said "there is no evidence whatsoever

indicating any adverse effect of radio broadcasts of outside games in the home territory of another club" and that such a broadcast "has no significant effect on attendance at football games." He rules the radio restrictions "illegal."

Baseball Ruling Not Considered

The decision came three days after the U. S. Supreme Court ruled that baseball is a sport and not subject to the interstate commerce law.

But Judge Grim said the decision in the baseball cases did not apply to the NFL's case because "the only restriction alleged in the baseball cases was in the internal operation of professional baseball itself.

"The present case on the other hand primarily concerns restrictions imposed by the NFL on the sale of radio and television rights. Therefore the present case basically concerns the league's restraint of interstate commerce in the radio television industries."

Graham Is Smothered As Cleveland Gridders Handed Worst Defeat

PHILADELPHIA, Dec. 13 (AP)—A fired-up flock of Philadelphia Eagles smothered pro football's master passer, Otto Graham, and unleashed a pulverizing offense of their own to snap the Cleveland Browns' 11-game winning streak 42-27.

A record home crowd of 38,654 roaring fans saw the Browns suffer their worst National Football League defeat in history.

The Eagles, in completely outplaying the 1953 Eastern Division champions, clinched second place in the division as a result of Washington's defeat by Pittsburgh. The Eagles and Redskins were tied for runnerup honors in the Eastern Division before today's competition.

TITTLE PASSES TO 4 SCORES IN PACING ATTACK

Young, Edwards Tally For Losers On Tosses From Mioduszewski

San Francisco, Dec. 13 (AP)— Quarterback Y. A. Tittle threw four touchdown passes and Fullback Joe Perry scored three six-pointers today as the San Francisco Forty-Niners overran the Baltimore Colts, 45 to 14, in the last game of the 1953 National Football League season.

The Forty-Niners set or tied four league offensive records for the season as they finished second in the Western Division, with a 9-3 record, compared to division champion Detroit's 10-2.

A crowd of 24,432 rooted the fast-finishing local club home as they scored touchdowns in every period, and two extra in the second quarter.

Soltau Scoring Leader

Gordon Soltau, rangy end and place-kicking specialist, booted in a 24-yard field goal in the second quarter, accounted for all six conversions and caught two touchdown passes, to become the league scoring leader for the season with 114 points. He replaced Lou Groza, Cleveland, who finished with 108 tallies.

The 45 points scored today also put the winners on top as the league's scoring leader with 372 points this year. Perry became the third player in league history to gain more than 1,000 yards in a single season. The other two to achieve that feat were Steve Van Buren, of Philadelphia and Tony Canadeo of Green Bay.

Perry wound up the season with 1,018 yards gained. His total of 108 today helped push the Forty-Niners to the top in league rushing offense. They finished with a net 2,230 yards on the ground compared with 2,148 for the Los Angeles Rams who are in second place.

Lions Retain Pro Grid Title By Beating Browns, 17-16

LION VICTORY DAZES PARKER

Detroit Coach Happy After Winning Pro Title

Detroit, Dec. 27 (AP)—"What a season!"

That was the Detroit Lions' coach, Buddy Parker, speaking today as he sat in the boss' cage of the Detroit dressing room, letting his nerves unwind after his squad's explosive 17-to-16 victory over the Cleveland Browns for the National Football League championship.

Parker was in happily dazed condition as well wishers filed through his office.

Shouts For Attention

The locker room itself was bedlam except for one moment when the Lions coach shouted for attention with a special announcement.

Parker's brief speech:

"This one is for the players. The game means $2,424.10 each."

The announcement brought a new crescendo of shouts.

End Jim Doran told interviewers the winning touchdown pass in the fourth period was set up when the Lions' bench noted Cleveland's secondary playing close up to slow the ends who were going out for passes.

"I went out and faked a block and then cut around a Cleveland defender. I raced toward the end zone and when I looked up, there was the ball," Doran said.

Browns Dress Silently

In contrast, the Brownie dressing room was morgue-like. The players dressed slowly, silently.

"It was the toughest game we've ever lost," said Paul Brown, the Brownies dejected coach.

"I doubt if any team ever lost a tougher one."

Brown refused to comment on the Lions' winning pass play. He just shook his head.

It was, in reality, a bitter defeat for him. He's never beaten a team coached by Buddy Parker and he's never won a football game in Detroit.

Statistics And Lineups

Cleveland		Detroit
11	First downs	18
182	Rushing yardage	129
9	Passing yardage	164
16	Passes attempted	25
3	Passes completed	12
2	Passes intercepted	2
5	Punts	4
42	Punting average	49
2	Fumbles lost	2
30	Yards penalized	50

Cleveland...... 0 3 7 6—16
Detroit........ 7 3 0 7—17

Cleveland scoring: Touchdown, Jagade. Conversion, Groza; Field goals, Groza (3).

Detroit scoring: Touchdowns, Walker, Doran. Conversions, Walker (2). Field goals, Walker.

Lineups

CLEVELAND

END—Brewster, Young Atkins, Lavelli, Gillion, Ford. TACKLE—Groza, Colo, Sandusky, Palmer, Helluin. GUARD—Gibron, Donaldson, Steinbrunner, Noll, Houston, Willis. CENTER—Gatski, Catlin. BACK—Graham, Ratterman, Gorgal, Renfro, Carpenter, Lahr, Reynolds, Jones, Konz, James, Jagade, Motley, Michaels, Howard.

DETROIT

END—Dibble, Box, Gande, Hart, Doran, Cain. TACKLE—Creekmur, Ane, McGraw, Spencer, Miller, Prchlik. GUARD—Sewell, Martin, Bingaman, Stanfel, Schmidt, CENTER—Banonis, Torgeson. BACK—Layne, Dublinski, Lary, Walker, Girard, David, Christiansen, Gedman, J. Smith, Jarilvacz, Hoernschemeyer, Klein, Cline, R. Smith, Carpenter.

LAYNE THROWS TO DORA[N] FOR WINNING TOUCHDOW[N] WITH 3 MINUTES TO G[O]

Detroit Comes From Behind 16-10 Score Wi[th] 80-Yard March To Defeat Cleveland For Second Straight Year

Detroit, Dec. 27 (AP)—Quarterback Bobby Lay[ne] pitched a dramatic 33-yard touchdown strike to E[nd] Jim Doran with less than three minutes to go to give t[he] Detroit Lions a 17-to-16 victory over the Clevela[nd] Browns today for the professional football champions[hip] of the world.

The Lions apparently beaten by the spectacu[lar] field-goal kicking of Cleveland's Lou Groza, marched 80 yards through the gloom in Brigg's Stadium in the closing minutes to become the third team in history to win two straight National Football League titles.

The winning pass play was an amazingly smooth operation but it shocked the 54,577 spectators from their seats.

Doran Scores

Layne lofted a soft pass into the end zone and it was just a matter of whether the speeding Doran would catch up to it.

He did. The former Iowa State end broke loose behind Ken Konz, Brownie halfback, and cradled the ball into his arms as he sped past the final money stripe.

Doak Walker kicked the winning extra point at 12.52—and for the third straight year the Browns, classed as one of the greatest organizations in the game, were shipped in the title game.

Won Last Year

Detroit defeated the Brow[ns] 17-to-7, in the play-off at Cl[eve]land last year. In 1951, the Cl[eve]landers were knocked off by [the] Los Angeles Rams, 24-to-17, in [the] title game.

So Brownie Coach Paul Br[own] must now go home and plan [for] the 1954 season. He's rated as [one] of the most successful coache[s in] history but he's never been [able] to beat a team coached by Bu[ddy] Parker, Lions coach. And t[his] was his seventh try.

It looked, however, as tho[ugh] the Browns would gain [long] awaited revenge. After being [al]most helpless in the first [half] they charged back after the in[ter]mission and played like an en[ti]rely different team.

Groza Puts Browns Ahead

Groza kicked two field goal[s in] the fourth quarter putting Cl[eve]land ahead for the first t[ime] 16 to 10.

But the Lions, who learne[d to] win the close ones during [the] regular season, marched for [the] winning touchdown.

Layne was a master signal [call]er in the final drive. He pa[ssed] twice to Doran for 17 and [33] yards putting the ball on Cl[eve]land's 45. The Lion quarter[back]

Bell Declares War As Giants Grid Star Joins Canadian League

PHILADELPHIA, Jan. 21 (AP)—"The war is on," Commissioner Bert Bell said today when informed that the Canadian League had signed Arnie Weinmeister of the New York Giants. "Weinmeister is under contract to the Giants," said Bell, adding "The Canadian League has again breached our contracts. They had beter start counting their players."

The NFL commissioner said that the National Football League would scan the roster of the new British Columbia Lions for any worthwhile native Canadian players who could make the pro league here. "We'll fight fire with fire," he said.

Asked if Weinmeister, one of the finest tackles ever to play in the NFL, had any mutual agreement with the Giants to permit him to go to Canada, Bell said, "Absolutely no. I wouldn't be at all surprised if the Giants take him into court, along with the Canadian team."

Actually, Weinmeister isn't under contract to the Giants, but rather is bound by a one-year renewal option. If the Giants fail to renew the player's option before May 1, 1954, he becomes a free agent and can play anywhere he chooses.

Bell said emphatically that it would be the NFL's policy to try to sign worthwhile players from any Canadian team which "stole" players from the American pro circuit. "We have a list of all Canadian players, some of whom could make some of our teams. We'll go after them if they go after our boys."

ACTION CONFORMS TO COURT DECISION

Local TV and Broadcasts in City Where Game Is Played Allowed Now by N. F. L.

PHILADELPHIA, Jan. 27 (AP)—The National Football League bowed to a court order today and rewrote its controversial rule concerning control of television of league games.

The N. F. L. club owners, in a preliminary to the opening of their annual meeting tomorrow, unanimously decided not to appeal the ruling handed down last fall by Judge Allan K. Grim in the United States District Court.

Some club owners, feeling that Judge Grim's ruling had vindicated to a certain extent their stand on television controls, wanted to appeal to a higher court in hope of getting a more favorable decision.

After hearing the league's lawyers explain and interpret the decision today, they agreed unanimously that there would be no appeal. Then they amended Article 10 of their constitution, the section that deals with radio and television, to bring it into line with the court order.

New Section Added

They also added a new section to Article 4 of the constitution, which binds each club to agree with the provisions of the court decision.

"Throughout the trial we expressed continuously our desire to learn to live with television. That's what we will try to do in this situation," said Commissioner Bert Bell.

Judge Grim's decision on the Government's anti-trust suit, which sought to wipe out all controls of TV by the league, was that the league could black out the immediate areas in which games were being played, but that it could not control television in a club's "home" territory when that club was playing away from home, nor could it control radio broadcasts.

During the trial, the league maintained that "reasonable" restraint was legal under the Sherman Anti-Trust Act. Bell emphasized that the rule changes made today were intended to conform with the court's decision and that if there were any complaints about the controls still exercised, the courts would decide whether or not they were reasonable.

The new sections of Article 10 permits local broadcasts and telecasts within the city where a game is being played, provided that part of the receipts from such broadcasts are added to the gross receipts of the game. The commissioner will determine the amount and also must approve the sponsors.

When a club is away from home, anyone can broadcast or telecast into its territory. Representatives of three major television networks were on hand to hear the league's decision and to start setting up plans for next season's telecasts.

With the touchy TV question settled, the clubs will turn to the annual "draft" of college players in an open meeting starting tomorrow morning. Before Saturday they also expect to deal with the impending "war" against Canadian football interests and with some changes in the playing rules.

Football Draft
Bobby Garrett Picked By Cleveland Browns As Bonus Selection

Rams and Forty-Niners Play to Deadlock Before 93,553

LOS ANGELES TEST ENDS IN 24-24 TIE

Rams Recover Fumble and Go Over in Last 2 Minutes to Gain Draw With 49ers

STATISTICS OF THE GAME

	49ers.	Rams.
First downs	23	17
Rushing yardage	181	148
Passing yardage	268	234
Passes attempted	35	26
Passes completed	23	12
Passes intercepted by	2	0
Punts	5	6
Punting avge., yds.	40.8	48
Fumbles lost	1	2
Yards penalized	30	65

LOS ANGELES, Oct. 3 (AP)— The San Francisco Forty-niners and the Los Angeles Rams fought to a 24-24 tie before a crowd of 93,553 in a National Football League game today.

BURK TIES RECORD

They Beat Redskins for 4th in Row—Star Back Hurls 7 Touchdown Passes

STATISTICS OF THE GAME

	Eagles	Rdskns
First downs	30	9
Rushing yardage	172	28
Passing yardage	257	87
Passes attempted	33	15
Passes completed	23	7
Passes intercepted by	4	1
Number of punts	6	6
Punting average, yds.	36.3	43.3
Fumbles lost	3	1
Yards penalized	40	15

WASHINGTON, Oct. 17 (AP)— Adrian Burk cut loose today with one of the greatest passing shows in football history, throwing a record-equalling seven touchdown strikes to drive the Philadelphia Eagles to a 49—21 victory over the Washington Redskins.

The former Baylor star, who hit for his seventh scoring pitch with only ten seconds left to play, tied the record for most touchdown passes thrown in a National Football League game, set in 1943 by Sid Luckman.

The unbeaten Eagles rolled to their fourth straight victory on the wings of Burk's strong right arm, handing the winless Redskins their fourth straight setback.

REDSKIN GRID PLAYER DIES

Dave Sparks, 26, Succumbs After Game With Browns

Washington, Dec. 5 (AP)—Dave Sparks, 26-year-old tackle for the Washington Redskins, collapsed and died tow hours after playing a National Football League game today.

Dick McCann, the football team's general manager, said an autopsy will be performed tomorrow but that the impression he gained from talking with doctors was that Sparks had died of a coronary attack.

Sparks, a resident of Lorain, Ohio, had player a good, hard game against the Cleveland Browns and was not injured except for hip bruises, McCann reported. He left the field to visit a Lorain school friend, Lieut. Domenick Colella, of suburban Arlington, Va.

Complains Of Chest Pains

McCann said Sparks complained of a pain in his chest, took a sedative and lay down for a while but then got up and had a spaghetti dinner with the Colellas. Shortly afterward he complained of the pain again and suddenly collapsed.

GARY KERKORIAN FAILS IN FIELD GOAL ATTEMPT TO TIE CLASH AT FINISH

Misses From 26-Yard Line After Late March; Perry, Kept From Rushing Record By Baltimore Line, Gets Decisive Touchdown

San Francisco, Dec. 11—The toe that gave the Colts a thrilling last-minute victory a week ago failed four times today as the Baltimore football team bowed, 10 to 7, to the Forty-niners in the final game of the 1954 season here at Kezar Stadium. A crowd of 26,956 saw the game.

Gary Kerkorian, hero of the Colts' 22-to-21 triumph over the Los Angeles Rams last week with a final-minute field goal, became the goat this afternoon when he missed place kicks from the 13, 32, 22 and 26.

Kerkorian's last miss, although no more important than the first, came in the final two minutes of play and, if made, would have gained the 18-point underdog Colts a tie with the powerful Forty-Niners.

Soltau Misses Attempts

The 26-yard boot, however, was off line and instead of a tie, the Colts ended their season with a loss—the ninth in the 12-game National Football League schedule.

The final result was actually a matter of percentage. Gordie Soltau wasn't much better than Kerkorian—just three points superior.

Soltau attempted four field goals, too, and, although they were on the whole, a great deal longer than Kerkorian's, he connected on the one that counted, a 10-yarder in the second period.

Perry Misses Record

It just wasn't in the books, maybe the five field goals the Colts made last week were supposed to be their quota. Gary missed again.

Although the Colts failed in their effort to win three straight games, they did stop Joe Perry, Forty-Niner fullback, from coming anywhere near the 140 yards he needed to break the all-time rushing record for one year.

The Jet, as Perry is called, was held to just 42 yards by the big, powerful Colt defensive line.

Steve Van Buren, of the Philadelphia Eagles, holds the rushing record with 1,146 yards in 1949.

Perry, who did register the deciding touchdown, ended the season with 1,049 yards.

Statistics And Lineups

Colts		San Francisco
17	First downs	18
96	Net yards rushing	98
177	Passing yardage	194
27	Passes attempted	26
17	Passes completed	17
2	Passes intercepted by	1
5	Punts	3
38	Punting average	42
1	Fumble lost	1
32	Yards penalized	32

Colts .... 7 0 0 0— 7
San Francisco 0 3 7 0—10

Baltimore scoring: Touchdown—Young. Conversion—Kerkorian. San Francisco scoring: Touchdown—Perry. Field goal—Soltau. Conversion—Soltau.

FORTY-NINERS
END—Soltau, Wilson, Babcock, Brumfield, Matthews. TACKLE—Hogland, St. Clair, Nomellini, Toneff, Carapelli. Campbell. GUARD—Feher, Banducci, Connolly, Hantla. CENTER—Johnson, T. Brown. BACK—Tittle, Johnson, Jesaup, Perry, Ducan, Arenas, Berry, Tidwell, Williams, H. Brown, Cason, Schabarum, Mixon, Cassara.

COLTS
END—Colteryahn, Edwards, Marchetti, Joyce, Langas, Cheatham, Mutscheller. TACKLE—Donovan, Finnin, Jackson, Little, Barwegen. GUARD—Sandusky, Spinney, Campanella, Eggers, Raiff. CENTER—Radosevich, Nutter, Pellington. BACK—Kerkorian, Davidson, Young, Taseff, Womble, Taliaferro, Shula, Rechichar, Keane, Leberman, Lesane, Toth.

Reprinted from
The Baltimore Sun

ANE PASSES TO GIRARD FOR TOUCHDOWN WHICH DECIDES LEAGUE FINALE

ou Groza Kicks 43-Yard Field Goal In Third Period On Snow-Covered Cleveland Field; Teams Meet Again Sunday For Pro Title

Cleveland, Dec. 19 (AP)—The World Champion De-oit Lions continued their mastery over the Cleveland owns here today with a last-minute touchdown for a -to-10 victory before 34,163 fans in a heavy snowstorm.

Cleveland has not beaten the Lions in four league mes and four exhibitions since Buddy Parker took over e Lions in 1951. Today's game, played under almost impossible conditions, could hardly be classed as a preview of next Sunday's world title contest between the same teams.

GRAHAM QUITS WHILE ON TOP

However, He'll Be In All-Star And Pro Bowl Games

Cleveland, Dec. 26 (AP)—Otto raham passed the Cleveland rowns to the National Football eague championship today and en announced again he was uitting professional football.

"That's the way to quit, go out n top," Graham remarked after e Browns upended the Detroit ions, 56 to 10, in the title game.

The fancy passing quarterback. ho came to Coach Paul Brown ter a standout career at North-estern University, said he would e around for the Pro Bowl game nd the College All-Star game, ut would then stop.

Passes For 163 Yards

Today, he completed nine of 12 asses for 163 yards and three uchdowns. He also ran over ree other touchdowns from dis-nces of 2 feet, 5 yards and 1 ard.

Beating the Lions, Graham ntinued, was a "thrill," but ere was one victory even weeter—the 30-28 victory over os Angeles in 1950, the first e Browns played in the Na-onal League.

"Detroit has a helluva team, but they got the breaks in those two other championship playoffs. This time we got them," Graham said.

Detroit won the playoffs from Cleveland in 1952 and 1953.

Second Only To Baugh

During his career since 1946, when the Browns were organized, Graham has completed 1,375 of 2,417 passes for 21,184 yards and 162 touchdowns.

His nine-year totals are second only to Sammy Baugh of Washington who played 16 years.

Coach Brown, who declared that "on any given day this was the best football team I ever saw," expressed hope Graham would be back next season. He admitted his hopes were based on the reaction of fall weather and the sound of a bouncing football on a veteran player.

Thinks Of His Family

Graham said the "mental pressure" was what prompted his decision to retire. "I hate that pre-game feeling," he said, "and it gets worse and worse as the years go by."

The 17-16 shading by the Lions of the Browns last year, he said, made him "feel worse than I ever have in my whole life."

Playing the games and getting into condition, he continued, do not bother him, but "being away from my family an awful lot is not so good."

'RETIRING' OTTO GRAHAM SCORES 3 TOUCHDOWNS AND PASSES FOR 3 MORE

43,827 See Second Highest Count In Playoff Contest; Winners Get $2,478.56 Each; Groza Sets Conversion Record.

Cleveland, Dec. 26 (AP)—Inspired Otto Graham, 33-year-old "retiring" quarterback, had a dramatic hand in six touchdowns as the pent-up Cleveland Browns annihilated the Detroit Lions and a long jinx, 56 to 10, to win the National Football League title today.

Before a Cleveland Stadium crowd of 43,827, Graham pitched three touchdown passes and ran to three touch-downs himself to personally smash Detroit's effort to win an unprecedented third straight league crown.

Groza Sets Record

The surprising attendance, after a poor advance sale of about 24,000, produced a record winning players' share of $2,478.56, while each of the Lions got $1,585.63. Last year's championship game at Detroit gave each winning Lion player $2,424.10.

Graham's three touchdowns gave him three championship game scoring records. 18 points on three touchdowns—never before scored by one player in a title game—and most touchdowns running. The eight extra points by Cleveland's Lou Groza also set a record for conversions in a title game.

The score was second highest in a playoff game, the most lop-sided previous game being the 73-to-0 rout by the Chicago Bears over the Washington Redskins in 1940.

Ovation For Graham

The Browns, 2½-point under-dogs, struck for five first-half touchdowns and a 35-10 intermission lead to score their first victory in nine meetings of all sorts with the Lions since 1951.

Graham, who had announced this was his last game after nine Brown seasons, thrilled the throng in the big lakeside bowl as well as a vast national TV audience with touchdown passes of 37, 10 and 31 yards and scoring smashes from the 1-yard line, 2-foot line and 5-yard line.

Graham, an inadequate figure last week as the Lions whipped the Browns, 14-10, here in the final league game, today completed 9 of 12 passes for 163 yards. He received a tremendous ovation as he left the game with three minutes left.

Bad Day For Layne

For the first time in pro football history at Cleveland, fans swarmed on the field—amid band tunes of "Auld Lange Syne"—and tore down the metal goal-posts.

The Browns had lost to the Lions, 17-16, in last year's playoff between the Western and Eastern divisional champions. In the 1952 title playoff, the Lions won, 17-7.

The closest the Browns previously had come to beating a Buddy Parker-coached Lion team was a 24-24 exhibition tie in 1953.

Graham never had thrown a touchdown pass in two previous title encounters and two league games against the Lions whose quarterback, Bobby Layne, was much manhandled by the bruising Browns today.

Statistics And Lineups

Detroit		Cleveland
16	First downs	17
135	Rushing yardage	146
195	Passing yardage	163
44	Passes attempted	12
19	Passes completed	9
	Passes intercepted by	6
	Punts	4
41	Punting average	43
	Fumbles lost	2
63	Yards penalized	40

Detroit .... 3 7 0 0—10
Cleveland ...... 14 21 14 7—56

Detroit scoring: Touchdown—Bowman; field goal—Walker. Conversion—Walker.

Cleveland scoring: Touchdowns—Ren-fro, 2; Brewster, Graham, 3; Morrison. Hanulak. Conversions—Groza, 8.

Prospects For Peace Fade In Pro Grid War

By JESSE A. LINTHICIM
[Sports Editor of The Sun]

New York, Jan. 29—With hope for peace with the Canadian League diminishing National Football League owners were set to send representatives to college campuses throughout the nation to sign their draftees, it was learned today.

This was the concluding day of the National's convention and the owners and coaches made an exit from the city as baseball men converged on it for baseball meetings and the annual banquet of the New York Baseball Writers Association.

The Colts have sent a telegram to every collegian they drafted Thursday. Some will be contacted personally and others will be invited to visit Baltimore for a talk.

Brown Leads Fight

The football war between the National League and Canada still is going strong. It appeared several days ago that an amicable agreement would be reached between the two circuits.

Paul Brown, general manager and coach of the championship Cleveland Browns, led the fight against making any deals with Canada, at least for the present, because there seemed no one in Canada could control all of the teams across the border.

Bert Bell, commissioner of the National Football League, has been given full authority to deal with the Canadians.

One faint hope for a peaceful settlement came tonight in the form of a telephone call to Bell from Harry Sunshine, of the Toronto club, who sought a meeting with the Commissioner in Philadelphia Tuesday. Another Canadian League official will accompany him.

Bell said he will deal with only one man representing the rival league, and then only if that man has the power to act for that circuit.

Giants Dislike Peace

Brown fought a long legal battle to regain John Kissell from the Canadian League, and in the National draft Thursday he picked three players who were reported to have signed with teams north of the border.

The New York Football Giants and one of the Chicago teams also are said to be urging their fellow-owners to continue the gridiron war.

Reprinted from
The Baltimore Sun

REDSKINS SIGN 'NO RAID' PACT

Enter Agreement With Calgary Over Players

Washington, Feb. 24 (AP)—The Washington Redskins and Canada's Calgary Stampeders today signed a precedent-making "no raid" agreement. The two football teams agreed to honor all contracts between players and the respective clubs.

The agreement was the first made between a National Football League team and a Canadian football club. Under it, a $50,000 suit brought against Calgary by the Redskins was settled out of court.

Offiials Hail Agreement

George Preston Marshall, the Redskins's owner, and Jack Hennemier, the Calgary coach, hailed the agreement "as a signal achievement in relations between teams in American and Canadian football."

They said they hoped it would serve as a precedent for similar agreements between other teams. Players have been scrapping contracts on both sides of the border for several years in a free-for-all scramble for talent.

The Redskins' $50,000 suit against Hennemier was scheduled to go to trial at Marlboro, Md., tomorrow.

Two Tackles Quit 'Skins

It was filed after Dick Modzelewski and Bob Morgan. tackles under contract to the Redskins, recently were signed by Hennemier to play for Calgary. The Redskins sued on charges Hennemier had induced the players to violate their contracts.

Under the agreement settling the suit. the Calgary contract with Morgan was recognized as valid but Modzelewski remains the property of the Redskins.

Bernard Nordlinger. attorney for the Redskins, said the suit was settled for a "substantial" amount, but would give no figure.

Former Maryland Coach

Hennemier, former line coach at the University of Maryland where Modzelewski and Morgan formerly played, had been seeking to sign two other former Maryland players, Quarterback Jack Scarbath and Fullback Ralph Felton. The agreement prohibits him from negotiating with those players.

Under the agreement, Quarterback Eddie LeBaron and End Gene Brito, who played for Calgary last season, were permitted to remain with the Redskins.

Trippi to Miss Half Season

CHICAGO, Sept. 16 (AP) — Charley Trippi, injured Chicago Cardinal halfback, will miss at least half, or perhaps the entire National Football League season, a club spokesman said today. Trippi suffered a smashed nose and a fractured skull in a 43-7 exhibition loss to the San Francisco Forty-Niners at San Francisco two weeks ago.

PACKERS TROUNCE CARDINALS, 31 TO 14

GREEN BAY, Wis., Nov. 13 (AP) — Quarterback Tobin Rote pitched three touchdown strikes and bucked for another score today as the Green Bay Packers broke a three-game losing streak by throttling the Chicago Cardinals, 31—14.

A crowd of 20,104 watched the Packers dominate the National Football League game until the fourth quarter. Then the Cards struck for two touchdowns, one on a spectacular 98-yard pass play from Ogden Compton to Dick Lane.

Rote, still groggy after a bout with intestinal flu, connected on touchdown passes of 25 yards to Gary Knafelc, and 15 yards to Bill Howton and Al Carmichael. He later tallied on a 1-yard plunge.

Fred Cone, the Packers' reliable kicker from Pineapple, Ala., made four conversions and booted a 42-yard field goal.

The Cards caught fire in the final period with Compton at quarterback.

Mal Hammack capped an 84-yard drive by plunging over from the 1. Shortly after Compton and Lane collaborated on their 98-yard pay-off pass—just one yard short of the N. F. L. record set by Andy Farkas and Frank Filchock of Washington against Pittsburgh on Oct. 15, 1939.

Green Bay Packers	7	17	7	0—31
Chicago Cardinals	0	0	0	14—14

Green Bay scoring—Touchdowns: Knafelc (25. pass from Rote); Howton (14. pass from Rote); Rote (1. plunge); Carmichael (15. pass-run from Rote). Conversions: Cone 4. Field goal: Cone (42).

Chicago scoring—Touchdowns: Hammack (1. plunge); Lane (98. pass-run from Compton). Conversions: Summerall 2.

Ameche Goes 79 Yards for Tally As Baltimore Trips Bears, 23-17

Former Wisconsin Ace Scores First Time He Carries Ball in Professional Debut

BALTIMORE, Sept. 25 (AP)—Alan (The Horse) Ameche galloped 79 yards for a touchdown the first time he carried the ball in regular season professional football today as the Baltimore Colts upset the Chicago Bears, 23—17.

Ameche, the Wisconsin All-America and Heisman Trophy winner of last year, broke through the big Bear line on the second play from scrimmage and went all the way after cutting to the sidelines.

Baltimore's entire offensive team was making its first start of any Colt game. This was the season opener.

An Impressive Debut

In all, Ameche carried the ball 21 times and gained 194 yards in one of the most impressive debuts in National Football League history.

George Shaw, the Colts' bonus selection from Oregon State, passed for the other Colt touchdown and Bert Rechichar, an otherwise defensive back, kicked three field goals and two extra points.

Redskins Check Eagles

DEFENSE EXCELS IN 31-30 TRIUMPH

Alert Redskins Capitalize on Lions Miscues—

STATISTICS OF THE GAME

	Wash.	Phil.
First downs	16	27
Rushing yardage	118	121
Passing yardage	136	344
Passes attempted	15	38
Passes completed	10	25
Passes intercepted by	0	0
Punts	5	3
Punting average, yds.	39	35
Fumbles lost	2	3
Yards penalized	50	42

PHILADELPHIA, Oct. 1 (AP)—The Washington Redskins scored four touchdowns—three in 2 minutes and 17 seconds in a fantastic third period—to upset the Philadelphia Eagles tonight, 31—30.

GLICK GOES FIRST IN FOOTBALL DRAW

Steelers Pick Star Colorado A. and M. Defensive Back as Their Bonus Choice

PHILADELPHIA, Nov. 28 (AP)—The Pittsburgh Steelers passed over the nation's top college football players to select a 25-year-old defensive quarterback as their bonus in the National Football League partial player draft today.

Coach Walter Kiesling of the Steelers named Gary Glick, a comparative unknown from Colorado A. and M., after Dan Rooney, club personnel director and son of Art Rooney, drew the lucky slip from the hat.

Green Bay and the Chicago Cardinals were the other participants in the annual bonus selection. However, their representatives never got a chance to put their hands in the hat held by Commissioner Bert Bell. Rooney was the first to pick and he came up with the winning slip.

Under league rules, each team winning the bonus choice—a gimmick initiated by Bell in 1947—drop out until every club has had a chance to become the lucky selector. Next year, the Cards and Green Bay will vie for the big prize.

Canadians Spur Draft

The clubs went through only three of the annual thirty rounds in the pro player draft. This early drafting was decided upon in order to meet competition from the Canadian League in signing the United States top gridiron talent.

After Pittsburgh picked Glick, the first three teams in the regular draft quickly grabbed the players everyone thought were surefire bonus material. San Francisco and Detroit, tied for last place in the league standings, tossed a coin for first choice and the 49ers won. Coach Red Strader named Earl Morrall, the brilliant quarterback in Michigan State's multiple offense.

Detroit wasted no time picking Howard (Hopalong) Cassady, running halfback from Ohio State's Big Ten champions. The Philadelphia Eagles grabbed Bob Pellegrini, the standout University of Maryland linebacker.

First-choices, as usual, went fast. Pittsburgh, with its bonus choice wound up with four players in the drafting, took Art Davis, the fine halfback of Mississippi State; the Los Angeles Rams, picking New York's first choice as part of a previous trade, named Joe Marconi, 220-pound West Virginia back.

Cards Take Childress

Then came the Chicago Cardinals, who took Joe Childress, Auburn fullback. Green Bay selected Jack Losch, University of Miami back; Baltimore took Penn State's fleet back, Lenny Moore; the Bears grabbed Menan Schriewer, Texas end; Los Angeles named Charley Horton, Vanderbilt halfback; Washington picked Ed Vereb, Maryland's halfback, and Cleveland took Preston Carpenter, Arkansas halfback.

Kiesling defended his choice of Glick, a native of La Porte, Colo. He said Glick was recommended highly by all who watched the Skyline quarterback in action.

In all, the pros drafted thirty-seven players from twenty-five colleges and universities. Four each were taken from West Virginia and Southern Methodist, three each from Auburn and Michigan State, and two each from Maryland and Arkansas.

Here are the team-by-team draft selections (with names listed in order of selection by each team):

San Francisco—Earl Morrall, Michigan State back; Bruce Bosley, West Virginia tackle; Bill Herschman, Texas Tech tackle.

Detroit—Howard Cassady, Ohio State back; Leon Clarke, Southern California end (handed to Los Angeles as part of previous trade); Don McIlhenny, S. M. U. back.

Philadelphia—Bob Pellegrini, Maryland center; Frank D'Agostino, Auburn tackle; Don Schaefer, Notre Dame back.

Pittsburgh—Gary Glick, Colorado A. and M. back (bonus selection); Art Davis, Mississippi State back; Joe Krupa, Purdue tackle; Jim Taylor, Baylor center.

New York—Joe Marconi, West Virginia back (turned over to Los Angeles as part of previous trade); Henry Moore, Arkansas back; Robert Lee Huff, West Virginia tackle.

Chicago Cardinals—Joe Childress, Auburn back; Norman Masters, Michigan State tackle; John Roach, S. M. U. back.

Green Bay—Jack Losch, Miami back; Forest Gregg, S. M. U. tackle; A. D. Williams, College of Pacific end (sent to Los Angeles to complete previous trade).

Baltimore—Lenny Moore, Penn State back; Dick Donlin, Hamline end; Bob Pascall, Duke back.

Chicago Bears—Menan Schriewer, Texas end; M. L. Brackett, Auburn tackle; Larry Ross, Denver end.

Los Angeles—Charley Horton, Vanderbilt back; Hugh Pitts, Texas Christian, end; John Marshall, S. M. U. back (traded to Cleveland to complete previous deal).

Washington—Ed Vereb, Maryland back; John Paluck, Pittsburgh end; Fred Wyant, West Virginia back.

Cleveland—Preston Carpenter, Arkansas back; Billy Kinard, Mississippi back; William Quinlan, Michigan State end.

INTERCEPTIONS AID IN 38-14 TRIUMPH

Browns Haul in 7 Ram Passes —Graham Excels as Record Play-Off Crowd Watches

STATISTICS OF THE GAME

	Browns.	Rams.
First downs	17	17
Rushing yardage	169	116
Passing yardage	202	143
Passes attempted	25	28
Passes completed	14	11
Passes intercepted by	7	3
Punts	3	4
Punting average, yds.	42.6	45
Fumbles lost	0	1
Yards penalized	74	10

LOS ANGELES, Dec. 26 (AP) — The Cleveland Browns trounced the Los Angeles Rams today as Otto Graham led the way to a 38-14 victory for the Browns' second straight National Football League championship.

A record play-off crowd of 87,695 saw the pro contest in Memorial Coliseum. For most of them the outcome was as gloomy as the leaden skies overhead. The turnout far exceeded the previous high of 58,346 fans who saw the 1946 Chicago Bears-New York Giants game in the Polo Grounds.

Cleveland intercepted seven passes. The Browns turned one interception into a sensational touchdown. Other intercepted aerials set the stage for two touchdowns and a field goal.

Lou Groza and his gold-plated toe sent the Browns into a lead in the first quarter with a 26-yard field goal. The champions scored five touchdowns before the rout ended. By that time thousands of fans had headed for home.

Quinlan Scores for Rams

Los Angeles scored on a 67-yard pass play from Norman Van Brocklin, its star quarterback, to Skeet Quinlan, a halfback, in the second quarter. It added its other touchdown in the closing minutes of the game with the assistance of a 40-yard penalty against Cleveland for interfering with a pass receiver.

Just as they had done against the Detroit Lions in last year's title game, the Browns started their touchdown parade when Don Paul, a defensive halfback, intercepted a pass. He raced 65 yards to the goal. The toss, made by Van Brocklin, had been intended for Quinlan.

Graham, who was to score two touchdowns later, started the next touchdown on its way with a 50-yard pass play late in the second quarter. The receiver was Dante Lavelli.

Ken Konz, defensive back, returned a punt 24 yards midway in the third quarter. Cleveland went 46 yards in five plays, with Graham going 15 yards around right end for the touchdown. Graham was making his last appearance as a football player in the play-off.

Sam Palumbo, a defensive player, was one of those who got into the pass burglary act in the third period. He stole a Van Brocklin toss and returned it 10. Soon the Browns were off again for 36 yards and a touchdown, with Graham slicing through for the final yard.

McLaughlin Sees Action

Late in the fourth quarter Graham connected with Halfback Ray Renfro for 35 yards and the final touchdown.

Leon McLaughlin, offensive center of the Rams who was bedded by the mumps last week, got into the starting line-up to help the Ram cause.

Twice in the first half Cleveland took a 10-point lead. While play was aggressive, it was relatively free of penalties.

Cleveland's first touchdown on Paul's pass theft found the former Washington State player with a clear view of the Ram goal line. Only Van Brocklin had a chance to overhaul him. However, the Flying Dutchman is not noted for his flying feet.

Quinlan's scoring play in the second quarter also was a case of speed and deception. He got behind the defensive man, Warren Lahr, and fielded Van Brocklin's throw on the dead run. Lahr caught Quinlan, but not until the little Texan was falling across the goal line.

Both teams had scoring threats ended by pass interceptions in the end zone in the first half. Ed Hughes of the Rams outwrestled Renfro for the ball on one occasion, and Konz took charge of a Van Brocklin pass that seemed earmarked for 6 points.

Konz Intercepts Pass

Groza's field goal followed an interception of a pass by Konz that halted a Ram touchdown drive.

The Cleveland defensive team was nothing short of superb. The Browns had been listed as only 5-point favorites going into the game. But Coach Paul Brown's workmen quickly showed their true class.

Van Brocklin completed eleven of twenty-five passes for a respectable 116 yards, but six were intercepted and the Browns stole another from the Dutchman's alternate, Billy Wade.

Len Ford and Carlton Massey, the huge defensive ends; Don Cole, tackle, and the rest of the interior of the line were just too much for a Ram outfit that tried to but never could contain the Browns.

Graham had a field day. He completed fourteen of twenty-five throws for 202 yards and two touchdowns, and was as slippery as a wet lollypop in his running plays. He received a big ovation when the Rams finally trapped him for a loss, which didn't occur until the second half.

Paul's runback of the interception set a record for yards on a runback in a title game. Ford returned 45 yards against Detroit a year ago.

The Rams' offensive stars who led them to a surprising Western conference title during the regular season could get nowhere this time.

Dan Towler, a fullback, who missed most of the season with injuries and who filled in for the bench-ridden Tank Younger, was the leading ground gainer for his team today. He gained only 64 yards in fourteen carries. Ron Waller, the rookie from Maryland who led the club in rushing, was held to forty-eight in eleven trips.

Cleveland's big gainer was Ed Modzelewski. The fullback got 61 yards before he went out with injuries early in the third quarter. His alternate, Maurice Bassett, proved an ample replacement. He powered 49 yards in eleven carries, and in one series he was the main gun in a scoring drive.

CLEVELAND BROWNS (38)
Left Ends—Brewster, Massey, Weber.
Left Tackles—Groza, Kissell.
Left Guards—Gibron, Gain.
Centers—Gatski, Noll, Palumbo.
Right Guards—Bradley, Forester.
Right Tackles—McCormack, Cole, Sandusky.
Right Ends—Lavelli, Ford, Gillom.
Quarterbacks—Graham, Ratterman.
Left Halfbacks—Renfro, Lahr, Konz, Smith.
Right Halfbacks — Morrison, Paul, James, Petitbon, Jones.
Fullbacks—Modzelewski, Michaels, Bassett, Perini.

LOS ANGELES (14)
Left Ends—Fears, Boyd, Miller, Fuller.
Left Tackles — Holtzman, McFadin, Lipscomb.
Left Guards—Putnam, Ellena, Paul, Fournet.
Centers—Cross, McLaughlin, Griffin.
Right Guards—Hock, Richter, Moris.
Right Tackles—Toogood, Hauser.
Right Ends—Hirsch, Lewis, Robuste'l.
Quarterbacks—Van Brocklin, Wade.
Left Halfbacks—Waller, McCormick, Hughes, Sherman, Burroughs.
Right Halfbacks—Quinlan, Cason.
Fullback—Towler.

Cleveland Browns	3 14 14	7—38
Los Angeles Rams	0 7 0	7—14

Cleveland scoring—Touchdowns: Paul, 65, pass interception (4:12, second period); Lavelli, 50, pass-run from Graham (14:21, second period); Graham, 15, run (8:06, third period); Graham, 1, plunge (12:44, third period); Renfro, 35, pass-run from Graham (9:11, fourth period). Conversions: Groza, 5. Field goal: Groza, 26 (12:38, first period).

Los Angeles scoring — Touchdowns: Quinlan, 67, pass-run from Van Brocklin (5:05, second period); Waller, 4, run (12:42, fourth period). Conversions: Richter 2.

The 1955 and 1954 attendance by clubs:

	1955	1954	
Cleveland Browns	251,444	183,476	+67,968
Washington Redskins	156,461	126,090	+30,371
New York Giants	163,847	190,447	—26,600
Chicago Cardinals	151,071	125,665	+25,406
Philadelphia Eagles	183,081	158,125	+24,956
Pittsburgh Steelers	176,877	184,177	— 7,300
Los Angeles Rams	397,995	326,586	+71,411
Chicago Bears	258,686	243,283	+15,405
Green Bay Packers	153,241	118,668	+34,573
Baltimore Colts	236,826	164,238	+72,588
San Francisco 49ers	281,780	268,153	+12,627
Detroit Lions	311,372	326,040	—14,668
Total	2,722,685	2,415,948	+306,737

CANADIAN FOOTBALL SEEKS TO END 'WAR'

WINNIPEG, Man., Jan. 23 (AP) — Canada's two professional football leagues are going all out in an effort to make peace with the National Football League.

The Big Four and the Western Interprovincial Football Union, through their controlling body—the newly formed Canadian Football Council—today empowered Chairman Ralph Cooper of Hamilton to try to work out an agreement with Commissioner Bert Bell of the N. F. L. whereby each group would respect the other's player contracts and options.

If the reciprocal agreement is drafted, it will mean the end of a war between the two groups that broke out in full force in 1951 when the Winnipeg Blue Bombers signed Tackle Dick Huffman of the Los Angeles Rams. The Bombers won the rights to Huffman through the Canadian courts.

The Canadian football council, composed of five representatives from each Canadian league, said its nine teams would continue to honor independently N. F. L. contracts and options until Cooper returned from a conference with Bell.

Cooper will meet with the N. F. L. commissioner "as soon as posible." If the N. F. L. rejects the reciprocal agreement, the council will meet again to give new instructions to Cooper for bringing the two groups closer together.

Lions' Court Action Dismissed

TORONTO, July 26 (AP)—Chief Justice J. C. McRuer of the Supreme Court of Ontario today dismissed an action by the Detroit Lions of the National Football League against Tom Dublinski, quarterback of the Toronto Argonauts. The Lions tried to restrain Dublinski from playing for Toronto last fall by claiming he was under contract to them until May 1, 1956. Detroit's claim for damages for breach of contract also was rejected.

NATIONAL FOOTBALL LEAGUE
STANDARD PLAYERS CONTRACT

BETWEEN

...BALTIMORE FOOTBALL INC....... A CORPORATION OF THE STATE OF MARYLAND which operates BALTIMORE COLTS FOOTBALL CLUB, and which is a member of the National Football League, and which is hereinafter called the "Club," and ....John Unitas........................ of ......Pittsburgh, Pennsylvania..... hereinafter called the "Player."

In consideration of the respective promises herein the parties hereto agree as follows:

1. The term of this contract shall be from the date of execution hereof until the first day of May following the close of the football season commencing in ...1956................, subject however, to rights of prior termination as specified herein.

2. The Player agrees that during the term of this contract he will play football and will engage in activities related to football only for the Club and as directed by the Club according to the Constitution, By-Laws, Rules and Regulations of the National Football League, hereinafter called the "League," and of the Club, and the Club, subject to the provisions hereof, agrees during such period to employ the Player as a skilled football player. The Player agrees during the term of this contract to report promptly for the Club's training seasons to render his full time services during the training seasons and at the Club's direction to participate in all practise sessions and in all League and other football games scheduled by the Club.

3. For the Player's services as a skilled football player during the term of this contract, and for his agreement not to play football or engage in activities related to football for any other person, firm, corporation or institution during the term of this contract, and for the option hereinafter set forth giving the Club the right to renew this contract, and for the other undertakings of the Player herein, the Club promises to pay the Player each football season during the term of this contract the sum of $..7,000......... to be payable as follows:

75% of said salary in weekly installments commencing with the first and ending with the last regularly scheduled League game played by the Club during such season and the balance of 25% of said sum at the end of said last regularly scheduled League game.

In addition, the Club promises and agrees to pay the reasonable board and lodging expenses of the Player incurred while playing games for the Club in other than the Club's home city and also to pay all proper and necessary travelling expenses of the Player and his meals en route to and from said games.

4. The Player agrees at all times to comply with and to be bound by all the provisions of the Constitution, By-Laws, Rules and Regulations of the League and of the Club, all of which are hereby made a part of this contract. If the Player fails to comply with said Constitution, By-Laws, Rules and Regulations the Club shall have the right to terminate this contract or to take such other action as may be specified in said Constitution, By-laws, Rules and Regulations, or as may be directed by the Commissioner of the League, hereinafter called the "Commissioner." The Player agrees to submit himself to the discipline of the League and of the Club for any violation of such Constitution, By-laws, Rules and Regulations subject however, to the right to a hearing by the Commissioner. All matters in dispute between the Player and the Club shall be referred to the Commissioner and his decision shall be accepted as final, complete, conclusive, binding and unappealable, by the Player and by the Club. The Player hereby waives any and all rights of action against the Commissioner, the League, the Club or any of its members or stockholders, and against any officer of the Club or of the League arising out of or in connection with decisions of the Commissioner, except to the extent of awards made by the Commissioner to the Player. The Player hereby acknowledges that he has read said Constitution, By-Laws, Rules and Regulations and that he understands their meaning.

5. The Player promises and agrees that during the term of this contract he will not play football or engage in activities related to football for any other person, firm, corporation or institution except with the prior written consent of the Club and the Commissioner, and that he will not during the term of this contract engage in any game or exhibition of baseball, basketball, hockey, wrestling boxing or any other sport which endangers his ability to perform his services hereunder, without the prior written consent of the Club. The Player likewise promises and agrees that during the term of this contract, when, as and if he shall receive an invitation to participate in any All-Star football game which is approved by the League, he will play in said game in accordance with all the terms and conditions relating thereto, including the player compensation therein set forth as ar agreed to between the League and the Sponsor of such game.

6. The Player represents and warrants that he is and will continue to be sufficiently highly skilled in all types of football team play to play professional football of the caliber required by the League and by the Club, that he is and will continue to be in excellent physical condition, and agrees to perform his services hereunder to the complete satisfaction of the Club and its Head Coach. If in the opinion of the Head Coach the Player does not maintain himself in excellent physical condition or fails at any time during the football seasons included in the term of this contract to demonstrate sufficient skill and capacity to play professional football of the caliber required by the League and by the Club, or if in the opinion of the Head Coach the Player's work or conduct in the performance of this contract is unsatisfactory as compared with the work and conduct of other members of the Club's squad of players, the Club shall have the right to terminate this contract upon written notice to the player of such termination.

7. Upon termination of this contract the Club shall pay the Player only the balance remaining due him for travelling and board and lodging expenses and any balance remaining due him for football seasons completed prior to termination, and, if termination takes place during a football season, any balance remaining due him on that portion of his total compensation for that season as provided in paragraph 3 hereof which the number of regularly scheduled League games already played by the Club during that season bears to the total number of League games scheduled for the Club for that season.

8. The Player hereby represents that he has special, exceptional and unique knowledge, skill and ability as a football player, the loss of which cannot be estimated with any certainty and cannot be fairly or adequately compensated by damages and therefore agrees that the Club shall have the right, in addition to any other rights which the Club may possess, to enjoin him by appropriate injunction proceedings against playing football or engaging in activities related to football for any person, firm, corporation or institution and against any other breach of this contract.

9. It is mutually agreed that the Club shall have the right to sell, exchange, assign and transfer this contract and the Player's services to any other Club of the League and the Player agrees to accept such assignment and to report promptly to the assignee club and faithfully to perform and carry out this contract with the assignee club as if it had been entered into by the Player with the assignee club instead of with this club.

10. On or before the date of expiration of this contract, the Club may, upon notice in writing to the Player, renew this contract for a further term until the first day of May following said expiration on the same terms as are provided by this contract, except that (1) the Club may fix the rate of compensation to be paid by the Club to the Player during said period of renewal, which compensation shall not be less than ninety percent (90%) of the amount paid by the Club to the Player during the preceding season, and (2) after such renewal this contract shall not include a further option to the Club to renew the contract; the phrase "rate of compensation" as above used shall not be understood to include bonus payments or payments of any nature whatsoever other than the precise sum set forth in Paragraph 3 hereof.

11. Player acknowledges the right and power of the Commissioner of the National Football League (a) to fine and suspend, (b) to fine and suspend for life or indefinitely, and/or (c) to cancel the contract of, any player who accepts a bribe or who agrees to throw or fix a game or who, having knowledge of the same, fails to report an offered bribe or an attempt to throw or fix a game, or who bets on a game, or who is guilty of any conduct detrimental to the welfare of the National Football League or of professional football; and the Player hereby releases the Commissioner of the National Football League, individually and in his official capacity, and also the National Football League and every club and every officer, director and stockholder of the League and of every club thereof, jointly, and severally, from all claims and demands for damages and every claim and demand whatsoever he may have arising out of or in connection with the decision of said Commissioner of the National Football League in any of the aforesaid cases.

12. Any payments made hereunder to the Player for a period during which he is entitled to workman's compensation benefits by reason of temporary total, permanent total, temporary partial, or permanent partial disability shall be deemed an advance payment of compensation benefits due the player, and the club shall be entitled to be reimbursed the amounts thereof out of any award of compensation.

13. This agreement contains the entire agreement between the parties and there are no oral or written inducements, promises or agreements except as contained herein. This agreement shall become valid and binding upon each party hereto only when, as and if it shall be approved by the Commissioner.

14. This agreement has been made under and shall be governed by the laws of the State of MARYLAND....
....

IN WITNESS WHEREOF the Player has hereunto set his hand and seal and the Club has caused this contract to be executed by its duly authorized officer on the date set opposite their respective names.

WITNESS:		...BALTIMORE FOOTBALL INC.......... Club
Margaret M. Madigan	1/26/56 Date	D. B. Kellett ...... President
Mrs. John C. Unitas	1/31/56 Date	...John C. Unitas... Player
Approved ......Bert Bell...... Commissioner	2/6/56 Date	1509 Creedmore Avenue....... Player's Address
		Pittsburgh, Pennsylvania

This Copy to be Sent to Commissioner for Approval
Return to Member Club

Cardinals Rout Redskins, 31-3, With Explosive Ground Attack

Matson Sprints 105 Yards on Kick-Off Return—Bernardi Goes 95 for Touchdown

WASHINGTON, Oct. 14 (AP)—Halfback Ollie Matson sprinted 105 yards on a kick off return that broke a Griffith Stadium record today and helped the Chicago Cardinals gain a 31-3 victory over the Washington Redskins.

Matson's spectacular run overshadowed another dazzling dash Frankie Bernardi's 95-yard return of a punt in the first period. It shot the undefeated Cards into a lead they proceeded to widen with an explosive ground game that kept the Redskins and 25,-794 fans gasping.

Statistics of the Game

	Cards	Redskins
First downs	13	15
Rushing yardage....	255	136
Passing yardage	55	100
Passes attempted....	9	23
Passes completed....	4	12
Passes intercepted by	2	1
Punts	3	7
Av. dist. of punts, yds.	47.6	44.3
Fumbles lost........	1	1
Yards penalized.....	70	30

Oct. 22

End Cracks Club Record for Yardage

Gains 257 Yards on Seven Catches; Team Rolls Up 498 From Scrimmage

By CHUCK JOHNSON

The Green Bay Packers ran the favored Los Angeles Rams right out of County Stadium Sunday. The score on a warm and sunny afternoon was 42-17. A crowd of 24,200 saw it and cheered.

On offense, the Packers were nearly perfect; on defense, extremely opportunistic. After a 7-7 first quarter, they completely crushed last year's western division champions.

Tobin Rote, Green Bay quarterback, had one of his finest days in seven seasons in the National Football league. Bill Howton, end, had his finest in five years.

Reprinted from
The Milwaukee Journal

Packers Roll 498 Yards

Rote, tall, lean and leathery Texan, passed for three touchdowns and ran for another. He picked Los Angeles' defense apart as Green Bay rolled up 498 yards from scrimmage, 342 of it on passes.

Howton, blond, frail looking Texan and like Rote a graduate of Rice Institute in Houston, broke one of Don Hutson's records and when you break one of Hutson's records you've had yourself a day.

All told, Howton caught seven passes for 257 yards gained. That

The Statistics

	Packers	Rams
First downs	26	18
Yards gained rushing	156	163
Yards gained passing	342	232
Passes	17–33	14–30
Passes intercepted by	4	0
Punting average	45	48
Yards penalized	46	54
Fumbles lost	0	1

is the third highest total in league history. Hutson held the old Green Bay record of 237 yards, set against Brooklyn in 1943. Only Jim Benton of the old Cleveland Rams and Cloyce Box of Detroit have done better in one game that Howton. Benton gained 303 yards and Box 302.

REACTION OF FANS CITED AS REASON

Their Objection to Electronic Devices Used by Coaches Brings Season's Ban

PHILADELPHIA, Oct. 18 (AP)—The National Football League is going back to the old-fashioned style of having quarterbacks either think for themselves or receive instructions by messengers on foot.

Commissioner Bert Bell said today that electronic devices used by some of the league teams for communication between the coaches on the sidelines and the quarterback had been outlawed for the balance of the season.

The action was taken in a telephone poll of N. F. L. teams and Bell said there was not one dissenting voice. Even Paul Brown, coach of the Cleveland Browns, who first supplied receiving sets to his quarterbacks, was happy to go along with the ban.

Permanent Action Expected

The commissioner said: "By unanimous consent of the twelve member clubs * * * all electronic devices, including walkie talkies * * * must be eliminated for the remainder of the season."

Bell thinks the action will become a permanent one. "All the clubs were cooperative and it is my opinion that at the next annual meeting something will be put in the league book to outlaw the things permanently," he said.

Bell said flatly that the action was initiated because reaction to the use of these coach-to-quarterback radios or transistors was bad. He said the fans, through the mail, and press, radio and television reporters had expressed disapproval. "I did not read or hear any favorable comments on it," Bell said.

Giants Snare Signals

The operation became almost a joke last Sunday when the New York Giants said they intercepted Brown's orders to his quarterbacks in the Browns-Giants game. According to the Giants, they had a coach stationed on the sidelines with an interceptor set and relayed the Cleveland plays to their defense.

Brown used the electronic system only for a few plays, as the roar of the crowd drowned out his voice in the quarterback's helmet receiving set.

The directive does not exclude a telephone line to the bench from the press box or scouting positions, or a telephone line with extra footage used by a coach on the sidelines.

Oct. 21

Vengeful Bears Maul Baltimore Colts, 58-27

Even the Surprise of Blanda's Missing a Kick Fails to Stop Chicago Team

From Press Dispatches

Chicago, Ill. — George Blanda missed his first extra point from placement in 157 attempts but the Chicago Bears ground the Baltimore Colts into a 58-27 defeat here Sunday to avenge their only setback of the National Football league season.

Blanda fired three touchdown passes and Ed Brown two as the Bears scored their most points since their 73-0 play-off victory over Washington in 1940.

The game was witnessed by 48,364 spectators.

Brown pitched touchdown passes covering 37 and 68 yards to Harlon Hill in the second period to put the Bears ahead, 20-14, at the intermission. But the Colts led by 21-20 in the third period when Carl Taseff returned Blanda's short try for a field goal 96 yards.

After that it was all Chicago.

Blanda had place kicked 156 successive extra points for a league record since 1951 but his boot after the third Chicago touchdown was wide to the left.

The Bears lost their rugged halfback, Bobby Watkins, who aggravated a leg injury. The Colts lost quarterback George Shaw in the second quarter and Taseff in the third through injuries.

	Colts	Bears
First downs	13	26
Rushing yardage	130	209
Passing yardage	148	268
Passes	13-24	16-21
Passes intercepted by	1	1
Punting average	36.7	49
Fumbles lost	4	1
Yards Penalized	70	55

| Baltimore Colts | 7 | 7 | 7 | 6—27 |
| Chicago Bears | 0 | 20 | 17 | 21—58 |

Colts Scoring—Touchdowns, Ameche (1 foot, plunge), Moore (56, run). Taseff (96, run). Mitscheller (36, pass from Unitas); conversions, Feamster 3. Bears Scoring—Touchdowns, Casares 2 (6, run; 14, run), Hill 2 (37, pass from Brown; 68, pass-run from Brown), Caroline (59, interception), Schroeder (9, pass from Blanda), McColl 2 (4 pass from Blanda; 9, pass from Blanda), conversions, Blanda 7; field goal, Blanda (50).

Bears Present Ball to Their 'Coast Chaplain'

[Chicago Tribune Press Service]

San Francisco, Oct. 28— The Chicago Bears gave the game ball used in today's 38 to 21 victory over the 49ers to the Rev. Charles Sullivan, pastor of St. Gabriel's church in San Francisco, a long-time Bear fan.

Accepting the football with a broad grin, the Rev. Sullivan described himself as "the Bear's west coast chaplain. But all I can do is pray for 'em. I am not allowed to suit up."

By CAMERON C. SNYDER

Philadelphia, Nov. 26 — The Colts, drafting in seventh position, picked two huge linemen, here today as the Green Bay Packers won the National Football League's bonus choice and selected Paul Hornung, Notre Dame quarterback.

Only 49 players were selected by the 12 member teams in today's abbreviated draft meeting. The other 26 rounds of the draft will be held in January along with the annual league meeting.

Van Brocklin's Passing Earns Triumph Before 45,209

Los Angeles, Dec. 16 (AP)—Defense Halfback Will Sherman sank Green Bay's hopes with a 95-yard runback of a pass interception and Quarterback Norman Van Brocklin, with his aerial wizardry, led the Los Angeles Rams to a 49-to-21 victory over the Packers today.

Sherman's spectacular theft of a Tobin Rote pass late in the first quarter broke a 7-7 tie just as Green Bay was about to take the lead itself.

The Rams were never behind from there, on in, much to the delight of 45,209 hometown fans who turned out to see the windup of the National Football League season here.

Van Brocklin Gets Big Ovation

Van Brocklin got a standing ovation, in contrast to the boos he heard earlier this season, when he left the game in the last quarter.

The Dutchman from Oregon completed 17 of 22 passes for 289 yards and three of the Rams' seven touchdowns.

Two of Van Brocklin's mighty throws were for 56 yards each, to speedy Bob Boyd.

Three Ram rookies were standouts. Fullback Joe Marconi scored three touchdowns on short plunges, End Leon Clarke scored a touchdown on a 9-yard pass from Van Brocklin, and Halfback Tom Wilson broke the N.F.L. record for yards gained in one game. The ex-Army flyer gained 223 yards in 23 carries, breaking the mark of 218 yards in 26 carries set in 1950 by Gene Roberts, of the New York Giants, against the Chicago Cardinals.

Green Bay, which defeated the Rams earlier in the season, came back after the half and went 69 yards for its second touchdown. Rote passed 13 yards to Al Carmichael for the TD.

Rams Get 33 First Downs

Early in the final quarter the Packers went 58 yards with second-string Quarterback Bart Starr at the helm. Fullback Fred Cone plunged the final 5 yards.

The Rams chalked up 33 first downs, one short of the club record.

Between halves the Rams' great end, Tom Fears, retiring from the game after nine years with the pro club, was given a tribute by the fans, fellow players, and the Ram management. Gifts included a 1957 station wagon.

Statistics

	Packers	Rams
First downs	19	33
Rushing yardage	181	314
Passing yardage	174	297
Passes	15-28	18-27
Passes intercepted by	0	0
Punts	5-46	80-0
Fumbles lost	0	2
Yards penalized	33	10

| Green Bay | 7 | 0 | 7 | 7—21 |
| Los Angeles | 14 | 21 | 14 | 0—49 |

Green Bay scoring: Touchdowns—Rote (1, plunge). Carmichael (13, pass from Rote), Cone (5, plunge). Conversions—Cone 3.

Los Angeles scoring: Touchdowns—Marconi 3 (1, 3, 2, plunges), Sherman (95, runback, pass interception), Boyd 2 (56, 56, pass-run from Van Brocklin), Clarke (9, pass from Van Brocklin). Conversions: Richter 7.

Chicago Team Sweeps Western Division In Taming Lions, 32-21

CHICAGO, Dec. 16 (P)—Full-back Rick Casares ripped off 190 yards including a 68-yard touchdown run today, powering the Chicago Bears to a 38 - 21 victory over the Detroit Lions and the Western Division title in the National Football League.

The triumph hoisted the Bears into a championship game against the New York Giants at New York Dec. 30.

It was sweet revenge for the Bears and the 225-pound Casares. Only two weeks ago the Lion tackle Gil Mains and held 42-10, at Detroit and limited Casares to 45 yards in 11 carries.

It was a rough, tough ball game in which several players were ejected for fighting and a free - for - all developed in the fourth quarter with players, fans and police engaging in the melee.

As best could be determined, the big battle featured Bear quarterback George Blanda and Litn tackle Gil Mains and held up play several minutes.

Casares Sets Record

Despite all their fury, the Lions couldn't contain Casares and his teammates. The 25-year-old former Florida star made his yardage in 17 plays but fell short of two league records. However, his 1,126 yards for the season bettered the Bear mark of 1,004 set by Beattie Feathers in 1934.

He missed the single game rushing mark of 218 set by Gene Roberts of New York in 1950 and was shy by 20 yards of Steve Van Buren's 1,146 season yards established with Philadelphia in 1949.

Except for a short - lived 7-3 lead in the second quarter, the Lions were never in the game. The Bears pushed out to a 17-7 halftime lead and pushed across three touchdowns in the second half to complete the rout.

Casares' brilliant touchdown run came in the second quarter and gave the Bears a 10-7 lead which they never relinquished.

Detroit's chances were dimmed early in the second quarter when star quarterback Bobby Layne was rocked by Bear tackle Ed Meadows and had to be carried off the field. Meadows later was thrown out of the game for fighting and Layne reportedly suffered a concussion and never returned to action.

Harry Gilmer replaced Layne and did a commendable job, tossing two touchdown passes, and setting up another one with a 12-yard completion.

Gilmer put the Lions ahead in the second quarter on an 18-yard touchdown pass to fullback Bill Bowman.

Three plays later Casares rambled for his 14th touchdown of the season and the Bears grabbed a 17-7 halftime lead on a nine-yard touchdown run by J. C. Caroline.

Lions Threaten

Detroit made its final threat early in the second half. Yale Lary intercepted a Bill McColl pass and ran 37 yards to the Bear 17. Two plays later Gilmer hit Dave Middleton with a 12-yard pass and Leon Hart carried over from the one for the touchdown.

Their lead chopped to only three points, the Bears unleashed one of their patent deEd Brown-Harlon Hill passes which was good for 44 yards and another touchdown. George Blanda, who had kicked a 37-yard field goal in the first quarter, made his third of five conversions.

The Bears added two more touchdowns in the fourth quarter on a seven-yard run by Bobby Watkins and a 27-yard pass interception returned by Joe Fortunato. Shortly before the game ended, Gilmer hit Doran Dibble with a nine-yard touchdown pass.

As soon as the game ended, thousands in the crowd of 49,086 swarmed down to the field and ripped down the metal goal posts.

It was the first divisional title for the Bears since 1946 when they went on to beat the New York Giants 24-14 for the championship.

Detroit   0 7 7 7 -21
Chicago Bears   3 14 7 14 -38
Detroit scoring—Touchdowns: Bowman (18, pass from Gilmer); Hart (1, plunge); Dibble (9, pass from Gilmer). Conversions: Martin 3.
Chicago Bears scoring—Touchdowns: Casares (68, run); Caroline (9, run); Hill (44, pass from Brown); Watkins (7, run); Fortunato (27, pass interception). Conversions: Blanda 5. Field goals: Blanda (37).

STATISTICS

	D	CB
First down	17	24
Rushing yardage	51	307
Passing yardage	181	137
Passes	15-30	8-17
Passes intercepted by	2	1
Punts	8-38.1	8-17
Fumbles lost	1	0
Yards penalized	58	67

Pro Grid Players Form Association

New York, Dec. 29 (P)—Pro football players of the National League today organized a National Football Players Association and retained Creighton Miller, former Notre Dame star, as legal counsel. The new organization appeared to be patterned on the same general outline as the Baseball Players' Association.

Norm van Brocklin, of Los Angeles, and Kyle Rote of New York, were selected by the player representatives to join with Miller in presenting their objectives to Commissioner Bert Bell and the owners.

Among the objectives was "training camp expenses" which included pay for exhibition games.

Miller said no date had been set for a meeting with Bell, who had been advised informally in advance of the meeting. Miller said Bell always has said, "The door is always open to the players."

Bell, in New York for the playoff game between the Chicago Bears and the New York Giants, said at his hotel he always was ready to meet with the players, but would have to consult his own counsel before meeting with the players' attorney.

Eastern Conference

	W	L	T	Pct.	Pts.	OP
N.Y. Giants	8	3	1	.727	264	197
Chi Cards	7	5	0	.583	240	182
Washington	6	6	0	.500	183	225
Cleveland	5	7	0	.417	167	177
Pittsburgh	5	7	0	.417	217	250
Philadelphia	3	8	1	.273	143	215

Western Conference

	W	L	T	Pct.	Pts.	OP
Chi Bears	9	2	1	.818	363	246
Detroit	9	3	0	.750	300	188
S Francisco	5	6	1	.455	233	284
Baltimore	5	7	0	.417	270	322
Green Bay	4	8	0	.333	264	342
Los Angeles	4	8	0	.333	291	307

Pro Football Crown

VICTORS RACE TO 10-0 LEAD IN FIVE MINUTES, SCORE IN EACH PERIOD

Crowd Of 56,836 Watches Gifford, Webster, Triplett Rip Chicago Line; Robustelli Paces Strong New York Defense

New York, Dec. 30 (AP)—A determined New York Giant team, striking furiously, chopped up the Chicago Bears today as they smashed their way to a 47-to-7 National League playoff victory and their first football championship since 1938.

Playing with the determination stemming from eighteen years of frustration, the Giants amazed a frozen but enthusiastic crowd of 56,836 Yankee Stadium fans with one of the greatest displays of power and pulverizing line play ever witnessed in a championship playoff.

Score Early And Often

Striking fast and furiously, the New Yorkers stunned the Bears by scoring a touchdown and a field goal for a 10-to-0 lead in less than five minutes after the opening kickoff, and went on to tally at least one touchdown in every period.

The powerful Bears, who had rolled up more than 4,500 yards during the regular season to easily capture the team ground gaining crown, never had a chance as the Giants burst into a 13-0 first quarter lead and added three more touchdowns in the second period for a 34-to-7 halftime lead to make the experts wonder why the Bears had been established as a three-point pregame favorite.

While New York's terrific backfield trio of Frank Gifford, Alex Webster and Mel Triplett was tearing the Bears' vaunted line to shreds, the Giants' defensive wall was holding the Bears' big guns completely in check.

Robustelli, Leads Defense

Led by Andy Robustelli, their brilliant defensive end, the Giants limited Rick Casares, the league's champion ground gainer, to 43 yards in 14 carries, contained Harlon Hill, the great end, to only six meaningless catches. They harried Ed Brown, the circuit's passing king, to such an extent, he was able to complete only eight of 19 passes, a majority of them in the final minutes when the game was no longer in doubt.

In the meantime, the Giant runners were tearing up the turf

Triplett scored the first touchdown on a 17-yard burst through the middle; Webster accounted for the next two on plunges of three and four yards. Gifford made the last one, grabbing a 14-yard pass from Chuck Conerly, who also threw a nine yard touchdown pass to Kyle Rote.

Blocked Kick Converted

The sixth Giants' touchdown came when Henry Moore recovered a blocked kick in the end zone

When Giants weren't scoring touchdowns they were kicking field goals Ben Agajanian booted two of them, both in the first period, one of 17 yards and one from 43 yards out. He also added five extra points

He missed his fifth conversion attempt, making the first time in his career as a Giant that he missed converting the point after touchdown

Won Title In 1938

The Giants' six-touchdown, two-field-goal explosion represented their highest point total in nine championship playoffs, on which this was only their third that ended in success.

It was the Giants' first title game since they were beaten, oddly enough, by the Bears, 24-14, in 1946, and their first championship since they defeated the Green Bay Packers, 23-17, in 1938.

Statistics

	Chi.	N. York
First downs	19	16
Rushing yardage	67	126
Passing yardage	213	222
Passes	20-47	11-20
Passes intercepted	0	2
Punting average	8-34	5-37
Fumbles lost	1	2
Yards penalized	50	40

Chicago Bears   0   7   0   0— 7
NY Giants   13 21   6   7—47

Chicago scoring: Touchdown—Casares (9 run) Conversion—Blanda.

New York scoring: Touchdowns—Triplett (17, run); Webster, 2 (4, plunge; 3, plunge); Moore (recovered blocked kick in end zone); Rote (9 yard pass from Conerly); Gifford (14-yard pass from Conerly). Field goals—Agajanian, 2 (17, 43) Conversions—Agajanian, 5.

Players Lack Recognition But Demands Are Granted

PHILADELPHIA, Feb. 20 (AP) —The National Football League tonight refused to recognize the Players' Association, but granted most of their demands.

Commissioner Bert Bell announced after an all-day session of the owners at their annual meeting that "we will not recognize anybody as a bargaining agent."

Bell said, however, that "any player or players have the right to meet with the commissioner at any time for the purpose of discussing any problems."

Different and Distinct

"The league believes that the circumstances and conditions affecting each club are different and distinct. It is submitted that if any problems now exist or hereafter arise, the player or players on each club should meet with their individual owners for the purpose of discussing and resolving their particular grievances."

Bell said that if such a meeting proves unsuccessful he is authorized to meet with the player or players and render a final and binding decision.

The Players Association was organized last December in New York and included all NFL players with the exception of the Chicago Bears. They asked the league for a minimum salary of $5,000, expense money in training camp, a $12 a day minimum for board and lodging while on the road an injury clause guaranteeing a full season's salary, a shorter training season, and formal recognition of the association.

The proposals were presented to Bell early this week by Kyle Rote, captain of the New York Giants, and Norman Van Brocklin of the Los Angeles Rams, and the association's attorney, former Notre Dame football star Creighton Miller. Bell outlined these proposals to the league owners here today.

Although the owners refused to recognize the group, they agreed to grant it most of the things requested. In announcing a standardized program on fringe benefits, Commissioner Bell said that the owners were putting in writing "what they

been doing, anyway over a period of years."

Five Point program

Bell outlined the following program:

1. All teams in the NFL will pay the transportation and expenses of all players to training camp. Any player who thereafter does not make the team shall be paid return transportation and expenses to his home.

2. All clubs, at the club's expense, shall provide all players with all game equipment for league games.

3. It is the declared policy of the league that whenever practical all players shall eat in a group. When such is impractical, the club shall advance each player, for meals and/or lodging, the following: $9 a day for meals and $12 a day for meals and lodging.

4. A player under contract may immediately, after each pre-season game, draw against his salary if he so desires an advance of $50 for each pre-season game. A player who fails to make the team need not repay the advance.

5. A player under contract may not be asked to report to training camp until nine weeks before the first league game, except in the case of the championship team preparing for the Chicago Tribune All-Star game in accordance with a league contract. (Previously, training camps had opened as early as the first week in July to prepare for the opening games, usually in the last week of September.)

No Need

Bell said the owners turned down the $5,000 minium salary demand because "there is no player in the National Football League who does not receive over this minium. If there is one, and he tells me about it, I'll see that it's corrected."

When the owners resumed their meeting the problem of league expansion was first on the agenda. The owners considered a plan to expand to 14 teams in 1958. Applications are on hand from eight cities, including Buffalo, N.Y., which presented its arguments yesterday.

Although Bell has denied it, there were reports in some quarters that a move may be afoot to transfer the Chicago Cardinals to Buffalo.

6-3 Decision Holds Pro League Subject To Anti-Trust Laws

WASHINGTON, Feb. 25 (AP)—The Supreme Court ruled 6-3 today that professional football, unlike professional baseball, is subject to the antitrust laws.

Speaking for the majority, Justice Tom Clark said the "orderly way to eliminate error or discrimination, if any there be" between baseball and football "is by legislation and not by court decision."

The three dissenting justices said they could see no difference between the two sports as regards the antitrust laws.

Clark wrote:

"If this ruling is unrealistic, inconsistent, or illogical, it is sufficient to answer, aside from the distinctions between the businesses, that were we considering the question of baseball for the first time upon a clean slate we would have no doubts."

Appeal By Radovich

Today's ruling was given on an appeal by William Radovich, one-time football star at the University of Southern California and later a pro player, who sued the National Football League for $105,000 damages. The suit charged violation of antitrust laws and said the league had boycotted Radovich.

The decision means Radovich's suit must be tried; it had been thrown out of lower courts. It does not mean that the Supreme Court is making any finding now as to whether the pro league has violated any law.

Clark noted that the court's 1922 decision in the Federal League baseball case held that the business of baseball was outside the scope of the Sherman Antitrust Act, but commented:

"No other business claiming the coverage of those cases has such an adjudication. We, therefore, conclude that the orderly way to eliminate error or discrimination, if any, is by legislation and not by court action.

More Accommodative

"Congressional processes are more accommodative, affording the whole industry hearings and an opportunity to assist in the formulation of new legislation.

"The resulting product is therefore more likely to protect the industry and the public alike. The whole scope of congressional action would be known long in advance and effective dates for the legislation could be set in the future without the injustices of retroactivity and surprise which might follow court action."

Clark said the doctrine of the 1922 decision and a 1953 decision adhering to it "must yield to any congressional action."

The 1922 decision was in the case of Baltimore a member of the old Federal League of Professional Baseball Clubs, against the National League. Today's opinions cited this case frequently as "federal" or "the federal case."

Clark said, too, the court was careful to restrict its 1953 decision to baseball and followed the judgment of the 1922 case only so far as it "determines that Congress had no intention of including the business of baseball within the scope of the federal antitrust laws."

Intended To Isolate

He also said the courts in 1953 made the observation that the decision "could not be relied upon as a basis of exemption for other segments of the entertainment business, athletic or otherwise."

It seems, Clark said, this language "would have made it clear that the court intended to isolate these cases by limiting them to baseball."

Clark said the court should adhere to, but not extend, the interpretation of the antitrust law made in the baseball cases "as long as the Congress continues to acquiesce."

"We did not extend them (exemptions) to boxing or the theater because we believed that the volume of interstate business in each ... was such that both activities were within the act," Clark said. "Likewise, the volume of interstate business involved in organized football places it within the provisions of the act."

Dissenting Opinion

Justice John M. Harlan wrote a dissenting opinion in which Justice William J. Brennan Jr. joined. Justice Felix Frankfurter wrote another dissenting opinion.

Joining Clark in the six-vote majority were Chief Justice Earl Warren, and Justices Hugo Black, Stanley Reed, William O. Douglas and Harold Burton.

Harlan said he was unable to distinguish football from baseball under the rationale of the 1922 and 1953 baseball decisions. And, Harlan said, he "can find no basis for attributing to Congress a purpose to put baseball in a class by itself."

"If the situation resulting from the baseball decisions is to be changed," Harlan said, "I think it far better to leave it to be dealt with by Congress than for this court to becloud the situation further either by making untenable distinctions between baseball and other professional sports, or by discriminatory fiat in favor of baseball."

Limited Competence

Frankfurter in his dissenting opinion described himself as a man of "limited competence in matters athletic."

But, Frankfurter said, he has yet to hear any consideration that led the court to hold baseball outside the scope of antitrust laws that is not equally applicable to football.

Radovich's suit charged the National Football League and others attempted to monopolize interstate commerce in the business of professional football, in violation of antitrust laws.

He alleged the defendants tied players to a particular club and prevented them, by use of a reserve clause similar to that used in professional baseball, from becoming free agents.

The Justice Department supported Radovich in arguments before the Supreme Court. Government counsel argued against a decision of the U. S. Court of Appeals in San Francisco holding football, like baseball, was not subject to antitrust laws.

Claimed Boycott

Radovich claimed the National Football League boycotted him after he jumped in 1946 from the Detroit Lions of the National Football League to the Los Angeles Dons of the All America Conference, now defunct.

In stating that Radovich is entitled to an opportunity to prove his charges, Clark said:

"Of course, we express no opinion as to whether or not respondents (defendants) have, in fact violated the antitrust laws, leaving that determination to the trial court after all the facts are in."

Shot by 'a Good Friend'

Barni, Football Star, Slain While in Peacemaker Role

SAN FRANCISCO, July 22 (AP)—Pro football star Roy Barni died in a hospital today from bullet wounds inflicted by a tragedy-haunted truck driver who later sobbed to police, "Roy and I were good friends."

Police said Mr. Barni, twenty-nine, defensive back for the Washington Redskins, was shot three times while trying to settle a dispute between two men outside his tavern, The Huddle, in the Marina district last night.

Police said the .38-caliber automatic was in the hand of James D. Invirnizzi, sixty-two, who they said had known Mr. Barni since the football player was a boy. He was charged with suspicion of murder.

"I'm sorry," said Invirnizzi. "I didn't know who I shot."

Police said it was an earlier tragedy in Invirnizzi's life that touched off last night's shooting. The truck driver said he had been arguing with another patron, Tom Botti, thirty-seven. Invirnizzi said his fifteen-year-old son had been shot accidentally by Mr. Botti in 1938. He said Mr. Botti kept talking about it despite his pleas to stop.

Finally the two men went outside. Mr. Barni followed as peacemaker. A witness, Lewis Chriskolm, eighteen, said he saw Invirnizzi draw the gun and fire at Mr. Barni. Mr. Chriskolm wrested the gun from the truck driver and beat him over the head with it. Mr. Barni staggered back into his tavern and collapsed.

Mr. Barni, who was to have reported to the Redskins next week for training, is survived by his pregnant wife and a three-year-old daughter, Pamela. He also had played with the Philadelphia Eagles and the Chicago Cardinals.

Grid Browns Pay Highest Wages

Washington, July 24 (AP)—The Cleveland Browns paid out more in salaries than any other team in the National Football League last season, the House Anti-Trust subcommittee was told today.

The Browns' pay roll, however, included compensation for the All-Star game at Chicago last summer against a team of college stars.

An N.F.L. breakdown presented the subcommittee in its study of the legal status of pro sports showed these figures:

	Total	Range
Cleveland	$368,031	$6,000-19,000
Los Angeles	352,958	5,500-20,000
Chicago Bears	342,525	6,500-14,200
San Francisco	332,614	5,600-20,100
Detroit	330,375	5,500-20,000
New York	324,258	5,200-16,000
Chicago Card'ls	318,441	5,500-20,000
Baltimore	294,392	6,000-17,500
Philadelphia	283,483	5,750-13,500
Green Bay	277,642	5,000-18,500
Pittsburgh	276,875	5,250-12,250
Washington	275,942	5,000-14,000

Sept. 27

Meet the Pack

Paul . . . !

Paul Hornung, quarterback, University of Notre Dame — First year in pro ball. . . . Packers bonus selection in NFL draft. . . . Hornung made just about every All-American team in the last two years. . . . Climaxed his career by winning the Heisman Trophy, given annually to the nation's top collegiate football player.

Hornung

. . . Ranked second in nation in total offense in 1956. . . . Hornung led the Irish in passing, rushing, scoring, kick-off returns and punt returns. . . . He also was second in number of tackles made and in pass interceptions. Can play halfback or fullback, as well as quarterback. . . . Most valuable collegian in the Hula Bowl game. . . . Played in the East-West Shrine game. . . . Also played basketball. . . . Single. . . . Residence: Louisville, Ky.

Reprinted from The Green Bay Press Gazette

Bert Bell Cites Elvis Presley As Reason To Monitor Pro Football TV

WASHINGTON, July 25 (AP)—Pro Football Commissioner Bert Bell cited beer commercials and Elvis Presley today as precedents for regulating what's shown on telecasts of football games.

Bell, as Commissioner of the National Football League, must give prior approval to sportscasters assigned to radio or television for NFL games.

He has cautioned announcers and cameramen against picking up fights that break out on the field, overstressing injuries or second-guessing officials.

The subject came up as Bell testified before the house anti-trust subcommittee in its sports inquiry. Chairman Celler (D-NY) and Rep. Rodino (D-NY) suggested the commissioner's radio-TV authority amounted to "censorship."

"You can play God, as it were," Celler commented. "You are top dog."

Bell said he acted only to "protect the game."

"I believe they should call the game as it is," he said. "They shouldn't criticize players or teach kids that a great ball player is fighting so they'll go out and copy him."

Bell, a former player and coach, said he was aghast one recent night to see TV cameras trained on a baseball player lying injured on the ground.

"His mother, father, sweethearts and friends at home were dying looking at that," the rotund Commissioner said.

Rodino asked if such incidents weren't really "part of the whole spectacle" and fair game for the camera.

"Well, they left it off beer," Bell said.

He later explained that he meant TV had shied away from showing beer-drinking scenes.

"They pour beer," noted Rep. Keating (R-NY).

"yes, but they don't drink it," Bell said.

"They sip it," Rodino put it.

"They don't drink it," Bell insisted.

Then the Commissioner testified someone decided "that Mr. Presley wasn't in the best interest of the public for kids looking in and they raised the camra on that, too."

Bell was referring to Elvis Presley, who wiggles while he warbles, and a TV show on which the sideburned rock 'n roller appeared several months ago. cameras focused only on the upper part of the Presley torso.

Buddy Parker Quits As Lions Coach

Resignation Is Made At Club Party

DETROIT, Aug. 12 (AP) — Raymond J. (Buddy) Parker resigned tonight as coach of the professional f o o t b a l l Detroit Lions in a sudden announcement that caught Lion officials by surprise.

Parker, starting his seventh season as head coach, made the startling announcement at the eighth annual "Meet The Lions" banquet at a downtown Detroit hotel. He said "When you get to a situation where you can't handle football players, it's time to get out — and that's what I'm doing tonight. I'm through with football in Detroit."

Dramatic Decision

Club President Edwin J. Anderson and General Manager W. N. Kerbawy immediately went into a huddle with Parker in an effort to talk him out of his dramatic decision.

Anderson returned to the speaker's rostrum a moment later and told the more than 500 fans that Parker "is emotionally upset about several matters that happened today."

"I am sure that when Buddy has slept on this thing and has realized what he has said in public that he will reconsider."

Parker, who guided the Lions to three Western Conference championships and who a year ago brought back a team that had finished last and wound up second to the Chicago Bears in the Western Division, refused to elaborate on his single statement.

He was summoned to the speaker's platform for his annual address about his team's prospects. That's when he announced his resignation, and sat down.

Asked by the master of ceremonies to return to the platform, Parker said "I just said what I thought and that's it."

Complete Confusion

There was complete confusion and the banquet broke up a few minutes later. Other Lion coaches were startled by the remark and said they had no idea that it was coming.

This is the second time in recent months that the veteran coach has talked of resigning.

After his club lost to the Chicago Bears in the game last December that decided the Western Conference championship, Parker announced "I've had enough. I'm getting out."

He said his decision at that time was prompted by alleged unsportsmanlike tactics by the Bears in the title game.

Parker's status with the club was unknown for a short period after that, but after a couple of meetings with President Anderson, Parker signed a new contract for the 1957 season.

The Lions' camp at nearby Cranbrook has been outwardly harmonious and the morale has seemed exceedingly high.

"I can't handle this team," Parker explained after his dramatic announcement. "It's the worst team I've ever seen in training camp. I don't mean material-wise. We've got good boys but there has been no life . . . no go . . . it's a completely dead team.

Parker refused to pin the blame on any individual. He made it clear that he was talking about the team as a whole.

"I'm not satisfied with the way the team is moving," he said. "I dont want to get in the middle of another losing season. I think somebody else could handle it better."

Parker said his decision had nothing to do with the squabble that preceded his signing a two-year contract. Parker had held out for the two year pact. The Lions had wanted to give him only one year.

Anderson said he planned to talk to Parker in the morning. "I hope we will prevail upon him to stay on as head coach," Anderson said. "I'm sure when Buddy sleeps on it he'll reconsider."

Parker said, however, "The meeting will make no difference."

Asked if he thought Anderson could hold him under his contract, Parker replied: "He (Anderson) can't make me coach if I don't want to."

Morabito Dies After Attack While Watching His 49'ers

San Francisco, Oct. 28 (AP)— Tony Morabito, 47, principal owner of the San Francisco Forty-Niners, died in a hospital today shortly after suffering a heart attack in the Kezar Stadium press box during today's National League Football game between the Forty-Niners and the Chicago Bears.

Morabito, watching the action along with a capacity crowd of 59,000, slumped from his chair in the press box to the floor in the second quarter while his Forty-Niners, co-leaders of the N.F.L.'s Western Division, were trailing the Bears, 7 to 14.

Died In Hospital

He died shortly after arriving at Mary's Help Hospital.

Morabito's wife was with him in the press box. As she bent over her unconscious husband, his brother, Victor, ran across the field and summoned the team physician, Dr. William O'Grady.

Tony and Victor brought major league pro football to San Francisco in 1946.

BROWNS BEAT RAMS, 45-31

Brown Sets Rushing Record With 237 Yards

Cleveland, Nov. 24 (AP)— Rookie Fullback Jim Brown scored four touchdowns and set a new National League rushing record today to trigger the Cleveland Browns to a 45-31 victory over Los Angeles before a crowd of 65,407.

The Syracuse All-American, a 220-pound bulldozer, piled up 237 yards rushing in 31 tries to erase the league record of 223 set a year ago by Tom Wilson of Los Angeles. The splurge boosted Browns' league-leading total to 769 yards in 161 tries and his four-touchdown effort hiked him to nine for the season.

Breaks Important

The Browns in retaining the Eastern Division lead by a half-game over the New York Giants came back from a 28-17 deficit in the last half of the wild and woolly contest.

Sept. 30

Biggest Crowd in Packer History—Turnstiles at new City Stadium checked off an attendance of 32,132 as the structure was dedicated Sunday, with the Packers edging out the traditional rival Chicago Bears by a 21-17 score. This aerial view, made by Emery Kroening of the Press-Gazette staff, looks to the southeast. The game, first here of the National Football League season, had an attendance of more than 7,000 over the capacity crowds at the old stadium. The 6,500-car parking lot was used to advantage by both cars and buses, as this picture shows. It is expected that another capacity crowd will be on hand for the game with the Detroit Lions next Sunday.

Reprinted from
The Green Bay Press Gazette

102,368 SEE LOS ANGELES WIN, 37-24

Pro Grid Attendance Record Set; 10,000 Turned Away

Los Angeles, Nov. 10 (AP)—The Los Angeles Rams, playing a bran dof football that produced five touchdowns and a safety before 102.368 fans, wrecked the winning streak of the San Francisco Forty-Niners today.

The Rams marched off the Memorial Coliseum turf with a 37-24 victory and a new attendance record for the National Football League. An estimated 10,000 were turned away.

Earlier Loss Avenged

Los Angeles, with a 2-4 win-loss this season, ended the five-game winning streak of the Forty-Niners and avenged an earlier loss to the Bay City club.

Quarterback Norman Van Brocklin capped his deadly aerial game with a throw that traveled 60 yards on a 50-yard touchdown pass to Bob Boyd in the second quarter.

The Rams and the Detroit Lions played before 3.751 in a league game here in 1953 that set a N.F.L. record at the time. The Rams and the Washington Redskins, in a *Times* charity game in 1951, drew 95,985.

Grid Pros Win Fight With Clubs

PHILADELPHIA, Dec. 2 (AP)—National Football League owners today unanimously granted all the demands of the players association—exhibition pay, minimum salary, injury protection clause and recognition.

The owners acted in executive session after completing the league's partial draft session.

Commissioner Bert Bell told a press conference that unanimous approval was given recommendations he had made to the owners on Oct. 16 and Nov. 4 that they write into the constitution and bylaws the various requests of the players association. The owners' action conformed exactly with an exlusive report by the Associated Press a week ago.

These recommendations provide a minimum annual salary of $5,000, $50 per game exhibition pay, protection for the players in event of injury in line of duty and recognition of the association as the formal representative of the players.

Injury Clause

The injury clause provides that if a player gives written notice to a team physician of an injury within 36 hours of its occurence, the club will provide medical and hospital care and continue the player's salary. If the player is not satisfied with the diagnosis of the club physician, he may within 72 hours after the initial examination, submit at his own expense to an examination by a physician of his own choice. If the diagnosis of the two doctors differ, the dispute shall be submitted to a third physician, whose opinion shall be binding on both the player and club.

In connection with recognition of the association, a point emphasized by Creighton Miller, attorney for the players' group, Bell said, 'I recognize the association before Congress and the owners today approved my action.'' He added that as commissioner he had the power to recognize the association without a vote by the owners.

On the subject of exhibition game play, Bell said that any private agreement between the players of an individual club and the team for such pay would be recognized.

Follow Congress Line

Bell emphasized that all of the actions taken here were in line with suggestions made by the Congressional committee before which he appeared last fall in Washington. The committee was investigating the possibility that some professional sports violated the anti-trust laws.

Bell said the language in the league's constitution and bylaws was changed to avoid any violations of the anti-trust act. The commissioner said that players, coaches and employes of the league may take any dispute with the NFL to court, if they disagree with his rulings as commissioner. He said this was not retroactive and would be in force as of Jan. 1, 1958.

The commissioner added that several rather technical items, such as fixing the price of tickets and limiting the amount of money a college player might receive as a member of a college all-star team playing an NFL team, were rephrased to comply with the law.

NFL STANDINGS

By the Associated Press

WESTERN DIVISION	W.	L.	T.	Pct.	Pts.	OP
Detroit	8	4	0	.667	251	231
San Francisco	8	4	0	.667	260	264
˙altimore	7	5	0	.583	303	235
Los Angeles	6	6	0	.500	307	278
Chicago Bears	5	7	0	.417	203	211
Green Bay	3	9	0	.250	218	311

EASTERN DIVISION	W.	L.	T.	Pct.	Pts.	OP
Cleveland	9	2	1	.818	269	172
New York	7	5	0	.583	254	211
Pittsburgh	5	6	0	.455	134	176
Washington	5	6	1	.455	251	230
Philadelphia	4	8	0	.333	173	230
Chicago Cards	3	8	0	.273	198	272

RESULT SATURDAY
Chicago Cards. 31; Philadelphia. 27.

RESULTS YESTERDAY
Cleveland. 34; New York. 28.
San Francisco. 27; Green Bay. 20.
Detroit. 21; Chicago Bears. 13.
Washington. 10; Pittsburgh. 3.
Los Angeles. 37; Baltimore. 21.

GAMES SUNDAY
Detroit at San Francisco (Western Division playoff.
Pittsburgh at Chicago Cardinals.

Detroit Comeback After Trailing 27-7 Captures Conference

SAN FRANCISCO, Dec. 22 (AP)—The Detroit Lions, refusing to quit when 20 points behind, staged a thrilling second half rally today and whipped the San Francisco 49ers 31-27 to win the Western Conference championship of the National Football League.

The victory in the playoff game before a capacity crowd of 60,118 in Kezar Stadium and a National television audience gave the Lions a date with the Cleveland Browns next Sunday in Detroit for the NFL title.

The Lions last held the league crown in 1953

Breakaway Back Tom Tracy provided the Lions with two touchdowns, his second on a brilliant 59 yard burst from scrimmage. Gene Gedman scored the fourth quarter touchdown which, combined with Jim Marth's fourth conversion, gave Detroit a 28-27 edge with the final period just 43 seconds old.

Field Goal Ends Scoring

Twice again the Lions threatened and added three more points on Martin's 13-yard field goal with two minutes left to play, as the 49ers failed in their bid for their first title in 12 years of trying.

San Francisco held a 24-7 half-time advantage on three touchdown passes by Y.A. Tittle and a 25-yard field goal by Gordy Soltau. As the third quarter started, Soltau added three more points on a 10-yard kick for a 27-7 lead.

The hard won conference title was the first for Lion Coach George Wilson, who took over when Buddy Parker quit at the start of the season.

Detroit	0	7 14 10—31	
San Francisco	14	10 3 0—27	

Detroit scoring: Touchdowns, Junker (4, pass from Rote), Tracy 2 (1 plunge; 59, run), Gedman (2, plunge). Field goal, Martin (13). Conversions, Martin 4.

San Francisco scoring: Touchdowns, Owens (34, pass from Tittle), McElhenny (47, pass-run from Tittle), Wilson (12 pass from Tittle). Field goals, Soltau 2 (25, 10). Conversions, Soltau 3.

STATISTICS

	D	S F
First downs	22	20
Rushing yardage	129	127
Passing yardage	195	224
Passes	16-30	18-31
Passes intercepted by	3	1
Punts	4-43.3	3-34.4
Fumbles lost	3	2
Yards penalized	.61	70

LIONS ROUT BROWNS FOR GRID TITLE

59-To-14 Defeat Is Cleveland's Worst As Tobin Rote Stars

Detroit, Dec. 29 (AP)—The Detroit Lions won the world's professional football championship today, burying the favored Cleveland Browns, 59 to 14.

It was the worst defeat ever suffered by the Cleveland club and brought the Lions a full measure of revenge for a 56-10 shellacking dealt them by the same Browns in the National Football League title contest three seasons back.

Tobin Rote directed the Lion attack flawlessly, throwing four touchdown passes—one a near-record pitch—and scoring another touchdown himself.

Detroit Record Set

The Lions captured their fourth world championship and set a new all-time team scoring record in doing it. The old Detroit record was 52 points, accomplished twice.

Rote, shouldering the quarterback duties all by himself over the last three crucial weeks of the campaign after a broken ankle sidelined veteran Bobby Layne, fired touchdown passes of 26, 78, 24 and 32 yards. He hit rookie End Steve Junker on two scoring pitches and connected with veterans Jim Doran and Dave Middleton on the others.

The one to Doran covered 78 yards, only 4 yards short of the record for a title game.

17 Points In First Period

A crowd of 55,263 sat in brilliant sunshine and 32-degree weather and watched the Lions turn the Browns team into a fumbling, ineffective giant from the very outset.

Striking for 17 points in the first period against the defense rated the finest in the league, the Lions never let the Browns threaten.

The Detroit club scored two touchdowns in every quarter and throttled a Cleveland offense headed by rookie Fullback Jim Brown, the league's leading ball carrier.

Ovation For Rote

The Browns and the Lions, whose rivalry is one of the most bitterly contested in all football, left little room for personal duels and fist fighting today. There were occasional flareups resulting in penalties late in the contest but officials never let it get out of hand.

Rote, given a tremendous standing ovation when he left the game with a 52-14 advantage, and Linebacker Captain Joe Schmidt were mobbed before they could get to the dugout tunnel leading to their dressing room.

Thousands of fans held them up 10 minutes before turning their attention to the goal posts. But cordons of police officers and stadium attendants managed to keep the big crowd away from the goal posts they wanted so badly to rip down.

$479,582 Net Receipts

The victory was worth $4,295.41 to each member of the victorious Lions team. The Cleveland shares were $2,750.30 apiece.

Brown Philosophical About 59-14 Licking

Detroit, Dec. 29 (AP)—Paul Brown, coach of the badly beaten Cleveland Browns, looks at his team's 59-14 licking about the only way he could.

"I'm philosophical about it," said Brown, managing a smile for the small knot of newsmen he'd let into the dressing room 25 minutes after the game with Detroit for the National Football League championship.

Assist For Fans

"The ball was just going to bounce that way and it did," he said. "The Lions were whetted to a fine competitive edge and we had been standing by waiting."

His reference was to the Western Division playoff between Detroit and San Francisco last week while the Browns took a week end off with their Eastern Division crown already sewed up

His passing of praise to the Detroiters included even an assist to wildly cheering fans that took up every seat in Briggs Stadium

Diving Catches Cited

"We couldn't hear our own signals," he said. "That crowd noise was terrific. There's something about this ball park that makes the crowd noise drown our signals. Finally we just gave up trying to defeat the confusion.

"Rote (Lions' Quarterback Tobin Rote) and his receivers had a great day They did everything right, guys diving and catching on their fingertips" Brown said.

"I've got to give them credit"

The Rote-to-Jim Doran pass play that covered 78 yards and got the Lions a touchdown early in the third period was the back-breaking blow for the Browns, said the veteran coach.

"We started the second half all right and got a touchdown," he said. "We were only 17 points behind and I thought we had a chance to come back. But they got the touchdown right back on that long pass."

The Statistics

	Cleveland	Detroit
First downs	17	22
Rushing yardage	218	137
Passing yardage	95	296
Passes	9-22	13-21
Passes intercepted by	0	5
Punts	4-35	4-36
Fumbles lost	2	1
Yards penalized	60	52

Cleveland	0 7 7	0—14
Detroit	17 14 14	14—59

Cleveland scoring: Touchdowns—Brown (29, end run), L. Carpenter (5, run). Conversions—Groza, 2.

Detroit scoring: Touchdowns—Rote (1, plunge), Gedman (1-foot plunge), Junker, 2 (26, pass-run from Rote, 24, pass-run from Rote), Barr (19, pass interception), Doran (78, pass-run from Rote), Middleton (32, pass from Rote), Cassady (17, pass run from Reichow), Field Goal—Martin, 31. Conversions—Martin, 8.

Oct. 7

Detroit Trades Bobby Layne To Pittsburgh Club

PITTSBURGH (P)— The Pittsburgh Steelers Monday obtained quarterback Bobby Layne from the Detroit Lions in exchange or quarterback Earl Morrall and two future draft choice—one in 1959 and one in 1960.

Steeler Coach Buddy Parker said he made the trade because Layne "is a top flight quarterback." Parker added:

"I don't think Morrall was a top flight quarterback. He may be in the future. But he isn't right now."

Parker said he wanted to give the Steelers more punch.

"Layne will help us immensely," Parker added. "We've got our running game going and we've got good receiving. With the addition of Layne, we might get back into the race."

Last year Morrall attempted 289 sses and completed 139 for 1,-900 yards and 11 touchdowns.

The Steelers acquired Morrall, a former Michigan State star, in 1957 from the San Francisco 49ers for lineman Marve Matuszak and two draft choices.

Layne, former Texas University star, is in his 11 season in professional football.

Played Under Parker

He was drafted by the Chicago Bears, later played for the old New York Bulldogs, then came to Detroit, where he played under Parker, former coach of the Lions.

In 10 seasons of pro ball, Layne has tossed 129 touchdown passes. He's attempted 2,518 passes and completed 1,233 or 17,567 yards. In 1956 he led the league in scoring with 99 points.

In Detroit, Lion coach George Wilson said:

"I believe we got a good deal on the trade. In Morrall we are getting a proven ball player and new blood."

Wilson, who took over the Detroit reins last year when Parker quit the Lions said he had known for a long time that he would trade either Layne or Tobin Rote.

Having two top quarterbacks, he said, neither of them got to play enough.

The one to go was Layne, he said, "because I would have been run out of town if we had traded Rote."

Oct. 27

101-YARD TOUCHDOWN SPRINT BY LYLES WITH KICKOFF IS TOP THRILL

Nearly-Flawless Unitas Increases Scoring-Pass Mark To 20 Games; Great Play Has Tilt Under Control After Three Periods

Victory

By CAMERON C. SNYDER

Leonard Lyles's 101-yard touchdown kickoff return early in the third period removed all anxiety about the outcome as the Colts coasted to their fifth straight victory, beating the Washington Redskins, 35 to 10, yesterday before a sellout of 54.403 at the stadium.

The comparatively easy victory kept the Colts atop the Western Division race of the National Football League with a 5-0 record.

Although Lyles's run was the highlight, the entire Colt squad helped make owner George Preston Marshall, of the Redskins, regret his "liar" charge hurled at a Baltimore player earlier this week.

Nutter Happiest Of All

And the man who was the subject of Marshall's abuse was the happiest of them all.

He helped make the Redskins eat Marshall's words, although suffering from a broken rib.

He is Buzz Nutter, Colt offensive center whose joking remark about having to hitchhike home after being released by the Redskins in 1953, caused Marshall to explode at a luncheon here last Monday.

The lanky West Virginian pleaded with the coaches and doctors to play yesterday, after an X-ray Friday night disclosed he had fractured his tenth rib. He had to play because he promised Marshall, "I'll see you on Sunday," and that meant on the playing field.

Reprinted from
The Baltimore Sun

	Colts	Redskins
First downs	21	11
First downs rushing	12	8
First downs passing	8	2
First dn. by penalty	1	1
Yards rushing (net)	186	175
Yards passing (net)	204	16
Total yards (net)	390	191
Forward passes	12-20	4-16
Passes interc'pt'd by	2	1
Yards interceptions returned	14	23
Yards passing	204	46
Yards lost attempting passes	0	30
Punts	5-31.5	6-47
Yards punts ret'ned	3-31	4-12
Yards kickoffs ret'd	3-155	5-156
Yards penalized	3-50	3-28
Fumbles	3	1
Opponents' fumbles recovered	1	1

Washington . 7 0 3 0—10
COLTS ...   7 14 14 0—35

W—Zagers, 4-yard run (Baker placement).
C—Moore, 12-yard run (Myhra placement).
C—Berry, 17-yard pass from Unitas (Myhra placement).
C—Ameche, 4-yard run (Myhra placement).
W—Baker, 31-yard field goal.
C—Lyles 101-yard run (Myhra placement).
C—Berry 48-yard pass from Unitas (Myhra placement).

Line-Ups
REDSKINS
END—Carson, Brito, Anderson, Dee, Walton, Ostrowski. TACKLE — Boll, Weatherall, Lemek, Renfro Miller. GUARD — Stephens, Flucher, Stanfel, Vovtek. CENTER — Schrader, Allen, Brueckman. BACK—LeBaron, Guglielmi, Bukich, Sutton, Watson, James, Nix Walters, Podoley, Zagers, Scudero, Lynch, Bosseler, Olszewski, Baker, Drazenovich, Felton.

COLTS
END—Marchetti, Braase, Berry, Mutscheller, Joyce, DeCarlo. TACKLE—Donovan, Lipscomb, Preas, Parker, Plunkett, Krouse. GUARD—Spinney, Sandusky, Myhra, Pellington, Shinnick, CENTER—Nutter, Szymanski, Sanford, BACK—Unitas, Moore, Dupre, Ameche, Call, Lyles, Taseff, Davis, Nelson, Brown, Rechichar, Horn, Sample, Shaw, Pricer.

Nov. 5

UNITAS DUE TO MISS 3 OR 4 GAMES

Ex - Stanford Gridder To Provide Depth Behind Shaw

By CAMERON C. SNYDER

Gary Kerkorian, the onetime Stanford signal caller, is coming out of retirement once again to give the Colts some insurance and depth in the now-critical quarterback position.

The loss of John Unitas for at least three weeks, and possibly more, reduces the Colt quarterback corps to just one experienced operator, George Shaw.

Colt players talking about Unitas's injury after watching films of the Green Bay game Sunday confirmed press box observations that he was kneed unnecessarily by John Symank of the Packers. The rough treatment accorded Johnny resulted in three fractured ribs and complications followed.

Reprinted from
The Baltimore Sun

CHICAGO TEAM HANDED FIRST SHUTOUT SINCE 1946, BEFORE 48,664

Shaw Completes 9 Straight Passes, Ameche Runs For 142 Yards; Both Touchdowns Are Scored In Second Quarter

By CAMERON C. SNYDER
[Sun Staff Correspondent]

Chicago, Nov. 16—Not satisfied with just beating the Bears, the Colts went all out and rubbed it in, handing the "Monsters of the Midway" their first shutout in 148 games, 17 to 0, before 48,664 disappointed fans at Wrigley Field today.

George Shaw, subbing for the injured John Unitas, parlayed a hot second quarter hand into Baltimore's two touchdowns, and the Colt defense had no trouble holding the margin while limiting the Bears to 161 yards.

The combination of a great defense plus 7 of Shaw's 9 straight completions in a ten-minute span lifted the Colts two games on top the Western Division race of the National Football League.

Rams Tie With Bears

The defeat dropped the Bears, Baltimore's closest competitor until today, into a second place tie with the Los Angeles Rams, next opponent for the Colts, with a 5-3 record with just four games left.

This was the big one for the Bears, the game they had to win, but the Colt defense made the Bruins play their game.

The Colts appeared to have suffered only one serious injury, that to Dick Szymanski who hurt his knee in the first period and did not get back into the game.

(In Baltimore, Dr. Erwin Mayer, team physician, was having x-rays taken of both Szymanski and Ray Berry late last night at Union Memorial Hospital after the team arrived by plane. "I think Berry merely has a bruised shoulder and will be okay," said Dr. Mayer. "We won't know the extent of Szymanski's injury until tomorrow."

Normally a high-scoring team which is willing to trade points with any opponent, the Colts, under the more conservative but just as effective handling of Shaw reverted to ball control today.

Ameche Gains 142 Yards

And in controlling the ball, aided by three interceptions and two fumble recoveries, the Colts did to the Bears what hadn't been done since the fifth game of the 1946 season when the New York Giants blanked the Chicagoans, 14-0.

Sharing offensive hero honors with Shaw were Alan Ameche and the Colt offensive line.

Ameche was more a bull than a horse today. He rumbled through and over the Bear defense for 142 yards on 26 ball carrying assignments.

Statistics

	Bears	Colts
First downs rushing	4	6
First downs passing	3	7
First downs by penalty	1	1
Total first downs	8	14
Yds. gained rushing (net)	107	159
Yds. gained passing (net)	54	126
Total yds. gained (net)	161	285
Forward passes attempted	26	23
Passes completed	8	10
Passes intercepted by	1	3
Yds. intercep. returned by	70	48
Yds. gained passing	72	131
Yds. lost attempted passes	18	5
Punts (number)	8	9
Average distance	46	45
Punts returned by	6	3
Yds. punts re..ned by	18	29
Kickoffs returned by (No.)	4	1
Yds. kickoffs returned by	162	28
Penalties (number)	6	8
Yds. penalized	72	75
Fumbles	2	1
Opp. fumbles recovered	1	2

Colts	0	14	0	3—17
Bears	0	0	0	0—0

C—Berry 7 yard pass from Shaw (Myhra placement)
C—Ameche 4 yard run (Myhra placement)
C—Myhra 12 yard field goal.

Line-Ups

COLTS
END—Berry, Mutscheller, Marchetti, Joyce, Braase, DeCarlo. TACKLE—Parker, Preas, Donovan, Lipscomb, Plunkett, Krouse. GUARD—Spinney, Sandusky, Myhra, Pellington, Shinnick. CENTER—Nutter, Szymanski, Sanford. BACK—Shaw, Taseff, Davis, Nelson, R. Brown, Ameche, Moore, Call, Lyles, Rechichar, Pricer, Sample.

BEARS
END—Hill, Jewett, Williams, Atkins, Carey, McColl, Cooke. TACKLE—Lee, Jones, Leggett, Bishop, Klein. GUARD—Gibron, Kilcullen, Healy, George, Roehnelt. CENTER—Strickland, Hansen, Howley. BACK—E. Brown, Caroline, Anderson, Casares, Fortunato, Zucco, Johnson, Wallace, Sumner, Bratkowski, Blanda, Barnes, Gallimore, Douglas, Morris.

48 GRIDDERS IN PRO DRAFT

Duncan, Of Iowa, Chosen First By Green Bay

Philadelphia, Dec. 1 (AP)—Here are the draft choices made today in the four rounds completed by National Football League teams. Randy Duncan, Iowa quarterback, was the first player to be chosen. He was the choice of the Green Bay Packers.

Colts — Jackie Burkett, Auburn center; Dave Sherer, S.M.U. end; Zeke Smith, Auburn guard.

Green Bay — Randy Duncan, Iowa quarterback; Alex Hawkins, South Carolina back; Boyd Dowler, Colorado back.

Chicago Cardinals — Bill Stacy, Mississippi State back; Jerry Wilson, Auburn end; James Butler, Vanderbilt back; Ken Beck, Texas A & M. tackle.

Philadelphia — J. 'D. Smith, Rice tackle; Wray Carlton, Duke back; Jim Grazione, Villanova quarterback.

Washington—Don Allard, Boston College quarterback; Emil Karas, Dayton tackle; Jim Wood, Oklahoma State end.

San Francisco — Dave Baker, Oklahoma back; Dan James, Ohio State center (first round choice from Pittsburgh); Bob Harrison, Oklahoma center; Ed Dove, Colorado back; Monte Clark, Southern California tackle.

Detroit — Nick Pietrosante, Notre Dame back; Charles Horton, Baylor guard; Mike Rabold, Indiana tackle (second round choice from Pittsburgh); Ron Koes, North Carolina center; Ron Luciano, Syracuse tackle (third round choice from Baltimore); Art Brandiff, V.M.I. back; Bob Grottkau, Oregon guard (fourth round choice from New York).

Chicago Bears — Don Clark, Ohio State back; Rich Petitbon, Tulane back; Pete Johnson, V.M.I. back.

Pittsburgh — All choices traded away.

Los Angeles — Dick Bass, College of Pacific back (first round choice from Philadelphia); Paul Dickson, Baylor tackle; Buddy Humphrey, Baylor quarterback (second round choice from Washington); Don Brown, Houston halfback; Larry Hickman, Baylor back; Tom Franckauser, Purdue end (third round choice from Pittsburgh); Blanche Martin, Michigan State back; John Tracey, Texas A & M. end (fourth round choice from Chicago Bears); Bob Reifsnyder, Navy tackle (fourth round choice from Pittsburgh)

New York — Lee Grosscup, Utah quarterback; Buddy Dial, Rice end; Joe Morrison, Cincinnati halfback.

Cleveland — Rich Kreitling, Illinois end; Dick Shafrath, Ohio State guard; Francis O'Brien, Michigan State tackle; Gary Prahst, Michigan end (fourth round choice from Green Bay); Dave Lloyd, Georgia center.

GIANTS DOWN BROWNS, 13-10

By EDWIN H. BRANDT
[Sun Staff Correspondent]

New York, Dec. 14—Pat Summerall's 49-yard field goal late in the fourth quarter brought the New York Giants a 13-to-10 victory over the Cleveland Browns today and deadlocked the two teams for the Eastern Division championship in Yankee Stadium.

The tremendous kick climaxed a bitter comeback struggle by the Giants which found them trailing, 10-3, with 11 minutes left to go in the game, and until then outplayed.

Teams Play Sunday

The New York triumph forces a playoff between the same two teams here next Sunday at 2.05 P.M. for the right to meet the Baltimore Colts December 28 for the National Football League championship.

Sunday's game will be televised nationally with the New York area blacked.

The final score overshadowed a fine performance by the Browns' Jimmy Brown on this cold, snowy day.

A crowd of 63,192 watched in dismay as Brown broke through the New York line on Cleveland's first scrimmage play for 65 yards and a touchdown, then proceeded to carry the Browns' ground attack most of the rest of the game in crashing through for 148 yards in 26 carries.

Groza Kicks 3-Pointer

The other Cleveland score came on a 22-yard field goal by Lou Groza in the second quarter. Summerall also had a 46-yard field goal, in addition to the game-winning boot, while Frank Gifford's 7-yard pass to End Bob Schnelker accounted for the Giants' only touchdown.

It was a pitchout pass that did most of the damage for the Giants today. New York used it effectively five weeks ago against the Colts, and today completely fooled the Browns with it in the waning minutes of the game.

Cleveland seemed to be in control of the contest from the opening moments until early in the fourth quarter; then, with the ball on the Cleveland 45, following a fumble by Plum, Quarterback Chuck Conerly pitched out to Halfback Frank Gifford, who started out around his right end.

Gifford Hurls Pass

He suddenly skidded to a halt, however, and threw diagonally across to the field to End Kyle Rote, alone on the ten. Don Paul came up quickly and dragged Rote down on the 6. Gifford lost a yard at center, then took an-other pitchout and passed to End Bob Schnelker in the middle of the end zone for the touchdown that tied the score at 10-10, with 4.40 gone in the fourth quarter.

This sudden surge seemed to bring the Giants alive, and the big New York line then proceeded to smother Plum trying to pass and began to do a reasonably good job stopping the line smashes of Jimmy Brown.

Cleveland didn't get a first down in the final ten minutes of the game as the Giants took control.

New York stopped the Browns following the kickoff and marched from its own 30 to the Brown 25, from where Summerall missed a field goal with five minutes left in the game.

Again the Browns were stopped and Dick Deschaine got off a poor kick that traveled 22 yards and went out of bounds on the Cleveland 44.

2 Passes Incomplete

Two passes by Conerly went incomplete, then Conerly passed to Gifford on the 35. Gifford appeared to catch it cleanly and take a step. He was hit hard and the ball fell loose, Cleveland recovering.

But the officials ruled it an incomplete pass, the Giants retaining possession on the Brown 42 with fourth down and 2.07 remaining to be played.

It was here that Summerall stepped into the ball and sent it straight through the goal posts. While Summerall had the wind at his back, it was a tremendous effort and clearly a last-ditch desperation try for the Giants, for a tie would have eliminated them from the title race just as effectively as a loss.

Giants Spill Plum

While Brown returned the ensuing kickoff to his own 45, the Giants were now a raging storm themselves and broke through to spill Plum for a 19-yard loss following a pass completion to Ray Renfro on the Giant 41.

With 25 seconds left, Groza attempted an almost impossible 55-yard field goal against the wind, which fell well short of the goal posts.

Jimmy Brown was a marvel in the losing cause. In his 65-yard touchdown run he caught the defense going the wrong way and simply outsprinted the Giant backfield to the goal line, actually pulling away the last 15 yards.

The tally tied him with Steve Van Buren for the most touchdowns in one season, 18. Most of the rest of the time he spent driving through the toughest part of the Giant line for consistent yardage, and he personally ate up most of the clock in the third quarter, carrying on 11 of 17 Cleveland plays.

Statistics

	Cleveland	New York
First downs	9	12
Rushing yardage	150	64
Passing yardage	140	170
Passes	6-12	15-37
Passes intercepted by	0	0
Punts	6-33	7-43
Fumbles lost	2	0
Yards penalized	55	63

Cleveland	7	3	0	0—10
New York	3	0	0	10—13

Cleveland scoring: touchdown, Brown (65-yd. run); field goal, Groza (22 yards), extra point, Groza; New York, touchdown, Schnelker (pass, 7); field goals, Summerall 2 (46, 49), extra point, Summerall.

GIANTS BEAT BROWNS, 10-0

Take Eastern Crown; To Face Colts For Title

By CAMERON C. SNYDER
[Sun Staff Correspondent]

New York, Dec. 21—"We did it on determination," said Dick Modzelewski, one of the Giants' defensive stalwarts, in the dressing room following New York's playoff victory over the Cleveland Browns.

"We knew we had to rush their passer and we were aroused for the job," explained the former University of Maryland tackle, who was better known as Little Mo.

"Kept Fighting All Way"

Big Mo was and is Ed Modzelewski, a fullback, who saw limited service with the Browns today.

"I never thought we would go so far," laughed Little Mo, "but we have just kept fighting all the way."

Roosevelt Brown, former Morgan State star and the Giants' best offensive lineman, said:

"It was a tough game and another tough one next week, but we'll take them, though," referring to the championship struggle with the Colts next Sunday.

Coach Jim Lee Howell led the victory parade of newspapermen into his dressing room smiling "thanks" to the numerous "congratulations, coach."

Triplett Fight View

He calmly doffed the winter clothes he was wearing on the field and then sank his lank frame into a chair before beginning his post-mortem.

Asked about the fight that resulted in his fullback, Mel Triplett, getting banished from the game in the second quarter, Howell quietly said:

"It takes two to make a fight. I tried to make the officials see my side of it, but they didn't."

"He (Triplett) said some one kicked him while he was down. He got a little riled. I thought he was kicked, too."

Don Colo, Brown tackle, was the object of Triplett's anger, but it appeared that even an official got clouted by the free swinging Mel in the ruckus.

Credits Tom Landry

Howell dished out credit to Tom Landry, his defensive coach, and the defensive unit for ruining the Browns.

"I have never seen a game where two equal teams were playing, where one defense overpowered the other team so completely.

"Landry and the defense deserves the credit. Andy Robustelli is a real money player and Dick Modzelewski played his heart out. Katcavage (Jim) and Huff (Sam) are newcomers, they don't know the meaning of defeat."

He tried to avoid talking about the championship game upcoming with the Colts.

Statistics

	Giants	Browns
First downs rushing	12	2
First downs passing	5	5
Total first downs	17	7
Y'ds gained rushing (net)	211	24
Y'ds gained passing (net)	106	62
Total yards gained	317	86
Y'ds lost att'pted passes	0	52
Passes	18	27
Completions	8	10
Intercepted by	3	1
Y'ds intercept's returned	23	24
Punts	7	8
Average distance	47	38
Punts returned	5	4
Yards punts returned by	6	11
Kickoffs returned	2	3
Penalties	4	2
Yards penalized	35	20
Yards kickoffs returned	2?	72
Fumbles	6	1
Ball lost fumbles	2	1

Cleveland	0	0	0	0—0
New York	3	7	0	0—10

New York scoring: TD, Conerly (18, lateral from Gifford). Field goal, Summerall (26). PAT, Summerall.

Reprinted from
The Baltimore Sun

Reprinted from
The Baltimore Sun

COLTS WIN CHAMPIONSHIP

Entire page reprinted from
The Baltimore Sun

DEFEAT GIANTS, 23-17, AS AMECHE SCORES IN SUDDEN-DEATH PERIOD

Myhra's Field Goal With Nine Seconds To Go In Regulation Game Ties Score, 17-17; Berry Breaks Playoff Record

By CAMERON C. SNYDER
(Sun Staff Correspondent)

New York, Dec. 28—Six years of sweat and frustration bore fruit today as the Colts stormed 80 yards in thirteen plays to win the National Football League championship, 23 to 17, in a sudden-death playoff with the New York Giants at Yankee Stadium.

Propelled by John Unitas's passes and Raymond Berry's catches, the Colts forced the game into the first sudden-death extra period in pro history when Steve Myhra place kicked a 20-yard field goal with nine seconds left in the regulation time.

Placekick Ties Score At 17-17

That placement evened the game at 17-17 and gave the Colts their winning chance, which Alan Ameche cashed on a 1-yard scoring plunge after 8.15 minutes had elapsed in the sudden-death period.

The first team to score in a sudden-death period is the winning team, no matter how the score is achieved.

Statistics

	Giants	COLTS
First downs rushing	3	9
First downs passing	7	17
First downs penalty	0	1
Total first downs	10	27
Yds. gained rushing (net)	88	138
Yds. gained passing (net)	178	322
Total yds. gained	266	460
Yds. lost attempt. passes	22	27
Passes attempted	18	40
Passes completed	12	26
Intercepted by	1	0
Yds. returned by	5	0
No. of punts	6	4
Average distance	48	51
Punts returned by	4	3
Yds. punts returned	14	10
Kick-offs returned	3	3
Penalties	1	4
Yds. penalized	5	32
Fumbles	6	2
Ball lost fumbles	4	2
Yds. kick-offs returned	52	62

Colts	0	14	0	3	6—23
Giants	3	0	7	7	0—17

Giants scoring: Touchdowns—Triplett (1-yard run), Gifford (15-yard pass from Conerly). Extra points—Summerall, 2 (placements). Field goal—Summerall (36-yards).

Colts scoring: Touchdowns—Ameche 2 (2-yard run; 1-yard run); Berry (15-yard pass from Unitas); Extra points—Myhra, 2 (placements); Field goal—Myhra (20 yards).

COLTS

END—Berry, Marchetti, Braase, Mutscheller, Joyce TACKLE—Parker Donovan, Lipscomb, Preas, Krouse GUARD—Spinney, Sandusky, Myhra, Plunkett, Thurston CENTER—Nutter Shinnick, Sanford BACK—Unitas, Shaw, Brown Rechichar, Dupre, Taseff, Nelson, Simpson, Sample, Moore, Davis, DeCarlo, Call, Lyles Ameche, Pellington, Pricer

GIANTS

END—Rote, Katcavage, Livingston Summerall, Schnelker, MacAfee, Robustelli, Svare. TACKLE—Brown, Modzelewski Youso, Grier, Stroud GUARD—Barry, Brackett, Mischak, Guy. CENTER—Wietecha, Huff, BACK—Heinrich Conerly, Kemp, Tunnell, Gifford, Maynard, Crow, Hughes, Lott Triplett, Svoboda, Chandler.

Individual Statistics

GIANTS RUSHING

	Att	Yds	Lg	Td		Att	Yds	Lg	Td
W'bster	12	24	38	0	Gifford	12	60	38	0
Triplett	5	12	8	1	Conerly	2	5	5	0
King	3	13	4	0					

COLTS RUSHING

	Att	Yds	Lg	Td		Att	Yds	Lg	Td
Ameche	14	65	23	2	Dupre	11	30	10	0
Moore	8	23	10	0	Unitas	6	20	15	0

GIANTS PASSING

	Att	Comp	Yds	LP	TD
Conerly	14	10	187	62	1
Heinrich	4	2	13	7	0

COLTS PASSING

	Att	Comp	Yds	LP	TD
Unitas	40	26	349	60	1

GIANTS RECEIVING

	No	Yds	Lg	Td		No	Yds	Lg	Td
Schnelker	2	63	46	0	Gifford	3	15	15	1
Rote	2	76	62	0	Triplett	2	15	9	0
Webster	2	16	9	0	Macafee	1	15	15	0

COLTS RECEIVING

	No	Yds	Lg	Td		No	Yds	Lg	Td
Moore	6	101	60	0	Dupre	2	7	4	0
Berry	12	178	25	1	Ameche	3	17	10	0
M'sch'er	3	46	32	0					

AMECHE SCORES THE TIE-BREAKER—This is a view from the Giants' side, showing Baltimore Colts' fullback Alan Ameche going through a big hole provided by teammates to score the winning touchdown in overtime period at New York's Yankee Stadium Dec. 28. Colts' Lenny Moore gets a good block on Giants' Emlen Tunnell (45) at left. Colt quarterback Johnny Unitas (19) is at right along with Giants' Jim Patton (20).

Pro Football Facts, Figures

New York, Dec 28 (AP) — Financial facts and figures of today's championship playoff game in the National Football League at Yankee Stadium.

Paid attendance — 64,185.

Gross receipts (including radio and television) $698,646.

Taxes and rental — $129,894.56.

Game operating expenses — $36,879.20.

Net receipts — $531,872.24.

Total player pool (70 per cent of the net) $372,310.57.

Each winning share — $4,718.77 (42½ shares).

Each losing share — $3,111.33 (42½ shares)

Pool for sectional second place clubs — $37,231.06.

6-Pointer Nearly Missed By TV

New York, Dec. 28 (AP) — Stirred-up fans attending today's National Football League title game almost cost television fans a chance to see the winning touchdown.

Onlookers pressing for a better view of the crucial overtime action jostled loose a connection of the TV power cable, and TV screens went blank for 2½ minutes before an NBC engineer located the trouble.

Sound was lost for two minutes. At the time of the trouble, the Baltimore Colts were inside New York Giants' 10-yard line and driving for the winning score in the 23-17 game.

"Fortunately, we missed none of the key action," an NBC spokesman said tonight. "There was time out on the field during much of our difficulty and it saved the day for our viewers." He emphasized that the time out was not called to accommodate the TV audience.

Transmission was restored in time to broadcast the winning touchdown.

Giant Coach

NOT ASHAMED OF N.Y. TEAM

Howell Cites Champs As Great Grid Squad

By CAMERON C. SNYDER
[Sun Staff Correspondent]

New York, Dec. 28—"They're a great ball club," said Jim Lee Howell, Giant coach, in the dressing room after his boys lost to the Colts in an unprecedent sudden death playoff.

"I mean the Colts," he explained, "We have a great bunch of boys."

"They (the Colts) didn't win by a fluke, but I am proud of my ball club," continued Howell, relaxing in his dressing room quarters.

Wasn't Disheartened

He wasn't disheartened although a little disappointed by the outcome.

"What can you say about players like mine who were up against people who outmanned and outgunned them.

"While we had to put out all the time to gain an inch, they had guys like that Jim Parker, who just took their stance and without expending too much effort did their jobs," said Howell.

Howell said he thought Unitas's call for a pass on the Giant 7-yard line was a smart play.

Plays Like That Win

"You have to do things like that to win," he avowed, "and Unitas is always doing them."

The situation on the play was this: Colt ball second down coming up on the 7 with Baltimore needing just a field goal to win the sudden death and the title. Unitas passes out to Jim Mutscheller, who is downed on the 1 from where Ameche bangs over for the winning points.

Many felt the chance of an interception was too great when a field goal could win it. Howell wasn't one of those.

Gave Team Spark

The Giant coach admitted the goal line stand by the Giants gave his team the spark it needed to move into the lead.

"It takes little things like that to spark a team. We have been sparked by such efforts before and a lot of times we have come from behind to win.

"It is that spark and desire that makes football such a great game," he sermonized.

The Giant players were disappointed but not downcast. They all felt they had played great ball against a great ball club.

They had given their best and it fell just a little short. Regrets, but no tears.

Sam Huff, great linebacker for the Giants, had only praise for the Colts, particularly Alan Ameche, Colt fullback.

Brown Is Faster

"Jim Brown (Cleveland Brown all-pro fullback) is faster, but Ameche hits quicker into the line. Both are tough boys, particularly Ameche," said Huff.

Andy Robustelli, Giant defensive end, said, "we played a good game against a great ball club. We have nothing to be ashamed of."

Concerning Jim Parker, who opposed Robustelli, Andy said, "He's a great one. They don't make better offensive tackles."

Reprinted from
The Baltimore Sun

Sunlight On Sports

BY JESSE A. LINTHICUM Sports Editor

From Rags To Riches
✰ ✰ ✰
Colts Win The Hard Way
✰ ✰ ✰
A Great Team Effort

THE COLTS offer a real rags-to-riches story. They came through the hard way on the field yesterday, but the big struggle—a losing one—came in the early fifties when the backers of the franchise were forced to bow out.

The Colts were reborn in January, 1953, and football fans, hungry after being without the sport two years, gave the club enthusiastic support. Season tickets were sold without great effort.

Baltimore had it made when Carroll Rosenbloom acquired 52 per cent of the club's stock in 1953. Rosenbloom, his associates, Zanvyl Krieger, Bill Hilgenberg, Tom Mullan and Bruce Livie, saw the franchise grow gradually into a power in the National Football League.

They almost made it last year, a slump at the tailend of the season robbing them of the Western Division championship.
✰ — ✰ — ✰

Greatest Day

YESTERDAY'S victory provided Baltimoreans with their greatest sports thrill. In almost a half century of sports reporting I can't recall anything comparable to the dramatic triumph over the New York Giants.

The Colts missed several scoring opportunities early in the game. With any kind of a break in luck they should have won without the sudden-death period. The Giants held the Colts with less than a yard to go in a great goal-line stand.

Earlier the Colts missed a field-goal attempt. But if the Colts had won in regulation time the fans would have lost a great deal of excitement. With only seconds of play remaining the Colts scored the field goal that tied matters, 17 to 17.
✰ — ✰ — ✰

No Accident

THE SUCCESS of the Colts cannot be regarded as an accident. When Rosenbloom took over control of the club he announced at a press conference that Baltimore would have a team in the title game, or else.

He explained what he meant by else. He said that he would turn the reins over to others if he could not make it.

And the coaches would have to produce.

He formed a solid organization to run the front office, the scouting system and such.

Rosenbloom set five years as the goal. The Colts produced. The Colt president took charge in 1953, and the world football championship came in the sixth season. That was close enough.
✰ — ✰ — ✰

The Best

YOU COULD feel the Colts growing in stature through the years, but there were many faint-hearted fans who would have fired Weeb Ewbank before he was given his big chance to turn out a winner.

Even before the present season started, the Monday morning quarterbacks were after Ewbank's scalp. This was especially true during the exhibition season when the Colts were far from impressive.

Ewbank explained his position, but not to the satisfaction of all the fans.

"I have to experiment with the new players we drafted," Ewbank said. "These games are for training. Don't take them too seriously. We'll try to win but we also will try to give all of the young men in uniform a chance to win jobs."
✰ — ✰ — ✰

Reprinted from
The Baltimore Sun

Chicago Cardinals Trade Matson

RAMS GIVE UP 9 GRIDDERS

Holtzman, Panfil, Hauser, Fuller Leave Coast Team

Chicago, Feb. 28 (AP)—In one of the biggest player trades in National Football League history, the Chicago Cardinals today exchanged Halfback Ollie Matson to the Los Angeles Rams for nine players.

The Rams gave up four first string veterans—defensive tackles Frank Fuller and Art Hauser, offensive tackle Ken Panfil and defensive end Glenn Holtzman. They also yielded three top draft choices—Halfback Don Brown of Houston (their No. 2 choice); Fullback Larry Hickman, Baylor (No. 3) and End John Tracey, Texas A.&M. (No. 4).

To Get Draft Choice

The Cards also will get another player to be selected prior to the 1959 season and also a high 1960 Ram draft choice.

"Our entire coaching staff feels that these additional top-flight players will, without a doubt, make the Cardinals a strong contender this year," said Walter Wolfner, managing director.

"We know we gave up a player who, in my opinion, is the greatest back ever to play in the league."

Was On Olympic Team

Matson was a member of the 1952 United States Olympic team as a middle distance star.

In six Cardinal seasons, Matson carried the ball 761 times for 3,331 yards, caught 130 passes for 2,150 yards, and scored 300 points. His career average in the N.F.L. to date is 4.38 for rushing, 16.5 for passes caught, 10.9 on punt returns and 28.5 for kick-off returns.

Rams' General Manager Pete Rozelle said in Los Angeles that he feels Matson is one of the finest backs in the history of the National Football League.

"Ollie has been alternating as both a full and halfback." Rozelle said. "Ultimately, it would be conceivable that he will be used as a flank end or as a defensive back."

American Grid Loop Organized

Chicago, Aug. 14 (AP)—A second professional football league, the American Football League, was formally organized today.

Lamar Hunt, of Dallas, said the league will begin play in 1960 with teams in Los Angeles, New York, Denver, Dallas, Houston and Minneapolis-St. Paul.

Representatives of the six sites met in Chicago to discuss such matters as player draft, league constitution, by-laws and working agreements.

The group hopes to have draft plans in operation by this fall to provide players for the new loop.

Hunt announced two weeks ago the league would be formed. He said each team probably will play 14 league games and four exhibitions.

Packers

Green Bay, Wis., Sept. 27 (AP)—The Green Bay Packers, frustrated for three periods in scoring bids, capitalized on Max McGee's booming punts for a touchdown and a safety in the final period to defeat the Chicago Bears, 9-6, today in a National Football League opener.

A fumble recovery on the return of a 54-yard punt by McGee set up the touchdown midway through the fourth quarter. Then, with the clock showing just 2:21 left, the veteran end stepped back and booted a 61-yard kick out of bounds on the Chicago two to set up the final two points.

Bears Get 6-0 Lead

The Bears held a 6-0 lead after John Aveni, a rookie from Indiana, kicked the second of two field goals with less than 14 minutes remaining. The Packers then appeared buried in their own end when McGee was forced to punt.

But John Petitbon fumbled after returning the kick nine yards and alert Jim Ringo, an all-pro offensive center, pounced on the ball for the Packers on the Bears' 26. Paul Hornung and Jim Taylor then alternated in carrying the ball, with Taylor skirting left end for the final five yards on the sixth play.

Packers Get Safety

After McGee's tremendous punt with the help of a wind with gusts up to 30 m.p.h., the Packers picked up the safety. Dave Hanner, a stalwart veteran, led a line charge and dumped Chicago's Ed Brown trying to find a receiver from his spot in the end zone.

As the gun sounded, the Packers, who finished with a 1-10-1 record in 1958, rushed to new Coach Vince Lombardi and carried him from the field.

Green Bay got down deep into Chicago territory several times, but was stymied on each occasion until Hornung and Taylor took charge after Ringo's fumble recovery.

Three Hornung Misses

Hornung, usually a sure-footed place-kicker, couldn't hit on three attempts. He was wide to left on boots from the 19 and 14 and had to look helplessly a third time because of a bad pass from center.

Aveni clicked on a 46-yard effort with the brisk wind in the thirteenth minute of the second period. He split the uprights with a 42-yarder on the third play of the fourth quarter after the Bears had reached the Green Bay 34 as the Packers missed two fine chances to intercept passes.

Green Bay's hard-charging line outplayed the Bears, who were seven-point favorites. The Packers held Chicago's running attack to just 2 first downs and 75 yards by rushing. The Packers picked up 176 yards overland, and added 101 by passing. The Bears had 96 in the air.

Statistics

	Bears	Packers
First downs	28	16
Rushing yardage	75	176
Passing yardage		
First downs	10	16
Rushing yardage	75	176
Passing yardage	96	101
Passes	10-23	4-14
Passes intercepted by	1	0
Punts	5-31.8	6-46
Fumbles lost	2	1
Yards penalized	65	51

Green Bay ..... 0 0 0 9—9
Chicago ..... 0 3 0 3—6
Chicago: Field goals; Aveni 2 (46, 42). Green bay; Touchdown, Taylor (5 run), Pat, Hornung. Safety Brown (tackled by Hanner).

N.F.L. Commissioner Bell Dies In Philadelphia At 65

Philadelphia, Oct. 11 (AP)—Commissioner Bert Bell, of the National Football League, died today of a heart attack. He collapsed in the seats of the very stadium in which he started his rise from college player to czar of professional football.

The 65-year-old Bell succumbed while doing the thing he loved best—watching a pro game. He was carried from the University of Pennsylvania's Franklin Field where the Pittsburgh Steelers and Philadelphia Eagles, teams he once owned and coached, were playing an N.F.L. game.

Bell's three children, Bert, Jr., 23; Upton, 21, and Jane, 17, were with their father when he was pronounced dead about 10 minutes after reaching University Hospital. The hospital is a stone's throw from where thousands once cheered him as Penn football captain.

Bell, under whose astute guidance professional football became a major sport instead of a road show, was sitting in end-zone seats

BERT BELL

with some friends when he keeled over.

GRID LEAGUE SET FOR '61

New American Loop Awards Seventh Franchise

New York, Oct. 28 (AP)—The embryo American Football League will begin operations in 1961 even if the long-established National Football League moves into Dallas and Houston, its founder, Lamar Hunt, said today.

Hunt, the multi-millionaire oil man and owner of the Dallas franchise in the newly proposed professional circuit, said he did not expect to get involved in a war with the older circuit but added:

"We won't be run over or stepped on.

Bell Wanted Competition

"Mr. Bert Bell (the late N.F.L. Commissioner) told me a second professional league was good for the National League and the players. He assured me his league was not anxious to run into another player war as it had with the All-America Conference some years ago.

"This threat to expand into Texas territory is not consistent with his thinking. However, as far as I am concerned, such a move would only change our promotional approach. It would not prevent us from going through with our plans."

Seek Commissioner

Hunt's remarks came during a press conference after a meeting of the seven franchise holders in which they explored the addition of an eighth member and proposed candidates for the job of commissioner. There is a strong possibility that Edgar (Rip) Miller, former Notre Dame star

and Navy line coach, will be named commissioner.

The six founding members—New York, Los Angeles, Denver, Minneapolis-St. Paul, Houston and Dallas — officially awarded a seventh franchise to Ralph C. Wilson, Jr., of Detroit, who hopes to place a team in Buffalo. Cincinnati, St. Louis, Philadelphia, Kansas City, Louisville, Jacksonville and New Orleans were named as possibilities for the eighth city.

No Raids Intended

Hunt declared the A.F.L. had no intention of raiding either the N.F.L. or the two professional circuits in Canada, but would compete with them in the college draft and for free agents.

"We will honor all players under contract to other leagues," he said, "even those only under option to clubs in another league. I have talked with the commissioner of the Canadian Football Leagues and we have verbally agreed to honor each other's contracts. He need have no fear on that score."

On the subject of a new commissioner, Hunt said:

'I'm disappointed we are not further along on the selection of a commissioner. We want to make sure we get the right fellow."

Crisler Rejects Job

Fritz Crisler, Athletic Director at Michigan, recently turned down the appointment.

In addition to Hunt, representing Dallas, other representatives at the meeting today were:

New York—Harry Wismer, Nash Dowdle, Donald O'Shaughnessy, Joseph Arcuni.

Los Angeles—Barron Hilton, Gregory Dillon, Frank Leahy.

Minneapolis-St. Paul — H. P. Skoglund, Max Winter.

Denver—Bob Howsam.

Houston—K. S. Adams, Jr., John W. Breen.

Buffalo—Ralph C. Wilson, Jr.

MEREDITH HEADS BIG-NAME DRAFT

Doubt on Twin Cities Clouds AFL's Start

MINNEAPOLIS, Nov. 23 (AP).—A tempest over the pro football future of Minneapolis-St. Paul got the American Football League off on a bewildering start today in its struggle to go into action by 1960.

An 11th-hour attempt to swing the Twin Cities into the National Football League failed, for the time being at least, to dislodge the Minneapolis-St. Paul entry from its membership in the new league.

Armed with a pledge by the cities' principal backers that they will stick with the AFL and field a team next year, league organizers went ahead with plans for a player draft begun last night.

But the possibility that a National League team may be operating in the Twin Cities in 1960 hung uncertainly in the background. The situation was tangled by unanswered questions about stadium commitments, contract obligations and financial backing.

Drafts Big Names

The American League sounded its challenge to the durable and successful NFL by drafting some of the most renowned names in college football in the opening round of its selections.

Undoubtedly, all of them also will be drafted by the NFL next Monday, raising the signal for an inevitable bidding fight to sign them to contracts.

The first player selected by the AFL was Southern Methodist's star quarterback, Don Meredith, picked by Dallas.

Houston drew All-America Halfback Billy Cannon of Louisiana State, and 'Buffalo drafted Quarterback Richie Lucas of Penn State. Quarterback George Izo of Notre Dame was picked off by the New York Titans in a coin flip with Los Angeles and Minneapolis-St. Paul.

Other first-round AFL draft choices were Gerhard Schwedes, Syracuse halfback, by Boston; Center Roger Leclerk of Trinity, by Denver; End Monte Stickles of Notre Dame, by Los Angeles, and Quarterback Dale Hackbart of Wisconsin by Minneapolis-St. Paul.

Overture to NFL Revealed

The Twin Cities hassle developed after Charles Johnson, executive sports editor of the Minneapolis Star and Tribune, disclosed that 10 of the National League's 12 clubs had agreed to accept a request by Minneapolis-St. Paul for membership in the NFL.

Johnson has acted as the negotiator for local football interests.

In revealing results of an NFL membership poll by the Chicago Bears' George Halas, chairman of the league expansion committee, Johnson made it clear that the approaches had been made by Minneapolis-St. Paul and not the NFL.

In Philadelphia, NFL Commissioner Austin Gunsel made the same point. "I suppose we're not going to try to put a team in any city," he said. "If the people come to us, that's up to them. And it's up to us to accept if the conditions are okay."

The NFL meets in January to act on expansion.

Johnson's statement yesterday said one other city, presumably Dallas, would be welcome as a new member to the NFL.

Deny Plan for Pullout

After the tense, six-hour session in which American League owners were advised of the NFL poll results, Dallas Owner Lamar Hunt quoted Minneapolis-St. Paul representatives as saying:

"We have no intention of pulling out of the AFL and we'll definitely field a team in the 1960 season."

Unclear was the position of Max Winter, Minneapolis-St. Paul acting general manager, who left the meeting early. There were some reports of a split in the Twin Cities ownership.

H. P. Skoglund, major investor, represented the Twin Cities in final talks.

Hunt refused to say whether Winter had left the Twin Cities combine.

Also uncertain is the stand of the Metropolitan Stadium Commission in the event it must choose between granting stadium rights to an NFL or AFL team here.

Hunt said that in the absence of a commission to make rulings, the league in its first year would have no territorial draft choices. A commissioner is expected to be named shortly.

A.F.L. DRAFTS 261 MORE

Additional Picks Added To 160 Picked Before

Dallas, Texas, Dec. 2 (AP)—Founder Lamar Hunt disclosed tonight the American Football League has completed its draft by naming 261 more college players.

Each of the eight clubs previously drafted twenty players.

Pro Football Player Draft

Philadelphia, Nov. 30 (AP)—Following are the National Football League draft choices made today:

First Round

Los Angeles, Billy Cannon, Louisiana State halfback; Chicago Cardinals, George Izo, Notre Dame quarterback; Detroit, John Robinson, Louisiana State halfback; Washington, Richie Lucas, Penn State quarterback; Green Bay, Tom Moore, Vanderbilt halfback; Pittsburgh, Jack Spikes, Texas Christian fullback; Chicago Bears, Roger Davis, Syracuse guard; Cleveland, Jim Houston, Ohio State end; Philadelphia, Ron Burton, Northwestern halfback; **BALTIMORE, RON MIX, SOUTHERN CALIFORNIA TACKLE**; San Francisco, Monte Stickles, Notre Dame end; New York, Lew Cordileone, Clemson tackle.

Second Round

Cardinals, Harold Olson, Clemson tackle; Los Angeles, choice traded to Cardinals, Mike McGee, Duke guard; Washington, choice traded to San Francisco, Mike Majac, Missouri guard; Detroit, Warren Rabb, L.S.U. quarterback; Green Bay, Robert Jeter, Iowa halfback; Pittsburgh, choice traded to Cleveland, Larry Stevens, Texas tackle; Cleveland, Prentice Gautt, Oklahoma back; Philadelphia, Max Baugham, Georgia Tech center; Chicago Bears, choice traded to Washington, Sam Horner, V.M.I. back; San Francisco, Carl Kammerer, College of Pacific guard; **BALTIMORE, DON FLOYD, TEXAS CHRISTIAN TACKLE**; New York, choice traded to Colts, Mervin Terrell, Mississippi guard.

Third Round

Los Angeles, Charles Britt, Georgia quarterback; Chicago Cardinals, Hugh McInnis, Mississippi Southern end; Detroit, Bob Scholtz, Notre Dame center; Washington, Andy Stynchula, Penn State tackle; Green Bay, choice traded to Cardinals, Charles Elizey, Mississippi Southern center; Pittsburgh, choice traded to Los Angeles, Pervis Atkins, New Mexico State back; Philadelphia, Curt Merz, Iowa end; Chicago Bears, Don Meredith, S.M.U. back; Cleveland, Ross Fichtner, Purdue back; **BALTIMORE, JAMES WELCH, S.M.U. BACK**; San Francisco, Rod Breedlove, Maryland guard; New York, Jim Leo, Cincinnati end.

Fourth Round

Chicago Cardinals, Willie West, Oregon back; Los Angeles, choice traded to Cardinals, Silas Woods, Marquette end; Detroit, Jim Andreotti, Northwestern center; Washington, choice traded to Philadelphia, Ted Dean, Wichita back; Green Bay, choice traded to Cleveland, John Brewer, Mississippi end; Pittsburgh, choice traded to Detroit, Roger Brown, Maryland State tackle; Chicago Bears, William Martin, Minnesota and San Diego Marines back; Cleveland, Jim Marshall, Ohio State tackle; Philadelphia, Jack Cummings, North Carolina back; San Francisco, Ray Norton, San Jose State back; **BALTIMORE, GERHARD SCHWEDES, SYRACUSE BACK**; New York, choice traded to Washington, Vince Promuto, Holy Cross guard.

Fifth Round

Los Angeles, Charles Janerette, Penn State tackle; Cardinals, Bill Burrell, Illinois center; Detroit, choice trade to Green Bay, Dale Hackbart, Wisconsin back; Washington, Don Stallings, North Carolina tackle; Green Bay, choice traded to Cleveland, Bob Jarus, Purdue back; Pittsburgh, choice traded to Cardinals, George Phelps, Cornell (Iowa) back; Cleveland, choice traded to Pittsburgh, Abner Haynes, North Texas State back; Philadelphia, Don Norton, Iowa end; Bears, Dick Norman, Stanford quarterback; **BALTIMORE, MARVIN LASATER, TEXAS CHRISTIAN BACK**; San Francisco, Lew Rohde, Utah State tackle; New York, choice traded to Cardinals, Ed Mazurek, Xavier (Ohio) tackle.

Sixth Round

Cardinals, Jack Lee, Cincinnati quarterback; Los Angeles, Jerry Stalcup, Wisconsin guard; Detroit, Gail Cogdill, Washington State end; Washington, Dave Hudson, Florida end; Green Bay, Michael Wright, Minnesota tackle; Pittsburgh, traded to Los Angeles, Don Ellersick, Washington State end; Philadelphia, Emmet Wilson, Georgia Tech tackle; Bears, Edward Kovac, Cincinnati end; Cleveland, Robert Khayat, Mississippi guard; San Francisco, Ola Murchison, College of Pacific end; **BALTIMORE, AL BANSAVAGE, SOUTHERN CALIFORNIA GUARD**; New York, George Blair, Mississippi back.

Rams Beaten By 21-Point Burst in 4th

LOS ANGELES, Dec. 12 (AP).— The Baltimore Colts locked up the Western Division title in the National Football League today, but it took a 21-point blast in the final quarter to stomp down the Los Angeles Rams, 45-26.

The Rams played their finest game of a sad season after Coach Sid Gillman announced

STATISTICS

	Colts	Rams
First downs	19	21
Rushing yardage	183	147
Passing yardage	99	289
Passes	13-27	17-37
Passes intercepted by	5	0
Punts	6-42	3-39
Fumbles lost	1	0
Yards penalized	54	58

before the game that he was quitting. The resignation was not unexpected, but the dramatic timing did come as a surprise.

The title-bound Colts, now headed for a December 27 game with the New York Giants in Baltimore for the league championship, could not be contained in a wierd final quarter.

A crowd of 65,528 saw the Rams wind up their season in the cellar, with 10 defeats and two victories. The game was televised nationally.

Rams Lead After Three

Whereas the fans booed the Rams against Green Bay last Sunday, they cheered them today as they went into the final period with a 26-24 lead.

The lead didn't last long.

Quarterback Johnny Unitas hit Jerry Richardson with his third scoring pass to put the Colts in front.

Then Linebacker Dick Szymanski intercepted a Billy Wade pass deep in Ram territory and romped 15 yards for another touchdown.

To wrap up Baltimore's second straight division title, Defensive Back Carl Taseff scooped up a Ram field goal attempt that fell short, bobbled it, and then took off for 99 yards and a final touchdown.

Taseff's run equaled an NFL record for such a play, established in 1951 by ex-Ram Jerry Williams against Green Bay. The runback was a letdown for the Rams' field goal kicker, Lou Michaels.

Unitas Improves Records

Unitas' scoring passes extended his league record for throwing touchdown passes to 37 straight games. He completed 13 out of 27 for 99 yards and three touchdowns, bringing his record for scoring passes in one season to 32. It was far from his best day, but the Colt rushing attack gained 183 yards. This, plus five interceptions, spelled doom for Los Angeles.

Fullback Alan Ameche went out of the game early with injuries and was replaced by Billy Pricer, who gained 63 yards, a figure matched by Sommer.

```
BALTIMORE    7 10  7 21—45
LOS ANGELES  7  6 10  0—26
```

Baltimore: TD. Sommer (53, run), Berry 2 (7 and 11 passes from Unitas), Richardson (9, pass from Unitas), Szymanski (15, interception return of Wade pass), Taseff (99, return of field goal kick attempt). PAT, Myhra 6. FG, Myhra (47).

Los Angeles: TD. Marconi (1, run), Arnett (27, run). PAT, Michaels 2. FG, Michaels 4 (15, 19, 40, 27).

Jim Brown Tops Rushers Again

Philadelphia, Dec. 13 (AP)—Jimmy Brown, of Cleveland, won his third straight National Football League ground-gaining title today and set a league record for rushing attempts. He has been in the league only three years.

The 228-pound fullback carried the ball 33 times against Philadelphia making his total for the season 290. Ed Price, of the New York Giants, set the old season record of 271 in 1951.

Brown scored twice and gained 152 yards in Cleveland's 28-21 victory. This gave him a season ground-gaining total of 1,329 yards. He did better last year when he rushed 1,527 yards on 257 carries.

Final Standings

Western Conference

	W.	L.	T.	Pct.	For	Agst.
COLTS	9	3	0	.750	374	251
Chicago Bears	8	4	0	.667	252	196
San Francisco	7	5	0	.583	255	237
Green Bay	7	5	0	.583	248	246
Detroit	3	8	1	.273	203	275
Los Angeles	2	10	0	.167	242	315

Eastern Conference

	W.	L.	T.	Pct.	For	Agst.
New York	10	2	0	.833	284	170
Philadelphia	7	5	0	.583	268	278
Cleveland	7	5	0	.583	270	214
Pittsburgh	6	5	1	.545	257	216
Washington	3	9	0	.250	185	350
Chicago Cards	2	10	0	.167	234	324

Playoff Facts And Figures

Financial facts and figures of yesterday's championship playoff game in the National Football League.

Paid attendance—57,545.

Gross receipts (including radio and television)—$666,281.

Taxes and rentals—$72,470.21.

Game operating expenses—$38,067.63.

Net receipts—$555,743.16.

Total players pool (70 per cent of net)—$389,020.21 (X).

Winning players pool — $210,070.91 (44 5-6 shares).

Losing players pool—$140,047.80 (45 shares).

Each winning player's share—$4,674.44.

Each losing player's share—$3,083.27.

Pool for sectional second place clubs—$38,902.02.

(X)—League record.

Reprinted from
The Baltimore Sun

COLTS WHIP GIANTS, 31-16; KEEP TITLE; 4TH PERIOD RALLY BREAKS GAME OPEN

3 INTERCEPTIONS HELP IN 24-POINT SPLURGE TO ERASE 9-7 DEFICIT

Marchetti And Sample Spark Defense Which Scores Or Sets Up Late Tallies; Unitas, Moore Are Baltimore Offensive Stars

By CAMERON C. SNYDER

Led by an inspired defense, the Colts defeated the New York Giants, 31 to 16, yesterday in the National Football League title rematch at the Stadium, removing all doubts about their superiority left over from last year's sudden-death thriller.

A fourth-quarter 24-point blaze, ignited by Defensemen Gino Marchetti and Johnny Sample, burned out any Giant hopes that this year it would be different.

The Colts' pyrotechnics proved that last year's winner is still the champ, but even more so.

If the Colt defense started the fire, John Unitas and Lenny Moore led the conflagration on offense much to the delight of 57,545 happy pyromaniacs.

During a ten-minute span, the Colts scored three touchdowns and a field goal to obliterate a 9-to-7 lead the New Yorkers carried into the final period.

Defense Accounts For 17

And to make the final-period rally even more impressive was the fact that seventeen of those 24 Colt points were scored or set up by the defense which caused Frank Gifford and Charley Conerly to throw three interceptions.

Marchetti led the rush all afternoon on Conerly, the aging Giant quarterback, but received great help from all other members of the Six Tons of Fun, particularly Ray Krouse.

While the Colt line caused the Giant passers to hurry their aerials, Sample was the man to take advantage of the awry throws, intercepting two, one for a 42-yard touchdown, the other a 34-yard return which brought on Steve Myhra's 25-yard field goal.

Nelson Starts Flame

It was Andy Nelson's interception, however, which started the flame in the fourth period, after Unitas had put the Colts ahead, 14 to 9, on a 4-yard roll-out run.

The turning point, so both coaches say, came in the third period when the Giants were leading, 9 to 7, by virtue of three Pat Summerall field goals.

Moving from their own 44, the Giants penetrated to the Colt 27, but a fourth-down plunge by Alex Webster for a needed foot was stopped by the Colts, and that was the Giants' last bid for a touchdown until the game was beyond recall in the final minute.

Krouse was on the bottom of the pile on Webster's plunge, but he received help from nearly the entire Colt defense, which ganged up the middle.

Recalls Last Year

This defensive action recalled the situation in last year's championship game when the Giants, leading 17 to 14, elected to punt on fourth down, needing a foot for a first down.

The Colts took that punt and marched from their 14 to a tie-clinching field goal and then a touchdown in the first sudden-death overtime game ever played for a title, which caused New York fans to holler tainted victory.

By this time Jim Lee Howell, Giant coach, must feel any situation is rigged against him from the start when he plays the Colts.

Unitas passed for two touchdowns besides fooling the Giants on his 4-yard scoring run.

His first scoring pass went to Moore, who sped 60 yards into paydirt to open the scoring early in the first quarter.

Colt Statistics And Scoring

	Colts	Giants
First downs rushing	3	4
First downs passing	10	11
First downs penalties	0	1
Total first downs	18	16
Net yards rushing	74	118
Net yards passing	207	205
Totals net yards	281	323
Passes complete	18-29	17-38
Passes intercepted by	3	0
Yards interception returned by	93	0
Number of rushing plays	25	30
Average gain per rushing play	2.9	3.9
Total offensive plays	61	73
Average gain per offensive play	4.6	4.4
Punts and average	6-37	6-48
Yard of punt returns	4-54	6-5
Yardage of kickoffs returned	4-64	5-135
Yards lost penalties	4-20	1-23
Fumbles	1	1
Ball lost on fumbles	0	0

New York   3   3   7   16
Baltimore   7   0   0   24   31

New York—T.D. Schnelker (32, pass from Conerly). P.A.T. Summerall. F G Summerall 3 (23, 37, 22).
Baltimore—T.D. Moore (60 pass from Unitas), Unitas (4, run), Richardson (12, pass from Unitas), Sample (42 pass interception). P.A.T. Myhra 4 F.G. Myhra (25).

Individual Statistics

Colts

INDIVIDUAL RECEIVING

Name	No.	Yds.	T.D.	Long Gain
Mutscheller	5	40	0	15
Moore	3	126	1	59
Berry	5	68	0	28
Ameche	1	12	0	12
Pricer	2	9	0	9
Sommer	1	-1	0	0
Richardson	1	12	1	12
Totals	18	264	2	59

COLTS RUSHING

	Nt	Yds.	Av.	L.G.
Unitas	2	6	3	4
Moore	4	7	1.7	3
Ameche	9	31	3.4	6
Sommer	6	15	2.5	5
Pricer	4	14	3.5	4
Totals	25	73	6	22

COLTS PASSING

	At.	C.	Int.	Yds.	Td.
Unitas	29	18	0	264	2

Giants

Name	No.	Yds.	T.D.	Long Gain
Rote	2	41	0	22
Schnelker	9	175	0	48
King	4	17	0	11
Gifford	1	19	0	19
Triplett	2	-2	0	0
Totals	17	250	1	48

GIANTS RUSHING

	Nt	Yds.	Av.	L.G.
Gifford	9	50	5.5	23
Webster	8	25	3.1	9
Triplett	5	37	7.4	28
King	3	6	2	4
Totals	30	118	18	64

GIANTS PASSING

	At.	C.	Int.	Yds.	Td.
Conerly	35	16	2	232	1
Gifford	2	1	1	18	0
King	1	0	0	0	0
Totals	38	17	3	250	1

New Young NFL Boss Just Breathes Football

LOS ANGELES, Jan. 26 (AP)—Alvin Ray (Pete) Rozelle has more than one good reason to remember the birth of his daughter.

Ann Marie Rozelle came into the world Sept. 28, 1958—at halftime of the Los Angeles Rams' league opener with Cleveland.

It was extremely convenient for Rozelle, a father for the first time, because he could hustle back to the Coliseum for the second half.

"We were ahead when she was born," Rozelle recalled later. "But I wasn't able to pass out cigars for a double victory. By the time I got to the game, we had wound up with a 30-27 loss.

That incident seems to sum up Rozelle, at 33 the new commissioner of the National Football League.

The tall, slim young man with the Ivy League manner eats, sleeps and breathes football.

The quiet-mannered Rozelle claims he works 13 months a year. And for the general manager of the colorful but controversial Los Angeles Rams, it sometimes seemed that wasn't enough.

His pretty wife, Jane, has recalled she once tried to get his mind off football. She took him to an art museum across the street from the huge Coliseum, home of the Rams.

"I bought a modernistic print of a shoe," she told an interviewer. "Pete took one look at the print and said, Now why did you buy that? It'll make me think of Lou Groza.'"

Pete never played football as a youngster but despite his lack of experience on the playing field, he had the temperament to handle 250-pound professional football players.

As general manager, the young executive heard players' grievances, collaborated with scouts, arranged television shows, handled the payroll, worked on the player draft, helped select the coach and — unpleasantly — sometimes fired the coach.

Pete was reared in Compton, Calif., where he played high school basketball and tennis. One day he saw a schoolmate pitch a no-hitter. Rozelle decided to get his chum on the all-league prep baseball selections. He called every newspaper in Los Angeles and his friend was named to the second string. The friend: Duke Snider, now of the Los Angeles Dodgers.

How does he feel about pro football?

"It's the most fascinating thing in the world," he says.

AFL Votes to Adopt 2-Point Conversion

DALLAS, Jan. 29 (AP).—The American Football League will use the 2-point conversion rule of the colleges this fall.

The league, which starts operations next season, voted 6-1 to use the rule that allows two points for passing or running the ball across from the 2-yard line.

N.F.L. ADDS DALLAS TEAM

Minneapolis-St. Paul Voted In For 1961 Season

By CAMERON C. SNYDER
[Sun Staff Correspondent]

Miami Beach, Fla., Jan. 28—The National Football League, feeling growing pains, added Dallas for the 1960 season and Minneapolis-St. Paul in 1961 today.

The vote for expansion was 11 to 0 with the Chicago Cards abstaining. This was a definite switch on the part of George Preston Marshall, owner of the Washington Redskins, the most avid non-expansionist here before today.

On Colt Schedule

Dallas will be a member of the Western Division in the standings, but will play all the other teams in the 13-team league.

To the Colts it means that one of their games will be played in Dallas since the inter-city rivalry with the Redskins will continue with Baltimore the host city in 1960.

Also, three players will be taken from each team in 1961 to bolster the Minneapolis squad.

Giving up three players in each of the years won't hurt the Colts' chances as much as the plan for the drafting of new players in the 1960 draft meeting.

Minneapolis will get the first choice in all 20 rounds of that draft and Dallas, with a year's experience, will get the second round.

With a minimum of good players around the draft could hurt the Colts, who are growing old in spots.

Others Encouraged

Miami and St. Louis franchise seekers got a word of encouragement, too, when it was decided that if conditions were practical, two more teams would be added within the next three years to raise the two divisions to eight members each.

Marshall said he wound up in an unusual spot.

"They were all for expansion without conditions," he laughed.

"I fought for the conditions and when they were passed, I found some of the members had slipped, so I had to talk in favor of expansion. It brought out the laughs."

$600,000 Payment

The big conditions imposed on new members was a total payment of $600,000 over a two-year period.

This was broken down to a $175,000 immediate payment by Dallas, which had already paid in $25,000 franchise retainer.

The other $400,000 will be paid over the next two years.

Minneapolis doesn't have to put up the $175,000 until next year.

Actually the league constitution calls for a payment of $50,000 for a franchise. The other $550,000 is in payment for veteran players to be assigned to the new member.

3-Year Condition

A three-year condition was imposed upon any new franchise, giving the league first option to buy at the same price the franchise as sold during that span.

Of less importance was the approval of an old amendment which continued the commissioner's control over management contracts and stock ownership.

The three veteran Colts will be picked from the 1959 roster for the Dallas team and from the 1960 roster for Minneapolis. The formula for selecting the three players from each team hasn't been devised as yet.

Another Marshall condition cut the new franchises from voting rights until the annual meeting following their admission.

To pacify the New York Giants, who wanted Baltimore in the Eastern Division, the Eastern Division will be able to select either one of the two franchises it wants following the 1960 season.

In the morning meeting today, an amendment was passed raising the minimum guarantee for league games from $20,000 to $30,000.

Reprinted from
The Baltimore Sun

Jan. 30

Oakland Given 8th Berth In American Grid League

DALLAS. Tex. (AP) — The American Football League filled its eighth franchise with Oakland, Calif., Saturday and looked toward its first season and a battle for the entertainment dollar with the long-established National Football League in four cities.

In what was obviously a great switch, the league picked Oakland to wind up its first annual meeting that struggled through five days.

Atlanta had fought Oakland for the last remaining spot but finally the California city came through mostly because of Barron Hilton, owner of the Los Angeles franchise.

Oakland, it was revealed, lead on the first ballot, but the vote switched until at one time Atlanta was reportedly ahead 5-2. Last night there was a caucus, as Hilton, who had gone home several days before, returned to speak for Oakland. He said he wanted that city because it would provide a natural rivalry for his Los Angeles club.

Close Vote

The club owners and commissioner Joe Foss would not reveal the vote on the four ballots that followed the first, but Lamar Hunt, Dallas owner and president of the league, said it was close. Foss merely announced that Oakland had been picked unanimously. A unanimous vote was necessary.

Oakland has Kezar Stadium and Candlestick Park in San Francisco, just across the bay, available, but Foss said the league had asked the California city to obtain a stadium in Oakland if possible. There are two that may be available, Foss said, but he was not certain that Oakland could get either for the first year.

Foss said the Oakland City council had decided to put the question of building a stadium on the ballot in June.

Discuss No-Raiding Policy

Rozelle, Foss Think Two Leagues Can Live Together Harmoniously

LOS ANGELES, Feb. 8 (AP) The commissioners of the two rival professional football leagues met for four hours Saturday and it appears that a "no-raiding" agreement has been reached.

National Football League Commissioner Pete Rozelle told a news conference today he had a meeting with Joe Foss, commissioner of the new American Football League at St. Louis airport.

"We agreed there should be no tampering with players in the two leagues," Rozelle told a news conference.

Asked if the discussion centered about a no-raiding agreement, Rozelle said:

"That's what it amounts to.

"Foss said his policy as commissioner would be to foster a policy in the AFL of no tampering with National League players—a policy I told him we would respect."

Then, Rozelle added:

"I was very impressed with Foss' sincerity and his whole outlook on how his new league should function. We talked about double contract signings.

"Foss told me he has not had an opportunity to investigate the double signings, but that he would look into it."

Brief mention was made of LSU backfield star Billy Cannon, who had signed contracts with both the Los Angeles Rams of the National League, and the Houston Oilers of the new conference, he said.

Rozelle said he interpreted "no tampering" to mean there would be no encouragement offered to players in another league to play out their options.

Rozelle said the meeting with Foss was mutually arranged by telephone. He said Foss told him he plans to be in Los Angeles next month and they agreed they would meet again if possible.

"The important thing," said Rozelle, "is that we get together on the basis that Bert Bell established with the Canadian League."

Rozelle said there was no talk of expansion in the NFL which some quarters have claimed was a move intended to kill off the new league before it started.

"Our talk was very friendly," said Rozelle. "The question of NFL expansion just never came up."

Rozelle, the 33-year-old compromise choice as the new commissioner, returned to Los Angeles where he plans to spend a month winding up his affairs as general manager of the Rams.

$10,625,000 TV Deal For New Football League

NEW YORK, June 9 (AP) The American Football League today closed an $10,625,000 five-year deal with the American Broadcasting Co., for the television rights to its games.

Under the terms of the contract, announced jointly today by Tom Moore, vice-president in charge of programming for ABC-TV, and commissioner Joe Foss of the league (AFL), the new pro league will collect $125,000 for each of 17 dates during the year.

This amounts to $2,125,000 a year. The AFL will divide the money equally among the eight clubs. Deducting agency fees and other expenses, each club will start the season with a $225,000 TV cushion.

The league starts its first season on Sept. 11 and closes with its championship contest on Dec. 31, a Saturday. There will be 15 Sunday afternoon dates, Thanksgiving Day, and the championship game.

The league is composed of the New York Titans, Buffalo Bills, Boston Patriots and Houston Oilers in the Eastern section, and the Oakland Raiders, Los Angeles Chargers, Dallas Texans and Denver Broncos in the Western Division.

Three months ago the ABC network won a two-year contract for the TV rights of the NCAA's college football program. ABC paid an estimated 6½-million-dollars in outbidding the National Broadcasting Co., which had been telecasting the college schedule for years.

In addition, ABC made a multi-million-dollar deal for the Friday night television fights, another long standing program at NBC. ABC will take over the Friday night show in October, shifting them to Saturday.

The pro football contract actually calls for the telecasting of 32 games this year. On the 15 Sundays one game will be telecast in the West and another in the East.

Moore said ABC has signed two sponsors (General Cigar Co., and Sinclair Refining Co.) for the football telecasts.

NFL Approves Move Of Cards to St. Louis

LOS ANGELES, March 13 (AP)—The National Football League tonight approved the transfer of the Chicago Cardinals to St. Louis for the 1960 season.

The transfer, which was emphatically denied just yesterday by Managing Director Walter Wolfner of the Cardinals, is subject to two conditions: The Cardinals must work out a satisfactory stadium lease at Busch Stadium, and television arrangements.

Commissioner Pete Rozelle said the league does not anticipate that either will be a problem.

The league agreed to pay the Cardinals $500,000 to move to St. Louis to relieve the club of the expense of the shift. Part of this is for the club's lease with Soldier Field.

Rozelle admitted that the rival Chicago Bears agreed to assume a large portion of the $500,000, realizing the now-open television territory will produce added revenue.

The Cardinals were a charter member of the NFL when it was organized in 1920. The club is a year older than the now more successful Bears.

Just yesterday Wolfner declared he was confident "no move would be made this year and I don't contemplate moving any time."

He then added: "It would cost the Cardinals too much money to move, and I don't think it is necessary to move."

Tonight Wolfner said that certain conditions which were requested of the league did not appear to have a chance of gaining approval yesterday.

He declared that the league unexpectedly agreed to meet these requests. "What they are is confidential," Wolfner added.

Mr. and Mrs. Wolfner still control the majority stock in the club. Yesterday the league approved Joseph Grieedieck, St. Louis brewer, as a minority owner.

Grieedieck and his brother Alvin have publicly campaigned to get the Cardinal franchise. Their brewery is one of the main television sponsors in the league.

Griesedieck said he and his associates had guaranteed the Cardinals 25,000 season ticket sales, adding a survey currently under way indicated St. Louis would support professional football. He pointed out the Missouri city was the largest town in the country that did not have a pro club.

Busch Stadium, home of the St. Louis Cardinal baseball team, can be augmented to handle about 32,000 for football. A giant project is under way in St. Louis for a new combined baseball-football stadium which will seat 55,000. It may be ready by 1963.

Sept. 10

Tripucka's Long Pass Beats Pats

BOSTON (AP) — Denver launched the American Football League on an upset note, beating Boston 13-10 Friday night on a sensational 79 yard punt return by Gene Mingo.

The tightrope, hula-hipped gallop just inside the chalk stripe in the third period decided the AFL inaugural though it took the unexpectedly tough Denver defense to preserve it.

The Broncos, doormats of the exhibition schedule when they lost all five starts, came alive with the quarterbacking of Frank Tripucka, the ball carrying and receiving of Al Carmichael and Mingo and a rushing wall which hurt Boston's vaunted passing game.

Carmichael scored on another picture play on the opening maneuver of the second period—a 59 yard flat pass from Tripucka. The 21,597 spectators were brought to their feet as Carmichael eluded two defenders about five yards beyond the line of scrimmage, twisted away from a third and cut back to the left sideline.

Picks Up Blockers

Picking up a cordon of blockers, Carmichael was on his way. The only pursuer having a chance to catch the former Southern California and Green Bay Packer ace was erased by Ken Adamson's block at the 30.

Boston scored on a 35-yard field goal by Gino Cappelletti in the first period and a 10-yard Tommy Greene to Jim Colclough pass near the end of the third quarter. A 46-yard return of an intercepted pass by Chuck Shonta set up the score.

Denver   0 7 6 0—13
Boston   3 0 7 0—10

Bos fg Cappelletti 35; Den Carmichael 59: pass from Tripucka (Mingo kick); Den Mingo 79 punt return (kick failed)

Bos Colclough 10 pass from Greene (Cappelletti kick).

	Denver	Boston
First Downs	15	13
Rushing Yardage	142	70
Passing Yardage	190	149
Passes	10-15	13-27
Passes Intercepted By	2	1
Punts	40.0	40.5
Fumbles Lost	1	1
Yards Penalized	55	15

Court Frees Cannon From Contract

JUDGE RULES PACT WITH CLUB INVALID

Cannon Now Is Free to Play With Oilers in New Loop —Flowers' Trial Starts

LOS ANGELES, June 20 (AP)—Billy Cannon, the all-America halfback from Louisiana State University, today won a court victory over the Los Angeles Rams of the National Football League that will enable him to fulfill a $110,000 contract with the Houston Oilers of the American Football League.

Federal Judge William J. Lindberg ruled the Ram contracts signed by Cannon were not valid and gave the A. F. L. its initial court triumph in the first of several test to be decided in its player war with the long-established N. F. L. He also criticized the N. F. L. commissioner, Pete Rozelle, who signed Cannon for the Rams.

Cannon was the most sought-after football player in the country last year. The Rams signed him first, but Cannon later signed with the Oilers' owner, K. S. (Bud) Adams Jr.

The key ruling was on an injunction suit filed by the Rams to prevent Cannon from playing with anyone else.

Ram President Shocked

The Rams' president, Dan Reeves, said he was shocked. He defended Rozelle, who was the Ram general manager when Cannon was signed, as "the most honest man in the world."

Judge Lindberg criticized Rozelle's handling of negotiations. He said it was hard to resolve the issues in the case because of a "shroud of secrecy" over Rozelle's operations. He called Cannon "exceptionally naive . . . a provincial lad untutored and unwise in the ways of the business world." He said Rozelle rushed him into signing on last Nov. 30, within forty-eight hours after first talking to him on the telephone.

The court did not dwell on the contracts Cannon signed with Adams, in Baton Rouge, La., on or about Dec. 22. Nor was there any comment from the bench on the fact that both the Adams' and Ram contracts were signed prior to Cannon's final collegiate game on Jan. 1, in the Sugar Bowl.

Cannon signed three Ram contracts—for the 1960, 1961 and 1962 seasons.

Wide World Photo
WINS COURT VICTORY: Billy Cannon, All-America Louisiana State halfback.

The court disposed first of the 1961-62 contracts. The judge ruled they were invalid because neither was signed nor filed with the N. F. L. Commissioner, a violation of the N. F. L. constitution, the judge said. The 1960 contract was signed and dated Dec. 1 by Austin Gunsel, the then acting commissioner.

Judge Lindberg said that Cannon did not have the benefit of advice of anyone other than Rozelle in their forty-five-minute signing session in Rozelle's hotel in Philadelphia.

Cannon did not endorse or cash the $10,000 bonus check nor the $500 expense check he received from Rozelle. The judge indicated he felt the reason Cannon did not cash either was because he knew it would impair his Sugar Bowl eligibility and that he (Cannon) felt the contract would not become effective until after the game.

Cannon testified in the trial last week that he did accept a $10,000 bonus from Adams, but in the final finding this was not accepted as evidence.

The Ram attorney said they would decide later whether to appeal. Cannon, who said he planned to return to Baton Rouge tonight or tomorrow, smiled for one of the rare times when general manager Elroy Hirsch of the Rams stepped over and shook hands after the verdict.

"Well, we wanted you anyhow," said Hirsch amiably.

Autopsy Shows Glenn Died of Broken Neck

HOUSTON, Tex., Oct. 10 (AP)—Howard Glenn, 24, New York Titan football player who died Sunday after an American Football League game, suffered a broken neck, an autopsy disclosed today.

Dr. Joseph Jachimczyk, Harris County medical examiner, officially listed the death as accidental caused by a broken neck. He said examinations showed no signs of brain injury or heart trouble.

Glenn, a native of Vancouver, B. C. and a graduate of Linfield College, was taken to a hospital in a coma after coming out of the game in the second half. He died shortly after.

Steelers Top Dallas, 35-28, on Late Rally

Long Pass to Tom Tracy Ends Hopes Of Successful Debut for Cowboys

By JACK SELL
Post-Gazette Sports Writer

DALLAS, Sept. 24—Coach Buddy Parker seems to be right in rating his present Pittsburgh Steeler offensive unit as the best in his four seasons at Rooney U.

Here tonight before an estimated 30,000 fans scattered around in the giant Cotton Bowl the attack clicked for five touchdowns but not until the final three minutes of play did they pass a determined bunch of Dallas Cowboys and notch a come from behind 35-28 victory in the first NFL game in history for the Texas team.

Big Homecoming

Those old buddies from the Detroit Lions, Bobby Layne and Tom (The Bomb) Tracy hooked up on the winning score, a sensational 65 yard pass, run play which climaxed great individual efforts by the pair of veterans all evening.

It was a fine homecoming for Layne, a college star here at Texas University who was starting his 13th season in pro football. He completed 16 of 25 passes for 288 yards, had one intercepted. He went far past Sammy Baugh's lifetime record of 22,063 yards, tops in the NFL prior to last night. Bob now has 22,351.

Shaw Passes for Four Scores

Giants Smash Cards

ST. LOUIS, Oct. 2 (AP)—Quarterback George Shaw fired four touchdown passes, good for 51, 6, 17 and 10 yards today as the New York Giants smashed St. Louis 35-14 in the Card's National Football League home opener before 26,089.

The 27-year-old veteran of six NFL campaigns took over from the ailing Charlie Conerly in the second quarter with the Eastern Division defending champions trailing 7-0. He quickly turned the tide.

Shaw pitched two touchdown passes to Joe Morrison in the last three and one-half minutes of the second quarter to stake the Giants to a lead they never relinquished. The one-time Baltimore Colt quarterback connected with Kyle Rote for 17 yards and a TD in the third quarter. He hit Rote for 10 and the Giants' final score in the fourth. Shaw completed 15 of 22 passes for 238 yards.

In between came a bull-like charge of 33 yards up the middle by Mel Triplett to give the Giants a 28-14 bulge.

The Cards, who transferred here last winter after 40 years in Chicago, took a 7-0 lead on John Roach's 26-yard scoring pass to John David Crow following a fumble recovery with the game 2:37 old.

The Cards also converted a fumble recovery into their second touchdown, King Hill plunging over from about six inches out in the fourth quarter.

The Giants' vaunted defense stiffened after the Cards' opening charge. A field goal try by Bobby Conrad was wide from the 29 after St. Louis stalled on New York's 22.

Lindon Crow stopped another Card drive early in the second, intercepting a pass by Crow on the Giants' 9.

Shaw then took command, directing the Giants' 80 yards in six plays for the tying touchdown. Moments later Dick Lynch stole the ball from the Cards' Crow on the St. Louis 29.

Two pass interference calls against the Cards' Bill Stacy helped the Giants move to the six where Shaw and Morrison collaborated for a 14-7 lead.

	STATISTICS	
Giants		Cardinals
18	First Downs	11
137	Rushing Yardage	107
256	Passing Yardage	??
19-33	Passes	3-27
3	Passes Intercepted	1
5-38	Punts	6-48
4	Fumbles Lost	2
65	Yards Penalized	24

| New York | 0 14 7 14—35 |
| St. Louis | 7 0 0 7—14 |

CARDS—Crow, 26 pass from Roach (Conrad, kick).
NY—Morrison, 51 pass from Shaw (Summerall, kick).
NY—Morrison, 6 pass from Shaw (Summerall, kick).
NY—Rote, 17 pass from Shaw (Summerall, kick).
CARDS—Hill, 1 run (Conrad, kick).
NY—Triplett, 33 run (Summerall, kick).
NY—Rote, 10 pass from Shaw (Summerall, kick).

Nov. 27

DIABETIC DEATH: Ralph Anderson, above, an end on the Los Angeles Chargers professional football team was found dead Saturday in his girlfriend's home. It was presumed he died of a diabetic attack.

Reprinted from
The Hartford Courant

LOSERS GET 6 YARDS NET BY RUSHING

Charley Conerly Directs Two Scoring Drives For New York

Cleveland, Nov. 6 (AP)—New York held the Cleveland Browns vaunted rushing attack to a net gain of 6 yards today as the Giants won, 17 to 13, for their sixth straight conquest of Cleveland.

Veteran Chuck Conerly, the 39-year-old Giant quarterback, came back to the football wars after a two-game absence to pilot the New Yorkers to the conquest.

The loss shoved the Browns out of a top-place tie and into third place in the National Football League's Eastern Conference.

Veteran Chuck Conerly, the 39-year-old Giant quarterback, came back to the football wars after a two-game absence to pilot the New Yorkers to the conquest.

The loss shoved the Browns out of a top-place tie and into third place in the National Football League's Eastern Conference.

Brown, Mitchell Stymied

Jim Brown, the league's leading ground-gainer, was held to 29 yards in eleven tries, and fleet-footed Bobby Mitchell gained only 14 in nine as the Giant line controlled play all the way.

Quarterback Milt Plum was thrown for 35 yards in losses, and although he completed 13 of 25 passes, they were good for a net of only 89 yards.

Mel Triplett gained 137 in 24 tries, and Frank Gifford got 71 in thirteen for the Giants.

It was a fumbling, stumbling game all the way and a multitude of passes were dropped as the game was staged in cold, snowy weather with a heavy wind blowing off Lake Erie. Despite the weather, a crowd of 82,672—largest ever to see the Browns' game here—witnessed the contest.

Nov. 22

LINEMAN IN DEMAND

AFL Drafts 40 Collegians, Will Select 8 More Today

By the Associated Press

American Football League teams have drafted 40 outstanding college stars and will announce the names of an additional eight selections today in their move to get a jump on the rival National Football League.

The early draft was conducted by telephone and will leave each of the eight teams with 24 choices to be made at a meeting in Dallas in mid-December.

One surprise in the early selections was the concentration on linemen. Six of the eight teams took linemen as their first choices.

Drafted in the first round were Ken Rice, Auburn tackle, by Buffalo; Tom Brown, Minnesota guard, by New York; Tommy Mason, Tulane halfback, by Boston; Bob Gaiters, New Mexico State halfback, by Denver; Joe Rutgens, Illinois tackle, by Oakland; E. J. Holub, Texas center, by Dallas; Earl Faison, Indiana end, by Los Angeles, and Mike Ditka, Pittsburgh end, by Houston.

Commissioner Joe Foss said no players could be signed to contracts before completing their college eligibility, including bowl games.

The draft selections:

BUFFALO.—Ken Rice, tackle, Auburn; Billy Shaw, tackle, Georgia Tech; Art Baker, fullback, Syracuse; Tom Gilburg, tackle, Syracuse, obtained in trade with New York for Sid Youngelman, tackle; Stewart Barber, tackle, Penn State; Norman Snead, quarterback, Wake Forest.

NEW YORK.—Tom Brown, guard, Minnesota; Herb Adderley, halfback, Michigan State; third draft choice. Tom Gilburg, tackle, Syracuse, traded to Buffalo; fourth draft choice, Arnold Davis, end, Baylor, traded to Denver; Tom Matte, quarterback, Ohio State.

BOSTON.—Tommy Mason, halfback, Tulane; Rip Hawkins, center, North Carolina; Danny Larose, end, Missouri; Mike Zeno, guard, Virginia Tech; Frank Tarkenton, quarterback, Georgia.

DENVER.—Bob Gaiters, halfback, New Mexico State; Jerry Hill, halfback, Wyoming; Charles Strange, center, Louisiana State. (Arnold Davis, end, Baylor, obtained from New York in trade for Joe Paglie); Roland McDole, tackle, Nebraska; Charles Cowan, end, New Mexico Highlands.

OAKLAND.—Joe Rutgens, tackle, Illinois; George Fleming, halfback, Washington; Myron Pottios, guard, Notre Dame; Elbert Kimbrough, end, Northwestern; Dick Norman, quarterback, Stanford.

DALLAS.—E. J. Holub, center, Texas Tech; Robert Lilly, tackle, Texas Christian; Jim Tyrer, tackle, Ohio State; Claude (Tee) Morrman, end, Duke; Jerry Mays, tackle, Southern Methodist.

LOS ANGELES.—Earl Faison, end, Indiana; Keith Lincoln, halfback, Washington State; Marlin McKeever, end, Southern California; James Johnson, halfback, UCLA; Bill Kilmer, halfback-quarterback, UCLA.

HOUSTON.—Mike Ditka, end, Pittsburgh; Tom Goode, center, Mississippi State; Walter Suggs, tackle, Mississippi State; Bobby Walden, halfback, Georgia; Monte Lee, guard, Texas.

BALTIMORE, 49ERS AND LIONS TIED

Touchdown Pass Record Of Unitas Ends In 48th Game

By CAMERON C. SNYDER
[Sun Staff Correspondent]

Los Angeles, Dec. 11—While there is life there is hope, but the Colts gave little evidence of being alive as they dropped a 10-3 decision to the Rams before 75,-461 Coliseum fans this afternoon.

Only the most optimistic can see a way for the twice National Football League champions to retain their title.

This would call for the resurrection of a Colt attack in the final game against the 49ers next Sunday in San Francisco, and the collapse of the Green Bay Packers here Saturday with the Rams.

A Full Game Behind

The Colts are now a full game behind the Packers (7-4) and tied for second with the Detroit Lions and the 49ers in the Western division race. All three have 6-5 records.

It is easier to foresee a collapse of the Packers, than the breathing of life into a Colt attack, that failed to score a touchdown for the first time since 1956.

Injuries to key offensive personnel, particularly end Raymond Berry, has sounded the death knell for Baltimore's hopes of an unprecedent third straight N.F.L. title.

Unitas Record Ends

These injuries will not miraculously improve this week.

Besides practically ending the Colt reign as grid champions, the Rams also stopped John Unitas's consecutive game record of throwing at least one touchdown at 47.

That is the Rams and Unitas cooperated in ending the string as John had another bad day on the passing line without constant use of his safety valve, Berry.

However, Unitas by completing 17 of 38 tosses for 182 yards broke a season record for the most yards gained passing, set by Sammy Baugh, Washington Redskin great, in 1947.

The Statistics

	Rams	COLTS
Total first downs	9	19
First downs rushing	2	5
First downs passing	7	11
First downs by penalty	0	3
Total yards gained (net)	248	272
Yards gained rushing (net)	113	91
Yards gained passing (net)	135	181
Passes attempted	23	38
Passes completed	12	17
Yards lost attempting to pass	29	1
Passes intercepted by	1	2
Yards interceptions returned	0	2
Number of punts	6	8
Average distance	48	42
Punts returned	4	2
Yards punts returned	9	1
Kickoffs returned	0	3
Yards kickoffs returned	0	45
Penalties	2	2
Yards penalized	10	10
Fumbles	0	5
Fumbles lost	0	3
No. of rushing plays	21	35
Average gain per rush	5.38	2.60
Total offensive plays (includes plays attempting to pass)	56	83
Average gain per play	4.43	3.28

COLTS				
	3	0	0	0—3
Los Angeles	0	0	7	3—10

C—Fg. Myhra, 9.
LA—Wade, 66 run (Villanueva kick).
LA—Fg. Villanueva, 32.
Attendance—75,461.

STARR HITS DOWLER ON 91-YARD PASS PLAY FOR LEAD TOUCHDOWN

Title Is First For Green Bay In 16 Years, Setting Up Title Game With Philadelphia; 53,445 See Game In Los Angeles

Los Angeles, Dec. 17 (AP)—The Green Bay Packers sailed into their first National Football League division title in sixteen years today, winging to a 35-to-21 victory over the Los Angeles Rams.

Performing before a crowd of 53,445 in Memorial Coliseum, plus a nation-wide television audience, the Packers' quarterback Bart Starr and right halfback Boyd Dowler connected with a spectacular 91-yard pass in the second quarter.

It was the go-ahead score for the long-starving Packers and the first of three explosive touchdowns by Green Bay in the second period.

The victory gave Green Bay the clear title to the Western Division, erasing any possible playoff with the San Francisco 49ers, Detroit Lions or the defending champion Baltimore Colts.

To Face Philadelphia

Green Bay now goes into a playoff December 26 with the Eastern champions, the Philadelphia Eagles, in Philadelphia.

A jubilant squad of Packers carried their coach, Vince Lombardi, halfway across the field after the final gun.

Hornung, who missed two field goal tries from 32 and 41 yards, a rare misfortune for him, added to his N.F.L. record of scoring the most points in a season. He added 11 to bring his total to 176.

Statistics

	Packers	Rams
First downs	12	24
Rushing yardage	58	143
Passing yardage	241	279
Passes	9-11	22-33
Passes intercepted by	3	0
Punts	5-47	4-30
Fumbles lost	0	1
Yards penalized	58	40

Green Bay	7	21	0	7	35
Los Angeles	7	0	0	14	21

LA—Wilson, 40, pass from Wade (Villanueva kick).
GB—McGee, 57, pass from Starr (Hornung kick).
GB—Dowler, 91, pass from Starr (Hornung kick).
GB—Winslow punt recovered in end zone (Hornung kick).
GB—McGee, 40, pass for Hornung (Hornung kick).
LA—Arnett, 1, pass from Wade (Richter kick).
GB—Hornung, 1, run (Hornung kick).
LA—Dale, 8, pass from Wade (Richter kick).
Attendance 53,445.

National Football League player draft:

FIRST ROUND

Minnesota, Tommy Mason, Tulane back; Washington (choice acquired from Dallas, Norman Snead Wake Forest quarterback, and then its regular choice, Joe Rutgens, Illinois tackle; Los Angeles, Marlin McKeever, Southern California linebacker; Chicago, Mike Ditka, Pitt end; San Francisco (choice from Pittsburgh) Jim Johnson, UCLA back; Baltimore, Tom Matte, Ohio State quarterback; St. Louis, Ken Rice, Auburn tackle; San Francisco, Bernie Casey, Bowling Green back; Cleveland (choice from Detroit) Bob Crespino, Mississippi end; San Francisco (choice from Baltimore, which had choice from New York) by Kilmer, UCLA back; Green Bay, Herb Adderly, Michigan State back; Dallas (choice from Cleveland) Bob Killy, Texas Christian tackle; Philadelphia, Art Baker, Syracuse back.

SECOND ROUND

Minnesota, Ross Hawkins, North Carolina back; Dallas, E. J. Holub, Texas Tech center; New York (choice from Washington), Bob Gaithers, New Mexico State back; Los Angeles, Elbert Kimbrough, Northwestern end; Pittsburgh, Myron Pottios, Notre Dame linebacker; Chicago, Bill Brown, Illinois back; Baltimore, Tom Gilburg, Syracuse tackle; St. Louis, Fred Abranas, Michigan State end; Detroit, Dan Larose, Missouri end; San Francisco, Ron Lakes, Wichita center; New York, Bruce Tarbox, Syracuse guard; Green Bay, Ron Kostelnik, Cincinnati tackle; Cleveland, Ed Nutting, Georgia Tech tackle; Philadelphia, Charles Strange, LSU center.

THIRD ROUND

Minnesota, Francis Tarkenton, Georgia quarterback; Dallas, Steve Barber, Penn State guard; Washington, Bill Wilson, Auburn tackle; Los Angeles, Harold Beaty, Oklahoma State guard; Chicago, Claude Gibson, North Carolina State back; Detroit (choice acquired from Pittsburgh), Dick Mills, Pittsburgh tackle; Baltimore, Jerry Hill, Wyoming back; Philadelphia (choice acquired from St. Louis), Jim Wright, Memphis State quarterback; San Francisco, Bill Cooper, Muskingum back; Detroit, Houston Antwine, Southern Illinois guard; Washington (choice acquired from New York), Jim Cunningham, Pitt back; Green Bay, Phil Nugent, Tulane back; Los Angeles (choice acquired from Cleveland), Ron Miller, Wisconsin quarterback; Philadelphia, Don Oakes, VPI tackle.

After Peak Seasons

Van Brocklin, Buck Shaw Retire

PHILADELPHIA, Dec. 26 (AP) — Coach Lawrence T. (Buck) Shaw and quarterback Norman Van Brocklin, retired today, officially, after bringing the Philadelphia Eagles a National League title.

"This is it for sure. I'm all through after today," Shaw said moments after the Eagles defeated Green Bay 17-13 in the NFL title game.

Shaw announced after last season that the would coach only one more year, regardless of what his team did.

Van Brocklin announced his retirement plans at the same time.

"What a way to go out," the quarterback kept repeating. "I can't think of a better way. Man, there just isn't any better way. This is the climax."

Van Brocklin refused to discuss his football future, which reportedly has him taking over Shaw's spot.

"I don't have the slightest idea of what I'm going to do," he said. "I'm just going to have me a quiet night and think about the future later. I'll talk about my plans later in the year (1961)."

This was the first NFL title for Shaw, who has been coach 39 years, 12 with pro teams. He coached the San Francisco 49ers for nine years and then had a stint at the Air Force Academy. The 61-year-old Californian took over the Eagles in 1958. He had a 2-9-1 record that year. His record with the 49ers was 71-39-4.

Last year Shaw guided the Birds to a 7-5 mark and a tie for second place with Cleveland in the Eastern Conference. He finished with a 10-2 mark this year, for the Eagles' first conference title since 1949, when they defeated Los Angeles for the NFL title.

Van Brocklin, 34, came into the NFL with the Los Angeles Rams in 1949 after starring for the University of Oregon. He played with them until differences of opinion with coach Sid Gillman caused him to "retire" after the 1957 season. He "unretired" soon after and came to Philadelphia with Shaw.

During the 1960 season, he completed 153 of 284 passes for 2471 yards and 24 touchdowns, and was directly responsible for the Eagles coming from behind to win seven games this year.

In today's title game, he completed nine of 20 passes for 204 yards. He passed to Tommy McDonald for the first touchdown, set up the clinching score with another and also helped get the Eagles into position for Bobby Waltson's 15-yard field goal.

He was awarded a sports car after being chosen the game's most valuable player.

PACKERS' FAILINGS COSTLY

Leaders of Eagles Bow Out in Glory

By LEWIS F. ATCHISON
Star Staff Writer

PHILADELPHIA, Dec. 27.— The Green Bay Packers ignored "the book" once and lost two races with the clock yesterday in their game with the Philadelphia Eagles, and these failings cost them the National Football League championship.

Performing before a sellout crowd of 67,325 at Franklin Field, the Eagles almost threw the game away with costly fumbles at the start. Then, propelled by the magnificent passing of old Norm Van Brocklin and aided by Green Bay's misplaced confidence, they twice came from behind to win, 17-13, and take their first NFL title since 1949.

For the Packers it was a day of missed oportunities. Twice they had the ball within the shadow of the Eagles' goalposts in the first period, but all they got was three points as Philadelphia's tough defense fought 'em off.

Even so, if they hadn't "thrown the book away" and gone for a touchdown the first time, instead of settling for three points, they might have won, the way the game unfolded.

The pro league's "book" says don't go away empty-handed when you get within scoring distance. Settle for 3 points if you must, but get something. The Packers were in range when Bill Quinlan grabbed an Eagle fumble on the 15-yard line on the first play of the game. But all they got were some lumps, for the Eagles took the ball away from them on the 6.

With three seconds left in the first half, the Packers tried a 13-yard field goal and the usually reliable Paul Hornung missed. This goal and an earlier 3-pointer would have meant the difference between victory and defeat, or between a $5,116 payoff per man and $3,105.

Seconds away from the end of the game the Packers once again were within range of the Philadelphia goalposts— on the 22-yard line.

This time they had to go for broke. With the Eagles leading by 4 points, a field goal wouldn't help. And now Hornung, the league's record-breaking scoring leader and the Packers' great clutch player, who had booted them to an early 6-0 lead, was on the bench with an injured shoulder.

Bednarik Halts Taylor

In this situation Bart Starr flipped a short pass to Green Bay's great runner, Jim Taylor. The big fullback threatened to get away, but finally he was smashed down on the 9-yard line by Chuck Bednarik, the ancient Eagle who was the defensive star of the game.

"They made the big play and we didn't," Coach Vince Lombardi of the Packers said, summing up the events of an afternoon that was bright and cheerful for everyone but the Packers and their supporters. He could have said field goals beat his team—the one it didn't try and the one it missed.

It was a game that had everything, despite the comparatively low score. It produced some good runs, excellent passing, vicious tackling and a minor riot between some exuberant citizens, who wanted to uproot the goalposts, and a small army of police.

It got pretty rough before word was passed to let the fans have the kindling.

Great Finish for Shaw

The championship was a triumphant finish to Buck Shaw's 39-year-old coaching career, but the 61-year-old Eagle coach admitted he didn't relax until the game-ending gun was fired.

"That was the turning point for me," he told reporters. "That's when I began to enjoy it."

STATISTICS

	Green Bay	Phila.
First downs	22	13
Rushing yardage	223	99
Passing yardage	178	197
Passes	21-35	9-20
Passes intercepted by	1	0
Punts	5-42.2	6-39.5
Fumbles lost	1	2
Yards penalized	27	0

INDIVIDUAL STATISTICS

RUSHING

Philadelphia	Atts.	Yds.	Lg.	Td.
Barnes	13	42	7	0
Dean	13	54	8	1
Van Brocklin	2	3	4	0
Totals	28	99	8	1
Green Bay	**Atts.**	**Yds.**	**Lg.**	**Td.**
Taylor	24	105	16	0
Hornung	11	61	16	0
Starr	1	0	0	0
McGee	1	35	35	0
Moore	5	22	12	0
Totals	42	223	35	0

FORWARD PASSING

Philadelphia	Atts.	Comp.	Yds.	Td.	Int.
Van Brocklin	20	9	204	1	1
Totals	20	9	204	1	1
Green Bay	**Atts.**	**Comp.**	**Yds.**	**Td.**	**Int.**
Starr	34	21	178	1	0
Hornung	1	0	0	0	0
Totals	35	21	178	1	0

PASS RECEIVING

Philadelphia	No.	Yds.	Lg.	Td.
Walston	3	38	25	0
McDonald	3	90	35	1
Retzlaff	1	41	41	0
Dean	1	22	22	0
Barnes	1	13	13	0
Totals	9	204	41	1
Green Bay	**No.**	**Yds.**	**Lg.**	**Td.**
Knafelc	6	76	20	0
Hornung	4	14	8	0
Taylor	6	46	15	0
Dowler	1	14	14	0
McGee	2	19	12	1
Moore	1	9	5	0
Totals	21	178	20	1

Taylor Gains 105

The Packers had plenty of ground speed, with Taylor pacing their offense with 105 yards, but the Eagles slowed them down when they got too close. And Starr was only 19 yards short of matching Van Brocklin's passing yardage. However, the old pro got his 197 yards on nine completions, while Starr completed 21 out of 35 to earn 178. Starr, one-time Alabama standout, couldn't match Van Brocklin when it came to throwing—and connecting—for distance.

CLICKS ON THIRD DOWN

Blanda Clutch Passes Give Oilers AFL Title

HOUSTON, Jan. 2 (AP).—The Houston Oilers are the first champions of the American Football League, thanks to the third-down passes of George Blanda and an out-of-character pass defense.

Blanda threw three touchdown passes and the Oiler pass defense was amazing as Houston took the championship yesterday with a 24-16 victory over the Los Angeles Chargers before a crowd of 32,183.

While Blanda's effectiveness on third down triggered the Oiler offense, the Houston defense was handing Jack Kemp, the league's No. 1 passer, his first touchdown shutout in five games.

All of Blanda's touchdowns came on third down, as did 11 of his 16 completions. The completions were good for 301 yards and all but 48 yards came on third-down plays.

Kemp Completes 21

Kemp had thrown six touchdowns in two regular season games against the Oilers, who won the Eastern Division title despite the leakiest pass defense in the league. Kemp's 21 completions yesterday were good for 171 yards but this was well below the 276.7-yard average Houston had allowed in 14 regular season games.

"It was our best defensive game of the season," said Blanda, who spent 10 years with the Chicago Bears before "retiring" two years ago.

Game officials thought play was too rough in spots. Second and fourth-quarter fist fights caused three players—Hogan Wharton and Julian Spence of Houston and Maury Schleicher of Los Angeles—to be ordered from the game.

Houston Takes Lead

Blanda did not get the Oiler offense under way until the second quarter, by which time Los Angeles had grabbed a 6-0 lead on field goals of 38 and 22 yards by Ben Agajanian.

Drives of 83 and 50 yards put Houston in front, 10-6, with Blanda passing 17 yards to Dave Smith for a touchdown and then kicking an 18-yard field goal. With nine seconds left in the half, a 19-yard punt by Houston's Charlie Milstead went out of bounds on the Oiler 31. Agajanian returned for a 27-yard kick that cut the Oiler halftime edge to 10-9.

Billy Cannon, the Heisman Trophy winner from Louisiana State, returned the second-half kickoff 42 yards to the Houston 45. It took the Oilers 10 players to move in front, 17-9, with Blanda passing to Bill Groman for the final 7 yards.

Kemp then teamed with Paul Lowe, the league's No. 2 rusher, for Los Angeles' only touchdown. Lowe carried over from the two, where Dave Kocourek had been knocked out of bounds after taking a 33-yard pass from Kemp.

This cut the Houston lead to one point a third time and it was not until early in the fourth quarter that Blanda threw his third strike of the day. With third down and 10 from his own 12, Blanda dropped back to his goal line before passing to Cannon at the 35. Cannon completed the 88-yard scoring play by out-racing Jim Sears, the Charger defensive back.

Cannon, whose three pass receptions totaled 128 yards, was voted the game's outstanding player. He received eight votes to seven each for Lowe and Kemp.

Lowe, whose 30-yard run to the 18 set up Agajanian's second field goal, gained 165 yards in 21 carries. Cannon led Houston with 50 in 18.

Oilers Total 401

Houston's 100 yards rushing gave the Oilers a total offense of 401 yards. A net of 162 yards rushing gave Los Angeles a 333 total.

Oiler players and coaches will receive 60 per cent of the game's net proceeds. The Chargers will split 40 per cent, but the facts and figures will not be released by the league office until later this week.

LOS ANGELES	6	3	7	0—16
HOUSTON	0	10	7	7—24

Los Angeles—FG, Agajanian 38.
Los Angeles—FG, Agajanian 27.
Houston—Smith 17, pass from Blanda (Blanda kick).
Houston—FG, Blanda 18.
Los Angeles—FG, Agajanian 22.
Houston—Groman 7, pass from Blanda (Blanda kick).
Los Angeles—Lowe 2, run (Agajanian kick).
Houston—Cannon 88, pass from Blanda (Blanda kick).

STATISTICS

	L. Angeles	Houston
First downs	21	17
Rushing yardage	162	100
Passing yardage	171	301
Passes	21-41	16-32
Passes intercepted by	0	2
Punts	4-41	5-34
Fumbles lost	0	0
Yards penalized	15	54

Canadian Football Czar Given Broader Powers

WINNIPEG, Feb. 10 (AP).—The Canadian Football League, prompted by the Sam Etcheverry case, has extended the powers of Commissioner Sydney Halter to enable him to interpret the validity of players' contracts.

Halter announced yesterday at the conclusion of the first day's sessions of the three-day meeting that the league's constitution had been amended by the unanimous vote of delegates to widen his powers in contract matters.

"I now am in the position to take the same type of action that Pete Rozelle (National Football League commissioner) took in the Etcheverry case," he said.

Touched Off Hassle

Etcheverry, former star quarterback of the Montreal Alouettes, touched off a controversy between the Canadians and the NFL when he signed with the St. Louis Cardinals after refusing to accept a trade to the Hamilton Tiger-Cats.

He claimed that Montreal's action in trading him without his consent breached his contract. He had a letter of agreement signed by the club, apart from his regular contract, which in part stipulated he could not be traded without his consent.

Rozelle, after seeking legal advice, upheld Etcheverry's claim and approved his signing with St. Louis.

Hit Rozelle's Action

Halter maintained that the player's contract reverted to Montreal when Etcheverry refused to accept the trade. The commissioner said Rozelle's action constituted a violation of the verbal agreement between the two leagues to honor each other's contract.

"Before today's amendment my powers were limited to determining the priority of agreement in the case where a player signed two contracts.

"This was the basis of the verbal agreement I negotiated with Bert Bell—that we would get together and decide the priority of contract in such a dispute and act accordingly."

Rozelle became commissioner of the NFL after Bell, the former commissioner, died.

The agreement between the two leagues was that if a player signed contracts with teams in both leagues, the commissioners would determine which was signed first and rule that it was the one in force.

"I now am free to judge any question of validity of contract that a player or his lawyer might raise," Halter said.

MODELL, SCHAEFER WILL KEEP COACH

Paul Brown Will Still Give Gridiron Orders Despite Change in Owners

CLEVELAND, March 22 (AP).—Controlling ownership of the Cleveland Browns of the National Football League went to two New York men today in a $4,000,000 deal. Coach Paul Brown received a new eight-year contract and a free hand to operate the team in the same winning way he has since 1946.

One of the New Yorkers, Arthur B. Modell, a 36-year-old advertising and television executive, will be the club's new board chairman and chief executive officer.

His chief associate in the purchase is R. J. Schaefer, a Brewery company president. He will be the Browns' vice-president.

MARSHALL'S GRID CONFLICT CLEARED UP

Udall Satisfied Owner Will Try To Draft Negro Players

Washington, Aug 14 (P)—A racial policy conflict apparently was cleared up today to let the Washington Redskins professional football team play in the newly completed, Government-owned Municipal Stadium.

The conflict has been between Redskins' club owner George Preston Marshall and Secretary of the Interior Stewart L. Udall.

Udall had threatened to bar the Redskins from the stadium unless it began hiring Negro players—something it has never done.

Letter To Rozelle

Marshall, in a letter to National Football League Commissioner Pete Rozelle in New York, released by Rozelle, said the Washington club did not discriminate against hiring Negro players and hoped to sign a number of Negro stars at the next player draft session.

Although this draft won't occur until late or after the coming pro gridiron season, Udall in statement said he is proceeding on the assumption that Marshall's assertion of nondiscrimination and intent to hire Negro players was made in good faith and will be honored.

Offer In Good Faith

"We are willing to proceed on the assumption that this offer has been made in good faith," Udall said. "If the Washington Redskin management follows through in implementing this new policy this should resolve the issue."

The practical situation is that Udall, who controls the new stadium, is going to let the Redskins play there this season—in belief Marshall will add Negro players to his squad at his earliest opportunity however, that opportunity may not come before the coming season is over.

Commends Rozelle

Udall's statement added:

"I should like to commend Commissioner Rozelle for his constructive action in this matter. He has performed a distinct service to American sports in his attempt to mediate the dispute which has existed between this department and the management of the Washington Redskins.

"The Kennedy Administration is determined that every American should have a full and equal opportunity to utilize his or her talents in the classroom, in industry, on the playing field and in all areas of our national life.

"If a new spirit is foreshadowed by Mr. Marshall's letter, which indicates clearly that individual merit will be the sole criterion in the future selection of talent, we of course welcome this development."

Marshall's letter to Rozelle said the Redskins hoped to sign such stars as Ernie Davis, of Syracuse, and Larry Ferguson, of Iowa, at the next selection meeting.

N.F.L. Gains Right To Pool TV Pacts

By The Associated Press

NEWPORT, R. I., Sept. 30—A bill permitting National Football League teams to pool their television rights in a single contract was signed into law today by President Kennedy.

Professional baseball, basketball and hockey leagues also will have the same privileges.

The new law marks a substantial victory for the National Football League over the Federal court, which last July threw out a pool contract negotiated with the Columbia Broadcasting System as a violation of the antitrust laws.

Instead of taking on the court, the league made an "end run" into Congress and had packaged contracts exempted from the antitrust laws. The original contract was for the 1962 season. Presumably, it will now be reinstated.

Under it, each N. F. L. team would get $325,000 for its television rights. Under the present individually negotiated contracts, teams in the smaller television markets get far less. For example, the Eastern Conference champion, Green Bay, is getting only $120,000 from television this season.

To protect college football, Congress wrote into the law a provision preventing the telecasting of professional football games on Friday night or Saturday within a seventy-five-mile radius of a college game.

The ban would be in force between the second Friday in September and the second Saturday in December.

VIKINGS TOP BEARS, 37-13

Rookie Tarkenton Stars In Team's Upset Debut

Minneapolis-St. Paul, Sept. 17 (P) — Fran Tarkenton, a rookie quarterback from Georgia, passed for four touchdowns and ran for another as Minnesota's Vikings walloped the Chicago Bears 37-13 in their National Football League debut today.

After the Vikings failed to capitalize on numerous first half scoring chances, Tarkenton got them rolling in the second 30 minutes—completing 8 of 11 passes in the third quarter alone, two for touchdowns. Then he rolled around right end for three yards and another touchdown to start the fourth period.

In all, Tarkenton fired 17 bullseyes in 23 attempts and moved the formerly sluggish Vikings' offense with abandon.

He was joined in the offensive show by newcomer Jerry Reichow and veteran Hugh McElhenny, both of whom turned in sparkling catches.

Bear Mistakes

A crowd of 32,236 watched the Vikings' NFL start.

The game also marked the NFL debut of Minnesota coach Norm Van Brocklin, who retired last year after 12 years as a pro quarterback. It was Van Brocklin's first coaching victory after losing five exhibition games.

Cowboys Top Steelers, 27-24, On Last-Second Field Goal

Dallas, Texas, Sept. 17 (P) — Allen Green, the rookie from Mississippi, kicked a field goal from the 27-yard line with one second left today as the Dallas Cowboys beat the Pittsburgh Steelers 27 to 24 to win their first National Football League victory.

Dallas scored twice in the final 56 seconds to get the triumph to the delight of a crowd of 23,500 in the Cotton Bowl.

Eddie LeBaron passed Dallas on two magnificent drives to gain the decision. First he engineered a 75-yard surge climaxed with a 17-yard pass to Dick Bielski for a touchdown. He completed five passes for all the yardage in this surge.

The next drive was from the Dallas 38 with LeBaron passing the Cowboys down to the Pittsburgh 22. Here, with just one second left on the clock, Green

The Statistics

	Dallas	Pittsb'gh
First downs	20	15
Rushing yardage	96	105
Passing yardage	327	252
Passes	19-39	16-26
Passes intercepted by	3	2
Punts	5-41.0	4-44.0
Fumbles lost	0	1
Yards penalized	46	20

Pittsburgh ... 0 14 0 10—24
Dallas .... 7 3 7 10—27

Dallas—Clarke 44 pass from Meredith (Green kick).
Pittsburgh—Johnson 1 run (Layne kick).
Pittsburgh—Dial 44 pass from Layne (Layne kick).
Dallas—FG Green 15.
Dallas—Howton 45 pass from LeBaron (Green kick).
Pittsburgh—FG Michaels 12.
Pittsburgh—Sample 39 pass interception (Layne kick).
Dallas—Bielski 17 pass from LeBaron (Green kick).
Dallas—FG Green 17.
Attendance—23,500.

booted the winning field goal.

Dallas had gotten the ball on a pass interception by Jerry Tubbs, the demon Dallas linebacker.

Oct. 9

HORNUNG SETS CLUB RECORD

Packer Halfback Scores Total Of 33 Points

Reprinted from
The Baltimore Sun

The Statistics Of Colt Game

	Packers	Colts
First downs rushing	13	10
First downs passing	9	
First downs penalties	3	
Total first downs	25	18
Yards gained rushing	211	153
Yards gained passing	157	147
Total yards gained	368	300
Passing: Attempted	29	29
Completed	13	12
Had intercepted	1	6
Yards intercepted		
passes returned	58	11
Yards lost on passing	11	11
Punts: Number by	3	2
Average distance	44	57
Number returned	3	
Yards punts returned	88	0
Kickoffs Number	5	6
Yards returned	42	127
Fumbles Number	0	2
Ball lost	10	2
Penalties Number		
against	10	8
Yards lost	69	73

Colts . . . . . 0 7 0 0—7
Green Bay . 7 10 14 14—45
G Bay—Hornung 54 run (Hornung kick).
Colts—Moore 1 run (Myhra kick).
G Bay F G Hornung 38.
G Bay—Hornung 1 plunge (Hornung kick).
G Bay—Hornung 8 pass from Starr (Hornung kick).
G Bay—Hornung 10 run (Hornung kick).
G Bay—Wood 72 punt return (Hornung kick).
G Bay—Taylor 3 run (Hornung kick).
Attendance—38,669.

Mike Holovak Takes Over Patriot Post

BOSTON, Oct. 11 (AP).—The Boston Patriots of the American Football League have fired Head Coach Lou Saban, former Western Illinois University coach, and hired Mike Holovak, ex-Boston College mentor, to replace him.

The Patriots' management lowered the boom suddenly last night by majority vote of the board of directors.

"I didn't know about it until they phoned me," Saban said. "They had to make a change. It just hit me and that's it."

Saban, 39, joined the Patriots last year, touted by the Boston club's general manager, Ed McKeever, as "the finest young coach I've seen in 15 years." His contract had one year to run.

Played With Bears

Holovak, an All-American fullback at Boston College and assistant Patriots coach, played professionally with the Chicago Bears.

OILERS BEAT BILLS, 28-16

Blanda Throws 4 Touchdown Passes In Victory

Buffalo, N.Y., Oct. 29 (AP)—Ageless George Blanda threw four touchdown passes enroute to a record-shattering passing yardage mark as his surging Houston Oilers battered Buffalo, 28 to 16, today in an American Football League game.

The 33-year-old former Chicago Bears quarterback connected on 18 of 32 passing attempts for 464 yards, seven better than his substitute, Jackie Lee, accounted for two weeks ago against Boston. Lee did not play today.

Oilers Leave Cellar

Blanda arched scoring heaves of 80, 68, 56 and 32 yards, finding flanker Charlie Hennigan and end Bill Groman for a pair each.

The triumph lifted the Oilers out of the Eastern Division cellar with a record of three victories, three losses and a tie. Buffalo took over the bottom run with a 3-5 record.

The first time he touched the ball, Blanda whipped a 56-yarder to Hennigan and then booted the first of his four conversions.

He connected with Groman for 32 yards and a score in the second period and then lofted the 80-yarder to Hennigan midway in the third. He closed his sensational performance with a 68-yard pitch to Groman.

Joe Hergert's 38-yard field goal in the second quarter opened Buffalo's scoring and punter Billy Atkins put the Bills in contention in the third when he raced 56 yards from punt formation, a maneuver he has been working with success much of the season.

M. C. Reynolds scored from the one in the last period to end a 9-play drive that carried 98 yards for Buffalo.

Statistics

	Houston	Buffalo
First downs	17	22
Yards rushing	50	99
Yards passing	464	274
Passes attempted	32	51
Passes completed	18	19
Passes intercepted by	4	4
Punts	4	5
Average yards punts	44	41.6
Fumbles lost	0	0
Yards penalized	70	30

Houston . 7 7 7 7—28
Buffalo . . 0 3 7 6—16
Hstn—Hennigan 56, pass from Blanda (Blanda kick).
Bflo—FG, Hergert 38.
Hstn—Groman 32, pass from Blanda (Blanda kick).
Bflo—Atkins 56, run (Atkins kick).
Hstn—Hennigan 80, pass from Blanda (Blanda kick).
Bflo—Reynolds 1, run (run failed).
Hstn—Groman 68, pass from Blanda (Blanda kick).
Attendance—21,237.

7 TD PASSES FOR BLANDA

Oiler Sets A.F.L. Record As Titans Bow, 49-13

Houston, Nov. 19 (AP)—Fists flew in every quarter today as George Blanda set an American Football League record by throwing seven touchdown passes as the Houston Oilers protected their Eastern Division lead by defeating the New York Titans, 49-13.

Three players were ejected from the game as officials and coaches kept busy halting frequent flareups that pleased a crowd of 33,428. The 193 yards in penalties tied a league record.

Accounts For All Points

Blanda, playing all but the final five minues, accounted for every Houston point while completing 20 of 32 passes for 418 yards. He kicked 7 extra points.

The seven Houston scoring passes covered a total of 241 yards and permitted Houston to win its fifth straight game since Wally Lemm took over as head coach October 16.

The old record of four touchdown passes for one game was set last year by Blanda.

After opening with a 28-yard scoring pass to Charley Hennigan, Blanda hit Billy Cannon and Bill Groman with three touchdown passes each. Cannon's were good for 6, 68 and 6 yards, while Groman's were good for 66, 46 and 11 yards.

Dorow Hits For Two

Al Dorow threw passes for both of New York's touchdowns, hitting Don Maynard with a 4-yarder in the second period and Thurlow Cooper with an 11 yards in the closing seconds.

Al Jamison of Houston and Sid Youngleman and Tom Saidock of New York got tossed from the game and socked with automatic $50 fines for the brawling.

Youngleman went out in the second quarter after squaring off with Jamison. Jamison and Saidock went out in the fourth after Saidock put a headlock on Jamison and the Houston tackle retaliated with a kick at Saidock's face. No one was badly hurt, but the action emptied both benches.

Statistics

	New York	Houston
First downs	25	24
Rushing yardage	107	148
Passing yardage	239	407
Passes	21-47	21-38
Passes intercepted by	3	1
Punts	5-49	5-39
Fumbles lost	1	0
Yards penalized	65	128

New York . . 0 6 0 7—13
Houston . . . 21 14 7 7—49
Houston—Hennigan 28, pass from Blanda (Blanda kick).
Houston—Cannon 6, pass from Blanda (Blanda kick).
Houston—Cannon 78, pass from Blanda (Blanda kick).
New York—Maynard 4, pass from Dorow (kick failed).
Houston—Groman 66, pass from Blanda (Blanda kick).
Houston—Cannon 6, pass from Blanda (Blanda kick).
Houston—Groman 46, pass from Blanda (Blanda kick).
Houston—Groman 11, pass from Blanda (Blanda kick).
New York—Cooper 11, pass from Dorow (Guesman kick).
Attendance—33,428.

Browns

Cleveland, Nov. 19 (AP)—Fullback Jim Brown set a new league rushing record and scored four touchdowns today as Cleveland's Browns banged back into contention in the National Football League's Eastern Division with a thumping 45-to-24 victory over the Philadelphia Eagles.

The former Syracuse All-America and the loop's No. 1 ground gainer the last four years blasted for 242 yards in 34 tries to erase the old mark of 237 yards he set in 31 jaunts against Los Angeles in 1957.

He also caught three passes for 52 yards to round his finest day as the Browns moved into a second place tie with the defending World Champion Eagles with a 7-to-3 record.

Private Bobby Mitchell, home from Fort Meade, Md., on a week-end pass, added to the game's fireworks as he caught a 28-yard scoring pass from Milt Plum and returned a kickoff 91 yards for a touchdown as Cleveland's closing gesture.

The Browns piled up 510 yards as they outclassed the Eagles, with Plum completing 16 of 21 passes for 246 yards and Mitchell adding 43 in eight ground plays to Brown's big total. The gain was more than that but Plum lost 21 yards on a fumble.

Philadelphia's Sonny Jurgensen connected on 18 of 32 passes for 230 yards and two touchdowns. Bobby Walston booted a 34-yard field goal to put the Eagles ahead and converted after the three Philadelphia scores. The Eagles touchdowns came on a two-yard plunge by Ted Dean, an 8-yard pass from Jurgensen to Tommy McDonald and a 39-yarder to Tim Brown. The last two Philadelphia scores came in the last four minutes after the Browns had the game tucked away.

Eagles Stopped On Ground

The Eagles picked up only 97 yards rushing, Brown leading the way with a total of that on one jaunt just before Jurgensen's touchdown pass to McDonald.

Brown's record breaking spree gives him a total of 1,094 yards for 225 tries this year. Lou Groza, the veteran Cleveland place kicker with the "Ph.D. toe," scored nine points to give him a N.F.L. total of 813—just a dozen short of the league's scoring record of 825 set by Don Hutson of Green Bay. The record has stood since 1945. Walston, with 6 points, crept up to 802.

Since starting in 1946 with the Browns in the old All-America Conference, Groza has booted 176 field goals, 551 extra points and has scored a lone touchdown for a grand total of 1,027 points.

The Statistics	Philadelphia	Cleveland
First Downs	19	30
Rushing Yardage	97	264
Passing yardage	230	246
Passes	18-32	16-22
Passes intercepted by	0	1
Punts	4-37	1-42
Fumbles lost	1	0
Yards penalized	0	32
Philadelphia	3 7 0 14—24	
Cleveland	0 14 10 21—45	

Phil.—F.G., Walston, 34.
Clev.—Brown, 2, run (Groza kick).
Phil.—Dean, 2, plunge (Walston kick).
Clev.—Brown, 4, run (Groza kick).
Clev.—Mitchell, 28, pass from Plum (Groza kick).
Clev.—F.G., Groza, 17.
Clev.—Brown, 1, run (Groza kick).
Clev.—Brown, 8, run (Groza kick).
Phil.—McDonald, 8, pass from Jurgensen (Walston kick).
Clev.—Mitchell, 91, kickoff return (Groza kick).
Phil.—Brown, 39, pass from Jurgensen (Walston kick).
Atendance—68,399.

FOSS CANCELS A.F.L. DRAFT

Wisner Attacks Action Of League's Commissioner

New York, Nov. 22 (AP)—The secret draft of the American Football League has been cancelled by commissioner Joe Foss, but the furor lingered on today.

Harry Wismer, president of the New York Titans, declared that "Foss knew about this early draft despite his denials," and said he would go right ahead trying to sign up the players he has selected, starting with star halfback Ernie Davis, of Syracuse.

The other owners generally were silent. Barron Hilton, president of the San Diego Chargers, said "he's the commissioner. I haven't any comment."

One Player Signed

At least one player, Jim Cadile, San Jose State end, said he had already signed with the Chargers at a $1,000 bonus.

The heart of the dispute is an agreement worked out between the American and National Football Leagues and the colleges, represented by Bill Reed, commissioner of the Big Ten, not to draft or approach college players until the end of the season.

Reed called the A.F.L. draft a "breach of faith," and Pete Rozelle, commissioner of the National Football League, termed it a "discredit to football."

Row Marks AFL Draft As Bills Claim Davis

DALLAS, Tex., Dec. 2 (AP). — The American Football League selected 200 collegians for service next season and shut off its annual draft at 25 rounds today.

Buffalo picked the prize of the lot, Ernie Davis, the Heisman Trophy winner from Syracuse, and got into an argument with New York over it.

New York claimed it had taken Davis in the late "secret draft" that had caused so much trouble, winding up with Commissioner Joe Foss declaring it void and running into a feud with Harry Wismer, New York owner, as a result.

Wismer said he would not abide by the Foss decision and his general manager, Steve Sebo, protested Buffalo's pick of Davis today. Wismer telephoned that he would pay $100,000 for three years and a $25,000 bonus to get Davis, but apparently he is out of luck unless he can swing a deal with Buffalo.

Foss said the secret draft was void and made them get on with things after it was held up for 45 minutes.

More tackles than any other position here were taken by the eight clubs. They picked 47 tackles, 44 ends, 23 guards, 14 centers, 16 quarterbacks, 14 fullbacks, 42 halfbacks and 21 redshirts.

The National Football League has its draft Monday at Chicago and undoubtedly will pick most of the same players as selected by the AFL today. Then will come the battle of the checkbooks.

The draft was cut to 25 rounds, lopping off five, because the coaches said the colleg crop was rather lean this year.

AFL Draft Selections

First Round
Oakland, Roman Gabriel, North Carolina State, quarterback; Denver, Merlin Olsen, Utah State, tackle; Dallas, Ron Bull, Baylor, halfback; Buffalo, Ernie Davis, Syracuse, halfback; New York, Sandy Stephens, Minnesota, quarterback; Boston, Gary Collins, Maryland, end; Houston, Ray Jacobs, Howard Payne, tackle; San Diego, Bob Ferguson, Ohio State, fullback.

Second Round
Oakland, Lance Alworth, Arkansas, halfback; Denver, Jerry Hillebrand, Colorado, end; Dallas, Bill Miller, Miami, end; Buffalo, Glenn Glass, Tennessee, halfback; New York, Alex Kroll, Rutgers, center; Boston, Leroy Jackson, Western Illinois, halfback; Houston, Earl Gros, Louisiana State, fullback; San Diego, Dick Hudson, Memphis State.

Third Round
Oakland, Ed Pine, Utah, center; Denver, Charles Holm, Maryland State, fullback; Dallas, Eddie Wilson, Arizona, quarterback; Buffalo, John Elwell, Purdue, end; New York, Fate Echols, Northwestern, tackle; Boston, Sherwyn Thorson, Iowa, guard; Houston, Ronald Case, Georgia, tackle; San Diego, John Hadl, Kansas, quarterback.

Fourth Round
Oakland, John Meyers, Washington, tackle; Denver, John Furman, Texas Western, quarterback; Dallas, Charles Hinton, North Carolina College, tackle; Buffalo, choice traded to Dallas previously, who chose Irv Goode, Kentucky, center; New York, Ed Blaine, Missouri, guard; Boston, choice traded previously to Houston, who chose Gary Cutsinger, Oklahoma State, tackle; Houston, choice traded previously to San Diego, who chose Bob Bill, Notre Dame, tackle; San Diego, Mack Burton, San Jose State, halfback.

Fifth Round
Oakland, Joe Hernandez, Arizona, halfback; Denver, choice traded previously to San Diego, who chose Bob Mitinger, Penn State, end; Dallas, Bobby Plummer, Texas Christian, tackle; Buffalo, Tom Bellinger, North Carolina State, halfback; New York, Bobby Ply, Baylor, quarterback; Boston, Bill Hull, Wake Forest, end; Houston, Bill Rice, Alabama, end; San Diego, John Cornett, Rice, tackle.

National Football League Draft Picks

CHICAGO, Dec. 4 (AP)—College players chosen today in the national football league draft:

WASHINGTON

1. Ernie Davis, halfback, Syracuse; 2. Joe Hernandez, halfback, Arizona; 3. Bob Mitinger, end, Penn State; 4. Billy Neighbors, tackle, Alabama; 5. traded to Chicago; 6. traded to San Francisco; 7. Bert Coan, halfback, Kansas; 8. Ron Hatcher, back, Michigan State.

9. Dave Viti, end, Boston U., 10; John Childress, guard, Arkansas; 11, Carl Palazzo, tackle, Adams State; 12, Terry Terrebonne, back, Tulane; 13, Bill Whisler, end, Iowa; 14, Jim Costen, back, South Carolina; 15, Len Vella, tackle, Georgia.

MINNESOTA

1. Traded to Los Angeles; 2. traded to Cleveland; 3. Bill Miller, end, Miami; 4. Roy Winston, guard, LSU; 5. traded to New York; 6. Larry Bowie, tackle, Purdue; 7. Jim Perkins, tackle, Colorado; 8. Paul White, back, Florida.

9. Marshall Shik, tackle, UCLA; 10, traded to Cleveland; 11, traded to Cleveland; 12, Gary Fallon, Syracuse, back; 13, Roger Van Cleef, tackle, Southwest Okla., 14, Pat Russ, tackle, Purdue; 15, Larry Guilford, end, Pacific U.

LOS ANGELES

1. Roman Gabriel, quarterback, N. C. State and Merlin Olsen, tackle, Utah State; 2. Joe Corollo, tackle, Notre Dame; 3. John Myers, tackle, Washington; 4. Art Perkins, fullback, North Texas State; 5. Ben Wilson, back, USC and Jim Smith, tackle, Penn State; 6. traded to New York; 7. Sherwin Thorsen, guard, Iowa; 8. Richard Farris, guard, North Texas State.

9. Isaac Lassiter, tackle, St. Augustine's; 10. James Norrts, tackle, Houston; 11. Bert Wilder, tackle, N. C. State; 12. Marv Martinovich, tackle, USC; 13. Bob Fearnside, back, Bowling Green; 14. Gary Henson, end, Colorado. 15. Walter Nikirk, tackle, Houston.

DALLAS

1. Traded to Cleveland; 2. Sonny Gibbs, quarterback, TCU; 3. traded to Chicago; 4. traded to San Francisco; 5. traded to Los Angeles; 6. Donnie Davis, end, Southern U.; 7. Jim Bakken, quarterback, Wisconsin; 8. Ken Tureaud, back, Michigan; 9. traded to Baltimore; 10. John Longmier, guard, Southern Illinois; 11. Larry Hudas, end, Michigan State; 12. traded to Green Bay; 13. Bob Moses, end, Texas; 14. Harold Hays, guard, Mississippi; 15. Guy Reece, tackle, SMU.

PITTSBURGH

1. Bob Ferguson, fullback, Ohio State; 2. traded to Chicago; 3. traded to Los Angeles; 4. traded to Detroit; 5. traded to Baltimore; 6. traded to San Francisco; 7. Jack Collins, halfback, Texas; 8. Gary Ballman, back, Michigan State.

9. John Power, end, Notre Dame; 10. Larry Vegnali, guard, Pitt.; 11. Bob Wills, end, California; 12. Sam Mudie, back, Rutgers; 13. Dave Woodward, Auburn; 14. Jim Whittaker, end, Nevada; 15. Vern Hatch, end, N. C. College.

ST. LOUIS

1. Fate Echols, tackle, Northwestern, and Irvin Goode, center, Kentucky; 2. Bob Jackson, fullback, N. Mex. State; 3. Charles Bryant, end, Ohio State; 4. Roger Kochman, halfback, Penn State; 5. Bill Rice, end, Alabama; 6. John Elwell, end, Purdue; 7. Bill Kirchiro, guard, Maryland; 8. George Gross, tackle, Auburn.

9. Willburn Hollis, quarterback, Iowa; 10. George Francovitch, guard, Syracuse; 11. James Saxton, halfback, Texas; 12. Bob O'Billovitch, back, Montana State; 13. Bill Diamond, guard, Miami, Fla.; 14. George Mans, end, Michigan; 15. Dick Barlund, end, Maryland.

CHICAGO

1. Ron Bull, halfback, Baylor; 2. Benny McRae, halfback, Michigan; 3. Jim Bates, end, USC, and Bill Hull, end, Wake Forest; 4. Jim Cadile, tackle, San Jose State; 5. end Mac Burton San Jose State, and Bill Tunnicliff, back, Michigan; 6. traded to Philadelphia; 7. Ed O'Bradovi, end, Illinois; 8. Ed Reynolds, tackle, Tulane, and Larry Onesti, center, Northwestern.

9. Kelton Winston, halfback, Wiley College; 10. Leroy Weaver, back, Adams State; 11. Jerry Robinson, back, Grambling; 12. Bill Watts, tackle, Miami, Fla.; 13. Joe Perkowski, back, Notre Dame; 14. Andrew Von Sonn, center, UCLA; 15. Kent Martin, tackle, Wake Forest.

SAN FRANCISCO

1. Lance Alworth halfback, Arkansas; 2. Ed Pine, center, Utah; 3. Billy Ray Adams, fullback, Mississippi; 4. Charles Sieminski, tackle, Penn State, and Floyd Dean, tackle, Florida; 5. Mike Lind, fullback, Notre Dame; 6. Bill Winter, tackle, West Virginia, Jerry Brown, guard, Mississippi, and Keith Luhnow, back, Santa Ana J. C.; 7. John Burrell, end, Rice; 8. Jim Vollenweider, back, Miami, Fla.

9. James Roberts, tackle Mississippi; 10. Regis Coustillac, guard Pitt; 11. Larry Jepson, center Furman; 12. Milton McPike, end Kirksville; 13. George Puerovich, back California; 14. Dick Easterly, back Syracuse; 15. Ray Osborne, tackle Mississippi State.

BALTIMORE

1. Wendell Harris, halfback, LSU; 2. Bill Saul, center, Penn State; 3. Dan Sullivan, tackle, Boston College; 4. James Dillard, back, Okla. State; 5. Jerry Croft, guard, Bowling Green, and Ted Woods, back, Colorado; 6. traded to Green Bay; 7. Fred Miller, tackle, LSU; 8. Peter Brokaw, back, Syracuse.

9. Walter Rappold, quarterback Duke, and Roy Walter, fullback Purdue; 10. Fred Moore, tackle Memphis State; 11. Scott Tyler, back Miami of Ohio; 12. Bob Turner, back Texas Tech; 13. Charles Holmes, back Maryland State; 14. Stinson Jones, back VMI; 15. Joe Monte, guard Furman.

DETROIT

1. John Hadl, quarterback, Kansas; 2. Ed Wilson, quarterback, Arizona; 3. Bobby Thompson, halfback, Arizona; 4. John Lomakoski, tackle, Western Michigan, and Larry Ferguson, back, Iowa; 5. Dan Birdwell, center, Houston; 6. Mike Bundra, tackle, USC; 7. Tom Hall, end, Minnesota; 8. George Hooper, tackle, Houston, and Frank Imperiale, guard, Southern Illinois.

9. Tod Grant, center Michigan; 10. Jerry Archer, center Pittsburg State; 11. Karl Anderson, tackle Bowling Green; 12. Gale Sprute, center Winona State; 13. Sherlock Knight, tackle Central State, Ohio; 14. Jim Davidson, back Maryland; 15. Dick Broadbent, end Delaware.

CLEVELAND

1. Gary Collins, end, Maryland, and Leroy Jackson, halfback, Western Illinois; 2. Charles Hinton, tackle, N. C. College, and Sandy Stephens, quarterback, Minnesota; 3. John Furman, quarterback, Texas Western; 4. Stan Sczurek, guard, Purdue; 5. Henry Rivera, back, Oregon State; 6. Sam Tidmore, end, Ohio State; 7. John Havlick, end, Ohio State; 8. traded to Detroit.

9. Charles Dickerson, tackle Illinois; 10. Albert White, back Capital, Ohio, and Gerald Goerlitz center N. Michigan; 11. Cliff McNeil, end Grambling, and Ronnie Meyers, end Villanova; 12. Ted Shute, end Ohio; 13. Fran Gardner, tackle N.C. College; 14. Jim Shorter, back Detroit; 15. Tom Goodby, guard Baldwin-Wallace.

PHILADELPHIA

1. traded to St. Louis; 2. Pete Case, tackle, Georgia; 3. Pat Holmes, tackle, Texas Tech; 4. Bill Byrne, guard, Boston College; 5. traded to Los Angeles; 6. John McGeever, back, Auburn, and Gus Gobzalez, guard, Tulane; 7. Bill Baird, halfback, Villanova; 8. Ralph Smith, end, Mississippi.

9. Bob Butler, tackle Kentucky; 10. Jim Skaggs, guard Washington; 11. George Horne, tackle Brigham Young; 12. Larry Thompson, center Tulane; 13. George McKinney, back Arkansas; 14. Jim Schwab, end Penn State; 15. Mike Woulfe, guard Colorado.

NEW YORK

1. Jerry Hillebrand, end, Colorado; 2. Bob Bill, tackle, Notre Dame; 3. traded to Green Bay; 4. Glynn Griffing, quarterback, Mississippi; 5. Bill Bolin, guard, Mississippi, and Curtis Miranda, center, Florida A&M; 6. Bill Triplett, back, Miami of Ohio; 7. Ken Buyers, tackle, Cincinnati; 8. traded to Chicago.

9. G. Reed Bohovich, tackle Lehigh; 10. J. R. Williams, tackle Fresno State; 11. Dave Bishop, back Connecticut; 12. Al Gursky, back Penn State; 13. Billy Joe Booth, tackle LSU; 14. Greg Mather, end Navy; 15. Joe Tayloe, back N. Carolina A&T.

GREEN BAY

1. Earl Gros, halfback, LSU; 2. Ed Blaine, guard, Missouri; 3. traded to Cleveland; 4. Ron Gassert, tackle, Virginia; 5. Chuck Morris, back, Mississippi, and John Schopf, guard, Michigan; 6. Oscar Donohue, end, San Jose State, and John Sutro, tackle, San Jose State; 7. Gary Cutsinger, tackle, Oklahoma State; 8. James Tullis, back, Florida A&M.

9. Peter Scheneck, halfback Washington State; 10. Gale Weidner, back Colorado; 11. Jim Thrush, tackle Xavier of Ohio; 12. Tom Pennington, back Georgia; Jack Joe Thorne, back, S. Dakota State; 13. Tom Kepner, tackle Villanova; 14. Ernest Green, back Louisville; 15. Roger Holdinsky, back West Virginia.

Future Big Concern

Davis Will Take Best Deal

NEW YORK, Dec. 4 (AP) Ernie Davis, Syracuse halfback who was the top pick today in the National Football League draft, says he has no particular preference where he plays.

"I'm going where I get the best deal," the Negro star, winner of the 1961 Heisman Trophy, said here today.

Davis was picked by the Washington Redskins in the NFL draft at Chicago.

On Saturday, Davis, who broke Jimmy Brown's career rushing record at Syracuse, was picked by the Buffalo Bills in the official American Football League draft.

"I want good money, sure, but I also want happiness and a guarantee of a future," Davis said. "I want to be able to do something constructive in the off-season so 10 or 15 years from now I can step out of pro football and into business."

Last week Harry Wismer, owner of the New York Titans who had drafted Davis in a "secret" AFL draft later voided by Commissioner Joe Foss, said he was willing to offer Davis a $100,000 three-year, no-cut contract plus a $25,000 bonus for signing. After the Bills picked Davis in the official AFL draft, Wismer indicated that he was willing to make a deal with Buffalo for the Syracuse halfback.

Davis will receive the Heisman Trophy, symbolizing the nation's outstanding college football player, here Wednesday.

Dec. 10

Cannon's Running

Rips New York's Defense In Scoring Five Times

NEW YORK (A) —Billy Cannon ripped apart the New York Titans' specially prepared defenses Sunday for a remarkable 330 yards and scored five touchdowns as the Houston Oilers clinched at least a tie for the American Football League's Eastern Division title with a 48-21 victory.

Cannon broke the league single game rushing record with 216 yards, scoring twice on runs of 61 and 53 yards in the second half. He scored twice in the first half on 67 and 15 yards passes from George Blanda. His other TD was a two-yard plunge with 17 seconds to play.

Blanda also passed 33 yards to Charlie Hennigan for another score, added 16 and 27-yard field goals and kicked the extra points after each of Houston's six touchdowns.

Mel West's 21-yard run and touchdown passes by Al Dorow of 43 yards to Don Maynard and 48 yards to Art Powell were all the Titans could do in this last gasp effort.

Cannon, the AFL's fourth best runner going into the game, got only 62 yards rushing in the first half but after the Titans had narrowed the gap to 20-14 with Maynard's TD, he zoomed on his 61-yard carry. His 53-yarder came midway in the last period.

Houston's victory was No. 8 in a row under coach Wally Lemm, who has yet to lose since taking over for Lou Rymkus. A ninth straight next week against Oakland means the Eastern title.

Cannon's great rushing performance broke the record of 158 set earlier this season by Abner Haynes of Dallas. He also scored eight touchdowns against the Titans this year.

Blanda didn't have such a bad day, either, completing 19 of 33 attempts for 287 yards.

Houston		10 10 7 21—48
New York		7 0 7 7—21

Houston—Cannon 67 pass from Blanda (Blanda ick).
N.Y.—West 21 run (Guesman kick).
Houston—FG Blanda 16.
Houston—Cannon 15 pass from Blanda (Blanda kick).
Houston—FG Blanda 27.
N.Y.—Maynard 43 pass from Dorow (Guesman kick).
Houston—Cannon 61 run (Blanda kick).
Houston—Hennigan 33 pass from Blanda (Blanda kick).
Houston—Cannon 53 run (Blanda kick).
N.Y. — Powell 48 pass from Dorow (Guesman kick).
Houston — Cannon 2 plunge (Blanda kick).
Attendance—9,462.

STATISTICS HOUSTON		NEW YORK
26	First downs	17
266	Rushing yardage	152
307	Passing yardage	152
19-38	Passes	9-28
1	Passes intercepted	2
3-33.3	Punts	6 42.1
0	Fumbles lost	2
66	Yards penalized	15

Dec. 11

DALLAS 49
DENVER 41

About the only bright spot for Denver was the performance of big Lionel Taylor. The sure-handed terminal came up with five grabs to give him an even 100 receptions' — the first time this feat has ever been accomplished in pro football. Taylor held the old AFL mark of 92 last year.

Score by quarters:
Denver   0 7 0 14—21
Dallas   7 14 14 14—49
Dallas—Dickinson 1 run (Davidson kick).
Dallas—Robinson 49 pass from Davidson (Davidson).
Dallas—Jackson 49 run (Davidson kick).
Denver—Stone 7 pass from Herring (Mingo kick).
Dallas—Jackson 8 run (Davidson kick).
Dallas—Jackson 20 pass from Davidson (Davidson kick).
Denver—Gavin 23 run with blocked punt (Mingo kick).
Denver—Frazier 18 pass from Stone (Mingo kick).
Dallas—Jackson 30 run (Davidson kick).
Dallas—Herdrick 31 pass interception (Davidson kick).

Reprinted from
The Rocky Mountain News

As NFL Leaders

Hornung, Brown Repeat

NEW YORK, Dec. 17 (AP) Pvt. Paul Hornung of the Green Bay Packers and fullback Jimmy Brown of the Cleveland Browns repeated as scoring and rushing champions of the National Football League, which ended its regular season Sunday.

Hornung, although he never left Fort Riley, Kan. (He couldn't get a weekend pass for Sunday's game with Los Angeles) won the scoring championship for the third straight year. The former Notre Dame ace finished the 14-game season with 146 points. Last year, Hornung set an NFL record of 176 points in 13 games.

Brown was the league's rushing champion for the fifth straight year. With 101 yards gained against New York, the Cleveland star finished with 1407 yards and a 100-yard edge over runnerup Jim Taylor of Green Bay. Taylor was held to 78 yards by Los Angeles Sunday and wound up with 1307.

Walston's Kicks Win For Eagles

DETROIT, Dec. 17 (AP) The 1960 world champion Philadelphia Eagles battled back to beat the Detroit Lions, 27-24, on Bobby Walston's 10-yard field goal with 25 seconds left today but missed out on tying for the National Football League's Eastern Division title.

The New York Giants captured the divisional crown by tying the Cleveland Browns, 7-7, in their finale at Yankee Stadium.

Philadelphia went into today's game one game behind the Giants and would have forced a playoff next week if New York had lost.

The Eagles scored 10 points in the final four minutes to come from behind for the victory.

Walston booted two field goals and added three extra points for nine points and became the National Football League's all-time high scorer with an 11-year total of 833 points.

Walston went from third to first on the NFL's all-time scoring list with his nine points. He bypassed Cleveland's Lou Groza, who booted only an extra point to run his 11-season total to 827 points. Last week Groza surpassed Don Hutson, the long-time leader who scored 825 points with the Green Bay Packer from 1935 to 1945.

GROMAN TIES RECORD WITH 18 RECEPTION TD'S

Blanda Hurls 4 Touchdown Passes As Oilers Win, 47-16

San Francisco. Dec. 17 (AP)—With George Blanda passing for four touchdowns. the Houston Oilers trounced the Oakland Raiders. 47-16. today and won their second straight Eastern Division championship in the American Football League.

It was the Oilers' ninth straight win and gave them a regular season record of 10-3-1. The Raiders. with their sixth straight loss, finished at 2-12.

Has 36 For Season

The Oilers needed the win for the division title as Boston trounced Western Division champion San Diego, 41-0, in San Diego today. The Oilers, defending A.F.L. champions, will play the San Diego Chargers for the 1961 league title in San Diego next Sunday.

Blanda's four touchdown passes gave the twelve-year professional

A.F.L. Standings

Scores Of Yesterday

Dallas, 35; New York, 24.
Houston at Oakland.
Boston, 41; San Diego, 0

(Only games scheduled)

Final Standings

EASTERN DIVISION

	W.	L.	T.	Pct.	Points For	Agts.
Houston	10	3	1	.769	513	242
Boston	9	4	1	.692	413	313
New York	7	7	0	.500	301	390
Buffalo	6	8	0	.429	294	342

WESTERN DIVISION

	W.	L.	T.	Pct.	Points For	Agts.
San Diego	12	2	0	.857	396	219
Dallas	6	8	0	.429	334	343
Denver	3	11	0	.214	251	432
Oakland	2	12	0	.167	237	458

veteran an A.F.L. record total of 36 for the season.

He connected with Willard Dewveall on scoring plays of 25 and 66 yards and with Bill Groman on strikes of 7 and 17 yards.

A crowd of 4,821 saw the Raiders' final game at Candlestick Park. They plan to play in Oakland for the first time next eason.

Grid Judge Mauled In Houston Title Win

San Diego, Cal., Dec. 25 (AP)—Holiday peace and quiet prevailed today after a stormy victory by the Houston Oilers over the San Diego Chargers for the American Football League championship.

Quarterback George Blanda kicked a 46-yard field goal, passed for 35 yards and a touchdown to halfback Billy Cannon and added the extra point, to give the Oilers their second straight league title.

Morrow Knocked Down

A crowd of 29,556 saw the game in Balboa Stadium and many of them today were still trying to piece together the weird scene that took place immediately after the final gun sounded.

The only certain fact was that a game official, field judge John Morrow, was suddenly knocked down as the players, coaches and a number of fans converged in the center of the field.

Morrow, of Oklahoma City, a veteran and highly respected grid official for many years, said

The Statistics

	Houston	San Diego
First downs	18	15
Rushing yardage	96	79
Passing yardage	160	177
Passes	18-41	17-32
Passes intercepted by	4	6
Punts	4-41	6-33
Fumbles lost	1	2
Yards penalized	68	106

Houston ..... 0 3 7 0—10
San Diego .... 0 0 0 3— 3
H—F.G.. Blanda. 46.
H—Cannon. 35. pass from Blanda. (Blanda kick).
SD—F.G.. Blair. 12.
Attendance. 29.556.
Players share of game receipts: Houston. $1.724 per player; San Diego. $1.069 per player.

league policy prohibited him from making any comment.

But he indicated a report will be forwarded to league commissioner Joe Foss. Foss left San Diego immediately after the game for his home in South Dakota and later will return to the league office in Dallas.

Gillman Makes Charge

It appeared, however, that Morrow was knocked off his feet when jostled by a Charger defensive halfback, Bob Zeman. Later Zeman admitted that he moved into closer quarters when he saw his head coach, Sid Gillman, charging across the field toward the officials.

Gillman was obviously enraged. His team had been penalized 10 times—7 in the last half—for a total of 106 yards. The coach said the officiating was the worst he had seen all season.

The Oilers were back home today and were promised a party tomorrow by their wealthy club owner, K. S. (Bud) Adams.

Final Pro Standings

National League

EASTERN DIVISION

	W	L	T	Pct.	Pts.	OP
New York	10	3	1	.769	368	220
Philadelphia	10	4	0	.714	361	297
Cleveland	8	5	1	.615	319	270
St. Louis	7	7	0	.500	279	267
Pittsburgh	6	8	0	.429	295	287
Dallas	4	9	1	.308	236	380
Washington	1	12	1	.077	174	392

WESTERN DIVISION

	W	L	T	Pct.	Pts.	OP
Green Bay	11	3	0	.786	391	223
Detroit	8	5	1	.615	270	258
Chicago	8	6	0	.571	326	302
Baltimore	8	6	0	.571	302	307
San Francisco	7	6	1	.538	346	272
Los Angeles	4	10	0	.286	263	333
Minnesota	3	11	0	.214	285	407

YESTERDAY'S RESULTS

Cleveland 7, New York 7 (tie).
Philadelphia 27, Detroit 24.
St. Louis 20, Pittsburgh 0.
Washington 34, Dallas 24.
Chicago 52, Minnesota 35.
Green Bay 24, Los Angeles 17.

CHAMPIONSHIP GAME

Sunday, Dec. 31
New York at Green Bay.

American League

EASTERN DIVISION

Team	W	L	T	Pct.	Pts	OP
Houston	10	3	1	.769	513	242
Boston	9	4	1	.692	413	313
New York	7	7	0	.500	301	390
Buffalo	6	8	0	.429	294	342

WESTERN DIVISION

Team	W	L	T	Pct.	Pts	OP
San Diego	12	2	0	.857	396	219
Dallas	6	8	0	.429	334	343
Denver	3	11	0	.214	251	432
Oakland	2	12	0	.143	237	458

YESTERDAY'S RESULTS

Boston, 41; San Diego, 0.
Houston, 47; Oakland, 16.
Dallas, 35; New York, 24.

CHAMPIONSHIP GAME

Sunday, Dec. 24
Houston at San Diego.

Packers Beat Giants, 37-0, For N.F.L. Championship

GREEN BAY PICKS OFF 4 PASSES

3 Interceptions Lead To 2 Touchdowns And Field Goal

By CAMERON C. SNYDER
(Sun Staff Correspondent)

Green Bay, Wis., Dec. 31—Last week this small city of 65,000 plastered its walls with the slogan "Title Town, U.S.A."

The Packers then made it stick by humbling the New York Giants, 37 to 0, in the National Football League's championship game today in frigid City Stadium.

A crowd of 39,029 shared the 21 degree weather and the victory with the Packers. This was Green Bay's largest crowd but scalpers were selling $10 tickets for $5 an hour before game time. The crowd was supposed to reach 41,000.

Apparently the city slickers from the big metropolis came to make the big pitch to their small town cousins.

But they stayed to absorb a lesson in elementary football, the art of blocking and tackling as demonstrated by masters of these techniques.

Reprinted from
The Baltimore Sun

It was a rout once the Packers dented the goal line on the first play of the second quarter. That was the starting point for Green Bay and the finish for the Giants.

The big pitch, a favorite weapon of the Giants in their drive to the Eastern Division title, became a boomerang because of the Packers' fierce rush of passer Y. A. Tittle and the alertness of the Green Bay secondary which picked off four interceptions.

Convert Breaks

Three of the four interceptions produced two touchdowns and a field goal as the Packers took advantage of every break while making the most of them.

Paul Hornung, the halfback star who has been dividing his time between Fort Riley, Kan., where he is in the army and here, was Green Bay's biggest hero today.

He received the plaudits and the automobile as the most valuable player of the game while setting a scoring record of 19 points in a championship game.

Broke Graham's Mark

His effort broke an 18-point mark put in the record books by Otto Graham in the 1954 championship game with the Lions.

Hornung scored one touchdown, kicked 4 extra points and three field goals to record the 19 points.

He also carried the ball 20 times, more than any other player, for 89 yards and caught 3 passes for 47 more yards.

It was the extra use of Hornung that may have caught the Giants off balance. Normally, Paul is second to Jim Taylor in ball toting assignments, but not today.

Taylor, who has been bothered by a bad back, was used mostly as a decoy.

Statistics

	Packers	Giants
First downs rushing	10	3
First downs passing	8	4
First downs by penalty	1	1
Total first downs	19	8
Yards gained rushing	181	31
Yards gained passing	164	119
Yards lost attempting to pass	0	20
Total yds gained (net)	345	130
Passing Attempted	19	29
Completed	10	10
Had intercepted	0	4
Yards interceptions returned	78	0
Punts Number	5	5
Average distance	42	39.2
Nbr punts returned	1	3
Yards punts returned	4	10
Kickoffs number returned	1	8
Yards kickoffs returned	18	119
Penalties number	4	4
Yards penalized	18	38
Fumbles number	1	5
Own fumbles recovered	1	0
Running plays from scrimmage	44	14
Average per play	4.1	2.2
Total offensive plays from scrimmage	63	43

Green Bay ... 0 24 10 3 37
New York ... 0   0   0 0   0
GB—Hornung 6 run (Hornung kick)
GB—Dowler 12, pass from Starr (Hornung kick)
GB—Kramer 13, pass from Starr (Hornung kick)
GB—FG. Hornung 17.
GB—FG. Hornung 22.
GB—Kramer 13, pass from Starr (Hornung kick)
GB—FG Hornung 19.
Attendance 39,029

Individual Statistics

Green Bay, Wis., Dec. 31 (P)—Leading individual statistics on today's National Football League championship game between Green Bay and New York:

Rushing

	Att.	Yds.	Long Gain
GREEN BAY			
Hornung	20	89	17
Taylor	14	69	33
Moore	6	25	11
NEW YORK			
Webster	7	19	7
Wells	3	9	8
King	2	8	7

Passing

	Att	Comp	Yds	Int	TD
GREEN BAY					
Starr	17	10	164	0	3
NEW YORK					
Tittle	20	6	65	4	0
Conerly	8	4	54	0	0

Pass Receiving

	No.	Yds	TD
GREEN BAY			
Dowler	3	37	1
Kramer	4	80	2
Hornung	3	47	0
NEW YORK			
Rote	3	54	0
Shofner	3	41	0
Webster	3	5	0
Walton	1	19	0

FANS CONFUSED BY 'FIFTH DOWN'

Packers Didn't Need Benefit Of Wild Sequence

Green Bay, Wis., Dec. 31 (P)—The play-by-play of today's Green Bay-New York N.F.L. title game indicated the officials had permitted the Packers five downs during one sequence in the third quarter.

There were several moments of wild confusion when quarterback Bart Starr ran from the Packers' 37 to the Giants' 40 on a keeper play and fumbled. Jimmy Patton of New York and several other players touched the ball before it went out of bounds.

Ball Ruled Dead

The officials ruled they had blown the ball dead before Starr fumbled. However, they also had called a penalty against the Packers for backfield in motion.

When the officials returned the ball, they made a mistake and marked off a 2-yard penalty instead of 5 yards. Apparently the sticks had been moved after the fumble and were not returned to the same position.

The ball was moved from the 37 to the 35. Then Green Bay ran three more plays — Paul Hornung and Jim Taylor running and Starr passing incomplete — before Boyd Dowler punted.

"The play was nullified by the officials," explained Jim Kensil, league public relations man. "However, the play-by-play indicated there probably was a fifth down."

N.F.L. TITLE ADDS TO GALA NEW YEAR EVE

Green Bay Stages Wild Party After Packers Beat Giants

Green Bay, Wis., Dec. 31 (P)—The Green Bay Packers' 38-0 trouncing of the New York Giants in today's National Football League title game set the stage for one of the wildest New Year's Eve whingdings in the history of the city.

Fans who poured out of the City Stadium stands after the final gun went off ripped the goal posts from their moorings, carted them downtown somehow, and joyously dragged them up and down the main streets of Green Bay.

Impromptu Rite

They were followed by a stream of cars, horns blaring in an impromptu victory rite, with people—teen-agers, mostly—hanging out the windows and hollering the Packers' praises.

Pedestrians jammed the streets, flipped firecrackers, and added their voices to the hubbub. The frosty weather prevented any victory marches but bars began filling rapidly and as the evening wore on, the celebration was on its way to a wild, wild peak.

All Kinds Of Signs

The cars filling the streets of the town were emblazoned with all kinds of signs, like "Wallop The Giants" (with "We Did!" painted in hastily) and "Titletown, U.S.A."

Harassed traffic officers tried to put the parade of cars in some semblance of order. At last report, there were no accidents beyond a couple of fender-benders.

But the Packers are the N.F.L. champs and the entire town joined in makin' whoopee as Green Bay exploded in appreciation of its team.

N.F.L. Title Game Facts, Figures

Green Bay, Wis., Dec. 31 (P)—Facts and figures on today's National Football League game between Green Bay and New York:

Paid attendance—39,029.
X-Gross receipts—$713,792.00.
Taxes & rental—$60,666.68.
Operating expense—$48,364.62.
Net receipts—$604,760.70.
Player pool (70 per cent of net) $423,332.49.
Winning players pool—$228,599.54.
Losing players pool—$152,399.70.
Each winning player's share—$5,195.44.
Each losing player's share—$3,339.99.
Pool for second place clubs in each conference—$42,333.25.

x-Gross receipts includ $215,000 from the $615,000 paid for radio-TV rights. Remaining $400,000 is not included because it goes directly into N.F.L. player benefit fund.

Mask Tackles in N.F.L. Will Cost 15 Yards—Test of New Timer Approved

MIAMI BEACH, Jan. 9 (AP) — The National Football League adopted its first playing-rule change in four years today in a safety move and approved, on an experimental basis, a new radio-controlled timing device.

Under the rule change, suggested by the Baltimore Colts, it will be illegal for any player to grab the face mask of an opponent, either in tackling or blocking. The penalty will be 15 yards. In the past, the ball-carrier was the only player whose mask could be grabbed.

"We didn't have any serious trouble with this in league play," said Pete Rozelle, the league's commissioner." Actually most of our injuries are of the knee or leg type. However, I did see one ball-carrier grabbed by his mask and thrown several yards. It scared me a little."

The new timing device meets the players' request that the scoreboard clock be made official in timing games. Often there has been a discrepancy between the official's watch and the clock on the field, as to the exact number of seconds remaining. Even a few seconds can change the thinking of a quarterback at a crucial stage.

FOSS IS AWARDED NEW 5-YEAR PACT

American Football League Head Gets Raise in Pay

SAN DIEGO, Jan. 10 (AP)— Directors of the American Football League ended their winter meeting on a harmonious note today by giving Commissioner Joe Foss a new five-year contract and pledging an all-out effort to stay alive.

The anticipated continuation of the clash between Foss, the ex-Marine flying ace of World War II, and Harry Wismer, the president of the New York Titans, failed to materialize.

The owners voted unanimously to tear up Foss' old contract, which was to expire this year, and give him a new one with an undisclosed raise in pay.

There was no demand by Wismer, as he had previously promised, to move the league headquarters from Dallas to New York. The only reference to this was a recommendation by one of the owners to add Chicago to the list of cities eligible as headquarters, but this was defeated without much discussion.

In a final session this morning, Foss named a committee composed of Wayne Valley of Oakland, Ralph Wilson of Buffalo and Lamar Hunt of Dallas to study ways of gaining a better balance among the eight clubs.

"We want competition within the league and our idea is to try to upgrade all clubs, not downgrade the stronger ones," said Foss.

The owners' consensus was that the A. F. L. and the National Football League were in for a long and costly price war over athletes. They said their rival television programs, beaming each other's games into areas on home-game dates, would be ruinous.

Hunt said the A. F. L.'s $10,-000,000 suit against the older league might solve the Dallas situation where both his club and the Cowboys of the N.F.L. were losing money. The suit is based on the alleged N. F. L. invasion of Dallas.

The directors decided that stadium scoreboard clocks would be the official game clocks. They also voted to increase the regular-season player limit from thirty-three to thirty-six and outlawed anyone tackling a ball-carrier by the face mask.

National Football League Signs 2-Year, $9,300,000 TV Pact With C.B.S.

EACH CLUB TO GET $320,000 A YEAR

Road Games of 14 Teams and Other N.F.L. Contests Involved in TV Deal

MIAMI BEACH, Jan. 10 (AP) The National Football League signed a $9,300,000 two-year contract with the Columbia Broadcasting System television network today. Under the terms each of the fourteen clubs will receive about $320,000 a year.

Commissioner Pete Rozelle said the only club that would receive less for its TV rights was the Baltimore Colts, who worked with another network last season. The Pittsburgh Steelers, who also had a separate deal, will receive about the same as last year, Rozelle said, adding:

"All the other clubs will receive appreciably more. All fourteen clubs are happy. Equality of competition has been the greatest single factor in the success of the league.

"This equal distribution of TV income will aid us appreciably in preserving a balanced league. It will enable teams like Dallas and Minnesota, both of which have made spectacular strides in their short existence, to compete on an even stronger level with the established clubs."

Rozelle said all the clubs, except the Dallas Cowboys, made money during the past season. He re-emphasized there was no talk of merger with the rival American Football League.

Under the old agreement, each club made separate TV deals with networks or sponsors. A league contract with C. B. S. was negotiated last April but was nullified in July when a Federal judge ruled it violated the antitrust law.

Separate Deals in 1961

The league then reverted to its policy of separate deals by each club in 1961. Eleven used C. B. S. facilities. Baltimore and Pittsburgh worked with the National Broadcasting Company and the Cleveland Browns worked with Sports Network. As a result, some nonleague cities had two games televised on the same day.

A bill, introduced by Representative Emanuel Celler, Democrat of Brooklyn, was signed in October by President Kennedy. The new law exempts pro football, baseball, basketball and hockey leagues from antitrust laws in the area of a single network TV contract.

Bill MacPhail, vice president of C. B. S. television sports, said the network would handle the road games of all fourteen clubs. It will also televise a network game on Thanksgiving Day and two late-season Saturday games from California.

In the event of a tie at the end of the season, C. B. S. will have the rights. However, the league championship game contract with N. B. C. still has one year to go at $615,000 a year.

"The bidding for the title game always will be separate from our regular-season package," said Rozelle.

MacPhail said C. B. S. had an option on pre-season games. The rights will revert to the individual clubs if the option is not exercised.

$10,000,000 Cost Likely

He said the total costs, including $4,650,000 a year from the rights, probably would come close to $10,000,000 a year with time and production costs taken into consideration.

Two sets of announcers will work each game, one for each of the regional networks, he said. When the football season starts, the network's Sunday baseball broadcasts will be preempted.

MacPhail said TV coverage would not change appreciably except in the deep South, where Washington and Baltimore, whose games were televised in the area last season, would share a network.

Rozelle said the $4,650,000 would be split fourteen ways annually after a deduction of $40,000 each for the two late-season Saturday games and league fees. He estimated each club would get about $320,000.

The league spent the balance of the day of its final session trying to agree on pre-season exhibition schedules. They will be announced later by individual clubs.

The regular championship schedule also will be drawn later. Each club again will play fourteen regular-season games.

New Justice Is 44, Has Had Varied Life

All-American Grid Star To Succeed Whittaker Who Is Retiring Due To Ill Health

By WILLIAM KNIGHTON, JR.
[Washington Bureau of The Sun]

Washington, March 30 — Byron R. White, Deputy Attorney General, tonight was named by President Kennedy to succeed Associate Justice Charles Evans Whittaker of the Supreme Court who is retiring Sunday due to ill health. He is 44.

The Justice-designate, known as "Whizzer," won his nickname as an All-American football player at the University of Colorado. It stayed with him during his varied career of scholar, beet picker, naval intelligence officer, law clerk to the late Chief Justice Fred M. Vinson, corporation lawyer and national chairman of the Citizens for Kennedy during the 1960 campaign.

Personal Announcement

President Kennedy said one of the "more exacting responsibilities" of the Chief Executive's office is the appointment of justices to the United States Supreme Court.

And to show how important he feels this task is, he called newsmen into his office early this eve-

Wide World Photo
BYRON R. WHITE
"A very large undertaking"

ning to personally announce his selection of the No. 2 man in the Department of Justice. It was his first Supreme Court appointment.

Mr. Kennedy said he was "delighted" to make the announcement that White had accepted.

"I have known Mr. White for over twenty years," the President said. "His character, experience and intellectual force qualify him superbly for service on the nation's highest tribunal.

Although he graduated first in his class of 1938 at the University of Colorado, he also was probably the best known college football player of that year—a halfback.

In order to pay his expenses through law school, he went into professional football, signing with the Pittsburgh Steelers at $15,000 —the highest salary a professional gridiron star had received up to that time.

In January, 1939, he went to England as a Rhodes scholar, returning to the United States in November to play football with the Detroit Lions and enter Yale Law School.

During the war, the Justice-designate served with a destroyer division and as an aide to Capt. Arleigh A. Burke, later chief of naval operations.

Reprinted from
The Baltimore Sun

IN THE

United States District Court

FOR THE DISTRICT OF MARYLAND

AMERICAN FOOTBALL LEAGUE, *et al.*	CIVIL No. 12559
v.	Filed: 5/21/62
NATIONAL FOOTBALL LEAGUE, *et al.*	

Warren E. Baker, of Washington, D. C., Richard S. Harrell, Thomas F. O'Toole, of New York, N. Y., and Chadbourne Park, Whiteside & Wolff, for plaintiffs.

Gerhard A. Gesell, Hamilton Carothers, Charles W. Havens, III, and Covington & Burling, of Washington, D. C., and William D. Macmillan, William A. Fisher, Jr., and Semmes, Bowen & Semmes, of Baltimore, Md., for defendants.

THOMSEN, Chief Judge

In this action for treble damages and injunctive relief under the antitrust laws, plaintiffs, the American Football League (AFL) and its members, charge defendants, the National Football League (NFL) and most of its members, with monopolization, attempted monopolization and conspiracy to monopolize major league professional football.

It is not disputed that all of the parties to the case are engaged in interstate commerce and subject to the provisions of the antitrust law, *Radovich* v. *National Football League*, 352 U. S. 445. See also *United States* v. *National Football League*, E. D. Pa., 116 F. Supp. 319. At a pretrial conference the parties agreed that the trial should be conducted in two stages: that the court first hear evidence on and determine the issue of liability (including the requirement that plaintiffs prove some injury from each of the alleged violations); and, if liability is found, that the court thereafter hear evidence on and consider the issue of relief (the amount of damages or the equitable relief to which the several plaintiffs may be entitled).

Monopoly Power

Plaintiffs contend that defendants had the power to prevent or exclude competition by plaintiffs in the business of major league professional football. As we have seen, the principal areas of competition are for (1) a sufficient number of cities capable of supporting teams to form a practicable league, (2) players, and (3) the sale of TV rights.

Conclusions

1. This court has jurisdiction over the defendants and the subject matter of this action.

2. Neither individually nor in concert have the defendants monopolized any part of the trade or commerce among the several states; particularly they have not monopolized major league professional football.

3. None of the defendants has attempted to monopolize or combined or conspired with any other person or persons to monopolize major league professional football.

4. None of the defendants has engaged in a combination or conspiracy in unreasonable restraint of trade or commerce among the several states in the presentation of major league professional football games.

5. None of the plaintiffs is entitled to relief in this case against any of the defendants.

Judgment will be entered in favor of the defendants, with costs.

....
Chief Judge, U. S. District Court

101, 100 YARD RUNS HELP COWBOYS WIN

DALLAS, Oct. 14. (AP) – Amos Marsh ran a kickoff back 101 yards to a touchdown and Mike Gaechter took an intercepted pass 100 yards to another today as the Dallas Cowboys crushed the Philadelphia Eagles, 41—19.

Marsh and Gaechter's runs were the longest of the year in the National Football League but were short of the records.

| Dallas Cowboys | 0 | 17 | 7 | 17—41 |
| Philadelphia Eagles | 6 | 0 | 0 | 13 -19 |

Phil.—FG, Walston, 36.
Phil.—FG, Walston, 9.
Dal.—FG, Baker, 40
Dal.—Marsh, 20, run (Baker, kick).
Dal.—Clarke, 8, pass from LeBaron (Baker, kick).
Dal.—Clarke, 57, pass from Meredith (Baker, kick).
Dal.—FG, Baker, 11.
Phil.—Hill, 1, run (kick failed).
Dal.—Marsh, 101, kickoff return (Baker, kick).
Phil.—Sapp, 5, run (Walston, kick).
Dal.—Gaechter, 100, pass interception (Baker, kick).
Attendance—18,645.

STATISTICS OF THE GAME
Cowboys Eagles

	Cowboys	Eagles
First downs	13	21
Rushing yardage	155	78
Passing yardage	199	253
Passes	10-12	17-32
Interceptions by	2	0
Punts	2-52	5-39
Fumbles lost	1	0
Yards penalized	55	25

Tittle Throws 7 Scores

WASHINGTON IS HANDED FIRST LOSS

Veteran Giant Leader Hits On 27 Of 39 Aerials For 505 Yards

New York, Oct. 28 ℗—Y. A. Tittle, the old "Bald Eagle" of the New York Giants, tied the National Football League record with seven touchdown passes today while the Giants clobbered the previously unbeaten Washington Redskins by a stunning 49-to-34 margin.

The 36-year-old Tittle hit Joe Walton with three touchdown passes, threw two to Joe Morrison and one each to Del Shofner and Frank Gifford in an awesome aerial display. At the end of this wild game, watched by another sellout crowd of 62,844, the Redskins' pass defense had been picked clean and only the bones were showing.

The two clubs scored a total of twelve touchdowns, all in the air except for one by Washington.

Tittle Hits On 12 In Row

Strange as it might seem from the final score, it was a ball game until Tittle started hitting in the third period. During one stretch that started in the second period and ran into the third, Tittle connected with twelve straight passes.

Despite this wild effort, Washington led once 7-0 and pulled within a point twice, 14-13 and 21-20. This only served to spur Tittle to more spectacular efforts.

Until Tittle put on his great show, the N.F.L. record for touchdown passes was held jointly by Sid Luckman of the Chicago Bears in 1943 and Adrian Burk of Philadelphia in 1954. The old Giant record was four, which Tittle shared with five others.

Record Threatened

Tittle even approached the all-time passing yardage in the league held by Norm Van Brocklin when the latter was with Los Angeles in 1951. He hit 27 of 39 passes for 505 yards. The record is 554.

Norm Snead, the Skins' fine sophomore quarterback, hit a personal high with four touchdown passes and also scored once on a 1-yard sneak.

The Statistics

	Wash.	New York
First downs	19	25
Rushing yardage	58	97
Passing yardage	316	505
Passes	17-40	27-39
Passes intercepted by	0	1
Punts	6-31	4-47
Fumbles lost		1
Yards penalized	35	127

| Washington | 7 | 6 | 7 | 14—34 |
| New York | 7 | 14 | 21 | 7—49 |

Washington—Mitchell, 44, pass from Snead (Khayat kick).
New York—Morrison, 22, pass from Tittle (Chandler kick).
New York—Walton, 5, pass from Tittle (Chandler kick).
Washington—Dugan, 24, pass from Tittle (Chandler kick).
Washington—Mitchell, 80, pass from Snead (Khayat kick).
New York—Shofner, 32, pass from Tittle (Chandler kick).
New York—Walton, 26, pass from Tittle (Chandler kick).
New York—Gifford, 63, pass from Tittle (Chandler kick).
Washington—Snead, 1, run (Khayat kick).
Washington—Junker, 35, pass from Snead (Khayat).
Attendance—62,844.

Detroit Lions Deal Packers First 1962 Loss, 26-14

GREEN BAY LEAD IS CUT TO 1 GAME

Plum's Passes, Rugged Defense Rout N.F.L. Champions Early

Detroit, Nov. 22 (AP)—The quick-striking Detroit Lions, armed by the Milt Plum-to-Gail Cogdill pass combination, conquered the previously unbeaten Green Bay Packers, 26 to 14, today with an overwhelming mixture of offense and defense.

The display that kept a capacity crowd of 57,598 in a constant uproar left the Packers leading the National Football League's Western division by only one game over the Lions. Each club has three games left.

Touchdown passes of 33 and 27 yards from Plum to Cogdill started the Packers down to their first defeat in eleven games this season. It was the Packers' first loss in thirteen games, including their championship victory last year.

Lions Strike Swiftly

The Lions, who lost their first game to Green Bay, 9 to 7, on a last-minute field goal, turned the nationally-televised rematch into a route early in the second quarter. They scored two touchdowns 21 seconds apart and ruined the Packers' chances of becoming the first team in twenty years to go through an N.F.L. schedule with a perfect record.

The Lions' defense stopped the Packers' proud offense at a virtual standstill until the fourth quarter. Jim Taylor, the N.F.L.'s leading ground-gainer, was held to 47 yards. And quarterback Bart Starr was dumped for a whopping 110 yards in losses while trying to pass under the heavy rush of the Lions defenders.

Packers Trail By 26-0

It wasn't until the Lions led, 26 to 0, in the fourth quarter that the Packers could get untracked, and their defense helped them to all their points.

Green Bay scored once when Bill Quinlan intercepted a pass, fumbled, and Willie Davis fell on the ball in the end zone for a touchdown. Another Davis recovery on Detroit's 14 set up Green Bay's second touchdown in the final three minutes on Taylor's 4-yard run.

A.F.L. Draft

Dallas, Dec. 1 (AP)—The American Football League's third annual draft ended at 6.12 P.M. today with San Diego selecting Heisman Trophy winner Terry Baker, of Oregon State, and Dallas grabbing off what it called the finest lineman in the country in Junious Buchanan.

Buchanan, the huge Grambling College tackle, was the first draft choice.

The clubs held off until the twelfth round to draft quarterback Baker, the nation's total offense leader, since they figured he might already be committed to the National Football League or Canada, which reportedly offered him a big contract.

The draft was heavy on the tackles, with 53 of them being chosen. Halfbacks were next with 45. There were 31 ends, 18 fullbacks, 17 guards, 17 linebackers, 11 quarterbacks and 8 centers.

Oakland Fares Poorly

Oakland, which traded away its first five choices, came out the worst.

Dallas, with the No. 1 choice, and Buffalo, which took such blue ribbon boys as tackle Jim Dunaway, of Mississippi, and Dave Behrman, of Michigan State, were considered to have come out of the draft to the best advantage.

Now, the scouts will hit the road trying to sign these players. They may have to wait a few days on most of them, however, because the National Football League draft is at Chicago Monday and most of the players selected here will be picked there, also. Then comes the signing war.

FIRST ROUND

Dallas—tackle Junious Buchanan, Grambling choice acquired from Oakland. San Diego — end Walt Sweeney, Syracuse. New York—halfback Jerry Stovall, L.S.U. Buffalo—center Dave Berrman, Michigan State. Denver — halfback Kermit Alexander. U.C.L.A. Houston—fullback Danny Brabham, Arkansas. Boston—end Art Graham, Boston College. Dallas—tackle Ed Budde, Michigan State.

SECOND ROUND

Buffalo — tackle Jim Dunaway, Mississippi choice acquired from Oakland. San Diego—linebacker Rufus Guthrie, Georgia Tech. Denver—fullback Ray Poage, Texas choice acquired from New York. Buffalo—end Tom Hutchinson, Kentucky. Denver —tackle Tom Nomina, Miami, Ohio. Boston—center Lee Roy Jordan, Alabama. Houston—tackle Don Estes, L.S.U. Dallas—tackle Walter Rock, Maryland.

THIRD ROUND

San Diego—end Dave Robinson, Penn State choice acquired from Oakland. San Diego—halfback Keith Kinderman, Florida State. New York—end Willie Richardson, Jackson State. Buffalo—halfback Tom Brown, Maryland. Denver—halfback Tommy Janik, Texas A.&I. Houston—halfback Jerry Cook, Texas. Boston—tackle Bob Vogel, Ohio State. Dallas—tackle Don Brumm, Purdue.

FOURTH ROUND

Houston—fullback Lee Roy Caffey, Texas A.&M. choice acquired from Oakland. San Diego—tackle Roy Williams, University of Pacific. New York—tackle John Contoulis, Connecticut. Buffalo—halfback Tom Woodeshick, West Virginia. Denver—linebacker Lou Slaby, Pittsburgh. Boston—tackle Bob Reynolds, Bowling Green. Houston—center Jerry Hopkins, Texas A.&M. Dallas—guard Daryl Sanders, Ohio State.

FIFTH ROUND

Oakland—choice to Houston. San Diego—halfback Larry Glueck, Villanova. New York—end John Mackey, Syracuse. Buffalo—end Bob Jencks, Miami, Ohio. Denver—center Ray Mansfield, Washington. Houston—halfback Homer Jones, Texas Southern, choice acquired from Oakland. Houston—tackle Don Chuy, Clemson. Boston—guard Lou Cioci, Boston College. Dallas—linebacker John Campbell, Minnesota.

N.F.L. Draft By Rounds

Chicago, Dec. 3 (AP)—The round-by-round selections of the National Football League college draft today:

FIRST ROUND

Los Angeles — quarterback Terry Baker, Oregon State. St. Louis—halfback Jerry Stovall, Louisiana State. Minnesota—tackle Jim Dunaway, Mississippi. Philadelphia tackle Ed Budde, Michigan State. COLTS—tackle Bob Vogel, Ohio State. Dallas—center Lee Roy Jordan, Alabama. Washington—end Pat Richter, Wisconsin. San Francisco—halfback Kermit Alexander, U.C.L.A. Cleveland—end Tom Hutchinson, Kentucky. Los Angeles, choice acquired from Chicago—guard Rufus Guthrie, Georgia Tech. Chicago, choice acquired from Pittsburgh—center Dave Behrman, Michigan State. Detroit tackle Daryl Sanders, Ohio State. St. Louis, choice acquired from New York—tackle Don Brumm, Purdue. Green Bay—end Dave Robinson, Penn State.

SECOND ROUND

Los Angeles—tackle Tom Nomina, Miami of Ohio. Minnesota—tackle Bobby Bell, Minnesota. St. Louis—tackle Bob Reynolds, Bowling Green, Ohio Philadelphia — tackle Ray Mansfield, Washington. COLTS—end John Mackey, Syracuse. Chicago, choice acquired from Dallas—tackle Steve Barnett, Oregon. San Francisco—guard Walter Rock, Maryland. Washington—halfback Lonnie Sanders, Michigan State. Cleveland—tackle Jim Kanicki, Michigan State. COLTS, choice acquired from Pittsburgh—halfback George Wilson, Alabama. Chicago — end Bob Jencks, Miami of Ohio. New York—tackle Frank Lasky, Florida. Detroit—tackle Roy Williams, University of Pacific. Green Bay—halfback Tom Brown, Maryland.

THIRD ROUND

Los Angeles—guard Dave Costa, Utah. St. Louis—fullback-defensive end Dan Brabham, Arkansas. St. Louis, choice acquired from Baltimore—back Mike Fracchia, Alabama. Minnesota—back Ray Poage, Texas. Philadelphia — back-center Dave Crossan, Maryland. COLTS—third choice traded to St. Louis. St. Louis—back Mike Frachia, Alabama. Dallas—lineback James Price, Auburn. Washington tackle Ron Snidow, Oregon. San Francisco—back Don Lisbon, Bowling Green. Cleveland, third choice traded to Green Bay. Green Bay—back Dennis Cla-

ridge, Nebraska. Detroit, third choice traded to Philadelphia. Philadelphia—back Louis Guy, Mississippi. New York—back Dick Skelly, Florida. Green Bay—tackle Tony Liscio, Tulsa.

FOURTH ROUND

Los Angeles—back John Griffin, Memphis State. Minnesota—end Paul Flatley, Northwestern. St. Louis—tackle Don Estes, Louisiana State. Philadelphia, fourth choice traded to San Francisco. San Francisco—guard Harrison Rosdahl, Penn State. COLTS—back Jack Jerry Logan, West Texas State. Dallas—tackle Whaley Hall, Mississippi. San Francisco, fourth choice traded to Chicago. Chicago—end Stan Sanders, Whittier. Washington, fourth choice traded to San Francisco. San Francisco—end Hugh Campbell, Washington State. Cleveland—back Bill Munsey, Minnesota. Pittsburgh, fourth choice traded to Chicago. Chicago—back Charley Mitchell, Washington. Chicago, fourth choice traded to Baltimore. COLTS—tackle Harlowe Fullwood, Virginia Union. New York choice traded to Green Bay. Green Bay—guard Lionel Aldridge, Utah State. Detroit—guard Dick Walton, Iowa State.

FIFTH ROUND

Los Angeles — back Joe Auer, Georgia Tech. St. Louis—back William Thornton, Nebraska. Minnesota—tackle Gary Kaltenbach, Pittsburgh. Philadelphia, fifth choice traded to Los Angeles. Los Angeles—tackle Roland Benson, Miami, Fla. COLTS—tackle Bill Ventura, Richmond. Dallas, fifth choice traded to New York. New York—tackle David Hill, Auburn. Washington, fifth choice traded to Green Bay. Green Bay—guard Jack Cvercko, Northwestern. San Francisco—end Vern Burke, Oregon State. Cleveland, fifth choice traded to Pittsburgh, then traded to San Francisco. San Francisco—back James Pilot, New Mexico State. Chicago, fifth choice traded to San Francisco. San Francisco—guard Gary Moeller, Ohio State. Pittsburgh, fifth choice traded to Los Angeles. Los Angeles—tackle Don Chuy, Clemson. Detroit, fifth choice traded to Cleveland. Cleveland—back Frank Baker, Toledo. New York—back Lou Slaby, Pittsburgh. Green Bay—tackle Dan Grimm, Colorado.

Tittle Throws 6 Touchdown Passes As Giants Beat Dallas

New York, Dec. 16 (P)—Y. A. Tittle, the old bald eagle of the New York Giants, set a National Football League season record of 33 touchdown passes by throwing for six scores today in a 41-to-31 victory by the Eastern Conference champions over the Dallas Cowboys.

Tittle hit Alex Webster, his favorite target all afternoon, with two TD passes and also threw three to Joe Walton and one to Frank Gifford. The old mark of 32 was set by Baltimore's Johnny Unitas in twelve games in 1959 and tied last year in the current fourteen-game season by Philadelphia's Sonny Jurgensen.

Another big crowd of 62,694, the seventh straight sell-out at Yankee Stadium, boosted the Giants' home attendance to a New York record of 439,456 for seven games.

Tittle, forced back into action when Ralph Guglielmi, his replacement, was injured in the fourth period, wound up by completing 21 of 42 passes for 341 yards and his six touchdowns. Earlier this year in a game with Washington, the 36-year-old quarterback threw for seven TDs.

The big crowd chanted "beat Green Bay" during the final seconds after Tittle had broken the record with an 8-yard pass to Walton with 1 minute, 8 seconds to play.

Long TD Pass To Gifford

Tittle's Giant mates greeted him like a collegian who had just won the Rose Bowl game, pounding him on the back and wringing his hands as he walked toward the bench. Walton ran over and handed him the football.

The Giants' quarterback started the day with a 47-yard pass to Gifford in the first period and hit Walton for 10 and Webster for 17 and 7 in the second quarter.

The Giants' passing ace hit Walton for a 20-yard TD in the third period, tying the old record. When Guglielmi replaced him early in the final period, it appeared Tittle's chances of setting a record were gone. However, Guglielmi was injured when thrown for a loss trying to pass and Tittle had to go back to work.

An interception of an Eddie LeBaron pass to Dick Lynch, Giants' corner back, gave Tittle his last chance with 1.29 to go. Tittle took care of things himself by rolling out and running 19 yards for a first down on the 8, and then hit Walton with the record breaking pass.

The Statistics

	Cowboys	Giants
First downs	16	23
Rushing yardage	166	153
Passing yardage	312	318
Passes	12-32	21-42
Passes intercepted by	2	1
Punts	3-50	4-37
Fumbles lost	3	2
Yards penalized	40	69

Dallas .... 3 21 0 - 7—31
New York .. 7 21 7 6—41

NY—Gifford 47, pass from Tittle (Chandler, kick).
Dal—FG, Baker, 35.
NY—Walton 10, pass from Tittle (Chandler, kick).
Dal—Marsh 8, run (Baker, kick).
NY—Webster 17, pass from Tittle (Chandler, kick).
Dal—Clark 53, pass from LeBaron (Baker, kick).
NY—Webster 7, pass from Tittle (Chandler, kick).
Dal—Howton 69, pass from Meredith (Baker, kick).
NY—Walton 20, pass from Tittle (Chandler, kick).
Dal—Howton 16, pass from Meredith (Baker, kick).
NY—Walton 8, pass from Tittle (kick failed).
Attendance—62,694.

GREEN BAY ENDS WITH SINGLE LOSS

News Of Lions' Loss Comes Early In Tilt; L.A. Rally Fails

Los Angeles, Dec. 16 (P)—The Green Bay Packers subdued the remarkably challenging Los Angeles Rams, 20 to 17, today and swept on automatically to their third straight Western Division title in the National Football League.

A crowd of 60,353 gathered in Memorial Coliseum under sunny skies watched the Packers wind up the regular season with their thirteenth victory and one defeat. The Packers now go into the N.F.L. championship game with the Eastern Division champions, the New York Giants, at New York December 30.

Bulldozing fullback Jim Taylor, the N.F.L.'s outstanding player, found a giant hole in the Ram line in the second quarter and stormed 28 yards for a touchdown. With it he established a record of 19 touchdowns scored in a single season. The try for extra point was blocked by David Jones.

The touchdown record of 18 for a season was established in 1945 in a ten-game season by Steve Van Buren of the Philadelphia Eagles. Jimmy Brown of the Cleveland Browns equaled the mark in 12 games in 1958.

The Packers also set another record for first downs in a season. They had 18 Sunday to boost their total to 281. The former record of 278 was set by a Ram team in 1950.

The Statistics

	Packers	Rams
First downs	18	16
Rushing yardage	181	207
Passing yardage	246	96
Passes	17-35	12-22
Passes intercepted by	0	1
Punts	4-35	3-46
Fumbles lost	5	1
Yards penalized	5	5

Green Bay ... 7 6 0 7 - 20
Los Angeles . 3 7 0 7 - 17

G.B.—R. Kramer, 45, pass from Moore (J. Kramer, kick).
L.A.—F.G. Villanueva, 39.
G.B.—Taylor, 28 (kick failed).
L.A.—Olsen, 20, return of pass interception (Villanueva, kick).
G.B.—Hornung, 83, pass from Starr (J. Kramer, kick).
L.A.—Dale, 15, pass from Arnett (Villanueva, kick).
Attendance—60,353.

Oakland Tops Boston, 20-0, Ends 19-Game Loss Streak

Oakland, Cal., Dec. 16 (AP)—Oakland's Raiders broke pro football's longest current losing streak with a 20-to-0 shutout of the Boston Patriots in mud and rain today.

The season-ending victory, viewed by 8,000 diehards, stopped a 19-game losing skein which included 13 defeats this year and 6 in 1961.

The last previous Oakland victory was a 26-to-20 triumph over the Buffalo Bills November 5, 1961.

Oakland's defensive team, which topped the American Football League in pass defense, recorded the first shutout in the Raiders' history.

Raider quarterback Cotton Davidson used long aerials to get his club in front, connecting with halfback Clem Daniels on a 75-yard hookup in the second period and setting up a 7-yard Daniels' touchdown run in the third period with a 34-yard completion to spread end Bo Roberson.

Placekicker Ben Agajanian opened and closed Oakland's scoring with field goals of 19 yards in the first period and 21 yards in the last quarter.

The Patriots' deepest penetration of the day was to Oakland's 16 in the fourth quarter, but they failed to score as Gino Cappelletti missed a field goal from the 28-yard-line.

The Statistics

	PATRIOTS	RAIDERS
First downs	11	10
Rushing yardage	82	71
Passing yardage	86	217
Passes	15-35	11-37
Passes intercepted by	1	2
Punts	5-40.4	7-37.3
Fumbles lost	3	1
Yards penalized	30	40

Boston .... 0 0 0 0— 0
Oakland ... 3 7 7 3—20

Oak—FG. Agajanian. 19.
Oak—Daniels. 75. pass from Davidson (Agajanian. kick).
Oak—FG. Agajanian. 21.

Blackout

New York, Dec. 28 (AP)—The National Football League's policy of blacking out home television in the New York metropolitan area of the championship game Sunday between the New York Giants and Green Bay Packers won and lost today in separate court cases.

A Federal judge in New York city ruled the National Broadcasting Co. was within its rights to prohibit TV within a 75-mile area of New York.

Injunction Denied

At New Haven, Conn., on the fringe of the 75-mile limit, a Superior Court judge denied a petition of the NBC and N.F.L. for an injunction to prohibit the New Haven Arena Co. from showing the game on a 10-foot screen at an indoor TV-barbecue. The arena can accommodate about 5,500 persons for an event of this type. A spokesman was unable to say how many tickets had been sold.

In Washington, Senator Thomas J. Dodd (D., Conn.) termed the blackout high-handed and promised to introduce legislation to prevent such blackouts in the future. Dodd is a member of the Senate anti-monopoly subcommittee. He said baseball does not black out the World Series, and "there is no reason why football should black out its play-off."

Yankee Stadium, scene of the title game, is a sellout and a crowd of almost 65,000 will see the game. Heavily populated areas of New York, New Jersey and Connecticut are blacked out.

In a seventeen-page decision, Judge Edward Weinfeld ruled in New York against three Long Island men who sought an injunction to force the league and NBC to lift the blackout.

Admitting that the plaintiffs "and millions of other football fans" in the restricted area desired to watch the game on television, he said:

"But their preferences cannot overcome the rights of these defendants, as authorized by Congress, to impose the local area restriction, believing as they do that serves their economic interests, however ill-advised the public may view their policy."

In New Haven, Judge Raymond J. Devlin refused to issue an injunction against the arena, which was filed late Thursday by NBC and N.F.L.

'Unfair Competition'

Plaintiffs claimed the arena was engaging in unfair competition and the indoor telecast would be interference with the NBC's exclusive contractual rights.

The only NBC network affiliate broadcasting the game in Connecticut is channel 30, an ultra high frequency station in West Hartford.

An attorney for the arena noted that many motels, hotels, restaurants and other places in the area "are doing precisely the same thing we are accused of doing, and none of them is being hauled into court."

Promises Action

Devlin said he was not deciding any questions of infringement of contractual rights, and said the legal problems raised "suggest a serious doubt as to the effectiveness of an injunctive action at this time."

Senator Dodd promised legislative action in a telegram to Pete Rozelle, the N.F.L. commissioner. He said that in 1961 when Congress passed a law granting certain exemptions from antitrust last it was done "in the hope that organized sports would use this privilege in the public interest."

'SKINS LOSE; SNEAD HURT

Steelers Edge Washington In 27-24 Game

Washington, Dec. 16 (AP)—Pittsburgh held off a fourth-quarter Washington rally today to preserve a 27-to-24 victory and wind up the National League football season with a 9-5 mark, best in the Steelers' history.

It was the fifth loss in a row and seventh in their last eight for the reeling Redskins, but they gave it a valiant try, despite the loss of star quarterback Norman Snead in the first quarter.

Michaels Has 26 3-Pointers

George Izo, who hadn't played at all this year, came off the bench to pitch for three touchdowns, two of them coming in the fourth quarter. The Skins finished the year with five wins, seven losses and two ties.

Lou Michaels, burly Steeler defensive end, kicked 38 and 33-yard field goals in the third quarter to run his N.F.L. record total to 26 for the season.

With Sneak connecting on two of his first three passes, Washington moved deep into Steeler territory after the opening kickoff, but faltered when Snead left the game with a shoulder separation and had to settle for a 33-yard field goal by Bob Khayat.

Bobby Layne put the Steelers in front to stay later in the first quarter with a 39-yard scoring pass to Buddy Dial.

The Steelers added a second touchdown on a 1-yard thrust by Dick Hoak, after Red Mack had set it up with a tumbling catch of a 40-yard pass from Layne. Redskin Claude Crabb came up with the ball and fans roundly booed when the officials gave it to the Steelers on the Washington 2.

Statistics

	Steelers	Redskins
First downs	14	17
Rushing yardage	117	22
Passing yardage	166	289
Passes	8-17	19-40
Passes intercepted by	4	2
Punts	7-36.5	4-31.5
Fumbles lost	1	1
Yards penalized	75	55

Pittsburgh ... 7 7 6 7—27
Washington ... 3 0 7 14—24

Washington—FG. Khayat. 33.
Pittsburgh—Dial 39. pass from Layne (Michaels. kick).
Pittsburgh—Hoak 1. run (Michaels. kick).
Washington—James 25. pass from Izo (Khayat. kick).
Pittsburgh—FG. Michaels. 38.
Pittsburgh—FG. Michaels. 33.
Pittsburgh—Carpenter 23. pass from Layne (Michaels. kick).
Washington—James 49. pass from Izo (Khayat. kick).
Washington — Anderson 27. pass from Izo (Khayat. kick).
Attendance—34.508.

Texans Win A.F.L. Crown In Sudden Death, 20-17

BROOKER'S FIELD GOAL BEATS OILERS AFTER 17.54 OF EXTRA TIME

25-Yard Kick Ends Houston's Reign For Two Years Of League's History; Losers Rally After 17-To-0 Deficit

Houston, Dec. 23 (AP)—Tommy Brooker's 25-yard field goal after 17 minutes, 54 seconds of a sudden-death play-off gave the Dallas Texans a 20-to-17 victory over the Houston Oilers today and the American Football League championship.

The Texans, who watched a 17-to-0 halftime advantage crumble before a second-half Houston comeback, were staked to their winning drive by a pass interception by Bill Hull shortly after the second overtime period started.

Defense Turns Vicious

The passing of Len Dawson and the running of Jack Spikes and Abner Haynes had jumped the Texans into their early lead but a vicious Houston defense and George Blanda, still something of a magician despite 13 years as a pro, forced the playoff with 10 points in the fourth quarter.

An overflow crowd of 37,981 and a national television audience saw the young Texans—there are ten rookies on the Dallas roster— take the A.F.L. championship away from the Oilers for the first time since the league was formed in 1960. Houston had entered the game a 6½-point favorite to win its third straight title.

Dawson Loses 43

The Oilers permitted Dallas to cross midfield only once in the second half while dominating play by tossing Dawson for losses totaling 43 yards.

The Oilers also were in control most of the way in overtime until Hull, a rookie defensive end from Wake Forest, intercepted a Blanda pass and returned 23 yards to midfield.

Spikes, named the game's most outstanding player, took a 10-yard pass from Dawson and then set up Brooker's winning three-pointer by breaking loose for a 19-yard run to the Oiler 19.

53-Yard Drive

Blanda's passing had sparked a 53-yard Houston drive to the Texan 35 before Hull moved in with the Texans' fifth interception of the day and second in overtime.

Johnny Robinson earlier had returned an interception 13 yards to permit the Texans to move to the Oiler 38 some 10 minutes in Oilers swarmed Dawson and the Texans were forced to punt from their own 49.

Brooker had given Dallas a 3-to-0 lead in the first period with a 16-yard field goal. Two second-period touchdowns jumped Dallas to a 17-to-0 lead at halftime. Dawson engineered an 80-yard drive, passing the final 28 yards to Abner Haynes.

Returned To 29

Haynes got his second touchdown from the 2-yard line minute later on the seventh play after Dave Grayson returned an interception 20 yards to the Oiler 29.

Houston took the second half kickoff and struck 67 yards in six plays for its first touchdown. Willard Dewveall scoring on a 15-yard Blanda pass.

The Oilers used a Blanda field goal and a 1-yard touchdown by Charlie Tolar for 10 points in the final period to gain the 17-to-17 tie.

Blanda's 31-yard field goal ended a 41-yard drive to the Texan 16. Tolar's run came on the sixth play of a 49-yard drive in which Blanda completed three of four pass attempts for 46 yards.

Each team had entered the league's third championship game with an 11-3 regular season record. Houston had clinched the Eastern Division championship by winning its last seven games.

The teams also ranked one-two in both total offense and total defense, Houston holding only an 8-yard-per-game advantage on offense and Dallas leading in defense by only a 13-yard-per-game margin.

The hard-running Texans, however, ripped the Oiler line for 199 net yards rushing and the Dallas defense limited Houston runners to 98 yards.

Photo Finish

Spikes and Curtis McClinton, who won the A.F.L.'s Rookie of the Year Award after taking over for the injured Spikes early in the season, had practically a photo finish as the game's top rusher. McClinton had 78 yards in 24 plays, while Spikes had 77 in 11.

Blanda, despite seeing his season intercepted-pass record boosted to 47, completed 23 of 46 attempts for 261 yards. Dawson attempted only 14 but completed nine for 88 yards.

Dawson had thrown two touchdown passes against Houston as the Texans crushed the Oilers 31-to-7 here October 28. Blanda threw two against the Texans a week later as the Oilers won in Dallas 14-to-6.

Won First Two

Houston won the A.F.L.'s first championship by defeating the Los Angeles Chargers, 24-to-16, in 1960.

The Chargers later moved to San Diego and Houston defeated them 14-to-3, in last year's title game.

Statistics

	Texans	Oilers
First downs	19	21
Rushing yardage	199	98
Passing yardage	88	261
Passes	9-14	23-46
Passes intercepted by	5	0
Punts	8-31	3-39
Fumbles lost	1	0
Yards penalized	42	50

Dallas 3 14 0 0 0 3—20
Houston 0 0 7 10 0 0—17

Dallas—FG, Brooker, 16.
Dallas—Haynes, 28, pass from Dawson (Brooker kick).
Dallas—Haynes, 2, run (Brooker kick).
Houston—Dewveall, 15, pass from Blanda (Blanda kick).
Houston—FG, Blanda, 31.
Houston—Tolar, 1, run (Blanda kick).
Dallas—FG, Brooker, 25.
Attendance—37,981.

N.F.L. Title

64,892 See Green Bay Defense Check N.Y. In Frigid Weather

You Wanna' Fight?

Boxing promoter Al Flora watched yesterday's National Football League play-off on TV and noticed Green Bay fullback Jim Taylor and linebacker Sam Huff engaging in several skirmishes during the game.

An idea struck.

Flora said he had sent a telegram to both players, guaranteeing each $2,000 to meet in a four-round fight here January 28.

It was expected he would be turned down.

By CAMERON C. SNYDER
[Sun Staff Correspondent]

New York, Dec. 30 — Jerry Kramer kicked three field goals. That was all the working margin the Packer defense needed to keep the National Football League title in Green Bay with a 16-to-7 victory over the New York Giants in frigid Yankee Stadium today.

Dispersed among Kramer's three successful field goals and two misses was a 7-yard touchdown run by Jim Taylor, showing that the Packer offense still wasn't completely frozen out of the end zone as was the Giants'.

Moral Victory

For the predominately Giant crowd of 64,892 the Packer edge of 9 points represented a moral victory. Last year in the championship game, held in Green Bay, the New Yorkers were smeared, 37 to 0.

Except for a blocked punt by the Giant defense which was converted into a touchdown by Jim Collier on his recovery in the Packer end zone, the Giants would have been shut out again.

Erich Barnes warmed up briefly the Giant fans with his block of Max McGee's punt, recovered by Collier in the third quarter, but the chill soon returned in the 17 degree temperature made more bitter by swirling wind gusts up to 30 m.p.h.

Heavy Wind Gusts

It wasn't a day fittin' for offenses and both the Packers and Giants failed to demonstrate any consistency in their attacks. The wind gusts played havoc with the passes and the frozen tundra spilled ball carriers and tacklers indiscriminately.

But the play on the field was every bit as bitter as the elements. Jim Taylor, Packer star fullback, never had it so tough. He was gang tackled nearly everytime he carried the ball and elbows and wild knees were his rewards.

The amazing thing is that Taylor survived the pounding during his 31 running trips that gained 85 yards. He was also thrown for 14 yards in losses by the Giant defense, berrated for its poor game in the 1961 championship game.

Not Tittle's Day

Then there is Y. A. Tittle, the spark at quarterback for the Giants. Y. A. has been around the league for 13 years, 15 years in pro ball including 2 years with the Colts of the old All-America Conference.

This wasn't Tittle's day. The bald brigadier had trouble controlling his pitches and that spelled finis for the Giants, who rode to the Eastern Division title on Y. A.'s passes.

Tittle threw 41 times, completed 18 for 197 yards, but failed to get his team closer to the Packer goal line than 15 yards until the last play of the game, a pass, was downed on the 7.

The Packer offense also wasn't good. It was adequate and controlled the game, making the Giant defense work overtime and the Giant defense is old, mighty old.

The Statistics

	Giant's	Green Bay
First downs rushing	5	11
First downs passing	11	6
First downs by penalty	2	1
Total first downs	18	18
Yards gained rushing (net)	94	148
Yards gained passing (net)	197	98
Total yards gained (net)	293	244
Forward passes attempted	41	22
Passes completed	18	10
Passes intercepted by	0	1
Yds. interceptions returned	0	30
Yds. gained passing (gross)	197	108
Yds. lost attempting to pass	0	10
Number of punts	5	6
Average distance	42	25.5
Punts returned by	1	2
Yds. punts returned by	0	36
Kickoffs returned	4	2
Yds. kickoffs returned	85	63
Number of penalties	4	5
Yards penalized	62	44
Fumbles	3	2
Ball lost on fumbles	2	0
Number of rushing plays	25	45
Average gain per rush	3.6	3.2
Total offensive plays	67	69
Rushing passing & plays	0	0
Attempting to pass	0	0
Average gain per play	4.4	3.5

Individual Statistics

Rushing

GREEN BAY

	Rushes	Yds.
Taylor	31	85
Hornung	8	35
Moore	6	24
Starr	1	4
Totals	46	148

NEW YORK

Webster	15	56
King	11	38
Totals	26	94

Passing

GREEN BAY

	Att.	Com.	Yds.
Starr	21	9	85
Hornung	1	1	21
Totals	22	10	106

NEW YORK

Tittle	41	18	197

Receiving

GREEN BAY

	P	Yds.	TDS
R. Kramer	2	25	0
Taylor	3	20	0
Dowler	4	48	0
McGee	1	13	0
Totals	10	106	0

NEW YORK

Walton	5	75	0
Shofner	5	69	0
King	2	14	0
Webster	1	5	0
Gifford	4	34	0
Morrison	1	0	0
Totals	18	197	

Cleveland Removes Paul Brown As Head Grid Coach

CLUB PRESIDENT SAYS HE HOPES TO ANNOUNCE SUCCESSOR IN 10 DAYS

News Jolts Fans But Wife Says He Knew It Was Coming

Cleveland, Jan. 9 (AP)—Paul E. Brown was removed today as head coach and general manager of the Cleveland Browns — positions he has held for seventeen seasons with the professional football club he founded.

Arthur B. Modell, president and principal owner of the National Football League club, refused to say in so many words that Brown had been fired, but there was no indication the veteran coach had resigned from a contract which had six years to go.

"Knew It Was Coming"

Brown was not immediately available for comment, but his wife said tearfully that he "knew it was coming." Brown was not at his club offices.

The announcement caught fans here by surprise, but Modell said he had been studying the change closely for about three weeks and had informed Brown of it Monday.

He said Brown was agreeable to remain as a vice president of the club and would perform other duties to finish out the balance of his contract at the agreed salary, believed to be in excess of $50,000 a year. Brown also will keep his minor stockholding in the club.

Ewbank Not On List

Modell said he hoped to announce a successor to Brown in about ten days, and added that several candidates were under consideration.

He would not identify the men, but did say Weeb Ewbank, onetime Brown's assistant coach fired yesterday as coach of the Baltimore Colts, was not now among those candidates.

"The only reason I will give for the change is that I believe it will serve the best interests of the Cleveland Browns," Modell said when he was pressed to explain the move.

He said he and Brown were agreed on the wording of the announcement and that it would be "unnecessary and irrelevent" to say more.

Modell said he looked forward to a "continuing good relationship" with the veteran coach.

5-Man Syndicate Buys Titans For $1,000,000

New York, March 15 (AP)—Five wealthy executives, all prominent in thoroughbred racing, obtained control of the bankrupt New York Titans of the American Football League today for $1,000,000.

Approval of the sale was made by John E. Joyce, Federal bankruptcy referee, to a group headed by David A. Werblin, president of Music Corporation of America-TV, and a director of Monmouth Park race track in Oceanport, New Jersey.

No Further Announcement

Harry Wismer, Titans' president and the team's principal stockholder, filed a bankruptcy petition in Federal court on February 6 listing the club's assets of $271,999 and liabilities of $1,341,000.

Werblin, of New York and Elberon, N.J., said he would head the Gotham Football Club, Inc., which will operate the Titans.

"We have nothing more to announce right now, because it will take several days to organize and the other members of the group are not in New York," Werblin said. "I expect it will be next Wednesday or Thursday before we can make any definite announcement about the football club organization."

The other four members are Donald C. Lillis, Pelham, N.Y., Wall Street broker and president of Bowie (Md.) race course; Townsend B. Martin, investment banker of Locust, N.J.; Leon Hess, of New York and Perth Amboy, N.J., head of the Hess Oil and Chemical Company, and Philip H. Iselin, of Oceanport, N.J., president of Korell Company, New York textile firm.

Martin, Hess and Iselin also are directors of the Monmouth Park Jockey Club, and Iselin is Monmouth's vice president and treasurer.

At a hearing earlier this week, George C. Levin, Wismer's attorney, said the Titans president had told him he was a creditor of the club "to the tune of $1,750,000."

Wismer told reporters in court today the agreement to sell the club to the Werblin group eliminated him as a creditor.

Levin made the formal motion for approval of the sale and said he would be retained as counsel for the Gotham Football Club. He told Joyce the proposed sale met with unanimous consent of the Titans' official creditor committee.

The $1,000,000 is to be deposited in a special account to be held in the name of the Titans at the Irving Trust Company and it will be used in formulation of a plan through which the creditors will be paid.

"The parties have been in continuous negotiations with the goal of arriving at a solution to this problem, and I am happy to report that we have come to what we think is a solution," Levin told Joyce.

In urging Joyce to approve the sale, Levin said, "We are dealing with a perishable asset whose franchise was on the verge of being canceled."

Wismer, after his full day in court and law offices, said he was "out, completely out" of the Titans operations after three seasons as head man.

Foss Is Happy

The dapper, voluble Wismer, who seemed to be relieved to be an ex-owner but still a little regretful at now being on the sidelines, added that he would not receive any of the $1,000,000 selling price.

"I'm out $1,750,000," he said, "and that's all I had to spend."

A.F.L. commissioner Joe Foss, here for the negotiations, said the league was "very enthusiastic about the sale. The new owners are a fine group, all well-respected."

N. F. L. Suspends Packers' Hornung, Lions' Karras

5 OTHER LION PLAYERS DRAW $2,000 FINES FOR BETTING ON PRO GAMES

Ban On Two Stars Will Be For At Least One Season

New York, April 17 (AP) — Paul Hornung, halfback star of the professional champion Green Bay Packers, and Alex Karras, bulwark of Detroit's defensive line, were suspended indefinitely today by the National Football League for betting on league games.

The league commissioner, Pete Rozelle, said there could be no review of their cases until after the 1963 season.

Five other Detroit players were fined $2,000 each for betting $50 each on Green Bay to beat the New York Giants last December in the 1962 title game. The players are John Gordy, guard; Gary Lowe, defensive back; Joe Schmidt, all-league middle linebacker; Wayne Walker, linebacker, and Sam Williams, defensive end.

The Detroit club was fined $4,000 because its coach, George Wilson, failed to forward to the proper authorities reports by Detroit police "of certain associations by members of the Detroit team," and because unauthorized individuals were permitted to sit on the Lions' bench.

When Karras heard the news in the Lions' office in Detroit he expressed shock. "I haven't done anything that I am ashamed of and I am not guilty of anything," he said. Asked if he planned any protest, he said "I sure do." He said he had retained a lawyer.

The Lions' management said that it would comply with the ruling but added that such compliance did not mean the club agreed with the nature or the extent of the penalty.

Owners Back Decision

Most of the other owners in the league backed Rozelle strongly. Art Modell, president of the Cleveland Browns, set the tone when he said "I'm certain the N.F.L. is a stronger organization today than it was yesterday. It is gratifying that Pete Rozelle took this decisive and forceful action."

In Washington, Senator McClellan, chairman of the Senate Investigating subcommittee, commended the league "for taking effective action to clean up conditions in professional football."

Rozelle said he had not completed an investigation of allegations that Carroll Rosenbloom, owner of the Baltimore Colts, had bet on league games.

Pointing out that Rosenbloom had denied the charges in a sworn affidavit, Rozelle said his investigation was delayed by legal proceedings involving the Colt owner. He promised that the inquiry would be completed in the near future.

Halas Started Inquiry

The suspensions and fines were announced at an afternoon news conference.

The case first broke into the newspapers January 3. At that time George Halas, owner of the Chicago Bears, asked the league to look into rumors involving a member of a Midwestern team.

In the course of the long investigation, Rozelle's office conducted 52 interviews with persons connected with eight of the fourteen clubs. The commissioner did not release any specific information obtained in the interviews.

However, he said, there was clear evidence that some players knowingly associated with undesirables, bet on their own club to win, bet on other games and had been too free in giving information about their clubs to friends.

Rozelle also found that not all clubs had been as diligent as league policy required in taking precautions against undesirable associates by players.

Rozelle said the league had heard rumors about Hornung's actions and had taken steps to explore them last spring. However, he said, Hornung was not directly questioned until January when enough evidence was in hand.

According to Rozelle's investigation, Hornung met an unidentified West Coast business man who bet on college and professional games, in San Francisco in 1956, before the East-West game. Hornung then had just finished his career at Notre Dame.

Size Of Bets Known

Rozelle said that the friend developed the habit of querying Hornung on football and that by the summer of 1959, Hornung was placing bets on N.F.L. and college games through his friend. The bets usually were $100 or $200 but on several instances reached $500, Rozelle said.

Rozelle refused to estimate how many bets Hornung had made. He said that the pattern continued through 1960 and 1961 but that Hornung stopped betting in 1962. He said the Packers' triple-threat halfback broke even most of the time but won $1,500 one year.

Hornung, 27, led the league in scoring during 1959, 1960 and 1961 and set a play-off record with nineteen points against the New York Giants in the 1961 title game at Green Bay.

He ws the league's most valuable player in 1961 as a runner, pass catcher, occasional passer and place kicker. Hobbled by a knee injury, he saw only part-time duty in 1962.

Asked if the betting rumors had anything to do with Hornung's sporadic appearances last fall, Rozelle said "Green Bay never was advised not to play Hornung. The injury to his knee was the only reason he didn't play."

Questioned about reports that Packer games often were not listed on the betting lines in many cities, Rozelle said "our people contacted certain persons and they concluded there was uncertainty about Hornung's condition and also the club is a team that runs up 49-0 scores."

Friends Called Hoodlums

Karras, called on the carpet in New York in mid-January after he had said during a televised interview that he sometimes bet on games, was suspended for betting and associating with people described by Detroit police as "known hoodlums."

Rozelle said Karras, a 250-pound tackle on the defensive unit, had made at least 6 significant bets since 1958 through a business associate.

Rozelle said the bets were for $50 until 1962 when Karras bet $100 on the Packers against the Giants in the title game and also $100 on the Lions at Green Bay.

The five other Lions who were fined were found to have bet $50 each on the Packers against the Giants after Karras had invited them to watch the game on television at a friend's home in Miami, Fla. The Lions were in Miami to play Pittsburgh the following Sunday in the Playoff Bowl game.

For this one isolated bet, each of the five was fined the $2,000 maximum under the league constitution. There were no suspensions for them.

Rozelle also found that several unnamed players played the $1 football cards and made token bets with friends. They got off with reprimands.

The fines against the Detroit club resulted from the passes to rove along the sidelines and the failure of coach Wilson to follow up the information from the Detroit police.

Asked why the club, and not Wilson, had been fined, Rozelle said "in a case like this I hold the club responsible for the action of its employees."

Rozelle said the players had admitted making the bets. He said he had talked to all but one of the seven men suspended or fined.

"They were disappointed," he said. "Karras was angry. I hope this will be a helpful deterrent for the future."

In answer to questions, Rozelle said Hornung and Karras would be "legally free to play in any league" while suspended. But they would be on the clubs' reserve lists. A spokesman for the American Football League in Dallas said there was no chance of their playing in the A.F.L.

As for the future of Hornung and Karras, Rozelle said, "Obviously their future conduct and attitude will have a bearing on the matter if I should choose to consider lifting the suspensions after the 1963 season.

May 11

Cause Of Big Daddy's Death Won't Be Known For Days

Exactly what killed Big Daddy Lipscomb, the fun-loving goliath of the gridiron, will not be known definitely until next week, Dr. Russell S. Fisher, chief medical examiner, said last night.

"We suspect that narcotics may have been involved," Dr. Fisher said, adding that the 34-year-old former Baltimore Colts all-pro tackle, had more than half a dozen needle marks on his arms.

The preliminary autopsy report showed the football star's alcoholic content was "quite low, at a non-intoxicating level," Dr. Fisher said.

More Tests Being Made

Additional tests are being made to determine exactly how the 6-foot-6, 290-pound grid star died. Dr. Fisher indicated it will be at least next Wednesday before a final report on test findings would be available.

Eugene Lipscomb was found slumped over in a chair in the kitchen of a friend's home in the 400 block North Brice street early

Reprinted from
The Baltimore Sun

yesterday and was pronounced dead on arrival at Lutheran Hospital at 7.55 A.M.

The ambulance crew found the man breathing heavily. He was wearing a polo shirt and trousers.

Timothy N. Black, 25, a laborer who lives at the Brice street address, told police both of them had been out on the town in the grid star's 1963 yellow Cadillac.

Mr. Black was taken to Northeastern district headquarters late yesterday for lie-detector tests, police said. Results of the tests were not made known.

$73 In Pockets

Capt. Wade H. Poole, who commands the Western district, said the gridiron star was unemployed during the off-season. He had wrestled on the West Coast during off-season but had not been wrestling for the last couple of years, the captain said.

He said police found $73 in the big man's pockets.

Mr. Black said he and the big Pittsburgh Steelers star went out about midnight in the big car. They returned with two women and a supply of beer.

They took the women home about 3 A.M. and drove around some more, returning to the apartment between 4 A.M. and 5 A.M.

Mr. Black said he went out for breakfast to a neighborhood lunch room and returned to the apartment about 7 A.M. to find the grid star slumped in the kitchen chair and breathing heavily.

He said he tried to slap the big man into consciousness but was unable to revive him.

The body was taken to the Morgue for the preliminary tests made yesterday.

Dr. Rudiger Breitenecker, assistant medical examiner, made the preliminary tests. He said at least three needle marks were found above the veins on both elbows.

A home-made syringe was found in the kitchen with the football star.

He was living with Sherman Plunkett, a former Colt now with the San Diego Chargers, and Mr. Plunkett's wife.

Police listed Mr. Lipscomb's address as the 3200 block Vickers road.

DAVIS DEAD OF LEUKEMIA

Ex-Syracuse Grid Great Succumbs After Battle

ERNIE DAVIS
Leukemia claims grid great

Cleveland, May 18 (P) — Ernie Davis, America's greatest collegiate football player of 1961 and a symbol of tremendous courage to all who knew him, died peacefully today in Lakeside Hospital after a thirteen-month battle against acute leukemia.

The 23-year-old former All-America halfback at Syracuse was the only Negro ever to win the Heisman Trophy, the highest honor accorded a college grid star. He was a member of the Cleveland Browns in the National Football League, but never played a game professionally.

He was stricken with the deadly blood disease at the College All-Star camp in Evanston, Ill., last July. However, doctors now have concluded the 6-foot-2, 212-pounder actually was afflicted in April, 1962.

For more than three months the news that Davis had leukemia was withheld from him and the general public. Then in October, doctors and Browns' officials told Davis his illness was in a remissive state, meaning the disease was arrested temporarily. That lasted for more than six months — or until ten weeks ago.

Davis entered the hospital Thursday afternoon. First he stopped by the Browns' office to talk to Arthur B. Modell, club president.

"He was here for one hour," Modell said. "He told me he had to go to the hospital, but that it was nothing serious and that he'd be out of there in a couple of days.

Saying His Goodbyes

"His neck was swollen considerably and we all knew what it meant. I think Ernie did, too.

"He was coming by to say goodby to me and the others.

"I asked him how he was feeling," Modell recalled. "All he would say was, 'I've felt better, but it's nothing to worry about. My throat hurts a little.' He was apologetic about having to go into the hospital."

Jim Brown, Cleveland's great fullback and the man who preceded Davis at Syracuse, was deeply touched by Ernie's death.

"This is a great personal loss," Brown said. "He was a tremendous invididual. He realized this was going to happen eventually, but he was courageous in the face of everything. He never

showed his feelings to any of the guys.

"I never caught him with his head down. He just carried on normally as if nothing was wrong. Football was his life and he wanted so badly to play for the Browns."

Modell, who knew Davis for eighteen months and went far beyond the normal relationship of owner-player in his association with Ernie, said he planned to start an Ernie Davis foundation for leukemia research.

Numbed By Death

"The Browns will make a substantial contribution to get the fund started," Modell said. "His mother has asked that instead of flowers, contributions should go to University Hospitals in Cleveland for the hospital's leukemia research projects."

In his hometown of Elmira, N.Y., Davis's mother, Mrs. Arthur Radford said the death was a "terrible shock." She said she was numbed by the loss of her only son. His father is dead.

The body was being shipped by airplane to Elmira. The Rev. Latta R. Thomas will officiate at funeral services Wednesday at 1 P.M., E.S.T., in the Monumental Baptist Church. Interment will be in the Woodlawn Cemetery in Elmira.

The Browns plan to charter a plane to take club officials and players to the funeral.

Worst Type

Dr. Austin S. Weisberger, Davis's personal physician and a blood specialist, said: "Ernie was a most impressive person. He was a real gentleman in all senses of the word. He had great courage and dignity. You couldn't help but admire him."

The doctor said Davis's form of the disease—acute monocytic leukemia—is the worst kind of all.

A.F.L. TO HELP 2 WEAK CLUBS

Jets And Raiders To Pick From Other Teams

Dallas, May 12 (AP)—Milt Woodward, assistant commissioner of the American Football League, said today the Oakland Raiders and the New York Jets will be allowed to pick players from the rosters of the other six teams in the loop.

Woodward said that the plan, approved in New York yesterday by the eight club owners, should strengthen the Raiders and Jets.

"At the same time, it should not hurt any of the other six clubs," Woodward said.

25 Jet Untouchables

The Jets and Raiders will start marking their choices June 1 and all selections should be completed by July 1, he said.

Woodward said that each of the other six teams would designate 25 veterans and half of their rookies draftees and free agents as unavailable.

In addition, New York is expected to be able to pick two available free agents from each roster and Oakland one from each. New York could take one available rookie from each team as well, under the plan.

Oakland was the weakest team in the league last year, losing its first twelve games, and finishing 1-13. The New York Titans, now renamed the Jets, were 5-9. They had financial troubles through the season, and were put into bankruptcy court in a reorganization effort before new owners took over the club.

Because of the delay in establishing the new ownership, the Titans had been unable to sign a single draft choice.

Sept. 7

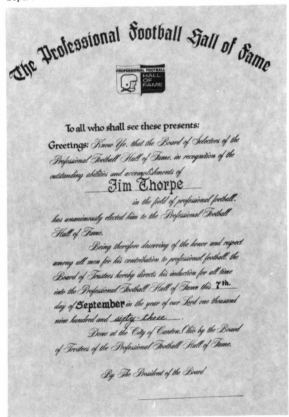

GRIDDER DIES FROM INJURY

Stone Johnson Was Hurt In Pro Exhibition Game

Wichita, Kan., Sept. 9 (AP)—Stone Johnson, promising rookie for the Kansas City Chiefs and a runner for the United States in the 1960 Olympics, died last night of a broken neck suffered in an exhibition football game eight days ago.

An attending physician attributed death to a fracture of the fifth cervical vertebra of the neck and spinal cord damage.

The physician, who declined use of his name, said an autopsy also revealed a blood clot in a lung artery. While this was a complication unknown previously, the physician said it was not the cause of death.

The 23-year-old halfback had been in serious condition since suffering a fractured neck vertebra in the game against the Houston Oilers. He was hurt on a first quarter kick-off when he dived to make a block in the game August 31.

Johnson, 6-foot-1 and 180 pounds, was left paralyzed in the lower part of his body and partially paralyzed in the arms.

He underwent surgery before the end of the game and was placed in traction. Johnson had been kept motionless on his back since the injury.

His parents, Mr. and Mrs. Jesse Johnson, of Dallas, Texas, had been at his bedside almost constantly.

Flowers and other remembrances had been sent to Johnson's room by friends, but he had been permitted no visitors.

Fifth In Olympics

A native of Dallas, Johnson attended Grambling College in Louisiana and after being drafted by the Chiefs—then the Dallas Texas—did not play out his college eligibility.

The Chiefs considered him one of the fastest men in football, pegged to his times of 9.3 seconds in the 100-yard dash and 20.5 seconds in the 220-yard dash.

In the 1960 Olympics at Rome, Italy, Johnson finished fifth in the 200-meter final with a time of 20.8 seconds. He was a member of the 400-meter relay team which finished first but was disqualified for illegally passing the baton.

Johnson was the seventh football player to die of game injuries this year and the first in professional ranks since 1960.

PASS PLAY MARK IS SET

Izo-To-Mitchell Aerial Clicks For 99 Yards

Cleveland, Sept. 15 (AP)—Jimmy Brown, Frank Ryan and Lou Groza unloosed a three-pronged attack for the Cleveland Browns and blasted Washington's Redskins, 37 to 14, today in each team's National League opener before a crowd of 57,618.

A 99-yard scoring pass from George Izo, to Bobby Mitchell, tying the league record which has stood since 1939, was far from enough to turn the tide in Washington's favor.

Brown, bidding for the ground-gaining title he lost last year after topping the list for five seasons, rushed for 162 yards in fifteen tries, caught three passes for 100, scored on runs of 80 and 10 yards and took an 83-yard pass for another.

Groza Kicks 3 Goals

Groza, greatest scorer in the history of the league, upped his career total to 915 with a 13-point effort as he converted four times and booted field goals from 42, 24 and 39 yards.

And Ryan, finally locking up the quarterback post, looked like the long-sought successor to Otto Graham as he completed 21 of 32 passes for 334 yards and two touchdowns.

All that added up to 534 yards for the Browns. Washington, which beat the Browns twice last year, was held to 71 rushing and 201 passing—almost half of the latter on Izo's first pass of the season to fleet-footed Mitchell.

Ryan Connects

Ryan passed four yards to Bob Crespino for the Brown's first marker, after Sam Tidmore recovered a fumble. Groza booted his 42-yard three-pointer to give Cleveland a 10-0 quarter lead.

Norm Snead hit Pat Richter with a seven-yard scoring pass on the first play of the second period to get the Redskins back in the game, but on the first play after the kick-off came the Ryan-to-Brown touchdown pass.

The big fullback was hit at least six times but kept going for the counter. Later in the period, big Jim went ten for another counter and a 27-7 halftime edge.

Statistics

	REDSKINS	BROWNS
First downs	14	23
Rushing yardage	71	217
Passing yardage	201	326
Passes	13-32	21-32
Passes intercepted by	2	2
Punts	7-43	1-26
Fumbles lost	1	0
Yards penalized	71	81

Washington 0 7 7 0—14
Cleveland 10 14 3 10—37

Cleveland—Crespino, 4, pass from Ryan. (Groza kick).
Cleveland—FG, Groza, 42.
Washington—Richter, 7, pass from Snead. (Khayat kick).
Cleveland—Brown, 83 yard pass from Ryan. (Groza kick).
Cleveland—Brown, 10, run. (Groza kick).
Cleveland—FG, Groza, 24.
Washington—Mitchell, 99, pass from Izo. (Khayat kick).
Cleveland—Brown, 80, run. (Groza kick).
Cleveland—FG, Groza, 39.
Attendance—57,618.

Redskins Edge Cowboys, 21-17, As Steffen Stars

Washington, Sept. 29 (AP)—Jim Steffen raced 78 yards after grabbing a Dallas pass in the first quarter to open Washington scoring today, then stymied the Cowboys with another pass interception in the closing minutes to preserve a 21-to-17 Redskins victory.

By winning, Washington boosted its National Football League record to 2-1. Dallas has lost all its three games.

Dallas recovered a Redskin fumble on the third play of the game deep in Washington territory, but a pass interference penalty cost the Cowboys a touchdown.

Steffen Scores TD

On the next play, Steffen picked off Don Meredith's pass and whizzed down the sidelines to put Washington ahead.

Midway in the second quarter, Bill Howton, Dallas' end, caught a 15-yard pass to break Don Hutson's career record for pass receiving.

For the game, Howton finished with four pass receptions for 82 yards, including a brilliant 43-yard pass-run play that put Dallas ahead 17-14 in the third period.

Howton Threatens Hutson

Howton now has a career yardage total of 8,067 yards, compared to the former Green Bay Packer end's total of 7,991 yards and is only ten behind Hutson's career mark of 488 pass receptions.

Bosseler Sparks Drive

Dallas tied the score late in the second quarter after Cornell Green intercepted a Redskin pass and ran it back 31 yards to midfield. Amos Marsh bucked over from the 1 after Howton caught two passes in the drive.

The Cowboys took the lead early

The Statistics

	Redskins	Cowboys
First downs	19	22
Rushing yardage	127	164
Passing yardage	175	191
Passes	13-26	14-30
Passes intercepted by	1	0
Punts	3-42	2-48.5
Fumbles lost	1	0
Yards penalized	61	77

Dallas 0 7 10 0—17
Washington 7 0 7 7—21

Wash.—Steffen 78, pass interception (Khayat kick).
Dallas—Marsh 1 run (Baker kick).
Dallas—FG Baker 41.
Wash.—James 1 run. (Khayat kick).
Dallas—Howton 38, pass from Meredith (Baker kick).
Wash.—Cunningham 1 run (Khayat kick).
Attendance—40,101.

in the third quarter on a 41-yard field goal by Sam Baker.

But the Redskins came back quickly with a 70-yard scoring drive. Don Bosseler led the way with a diving catch of a 33-yard pass, then took the ball 18 yards on a draw play to the 3-yard line. Dick James drove over from the 1 for the score.

Howton put the Cowboys ahead again a few minutes later with a dazzling run after taking a short pass from Meredith.

Then the Redskins meshed their air and ground attacks and marched 80 yards for the winning touchdown.

Norman Snead completed a 12-yard toss to Bobby Mitchell and an 18-yard pass to Pat Richter to move Washington to the Dallas 27.

Bill Barnes and Don Bosseler then moved the ball inside the 5 and Jim Cunningham buck over from the 1.

Houston Beaten By Kansas City

Kansas City, Oct. 6 (AP)—The Kansas City Chiefs combined quarterback Len Dawson's four touchdown passes with a crunching ground game and bruising defense for a 28-to-7 victory over Houston in an American Football League game today.

The crowd of 27,801 paid at the Chiefs first game in Kansas City turned out in 92-degree weather on a World Series day to watch the defending champion A.F.L. champions.

The club averaged about 22,000 last season in Dallas in a bitter attendance duel with the National Football League Cowboys before moving the A.F.L. franchise to Kansas City.

Dawson brought his season total to 12 touchdown passes by firing scoring strikes of 14 and 4 yards to tight end Fred Arbanas, 69 yards to split end Chris Burford, and 12 yards to flanker Frank Jackson.

Balanced Attack

The Kansas City running attack, impotent the past two games, came to life with Abner Haynes and Curtis McClinton. This gave the Chiefs' offense the balance it has needed. Dawson got near-perfect protection as he hit 14 of 22 pass attempts for 225 yards and had none intercepted.

George Blanda, 36-year-old quarterback of the Oilers, was frustrated by four interceptions and two lost fumbles. Down 21-0, he pulled Houston together for an 84-yard scoring drive climaxed by a four-yard pass to halfback Dave Smith in the final period.

Kansas City is the only A.F.L. club with a series edge over the three-time eastern division champion Oilers. The margin between the clubs is now 5-3.

Statistics

	OILERS	CHIEFS
First downs	12	21
Rushing yardage	46	125
Passing yardage	241	212
Passes	20-39	14-23
Passes intercepted by	0	4
Punts	3-49.3	5-50.6
Fumbles lost	2	2
Yards penalized	5	20

Houston .... 0 0 0 7— 7
Kansas City .... 0 14 7 7—28

K.C.—Arbanas, 14, pass from Dawson (Brooker kick).
K.C.—Burford, 69, pass from Dawson (Brooker kick).
K.C.—Arbanas, 4, pass from Dawson (Brooker kick).
Hou.—Smith, 4, pass from Blanda (Blanda kick).
K.C.—Jackson, 12, pass from Dawson (Brooker kick).
Attendance, 27,801.

A.F.L. Draft

FIRST ROUND

Boston—Jack Concannon, Boston College quarterback choice acquired from Denver; Kansas City—Pete Beathard, Southern California quarterback; New York—Matt Snell, Ohio State fullback. Denver—Bob Brown, Nebraska guard, choice acquired from Boston; Buffalo—Carl Eller, Minnesota tackle; Houston—Scott Appleton, Texas tackle; Oakland—Tony Lorick, Arizona State fullback; San Diego—Ted Davis, Georgia Tech

SECOND ROUND

Houston — Charles Taylor, Arizona State halfback choice acquired from Denver; Kansas City—Billy Martin, Georgia Tech end; New York—Lloyd Voss, Nebraska tackle; Buffalo—Dick Evey, Tennessee tackle; Boston—Jim Kelly, Notre Dame end; Houston—Billy Truax, L.S.U. end; Oakland—Dan Conners, Miami (Fla.) tackle; San Diego—John Kirby, Nebraska linebacker.

THIRD ROUND

Denver—Marv Woodson, Indiana halfback; Kansas City—Ken Kortas, Louisville tackle; New York—Gerald Philbin, University of Buffalo guard; Denver—Matt Snorton, Michigan State end (choice acquired from Boston); Buffalo—George Rose, Auburn back; Houston—Bob Crenshaw, Baylor tackle; Oakland—George Bednar, Notre Dame tackle; San Diego—Perry Lee Dunn, Mississippi quarterback.

Contractor From D.C. Buys Eagles; Keeltys Lose Out

Philadelphia, Dec. 5 (AP)—The Philadelphia Eagles were sold tonight for $5,505,500 to Washington contractor Jerry Wolman. The sale is contingent on approval of the National Football League and other club owners.

Approval of at least eleven of the remaining thirteen owners is necessary to complete the sale.

After four hours of sometimes heated debate over offers that ranged from $5,100,000 to the Wolman bid, 50 of the 91 shares of stock voted to sell to Wolman, a native of Shenandoah, Pa. who moved to Washington some ten years ago.

A bid by Joseph McCrane, son-in-law of Garden State race track owner Eugene Mori, of $5,105,000 received the vote of 23 shares, while 9 shares favored Jack Wolgin, a credit corporation executive, who offered $5,100,000.

Nine shares were not represented at the meeting.

There were no votes for a $5,120,000 offer by James and Joseph Keelty, Baltimore house builders.

The stockholders voted Wolgin second choice in the event that the league and/or the owners should turn down Wolman. McCrane was voted third choice.

Wolman is in line to be the fourth owner in the 33-year history of the Philadelphia franchise. The late Bert Bell, former N.F.L. commissioner, headed a group which bought the team for $2,500 in 1933. Bell became sole owner in 1936 on a $4,000 investment.

In 1941, Bell sold out to Alexis Thompson, late New York millionaire. In 1949 the present syndicate took over for $300,000.

The 65 present owners who bought the club's stock 14 years ago for $3,000 a share thus sold their interests for $60,500 per share.

N.F.L. Choices

FIRST ROUND

San Francisco 49ers—Dave Parks, Texas Tech end. Philadelphia Eagles—Bob Brown, Nebraska guard. Washington Redskins—Charley Taylor, Arizona State halfback. Dallas Cowboys—Scott Appleton, Texas tackle. Detroit Lions—Pete Beathard, U.S.C. quarterback. Minnesota Vikings—Carl Eller, Minnesota tackle. Los Angeles Rams—Bill Munson, Utah State quarterback. Baltimore Colts—Marvin Woodson, Indiana halfback. St. Louis Cards—Ken Kortas, Louisville tackle. Pittsburgh Steelers—Paul Martha, Pittsburgh halfback. Cleveland Browns—Paul Warfield, Ohio State halfback. New York Giants—Joe Don Looney, Oklahoma halfback. Green Bay Packers—Lloyd Voss, Nebraska tackle. Chicago Bears—Dick Evey, Tennessee tackle.

SECOND ROUND

San Francisco—George Mira, Miami, Fla. quarterback. Philadelphia—Jack Concannon, Boston College, quarterback. Dallas—Mel Renfree, Oregon, halfback. Washington—Paul Krause, Iowa, halfback. Minnesota—Hal Bedsole, Southern California end. Detroit—Matt Snorten, Michigan State, end. Chicago — Billy Martin, Georgia Tech, end. (Choice acquired from Los Angeles). Colts—Tony Lorick, Arizona State, fullback. Chicago—Pat Crain, Clemson, fullback. (choice acquired from Pittsburgh). St. Louis—Herschel Turner, Kentucky, tackle. New York—Steve Thurlow, Stanford, halfback. Cleveland—Bill Truax, Louisiana State, end. Green Bay—Jon Morris, Holy Cross, center. Pittsburgh—Jim Kelly, Notre Dame, end (choice acquired from Chicago).

THIRD ROUND

San Francisco—Dave Wilcox, Oregon end. Detroit—Pat Batten, Hardin-Simmons back (choice acquired from Philadelphia); Los Angeles—John Mims, Rice tackle (choice acquired from Washington); Los Angeles—Willie Brown, Southern California back (choice acquired from Dallas); Minnesota — George Rose, Auburn back. Detroit—Gerald Philbin Buffalo tackle; Los Angeles—Jerry Richardson, West Texas State back; Green Bay—Ode Burrell, Mississippi State back (choice acquired from Dallas and Baltimore); St. Louis—Rene Prudhomme, Louisiana State tackle; Pittsburgh — Ralph Baker, Penn State linebacker; Los Angeles—Roger Pillath, Wisconsin tackle (choice acquired from Cleveland); Green Bay—Joe O'Donnell, Michigan guard (choice acquired from New York); Green Bay—Tommy Crutcher, Texas Christian back; Chicago—Sid Blanks, Texas A&I back.

BILLS ROUT JETS, 45-14

Gilchrist Scores 5 Times, Gains 243 Yards

Buffalo, N.Y., Dec. 8 (AP) — Cookie Gilchrist riddled the New York Jets line today for 243 yards and scored 5 touchdowns —American Football League records — as the Buffalo Bills crushed the Jets, 45-14, before 30,222 fans in War Memorial stadium.

Gilchrist, the A.F.L.'s most valuable player last year and unable to break away consistently this season until today, set three league records and four team records and equaled three league marks.

His 243 yards surpassed the 216 ripped off by Houston's Billy Cannon in a 1961 game against New York. Abner Haynes, playing for Dallas in 1961 against Oaklan, had scored 4 touchdowns rushing.

Wood In Flight

Buffalo virtually crippled New York's attack on the first play from scrimmage after the opening kick-off. Sid Youngleman chased quarterback Dick Wood from his 21 to the 4, where Wood went down and, at the same time, stretched the muscles in his left leg.

The signal-calling duties were turned over to Galen Hall, who tossed a 23-yard fourth-period touchdown pass to Don Maynard. Hall could engineer only 38 yards rushing for the Jets.

Gilchrist scored his first touchdown from the 4-yard line after three minutes of play. His others came on a pair of 1-yard smashes, and runs of 4 and 19 yards.

He carried the ball 36 times.

Jets Drop To Cellar

Rookie Daryle Lamonica, who started his first game at quarterback for the Bills, hit Elbert Dubenion with a 23-yard scoring pass with 26 seconds left in the second period.

Mark Smolinski, New York fullback, tallied the Jets first touchdown on a 1-yard plunge at 13.40 of the first period.

The victory evened Buffalo's season record at 6-6 with one tie. New York, now 5-6-1, replaced Buffalo as the Eastern Division's cellar-dweller.

Besides setting league records for one-game rushing yardage and touchdowns rushing, Gilchrist's 36 carries set a new A.F.L. one-game record.

He tied individual one-game league marks for most touchdowns scored by both rushing and pass-receiving, and for most points scored, 30.

His new one-game team records are for most carries, most touchdowns, most points and most rushing yardage.

Statistics

	New York	Buffalo
First downs	14	22
Rushing yardage	38	285
Passing yardage	130	85
Passes	15-37	10-16
Passes int'rcptd by	0	2
Punts	4-33.7	2-46.5
Fumbles lost	2	0
Yards penalized	27	37

New York .... 7 0 0 7—14
Buffalo .... 10 14 7 14—45

Buf.—Gilchrist 4, run (Yoho kick).
Buf.—FG Yoho 13.
NY—Smolinski 1, run (Guesman kick).
Buf.—Gilchrist 1, run (Yoho kick).
Buf.—Dubenion 23, pass from Lamonica (Yoho kick).
Buf.—Gilchrist 1, run (Yoho kick).
Buf.—Gilchrist 19, run (Yoho kick).
Buf.—Gilchrist 4, run (Yoho kick).
NY—Maynard 23, pass from Hall (Guesman kick).
Attendance 20,222.

Browns Whip 'Skins, 27-20; Brown Hits Mile In Rushing

The Statistics

Washington, Dec. 15 (AP)—Jimmy Brown ran his season's rushing total past the mile mark and Frank Ryan pierced the Washington defense for three touchdown passes today as Cleveland scored a 27-to-20 National Football League victory over the Redskins.

With 125 yards in 28 carries, Brown pushed his total yardage for the year to 1,863 yards and became the first N.F.L. player to gain more than a mile on the ground in one season.

	Browns	Skins
First downs	22	12
Rushing yardage	176	56
Passing yardage	192	215
Passes	14-30	12-28
Passes int. by	1	1
Punts	4-48	6-37
Fumbles lost	2	0
Yards penalized	53	34

Cleveland 10 10 0 7 27
Washington 0 7 7 6—20
Clev.—F G , Groza 42
Clev.—Collins 34, pass from Ryan (Groza, kick)
Clev.—F G , Groza 42
Wash.—Mitchell 92, kickoff return (Khayat, kick)
Clev.—Green 33, pass from Ryan (Groza, kick)
Wash.—Barnes 1, run (Khayat kick)
Clev.—Collins 9, pass from Ryan (Groza, kick)
Wash.—Barnes 23, pass from Snead (kick missed).
Attendance. 40,865.

Dec. 15

Unitas-To-Matte Aerial Gives Baltimore Victory In Finale

By CAMERON C. SNYDER

John Unitas flipped a 14-yard touchdown pass to Tom Matte with 33 seconds left and the Colts wrapped up the season and the Los Angeles Rams, 19 to 16, yesterday at the Stadium.

It was a typical Colt and Unitas finish and gave 52,834 fans a tingle which wasn't produced from the 26-degree temperature.

The crowd was stirring from frozen seats, visualizing a Colt lost of 16-13 when Jim Welch, Colt defensive halfback, first jarred the ball loose from Ben Wilson, Ram fullback, and then recovered it on the L.A. 39.

Unitas broke Sonny Jurgensen's mark of 235 completions in a season by 2 with 237. Jurgensen's league mark had been set in 1961 with the Philadelphia Eagles.

Also Martin's 2 field goals and one extra point, the last one was blocked, gave him a total of 104 points for the season, second to the Giants' Don Chandler, who had 106.

The surprising thing about the game was that the Rams, who had trained in warm California and were then subjected to the freezing climate here, were more sure-fingered than the supposedly acclimated Colts.

Although they were statistically outplayed most of the game, the Rams came within 33 seconds of winning over a team that gained 526 yards for the afternoon.

TITTLE SETS TD PASS MARK AS N.Y. DEFEATS PITTSBURGH BY 33-17

New York, Dec. 15 (AP)—Y. A. Tittle pitched the New York Giants to the National Football League's Eastern Conference title with three record-breaking touchdown passes in a 33-to-17 victory over the fired-up Pittsburgh Steelers today in a winner-take-all showdown in the final game of the regular season.

Joe Morrison, the handyman of the Giants who was filling in for injured Alex Webster, caught two of Tittle's scoring passes and dove over from the one for three big touchdowns.

The season's largest crowd at Yankee Stadium, 63,240, sensed the Steelers' second half bid was dead when Frank Gifford made two sensational catches of Tittle's passes midway in the third period. The first catch came on a third and eight situation and was a one-hander that gained 3 yards to the Steelers' 47.

Giants Against Bears

The victory sent the Giants into a National Football League championship game December 29 against the Chicago Bears at Chicago's Wrigley Field. The Bears beat the Detroit Lions, 24 to 14, today for the Western title.

Tittle, voted the most valuable player in the league earlier in the week in an Associated Press poll, proved it all over again with another fine performance on a bitterly cold day with a chill wind whipping across the stadium. Tittle had not played when the Steelers shut out the Giants 31-0 September 22 at Pittsburgh.

It was the end of the line for the Steelers, who never have won a division title but had a chance to take it all with a victory because of three ties. The Giants finished with an 11-to-3 record. Pittsburgh wound up 7-4-3.

Oakland Beats Houston, 52-49, On 39-Yard 3-Pointer

Oakland, Cal., Dec. 22 (AP)—Mike Mercer's 39-yard field goal in the fourth quarter brought the Oakland Raiders a 52-to-49 victory over the Houston Oilers today in the highest scoring game of the four-year American Football League history.

The Raiders, who kept their Western Division title hopes alive until the final day of the regular season, finished in second place with a 10-4 record, one game behind San Diego.

The Chargers won the title with an 11-3 record after defeating Denver 58-20 Sunday.

In a wild game that saw the Cinderella Raiders capture their eighth straight victory, the score stood 49-49 before Mercer booted his decisive three-pointer with four minutes, 37 seconds remaining to end the scoring orgy.

Oakland's Clem Daniels on the final play of the game plunged for three yards to break unofficially the league rushing record with 1,098 yards for the season, two more than Cookie Gilchrist had with Buffalo a year ago.

The 101 points were eight more than the record high of 93 set when the Chargers, then in Los Angeles, beat New York 50-43 in 1960.

Powell Catches 4 Scores

Raider end Art Powell caught four touchdown passes, setting a single game record.

The offensive show highlighted the passing of Oakland's Tom Flores and George Blanda of the Oilers. Flores hit 17 of 29 passes for 407 yards and six touchdowns.

Blanda hit 20 of 32 pass attempts for 342 yards and five touchdowns. Blanda holds the league record for touchdown passes in a game with seven.

All told, the Raiders gained 588 yards today after going through the first quarter without a first down. They needed 1 point in the final quarter to win.

Flores threw touchdown passes of seven yards to Ken Herock, 56 to Daniels and 81, 20 45 and 22 to Powell.

The Statistics

	Oilers	Raiders
First downs	27	21
Rushing yardage	133	181
Passing yardage	342	407
Passes	20-32	17-29
Passes intercepted by	2	2
Punts	5-42.0	4-42.0
Fumbles lost	0	0
Yards penalized	60	88

Houston .... 14 21 14 0—49
Oakland .... 7 28 7 10—52

Oak.—Gibson, 68 punt return (Mercer, kick).
Hou.—Hennigan, 4 pass from Blanda (Blanda, kick).
Hou.—Smith, 2 run (Blanda, kick).
Hou.—Dewveall, 12 pass from Blanda (Blanda, kick).
Oak.—Herock, 7 pass from Flores (Mercer, kick).
Oak.—Daniels, 56 pass from Flores (Mercer, kick).
Hou.—Smith, 25 pass from Blanda (Blanda, kick).
Oak.—Powell, 81 pass from Flores (Mercer, kick).
Hou.—Tolar, 1 run (Blanda, kick).
Oak.—Powell, 20 pass from Flores (Mercer, kick).
Oak.—Powell, 45 pass from Flores (Mercer, kick).
Hou.—Dewveall, 26 pass from Blanda (Blanda, kick).
Hou.—McLeod, 7 pass from Blanda (Blanda, kick).
Oak.—Powell, 22 pass from Flores (Mercer, kick).
Oak.—F.G., Mercer, 39.
Attendance, 17,401.

Blanda's strikes covered four yards to Charlie Hennigan, 12 and 26 to Willard Dewveall, 25 to Dave Smith and 21 to Bob McLeod.

Claude Gibson raced a punt back 68 yards the first time an Oakland player got his hands on the ball.

Houston promptly surged back to lead 14-7 at the first quarter.

The wild first half ended in a 35-35 deadlock with 21 points scored in the final minute and 49 seconds.

Houston led 28-21 when Flores hit Powell on the 81-yarder, tying it at 28-28. The Oilers snapped back 54 yards in four plays, including pass interference in the end zone. Charlie Tolar then scored from the one for 35-28 on Blanda's conversion.

The clock showed 1:09, enough it proved for six plays, including four Flores completions, the finale to Powell from 2 yards out with six seconds remaining. Mercer's conversion knotted it 35-35 at intermission.

Each quarterback connected on a dozen throws in the first half with Flores gaining 277 yards on his passes and Blanda 222.

BOSTON TRIPS BILLS, 26 TO 8

Takes Play-Off Game In Eastern Half Of A.F.L.

A.F.L. Standings

Saturday's Result

Boston 26, Buffalo 8, Eastern Division playoff.

Championship Game, Jan. 5

Boston at San Diego.

(Final Standings)

EASTERN DIVISION	W.	L.	T.	Pct.	Pts.	Op.
Boston	8	6	1	.571	353	265
Buffalo	7	7	1	.500	312	317
Houston	6	8	0	.429	302	372
New York	5	8	1	.385	249	399
WESTERN DIVISION						
San Diego	11	3	0	.786	399	255
Oakland	10	4	0	.714	363	282
Kansas City	5	7	2	.417	347	263
Denver	2	11	1	.154	291	473

Buffalo, N.Y., Dec. 28 (AP)—Boston quarterback Babe Parilli passed for two touchdowns and Gino Cappelletti kicked four field goals as the Patriots defeated the Buffalo Bills today, 26-to-8, and won the Eastern Division title in the first playoff in American Football League history.

The Patriots, bringing their record to 8-6-1 in this showdown struggle on a slippery field covered with a one-inch snowfall, will meet the Western Division champion San Diego Chargers at San Diego Sunday, January 5, for the A.F.L. championship.

Parilli and Ron Burton, the center of a heated controversy before the game, were the keys to the victory as the Patriots struck for a 16-0 lead in the first half, then wrapped it up after Buffalo battled back on a 93-yard pass from Daryle Lamonica to El Dubenion—the most dramatic play of the game.

Burton was activated despite the protests of Buffalo owner Ralph Wilson, who contended the move was a violation of the league constitution. Commissioner Joe Foss ruled otherwise and Burton, sidelined since last August with a slipped disc, proved effective both in rushing and pass receiving.

WADE GETS TWO TDS TO WIN IT

Chicago Picks Off Five Tittle Passes; Morris Is Outstanding

By CAMERON C. SNYDER
[Sun Staff Correspondent]

Chicago, Dec. 29 — The Chicago Bears rode to their first National Football League championship in 17 years on a stout defense which set up both touchdowns in the 14-to-10 victory over the New York Giants and made a one-legged passer out of Y. A. Tittle this cold afternoon at Wrigley Field.

For the Giants, the perennial champions of the Eastern Division, this was another one so-close-but-not-enough effort which has dogged them since the Baltimore Colts' famous "sudden death" victory in 1958.

Reprinted from
The Baltimore Sun

Five Straight Losses

Since then the Giants have been the party of the second part four times, missing only the 1960 title game. And the results have all been the same against three different teams—the Colts again in 1959, the Green Bay Packers in 1961 and 1962 and now the Bears.

If it were possible to do so, the goat of this game would also wear the hero's mantle, because Tittle, the ageless veteran, was both a goat and a hero, carrying on despite a left leg he could hardly stand on.

One of his screen passes was picked off by Larry Morris, Bear linebacking star, in the first quarter and returned 61 yards to the Giant 5. Wade on second-down then sneaked in from the 2-yard-line for the equalizing touchdown.

Interception Is Costly

In the third quarter, after Tittle had been half-carried from the field with seven minutes left in the second period, Ed O'Bradovich, Bear defensive end, stepped in the way of another Tittle screen pass and returned 10 yards to the Giant 14.

It took the Bears five plays, including a 12-yard Wade-to-Mike-Ditka pass to the one, for the Bears to push it across with Wade again doing the honors on a sneak of an inch.

That was it for both the Bears, whose best offense was a tough defense, and the Giants whose offense was left in the hands of a cripple.

Gifford Scores

Tittle, before his injury, had directed a 59-yard touchdown drive, featuring draw plays up the middle by Phil King and Joe Morrison and climaxed when the Bears drew in their defense with a 14-yard pass to Frank Gifford in the Bear end zone.

After giving up the equalizing touchdown on the screen interception in the opening quarter, Tittle guided the Giants on a 62-yard march which produced a field goal instead of a touchdown after Del Shofner dropped a perfect pass in the end zone.

Settle For Field Goal

The Giants settled for a 13-yard placement by Don Chandler and there went their chances for victory.

Lincoln Hauls Chargers To 51-10 Rout Of Patriots In Title Game

San Diego, Cal., Jan. 5 (P). Keith Lincoln, a thunderbolt fullback, stunned Boston today with two spectacular first quarter runs and then blitzed to a record individual performance in leading San Diego's Chargers to a 51-to-10 rout of the Patriots and to the American Football League championship.

It was the highest scoring title game in the A.F.L.'s four-year history.

Lincoln, who runs like a halfback and catches passes like an end, set up San Diego's first touchdown with a 56-yard run, streaked 67 yards for his own first touchdown and scored a second touchdown on a 25-yard pass from Tobin Rote.

21 Point First Period

San Diego's first league title in the three tries actual y was settled with a 21-point first quarter against the best defense in the four-season old A.F.L.

But Lincoln, three-season veteran from Washington State, didn't let up after his first period fireworks thrilled a crowd of 30,127 in Balboa Stadium.

He kept pounding away for a title game record of 349 yards -- by rushing, receiving and pass-

LINCOLN STEPS OUT—Keith Lincoln (22), of San Diego Chargers, gallops 65-yards to the Boston Patriots' 1-yard line to set up the first touchdown in this A.F.L. title game.

ing — to get the unanimous vote as the game's outstanding player.

The only time the Patriots, beaten by San Diego in regular season play 17-14 and 7-6, were in the game was when Larry Garron smashed seven yards for a touchdown which trimmed the Charger lead to 14-7 with the opening period eight minutes old.

But when San Diego halfback Paul Lowe uncorked another 58-yard scoring run two minutes later against the Boston blitz, that made it 21-7 for the Chargers and the game was locked up.

Boston, A.F.L. defensive leader despite the meager 8-6-1 record it carried into the game, made the mistake of red-dogging too hard on San Diego's opening plays.

That set up Lincoln's sweep around end for 56 yards on his first carry and enabled Rote's two-yard sneak for a touchdown with the game 89 seconds old.

The red-dogging Patriots also saw Lincoln take a Rote pitchout on his second carry of the game and explode 67 yards down the sidelines for a 14-0 San Diego lead.

Almost the same thing happened on Lowe's 58-yard scoring spring.

Thus, on their first ten plays of the game, the Chargers had three touchdowns.

Norton Scores

The only other Boston score after Garron's touchdown smash was Gino Cappelletti's 15-yard field goal in he second period, which left San Diego ahead, 24-10.

Forty-eight seconds before halftime Rote, who threw two touch-

down passes and directed a withering attack, connected on a 14-yard pay-off shot to Don Norton.

That made it 31-10, and Boston might just as well have stayed in te dressing room after the intermission.

Lincoln averaged more than 15 yards in carrying thirteen times for 206 rushing yards and had 123 yards on his seven pass catches.

Placekicker George Blair, who booted an 11-yard field goal to make it 24-7 in the third quarter, also converted after six of San Diego's seven touchdowns.

In the third quarter, Lance Alworth grabbed a 48-yard touchdown pass from ote, wresting the ball from Patriot defender Bob Suci on the Boston 20 and galloping across all alone.

That made it 38-10. But still to come was sub quarterback John Hadl's 1-yard touchdown sneak in the fourth quarter to cap an 80-yard San Diego strike, with Hadl's passing moving the Chargers down the field.

Third Time, Victory

San Diego's title conquest followed two previous futile tries. In the 1960 play-off, as the Los Angeles entry, the Chargers lost to Houston's Oilers 24-16. In the battle for the 1961 crown, they lost to Houston again 10-3.

The 1962 A.F.L. title went to Dallas, now Kansas City, over Houston, 20-17.

"My legs sort of went out after I made those first couple of runs," Lincoln said. "The heat got me. I just didn't seem to have life in my legs. I felt I might have trouble running the 100 as fast as Ernie Ladd"—the 320-pound San Diego lineman.

"Lincoln is the best all-around back we've had on the squad," Gillman said.

"And that Tobin Rote called a great game. I didn't call any of the plays. Rote calls plays better than I could ever hope to call them."

"They left nothing untouched," said Boston Coach Mike Holovak.

"Give them all the credit in the world and give me hell for not getting 'em ready. I thought we were ready."

Statistics

	Patriots	Chargers
First downs	14	21
Rushing yardage	75	328
Passing yardage	186	292
Passes	17-37	17-26
Passes intercepted by	0	2
Punts	7-47	2-44
Fumbles lost	0	1
Yards penalized	18	30

Boston .... 7 3 0 0—10
San Diego ...... 21 10 7 13—51

S.D.—Rote, 2 run (Blair kick).
S.D.—Lincoln, 67 run (Blair kick).
Bos.—Garron, 7 run (Cappelletti kick).
S.D.—Lowe, 58 run (Blair kick).
S.D.—FG, Blair 11.
Bos.—FG, Cappelletti 15.
S.D.—Norton, 14 pass from Rote (Blair kick).
S.D.—Alworth, 48 pass from Rote (Blair kick).
S.D.—Lincoln, 25 pass from Hadl (pass failed).
S.D.—Hadl, 1 run (Blair kick).
Attendance—30,127.

N.F.L. Regular-Season Attendance Mark Set

98 GAMES IN 1963 DREW 4,163,643

Clubs' Player Limits Raised From 37 to 40—Move to Count Ties Voted Down

MIAMI BEACH, Jan. 28 (AP)—The National Football League, which completed a $28.2 million television deal last week, announced today that regular-season games in 1963 drew 4,163,643 fans, a record.

In view of such prosperity, the league decided not to change its rule about tie games.

The owners did vote, however, to increase the player limit for each club from 37 to 40, adding 52 players over all.

They also gave each club permission to experiment with closed-circuit television on home games in the team's blackout area of about 75 miles around the city. Receipts would be considered as part of the game's receipts and would be split on the same basis of 60 per cent for the home team and 40 for the visiting club.

An amendment to count tie games as half a game won and half a game lost was withdrawn after discussion, and the league will continue to determine standings on a percentage basis of games won and lost.

HUNT BACKS TITLE GAME

A.F.L. Founder Sees Event Creating Great Interest

San Diego, Cal., Jan. 17 (AP)—A championship game between the title winners in the National and American Football League would create tremendous interest, says Lamar Hunt.

But the over-all effect would not be too significant, the president of the Kansas City Chiefs said today.

The man who founded the 5-year-old A.F.L. said he is in favor of such a game, as well as interleague play of one type or another and a common draft of players.

Hunt Explains Position

But his point—as he explained it—is this:

Suppose the San Diego Chargers of the A.F.L. played the Chicago Bears of the N.F.L.:

If San Diego defeated the Bears, it might sell a few more tickets next year in San Diego-but it would not help ticket sales, say, in Denver or Kansas City. Nor would it decrease interest in the Bears in Chicago.

If the Bears defeated the Chargers it would not increase interest in Chicago. Nor would it hurt the ticket sales in Denver or Kansas City—or even San Diego.

Annual Meeting Continues

Hunt added, smiling, that if the Bears won, a lot of people would say, "I told you so."

There has been increasing speculation over a possible title game between the two rivals, but no one within the A.F.L. cares to hazard a guess when it will ever come about.

Late in the day representatives of the newly formed Players Association—Tom Addison, of the Boston Patriots, Jim Tyrer, of Kansas City, and Jack Kemp, of the Buffalo Bills—went before the owners to present several recommendations.

Addison said they were not demanding — "because the owners have been very good to us"—and that the matters were in the form of requests for recommendations.

Clearer Ruling Sought

In the only final action of the day, the owners voted unanimously to recognize the players' association.

League officials said they will discuss in detail the other requests of the players.

Commissioner Joe Foss said that the players' question was a request for a clearer ruling on judgment calls.

Contrary to the views of some of the other owners, Hunt said he does not believe that all clubs in the league will be in the black by 1965. He said the league is developing but some teams have trailed financially and cannot catch up with the others until a later date.

Hunt, who moved his club from Dallas in 1963, predicted that he will finish in the black in his first year at Kansas City.

A.F.L. MAKES BIG TV DEAL

Signs 5-Year Contract With NBC For $36 Million

New York, Jan. 29 (P)—The American Football League, barreling into a stronger competitive position with the rival National League, grabbed a $36,000,000 television package with both hands today and said it will start exploring expansion possibilities immediately.

The five-year contract with the National Broadcasting Company becomes effective with the 1965 season, after the present A.F.L. pact with the American Broadcasting Company expires.

"This is another step forward for the American Football League which has improved its position yearly since its formation in 1960," said Commissioner Joe Foss.

Each Club Due $900,000

The A.F.L. contract is comparable to the $28,200,000 two-year agreement signed by the National Football League with the Columbia Broadcasting System last Friday.

The N.F.L. pact breaks down to slightly more than $1,000,000 a year for each of its fourteen teams. Each of the eight A.F.L. clubs will receive approximately $900,000 a year from NBC.

"It's a great thing for the prestige of the league and the greatest day in our history," said Billy Sullivan, president of the A.F.L. and the Boston Patriots. "We haven't signed as many draft choices this year as in the past and this will allow our owners to be in a stronger position from now on."

Franchises Sought

An A.F.L. spokesman said that the National League has signed or has commitments from 61 and the A.F.L. 53 of the players drafted by the American League in 1963.

Foss disclosed that at least a dozen groups have applied for franchises.

"I'm sure that this will be increased soon," he said. "We have received applications from four groups in Philadelphia, also others from Chicago, Los Angeles, Cincinnati, Columbus, Montreal, Atlanta and Portland, Ore.

"I don't know how far away expansion is, maybe three or four years but now we can really start

thinking about it. This contract puts all of our present clubs in the black."

Payment Graduated

The NBC payment to the American League will be on a graduated scale over the five years and the A.F.L. said it will guarantee each club, approximately $1,000,000 for 1969, the last year of the contract.

In Miami, Fla. where the N.F.L. is holding its annual meeting, there was no official comment on the new A.F.L. deal.

However, a club owner who did not wish to be identified said, "the new contract gives the other league substance. It makes them big league." A representative of another team commented that the five-year deal indicated that the A.F.L. was in the field to stay.

The new contract does not cover the league's championship play-off game nor the All-Star game. Provision is also made for A.F.L. expansion, guaranteeing additional television revenue to any new clubs.

Bought College Rights

The ABC Network has a holdover contract for 1964 which will pay $2,350,000 for the season with an additional payment for the circuit's All-Star game.

NBC, which also bought the rights to college football television for 1964 and 1965 for $13,000,000, lost out in the recent bidding for the N.F.L. television right. NBC bid $21,000,000 and ABC $26,000,000 to the $28,200,000 by CBS.

PRO FOOTBALL PICKS 7 FOR HALL OF FAME

CANTON, Ohio, Feb. 27 (AP)—
Seven new members of the professional football Hall of Fame were announced today. They join the 17 charter members installed last year in this city, where the National Football League was founded in 1920.

Six players from the nineteen-twenties and nineteen-thirties, and Art Rooney, the founder and owner of the Pittsburgh Steelers, will be inducted formally Sept. 8 in ceremonies preceding the annual Hall of Fame game.

This year's game will be played between the Steelers and the Baltimore Colts.

All seven of the new members are living and are expected to participate in the ceremonies in September.

Four linemen, George Trafton, a center; Ed Healey, and Roy Link Lyman, tackles, and August Mike Michalske, a guard, were named along with two backs, Clarke Hinkle and Jimmy Conzelman.

Conzelman's selection posed a problem. The former coach of the Providence Steamrollers, Detroit Lions and Chicago Cardinals is a member of the 14-man board of newsmen and officials who pick the new members.

By coupling Conzelman's name with Rooney, both were accepted by acclamation, before Conzelman realized what was happening.

N.F.L. Lifts Suspensions Of Hornung And Karras

GRID STARS HAD BET ON PRO GAMES

Reinstatement Comes After Sitting Out Full Season

New York, March 16 (AP)—Paul Hornung and Alex Karras, two top pro football stars whose suspension last year for betting on games shook the National Football League to its foundations, were reinstated today after sitting out one full season.

Hornung, the Green Bay Packers' Golden Boy who led the N.F.L. in scoring three years, and Karras, the Detroit Lions' tough defensive tackle, were suspended indefinitely last April 17.

Bet On Own Team

Both had admitted to betting on their own teams to win games and on games in which they were not involved.

Commissioner Pete Rozelle announced their reinstatement, effective immediately, in a prepared statement which emphasized that neither had been charged with betting against his own team or with giving less than his best effort in any game.

Rozelle said he had talked to Karras last Saturday and to Hornung a week before "to explore their attitude and thinking" before he reached his decision to end the suspensions. He said he had not told either player of his decision before he released the news.

Plans Early Training

Hornung, vacationing in Miami Beach, Fla., said he would report to the Packers early in May for a special training program to regain his playing form.

"That's wonderful news. I feel very good about it," Hornung said when he was told of his reinstatement.

When the two players were suspended, five other Detroit players were fined $2,000 each for betting on one game and the Detroit club was fined a total of $4,000. The club was fined for failure to give the commissioner reports on the associates of some Detroit players and for giving sideline passes to unauthorized persons.

Contracts Ban Betting

The five players fined were Joe Schmidt, Wayne Walker, John Gordy, Gary Lowe and Sam Williams. They and Karras had made bets on the Packers to beat the New York Giants in the 1962 championship game, which the group was watching on television.

Rozelle indicated that the severity of the penalties was based on the fact that player contracts specifically prohibit betting and that players repeatedly have been warned against betting.

The statement said: "There was no evidence that either ever bet against his own team or performed less than his best in any football game. Further, there was nothing in the record of the cases to reflect on their competitive excellence or on their intense pride in winning.

"Personal disussions with Hornung and Karras have established to the satisfaction of the commissioner that each now has a clear understanding of the seriousness of the offenses and the circumstances that brought them about.

"Therefore, taking into prime consideration the extent of their violations and also their conduct during the period of suspension, it is felt the interests of the league will be best served by the termination of the suspensions."

William A. Shea Stadium — New Home of the New York JETS

2 FOOTBALL STARS DIE IN AUTO CRASH

Galimore and Farrington of Bears Victims in Indiana

By The Associated Press

RENSSELAER, Ind., July 26—Two Chicago Bear players —Willie Galimore and John Farrington—were killed tonight when their car crashed on a Jasper County road about 2½ miles west of here.

Coach George Halas announced at the Jasper County Hospital that the the two players had been killed. No other details of the accident were disclosed immediately.

Galimore, a graduate of Florida A. and M. University, joined the Bears in 1957 and had been a starting offensive halfback through most of his seven years with the National Football League champions.

However, an offseason operation to repair knee injuries kept him on the bench much of last season. Galimore's best season with the Bears was in 1961 when he gained 707 yards in rushing.

The 29-year-old Galimore, rated one of the fastest running backs in professional football, gained 2,985 yards in 670 carries during his career with the Bears, a total exceeded only by Rick Casares among the active Chicago backs. Last season the fleet 187-pounder carried the ball 85 times for 321 yards after a slow start.

Galimore won all-league honors at halfback in 1959. He was named the winner of the Eisenhower Trophy as the most valuable player in the 1958 Armed Forces Game. He shares the team record of four touchdowns in one game.

Farrington, 28, an offensive end from Prairie View (Tex.) College joined the Bears in 1961. Playing in all 14 regular-season games last year, the 217-pound 6-foot-3-inch end caught 21 passes for 335 yards and two touchdowns.

Farrington set a team record for the longest pass play—98 yards—with Bill Wade. The play was made against the Detroit Lions in 1961 and is only one yard under the league mark. Farrington lived in Houston.

The tragedy recalled other recent accidental deaths of pro football players. Only a few months ago Terry Dillon, halfback for the Minnesota Vikings, drowned in Montana.

Don Fleming, a back for the Cleveland Browns, was electrocuted during the offseason while working in Florida a year ago. Tom Bloom, a former Purdue back who had bbeen signed by the Browns, was killed in an auto mishap a year ago before he played a game.

Phil Handler, Bears' assistant coach, said Galimore, a halfback, had recovered from his knee injuries and was "doing wonderful" in practice this summer at St. Joseph's College here.

"Willie was looking better than ever before since he's been with us," Handler said.

Galimore is survived by his wife and three children.

State Trooper Ivan Finch said the accident occurred about 10:25 P.M. on Bunkum Road. Finch said the auto missed a curve and went off the road, throwing both players from the vehicle.

The car was not equipped with seat belts, Finch said. The trooper believed if belts had been installed they might have saved the pair from death.

The state police said the two players were returning to the Bear training camp after a round of golf.

The accident occurred at about 10:30 P.M. when Galimore's Volkswagen hit the shoulder of the road and the rear wheel collapsed. No other persons were involved in the accident.

Dan Desmond, public relations spokesman for the Bears, said the two were trying to make it back to camp for an 11 P.M. curfew.

A farming couple was the first to reach the scene of the accident. The police quoted them as having said Galimore and Farrington had been killed instantly.

The Jasper County coroner, E. R. Beaver, said both men had suffered multiple skull fractures and internal injuries. He said the men had been thrown out from the top of the auto and the car had rolled over on them.

Deputy Yayne Calloway said the car, driven by Galimore, had been traveling about 55 miles an hour. Had the men been familiar with the country road, Calloway said, they could have made the curve at an even higher speed.

Buffalo Rallies To Beat Houston

Buffalo, N.Y., Nov. 1 (AP) — The undefeated Buffalo Bills, minus an effective aerial attack, put across two fourth period touchdowns to come from behind today and defeat the Houston Oilers, 24 to 10, in an American Football League game.

Until rookie Bob Smith and veteran Cookie Gilchrist raced into the Houston end zone for scores, the Oilers pass defense and quarterback George Blanda's passing ketp Buffalo in check.

Blanda tossed 68 passes, an A.F.L. game record, and completed 37 for 393 yards. One, an 11-yarder to Willard Dewvall, produced a touchdown at 8.58 of the first period.

Gilchrist, who scored on a 6-yard burst midway in the last period, gained 139 yards in 15 carries to take over the league rushing lead from New York's Matt Snell. Gilchrist now has a total of 621 yards gained.

Statistics

	Oilers	Bills
First downs	27	18
Rushing yardage	35	290
Passing yardage	293	107
Passes	37-68	7-18
Passes intercepted	3	3
Punts	2-44	3-38
Fumbles lost	1	1
Yards penalized	0	28
Houston	10 0 0 0—10	
Buffalo	7 0 0 17—24	

Hou.—Dewvall, 11 pass from (Blanda kick).
Buf.—Smith 37 run (Gogolak kick).
Hou.—FG Blanda 49.
Buf.—Smith 3 run (Gogolak kick).
Buf.—Gilchrist 60 run (Gogolak kick).
Buf.—FG Gogolak 17.
Attendance—40,119.

Buffalo Beats Jets, 20-7, To Remain Undefeated

New York, Nov. 8 (AP) — Pete Gogolak, Buffalo's soccer-style kicking specialist, booted field goals of 47 and 33 yards in the second half as the Bills defeated the New York Jets 20 to 7 today and remained undefeated in the American Football League.

Gogolak's two field goals, after the teams had battled to a 7-to-7 halftime tie, brought the Bills their ninth victory and kept them well in front of second-place Boston, 6-2-1, in the Eastern title race.

The Jets, meanwhile, dropped to 4-3-1 but proved a point at the turnstiles, drawing a league record crowd of 60,300 in direct competition with the New York-Dallas National Football League game at Yankee Stadium.

A.F.L. Standings

Scores Of Yesterday

Buffalo, 20; New York, 7.
Kansas City, 42; Oakland, 7.
San Diego, 31; Denver, 20.

Where They Play Sunday

Boston at Buffalo.
Houston at Oakland.
New York at Denver.
San Diego at Kansas City.

Standings Of The Clubs

EASTERN DIVISION

	W.	L.	T.	Pct.	Points For	Ag't
Buffalo	9	0	0	1.000	278	133
Boston	6	2	1	.750	238	197
New York	4	3	1	.571	182	151
Houston	2	7	0	.222	197	241

WESTERN DIVISION

	W.	L.	T.	Pct.	Points For	Ag't
San Diego	6	2	0	.750	225	200
Kansas City	4	4	0	.500	213	188
Oakland	1	7	1	.125	187	252
Denver	1	8	0	.111	159	326

Pro Football Draft Selections

National League

FIRST ROUND

NEW YORK GIANTS — Tucker Frederickson, Auburn fullback.
SAN FRANCISCO 49ers—Ken Willard, North Carolina halfback.
CHICAGO BEARS—Dick Butkus, Illinois linebacker rights acquired from Pittsburgh); Gale Sayers, Kansas halfback; Steve De Long, Tennessee, guard (rights acquired from Washington).
DALLAS COWBOYS—Craig Morton, California quarterback.
GREEN BAY PACKERS — Donny Anderson, Texas Tech halfback (future choice); Larry Elkins, Baylor end.
MINNESOTA VIKINGS — Jack Snow, Notre Dame end.
LOS ANGELES RAMS — Clarence Williams, Washington State defensive halfback.
DETROIT LIONS — Tom Nowatzke, Indiana fullback.
ST. LOUIS CARDINALS — Joe Namath, Alabama quarterback.

American League

FIRST ROUND

HOUSTON—Larry Elkins, Baylor flanker.
NEW YORK JETS—(rights acquired from Houston), Joe Namath, Alabama quarterback.
OAKLAND—Harry Schuh, Memphis State tackle.
NEW YORK JETS—Tom Nowatzke, Indiana fullback.
KANSAS CITY—Gale Sayers, Kansas halfback.

SAN DIEGO—Steve DeLong, Tennessee guard.
BOSTON—Jerry Rush, Michigan State tackle.
BUFFALO—Jim Davidson, Ohio State tackle.

SECOND ROUND

DENVER—Dick Butkus, Illinois linebacker.
HOUSTON—Malcolm Walker, Rice linebacker.
OAKLAND—Fred Biletnikoff, Florida State end.
NEW YORK JETS—John Huarte, Notre Dame quarterback.
KANSAS CITY—Jack Chapple, Stanford guard-linebacker.
SAN DIEGO—Roy Jefferson, Utah end.

THIRD ROUND

HOUSTON—Ernie Koy, Texas fullback—kicker.
DENVER—Glenn Ressler, Penn State center-linebacker.
OAKLAND—Bob Svihus, Southern California tackle.
NEW YORK Jets—Vernon Biggs, Jackson State end.
KANSAS CITY—Mike Curtis, Duke fullback.
SAN DIEGO—Allen Brown, Mississippi end.
BOSTON—Jim Whalen, Boston College end.
BUFFALO—Al Atkinson, Villanova tackle.

JIM BROWN RUSHING VS. the BALTIMORE COLTS

Courtesy
Football Hall of Fame

93RD RECEPTION FOR MORRIS

Brown Scores 3 Times

CHICAGO, Dec. 13 (AP)—
The Minnesota Vikings, led by
Bill Brown's three touchdowns,
today crushed the Chicago
Bears, 41—14, to close the worst
season for a George Halas team
in the 45-year history of the
National Football League.

The Bears skidded from their
1963 championship season to a
5-9 won-lost record. The Vikings ended with an 8-5-1 record.

The Vikings, clicking methodically behind Brown, Frank
Tarkenton and Tom Mason,
rolled to a 31-0 half-time lead
while holding the Bears to a
total gain of 19 yards.

Runs of 47 yards by Brown
and Tarkenton's 22-yard pass
to Mason set up the first touchdown, with Brown going over
from the 1.

A 19-year-old rookie, Andy
Livingston, returned a kickoff
86 yards for the Bears' first
touchdown. In the fourth period,
Billy Wade of Chicago completed five of six passes on a
76-yard drive that was capped
by Ron Bull's 10-yard touchdown run.

Minnesota Vikings .....14 17   7   3—41
Chicago Bears 0   0   7   7—14
Min.—Brown, 1, run (Cox, kick).
Min.—Mason, 1, run (Cox, kick).
Min.—FG, Cox, 15.
Min.—Brown, 20, pass from Tarkenton
(Cox, kick).
Min.—Hawkins, 29, interception (Cox, kick).
Min.—Brown, 1, run (Cox, kick).
Chi.—Livingston, 86, kickoff return (Jencks,
kick).
Min.—FG, Cox, 32.
Chi.—Bull, 10, run (Jencks, kick).
Attendance—46,000.

COLTS TURN BACK REDSKINS, 45 TO 17

Moore and Berry Set Marks for Scoring, Completions

STATISTICS OF THE GAME

	Colts	R'skins
First downs	21	9
Rushing yardage	118	66
Passing yardage	269	174
Passes	16-26	13-23
Interceptions by	1	1
Punts	3-42	8-42
Fumbles lost	4	2
Yards penalized	47	116

BALTIMORE, Dec. 13 (AP)
—The Baltimore Colts, champions of the Western Con-
ference, finished the regular
season today with a 45-17 victory over the Washington Redskins as National Football
League records were set by
Lenny Moore and Raymond
Berry.

Moore's two short runs for
scores in the last quarter gave
him 20 touchdowns this season,
one more than the previous
mark set by Jim Taylor of
Green Bay in 1962. It also was
the 18th game in which Moore
had scored, another N.F.L. record.

Berry caught five passes, one
for a 30-yard touchdown, to
raise his career total of 506
completions, three more than
the previous career record held
by Jim Howton.

The Colts overcame a rash
of fumbles and a costly pass
interception. They lost the ball
four times on fumbles. Washington recovered the opening kickoff fumble on the Colts 27 and
three plays later Pervis Atkins
ran 17 yards for a touchdown.

With John Unitas completing
13 of 20 passes for 226 yards
and two touchdowns, the Colts
overcame their troubles in the
second half, scoring two touchdowns in the third period and
three in the final.

Baltimore Colts 3   7 14 21—45
Washington Redskins ...7   3   7   0—17
Wash.—Atkins, 17, run (Martin, kick).
Balt.—FG, Michaels, 25.
Balt.—Berry, 30, pass from Unitas (Mi-
chaels, kick).
Wash.—FG, Martin, 25.
Balt.—Hill 7, run (Michaels, kick).
Wash.—Jurgensen, 2, run (Martin, kick).
Balt.—Mackey, 22, pass from Unitas
(Michaels, kick).
Balt.—Moore, 3, run (Michaels, kick).
Balt.—Moore, 1, plunge (Michaels, kick).
Balt.—Petties, 15, pass from Matte
(Michaels, kick).
Attendance—60,213.

Vikings Refuse To Enter Bidding

By SEYMOUR S. SMITH
[Assistant Sports Editor of The Sun]

Land of opportunity? Sure is.
Just ask any collegiate senior
being pursued by the National and
American Football Leagues or
one-time all-pros Leo Nomellini
and Clayton Tonnemaker, signed
for $14,000 fifteen years ago, or
Jim Finks, Minnesota's general
manager, who refuses to enter the
skyrocketing bidding for draft
choices.

"We're offering oustanding contracts to our selections, but at the
same time we don't plan to go
way off base in our offers," Finks,
only two months on the job when
the player war began, declares.
"A lot of the players are demanding unrealistic contracts with big
bonuses and lock-in contracts.

"We lost our fourth pick, Jim
Harris, of Utah State, the nine-
teenth, Ellis Johnson, from Southeast Lousiana, and the twentieth,
Princeton's Cosmo Icavazzi, because we insisted on a contract
where the player had to make the
team. We're not going to give no-
cut contracts to our top choices,
so we're sure not going to give it
to them."

The Vikings did lose their No. 1
selection, Jack Snow, swapping
the Notre Dame end for two Los
Angeles Rams when he gave hints
of signing with San Diego, of the
A.F.L. "It'll be a few weeks before the names are released,"
Finks says, "but our fans will be
happy." Reports have the new
Vikings being end Red Phillips
and tackle Gary Larsen.

Tonnemaker recalls he and
Nomellini both came out of Minnesota when the N.F.L. was then
bidding for talent against the All-
America Conference. Tonnemaker
received a $500 bonus and a $7,500
contract to sign with San Francisco, then of the A.A.C., and
Nomellini $6.500. Then the two
leagues merged and contracts
were not valid.

"They held a joint draft,"
Tonnemaker, now part of the network team airing N.F.L. telecasts, continues, "and Green
Bay took me on the first round
and I was the third player picked
that year. I finally signed for $8,-
000 without a bonus. My salary
sounds like part of the bonuses
they're handing out now."

Reprinted from
The Baltimore Sun papers

[CAPPELLETTI SCORES 155 POINTS]

KEMP LEADS BUFFALO IN SNOWSTORM

Scores Twice, Passes For 3d; Victors Face Chargers Saturday

Boston, Dec. 20 (AP) — Jack Kemp, demoted a week ago, led the Buffalo Bills to the Eastern Division title of the American Football League today by scoring twice and throwing a touchdown pass in a 24-14 victory over the Boston Patriots in a whirling snowstorm.

The field was covered with snow and the yard lines had been obliterated before the game started one-half hour late. As soon as the ground crew removed the tarpaulin new snow fell. As the game ended a miniature blizzard whirled down on the 38,021 fans at Fenway Park.

Good Football Played

Despite the miserable playing conditions, falling temperatures and the wind-blown snow, the teams played good football. Buffalo's victory sent coach Lou Saban's Bills into an A.F.L. title game with San Diego Saturday at Buffalo.

Kemp, who sat out last week while Daryle Lamonica ran the show, put the Bills out front early with a 57-yard touchdown pass to Elbert Dubenion. Kemp later scored twice from the one on quarterback sneaks. Pete Gogolak, the rookie from Cornell who kicks soccer style, added a 12-yard field goal.

Parilli To Romeo

Babe Parilli, the 34-year-old former Kentucky ace, found the cold weather a little tough but he hit Tony Romeo with a 37-yard scoring pass in the first period.

Coach Mike Holovak gambled on a try for two points and the lead, but lost. Parilli's attempted two-point conversion pass to Gino Cappelletti failed when Cappy slipped and fell in a corner of the end zone.

Boston Was Favored

The Patriots didn't score again until the final minutes when Parilli connected with Romeo for another score from 15 yards out. Romeo passed to Jim Colclough for a two-point conversion.

Buffalo went into the game with a half game lead over favored Boston, which could have won the division title by a victory. The Patriots beat Buffalo a year ago in a tie play-off for the division crown and then were routed by San Diego 51 to 10.

Mike Stratton, Buffalo's All-Star linebacker, played a tremendous defensive game and Ron Hall, a Boston All-Star safety, intercepted two of Kemp's passes as both receivers and defenders skidded around the slippery field.

Players Wear Gloves

Many of the players wore gloves, and the fans amused themselves by throwing snowballs at each other and the players. A small delegation of Buffalo visitors who carried a banner around the field were pelted with a barrage of snow balls before the police made them break up their demonstration.

The field looked like a setting for a Santa Clause pagenat at the end. The second half was played under lights, with the temperature falling.

Kemp completed 12 of 25 passes for 286 yards despite the weather. Parilli hit with 19 of 39 for 294 yards. Glenn Bass, Kemp's favorite target after the Pats started to double-team Dubenion, caught 6 passes for 103 yards. Dubenion got away with 3 for 127 yards.

Colclough grabbed 6 for 134 yards for Boston. The Bills' top runner was Cookie Gilchrist with 52 yards on 20 carries, leaving him just short of a 1,000-yard season. Cookie, the league's All-Star fullback, wound up with 981 for the year.

Statistics

	Bills	Pats
First downs	17	15
Rushing yardage	94	33
Passing yardage	286	294
Passes	12-24	19-40
Pases intercepted by	2	3
Punts	5-38	5-30
Fumbles lost	0	1
Yards penalized	40	20
Buffalo	7 10 0 7—24	
Boston	6 0 0 8—14	

Buff.—Dubenion, 57, pass from Kemp (Gogolak kick).
Bos.—Romeo, 37, pass from Parilli (pass failed).
Buff.—Kemp, 1 run (Gogolak kick).
Buff.—FG. Gogolak, 12.
Buff.—Kemp, 1 run (Gogolak kick).
Bos.—Romeo, 15, pass from Parilli. Colclough, pass from Parilli.
Attendance—38,021.

Oilers Whip Denver, 34-15, As Blanda Sets Pass Mark

Houston, Dec. 20 (AP)—Veteran Houston quarterback George Blanda set an American Football League pass attempt record today as he engineered the Oilers to a 34-to-15 victory over the Denver Broncos.

The 15-year veteran became the passingest quarterback in A.F.L. history the first time he tossed the ball—a 52-yard aerial to Charlie Tolar which set up the first Oiler touchdown.

It was his 479th pass attempt this year, which put him one ahead of the mark set by Denver's Frank Tripucka in 1960.

262 Completions

Blanda completed 16 of 27 passes for 204 yards for a season total of 505 attempts and 262 completions.

The fourth time he hit a receiver he set the league mark for single season completions. Tripucka also set that record in 1960.

Blanda was replaced by rookie quarterback Don Trull midway through the third period after a tussle with Denver defensive back Jerry Hopkins.

Houston's Charlie Hennigan caught 8 passes in the game, exactly enough for a season total of 101 and a new A.F.L. pass receiving mark. Denver's Lionel Taylor set the old one in 1961.

Hennigan snagged a total of 8 aerials for 75 yards and a touchdown.

The battle of the divisional cellar dwellers left Denver with a 2-11-1 mark and Houston 4-10, the

The Statistics

	Broncos	Oilers
First downs	26	16
Rushing yardage	67	80
Passing yardage	280	218
Passes	35-55	18-35
Passes intercepted by	3	3
Punts	5-40	1-16
Fumbles lost	0	3
Yards penalized	58	28
Denver	0 8 0 7—15	
Houston	17 7 7 3—34	

Hous.—Blanks, 2, run (Blanda kick).
Hous.—F.G. Blanda, 26.
Hous.—Jancik, 82, punt return. (Blanda kick).
Hous.—Hennigan, 25, pass from Blanda, (Blanda kick).
Denv.—Scarpitto, 15, pass from Slaughter, (Joe pass from Slaughter).
Hous.—Hoffman, 1, run (Blanda kick).
Denv.—Mitchell, 1, run (Guesman kick).
Hous.—F.G Blanda, 18.
Attendance—15,833.

Oilers' most dismal season in their five-year history.

The Oilers moved quickly into the lead with Sid Blanks scoring the first touchdown on a 2-yard rush.

Within seven minutes of the opening period the Oilers had 17 points on the scoreboard. Blanda booted a 26-yard field goal and Bobby Jancik made a magnificent 82-yard punt return for a touchdown.

Houston went ahead 24-0 midway in the second period when Blanda passed to Hennigan for 25 yards and a touchdown.

Denver's first sustained drive came late in the second quarter when quarterback Mickey Slaughter tossed a 15-yard scoring pass to Bob Scarpitto.

Houston scored a final touchdown in the third period when Dalton Hoffman plunged over from the one.

Buffalo Topples San Diego, 20-7, For A.F.L. Crown

GILCHRIST, KEMP SPARK BILL ATTACK

Former Charger QB Brings First Title To Buffalo

Buffalo, N.Y., Dec. 26 (P)—Each member of the Buffalo Bills will receive a record $2,668.60 for winning the American Football League championship today against San Diego. Each Charger will receive $1,738.63.

Buffalo, N.Y., Dec. 26 (P) — Cookie Gilchrist, Buffalo's repentent bad boy, gained 144 yards and combined with revenge-minded Jackie Kemp to bring the Bills their first American Football League championship with a 29-to-7 victory today over San Diego's defending champions.

Gilchrist and Kemp, who was claimed from San Diego in 1962 for the $100 waiver price, thus ended a long title search for this football-crazy city that supported the now defunct All-American Conference in the late 1940's and began looking again when the A.F.L. was formed five years ago.

Kemp 10 For 20

Gilchrist, the prime mover in Buffalo's grind-it-out-offense, gained 122 yards rushing and grabbed 2 of Kemp's passes for 22 yards. Kemp, meanwhile, completed 10 for 20 passes for 168 yards.

Oddly, Gilchrist did not score and Kemp did not pass for a touchdown but the 29-year-old signal-caller managed to sneak a couple of inches for the final touchdown in the last quarter.

Wray Carlton, Gilchrist's running mate, scored one touchdown on a 4-yard run and soccer-style Pete Gogolak kicked a pair of field goals from 12 and 17 yards out.

Fog Shrouds Stands

Gilchrist made his rushing yardage on 16 carries before being forced out of the bruising game with banged-up ribs in the fourth quarter as the fog that hung over War Memorial Stadium all day dipped lower and lower into the stands crowded with a sellout throng of 40,242.

Then, with 26 seconds left, Buffalo's impassioned fans broke through police restraining lines, took down both goalposts and continued to run and circle the field while San Diego tried to get off its last play.

The final break-out of emotions came at the end of a dramatic season in which the Bills whipped San Diego twice, put together an unbeaten nine-game string but still had to beat Boston last week in the final regular season game to win the Eastern crown.

Rote, the veteran signal-caller who was retiring after a 15-year pro career in 3 pro leagues and 2 countries, was unable to get the Chargers moving after the first drive and eventually was pulled out in favor of young John Hadl late in the third quarter.

Statistics

	Chargers	Bills
First downs	15	20
Rushing yardage	124	219
Passing yardage	135	168
Passes	13-36	10-20
Passes intercepted by	0	3
Punts	5-36	5-46
Fumbles lost	0	0
Yards penalized	20	45

San Diego	7	0	0	0	7
Buffalo	3	10	0	7	20

San Deigo—Kocourek, 26, pass from Rote (Lincoln, kick).
Buffalo—Field Goal, Gogolak, 12.
Buffalo—Carlton, 4, run (Gogolak, kick).
Buffalo—Field Goal, Gogolak, 17.
Buffalo—Kemp, 1, plunge (Gogolak, kick).
Attendance, 40,242.

Browns Shut Out Colts, 27 To 0, To Capture N.F.L. Championship

17-POINT 3D QUARTER KILLS LOSERS' HOPES

Ryan Hits Collins For 3 TD's; Brown Stars Before 79,544

The Statistics

	Browns	Colts
Total first downs	20	11
First downs rushing	8	5
First downs passing	9	4
First downs by penalty	3	2
Total yards gained (net)	339	171
Yards gained rushing (net)	142	82
Yards gained passing (net)	197	89
Gross yards gained passing	206	95
Times thrown & yards lost attempting to pass	1-9	2-6
Passes attempted	18	20
Passes completed	11	12
Average gain per pass attempt	10.9	4.4
Passes intercepted by & yds. interc. returned	2-10	1-14
Number and total yardage of punts	3-132	4-135
Average distance of punts	44	33.9
Number & total yards punts returned	1-13	2-18
Number & total yards kickoffs returned	1-21	3-29
Number of penalties & total yds penalized	7-59	5-48
Number of fumbles & fumbles lost	0-0	0-2
Number of rushing plays	41	28
Average gain per rushing play	3.45	3.5
Total offensive plays inc. times thrown passing	60	45
Average gain per offensive play	5.7	3.8

Colts	0 0 0	0—	0	
Cleveland	0 0 17	10—	27	

Scoring Plays:
Cleveland—Third period time. 11.39 Groza (43-yd. field goal).
Cleveland—Third period time 8.34. Collins (18-yd. pass from Ryan) Groza converts.
Cleveland—Third period time. 6.12. Collins (42-yd. pass from Ryan) Groza converts.
Cleveland—Fourth period time. 11.53 Groza converts.
Cleveland—Fourth period time. 11.35 Groza (10-yd. field goal).
Cleveland—Fourth period time. 6.10. Collins (51-yd. pass for Ryan) Groza converts.
Attendance 79,544; time of game 2 hours, 15 minutes.

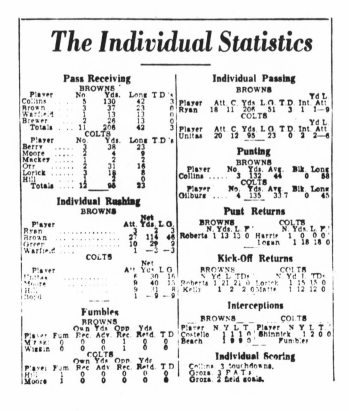

The Individual Statistics

Pass Receiving

BROWNS

Player	No.	Yds.	Long	T.D.'s
Collins	5	130	42	3
Brown	3	37	23	0
Warfield	1	13	13	0
Brewer	2	26	13	0
Totals	11	206	42	3

COLTS

Player	No.	Yds.	Long	T.D.'s
Berry	3	38	23	
Moore	2	4	9	
Mackey	1	2	2	
Orr	2	31	16	
Lorick	3	18	8	
Hill	1	2	0	
Totals	12	95	23	

Individual Rushing

BROWNS

Player	Att.	Net Yds.	L.G.
Ryan	3	2	3
Brown	27	114	46
Green	10	29	9
Warfield	1	-3	-3

COLTS

Player	Att.	Net Yds.	L.G.
Unitas	5	30	16
Moore	9	40	15
Hill	9	31	8
Boyd	1	-9	-9

Fumbles

BROWNS

Player	Fum	Own Rec.	Yds Adv.	Opp Rec.	Yds Retd.	T.D.
Mirski	0	0	0	1	0	0
Wiggin	0	0	0	1	0	0

COLTS

Player	Fum	Own Rec.	Yds Adv.	Opp Rec.	Yds Retd.	T.D.
Hill	1	0	0	0	0	0
Moore	1	0	0	0	0	0

Individual Passing

BROWNS

Player	Att.	C.	Yds.	L.G.	T.D.	Int.	Yd L. Att.
Ryan	18	11	206	51	3	1	1—9

COLTS

Player	Att.	C.	Yds.	L.G.	T.D.	Int.	Yd L. Att.
Unitas	20	12	95	23	0	2	2—6

Punting

BROWNS

Player	No.	Yds.	Avg.	Blk.	Long
Collins	3	132	44	0	58

COLTS

Player	No.	Yds.	Avg.	Blk.	Long
Gilburg	4	135	33.7	0	45

Punt Returns

BROWNS				COLTS			
	N.	Yds.	L.P.		N.	Yds.	L.P.
Roberts	1	13	13	Harris	1	0	0
			0	Logan	1	18	18 0

Kick-Off Returns

BROWNS				COLTS			
	N.	Yd.	L	TDs		N.	Yd. L	TDs
Roberts	1	21	21	0	Lorick	1	15 15	0
Kelly	1	2	2	0	Matte	1	12 12	0

Interceptions

BROWNS					COLTS				
Player	N.	Y.	L.	T.	Player	N.	Y.	L.	T.
Costello	1	1	1	0	Shinnick	1	2	0	0
Beach	1	9	9	0					

Individual Scoring

Collins 3 touchdowns.
Groza 3 PATs.
Groza 2 field goals.

Entire page reprinted from
The Baltimore Sun

Jets Sign Joe Namath For Record $400,000

Miami Beach, Fla., Jan. 2 (P)— Brawny Joe Namath, son of a struggling Beaver Falls (Pa.) steelworker, signed the contract today that made him the richest rookie in the history of pro football—and probably any other sport.

The Horatio Alger story of the former shoeshine boy who led Alabama to the national college championship was climaxed at a luxury hotel at Miami Beach. Here, he concluded a deal with the New York Jets, of the American Football League, that reportedly will bring him $400,000 for three years' work.

Retirement Plan, Too?

This is said to include $100,000 a year in salary and some $100,000 in bonuses. There also were unconfirmed reports of a fringe benefit retirement plan giving Namath $5,000 a year for life after his playing days.

Sonny Werblin, president of the Jets, said the details of the fabulous contract were considered privileged information but he added that, "I'm sure it pays the largest amount ever given to a young athlete in any sport."

And the cat-quick Namath, he said, was a bargain at the price.

"We feel that in getting Joe," Werblin told a news conference, "we got the No. 1 college football player in America, and with him we will give New York fans the finest football team in America.

"Start To Championship"

"This is the start toward many championship years for the Jets."

Namath disclosed that the Jets and the St. Louis Cardinals, who drafted him in the American Football League, made "about the same" offers. It had been reported that St. Louis dropped out when the bidding reached $400,000.

"I took both teams into consideration," said the 6-foot-2, 194-pound quarterback who is one of the most promising passers to enter pro ranks. "I wanted more than money. I was interested in the coach and the organization.

"New York city is a fine place. The sports fans are great and Weeb Ewbank is an outstanding coach."

Ewbank was beaming as he announced the signing of a quarterback he believes has all the potential of Johnny Unitas, of the Baltimore Colts.

"I see in this young man the same qualities that are found in Unitas," Ewbank said. "He has size, quickness, a wonderful arm, a quick delivery, courage and the ability to make the big play.

"We say in the pros that it takes three or more years to make a quarterback out of a college boy, but it won't take that long for Joe. There are veteran pros who can't react the way he does right now. He has reactions a lot of quarterbacks could never learn.

Limps To Conference

"In the Orange Bowl last night, even with his bad leg, Joe murdered Texas when they tried to rush him. If he had been in normal condition he would have busted that game open."

Namath, limping into the conference room, had come a long way from the days when he shined shoes on the street corners of Beaver Falls for nickels and dimes. Dressed in a natty pink sports jacket, he looked like anyone but the youth who showed up on the Alabama campus four years ago dressed like a beatnik.

His father's salary from the steel mill was stretched thin as he put five children, including Joe, through high school.

Knee Surgery Due

"A steelworker's pay wasn't that good," Namath said. "Dad did the best he could, but football had to get me into college."

After completing work for his degree, Namath's next stop will be a hospital probably in New York, where the Jets will have surgery performed on the knee that kept him out of action part of the past season.

He had ignored the handicap and the pain the night before in a courageous but losing effort to lead Alabama to victory over Texas in the Orange Bowl. Great defensive play by the Longhorns spoiled Alabama's comeback bid, but Namath was a landslide choice as the best player on the field.

Jets

New York, Jan. 9 (P) — John Huarte, Notre Dame's star quarterback and the 1964 Heisman Trophy winner, signed to play for the New York Jets of the American Football League today, and siid he was ready to get into the high-priced quarterback derby the team will run next season.

The Jets wouldn't say how much it cost to land Huarte but guesses around town are putting the figure at $200,000, or just half of what the Jets reportedly shelled out for Joe Namath, the gimpy-kneed quarterback from Alabama.

Jets Not Saying How Much

Actually, both figures contain a lot of fringe benefits such as insurance policies and annuities, which can be listed at cash or face value, sources said.

"We've never said how much Namath got," said one Jet official, "and we aren't saying how much we paid for Huarte."

Sonny Werblin, the show business tycoon who owns the Jets, said the figure on the Huarte contract was "privileged information." He said the length of the contract was, too.

That led to speculation that the pact took all possible advantage of long-term tax write-offs.

Huarte said money wasn't everything in his choise of the Jets over the Philadelphia Eagles, who are coached by Joe Kiuharich, the man who imported the Californian to Notre Dame in the first place.

STEP FORCED BY WALKOUT OF NEGROES

Foss Takes Action As Players Complain Of Discrimination

Houston, Jan. 11 (AP)—Saturday's American Football League All-Star game was transferred today from New Orleans to Houston after Negro players complained of discrimination in the Louisiana city.

The nationally televised game will be played in the 37,000-seat Jeppeson Stadium, home of the Houston Oilers since the league was founded in 1960.

No discrimination incidents involving athletes have developed in Houston since the Oilers began play in 1960 and the Houston Astros became members of the National Baseball League in 1962.

Forces Late Ticket Sales

All major hotels and most restaurants and taverns integrated several years ago. Under State law, selling liquor by the drink is illegal in Texas except in private membership clubs.

A crowd of 60,000 had been expected at New Orleans. Joe Foss, the A.F.L. commissioner, and other Oiler officials side-stepped crowd estimates for the game, but everyone acknowledged the late shift would hinder the sale of the tickets ranging in price from $2.50 to $7.50.

Also switched to Houston was the league's winter meeting that begins Wednesday and continues through Friday.

Situation Seen Regrettable

Foss, in Chicago, said the New Orleans situation was regrettable, but the Negro players seemed to have adequate reason for deciding to walk out.

The 21 Negro players on the East and West squads met yesterday and voted to pack their bags because some were refused taxicab service and admittance to French Quarter clubs.

"The players called me from the meeting—Ernie Warlick, of the Buffalo Bills, was the spokesman—and told me about their decision," Foss said. "I'm not critical of their action."

16,000 Tickets Sold

Foss said the league had no choice but transfer the game even though David F. Dixon, promoter of the New Orleans game, would have to take a terrible beating financially.

Some 16,000 tickets already had been sold by Dixon, who has headed a group seeking a pro football team for New Orleans for several years.

Dixon called the walkout a "grievous injury . . . on a city that has struggled sincerely not only to comply with the provisions of the Civil Rights Act of 1964 . . . before that, to reach a voluntary accommodation of the races."

"Seriously Question Action"

"We seriously question the wisdom of the peremptory action which they took to redress these alleged grievances," Dixon said.

". . . We consider it both unfortunate and erroneous New Orleans be judged and condemned by the actions, if these actions be substantiated by proper investigation, of a few."

Oddly enough, when Syracuse played in the Sugar Bowl on New Year's Day with half a dozen Negro players on the squad, the players were quoted after the game as saying they found no discrimination.

Jim Nance, one of the Syracuse backs, said: "I'm going back and tell everybody about the splendid treatment we received down here."

CURLY LAMBEAU, EX-COACH, 67, DIES

Head of Green Bay Packers Helped to Found Team

STURGEON BAY, Wis., June 1 (AP)—Curly Lambeau, former coach of the Green Bay Packers and one of the founders of the professional football team, died today. He was 67 years old.

Mr. Lambeau collapsed after an apparent heart attack and died while cutting grass at a friend's home in Sturgeon Bay.

Start of the Packers

On a chilly autumn morning in 1918, a curly-haired young man of 20 entered the office of Frank Peck, the owner of the Indian Packing Company of Green Bay.

"Mr. Peck," he said, "I've been talking to some of the other young fellows and we think we could get together a football team. It will be a great thing for Green Bay and the company. Will you back us?"

"Okay, Curly," said Mr. Peck to the boy, whose real name was Earl, "I'll let you have $500."

For Curly Lambeau, a fullback who adored football with a consuming passion, the creation of the Green Bay Packers was the start of a brilliant and dazzling career a career that spanned 31 years in Green Bay, producing dozens of football stars, and making him the dean of professional football coaches.

"During Curly's long leadership, the Packers put Green Bay on the map as the home of rough, rugged football, boasting some of the best players in football history," the Encyclopedia of Football declares.

"What he's done for Green Bay borders on the miraculous," Tony Canadeo, the "Gray Ghost of Gonzaga," who played with the Packers from 1941 to 1949, said last night. "He brought a small town into the big leagues."

Explosive Personality

Restless, impatient, mercurial, explosive and — at times — conversationally violent, he left Green Bay in 1950 in the same swirl of publicity and controversy that marked his career. In his 31 years at Green Bay, Mr. Lambeau's record included six National League titles, seven divisional championships and one first-place tie. In all, his Packers won 236 games, lost 111 and tied 23 in league competition.

After his departure in a factional fight with the Packers' management, Mr. Lambeau coached the old Chicago Cardinals for two years before finishing his pro-career in Washington in 1954.

"Curly never has been just another coach in pro football," wrote Arthur Daley, sports columnist for The New York Times, in 1951. "He was one of the pioneers, the man who founded the dynasty of the Green Bay Packers. . . . He left his heart in Green Bay, however, and the adjustment apparently never could be made. Yet even in Green Bay he had outlived his usefulness as the town split into anti-Lambeau and pro-Lambeau camps. Now he has nothing left but his memories."

His memories doubtlessly included his early years with the Green Bay team—when he was quarterback from 1919 to 1928, when he threw 45 forward passes in one game in an era when teams used aerial offense sparingly, and when the Packers won three consecutive championships (1929-31), a feat never duplicated.

Mr. Lambeau's playing days ended in his 10th season, when, typically, he roared at his team between halves for the fumbles and errors it had made in the first half.

"I'll show you bums how to pass," he raged.

"Let's open the gates on Curly," suggested huge Cal Hubbard in an aside to his mates. They did. Eleven Packers stepped aside and let the enemy's line smash Mr. Lambeau at once. He never played again.

During his years at Green Bay he became head coach, a vice president and general manager of the team. The Packers finished out of the first division only twice while he was coach, in 1948 and 1949.

Bellicose Belgian

Mr. Lambeau was considered one of the original salesmen—called the Bellicose Belgian by sports writers—of professional football. He realized early that the game had to be colorful to attract fans, and he developed a spectacular passing game led by Arnie Herber and Don Hutson.

Mr. Lambeau, himself, had never gone to college though most of the Green Bay team had. He enrolled at the University of Notre Dame in 1918 and was one of the 13 players to win a monogram on Knute Rockne's first team. He left school in midyear, however, to have an operation and never returned to the campus.

With George Calhoun, then sports editor of The Green Bay Press Gazette, Mr. Lambeau developed the idea of starting a football team in Green Bay and, after receiving the initial financial help, began lining up players from the area, among them Henry (Tubby) Bero and Jimmy Coffeen.

In 1921, Mr. Lambeau, backed by two packing plant officials, obtained a franchise in the new National Football League. The league forfeited the franchise after the first season because of poor attendance. He talked other businessmen into backing the team, and in 1922, he bought the franchise back for $250.

Mr. Lambeau is survived by a brother, Oliver, and a sister, Mrs. Francis Evrard, both of Green Bay.

A.F.L. SEEN HAVING LOST DIXIE PRIZE

Unanimous Franchise Approval Contingent On Stadium Rights

New York, June 21 /—The National Football League staked its fist claim in the Deep South today, voting a franchise to Atlanta for 1966 and apparently taking the prized Dixie metropolis away from the rival American Football League.

In a unanimous vote, the fourteen N.F.L. club owners approved —as expected—the initial step in the league's second major expansion project in five years.

"Our goal still is sixteen teams in 1967," said an obviously pleased Pete Rozelle, the N.F.L. commissioner. He added, however, that nothing definite on further expansion would be done until the league meeting next February.

One Proviso

The N.F.L. did not say which of several interested Atlanta groups would be given the new francise. But it did attach one proviso to the awarding of the franchise: Whoever gets it is in business only if a lease on the city's new $18,000,000 stadium is acquired.

SYNDICATE HEADED BY TV STAR

First Team In South To Play In Loop In 1966

Miami, Fla., Aug. 16 (AP)—Miami became the ninth member of the American Football League and first in the Deep South today when a franchise for 1966 was sold to a group headed by television star Danny Tnomas for more than $7,500,000.

Announcement was made by Miami Mayor Robert King High, who has been active in bringing professional football to this city. A.F.L. Commissioner Joe Foss signed the papers in the mayor's office.

Joseph Robbie, Minneapolis attorney who helped put the deal together, and Thomas are owners of the new franchise. It was agreed that they can take in partners later, but presently they are the only stockholders.

Ninth Team In League

Miami will join New York, Buffalo, Boston, Kansas City, Houston, San Diego, Denver and Oakland in the league.

"We're not prepared to make an anouncement on the details of the financing," Robbie told a news conference. "Let's just say we started at $7,500,000.

"We've bet a lot of money on Miami as a major league city and we think we've won. We think we've picked the best potential American Football League city in America."

Big Stadium Helped

Foss said a major factor in selecting Miami was availability of the 70,000-plus seat Orange Bowl Stadium.

"Our group feels that Miami is the right place and that Danny Thomas is the right person to hold this franchise," Foss said.

The Miami team—as yet unnamed—will obtain players this way:

Each of the present teams will "freeze" 23 players on its roster. Miami then can select two from the remaining roster. After this, one more player will be frozen, and Miami will select two more from each squad.

32 Players On Roster

After this, with 32 players on its roster, Miami will get first choice of the two top college draft choices of the league at its meeting in November and first choice in each following round.

Foss said the player limit for A.F.L. teams will be raised from 3C to 38 this season to give the incumbents more of a cushion when the Miami team is put together.

Most Miami games will be played on Sunday afternoons, with local games blacked out on television in a 75-mile radius. Games away from Miami probably will be televised back, some on a nationwide hookup, he said.

Rental $150,000

The Orange Bowl rental will be $150,000 from 1966 to 1968, $160,000 in 1969 and $170,000 in 1970. The A.F.L. will extend the lease for another five years starting in 1971, at $200,000 annually.

Miami probably would be in the Eastern Division. "We'd prefer to keep it on a general geographical basis, but this is something the owners will have to hash out," Foss said.

DRAFT

N.F.L.

New York, Nov. 27 (AP)—Round-by-round selections in today's National Football League draft:

FIRST ROUND

1. Atlanta, Tommy Nobis, Texas linebacker. 2. Los Angeles, Tom Mack, Michigan tackle; 3. Pittsburgh passed; 4. Philadelphia, Randy Beisler, Indiana defensive end; 5. Dallas, John Niland, Iowa guard; 6. Washington, Charlie Gogolak, Princeton placekicker; 7. Minnesota, Jerry Shay, Purdue tackle; 8. St. Louis, Carl McAdams, Oklahoma line-backer; 9. Green Bay (choice acquired from Detroit). Jim Grabowski, Illinois fullback; 10. New York, Francis Peay, Missouri tackle; 11. San Francisco, Stan Hindman, Mississippi tackle; 12. Chicago, George Rice, Louisiana State tackle; 13. Pittsburgh, Dick Leftridge, West Virginia fullback; 14. Green Bay, Gale Gillingham, Minnesota tackle; 15. Cleveland, Milt Morin, Massachusetts end; 16. Colts, Sam Ball, Kentucky tackle; 17. Atlanta, Randy Johnson, Texas A&I quarterback.

SECOND ROUND

1. Atlanta, Nick Rassas, Notre Dame defensive back. 2. Los Angeles, Mike Garrett, Southern California halfback. 3. Pittsburgh, Larry Gagner, Florida tackle. 4. Philadelphia, Gary Pettigrew, Stanford defensive end. 5. Washington, Walter Barnes, Nebraska tackle. 6. Dallas, Willie Townes, Tulsa tackle future. 7. St. Louis, Harold Lucas, Michigan State tackle. 8. Detroit, Nick Eddy, Notre Dame halfback, future. 9. New York, Don Davis, Los Angeles State tackle. 10. San Francisco, Bob Windsor, Kentucky end, future. 11. Minnesota, Jim Lindsey, Arkansas Halfback. 12. Chicago, Charley Brown, Syracuse defensive back. 13. Cleveland, Rick Norton, Kentucky quarterback. 14. Green Bay, Tom Cichowski, Maryland tackle, future. 15. COLTS, Burford Allison, Missouri tackle. 16. Atlanta, Jerry Jones, Bowling Green tackle.

THIRD ROUND

1. Atlanta, Mike Dennis, Mississippi halfback. 2. Los Angeles, Richard Tyson, Tulsa guard. 3. Pittsburgh, Pat Killorin, Syracuse center. 4. Philadelphia, Ben Hawkins, Arizona State fullback. 5. San Francisco, choice acquired from Dallas, A. Randolph, Iowa, halfback. 6. Washington, T. Barrington, Ohio St. fullback. 7. Detroit, Bob Malinchak, Indiana end. 8. New York, Tom Fisher, Tennessee linebacker, future. 9. San Francisco, Dan Bland, Mississippi State defensive halfback. 10. Minnesota, Don Hansen, Illinois linebacker. 11. St. Louis, Dave Long, Iowa defensive end. 12. Chicago, Bob Pickens, Nebraska tackle, future. 13. Green Bay, Fred Heron, San Jose tackle, on regular choice and Tony Jeter, Nebraska end, on choice acquired from Cleveland. 14. Colts, Rick Kestner, Kentucky flanker. 15. Atlanta, Phil Sheridan, Notre Dame end.

FOURTH ROUND

1. Atlanta, Ken Reaves, Norfolk State defensive back. 2. Los Angeles, Henry Dyer, Grambling fullback. 3. Chicago, choice acquired from Pittsburgh, Randy Jackson, Florida tackle. 4. Philadelphia, Frank Emanuel, Tennessee linebacker. 5. Washington, Bill Clay, Mississippi defensive back. 6. Colts, choice acquired from Dallas, Rod Sherman, Southern California flanker, future. 7. Detroit, choice acquired from New York, Doug Van Horn, Ohio State guard. 8. San Francisco, Don Parker, Virginia guard. 9. Minnesota, Ron Acks, Illinois defensive end. 10. St. Louis, Gary Snook, Iowa quarterback. 11. Detroit, Willie Walker, Tennessee A&I flanker. 12. Chicago, Doug Buffone, Louisville linebacker. 13. Cleveland, Pete Duranko, Notre Dame defensive end, future. 14. Green Bay, John Roderick, Southern Methodist flanker, future. 15. Colts, Hoyle Granger, Mississippi State fullback. 16. Atlanta, Willie Asbury, Kent State halfback.

A.F.L.

FIRST ROUND

Bonus, Miami, Jim Grabowski, Illinois fullback. 1. Miami, Rich Morton, Kentucky quarterback. 2. Boston, Karl Singer, Purdue tackle. 3. Denver, Jerry Shay, Purdue tackle. 4. Houston, Tommy Nobis, Texas linebacker. 5. New York passed. 6. Kansas City, Aaron Brown, Minnesota end. 7. Oakland passed. 8. San Diego, Don Davis, Los Angeles State tackle. 9. Buffalo, Mike Dennis, Mississippi halfback.

SECOND ROUND

1. Miami, Frank Emanuel, Tennessee linebacker. 2. Boston, Jim Boudreaux, Louisiana Tech end. 3. Denver, Freeman White, Nebraska end. 4. Houston, Stan Hindman, Mississippi guard. 5. New York, Bill Yearby, Michigan tackle for first round and Sam Ball, Kentucky tackle for the second round. 6. Kansas City, Francis Peay, Missouri tackle. 7. Oakland passed. 8. San Diego, Nick Rassas, Notre Dame halfback. 9. Buffalo, Jim Lindsey, Arkansas halfback.

THIRD ROUND

1. Miami, Larry Gagner, Florida guard. 2. Boston, Harold Lucas, Michigan State tackle. 3. Denver, Bob Hadrick, Purdue end. 4. Houston, George Rice, Louisiana State tackle. 5. New York, Carl McAdams, Oklahoma linebacker. 6. Kansas City, Walt Barnes, Nebraska guard. 7. Oakland passed. 8. San Diego, Milt Morin, Massachusetts end. 9. Buffalo, Randy Jackson, Florida tackle.

FOURTH ROUND

1. Miami, Dick Leftridge, West Virginia fullback. 2. Boston traded choice to New York for future consideration. 3. Denver, Randy Johnson, Texas A&I quarterback. 4. Houston, George Allen, West Texas State tackle. 5. New York, James Waskiewicz, Wichita center on choice acquired from Boston and Phil Sheridan, Notre Dame end, on regular choice. 6. Kansas City, Elijah Gibson, Bethune-Cookman halfback. 7. Oakland passed. 8. San Diego, Charlie Brown, Syracuse defensive back. 9. Buffalo, Bobby Burnett, Arkansas halfback.

49ERS VANQUISHED IN CHICAGO, 61-20

Sayers Sets Season Mark With 21 Touchdowns and Ties Record for Game

STATISTICS OF THE GAME

	Bears	49ers
First downs	21	19
Rushing yardage	183	58
Passing yardage	401	272
Passes	17-33	23-44
Interceptions by	2	0
Punts	3-33	6-49
Fumbles lost	0	0
Yards penalized	30	14

CHICAGO, Dec. 12 (AP)—Gale Sayers scored six touchdowns today, raising his season total to 21—a National Football League record—as the Chicago Bears routed the San Francisco 49ers, 61-20.

Sayers established a Bear scoring record for one game and also matched the single game N.F.L. mark for touchdowns set by Ernie Nevers in 1929 and matched by Dub Jones in 1951.

Sayers's season total bettered the league record of 20 by Lenny Moore of the Baltimore Colts and matched this year by Jimmy Brown of the Cleveland Browns.

The triumph, avenging an opening-game 52-24 defeat at San Francisco, kept alive the Bears' chances of sharing the Western Conference title. They now have a 9-4 won-lost mark.

The remarkable rookie from Kansas scored in the first quarter, taking a screen pass from Rudy Bukich and running 80 yards.

In the second period, Sayers scored on runs of 21 and 7 yards.

Sayers cut through tackle and raced 50 yards in the third period. Later in this quarter, he dived over from the 1. His final touchdown, in the fourth quarter, came on a punt return of 85 yards.

```
Chicago Bears.........13  14  13  21—61
San Francisco 49ers....  0  13   0   7—20
```

Chi—Sayers, 80, pass from Bukich (pass failed).

Chi—Ditka, 29, pass from Bukich (Leclerc, kick).

S.F.—Parks, 9, pass from Brodie (Davis, kick).

Chi—Sayers, 21, (Leclerc, kick).

S.F.—Crow, 15, pass from Brodie (kick failed).

Chi—Sayers, 7, run (Leclerc, kick).

Chi—Sayers, 50, run (Leclerc, kick).

Chi—Sayers, 1, run (run failed).

S.F.—Kopay, 2, run (Davis, kick).

Chi—Jones, 8, pass from Bukich (Leclerc, kick).

Chi—Sayers, 85, punt return (Leclerc, kick).

Chi—Arnett, 2, run (Leclerc, kick).

Attendance—46,278.

Mack Hill Of Chiefs Dies After Operation On Knee

Kansas City, M. Dec. 14 (P)— Mack Lee Hill, a second-year fullback with the Kansas City Chiefs, died following surgery today in Kansas City's Menorah Medical Center.

A spokesman for the Chiefs said the surgery for the repair of torn knee ligaments ended about 3 p.m., C.S.T. Following surgery, the 25-year-old Hill went into convulsions. His temperature shot up to 105.

He died at 4.35 P.M.

Hill suffered a ruptured ligament in his right knee last Sunday when the Chiefs played at Buffalo in an American Football League game.

He entered the hospital last evening.

The cause of death, according to the team's spokesman, was a "Sudden and massive embolism lbood clot after surgery."

Scouts Liked Him

Roger Valdiserri, Chiefs' publicity director, said, "The doctors reported that this type of thing is not common, there is no known treatment, it is entirely unpredictable and unpreventable."

Born in Quincy, Fla., Hill was a halfback on his high school team and received a scholarship to Southern University in Baton Rouge, La.

Hill, known as "Mack the Truck," caught the eyes of pro scouts as a freshman at Southern, where he was a 225-pound halfback. He had a great year as a sophomore, then tapered off, because of injuries, in his final two years.

He came to the Chiefs' preseason training camp as a free agent because Kansas City was the only club that showed any interest at all.

He ran with power, a quickness that belied his 235 pounds spread over a 5-11 frame, and a balance that was the key to his success.

Hill earned his way into the starting line-up and became so valuable that when the Chiefs' staff had to decide between keeping the rookie or the veteran Jack Spikes, Spikes was sent to Houston.

As a rookie, Hill finished with the best average per carry among A.F.L. backs, 5.4 yards. He scored 6 touchdowns and had one run of 71 yards. He carried the ball 105 times and gained 576 yards.

This season the stocky fullback picked up 673 yards rushing, making him the sixth best runner in the league. His 5.0 average per carry was tops.

"Mack Lee Hill was a fine gentleman and a great football player," Stram said. "He came to us a virtual unknown and became a rookie sensation last year. He fulfilled every expectation this year and earned the respect and admiration of his coaches, teammates and every team in the American Football League.

"He was probably one of the most unselfish players I have ever coached," Stram continued. "He was completely dedicated to the team. Football was his life."

VIKINGS TRIP BEARS, 24-17

Sayers Scores For Record 22 TD's In Defeat

Chicago, Dec. 19 (P)—Brilliant rookie Gale Sayers established a National Football League touchdown-making record at 22, but it failed to stop the rallying Minnesota Vikings from upsetting the Chicago Bears 24-to-17 in the season finals for both today.

The Vikings exploded for 21 points in the final quarter, moving ahead for the first time on Rip Hawkins's 35-yard touchdown run with a pass interception with 65 seconds left.

Only 21 seconds before, a 22-yard scoring pass from Fran Tarkenton to Gordon Smith pulled the Vikings into a 17-17 tie.

Minnesota, closing with a 7-7 N.F.L. record, thus snapped a five-game winning streak by the Bears, who had won nine of their 10 previous starts.

The Bears, who dropped their first three starts of the season, wound up with a 9-5 record.

Sayers plunged two yards for the second touchdown which gave the Bears a 14-3 lead at the start of the fourth quarter.

Says Rolls In 2d Half

Sayers, who last week scored six touchdowns against the San Francisco 49ers and broke Baltimore Colt Lenny Moore's former N.F.L. season TD mark of 20, also wound up the year with a league rookie scoring record of 132 points.

The flashy rookie from the University of Kansas, effectively checked by the Vikings in the first half, got rolling somewhat in the second half. He finished with 82 yards on 14 carries and returned three kickoffs 41, 26 and 14 yards.

Statistics

	Vikings	Bears
First downs	17	17
Rushing yardage	103	167
Passing yardage	181	164
Passes	13-29	11-29
Passes intercepted by	3	1
Punts	5-41	5-36
Fumbles lost	2	0
Yards penalized	38	73

Minnesota .. 0 0 3 21—24
Chicago .... 0 0 7 10—17
Chi.—Bull, 23, run (Leclerc kick).
Minn.—F.G., Cox, 33.
Chi.—Sayers, 2, run (Leclerc kick).
Minn.—Hall, 17, pass from Tarkenton (Cox kick).
Chi.—F.G., Leclerc, 20.
Minn.—Smith, 22, pass from Tarkenton (Cox kick).
Minn.—Hawkins, 35, pass interception (Cox kick).
Attendance—46,604.

Jim Brown Ejected As Browns Nip Cards

Cleveland Owner Modell Storms At 'Gross Injustice' As Stars Misses Shot Record

Brown

St. Louis, Dec. 19 (P)—Cleveland Browns owner Art Modell was an angry man today although his club defeated the St. Louis Cardinals, 27 to 24, despite the loss of star fullback Jim Brown, who was ejected for fighting at the end of the first half.

"It was a gross injustice," Modell stormed after his prize star and defensive end Lee Robb of the Cardinals were given the boot.

"To rob Brown of a cnahce to win the scoring title on such an incident is ridiculous. He's been kicked, beaten and gouged for many seasons and has never complained, and now when it mattered to him, he has to be kicked out after years of injustice."

Brown had scored on a three-yard run in the first half, giving him 21 touchdowns for the season. Chicago's Gale Sayers scored his twenty-second touchdown in the Bears' loss to Minnesota and won the scoring crown.

There were different versions of what occurred between Robb and Brown, who said he had only been ejected one other time in his long career in the N.F.L.

"He hit me once before," Brown said of Robb, "and when he did it the second time, I came back at him. He hit me on the jaw, but it was one of those quick things, and we shook hands, almost immediately. But the officials took it more seriously."

Robb was quoted by teammates as saying Brown threatened him before the play and came at him with elbow high and kicked him.

Brown was reluctant to say more and was more concerned with what his absence meant to the Cleveland offense, which lost a 17-7 lead in the second half before coming back with the winning field goal and touchdown in the final six minutes.

His coach, Blanton Collier, saw it the same way.

"We counted so much on Jim and when he goes out, the tendency was to let down," Collier said, "but the players realized in the fourth quarter they had to play harder to pick up the slack."

The Browns also played the second half without star flanker Gary Collins, who suffered bruised ribs. However, he is expected to be ready for the championship game January 2.

Jimmy Brown's Last Game

Browns

St. Louis, Dec. 19 (P)—Linebacker Vince Costello's interception set up Frank Ryan's 24-yard scoring pass to Tom Hutchinson with 4½ minutes left and carried the Cleveland Browns to a 27-to-24 victory over the St. Louis Cardinals today in their National Football League regular season finale.

The Eastern Division champion Browns, playing without Jimmy Brown, who was ejected for fighting at the end of the first half, had lost a 17-to-0 lead to the heroics of St. Louis safety Larry Wilson.

Wilson Intercepts Three

Wilson intercepted three Ryan passes, returning one 95 yards for a touchdown and setting up two other scores that brought the Cardinals back to a 24-to-17 lead under the direction of third-string quarterback Terry Nofsinger.

The Cardinal defense gave them one last chance when it blocked a field goal attempt by Lou Groza and Pat Fisher picked up the ball at the 50 and raced to the Cleveland 24 with 1½ minutes left. But Jackie Smith dropped a pass in the end zone and Nofsinger was unable to connect on a fourth-down pass.

The Brows, who averaged an earlier 49-to-13 loss to the Cardinals, built their early lead on three interceptions of Buddy Humphrey passes. Larry Benz grabbed one, setting up the first of Lou Groza's two field goals, and Jim Houston nabbed two, putting Cleveland in position for Ryan's 13-yard loss to Gary Collins and Brown's three-yard scoring run.

Brown's touchdown gave him 21 for the season, but the ejection from the game ruined his chance to overtake Chicago's Gale Sayers, who won the scoring title with 22 touchdowns. St. Louis defensive end Joe Robb also was ejected from the game.

Wilson's interceptions set up Nofsinger's one-yard plunge and Jim Bakken's 23-yard field goal. Nofsinger threw five yards to Bill Triplett midway through the final period to give the Cardinals their only lead.

The Browns will take an 11-3 record into the championship game. St. Louis finished with a 5-9 mark.

Statistics

	Browns	Cards
First downs	16	14
Rushing yardage	141	110
Passing yardage	146	50
Passes	16-33	13-34
Passes intercepted by	4	3
Punts	5-37	7-38
Fumbles lost	0	0
Yards penalized	75	15

Cleveland .... 7 10 0 10—27
St. Louis .... 0 7 10 7—24

Clev.—Collins, 13, pass from Ryan (Groza kick).
Clev.—Brown, 3, run (Groza kick).
Clev.—F.G., Groza, 44.
St. L.—Wilson, 95, pass interception (Bakken kick).
St. L.—Hofsinger, 1, run (Bakken kick).
St. L.—F.G., Bakken, 23.
St. L.—Triplett, 5, pass fro Nofsinger (Bakken kick).
Clev.—F.G., Groza, 45.
Clev.—Hutchinson, 24, pass from Ryan (Groza kick).
Attendance—29,348.

BILLS TAKE A.F.L. TITLE

Champs Repeat By Blanking San Diego, 23-0

San Diego, Cal., Dec. 26 (AP) — Buffalo struck for two quick touchdowns in the second quarter, one on a spectacular 74-yard punt return, and the Bills rolled on' to defeat the San Diego Chargers, 23 to 0, and win the American Football League championship today for the second straight year.

Butch Byrd took a 40-yard punt from the Chargers' John Hadl on his own 26 and streaked down the San Diego sideline 74 yards, the first punt runback for a score in the A.F.L. championship series.

Moments earlier, Jack Kemp, whom the Chargers let go for $100 on waivers in 1962, fired a bullet pass down the middle for 18 yards into the end zone to Ernie Warlick, and the underdog Bills took a 14-0 lead at the half.

Place-kicking specialist Pete Gogolak, the soccer style booter, added three field goals in the second half with kicks of 11, 39 and 32 yards to further the Chargers' woes.

A crowd of 30,361 highly partisan fans gathered in 60-degree clear weather to witness the contest in Balboa Stadium.

The Chargers went into the game favored by 6½ points to avenge their 20-7 defeat in the championship game in Buffalo last year.

The first quarter was scoreless, and it was not until late in the second that Buffalo broke up what was a tremendous defensive battle. Kemp directed the Bills 60 yards in six plays.

Fullback Wray Carlton started it with two eight-yard smashes through the huge Charger line, which had the best record in the A.F.L. this year, and Kemp's 22-yard pass to Paul Costa put Buffalo in scoring position.

Kemp's rifle shot to Warlick went through the goal posts to find its target.

Offense Stopped

San Diego, with the best offensive record in the league—Hadl the leading rusher — was completely stymied. It was the first time San Diego had been held scoreless since Boston defeated the Chargers 41-0 December 17, 1961. And this was the first shutout for any team in the title history of the league.

Gogolak's three field goals tied a title game record set by Ben Agajanian for the old Los Angeles Chargers against Hosston in 1960.

Kemp, who was named the most valuable player in the game, hurled a 49-yard pass to Bo Roberson to the Chargers' 24 to set up Gogolak's first field goal from the 11.

The relentless ball hawk, Byrd, intercepted a Hadl pass, rushed it back 24 to the Chargers's 23, and Gogolak came through from a difficult angle from 39 yards out.

Buffalo got the ball on downs for the second time, with less than a yard to make, and again it was Gogolack from the 32. Gogolak barely missed from the 32 for a fourth field goal. He kicked the extra points on the touchdowns to score 11 points.

The Buffalo defensive team proved to be tremendous, with 270-pound Tom Sestak and 250-pound Tom Day as standouts throttling the Chargers' offense. The flashy running Lowe was held to a net 57 yards in 12 carries, but he got off one sparkler of 47 yards to pull San Diego out of the temporary hole temporarily.

Mainstays of the Bills' running team were Billy Joe and Carlton.

COACH CITES 3 LOSSES TO GREEN BAY

Owner Rosenbloom Is 'Proud' Of Team Despite Defeat

By CAMERON C. SNYDER
[Sun Staff Correspondent]

Green Bay, Wis., Dec. 26 — Their coach had told them to hold their heads high, but disappointment weighed more than praise and te Colts were bowed under it.

Phrases like "great game," "well done," "tremendous effort" fell on unflattered ears when the press corps was finally admitted after a 30-minute wait into the mortuary called the Colt dressing room.

Colt Lament

"We lost. That's all that matters," groaned Bobby Boyd. think I'd rather get beat 503 to than this way."

The score was 13-10 in overtime.

	Colts	Packers
First downs	9	23
Rushing yardage	143	112
Passing yardage	32	250
Passes	5-12	23-41
Passes intercepted by	2	0
Punts	8-41	5-42
Fumbles lost	1	2
Yards penalized	59	40

Colts   0 7 3 0 0—10
Green Bay 0 0 7 3 3—13

Colts—Shinnick, 25, fumble recovery (Michaels, kick).
Colts—Michaels, 15, field goal.
Green Bay—Chandler, 22, field goal.
Green Bay—Chandler, 25, field goal.
Attendance—50,484.

Individual Statistics:

Rushing

Player, Club	Att.	Yards
Taylor, Green Bay	23	61
Hornung, Green Bay	10	33
Pitts, Green Bay	3	14
Moore, Green Bay	3	5
Mette, Baltimore	17	57
Hill, Baltimore	16	57
Moore, Baltimore	12	33
Gilburg, Baltimore	1	5
Lorick, Baltimore	1	1

Passing

	Att.	Comp.	Yds.
Brat'ski, Green Bay	39	22	248
Starr, Green Bay	1	1	10
Mornung, Green Bay	1	0	0
Matte, Baltimore	12	5	40

Pass Receptions

	No.	Yards
Anderson, Green Bay	8	78
Dowler, Green Bay	5	50
Dale, Green Bay	3	63
Hornung, Green Bay	4	42
Taylor, Green Bay	2	29
Moore, Green Bay	1	-4
Mackey, Baltimore	3	25
Moore, Baltimore	2	15

N.F.L. Signs Two-Year, $37.6 Million Television Contract With CBS

TITLE GAME EXCLUDED FROM PACT

Home Blackout Plan Modified; Game On TV Every Week

New York, Dec. 29 —The Columbia Broadcasting System announced today that it has signed a new contract to continue televising National Football League games for two years for a total of $37,600,000.

The old two-year contract between the network and the N.F.L., calling for $14,000,000 a year, expired at the end of the season.

The two-year contract for the championship game, calling for $ .800,000 annually, ends after Sunday's game in Green Bay, Wis., between the Packers and Cleveland Browns.

The pact was described by CBS as "the largest sports contract in television history."

Under the contract, announced jointly by Pete Rozelle, commissioner of the N.F.L. and Bill MacPhail, vice president in charge of sports for CBS-TV, CBS gets the rights for regular and pre-season games.

Expect Agreement

Rozelle and MacPhail said that negotiations are being conducted for the N.F.L. championship game Playoff Bowl and Pro Bowl games with the expectations that an agreement will be reached shortly.

They also announced that CBS has an option for a third year. The contract includes the new team, the Atlanta Falcons, who will start operating next year, and provides for the possibility of a sixteenth team in 1967 as well as divisional playoffs at the end of the season.

If the N.F.L. goes to 16 teams, it is expected to form four divisions with two playoffs leading to the championship game.

Three Night Games

The new contract calls for the televising of three games during the season at night and in prime TV time.

There also was a modification of the blackout restrictions on television. Television viewers in home cities will be able to see another N.F.L. game on their sets.

That means that if the Chicago Bears, for example, were home to the Green Bay Packers, the Chicago television station could show a game between the New York Giants and Philadelphia Eagles.

In past contracts, no N.F.L. game could be televised into the city of a team that was playing a home game at the time.

Win N.F.L. Crown

GREEN BAY CAVORTS ON WET FIELD

Taylor And Hornung Splash Through Losers' Line

By CAMERON C. SNYDER
Staff Correspondent

Green Bay, Wis., Jan. 2—While the Cleveland Browns slipped and slithered and finally fell, the Green Bay Packers cavorted like happy hogs in the muck and mire of Lambeau Field to wrest the National Football League crown from the defending champions, 23 to 12, today.

The Packers came equipped with non-skid tires in the persons of Jim Taylor and Paul Hornung, who waded through the slippery mud for 96 and 105 yards, respectively.

These two, disdaining injuries, carried the fight to the Browns, whose attack bogged down under the load of mud on Jim Brown's feet.

Ball Control Display

Leading only 13 to 12 at halftime and apparently having trouble keeping their feet, the Packers, particularly the offensive line, played root hog in the second half for 10 more points in a great ball control display.

Meanwhile, the Browns' attack was choked off in the air by a good Packer secondary and a slippery ball and on the ground by a good Packer defense and the slippery field.

The mud and a great Packer pursuit took away Jim Brown's forte, the run around end, and with it most of Cleveland's attack.

Line Open Holes

But Hornung and Taylor, not nearly as fast as Brown, used the direct routes through the line and kept their feet as their teammates gouged out huge holes in the Cleveland defense.

Meanwhile, kicker Don Chandler tied a title game record by booting three field goals.

The field conditions were caused by a three inch snow which ended just before kickoff. The Packer ground crew did a fine job of cleaning up the playing surface, which then suffered further damage by a light but steady drizzle throughout most of the game.

The field conditions played a most important part in the Packer success and the Brown failure. It was made to order for Vince Lombardi's unfancy attack which puts a premium on execution of simple assignments.

Too Big An Obstacle

For the Browns the playing conditions plus the Packers were too much of an obstacle. Frank Ryan, Cleveland quarterback, couldn't open up the Packer defense with passes as his receivers had trouble making cuts.

As it was Ryan threw for one touchdown, in the first period when the surface was just slick, not slick and slimey, and that the extent of the Brown attack except for two field goals by the ageless Lou Groza, one in the first and the other at the end of the second period.

After Ryan's scoring pass to Gary Collins, a former Maryland star, came the play that might have been the key to the entire game.

Bad Snapback

Groza, who has kicked 96 straight extra points, didn't get a chance as the snapback from center was wide of the holder, Bob Franklin, on the conversion attempt.

The ball rolled loose for a moment. Then Groza picked it up like a hot potato, looked at the Packers pouring in on him and for the first time probably in his life threw a pass to Franklin, who

was immediately tackled six yards from the goal line.

So the Browns, who usually are willing to trade scores, found themselves on the short end of an exchange of touchdowns, 7-6, after 5 minutes of play.

The Packers had scored on the kickoff series via a 47-yard pass from Bart Starr to Carroll Dale. And just as important, Don Chandler converted.

The Browns later took over the lead for short time on a 24-yard field goal by Groza, a 42-year-old veteran of the 1946 Browns.

However, when the Packers came back to equalize Groza's field goal with one of 15 yards by Chandler, the Browns found themselves a point behind, although each club had scored a touchdown and a field goal.

Still Trailed

Chandler's second field goal of the second period moved the Packers ahead 13 to 9 and even after the Browns countered with a 28-yard field goal in the last minute of the first half, they went into the dressing room one point behind.

That was as close as they were ever to get. On the first Packer series, Hornung and Taylor took over and 90 yards and 11 plays later, which consumed over 5 minutes, the Packers scored their second and final touchdown.

The Statistics

	Browns	Packers
First downs	8	21
Rushing yardage	64	204
Passing	8-18	10-19
Passing yardage	97	128
Passes int'cepted by	1	2
Punts	4 46	3 38
Fumbles lost	0	0
Yards penalized	35	20

Cleveland 9 3 0 0 — 12
Green Bay 7 6 7 3 — 23

G B Dale, 47, pass from Starr (Chandler, kick)
Cleve Collins, 17, pass from Ryan (pass failed)
Clev FG, Groza, 24
G B FG, Chandler, 15
G B FG, Chandler, 23
Clev FG, Groza, 28
G B Hornung, 13, run (Chandler, kick)
G B FG, Chandler, 29
Attendance— 50,852

RUSHING

Green Bay

Player	Att.	Net Yards
Taylor	27	96
Hornung	18	105
Moore	2	3

Cleveland

Brown	12	50
Green	3	5
Ryan	3	9

PASSING

Green Bay

	Att	Comp	Yds	TDs	Int
Starr	18	10	147	1	1
Hornung	1	0	0	0	0

Cleveland

Ryan	18	8	115	1	2

PASS RECEPTIONS

Green Bay

	No.	Yards
Dowler	5	59
Dale	2	60
Taylor	2	20
Hornung	1	8

Cleveland

Brown	3	44
Collins	3	41
Warfield	2	30

PUNT RETURNS

Green Bay

	No.	Yards
Pitts	1	-10
Wood	1	0

Cleveland

Roberts	1	11

KICKOFF RETURNS

Green Bay

	No.	Yards
Moore	3	66

Cleveland

Scales	1	14
Roberts	1	95
Kells	1	46

Reprinted from
The Baltimore Sun

Wis. Governor Snowed Out

Green Bay, Wis., Jan. 2 (AP)—Wisconsin Gov. Warren P. Knowles had to settle for the televised version of the National Football League championship game between the Green Bay Packers and the Cleveland Browns today.

He flew to Green Bay from Madison today but his plane couldn't land because of the heavy snowstorm and was forced to return to Madison.

How Draft Choices Chose

New York, Jan. 3 (P)—The National Football League won the annual signing game between the two leagues, both in quality and quantity, but the biggest news turned out to be the sums of money handed out to untried, untested players. If the figures tossed around can be believed, some twenty top players cost upwards of $7,000,000.

Over-all, the N.F.L. has signed 75 per cent of the 232 eligibles it drafted, 174 players deciding to go with N.F.L. teams and 40 with A.F.L. teams, while 18 remained unsigned. The A.F.L., meanwhile, has signed 46 per cent of its 181 draftees, getting 84 players and losing 78 to the N.F.L., while 19 remain unsigned.

Of 111 players drafted by both leagues, the N.F.L. outsigned the A.F.L., 79-28, with 4 unsigned.

National League

Atlanta (Two picks on each round)—Signed Texas linebacker Tomy Nobis, signed Texas A & I quarterback Randy Johnson, signed Notre Dame defensive back Nick Rassas, signed Bowling Green tackle Jerry Jones, sent rights to Mississippi halfback Mike Dennis to Los Angeles, which signed him, signed Notre Dame end Phil Sheridan.

Los Angeles—Signed Michigan tackle Tom Mack, lost Southern California halfback Mike Garrett to Kansas City, lost Tulsa guard Dick Tyson to Oakland.

Pittsburgh.—Signed West Virginia fullback Dick Leftridge, signed Florida guard Larry Gagner, signed Syracuse center Pat Killorin.

Philadelphia—Signed Indiana defensive end Randy Beisler, signed Stanford defensive end Gary Pettigrew, signed Arizona State back Ben Hawkins.

Dallas—Signed Iowa guard John Niland, signed Tulsa tackle Willie Townes, no third-round pick.

Washington—Signed Princeton kicker Charlie Gogolak, signed Nebraska tackle Walt Barnes, signed Ohio State fullback Tom Barrington.

Minnesota — Signed Purdue tackle [...] tackle Bob Pickens as a future on third round.

Green Bay (Two first-round picks)—Signed Illinois fullback Jim Grabowski, signed Minnesota tackle Gale Gillingham, selected Maryland tackle Tom Chichowski as a future on second round, signed San Jose tackle Fred Heron and Nebraska end Tony Jeter, both third-round selections.

Cleveland—Signed Massachusetts end Milt Morin, lost Kentucky quarterback Rick Norton to Miami, no third-round pick.

Baltimore—Signed Kentucky tackle Sam Ball, signed Missouri tackle Butch Allison, signed Kentucky flanker Rick Kestner.

American League

Miami (Two first round picks)—Lost Illinois fullback Jim Grabowski to Green Bay, singed Kentucky quarterback Rick Norton, signed Tennessee linebacker Frank Emanuel, lost Florida guard Larry Gagner to Pittsburgh.

Boston—Signed Purdue tackle Karl Singer, signed Louisiana Tech tackle Jim Boudreax, lost Michigan State tackle Hal Lucas to St. Louis.

Denver—Lost Purdue tackle Jerry Shay to Minnesota, lost Nebraska end Freeman White to New York, signed [...]

Rams Invite Allen To Discuss Post

Los Angeles, Jan. 9 (P)—George Allen, defensive coach of the Chicago Bears, has been invited to consider taking over coaching chors of the Los Angeles Rams of the National Football League, a Ram spokesman said today.

Allen is expected in Los Angeles tomorrow, the spokesman said, to discuss the post with Ram owner Dan Reeves.

It was vacated when Reeves fired former head coach Harland Svare, 34, just before Christmas.

Winning, says Reeves, is a condition to being a long-time Ram coach. Svare's 3½-year record was 14-31-3, and last season his team won 4 and lost 10, to finish in the cellar of the N.F.L.'s Western Division.

GRID 'FAME' LIST GROWS

N.F.L. Enshrines Eight Former Stars Of Game

Canton, Ohio, March 22 (P)—Bulldog Turner, George McAfee and Bill Dudley are among eight celebrated figures voted into the National Professional Football Hall of Fame it was announced today.

Steve Owen, Joe Guyon, Arnie Herber, Walt Kiesling and Shorty Ray also were selected for the honor by a panel of fourteen sports writers and broadcasters.

Ceremonies Aug. 27

They will be enshrined at special ceremonies tentatively scheduled for August 27, joining 31 others previously voted into the Hall.

Turner was a center and McAfee a halfback for the Chicago Bears, hitting the peak of their careers in the 1940's, and Dudley played halfback for the Pittsburgh Steelers, Detroit Lions and Washington Redskins in the same era.

Owen was a long-time coach in the National Football League, including a span of 23 years with the New York Giants. Kiesling also was a coach for many years, with several pro teams.

Teamed With Hutson

Guyon, an Indian who was a teammate of Jim Thorpe's at Carlisle, played both tackle and halfback as a pro in the 1920's. Herber, the N.F.L.'s leading passer for three years, teamed with Don Hutson to give the Green Bay Packers a legendary aerial attack.

Ray spent eighteen years as the N.F.L.'s technical advisor and supervisor of officials, 1938-1956.

BEARS' AIDE HIRED, N.F.L. FEUD ERUPTS

Halas Accuses L.A. Of 'Tampering' And Issues Threat

Los Angeles, Jan. 10 (P)—Assistant coach George Allen of the Chicago Bears today accepted the head coaching position with the Los Angeles Rams and triggered a bitter controversy between the owners of the two National Football League teams.

In Chicago, owner-coach George Halas blasted the deal as "a flagrant case of tampering with a coach under contract" and indicated he might attempt to nullify the Allen-Rams agreement.

Allen has two years remaining on his Chicago contract.

Negotiations Defended

President Daniel F. Reeves of the Rams, at a press conference which followed the announcement of Allen's acceptance, vehemently defended the negotiations.

"Last Christmas, George Allen called one of our staff men, Johnny Sanders, and asked if the Rams might be interested in him as a head coach," Reeves related.

"Sanders called me the following Monday after Christmas and I instructed him to tell George Allen to ask George Halas for permission to talk to us," Reeves added. "Mr. Halas gave him this permission.

Permission Rescinded

"Later, George Halas rescinded this permission and his objection was quite strong. Mr. Halas said he didn't want me to take Mr. Allen, or, if you prefer, Mr. Allen to take me."

Reeves said the history of the N.F.L. has numerous parallels of assistant coaches going to other teams as head coaches.

"I can't believe George Halas will stand in his way," added Reeves.

Allen, sitting beside Reeves, declared that Halas at first told him to go ahead and talk to the Rams and that he had no objection.

SUCCEEDS JOE FOSS, WHO QUIT

'Not So Worried About N.F.L. As Making A.F.L. No. 1'

Houston, April 8 (P)—Al Davis, a dynamic young man in the American Football League, was named today to succeed Joe Foss as the A.F.L. commissioner.

Davis gave up a long-term contract as coach and general manager of the Oakland Raiders in accepting the post, a move that had been more or less expected.

After guiding the A.F.L. since its inception in 1959, Foss stepped aside yesterday with a resignation reportedly resulting in part from smoldering club owner dissatisfaction over loss of the Atlanta (Ga.) area to the National Football League.

Not N.F.L. Minded

Davis, 36, told newsmen repeatedly today that solutions to problems involving the N.F.L. are not among his immediate goals and objectives.

"My goal is to make the A.F.L. the best league in pro football," he said. "My first job is dedication to the growth of this league."

Unexpectedly, one of Davis's first acts as commissioner of the league was to help break up a scuffle between one of the A.F.L. owners and a newsman.

It developed between Bud Adams, Jr., owner of the Houston Oilers, and Jack Gallagher, Houston Post sports writer, when Gallagher and a photographer attempted to get pictures of Davis and some A.F.L. officials during an executive committee meeting.

A Misunderstanding

Gallagher said a misunderstanding developed between himself and Adams over who would be in the picture. A scuffle followed, and Davis and the A.F.L. owners separated the two.

'Giants Get Best Kicker Available'

Princeton, N.J., May 17 (P)—"I'd like to see him kick every field goal he tries as long as we win the game," Charlie Gogolak said today after learning that his older brother, Pete, had left the Buffalo Bills of the American Football League and signed with the New York Giants of the National Football League.

EX-BUFFALO ACE PLAYED OUT OPTION

Action Opens Way For N.F.L. Clubs To Talk To Ladd, Faison

By CAMERON C. SNYDER
[Sun Staff Correspondent]

Washington, May 17—Al Davis declared war on the National Football League after his recent appointment as Commissioner of the American Football League.

But the older circuit fired the first shot, a 10-megaton bomb, with the announcement today that the New York Giants had signed Peter Gogolak as a free agent.

Gogolak, former Cornell side-swiping place kicker, has been a star in his specialty with the A.F.L. champion Buffalo Bills for several years.

Wellington Mara, president of the Giants, made the announcement of the signing after this morning's meeting of league owners.

Pete Makes Move

He said Goglak, whose brother Chrley was the No. 1 draft choice of the Washington Redskins in the winter draft as a side-footed place-kicker from Princeton, reached the Giants through his lawyer and his manager.

"He sought us out," Wellington informed the press gathering, "through attorney Michael Mooney and manager Fred Cocoran," (Corcoran is bettern known as the former P.G.A. tourney director).

"There was no bonus involved," Wellington continued. "We are not going to announce what he signed for because of club policy."

Later, he admitted, almost too readily, that Gogolak's contract wasn't astronomical. Pete's brother Charley however, was a high-priced bonus baby, of the Redskins although just a rookie.

Opens The Gates

The signing of Gogolak opens the way, which has apparently been shut by owners, to other raids between the leagues and offers players in either circuit a better future in the event they wish to play out their option as Gogolak did.

The vista this signing opens includes two huge hunks of men by the name of Earl Faison and Eernie Ladd, defensive end and tackle for the A.F.L.'s San Diego Chargers. These two played out their options in 1965 and became free-agents May 1, the same day as Gogolak.

Since then they have been wandering, looking for a berth in football. For some strange reason the N.F.L. teams have steered clear of them, probably fearing a rash of free agents coming out of their own league if the way was cleared for player stealing between the circuits.

Now that door has been open, which was left ajar when offensive end Willard Dewveall, of the Chicago Bears, played out his option and joined the Houston Oilers for the first season of A.F.L. competition in 1960.

Faison belongs through prior draft rights to the Detroit Lions of the N.F.L. and Ladd to the Bears. No other N.F.L. club besides these two can contact Faison or Ladd unless an agreement is reached with the teams holding the draft rights.

When asked what the Lions' position would be on Faison now that the Giants have broken the "co-existent" policy, general manager Edward Anderson said:

"This came about suddenly. We will have to do some thinking about it."

Asked why the Lions hadn't made some move to obtain Faison earlier, he replied, "We felt it wasn't a good policy and that it could trigger something."

Real Shootint Next?

Just what it can trigger is now done. The cold war should be over and the real shooting underway.

Muggs Halas, son of George, said pretty much the same as Anderson.

"This came about suddenly," said Muggs. "We aren't prepared to say anything about Ladd and our situation now. We have to think it over and after we do we'll issue a statement in a couple of days."

Both Anderson and Halas made a point of it that Faison and Ladd hadn't approached their clubs. The feeling here was that in such circumstances the clubs would go to the mountains if the mountains wouldn't make the first move.

No Colt Comment

This standoffish attitude apparently is a conciliatory measure adopted by some of the N.F.L. owners.

Don Kellett, Colt general manager, was asked if his team would be interested in obtaining either Ladd or Faison or both.

He avoided a direct answer, pointing out the draft rights of the pair belonged to other teams.

Reprinted from
The Baltimore Sun

Dove Of Grid Peace Arrived Weary

New York, June 9 — The dove of peace in the pro football war limped home on weary wings today after shadowing Tex Schramm and Lamar Hunt for ten weeks.

Peace finally was declared last night between the National Football League and the American Football League after a series of cloak - and - dagger meetings between Schramm, general manager of Dallas in the N.F.L., and Hunt, owner of Kansas City of the A.F.L.

Sentiment Was There

Informal peace feelers had been exchanged for several years between various owners in both leagues. Actually, Hunt had talked to the late Bert Bell, N.F.L. commissioner in 1959 before the A.F.L. ever got off the ground. At various times there had been talks of a common draft between Ralph Wilson, Buffalo owner, and various N.F.L. clubs. Former A.F.L. commissioner Joe Foss often spoke out in favor of a common draft. There never was a formal reply from the N.F.L.

Sentiment for an agreement between the two leagues was evident after the 1964 season and there were informal talks in the spring of 1965.

The matter came to a head in late February or early March of this year when N.F.L. commissioner Pete Rozelle and Schramm drew up a suggested format for peace. Three owners, never identified, were briefed.

The big bonus splurge of the 1965 draft had piqued the interest of the owners in curbing the wave of spending. The war was costing money. There was public demand for peace. There was concern about squad morale, invasion of territory and run-away inflation.

Meet In Parking Lot

Schramm was selected as the liaison man for the N.F.L. It was decided that the man to contact in the A.F.L. was Hunt, founder of the league and one who desired to work on the problem.

The first actual meeting was about April 1. It happened at the Dallas Airport and was held in Schramm's sedan in the parking lot.

Schramm outlined the N.F.L.'s concept of a settlement. Hunt was interested. The original plan contained several variations from the peace that finally was adopted.

More Meetings

After the initial meeting, each man agreed to go to a small group in his own league. Hunt discussed the proposal with at least three A.F.L. clubowners. He came back to Schramm with the suggestion that maybe something could be worked out.

N.F.L. Will Add Sixteenth Franchise For 1967 Season

New York, June 10 — The National Football League still plans to go ahead with a sixteenth team in 1967 as originally outlined before peace came to professional football.

New Orleans, Cincinnati, Seattle, Portland, Ore., and Phoenix are the leading possibilities. Unless some other cities move into the picture before 1970, four of this quartet could be in the league by that time.

Boston and Houston also made a pitch for an N.F.L. franchise at the May meetings in Washington. Although the peace announcement did not rule out future two-club cities, it was believed that would be the case.

Oilers Snub Astrodome

The Houston Oilers, unable to agree on terms with Judge Roy Hofheinz, principal owner of the Astrodome, played in Rice Stadium last year. Owner Bud Adams of the Oilers insists he is sticking with that deal under a contract that has four years to run.

Hofheinz urged the N.F.L. to move into the Astrodome during the recent Washington meetings.

Boston presumably will be left to the Patriots, who are hopeful that the recent presentation of a civic group before the N.F.L. will spur the building of a new stadium.

A.F.L. In No Hurry

New Orleans is regarded a strong possibility for 1967 along with Cincinnati. The N.F.L. is committed to expanding to sixteen clubs by 1967. The American Football League reportedly is willing to wait until 1968 before adding a tenth team.

When the two leagues start playing regular season interleague games in 1970, there probably will be 28 teams, 14 in each league. This could involve adding an eleventh and twelfth team to the present A.F.L. and shifting two N.F.L. clubs. The mechanics of dividing the league into two divisions or conferences in 1970 have yet to be worked out.

It is the current thinking of the N.F.L. that the fourteen-game season will continue indefinitely. The problems of sharing several parks with baseball clubs precludes an earlier start.

N.F.L. Plans Divisions

When the N.F.L. goes to 16 teams in 1967, there will be two 8-club conferences, each divided into 4-club divisions.

The division champions will play for the right to meet in the league championship game and the winner will go on to play the A.F.L. winners. Eventually, under the 28-team setup, there will be two 14-club leagues, split into two 7-club conferences.

No date has been set for the first N.F.L.-A.F.L. championship game. However, Saturday, January 7 in regarded as a strong possibility. The A.F.L. title game will be played December 26 and the N.F.L.'s January 1

The Play-Off Bowl between the N.F.L. second-place teams already is set for Miami, Sunday, January 8, and the Pro Bowl game of N.F.L. all-star teams for Sunday, January 15.

The site of the A.F.L.-N.F.L. game is yet to be determined but it is considered likely that it will be played at a neutral site in the warm weather belt.

Aug. 6

Pro Football Merger in Jeopardy

By BOB HOOBING

CHICAGO — If pro football doesn't get quick Congressional action, the 1970 merger may not materalize. Time is running out.

Confident Commissioner Pete Rozelle dropped this bomb at a meeting Friday of the Football Writers of America.

Rozelle feels aid from Capitol Hill will be forthcoming after a two-day visit to Washington earlier in the week. MAY RE-

May Re-evaluate

But he warned if legislation is not passed this summer clarifying the present vagueness in anti-trust statutes, Washington legal advisors will be consulted and "we may have to re-evaluate."

Rozelle stressed the National and American League's common draft and title game next January, with the merger to come later, is an "All or nothing" plan. He added, "We have every intention to go through with it. I see no reason why we can't."

But legal roadblocks must be cleared.

Rep. Emmanuel Celler, (D-N.Y.), chairman of the House Judiciary Committee, could prove the toughest linebacker the game has ever known.

With the so-called "Sports Bill" apparently dead, Rozelle has asked Celler and his committee to consider legislation dealing specifically with the pro football merger agreement of June 8.

Such a bill would give anti-trust exemptions "to enable us to fully implement the merger plan we set forth," Rozelle explained. Last year the "Sports Bill" passed the Senate. It would have given other pro sports the same anti-trust exemptions baseball enjoys. The legislation will not get past Celler.

Favors Football

Rozelle expressed privately the feeling that Celler is in sympathy with pro football's need and position. But it is known that the Congressional leader is against giving baseball more privileges than it has and is questioning the hockey structure.

What this means specifically in Boston terms is that Celler would like to see the Patriots in the new super-league but questions giving added legal advantages to the Red Sox and Bruins.

That's why the special appeal for special legislation by the N.F.L. head.

"Time is our problem," said Rozelle. "It still may be possible to get legislation this seassion, but the lengthy debate on the Civil Rights Bill and the airline strike have occupied everyone's time.

So Rozelle felt it necessary to put in a separate pitch. He feels public support is with the merger. Congressman Celler has now been asked to carry the ball.

On another subject, Rozelle said much has been made of the so-called club management holds over an athlete, particularly in light of the merger. The Commissioner stressed the inherent advantage the player has, because if he and his term aren't satisfied they won't be successfu on the field. From this, Rozelle concludes, salaries will continut to escalate in pro ball.

Stadiums Vital

The Commissioner, obviously referring to Boston and Denver, said, "new stadiums in some areas are mot important to provide the proper minimum seating by 1970."

"They may be necessary to have the ownership continue in those cities," he added.

Rozelle also said he personally feels expansion franchises should be granted to accommodate those areas which do not now have pro ball. New Orleans, Cincinnati and Seattle thus top the N.F.L. list for '67 expansion. The feeling is Pheonix, Arizona, will be a candidate in about five years.

"I feel we're going to hit. But this legislation is very important to us. If it doesn't pass, it doesn't necessarily mean the merger is dead. But we have to look at it again and be responsible to the future of pro football."

Unwelcome Words

Obviusly pro game leaders were concerned with the John Brodie case. The San Francisco 49'ers quarterback also had signed an agreement with Houston's A.F.L. entry prior to the merger announcement. The recent "settlement" with Brodie by the 49'ers was made to insure the player was happy and would not bring legal action.

Restraint of trade and inter-state commerce are unwelcome words until the full legal position of football is clarified once and for all. Brodie had a case and good lawyers. The 49'ers settled. Rozelle assured everyone that no matter what the press said, Houston was not footing part of Brodie's longterm salary, reportedly $750,000 over four years.

Meanwhile, the N.F.L. AND A.F.L. offices and staffs are being carefully kept as separate entities. Both sides are walking softly so as not to stir any adverse legislative feeling or court action.

The Wisconsin State Supreme Court's reversal of a district court decision that the Braves and baseball vilated anti-trust laws by moving to Atlanta hurt pro football's cause. It tomok the pressure off the question.

Reprinted from the **Boston Herald**, courtesy the **Boston Herald American**

Falcons' Coming Out Ruined By Toe Of Rams, 19-14

Atlanta, Sept. 11 (AP)—Bruce Gossett kicked four field goals for Los Angeles today, pushing the Rams to a 19-to-14 victory over ambitious Atlanta in the Falcons' first National Football League game.

The Rams rolled to a 16-0 lead in the second quarter before rookie quarterback Randy Johnson brought Atlanta back by throwing a 53-yard touchdown pass to Gary Barnes and scoring himself on a three-yard run.

The Texas A.&I. newcomer's touchdown was set up by a 65-yard run on the first play of the second half by fullback Ernie Wheelwright, a castoff from the New York Giants.

Johnson's score cut the Rams' lead to 16-14, but Gossett booted his fourth field goal midway in the third period to assure Los Angeles' new coach, George Allen, of a victorious debut.

Roman Gabriel hit 15 of 22 passes for 233 yards in the first half and provided the Rams with their only touchdown when he threw a 51-yard scoring strike to end Jack Snow.

Atlanta's pass defense tightened in the second half as Gabriel hit only 6 of 12 for 51 yards, but the Rams never had to punt until late in the fourth quarter.

Gossett, the Rams' leading scorer in 1965, hit on field goals of 15, 15 and 23 yards before his

The Statistics

	Rams	Falcons
First downs	23	10
Rushing yardage	146	121
Passing yardage	294	154
Passes	21-35	9-25
Passes intercepted by	2	1
Punts	2-38	7-45
Fumbles lost	1	0
Yards penalized	20	35

Los Angeles ...... 3 13 3 0—19
Atlanta ...... 0 7 7 0—14
Los Angeles—Field goal. Gossett, 15.
Los Angeles—Snow, 51, pass from Gabriel (Gossett kick).
Los Angeles—Field goal. Gossett, 15.
Los Angeles—Field goal. Gossett, 23.
Atlanta—Barnes, 53, pass from Johnson (Trayham, kick).
Atlanta—Johnson, 3, run (Trayham, kick).
Los Angeles—Field goal. Gossett, 22.
Attendance, 54,418.

third quarter boot from the 22.

A crowd of 54,418 watched the game.

Cut Player Gave Team Plays To L.A.: Hecker

Atlanta Sept. 11 (AP)—Coach Norb Hecker charged today a disappointed player cut last week disclosed Atlanta's offensive plans to Los Angeles before the Falcons' National Football League debut.

Hecker did not name the player, but Los Angeles Coach George Allen admitted that former Falcon kicker Bob Jencks had talked with the Rams.

"Jencs came over to try to get a job with us," Allen said. "He was disappointed about being cut and he talked to Bill George a while."

George is a Los Angeles linebacker, but Allen denied knowing all about the Falcons' offense.

"If we knew what they were going to do, we wouldn't have gone down to the last minute of the game in a position to lose," Allen said.

Raiders Open A.F.L. Season By Whipping Miami 23-14

Miami, Fla., Sept. 2 (AP)—The Oakland Raiders had to steal their old teammate, Dick Wood, blind tonight to beat the amazing young Miami Dolphins 23 to 14 in the kickoff game of the American Football League season.

Howie Williams and Dave Grayson each snagged two of Wood's passes in the second period and the Raiders turned the first two thefts into 10 points in a three-minute span.

Auer Scores TD

Except for this wholesale thievery against Wood, who was claimed by the Dolphins from Oakland in the A.F.L. expansion draft, the new Miami team may have pulled off a real shocker by winning its first time out in league combat.

Joe Auer, a Miami boy who left the Los Angeles Rams to come home and join the Dolphins, gave Oakland's 17-point favorites a warning that a rough night was ahead when he raced 95 yards to a touchdown with the opening kickoff.

Only one Raider, Rodger Bird, got a shot at the fleet Auer. He missed at the 10 as Auer dove into the end zone.

Then interceptions put the Raiders twice on the Dolphin 16, from where they scored on a two-yard run by Hewritt Dixon and a 16-yard field goal by Mike Mercer.

2 Interceptions

The two other pass thefts in the fatal second period stopped the Dolphins after they had penetrated deep into Oakland territory or Wood's passes to Auer.

Gene Mingo, another Miami draftee from Oakland, missed an opportunity to put the Dolphins in a tie when he failed on a 19-yard field goal try early in the second half. Auer and Billy Joe had set it up by ripping off solid gains on the ground after Jim Warren intercepted a pass from Cotton Davidson.

Tom Flores, coming in for Davidson, then took the Raiders 81 yards to a touchdown on passes to Art Powell, Clem Daniels, Roger Hagberg and Tom Mitchell. The payoff pitch went 15 yards to Powell.

Mingo missed another field goal try from 15 yards out but Miami cut the margin to 17-14 on a two-yard pass from Norton to the aging former Chicago Bear star, Rick Casares.

	Oakland	Miami
First downs	16	12
Rushing yardage	16	104
Passing yardage	241	91
Passes	18-39	9-30
Passes intercepted	5	4
Punts	3-42.8	5-35.5
Fumbles lost	2	0
Yards penalized	49	20

Oakland — Dixon, 2, run (Mercer kick).
Oakland — Powell, 15, pass from Flores (Mercer kick).
Miami — Casares, 2, pass from Norton (Mingo kick).
Oakland — Mitchell, 16, pass from Flores (kick failed).
Attendance, 26,776.

Oakland ...... 0 10 7 6—23
Miami ...... 7 0 0 7—14
Miami — Auer, 95, kickoff return (Mingo kick).
Oakland—Mercer, FG, 16.

Oct. 10

BALTIMORE LINE STOPS PASS RUSH

Detroit Rookie QB Passes 99 Yards To Studstill

By CAMERON C. SNYDER

It was a discotheque "Home Sweet Home" for the Colts yesterday as they twisted, shook, rattled and bumped out a 45-to-14 victory over the Detroit Lions in their return to friendly Memorial Stadium.

John Unitas set the beat with four touchdown passes but everyone was in tune, particularly the offensive line which drowned out the ferocious Lion defense with deafening blocks.

A capacity crowd of 60,238 benevolent and tolerant fans added their voices to the homecoming rock and roll session that kept the Colts in contention in the West.

Baltimore's record is now 3-2, while Detroit must now be considered a spoiler with a 2-4 record. Both Colt losses were on the road.

99-Yard Pass

There were only minor discordant notes heard during the afternoon, including a record tying 99 yard touchdown pass from rookie Karl Sweetan to Pat Studstill while the Colts were changing their music.

Reprinted from
The Baltimore Sun

NEELY STAYS WITH DALLAS

Oilers Get Top '67 Draft Choice, 2 Others Later

Houston, Nov. 17 (AP)—The Houston Oilers and the Dallas Cowboys settled their dispute over tackle Ralph Neely today by agreeing he will remain with Dallas.

The Oilers, in return, will get Dallas's first draft choice in the upcoming draft plus two other draft choices to be named later.

Neely, who signed contracts with both the Oilers of the American Football League and Dallas of the National Football League, had been adjudged Oiler property by the courts.

However, the Cowboys, in the thick of the N.F.L. Eastern Division title race, had asked for the meeting with Oiler officials to work out an agreement to keep the former University of Oklahoma lineman.

At Dallas, Coach Tom Landry of the Cowboys said, "We are pleased indeed that Tex Schramm was able to work this out and that we are going to have Neely from now on. He has done an excellent job in the offensive line and been a major factor in the big improvement in our offense."

Statistics

	New York	Washington
First downs	25	16
Rushing yardage	111	209
Passing yardage	278	132
Passes	20-33	10-18
Passes inte'ted by	1	5
Punts	4-38	6-46
Fumbles lost	1	1
Yards penalized	119	107
New York	0 14 14 13—41
Washington	13 21 14 24—72

Wash.—Whitfield, 5 pass from Jurgensen (kick failed).
Wash.—Whitfield, 62 run (C. Gogolak).
Wash.—Owens, 62 run on recovered fumble (C. Gogolak kick).
NY—Jacobs, 6 run (P. Gogolak kick).
Wash.—Whitfield, 1 run (C. Gogolak kick).
Wash.—Looney, 9 run (C. Gogolak kick).
NY—Wood, 1 run (P. Gogolak kick).
NY—Morrison, 41 pass from Wood (P. Gogolak kick).
Wash.—Taylor, 32 pass from Jurgensen (C. Gogolak kick).
NY—Jones, 50 pass from Wood (P. Gogolak kick).
Wash.—Taylor, 74 pass from Jurgensen (C. Gogolak kick).
Wash.—Harris, 52 punt return (C. Gogolak kick).
Wash.—Owens, 60 pass interception (C. Gogolak kick).
NY—Thomas, 18 pass from Kennedy (kick failed).
NY—Lewis, 1 run (P. Gogolak kick).
Wash.—Mitchell, 45 pass from Shiner (C. Gogolak kick).
Wash.—F.G. C. Gogolak kick.
Attendance 50,439.

New Records Made As Skins Rip Giants, 72-41

Washington, Nov. 27 (AP) — The Washington Redskins set a National football League scoring record today, as they trounced the New York Giants, 72-to-41, in a wild game.

The 72 Redskins points topped the 70 scored by Los Angeles against Baltimore October 22, 1950.

The record was for regular season play. The Chicago Bears set the playoff record when they walloped the Redskins 73-0 for the 1940 championship.

Coach Wants Record

The 113 points for both teams also set a N.F.L. record, topping the 98 points run up on October 17, 1948, when the Chicago Cardinals defeated the Giants, 63-35.

Coach Otto Graham definitely was going for the team scoring record as he sent in place kicker Charlie Gogolack to kick a 29-yard field goal with 3 seconds remaining in the game even though Washington was leading, 69 to 41.

Defensive back Brig Owens scored two touchdowns and set up two others as the Redskins crossed the Giants' goal at will.

Owens scored 1 touchdown when he picked up a Giant fumble and ran 62 yards. He also went over after picking off a Gary Wood pass and returning it 60 yards.

Sets Up First TD

The 5-foot-11, 190-pounder also intercepted New York starting quarterback Tom Kennedy's initial pass of the day, setting up the Redskins first touchdown six plays later.

In the second quarter, he intercepted another Kennedy pass. The Redskins converted it into a touchdown on the next play.

Halfback A. D. Whitfield scored three times, end Charley Taylor twice, and fullback Joe Don Looney and Bobby Mitchell once each.

Washington picked up a touchdown on a 52-yard punt return by Rickie Harris.

Whitfield scored on a 63-yard run and a one-yard plunge and on a five-yard pass from quarterback Sonny Jurgensen. Taylor scored on passes of 74 and 32 yards from Jurgensen. Looney ran over from the nine and Mitchell scored on a 45-yard pass from Dick Shiner with 48 seconds left in the game.

The day's scoring output was the most for a Redskin team since Washington defeated the old New York Yankees, 59-21, in 1939.

HOUSE VOTES GRID LOOPS IMMUNITY

Celler Fails To Block Move; Passage By Senate Assured

Washington, Oct. 20 (AP)—The House today granted the National and American Football Leagues the antitrust immunity they wanted to go ahead with their merger into one league.

In approving the merger, the House turned down a final protest by Representative Emanuel Celler (D., N.Y.), chairman of the Judiciary Committee, who wanted to probe its possible repercussions in extensive hearings.

Celler and hoped to get a vote on a motion to separate the merger provision from the tax exemption bill but was blocked when Rep. Jackson E. Betts (R-Ohio) a member of the committee handling the bill, offered a motion that would have killed the entire measure.

It was defeated 184, to 57. Celler and some of his supporters voted for the motion, but it was not a clear test of the merger issue. The House then passed the entire bill, merger and all, by a vote of 161 to 76.

Final Senate approval is needed to send the measure to the White House, but that will just be a formality. The Senate has already passed the legislation twice unanimously and overcame Celler's opposition by tacking it on to an anti-inflation bill requested by President Johnson.

Competition Ended

As outlined by the leagues last June, the merger plan calls for expansion of the present 24-team operation into a 26-team league by 1968, with possibly two more franchises to be awarded before the merger is actually completed in 1970.

There would be two immediate developments, however. The cutthroat competition for the top college players would be ended, so the combined leagues could operate a common draft of talent this winter. And on January 7, the champions of the two leagues would meet in a play-off game, probably in either Southern California or Florida.

In New York, president Milt Woodard of the American League was pleased to hear of the victory.

Commissioner Pete Rozelle of the National League was in Washington for the passage and said afterward:

"We're very pleased with the action taken by the House today and are hopeful of final approval in the Senate tomorrow."

Celler said it was the war between the leagues to sign the outstanding college players that led to the merger. Bonuses as high as $750,000 were paid to a single player, he said.

Help For Boggs

"They are poor labor negotiators and are asking Congress to rescue them from their own ineptitude and folly," said Celler.

Celler also criticized the Senate, first for rushing the bill through without hearings or debate, and then for adding it to an important tax measure in order to get around the House hearings.

"Wh the haste?" he asked. There was no audible answer but it was believed among House members that the bill was hurried along to help Representative Hale Boggs (D., La.) who is in a tough reelection fight in New Orleans under the expansion of the combined league. Boggs is the acting House majority leader and his bined league.

New Orleans is bidding for one of the franchises to be granted Louisiana colleague, Senator Russell Long, is the assistant Senate Democratic leader. Long introduced the merger bill in the Senate and helped tack it on to the tax bill.

"The end run was made not around me," said Celler, "but around the public, who now have no way of knowing the whys and the wherefores and the result that may flow from this football merger."

During three appearances before Celler's Antitrust subcommittee, commissioner Pete Rozelle, of the National Football League, said the antitrust exemption would extend only the mechanics of putting the two leagues together.

He repeatedly assured Celler that the bill would not extend to the combined league any greater antitrust immunity than the National and American Football Leagues now have as single leagues.

However, Rozelle declined Celler's suggestion that the bill state specifically that such things as the player draft, pay television, and the award of franchises would be outside the grant of immunity.

The report written by the House and Senate conferees, who agreed to include the merger provision in the anti-inflation bill, spelled out the limited nature of the exemption being granted."

"It is the intent of the conferees," the report said, "that the new league will commence operations with no greater anti-trust immunity than the existing individual leagues now enjoy."

Schools Protected

The bill also extends to high school football games on Friday nights the same protection against televised pro football games now enjoyed by colleges on Saturday afternoons. It would prohibit the telecasting of a pro game within 75 miles of a high school or college game played after 6 P.M. Friday between the second Friday in September and second Saturday in December.

Celler told the House, "I may lose this game, but I won't lose the series. I am going to continue this inquiry. I can assure you that a great deal will be made manifest that if you knew it now you would not vote for this bill."

Celler found a few supporters, including Rep. William T. Cahill (R., N. J.), who said Celler had not been the victim of an end run but had been clipped from the rear.

"The Judiciary Committee was mousetrapped," Cahill said "and every member of the House has been subjected to unnecessary roughness. I think the commissioner should be penalized half the distance and the game should be postponed until next year."

COLTS PUT IN WEAKER 4-TEAM WEST CIRCUIT IN N.F.L. REALIGNMENT

Baltimore Joins San Francisco, Los Angeles And Atlanta For 1967-68 In Division Of New Western Conference

By CAMERON C. SNYDER
[Sun Staff Correspondent]

New York, Nov. 30—Christmas came early for the Baltimore Colts. They were put into the weaker four-team division of the eight-team Western Conference of the National Football League during realignment of the whole circuit today.

After a long drawn-out debate that has been raging since Monday's opening session, commissioner Pete Rozelle was able to announce the alignment for a 2-year period of 1967-1968, this afternoon.

Each four-team segment is to be considered a division within the Eastern and Western Conferences. The owners thought names were needed for the divisions and decided to call them Coastal, Central, Federal and Capitol. The new alignment:

The alignment:

Western Conference

Coastal Division	Central Division
Baltimore	Chicago
San Francisco	Green Bay
Los Angeles	Minnesota
Atlanta	Detroit

Eastern Conference

Federal Division	Capitol Division
Cleveland	Philadelphia
Pittsburgh	Washington
St. Louis	Dallas
*New York	*New Orleans

(New Orleans and New York will switch divisions in the Eastern Conference in 1968 with the Giants going to the Capital Division and New Orleans to the Federal.

It was decided there would be no play-offs in the event of ties within the divisions.

In the case of ties between two clubs, say in the Coastal Division, the winner of the division shall be decided on point differential. That is, if Baltimore beats San Francisco, 14-0, and loses to San Francisco, 7-0, in the two-game series and both are tied in the standings, Baltimore, because of the 14-7 point differential, would be the Coastal Division Representative.

Coin Flip To Decide

If both clubs are tied in point differential—Baltimore wins, 14-0 and loses to San Francisco, 14,0, then the winner of the division will be decided against the last to go to a title game. If this can't break the deadlock a coin will be flipped.

In the event of a 3 or 4 team tie in a division, a remote possibility, the standings among the 4 teams on percentage will be used to break the deadlock.

If this can't do it, then the point differential will be used and finally a coin flip.

Compromise Reached

Commissioner Rozelle, who hopes to become commissioner of both leagues, if the N.F.L. can ever finish its business, said the flip-flopping of New York and New Orleans was a compromise.

So many teams considered New York a "traditional rival" that by switching the Giants from Federal to Capital division will give everyone a shot at probably the weakest established team in the N.F.L.

Reprinted from
The Baltimore Sun papers

N.F.L. Names Mecom Owner Of New Orleans Franchise

New Orleans, Dec. 15 (AP)—John W. Mecom Jr., 27-year-old scion of the Texas oil millionaire family, was formally granted ownership of New Orleans National Football League team Thursday.

It took the N.F.L. 45 days to make up its mind, officially, about an owner for the team after announcing November 1 that New Orleans would get the league's sixteenth team.

Mecom, however, is believed to have been N.F.L. Commissioner Pete Rozelle's choice for some time.

Impressive List

As minority stockholders in the team, Mecom, at Rozelle's urging, took on an impressive list of New Orleanians including some who had been affiliated with others seeking the franchise at one time.

Rozelle, in a late afternoon news conference at Mecom's office here, said the choice "was a most difficult decision" reached after considerable study. He said the N.F.L. felt that since the Mecom family had 90 per cent of their business "at least their oil business, in Louisiana," that qualified them for home ownership.

One minority stockholder will be jazz trumpeter Al Hirt, the bearded virtuoso who owns a Bourbon Street nitery.

Also in the group is David Dixon, who started the campaign six years ago to lure professional football to the city.

Mecom will shell out an estimated $8,500,000 to the N.F.L. for the franchise. The money will go to 14 teams for the 42 players New Orleans will take in a draft of veterans.

New Orleans will also participate in the collegiate draft, scheduled for next month.

JETS BURST PATS' BUBBLE

38-28 N.Y. Upset Gives Buffalo Title Chance Today

Nance, who went into the game with 1,380 yards, rushed 17 times for 78 yards and wound up the season with 1,458. Namath, meanwhile, completed 14 of 21 passes for 287 yards.

Statistics

	Patriots	Jets
First downs	21	26
Rushing yardage	82	241
Passing yardage	379	287
Passes	21-38	14-21
Passes intercepted by	0	2
Punts	2-43	4-38
Fumbles lost	1	0
Yards penalized	71	86
Boston	7 0 6 15—28
New York	7 10 14 7—38

Bos—Cappelletti, 18, pass from Parilli (Cappelletti kick).
N.Y.—Maynard, 20, pass from Namath (J. Turner kick).
N.Y.—Boozer, 1, run (J. Turner kick).
N.Y. F.G. J. Turner 12.
N.Y.—Maynard, 8, pass from Namath (J. Turner kick).
Bos—Whalen, 18, pass from Parilli (kick failed).
N.Y.—Sauer, 77, pass from Namath (J. Turner kick).
Bos—Nance, 1, run, Cappelletti pass from Parilli.
N.Y.—Snell, 25, run (J. Turner kick).
Bos—Graham, 15, pass from Parilli (Cappelletti kick).
Attendance, 58,921.

BILLS OWNER IS THANKFUL

'Anything I Can Send You?' Jets Are Asked

New York, Dec. 17 (AP)—Ralph Wilson, owner of the Buffalo Bills, bent down on one knee on the green carpet in the New York dressing room and bowed down to Sonny Werblin, owner of the Jets.

In the Boston dressing room, coach Mike Holovak of the Boston Patriots sat slumped in a green leather chair and repeated over and over: "I wish I knew. I wish I knew."

What Holovak wanted to know was how the Patriots lost to the Jets 38 to 28 today, all but losing a chance for the Eastern Division title in the American Football League.

"Anything I Can Send You?"

Wilson, on the other hand, was delighted because now his Bills can wrap up their third straight Eastern crown by beating weak Denver tomorrow.

"Anything I can send you? Champagne? I'll give them anything they want," Wilson said, referring to Werblin, coach Weeb Ewbank and quarterback Joe Namath.

Holovak, meanwhile, wasn't giving anything away. His team just had.

Poor Defense

"We lost it, that's all," Holovak, said, slowly pulling a blue sock on his left foot. "If I knew what we were doing wrong, I'd have done something about it. We got 28 points. I'll take 28 points every game I ever play. We just played a lousy defensive game. It was the worst defense.

"Every team has thrown against us, but this team ran, too. That helped them. Other teams haven't been able to run against us. This is the first team that's done it. This is the only game we've lost to an Eastern club this year. It cost us."

The Patriots' defense was so weak the Jets were able to set a club record for total offense—Namath completing 14 of 21 passes for 287 yards and the other backs rushing for 241.

As tough as the loss was, Holovak found another fact just as tough.

"We beat Buffalo twice," he said. "That's the toughest part about it. We beat them twice and still lose. Basically, they don't deserve to win, but you have to beat everybody if you want to win."

'Hasn't Sunk In Yet' Says Cowboys' Landry

New York, Dec. 17—The Dallas Cowboys had their first National Football League division title tucked neatly away tonight, but they were still trying to digest the glad tidings.

"I don't feel as elated as I thought I would," Coach Tom Landry said after watching Cleveland eliminate the St. Louis Cardinals 38-10 in today's televised game at St. Louis. "I'm sure it just hasn't sunk in yet."

The Browns' victory nailed the Eastern Conference championship for the Cowboys, who wind up their seventh N.F.L. season tomorrow against the dangerous New York Giants at Yankee Stadium.

The Cowboys watched the Cleveland-St. Louis game on television at their mid-town hotel but put off a full-scale celebration until tomorrow's unfinished business is taken care of.

"This doesn't affect how we feel about our game with the Giants," said All-N.F.L. defensive tackle Bob Lilly. "We still want to win this one."

"I feel kind of numb," said Don Meredith, the quarterback who sparked the Cowboys' title drive but will sit out the finale against the Giants. "The thing hasn't really sunk in. It'll take a few days, I guess."

Meredith, who suffered a mild concussion in last Sunday's game against Washington, had been pronounced fit for the New York game. But Landry switched signals after the Cards' loss to Cleveland assured Dallas of the host spot in the N.F.L. championship game against Green Bay, January 1.

"Meredith won't play," Landry said. "Jerry Rhome will start at quarterback and probably will split the game with Craig Morton."

Landry said Cleveland "did a great job of hitting the big play against the Cardinals' blitz," adding he thought Frank Ryan, the Browns' quarterback who threw four touchdown passes, was outstanding.

The Dallas pilot said his club would not be coasting against the last-place but ever tough Giants. "You have to keep winning to keep momentum," he said, "and we intend to win."

SAYERS WINS RUSHING TITLE

Gale Is 1st Halfback Champ Since Van Buren In '49

New York, Dec. 18 (AP)—Halfback Gale Sayers's 197 yards running against Minnesota in Chicago's 41-to-28 victory today gave him 1,231 for the season and the National Football League rushing championship for 1966.

The last halfback to win the title was Philadelphia's Steve Van Buren in 1949.

Sayers, who gained a total of 339 yards today, including 90 with the return of the opening kick-off for a touchdown, also set a new combined net yardage season record of 2,440. The old mark of 2,428 was set in 1963 by Timmy Brown, of Philadelphia, who holds the single game record of 341 set in 1962.

Kelly Finishes Second

Sayers's 1,231 yards rushing left him ahead of Cleveland fullback Leroy Kelly, with 1,141, and Los Angeles' fullback Dick Bass, with 1,090.

Several other N.F.L. records were set today as the regular season came to a close.

Bruce Gossett, of Los Angeles, kicked 3 field goals for a season record of 28, breaking the mark of 26 set by Lou Michaels, then with Pittsburgh, in 1962.

Jurgensen Breaks Record

Washington quarterback Sonny Jurgensen finished with 254 completions, eclipsing the record of 242 set last year by John Brodie, of San Francisco.

Danny Villanueva broke the record of most consecutive extra points in one season by finishing with 56. Bob Waterfield had kicked 54 for Los Angeles in 1950. Tommy Davis, of San Francisco, holds the record of consecutive conversions over more than one season—234.

Starr's 4 TD Passes Help Put Green Bay In Super Bowl

By CAMERON C. SNYDER
(Sun Staff Correspondent)

Dallas, Jan. 1—The Green Bay Packers hitched their wagon to a brilliant Bart Starr but still had to rely on one of their patented breaks in defeating the Cowboys, 34 to 27, at the Cotton Bowl today.

It was the most exciting National Football League title game since Baltimore's 1958 sudden death triumph over the New York Giants.

For some strange reason, the Packers, whose Stars threw four touchdown passes today, have the unhappy facility of making losers look like winners.

Packers Rely On "Bomb"

Known for their ball control tactics, the Packers had to rely on the "bomb" to hold the Cowboys in check and fortunately, Green Bay had Starr for that work.

He pitched scoring strikes of 17 yards to Elijah Pitts, 51 yards to Carroll Dale, 16 yards to Boyd Dowler and 28 yards to Max McGee.

Yet it wasn't enough, particularly after Don Chandler's conversion attempt after that last touchdown was blocked by Bob Lilly, the Cowboys' all-pro defensive tackle.

After that final Packer touchdown that boosted them to a 34-20 lead with just about 5 minutes left to play, the Cowboys staged one of the greatest comebacks ever seen in pro ranks.

Meredith cut the Packer lead to just 7 points with a 68-yard pass-and-run play to Frank Clarke with 4 minutes left, and then the Cowboy defense took the Packer offense apart to give their attack one more chance.

In fact, the defense almost accomplished the task by itself, by nearly blocking Chandler's punt which squirted off the side of his foot for only 16 yards.

Brown Interferes On Pass

That gave the Cowboys their big chance to tie it with 2.19 minutes left to play. Meredith started the Cowboys on their way with a 27-yard pass to Clarke on the Green Bay 20.

A play later Tom Brown was guilty of pass interference on Clarke at the 2-yard line and a sudden death looked like a certainty.

Then, a defense which had been manhandled suddenly got together ("We said to each other," reported Ray Nitschke, Packer middle linebacker, "that we had come too far to blow it now and that we owed Starr a favor.")

Dan Reeves tried the right side on a smash and gained just one yard. This particular side has been producing most of the rushing yards for the Cowboys behind the superlative blocking of offensive tackle Ralph Neely, who knocked all-pro defensive end Willie Davis all over the lot most of the day.

Offsides Penalty Hurts

Meredith then apparently became panicky. Instead of hitting the line again, he tried a pass. Unfortunately, a Cowboy interior lineman jumped offsides and the ball was back on the 6.

Another pass fell incomplete and then on third down, a pass to Pettis Norman took the Cowboys back to the 2.

Faced with a fourth-down situation and just 42 seconds left to play, Meredith rolled out to his right. Dave Robinson, left linebacker, smelled the play, rushed in and grabbed Meredith by the left arm.

In a great individual effort Meredith still managed to fling the ball in the general direction of two Cowboy receivers in the end zone. However, the pass was in the specific direction of Tom Brown, Packer safetyman who intercepted.

Statistics

	P'ers	C'boys
First downs	19	23
Rushing yardage	102	187
Passing yardage	265	233
Passes	19-28	15-31
Passes intercepted by	1	0
Punts	4-40	4-32
Fumbles lost	1	1
Yards penalized	23	29
Green Bay	14 7 7 6—34
Dallas	14 3 3 7—27

G.B.—Pitts. 17. pass from Starr (Chandler kick).
G.B.—Grabowski. 18. run with fumble recovery (Chandler kick).
Dal.—Reeves. 3. run (Villanueva kick).
Dal.—Perkins. 23. run (Villanueva kick).
G.B.—Dale. 51. pass from Starr (Chandler kick).
Dal.—FG. Villanueva. 11.
Dal.—FG. Villanueva. 32.
G.B.—Dowler. 16. pass from Starr (Chandler kick).
G.B.—McGee. 28. pass from Starr (kick failed).
Dal.—Clarke. 68. pass from Meredith (Villanueva kick).
Attendance. 75,504.

Reprinted from
The Baltimore Sun

Posts Are Goal Of Packer Fans

Green Bay, Wis., Jan. 1 (AP)—Never let it be said that supporters of the Green Bay Packers didn't tear the goal posts down in traditional fashion after their team defeated the Dallas Cowboys a Dallas 34 to 27 today for the National Football League title.

The unusual feature was that the goal posts were located at Lambeau Field in Green Bay, the home of the Packers, more than a thousand miles away from the scene of the title game. And one of the pair of uprights was missing.

Green Bay police said they were investigating a report that a truck was seen leaving the field this evening carrying one of the goal posts.

Garrett Runs For Pair To Put Chiefs Into Super Bowl Tilt

Buffalo, N.Y., Jan. 1 (AP)—The Kansas City Chiefs ended Buffalo's two-year domination of the American Football League today on Len Dawson's unerring passes and Mike Garrett's two touchdown runs, whipping the Bills, 31 to 7, in the league's championship game.

The victory, worth an A.F.L. championship record of $5,308.39 to each Chief, sent Kansas City into the first Super Bowl game at Los Angeles January 15 against the National League champion Green Bay Packers.

A slight drizzle fell throughout the dismal, overcast day as the Bills sought an unprecedented third straight title and the Chiefs went after their first title since 1962 when they stopped Houston's bid for three straight crowns.

Targets Elude Kemp

History virtually repeated as Dawson consistently hit his receivers while Buffalo quarterback Jack Kemp had difficulty finding his targets.

Dawson actually put the game out of Buffalo's reach in the first half when he completed nine of fourteen passes for 109 yards and two touchdowns—duplicate 29-yard throws to right end Fred Arbanas and flanker Otis Taylor.

Mike Mercer added a 32-yard field goal for a 17-7 halftime lead before the Chiefs broke it open in the final quarter on Garrett's one-yard plunge and 18-yard run.

Kansas City ran its plays out of the "I" formation with the backs lining up behind Dawson before shifting into a normal formation.

Buffalo Timing Off

That apparently threw off the timing of the Buffalo defense enough to make the difference.

In addition, the Bills contributed several times to Kansas City's offense, particularly in the first half when Dudley Meredith fumbled a kickoff, Tom Janik dropped two apparent interceptions and Kemp missed a chance to put Buffalo on the scoreboard when his pass attempt near the end of the period was intercepted by Johnny Robinson.

Kemp, hard-pressed to find his receivers most of the game, finished with only 12 completions in 27 attempts. He did hit Elbert Dubenion on a 69-yard scoring play and wound up with 253 yards gained.

Dawson was more effective, hitting on 16 of 24 attempts for 227 yards. That, and Garrett's late runs, were enough to send the Chiefs into the Super Bowl and a bid for the $15,000 winner's prize.

The Statistics

	Chiefs	Bills
First downs	14	9
Rushing yardage	113	40
Passing yardage	164	215
Passes	16-24	12-27
Passes intercepted by	2	0
Fumbles lost	0	2
Punts	4-42	6-39
Yards penalized	40	33
Kansas City	7 10 0 14—31
Buffalo	7 0 0 0—7

KC—Arbanas 29 pass from Dawson (Mercer kick).
Buff—Dubenion 69 pass from Kemp (Lusteg kick).
KC—Taylor 29 pass from Dawson (Mercer kick).
KC—FG Mercer 32.
KC—Garrett 1 run (Mercer kick).
KC—Garrett 18 run (Mercer kick).
Attendance. 42,080.

Green Bay Rips Chiefs In First Super Bowl, 35-10

PACKERS BREAK GAME OPEN WITH 3 TD'S IN LAST TWO QUARTERS

Starr Leads N.F.L. Champs After Kansas City Trails By Only 14-10 At Half; Crowd Of 63,036 Watches Game In L.A.

By CAMERON C. SNYDER
[Sun Staff Correspondent]

Los Angeles, Jan. 15—Green Bay, behind the direction of Bart Starr, romped to a 35-to-10 victory over the Kansas City Chiefs of the American League today in the first Super Bowl.

In the first half, however, it appeared this game—misnamed the Super Bowl—was going to be something super. The Chiefs stayed close, 14-10, to their overwhelmingly favored opponents.

But as they say in horse racing "class will tell." With a little larceny by Willie Wood as a spur, the aristocrats of the professional football world won going away.

Only 63,036 fans showed up for what was probably the most publicized football game in history, and those who stayed away missed a great show—before the game and at half time—and some good football.

Despite the lopsidedness of the score, the much maligned A.F.L. proved by Kansas City's performance it plays football—which had been doubted—although it is still three or four years away from the N.F.L.'s top teams.

McGee Comes Through

Wood's third period interception and run of 50 yards was the obvious turning point. It set up the Packers' third touchdown which left the Chiefs floundering.

But the undetectable turning points were two men—Starr and the seldom-used 34-year-old veteran Max McGee—and Packer defense.

McGee, subbing for Boyd Dowler who was injured early in the first period, demonstrated for A.F.L. fans and the Chiefs the strength of the Packer bench.

Max, who caught only 4 passes in infrequent appearances in the 14 regular season games and only one—a touchdown—in the N.F.L. title game with the Dallas Cowboys, grabbed 7 today, 2 for touchdowns.

16 Pass Completions

Starr, as he had demonstrated so convincingly in the 34-27 victory over the Cowboys, is a great passer and even more important a great leader with an excellent football mind.

Bart completed 16 of 23 aerials for 250 yards and 2 McGee touchdowns and picked the K.C. defense apart.

But just as important as Starr, McGee and offensive mates were to the Packer cause, was the Green Bay defense, which pulled itself together for a typical Packer performance in the second half.

Whatever coach Vince Lombardi said to the defense, which had allowed the Kansas City offense 181 yards in the first half, did the job. In the second half the Chiefs netted only 48 yards.

G. B. BLASE ABOUT WIN

Lombardi, And Players Take $15,000 In Stride

By CAMERON C. SNYDER

Los Angeles, Jan. 15—As they trooped into their dressing room, one of a multitude of reporters waiting outside, yelled to the World professional football champion Green Bay Packers:

"Another day and another dollar."

The inference was to the $15,000 each member of the National Football League champions will collect for trampling the American Football League titlists from Kansas City, 35 to 10, here today.

But the Packers displayed about as much emotion as the third shift at the nut and bolt factory on pay day.

The Statistics

	Chiefs	Packers
First downs	17	21
Rushing yardage	72	130
Passing yardage	167	228
Passes	17-32	16-24
Passes intercepted by	1	1
Punts	7-45	4-23
Fumbles lost	1	1
Yards penalized	26	40
Kansas City	0 10 0 0—10	
Green Bay	7 7 14 7—35	

G.B.—McGee, 37, pass from Starr (Chandler kick).
K.C.—McClinton, 7 pass from Dawon (Mercer kick).
G.B.—Taylor, 14 run (Chandler kick).
K.C.—FG, Mercer, 31.
G.B.—Pitts, 5 run (Chandler kick).
G.B.—McGee, 13 pass from Starr (Chandler kick).
G.B.—Pitts, 1 run (Chandler kick).
Attendance—63,036.

Entire page reprinted from
The Baltimore Sun

STRAM BLAMES PASS PROTECTION

'Broke Down' In 2d Half, K.C. Coach Deplores

By W. LAWRENCE NULL
[Sun Staff Correspondent]

Los Angeles, Jan. 15—"You can't make mistakes like we did and expect to win," said Kansas City coach Hank Stram, his back to the wall of a quiet but not unhappy locker room.

"We were hoping we could play our kind of football and we were doing it in the first half, but we broke down on pass protection in the second half and Green Bay was quick to capitalize' on it."

Overriding all of Stram's comments on his team's 35-to-10 loss to the Packers in the first Super Bowl game between the American and National football leagues was the conviction, shared by his players, that despite the score, the N.F.L. representative did not display any great superiority.

Can't Tell By One Game

"We respect every team we play," Stram stated, "and I'll just repeat what I have said all along. I don't think you can measure the abilities of the two leagues on the result of one game. We think we played well early in the game and who knows what would happen if we played again."

As far as the game's key play was concerned, that was obvious to the disappointing crowd of 63,036 fans who witnessed the live action as well as the millions who sat in at home. It was the interception and 50-yard runback by Willie Wood early in the third period that enabled the Packers to break the game open with their third T.D.

"That changed the personality of the game," Stram continued. "They're an excellent team and it is imperative not to give them anything easy. We did it and it cost us."

He insisted that the Packers did not do anything either offensively or defensively that he didn't expect. Even the fact that the Packers blitzed much more than usual in the second half did not appear to surprise him.

"Our pass protection just broke down in that second half and at the same time they were picking up some of our moves," Stram added.

Super Bowl Statistics

Taylor And Buchman Involved In Flareup

[By a Sun Staff Correspondent]

Los Angeles, Jan. 15 — Although both the Kansas City Chiefs and Green Bay Packers were keyed up sky high for the lucrative Super Bowl game, there was only one flareup among the players that required intervention by the officials.

Not surprisingly, Packer fullback Jim Taylor was involved in the brief flurry of temperament.

On a first down at the Chiefs 28 in the third quarter, Taylor picked up two yards, resisted the tackler as usual and was unceremoniously dumped to the turf by 6-7, 287-pound defensive tackle Buck Buchanan.

"I don't even remember what I said," Buchanan laughed later. "But I know it wasn't very nice. He (Taylor) didn't say anything. He had his hand in my face and I just pushed him down."

Did he talk to Taylor later? "Sure," Buchanan replied. "You forget things like that in a hurry."

Did you apologize? "No. I didn't think any apologies were necessary." W.L.N.

Entire page reprinted from
The Baltimore Sun

Pro Football's Collegiate Draft

First Round

1. COLTS—(Traded by New Orleans) Defensive end Bubba Smith, Michigan State.
2. Minnesota—(Traded by New York Giants) Halfback Clint Jones, Michigan State.
3. San Francisco—(Traded by Atlanta) Quarterback Steve Spurrier, Florida.
4. Miami — Quarterback Bob Griese, Purdue.
5. Houston—Lineback George Webster, Michigan State.
6. Denver—Halfback Floyd Little, Syracuse.
7. Detroit—Halfback Mel Farr, U.C.L.A.
8. Minnesota—End Gene Washington, Michigan State.
9. Green Bay—(Traded by Pittsburgh) Guard Bob Hyland, Boston College.
10. Chicago—Defensive Tackle Lloyd Phillips, Arkansas.
11. San Francisco—End Cas Banaszek, Northwestern.
12. New York Jets—Guard Paul Seiler, Notre Dame.
13. Washington—Fullback Ray McDonald, Idaho.
14. San Diego—Defensive Tackle Ron Billingsley, Wyoming.
15. Minnesota (traded by Los Angeles)—Defensive end Alan Page, Notre Dame.
16. St Louis—End Dave Williams, Washington.
17. Oakland—Tackle Gene Upshaw, Texas A&I.
18. Cleveland—Linebacker Bob Matheson, Duke.
19. Philadelphia — Halfback Harry Jones, Arkansas.
20. COLTS—Halfback Jim Detwiler, Michigan.
21. Boston—Defensive back John Charles.
22. Buffalo -- Defensive back John Pitts, Arizona State.
23. Houston (Traded from Dallas)—Guard Tom Regner, Notre Dame.
24. Kansas City, Eugene Trosch, Miami, tackle.
25. Green Bay—Don Horn, San Diego State, quarterback.
26. New Orleans, Lesley Kelly, Alabama, halfback.

Second Round

1. New Orleans, James Burris, Houston, quarterback.
2. Minnesota choice acquired from New York, Bob Grim, Oregon State, halfback.
3. Miami, Jim Riley, Oklahoma, tackle.
4. Houston, Bob Davis, Virginia, quarterback.
5. Atlanta, Leo Carroll, San Diego State, end.
6. Denver, Tom Beer, Houston, end.
7. Los Angeles choice acquired from Minnesota, Willie Ellison, Texas Southern, back.
8. Detroit, Lem Barney, Jackson State, defensive back.
9. Pittsburgh, Don Shy, San Diego, halfback.
10. Chicago, Bob Jones, San Diego State, defensive back.
11. New York Jets, Rich Sheron, Washington State, end.
12. Washington, Spain Musgrove, Utah State, tackle.
13. San Francisco, Tom Holzer, Louisville, tackle.
14. San Diego, Ron McCall, Weber State, linebacker.
15. Green Bay (choice acquired from Los Angeles), Dave Dunaway, Duke, flanker.
16. Buffalo (choice acquired from Oakland), Jim LeMoine, Utah State, end.
17. St. Louis, Bob Rowe, Western Michigan, end.
18. Philadelphia, Jon Brooks, Kent State, guard.
19. COLTS, Rick Volk, Michigan, defensive back.
20. Cleveland, Larry Conjar, Notre Dame, fullback.
21. Kansas City (choice acquired from Boston), Jim Lynch, Notre Dame, linebacker.
22. San Diego (choice acquired from Buffalo), Bob Howard, San Diego State, defensive back.
23. Houston (choice acquired from Dallas), Roy Hopkins, Texas Southern, halfback.
24. Kansas City, Willie Lanier, Morgan State, linebacker.
25. Green Bay, James Flannigan, Pittsburgh, linebacker.
26. New Orleans, John Gilliam, South Carolina State, flanker.
27. New Orleans, David Rowe, Penn State, tackle.

Third Round

1. COLTS (choice acquired from New Orleans), Norman Davis, Grambling, tackle.
2. Cleveland (choice acquired from New York Giants), Don Cockroft, Adams State, Col., kicker.
3. Houston, Larry Carwell, Iowa State, defensive back.
4. Atlanta, Jim Jordan, Florida, halfback.
5. Denver (choice acquired from Miami), Mike Current, Ohio State, tackle.
6. Denver, George Goeddeke, Notre Dame, center.
7. Detroit, Paul Naumoff, Tennessee.
8. Minnesota, Earl Denny, Missouri, flanker.
9. San Francisco (choice acquired from Pittsburgh), Frank Nunley, linebacker, Michigan.
10. Chicago, Gary Lyle, George Washington, halfback.
11. Washington, Curt Belcher, Brigham Young, defensive back.
12. San Francisco, Bill Tucker, Tennessee A&I., halfback.
13. New York Jets, Dennis Randall, Oklahoma State, defensive end.
14. San Diego, Harold Akin, Oklahoma State, offensive tackle.
15. Philadelphia (choice acquired from Los Angeles), Harry Wilson, Nebraska, halfback.
16. St. Louis, Vidal Carlin, North Texas State, quarterback.
17. Buffalo (choice acquired from Oakland through Denver), Tom Rhodes, Notre Dame, defensive end.
18. Colts, Leon Ward, Oklahoma State, linebacker.
19. Cleveland, Ennie Barney, Iowa State, linebacker.
20. Pittsburgh (choice acquired from Philadelphia), Rodney Firetas, Oregon State, center.
21. New York Jets choice acquired from Boston), Henry King, Utah State, defensive back.
22. Oakland (choice acquired from Buffalo), Bill Fairband, Colorado, linebacker.
23. Dallas, Phil Clark, Northwestern, defensive back.
24. Kansas City, Billy Masters, Louisiana State, tight end.
25. Green Bay, John Rowser, Michigan, defensive back.
26. New Orleans, Del Williams, Florida State, center.
27. New Orleans, Ben Hart, Oklahoma, halfback.

Reprinted from
The Baltimore Sun

BROWN JOINS HALL OF FAME

Ex-Cleveland Coach, Seven Others Bet Grid Honor

Canton, Ohio, Aug. 5 (AP)—Eight new members were inducted into the National Professional Football Hall of Fame here today in what Paul Brown, one of the inductees, called "a red letter day."

Brown is a former coach and general manager of the Cleveland Browns who met the Philadelphia Eagles in an exhibition game at Fawcett Stadium tonight to end the day's festivities.

Others enshrined in the Hall of Fame with him were Chuck Bednarik, Bobby Layne, Ken Strong, Joe Stydahar, Emlen Tunnell, Dan Reeves and the late Charles Bidwill, Sr.

'Red Letter Day'

"This is a red letter day for yours truly and the the Brown family," Brown told the crowd gathered in front of the Hall of Fame building.

"I guess everybody in football thinks about this honor, but not too much for fear of being disappointed."

The enshrinement served as a reunion for Brown and Otto Graham, his former quarterback on the Browns and now head coach of the Washington Redskins. Graham presented Brown at the ceremonies. Brown did the honors when Graham was inducted two years ago.

47 Members

The eight new Hall of Fame members brought the total membership to 47 in five years.

Other presenters were Pittsburgh Steelers owner Art Rooney for Bidwill, Bob Waterfield for Reeves, Dr. Dan Fortmann for Stydahar, Greasy Neale for Bednarik, the Rev. Benedict Dudley for Tunnell, Chick Meehan for Strong and Buddy Parker for Layne.

Each of the new members received a bronze bust replica of himself, similar to the one that went into the Hall, and a ring.

Chuck The Clutch

Bednarik, 42, played 14 seasons at center and linebacker for the Eagles before retiring. He was an All-Pro lineman nine times.

Layne, 41, led the Detroit Lions to a National Football League championship and four division titles as quarterback. He went from the Lions to the Steelers and retired after the 1962 season.

Strong, who was a fullback for the New York Giants, played on four world championship teams and led the N.F.L. in scoring three times. He is 60.

Stydahar, 55, a tackle, played with the Chicago Bears from 1936 to 1939 and later coached the Los Angeles Rams and Chicago Cardinals.

Giant Great

Tunnell, former defensive back for the Giants, joined the team as a free agent and was an All-Pro selection four times. He later played with the Green Bay Packers.

Reeves owned the Cleveland Rams, who won the N.F.L. championship in 1945, and moved the club to Los Angeles the following year.

Bidwill, who bought the Chicago Cardinals in 1933, died April 19, 1947. The Cardinals moved to St. Louis in 1960.

Jets Plan Fine For Joe Namath

Oceanport, N.J., Aug. 5 (AP)—Joe Namath, star quarterback of the New York Jets in the American Football League, will receive a stiff fine for his early morning escapade yesterday along Second Avenue in New York, Sonny Werblin, owner of the club, said today.

Namath was seen in New York's East Side bars long after the club's curfew.

"I do not know how much it will be. That is up to coach Weeb Ewbank," said Werblin.

"Weeb told me he was going to think about it over the weekend before setting the amount."

Werblin, the man who paid a reported $400,000 to the Alabama star to sign with the Jets, added that if it were his decision to make he would not fine Namath.

"It was an emotional upset, and I do not believe any player should be fined for such a thing. But Weeb runs the club."

Werblin explained that Namath, who apologized to his teammates a few hours before the Jets defeated Boston, 58-13, in an exhibition game at Bridgeport, Conn., had become emotionally upset over family problems.

BRONCOS' WIN STUNS LIONS

A.F.L. Gets First Victory Over An N.F.L. Club

Denver, Aug. 6 (P)—"We want to win football games," Lou Saban said last December when he took over as general manager and head coach of the Denver Broncos in the American Football League.

The Broncos, who won only four games during the 1966 season, stunned the Detroit Lions of the National League, 13-to-7, last night and marked up the first victory ever by an A.F.L. team over an N.F.L. team.

A surprise run by Bob Scarpitto, back to punt on a fourth-and-11 situation, paved the way for a touchdown that provided the winning points before a crowd of 21,228 here.

28-Yard Run

The ball was on the Detroit 44 when Scarpitto dropped back as if to punt. Instead he broke for the right sideline and scampered 28 yards to the Lions 16 for a vital first down. Six plays later, Cookie Gilchrist bucked over from the one.

That gave the Broncos a 10-0 edge, more than enough to offset Detroit's last period score on a 15-yard pass from Milt Plum to Bill Malinchak.

DENVER WINS GRID OPENER

Denson Foregoes Tragedy To Help Beat Boston

Denver, Colo., Sept. 3 (P) — Remarkable catches by flanker Al Denson, playing despite a deep personal tragedy, and some spectacular interceptions carried Denver to a 26-to-21 victory over Boston in the American Football League opener today and preserved the Cinderella tradition being built this season by the former A.F.L. doormat.

The all-new Broncos, scoring first on a Steve Tensi-to-Denson pass for 12 yards, fell behind only once—in Boston's 14-point third period—and delighted a record crowd of 35,488 with long distance passes, those interceptions and two punts of 73 and 72 yards by Bob Scarpitto.

3-Year-Old Son Dies

Denson, who left immediately after the game for Jacksonville, Fla., where his 3-year-old son, Al Denson, Jr., died over the weekend, also caught a 55-yard scoring pass from Tensi and a 58-yard throw that set up a important field goal early in the fourth period.

RAMS WIN OVER SAINTS BY 27-13

L.A. Survives 94-Yard Run By Rookie Gilliam

New Orleans, Sept. 17 (P)— Stunned by a 94-yard run with the opening kickoff by New Orleans' rookie John Gilliam, the Los Angeles Rams pulled away in the second half today for a 27-to-13 victory over the Saints.

Gilliam scored for New Orleans and Charlie Durkee converted to give the Saints a 7-0 lead before a frenzied sellout crowd of 80,879 was fully seated.

The Rams went ahead with one second left in the first half, 13-10, on a two-yard run by quarterback Roman Gabriel. Gabriel threw to Bernie Casey for 48 yards and on the next play hit Casey for 20 yards, then carried it over himself on the following play.

Rams Stop Saints

Midway through the third period, the Rams' defensive line stopped the Saints deep in their own territory. Tom McNeil couldn't get off a punt from the end zone but ran the ball out to the 17. It was not enough for a first down and two plays later, Dick Bass broke through on a 13-yard touchdown run to put the Rams out front.

```
Los Angeles ............... 6 7 7 7—27
New Orleans ............... 7 3 3 0—13
NO—Gilliam 94 kickoff return (Durkee kick).
LA—FG 10 Gossett.
LA—FG 21 Gossett.
NO—FG 44 Durkee.
LA—Gabriel 2 run (Gossett kick).
NO—FG 25 Durkee.
LA—Bass 13 run (Gossett kick).
LA—Josephson 15 pass from Gabriel (Gossett kick).
Attendance—80,879.
```

CARDINALS KICK STEELERS, 28-14

Bakken Hits Record Seven Field Goals In Triumph

Pittsburgh, Sept. 24 (P)—Jim Bakken overcame 14 - mile - an-hour winds and a switch in holders today to kick a record-smashing seven field goals and boost the St. Louis Cardinals to a 28 - to - 14 National Football League upset of Pittsburgh.

Bakken's performance bettered the league mark of six set by soccer-style kicker Garo Yepremian of Detroit last season.

Five of Bakken's kicks—18, 24, 24, 32 and 23 yards long—went into the wind swirling around Pitt Stadium. The other two, 33 and 29 yards, were with the wind. His last three came as holder Larry Wilson abandoned his job because of a cut hand.

Bakken, who once kicked five field goals in a game, said that, ironically, Bobby Conrad, who held for the last three, hadn't held for two years but began working at it earlier in the week.

Three Key Players

"Larry wanted to get in a little tackling practice," said six-year-veteran Bakken. "So I worked with Bobby the last two days of the week."

Bakken said he feels the holder is as important as the kicker.

"I don't think you can make any distinction between the holder, the kicker and the center," he said. "If any one of them doesn't do his job, the kick won't be any good.

"I knew about the record and it almost cost me," Bakken added. "When I kicked the seventh one, I wanted to see if it was any good almost before I kicked it. So I looked up and almost dubbed it. It just made it."

Misses Twice

Bakken missed field goal attempts of 50 and 45 yards, setting a league record with his nine attempts.

The Cardinals 10-point underdogs, converted three interceptions and a fumble recovery into 16 points and kept Steelers off balance with an assortment of blitzing defenses.

Quarterback Bill Nelsen of Pittsburgh, who was helped from the field with a knee injury in the last five minutes of the game, didn't complete a pass until a little over five minutes remained in the first half. The injury wasn't believed to be serious.

62-Yard TD Drive

He then connected on three straight, the last one for five yards and a touchdown to Chet Anderson. The big play in the 62-yard drive was a 48-yard pass to Anderson.

Quarterback Jim Hart scored the only St. Louis touchdown on a 23-yard run near the end of the first quarter.

Pittsburgh went for 33 yards and another touchdown on Bill Asburry's one-yard plunge in the third period. Marv Woodson set up the series with an interception.

That brought the Steelers to within five points, but Bakken tacked on three more field goals in the final period.

Charley Johnson, who joins the Cardinals as quarterback only on weekend passes from the Army, made his first appearance of the season in the final 2½ minutes.

Statistics

	Cards	Steelers
First downs	12	17
Rushing yardage	146	94
Passing yardage	137	143
Return yardage	127	131
Passes	8-26-1	11-30-3
Punts	3-36	4-36
Fumbles lost	0	3
Yards penalized	87	20

St. Louis .... 13 6 0 6—28
Pittsburgh .... 0 7 7 0—14

St. Louis—F.G. Bakken, 18.
St. Louis—F.G., Bakken, 24.
St. Louis—Hart, 23, run (Bakken kick).
St. Louis—F.G., Bakken, 33.
Pitt—Anderson 5' pass from Nelson (Clark kick).
St. Louis—F.G. Bakken, 29.
Pitt—Asbury 1 run (Clark kick).
St. Louis—F.G., Bakken, 24.
St. Louis—F.G., Bakken, 32.
St. Louis—F.G., Bakken, 23.
Attendance—45,579.

A.F.L. AWARD TO CINCINNATI

Paul Brown Group Gets 1968 Grid Franchise

Cincinnati, Sept. 26 (P)—Milt Woodard, president of the American Football League, announced tonight that Cincinnati has been awarded officially an A.F.L. franchise, beginning in 1968, and it goes to Paul Brown and his associates.

Woodard said that it was purely "an academic situation," the the proposed Cincinnati Stadium might not be available until the 1970 season.

Agreement Delayed

The A.F.L. previously had picked Brown and his group unofficially for the franchise but signing of the agreement was held up because of objections to its terms.

For three days Brown and his associates have been meeting here and today they were joined by Woodard.

Brown is a former coach of the Cleveland Browns, of the National Football League. He has been out of football since 1963 after being relieved of his duties at Cleveland.

Brown To Coach

Brown, who said he probably will coach the team at least for the first year, disclosed there was little change in the agreement terms, originally proposed.

Under those terms, each of the clubs in the A.F.L., excluding the new Miami team, will freeze 29 players and the Cincinnati club can pick one of those remaining.

Each of the other clubs then may greeze two more and Cincinnati can select two of those remaining.

The final stage will find each club freezing one more player with Cincinnati selecting one from those remaining.

In addition, Cincinnati will have the sixth round college draft choice except for that of Miami.

FIRST LOSS ELIMINATES BALTIMORE

L.A. Front Foursome Dominates Game In Second Half

By CAMERON C. SNYDER
[Sun Staff Correspondent]

Los Angeles, Dec. 17—The Los Angeles Rams won the Coastal Division title here today, trouncing the Colts, 34 to 10, before 72,277 Coliseum fans.

It was no contest after the second half began as the famous fearsome foursome of the Ram defense battered and banged the Colts, particularly John Unitas, from goal post to goal post.

It was Baltimore's first loss of the year, and although the Colts finished with the same record as the Rams, 11-1-2, the L.A. team will be the Coastal Division representative because it scored more points in the two games played between the clubs.

Rams To Play Packers

The Rams will play the Green Bay Packers next Saturday for the Western Conference title. Baltimore and Los Angeles battled to a 24-24 deadlock in October, therefore the Rams gained the right to meet the Packers by compiling 58 points to Baltimore's 34 in the two game series.

The Colts entered this final regular season game with visions of sugar plums dancing in their heads. The visions became nightmares, the sugar plums sour tarts and their heads were reeling under a relentless Ram defense and a jarring Ram offense.

For most of the first half the Colts made a game of it, but Roman Gabriel's two touchdown passes of 80 yards to Jack Snow and 23 yards to Bernie Casey in the second quarter changed the game's complexion completely.

SAINTS STUN 'SKINS, 30-14

Sub Quarterback Kilmer, Abramowicz Lead Upset

Washington, Dec. 17 (P)—Quarterback Bill Kilmer passed to split end Dan Abramowicz for two touchdowns—one going 80 yards—today as New Orleans upset favored Washington, 30 to 14.

The victory gave the Saints a 3-11 record for their inaugural season while the Redskins, who had hoped to finish with their first winning year since 1955, wound up 5-6-3.

Jurgensen broke a National Football League passing yardage mark in a losing cause, throwing for 214 yards for a total 3,747. He held the previous record of 3,723, a mark he set as a Philadelphia Eagle in 1961.

Statistics

	Saints	Redskins
First downs	15	19
Rushing vardage	116	58
Passing vardage	279	273
Return vardage	133	126
Passes	28-17-2	49-26-2
Punts	7-41	6-44
Fumbles lost	0	1
Yards penalized	36	30
New Orleans	0 7 9 14—30
Washington	0 0 7 7—14

N.O.—Abramowicz, 80, pass from Kilmer (Durkee, kick).
Wash.—Taylor, 6, pass from Jurgensen (Alford, kick).
N.O.—Safety Love tackled by Anderson.
N.O.—Schultz, 1, run (Durkee, kick).
N.O.—Abramowicz, 13, pass from Kilmer (Durkee, kick).
Wash.—Whitfield, 23, pass from Jurgensen (Alford, kick).
N.O.—McCall, 49, run (Durkee, kick).
Attendance—30,486.

Dec. 24

Namath's Passes Topple Chargers

SAN DIEGO, Calif. (P)—Quarterback Joe Namath passed for four touchdowns and rolled up 343 yards through the air yesterday to set a pro football season passing record in leading the New York Jets to a 42-31 victory over the San Diego Chargers.

Namath finished the day with a season total of 4,007 yards, breaking the mark of 3,746 yards set last week by Sonny Jurgensen of the National League Washington Redskins. Namath previously had broken the American League mark.

THE CHARGERS struck first with the game only a minute and 24 seconds old on a 72-yard pass play from John Hadl to Willie Frazier, but Namath quickly tied it on a 13-yard pass to Don Maynard.

Bill Mathis put the Jets ahead with a one-yard plunge following Bill Baird's interception of a Hadl pass on the Charger 39, but the hosts came right back on the ground.

Brad Hubbert regained the lead for the Chargers early in the second by breaking loose twice within two minutes on sweeps of 46 and 80 yards around right end.

A 36-YARD pass from Namath to George Sauer quickly tied it, but Dick Van Raaphorst's 13-yard field goal put the Chargers on top again 24-21.

Maynard's second TD reception, a 36-yard bomb from Namath, ended the first half scoring and sent the Jets to the locker room leading 28-24.

After the break the Jets extended their lead to 42-24 after Mathis' second one-yard scoring plunge and Maynard's third TD catch, a 37-yarder from Namath.

The Chargers' final score came on an eight-yard pass from reserve quarterback Kay Stephenson to Jacque Mackinnon with 2:17 left.

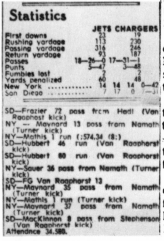

Statistics

	JETS	CHARGERS
First downs	23	19
Rushing yardage	113	230
Passing yardage	316	246
Return yardage	93	187
Passes	18-26-2	17-31-1
Punts	3-47	3-48
Fumbles lost	2	2
Yards penalized	60	48
New York	14 14 14 0—42
San Diego	7 17 0 7—31

SD—Frazier 72 pass from Hadl (Van Raaphorst kick).
NY—Maynard 13 pass from Namath (Turner kick).
NY—Mathis 1 run (;574,34 (8;)
SD—Hubbert 46 run (Van Raaphorst kick).
NY—Sauer 36 pass from Namath (Turner kick).
SD—FG Van Raaphorst 13
NY—Maynard 35 pass from Namath (Turner kick).
NY—Mathis 1 run (Turner kick).
NY—Maynard 37 pass from Namath (Turner kick).
SD—MacKinnon 8 pass from Stephenson (Van Raaphorst kick).
Attendance 34,580.

GREEN BAY WINS WEST TITLE, 28-7

Starr, Williams Lead Rout Of Los Angeles In Cold Weather

By CAMERON C. SNYDER
[Sun Staff Correspondent]

Milwaukee, Dec. 23—Green Bay's heady oldy old pros and a foot-loose rookie sent the Rams reeling and won the Western Conference Championship, 28 to 7, before 49,861 frozen fans in County Stadium today.

The scrooges of the northland tried to play Santa Claus on offense early in the game, but the Rams returned all but one present unopened while trying to buck the stout Packer defense.

Then Bart Starr hitched his sled to a speedy rookie named Travis Williams, and the demise of the Rams was on.

Reprinted from
The Baltimore Sun

Final Round

By winning, the Packers move into the National Football League championship round, meeting the Eastern Conference champions New Year's eve at Green Bay.

The Eastern title will be decided tomorrow when the Cleveland Browns play the Cowboys in Dallas.

The Rams, who gained the right to meet the Packers for the conference title by whipping Baltimore Colts last week for the Coastal Division title, lost their spark when Williams sped through a large hole at right tackle for a 46-yard touchdown run.

The Statistics

	Los Angeles	Green Bay
First downs	12	20
First downs rushing	2	11
First downs passing	9	8
First downs by penalty	1	1
Yards gained (net)	217	374
Yards gained rushing (net)	75	163
Yards gained passing	186	222
Times thrown & yards lost attempting to pass	5-44	1-12
Passes	11-31	17-23
Average gain per pass	4-7	6-0
Passes intercepted by & yds interc. returned	1-24	1-2
Punts	6-39.3	3-32.6
Punts returned	1-0	3-46
Kickoff	4-80	2-16
Penalties	3-25	7-61
Fumbles, lost	0-0	3-1
Number of rushing plays	28	46
Average gain per rushing play	2.7	3.5
Total offensive plays	64	76
Average gain per offensive play	3.4	5.3
Los Angeles	7 0 0 0—7
Green Bay	0 14 7 7—28

L.A.—Casey, 29, pass from Gabriel (Gossett, kick).
G.B.—Williams, 46, run (Chandler kick).
G.B.—Dale, 17, pass from Starr (Chandler, kick).
G.B.—Mercein, 6, run (Chandler, kick).
G.B.—Williams, 2, run (Chandler, kick).
Attendance—49,861.

GREEN BAY HELPS DALLAS VICTORY

Romp Inspired Cowboys To Rout Cleveland, 52-14

Dallas, Dec. 25 (P) — The Dallas Cowboys demolished the Cleveland Browns, 52 to 14, yesterday and the Green Bay Packers, next Sunday's opponent for the National Football League championship, may have provided some inspiration.

Green Bay beat the Los Angeles Rams, 28 to 7, Saturday for the N.F.L.'s Western Conference title. Dallas repeated as Eastern champions.

Play Sealed Fate

"After watching the Packers, I felt what they did carried over into this game for us," Dallas Coach Tom Landry said.

"I never expected to win the game this big. I don't think it hurts you to win big."

The play that probably sealed the Browns' fate was the 86-yard touchdown pass from Don Meredith to Bob Hayes that gave Dallas a 21-to-0 lead with the second quarter only four minutes gone.

'It's To Be Expected'

"We called an audible," Hayes said, meaning the Cowboys changed plays at the line of scrimmage. "They had a blitz look. Don threw a perfect pass. It coudln't have been more perfect."

Mike Howell, the Cleveland cornerback who was the victim of the N.F.L. playoff record scoring pass, said, "I don't feel badly. It's to be expected with that guy. "I can't compare him with anyone. He has everything a receiver needs, but his speed sets him apart."

Hayes said he was disappointed that he did not score on his punt returns of 64 and 68 yards "since I got as far as I did. They had me penned in on the first one, but the second one I stumbled and fell."

Statistics

	Browns	Cowboys
First downs	15	22
Rushing yardage	159	178
Passing yardage	163	223
Return yardage	419	219
Passes	14-30-1	11-15-1
Punts	7-39	2-44
Fumbles lost	0	1
Yards penalized	18	10
Cleveland	0 7 0 7—14	
Dallas	14 10 21 7—52	

Dal.—Baynham. 3. pass from Meredith (Villanueva kick).
Dal.—Perkins. 4. run (Villanueva kick).
Dal.—Hayes. 86. pass from Meredith (Villanueva kick).
Dal.—FG. Villanueva. 10.
Cle.—Morin. 13. pass from Ryan (Groza kick).
Dal.—Baynham. 1. run (Villanueva kick).
Dal.—Perkins. 1. run (Villanueva kick).
Dal.—Green. 60. pass interception (Villanueva kick).
Dal.—Baynham. 1. run (Villanueva kick).
Cle.—Warfield. 75. pass from Ryan (Groza kick).
Attendance. 70.786.

RAIDERS RIP OILERS FOR A.F.L. TITLE

Dixon And Banaszak Lead 40-To-7 Rout; Blanda Kicks Four

Oakland, Cal., Dec. 31 (P) — The Oakland Raiders romped to their first American Football League championship today, demolishing the Houston Oilers, 40 to 7.

Hewritt Dixon softened the Oilers up with a 69-yard touchdown sprint on the first play of the second period, and after that it was all Oakland.

The Raiders, who will play National League champion Green Bay in the Super Bowl at Miami, January 14, ran up a 30-to-0 lead before the Oilers scored in the fourth period. They will go into the Green Bay game with an 11-game winning streak.

Lamonica Scores

Dixon and Pete Banaszak shredded the Houston defenses along the ground while quarterback Daryle Lamonica plunged for one TD and passed for two more.

Dixon finished with 144 yards on 21 carries while Banaszak picked up 116 on 15 carries.

George Blanda had kicked the first of his record four field goals for the only points of the first period.

Final Block

On the first play of the second quarter, Dixon took off around left end. Rookie guard Gene Upshaw pulled in front of him and threw a devastating block on defensive back W. K. Hicks that gave Dixon a clear path.

The run set a championship game record for the longest TD run from scrimmage. And it set the tone for the game. After that, the Raiders had things pretty much their own way.

Houston's Hoyle Granger, the A.F.L.'s second leading rusher with 1,194 yards during the regular season, never got loose against the Raider front four and several times the record crowd of 53.330 gave the Oakland defense a standing ovation as it came off the field.

The Statistics

	Oilers	Raiders
First downs	11	18
Rushing yardage	38	263
Passing yardage	108	101
Return yardage	215	135
Passes	15-35-1	10-26-0
Punts	11-38.6	4-44.3
Fumbles lost	2	0
Yards penalized	7-45	4-69
Houston	0 0 0 7—7	
Oakland	3 14 10 13—40	

Oakland—F.G. Blanda. 37.
Oakland—Dixon. 69 run (Blanda kick).
Oakland—Kocourek. 18. pass from Lamonica (Blanda kick).
Oakland—Lamonica. 1 run (Blanda kick).
Oakland—F.G. Blanda. 40.
Oakland—F.G. Blanda. 42.
Houston—Frazier. 5 pass from Beathard (Wittenborn kick).
Oakland—F.G. Blanda 36
Oakland—Miller. 12 pass from Lamonica (Blanda kick).
Attendance. 53.330.
Rushing—Oakland. Dixon 21 for 144. Banaszak 15 for 116. Lamonica 5 for 22. Houston. Granger 14 for 19. Campbell 6 for 15.
Passing—Oakland. Lamonica 10 of 24 for 111 yards and 2 touchdowns; Houston. Beathard 15 of 35 for 142 yards and 1 TD. Receiving—Oakland. Miller 3 for 32 and 1 TD. Biletnikoff 2 for 19. Cannon 2 for 31. Banaszak 1 for 4. Kocourek 1 for 17 and 1 TD. Dixon 1 for 8; Houston. Taylor 1 for 6. Frazier 7 for 81 and 1 TD. Campbell 6 for 60; Granger 1 for minus 10.

Nance Repeats

Two Oakland Retreads Nab AFL Crowns

NEW YORK (AP) — Two retreads who helped Oakland win its first American Football League Western Division title this season, led statistical races as well.

Figures released by the AFL today showed veteran place kicker George Blanda winning the scoring crown with 116 points and quarterback Daryle Lamonica finishing first among the league's passers.

Blanda, cast off by Houston before the season, hooked on with the Raiders and kicked 20 of 30 field goal attempts and 56 of 57 conversion attempts, finishing eight points ahead of Kansas City's kicking specialist, Jan Stenerud.

Lamonica, who was a bench-warmer for four years at Buffalo before being traded to Oakland, hurled 30 touchdown passes and completed 220 of 425 passes for 3,228 yards.

Boston's Jim Nance won his second straight rushing title, gaining 1,216 yards and New York's George Sauer led the league's pass catchers with 75 receptions.

LEADING GROUND GAINERS

	Att.	Yards	Avg. Gain	TDs
Nance, Bos.	269	1,216	4.5	7
Granger, Hou.	236	1,194	5.0	6
Garrett, K.C.	236	1,087	4.6	9
Post, S.D.	161	663	4.1	7
Hubbert, S.D.	116	643	5.5	2
Lincoln, Buff.	159	601	3.8	4
Daniels, Oak.	130	575	4.4	4
Dixon, Oak.	153	559	3.7	5
Campbell, Hou.	110	511	4.6	4
Carlton, Buff.	107	467	4.4	3

LEADING PASSERS

	Att.	Com.	Yds.	TDs	Avg. Gain
Lamonica, Oak.	425	220	3,228	30	7.60
Dawson, K.C.	357	206	2,651	24	7.43
Namath, N.Y.	491	258	4,007	26	8.16
Hadl, S.D.	427	217	3,365	24	7.88
Griese, Mia.	331	166	2,005	15	6.06
Parilli, Bos.	344	161	2,317	19	6.74
Tensi, Den.	325	131	1,915	16	5.89
Kemp, Buff.	369	161	2,503	14	6.78
Beathd. K.C.-Hou.	231	94	1,114	9	4.82

LEADING PASS RECEIVERS

	Recd.	Yds.	Avg. Gain	TDs
Sauer, N.Y.	75	1,189	15.9	6
Maynard, N.Y.	71	1,434	20.2	10
Clancy, Mia.	67	868	13.0	2
Taylor, K.C.	59	958	16.2	11
Dixon, Oak.	59	563	9.5	2
Frazier, S.D.	57	922	16.2	10
Alworth, S.D	52	1,010	19.4	9
Denson, Den.	46	899	19.5	11
Crabtree, Den.	46	716	15.6	5
Garrett, K.C.	46	261	5.7	1

LEADING SCORERS

	TDs	FG	PAT	TP
Blanda, Oak.	0	20	56	116
Stenerud, K.C.	0	21	45	108
Cappelletti, Bos.	3	16	29	95
VanRaaphorst, S.D.	0	15	45	90
J.Turner, N.Y.	0	17	36	87
Boozer, N.Y.	13	0	0	78
Mercer, Buff.	0	16	25	73
Taylor, K.C.	12	0	0	72
Wittenborn, Hou.	0	14	30	72
Denson, Den.	11	0	0	66

N.F.L. Title

YAHOO—Green Bay Packer coach Vince Lombardi reacts like typical fan as charges score winning TD late in game.

VINCE DISPLAYS "HEART" AT LAST

Gambled On Touchdown So Fans Could Leave

By ALAN GOLDSTEIN
(Sun Staff Correspondent)

Green Bay, Wis., Dec. 31—Vince Lombardi, who has been called the Scrooge of the northlands and accused of having a heart about as warm as the sub-zero weather here today, proved he really is a man of compassion.

"I couldn't see going for a tie and making all those people in the stands suffer through a sudden death in this weather," said the Packers' dictatorial genius. "That's why we gambled for the touchdown."

Viscount Vince, of course, was referring to Bart Starr's dramatic quarterback sneak for the final foot to climax Green Bay's 21-to-17 victory over the unfortunate Dallas Cowboys.

No Time Outs

Only 16 seconds remained in the N.F.L. championship game when Starr decided to take matters into his own hands following two unsuccessful cracks at the line by halfback Donny Anderson from 1 yard out.

"We didn't have any time outs left," Lombardi explained, "so we had to gamble that Starr would make it. I had the field goal team ready on the sidelines in case he didn't, but I'm not sure if they would have had time to run out on the field and get the kick off."

In last year's dramatic classic between the same two teams, the shoe was on the other foot. Dallas had four cracks from the 2-yard line and failed to make it and Green Bay triumphed, 34 to 27.

Reprinted from
The Baltimore Sun

LAST-DITCH TD BY STARR IS CLINCHER

Crown Is 3d Straight For Green Bay And Lombardi

By CAMERON C. SNYDER
(Sun Staff Correspondent)

Green Bay, Wis., Dec. 31—A southerner from Alabama with nerves as cold as the weather on this coldest day in National Football League history, gambled an unprecedented - third straight championship and a possible Super Bowl winners' share of $735,000 on a quarterback sneak . . . and won, 21 to 17.

It was Packer weather, on a Packer field before a Packer crowd of 50,961, but it didn't become a Packer victory until Bart Starr leaped over the Dallas Cowboy line from one yard out with 13 seconds left to play.

It was a blue chip effort (what other color could it have been in the 13 below zero weather) which if it had failed probably would have cost the Packers everything including the $15,000 per man share for 49 persons—the winning Super Bowl team.

Starr's Gamble

Starr took his gamble on a third and one situation with no Green Bay timeouts left. It appeared if the Dallas defense had held on the sneak, the Packers wouldn't have had a chance to get their field goal team in for the tying placement attempt.

Reprinted from
The Baltimore Sun

The Packers, winners of the N.F.L. title in 1965, 1966 and now this year, will meet the Oakland Raiders of the American Football League two weeks from today in Miami, Fla.

The playing conditions were atrocious today. The Cowboys expected cold weather, but not a record reading in Green Bay for this day. They also expected a good field.

Packers Final Rally

With 4.40 left to play, the Packers staged their final rally. Starr, attempting to beat the rush, went to the short pass and down the field Green Bay rolled.

Critical situations kept cropping up, but Starr and his mates got over them, like a third and 7 pass to Anderson that went for 9 yards and a 19-yard flare pass to Chuck Mercein to put the ball on the Cowboy 11.

From the 11, Mercein went to the 3. Anderson then picked up a first down at the 2, but two more shots by him moved the ball only to the one.

Starr called time out after the last Anderson try. The clock had just 20 seconds to run.

The Statistics

	Dallas	G. B.
Total first downs	11	18
First downs rushing	4	5
First downs passing	6	10
First downs by penalty	1	3
Total yards gained (net)	192	195
Yards gained rushing (net)	92	80
Yards gained passing (net)	100	115
Gross yards gained passing	109	191
Times thrown and yards lost attempting to pass	1.9	8.76
Passes attempted	26	24
Passes completed	11	14
Average gain per pass attempt	3.8	4.8
Passes intercepted by and yards intercepted returned	0-0	1-13
Number and total yardage of punts	8-313	8-230
Average distance of punts	39.1	29
Number and total yards punts returned	0-0	5-19
Number and total yards kickoffs returned	3-43	1-13
Number of penalties and total yards penalized	7-58	2-10
Number of fumbles and tumbles post	3-1	3-2
Number of rushing plays	33	32
Average gain per rushing play	2.8	2.5
Total offensive plays (include times thrown passing)	60	64
Average gain per offensive play	3.2	3.1
Cowboys	0 10 0 7 17	
Packers	7 7 0 7 21	

	Dallas	G. B.
Packers 1 8:50 Dowler, on eight-yard Starr pass	0	6
Packers 1 8:50 Chandler, Pat	0	7
Packers 2 2:41 Dowler, on 46-yard Starr pass	0	13
Packers 2 2:41 Chandler, Pat	0	14
Cowboys 2 10:56 Andrie, recovered Starr fumble and ran 7 yds.	6	14
Cowboys 2 10:56 Villanueva, Pat	7	14
Cowboys 2 14:28 Villanueva, on 21-yard field goal	10	14
Cowboys 4 08 Rentzel, on 50-yard pass from Reeves	16	14
Cowboys 4 08 Villanueva, Pat	17	14
Packers 4 14:47 Starr on one-yard quarterback sneak	17	20
Packers 4 14:47 Chandler, Pat	18	21
Packers 4 14:47 Chandler, Pat	17	21

Packers Crush Raiders, 33 To 14, In Super Bowl

CHANDLER KICKS FOUR FIELD GOALS

Starr Directs Attack As Winners Roll To 2d Crown In Row

By CAMERON C. SNYDER
[Sun Staff Correspondent]

Miami, Fla., Jan. 14—The Green Bay Packers started with Don Chandler's toe, added the legs of Donny Anderson and Ben Wilson and the hands of Boyd Dowler to the right arm of Bart Starr and handed the Oakland Raiders their heads, 33 to 14, in the Super Bowl today at the Orange Bowl.

It was the second consecutive pro football championship in the two years of competition for the Packers. Green Bay last January defeated the Kansas City Chiefs, 35 to 10, in the Los Angeles inaugural of the National vs. American Football League rivalry.

Deep Six Treatment

In foul weather or fair, the Packers always cool off their opponents. Two weeks ago in Green Bay, Vince Lombardi's Eskimos put the Dallas Cowboys into a 13-below-zero deep freeze, 21 to 17, to ice down the N.F.L. title.

Today in warm and sunny Florida where the temperature was 68, 81 degrees higher than the Green Bay game, Lombardi's surfers gave the Raiders the deep six treatment.

Reprinted from
The Baltimore Sun

The Packers made Oakland go under with their usually steady and sometimes boring brand of game where they hogged the ball for minutes on end.

It was just such ball control in the third period that added the Raiders to the long list of Packer victims. In that 15-minute span, Green Bay scored 10 points while running off 25 plays to Oakland's 9 plays and one first down.

Field Goal Opens Scoring

The score at the start of the second half was a respectable one for the Raiders, 16 to 7, which the Packers had forged on 3 Chandler field goals and a 62-yard touchdown pass from Starr to Dowler.

MCGEE ENDS GRID CAREER

12-Year Green Bay Veteran Bows Out In Style

Miami, Fla., Jan. 14 [P]—Max McGee closed out his sparkling 12-year National Football League career in typical fashion today.

With a third and one situation on the Green Bay 40, Packer quarterback Bart Starr flipped one of his patented third down aerials into the waiting arms of McGee, who raced to the Oakland 25. The play set up a Don Chandler field goal and gave Green Bay a 23-7 lead.

The pass was the only one McGee caught during his final game and he probably wouldn't have been on the field if Boyd Dowler hadn't been hurt.

"I really didn't expect to play," he said afterwards in the Packer dressing room. "I kiddingly told Boyd to get hurt so I could catch a pass and darned if he didn't."

The Statistics

	Oakland	Green Bay
Total first downs	16	9
First downs rushing	5	1
First downs passing	10	1
First downs by penalty	1	1
Total yards gained (net)	291	322
Yards gained rushing (net)	105	163
Yards gained passing (net)	186	162
Gross yards gained passing	208	202
Times thrown and yards lost attempting to pass	3-22	4-40
Passes attempted	34	24
Passes completed	15	13
Average gain per pass attempt	5.0	5.3
Passes intercepted by and yards intercept returned	0.0	1.60
Number and total yardage of punts	6-264	6-234
Average distance of punts	44.0	39.0
Number and total yards punts net	3-12	3-35
Number and total yards kickoffs returned	7-127	3-49
Number of penalties and total yards penalized	4-31	1-12
Number of fumbles and fumbles lost	3-2	0-0
Number of rushing plays	20	41
Average gain per rushing play	5.2	4.0
Total offensive plays (including times thrown passing)	57	69
Average gain per offensive play	5.1	4.7

			Oakland	Green Bay
Oakland			0 7 0 7	—14
Green Bay			3 13 10 7	—33

Team	Pd.	Time	Detail	Oak.	G.B.
GB	1	5.07	FG Chandler 39	0	3
GB	2	3.08	FG Chandler 20	0	6
GB	2	4.10	Dowler, 62 pass from Starr (Chandler kick)	0	13
OK	2	8.45	Miller, 23 pass from Lamonica (Blanda kick)	7	13
GB	2	14.59	FG Chandler 43	7	13
GB	3	9.06	Anderson 2 (Chandler kick)	7	23
GB	3	14.56	FG Chandler 31	7	26
GB	4	3.57	Adderly 60 interception (Chandler kick)	7	33
OK	4	4.47	Miller, 23 pass from Lamonica (Blanda kick)	14	33

Attendance, 75,546.

Reprinted from
The Baltimore Sun

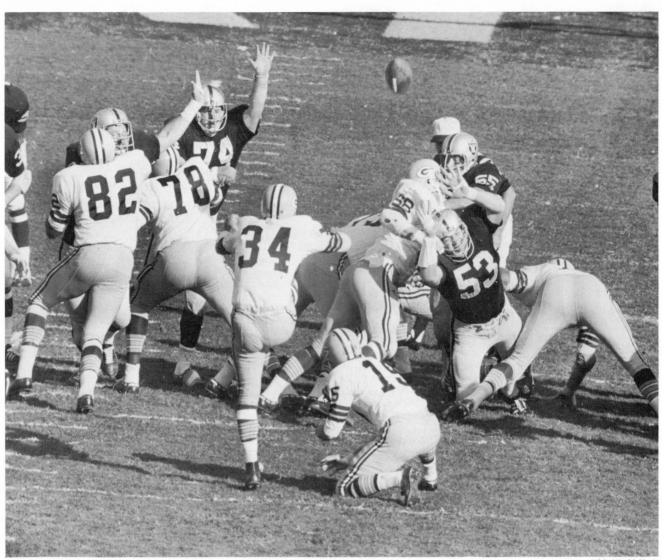

DON CHANDLER (34) BOOTS A 39-YARD FIELD GOAL

Wide World Photo

RAUCH CALM, GRACIOUS IN RAIDER LOSS

Calls Packer Control Of Third Quarter Turning Point

By W. LAWRENCE NULL
(Sun Staff Correspondent)

Miami, Fla., Jan. 14—"It's always tough to accept a beating, especially when you're not used to it."

Raider coach Johnny Rauch, who called the Super Bowl the high point in his 15-year coaching career, calmly discussed the defeat with reporters.

"I don't think there was ever a point in the game when our players gave up," he said quietly. "We were losing at the half (16-7), but several times during the season we were down at the half and we came back to win.

"We thought we could do it today. We went out there in the second half with quiet confidence that we could win without hysteria or long bombs. But the Packers don't give you many openings."

Third Quarter Hurt

Rauch felt the turning point in the contest was the complete dominance of the third quarter by the Packers, who boosted their lead to 26-7. "The breaks went against us in that quarter and that's the name of the game."

Green Bay receivers repeatedly got behind Oakland defenders for long gains and the first touchdown to Boyd Dowler. Rauch cited the breakdown in pass coverage as "one of those mistakes that lose games for you."

Reprinted from
The Baltimore Sun

LOMBARDI QUITS JOB AS COACH

Remains Packer G.M. Names Phil Bengtson As Successor

Green Bay, Wis., Feb. 1 (P)—Iron-willed Vince Lombardi stepped down otnight as coach of the world-champion Green Bay Packers and named long-time assistant Phil Bengtson to succeed him.

Lombardi said he would remain in Green Bay as the National Football League club's general manager.

Double Duties Too Much

The decision came only a month after Lombardi guided the Packers to a third straight N.F.L. title and a second straight Super Bowl triumph.

The coach told a gathering of Packer directors and newsmen that the responsibilities of both coaching and running the team as general manager had become too much for one man.

The growth of professional football, the problems created by the merger of the National and American Football Leagues and the increasing burden of player relations demanded a full-time genesal manager, Lombardi said.

"I must relinquish one of the jobs," Lombardi said.

Praises Bengtson

He then announced he was turning over head coaching duties to Bengtson, whom he described as a "loyal and dedicated assistant."

"Under his leadership and direition, Green Bay football will continue to be excellent. Green Bay football will continue to grow," Lombardi said.

Bengtson, 56, has been Lombardi's defensive coach since Lombardi took over the ailing Green Bay franchise and turned it into a winner 1959.

Defensive Genius

The former Minnesota athlete has long held the reputation of being one of football's foremost defensive coaches.

As Packer coach Limbardi won as no other coach in professional football ever had won.

Winning Only Thing

"Winning isn't everything," Lombardi once said. "It's the only thing." With the Packers under Lombardi, it almost was.

In none seasons as Packer coach, Lombardi's teams won 89 regular season games, lost only 29, and tied 4. The Packers captured five N.F.L. titles, six Western Conference titles, and two World Titles in two games with the American Football League champions.

The last three N.F.L. crowns came in succession. No other team since 1933 when the N.F.L. went to a play-off system to determine its champion ever won three straight titles.

Players Give Demands To N.F.L.

Bargaining Session Includes Minimum $15,000 salary

Chicago, March 19 (P)—The National Football League's Players Association presented a list of demands to management today and some of them met with objection.

It was the first formal collective bargaining session in pro football history.

The demands covered a 25-page agreement with amplification on these points:

A grievance and arbitration procedure.

No Discrimination

No discrimination to any athlete because of race, religion or national origin.

The right to negotiate individual player salaries shall be reserved to the individual player and the individual club owner.

A minimum yearly salary of $15,000. Such a minimum on a standard contract is $5,500, but has gone as high as $12,000.

1Interleague Game

A pension contribution of $5 million annually to provide increased pension benefits, increased widow benefits, and increased insurance benefits.

An NFL—American Football League All-Star game, not necessarily an extra game, with the major portion of the receipts going to the benefit funds.

A complete review of the option clause to work out an equitable settlement.

Exhibition game pay of $500. Basic pay now is $10 per day during the exhibition season.

No player shall be required to report to camp, or fined for failure to report, unless he has signed his contract.

Share of gate receipts and post-season playoff games.

Severance pay in event a player is cut from the squad when the season is underway.

Moving Expenses

A player who is traded shall be reimbursed for his moving expenses.

"It should be understood that we are not out to disrupt the normal functions of the league," said John Gordy of the Detroit Lions, president of the N.F.L.P.A.

n the past, our owners have demonstrated an enlightened attitude and we have every reason to hope that this will continue."

Pro Football Draft Picks

New York, Jan. 30 (AP)—Here are the selections, by round, in the combined American and National Football Leagues draft of college players.

First Round

1. Minnesota from New York Giants, Ron Yary, Southern California offensive tackle. 2, Cincinnati, Bob Johnson, Tennessee center. 3, Atlanta, Claude Humphrey, Tennessee A.& I. defensive tackle. 4, San Diego from Denver, Russ Washington, Missouri offensive tackle. 5, Green Bay from New Orleans, Fred Carr, Texas El-Paso linebacker. 6, Boston, Dennis Byrd, North Carolina State defensive tackle. 7, New Orleans from Minnesota, Kevin Hardy, Notre Dame defensive end. 8, Miami, Larry Csonka, Syracuse fullback. 9, Buffalo, Haven Moses, San Diego State offensive end.

10, Pittsburgh, Mike Taylor, Southern California offensive tackle. 11, Detroit, Greg Landry, Massachusetts quarterback. 12, Washington, Jim Smith, Oregon defensive back. 13, St. Louis, MacArthur Lane, Utah State running back. 14, Tim Rossovich, Southern California defensive end.

15, San Francisco, Forrest Blue, Auburn center. 16, Chicago, Mike Hull, Southern California running back. 17, New York Jets, Lee White, Weber State running back. 18, San Diego, James Hill, Texas A.& I. defensive back. 19, Kansas City, Maurice Moorman, Texas A.& M. guard.

20, Dallas, Dennis Homan, Alabama end. 21, Cleveland, Marvin Upshaw, Trinity (Texas) defensive end. 22, Kansas City from Houston George Daney, Texas El-Paso guard. 23, COLTS, JOHN WILLIAM, MINNESOTA OFFENSIVE TACKLE. 24, Detroit from Los Angeles, Earl McCullouch, Southern California flanker. 25, Oakland, Eldrige Dickey, Tennessee A.& I. quarterback. 26, Green Bay, Bill Lueck, Arizona guard. 27, Miami from Cincinnati Doug Crusan, Indiana offensive tackle.

Second Round

1, Cincinnati, Bill Staley, Utah defensive end. 2, Atlanta, Carlton Dabney, Morgan State, defensive end. 3, Los Angeles from New Orleans, Gary Beban, U.C.L.A. quarterback. 4, Denver, Curley Culp, Arizona State defensive end. 5, Boston, Tom Funchess, Jackson (Miss.) State offensive tackle. 6, Minnesota, Charles Wet. Texas-El Paso defensive back. 7, Buffalo, Bob Tatarek, Miami, (Fla.) defensive tackle. 8, Miami, James Keyes, Mississippi linebacker. 9, Pittsburgh, Ernest Rupel, Arkansas offensive tackle.

10, Detroit, Jerry DePoyster, Wyoming kicker. 11, Washington, Tom Roussel, Southern Mississippi linebacker. 12, Philadelphia, Cyril Pinder, Illinois running back. 13, St. Louis, Fred Hyatt, Auburn flanker. 14, New York Giants, Dick Buzin, Penn State offensive tackle. 15, St. Louis from San Francisco, Bob Atkins, Grambling defensive back. 16, San Diego, Bill Lenkaitis. Penn State center. 17, New York Jets, Steve Thompson, Washington defensive tackle. 18, Dallas, David McDaniels. Mississippi Valley end.

19, Chicago, Bob Wallace, Texas-El Paso end. 20, Cleveland, John Garlington, Louisiana State linebacker. 21, Kansas City, Mike Livingston, Southern Methodist quarterback. 22, Houston, Mac Haik. Mississippi end. 23, COLTS. BOB GRANT, WAKE FOREST LINEBACKER. 24. LOS Angeles, Mike LaHood. Wyoming guard. 25, Oakland, Ken Stabler, Alabama quarterback. 26, Atlanta, from Green Bay through Los Angeles, John Wright. Illinois flanker. 27, Miami from Cincinnati, James Cox, Miami, Fla., end. 28, Cincinnati, Tom Smiley, Lamar Tech fullback.

Third Round

1, Cincinnati. Gary Davis, Vanderbilt quarterback. 2, Chicago from Atlanta, Major Hazelton, Florida A.&M. defensive back. 3, Denver, Garrett Ford, West Virginia running back. 4, New Orleans. Dave Szymakowski, West Texas State end. 5, Boston. Aaron Marsh. Eastern Kentucky flanker. 6, Pittsburgh from Minnesota. Jon Henderson, Colorado State defensive back. 7, Miami, Jim Urbanek, Mississippi tackle. 8, Buffalo, Richard Trapp, Florida end. 9, Cleveland from Pittsburgh, Harry Olszewski, Clemson guard. 10, San Francisco from Detroit. Lance Olssen, Purdue tackle. 11, Cleveland from Washington, Reese Morrison, Southwest Texas State running back.

12, Green Bay from St. Louis, Billy Stevens. Texas-El Paso quarterback. 13, Philadelphia, Adrian Young, South California linebacker. 14, San Francisco, Skip Vanderbundt. Oregon State linebacker. 15, New York Giants, Bob Duhon, Tulane running back. 16, Dallas from Chicago, Ed Hamon, Louisville linebacker. 17, New York Jets, Sam Walton, East Texas State tackle.

18, Miami from San Diego. Dick Anderson, Colorado defensive back. 19, Detroit from Cleveland, through Los Angeles, Charles Sanders, Minnesota tight end. 20, Denver from Kansas City. Robert Vaugh, Mississippi tackle. 21, Minnesota from Dallas, Mike McGill, Notre Dame linebacker. 22, Houston, Elvin Beathea, North Carolina A.& T. tackle. 23, COLTS, RICH O'HARA, NORTHERN ARIZONA FLANKER. 24, Pittsburgh from Los Angeles, Ken Hebert, Houston flanker-kicker. 25, Oakland, Arthur Shell, Maryland State tackle. 26, Green Bay, Richard Himes, Ohio State tackle. 27, Cincinnati, Paul Robinson, Arizona running back. 28, Cincinnati. Dale Lvingston. Western Michigan kicker.

WERBLIN'S 4 PARTNERS BUY HIM OUT

Don Lillis Becomes New President Of New York Jets

New York, May 21 — Sonny Werblin has sold his share of the New York Jets of the American Football League to his four partners, one of the partners confirmed tonight.

"The deal has been made," Townsend B. Martin said. "We offered Sonny a price and he accepted. There will be four equal partners and Don Lillis will be the new president.

Weeb Ewbank will remain as general manager and head coach "as far as I know," Martin said. He added that he knew nothing of rumors to try and persuade Vince Lombardi to leave the Green Bay Packers to coach the Jets.

Big A.F.L. Hike No Solace For N.F.L. Cousins

New York, July 11 (P)—A sharp increase in American Football League pension benefits added fuel to the simmering dispute that has kept veterans out of all National Football League camps and threatens schedule dislocations.

Until now, the two merged leagues have had equal pension plans under which a five-year veteran would receive $500 monthly at 65, a ten-year man $775 and a fifteen-year man $990.

Agreement has been reached between the A.F.L. Players Association and league owners to increase this to $689 for a five-year man, $1,132 for ten years, and $1,497 for fifteen.

Behind Closed Doors

Presumably N.F.L. players are asking more, but all negotiations have been behind closed doors and nothing has been revealed beyond the fact that 21 of the 22 players' demands have been met.

Both football pension plans are non-contributory, that is to say, the owners foot the bill.

Before the negotiations started, the N.F.L. players talked of demanding an increase in the owners' contributions to the pension fund from the current $1,400,000 annually to $5,000,000.

The owners offered a 25 per cent increase in their contributions this year and a similar increase next year.

There was speculation that the break between the NFL players and the owners came because the NFL demands considerably exceeded the scale granted by the AFL.

Under the terms of the merger of the two leagues, the pension plans would be made equal by 1970 when the merger is to be completed. However, the AFL last year brought its pension plan to parity with the NFL.

Behind Baseball

Football is only now catching up with baseball. A man with five years in the majors gets $643 monthly at 65, or if he wishes $250 monthly at 50. A 20-year man gets $1,487 at 65. Sixteen years is the record for playing professional football, but baseball players have longer careers.

Hockey has the highest pension ceiling. A 20-year player in the National Hockey League who waits until 65 to draw a pension gets $1,640 per month.

Hockey also has lower entrance requirements than baseball and football, both of which start at five years. A man with only three years service in the N.H.L. can look forward to $75 monthly at 45 or $246 monthly at 65.

Strike Threat Over; Owners Will Pay $3 Million

New York July 14 (P) — National Football League club owners and the N.F.L. Players Association agreed on a new pension plan today, ending a dispute which threatened to wreck the 1968 season.

The agreement will cost the club owners $3 million for 1968 and 1969.

The settlement, which broke a stalemate of several weeks, came in fourth-down-and-one-fashion. The main N.F.L. training camp activity is scheduled to get under way this week.

Furthur delay could have affected the exhibition schedule, knocked out the College All-Star Game and produced negative effects on the regular season.

4½—Hour Meeting

Following a meeting of about 4½ hours at a midtown hotel, the agreement was announced at a news conference by N.F.L. President Arthur Modell, owner of the Cleveland Browns, and Detroit Lion guard John Gordy, head of the N.F.L. Players Association.

Part of a statement read by Modell said:

"Under this agreement, the league club owners will contribute a total of $3 million for the years 1968 and 1969 for pension benefits, administrative costs, and the cost of a joint study to be conducted in anticipation of the merger of the N.F.L. and A.F.L. pension plan by 1970. "It is estimated that administrative costs will amount to $144,000 and that the joint study will cost about $40,000. No commitment was made by the owners regarding pension contributions beyond 1968 or 1969.

In a departure from past practice in this area, the parties agreed that in view of the owners' guarantee as to the amount of contribution, any reference to the source of revenue shall be dropped and the owners shall have exclusive control over determining how best to meet the guarantee."

Gordy said he was proud "that we as professional athletes can settle our differences across the bargaining table as gentlemen.

"We wanted to be heard and we wanted voice but never, never wanted to use our own strength unjustly."

Retroactive To 1959

Gordy said the new pension plan is retroactive to 1959 and guarantees 10-year veterans $1,600 a month after reaching the age of 65. Under the old plan, a 10-year veteran received $775 monthly. A 10-year American Football League veteran, under an agreement reached last Wednesday, gets $1,132.

A breakdown for five-year and 15-year veterans under the new N.F.L. plan was not available.

The pension agreement was the last of 21 points to be settled by the negotiations which started last March 19.

49ers Awarded Hardy, No. 1 Pick

Santa Barbara, Cal., July 26 (P) — The San Francisco 49ers announced tonight they have been awarded rookie lineman Kevin Hardy of Notre Dame and a first round draft choice next year for their former ace pass catcher, Dave Parks, who went to New Orleans.

The award was made by Commissioner Pete Rozelle of the National Football League after Parks made a deal for himself with the Saints.

Parks, who failed to agree on terms with the 49ers last year, played out his option, then signed with New Orleans for a reported $60,000.

KANSAS CITY NIPS HOUSTON, 26-21

Chiefs Stop Late Threat With Tough Defense

Houston, Sept. 9 (P) — Mike Garrett and Wendell Hayes provided the speed and Len Dawson the effective passing tonight as the Kansas City Chiefs defeated the Houston Oilers, 26-to-21, in an American Football League opener in the Astrodome.

The Chiefs overcame an early Houston lead by backing Dawson's attack with a stingy defense that limited the Oilers to a net rushing gain of only 29 yards the first two quarters.

Pete Beathard completed his first six passes for 129 yards as Houston jumped to a quick 7-0 advantage on a five-yard run by Hoyle Granger.

Chiefs Go 65 Yards

The chiefs, using only two short Dawson passes, then moved 65 yards to set up a 27-yard fiel dgoal, the first of four by Jan Stenerud. Kansas City pass interceptions by Jim Kearney and big Ernie Ladd thwarted other Houston threats until lat in the fourth quarter.

Kansas City ....3 14 3 6—26
Houston 7   0 0 14—21

Hous—Granger 5 run (Wittenborn kick).
KC—fg Stenerud 27.
KC—Hayes 1 run (Stenerud kick).
KC—Taylor 6 run (Stenerud kick).
KC—FG Stenerud 33.
KC—FG Stenerud 26.
KC—FG Stenerud 32.
Hous—Haik 5 pass from Beathard (Wittenborn kick).
Hous—Kaik 59 pass from Beathard (Wittenborn kick).
Attendance—45,083.

REDSKINS DOWN BEARS BY 38-28

Jurgensen Fires 4 TDs. In N.F.L. Upset

Chicago, Sept. 15 (P)—Sonny Jurgensen, using the exhibition season to recover from an elbow operation, fired four touchdown passes including a 99-yarder to Gerry Allen today and guided the Washington Redskins to an upset 38-to-28 victory over the Chicago Bears in a National Football League opener.

BENGALS DEFEAT BRONCOS, 24-10

A.F.L. Expansion Team Wins Home Debut

Cincinnati, Sept. 15 (P)—John Stofa fired two long touchdown passes today, leading Cincinnati to a successful home professional debut with a 24-to-10 American Football League victory over the Denver Broncos.

The Bengals, who ten days ago lost their opener to San Diego, blew a 10-0 advantage but roared back with two fourth quarter touchdowns to seal the decision.

Statistics

	Bronces	Bengals
First downs	15	11
Rushing vardage	78	99
Passing vardage	106	185
Return yardage	13	34
Passes	16-35-1	12-22-0
Punts	6-47	6-44
Fumbles lost	0	0
Yards penalized	15	24

Denver 0   0   3   7—10
Cincinnati 0   0 10 14—24
Cin—FG Livingston 49.
Cin—Trumpy 58 pass from Stofa (Livingston kick).
Den—FG Humphrevs 33.
Den—Crabtree 5 pass from Leclair (Humphreys kick).
Cin—McVea 54 pass from Stofa (Livingston kick).
Cin—Johnson 34 run (Livingston kick).
A—25,049.

FALCONS HIRE VAN BROCKLIN

New Coach Will Be Given Free Hand At Atlanta

Atlanta, Oct. 1 (P)—Norm Van Brocklin, one of pro football's most colorful characters, today was given the job of building the hapless Atlanta Falcons into a National Football League contender.

"Van Brocklin has been controversial" Atlanta owner Rankin Smith said in announcing the firing of Norb Hecker as coach and hiring of Van Brocklin. "But he has one of the finest minds in pro football."

Free Hand

Van Brocklin, 42, has been given a long-term contract and promised a free hand in trading and drafting players, Smith said. Terms of the contract were not disclosed.

The former N.F.L. quarterback and coach of the Minnesota Vikings for six years was still at his home in Medicine Lake, Minn., when the Falcons announced the coaching change.

"I've got a house for sale," Van Brocklin said before leaving for Atlanta, adding that he had not had time to think about changes he planned for the Falcons, who have won but four games since joining the N.F.L. in 1966.

Raiders Fall To Chargers As Win Skein Ends, 23-14

Oakland, Oct. 13 (P)—Lance Alworth and place kicker Dennis Partee sparked the offense and San Diego's defense throttled the Oakland Raiders in the second half today as the Chargers won, 23 to 14.

The loss dropped the Raiders out of first place in the American Football League's Western Division.

lippery Alworth

A capacity crowd of 53,257 sat through a light drizzle, as the Chargers snapped Oakland's 14-game winning streak in A.F.L. regular season play.

It was Oakland's first regular season loss since a 27-14 defeat by New York October 7, 1967.

AP REPORTS EAGLES NOW UNDER N.F.L.

But Owner Wolman, In Financial Jam, Enters Denial

Philadelphia Oct. 10 (AP) — The National Football League reportedly has taken over administration of the Philadelphia Eagles franchise from financially-pressed owner Jerry Wolman, the Associated Press learned tonight.

The club reportedly is being run for Commissioner Pete Rozelle by Bert Rose, former general manager of the Minnesota Vikings.

But Wolman said Rose was hired by the Eagles last month "to help out personnel and the player draft and for any other job that I might see fit to use him in."

"He (Rose) was invited by me into our organization and he's experienced in personnel, so I brought him in to help with our personnel ..." said Wolman, who owns 52 per cent of the team.

Hearing Set For Baltimore

In New York, Rozelle was unavailable for comment but Jim Kensil, executive director of the commissioner's office, said the story was "absolutely without foundation."

Wolman is scheduled for a hearing before a bankruptcy referee in Baltimore in a few weeks. At that time, he has to present a new plan to pay off some $75 million worth of creditors or be thrown into bankruptcy.

Rozelle is believed to have acted to protect the league in the event that Wolman is unable to come up with a substitute plan.

The 41-year-old Wolman has been under financial pressure for more than a year. His multimillion dollar construction business began to crumble when he suffered an $11 million loss in a Chicago building project.

Wolman has been trying to organize some sort of operation which would incorporate the Eagles, the $10 million Spectrum arena which he built in Philadelphia, Connie Mack Stadium and the Yellow Cab Co. of Philadelphia and Camden, N.J.

Bought Eagles In 1964

Wolman purchased the Eagles for $5,505,500 in 1964 from a syndicate of Philadelphians who had owned the team for sixteen years. The building contractor from Washington, outbid three other groups in closed bidding for the team.

Wolman has been fighting bankruptcy in order to hold onto the football team. He reportedly verbally agreed to sell it last year to partners in a clothing manufacturing business, but backed out before it was legally consummated.

The Morgan Guaranty Trust Company of New York holds a lien in excess of $5,000,000 against Wolman and the Eagles while the Fidelity Philadelphia Trust Company holds one for more than $2,500,000.

Wolman, Foreman and Snider formed the group which bought the team in 1964.

BEARS WIN, 27-19, BUT LOSE SAYERS

Back Lost For Season In Victory Over 49ers

Chicago, Nov. 10 (AP)—Rookie quarterback Virgil Carter ran for two touchdowns and passed for a third as the Chicago Bears won their fourth straight game by dropping the San Francisco 49ers, 27-to-19, today.

The Bears remained tied with Minnesota for the lead in the National Football League's Central Division, each with 5-4 records.

But the victory was costly for the Bears. They lost star ball carrier Gale Sayers for the season. The league's number one rusher left the game early in the second quarter with torn ligaments in the right knee and was to undergo surgery.

The Bears led 14-0 at the time and the remarkable Sayers had carried 11 times for 32 yards, boosting his season total to 856. He was injured after a short run when he was stopped near the sidelines.

The Bears' Bennie McRae, Lloyd Phillips, and Dick Butkus stole three John Brodie passes.

One was converted into a touchdown and two of them eventually resulted in 42 and 15-yard field goals by Mac Percival. Percival missed three other field goal attempts and had one blocked.

Statistics

	49ers	Bears
First downs	11	26
Rushing yardage	56	215
Passing yardage	199	231
Return yardage	69	12
Passes	9-26-4	16-30-1
Punts	5-36	2-26
Fumbles lost	0	0
Yards penalized	60	100

Chicago	7	13	3	0	27
San Francisco	0	6	13	0	19

Chi—Carter 7 run (Percival kick)
Chi—Carter 1 run (Percival kick)
Chi—FG Percival 42
Chi—Wallace 18 pass from Carter (Percival kick)
SF—Lewis 1 run kick failed
Chi—FG Percival 15
SF—Windsor 18 pass from Brodie (Patera kick)
SF—McNeil 28 pass from Brodie (kick failed)
A—46,978.

Oakland Rally Buries Jets, 43-32

Oakland. Nov. 17 —Oakland rookie Charlie Smith grabbed a 42-yard scoring pass from Daryl Lamonica with 42 seconds left in the game for the go-ahead touchdown and Oakland scored again nine seconds later on a fumble recovery of the kickoff in the end zone to beat the New York Jets, 43-to-32, in d Americ n Football League game.

The Jets took the lead with 1.05 remaining on Jim Turner's fourth field goal of the game, a 26-yarder. Smith took the kickoff to the Oakland 22. Lamonica then threw him a screen pass, good for 20 yards.

Ridlehuber On The Spot.

The Jets were penalized for grabbing a face mask and, with Oakland in possession at the New York 42, Lamonica hit Smith on the right sideline. The 21-year-old Morris Brown graduate dashed into the end zone untouched.

Nine seconds later, New York's Earl Christy fumbled the kickoff, and Oakland's Preston Ridlehuber recovered for the score.

New York trailed going into the fourth quarter, but in two passes, Joe Namath covered 97 yards, both of them going to Don Maynard, and New York went ahead 26-22.

Then Turner kicked a 12-yard field goal to widen the lead to 29-22.

Lamonica followed with a 65-yard touchdown pass to Smith that was called back when Oakland's Jim Harvey was charged with offensive holding. But later in the series, Lamonica tried the score with a 22-yard touchdown pass to Fred Biletnikoff.

Beteran Back Out

The Namath-Maynard combination nearly did in the Raiders, especially in the fourth quarter, as they ran rookie defender George Atkinson ragged. Atkinson was replacing the Raiders' veteran cornerback Kent McCloughan, who was placed on the reserve list before the game.

Both teams were close to putting the game away in the third period. After the Jets took a 19-14 lead on Bill Mathis's four-yard plunge, Namath brought New York down to the Oakland 15, but Raider defensive end Ben Davidson and Ike Lassiter caught him behind the line. Turner then missed a 33-yard field goal attempt.

Statistics

	Jets	Raiders
First downs	18	21
Rushing yardage	68	136
Passing yardage	345	29?
Return yardage	46	69
Passes	19-37-0	21-34-2
Punts	7-39	5-43
Fumbles lost	1	2
Yards penalized	145	92

New York	6	6	7	11—32
Oakland	7	7	8	21—43

New York—FG Turner 18.
Oakland—Wells 9 pass from Lamonica (Blanda kick).
Oakland—Cannon 48 pass from Lamonica (Blanda kick).
New York—Namath 1 run (pass failed)
New York—Mathis 4 run (Turner kick)
Oakland—Smith 3 run (Dixon pass from Lamonica).
New York—Maynard 50 pass from Namath (Turner kick).
New York—FG Turner 12.
Oakland—Biletnikoff 22 pass from Lamonica (Blanda kick).
New York—FG Turner 26
Oakland—Smith 42 pass from Lamonica (Blanda kick).
Oakland—Ridlehuber 4 fumble recovery (Blanda kick).
Attendance—53,318

Lovable Little Heidi Enrages Grid Fans

New York, Nov. 17 — Thousands of kids settled happily into their chairs to watch Heidi tonight just moments after their fuming, football-loving fathers leaped to their feet in outrage and reached for the telephone.

The start of Heidi at 7 P.M. cut off to most of the country the final minute of the New York Jets-Oakland Raiders game being telecast by NBC from Oakland.

New York went ahead, 32-29, with 1.05 minutes left, and the fans at home saw the Raiders return the kickoff and run one play.

What they didn't see were two Oakland touchdowns.

Julian Goodman, president of N.B.C., said in a statement:

"It was a forgiveable error committed by human beings who were concerned about the children expecting to see Heidi at 7 P.M. I missed the end of the game as much as anyone else."

ROZELLE SUSPENDS OFFICIALS

Referees Who 'Erred' In Ram Game Lose 1968 Assignments

New York, Dec. 9 —Pete Rozelle, commissioner of pro football, announced today the suspension of the six game officials whose mistake cost Los Angeles a down in the Rams' crucial 17-to-16 National Football League loss to Chicago yesterday.

The officials were referee Norm Schachter, umpire Joe Connell, head linesman Burl Toler, line judge Jack Fette, back judge Adrian Burk and field judge George Ellis.

Rozelle issued the following statement:

"National Football League game officials erred in not permitting Los Angeles one more down near the end of the Rams' game with the Chicago Bears Sunday.

"A penalty against Los Angeles on the first down of its final series nullified an incomplete pass play. Following three additional incomplete passes by Los Angeles, the ball was turned over to Chicago, thus depriving Los Angeles of a fourth down play to which it was entitled.

No More Assignments

"Los Angeles would have started the fourth down from its own 47-yard line with five seconds to play and 31 yards needed for a first down.

"All six game officials are equally responsible for keeping track of the downs.

"The crew which officiated the Los Angeles-Chicago game is considered among the most competent in pro football. However, because all six must bear responsibility for the error, the entire crew will receive no assignments for the remainder of the 1968 NFL season, including post-season games."

The series started on first down at the Chicago 32, with time running out. Los Angeles right tackle Charlie Cowan was cited for holding as a Roman Gabriel pass meant for Jack Snow went incomplete.

Holding costs 15 yards from the point of the infraction and referee Schachter marched off the yardage to the Rams' 47. The down should have remained the same, but unaccountably, it became second down.

Three incomplete passes by the Rams and the Bears took over five seconds before the game was over.

So Baltimore became the Coastal Division winner with 12-1 to 10-2-1 for the Rams. The meeting between those two clubs next Sunday can't alter their positions.

Demands Explanation

Sports Editor Bud Furillo, of the Los Angeles *Herald-Examiner*, wrote today that he was present in the officials' dressing room when Ram official Elroy Hirsch demanded an explanation.

Burr Beardsley, who operates the down marker, said, "I left it on first down when we moved back after the penalty, but Burl told me to change it to second."

Burl Toler was the head linesman. He made no comment pending the official report to the league.

"It would do no good to protest in a situation such as this," a Rams spokesman said.

Coach George Allen of the Rams said. "We have no excuses, no alibis. We've drained ourselves dry . . . three years of working and everything is down the drain. The Rams lost because they beat themselves."

Full credit was given a fine Chicago defense but in a game which included 22 penalties, the Bears were called for a dozen infractions and set back 105 yards. The Rams lost 116 on 10.

EASTERN DIVISION						
	W	L	T	Pct.	Pts.	OP
New York	11	3	0	.786	419	280
Houston	7	7	0	.500	303	248
Miami	5	8	1	.385	276	355
Boston	4	10	0	.286	229	406
Buffalo	1	12	1	.077	199	367

WESTERN DIVISION						
	W	L	T	Pct.	Pts.	OP
Oakland···	12	2	0	.857	453	233
Kansas City	12	2	0	.857	371	170
San Diego	9	5	0	.643	382	310
Denver	5	9	0	.357	255	404
Cincinnati	3	11	0	.214	215	329

Jim Turner's record 34th field goal

JETS SUBDUE MIAMI, 31-7

Namath Puts N.Y. Ahead, Parilli Mops Up

Miami, Fla., Dec. 15 (P)—The New York Jets, catching a Miami team crippled by the absence of injured quarterback B Griese, coasted into the American Football League division playoff today with a 31 to 7 victory over the Dolphins.

Joe Namath directed the Eastern Division champions to a 17-7 lead at halftime, then retired in favor of Babe Parilli, while Miami was alternating Rich Norton and rookie Kim Hammond at quarterback.

On New York's first offensive formation, Namath connected with Bake Turner on a 71-yard pass play to the Dolphin nine and, on the third play, Matt Snell banged six yards for the opening touchdown.

Boozer Scores

Jim Turner booted a 49-yard field goal and the Jets ran the margin to 17-0 on Emerson Boozer's one yard run after Ralph Baker intercepted Norton's deflected pass and returned it 29 yards to the Dolphin four.

Two successive mistakes by the Jets led to Miami's only touchdown in the second period. Clobbered after catching a Namath pass, George Sauer fumbled. John Bramlett snatched up the loose ball and ran 15 yards to the Jets' nine.

Then Randy Beverly cracked into Karl Noonan as Noonan reached for Norton's pass in the end zone and the penalty set the Dolphins up for Larry Csonka's one-yard scoring run.

Parilli Paves Way

Parilli led the Jets 82 yards to a touchdown on the first drive of the second half, hitting Turner for 29 yards to the Dolphin three and Pete Lammons for the score.

Bill Mathis ran two yards for the final touchdown in the fourth quarter.

Statistics

	Jets	Dolphins
First downs	19	12
Rushing yardage	136	41
Passing yardage	221	96
Return yardage	80	195
Passes	15-25-1	15-34-2
Punts	2-37	6-41
Fumbles lost	2	0
Yardage penalized	42	30

New York .... 10 7 7 7—31
Miami .... 0 7 0 0— 7

NY—Snell 6 run (Turner kick).
NY—FG Turner 49.
NY—Boozer 1 run (Turner kick).
MIA—Csonka 1 run (Moreau kick).
NY—Lammons 3 pass from Parilli (Turner kick).
NY—Mathis 2 run (Turner kick).
A—32,843.

RAIDERS RIP CHIEFS; GAIN AFL FINAL

Lamonica Aerials Give Oakland 41-6 Victory; Now Face Jets

Oakland, Dec. 22 (P) — Oakland quarterback Daryle Lamonica blitzed favored Kansas City with four touchdown passes in the first half, three of them to Fred Biletnikoff, as the Raiders smashed the Chiefs, 41 to 6, in their American Football League Western Division playoff today.

Lamonica wound up the chilly, sometimes rainy afternoon with five scoring pitches — the other two going to Warren Wells — before a record Oakland Coliseum throng of 53,605.

Title Game Sunday

Victory for the defending AFL champions sends them against the Jets of the Eastern Division in New York next Sunday for this season's title and the trip to the Super Bowl.

While Lamonica and his receivers glowed on offense, the Raider defensive corps was shutting off the Chiefs without a touchdown for the first time since the Jets did it five years ago.

In the last few minutes of the game, minor skirmishes broke out among the frustrated Chiefs and happy Raiders and for a while, it appeared that it might escalate into a full-fledged battle. But referees separated the opposing forces and the game ended without further incident.

Lamonica, a former Notre Dame star, pulled the trigger on touchdown passes three times in the first quarter to build a 21-0 lead over a team favored by from three to six points.

NAMATH-LED JETS REACH SUPER BOWL

Edge Raiders, 27-23, For AFL Title, Colt Date

By Ken Nigro
[Sun Staff Correspondent]

New York, Dec. 29—Joe Namath, almost the goat of the game a few minutes earlier, put his magic arm to work and calmly guided New York 68 yards in three lightning plays for the winning touchdown as the Jets edged the Oakland Raiders, 27 to 23, today to capture their first American Football League Championship.

Namath threw three successive complete passes in the last quarter drive with the final two going to veteran flanker Don Maynard. Both times Maynard outsmarted rookie defensive back George Atkinson.

Late Bid Fails

The touchdown pass, Namath's third of the afternoon, was a six-yarder and came with 6:47 remaining. It finally put the Jets ahead for good after they had lost the lead for the first time early in the quarter when Namath had his only pass interception.

Oakland, trying for its second straight AFL title, made one last bid in the closing minutes, but failed because of one of the rarest plays in football—a fumble recovery on a lateral pass.

It was a wild ending to a wild fourth period and the 62,627 fans braved bone-chilling temperatures and wind gusts up to 35 mph to watch their heroes complete a story book ending

Ewbank Pleased

Only seven years ago the Jets were on the verge of bankruptcy, but now they come out of it all with a cool $25,000 apiece if they beat the Baltimore Colts in the Super Bowl two weeks hence.

Today's victory was especially pleasing to coach Weeb Ewbank, who became the first man in history to coach a champion in both leagues. Ten years ago yesterday he guided the Colts to their first NFL title.

ALERT DEFENSE STOPS NELSEN AND KELLY; NFL TITLE IS FIRST SINCE 1959

17-Point Second Quarter Puts Baltimore In Command; Missed Field Goals Pose Cleveland's Only Threats

By Cameron C. Snyder
[Sun Staff Correspondent]

Cleveland, Dec. 29—Methodically, almost disdainfully, the Colts took apart a fine Cleveland Brown football team and scattered the pieces all over Municipal Stadium while registering a 34-to-0 National Football League championship victory today.

So, it is on to the Super Bowl engagement with the New York Jets for the brutally efficient Colts, who played as though there was no tomorrow.

The Browns made two mistakes that not only cost them the championship but very nearly their lives: they beat the Colts in the 1964 championship game, 27 to 0, and then handed Baltimore its only loss during the 1968 season, 30-20.

Honors Are Shared

These two losses have been festering under the Colts' hides for a long time and erupted today in one of the finest displays of power football seen in pro ranks for a decade or more.

Tom Matte emerged as the star, scoring three touchdowns, all running, to equal the championship game record, held jointly by former Brown Otto Graham in 1954 and end Gary Collins, who scored all three touchdowns in the Browns' 1964 victory over the Colts.

But, Matte, who scored on runs of 1, 12 and 2 yards, had to share all his honors with an offensive line that pounded the Brown defense into the spongy turf and Jerry Hill, the fullback who blocked like three men.

There were others too. Earl Morrall directed the assault and gave his runners the best possible lanes to speed down on the scarred turf which was muddy in some spots and concrete-hard in others.

Namath Leads Jets To 16-7 Super Bowl Victory Over Heavily-Favored Colts For Pro Grid Title

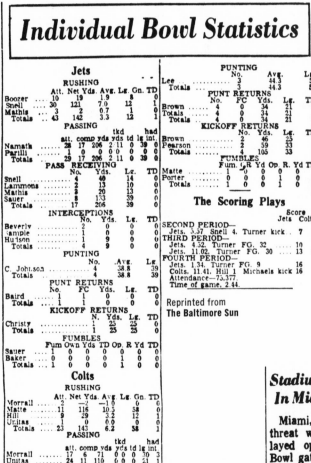

Individual Bowl Statistics

Jets

RUSHING

	Att.	Net Yds.	Avg.	Lg. Gn.	TD
Boozer	10	19	1.9	8	0
Snell	30	121	7.0	12	1
Mathis	3	2	0.7	1	0
Totals	43	142	3.3	12	1

PASSING

	att.	comp	yds	tkd yds	td	lg	int.
Namath	28	17	206	2 11	0	39	0
Parilli	1	0	0	0 0	0	0	0
Totals	29	17	206	2 11	0	39	0

PASS RECEIVING

	No.	Yds.	Lg.	TD
Snell	4	40	14	0
Lammons	2	13	10	0
Mathis	3	20	13	0
Sauer	8	133	39	0
Totals	17	206	39	0

INTERCEPTIONS

	No.	Yds.	Lg.	TD
Beverly	2	0	0	0
Sample	1	0	0	0
Hudson	1	9	0	0
Totals	4	9	0	0

PUNTING

	No.	Avg.	Lg.
C. Johnson	4	38.8	39
Totals	4	38.8	39

PUNT RETURNS

	No.	FC	Yds.	Lg.	TD
Baird	1	1	0	0	0
Totals	1	1	0	0	0

KICKOFF RETURNS

	N.	Yds.	Lg.	TD
Christy	1	25	25	0
Totals	1	25	25	0

FUMBLES

	Fum	Own Yds	TD	Op. R Yd	TD
Sauer	1	0 0	0	0 0	0
Baker	0	0 0	0	1 0	0
Totals	1	0 0	0	1 0	0

Colts

RUSHING

	Att.	Net Yds.	Avg.	Lg. Gn.	TD
Morrall	2	-2	-1.0	0	0
Matte	11	116	10.5	58	0
Hill	9	29	3.2	12	1
Unitas	1	0	0.0	0	0
Totals	23	143	6.2	58	1

PASSING

	att.	comp	yds	tkd yds	td	lg	int.
Morrall	17	6	71	0 0	0	30	3
Unitas	24	11	110	0 0	0	30	1
Totals	41	17	181	0 0	0	30	4

PASS RECEIVING

	No.	Yds.	Lg.	TD
Mackey	3	35	19	0
Mitchell	1	15	15	0
Richardson	6	58	21	0
Matte	2	30	30	0
Hill	2	1	1	0
Orr	3	42	17	0
Totals	17	181	30	0

PUNTING

	No.	Avg.	Lg.
Lee	3	44.3	51
Totals	3	44.3	51

PUNT RETURNS

	No.	FC	Yds.	Lg.	TD
Brown	4	0	34	21	0
Totals	4	0	34	21	0
Totals	4	0	34	21	0

KICKOFF RETURNS

	No.	Yds.	Lg.	TD
Brown	2	46	25	0
Pearson	2	59	33	0
Totals	4	105	33	0

FUMBLES

	Fum.	O R Yd	Op. R. Yd	TD
Matte	1	0 0	0 0	0
Porter	0	0 0	1 0	0
Totals	1	0 0	1 0	0

The Scoring Plays

	Score Jets	Colts
SECOND PERIOD—		
Jets, 5.57 Snell 4, Turner kick .	7	0
THIRD PERIOD—		
Jets, 4.52, Turner FG. 32	10	0
Jets, 11.02, Turner FG. 30	13	0
FOURTH PERIOD—		
Jets, 1.34, Turner FG. 9	16	0
Colts, 11.41, Hill 1 Michaels kick	16	7

Attendance—75,377.
Time of game, 2.44.

Reprinted from
The Baltimore Sun

Stadium Bomb Threat In Miami Proves False

Miami, Jan. 12 (AP)—A bomb threat which proved false delayed opening of the Orange Bowl gates today for the Super Bowl football game, but most of the 73,377 fans knew nothing of the threat.

Miami Police Maj. Newell Horne said a man called local radio and television stations, said he was associated with the Black Power movement and warned that 500 pounds of plastic explosive were hidden in the stadium.

More than 100 uniformed Miami police and firemen, FBI agents and county bomb squad experts searched 90 minutes, Horne said. The gates were opened 30 minutes later.

JETS LET ALL KNOW WHO WON

Many Players Come In For Their Share Of Plaudits

Miami, Jan. 12 (AP)—Eighteen point underdogs?

That was the cry that resounded through the New York Jet's dressing room after the American Football League champions had trimmed the Baltimore Colts, 16 to 7, today and broke the National Football League's domination of the Super Bowl since its inception three years ago.

Not once did the American League representatives fail to let everybody in the steaming hot, humid quarters know that they were the best. They were the champions just as they said they would be despite the great record of the Colts and the odds favoring the NFL champs.

Joe Is Coaxed

"It is a victory for the entire American Football League," said quarterback Joe Namath, who goaded the Colts' all week and then made his words stick by completing 17 of 28 passes for 206 yards and calling what coach Weeb Ewbank described as an almost perfect game.

Namath had to be coaxed by Phil Iselin, to appear on television. Then the controversial quarterback said "never were so many people wrong."

There was hardly a player in the steaming dressing room who didn't come in for a share of the plaudits.

ALLEN GETS JOB BACK WITH RAMS

Coach, Owner Reeves Pledge Each Other Closer Support

Los Angeles, Jan. 6 (AP)—A peace came to th embattled Los Angeles Rams today when Coach George Allen, abruptly fired the day after Christmas, was rehired by owner-president Daniel F. Reeves.

The two appeared together at a mid-afternoon news confernece in a West Los Angeles hotel several hours after the club had announced that Allen was returning to the team.

The session lasted 30 minutes, during which Reeves announced that Allen's contract, which had two years left to run, remains the same and with the same salary, reportedly $40,000 a year.

Pro Football Draft Picks

FIRST ROUND

Buffalo—O. J. Simpson, Southern Cal. halfback, 6-1, 207. Atlanta—George Kunz, Notre Dame tackle, 6-5, 245. Philadelphia—Leroy Keyes, Purdue halfback, 6-3, 205. Pittsburgh—Joe Greene, North Texas State tackle, 6-4, 274. Cincinnati—Greg Cook, Cincinnati quarterback, 6-4, 200. Boston—Ron Sellers, Florida State split end, 6-4, 187. San Francisco (from New Orleans)—Ted Kwalick, Penn Stae split end, 6-4, 230. Los Angeles (from Detroit)—Larry Smith, Florida halfback, 6-4, 221. San Diego (from Denver) Marty Domres, Columbia quarterback, 6-4, 212. Los Angeles (from Washington)—Jim Seymour, Notre Dame split end, 6-4, 205. Miami—Bill Stanill, Georgia tackle, 6-5, 245.

Green Bay—Richie Moore, Villanova tackle, 6-7, 291. Chicago—Rufus Mayes, Ohio State tackle, 6-5, 250. N.Y. Giants—Fred Dryer, San Diego State defensive end. Houston—Ron Pritchard, Arizona State linebacker, 6-0, 230. San Francisco—Gene Washington, Stanford flanker, 6-1, 182. New Orleans (from Minnesota)—John Shinners, Xavier guard, 6-3, 255. San Diego—Bob Babich, Miami of Ohio linebacker, 6-2, 225. St. Louis—Roger Wehrli, Missouri defensive back, 6-0, 184. Cleveland—Ron Johnson, Michigan running back, 6-1, 196. Los Angeles—Bob Klein, Southern Cal tight end, 6-5, 238. Oakland—Art Thomas, Syracuse defensive tackle, 6-5, 236. Kansas City—Jim Matsalis, Tennessee State defensive back. Dallas—Calvin Hill, Yale running back, 6-3, 210. COLTS—Eddie Hinton, Oklahoma flanker, 6-0, 201. N.Y. Jets—Dave Foley, Ohio State tackle, 6-5, 255.

SECOND ROUND

Buffalo, running back Bill Enyart, Oregon State; Philadelphia, Ernest Calloway, linebacker, Texas Southern; Atlanta, Paul Gipson, running back, Houston; Pittsburgh, Terry Hanratty, Notre Dame quarterback; Cincinnati, Bill Bergey, linebacker, Arkansas State; Boston, Mike Montler, offensive tackle, Colorado; Colts, from New Orleans, Ted Hendricks, defensive end, Miami; Detroit, Altie Taylor, running back. Utah State; St. Louis, from Washington, Rolf Krueger, defensive tackle, Texas A&M; Denver, Grady Cavness, defensive back, Texas-El Paso; Miami, Bob Heinz, defensive end, Pacific; Green Bay, Dave Bradley, tackle, Penn State; Minnesota, from Giants, Ed White, defensive guard, California; Houston, Jerry Levias, flanker, Southern Methodist; Chicago, Bob Douglass, quarterback, Kansas; Pittsburgh, from San Francisco through Cleveland, Warren Bankston, running back, Tulane; Minnesota, Volly Murphy, flanker, Texas-El Paso.

San Diego, Ron Sayers, running back, Omaha; New Orleans, from St. Louis, Rich Neal, defensive end, Southern University; Washington, from Cleveland, Eugene Epps, defensive back, Texas-El Paso; Detroit, from Los Angeles, Jim Yarbrough, tight end, Florida; Kansas City, Ed Podolak, running back, Iowa; Dallas, Richmond Flowers, flanker, Tennessee; Oakland, George Buehler, guard, Stanford; Colts, Tommy Maxwell, defensive back, Texas A&M; New York Jets, Al Woodall, quarterback, Duke.

THIRD ROUND

Buffalo, Julian Nunamaker, defensive end, Tennessee-Martin; Atlanta, Malcom Snider, Tackle, Stanford; Cleveland, from Philadelphia, Al Jenkins, guard, Tulsa; Pittsburgh, Jon Kolb, center, Oklahoma State; Cincinnati, Louis Thomas, split end, Utah; Boston, Carl Garrett, running back, New Mexico Highlands; Detroit, from New Orleans, Larry Walton, flanker, Arizona State; New York Giants, from Detroit, Vernon Vanoy, defensive end, Kansas.

Denver, Bill Thompson, defensive back, Maryland State; Washington, Ed Cross, running back, Arkansas A&M; Miami, Eugene Morris, running back, West Texas State; Green Bay, John Spilis, flanker, Northern Illinois; Houston, Elbert Drungo, tackle, Tennessee State; Chicago, Russ Montgomery, running back, Texas Christian; Atlanta, from Giants through Los Angeles, Jon Sandstrom, guard, Oregon State; Dallas, from San Francisco, Tom Stincic, linebacker, Michigan; Philadelphia, from Minnesota, Bill Bradley, defensive back, Texas; San Diego, Eugene Ferguson, tackle, Norfolk State.

St. Louis, Chip Healey, linebacker, Vanderbilt; Cleveland, Charles Glass, tight end, Florida State; St. Louis, from Los Angeles through Detroit, Terry Brown, defensive back, Oklahoma State; Dallas, Halvor Hagen, defensive tackle, Weber state; Oakland, Lloyd Edwards, tight end, San Diego State; Kansas City, Morris Streud, tight end, Clark; Colts, Dennis Nelson, tackle, Illinois Normal; Houston, from Jets, Rich Johnson, running back, Illinois.

FOURTH ROUND

Buffalo, Mike Richey, tackle, North Carolina; Philadelphia, Bob Kuechenberg, guard, Notre Dame; Atlanta, Jim Mitchell, tight end, Prairie View; Pittsburgh, Bob Campbell, running back, Penn State; Cincinnati, Clem Turner, running back, Cincinnati; Denver, from Boston through Kansas City, Mike Schnitker, linebacker, Colorado; New Orleans, Dennis Hale, defensive back, Minnesota.

San Francisco, from Detroit, Jim Sniadecki, linebacker, Indiana; Colts, from Washington, Jacky Stewart, running back, Texas Tech; Denver, Ed Hayes, defensive back, Morgan State; Miami, Norman McBride, linebacker, Utah; Green Bay, Perry Williams, running back, Purdue; Chicago, Rudy Redmond, defensive back, Pacific.

New York Giants, Rich Houston, flanker, East Texas State; Houston, Charles Joiner, defensive back, Grambling; San Francisco, Gene Moore, running back, Occidental; Minnesota, Mike McCaffrey, linebacker, California; Houston, from San Diego, Roy Gerela, punter, New Mexico State; St. Louis, Bill Rhodes, guard, Florida State; Cleveland, Fred Summers, defensive back, Wake Forest.

Los Angeles, John Zook, defensive end, Kansas; Oakland, Ruby Jackson, tackle, New Mexico State; Kansas City, Jack Rudnay, center, Northwestern; New Orleans, from Dallas, Bob Hudspeth, tackle, Southern Illinois; Atlanta, from Baltimore, Dickie Lyons, defensive back, Kentucky; New York Jets, Ezell Jones, tackle, Minnesota.

FIFTH ROUND

Buffalo, Ben Mayes, defensive tackle, Drake; Minnesota, from Atlanta, Jim Barnes, Guard, Arkansas; Philadelphia, Jim Anderson, guard, Missouri; St. Louis, from Pittsburgh, Walt Shockley, running back San Jose State; Cincinnati, Guy Dennis, guard, Florida; Boston, Onree Jackson, quarterback, Alabama A&M; New Orleans, Tony Kvasky, defensive back, Syracuse; Minnesota, from Detroit through Pittsburgh, Mike O'Shea, split end, Utah State.

Denver, Frank Quayle, running back, Virginia; Washington, Bill Kishman, defensive back, Colorado State; Miami, Willie Pearson, defensive back, North Carolina A.&T.; Green Bay, Bill Hayhoe, defensive tackle, Southern California; New Orleans, from Giants, Keith Christensen, tackle, Kansas; Houston, John Peacock, defensive back, Houston; Chicago, Jim Winegardner, tight end, Notre Dame; San Francisco, Earl Edwards, defensive tackle, Wichita; Minnesota, Corny Davis, running back, Kansas State.

San Diego, Harry Orszulak, flanker, Pitt; St. Louis, Gene Huey, flanker, Wyoming; Cleveland, Fair Hooker, flanker, Arizona State; Dallas, from Los Angeles, Chuck Kyle, linebacker, Purdue; Kansas City, Bob Stein, linebacker, Minnesota; Atlanta, from Dallas through Baltimore, Tony Pleviak, defensive end, Illinois; Miami, Karl Kremser, kicker, Tennessee; Colts, Keith Dunlap, defensive tackle, Tennessee State; New York Jets, Chris Gilbert, running back, Texas.

Reprinted from
The Baltimore Sun

NFL Keeps Out Of Lombardi Case

But Redskin President Is Quoted as Saying That Commissioner Had Intervened

New York, Feb. 4 (AP) — The National Football League is keeping hands off in the tug-of-war between the Redskins and Packers for the services of Vince Lombardi.

"The NFL is not involved at this time," Commissioner Pete Rozelle said today, speaking from his office at the league headquarters.

"Our understanding is that Mr. Lombardi's request for release from his contract is being reviewed by the Green Bay Board of Directors."

Says Rozelle Intervened

Despite Rozelle's statement, a Washington newspaper quoted the Redskins' club president as saying the football commissioner had intervened to nip an announcement that the Lombardi deal was sealed.

The executive, Edward Bennett Williams, was quoted as saying Rozelle telephoned him only five minutes before his news conference late yesterday.

"I told him what I was going to say and he told me not to," Williams said. "He told me that I could have the deal or the press conference, but not both."

So a tight-lipped Williams walked into the news conference and said he had nothing to say.

The Washington *Daily News* quoted Williams as saying, "I was never more humiliated .. I was set to walk in there and break the news ... but I was warned."

Rozelle acknowledged after Williams' revelation that he had phoned the Redskins' president. "Yes, I talked with both sides and offered counsel," the NFL executive said.

Lombardi, unruffled by the mounting furor over his proposed defection, arrived here tonight to wait out the tug-of-war. Lombardi, seeking release as general manager of the Packers so that he can move in as general manager, coach and part owner of the Washington club, flew here to attend an awards banquet tomorrow night.

The Packers' board of directors is scheduled to meet at the same time in Green Bay to decide whether or not to let him out of the pact, which runs through Jan. 31, 1974.

'No Ill Feelings'

"I would hope they will release me, of course." Lombardi said at the airport. "If they don't—then I'll be back in Green Bay next year."

Lombardi, who stepped down from his dual role as manager-coach of the Packers last year, repeated his earlier statements that there has been, and will be, "no ill feelings" between himself and the Green Bay organization regardless of the directors' decision.

"The Packers have contributed much to Vince Lombardi in the last 10 years," he said, "and I feel Vince Lombardi has contributed something to the Packers."

Willing To Go Back

"There hasn't been a single instance of ill feeling toward me from the Packers' management."

Asked if it wouldn't be human for him to feel resentment toward the Green Bay club if it refused to let him out of his contract, Lombardi replied: "Well, I've been accused o being inhuman before. Maybe this is part of it."

Special Packer Meeting

The special board meeting is the first called since Lombardi arrived in Green Bay in 1959 as coach and general manager. According to the Milwaukee Sentinel tonight, the meeting was called because the executive committee felt a decision of this importance should be explained to the 45-member board because of the many ramifications.

"If I were the owner of the club, there would be no question about telling what my feelings are," said Dominic Olejniczak, Packer president. "But we operate as a team in Green Bay and we owe the directors the courtesy of this meeting."

Coached 5 Champions

Lombardi, a stern disciplinarian who coached Green Bay to five championships before turning over the reins last fall to Phil Bengston, announced yesterday that he had asked for his release to take a position with the Washington Redskins.

Lombardi Released To Take 'Skins Post

Green Bay, Wis., Feb. 5 (AP)—The Green Bay Packers said tonight its board of directors agreed to release Vince Lombardi from his contract, allowing him to take command of the Washington Redskins. Directors had met in emergency session for the first time in a decade to discuss Lombardi's request.

Lombardi, now general manager of the National Football League team, requested Monday to be freed from his contract to join the Redskins as part owner, executive vice president and head coach.

With Regret

"With regret, the resolution was unanimously adopted," Dominic Olejniczak, president of the Packers, said after the first emergency meeting of the Board of Directors in 10 years.

"To a man, the entire board felt like the executive committee had felt that there wasn't anything we would not have done to have kept Vince Lombardi," Olejniczaksaid.

The prseident of the Packe. corporation said there was considerable discussion among board members on whether the club should be reimbursed by the Redskins. He said no terms are being asked.

Difficult To Measure

"It is difficult to measure the true value of compensation," he said. "I would not cheapen this deal by measuring it in money or a couple of players."

Lombardi, general manager of the National Football League club for 10 years and coach until last year, had asked for cancellation of the final five years of his Green Bay contract to become executive vice president, coach and stockholder with the Washington club.

Olejniczak said one basic reason for the board's decision to agree was to allow Lombardi, 55, to acquire stock in a pro football team, a desire Lombardi had often expressed.

Has Opportunity

"Perhaps the most dominant motivation in our coming to this conclusion was the fact that Vince Lombardi had an opportunity to purchase from the Washington Redskins a substantial block of stock," Olejniczak told the board.

"Stock in football corporations is difficult to obtain and, in all probability, this would be the chance of a lifetime for Mr. Lombardi," he said.

"Lombardi has served us well, far and above the call of duty, and we felt it would be a dog-in-the-manger attitude if we were to stand in his way of obtaining a very profitable and substantial interest in the Washington ball club," he said, speaking as a member of the Green Bay executive committee.

After leading the Packers to a nine-year record of 141-39-4, five NFL championships and two Super Bowl titles, Lombardi stepped down as coach last year, saying both jobs were too much for one man.

WOLMAN SEEKS TO SELL EAGLES

Philadelphia Owner Would Make $15.6 Million Deal

By GERALD A. FITZGERALD

Jerry Wolman, majority owner of the Philadelphia Eagles, asked the Federal bankruptcy referee in Baltimore yesterday to authorize the sale of the football team for $15.6 million.

A contract filed with Joseph O. Kaiser, the referee, called for the sale of the club to Leonard M. Tose, a Norristown, Pa. trucking executive, on May 1.

The agreement also provides that if Wolman can raise approximately $11.2 million before that date to pay outstanding claims against the club by secured creditors, the sale will not be valid.

Others Seek Eagles

At least four other individuals or groups have also expressed interest in buying the National League team, but Kaiser would not give their identities.

"The exact procedures I haven't worked out," Kaiser said, but all interested parties will be given a chance to bid on the team before a hearing is held on the Wolman petition later this month.

Earlier Agreement

Kaiser said he plans to meet tomorrow with Wolman's lawyers to settle on the procedures to be followed, and after that he said he will announce a hearing date.

Kaiser meanwhile confirmed that Wolman earlier had worked out another agreement with Tose by which Wolman was to have obtained through a loan, funds that he needed to shore up his troubled financial empire.

The agreement fell through, Kaiser said, when the First Pennsylvania Banking and Trust Company, of Philadelphia, refused to go along with the arrangement.

Kaiser said that the contract filed with him yesterday provides for the sale of all the club's assets, including the franchise, equipment and player contracts.

The contract provides that up to $2 million of the $15.6 million conditional sales price may be used to pay off corporate debt associated with the club's past operations, including a $100,000 broker's fee to Robert Melnick, of Washington, D.C.

RAIDERS NAME MADDEN COACH

Aide, 33, Steps Up To Top Job At Oakland

Oakland, Feb. 4 P—The Oakland Raiders once again dipped into their own ranks for a head coach today, naming assistant John Madden to the job.

Madden, who at 33 becomes professional football's youngest coach, replaces John Rauch at the helm of the American Football League club which won the championship in 1967 and the Western Division title in '68. Rauch resigned after the 1968 season to become coach of the Buffalo Bills.

Al Davis, managing general partner of the Raiders and boss of certainly the most tightlipped, close-knit front office in the sport, made the announcement in a brief press release.

Madden Out Of Town

Madden was out of town on personal business.

Davis said he would have no comment on the new coach until a news conference tomorrow morning at which Madden is to be present.

"Al moves in mysterious way his wonders to perform," said an onlooker of Davis, who was head coach of the Raiders before becoming commissioner of the AFL and then returning to Oakland. Rauch was an Oakland assistant before taking over for Davis in 1966.

Madden was the youngest assistant on the staff last year and for the past two years has worked with the Raiders' linebacking corps, developing such outstanding players as Dan Connors, Gus Otto and Ralph Oliver.

NOLL PLUNGES INTO BIG TASK

Knows Steelers Would Not Change If Doing Well

By SEYMOUR S. SMITH
[Assistant Sports Editor of The Sun]

It's been a week for making promises, some of which may even be kept, few of which will be remembered. It's been a week for promises and hopes and dreams as Chuck Noll, only eight days ago one of Don Shula's aides on the Colts, attempts to pump new life into one of pro football's most consistent losers — the Pittsburgh Steelers.

"Let's face it, if the Steelers were doing well, I wouldn't be here," the 37-year-old Noll was saying on the anniversary of his first week as coach. "One of the reporters at the press conference said Pittsburgh is 'the City of Losers.' Well, maybe we'll change history. I'm prepared as I'll ever be. It's as good a time as any to find out."

Noll Seeking Assistants

"Our immediate task is to start building a staff. We'll try to build up a team, a congenial group which works together. All of the aides will enjoy equal status with each in charge of a specific area of responsibility. No single assistant will be in charge of the overall defense or offense. The overall operation of the team is my responsibility.

"I'm pleased with what we got in the draft. We picked the best football player available in every round, regardless of what position he played. I think the first choice (Joe Greene, of North Texas State) worked out real well for us. Pass defense begins with the rush on the passer and Greene is a big strong tough boy who wants to play real bad.

"I was really surprised at the efficiency of the organization. Art Rooney deserves a pat on the back. We had just as much information as the Colts had. I saw Greene play two years and the reports by the Pittsburgh scouts substantiated my feeling about him. We did have one advantage—drafting fourth. But I don't want that advantage again."

Colts, Browns And Steelers Move To AFL In Merger

Reprinted from
The Baltimore Sun papers

March 25

—Buoniconti to Miami

By JACK CLARY

The Patriots made two bold moves to strengthen themselves yesterday when they traded away all-star defensive players Nick Buoniconti, their all-league middle linebacker, and top defensive back Leroy Mitchell. Six players were received, in return.

Buoniconti went to the Miami Dolphins for quarterback Kim Hammond, linebacker John Bramlett and an undisclosed draft choice.

Earlier in the day, Mitchell and a high draft pick wound up in Houston. The return was running back Sid Blanks, flanker Charley Frazier, cornerback Larry Carwell and linebacker Ron Caveness.

THE MOVES WERE THE FIRST to be made by new head coach Clive Rush. Both were shockers in that no one really wanted to see Buonicotni leave the Patriots and just as many didn't expect that Mitchell, probably the team's best defensive back, would leave.

"We considered Mitchell one of the finest cornerbacks in pro football," Rush said. "But we had the chance to get a good amount of talent in return for him. We felt we couldn't afford to pass up that opportunity. It took a man of his caliber to get four players we hope will help us right away."

In trading Buoniconti, Rush noted:

"This was the best chance to get the man everyone in the league considers the best back-up quarterback."

That would be Hammond, a rookie with the Dolphins last year who threw a grand total of 26 passes and completed half of them while playing behind Bob Griese. In effect, what the Patriots have obtained is a rookie quarterback and a linebacker whom they could have had two years ago off the waiver list for one of the league's best middle linebackers.

The plus points in Hammond's favor are that he was the batterymate for the Pats new No .1 draft pick, Ron Sellers, for two years at Florida State. In their last year together, they led their team to the Gator Bowl, tieing Penn State which was quarterbacked by Tom Sherman, also a Patriots' QB.

The trade didn't surprise Buoniconti. seven years a Patriot and five of which he was all-league selection at middle linebacker.

eprinted from the **Boston Herald Traveler**, ourtesy the **Boston Herald American**

EAGLE SALE COMPLETED

Club Ownership Is Turned Over To Tose

Philadelphia, May 1 ℗—The Philadelphia Eagles of the National Football League were sold tonight with one string attached to the $16,055,000 deal.

The ownership of the club was turned over by financially pressed Jerry Wolman to Leonard Tose, Norristown, Pa., trucking magnate. The deal was completed in a mid-city bank building. Wolman paid $5,505,000 for the team in 1964.

The one string is the private agreement between Tose and Wolman that if Wolman can raise the $16,055,000 by August 1, he can repurchase the team. In the interim, Tese is expected to completely revamp the club from general manager and coach down to the lowest executive.

Tose is expected to fire general manager-coach Joe Kuharich, buying up the last 11-years of Kuharich's 15-year contract valued at an estimated $50,000 a year. The new owner then is believed to name Peet Retzlaff, one-time all-pro end of the Eagles, as the new general manager.

TRANSFERS BEGIN WITH 1970 SLATE

By CAMERON C. SNYDER
(Sun Staff Correspondent)

New York, May 10—The Baltimore Colts, champions of the National Football League, will in 1970 try to become the kings of the American Football League, which means beating their Super Bowl conquerors, the New York Jets, twice each season.

Joining the Colts from the old circuit were Eastern Conference champions Cleveland Browns and the long-established Pittsburgh Steelers.

Colts With Jets

The Colts will be in Division II of what now is the American Conference under the banner of the National Football League. Joining Baltimore in the second division are Boston, Buffalo (with O. J. Simpson), Miami and, of course, the Jets.

The first division will have Cincinnati, Cleveland, Houston and Pittsburgh. This refuted a statement by Commissioner Pete Rozelle made earlier that each one of the three teams moving into the AFL would go into separate divisions. He explained that the reasons were the long-time rivalry between Cleveland and Pittsburgh and a favorable setup for a home-state rivalry between the Browns and Bengals.

The third division includes Denver, Kansas City, Oakland and San Diego.

It took the 26 owners of pro football franchises 35 hours and 45 minutes of marathon session to arrive at the agreement. Rozelle made sure he wore down any opposition to the three-team move from what was the 16-team NFL by keeping the owners secluded and without sleep in the pro football leagues headquarters on Park avenue.

JOE NAMATH RETURNS TO GRID WARS

Jet QB Agrees To Bow Out Of Bar Business At Rozelle Order

New York, July 18 (P)—Joe Namath bowed to pressure and agreed today to sell his interest in a swinging East Side night club so he could return as quarterback of the New York Jets.

The decision came after a near all-day conference with commissioner Pete Rozelle in the National Football League headquarters.

The announcement was made by Rozelle at a mammoth press conference with scores of newsmen, cameramen and television cameramen.

Total Accord

"I'm happy to announce Joe will be back with the Jets," the commissioner said. "He and I have privately reached total accord. He is selling his interest in Bachelors III and we consider the entire matter closed."

Although Rozelle would neither confirm nor deny it, there almost certainly were conditions attached to Namath's returning to the Jets, other than selling Bachelors III. "But," Rozelle pointed out, "he's not on probation."

Namath did not comment on that aspect of the situation either and said he was leaving almost immediately for Los Angeles on business, but "I'll definitely be back in camp Sunday."

amath announced his retirement in a tearful news conference June 6, refusing to sell his half-interest in Bachelors III as ordered by Rozelle.

Namath returned from California, where he was making a movie, last Saturday night, but did not show at the opening of the Jets' training Sunday at Hofstra University campus in Hempstead, N.Y.

Met Teammates

Wednesday night, Namath met secretly with veteran teammates of the Super Bowl champions in the training room at Hofstra and told them he thought the situation might be resolved this weekend. Namath has been meeting all week long with Rozelle. Namath's attorney, James Walsh, also has been in on the conferences.

When he made his announcement June 6, the former University of Alabama quarterback, star of the Jets' Super Bowl victory over Baltimore in January, said he had been threatened with suspension if he did not dispose of his interest in the night club.

Rozelle insisted the place was frequented by unsavory characters and, while Namath himself had not been found guilty of wrong-doing, pro football had to avoid the "appearance of evil."

REDSKIN OWNER MARSHALL DEAD

'Skins President Emeritus Had Colorful Career

Washington, Aug 9 (P)—George Preston Marshall, the caustic, flamboyant, controversial football pioneer and president emeritus of the Washington Redskins, died at his home in illness. He was 72.

Marshall, whose stormy career as businessman, showman and promoter was capped with his right-fisted, one-man rule of the National Football League Redskins, had been in declining health since a henria operation in the summer of 1962.

A light stroke in July, 1963 hospitalized him for a time but after he went home a few weeks later he seldom left his bed again.

Son of a West Virginia newspaper publisher who later operated a lundry in Washington, Marshall made a fortune from laundry operations, then turned to sports promotion.

Complete Showman

A showman to his fingertips, Marshall built the Redskins into a solid attraction in Washington. He liked to boast that since he moved the Redskins here in 1937, he never had a losing year at the gate.

Marshall also left his mark on the NFL with such brain children as the interdivisional playoff for the NFL championship and the Pro Bowl.

As a promotor, Marshall was inventive and successful. He was the first professional owner to hire a marching band and to have his own team song, "Hail to the Redskins."

GEORGE P. MARSHALL
Redskin founder dies at 72

O.J. SIMPSON, BILLS AGREE TO TERMS

Contract to Run Four Years—Undisclosed Figure Called Highest Since Merger

By The Associated Press

BUFFALO, Aug. 9—O. J. Simpson, possibly the most prized collegian to enter pro football, agreed to terms with the Buffalo Bills of the American Football League today for a contract that the club said would make him the highest paid rookie since the merger between the American and National Leagues. The contract will run for four years.

In a statement issued by the Bills' owner, Ralph C. Wilson, terms of the contract for the former Southern California halfback were not announced, but it was disclosed that "Simpson will be getting more than any rookie has been paid since the merger." That would exceed $80,000 a year.

It has been reported that the highest paid rookie since the merger of the two leagues in 1966 was Steve Spurrier, San Francisco quarterback who was believed to have signed a three-year contract for approximately $250,000.

Simpson originally sought a five-year contract for $600,000 plus a $500,000 loan, but withdrew his request for a loan recently while raising his money demands to $650,000. The Bills had countered with an offer of a $250,000 contract over five years.

The statement by Wilson said: "On behalf of the Buffalo management, I am delighted to announce a contract agreement has been reached with O. J. Simpson. It covers a four-year period.

"In deference to O. J., we are not disclosing the financial figures, but they represent what we feel is a fair and sensible compromise.

"Simpson will be getting more than any rookie has been paid since the merger, and Buffalo will be getting what it feels is an outstanding football player who one day may take a place among the great running backs of this game."

Through Front Office Error

BROWNS LOSE SABATINO

By CHUCK HEATON, Staff Writer

TACOMA, WASH. — Bill Sabatino is gone from the rowns again — and this time for good.

The big defensive tackle, who walked out of the Hiram ollege training camp a couple of weeks ago for no apparat reason and then returned three days later, now is the roperty of the Atlanta Falcons.

Through an administrative misinterpretation by the rowns' front office, the 6-3, 250-pound lineman was placed a the team's reserve list when he left camp. Thus waivers d to be asked on him with no recall possible when he eturned.

THREE TEAMS CLAIMED the second-year gridder he was born in Alliance, O., but played his college football at the University of Colorado. Two of them withdrew men they learned the circumstances of the case.

Atlanta was the third and Coach Norm Van Brocklin efused to relinquish his claim.

BLANTON COLLIER, UPSET about the loss, wanted make it clear that Sabatino's departure had nothing to o with his earlier AWOL.

"Bill played well before he left and has continued to do since his return," the coach asserted. "He's a fine young man and I hate to see him go. He had a chance to be a egular defensive tackle."

Big Sabo, very well liked by his teammates, blamed his arlier departure on "pressure."

"I SIMPLY WAS mixed up then and made a mistake," e recalled last night before departing for the Falcon's raining camp in Tennessee. "This thing wouldn't have appened if I hadn't left the Brown's camp earlier.

"I like the Browns and am sorry about this. I wish hem the best of luck. I made my bed, though, and I guess 'll just have to lie in it."

Bill's departure could necessitate some juggling of the efensive line. The third tackle now is Joe Righetti, a rook-e from Waynesburg College.

THERE IS A DISTINCT possibility that either Ron Snidow, veteran obtained from Washington a year ago or Bob Oliver, first-year man from Abiline Christian, will be shift-d. They are defensive ends.

This probably will not be done, however, until after omorrow night's second exhibition game against the Rams n Los Angeles.

rinted from
e Cleveland Plain Dealer

BENGALS TOP MIAMI, 27-21

QB Cook Returns Home To Spark Victory

Cincinnati, Sept. 14 (P) — Rookie Greg Cook fired two touchdown passes and Cincinnati's defense withstood a late Miami thrust as the Bengals whipped the Dolphins, 27 to 21, today in the American Football League opener for both teams.

The victory for coach Paul Brown was his 300th in a coaching career spanning 35 years. But it was marred by the sudden death this morning of Bengal linebacker Frank Buncom.

Buncom, 29, an eight-year pro from Southern California, died of a blood clot on the left lung.

Returns Home

A crowd of 25,335 watched Cook return to Nippert Stadium, where he had starred at University of Cincinnati, and connect with Eric Crabtree for two second quarter scores.

The first touchdown strike covered 69 yards. Three minutes later Crabtree made a diving catch in the end zone on a 25-yard pass.

Rookie linebacker Bill Bergey intercepted Bob Griese's pass midway through the first period and rambled 58 yards to set up Cincinnati's first touchdown.

Morris Scores

Paul Robinson bolted across from the 4-yard line for the score which was wiped out 7 seconds later when Miami's Mercury Morris sped 105 yards on the ensuing kickoff.

Cincinnati charged ahead, 21 to 7, but Griese hit Karl Noonan with a 15-yard TD pass with 3 seconds remaining in the half.

Horst Muhlmann booted a pair of third-period field goals, both from 21 yards to boost the Bengals' advantage to 27 to 14.

But Griese brought the Dolphins back late in the fourth quarter on a 62-yard march in seven plays. Jim Kiick scored the touchdown from two yards out.

Statistics

DOLPHINS	BENGALS	
First Downs	19	11
Rushing yardage	79	101
Passing yardage	94	165
Return yardage	94	105
Passes	19-39-2	11-21-1
Punts	7-39	9-42
Fumbles lost	0	0
Yards penalized	78	52

Miami	7	7	0	7—21
Cincinnati	7	14	6	0—27

CIN—Robinson 4 run (Muhlmann kick).
MIA—Morris 105 run (Kremser kick).
CIN—Crabtree 69 pass from Cook (Muhlmann kick).
CIN—Crabtree 25 pass from Cook (Muhlmann kick).
MIA—Noonan 13 pass from Griese (Kremser kick).
CIN—FG Muhlmann 21.
CIN—FG Muhlmann 21.
MIA—Kiick 2 run (Kremser kick).
A—25,335.

FRANK BUNCOM, OF BENGALS, DIES

Heart Attack Fells AFL All-Star Linebacker

Cincinnati, Sept. 14 (P)—Frank Buncom, 29-year-old linebacker for the Cincinnati Bengals of the American Football League, died early today in his hotel room, apparently of a heart attack.

Doctors said a blood clot on the left lung caused severe shock to his body resulting in heart failure.

Buncom, an eight-year veteran of pro football, and an all-league in 1967, was acquired last year from the San Diego Chargers in the expansion draft when the Bengals entered the league.

San Diego Resident

He lived in San Diego, was married and the father of one.

Buncom's death came on the day the Bengals opened their 1969 AFL regular season against the Miami Dolphins.

Buncom was a graduate of the University of Southern California and was the sixth round draft choice of the Chargers in 1961. He played in the East-West and College All-Star football games after his graduation.

It was reported that Buncom had not practiced with the Bengals during the week.

Roommate Alarmed

Ernie Rice, Buncom's roommate, said he was awakened about 7 A.M. by Buncom's heavy breathing.

Rice called the Bengals trainer and the Cincinnati life squad but the player was dead before either could arrive.

Buncom, 6-foot-2 and 246, was a strong performer for the Bengals last year in their opening pro season.

While with San Diego he was an All-AFL line backer in 1967 and a second team member in 1964, 1965 and 1966.

Bengal officials said Buncom's wife was here at the time of death.

What's $5 to Big Jet Loser

Denver's rabid pro football fans often have been called the most fanatical followers in the game.

But while 50,583 Bronco leathernecks cheered their heroes in victory Sunday, one loyal New York Jet fan was willing to stand up and be counted in defeat.

Shortly after the Broncos had scored a 21-19 victory over the Jets Sunday, a long distance call from New York City jangled the

Reprinted from
The Rocky Mountain News

phone off the hook at The Rocky Mountain News.

The call came from Robert W. Smith, 131 W. 121st St., New York City.

"I want all of you folks in Denver to know that the New York Jets are still the best football team in the world," the caller said politely but with fervent certainty.

"Just tell those referees who walked off three 15-yard penalties against the Jets with four seconds left never to show up in New York. Everybody knows the Jets have the best players in the world and those three unsportsmanlike conduct penalties were ridiculous.

"As far as football is concerned Denver played a good game. But when the Broncos come back to New York we'll get even."

The Broncos, who whipped the Jets on their home grounds the

last two years, do not play a return game in New York this year.

As the conversation continued, the harried News reporter became skeptical that a Robert W. Smith could indeed be calling from New York.

A return call, placed to a number left by the caller, revealed the call indeed had come from New York and the "hot line" again was on.

"So you couldn't believe anyone would call from New York." Smith said. "I can't help it if my mother married a fellow named Smith. But what's a lousey $5 phone call when I just lost a $300 wager on the game? Anyway, the Jets will come back—and you can bet on that," Smith chuckled.

With that, the conversation came to an abrupt halt and office clerks got back to the revelry of celebrating a big, big Bronco win.

Quarterback Equals League Mark for Scoring Tosses

BLOOMINGTON, Minn., Sept. 28 (AP)—Joe Kapp shredded the Baltimore defense for a league record-tying seven touchdown passes today as the Minnesota Vikings smashed the defending National Football League champion Colts, 52-14.

Kapp, whose play elicited boos the last two seasons, joined the elite group of Sid Luckman, Y. A. Tittle and Adrian Burk for throwing the most scoring passes in a single game. Burk helped officate the game as the back judge.

A sellout crowd of 47,644, which included Vice President Spiro Agnew, saw Kapp hit 12 different receivers for a Viking record of 449 yards.

6 Different Receivers

His scoring strikes of 18, 83, 21, 13, 41, 1 and 15 yards went to six different men, with Gene Washington taking in the 83 and 41-yard bombs.

It was Baltimore's worst loss since the Colts fell, 57-0, to Chicago in 1962 and the first time since 1950 that the Colts had lost their first two regular season games.

Kapp completed his first six passes of the game, the first score coming on an 18-yarder to Dave Osborn when the game was just two minutes old.

Penalties Hurt Colts

In contrast, Minnesota's hard rush made the Colt quarterbacks, Johnny Unitas and Earl Morrall, almost ineffective. Unitas completed only two of his first 13 passes and Morrall had two passes intercepted.

The Colts hurt themselves with numerous penalties, including a defensive holding call against linebacker Don Shinnick, nullifying Roy Hilton's 58-yard touchdown run with a recovered fumble after Bubba Smith slammed into Kapp.

Tom Matte scored both Baltimore touchdowns, on a 42-yard pass from Morrall and a four-yard run.

Minnesota Vikings	14	17	14	7—52
Baltimore Colts	0	7	7	0—14

Minn.—Osborn, 18, pass from Kapp (Cox, kick).
Minn.—Washington, 83, pass from Kapp (Cox, kick).
Balt.—Matte, 42, pass from Morrall (Michaels, kick).
Minn.—Grim, 21, pass from Kapp (Cox, kick).
Minn.—F.G., Cox, 41.
Minn.—Kramer, 13, pass from Kapp (Cox, kick).
Minn.—Washington, 41, pass from Kapp (Cox, kick).
Balt.—Matte, 4, run (Michaels, kick).
Minn.—Beasley, 1, pass from Kapp (Cox, kick).
Minn.—Lindsey, 15, pass from Kapp (Cox, kick).
Attendance—47,644.

STATISTICS OF THE GAME

	Vikings	Colts
First downs	34	15
Rushing yardage	92	56
Passing yardage	530	179
Return yardage	55	35
Passes	36-56	20-42
Interceptions by	3	2
Punts	4-39	6-42
Fumbles lost	1	0
Yards penalized	128	62

Jets Edge Dolphins

New York, Nov. 2 — Jim Turner's 36-yard field goal with less than three minutes to capped a fourth period comeback and carried the New York Jets past Miami's aroused Dolphins, 34-to-31, today for their fifth straight American Football League victory.

Joe Namath led the Jets from behind with scoring passes to George Sauer and Don Maynard in the final period before John Elliott blocked a Miami punt and Turner, the AFL scoring leader, snapped a 31-31 deadlock with his 20th field goal of the season.

Bob Griese, whose fourth touchdown pass of the game, had sent the Dolphins ahead 31-24 with 9.22 to play, then combined with reserve quarterback Rick Norton to lead the visitors back to the Jets' 35-yard line. But Bill Baird intercepted Griese on the 17 in the final minute of play, sealing New York's sixth victory in eight starts.

Maynard Hits 10,000

But Namath and Maynard clicked for 37 yards, pushing the Jet receiver over the 10,000 mark in career yardage, then teamed up again on a 25-yard scoring play.

The Jets defense held after the ensuing kickoff and Elliott broke through to block Seiple's punt, Randy Beverly recovering for New York on the 31. After three running plays netted only seven yards and an offside penalty set the Jets back to the 29, Turner booted the decisive three pointer.

Maynard caught four passes for the Jets and his two touchdowns gave him an all-time AFL career mark of 83.

Statistics

	Dolphins	Jets
First downs	23	15
Rushing yardage	185	85
Passing yardage	236	221
Return yardage	10	1
Passes	20-30-1	13-26-1
Punts	4-44	4-46
Fumbles lost	3	1
Yards penalized	46	17

Miami	7	14	3	7—31
New York	10	0	6	18—34

NY—FG J Turner 14
NY—Maynard 42 pass from Namath (J. Turner kick)
Mia—Clancy 5 pass from Griese (Kremser kick)
Mia—Seiple 29 pass from Griese (Kremser kick)
Mia—Csonka 11 pass from Griese (Kremser kick)
NY—Snell 1 run (pass failed)
MIA—FG Kremser 22
NY—Sauer 27 pass from Namath (Maynard pass from Snell)
Mia—Seiple 9 pass from Griese (Kremser kick)
NY—Maynard 25 pass from Namath (J. Turner kick)
NY—FG J. Turner 36.
A—61,761.

SAINTS TRIP CARDS IN AERIAL BATTLE

Win, 51-42, as Each Team Counts 6 Times on Passes

STATISTICS OF THE GAME

	Saints	Cards
First downs	26	19
Rushing yardage	163	99
Passing yardage	345	374
Return yardage	185	158
Passes	22-34	20-37
Interceptions by	1	1
Punts	2-45	5-34
Fumbles lost	0	2
Yards penalized	48	75

ST. LOUIS, Nov. 2 (AP)—Bill Kilmer's six touchdown passes led New Orleans to the biggest point production in its history today and the Saints tripped the St. Louis Cardinals, 51-42, for their first National Football League victory of the campaign.

Charlie Johnson of the Cards also threw six scoring passes in the wild offensive show, but the Saints added tallies on a short run and a field goal for their margin.

The game's 12 touchdown passes erased the N.F.L. record of 11 set by the New York Giants (7) and Washington Redskins (4) in 1962.

The 51 points represented the most scored on a Cardinal team since it moved to St. Louis from Chicago in 1960.

New Orleans Saints ... 7 16 21 7—51
St. Louis Cardinals ... 7 7 7 21—42
N.O.—Parks, 25, pass from Kilmer (Dempsey, kick).
St. L.—Williams, 32, pass from Johnson (Bakken, kick).
St. L.—Williams, 14, pass from Johnson (Bakken, kick).
N.O.—FG, Dempsey, 43.
N.O.—Wheelwright, 20, pass from Kilmer (Dempsey, kick).
N.O.—Abramowicz, 5, pass from Kilmer (kick failed).
N.O.—Shy, 28, pass from Kilmer (Dempsey, kick).
N.O.—Wheelwright, 1, run (Dempsey, kick).
St. L.—Gilliam, 28, pass from Johnson (Bakken, kick).
N.O.—Abramowicz, 11, pass from Kilmer (Dempsey, kick).
N.O.—Parks, 13, pass from Kilmer (Dempsey, kick).
St. L.—Williams, 31, pass from Johnson (Bakken, kick).
St. L.—Williams, 26, pass from Johnson (Bakken, kick).
St. L.—Shivers, 14, pass from Johnson (Bakken, kick).
Attendance—46,718.

VIKINGS SNAP RAM STREAK AT 11 GAMES

Unbeaten Season For Los Angeles Ends In 20-13 Defeat

Los Angeles, Dec. 7 (AP)—Hard-hitting Minnesota shattered the dream of an unbeaten season by the Los Angeles Rams and ended their 11-game winning streak today, 20-to-13, and set the stage for the title game in the Western Conference of the National Football League in three weeks.

A sellout crowd of 80,430, including Vice President Spiro T. Agnew and former Vice President Hubert H. Humphrey, was on hand in sunny 70-degree weather in Memorial Coliseum, for the game between the Central and Coastal Divisions of the NFL.

West Starts Viking Surge

The Rams put on a belated rally in the final three minutes in an attempt to catch the Vikings but couldn't make it and Minnesota, which lost its first game of the season to New York, registered its eleventh straight victory of the campaign.

Viking Charlie West returned the opening kickoff 78 yards to the Rams' 22 to set up the first touchdown, a four-yard plunge by Dave Osborn, and Minnesota was in command from then until the spirited final minute.

Running back Bill Brown scored from the one in the second quarter and Fred Cox, the leading scorer in the National League, kicked a 39-yard field goal to give the Vikings a 17-3 lead at half time.

Gabriel Harrassed

The solid-hitting Minnesota defense limited the Rams to a field goal in the second and third quarters — kicks of 37 and 27 yards by Bruce Gossett — and the Rams only touchdown came with 2.59 left in the game.

Quarterback Joe Kapp was in the driver's seat for Minnesota all the way. The Rams' Roman Gabriel, constantly harrassed by the defensive troops, did not get hot until the closing phases when he passed the Rams on a 77-yard march for their only touchdown.

Gabriel in this series completed seven of nine throws for 59 yards, the final a four-yard shot to Larry Smith for the touchdown.

Minnesota did not score in the third quarter but Cox booted his second field goal some 29 yards midway in the final quarter to end the scoring by the visitors.

The Vice President, who was accompanied to the game by Governor Ronald Reagan and U.S. Senator George Murphy, sat on the Rams's side of the field and the group left with about two minutes remaining. Humphery, a former U.S. Senator from Minnesota, naturally sat on the Vikings' side of the field.

Rams Race Against Clock

The Rams got possession of the ball with one minute 32 seconds left and began a frantic race against the clock. Gabriel moved them from their own 14 to midfield but the threat which could have tied the score frittered away on four incomplete passes.

Minnesota got its first touchdown following West's runback on five plays which covered only 22 yards as Brown and Osborne knocked off short yardage gains.

The Vikings put together an 88-yard drive in 12 plays, with Brown scoring from the one. It was longest sustained drive of the afternoon.

On a keeper, Kapp gained 18 yards in the parade, and the key play was a 28-yard pass to the Rams' one to John Henderson.

Statistics

First downs	15	15
Rushing yardage	177	61
Passing yardage	69	186
Return yardage	51	86
Passes	8-16-0	21-38-1
Punts	7-39	4-32
Fumbles lost	0	0
Yards penalized	52	31

Minnesota .... 7 10 0 3—20
Los Angeles .... 0 3 3 7—13
Min—Osborne 4 run (Cox kick).
Min—Brown 1 run (Cox kick).
LA—FG Gossett 37.
Minn—FG Cox 39.
LA—FG Gossett 27.
Min—FG Cox 29.
LA—L. Smith 4 pass from Gabriel (Gossett kick)
A—80,430.

Stenerud's 5th Field Goal Gives Chiefs 22-19 Victory

Kansas City (AP) — Jan Stenerud kicked his fourth field goal with two minutes to go today snapping a tie and lifting the Kansas City Chiefs to a 22-to-19 American Football League victory over Buffalo.

The 25-yard kick was Stenerud's 16th straight field goal without a miss, setting a professional football record. Stenerud broke the record earlier in the game when he notched his second of the afternoon and 13th in a row. Lou Groza set the pro record of 12 field goals with the Cleveland Browns in 1953.

Simpson Scores

Buffalo, trailing by 10 points much of the game, tied the score 19-19 with eight minutes left when O. J. Simpson uncorked his longest run as a pro skirting left end for 32 yards and a touchdown.

For the Bills' publicized rookie it was only his second touchdown run of the season. Simpson danced by tacklers, then ran over two Chiefs when he got near the goal.

Buffalo missed a chance to go ahead by one point when the snap from center on the extra point attempt was bad. Placement holder Marlin Briscoe had his frantic pass on the broken conversion batted down.

The Chiefs stormed back to ten on Stenerud's 27th field goal in 34 tries this season. Stenerud tied Groza's record with a 52-yard field goal early in the second quarter, then broke the mark with an eight-yarder three minutes later

Statistics

	Bills	Chiefs
First downs	17	17
Rushing vardage	93	146
Passing vardage	144	131
Return yardage	128	180
Passes	13-32-0	13-23-0
Punts	6-50	4-51
Fumbles lost	2	3
Yards penalized	26	10

Buffalo .... 3 0 10 6—19
Kansas City ...... 7 6 3 6—22
Buff—FG Alford 16
KC—Holmes 3 run (Stenerud kick)
KC—FG Stenerud 52
KC—FG Stenerud 8
Buff—FG Alford 34
KC—FG Stenerud 47
Buff—Briscoe 17 pass from Kemp (Alford kick)
KC—FG Stenerud 20
Buff—Simpson 32 run (pass failed)
KC—FG Stenerud 25
Attendance—47,112.

Pass-Catching Record Set By Alworth; Chargers Win

SAN DIEGO, Dec. 14 (AP)— Lance Alworth set a pass-catching record today as the San Diego Chargers rolled to a 45-6 victory over the Buffalo Bills in the American Football League.

Alworth caught a 9-yard pass from John Hadl in San Diego's second offensive series to break Don Hutson's record of receptions in 96 consecutive games. Hutson, of Green Bay, set the mark 27 years ago.

Alworth finished with seven catches for 122 yards, gaining more than 1,000 for the seventh straight season. A 27-yarder in the second quarter was his 453d, moving him into ninth place in the all-time reception list.

The Chargers poured it on with Dick Post, the league's rushing leader, scoring on runs of 34 and 3 yards. He gained 106 yards in 19 carries.

It was the fifth game in which the 5-foot-9-inch, 190-pounder had rushed for more than 100 yards.

The rookie quarterback, Marty Domres of Columbia, re-

placed Hadl and scored the Chargers' sixth touchdown on a 9-yard run before Buffalo got on the scoreboard in the waning moments.

The Chargers ended the season with eight victories and six defeats. The Bills were 4-10.

O. J. Simpson, Buffalo's rookie back, managed only 27 yards in seven carries. He lost 8 yards on three pass receptions.

STATISTICS OF THE GAME

	Charg.	Bills
First downs	30	15
Rushing yardage	242	58
Passing yardage	305	180
Return yardage	74	46
Passes	19-32	18-35
Interceptions by	2	0
Punts	2-54	8-45
Fumbles lost	1	0
Yards penalized	21	55

San Diego Chargers	10	14	7	14	45
Buffalo Bills	0	0	0	6	6

S.D.—Garrison, 41, pass from Hadl (Partee, kick).
S.D.—FG, Partee, 33.
S.D.—Ever, 20, pass from Hadl (Partee, kick).
S.D.—Alworth, 1, pass from Hadl (Partee, kick).
S.D.—Post, 34, run (Partee, kick).
S.D.—Post, 3, run (Partee, kick).
S.D.—Domres, 9, run (Partee, kick).
Buf.—Grate, 19, pass from Sherman (kick failed).
Attendance—47,582.

RAIDERS SLAUGHTER OILERS, 56-7

Lamonica Fires Six TD Passes In AFL Play-Off Tilt

Oakland, Dec. 21 (AP) — The Oakland Raiders, who had been saying all along they thought the American Football League's play-off system was silly, proved their point today by crushing the Houston Oilers, 56 to 7, on six touchdown passes by Daryle Lamonica

The Raiders, who will play the Kansas City Chiefs for the AFL title January 4 in Oakland, took advantage of repeated Oiler mistakes as they scored four touchdowns within four minutes and 22 seconds of the first quarter and handed the Oilers the worst defeat in their history.

Four In First Half

Lamonica threw four scoring passes in the first half and added two more in the third period before leaving the game early in the final frame.

Two of his touchdown passes went to Fred Biletnikoff, for 13 and 31 yards; two more were caught by Rod Sherman, for 24 and 23 yards; one went to Charlie Smith for 60 yards and the last was a three-yarder to Billy Cannon.

Lamonica, voted the AFL's Most Valuable Player for the second time in three years, finished the game with 13 completions out of 17 attempts for 276 yards.

Strong Wind, Fierce K.C. Defense Freeze Out Namath

New York, Dec. 20 (AP)—"Right now, I feel like I was in a gang fight all by myself," a battered Joe Namath said while trying to explain the big one that got away.

Namath, rebuffed by a cruel wind in chilly Shea Stadium and buffeted by Kansas City's ferocious defenders, was shut off the scoreboard as the New York Jets bowed to the Chiefs, 13 to 6, in today's American Football League play-off game.

Tought Wind

"It was the wind—and Kansas City's defense," said the Jets gifted quarterback, who completed only 14 of 40 passes, was flattened half a dozen times by the Chiefs' front four and failed for the first time this year to put the ball over the enemy goal line.

"The wind was a major factor," Namath said. "The ball was going end-over-end and every direction. The timing was

The Statistics

	Chiefs	Jets
First downs	14	19
Rushing yardage	19	87
Passing yardage	177	148
Return Yardage	56	10
Passes	12-27-0	14-40-3
Punts	6-33	5-37
Fumbles lost	0	1
Yards penalized	63	15

Kansas City	0	3	3	7	13
New York	3	0	0	3	6

NY—FG, J. Turner 27.
KC—FG Stenerud 23.
KC—FG Stenerud 25.
NY—FG J. Turner 7.
KC—Richardson 19 pass from Dawson (Stenerud kick).
Attendance—62,977.

Individual Leaders

Rushing—Kansas City, Garrett 18—67; Hayes 10—32. New York, Snell 12—61; Mathis 6—11; Boozer 3—13.
Receiving—Kansas City, Hayes 5—46; Arbanas 2—39; Taylor 2—74; Holmes 1—29; Richardson 1—19; New York, Sauer 5—61; Lammons 3—37; B. Turner 2—25.
Passing—Kansas City Dawson 12—27—0, 261 yards. New York, Namath, 14—24—3, 164 yards.

gone with the receivers. You could throw up the middle, but even when I'd throw an 8-yard out pattern to Matt Snell, the ball would sail away."

"I'm not gonna knock the Chiefs," said defensive end Gerry Philbin, who played a strong game with a harness protecting his dislocated left shoulder. "We played our best and they won, so they were the better team. They had a great game defensively."

"I think we would have had a better chance without the wind," sid George Sauer, who just missed a tying touchdown catch in the next-to-last Jet drive wind for them."

Cornerback Cornell Gordon was beaten by Gloster Richardson for the winning touchdown after Len Dawson and tis Taylor clicked on a 61-yard pass-run play to the Jets' 19.

"Richardson got a step on me and just went all the way," said Gordon, who played an otherwise airtight defensive game going head-to-heat with Taylor.

Falcons Upset Vikings In Rain, 10-3

Atlanta, Dec. 21 (P)—A 24-yard touchdown run with a recovered fumble by defensive end Claude Humphrey gave the Atlanta Falcons a 10-to-3 upset victory over Minnesota today, ending the Vikings' hope of tying a National Football League record for consecutive wins.

The Vikings, champions of the Central Division in the Western Conference, were trying to equal the single-season streak of 13 straight victories set by Chicago in 1934. Minnesota had won 12 in a row after losing the season opener to New York.

Coach Bud Grant's team did get one record, this year's Vikings allowed 133 points to 14 foes, breaking the previous mark of 144 shared by the 1963 Chicago Bears and the 1968 Colts.

Minnesota had taken a 3-0 lead on a 19-yard field goal by Fred Cox in the first period and the two teams exchanged fumbles and pass interceptions the rest of the half in an icy rain, occasionally mixed with snow and sleet.

But with 25 seconds left in the half, defensive end John Zook forced Viking quarterback Gary Cuozzo to fumble at the Minnesota 24 and Humphrey, last season's defensive rookie of the year, picked up the loose ball and scampered into the end zone to give Atlanta a 7-3 halftime lead.

NELSEN HOT AS BROWNS RIP DALLAS

Cleveland QB Riddles Cowboys, 38 To 14, For East Title

By CAMERON C. SNYDER
[Sun Staff Correspondent]

Dallas, Dec. 28—Bill Nelsen, like the famous admiral, caught the enemy crossing his sights and fired Salvo after Salvo to sink the land locked Cowboys, 38-to-14, while hoisting the Eastern Conference title flag above the Cleveland Browns in the rain soaked Cotton Bowl today.

The next port of call for the trim skipper and his band of piratical Brownies will be Minnesota, frozen fortress of the Vikings.

The treasure trove awaiting there is the National Football League championship and a chance for a Super Bowl voyage against the American Football League titlists.

No Weather Edge

Acclimatization to Minnesota's cold, snow and ice will present no more problems for the Browns than it does for the Vikings. Neither team is considered fair-weather sailors and there will be no weather advantage on either side.

Today's weather was more like Cleveland's than supposedly Dallas' warm clime, and the Browns reveled in the cold rain against the Cowboys, who ruled a touchdown choice before the game.

Nelsen came up with key third-down passes and baffled the Cowboy defense with screens and draws to control the ball and the tempo of the game throughout.

The Statistics

	Browns	Cowboys
First downs	22	17
Rushing yardage	97	100
Passing yardage	247	117
Return yardage	134	0
Passes	20-29-0	12-29-2
Punts	1-34	5-36
Fumbles lost	0	1
Yards penalized	50	51

Cleveland	7	10	7	14—38
Dallas	0	0	7	7—14

Clev—Scott. 2 run (Cockroft kick).
Clev—Morin. 6 pass from Nelsen (Cockroft kick).
Clev—FG. Cockroft 29
Clev—Scott. 2 run (Cockroft kick).
Dal—Morton. 2 run (Clark kick).
Clev—Kelly. 1 run (Cockroft kick).
Clev—Summer. 88 pass interception (Cockroft kick).
Dal—Rentzel. 5 pass from Staubach (Clark kick).
A—69,321.

KAPP STARS AS VIKINGS CATCH RAMS

Minnesota Wipes Out 17-7 Deficit, Gains Title Game, 23-20

By CAMERON C. SNYDER
[Sun Staff Correspondent]

Minneapolis-St. Paul. Dec. 27—That abominable snowman the Vikings imported from Canada became acclimated to the 21-degree weather in the second half and mushed Minnesota to a 23-to-20 come-from-behind victory over the Los Angeles Rams in the Western Conference play-off at Metropolitan Stadium today.

Joe Kapp apparently gets hotter as the temperature dips and the pressure rises. He rallied his mates from a 17-7 deficit at halftime with two second half touchdowns. The other two points came on a safety.

Coach Bud Grant, of the Vikings, must have turned on the air-conditioner in the dressing room because the Vikings became cold-blooded killers in the last two periods after being just another football team in the first 30 minutes.

Gain Title Game

The rally pushed the Vikings into the National Football League championship game against the winner of tomorrow's Dallas Cowboy-Cleveland Brown encounter. The NFL title game also will be played here next Sunday.

For awhile it seemed that Roman Gabriel, Los Angeles' huge Filipino quarterback, had a little Eskimo in his blood as he poured hot coals all over the famed Viking defense.

But Gabriel and his warm-blooded mates couldn't stand up to the cold shoulders of the Vikings in the second half, as Kapp, despite two interceptions, warmed to his task.

The Statistics

	LA	Minn
First downs	19	18
Rushing yardage	126	97
Passing yardage	129	178
Return yardage	32	55
Passes	22-32-1	12-19-2
Punts	3-36	3-39
Fumbles lost	0	1
Yards penalized	37	36

Los Angeles	7	10	0	3—20
Minnesota	7	0	7	9—23

Scoring Plays

	Rams	Vikings
FIRST PERIOD		
LA—6.06. Klein 3 pass from Gabriel (Gossett kick)	7	0
Minn—11.31. Osborn 1 run (Cox kick)	7	7
SECOND PERIOD		
LA—10.27 FG Gossett 20	10	7
LA—14.21. Truax 2 pass from Gabriel (Gossett kick)	17	7
THIRD PERIOD		
Minn—5.40. Osborn 1 run (Cox kick)	17	14
FOURTH PERIOD		
LA—0.22. FG Gossett 27	20	14
Minn—6.36. Kapp 2 run (Cox kick)	20	21
Minn—7.11. Safety. Eller. tackled Gabriel in end zone	20	23

Rams

RUSHING

	Att.	Net Yds.	Avg.	Lg. Gn.	TD
Gabriel	5	26	6.5	13	0
L. Smith	11	60	5.5	12	0
Josephson	10	16	1.6	7	0
Ellison	4	22	5.5	17	0
Mason	1	2	2.0	2	0
Totals	30	126	4.2	17	0

PASSING

	att.	comp.	yds.	tkd. yds.	td.	lg.	int.
Gabriel	32	22	150	3/21	2	18	1
Totals	32	22	150	3/21	2	18	1

PASS RECEIVING

	No.	Yds.	Lg.	TD
Tucker	3	23	9	0
Klein	1	3	3	1
L. Smith	6	36	10	0
Josephson	7	41	13	0
Truax	5	47	18	1
Totals	22	150	18	2

Vikings

RUSHING

	Att.	Net Yds.	Avg.	Lg. Gn.	TD
Brown	8	22	2.7	6	0
Osborn	13	30	2.3	12	2
Reed	1	3	3.0	3	0
Kapp	7	42	6.0	15	1
Totals	29	97	3.3	15	3

PASSING

	att.	comp.	yds.	tkd. yds.	td.	lg.	int.
Kapp	19	12	196	2/18	0	41	2
Totals	19	12	196	2/18	0	41	2

PASS RECEIVING

	No.	Yds.	Lg.	TD
Washington	4	90	41	0
Henderson	4	68	24	0
Reed	2	18	12	0
Brown	2	20	12	0
Totals	12	196	41	0

Jan. 5

Chiefs Win AFL Title, 17-7

From Press Dispatches

Oakland, Calif. – The Kansas City Chiefs and the Oakland Raiders played a high stakes game of giveaway in the fourth period here Sunday, but it didn't keep the Chiefs from a 17-7 victory and the American Football League championship.

The Chiefs began the period with a 14-7 lead and added a field goal to it. but the victory wasn't nearly that easy. Three times in the fourth period the Chiefs lost the ball in their own territory on fumbles; three times Oakland quarterback Daryle Lamonica threw interceptions to frustrate Raider attempts to catch up.

Super Bowl Next

So the Chiefs, who played in the first Super Bowl in 1967 — and lost to the Green Bay Packers, 35-10 — will now play in the last under the present setup, against the Minnesota Vikings at New Orleans next Sunday.

Next year, with the two pro leagues merged, the Super Bowl will merely be a meeting of conference champions.

Lamonica threw the interceptions, the only ones he suffered all day, after bruising his hand badly in the third period.

He threw an incomplete pass, and on the followthrough rammed his passing hand against the shoulder pads and helmet of Chiefs' defensive tackle Aaron Brown.

"I thought I'd broken it," Lamonica said later. "I jammed three fingers."

Injury Is Handicap

It was reported after the game that Lamonica had suf-

Daryle Lamonica

fered no fracture, but by then it didn't do the Raiders much good. He was out of the game for eight minutes after being hurt, and when he returned, he was ineffective. He completed only 3 of 18 passes after his injury.

"I could grip the ball, but I didn't have the zing on my followthrough," Lamonica said.

There was more to it than that, though. Lamonica was hounded all day by a superb pass rush, especially from Brown, and the beating he took in the second half was fearsome.

He was caught trying to pass four times — he had been nailed only 12 times in the entire regular season — and a dozen other times he got rid of the ball a moment before the Chiefs knocked him galley west.

Chiefs Start Slowly

The Kansas City command at the end of the game was a situation quite different from the beginning. For almost all the first half the Chiefs were struggling to get going, and the 7-0 lead the Raiders had taken on Charlie Smith's three yard run in the first period grew in importance as the game went on.

But then the Chiefs' Len Dawson threw a pass to Frank Pitts, who turned it into a 41 yard gain to the one yard line, and Wendell Hayes rammed into the end zone with three minutes left in the half. Jan Stenerud's kick tied the score,

and the tide of the game had turned for good.

Another long pass helped the Chiefs make sure of that.

In the third quarter, with the ball on the Kansas City two and third down coming up, Dawson retreated into the end zone and threw far downfield.

Catch Starts Drive

Otis Taylor caught the ball over his head and plunged out of bounds at the 37 yard line and, once started, the Chiefs didn't stop until Robert Holmes had run five yards into the end zone.

Stenerud added the point, and a 22 yard field goal in the fourth quarter, and Kansas City had won.

"Otis wasn't the primary receiver," Dawson said. "I was looking for Holmes coming across the middle, but he got banged.

"I was in the end zone and couldn't wait any longer, so I threw it so it would have gone out of bounds if he didn't catch it. It was a great catch."

It was a profitable one, too. The touchdown drive it began earned the Chiefs an estimated $7,000 apiece, plus a trip to the Super Bowl

Reprinted from
The Milwaukee Journal

Vikings and Weather Refrigerate Browns

By Chuck Johnson
of The Journal Staff

Minneapolis, Minn. – This time it would be different, Bud Grant kept insisting all week long. The 51-3 victory that his Minnesota Vikings had scored over the Cleveland Browns here two months ago in the regular season was not a true measure of the two teams.

Grant was right. Sunday it was different. The Minnesota Vikings called off the dogs after opening a 14-0 lead in the first 7 minutes 7 seconds and settled for a 27-7 victory in the National Football league's championship game.

The feeling persisted, though, that Joe Kapp, the unconventional quarterback, the refugee from Canada, and his purple clad teammates could almost have named the score. Cleveland really was never in the game.

Perhaps there was luck involved in Minnesota's quick getaway, for Kapp scored the first touchdown himself on a seven yard run after fullback Bill Brown slipped and the quarterback couldn't hand him the ball. So Kapp turned and chugged through the middle, dragging a couple of the other kind of Browns with him the last few yards.

Barnes Slips, Falls

And then Kapp arched a long pass up the middle a few plays later and end Gene Washington was all by himself on Cleveland's 40 because defender Erich Barnes had tried to bump the receiver and slipped and fell when he missed most of him. So Washington caught the ball — he almost dropped it because it was such an easy play — and the result was a 75 yard touchdown and Minnesota led, 14-0.

But the good teams are lucky and the lucky teams are good, and the Vikings fit both descriptions Sunday.

"You saw a pretty good facsimile of our team today," said Grant afterward, in a strange choice of words. "That's what we've done most of the season — gotten a quick jump on the other team and then our defense goes to work."

Alan Page, one of the Four Norsemen who put so much pressure on the other quarterback, agreed. "Once our offense put 14 points on the board, we could do a lot of things on defense," he said. "We needed whatever edge we could get, because Cleveland can do so many things." But never on Sunday, Jan. 4, 1970.

Minnesota gradually built its lead, to 24-0 at the half and 27-0 after three quarters, a n d then Cleveland got a consolation touchdown after it didn't matter.

D a v e Osborn, who averaged six yards for each of his 18 carries, made the third Minnesota touchdown on a 20 yard run, shedding Browns as he went, and Fred Cox kicked the three extra points and made both field goals he tried, from 30 and 32 yards.

Quarterback Bill N e l s e n, who seemed to have trouble throwing — perhaps Minnesota's constant pressure had something to do with it as well as an early bump on the head which made his right arm go numb — finally connected with end Gary Collins for a three yard touchdown pass early in the fourth quarter, and Don Cockroft kicked the extra point.

This was a cold day — but everybody expected that ahead of time, and the field was playable. The Browns, however, seemed to make more of the seven degree temperature with a 12 mile an hour wind — for a chill index of 20 below zero. Both teams came out wearing football cleats b u t as the game went on, more and more Browns switched to tennis shoes.

On the sidelines, the Browns huddled in their capes and stood on the benches so as to get full benefit of the h o t air blowers. The Vikings stood around, some wearing short sleeves, with no heaters at their backs.

The Cold Facts

"We generate our own heat," said Grant, coldly.

Along with scoring the first touchdown and passing for the second, Kapp exhibited another kind of leadership when he fairly leaped into a collision with Cleveland linebacker J i m Houston in the third quarter. Kapp got up and walked back to the Minnesota huddle. Houston was out cold, was helped to t h e bench and never returned.

"Maybe I got a lucky hit," Kapp said afterward. "Or maybe he got hit wrong."

Said Houston, "I hit Unitas like that once, and he didn't get up."

While it mattered, the Vikings had complete control. T h e y gained 171 yards f r o m scrimmage in the first quarter to Cleveland's 31, had seven first downs to one and a 14-0 lead and were on the way to more points as the quarter ended.

What the offense didn't accomplish, the defense did. Right linebacker Wally Hilgenberg, a reject of both Detroit and Pittsburgh, had an especially good day, with a fumble recovery and the first interception of his entire football career.

Vikings vs. Browns

	Cleveland	Minnesota
First downs	14	18
Yards rushing	97	222
Yards passing	171	161
Total yards	268	383
Passes	17—33—2	7—13—0
Punts	3—33	3—41
Fumbles lost	1	0
Yards penalized	5	33

Cleveland	0	0	0	7 — 7
Minnesota	14	10	3	0 — 27

Minnesota—Kapp, 7, run (Cox, kick).
Minnesota—Washington, 75, pass from Kapp (Cox, kick).
Minnesota—Field goal, Cox, 30.
Minnesota—Osborn, 20, r u n (Cox, kick).
Minnesota—Field goal, Cox, 32.
Cleveland—Collins, 3, pass from Nelsen (Cockroft, kick).
A—47,900.

RUSHING
(Attempts, Yards)
Cleveland — Kelly, 15-50; Scott, 6-17.
Minnesota — Osborn, 18-108; Kapp, 8-57; Brown, 12-43; Reed, 5-7; Jones, 2-7.

PASSING
(Attempts, Completions, Interceptions, Yards)
Cleveland — Nelsen, 33-17-2-181.
Minnesota — Kapp, 13-7-0-169.

RECEIVING
(Catches, Yards)
Cleveland — Scott, 5-56; Collins, 5-43; Warfield, 4-47; Kelly, 2-17; Morin, 1-18.
Minnesota — Washington, 3-120; Henderson, 2-17; Beasley, 1-12; Brown, 1-20.

INTERCEPTIONS
Cleveland — None.
Minnesota — Hilgenberg, Krause.

FUMBLES RECOVERED
Cleveland — None.
Minnesota — Hilgenberg.

Entire page reprinted from
The Milwaukee Journal

Super Chiefs Beat Vikings in Every Way

AFL Pulls Even, 23-7; Errors Hurt

By Chuck Johnson
of The Journal Staff

New Orleans, La. – Grady Alderman, Minnesota's offensive captain, probably summed it up best after the Kansas City Chiefs had finished taking the Vikings apart in the fourth and last Super Bowl in the Sugar Bowl here Sunday, 23-7.

"They beat us on offense and they beat us on defense and they beat us in every way," Alderman said.

And that, folks, was exactly what happened, as the Chiefs achieved parity for the American Football League against the National Football League,

The Statistics

	Minnesota	Kansas City
First downs	13	18
Yards rushing	67	151
Yards passing	172	122
Total yards	239	273
Passes	17 28—3	12 17 1
Punts	3 37	4 48
Fumbles lost	2	0
Yards penalized	67	47

and as Kansas City also got even for the 35-10 beating that Green Bay handed out in the first Super Bowl in Los Angeles three years ago.

"We made more mistakes today than we made in 22 games," said Karl Kassulke, the Vikings' safety man from West Milwaukee, referring to Minnesota's 14 regular season games, two playoff victories and six exhibitions.

Coach Bud Grant saw it the same way. "The mistakes were cumulative," Grant said. "Eventually, someone had to pay the piper."

High Cost of Erring

And the Vikings paid, and paid, and paid. And the AFL

caught up with the NFL — or rather, with the Green Bay Packers, who won the first two Super Bowls under Vince Lombardi, including the aforementioned whomping of the Chiefs.

For those looking for portents, there were many. It started with heavy rain in the morning, continued through a tornado alert before game time, and then in the pregame show there was that ill fated balloon race.

Something probably could have been made of the AFL balloon never getting off the ground, but the NFL balloon crashed into the stands, landing among the beauties who graced Super Sunday. And then at halftime there was a re-enactment of the battle of New Orleans. When the cannon fire had subsided, there was the definite impression that the British had won. They wore the red uniforms, even as the Chiefs did.

But, back to the game.

The Upper Hand

Hank Stram's Chiefs got an early upper hand when Jan Stenerud, their Norwegian born soccer style kicker, made three field goals in three attempts, from 48 yards (a Super Bowl record) bettering the 43 yard kick of the Packers' Don Chandler two years ago, and from 32 and 25 yards. That made it 9-0.

The situation, from Minnesota's standpoint, immediately became more desperate when Charlie West let the subsequent kickoff slip through his hands and bounce off his thigh pad. The Chiefs' Remi Prudhomme recovered on Minnesota's 19, and six plays later, halfback Mike Garrett ran five yards over left tackle for a touchdown and a 16-0 lead at the half.

The Vikings tried to get back in the game as halfback Dave Osborn scored on a four yard run in the third period, but then quarterback Lenny Dawson threw a short pass to end Otis Taylor, and Taylor

broke tackles by corner back Earsell Mackbee and Kassulke on the way to a 46 yard touchdown and it was all over.

Dawson and Defense

Kansas City's victory was predicated chiefly on Dawson and defense.

Dawson on this day was a great quarterback. He called a fine game and threw the passes that could beat Minnesota — short quickies in front of the cornerback, who let the receivers have such passes. The big thing was that Dawson did not make the mistakes that some quarterbacks make, and so his ball control offense worked well against Minnesota's usually sturdy defense. To no one's surprise, he was named winner of a sports car as the most valuable player.

Garrett was an excellent runner on this mostly cloudy, cool afternoon, as a capacity crowd of **80,977** sat in and a national television audience looked on. And the Chiefs made use of Minnesota's fast pursuit by springing Frank Pitts on three end around plays which netted 37 yards.

"That Big Line"

"They've got that big line," said Grant afterward. "And they have those little runners and Dawson isn't too big, either. They do a good job of hiding the ball and faking the run when they're going to pass, and of faking the pass when they're going to use the draw play."

Added Viking linebacker Roy Winston, "There were so many guys running around there in the backfield it was hard to figure out what was going on."

Dawson had a tough time in a season in which the Chiefs wound up second in their division, but then won the title by beating both the New York Jets, last year's Super Bowl winners, and the Oakland Raiders, who finished ahead of them by beating them twice in the season. And the Chiefs did all these things on the other people's fields.

Dawson also postponed surgery on his knee — he will have to undergo the operation soon now. And he overcame a reputation as a very ordinary quarterback, one who had been discarded by both Pittsburgh and Cleveland of the NFL before he found a home with the Chiefs in the AFL.

Tarkenton's View

Fran Tarkenton, the New York Giants' quarterback, was talking about Dawson afterward, and he may have put some things in perspective.

"That's the first time I'd seen Dawson play," Tarkenton said. "All I'd heard — from players, coaches and writers — was that Lenny wasn't much of a quarterback. I never heard a good word about him. But off what I saw today, he's one fine quarterback."

Kansas City	3 13 7	0—23
Minnesota	0 0 7	0—7

Kansas City—Field goal, Stenerud, 48.
Kansas City—Field goal, Stenerud, 32.
Kansas City—Field goal, Stenerud, 25.
Kansas City—Garrett, 5, run (Stenerud, kick).
Minnesota—Osborn, 4, run (Cox, kick).
Kansas City—Taylor, 47, pass from Dawson (Stenerud, kick).
A—80,897.

Vikings vs. Chiefs

RUSHING
Attempts, Yards

Vikings — Brown, 6-26, Read, 4-17, Osborn, 7-15; Kapp, 2-9.

Chiefs — Garrett, 11-39; Pitts, 3-37, Hayes, 8-31; McVea, 12-26, Dawson, 3-11, Holmes, 5-7.

PASSING
Attempts, Completions, Yards, Interceptions

Vikings — Kapp, 25-16-183-2; Cuozzo, 3-16-1

Chiefs — Dawson, 17-12-142 1.

RECEIVING
Number, Yards

Vikings — Henderson, 7-111, Brown, 3-, Beasley, 2-41, Reed, 2-16, Osborn, 2-, Washington, 1-9.

Chiefs — Taylor, 6-81, Pitts 3-33, Garrett, 2-25, Hayes, 1-3.

INTERCEPTIONS

Vikings — Krause.

Kansas City — Lanier, Robinson, Thomas.

OPPONENTS FUMBLES RECOVERED

Vikings — None.

Kansas City — Robinson, Prudhomme.

Reprinted from
The Milwaukee Journal

Tarkenton Convinced by Chiefs

Staff Correspondence

New Orleans, La. - Questions and answers from Sunday's Super Bowl:

Q. As the two leagues merge, has the American Football League really gained parity, or perhaps more?

A. Fran Tarkenton, New York Giants quarterback: "I think maybe the AFL has passed the NFL. Really. Kansas City, Oakland, the New York Jets — they would be great in our league. Our league doesn't have the good teams it used to. Who's got the good defenses any more in the NFL — Los Angeles, Minnesota, Detroit, Green Bay? Our league isn't as good as it used to be."

Bill Curry, Baltimore Colts center, who played in the ● Super Bowl against Kanity when he was with ● Bay and in the third Super Bowl against the Jets: "I still think that if we (the Colts) played the Jets 10 times, we'd win nine. I don't think that about the Vikings and the Chiefs. The Chiefs are a lot better team than the Jets, and they're vastly improved over when the Packers played them three years ago. Look at their defense— they've got seven new men and all are better than what

they had. I thought going in that the Vikings would win, but I don't think like that any more, after watching the Chiefs execute. They're a very fine football team."

Joe Foss, former commissioner of the AFL: "Hell, maybe we shouldn't have merged."

Q. Jan Stenerud had a big day as a field goal kicker for the Chiefs. How important was his contribution of three field goals for a 9-0 lead?

A. Carl Eller, Minnesota defensive end: "Give the car to the kicker, baby, he won the game for them. After he kicked that first one, we had to know that any time they got inside the 50 they were in scoring range."

Stenerud: "I had trouble warming up with all that commotion going on. But I kicked all right once the game started."

Q. Why was Kansas City's end around play so effective?

A. Hank Stram, Kansas City coach: "We hadn't used it for the last two months, so it wasn't on the films. We put it in for them because they are a great pursuit team and we figured a 'misdirection' play would be effective. We got the flow going to the left and then brought Pitts

around the other way and they weren't in position to handle it."

Wally Hilgenberg, Minnesota linebacker: "We went with the keys, and they did a good job of fooling us. That's all."

Q. How good is Kansas City's defense?

A. Joe Kapp, Minnesota quarterback, as quoted by Bill McGrane, Minnesota

Fran Tarkenton

publicity man: "The Kansas City defensive line looked like a redwood forest. They took the running game away from us. That line — like a redwood forest in California — seemed to block things out sometimes."

Dave Osborn, Minnesota

running back: "They took everything away from us. We thought there were some things we could do, but on this day, they were the better team."

Q. Hilgenberg was called for unnecessary roughness on the play before Kansas City's last touchdown and Minnesota was penalized 15 yards on an incomplete pass. What happened?

A. Hilgenberg: "Mike Garrett was my man, and I just gave him a forearm, that's all. The official said, 'You can't use your forearm,' and he penalized us. I didn't try to take his head off or anything like that. If I had, I could see the penalty.

Garrett: "He clotheslined me."

Magazines Report Calls of Gamblers

From Press Dispatches

New York, N. Y. - Two national magazines reported Sunday that at least three professional football quarterbacks had received calls from a Detroit gambler.

Time and Newsweek, in independent reports, said Dave Dawson of Detroit had called Len Dawson — no relation — of the Kansas City Chiefs, Bill Munson of the Detroit Lions and Karl Sweetan of the Los Angeles Rams. Newsweek said Dawson had also called the

home of a fourth quarterback. Joe Namath of the New York Jets, and Time said calls had gone to the home of Frank Kush, football coach at Arizona State.

Donald Dawson was among 14 persons arrested by federal agents in a series of raids New Year's Day. The raids were said to be aimed at a nationwide betting ring.

Time contended that Jerome (Dizzy) Dean, former major league pitcher, had introduced Howard Sober, a Michigan trucking executive, to Donald Dawson in 1967. The magazine

said Sober had since "lost roughly $1 million" in bets.

Both magazines said the investigations had begun when Sober, fearing he might miss an airplane connection, gave an airport clerk $50 to make a phone call and ●●●. The clerk notified FBI agents, who gave him permission to make the call. They discovered the number belonged to Donald Dawson, the magazines said.

Added Time, "The agents were particularly curious about Dawson's telephone calls, many of which were charged to Sober's credit card. On the list of 1,900 calls were

hundreds to horse owners, jockeys and trainers, some to bookies and mobsters, others to universities."

Time said investigators could not learn what was said in any of the conversations. It said requests to tap Dawson's telephone were denied by the Justice Department's "top echelon."

Jan. 27

By BILL SCHOLL
Repository Special Writer

CLEVELAND—The Cleveland Browns today drafted Purdue Quarterback Mike Phipps to fit the final piece into place in the wheeling and dealing of players begun late Monday.

Pittsburgh opened the annual drafting of collegiate players by selecting Louisiana Tech Quarterback Terry Bradshaw. Green Bay then chose Notre Dame defensive tackle Mike McCoy.

That left Phipps, the young passer the Browns maneuvered to get with Monday's trades with New York and Miami, and Cleveland grabbed him.

"Phipps is one of the greatest passers I've seen in the college ranks since I became personnel director," said the Browns' Paul Bixler.

-:-

THE HANDSOME 22-year-old native of Shelbyville, Ind. stands 6 feet 3' inches and weighs 206 pounds. He attended high school in Columbus, Ind.

Phipps was the Big Ten's most valuable player in 1969 as he completed his collegiate career with 24 Purdue season and game records. He also was a concensus All-American.

Purdue won 22 of 27 games Phipps started. His three-year totals were 375 completions in 733 attempts for 5,423 yards and 37 touchdowns.

Art Modell made countless phone calls before becoming convinced the Steelers would

take Bradshaw and the Packers would go for McCoy. Final confirmation came Sunday night and Monday he swung the trades which have stirred up much controversy among Browns' fans.

The swapping of defensive tackle Jim Kanicki, running back Ron Johnson and linebacker Wayne Meylan to the Giants for Homer Jones was almost lost in the furor caused by the second half of swapping. That was the one sending popular and talented receiver Paul Warfield to Miami's early first round draft choice.

"A lot of thought went into this, a lot of soul searching," said Modell. "Every member of our coaching staff and everyone in the front office had a voice.

-:-

"THE FINAL decision, of course, was mine and the clincher to me was obtaining Jones. The net deal was Warfield, an outstanding receiver, for Jones, also an outstanding receiver, and a college passer."

April 14

Patriots Assured Of Foxboro Home

FOXBORO, Mass. (AP) — The Boston Patriots, who were driven from that city for lack of a large enough stadium, will have a home in Foxboro, about midway between Boston and Providence.

More than 3,000 residents of Foxboro packed a special town meeting Monday to vote overwhelmingly in favor of a plan to build a 57,000-seat stadium.

The vote was 1,933 in favor, 84 opposed, on a show of hands.

The privately financed stadium would go up on land near the Bay State Raceway track on Route 1.

Patriots President William

Sullivan was at the meeting to argue in favor of the plan.

Gratified by the vote after months of unsuccessful efforts to get a stadium elsewhere, Sullivan told the townspeople, "With a heart overflowing with gratitude, I thank everyone that had anything to do with this."

The stadium site belongs to E. M. Loew, who will transfer 15 acres of land to the stadium corporation. The stadium will have access to Loew's 10,000-car parking lot next to the race track.

Instead of taxes, the town will get 25 cents on each ticket sold, with a limit of $100,000 a year.

The agreement will be reviewed every five yeras.

After 50 years title to the land would pass to the town.

Pro Draft List

FIRST ROUND

1. Pittsburgh, Terry Bradshaw, qb, Louisiana Tech; 2. Green Bay (choice from Chicago), Mike McCoy, dt, Notre Dame; 3. Cleveland (choice from Miami), Mike Phipps, qb, Purdue; 4. Boston, Phil Olsen, de, Utah State; 5. Buffalo, Al Cowlings, dt, Southern California.

6. Philadelphia, Steve Zabel, te, Oklahoma; 7. Cincinnati, Mike Reid, dt, Penn State; 8. St. Louis, Larry Stegent, rb, Texas A. and M.; San Francisco, Cedrick Hardman, de, North Texas State; 10. New Orleans, Kenny Burroughs, wr, Texas Southern.

11. Denver, Bob Anderson, rb, Colorado; 12. Atlanta, John Small, lb, The Citadel; 13. New York Giants, Jim Files, lb, Oklahoma; 14. Houston, Doug Wilkerson, g, North Carolina Central; 15. San Diego, Walker Gillette, wr, Richmond.

16. Green Bay, Rich McGeorge, te, Elon (N.C.) College; 17. San Francisco (choice from Washington), Bruce Taylor, db, Boston University; 18. Baltimore, Norm Bulaich, rb, Texas Christian; 19. Detroit, Steve Owens, rb, Oklahoma; 20. New York Jets, Steve Tannen, db, Florida.

21. Cleveland, Bob McKay, ot, Texas; 22. Los Angeles, Jack Reynolds, lb, Tennessee; 23. Dallas, Duane Thomas, rb, West Texas State; 24. Oakland, Raymond Chester, wr, Morgan State; 25. Minnesota, John Ward, ot, Oklahoma State; 26. Kansas City, Sid Smith, ot, Southern California.

SECOND ROUND

1. Dallas (choice from Chicago), Bob Asher, ot, Vanderbilt; 2. Pittsburgh, Ronnie Shanklin, wr, North Texas State; 3. Miami, Jim Mandich, te, Michigan; 4. Buffalo, Dennis Shaw, qb, San Diego State; 5. Houston (from Boston), Leo Brooks, dt, Texas.

6. Cincinnati, Ron Carpenter, dt, North Carolina State; 7. St. Louis, James Corrigall, lb, Kent State; 8. Philadelphia, Raymond Jones, db, Southern, La., University; 9. Los Angeles (from San Francisco), Charlie Williams, wr, Prairie View A & M. 10. Cleveland (from New Orleans), Joe Jones, de, Tennessee State; 11. Denver, Alden Roche, de, Southern, La., University.

12. St. Louis (from New York Giants), Charlie Hutchinson, g, Ohio State; 13. Atlanta, Art Malone, rb, Arizona State; 14. Houston, William Dusenberry, rb, J. C. Smith; 15 Green Bay, Al Matthews, db, Texas A. and J.; 16. San Diego, Tom Williams, dt, Un. California at Davis; 17. Washington, Bill Brundige, de, Colorado.

18. Baltimore, James Bailey, dt, Kansas; 19. Detroit, Ray Parson, de, Minnesota; 20. New York Jets, Richard Caster, wr, Jackson State; 21. Cleveland, Jerry Sherk, dt, Oklahoma State; 22. San Francisco (from Los Angeles through Philadelphia), John Isenbarger, rb, Indiana; 23. Dallas, Margene Adkins, wr, Henderson, J. C.;

24. Oakland, Ted Koy, rb, Texas; 25. Minnesota, Bill Cappleman, qb, Florida State; 26. Clyde Werner, lb, Washington.

THIRD ROUND

1. Pittsburgh, Mel Blount, db, Southern University; 2. Chicago, George Farmer, wr, UCLA; 3. Miami, Tim Foley, db, Purdue; 4. Boston, Mike Ballou, lb, UCLA; 5. Buffalo, Jim Reilly, g, Notre Dame. 6. St. Louis, Charlie Pittman, rb, Penn State; 7. Philadelphia, Lee Bouggess, rb, Louisville; 8. Cincinnati, Chip Bennett, lb, Abilene Christian; 9. Kansas City (from San Francisco), Billy Bob Barnett, de, Texas A. and M.

10. New Orleans, Clovis Swinney, de, Arkansas State; 11. Denver, John Kohler, t, South Dakota; 12. Atlanta, Andy Maurer, g, Oregon; 13. Atlanta (from New York Giants), Todd Snyder, wr, Ohio University.

14. Dallas (from Houston through Cleveland), Charlie Waters, db, Clemson; 15. Buffalo (from San Diego), Glen Alexander, db, Grambling; 16. Green Bay, James Carter, lb, Minnesota; 17. St. Louis (from Washington), Eric Harris, db, Colorado; 18. Baltimore, Jim O'Brien, wr, Cincinnati, 19. Detroit, Jim Mitchell, de, Virginia State.

20. New York Jets, Dennis Onkotz, lb, Penn State; 21. Dallas (from Cleveland), Steve Kiner, lb, Tennessee; 22. Baltimore (from Los Angeles through Philadelphia), Ara Pearson, te, Morgan State; 23. Dallas, Denton Fox, db, Texas Tech; 24. Oakland, Gerald Irons, de, Maryland State; 25. Minnesota, Chuck Burgoon, lb, North Park, 26. Kansas City, David Hadley, db, Alcorn A. and M.

FOURTH ROUND

1. Chicago, Lynn Larson, t, Kansas State; 2. Pittsburgh, Ed George, t, Wake Forest; 3. Miami, Curtis Johnson, db, Toledo; 4. Buffalo, Jerome Gantt, de, North Carolina Central; 5. Boston, Eddie Ray, rb, Louisiana State University; 6. Atlanta (from Philadelphia), Paul Reed, T, J. C. Smith; 7. Cincinnati, Joe Stephen, g, Jackson State; 8. St. Louis, Greg Lens, dt, Trinity, Tex.

9. San Francisco, Vic Washington, wr, Wyoming. 10. New Orleans, Delles Howell, db, Grambling; 11. Denver, Jerry Hendren, wr, Idaho; 12. Pittsburgh (from New York Giants), Jim Evenson, rb, Oregon; 13. St. Louis (from Atlanta), Don Parish, lb, Stanford.

14. Houston, John Jones, k, Georgia; 15. Green Bay, Ken Ellis, wr, Southern University; 16. San Diego, Bill Maddox, te, Syracuse; 17. Baltimore (from Washington), Steve Smear, lb, Penn State; 18. Green Bay (from Baltimore), Skip Butler, k, Texas-Arlington; 19. New York Giants (from Detroit), Wesley Grant, de, UCLA; 20. New York Jets, John Ebersole, de, Penn State. 21. Cleveland, Ricky Stevenson, db, Arizona; 22. Chicago (from Los Angeles), Ross Brubacher, lb, Texas A. and M. 23. Dallas, John Fitzgerald, t, Boston College; 24. Oakland, Tony Cline, lb, Miami.

25. Washington (from Minnesota through Los Angeles and New Orleans), Paul Laaveg, t, Iowa. 26. Cincinnati (from Kansas City), Billy Hayes, db, South Dakota State.

FIFTH ROUND

Pittsburgh, Jon Staggers, DB, Missouri; New Orleans (from Chicago), Glenn Cannon, DB, Mississippi; Boston (from Miami), Bob Olson, LB, Notre Dame. New York Jets (from Boston), Cliff McClain, RB, South Carolina State; Buffalo, Steve Starnes, LB, Tampa; Houston (from Cincinnati through New York Jets), Ron Saul, G, Michigan State; St. Louis, Tom Lloyd, OT, Bowling Green. Atlanta (from Philadelphia through New York Giants), Bruce Van Ness, RB, Rutgers; San Francisco, Gary McArthur, RB, Southern California; Washington (from New Orleans), Manuel Sistrunk, DT, Arkansas A. M. and N.; Denver, Billy McKoy, LB, Purdue; Atlanta, Ken Mendenhall, C, Oklahoma; New York Giants, Claude Brumfield, G, Tennessee State; Houston, Ed Dooley, DT, Northern Arizona; San Diego, Pettus Farrar, RB, Norfolk State; Green Bay, Cecil Pryor, DE, Michigan; Washington, Danny Pierce, RB, Michigan State; Baltimore, Billy Newsome, DE, Grambling; Detroit, Bob Parker, C, Memphis State; New York Jets, Gary Arthur, TE, Miami Ohio; Cleveland, Steve Engel, RB, Colorado; New Orleans (from Los Angeles), Steve Ramsey, QB, North Texas State; St. Louis (from Dallas), Barry Pierson, DB, Michigan; Oakland, Bart Laster, OT, Maryland State; Minnesota, Greg Jones, RB, UCLA; Kansas City, Mike Oriard, C, Notre Dame.

Gridder Quits For Life With Hippies

April 14

COLTS GET DOLPHINS' NO. 1 PICK

Rozelle Charges Miami With Tampering In Luring Shula

By CAMERON C. SNYDER

The Colts will receive a first round draft choice in 1971 from the Miami Dolphins for violating the National Football League rule on tampering in the Don Shula affair.

Shula, Baltimore's head coach and a vice president, quit the Colts on February 18 to accept a similar position with the Dolphins plus a part of the club's stock.

In making the announcement yesterday, Commissioner Pete Rozelle showed that pro football also washes its soiled linen on Mondays.

Expected More

Soaking Miami a draft choice proved that the Colts' contention of illegal tampering in the Shula case was well founded.

At first glance it would appear the Colts got full payment for Shula's contract breaking.

But the Colts aren't talking about the Commissioner's ruling until they study the full statement. This seems to indicated they might have expected more.

Reprinted from
The Baltimore Sun

Contacted in Miami, Shula said:

"I am unhappy with the commissioner's decision to take our number one draft choice next season. It will retard our program for the future."

Don was mostly concerned that the action would reflect unfavorably upon his integrity.

"I acted in good faith all through the negotiations. I asked for and was granted permission from Steve (Rosenbloom) to talk with Miami. Throughout the negotiations I kept Steve abreast of what was happening."

Joe Robbie, managing director of the Dolphins, said: "The commissioner has completely vindicated our honesty and integrity. . . . Coach Shula and I have acted in a completely honest and forthright manner. My partners and I will meet and decide on a course of action. We'll have nothing further to say until then."

The Commissioner listed three violations of the league's tampering provisions by the Dolphins:

1. Permitting an outsider to initiate talks with Shula; 2. Continuing direct negotiations with Shula without first contacting the Colts for approval to talk with him. 3. Failing to make direct contact with Colt ownership until February 18, the day Shula was hired by the Dolphins.

Colt owner Carroll Rosenbloom commented on the situation last Monday when he hired Don McCafferty as head coach, saying, "I believe they (the Dolphins) contacted Shula around Super Bowl time and waited until after I left on a tour of the Orient to consummate it."

Mill Valley, Calif., May 12 (P)—The scene was an old Victorian house on a Marin County hillside a few miles north of here.

In the basement, a girl washed clothes. In the kitchen, two young men baked bread for two health food restaurants. In the backyard, a girl sun-bathed in the nude.

In his drab room, Ralph (Chip) Oliver sat on his bed—three mattresses stacked on the floor—and tried to explain why he traded the violent but lucrative world of professional football for long hair, a beard and life in a 13-member hippied commune.

Won't Be Back

"There's no way I'll return to training camp," the 26-year-old, first-string Oakland Raiders linebacker vowed today in an interview.

The story of Oliver's transition from linebacker to hippie was revealed Sunday by the Oakland *Tribune* in a copyrighted article.

"Football dehumanizes people," Oliver was quoted by the *Tribune*. "They've taken the players and made them into slabs of beef that can charge around and hit each other."

"A Silly Game"

Oliver said he told Raiders' general manager Al Davis and coach John Madden that football "is a silly game. It's irrelevant and I don't need it anymore."

"He's been saying he's going to quit," Madden said. "I'll believe it when he doesn't show up for training camp in July."

Oliver, a member of the 1967 national championship team at the University of Southern California, said he started his transition last November.

Lost 50 Pounds

He went on a vegetarian diet and dropped from 230 to 200 pounds. Now the 6-foot-2 Oliver s down to 180.

A native of Winona, Miss., Oliver played seven different positions in high school in San Diego and Centralia, Wash.

At 19, he moved to Las Vegas and married a show girl. Eight months later he was divorced and playing football for San Diego City College. From there he went to USC and was drafted by the Raiders on the 11th round in 1968.

He joined the commune, called the One World Family, last January.

$5,000 For "Messiah"

In two years with the Raiders, Oliver says, he earned $50,000, counting playoff bonuses.

He gave $5,000 to a 54-year-old man named Allen, the commune's "messiah," Oliver said.

The commune members run two health food restaurants, Mustard Seed No. 1 in Mill Valley, in which Oliver works from 3.30 P.M. to midnight, and Mustard Seed No. 2 in Berkeley.

He won't miss the money from football, Oliver says.

"Material things just hold you back," he said. "Give me a couple of pairs of jeans and a good pair of boots. That's all I need."

Only Two Souvenirs

He keeps two souvenirs—a pair of old football shoes and a balnket inscribed "Elks Club Bowl 1964."

He is dead serious about the hippie life, Oliver says.

"What I'm saying is the truth," he said.

"I would look up at the people in the Coliseum and realize I wasn't helping them. . . . All we're doing in professional football is entertaining these people and they don't need to be entertained. They need to do their own creative thing.

"I tried to talk to my teammates about this, about getting into a higher state of consciousness. But it was 45 to one.

"All I got for it was my nickname, 'Loose Wire.'"

Aug. 1

Jim Conzelman—as a player . . .

named to Pro Football's Hall of Fame

BEARS' PICCOLO DIES OF CANCER

Back Recently Eulogized For Courage By Sayers

New York, June 16 (P)—Running back Brian Piccolo of the Chicago Bears, saluted recently by teammate Gale Sayers as "a friend who spells out the word courage 24 hours a day every day of his life," died today of cancer at the age of 26.

Survivors include his widow, Joy, and three small daughters. Funeral arrangements were incomplete.

Death came shortly before 4 A.M., E.D.T., at Memorial Hospital for Cancer and Allied Diseases to the courageous athlete who was an unspectacular football player but left a lasting inmark because of his bravery in the face of the dread killer.

Eulogized By Halas

"He was so young to die, with a future that held so much for him," said George Halas, the owner of the Chicago Bears.

"But Brian made the most of the brief 26 years allotted to him, and he will not be forgotten."

One of those who will not forget the former Wake Forest star who was the country's top ground gainer and leading scorer in 1964 is Sayers, who Piccolo began rooming with when the Bears decided on a policy of integrated rooming three years ago.

Man Of Courage

Just three weeks ago, at a dinner in New York at which Sayers was honored as pro football's Most Courageous Athlete for his comeback from a knee injury, Sayers had the audience in tears with an emotional speech in which he paid tribute to Piccolo.

"You flatter me by giving me this award," said Sayers, "but I tell you here and now that I accept it for Brian Piccolo. Brian Piccolo is the man of courage who should receive the award. It is mine tonight. It is Brian Piccolo's tomorrow.

"I love Brian Piccolo and I'd like all of you to love him too. When you hit your knees to pray tonight please ask God to love him too."

Sayers credited Piccolo with being one of the people who had urged him on as he made his comeback and asked the audience "to compare his courage with that which I am supposed to possess.

"Think of Brian and his courage and fortitude shown in the months since last November, in and out of hospitals, hoping to play football again but not too sure at any time what the score was or might be. Brian Piccolo has never given up.

"He has the heart of a giant and that rare form of courage that allows him to kid himself and his opponent — cancer. He has the mental attitude that makes me proud to have a friend who spells out the word courage 24 hours a day every day of his life."

Free Agent

Piccolo began displaying the inner man when he left Wake Forest and was not drafted by any pro team because he was supposedly too small.

However, he signed as a free agent with the Bears, and made many contributions, particularly when Sayers was injured in 1968.

Piccolo took over for the final five games of the season and carried 76 times for 269 yards, finishing with 450 yards—the best of his career. He played during the 1969 season until November 23 when he was declared out of a game against Baltimore because of a cough.

The cough turned out to be cancer, and Piccolo underwent a 4½-hour operation at the end of last November for the removal of a malignant tumor on his chest. Three months later he underwent further treatment and this month again returned to Memorial Hospital.

Woman Signs Grid Contract

Orlando, Fla., July 31 (P)—Pat Palinkas traded her hair curlers for cleats today by signing a standard one-year player's contract with Orlando's professional football team.

The 27-year-old, 35-25-34 Tampa housewife will hold the ball for her placekicker husband, Steve, who also signed a contract with Orlando.

"It feels fine to have them," head coach Paul Massey said after signing the husband-wife combo.

"We told the squad last night we were going to do this. And I didn't hear any adverse reaction at all."

ROOKIES REPORT TO NFL CAMPS

Vets Barred As Owners, Players Remain At Odds

New York, July 14 (P)—The National Football League club owners and players remained at odds today as several rookie camps opned with veterans barred.

"They are still negotiating," was the word from NFL headquarters.

The veteran players have been asked by their own association not to report to camp and the NFL has barred the camps to all but rookies.

Camps are scheduled to open daily until July 26 when Denver, the last to report, will be at work.

George Halas, president of the National Conference, and Lamar Hunt, president of the American Conference, made a joint announcement in Chicago yesterday in which they said camps would open only to rookies.

"Oittle Progress"

However, the players, countering the action to bar veterans from camp, will request members of the College All-Star team to leave their Evanston (Ill.) training camp tomorrow the New York Times said. The All-Stars are preparing to meet the world champion Kansas City Chiefs at the annual Chicago Tribune charity game July 31.

"We're not trying to hurt the Chicago Tribune charity," the Times quoted a players association spokesman as saying, "but if the Chiefs can't practice, the All-Stars shouldn't. The Chiefs voted to support us by giving up their one-game salary for the game, if necessary. And even though the All-Stars are rookies, we're representing them."

John Mackey, of the Colts, president of the NFL Players Association, released a statement early this morning in which he said, "Little progress had been made on NFL player rights and economic issues."

Aug. 3

Exhibition Openers To Go On

[By the Associated Press]

With the strike settled and the players reporting to training camps yesterday, the National Football League will open its pre-season exhibition schedule Saturday. Only one change was made in the 10-game program.

The game between the Cleveland Browns and the Los Angeles Rams, originally scheduled for Friday night at the Los Angeles Coliseum, has been set back 24 hours to Saturday night, in order to give both teams an extra practice day.

Reduction Of Guarantee

After considering a delay of one or two days, the Green Bay Packers decided to play the New York Giants Saturday night as scheduled in their annual Bishop's charity game. There had been some talk of Sunday afternoon or Monday night.

The Miami-Pittsburgh game in Jacksonville's Gator Bowl was believed in danger while the strike still was on but Abe Fletcher, promoter of the game, said the Dolphins and Steelers had agreed to a reduction of their $25,000 guarantees because of the short time left to sell tickets.

Hank Stram, coach of the world champion Kansas City Chiefs who already have beaten the College All-Stars in their first game, was elated over the settlement. His Chiefs will be in Detroit Saturday night to play the Lions.

Gaubatz Arrives

The Minnesota Vikings, beaten by the Chiefs in last January's Super Bowl, will make their bow at the Hall of Fame game in Canton, Ohio, Saturday afternoon against the New Orleans Saints. This game was to have been played anyhow, strike settlement or not, with rookies but now will have most of the veterans in the lineup.

Denny Gaubatz, a former Baltimore linebacker who was traded to Washington during the winter, was the first of the veteran Redskins to show up at Carlisle, Pa., to get ready for Saturday night's game with the Bengals at Cincinnati.

Promoters in Birmingham, Ala., heaved a sigh of relief at the strike ending because they had sold 30,000 seats for Saturday night's game between the New York Jets and the Buffalo Bills. Officials said the game definitely would be played.

Like many of the other coaches, Jim Dooley of the Chicago Bears planned three-a-day workouts to get his men ready for Saturday night's game with the Houston Oilers in Houston. Most of the veterans had been drilling privately at Soldier Field.

Baltimore's Butch Riley, a second year linebacker, popped into camp within minutes after the settlement was announced, prompting a team spokesman to say, "He must have been hovering over the field in a helicopter." Riley and the other Colts started preparing for Saturday night's game at Oakland.

The Dallas Cowboys expected all 41 veterans to show up at Thousand Oaks, Calif., as soon as possible to get ready for Saturday night's game with the San Diego Chargers at San Diego.

Six teams get a break because they have no exhibitions games until next week. The six who draw a bye Saturday are the Boston Patriots, Denver Broncos, Philadelphia Eagles, St. Louis Cards, Atlanta Falcons and San Francisco 49ers.

Aug. 3

GRID WIDOWS SOUND OFF

Many Are Upset By News Of Strike Settlement

[By the Associated Press]

"Most wives watch football in self-defense," said Lucille Waite, of Chicago, but Monie Pallats, an Atlanta housewife, plans to play offense.

"Organized football is unfair to wives," Mrs. Pallats protested today upon hearing the professional football players' strike against club owners had been settled.

"I just might go out and picket the stadium this year."

Varied Reactions

Reaction by Sunday afternoon football widows to the go-ahead for the 1970 pro football season ranged from militancy to resignation and from disappointment to glee.

"I think it's terrible they're going to play," said Mrs. Pallats, adding that she had hoped the season would be canceled.

"If you can't beat em, join 'em," said Mrs. Waite, who was a football widow until she adopted that philosophy. Now she's looking forward to the Bears' games either on television "or in person when we can get tickets."

"I'm really pretty happy about it," beamed Mrs. Ron Erickson, a Minnesota Vikings' fan from Long Beach, Calif. "Before last year it wouldn't have mattered, but now I've really become interested in the games."

"I'm disappointed," lamented Lynda Carruthers, of Los Angeles. "My boy friend, my two brothers, five of their friends and my father all watch the games . . . in my bedroom. It's the only color TV in the house. I like to watch the other programs but they outnumber me."

Out-Numbered 7-1

Joe Gully, of Wantagh, L.I., is out-numbered in his home seven to one, but that doesn't stop him from his Sunday afternoon pastime.

"Mother hates football," said 21-year-old Ellen Gully, a Manhattan secretary. "She tried to break the TV set last season. Well, not really. It's color and she just touched the knobs on the back that aren't supposed to be touched. Both teams turned out red and green but Dad just went to the back porch and turned on the black and white set."

"I'm really looking forward to this season," said Ellen's mother, Eileen, "especially after what happened yesterday."

It seems that Joe decided to tear himself away from the baseball game long enough yesterday to launch his boat at the shore but it was Mrs. Gully's car that ended up in the water with only the radio antenna in view.

Death Closes Era Of Lombardi

Washington, Sept. 3 (P)—An era of professional football ended today with the death from cancer of Vince Lombardi, the Washington Redskins' coach who reached legendary heights in the 1960's with the teams he led at Green Bay.

Lombardi, 57, believed deeply in the old-fashioned virtues which were stamped over all his teams--hard work, dedication and never give up.

"Any man's finest hour," he once said, "is when he has worked his heart out, exhausted on the field of battle, victorious."

He believed that football was basically a game of blocking and tackling, with no fancy frills intruding.

Flawless Execution

He won five National Football League and two world championships with Packer teams that ran the fundamental power sweep and the off-tackle plays with monotonous regularity but made them work with flawless execution.

Lombardi died at Georgetown University Hospital after a two-month bout with intestinal cancer. His wife of 30 years, Marie, and son, Vincent, were at his side.

Although friends knew of his ailment for which he underwent two operations, no public announcement on the gravity of his condition was made until yesterday when Mrs. Lombardi authorized a statement which described him as suffering from "an extraordinarily virulent form of cancer."

Services In New York

Mass will be said at St. Patrick's Cathedral in New York Monday morning by Terence Cardinal Cook, described as "a great personal admirer and an old friend."

Lombardi will be buried Monday at Mount Olivet cemetery in Middletown Township near Red Bank, N.J., home of his widow.

Football fans who thrilled to the skill and precision of his teams mourned the death of Lombardi.

"He had a covenant with greatness, more than any man I have ever known," said Redskins president Edward Bennett Williams. "He was committed to excellence in everything he attempted."

Influenced By Blaik

The man who had a marked influence on Lombardi himself, the coach whom Lombardi called the greatest he had ever known, was Earl (Red) Blaik. Lombardi was an assistant to Blaik at West Point in the 1950s.

"Vince Lombardi epitomized Twentieth Century America by his devotion to his family and dedication to his church and country," said Blaik.

"He was recognized as a strong-willed man whose extraordinary success in life came from a seriousness of purpose and hard work.

"This coupled with a remarkable intellect, made him the peer of his profession. He was a volatile, sometimes gruff but a lovable, loyal friend who somehow seemed indestructible."

Drawn To Gridiron

The son of an immigrant Italian butcher, Lombardi started out as a boy studying for the Roman Catholic priesthood but football drew him away.

He was a star fullback at Brooklyn's St. Francis Prep and went to Fordham University, where he switched to guard and quickly earned a reputation as a short-fused scrapper whose violent charges made him seem twice his 182 pounds. In 1935-1936, he was one of Fordham's famed "Seven Blocks of Granite."

After graduation, Lombardi worked days as an insurance investigator, studied law at night at Fordham because his father wanted him to, and played weekend football for a minor league pro team that called itself the Brooklyn Eagles.

In 1939, he took his first coaching job as an assistant at 600-student St. Cecilia High School in Englewood, N.J. Three years later, he was head football, basketball and baseball coach.

Back To Fordham

He returned to Fordham as an assistant in 1947 and two years later joined Blaik at Army where he handled the offense.

Lombardi went to the New York Giants as an assistant in 1954 to put some offensive thrust into a team that had lost nine games the season before. Two years later the Giants won the NFL championship. Then came Green Bay.

He became head coach and general manager in 1959 with absolute authority—the power to hire and fire, even to design Packer uniforms.

He took them from a 1-10-1 record to 7-5 and a third-place finish his first year. In his second season the Packers won the first of their six division titles in eight years.

3 Straight Titles

Lombardi was the only coach to win three consecutive NFL titles.

His success in nine years was so phenomenal that he was sought as an authority on other matters and even urged to enter politics. He authorized a best seller, "Run to Daylight," and produced a film, "Second Effort," that inspired sales groups and still remains heavily in demand.

Lions Deal Packers First Shutout, 40-0, Since 1958

Green Bay, Wis., Sept. 20 (P)—Mel Farr scored two touchdowns and Errol Mann kicked four field goals as the Detroit Lions crushed the Green Bay Packers, 40 to 0, in a National Football League opener this afternoon.

It was the first time the Packers have been shut out since 1958, when the Baltimore Colts stomped Green Bay, 53 to 0.

The last time the Packers were blanked in Green Bay was the opening game of the 1949 season when the Chicago Bears turned the trick, 17 to 0.

FIRST MONDAY NIGHT
TV GAME

BROWNS TOPPLE JETS, 31 TO 21

Cleveland Gets AFC Grid Indoctrination

Cleveland, Sept. 21 (AP)—A spectacular 96-yard touchdown runback of the second-half kickoff by Homer Jones and a 65-yard punt in the final two minutes led Cleveland to a 31-to-21 victory over the New York Jets in the Browns' American Football Conference debut tonight.

A record Cleveland crowd of 85.703 watched the Browns take an early lead and hold it.

Substitute linebacker Billy Andrews iced the victory with 35 seconds left when he intercepted a Joe Namath pass at the New York 25, fell down, got up and scampered in for a touchdown.

Fumble Is Critical

Jones's touchdown gave the Browns a 21-7 lead. Then, with the Browns leading 24-14 in the fourth quarter, Jack Gregory pounced on a fumble by the Jets' Matt Snell on the Cleveland seven-yard line.

The Browns used up almost six minutes after that before giving up the ball when Don Cockroft missed an 18-yard field goal.

Namath then passed the Jets back into contention with 3.22 left when he completed an 80-yard, four-play drive with a 33-yard touchdown pass to George Sauer.

The Browns failed to move, but Cockroft uncorked a 65-yard punt that drove the Jets back to the four-yard-line.

New York's Ed Bell called for a fair catch at the 30 but the ball bounced past him and he was nailed at the four.

Andrews's clinching touchdown came four plays later.

Kapp Signs With Boston

Boston, Oct. 2 (AP) Fiery Joe Kapp. who led the Minnesota Vikings to glory last year but couldn't resolve his contract differences with the management. joined the Boston Patriots today and immediately predicted: "We're going to be a winner."

The star quarterback, who played out his option while helping the Vikings win the National Football League championship. was technically a free agent when signed by Boston.

The Patriots, however. gave up strong safety John Charles and an undisclosed 1972 draft pick for Kapp in keeping with the league policy of providing compensation in such cases.

Head coach Clive Rush said Kapp would be activated immediately but would not start Sunday against the Baltimore Colts here. He said he did not know whether the 6-foot-3, 215-pound veteran would see any action in the game.

Kapp, who reportedly had been demanding a five-year, $1.25 million pact from the Vikings, also refused to answer questions about his agreement with Boston or his differences with Minnesota.

"I'm here to play football," he said. "All the rest is ancient history. I don't know how it happened, but it happened. Now I'm here to help this club."

Oct. 18

Cleveland Stadium Tops in Pro Football Attendance

Browns' Turnstiles Are Keeping Up Steady Click, Click

BY BILL SCHOLL
Repository Special Writer

CLEVELAND — Back in 1934 when the National Football League began keeping attendance figures, the entire 60-game schedule drew 492,684 spectators.

Compare that with last year when the Browns alone pulled in 578.360 for their seven regular season games at the stadium. It was the largest total for any club in NFL history.

And the magnetism of the Browns at the turnstiles goes on and on.

When the Detroit Lions drop in for a visit today, the stadium will house its 16th consecutive standing-room-only crowd of more than 80,000 for a Browns game. No other pro club has come close to matching that accomplishment.

Dan Rooney, vice president of the Pittsburgh Steelers, said, "Cleveland's attendance is one of the real phenomenons of pro football. It's fantastic.

"We have a brand new stadium in Pittsburgh with a capacity of 51,000 and that's not much more than half of what the Browns draw for every game."

Pete Rozelle, commissioner of the NFL, said, "It's a wonderful tribute to the Cleveland organization under Art Modell.

"The Browns have maintained a winning tradition going back to 1946 and it has become a weekend habit for fans in Central and northern Ohio to watch the Browns.

"Ohio has a great background of football interest, and looking at it from the other side, it's great for a team to have backing like that."

The biggest single spur to the current remarkable fan interest was having the Browns win the league championship in 1964. The team has had 47 home crowds of 80,000 in its 25-year history and 33 of them have come since trimming Baltimore that December day.

Cleveland stadium seats 79,282 for football. Yet last year's average for seven league games was 82,623. That could be surpassed this season, since every crowd so far has been above that figure.

Park limitations prevent most other pro clubs from having a chance to match the Browns' turnouts. Only Tulane Stadium in New Orleans, the Coliseum in Los Angeles, the Cotton Bowl in Dallas and the Orange Bowl in Miami are close in size.

New Orleans has had outstanding throngs in what more commonly is called the Sugar Bowl. Capacity is 80,997 and the Saints, 528,242 season total three years ago ranks next behind Browns totals since 1963.

Before the Coliseum was modernized, the Rams set single game records which are unbeatable at the present time. Three crowds were in excess of 100,000 and seven others topped 90,000.

But attendance was uneven in Los Angeles and the club's best year was 1958 when 502,084 for six games. Given a seventh game, as played now, they might own the record today. Yet in the last nine years of seven-game home cards, the Rams' peak was 498,693.

By the close of this season, the Browns will have drawn approximately 11,000,000 people to the stadium since the club was born in 1946.

Politics Tougher Than Grid, Kemp Says After Triumph

Washington, Nov. 4 (*P*)—Jack Kemp, pro football quarterback who ran successfully for Congress, said today politics is tougher on an individual than sports.

"Politics is far more challenging intellectually," said Kemp from his home in Buffalo, N.Y., where he last played with the Bills in 1969. "And campaigning is as physically demanding as football."

N.Y.'s 39th District

Kemp, a Republican-Conservative who had campaigned in the past for Barry Goldwater, Ronald Reagan and President Nixon, easily defeated attorney Thomas P. Flaherty, a Democrat-Liberal, for New York's 39th District seat vacated by Richard D. McCarthy, a Democrat.

The 35-year-old Kemp won't be as lost in the halls of Congress as many newcomers because he worked in Washington in the off season for Republican National Chairman Rogers C. B. Morton.

"But I've got a lot to learn," he said.

Other former athletes who scored victories in yesterday's election include Ralph Metcalfe, 1932 Olympic sprinter from Chicago who joins Kemp in the House, and Wendell Anderson, a member of the 1956 Olympic hockey team who will be Minnesota governor.

Mizell Returns To House

Returning to the House will be Reps. Wilmer (Vineger Bend) Mizell (R., N.C.), former pitcher for St. Louis and Pittsburgh, and Bob Mathis (R., Calif.), Olympic decathalon champion in 1948 and 1952.

Other former athletic luminaries in the 92nd Congress will be Reps. Gerald R. Ford (R., Mich.), a football player at the University of Michigan: Morris ty of Michigan; Morris K. Udall (D., Ariz.) co-captain of the University of Arizona basketball team and pro player with the Denver Nuggets; Rep. John L. McMillan (D., S.C.), All-Southern choice while playing football at the University of South Carolina; Rep. Bill Nichols (D., Ala.), captain of the 1940 Auburn football team, and Rep. Torbert MacDonald, (D., Mass.), three-letter man at Harvard who also was a New York Yankee farmhand.

But several former athletes might well be reflecting the post-election woes of pro football linebacker Sam Huff who was unsuccessful last spring in his bid to win the Democratic primary for a West Virginia House seat.

Opponents Are Everywhere

"In football, your opponents are right across the scrimmage line where you can see them," he said. "In politics, your opponents are everywhere. It is like fighting shadows."

Jay Wilkinson, former Duke football player, followed in the steps of his father, Bud Wilkinson, in losing his first attempt at political office.

The younger Wilkinson was defeated in an Oklahoma House race by incumbent Tom Steed. The elder Wilkinson, former Oklahoma football coach, sought a Senate seat in 1966 and lost.

Another loser in yesterday's election was John Erickson, former Wisconsin basketball coach and general manager of the Milwaukee Bucks, who was defeated in his bid to unseat Sen. William Proxmire (D., Wis.).

SAINTS NIP LIONS ON RECORD KICK

Last-Second 63-Yard Field Goal Decisive, 19-17

New Orleans, Nov. 8 (*P*)—Tom Dempsey kicked a record 63-yard field goal on the last play of the game to give the New Orleans Saints a 19-to-17 upset of the Detroit Lions in a National Football League game today.

Detroit appeared to have won the game when Erroll Mann kicked an 18-yard field goal with 11 seconds to give the Lions a two-point lead.

But Saint quarterback Billy Kilmer completed a pass to Al Dodd after the enusing kickoff and Dodd went out of bounds at the New Orleans 45 with two seconds left on the clock.

Only Chance

The out-of-bounds play gave the Saints time to get Dempsey and the rest of the field goal team onto the field. Then Dempsey, whose kicking foot is partially missing, booted the 63-yarder.

It bettered the NFL record by seven yards.

The previous distance record for field goals, 56 yards, was a kick by Bert Rechichar of the Baltimore Colts against the Chicago Bears on September 27, 1953. Dempsey had booted a 55-yarder against the Los Angeles Rams a year ago.

Dempsey's boot was not a thing of beauty but it cleared the cross-bar by scant inches, sending a crowd of 66,910 into an unbelievable frenzy.

Earlier, Dempsey had kept the Saints, decided underdogs in J. D. Roberts's debut as head coach, within striking distance with field goals of 29, 27, and 8 yards. Roberts replaced Tom Fears, fired last week.

Barrington Scores

The other New Orleans points came on a three-yard touchdown run by Tom Barrington with just under seven minutes to play. Dempsey converted to give the Saints a 16-14 lead.

The Lions, aided by an extra down and an interference panalty drove from their 14 to the 10 where Mann's field goal apparently gave Detroit the victory. Detroit had scored on a 10-yard run in the second period by Mel Farr and a two-yard Bill Munson-to-Charlie Sanders pass in the third.

Dempsey, in his second year with the Saints, was born with part of his right foot missing.

"I knew I could kick the ball that far, but whether or not I could kick it straight that far kept running through my mind," said Dempsey.

"I knew I had to hit the ball awfully hard and would need a little extra time. But they held up perfectly and I got a perfect snap."

Dempsey said he was so far back he couldn't see the ball clear the crossbar. "I saw the referees hands go up and heard everybody start yelling and I knew it was good. It's quite a thrill. I'm still kind of shook up."

Statistics

	Lions	Saints
First downs	18	15
Rushing yardage	135	131
Passing yardage	143	141
Return yardage	51	42
Passes	13-25-2	15-28-0
Punts	3-31	6-44
Fumbles lost	3	0
Yards penalized	31	124

Detroit	0	7	7	3—17
New Orleans	3	3	3	10—19

NO—FG Dempsey 29
Det—Farr 10 run (Mann kick)
NO—FG Dempsey 27
Det—Sanders 2 pass from Munson (Mann kick)
NO—FG Dempsey 8
NO—Barrington 3 run (Dempsey kick)
Det—FG Mann 18
NO—FG Dempsey 63
A—66,910

COWBOYS SHUT OUT LIONS, 5-0

Dallas Defense Superb; Clark Boots 26-Yard Field Goal

Dallas, Dec. 26 (*P*)—Dallas' savage Doomsday Defense victimized Detroit quarterback Greg Landry for a safety and intercepted a pass on a desperation last-minute Lion drive today for a 5-to-0 victory in the National Football League play-offs.

The victory pushed the Cowboys into the National Football Conference final next week against the survivor of tomorrow's San Francisco-Minnesota clash.

The safety came with 4.45 remaining in the game.

Clark Hits

Dallas held a 3-0 lead at the time on a 26-yard field goal by Mike Clark in the first period.

It was the first NFL play-off game without a touchdown since 1950 when Cleveland downed the New York Giants 8-3.

How Much Is Too Much?

THE COMMISSIONER'S WHITE PAPER

Now and then you'll read that America is saturated with televised football, and that it won't be long before professional football will be so diluted that its popularity and appeal will drop.

The fact that we are now televising nationally a game every Monday night, in addition to the traditional Sunday coverage, has rekindled these observations.

It might be pertinent, then, to ask the question: Is there a danger of overexposure in football television?

I'd answer, yes, unequivocally.

But has the saturation point been reached?

To that, I'd answer, no, just as unequivocally.

If anything, our surveys—and we look into this regularly and have for several years—indicate that the public wants even more games than are now on television.

I know it may sound strange, particularly after having said that we are concerned about overexposure, but we felt that by adding the Monday night weekly series we had a better chance of stabilizing our sport for the future.

For one thing, there are more sets automatically in use in the evening hours than there are on Sunday afternoon. We have a large, regular viewing audience on Sunday but week after week and, actually, year after year, they are mostly the same people. Compared with the overall viewing audience—the vast group of television watchers—this Sunday group is relatively small. We felt that reaching this broader market on Monday night gave us a chance to make new fans on television, fans who eventually will want to come out to our games. And by reaching this broad market, we created a still broader market for television sponsors. And this, in turn, would help us insure that pro football on television would continue as it had in the past.

Our early ratings have indicated that we are, in fact, reaching a broader market than we normally do on Sunday, including more women. A survey made early in the season turned up some very favorable comments from wives concerning the Monday night telecasts. Several said at least they knew where their husbands were.

To reach this market was a major goal of the Monday night series. But as far as overexposure is concerned there was another major reason, and that was that we did feel the saturation point might have been reached on Sunday.

In order to get the necessary monies for our 26 clubs from the two networks handling the Sunday telecasts—CBS and NBC—both of those networks would have been required to have a doubleheader every week. With four Sunday games every week for 14 weeks, we recognized the fact that we could soon have overexposure.

We still have a lot of football on Sunday—generally one game on each network in NFL franchise cities, and one game on one network and two on the other network outside of franchise areas, and when the team is playing at home.

But you don't have two doubleheaders every week, as we had for most of the last few years. The Monday night series lessens the money we need from Sunday, which in turn lessens utilization of our product.

By going to Monday night, we hoped to reduce the danger of overexposure on the simple premise that it is hard to overexpose an audience that includes many who have never been exposed at all.

There is little question that television has been an important factor in professional football's growth and popularity. It is a game particularly well suited to television—it is colorful, active, and not difficult to understand.

Similar to other news media, including the newspapers and less frequent publications which continue to devote s much space and attention to our sport, television is a means through which millions of people can enjoy professional football.

And that is what a professional sport is mostly all about.

Dec. 26

NFL Named in Antitrust Action

Alworth Sues— a la Flood

BY JERRY MAGEE

SAN DIEGO—The fawn known as "Bambi" who has tripped through the football forest so appealingly these last nine years, Lance Alworth, has decided he wants to cut down all the trees.

In one of two suits he has filed, Alworth is challenging the very touchstone of the game, the player contract, in an action similar to the one Curt Flood initiated against baseball.

In a separate action, taken in San Diego's Superior Court, Alworth, alleging breach of contract and violation of state antitrust laws, has sued the Chargers for $5.6 million.

San Diego may not be much on the football field but it leads the league in litigation. Earlier, Houston Ridge, a defensive lineman, entered a $1.25 million action against the Chargers, alleging improper medical treatment that included use of drugs. The suits of Alworth and Ridge add up to over $6.8 million.

ALWORTH'S FEDERAL COURT suit is the one which could be of greatest consequence to football. It named the Chargers, the National Football League and all the 26 NFL teams. It charged violations of the federal antitrust laws.

After filing suits, Alworth showed up the next day for practice and coach Charlie Waller said he planned to continue to utilize him. Earlier, however, Alworth's name figured in trade speculation and his legal move against the club likely means this season, his ninth, will be his last here.

After catching more than 1,000 yards for a record seven straight seasons, Lance had little more than half that with two games to go. When he was asked if his tangled affairs had influenced his performance, he answered, "I don't know."

Alworth, who has entered a petition for bankruptcy in a federal court, intends to continue his career, said one of his attorneys, Don Augustine. Augustine may be remembered as the onetime counsel for the American Football League Players Association and as the man who signed O.J. Simpson.

Alworth is in his final year of a three-year contract with San Diego with an option year still to go. In his state court suit, he claimed he signed a contract for $35,000 a year in 1967 for three years with an understanding with Eugene Klein (president of the Chargers) that the club would provide financing to construct a $1.5 million apartment project in Little Rock, Ark.

Alworth contended he also was to receive insurance business which would have provided about $10,000 a year in commission until one year after his retirement.

Alworth's suit claims Klein had no intention of carrying out the team's part of the agreement.

In another allegation, Alworth contends he met with Sid Gillman (general manager of the Chargers) in January of 1970 to sign a three-year contract with 1974 an option year with the agreement the team would enable Alworth to obtain a $50,000 personal use loan.

HE CONTENDS GILLMAN signed the agreement on behalf of Klein which would have allowed him a reasonable time to repay the loan. Alworth said the team agreed not to file the contracts with the commissioner's office to make them valid contracts and that upon repaying the loan, the team had agreed to destroy and cancel the contracts.

He alleges Klein and the Chargers had no intent to allow him reasonable time to repay the money and did file the contracts as valid.

In his federal court action, Alworth charges that since 1967 (when the NFL-AFL merger was consummated) that the NFL has exercised an unlawful power of monopoly enabling the teams to retain players for far less compensation than they would have gotten with open competition in the player market.

Alworth also challenged Commissioner Pete Rozelle's authority given him by the league.

Under state and federal laws, Alworth, should he win the anti-trust case, could be awarded treble damages. However, in the suit, there was no figure listed regarding damages incurred to date. The figure will be determined on what he might have earned in a free and open market, the suit said.

Alworth's attorneys have indicated it could be three to five years before his actions have gone through the legal process.

49ers Stun Vikings, 17-1

Dec. 27

Colt Defense Stops Bengals, Unitas Engineers 17-0 Win

By CAMERON C. SNYDER

Cincinnati's Cinderellas ran into the Colts' witching-hour defense yesterday and changed back into what they were, a young expansion team.

Prince charming John Unitas waved his magic right arm twice for touchdown passes of 45 and 53 yards, but used battering Ram Norm Bulaich for most of the pounding in the 17-to-0 Colt victory at cold and windy Memorial Stadium.

Now the Colts will meet today's winner of the Miami Dolphin-Oakland Raider game here next Sunday for the right to represent the American Conference in the Super Bowl against the National Conference champions.

Scoring Plays
FIRST PERIOD
	Bengals	Colts
Colts—11.01. Jefferson 45 pass from Unitas (O'Brien kick)	0	7
SECOND PERIOD		
Colts—7.23. FG O'Brien 44	0	10
FOURTH PERIOD		
Colts—7.53. Hinton 53 pass from Unitas (O'Brien kick)	0	17

Attendance—31.137. Time of game—2 hours, 19 minutes.

John Brodie's Passing, Gossett's Field Goal Spark Win

Minneapolis-St. Paul, Dec. 27 (P)—The San Francisco 49ers, overcoming their own adversity, stunned the Minnesota Vikings, 17 to 14, today in a National Football Conference semi-final play-off on Bruce Gossett's 40-yard field goal and John Brodie's touchdown pass and run.

Cox Misses

The victory, in nine degree weather, that contributed to the game's eight fumbles, sends the 49ers into the NFC championship game next Sunday in San Francisco against the Dallas Cowboys.

Gossett's field goal broke a 7-7 tie in the second period and San Francisco's unheralded defense helped save it in the fourth period when defensive end Tommy Hart spilled Gary Cuozzo for a seven yard loss at the 49er 37.

Fred Cox, who had missed a 33-yard field goal earlier, was short this time on a 43 yarder that would have tied the game with 10 minutes to play.

Brodie, himself, capped the victory with a one-yard sneak with 1.20 left in the game to complete San Francisco's upset of professional football's winningest team.

With one second to play, Cuozzo passed 24 yards to Gene Washington for the game's final touchdown.

The Statistics

	Dolphins	Raiders
First downs	16	12
Rushing yardage	118	114
Passing yardage	124	187
Return yardage	5	19
Passes	13-27-1	8-16-0
Punts	5-39	4-32
Fumbles lost	0	2
Yards penalized	0	30
Miami	0 7 0	7—14
Oakland	0 7 7	7—21

Mia—Warfield 16 pass from Griese (Yepremian kick).
Oak—Biletnikoff 22 pass from Lamonica (Blanda kick).
Oak—Brown 50 pass interception (Blanda kick).
Oak—Sherman 82 pass from Lamonica (Blanda kick).
Mia—W. Richardson 7 pass from Griese (Yepremian kick).
Attendance—54.401.
Rushing—Miami. Kiick 14-64. Csonka 10-33. Morris 8-29. Oakland. Hubbard 18-36. Smith 9-37. Dixon 8-31.
Receiving—Miami. Warfield 4-62. Kiick 4-34. Richardson 2-30. Morris 2-15. Twilley 1-14. Oakland. Biletnikoff 3-46. Chester 2-47. Sherman 1-82. Smith 1-9. Dixon 1-3.
Passing—Miami. Griese 13-27-1. 155 yards: Oakland. Lamonica 8-16-0. 187.

RAIDERS TOP DOLPHINS IN SEMI-FINAL

Brown, Sherman Score In Second Half Of 21-14 Victory

By KEN NIGRO
Sun Staff Correspondent

Oakland, Calif., Dec. 27—The Oakland Raiders needed no miracle from George Blanda today. Instead, they relied on an electrifying 82-yard pass play in the fourth quarter to defeat the stubborn Miami Dolphins. 21 to 14.

The picture pass went from Daryle Lamonica to wide receiver Rod Sherman on a third-and-12 situation with the Raiders clinging to a 14-to-7 lead. Sherman caught the ball on the Miami 35 a few steps beyond defender Curtis Johnson and went the rest of the way untouched.

The Dolphins, who had played a near-flawless game to that point, came back with a touchdown of their own on a seven-yard pass from Bob Griese to ex-Colt Willie Richardson, but then ran out of time.

Shula Disappointed

It was an especially tough loss for Miami coach Don Shula who was looking forward to another trip to Baltimore next week to face his old team for the American Conference championship. Instead it is the Raiders who will be playing the conference title game for the fourth straight year.

"We were disappointed, naturally," said Shula. "We worked hard and accomplished a lot but suddenly our whole season comes to a screeching halt.

"I'm not making any predictions on next week. Oakland is really a solid team but if Baltimore can run the ball like they did against Cincinnati, they'll be awfully tough."

	49ers	Vikings
First downs	14	14
Rushing yardage	96	117
Passing yardage	193	124
Return yardage	28	34
Punts	8-34	7-39
Fumbles lost	3	5
Yards penalized	37	5
San Francisco	7 3 0	7—17
Minnesota	7 0 0	7—14

Minn—Krause fumble return 22 (Cox kick).
SF—Witcher 24 pass from Brodie (Gossett kick).
SF—FG Gossett 40.
SF—Brodie 1 (Gossett kick).
Minn—Washington 24 pass from Cuozzo (Cox kick).
Attendance—46.050.

To Super Bowl

Raiders Bow, 27-17, In AFC Showdown

Unitas's TD Pass To Perkins Clinches Victory After Blanda Rallies Raiders

By CAMERON C. SNYDER

John Unitas and his offensive troops atoned for wasted opportunities in the first half with a 17-point output in the last 30 minutes and the Colts hitched a ride to the Super Bowl with a 27-to-17 victory over the Oakland Raiders in the American Football Conference title game yesterday at the Stadium.

Opponents for the Colts will be the Dallas Cowboys in the January 17 classic in Miami. Dallas defeated San Francisco, 17-10.

As has been the case so often this season, the Colts played just well enough to win, but for once they quieted the scoffers who kept repeating during the year "They didn't play anybody."

Oakland was a good team, a true representative for this championship game. But the Colts were better and could just as easily have won big with a few pass connections in the first half. Instead, they won with a drive after the Raiders had tied it 10-10 in the third period and crept to within 20-17 in the first two minutes of the last quarter.

Blanda At Quarterback

But the Colts don't know how to take the easy road. While the so-called good teams chartered limousines in reaching the playoff, the Colts used their thumbs to get to the same destination.

If anything, the hard road and the ridicule toughened the Colts and that was evident yesterday to the 56,368 fans who watched under sunny skies.

Baltimore was just too physical for the Raiders on offense and defense. The Colt zone defense bent but never broke against the Raider air assault which had to be carried on by the 43-year-old George Blanda after Daryle Lamonica, Oakland's starting quarterback, was sent to the sidelines with an injury midway of the second quarter.

Colt Statistics

	Oakland	Colts
Total first downs	16	18
First downs rushing	5	7
First downs passing	10	11
First downs by penalty	1	0
Total offensive yardage	336	363
Total No. offensive plays (inc. times thrown passing)	52	70
Average gain per offensive play	6.4	5.2
Net rushing yardage	107	126
Total rushing plays	22	38
Average gain per rushing play	4.9	3.3
Net passing yardage	229	237
Gross yds. gained passing	277	245
Times thrown and yards lost attempting to pass	5-48	2-8
Passes attempted, completed, had intercepted	35-18-3	29-11-0
Average gain per pass play (inc. times thrown passing)	5.5	7.6
Punts — number, average, had blocked	5-40-0	6-47-0
Fumbles—number and lost	1-1	0-0
Penalties—number & yards	2-20	2-10
Total return yardage	5-70	9-122
No. & yds. punt returns	2-10	2-1
No. & yds. kickoff returns	3-60	4-105
No. & yds. interception returns	0-0	3-16

Oakland	0	3	7	7—17
Colts	3	7	10	7—27

FIRST PERIOD

	Oak.	Colts
Colts—9.46. Field Goal O'Brien 16 yds.	0	3

SECOND PERIOD

Colts—7.18 Rush Bulaich 2 yds. (O'Brien k'ck)	0	10
Oakland—11.39 Field Goal - Blanda 48 yds.	3	10

THIRD PERIOD

Oakland—4.58 Pass Blanda To Biletnikoff 38 yds. (Blanda k'ck)	10	10
Colts—8.38. Field Goal O'Brien 23 yds.	10	13
Colts—13.32. Rush Bulaich 11 yds. (O'Brien k'ck)	10	20

FOURTH PERIOD

Oakland—1.54. Pass Blanda to Wells 15 yds. (Blanda kick)	17	20
Colts—3.29. Pass Unitas to Perkins 68 yds. (O'Brien kick)	17	27

Attendance—56,368
Time—2 hrs. 29 min.

49ERS LOSE NFC TEST TO DALLAS

Jordan, Renfro Thefts And Thomas's Runs Spark 17-10 Win

By KEN NIGRO
Sun Staff Correspondent

San Francisco, Jan. 3 — The Dallas Cowboys ended four years of frustration and failure today, defeating the San Francisco 49ers, 17 to 10, to win the National Football League Championship.

The game was expected to be a duel between the passing of John Brodie against the running of rookie Duane Thomas and Walt Garrison. The Cowboys did indeed feature a punishing ground attack, grinding out 229 yards to only 61 for the 49ers.

But, today, at least, Brodie was not on target. He threw just one touchdown pass and completed only 19 of 40. More importantly, he was intercepted twice and both led to Dallas touchdowns in the third quarter.

Defense Protects Lead

These two scores put the Cowboys on top, 17-3, and their ferocious defense protected the lead the rest of the way. Brodie did manage to complete a 26-yard TD pass to Dick Wichter late in the third period but he could not rally the 49ers in the last 15 minutes.

The 49er touchdown, incidentally, was the first the Dallas defense had allowed in the last five games. Houston did score in the final regular-season game but that came on a 41-yard run after a fumble recovery.

The victory erased some bitter Cowboy defeats over the last four years and now it can no longer be said that they always lose the big ones. They had been defeated for the NFL title by Green Bay in both 1966 and 1967 and had lost to Cleveland in 1968 and 1969 in the Eastern Conference final.

Now the Cowboys find themselves in the biggest game of them all—the Super Bowl—against the Baltimore Colts who at one time also called Dallas home.

Statistics

	Cowboys	49ers
First downs	22	15
Yards rushing	229	61
Yards passing	90	246
Return yardage	31	5
Passes	7-22-0	19-40-2
Punts	6-40	5-41
Fumbles lost	0	1
Penalties	75	51

Dallas	0	3	14	0—17
San Francisco	3	0	7	0—10

SF—FG Gossett 16.
DAL—FG Clark 21.
DAL—Thomas 13 run (Clark kick).
DAL—Garrison 5 pass from Morton (Clark kick).
SF—Witcher 26 pass from Brodie (Gossett kick).
Attendance—59,625.

Individual Statistics

RUSHING—Dallas, Thomas 27-143; Garrison, 17-71; Welch, 5-27. San Francisco, Willard 13-42; Cunningham, 8-14.
PASSING—Dallas, Morton 7-22-0, 101 yards. San Francisco, Brodie, 19-40-2, 262.
RECEIVING—Dallas, Garrison, 43-51; Thomas, 3-24; Rucker, 1-21. San Francisco, Washington 6-68; Cunningham, 4-34; Windsor 3-70; Witcher, 1-41; Willard, 2-1.

Colts Top Cowboys, 16-13, In Super Bowl

O'BRIEN KICK DECISIVE IN LAST MINUTE

Loss To Jets Redeemed As Morrall Steps In For Injured Unitas

The Baltimore Colts captured pro football's biggest prize—the Super Bowl—in Miami yesterday when rookie Jim O'Brien kicked a 32-yard field goal with 5 seconds remaining to defeat the Dallas Cowboys, 16 to 13.

Until the 22-year-old O'Brien's boot settled the issue, the contest appeared to be heading for the first sudden-death finish in Super Bowl history.

But the Colts salvaged the victory in regulation time to redeem themselves for their 16-to-7 upset by the New York Jets in the third Super Bowl two years ago.

Reprinted from
The Baltimore Sun

Morrall At Helm

Backup quarterback Earl Morrall was at the controls in place of the injured John Unitas as Baltimore fought back from a 13-to-6 deficit to earn the $15,000 pay-off that goes to each member of the world-championship team. Unitas was sitting on the bench with a rib injury suffered in the first half, but was ready to play if needed.

The Colts, who lost the ball 7 times on turnovers, rallied for 10 points in the fourth quarter with Tom Nowatzke's 2-yard touchdown run and O'Brien's conversion tying the score at 13-13.

Just over a minute remained when Colts' middle linebacker Mike Curtis intercepted Craig Morton's pass at the Dallas 40 and ran to the 28-yard line. Norm Bulaich gained three yards in two carries as Morrall positioned the Colts for O'Brien's winning field goal.

2 Cowboy Field Goals

The Cowboys had used field goals of 14 and 30 yards by Mike Clark and Morton's 7-yard touchdown pass to Duane Thomas to establish a 13-to-6 halftime advantage.

Baltimore's only score in the first half was produced by Unitas's 75-yard touchdown pass to John Mackey, but O'Brien's extra-point attempt was blocked.

Unitas completed three of nine passes, had two intercepted and fumbled once before giving way to Morrall. The Colts' relief quarterback found the target on 7 of 15 passes for 147 yards with one interception.

Thomas Stifled

The Baltimore defense limited Thomas, the Cowboys' rookie star, to 37 yards in 18 carries while Morton was limited to 12 completions in 26 attempts for 126 yards.

Nowatzke was the Colts' top ground gainer with 33 yards in 10 tries. Bulaich contributed 28 yards in 18 carries. Both trailed the Cowboys' Walt Garrison, most productive ground gainer of the day, who gained 65 yards in 12 attempts.

Super Bowl Statistics

	Colts	Dallas
First downs	14	9
Rushing yardage	69	104
Passing yardage	260	113
Return yardage	69	31
Passes	25-11-3	26-12-3
Punts	4-41	9-38
Fumbles lost	4	1
Yards penalized	44	120

Colts	0	6	0	10—16
Dallas	3	10	0	0—13

Dal—FG Clark 14.
Dal—FG Clark 30.
Colts—Mackey 75 pass from Unitas (kick blocked).
Dal—Thomas 7 pass from Morton (Clark kick).
Colts—Nowatzke 2 run (O'Brien kick).
Colts—FG O'Brien 32.
Attendance—80,055.

Austin

Washington, Jan. 6 (AP)—Bill Austin was fired as head coach of the Washington Redskins today by club president Edward Bennett Williams. Williams hinted he would name a new coach later this week.

Most prominently mentioned to succeed Austin is George Allen, just let go by the Los Angeles Rams after five years as head coach for the West Coast team.

Austin took over as the Redskins' head coach when Vince Lombardi died last summer, but he failed to produce a winning season for the team, something Lombardi accomplished in his first hear here.

Williams said in a statement that Austin's contract will not be renewed for 1971 and "I expect to have a further announcement on the Redskins' 1971 plans later this week."

The Washington *Post* reported today that Allen had a solid offer to take over as head coach and general manager of the Washington team and was expected to reply to the proposal in a day or two.

"At present I'm out of a job, but I will be in the league,' Austin said in confirming that his contract had not been renewed.

Not Flamboyant

Despite high hopes for the Washington team early in the season, the Redskins ended the year with a 6-8 record.

Allen had a 49-17-4 record in his five years with the Rams, a period marked by continued feuding with owner Dan Reeves.

Reeves refused to pick up Allen's contract when it expired December 31.

Austin, 42, apparently has been expecting his dismissal, especially after the Redskins went into a five-game losing streak midway through the 1970 season.

"I felt he (Williams) was looking for a big name, a flamboyant coach," Austin said after the announcement, "and that if he couldn't get one he would come back to me.

"I'm not a big name and I'm not flamboyant. I'm a football coach, and I think I'm a good one."

Allen Offered Coach-GM Job With Packers

Milwaukee, Jan. 6 (AP)—George Allen, fired as head coach of the Los Angeles Rams December 31, has been offered the dual post of coach and general manager of the Green Bay Packers, the Milwaukee *Journal* reported today.

Allen also has been offered a similar package by the Washington Redskins.

Allen said he had not rejected Green Bay's porposal but declined further comment, the *Journal* reported.

Dominic Olejniczak, Packer president, refused to say whether the club had made offers to any prospective coach.

Phil Bengtson resigned as the Packers' coach and general manager, effective February 1, following Green Bay's 6-8 season.

The Draft Selections

New York, Jan. 28 (AP)—Order of picks today in the National Football League college draft:

First Round

Boston—Jim Plunkett, quarterback, Stanford; New Orleans—Archie Manning, quarterback, Mississippi; Houston—Dan Pastorini, quarterback, Santa Clara; Buffalo—J. D. Hill, wide receiver, Arizona State; Philadelphia—Richard Harris, def. tackle, Grambling.

New York Jets—John Riggins, running back, Kansas; Atlanta—Joe Profit, running back, Northeast Louisiana; Pittsburgh—Frank Lewis, wide receiver, Grambling; Green Bay from Denver—John Brockington, running back, Ohio State; Los Angeles from Washington—Isiah Robertson, Southern University.

Chicago—Joe Moore, running back, Missouri; Denver—Marv Montgomery, off. tackle, Southern California; San Diego—Leon Burns, running back, Long Beach State; Cleveland—Clarence Scott, defensive back, Kansas State; Cincinnati—Vernon Holland, defensive tackle, Tennessee State.

Kansas City—Elmo Wright, wide receiver, Houston; St. Louis—Norm Thompson, defensive back, Utah; New York Giants—Ralph (Rocky) Thompson, wide receiver, West Texas State; Oakland—Jack Tatum, corner back, Ohio State; Los Angeles—Jack Youngblood, def. end, Florida.

Detroit—Bob Bell, def. tackle, Cincinnati; Colts—for Miami—Don McCauley, running back, North Carolina; San Francisco—Tim Anderson, def. back, Ohio State; Minnesota—Leo Hayden, running back, Ohio State; Dallas—Poly Smith, def. end, Southern California; Colts—Leonard Dunlap, def. back, North Texas State.

Second Round

Boston—Julius Adams, defensive tackle, Texas Southern; Chicago from New Orleans—James Harrison, running back, Missouri; Buffalo—Jan White, tight end, Ohio State; Detroit from Philadelphia—David Thompson, center-guard, Clemson; New Orleans from Houston—Sam Holden, guard, Grambling.

Miami—Otto Stowe, wide receiver, Iowa State; Detroit—Charlie Weaver, linebacker, Southern California. San Francisco, Joe Orduna, running back, Nebraska; Philadelphia from Minnesota—Henry Allison, guard, San Diego St.; Dallas, Isaac Thomas, defensive back, Bishop, (Texas); Colts, Bill Atessis, defensive end, Texas.

Kansas City—Scott Lewis, defensive end, Grambling; St. Louis—Daniel Dierdorf, tackle, Michigan, New York Giants—Wayne Walton, tackle, Abilene Christian; Oakland—Phil Villapiano, linebacker, Bowling Green; Green Bay from Los Angeles—Virgil Robinson, running back, Grambling.

San Francisco from Green Bay—Ernie Janet, guard, Washington; Washington—Cotton Speyrer, wide receiver, Texas; Kansas City from San Diego—Wilber Young, def. tackle, William Penn; Cleveland—Bo Cornell, running back, Washington; Cincinnati—Steve Lawson, guard, Kansas.

Third Round

Buffalo from Boston through Oakland—Bruce Jarvis, center, Washington; New Orleans—Bivian Lee, defensive back Prairie View; San Francisco from Philadelphia—Sam Dickerson, wide receiver, Southern California; Houston—Lynn Dickey, quarterback, Kansas State; Buffalo—Jim Braxton, running back, West Virginia.

New York Jets—Chris Farasopoulos, defensive back, Brigham Young; Atlanta—Leo Hart, quarterback, Duke; Pittsburgh—Steve Davis, running back, Delaware State; St. Louis from Denver—James Livesay, wide receiver, Richmond, Green Bay—Charles Hall, defensive back, Pittsburgh.

Los Angeles from Washington—Dave Elmendorf, defensive back, Texas A&M; Chicago—Tony McGee, defensive end, Bishop, (Texas) San Diego—Mike Montgomery, running back, Kansas State.

Cleveland—Paul Staroba, wide receiver, Michigan; Cincinnati, Ken Anderson, quarterback, Augustana, Ill; Cleveland from Kansas City, Charles Hall, linebacker, Houston; Dallas from St. Louis Sam Scriber, running back, New Mexico; New York Giants, Ronnie Hornsby, linebacker, Southeastern Louisiana.

Oakland, Warren Coegel, center, Penn State; Chicago from Los Angeles Bob Newton, tackle, Nebraska; Detroit, Al Clark, defensive back, Eastern Michigan; Miami, Dale Farley, linebacker, West Virginia; San Francisco, Willie Parker, center, North Texas St.

Minnesota, Eddie Hackett, wide receiver, Alcorn A&M.; Dallas, Bill Gregory, defensive tackle, Wisconsin; Colts, Karl Douglas, quarterback, Texas A&I.

Fourth Round

Denver from Boston, Lyle Alzado, defensive end, Yankton, S.D.; Dallas from New Orleans, Joe Carter, defensive end, Grambling; Houston, Lrron Johnson, tackle, Missouri; New Orleans from Buffalo Carlos Bell, running back, Houston; Philadelphia, Happy Feller, place kicker, Texas; New York Jets, Bill Zapalac, linebacker, Texas; Atlanta, Mike Potchad, tackle, Pittsburg,Kansas; Pittsburgh, Gerry Mullins, tight end, Southern Cal.; Denver, Cleo Johnson, defensive back, Alcorn A&M.; New Orleans from Washington, Richard Winther, center, Mississippi.

Los Angeles from Green Bay, Steve Worster, running back, Texas; New Orleans from San Diego, D'Artagnan Martin, defensive back, Kentucky St.

Cleveland, Robert Pena, guard, Massachusetts; Cincinnati, Fred Willis, running back, Boston College; Kansas City, David Robinson, tight end, Jacksonville, Ala., St.; St. Louis, Larry Willingham, defensive back, Auburn; New York Giants, David Tipton, defensive tackle, Stanford.

Oakland, Clarence Davis, running back, Southern Cal.; New Orleans from Los Angeles, Don Morrison, tackle, Texas, Arlington; Miami, Joe Theismann, quarterback, Notre Dame; Detroit, Larry Woods, defensive tackle, Tennesse St.; San Francisco, Tony Harris, running back, Toledo.

Minnesota, Vince Clements, running back, Connecticut; Dallas, Adam Mitchell, tackle, Mississippi; Pittsburgh from Baltimore, Dwight Wight, defensive end, E. Texas St.

Jan. 28

'Skins Get Talbert, Linebacking Corps From Rams For 7 High Draft Choices

By The Associated Press

The Washington Redskins, hoping to hitch their wagon to stars, landed almost half of the Los Angeles Rams' defense today in the biggest trade of a free-wheeling flurry in the National Football League.

Making his intentions known for instant success, Washington coach, George A.len collected some of the squad he led for several years—linebackers Myron Pottios, Jack Pardee and Maxie Baughan, defensive tackle Diron Talbert, guard John Wilbur and runner Jeff Jordan.

In addition, the Redskins gained the Rams' fifth round choice in the college draft.

Looking Ahead

Los Angeles, apparently looking ahead under new coach Tommy Prothro, received linebacker Marlin McKeever, the Redskins' No. 1 and No. 3 draft picks this year and five more picks—No. 3 through No. 7 in 1972.

"The future is now," said Allen, who built the Rams into a contender by swapping for veterans. "We want to win in 1971."

The trade is "good for both teams," exclaimed Prothro, who said he "hated to give up Talbert," one of the keys the deal for the Redskins.

Rams Get Williams

Prothro wasn't dealing entirely for the future, however. The Rams, in addition to the Washington trade, also went to Green Bay to nail surefooted back Travis Williams. Los Angeles coughed up its second round draft choice this year and an undisclosed pick next year for Williams and a fourth-round pick in 1971.

The active Allen later made another deal with Green Bay obtaining the rights to former receiver Boyd Dowler. He retired last season and spent the season as an assistant to Allen at Los Angeles.

The Packers, a recent disappointment after years of glory, also made deals with the Denver Broncos and Minnesota Vikings.

Choices Swapped

They shipped quarterback Don Horn to Denver for defensive end Alden Roche and the clubs also swapped positions in the first round of the draft, Green Bay getting No. 9 and Denver No. 12.

Green Bay also gave up an undisclosed 1972 draft choice to Minnesota for the rights to former Packer Zeke Bratkowski. He has been a coach for Green Bay for the past two years, although Minnesota held the rights to him as a player.

The Philadelphia Eagles were busy too, swinging a couple of deals with Detroit and Minnesota.

Philadelphia, waiting years for Norm Snead to blossom into a winner, traded their No. 1 quarterback to Minnesota for tackle Steve Smith, and the Vikings' second and sixth picks in the draft in 1971 and a third-round choice in 1972.

The Eagles then got another quarterback, Greg Barton, of the Detroit Lions, for their No. 2 draft pick this year and two choices in 1972.

Diron Talbert Happy Redskins Drafted Him

Los Angeles, Jan. 28 (AP)—The phone rang and the first booming words of the answering party were:

"Washington Redskins!"

It was defensive tackle Diron Talbert, who earlier had been tabbed by new Washington coach George Allen as the key man in the Redskins' multiple trade with the Los Angeles Rams.

Allen was dismissed as Rams coach at the end of last season.

Said Talbert, a member of the Rams' Fearsome Foursome, "This is the happiest moment in my entire football career. I've been callin' my mother and my daddy and all my relatives and friends all over."

The 6-5, 255-pounder from the University of Texas, four years with the Rams, reminded his caller that he had played out his option with the Rams "and I had no intention of coming back."

It was purely a financial beef with the Rams.

"I hate to leave the guys I played with on the Rams. I've enjoyed every minute and I learned a lot from Rosie, Lamar Lundy—and of course Marlin Olsen was just the greatest."

Rosie is Roosevelt Grier, who with Lamar Lundy, was one of the original Fearsome Foursome.

Talbert, a handsome bachelor, said he and Myron Pattios, another departee for Washington, spent the day celebrating the trade. And told that Allen had called him the key factor and, in effect, his No. 1 draft choice, Talbert concluded:

"I just hope I pan out. And I honestly believe the Redskins can win the National Football Conference. Wouldn't it be something if the Redskins and Rams met for the championship?"

LEGAL PROBLEM SEEN BY ROZELLE

Palm Beach, Fla., March 22 (AP)—Commissioner Pete Rozelle said today as the National Football League meetings opened that pro football could be faced with a problem by the ultimate legal ruling in the controversial Spencer Haywood basketball case.

"In today's climate, any adverse litigation in any phase of sports could have a ruboff on any other sport," Rozelle acknowledged.

"It could be a problem for us. We'd have to find a way out."

The Haywood case is being watched closely by all sports, involving as it does the question of whether it is illegal to prevent a college athlete from turning pro before his college class graduates.

Trial Going On

Haywood, who did just that by signing before his class graduated, currently is involved in a court trial testing that principle. He has sued the National Basketball Association for voiding his contract with the Seattle SuperSonices.

The court, issuing a temporary injunction that permits Haywood to continue playing while the issue is decided, expressed the opinion that the rule prohibiting Haywood's playing in the NBA violated his rights.

Should that be upheld, it is considered likely the NFL, as well as the NBA, would have to do away with that provision of its rules, creating a situation that might cause chaos in the battle among teams to sign college stars.

Rozelle, however, said he did not think the ultimate ruling would be along the same lines as the opinion expressed in the temporary injunction.

To Keep Same Rule

"We're going to continue with our present rule, which was started with Red Grange in 1926," Rozelle said. "I can't feel something like that would hold up. I can't believe a practice for the protection of the colleges would be legally ruled invalid.

"It would destroy college football—all sports in the colleges."

Asked pointedly what he would do if a contract were submitted to him of a player whose class was not graduated, Rozelle said frankly "The contract would not be approved."

Rozelle made his comments about the Haywood case at an afternoon news conference, during which he disclosed he had recommended to the owners that they hang less of their dirty wash in public.

He said he had asked that "more discipline be handled at the club level" and admitted that he had been forced to talk to Los Angeles owner Dan Reeves and former Ram coach George Allen, now with Washington, about curtailing their public feud.

"I told them it was unhealthy for the sport and told them to cease their comments," Rozelle said. Asked if he had fined either, Rozelle answered, "Not yet."

Rozelle declined to disclose whether he had fined Colts' owner Carroll Rosenbloom in a similar case involving comments made when Don Shula left the Colts for the Miami coaching job.

Grid Giants Make It Official, Will Shift To N.J. By 1975

New York (AP)—"New York fans are not losing a football team, they are gaining a stadium," Wellington Mara, president of the Giants, said yesterday in announcing that the NFL team was moving across the river to New Jersey no later than 1975.

"We are still the New York Giants—we always will be," Mara added. "A family always dreams of moving into a house of its own. It's sometimes good to get away from one's in-laws."

The Giants, who played 31 years in the old Polo Grounds, have been playing home games in Yankee Stadium for 15 years, sharing the famous old ball park with the baseball Yankees. Their present lease runs through 1974.

Bitter Reaction

The announcement of the move, made at a hastily called news conference in New York, drew a bitter reaction from New York's Mayor John Lindsay, who has proposed a $24 million renovation of Yankee Stadium to keep both the Yankees and Giants playing in New York.

Lindsay said he would continue plans for such a renovation but added that he also would seek a new National Football League franchise for the city and take legal steps to keep the Giants from using the name "New York."

"I have asked Chairman Emanuel Celler, (D.-N.Y.) of the House Judiciary Committee to conduct an inquiry into this matter by his sub-committee on anti-trust matters," the mayor added.

15 Minutes Away

The Giants' future home is a projected 80,000-seat complex to be built in the Hackensack Meadows in East Rutherford, N.J., only about 15 minutes by car from the western end of the Holland Tunnel.

The plant, with parking space for 25,000 cars and 400 buses and all the features of a modern stadium, will be financed by bonds under the supervision of the New Jersey Sports and Exposition Authority.

This Authority is headed by David A. (Sonny) Werblin, former owner of the New York Jets, who with New Jersey Gov. William Cahill and leading New Jersey officials joined Mara at the news conference.

"You might just call it another bridge across the river, linking New York and New Jersey," said Gov. Cahill.

Mike Burke, president and chairman of the board of the Yankees, greeted the news without rancor.

"We are sad to see the Giants go," he said in a formal statement. "It's rather like having a member of the family leave home, but we wish them good luck."

He added:

"My overriding concern remains the future of the Yankees. We shall now have to take a new and realistic reading of our option."

No Baseball

The new New Jersey complex—to be known as Giant Stadium—will not be geared for baseball. Plans are for future construction of a race track and recreation facilities in the 20,000-acre area.

The lease between the Giants and the New Jersey Sports and Exposition Authority is for 30 years, with the Giants to pay an annual rental of 15 per cent of the gross revenue obtained from ticket sales.

Sept. 20

Patriots Shock Raiders, 20-6, In Plunkett's Debut

Foxboro, Mass. (AP)—Heisman Trophy winner Jim Plunkett made a spectacular National Football League debut with a pair of second half touchdown passes and the New Englnad Patriots upset the Oakland Raiders, 20 to 6, yesterday.

Oakland managed to get a sputtering attack in gear against the Patriots' tough defense late in the first half and took a 6-0 lead on Pete Banaszak's four-yard touchdown run.

Oakland managed to get a sputtering attack in gear against the patriots tough defense late in the first half and took a led on Pete Banaszak's four-yeard touchdown run.

Then Plunkett, who threw only four times in the first two periods, took charge after the intermission and flashed the form which earned him All-America honors at Stanford in rallying the Patriots.

New England, which lost 5 of 6, pre-season games after finishing last with a 2-12 record in 1970, went in front to stay as Plunkett hit Ron Sellers with a perfect pass on a scoring play of 33 yards.

Later in the third period, Plunkett directed the Patriots on a 70-yard scoring drive. On the sixth play he caught the Raiders by surprise and passed to tight end Tom Beer on a 20-yard touchdown maneuver.

| Oakland | 0 6 0 0— 6 |
| New England | 0 0 14 6—20 |

Oak—Banaszak 4 run (kick failed).
NE.—Sellers 33 pass from Plunkett (Gogolak kick).
NE.—Beer 20 pass from Plunkett (Gogolak kick).
NE.—FG Gogolak 46.
NE.—FG Gogolak 22.
Attendance—55,105.

Sept. 28

U.S. FILES SUIT AGAINST FALCONS

Atlanta's Rise In Ticket Price Charged Violation

Washingtin (AP)—The Justice Department filed suit yesterday against the Atlanta Falcons for allegedly violating President Nixon's wage-price freeze by raising the price of football tickets.

According to a suit filed in U.S. District Court in Atlanta, regular-game admission prices were raised by $1.50 after the freeze took effect Aug. 15.

The action against the National Football League club is the third to be taken by the Justice Department to enforce the 90-day wage-price freeze.

In its suit against the Falcons, the government seeks a court order rolling back the ticket prices and requiring refunds to purchasers of the $1.50 increase.

The Justice Department disclosed that the football team had filed suit earlier in the day in the same court seeking a declaratory judgment that the ticket price increase is not a violation of the wage-price freeze order.

Connally Disappointed

The two previous legal actions were taken against a Louisiana school district that granted a raise to its teachers and against a Texas landlord who increased the rent on two apartments.

Secretary of the Treasury John B. Connally, chairman of the Cost of Living Council, said in a statement, "I am indeed disappointed that such a flagrant violation of the wage-price freeze should occur in the world of professional sports, which has benefited from widespread public support. I am hopeful that the owners of the Falcons will not prolong this case and will quickly make restitution to their many loyal supporters."

The Falcons raised ticket prices from $6 to $7.50 this year. The suit filed by the government maintains the team should make refunds to approximately 58,000 ticket-holders for Falcon home games of August 29, September 19, October 10, October 17, and October 24.

Meanwhile, in Tempe, Ariz., the Arizona State University director of athletics said the school will have to refund $175,-000 because of the price freeze on football tickets.

Sept. 20

Giants Nip Packers In 42-40 Thriller

Green Bay, Wis. (AP)—Fran Tarkenton threw touchdown passes of six, 39 and 81 yards to Dick Houston and the New York Giants recovered two fumbles in the Green Bay end zone for two other scores yesterday, then held off a furious Packer comeback for a 42-to-40 National Football League victory.

The Giants built up a 42-24 lead, only to see rookie quarterback Scott Hunter direct the Packers to a 19-yard touchdown run by Donny Anderson and pass 18 yards to Carroll Dale for another touchdown in the fourth quarter.

The Packers made it, 42-40, when Doug Hart tackled Giant punter Tom Blanchard in the end zone with 2:38 left.

Drive Halted

The Packers took over on a punt following the safety and drove to the New York 36 with 1:14 left, but linebacker Jim Files saved the Giants' victory when he intercepted a Hunter pass.

Recover 4 Fumbles

The Packers' last touchdown was set up by a Hart interception with 7.02 left on front of the Packer bench. The Packers' Dan Devine, making his regular season pro coaching debut, suffered an apparent broken left leg in the pileup out of bounds.

The clinching touchdown was a 20-yard Tarkenton to Tucker

Statistics

	Giants	Packers
First downs	12	17
Rushes-yards	3-102	30-124
Passing yardage	221	224
Return yardage	71	119
Passes	12-21-1	15-26-1
Punts	5-33	4-35
Fumbles lost	0	4
Yards penalized	25	28

New York	0 28 14	0—42
G. B.	7 7 10	16—40

GB—Ellis 1-00 returned field goal attempt (Conway kick).
NY—Houston 6 pass from Tarkenton (Gogolak kick).
NY—Houston 39 pass from Tarkenton (Gogolak kick).
NY—Heck fumble recovery end zone (Gogolak kick).
NY—Green fumble recovery end zone (Gogolak kick).
GB—Hampton 19 pass from Bratkowski. (Conway kick).
GB—FG Michaels 28.
NY—Houston 81 pass from Terkenton. (Gogolak kick).
GB—McGeorge 21 pass from Hunter (Conway kick).
NY—Frederickson 20 pass from Tarkenton (Gogolak kick).
GB—Anderson 19 run (Conway kick).
GB—Dale 18 pass from Hunter (Conway kick).
GB—Safety pass from center out of end zone.
Attendance—56,263.

Frederickson pass which gave the Giants a 42-24 lead late in the third period.

The Giants, who had scored only 58 points in losing all six of their pre-season games, recovered four Green Bay fumbles on rainy Lambeau Field and each resulted in a touchdown.

The Packers took a 7-0 lead on Ken Ellis's record-tying 100-yard runback with a short field goal attempt, but New York struck back with four touchdowns in the second quarter, two of them by Houston.

Ralph Heck and Joe Green scored the others when Hampton fumbled on a handoff and a kickoff in his end zone.

The Packers, down 28-7 late in the second quarter, came back to make it, 28-14, at halftime on a 19-yard touchdown pass from Zeke Bratkowski to Hampton. Their other scores came on a 28-yard field goal by Lou Michaels and a 21-yard touchdown pass from Hunter to Rich McGeorge in the third quarter.

pic up agate

Oct. 25

Lion receiver Hughes dies after Bears' game

Detroit (P)—Wide receiver Chuck Hughes of the Detroit Lions died of an apparent heart attack yesterday following a National Football League game with the Chicago Bears, Henry Ford Hospital reported.

Hughes collapsed as he returned to the Lions' huddle minutes before the end of the game. Artificial respiration and heart massage were applied as Hughes lay on the field.

He was rushed off the field on a stretcher and taken to the hospital, where he was pronounced dead about an hour after the game.

Death was attributed to a ruptured vessel in the aorta.

An autopsy will be performed this morning, doctors said.

It was pro football's first game-related death since December, 1965 when Mack Lee Hill died following surgery for a knee injury.

Hill, a fullback with the Kansas City Chiefs, had suffered torn knee ligaments in a game against Buffalo. He underwent the operation two days later and died of what a Chiefs' spokesman described as a "sudden and massive embolism blood clot after surgery."

Nov. 15

Bears stun 'Skins on weird play

Chicago (P)—Burly Dick Butkus speared a desperate conversion pass for the game-deciding point as the Chicago Bears rallied to shade the Washington Redskins, 16 to 15, yesterday in a thriller which produced a National Football League game record of eight field goals.

Washington, Eastern Division leader of the National Conference, led on five Curt Knight field goals until the game's only touchdown came on an explosive 40-yard run by Chicago's Cyril Pinder at 3.41 of the fourth quarter.

On the Bears' extra point kick attempt to break a 15-15 tie, a bad center snap sailed over holder Bobby Douglass's head, but he recovered on the Redskins 30 and flipped it to Butkus all along in the end zone. Linebacker Butkus was eligible for the pass because he was a backfield blocker on the point try.

TEXAS STADIUM OPENS

Oct. 25

Irving, Texas (P) — The Dallas Cowboys celebrated the opening of Texas Stadium with a 44-to-21 National Football League romp over New England yesterday, behind the running of Duane Thomas and the passing of Roger Staubach.

Thomas, who was traded to the Patriots in the off-season but given back because he refused to take a physical, burst 56 yards for a touchdown on Dallas' fourth offensive play and the rout was on.

Staubach dashed two yards for a touchdown and found Boy Hayes on touchdown bullets of 35 and 28 yards as Dallas piled up a 34-7 halftime lead. Mike Clark kicked field goals of 16, 17, and 12 yards.

Staubach completed 13 of 21 passes for 197 yards as he riddled the patched-up Patriot secondary.

Plunkett badgered

Rookie quarterback Jim Plunkett was badgered by a strong Dallas rush and dumped for losses five time. He completed a 33-yard touchdown pass to Randy Vataha and a 31-yard scoring pass to Tom Beer in the second half. Jim Nance scored on a one-yard run for the Patriots.

A crowd of 65,708 fans watched at the professional opener in the new $25 million stadium which features a two and one-half acre opening in the roof.

Thomas hardly let the fans get settled in their seats when he roared around right end, cut back against the grain and followed a crushing block by Lance Alworth to the end zone.

After Clark's first field goal, New England fought back to make it 10-7 on Nance's one-yard run. But two fumbles and an interception put the Cowboys in excellent position for the kayo punches and Staubach delivered them to Hayes.

Frustrated offense

The Patriot offense was so frustrated in the first half that at one point they faced a fourth-and-63 situation.

Dallas shut down its offense in the second half with Craig Morton taking over for Staubach in the fourth period. Joe Williams scored on a two-yard run for Dallas' only second half touchdown.

Plunkett completed 16 of 29 passes for 228 yards in the face of the fierce Dallas rush.

Statistics

	Patriots	Cowboys
First downs	17	20
Rushes—yardage	24-76	34-168
Passing yardage	183	238
Return yardage	16	26
Passes	16-29-1	16-25-0
Punts	6-41	3-47
Fumbles lost	2	0
Yards penalized	59	58

New England	7	0	0	14—21
Dallas	10	24	0	10—44

DAL—Thomas 56 run (Clark kick).
DAL—FG Clark 16.
NE—Nance 1 run (Gogolak kick).
DAL—Staubach 2 run (Clark kick).
DAL—FG Clark 17.
DAL—Hayes 35 pass from Staubach (Clark kick).
DAL—Hayes 28 pass from Staubach (Clark kick).
DAL—FG Clark 12.
NE—Vataha 33 pass from Plunkett (Gogolak kick).
DAL—Williams 2 run (Clark kick).
NE—Beer 31 pass from Plunkett (Gogolak kick).
Attendance—65,708.

Nov. 1

Raiders tie KC, 20-20, Blanda sets point mark

Oakland, Calif. (AP) — George Blanda, after throwing a fourth-quarter touchdown pass to Fred Biletnikoff, became the leading scorer in pro football history with an 8-yard field goal that gave the Oakland Raiders a 20-to-20 National Football League tie with the Kansas City Chiefs yesterday.

The tie kept the arch-rivals deadlocked for first place in the American Conference's Western Division. Each team is 5-1-1.

The 44-year-old Blanda, who broke into the NFL in 1949, had eight points on two field goals and two extra points against the Chiefs, giving him 1,609 career points, one more than former Cleveland Browns' kicker Lou Groza.

Blanda replaced starting quarterback Daryle Lamonica in the fourth period after the Chiefs had taken a 20-10 lead.

He threw a 24-yard touchdown pass to Biletnikoff to end a 66-yard drive, then kicked the tying field goal with 2½ minutes left after a 55-yard drive stopped inches short of the Chiefs' goal line.

Ed Podolak scored both Kansas City touchdowns, one on a 1-yard run and the other on a 2-yarder that completed long scoring drives in the first half.

Podolak's second touchdown put Kansas City ahead, 14-10, in the second quarter, and Jan Stenerud kicked field goals from 12 and 37 yards in the second half.

Blanda's first field goal of the game, from 17 yards out, came after the Chiefs stopped a first-period Oakland drive. Fullback Marv Hubbard scored on a 1-yard run as the Raiders took a 10-7 lead early in the second period.

Statistics

	Chiefs	Raiders
First downs	18	19
Rushes-yards	37-161	28-111
Passing yardage	87	141
Return yardage	37	97
Passes	7-13-1	12-25-2
Punts	4-47	5-35
Fumbles lost	1	0
Yards penalized	66	31

Kansas City	7	7	3	3—20
Oakland	3	7	0	10—20

KC—Podolak 1 run (Stenerud kick)
Oak—FG Blanda 17
Oak—Hubbard 1 run (Blanda kick)
KC—Podolak 2 run (Stenerud kick)
KC—FG Stenerud 12
KC—Stenerud 37
Oak—Biletnikoff 24 pass from Blanda (Blanda kick)
Oak—FG Blanda 8
A—54,715.

Dec. 5

Ellison sets rushing mark

Los Angeles (AP)—Running back Willie Ellison opened the Los Angeles scoring with an 80-yard burst from scrimmage and wound up the afternoon with a National Football League rushing record of 247 yards in 26 carries yesterday as the Rams whipped New Orleans, 45-to-28.

The smashing show of the 200-pound veteran from Texas Southern overshadowed three touchdown passes by Roman Gabriel and a 105-yard kickoff return by Los Angeles' Travis Williams.

Ellison surpassed the pro record of 243 yards set by Cookie Gilchrist of Buffalo against the New York Jets in the American Football League on December 8, 1963, and the 237 yards by former Cleveland star Jim Brown on two occasions.

Only 1:59 remained in the game when Ellison bettered the Gilchrist record.

Statistics

	Saints	Rams
First downs	20	22
Rushes-yards	23-56	39-293
Passing yardage	207	128
Return yardage	15	40
Passes	19-36-1	10-18-1
Punts	6-34	3-29
Fumbles lost	0	1
Yards penalized	67	119

New Orleans	7	0	14	7—28
Los Angeles	21	10	0	10—45

LA—Ellison 80 run (Ray kick)
LA—Snow 37 pass from Gabriel (Ray kick)
NO—Abramowicz 25 pass from Hargett (Durkee kick)
LA—T. Williams 105 kickoff return (Ray kick)
LA—Smith 5 run (Ray kick)
LA—Rentzell 8 pass from Gabriel (Ray kick)
NO—Gresham 1 run (Durkee kick)
NO—Hargett 1 run (Durkee kick)
LA—Rentzell 39 pass from Gabriel (Ray kick)
NO—Gresham 1 run (Durkee kick)
LA—FG Ray 12
Attendance—73,610.

Dec. 14

Grid Cards bar Lane for rap at team V.P.

St. Louis (AP)—Star running back MacArthur Lane has been suspended for the St. Louis Cardinals' final game of the regular National Football League season.

Suspension of the 6-foot-1, 229-pound Lane followed remarks attributed to him after the Cardinals 19-to-7 loss Sunday to the Philadelphia Eagles in Philadelphia.

Foot in mouth

The *Globe Democrat*, in its morning editions, quoted Lane as blaming Cards vice-president William V. Bidwill for the team's troubles.

"All his money's right there in his stomach," Lane was quoted as saying.

Lane, thought to be among about 12 Cardinals playing without contracts because of the wage-price freeze, partially retracted the statement and apologized in the *Post-Dispatch's* afternoon editions.

"I put my foot in my mouth," he said.

Lane's frustrations evidently stemmed from the Cardinals' poor record and his decline from 977 yards rushing last season.

Held to nine yards on eight carries against the Eagles, the four-year veteran has a 1971 total of 592 yards rushing on 150 carries.

Why is the question

"Everybody wants to know why I don't carry the ball anymore," Lane was quoted by the *Globe-Democrat* as saying.

"It's a good question. I wish I knew the answer."

The newspaper also quoted Lane as saying, "I'm on my option year. I really don't know if I'll be here next year. Sometimes it makes you wonder if you wouldn't be a lot better off playing somewhere else."

The announcement of Lane's suspension for the game Saturday against the Dallas Cowboys in Dallas came from Bidwill and cocah Bob Hollway.

Dec. 8

Falcons' Berry held on assault charge

Marietta, Ga. ℗ — Atlanta Falcons quarterback Bob Berry and Randy Marshall, a defensive end, were arrested by police who raided Marshall's apartment Monday night.

A spokesman for the Falcons said a statement would be issued later.

Berry was charged with assaulting a police officer and Marshall was charged with keeping a disorderly house, Cobb County police reported.

Police also arrested Carol Nichols, 20, of Marietta, on marijuana charges but released her on $300 bond. Berry and Marshall both were freed on $500 bond.

Deputy Sheriff Carl Price said the three were arrested after about 10 deputies and county police raided Marshall's apartment, where a party was in progress.

The sheriff said less than an ounce of marijuana was recovered and said it had not been determined who was smoking it.

"Whoever had been smoking it was using a coffee pot, like a water pipe," he said.

Berry, who has been the Falcon starter at quarterback for three seasons, said later, "I've never been involved with marijuana or any kind of dope. I've never smoked it. I'm a little shook up and very upset about the whole thing."

The 29-year-old quarterback said he was in Marshall's apartment when "all of a sudden people were all around . . . People were pushing and telling people to clear out. A few minutes later, they had Randy Marshall in a police car."

He said he went to talk to Marshall, and "the first thing I know, people are throwing me on the ground, wrestling me . . . Naturally, I fought back and before I knew it, I was in the back seat of a car handcuffed.

Marshall, 25, is a reserve defensive lineman who has seen little action this year because of injury and illness.

Their hearing in court is scheduled December 23.

The deputy sheriff said Miss Nichols told officers she was the only person at the party smoking marijuana and that she should be arrested.

He said Marshall was taken into custody because the marijuana was found in his apartment.

The deputy said officers were escorting Marshall and Miss Nichols to a squad car when Berry approached them. "I don't know what he was trying to do," the officer said. "He was placed under arrest for assault. He struck an officer on the chin."

The officer said there were between eight and 12 persons in the apartment at the time.

Dec. 26

Chiefs fall in overtime

Yepremian's FG decides longest game, 27-24

By KEN NIGRO
Sun Staff Correspondent

Kansas City—Garo Yepremian, the balding ex-soccer player from the island of Cyprus, put an end to the longest football game ever played late yesterday afternoon with a 37-yard field goal as the Miami Dolphins defeated the Kansas City Chiefs, 27 to 24.

By the time the 5-8 Yepremian booted the ball squarely through the uprights, darkness had descended upon Municipal Stadium and the 50,374 fans were wondering if they were ever going to get home for Christmas dinner.

In all, the game consumed 82 minutes and 40 seconds which broke the old mark of 77.54 set in the 1962 American Football League championship game between these same Chiefs (then in Dallas) and the Houston Oilers. The last sudden death game was in 1965 when the Green Bay Packers beat the Colts, 13-10, on that disputed field goal by Don Chandler.

Colts key to site

The big victory enabled Don Shula's club to advance to next Sunday's American Conference final. Miami will be at home if the Colts beat the Browns today but must travel to Cleveland should the rBowns triumph.

Yesterday's game featured a little bit of everything, but in the end it boiled down to a kicking duel between Yepremian and Kansas City's Jan Stenerud, the Norwegian skier.

Stenerud, who was chosen to the Pro Bowl instead of Yepremian, missed an easy 31-yard field goal with just 35 seconds left in regulation time that would have won the game for the Chiefs. He also had a 42-yard attempt blocked in the first overtime period.

Yepremian had missed on a 52-yarder late in the first overtime but he was ready when his second chance came.

It came just when it looked like everyone, including the players, might be ready for a little bit of sleep.

Csonka's big play

The Dolphins took over on their own 30 following a punt and Jim Kiick gained five yards on the first play. Then came the big gainer in the drive—a 29-yard run by bruising fullback Larry Csonka that brought the ball all the way to Kansas City's 36. Three running plays moved the ball to the 30 and on came Garo, who makes ties in his spare time and has become something of a national hero in Miami.

"I knew before I kicked it that it was good," Yepremian said later. "As soon as I hit the ball, I put my arms up. But I had to wait a little for the referee's signal because my ball travels so slowly."

The field goal capped a remarkable comeback by the Dolphins who spent the first 60 minutes just trying to catch up Each time they did manage a tie, Kansas City would jump on top again, thanks mainly to some great running by Ed Podolak and Wendell Hayes.

Podolak, in particular, was devastating. In addition to gaining 85 yards on the ground, he caught eight passes for another 110 yards and scored two of Kansas City's touchdowns.

The statistics

	Dolphins	Chiefs
First downs	22	23
Rushes-yards	43-144	44-213
Passing yardage	2-3	238
Return yardage	31	18
Passes	20-33-2	18-26-3
Punts	6-40	3-31
Fumbles lost	0	3
Yards penalized	26	44

Miami	0	10	7	7	3
Kansas City	10	0	7	7	0

K.C.—FG Stenerud 24
K.C.—Podolak 7 pass from Dawson (Stenerud kick)
Mia—Csonka 1 run (Yepremian kick)
Mia—FG Yepremian 14
K.C.—Otis 1 run (Stenerud kick)
Mia—Kiick 1 run (Yepremian kick)
K.C.—Podolak 3 run (Stenerud kick)
Mia—Fleming 5 pass from Griese (Yepremian kick)
Mia—FG Yepremian 37
Attendance—50,374.

Reprinted from
The Baltimore Sun

Dec. 26

Vikings toppled by 20-12

Opportunistic defense keys NFC victory

Minneapolis-St. Paul (P) — The Dallas Doomsday Defense dazed the Minnesota Vikings and with Roger Staubach igniting the offense, the Cowboys powered to a 20-to-12 victory in a National Football Conference semi-final play-off game yesterday.

The Cowboys. intercepting four passes and recovering a fumble. advanced to the NFC championship game in Dallas January 2 against the winner of today's San Francisco-Washington game.

Cliff Harris. the youngest member of the Dallas defense. made the key interception on the third play of the second half.

With the Cowboys leading by 6-3, he swiped Bob Lee's pass at the Vikings' 43 and scrambled back to the Minnesota 13.

On the next play, Duane Thomas slammed 13 yards up the middle for a touchdown with 13.31 left in the third quarter.

Staubach then drove the Cowboys 52 yards. capping the march with a nine-yard scrambling touchdown pass to Bob Hayes that gave Dallas a 20-3 lead with 1.38 left in the period.

Fred Cox kicked a 27-yard field goal in the second period, the Vikings' front four smeared Staubach for a safety in the fourth quarter and Gary Cuozzo passed six yards to Stu Voigt for Minnesota's only touchdown with 2.08 left to play in the game.

Mike Clark. who had been demoted to the taxi squad earlier in the season. booted Cowboy field goals of 26 and 44 yards.

Chuck Howley. setting up one field goal. and Lee Roy Jordan, stopping a Viking drive at the Dallas 15 in the fourth period, also intercepted passes.

Dec. 27

Nottingham scores twice in 20-3 win

By CAMERON C. SNYDER
Sun Staff Correspondent

Cleveland--With the Baltimore defense pointing the way, the Colts advanced to the American Football Conference championship game with a 20-to-3 manhandling of the Cleveland Browns at fog-shrouded Municipal Stadium yesterday.

The victory sends the Colts to Miami next Sunday where they meet the Eastern Division champion Dolphins for the right to represent the American Conference in Super Bowl VI on January 16.

The Colts were runners-up to the Dolphins in the East and gained a play-off berth by having the best second-place record in the 13-team conference.

11 surgeons

The Colt defense, led by 11 fanatical surgeons, first anesthesized the Browns with a senses-dulling goal line stand and then calmly and professionally continued the dissection of the Central Division titlists the rest of the way.

It was an overpowering display of defense and it was needed because the Colt offense wasn't all that good. It was good enough to put points on the scoreboard, but it constantly left the defense in what should have been precarious positions.

They weren't precarious spots because the Browns' Leroy Kelly couldn't find anywhere to run and quarterback Bill Nelsen couldn't locate his receivers under a ton of Colts.

John Unitas did ignite one long touchdown march, 93 yards in 17 plays with Don Nottingham going over from the one for the touchdown.

Volk steals two

That and a 3-play 15-yard TD drive, set up on Rick Volk's first of two interceptions and climaxed by Nottingham's 7-yard scoring run, were the only 7-point plays of the day.

To round out the Colt scoring. Jim O'Brien kicked third and fourth-period field goals of 42 and 15 yards.

Dec. 27

49ers topple 'Skins

24-20 success sends victors against Dallas

San Francisco (P) — Quarterback John Brodie connected on an unexpected 78-yard touchdown pass play to fleet wide receiver Gene Washington to turn the tide yesterday and fire the San Francisco 49ers to a 24-to-20 victory over the Washington Redskins in their National Football Conference semi-final play-off game.

The triumph sends the 49ers against the Cowboys in Dallas next Sunday to decide which NFC team goes to the National Football League's Super Bowl VI.

Washington, the "wild card" entry in the NFC play-offs, led the Western Division champions, 10-3, at the half and threatened to boost the count at the start of the third quarter after Speedy Duncan carried the kickoff back 66 yards to the 49ers' 34 yard line.

Brown stopped

In six plays, Washington reached the 11, where a gamble by Redskins' coach George Allen failed.

On fourth down and less than a yard to go, he called a running play instead of settling for a field goal, only to have Frank Nunley and Jim Sniadecki throw Larry Brown for a two-yard loss.

San Francisco gained nine yards in two plays and the Redskins expected another running play. Instead, Brodie called a play-action pass and hit Washington in the clear at the Redskins' 40.

San Francisco turned an intercepted pass into another third-period score and, in the fourth quarter, Bob Hoskins of the 49ers' special team recovered a fumble in the end zone after Washington punter Mike Bragg failed to handle the low snap from center on this windy, rainy day in Candlestick Park.

The Redskins fought back to score a touchdown late in the game on a Billy Kilmer-to-Brown pass for 16 yards, but the comeback came too late.

The lone 3-pointer for the Browns was a gift by the Colt offense when Ron Snidow intercepetd a Unitas pass and lateralled it to Clarence Scott for a return to the Colt 30.

Finally, after getting to the 8, the Browns called on Don Cockroft for a 14-yard field goal. He made it this time but twice before he had field goal tries blocked by Bubba Smith from the 16 and the 44.

Reprinted from
The Baltimore Sun

Jan. 3

49ers fall in NFC title game, 14-3

By ED WINSTEN
Sun Staff Correspondent

Dallas—The Dallas Cowboys put together marches of 2 and 80 yards yesterday in Texas Stadium to march into the January 16 Super Bowl, a place that caused them much embarrassment last-season.

The Cowboys didn't especially distinguish themselves yesterday in the National Conference title game but they had enough to down the bumbling San Francisco 49ers, 14 to 3.

It was the second time this season that the John Brodie-led 49ers had been shut off without a touchdown. Los Angeles did it in a 17-6 regular-season game.

Whether it was due to the vaunted Doomsday Defense or an off day by Brodie, a 15-year veteran, the 49ers just couldn't put anything together.

"It was our worst offensive performance in as long as I can remember," Brodie said.

Andrie gets a gift

Brodie gave Dallas its first scoring chance, throwing a screen pass cleanly into the hands of defensive end George Andrie at the eight-yard line in the second quarter. Andrie returned the theft six yards.

After two cracks at the line, the Cowboys had a lead they never lost.

That took care of the offense until Roger Staubach engineered an 80-yard drive that used up 7 minutes 43 seconds in the second half. When Duane Thomas dashed around left end, it gave Dallas a 14-3 lead with 9.15 to go.

Brodie and the 49ers were not up to rallying in this game.

Dallas did need two big defensive plays, getting last-second deflections on possible touchdown passes from safety Cornell Green and linebacker Dave Edwards.

In the third quarter, Brodie led the 49ers to the Dallas 21, from where he lifted a pass to wide receiver Gene Washington. Green dashed over to deflect the pass just inside the end zone.

"I didn't have him," Green explained. "I was just playing the ball. We had a combination defense and I was playing an area. I thought I was going to intercept it, but I misjudged it."

Bruce Gossett kicked a 28-yard field goal on the next play, giving San Francisco its points for the afternoon. It made the score 7-3.

Later, in the fourth quarter, Brodie tossed one up the middle for Larry Schreiber, a substitute at fullback. Edwards seemed to be beaten but he stuck up a hand and knocked the ball away.

"That was a touchdown if I could have gotten the ball to him," said Brodie.

"I had him covered pretty good," Edwards said. "We'd been playing that defense all day and I just knew it was coming. They'd been sending their fullback at me.

"I figured he was going inside. I had to give him a step so I could get in front of him."

There was no interception on his mind, he said, adding, "I just wanted to get a hand on it; that's all you need. It worked out great."

For the day, Dallas held Brodie to 184 yards on 30 tries. The Cowboys also picked off three passes including two late ones when Brodie was throwing them up for grabs.

Staubach looks unsure

Staubach has directed Dallas to nine consecutive victories, but this wasn't one of his masterpieces. He gained 103 yards passing and 55 more on eight scrambles, but, all in all, he seemed unsure of himself in the face of the good San Francisco pass rush.

"Roger wasn't as sharp as he normally is," Dallas coach Tom Landry said. "He was holding the ball back there too long."

On the 49er pass rush, Landry offered: "We weren't reading our keys." The key to the pass rush was end Cedrick Hardman, who sacked Roger twice and got him several times downfield.

Calvin Hill's knee collapsed in the first half, sending the Yale graduate to the sidelines. Runner rich Dallas simply substituted rodeo vet Walt Garrison, and he rambled for 52 yards on 14 carries.

Reprinted from
The Baltimore Sun

Jan. 3

AFC title

Griese's bombs to Warfield trigger Miami

By CAMERON C. SNYDER
Sun Staff Correspondent

Miami—It was New Year's Eve all over again for 78,629 Miami fans—intoxicated with joy—who rung in the new American Conference champs and booed out the old as the Dolphins defeated the Colts, 21 to 0, yesterday.

Thus Baltimore's one-year reign as world champion came to an end against a team that previously had ousted it from the Eastern Division title.

The game itself was more like the Fourth of July than a chaotic New Year's affair, because of the skyrockets.

Setting off two of these skyrockets was Dolphin quarterback Bob Griese, who had a spin wheel target in Paul Warfield. This pair accounted for a 75-yard touchdown and set up a third TD with a 50-yard cherry bomb which exploded in the end zone one play later as Larry Csonka plunged over from the Colt five.

The other Dolphin touchdown, the middle one of the three, was set off by the Colt quarterback John Unitas. Unfortunately, it was a boomerang skyrocket that came back past Unitas like a shot and was named Dick Anderson, who returned the deflected interception 62 yards for a touchdown.

The one that hurt the most

That TD probably was the one that hurt the Colts most, but a safety or a field goal by the Dolphins would have been just as conclusive against a team that couldn't score a point.

This was the first time the Colts have been shut out in 81 games including regular and post season games. The Chicago Bears were the villains that time, 13-0.

The last time the Colts were shut out in a championship game was in 1964. The Cleveland Browns did it, 27 to 0, to win the National Football League title.

Reprinted from
The Baltimore Sun

It was a 20-3 victory over the Browns last week that sent the Colts against Miami for the AFC title and a chance at the Super Bowl crown.

The Dolphins, as division champs, had to play the tougher Western bracket titlists, the Kansas City Chiefs, and won in the longest game on record, one hour and 20.40 minutes of playing time, 27-24.

The Colts now have failed to win in the Orange Bowl against the home team in three outings and Unitas has put only 31 points on the board in those games.

Not all the fault should be put on Unitas, who was intercepted three times while completing 20 to 36 passes for 224 yards.

He started with two rookies in his backfield, Don Nottingham and Don McCauley, and with these two he kept the pressure on the Miami defense, but wasn't able to come up with the big play enough on third and fourth down with short yardage.

It was a failure on a fourth and one play at the Dolphin nine that was the key to the Colt offensive failure and the lock to the Miami shutout.

Nottingham was the man Unitas selected for this crucial lunge at the line but the Human Bowling Ball ran into a crusty old middle linebacker named Nick Buoniconti and missed the first down by a foot.

A turning point? Definitely. There was still enough time and still enough talent, but that stand by the Dolphins made them tougher defensively thereafter.

Jim O'Brien tried three field goals after promising Colt drives fizzled on third down failures. He missed from the 46 and 48 and had the other, a 35-yarder, blocked by Lloyd Mumford. All these attempts were in the first half, while the Colts were dominating play but trailing, 7-0.

Interceptions stopped any Colt rally in the second half and the first steal by Anderson went for the TD. That put the Dolphins up 14-0 and marked only the second deep penetration of the Colt end of the field.

The first was the Griese to Warfield aerial of 75 yards. Baltimore's defense, the best in the American Conference, was excellent again.

Besides the Warfield touchdown they got past midfield just one other time in the first half and that was to the 48 where on the next play Griese's bomb was intercepted by Jerry Logan.

In the third quarter, before Anderson's interception touchdown, the Dolphins reached the Colt 49 only to be thrown back to their own 39 and forced to punt.

Miami's third touchdown, in the fourth quarter, was the first penetration of Colt terriory since the third period TD, but this time it was earned, not stolen.

Jan. 4

Sayers Undergoes 4th Knee Surgery

Jan. 17

Cowboy stampede sinks Dolphins, 24-3

QB Staubach, Thomas pace Super romp

By CAMERON C. SNYDER

Sun Staff Correspondent

New Orleans—Jolly Roger Staubach and silent Duane Thomas were featured performers, but it was a bruising Dallas Cowboy chorus line which kicked the Miami Dolphins into the second balcony, 24 to 3, during the four-act Super Bowl VI play at Tulane Stadium yesterday.

A crowd of 81,023 was on hand and was sitting on its hands before it was over to keep warm in the 30-degree weather at this supposedly warm weather city.

Before Thomas broke his season-long vow of silence for television after the game, he broke a Miami defense, which two weeks ago shut out the Colts, with his running—95 yards in 19 carries. He also scored once.

For variation, Staubach, most of the time staying in the pocket in the tradition of a captain on a sinking ship, tossed 12 completions, 2 for touchdowns against a thoroughly demoralized and beaten Miami team.

Cowboys set tempo

But the act of these two couldn't have turned the game into a burlesque without the overpowering Cowboy offensive line, whose watchword was to wall off Nick Buoniconti, Miami's swift, hard tackling but little middle linebacker.

It was Buoniconti who led the Dolphins over the Colts in the American Conference title game, but old Nick was crossed off effectively by one of three interior linemen, guards John Niland and Blaine Nye and center Dave Manders.

Once Dallas established the tempo of running mostly to the right side and Miami failed to adjust, it was just a matter of waiting for the final whistle before offering coach Tom Landry and the Cowboys an apology.

Losers to the Colts, 16-13, in last season's Super Bowl, the Cowboys were being called a team that couldn't win the big one after previous disappointments in several old National Football League championship games.

The game probably would have been stowed away much sooner than the third period, when the Cowboys went 71 yards in 8 plays with the second half kick-off for a 17-3 lead, if Staubach, a former Navy officer and a graduate of the Naval Academy, had picked out open receivers in the first half

Roger the Dodger was chased and clobbered by the Dolphin rush while Bob Hayes, Lance Alworth and Thomas were wide open.

Common coaching error

But, Staubach, who didn't become a starter until midway in the season and then piloted the Cowboys to 10 straight victories, including yesterday's, anchored himself behind his convoy of cruisers and fired guided missiles.

Roger threw touchdown passes of seven yards each to Alworth and Mike Dikta.

The first of these, to Alworth, in the second period climaxed a 76-yard drive in 11 plays and was enough to bring the Super Bowl Trophy safely to Dallas.

Earlier, the Cowboys had landed on the scoreboard with a 9-yard field goal by Mike Clark. An 11-play, 53-yard drive ran out of steam at the Miami 2, when Thomas, on third down, tried to be cute instead of just running for the end zone.

The field goal and the touchdown should have given the Cowboys a 10-point advantage at halftime, but Landry made a common coaching mistake and had his defense go into a prevent line-up. As happens so often in the prevent, Bob Griese drilled it full of holes while racing against the clock.

In five plays, starting from their own 32, the Dolphins were able to score on a Garo Yepremian field goal of 31 yards.

It made the predominantly Miami crowd hopeful and eager for the second half, but it was false hope.

Landry said the second half kickoff drive by his Dallas offense was the decisive series in the game.

On the clinching drive, the Cowboys changed emphasis and came out with wide pitchouts to Thomas running, as before, to the right.

"They had adjusted to the inside plays," explained Niland, "so we had to start running outside and running as quickly as we could. The pitchout is the fastest method."

Thomas ran 3 times with pitchouts for 4, 7, and 22 yards, Hayes, on an end-around, carried, after Thomas's 22-yard run, 18 yards around right end to the Miami 5 and on second down at the 3, Thomas, crossing up the Dolphins, went off left end, cutting into the end zone.

Drive thwarted

The third touchdown was set up by Chuck Howley's interception and return of 41 yards of a Griese pass to the Miami 10. Thomas and Calvin Hill were held to three yards in two tries, but Staubach lofted a touchdown pass to Ditka on third down as the tight end crossed the end zone from left to right.

The Cowboys almost scored again in the late stages with a 79-yard march that was halted on the Miami 1 when Hill, who played infrequently as Thomas's replacement because of a knee injury, fumbled and Manny Fernandez, best of the Dolphin defenders yesterday, recovered.

Howley, who won the automobile last year as the outstanding player of Super Bowl V despite being on the losing side, also started the Cowboys on the way to victory with a recovery of a Larry Csonka fumble. This recovery resulted in Clark's field goal.

Overwhelming statistics

If this replay of the game seems overly weighted with Cowboy doings, it was because the Cowboys were doing it.

Coach Don Shula's young team wasn't able to cope with the more experienced Dallas club either offensively or defensively.

The Cowboys gained 352 yards to the Dolphins' 185, had 23 first downs to Miami's 10 and set two Super Bowl records, 252 yards rushing and the 23 first downs. Green Bay was the rushing leader with 160 in 1968 and with 21 first downs in 1967, shared by the New York Jets who defeated the Colts in 1969. That Jet victory was also Shula's loss.

Reprinted from
The Baltimore Sun

Individual Statistics
COWBOYS
RUSHING

	Att.	Yds.	Avg.	Lg. Gn.	TD
Thomas	19	95	5.0	23	1
Garrison	14	74	5.3	17	0
Staubach	5	18	3.6	5	0
Hill	7	25	3.6	13	0
Hayes	1	16	16.0	16	0
Reeves	1	7	7.0	7	0
Ditka	1	17	17.0	17	0
Totals	48	252	5.3	23	1

PASSING

	Att.	Cmp.	Yds.	T. Yds.	H.	Int.
Staubach	19	12	119	2	19	0
Totals	19	12	119	2	19	0

PASS RECEIVING

	No.	Yds.	LG.	TD
Hayes	2	23	18	0
Thomas	3	17	11	0
Garrison	2	11	7	0
Alworth	2	28	21	1
Hill	1	12	12	0
Ditka	2	28	21	1
Totals	12	119	21	2

INTERCEPTIONS

	No.	Yds.	LG.	TD
Howley	1	41	41	0

PUNTING

	No.	Yds.	Avg.	Lg.
Widby	5	186	372	47

PUNT RETURNS

	No.	Fc.	Yds.	Lg.
Hayes	1		1	1
Harris	0	2	0	0
Totals	1		1	1

KICKOFF RETURNS

	No.	Yds.	Lg.	TD
Waters	1	11	11	0
I. Thomas	1	23	23	0
Totals	2	34	23	0

FUMBLES

	Fum.	Opp. Rec.
Howley	0	1
Cole	0	1
Hill	1	0
Totals	1	2

DOLPHINS
RUSHING

	Att.	Yards	Avg.	Long Gain	TD
Kiick	7	40	5.7	9	0
Csonka	9	40	4.4	12	0
Griese	1	0	0.0	0	0
Totals	17	80	4.2	12	0

PASSING

	Att.	Comp.	Yds.	Yds.	TD	LG.	Int.
Griese	23	12	134	1	21	0	27	1

PASS RECEIVING

	No.	Yards	LG.	TD
Twilley	1	20	20	0
Kiick	3	21	11	0
Warfield	4	39	23	0
Csonka	2	18	16	0
Fleming	1	27	27	0
Mandich	1	9	9	0
Totals	12	134	27	0

PUNTING

	No.	Yds.	Avg.	Lg.
Seiple	5	288	46.0	45

PUNT RETURNS

	No.	Fc.	Yds.	LG.	TD
Scott	1	0	21	21	0

KICKOFF RETURNS

	No.	Yds.	LG.	TD
Morris	4	90	37	0
Ginn	1	32	32	0
Totals	5	122	37	0

FUMBLES

	Fum.	Own Rec.	Opp. rec.
Csonka	1	0	
Griese	1	0	
Fernandes	0		1

Statistics

	Cowboys	Dolphins
First downs	23	10
Rushes, yards	48—252	20—80
Passing yardage	119	134
Return yardage	42	21
Passes	12-19-0	12-23-1
Punts	5-37	5-46
Fumbles lost	1	2
Yards penalized	15	0

Dallas	3	7	7	7	24
Miami	0	3	0	0	3

Dal—FG Clark 9.
Dal—Alworth 7 pass from Staubach (Clark kick).
Mia—FG Yepremian 31.
Dal—Thomas 3 run (Clark kick).
Dal—Ditka 7 pass from Staubach (Clark kick).
Attendance—81,023.

Reprinted from
The Baltimore Sun

VICTORY   Wide World Photo

New Orleans. . . . Coach Tom Landry of Dallas is carried from the field on the shoulders of his players. Players are Bob Hayes (22), Rayfield Wright (70), and Mel Renfro (20).

Thomas breaks silence after Cowboy victory

By CAMERON C. SNYDER

New Orleans—The sphinx spoke.

Duane Thomas, who covered himself in silence for most of the season, uttered a few words in the happy Cowboy dressing room after Dallas's 24-to-3 victory over the Miami Dolphins.

What Duane, who also was quiet around his teammates and coaches, said was much shorter and nowhere near as noteworthy as the Gettysburg Address. But he spoke.

His first words were: "Pardon me"? He was confused when someone told him he was in the running for the automobile that a sports magazine gives to the most valuable player in the Super Bowl.

Then when asked whether he was going to the Pro Bowl game he said, "Yea, excuse me I have to go up front for a moment."

Up front was before the television cameras. He was persuaded to do this by his adviser Jim Brown, one of the all-time running back greats with the Cleveland Browns.

It was Brown who told Thomas after Duane's contract disputes with the Cowboys, to "go back there, give the team 100 per cent but don't say a word."

And Thomas took him literally and didn't say a word until yesterday.

Tom Brookshire, a former pro defensive back star with the Philadelphia Eagles, was the TV MC. He told Thomas that the Cowboy's speed surprised him and that Duane was faster than he thought.

"Evidently," came the terse reply.

Asked if he were happy, Duane said:

"I never said I was sad."

Taking over for his protege, Brown said, "He's one of the greatest backs who ever lived. He should get more money."

Money talks. The $15,000 winner's share for the Super Bowl even got Thomas to speak.

Reprinted from
The Baltimore Sun

Team-by-Team

Atlanta Falcons
Clarence Ellis, defensive back, Notre Dame; Pat Sullivan, quarterback, Auburn; Steve Okoniewski, offensive tackle, Montana; Roosevelt Manning, defensive tackle, Northeastern Oklahoma State; Les Goodman, running back, Yankton, S.D.; Andrew Howard, defensive tackle, Grambling; Billy Taylor, running back, Michigan; Ralph Cindrich, linebacker, Pittsburgh; Mike Perfetti, defensive back, Minnesota; Fred Riley, wide receiver, Idaho; Lance Moon, running back, Wisconsin.

Baltimore Colts
Tom Drougas, offensive tackle, Oregon; Jack Mildren, defensive back, Oklahoma; Glenn Doughty wide receiver, Michigan; Lydell Mitchell, running back, Penn State; Eric Allen, wide receiver, Michigan State; Don Croft, defensive tackle, Texas-El Paso; Bruce Laird, defensive back, American International; John Sykes, running back, Morgan State.

Buffalo Bills
Walt Patulski, defensive end, Notre Dame; Reggie McKenzie, guard, Michigan; Fred Swendsen, defensive end, Notre Dame; Randy Jackson, running back, Wichita State; Leon Garror, defensive back, Alcorn A&M; Robert Penchion, guard, Alcorn A&M; Ralph Stepaniak, defensive back, Notre Dame.

Chicago Bears
Lionel Antoine, offensive tackle, Southern Illinois; Craig Clemons, defensive back, Iowa; Johnny Musso, running back, Alabama; Bob Parsons, tight end, Penn State; Bob Pifferini, linebacker, UCLA; Jim Fassel, quarterback, Long Beach State; James Osborne, defensive tackle, Southern U.

Cincinnati Bengals
Sherman White, defensive end, California; Tommy Casanova, defensive back, Louisiana State; Jim LeClair, linebacker, North Dakota; Bernard Jackson, defensive back, Washington State; Tom DeLeone, center, Ohio State; Steve Conley, running back, Kansas.

Kansas City Chiefs
Jeff Kinney, running back, Nebraska; Andy Hamilton, wide receiver, Louisiana State; Milt Davis, defensive end, Texas-Arlington; John Kahler, defensive end, Long Beach State; Dean Carlson, quarterback, Iowa State.

Los Angeles Rams
Jim Bertelsen, running back, Texas; Larry McCutcheon, running back, Colorado State; John Saunders, defensive back, Toledo; Eddie Phillips, defensive back, Texas; Bob Childs, guard, Kansas; Bob Christiansen, tight end, UCLA; Edward Hebert, defensive tackle, Texas Southern;

Miami Dolphins
Mike Kadish, defensive tackle, Notre Dame; Gary Kosins, running back, Dayton; Larry Ball, defensive end, Louisville; Al Benton, tackle, Ohio University; Charles Babb, defensive back, Memphis State; Ray Nettles, linebacker, Tennessee; Bill Adams, guard, Holy Cross; Calvin Harrell, running back, Arkansas State.

Minnesota Vikings
Jeff Siemon, linebacker, Stanford; Ed Marinaro, running back, Cornell; Bart Butow, tackle, Minnesota; Anthony Martin, linebacker, Louisville; Bill Slater, defensive end, Western Michigan.

New England Patriots
Tom Reynolds, wide receiver, San Diego State; Jim White, defensive end, Colorado State; Ron Bolton, defensive back, Norfolk State; Clark Hoss, tight end, Oregon State; John Traver, running back, Colorado.

New Orleans Saints
Royce Smith, guard, Georgia; Willie Hall, linebacker, Southern California; Bob Kuziel, center, Pittsburgh; Tom Myers, defensive back, Syracuse; Mike Crangle, defensive end, Tennessee-Martin; Joe Senderspiel, linebacker, Kentucky; Mike Colman, defensive end, Knoxville College; Bill Butler, running back, Kansas State; Carl Johnson, tackle, Nebraska; Bob Davies, defensive back, South Carolina; Wayne Dorton, guard, Arkansas State; Curt Watson, running back, Tennessee; Ernie Jackson, defensive back, Duke.

New York Giants
Eldridge Small, defensive back, Texas A&I; Larry Jacobson, defensive end, Nebraska; John Mendenhall, tackle, Grambling; Tom Mozisek, running back, Houston; Tom Gatewood, wide receiver, Notre Dame; Larry Edwards, linebacker, Texas A&I; John Hill, center, Lehigh; Mike Zikas, defensive tackle, Notre Dame.

Cleveland Browns
Tom Darden, defensive back, Michigan; Clifford Brooks, defensive back, Tennessee State; Lester Sims, defensive end, Alabama State; George Hunt, kicker, Tennessee; Greg Kucera, running back, North Colorado; Leonard Forey, guard, Texas A&M; Jorn Wesley, tackle, Maryland State.

Dallas Cowboys
Bill Thomas, running back, Boston College; Robert Newhouse, running back, Houston; John Babinecz, linebacker, Villanova; Charlie McKee, wide receiver, Arizona; Mike Keller, linebacker, Michigan; Marv Bateman, kicker, Utah; Tim Kearney, linebacker, Northern Michigan; Robert West, wide receiver, San Diego State; Charles Zapiec, linebacker, Penn State; Charles Bolden, defensive back, Iowa.

Denver Broncos
Riley Odoms, tight end, Houston; Bill Phillips, linebacker, Arkansas State; Tom Graham, linebacker, Oregon; Jim Kreig, wide receiver, Washington.

Detroit Lions
Herb Orvis, defensive end, Colorado; Ken Sanders, defensive end, Howard Payne; Charles Potts, defensive back, Purdue; Chrales Stoudamire, wide receiver, Portland State.

Green Bay Packers
Willie Buchanon, cornerback, San Diego State; Jerry Tagge, quarterback, Nebraska; Chester Malcol, kicker, Hillsdale; Eric Patton, linebacker, Notre Dame; Nathaniel Ross, defensive back, Bethune-Cookman; Dave Pureifory, linebacker, Eastern Michigan; Robert Hudson, running back, Northeastern Oklahoma; Bill Busrong, defensive tackle, Kentucky.

Houston Oilers
Greg Sampson, defensive end, Stanford; Lewis Jolley, running back, North Carolina; Solomon Freelon, guard, Grambling; Joe Bullard, defensive back, Tulane; Elmer Allen, linebacker, Mississippi; Eric Hutchinson, defensive back, Northwestern.

New York Jets
Jerome Barkum, wide receiver, Jackson State; Mike Taylor, linebacker, Michigan; Gary Hammond, wide receiver, Southern Methodist; Ed Galigher, defensive end, UCLA; Dickie Harris, defensive back, South Carolina; Joe Jackson, defensive end, New Mexico State.

Oakland Raiders
Mike Siani, wide receiver, Villanova; Kelvin Korver, defensive tackle, Northwestern, Iowa; John Vella, offensive tackle, Southern California; Mel Lunsford, defensive tackle, Central State, Ohio; Cliff Branch, wide receiver, Colorado; Dave Dalby, center, UCLA; Dan Medlin, defensive tackle, North Carolina State; Ray Jamieson, running back, Memphis State; Alonzo Thomas, defensive back, Southern California; Dennis Pete, defensive back, San Francisco State.

Philadelphia Eagles
John Reaves, quarterback, Florida; Dan Yochum, offensive tackle, Syracuse; Tom Luken, guard, Purdue; Bobby Majors, defensive back, Tennessee; Ron (Poe) James, running back, New Mexico State; Vern Winfield, guard, Minnesota; Will Foster, linebacker, Eastern Michigan.

Pittsburgh Steelers
Franco Harris, running back, Penn State; Gordon Gravelle, offensive tackle, Brigham Young; John McMakin, tight end, Clemson; Lorenzo Brinkley, defensive back, Missouri; Ed Bradley, linebacker, Wake Forest; Steve Furness, defensive end, Rhode Island; Dennis Meyer, defensive back, Arkansas State; Joe Colquitt, defensive end, Kansas State; Robert Kelley, defensive back, Jackson State.

St. Louis Cardinals
Bobby Moore, running back-wide receiver, Oregon; Mark Arneson, linebacker, Arizona; Tom Beckman, defensive end, Michigan; Jeff Lyman, linebacker, Brigham Young; Martin Imhof, defensive tackle, San Diego State; Conrad Dobler, guard, Wyoming; Don Heater, running back, Montana Tech; Council Tudolph, defensive end, Kentucky State.

San Diego Chargers
Pete Lazetich, defensive end, Stanford; Bill Clard, kicker, Argansas; Jim Bishop, tight end, Tennessee Tech; Harry Gooden, defensive end, Alcorn A&M; Bruce Ward, guard, San Diego State.

San Francisco 49ers
Terry Beasley, wide receiver, Auburn; Ralph McGill, defensive back, Tulsa; Jean Barrett, offensive tackle, Tulsa; Allen Dunbar, wide receiver, Southern University; Windlam Hall, defensive back, Arizona State; Mike Greene, linebacker, Georgia; Jackie Walker, defensive back, Tennessee; Edgar Hardy, guard, Jackson State.

March 23

NFL moves hash marks in to perk up attack

Honolulu —National Football League owners moved to put more offense in the game yesterday, adopting a rule change concerning the placement of the markings on the field that aids all three phases of the offense-run, pass and kick—and destroys one of the keys employed by some zone defense teams.

The actual rule change adopted moves the hash marks in from the sidelines by 3½ yards, from 20 yards from the sideline to 23½, and calls for uniform marking of the yardlines on the field just one yard from these new hash marks.

While the rule change is very technical in nature, Commissioner Pete Rozelle said: "We feel it will help open things up for the offense more than it would appear to do."

Aim to help offense

The change was adopted after a recommendation by the Competition Committee which has been studying the drop in scoring in recent years. There has been concern because teams last year scored 100 fewer touchdowns than in 1969 which, said Rozelle, made the committee feel "there was a potential danger."

According to Mark Duncan, the head of officials for the NFL, moving the hash marks in from the sidelines will aid the run, the pass and the kick, while the uniform marking of the field will handicap zone defense teams who previously marked their fields in a manner that provided keys for their defensive backs.

"Defensive players are so big and fast they're consuming a lot of space," Duncan explained. "We can't widen the field, but this is one way to accomplish the same thing."

More running room

It will help running backs because it will give them more room to run toward either sideline.

It will help passers against the zone because it stretches the areas of responsibility for defensive backs.

It will help field goal kickers because it will cut down the angle on long field goal attempts.

One other rule change was adopted by the owners to help aid the offense. That permits a punt to be run out of the end zone. Previously it was an automatic touchback. The same rule change applying to the field goal was adopted by the owners last year.

2 points defeated

Two other rule changes adopted concerned penalties. They were:

The penalty for a receiver going out of bounds and coming back in to catch a pass was changed from 15 yards and loss of down to just loss of down.

The penalty for grabbing a face mask was made five yards and a first down unless its flagrant, when it still will be 15 yards and a first down.

May 25

Rozelle target of suit

Owners vote to count tie in standings

BY CAMERON C. SNYDER
Sun Staff Correspondent

New York—Professional football has become the plaything of mathematicians and legal beagles; at least that is the impression given yesterday.

First of all the NFL owners meeting here gave unanimous approval to a change in keeping the standings of the clubs. From now on a tie game, which previously had counted for nothing in the standings, will be counted as a half game won and a half game lost.

But that news was overshadowed by an anti-trust suit filed against the NFL club owners and Commissioner Pete Rozelle, attacking Rozelle's compensation rule but also seeking separate damages for eight free agent players.

Complete surprise

The Rozelle rule for compensation simply gives the team from which a player has played out his option equal compensation from the team that signs the free agent player.

Among the eight was John Williams, Colt guard, who played out his option last season and became a free agent as of May 1.

Don Klosterman, Colt general manager, was one of four GM's to be interviewed in defense of the league and the compensation rule by the press yesterday.

"It came as a complete surprise to me," said Klosterman of Williams's suit. "I talked with Williams's agent (Bob Woolf) last week and he said nothing about such a suit.

"I think it is significant that our other free agent player, Charlie Stukes, was not among the group filing against the NFL."

The other free agents suing for what could be treble damages under anti-trust laws were John Henderson, Clint Jones, Gene Washington, Charlie West and Nate Wright, all from the Minnesota Vikings, Buffalo's Marlin Briscoe and Oakland's Dan Connors.

Rozelle responds

Twenty-nine players played out their options last season, which means 21 have not joined in the suit.

However, they are indirectly involved because the plaintiffs were not only the eight players but also officials of the National Football League Players Association.

Incidentally, the players' lawyer, Edward Glennon, was a law partner to Ed Garvey, now executive director of the NFLPA.

Rozelle had only a brief comment to offer in response:

"We would have hoped that could be resolved through the process of collective bargaining as is the case in normal union-management relationships. This process is, of course, currently available to both the players and the clubs and both certainly are aware that the rules of professional football offer players a greater freedom of movement than the rules of any other professional sport. The record of player rtansfers in the NFL documents that fact."

Tex Schramm, general manager and president of the Dallas Cowboys, was the principal speaker for the general managers yesterday because of his long tenure.

He pointed out that the compensation rule was established to keep alive the competitiveness of the game, and that wiping it out "would make the strong teams stronger and the weak teams weaker."

Give up something

"It would end the college draft," he said. "What team would draft a college player and then run the chance of losing him after one year. The draft is the equalizer among the clubs. A weaker team, lower in the standings, selects players earlier than a stronger team and eventually the better choices should even the competition."

The reason the owners changed the method of ranking the clubs was because under the old rule, theoretically, one team could have a 13-1 record and lose to a team that won one game and tied 13.

Ties didn't count for or against a team under the old method. Now a tie will count as one-half a win.

This means a team with a 10-3-1 record, whose percentage was .769 would have a .750 percentage under the new method.

Reprinted from
The Baltimore Sun

Joe, Jets dazzle Colts

Namath burns zone for 6 TDs in 44-34 win

By CAMERON C. SNYDER

Joe Namath made a liar out of John Unitas by attacking Baltimore's famed zone defense and puncturing it with 6 touchdown passes as the New York Jets flattened the bomb-shocked Colts, 44 to 34, yesterday at the Stadium.

Unitas, who also had a good afternoon with the pass, has frequently said, "You can't throw long against the zone."

Either Namath didn't hear the old master or didn't pay any attention to Unitas as he threw touchdowns of 65 yards to Ed Bell, 67 yards to John Riggins, 21 yards to Don Maynard and 10, 79 and 80 yards to Rich Caster.

Thrill-a-minute game

He completed only 15 of 28 passes, but gained 496 yards, a personal best for himself and a Jet record although only third on the all-time list. Norm Van Brocklin's 554 yards against the New York Yanks in 1951 is tops, and Y. A. Tittle's 505 in 1962 Giant-Redskin game is second.

Unitas was busy on his end of the offense, too. He set a personal and a Colt record with 26 completions. His old mark was 25 against the Redskins in 1962 and 1966. His 376 yards passing was the 27th time he has pitched for 300 or more yards.

Unitas hot

He threw for 2 touchdowns, a 8-yard flea flicker to Sam Havrilak and a 21-yard pass to Tom Matte.

The combined total of 872 yards by the two quarterbacks set a National Football League record.

reprinted from the Baltimore Sun

Rosenbloom sole owner of Rams; plans to keep Prothro as field boss

Los Angeles (AP)—Carroll Rosenbloom, the new owner of the Los Angeles Rams, flew into town yesterday and held a press conference in which he explained the deal in which he swapped the Baltimore Colts for the Rams.

"We avoided capital gains taxes by doing it this way," said Rosenbloom, who had flown all night to be at a news conference announcing the financial move.

Rosenbloom had demanded 80 per cent of the Rams' stock before he would entertain a switch. As things turned out, he got 100 per cent, and made it abundantly clear that Tommy Prothro would remain as coach.

"I am the sole owner, that's the only way I would have it," he told newsmen. Asked why the move from East to West, he said, "There is a great challenge here. We have won the Super Bowl in Baltimore. I like a challenge. I loved Dan Reeves. He loved to win and so do I."

Rosenbloom also said he had some financial interests on the West Coast—Warner Bros. Pictures and some others.

Bill Barnes, president of the Rams since the death of Reeves, had been seeking a buyer for more than a year. He said the negotiations leading to this deal began early last month.

Likes Prothro

Asked if he would honor the five-year contract given Prothro last year, Rosenbloom answered, "One of the reasons I wanted the Rams is because he's tied up for five years."

Rosenbloom said that Robert Irsay and Willard Keland, a former part-owner of Miami's Dolphins, wanted a club in the East.

"I didn't want to get out of professional football, so I wouldn't sell the club outright," he explained. "Then came the idea of the switch."

Rosenbloom said he didn't know how much the Midwesterners paid for the Rams' stock. Barnes, however, gave a $19 million figure.

Raider rally nips Packers

Green Bay, Wis (AP)—The Oakland Raiders, bogged down by penalties most of the way, struck back to defeat Green Bay, 20 to 14, yesterday with the help of two calls disputed by the Packers.

Jack Tatum returned a Green Bay fumble 104 yards, breaking a 49-year-old National Football League record by six yards. Oakland's other touchdown, on Charlie Smith's one-yard run, came one play after a 32-yard pass interference penalty against Packer rookie Willie Buchanon moved the ball to the Green Bay one.

Phil Villapiano set up Oakland's lead touchdown by recovering Scott Hunter's fumble at the Packer 45 late in the third quarter. Three plays later, Darryl Lamonica's long pass for Fred Biletnikoff was picked off by Jim Hill, but the interference call negated the interception.

The Raiders' other scores came on field goals of 43 and 14-yards by George Blanda, and Tatum's spectacular fumble runback.

Statistics

	Raiders	Packers
First downs	21	15
Rushes-yards	46-196	36-143
Passing yards	117	64
Return yards	133	41
Passes	8-21-0	5-13-0
Punts	4-45	6-46
Fumbles—lost	2-1	2-2
Penalties—yards	7-102	4-55

Oakland	10	0	10	0—	20
Green Bay	7	7	0	0—	14

Oak—FG Blanda 42.
Bay—Brockington 1 run (Marcol kick).
Oak—Tatum 104 fumble runback (Blanda kick).
Bay—Brockington 1 run (Marcol kick).
Oak—FG Blanda 14.
Oak—Smith 1 run (Blanda kick).

Oct. 22

Youth-oriented Colts face Jets today with new coach

By CAMERON C. SNYDER
Sun Staff Correspondent

New York—The Baltimore Colts take their new look, featuring a new coach and a new quarterback, into Shea Stadium at 1 o'clock this afternoon for a rematch with Joe Namath and the New York Jets

Making his debut as head coach is John Sandusky who took the job Monday after the firing of Don McCafferty. And the quarterback is Marty Domres, who is in his fourth year but only his first season as a Colt after being acquired from the San Diego Chargers in a pre-season deal.

Domres, who has never started before as a Colt and whose last starting assignment was two years ago with the Chargers, replaces Baltimore's superstar, John Unitas.

Unitas, whose statistics are impressive but whose ability to get points on the scoreboard is unimpressive, will warm the bench and not get in the game unless Domres is injured. The Colt record is 1-4; the Jets are 3-2.

It is a bitter letdown for the 17-year veteran who holds all the passing records in pro football, but as he said, "I have been benched before."

Reprinted from
The Baltimore Sun

Dec. 12

Raiders win, 24-16

Jets lose play-off chance

Oakland ℗ — Oakland's Daryle Lamonica threw long touchdown passes to Fred Biletnikoff and Raymond Chester last night and Marv Hubbard became the ninth National Football League player to rush for 1,000 yards this season in a 24-to-16 victory over New York which killed the Jets' playoff hopes.

The loss also spoiled a record-breaking night for Jets' receiver Don Maynard, who caught seven of Joe Namath's passes for 132 yards to establish an NFL mark of 632 career receptions, one more than Baltimore's Raymond Berry.

Nov. 13

Dolphins humiliate Patriots

Miami ℗—Mercury Morris ran for three first half touchdowns Sunday as the Miami Dolphins crushed the New England Patriots, 52 to 0, at the Orange Bowl to make Don Shula the first National Football League coach to ever win 100 games in his first 10 seasons.

The victory put the Dolphins in a position to clinch a play-off spot in their home game next week against the New York Jets.

The defending American Football Conference champions boosted their record to 9-0 by scoring every time they got their hands on the ball in the first half for a 31-0 lead.

Morris scored twice on four-yard sweeps around left end for a 14-0 lead after the Dolphins' first five offensive plays. A six-yard run by Morris concluded the first-half scoring aginst the hapless Patriots, now 2-7.

No fumble ruled

"I'm grateful to a lot of people over the 10 years," Shula said. "I'm grateful to two wonderful coaching staffs and the great players in Baltimore and here in Miami.

"I'm proud to get 100 wins but it is only really meaningful if it happened in a year we get a world championship."

Dolphin players presented him with the game ball after their record stretched to 9-0 but Shula said, "I'm happy to have received the game ball but the one I want is at the end of the year."

Dec. 18

'Skins stunned by Bills

Interceptions, Simpson pace 24-17 upset

Washington ℗—Two key interceptions and the running of O.J. Simpson gave the lowly Buffalo Bills a 24-to-17 upset victory over the Washington Redskins in a National Football League game yesterday.

Simpson captured the NFL rushing title by gaining 101 yards in 26 carries, giving him 1,251 yards for the season. Washington's Larry Brown, sitting on the bench for the second straight week, finished with 1,216.

Dec. 18

Dawson's 2 TD passes lead K.C. past Atlanta

Atlanta (P)—Veteran Len Dawson tossed two scoring passes in peppering Atlanta's pass defense with amazing accuracy, guiding the Kansas City Chiefs to a 17-to-14 National Football League victory over the Falcons yesterday in the season finale for both clubs.

The Chiefs closed out the season with an 8-6 mark and second place in the American Conference West, while Atlanta, eliminated a day earlier from the National Conference West, ended at 7-7.

Dawson fired a seven-yard winning touchdown pass to Ed Podolak with 2.19 left to play. Earlier, Dawson put the Chiefs ahead 10-7 when he hit Otis Taylor with a 15-yard touchdown pass with 59 seconds remaining in the third period.

Atlanta had gone ahead 14-10 early in the final period on Bob Berry's 17-yard TD strike to Ken Burrow before Dawson took Kansas City on its winning 81-yard, 13-play march.

The Falcons led 7-3 at halftime on a one-yard scoring run by Art Malone 2½ minutes before the intermission. Jan Stenerud had booted a 28-yard field goal for the Chiefs earlier in the period.

Atlanta's Dave Hampton, honored at halftime as the Falcons' most valuable player, fell five yards short of reaching the 1,000-yard rushing plateau this season. He needed 70 yards but got only 65 in 19 carries to close with 995.

In Kansas City's first touchdown drive, Dawson connected for eight consecutive passes, capping the 71-yard drive with his scoring toss to Taylor.

Dawson hit on three more passes on the next drive before ending his string at 11 straight completions, four short of his own record set in 1967.

Actually, Hampton reached the 1,000 yard plateau when he ran one yard on the second play of the final quarter. The game was stopped and he was presented with the ball.

However, on the Falcons' final scoring drive, Hampton lost six yards on a pitchout, which he fumbled, then recovered, before he was tackled. He only ran the ball one more time, gaining a yard.

Statistics

	Chiefs	Falcons
First downs	19	16
Rushes—yards	43-182	31-85
Passing—yards	108	166
Return yards	—1	67
Passes	18-36-1	11-25-2
Punts	4-38	5-39
Fumbles—lost	0-0	3-1
Penalties—yards	2-20	3-25

Kansas City	0	3	7	7—	17
Atlanta	0	7	0	7—	14

KC—FG Stenerud 28
Atl—Malone 1 run (Bell kick)
KC—Taylor 15 pass from Dawson (Stenerud kick)
Atl—Burrow 17 pass from Berry (Bell kick)
KC—Podolak 7 pass from Dawson (Stenerud kick)
Attendance—38,850.

1972

AMERICAN CONFERENCE							NATIONAL CONFERENCE						
EASTERN DIVISION							**EASTERN DIVISION**						
	W	L	T	Pct.	Pts.	OP		W	L	T	Pct.	Pts.	OP
Miami	14	0	0	1.000	385	171	Washington	11	3	0	.786	336	218
N.Y. Jets	7	7	0	.500	367	324	Dallas*	10	4	0	.714	319	240
Baltimore	5	9	0	.357	235	252	N.Y. Giants	8	6	0	.571	331	247
Buffalo	4	9	1	.321	257	377	St. Louis	4	9	1	.321	193	303
New England	3	11	0	.214	192	446	Philadelphia	2	11	1	.179	145	352
CENTRAL DIVISION							**CENTRAL DIVISION**						
	W	L	T	Pct.	Pts.	OP		W	L	T	Pct.	Pts.	OP
Pittsburgh	11	3	0	.786	343	175	Green Bay	10	4	0	.714	304	226
Cleveland*	10	4	0	.714	268	249	Detroit	8	5	1	.607	339	290
Cincinnati	8	6	0	.571	299	229	Minnesota	7	7	0	.500	301	252
Houston	1	13	0	.071	164	380	Chicago	4	9	1	.321	225	275
WESTERN DIVISION							**WESTERN DIVISION**						
	W	L	T	Pct.	PTS.	OP		W	L	T	Pct.	Pts.	OP
Oakland	10	3	1	.750	365	248	San Francisco	8	5	1	.607	353	249
Kansas City	8	6	0	.571	287	254	Atlanta	7	7	0	.500	269	274
Denver	5	9	0	.357	325	350	Los Angeles	6	7	1	.464	291	286
San Diego	4	9	1	.321	264	344	New Orleans	2	11	1	.179	215	361

*Wild card qualifier for playoffs

All-Rookie Team

OFFENSE

WR—Mike Siani, Oakland; Bobby Moore, St. Louis.
T—Tom Drougas, Baltimore; Gordon Gravelle, Steelers.
G—Dennis Havig, Atlanta; Reggie McKenzie, Buffalo.
C—Guy Murdock, Houston.
QB—John Reaves, Philadelphia.
RB—Franco Harris, Steelers; Jim Bertelsen, Los Angeles.
TE—John McMakin, Steelers.

DEFENSE

E—Walt Patulski, Buffalo; Sherman White, Cincinnati.
T—John Mendenhall, New York Giants; Otis Sistrunk, Oakland.
LB—Jeff Siemon, Minnesota; Joe Federspiel, New Orleans; Tom Graham, Denver.
CB—Willie Buchanon, Green Bay; Ernie Jackson, New Orleans.
S—Tom Darden, Cleveland; Tommy Casanova, Cincinnati.

Dec. 22

'Error' gives Morris 1,000 yards

Miami (P)—The unbeaten Miami Dolphins yesterday became the first professional football team in history to have two 1,000-yard rushers in one season after the National Football League reviewed films of an October 22 game and gave Dolphin running back Mercury Morris nine more yards.

A spokesman for the Dolphins said NFL Commissioner Pete Rozelle had reviewed the films of the Dolphins' October 22 victory over Buffalo and ruled that a nine-yard loss charged against Morris should have been charged as a fumble against Dolphin quarterback Earl Morrall.

In that play, Morrall attempted to pass to Morris, but the ball was tipped by Buffalo defensive lineman Dave Washington and ultimately was recovered by Buffalo.

The game officials at that time said the pass was a lateral and charged the loss to Morris. But a spokesman for the Dolphins said Rozelle had ruled that the play was incorrectly scored and should have been recorded as a fumble by Morrall.

The ruling gave Morris a season rushing total of exactly 1,000 yards, the spokesman said, pushing him into the ranks already occupied by Dolphin running back Larry Csonka who ended the season with 1,117 yards.

The Dolphins went through the regular 1972 season with a 14-0 record, the best in history, and Morris's yardage boost also raised the all-time team rushing record set by the Dolphins to 2,960 yards.

Miami meets the Cleveland Browns Sunday in the Orange Bowl in an American Football Conference playoff game.

Dec. 24

Dallas stuns 49ers

By KEN NIGRO
Sun Staff Correspondent

San Francisco — Today, the Bay area lies in a state of shock. From Oakland to San Francisco, not a creature is stirring.

The final, crushing jolt came late yesterday afternoon in the shadows of Candlestick Park when the defending Super Bowl champion Dallas Cowboys staged an incredible comeback in the final two minutes to defeat the 49ers, 30 to 28.

In snatching victory from almost certain defeat, the Cowboys scored two touchdowns in the unbelievable span of 38 seconds. Both came on passes from Roger Staubach, the forgotten man for the champs during the regular season.

2 action-filled minutes

Staubach, who relieved ineffective starter Craig Morton late in the third quarter, completed six straight passes and ran once for 21 yards during the two TD blitzes that left the 49ers and their fans—most of whom had long since departed to beat the traffic—in a coma.

It marked the third straight year San Francisco had lost to the Cowboys in the play-offs and the latest defeat came only a few hours after the Oakland Raiders had suffered the same kind of fate at Pittsburgh.

"It was unreal," said Cowboy coach Tom Landry, who actually was smiling. "I think it was the best comeback we've ever made. It looked like it was out of our hands but Roger pulled it out.

"You can't give up because you never know what's going to happen. Pittsburgh will tell you that."

If Landry hadn't given up, almost everyone else in the park had conceded the win to the 49ers. For 58 minutes the oft-maligned Cowboys had confirmed every suspicion that they weren't about to get very far in this year's NFL post-season extravaganza.

Reprinted from
The Baltimore Sun

Dec. 24

Steelers win on late TD

Raiders fall in last five seconds, 13-7

By CAMERON C. SNYDER
Sun Staff Correspondent

Pittsburgh—Franco Harris thundered 42 yards for a touchdown to snatch victory from the Oakland Raiders, who were envisioning Super Bowl plums with just five seconds to play yesterday at Three Rivers Stadium.

Art Rooney's Pittsburgh Steelers needed not only his luck of the Irish to prevail, 13 to 7, in the American Conference divisional play-off, but the combined luck of the Italians and Negroes to achieve their first play-off victory after 40 frustrating years of trying.

Harris is the son of an Italian-born mother and an American black father. His scoring run on the incredible last-ditch, deflected reception from quarterback Terry Bradshaw gave the 50,350 screaming Steeler fans a Christmas cake of meat balls and soul food, topped by a big shamrock.

For 54 of the 60 minutes the game was as dull as the steel grey sky as defense completely thwarted every offensive move.

Gerela boots two

The Steelers led, 6-0, on two Roy Gerela field goals of 18 and 29 yards with 4.10 left and the way the Raider offense had been functioning it looked like an insurmountable lead.

Reprinted from
The Baltimore Sun

Then Kenny Stabler, subbing for starting quarterback Daryle Lamonica, rallied the West Coast team for an 80-yard touchdown drive, climaxed by a fine 30-yard touchdown run by the left handed quarterback from Alabama.

The ensuing extra point put the Raiders ahead 7-6, with just 1.13 left on the scoreboard clock.

The after-touchdown kickoff to the Steelers was downed in the end zone, which meant the Pittsburghers had 80 long yards to go.

It was luck coupled with an alert and opportunistic Harris that covered the distance.

It looked like it was all over at the Steeler 40. Bradshaw was facing a fourth and 10 situation there with 22 seconds on the clock.

Starts to scramble

Bradshaw dropped back in the pocket to pass. He said he felt pressure and started to scramble, looking for his wide receiver, Barry Pearson.

He couldn't find him and threw a hard, fast one to John Fuqua, the Morgan State graduate. The pass was low, under the knees of the 5-11 Fuqua, who dove for it at the Raider 35. Also getting into the diving act was Oakland's Jack Tatum.

The ball was hit, whether by Tatum or Fuqua no one is sure, and caromed backward and to the left side.

Streaking down the field from his pass protection blocking assignment for Bradshaw, when Terry started to scramble, came Harris. He reached out with extended arms, bending to scoop up the low trajectory ball, cuddled it in his arm and zoomed in at the goal line and out-of-bounds flag.

He made it, and the Steelers moved into the American Conference championship game next Sunday here against the winners of the Cleveland Brown-Miami Dolphin game today in Miami.

Dec. 25

Kilmer ponders Cowboys

Washington (AP) — Quarterback Bill Kilmer of the Washington Redskins had just beaten the Green Bay Packers, but the Dallas Cowboys were on his mind.

"It's gonna be a helluva ballgame," said Kilmer after the Redskins defeated Green Bay, 16 to 3, Sunday to win the opportunity to meet the world champion Cowboys next weekend for the National Conference title.

"We're ready for Dallas," said Kilmer. "We know the Cowboys, and they know us. I don't look for a lot of shocks. We've just got to out-hit them."

Five-man line

The Dallas-Washington clash Sunday may be a brutally physical one because of the game two weeks ago, when the Cowboys defeated the Redskins, 34-24, after which bitter words were exchanged between the teams over the so-called crack-back blocking against Washington linebacker Jack Pardee.

The Cowboys, of course, called it good defense, while the Redskins said it was illegal.

"We know them," said a happy coach George Allen yesterday. "We played them twice this year. We know what we have to do. They know what we can do.

"We felt all along that we would have to play Dallas," said Allen, whose club downed the Cowboys, 24-20, at midseason.

On Green Bay, Allen used a five-man defensive line that he said was necessary to stop the Packer rushing game. The Pack was held to only 78 yards on the ground.

Dec. 25

Rally pleases Miami

Miami (AP)—"The best thing for us," said Miami's Larry Csonka, "was to get behind. It got very quiet and somebody said, 'If we're gonna get anything done, now's the time to do it.' It got done."

The Dolphins, heavy favorites to beat Cleveland, had to come from one point back in the fourth quarter to down the Browns, 20-to-14, Sunday in their National Football League Play-off game.

The victory carried Miami into the American Football Conference championship game next Sunday aginst the Steelers in Pittsburgh and lifted their record perfect to 15-0.

The Browns were brutal in shutting down the Dolphins' high-powered offense—until about eight minutes remained in the game.

Then Earl Morrall's passing and Mercury Morris's running started things for Miami and Jim Kiick finished matters, plowing over from eight yards behind the blocking of tackle Norm Evans and guard Bob Kuechenberg for the winning score with 4 minutes and 54 seconds to go.

"I'm glad I had the opportunity to redeem myself," said Kiick, who had spent the season in Morris's shadow.

The Browns weren't really finished, though, until linebacker Doug Swift made Miami's fifth interception off quarterback Mike Phipps—a drive-killing pickoff in the closing seconds deep in Miami territory.

"We thought we would win," said Browns coach Nick Skorich when asked of the team's feeling at halftime. Other Browns said the feeling of victory remained until the interception by Swift.

Statistics

	Browns	Miami
First downs	15	17
Rushes yards	32-165	47-198
Passing yards	118	71
Return yards	102	68
Passes	9-23-5	6-13-0
Punts	6-35	3-45
Fumbles lost	2-0	2-2
Penalties yards	3-25	3-25

Cleveland	0	0	7	7	14
Miami	10	0	0	10	20

Miami—Babb 7 blocked punt recovery (Yepremian kick)
Miami—FG Yepremian 40
Clev - Phipps 5 run (Cockroft kick)
Miami—FG Yepremian 46
Clev - Hooker 27 pass from Phipps (Cockroft kick)
Miami - Kiick 8 run (Yepremian kick)
Attendance 80,010.

Individual Leaders

RUSHING—Cleveland, Scott 16-94, Phipps 8-47. Miami, Morris 15-72, Kiick 14-50, Warfield 2-41, Csonka 12-32.
RECEIVING—Cleveland, Scott 4-30, Hooker 3-53. Miami, Twilley 3-33, Warfield 2-50.
PASSING Cleveland, Phipps 9-23-5, 131 yards. Miami, Morrall 6-13-0, 88.

Dec. 25

Rooney gave up hope, missed Steeler 'miracle'

Pittsburgh (AP) — It was the most miraculous play in Pittsburgh Steeler history, and Art Rooney didn't see it.

The 71-year-old team owner left his private box in the waning seconds Saturday with Pittsburgh trailing Oakland, 7-6, and facing a seemingly hopeless fourth-down situation.

"I figured we had lost, and I wanted to get to the locker room early so I could personally thank the players for the fine job they'd done all season," said Rooney, who waited four decades for the Steelers' first division title.

Heard the shouting

"I was standing by the elevator when one of the stadium guards came running at me yelling, 'You won it. You won it,' " he added. "I asked him if he was kidding and he screamed, 'No, no. Listen to the crowd!' "

The crowd was indeed in a state of joyous frenzy after watching a one-in-a-million touchdown play that gave Pittsburgh a 13-7 play-off victory over the Raiders and sent the Steelers into the American Football Conference title game against Miami.

Dec. 31

NFC

By JOE SNYDER
Sun Staff Correspondent

Washington — Washington's irrepressible Redskins rang out the old year in grandiose style yesterday, annihilating the Dallas Cowboys to win the National Football Conference championship with astonishing ease.

Quarterback Billy Kilmer pitched touchdown strikes of 15 and 45 yards to Charley Taylor and Curt Knight kicked four field goals as the Redskins left the Cowboys gasping, 26 to 3, before an RFK Stadium audience that burst into unrestrained joy at the finish.

The prize for Washington's old-timer brigade was a January 14 Super Bowl shot against the Miami Dolphins, who leapfrogged over the Pittsburgh Steelers to capture the American Conference crown. The Super Bowl appearance will be Washington's first.

Kilmer 14 of 18

For the Cowboys, deprived of an opportunity to defend the world championship they won last year, the afternoon was one of frustration. They fell behind, 10-0, two-thirds of the way through the second quarter and never got untracked against a ferocious Redskin defense that kept the pressure on the full 60 minutes. Even Roger Staubach was powerless to pull off anything resembling the miracles he produced at San Francisco in the conference semi-finals a week ago.

The Redskins, who controlled the football for 62 offensive plays against 20 fewer for the Cowboys, rationed Dallas to 96 rushing yards—59 of those by Staubach—and 73 net passing yards. All the while, Washington accumulated 194 yards on Kilmer's near-perfect passing—he was 14-for-18—and 122 on the ground where Larry Brown once more was the standout with 88 yards in 30 carries.

Taylor, the Redskins' 9-year veteran, was in a class by himself as a receiver with 7 catches for 146 yards, including a magnificent 51-yard collaboration with Kilmer to set up Washington's first touchdown.

Reprinted from
The Baltimore Sun

53,129 on hand

And Knight had perhaps his greatest day with field goals of 18, 39, 46 and 45 yards as he redeemed himself for what had been a disappointing regular season.

Washington coach George Allen labeled his club's performance "very nearly perfect," and indeed it was. Only a Toni Fritsch field goal from 35 yards away saved Dallas the humiliation of being shut out.

The Cowboys' usually devastating tandem of Calvin Hill and Walt Garrison met their match against the revved-up Redskin defense. Hill managed a measly 22 yards in 9 trips and Garrison 15 in 7 carries.

Staubach, who started for the first time this season and went the distance at quarterback for Dallas, hit 9 of 20 and, like Kilmer, escaped without an interception.

Redskins Summary

How They Scored

Cowboys	0	3	0	0	— 3
Redskins	0	10	0	16	—26

SECOND QUARTER

Wash. Dal.

5:15—Knight kicked 18-yard field goal, capping 62-yard drive in which Brown ran for 31 yards and caught a pass for nine. — 3 0

9:27—Taylor took Kilmer's 15-yard scoring pitch, ending six-play, 72-yard march. Big play was Kilmer's 51-yard pass to Taylor over cornerback Waters. Knight converted. — 10 0

12:28—Fritsch's 35-yard field goal hit left upright and bounced across, ending 52-yard advance in which Staubach provided big-gainer with 29-yard run. — 10 3

FOURTH QUARTER

:48—Taylor took Kilmer's 45-pass down the sidelines, beating cornerback Washington, to cap 78-yard, 11-play drive. Knight converted. — 17 3

4:39—Knight kicked 39-yard field goal after Hill's fumble on completed pass was recovered by McDole on Dallas 38. — 20 3

8:47—Knight kicked 46-yard field goal after Redskins took possession on Dallas 46 following Bateman's short 35-yard punt. — 23 3

13:44—Knight kicked 45-yard field goal after Cowboys lost ball on downs on Dallas 38. — 26 3

Team Statistics

	Dallas	Wash.
First Downs	8	16
Rushing Yardage	96	122
Passing Yardage	73	194
Return Yardage	49	10
Passes	9-21-0	13-18-0
Punts	7-43.1	4-35
Fumbles Lost	1	1
Yards Penalized	30	38

Individual Statistics

RUSHING

	Att.	Yds.	Avg.
Brown, Wash.	30	88	2.7
Harraway, Wash.	11	19	1.7
Kilmer, Wash.	3	15	5.0
Hill, Dal.	9	22	2.4
Garrison, Dal.	7	15	2.1
Staubach, Dal.	5	59	11.8

PASSING

	Att.	Com.	Yds.	TD	Int.
Kilmer, Wash.	18	14	194	2	0
Staubach, Dal.	20	9	98	0	0
Hill, Dall.	1	0	0	0	0

PASS RECEIVING

	No.	Yds.	TD
Taylor, Wash.	7	146	2
Jefferson, Wash.	2	13	0
Brown, Wash.	2	16	0
Harraway, Wash.	3	13	0
Sellers, Dal.	2	29	0
Alworth, Dal.	1	15	0
Parks, Dal.	1	21	0
Hill, Dal.	2	11	0
Ditka, Dal.	1	4	0
Garrison, Dal.	2	18	0

REDSKIN 1-POINT SUPER BOWL PICK

Three betting outlets in Nevada decided to go with George Allen after his team's 26-3 victory over Dallas and quoted the Redskins as one-point favorites to defeat the Miami Dolphins in pro football's Super Bowl Jan. 14.

The Sports Book at Churchill Downs here in Las Vegas, Harrah's Race Book at Lake Tahoe and the Reno Turf Club all listed Washington as a one-point favorite to take the National Football League title, despite the undefeated season of Don Shula's Dolphins.

Allen cites two key plays for 'Skins

By JOE SNYDER

Washington — The Redskins found Mayor Walter Washington waiting to greet them when they trudged into their RFK Stadium dressing quarters after corraling the Dallas Cowboys yesterday.

"This city has needed a champion for a long time," beamed the mayor, "and now we have a great, great champion."

Then the Rev. James Skinner, the team chaplain, led the Redskins in prayer as television cameras recorded the scene on film.

Celebration time

With those niceties out of the way, it was celebration time for the Redskins, frustrated so many times over the years. Their unbridled joy led one to believe they had already won the Super Bowl, rather than just having hurdled the last obstacle to the Los Angeles classic two weeks hence.

"A lot of people wrote our guys off as too old, too slow and too heavy," said coach George Allen as he mounted a platform, seated himself in a chair and faced a battery of newsmen. "Well, I'll take the old guys anytime. These fellows believe in each other, they respect each other. There is no other team quite like this one."

Allen considered two plays important to the victory. "First, was (Bill) Kilmer's bomb to (Charley) Taylor (the 51-yarder) in the second quarter. We were struggling up to that point and it gave us some needed spark.

"Second, the missed field goal by Fritsch (Toni Fritsch, the Cowboys' place-kicking specialist) just before the half. That let us take a 10-3 lead at halftime rather than 10-6."

Allen said the Redskins "knew we had to shut off the Cowboys' running game, and I can't give the defense too much credit for the job they did.

"Offensively, we felt we could make the big play to Taylor when we needed to. Everything worked out perfectly. This was my biggest thrill, and I'm sure the players feel the same way."

Quarterback Kilmer, who made believers of any detractors he might have left in Washington, credited Taylor for "two super catches. That guy is a great athlete.

"We didn't want to take any chances against Renfro (Mel Renfro Cowboy right cornerback) and things were working well for us to the other side so we just kept it going. They tried double coverage on Taylor with the left linebacker and cornerback but he broke the coverage. The first touchdown pass was a post pattern and the second, the 45-yarder, what we call a "go" pattern.

"We played our game, concentrating on not making mistakes. I've been so tense I haven't had a good night's sleep all week. I just want to sleep for about two days now."

"The cornerbacks were playing me to the inside," explained Taylor, "so I took the outside route. Billy read the defenses perfectly and our execution was great. This was our third game against the Cowboys so we knew their personnel and what they did best."

AFC

By CAMERON C. SNYDER
Sun Staff Correspondent

Pittsburgh—It was Miami weather. But that wasn't as surprising as the surprises the Miami Dolphins popped out of the bottle to leave the 50,350 Pittsburgh fans and the Steelers with the greatest morning after hangover ever seen on New Year's Eve.

The 63-degree temperature and sunny skies portended another trip to the Sugar Bowl for the Dolphins. And coach Don Shula wasn't about to ignore the signs. He gambled on a fake punt, several fourth and short yardage rushes and a switch of quarterbacks to confound the Steelers, 21 to 17, yesterday at Three Rivers Stadium.

These gambles left the home folk as chilled as they normally would be in normal Western Pennsylvania weather at this time of the year and spun the unbeaten Dolphins

into their second straight Super Bowl against the Washington Redskins two weeks hence in Los Angeles.

The Dolphins have now won 16 straight games, including two play-offs and 14 regular season games, a feat no team has accomplished in 53 National Football League seasons.

The Steelers and their wild, mad fans have nothing to be ashamed of. Coach Chuck Noll, once Shula's aide with the Baltimore Colts, had a ready and willing team to send against the Dolphins.

Griese takes over

Because no Steeler team had ever gotten this far before in Pittsburgh's 40 year history, Noll's brave squad lacked the poise and the maturity to meet the pressure situations.

And the Dolphins gave them pressure situations throughout the game.

The Steelers cracked just a couple of times, but that was all the "we have been here before" Dolphins needed as they broke away from a 7-7 halftime deadlock in the last two periods.

Shula decided at halftime to replace Earl Morrall with Bob Griese, who started the season for the Dolphins but was sidelined during the fifth game with a dislocated ankle.

"We hadn't established our offense," explained Shula. "I thought Griese might get us going."

So, Morrall, the 38-year-old quarterback who took over for the 27-year-old Griese after the injury and directed them unbeaten to the American Conference title game, was benched.

It is true Morrall hadn't sustained a ball-control drive which is the basis of the Dolphin attack, but he hadn't played poorly, either.

DOLPHINS 21, STEELERS 17

STATISTICS

	Dolphins	Steelers
First Downs	19	13
Rushes-Yards	49-193	26-128
Passing Yards	121	122
Return Yards	34	113
Passes	10-16-1	10-20-2
Punts	4-36	4-51
Fumbles-Lost	0-0	2-0
Penalties-yards	2-19	4-30

Miami	0	7	7	7—21
Pittsburgh	7	0	3	7—17

Pit—Mullins recovered fumble in end zone (Gerela kick)
Mia—Csonka 9 pass from Morrall (Yepremian kick)
Pit—FG Gerela 14
Mia—Kiick 2 run (Yepremian kick)
Mia—Kiick 3 run (Yepremian kick)
Pit—Young 13 pass from Bradshaw (Gerela kick)
A—50,350

INDIVIDUAL LEADERS

RUSHING—Miami, Csonka 24-68, Morris 18-76, Kiick, 8-12, Seiple, 1-37. Pittsburgh, Harris 16-76, Fuqua 8-47.
RECEIVING — Miami, Fleming 5-50, Warfield 2-63. Pittsburgh, Young 4-54, Shanklin 2-49.
PASSING—Miami, Morrall 7-11-1, 51 yards; Griese 3-5-0, 70. Pittsburgh, Bradshaw 5-10-3, 80; Hanratty 5-10-0, 57.

Morrall upset by Shula's switch

By CAMERON C. SNYDER

Pittsburgh — Don Shula switched quarterbacks and won a game as his Miami Dolphins moved into the Super Bowl with a 21-to-17 victory over the Steelers yesterday.

But he not only disappointed the Steelers and their fans, but Earl Morrall as well.

It was Morrall—who led the Colts to the Super Bowl in 1968—who was replaced by Bob Griese in the second half as the Dolphins rallied to score two touchdowns and gain the victory.

Morrall, who had taken over for Griese in the fifth regular season game when Bob wrecked his ankle, was as miffed as such a gentleman can get.

Two drives

"I wasn't jumping for joy, if that is what you mean," he said to reporters searching for his feelings.

Later, "I wasn't overjoyed. No, I didn't think I was having a bad game. We weren't getting a good drive going, but we didn't have good field position.

"No, I'm not going to second-guess the coach. He felt that Bob might get the attack moving, but that doesn't mean I'm overjoyed by it."

Griese directed two sustained drives in the last half. Morrall was the quarterback for one first-half TD, helped considerably by a 37-yard-run from punt formation by Larry Seiple.

After that run Morrall pitched to Csonka for a 9-yard TD.

"The play was called from the bench," explained Earl, "but they covered perfectly, I was suppose to go to Warfield. I had to go to the alternate. Csonka made a great catch and then ran over his defender (Mel Blount).

"I don't think I ran over him in the true sense of the word," said Csonka. "Rather, he was trying to recover from inching over on Warfield and wasn't in position.

"Deserved chance"

"Let me tell you, those Steeler backs come up and hit. They are much better at doing that than I expected. They nailed Mercury Morris and myself a couple of times."

Shula said of the quarterback switch, "We weren't getting sustained drives and Griese has been working well in practices so I thought he might get our offense moving. He deserved the chance."

"Don came up to me at halftime and said, "You're going in." The one thing in this game is a player has to be ready. If he isn't then he doesn't belong on the team," Griese said.

Griese was ready and the Dolphins were ready to move. They complemented each other.

"No, I don't care who we meet in the Super Bowl. The object is to get there and to win that, too," said Griese.

"Yes, that is the main thing," said Morrall, "Getting to and winning the Super Bowl even if it takes a switch of quarterbacks."

Key Dolphin play

Shula cited a 37-yard fake-punt run as the play that got the Dolphins going.

"They (the Steelers) came out at us and were pushing us around in the first quarter.

"No, I didn't tell Seiple to run, but we have an understanding. He can run anytime he can make the first down, but he better make it.

'He wanted to do it last week (in the divisional play-off victory over the Cleveland). I told him I'm glad he saved it for this game. But he is a smart player and has my sanction to run whenever he feels he can get the yards. No, I won't second-guess him. He has done it four or five times and missed only one. That's not a bad percentage."

Dolphins down Redskins in Super Bowl, 14-7

Become first NFL team to go undefeated

By CAMERON C. SNYDER
Sun Staff Correspondent

Los Angeles—The Miami Dolphins made their impossible dream come true yesterday, beating the Washington Redskins a lot easier than the 14-to-7 score would indicate in Super Bowl VII at the Coliseum, and completing the first perfect season in National Football League history.

A great game it wasn't. But it was vindication for coach Don Shula, who has suffered under the "can't win the big one" tab after being the loser in Super Bowl III and VI.

In the final analysis, Shula's once-denied Dolphins in Super Bowl VI had too much maturity for coach George Allen's "Over-the-Hill Gang" from Washington.

For the biggest Super Bowl crowd ever, 90,182, the game went routinely most of the way with the Dolphins forcing the breaks, until the final three minutes.

Field goal attempt spoiled

Leading by 14 to 0 and in complete control with time against a Washington club which seriously threatened only twice, in the third and fourth quarters, the Dolphins decided to put the game out of reach of even the most diehard Redskin fan.

The expected clincher was a field goal attempt from the Redskin 42, not an impossible feat for the little, balding Cypriot, Garo Yepremian.

But the Redskins, who escaped a rout on Dolphin penalties, tried once more for their fans, including President Nixon.

They blocked Yepremian's attempt with help from Garo, who didn't get his kick up. Garo then helped them more, scampering back to pick up the loose ball and attempting to pass. The ball went 6 inches above his head and 2 feet in front on his face.

Cornerback Mike Bass picked it off in the air at the Dolphin 49 and raced in for Washington's only score.

No chance for heroics

There were 2 minutes, 7 seconds left on the scoreboard clock, enough time if Washington could get the ball back quickly.

Allen then had Curt Knight kick long on the kickoff. The Dolphins got a first down as the Redskins used up their time-outs, and then Miami was forced to punt.

Larry Seiple, whose punting far overshadowed that of his opponent, Mike Bragg, punted to the 24; Alvin Haymond returned to the 30 but the clock was down to 1:14.

Kilmer tried four passes. The last one he didn't get off as the fine Miami line poured over him with Bill Stanfill getting credit for the sack on what was the last play of the game.

Both teams were noted for their cautious attacks, featuring running, and they played back to their history.

But Miami Bob Griese was a little more daring and much more successful with the pass than Washington's Bill Kilmer. Griese connected with Howard Twilley in the first quarter for a 28-yard touchdown and set up Jim Kiick's one-yard plunge in the second quarter with a 19-yard pass to Jim Mandich to the Redskin 2.

Although it was Miami weather—bright sunshine and the temperature reaching 84—it appeared the old fellows from Washington were the fresher at the end.

Shula denied this. "Who won?" was his retort.

Missed opportunities

The coaches predicted that the game would be won on turnovers—interceptions and fumble recoveries—but each team scored only once as the result of a turnover.

The Dolphins' winning touchdown was set up by Nick Buoniconti on a 32-yard interception return of a Kilmer pass. Five plays later Kiick crushed over from the one.

And Washington scored on the blocked field goal.

The Dolphins, who have been so opportunistic in winning a record number of games, failed several times to capitalize on interceptions and the short punts by Bragg.

These failures, at least, gave the crowd the final-minutes thrills which otherwise would have been meaningless.

One apparent Dolphin touchdown was nullified on an illegal procedure penalty by Marlin Briscoe, who was substituting for touchdown catcher Twilley. Griese's apparent touchdown pass went 47 yards to Paul Warfield.

Another touchdown or at least a field goal was lost in the third quarter after a long drive when on a second-and-five at the Washington 5, Griese's pass to Merv Fleming was intercepted in the end zone by Brig Owens.

And a promising drive, set up by an early second-quarter interception by Jake Scott, fizzled when a 20-yard pass to Fleming to the Redskin 26 was nullified by a 15-yard holding penalty.

Csonka sets rushing pace

Excitement in this game was expected to come from the flashing feet of Larry Brown, of Washington, and Mercury Morris, of Miami. Both were 1,000-yard rushers during the season and both were capable of breaking a game open.

But the human rhino, Larry Csonka, horned his way into the top rushing spot, grinding out 112 yards for Miami in 15 carries. The 235-pounder, also a 1,000-yard rusher, had the longest run from scrimmage and the longest play of the game, a 49-yard gallop down the middle of the field, tossing Redskins on their ears on his thundering gallop.

The Redskins had no one to compare with Csonka, who kept Washington's defense honest. Nor had they a quarterback the equal of Griese, who completed just 8, but threw only 11 times.

Reprinted from
The Baltimore Sun

Super Bowl statistics

	Dolphins	Redskins
First downs	12	16
Rushes-yards	37-184	36-141
Passing yards	69	87
Return yards	129	59
Passes	8-11-1	14-28-3
Punts	7-43	5-31
Fumbles-lost	2-1	1-0
Penalties-yards	3-35	2-25

INDIVIDUAL LEADERS

RUSHING—Miami, Kiick 12-38. Csonka 15-112. Morris 10-34. Washington, Brown 22-72. Harraway 10-37. Kilmer 2-18. C. Taylor 1-8. Smith 1-6.

RECEIVING—Miami, Warfield 3-36. Twilley 1-28. Kiick 2-6. Mandich 1-19. Washington. Brown 5-26. Jefferson 5-50. Smith 1-11. C. Taylor 2-20.

PASSING—Miami. Griese 8-11-1, 88 yards. Washington, Kilmer 14-28-3, 104.

Miami	7	7	0—14
Washington	0	0	0	7—7

Mia-Twilley 28 pass from Griese (Yepremian kick).
Mia-Kiick 1 run (Yepremian kick).
Wash-Bass 49 fumble recovery return (Knight kick).
Attendance—90,182.

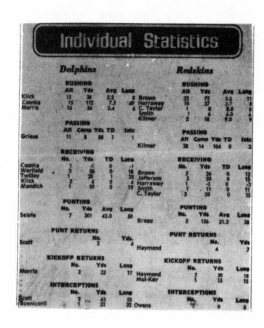

Individual Statistics

Dolphins

RUSHING

	Att	Yds	Avg	Long
Kiick	12	38	3.2	
Csonka	15	112	7.5	49
Morris	10	34	3.4	

PASSING

	Att	Comp	Yds	TD	Intc
Griese	11	8	88	1	1

RECEIVING

	No.	Yds	TD	Long
Csonka	3	-1	0	-1
Warfield	3	36	0	18
Twilley	1	28	1	28
Kiick	2	6	0	
Mandich	1	19	0	19

PUNTING

	No.	Yds	Avg	Long
Seiple	7	301	43.0	50

PUNT RETURNS

	No.	Yds.
Scott	2	4

KICKOFF RETURNS

	No.	Yds	Long
Morris	2	33	17

INTERCEPTIONS

	No.	Yds	Long
Scott	2	63	55
Buoniconti	1	32	32

Redskins

RUSHING

	Att	Yds	Avg	Long
Brown	22	72	3.3	11
Harraway	10	37	3.7	8
C. Taylor	1	8	8.0	8
Smith	1	6	6.0	6
Kilmer	2	18	9.0	9

PASSING

	Att	Comp	Yds	TD	Intc
Kilmer	28	14	104	0	3

RECEIVING

	No.	Yds	TD	Long
Brown	5	26	0	12
Jefferson	5	50	0	15
Harraway	1	-3	0	-3
Smith	1	11	0	11
C. Taylor	2	20	0	13

PUNTING

	No.	Yds	Avg	Long
Bragg	5	156	31.2	36

PUNT RETURNS

	No.	Yds
Haymond	4	7

KICKOFF RETURNS

	No.	Yds	Long
Haymond	2	30	18
Mul-Key	2	15	15

INTERCEPTIONS

	No.	Yds	Long
Owens	1	0	

Pressure on Kilmer called key factor

Los Angeles (AP)—Washington Coach George Allen said yesterday Miami's pressuring of quarterback Billy Kilmer was probably the key factor in the Redskins' 14-to-7 Super Bowl loss to the unbeaten Dolphins.

"We felt we had to run on them consistently," said Allen in a steamy, jammed locker room. "But they did a good job on the run and they put pressure on Billy. They stopped our run and forced us to make mistakes."

Allen refused to single out any Dolphin as the key to the fine defense but admitted that massive Manny Fernandez led the Miami charge.

Kilmer also indicated that the pressure on him was terrific.

Wilbur disagrees

"I didn't throw well and there was pressure on me, too. A couple of times, they red-dogged and I didn't have anybody pick him up," he said.

John Wilbur, the Washington guard assigned to Fernandez, said he "didn't think Fernandez was really a factor" in the game. But he admitted, "He's a hell of a tackle . . . very quick, and very fast laterally."

Miami's famed "53 defense" —named because linebacker Bob Matheson, who wears No. 53, comes into the game to play either on the line or as a linebacker—was most effective, Allen noted.

"I think the statistics will show that we didn't do much against it. It didn't surprise us because we knew what it was.

"Miami simply executes real well. Oh, it's nothing that'll impress you on film, but they don't make mistakes."

President sees 'Skins bow on TV

Key Biscayne, Fla. (AP)—President Nixon watched with dismay yesterday as his favorite football team, the Washington Redskins, lost to Miami, 14-to-7, in what he called "one of the best Super Bowls ever."

"That was a fine game," Nixon said, in comments relayed by deputy press secretary Neal Ball, "because there was suspense right up to the end."

"The people of Washington and the people of Miami can both be proud of their teams," Nixon said. "They played well."

Aides said they expected that Nixon would telephone the coaches of the rival teams today.

The chief executive watched the game on television with his close friend and neighbor, C. G. (Bebe) Rebozo, a Key Biscayne banker.

The two drove to Rebozo's second home on this island south of Miami to watch the game.

While the game was in progress, aides said Nixon and Rebozo ate a seafood dinner.

Jan. 23

17-year era ends with Colts trading Unitas to Chargers

By CAMERON C. SNYDER

John Unitas, who made the Baltimore Colt franchise successful and was largely responsible for the growth of professional football, has been traded to the San Diego Chargers for "future considerations."

What these future considerations consist of probably is money and only money.

So the greatest quarterback of pro football history, so named by the Associated Press several years ago, will wind up his brilliant career on the West Coast where the sunshine and warmth should be beneficial to his 40 year old bones, particularly to the right elbow. John will be 40 in May.

Unitas, a legend in Baltimore after 17 years of service to the Colts, left some doubt about reporting to San Diego.

"Just because I've been traded," he said, "doesn't mean I'll be going to the West Coast. For one thing, I don't know if it's legal. I'll just have to sit down and look at things, and then talk with the San Diego people."

That could be just talk. Unitas, who wants to play "two or three more years," couldn't have picked a better spot to wind up his illustrious career than San Diego, and the Chargers, knee deep in talent, could be contenders with Unitas's knowledge and leadership. They were 4-9-1 in 1972.

Unitas laid down three conditions when he said he wouldn't play again for the Colts but wanted to play football for a couple more years. They were:

1. To have a chance at starting.
2. To be with a good team.
3. To be close to Baltimore.

Only the last consideration is out of line and a $125,000 salary can make distances between Baltimore and San Diego seem as close as Baltimore and Washington.

John will be the starting quarterback with the Chargers. San Diego's No. 1, John Hadl, has asked to be traded and the acquisition of Unitas apparently confirms his request.

Reprinted from
The Baltimore Sun

Hadl Traded For Ram Pair

LOS ANGELES, Jan. 25 (AP) — The Los Angeles Rams, who suffered through a mediocre season with sore-armed quarterback Roman Gabriel, today acquired veteran quarterback John Hadl from the San Diego Chargers for defensive end Coy Bacon and running back Bob Thomas.

Jan. 31

The First to Go in the Draft

TEAM	PLAYER	POS.	COLLEGE				
1—Houston	John Matuszak	DT	Tampa	14—Houston (from Atl.)	George Amundson	RB	Iowa St.
2—Baltimore (from NO)	Bert Jones	QB	LSU	15—Cincinnati	Isaac Curtis	WR	S.D. St.
3—Philadelphia	Jerry Sisemore	OT	Texas	16—Clev. (from Giants)	Steve Holden	WR	Arizona St.
4—New England	John Hannah	OG	Alabama	17—Detroit (from KC)	Ernest Price	DE	Texas A&I
5—St. Louis	Dave Butz	DT	Purdue	18—San Francisco	Mike Holmes	DB	Texas Sou.
6—Phila. (from SD)	Charles Young	TE	USC	19—New Eng. from Det.)	Darryl Stingley	WR	Purdue
7—Buffalo	Paul Seymour	OT	Michigan	20—Dallas	Billy Joe DuPree	TE	Mich. St.
8—Chicago	Wally Chambers	DE	E.Kentucky	21—Green Bay	Barry Smith	WR	Florida St.
9—Denver	Otis Armstrong	RB	Purdue	22—Cleveland	Pete Adams	OT	USC
10—Baltimore	Joe Ehrmann	DT	Syracuse	23—Oakland	Ray Guy	P-K	Sou. Mich.
11—New Eng. (from LA)	Sam Cunningham	RB	USC	24—Pittsburgh	James Thomas	DB	Florida St.
12—Minnesota	Chuck Foreman	RB	Miami	25—S. Diego (from Wash.)	Johnny Rodgers	WR	Nebraska
13—N.Y. Jets	Burgess Owens	DB	Miami	26—Buffalo (from Miami)	Joe DeLamielleure	OG	Mich. St.

Reprinted from
The Washington Star-News

June 8

Eagles pay heavily to get Rams' Gabriel

Los Angeles (AP)—Discontented quarterback Roman Gabriel was traded yesterday by the Los Angeles Rams to the Philadelphia Eagles for two top offensive stars and three draft choices, the Rams announced.

The Rams receive in return for Gabriel all-pro wide receiver Harold Jackson, running back Tony Baker, the Eagles' first draft choice in 1974 and the Eagles' first and third choices in the 1975 draft.

The Ram spokesman said Gabriel's contract would be transferred to the Eagles intact and any changes in it would have to be made by the Eagles.

Gabriel, former National Football League most valuable player, became upset at the new Ram management following the 1972 season when the Rams acquired San Diego Charger quarterback John Hadl.

The trade brought to an end a bitter feud between Gabriel and Rams management. He attacked them as recently as Wednesday with a lengthy statement in which the quarterback accused the Rams of not bargaining in good faith.

Gabriel, 32 years old, 11-year pro who was the NFL's most valuable player in 1969, suffered from elbow tendonitis last season but has said he had fully recovered. After the season, he criticized some teammates for not putting out full effort, statements which he since has disclaimed.

Gabriel, who signed with the Rams after a brilliant career at North Carolina State, said he was upset because he had no advance knowledge of the Rams' plan to acquire Hadl.

Roman initially demanded to be traded to the Washington Redskins, but when the Rams could not gain satisfactory terms with the 'Skins, he agreed to be sent elsewhere. A clause in his contract allowed him to approve his destination in a trade.

Gabriel had one of his first games of the year last season against the Eagles in Philadelphia and has said he appreciated the Philadelphia fans' reaction to his play.

July 21

Thomas to join 'Skins Monday

Carlisle, Pa. ⒫—Controversial running back Duane Thomas will report to the Washington Redskin's training camp at Dickinson College on Monday afternoon, coach George Allen reported last night.

After talking by telephone with Thomas, whom the Redskins acquired from San Diego in a trade Thursday, Allen said the running back is "looking forward to being with us" after he has taken care of some personal business in Texas.

"I'm not going to press him.

It's not that urgent," the Redskins coach said. "I want him to come in with all his personal problems cleared up."

Allen quoted Thomas, who has been on four teams in the last four years, as saying he is looking forward to playing with the Redskins."

"I'm kind of excited about it," the coach continued. "It's more than just a football player. It's a chance to help a guy."

Allen also said that if for any reason Thomas is unable to arrive at the Redskins' camp on Monday, he will not be concerned about it.

"I'm just not going to give him a deadline," he said. "He has a chance to be a great football player. I hope he wants to play as much as we want him to succeed."

July 26

Kassulke condition slipping

Minneapolis ⒫—Minnesota Viking defensive back Karl Kassulke, known around the National Football League as one of the game's fiercest tacklers and competitors, has slipped into what attending doctors describe as a "very critical condition" yesterday.

Kassulke, injured Tuesday in a car-motorcycle collision, was listed in serious condition prior to three hours of surgery late Tuesday. But his condition worsened during the night and an attending physician, Dr. Paul Blake, said yesterday that Kassulke probably will never regain normal use of his legs.

The driver of the motorcycle on which Kassulke was a passenger, Monty Crizan, 29, was reported in good condition yesterday. The car driver was not seriously hurt.

A Minnesota Highway Patrol officer who investigated the accident said Kassulke was thrown 100 feet by the impact.

Kassulke is hospitalized in suburban St. Louis Park. Doctors said he was moved to a respirator yesterday to ease his breathing. A hospital spokesman said at the time of surgery Kassulke's spinal cord was badly compressed.

A hospital spokesman said Kassulke suffered a fractured right lower leg, fractured left wrist, farctured shoulder and fractured spine at the seventh thoracic vertebra.

July 21

Unitas agrees to 2-year contract to quarterback San Diego club

San Diego ⒫—Quarterback Johnny Unitas, whose 40th birthday was a month ago, signed a two-year contract yesterday to play for the San Diego Chargers of the National Football League after 16 years as Mr. Baltimore Colt.

"I'm delighted to say we have signed the greatest quarterback in football history,"

Charger owner Eugene V. Klein told a news conference. No salary terms made were disclosed.

Unitas, smiling and fit-looking, said his throwing arm feels "just fine" and after the two years are up "we can sit down and evaluate where we are."

Unitas, one of the all-time

quarterback greats of pro football, said: "I feel the Chargers are a good team with a good chance to go all the way.

"I'm not demanding to be a No. 1 quarterback—I just want an opportunity to play."

NFL 'Penalized' Gillman Over Drugs

From News Dispatches

The National Football League acknowledged yesterday that it placed Houston Oilers' general manager Sid Gillman on "probation" stemming from charges that he was involved with improper dispensing of drugs while coach and general manager of the San Diego Chargers.

An NFL spokesman insisted, however, that the probation was "a routine procedure after matters of this type" and that the action only means that Gillman "is expected to live up to the highest standards of conduct throughout his NFL career."

The action, the spokesman said, was taken by commissioner Pete Rozelle "months ago," while testimony was being gathered for a $1.25

SID GILLMAN
. . . 'routine' probation

million suit by former Chargers' defensive lineman Houston Ridge.

Gillman, who resigned his San Diego posts in November, 1971, after being with the team since its inception in 1960, was named in the Ridge suit along with the Chargers' team physician and trainer, the NFL and AFL. The suit was settled four months ago and Ridge collected $295,000.

From San Diego, Ridge said he had "no comment until I talk to my lawyer." His attorney, Robert Baxley, was not avaalable.

Ridge's suit arose out of a broken left hip he sustained in an Oct. 11, 1969, game against tae Miami Dolphins. He testified that he had taken nine pills—including three amphetamines and three muscle relaxants—either before the game or at halftime.

PETE ROZELLE
. . . takes action

Ridge, who had undergone two operations on the hip, is permanently disabled and

must use a crutch. He claimed the drugs dulled his awareness of pain.

The NFL spokesman explained that the Gillman Probation is the same issued to Redskin running back Duane Thomas after he and his brother pleaded guilty to marijuana possession and the same Lance Rentzel received after pleading guilty to indecent exposure in 1971.

Rentzel later pleaded guilty to possession of marijuana and was suspended by Rozelle on July 20.

"Anybody who has been involved in problems such as these is in effect on (NFL) probation as a routine procedure," the league spokesman said. "Anything further would perhaps require a review or further action."

Sept. 14

Congress rushes approval of TV sports blackout ban

By ALBERT SEHLSTEDT, JR.
Washington Bureau of The Sun

Washington—Congress approved a bill yesterday lifting home-town blackouts of televised professional football games sold out 72 hours before kickoff.

The bill, hurriedly approved by the House and Senate just three days before the opening of the National Football League's regular season, also applies to telecasts of home games of professional baseball, basketball and hockey teams.

First to act yesterday on the blackout legislation was the House, which passed the measure on a roll-call vote, 346 to 37, at 5:31 P.M.

Then the bill was sent over to the Senate side of the Capitol, where it was taken up on the floor at 5:43 P.M. and approved on a voice vote without a roll-call at 5:58 P.M.

Pete Rozelle, National Football League commissioner, announced in New York shortly before yesterday's action by Congress came, he would inform the major television networks that "we no longer consider them bound by contractual provisions with the NFL prohibiting local telecasts of games, provided that all seats are sold 72 hours before kickoff."

He is taking that action although President Nixon has not yet signed the act into law and despite the fact that the major league sports had opposed the bill.

President Nixon is expected to sign the measure soon. The blackout ban is supported by the administration and the Federal Communications Commission.

Aug. 5

Sniper Wounds 2 At 3 Rivers Stadium
Eludes Cops At Steeler Game; Ex-Duke Cooper, Woman Hit

By WILLIAM ALLAN JR.

A sniper dressed in white and posing as a Liquor Control Board (LCB) agent shot and wounded two persons including former All-America basketball player Charles H. "Charlie" Cooper at last night's Steelers-Colts football game in Three Rivers Stadium.

Cooper and the other victim, Rose Marie Dell, 38, of Alverton, Westmoreland County, were not seriously hurt. A search for their assailant was being continued.

Shot In Thigh

Cooper was taken to Allegheny General Hospital with a wound of the thigh.

Mrs. Dell, who was shot in the foot, was taken home after the slug was removed at the stadium emergency station.

Police said the gunman, described as about 40 years old, with short brown hair, was dressed completely in white, and had passed himself off as an LCB man. They said the weapon was a .45-caliber automatic.

Police rushed to the stadium immediately after the halftime shootings, but the gunman eluded them. They checked spectators leaving the stadium in the event the sniper attempted to melt into he crowd.

All but two of the exits were closed by police as the crowd of 50,000 left the stadium, most of them unaware of the shootings.

Cooper was in Section 282 near Gate C, and Mrs. Dell was in the Gate B area when they were shot.

"It's just a weird thing," Cooper said as he awaited a decision on surgery. The bullet lodged in the fleshy section of his leg and the bone was not broken.

All-America Pick

Cooper was an All-America selection at Duquesne University in 1950, later played with the Boston Celtics, and then became director of parks and recreation with the City of Pittsburgh. He currently is deputy director of Community Action Pittsburgh (CAP).

Simpson Sets Rush Mark

FOXBORO, Mass., Sept. 16 (AP)—Buffalo's O. J. Simpson set an NFL rushing record by gaining 250 yards today in sparking the Bills to a 31-13 victory over the New England Patriots.

Simpson, the 1968 Heisman Trophy winner from southern California, picked up where he left off last year, when he led the league in rushing with 1,251 yards.

He carried 29 times today in shattering the league record of 247 yards set by Willie Ellison of the Los Angeles Rams against New Orleans in 1971.

Simpson scored on an 80-yard spring in the first period and on a 22-yard jaunt in the third as the Bills, winless in six preseason games, spoiled Chuck Fairbanks' debut as New England coach.

Larry Watkins, a five-year pro acquired from the Philadelphia Eagles, gave Simpson plenty of help, carrying 15 times for 105 yards and two touchdowns.

The Patriots drove 90 yards in eight plays to take the lead in the first period. Sam Cunningham, a No. 1 draft choice from Southern California, capped the drive by bulling eight yards into the end zone. The conversion kick was blocked after a poor snap, signalling a bad day the rest of the way for New England.

"It looked a track meet out there," Fairbanks said after his debut.

"It looked like Grant going through Richmond. We were helpless and couldn't slow him down. Give Simpson's blocking a lot of credit. And we gave him a lot too."

"He had more yardage than Secretariat," said New England linebacker Edgar Chandler, who played with Simpson for four years in Buffalo before being traded to the Patriots this summer. "He has that deceptive speed. You think you have the angle on him, then he's gone. It was embarrassing."

"I didn't know until late in the game that he was nearing the record," Buffalo coach Lou Saban said. "Then someone said he needed about 15 yards to break it. I was reluctant to put him back in because of the risk of injury.

"So he gets 15 yards and they tell me he needs 15 more. I was really exasperated then, but I'm glad he got the record. You don't find many like him. He's a man, a great team man."

First downs	23	17
Rushes—yards	51-360	26-107
Passing yards	99	190
Return yards	38	15
Passes	9-12-1	16-27-1
Punts	2-43	2-40
Fumbles lost	1-1	3-3
Penalties—yards	11-95	4-40

Buffalo	7 3 7 14—	31
New England	6 0 7 0—	13

NE—Cunningham (8, run); kick failed.
BU—Simpson (80, run); Leypoldt (kick).
BU—FG, Leypoldt, 48.
BU—Watkins (4, run); Leypoldt (kick).
NE—Herron (10, run); Bell (kick).
BU—Simpson (22, run); Leypoldt (kick).
BU—Watkins (15, run); Leypoldt (kick).
A—56,119.

Individual Leaders

RUSHING: Buffalo—Simpson, 29-250; Watkins, 18-105; New England—Cunningham, 12-53; Ashton, 9-33.
RECEIVING: Buffalo—Chandler, 3-44; J. D. Hill, 3-37; Watkins, 2-38. New England—Cunningham, 3-39; Adams, 3-35; Ashton, 2-55.
PASSING: Buffalo—Ferguson, 1-2-0, 10 yards; Shaw, 7-9-1, 109 yards. New England—Plunkett, 16-26-1, 226 yards.

Oct. 3

World Football League Being Formed for 1974

By Cooper Rollow
Chicago Tribune News Service

CHICAGO — A second major professional football league is being formed to open play in 1974.

The new league will be called the World Football League, and will have 12 franchises, six of which have already been awarded it will challenge the National Football League for players, television money and fans.

Heading the league is Gary Davidson, who is using the same formula he employed in forming the American Basketball Association and the World Hockey Association.

Davidson is president of the WHA. He apparently will retain that post while also becoming president of the World Football League and will be owner of a West Coast franchise in either Los Angeles or Anaheim.

The six charter cities and their owners, each of whom have posted $250,000 for the franchises:

Los Angeles-Anaheim: Gary Davidson.

New York: Bob Schmertz, owner of the Boston Celtics and New England Whalers.

Honolulu: Ben Hatskin, owner of the Winnipeg Jets.

Tampa: Nick Mileti, owner of the Cleveland Indians, Cavaliers and Crusaders.

Tokyo: Steve Arnold, director of player personnel for the WHA.

Toronto: John Basseft Jr., whose father owns the Canadian Football League Toronto Argonauts, and owner of the WHA Toronto Toros

In addition to Chicago other cities under consideragion include Boston, Houston, Memphis, Norfolk or Richmond, Va., Birmingham, Charlotte, Mexico City, London, and Osaka, Japan.

The NFL plans to expand within the next three years, either league reportedly leaning towards Seattle and a Florida city — Jacksonville or a Tampa-Orlando combination.

Franchises will be awarded, the source said, "on a graduated scale" as they become approved. The price, which started at $250,000 for the six charter teams, already has reached $500,000 and the last couple of teams may go for approximately $750,000.

"This is a very modest price when you consider that the average NFL franchise is said to be worth $12 million," the source said. "But we want to keep the cost of the franchise down so the owners can put their money into player contracts.

"We respect the validity of the NFL contract," the spokesman added. But he also made it clear that any athlete who has played out his NFL option becomes a free agent and thus a target of the new league.

The new league plans to play a schedule of 14 games next fall with no exhibitions. Travel between such distant franchise spots as Tokyo and London is not seen as an obstacle. Transportation costs will be divided among the league, which will have its own travel bureau.

Reprinted from
The Chicago Tribune

Nov. 5

Oiler'Characters' Show Up the Colts

Special to The Star-News
BALTIMORE — Most neutral observers expected the young Baltimore Colts to be bad at times this season.

Now it turns out they were wrong. The Colts, struggling along with a 2-6 record, aren't bad. They're atrocious, particularly on defense.

How atrocious? Well, the Houston Oilers did something yesterday they hadn't done in the past 18 games — win. The Colts became 31-27 victims when Lynn Dickey threw his third touchdown of the game, a 13-yarder to Fred Willis with 32 seconds left.

Afterwards Dickey rubbed it in.

"I couldn't believe the Colts' (lack of) pass rush when I saw the movies last week," Dickey said. "When you've got time like that, it's easy to be a quarterback."

Dickey, the former Kansas State superstar, discovered Saturday that Coach Sid Gillman wanted him to start instead of Dan Pastorini. Dickey responded by completing 22 of 32 passes for a whopping 340 yards. A week earlier, Oakland's Ken Stabler set a pro record by competing 25 of 29 against the Colts.

Gillman, the veteran who fired Bill Peterson as Houston's coach two weeks ago and took the job himself, admitted he was grateful for the Colts' imeptitude.

"This should give us some character," Gillman added. "We haven't been a team of character. We've been a team of characters."

PRO FOOTBALL
Steelers Request a Probe

Nov. 13

The Pittsburgh Steelers, upset by some alleged dirty tricks encountered in their 17-9 victory over the Oakland Raiders, have asked the National Football League office to investigate.

Did a slow clock help the Raiders? Were the Oakland offensive linemen wearing greased jerseys so they couldn't be grabbed? How did a ball handed the Steeler center before a field goal try get deflated?

"I'm a little bit shocked at these things, but I don't want to say much until I hear an explanation," Steeler Vice President Dan Rooney said yesterday after phoning Art McNally, NFL supervisor of officials.

A reporter called the Raider office late yesterday afternoon and asked to speak to Al Davis, managing general partner of the club.

Tom Grimes, Oakland's director of public relations, came to the phone instead, but he declined to discuss the matter.

"You don't need any comment from us. You need it from the league office," Grimes said. "We have nothing to say."

Nonetheless, Raider Coach John Madden confronted the accusations earlier in the day and said, "There's nothing to them.

"In the first place," Madden added, "all the things they're talking about are in the officials' jurisdiction. If the Steelers claimed there was anything wrong, it was the officials' job to check it."

Steeler Coach Chuck Noll was particularly upset by the allegedly slow clock, which was the responsibility of the NFL timekeeper assigned to Oakland.

"There were 12 seconds left in the second quarter when Daryle Lamonica threw a pass to Mike Siani and he was tackled in the middle of the field at the 16-yard line," Noll said.

"We thought time had run out, but the clock was stopped with one second left on a supposed timeout," he added. "We didn't see anybody on the field call it, and if it was called from the bench it was illegal."

The timeout enabled the Raiders to kick a field goal on the last play of the first half, and Noll also claimed the Raiders were given precious extra seconds late in the game.

The Steelers' front four sacked Raider quarterbacks five times and forced four interceptions, but the Pittsburgh players insisted Oakland's linemen had something slippery on their shoulders.

"You couldn't grab them," said Steeler tackle Joe Greene.

Madden, the Raider coach, countered by saying, "It was so wet and muddy out there, I'm sure everything was slippery."

Reprinted from
The Washington Star-News

"But," said Steeler end Dwight White, "it seemed too slick to be just water. I don't know what it was, but it might be worth an investigation."

Elsewhere in the NFL:

* * * *

INJURED quarterback dept.: Detroit's Greg Landry undergoes surgery on his left knee tomorrow in Detroit. He won't return to the Lions until next season. Pittsburgh's Terry Bradshaw, however, is working out in an effort to get his separated right shoulder in shape to play within two weeks. Oakland's Ken Stabler, who incurred strained ligaments in his right knee Sunday, is a questionable starter this weekend. A final decision on Stabler's status won't be known until the middle of the week.

PACKERS: Coach Dan Devine announced he'll stick with Jerry Tagge for Sunday's game against New England. Tagge won the job by directing the Packers to a 25-21 victory over St. Louis.

* * * *

FALCONS: When Atlanta squares off against Minnesota next Monday night Art Malone may be back in the line-up. The fullback has missed the last two Falcons' games because of a knee injury, but Coach Norm Van Brocklin thinks Malone will be available.

* * * *

49ERS: Offensive tackle Cas Banaszek, who tore a thigh muscle against the Redskins, will miss Sunday's game at Los Angeles.

Dec. 17

Raiders repulse Broncos, 21-17, win division title

Oakland, Calif. (P)—Oakland quarterback Ken Stabler threw a 31-yard touchdown pass to Mike Siani soon after a daring fourth-quarter gamble blew up in the faces of the Denver Broncos yesterday and the Raiders scored a 21-to-17 triumph that gave them another division championship and a spot in the National Football League playoffs.

The underdog Broncos, outclassed early in the game, trailed only 14-10 when their dreams of a first division title were virtually dashed by two quick setbacks.

First, starting quarterback Charley Johnson, who had thrown a 13-yard touchdown pass to Haven Moses in the third quarter, was injured and forced out of the game. Two plays later, coach John Ralston called for a run on a fake punt play at the Denver 48-yard line and linebacker Monte Johnson stopped Joe Dawkins at the line of scrimmage.

The Raiders moved to the Denver 31 on runs by Marv Hubbard and Clarence David before Stabler threw on a first-down play and hit Siani in the end zone, a step behind defender Calvin Jones.

"We were ready for it," Oakland coach John Madden said. "We remembered that Ralston [Denver coach, John Ralston] used that play for Stanford against Ohio State in the Rose Bowl three years ago and got away with it. The Broncos have used it three times this season."

Johnson, a rookie linebacker, said, "We worked on it all week."

"It was supposed to be an inside reverse," Ralston explained, "but the execution was all wrong. The snap was bad and we didn't get the handoff to Otis Armstrong."

The Raiders, American Football Conference Western Division titlists, finished the regular season with a 9-4-1 record and will play the Pittsburgh Steelers here next Saturday in a play-off opener.

O. J. clears 2,000 as Bills win, 34-14

New York ⑨—O. J. Simpson bulldozed his way through the snow for 200 yards and crashed the 2,000-yard barrier, shattering a spate of National Football League records and powering the Buffalo Bills to a 34-to-14 victory over the New York Jets yesterday.

Simpson, a former Heisman Trophy winner from Southern California, finished the game with 2,003 yards for the season. He carried 34 times against the helpless Jets, giving him a season total of 332 carries. Both his total yardage and total carries bettered records by Jim Brown, the former Cleveland star.

At first Simpson's yardage for the game was announced at 198. But NFL statisticians later announced that a recheck of each play showed Simpson had gained an additional 2 yards.

Brown, considered one of the greatest running backs of all-time, had held the previous record of single-season yardage at 1,863 set 10 years ago. Simpson broke that midway through the first period

Goes for 2,000

Then he set his sights on the seemingly unattainable 2,000-yard barrier. And he got it with 5:56 remaining in the game on a 7-yard sweep around left end.

For the second time in the game, play was halted as his jubilant teammates rushed onto the icy field and hoisted him to their shoulders while the Shea Stadium crowd again thundered its approval.

It was Simpson's final play of the game, and gave him his 332 rushes for the season, far out-stripping Brown's mark of 305 set 12 years ago.

The corrected yardage total made Simpson the first player in NFL history to rush for 200 yards three times in a season.

Simpson blazed 13 yards for one Buffalo touchdown. The Bills got two more touchdowns from Jim Braxton on one-yard runs, and Bill Cahill ran 51 yards with a punt for another score, while John Leypoldt kicked field goals from 12 and 11 yards out.

The Jets' only touchdowns came on Joe Namath passes of 48 yards to Jerome Barkum and 16 yards to Rich Caster.

But it was Simpson who brought 47,740 fans into snow-swept, freezing Shea Stadium. And it was Simpson they got, right from the outset.

He carried on Buffalo's first three plays, the second one a 30-yard sweep around right end that made it obvious he was going to be a record-breaker.

After Braxton carried once, Simpson rushed four more times. Then, with the ball on the New York three, Braxton carried three straight times for the touchdown that capped a 71-yard march.

Passes Brown

When the Bills got the ball back, Simpson belted over left tackle for the **6 yards that surpassed Brown's previous single-season rushing record. On the next play, though, he fumbled after a 3-yard gain.

The Jets capitalized, with Namath hitting Emerson Boozer for 11 yards, then connecting with Barkum, who caught the ball racing down the left sideline en route to a touchdown.

The Bills, who finished the season at 9-5 and ended with 3,096 rushing yards, breaking Miami's one-year-old **record of 2,960 yards**, put the game away in the second quarter.

Wide World Photo

O. J. Simpson surpasses Jim Brown's NFL single season rushing record of 1,863 years on this run vs. the Jets.

AMERICAN CONFERENCE						
EASTERN DIVISION						
	W	L	T	Pct.	Pts.	OP
Miami	12	2	0	.857	343	150
Buffalo	9	5	0	.643	259	230
New England	5	9	0	.357	258	300
Baltimore	4	10	0	.286	226	341
N Y Jets	4	10	0	.286	240	306
CENTRAL DIVISION						
	W	L	T	Pct.	Pts.	OP
Cincinnati	10	4	0	.714	286	231
Pittsburgh*	10	4	0	.714	347	210
Cleveland	7	5	2	.571	234	255
Houston	1	13	0	.071	199	447
WESTERN DIVISION						
	W	L	T	Pct.	Pts.	OP
Oakland	9	4	1	.679	292	175
Denver	7	5	2	.571	354	296
Kansas City	7	5	2	.571	231	192
San Diego	2	11	1	.179	188	386

*Wild card qualifier for playoffs.

NATIONAL CONFERENCE						
EASTERN DIVISION						
	W	L	T	Pct.	Pts.	OP
Dallas	10	4	0	.714	382	203
Washington*	10	4	0	.714	325	198
Philadelphia	5	8	1	.393	310	393
St Louis	4	9	1	.321	286	365
N Y Giants	2	11	1	.179	226	362
CENTRAL DIVISION						
	W	L	T	Pct.	Pts.	OP
Minnesota	12	2	0	.857	296	168
Detroit	6	7	1	.464	271	247
Green Bay	5	7	2	.429	202	259
Chicago	3	11	0	.214	195	334
WESTERN DIVISION						
	W	L	T	Pct.	PTS.	OP
Los Angeles	12	2	0	.857	388	178
Atlanta	9	5	0	.643	318	224
New Orleans	5	9	0	.357	163	312
San Francisco	5	9	0	.357	262	319

Dec. 23

Vikings top Redskins in NFC play-off, 27-20

By KENT BAKER
Sun Staff Correspondent

Bloomington, Minn.—The Minnesota Vikings recovered from a lethargic first half, crammed two decisive touchdowns into 65 seconds and fought off Washington, 27 to 20, in the National Football Conference semi-final play-off yesterday.

The victory, eliminating the defending NFC champions before 45,475 Metropolitan Stadium customers, sends the Vikings into the conference title game next weekend against the winner of today's Dallas-Los Angeles struggle.

Minnesota combined the passing tandem of Fran Tarkenton and John Gilliam, a timely interception and a late field goal as the principal ele-

ments in the triumph, its 13th of the season against two losses.

Fred Cox's 30-yard field goal with 1.40 to play ended the scoring, but the sudden two-TD salvo earlier in the quarter actually locked up the outcome.

Curt Knight's 42-yard three-pointer on the first play of the last period gave the Redskins their final advantage, 13-10, and ended a topsy-turvy format in which the lead changed hands four times.

Fischer injured

Then the Vikings took charge.

Tarkenton steered them 71 yards in eight plays into the end zone, passing the last 28 yards to Gilliam, who beat defender Speedy Duncan in the deep corner. Cox's placement made it 17-13 with 10.27 left.

Duncan had replaced Pat Fischer at cornerback in the second period after Fischer was hurt while tackling Oscar Reed. Fischer returned only briefly in the second half.

"The loss of Fischer was extremely costly," evaluated Redskin coach George Allen. "He suffered busted ribs and attempted to play, but it was simply too painful. We also lost Ted Vactor at this same position and we were playing with our third man in a key spot."

On the next series, Billy Kilmer, who turned in a superb performance overall just two days after leaving a hospital bed, was intercepted.

Nate Wright returned the

theft to the Redskin 8 and, following a plunge, Tarkenton darted about until Gilliam shook loose to nab a 6-yard scoring throw. Cox's kick at 9.22 made it 24-13.

NFC statistics

	Wash.	Minn.
First downs	18	17
Rushes yards	42-155	34-111
Passing yards	159	218
Return yards	46	29
Passes	13-24-1	16-28-1
Punts	4-37	6-32
Fumbles lost	2-1	2-1
Penalties yards	0-0	2-9

Individual leaders

RUSHING—Washington, L. Brown 29-115, Harraway 13-90; Minnesota, Reed 17-95, Foreman 11-90.
RECEIVING — Washington, Jefferson 6-48, Taylor 4-56; Minnesota, Reed 5-76, Voigt 3-39, Gilliam 2-36, Dale 2-31.
PASSING—Washington, Kilmer 13-24-1, 159 yards; Minnesota, Tarkenton 16-28-1, 222.

Washington	0 7 3 10	—20
Minnesota	0 3 7 17	—27

Minn—FG Cox 19
Wash—L. Brown 3 run (Knight kick)
Minn—B. Brown 2 run (Cox kick)
Wash—FG Knight 52
Wash—FG Knight 42
Minn—Gilliam 28 pass from Tarkenton (Cox kick)
Minn—Gilliam 6 pass from Tarkenton (Cox kick)
Wash—Jefferson 28 pass from Kilmer (Knight kick)
Minn—FG Cox 30
Attendance—45,475.

Dec. 24

Cowboys halt Rams' rally for 27-16 win

By JIM CAFFREY
Sun Staff Correspondent

Dallas—An electrifying 83-yard touchdown pass from Roger Staubach to Drew Pearson catapulted the Dallas Cowboys to a 27-to-16 play-off victory over the Los Angeles Rams yesterday and into Sunday's National Football Conference championship game with the Minnesota Vikings.

The opportunistic Cowboys had turned two early Los Angeles turnovers into a 17-0 lead before the Rams battled back to cut the deficit to 17-16 in the fourth quarter.

Dallas faced a desperate third and 14 situation at its own 17 when Staubach heaved a bomb to the speedy rookie Pearson at midfield

Rally stopped

Pearson had split the Rams' zone defense and took the ball away from defenders Steve Preece and Eddie McMillan and then legged it 50 yards to the end zone, goose stepping joyously and untouched the final 20 yards.

In that instant the Cowboys throttled a brave Los Angeles rally which seemed on the verge of snatching the victory.

Toni Fritsch's subsequent field goal placed the Rams in the position of needing two touchdowns to win and the Dallas Doomsday Defense smothered L.A. quarterback John Hadl's every effort to recover from the devastating effects of the bomb.

NFC statistics

	Los Angeles	Dallas
First downs	11	15
Rushes—yards	30-93	45-162
Passing yards	99	136
Return yards	12	49
Passes	7-23-1	8-15-2
Punts	5-43	7-46
Fumbles—lost	2-2	2-2
Penalties—yards	2-20	5-44

Individual leaders

RUSHING—Los Angeles, McCutcheon 13-48, Bertelsen 12-37; Dallas, Hill 25-97, Garrison 10-30, Staubach 4-30.
RECEIVING—Los Angeles, Snow 3-77, L. Smith 2-13, Jackson 1-40; Dallas, Pearson 2-87, Hill 2-21, Fugett 1-38.
PASSING—Los Angeles, Hadl 2-23-1, 133 yards; McCutcheon 0-1-0; Dallas, Staubach 8-16-2, 180.

Los Angeles	0 6 0 10	—16
Dallas	14 3 0 10	—27

Dal—Hill 3 run (Fritsch kick)
Dal—Pearson 4 pass from Staubach (Fritsch kick)
Dal—FG Fritsch 39
LA—FG Ray 33
LA—FG Ray 37
LA—FG Ray 40
LA—Baker 5 run (Ray kick)
Dal—Pearson 83 pass from Staubach (Fritsch kick)
Dal—FG Fritsch 12
Attendance—64,291.

Dec. 23

Raiders trounce Steelers, 33 to 14

By ALAN GOLDSTEIN
Sun Staff Correspondent

Oakland, Calif.—The revenge-bent Oakland Raiders left no room for miracles yesterday.

Stirred by the memory of last year's last-second loss to Pittsburgh on Franco Harris's incredible touchdown catch, the Raiders played a near per-fect game in obliterating the Steelers, 33 to 14, before 51,110 raucous fans at the Oakland Coliseum.

The Raiders, who have worn a "choke tag" for failing to win the Super Bowl despite six previous play-off appearances, advanced to the American Football Conference finals next Sunday against the winner of the Miami-Cincinnati game today.

Steelers won last three

The Steelers had whipped Oakland in three previous encounters, including last year's storybook play-off victory, but yesterday they were beaten in every phase of the game. There was no chance for excuses or alibis.

Pittsburgh, capitalizing on a late second-quarter touchdown pass from Terry Bradshaw to Barry Pearson, trailed by only 10-7 at halftime. But the Raiders, under the flawless leadership of southpaw quarterback Ken Stabler, completely dominated the second half.

Two field goals by that ageless wonder, George Blanda, who kicked four in the game, increased Oakland's lead to 16-7 in the third quarter before defensive back Willie Brown provided the game-breaking play by picking off a Bradshaw pass in the flat and scampering 54 yards for a touchdown. Three minutes later, Blanda split the uprights again from 10 yards out for a 26-7 advantage.

Bradshaw gave the Steelers a ghost of a chance with another TD toss of 26 yards to Frank Lewis with 5.48 left to play, but that was their dying gasp.

Hubbard scores

Brawny fullback Marv Hubbard, who led the Raiders' savage running game with 91 yards in 20 carries, leaped over from the 1-yard line in the closing seconds to add to the Steelers' humiliation.

The Raiders had blamed their past failings against the Steelers on their own costly mistakes. This time they made certain they would not beat themselves, playing an error-free game without a single fumble or interception.

Reprinted from
The Baltimore Sun

AFC statistics

	Pittsburgh	Oakland
First downs	13	24
Rushes—yards	29-65	58-225
Passing—yards	139	129
Return—yards	28	73
Passes	12-25-3	14-17-0
Punts	5-42	2-30
Fumbles—lost	1-0	0-0
Penalties—yards	4-60	9-75

Individual leaders

RUSHING—Pittsburgh. Harris 19-29; P. Pearson, 4-14; Fuqua, 3-13. Oakland. Hubbard, 20-91; Smith, 17-73; Davis, 12-48.

RECEIVING—Pittsburgh. Lewis, 4-70; Fuqua, 4-52; B. Pearson, 2-7. Oakland. Siani, 5-68; Moore, 3-26; Smith, 2-10.

PASSING—Pittsburgh. Bradshaw, 12-25-3, 167 yards; Oakland. Stabler, 14-17-0, 142 yards.

Pittsburgh	0	7	0	7	—14
Oakland	7	3	13	10	—33

Oak—Hubbard 1. run (Blanda kick).
Oak—FG Blanda 25.
Pit—B. Pearson 4. pass from Bradshaw (Gerela kick).
Oak—FG Blanda 31.
Oak—FG Blanda 22.
Oak—W. Brown 54. interception return (Blanda kick).
Oak—FG Blanda 10.
Pit—Lewis 26. pass from Bradshaw (Gerela kick).
Oak—Hubbard 1. run (Blanda kick).

AFC statistics

	Cincinnati	Miami
First downs	11	27
Rushes—yards	20-97	52-241
Passing yards	109	159
Return yards	71	25
Passes	11-27-1	11-19-2
Punts	7-36	2-49
Fumbles lost	0-0	2-1
Penalties—yards	2-19	1-5

Individual leaders

RUSHING Cincinnati Clark 7-40. Anderson 3-26. Johnson 2-17. Elliott 7-15; Miami—Morris 20-106. Csonka 20-71. Kiick 10-51.

RECEIVING Cincinnati—Elliott 3-53. Joiner 2-33. Clark 2-18. Miami—Warfield 4-93. Mandich 3-28 Kiick 3-19.

PASSING Cincinnati—Anderson 14-27-1, 113 yards. Miami—Griese, 11-18-1, 159.

Cincinnati	3	13	0	0	—16
Miami	14	7	10	3	—34

Mia—Warfield 13 pass from Griese (Yepremian kick)
Cin—FG Muhlmann 24
Mia—Csonka 1 run (Yepremian kick)
Mia—Morris 4 run (Yepremian kick).
Cin—Craig 45 interception return (Muhlmann kick).
Cin—FG Muhlmann 46.
Cin—FG Muhlmann 12
Mia—Mandich 7 pass from Griese (Yepremian kick)
Mia—FG Yepremian 50
Mia—FG Yepremian 46
Attendance—74.770.

Dec. 24

Dolphins blast Bengals, 34-16, gain AFC final

By CAMERON C. SNYDER
Sun Staff Correspondent

Miami—Only for a moment yesterday were Miami's irresistible Dolphins slowed on their march to a 34-to-16 divisional play-off victory, but they had too much talent to be delayed too long by outmanned Cincinnati in the warm, sunny Orange Bowl.

The hesitation came in the last minutes of the first half and was more the doings of the Dolphins than the play of the Bengals.

Bob Griese, who received the game ball, started the Dolphin slowdown with one of his three touchdown passes for the day. Unfortunately, this pass went to Neal Craig of the Bengals who returned it for a 45-yard touchdown interception.

Even that was insignificant to the Dolphins, who then held a 21-10 lead, but with less than 14 seconds remaining until intermission, Horst Muhlmann kicked a 46-yard Bengal field goal to cut the margin to eight points.

Morris fumbles

Then on the next kickoff Mercury Morris, whose sharp cuts on rushing plays accounted for 106 yards and one Miami touchdown, fumbled a twisting grounder and Jim LeClair recovered for the eventual losers.

Muhlmann was hustled into the game with 4 seconds left and booted a 12-yard field goal, cutting the Miami lead to an uncomfortable 5 points.

That was the end for the Bengals as Miami came out storming offensively and defensively, making sure Sunday's American Conference title game with the Oakland Raiders would be staged in the Orange Bowl.

Griese deserved the game ball. So did the Dolphin offensive line and the entire defense. Griese mixed his plays with great skill.

He threw two Dolphin touchdown passes to Paul Warfield and Jim Mandich and called on Larry Csonka and Morris for TDs on the ground. Csonka scored from 1 yard out and Morris from the 4.

In the second half, when a drive would stall, Garo Yepremenian, the bald little side-winding place kicker, would shuffle in and do his thing, booting field goals from the 50 and 46 yard lines.

Reprinted from
The Baltimore Sun

Dec. 31

Miami beats Oakland, 27-10

AFC

By CAMERON C. SNYDER
Sun Staff Correspondent

Miami—For the most part yesterday, quarterback Bob Griese was just the middleman in the exchange from center to him to Larry Csonka, but he still came up with the two door opening plays that allowed the Miami Dolphins to walk through the Oakland Raiders, 27 to 10, in the American Football Conference title game here.

Although Csonka rammed for three touchdowns and 117 yards, and received the game ball, Griese chipped in two long runs at critical junctures to ease the Dolphins into the Super Bowl against the Minnesota Vikings, January 13 in Houston.

Bob threw only six times and completed three for just 34 yards, but his play calling was masterful, recalling another quarterback, Bart Starr, whose main function was to handoff and watch his backs run to daylight during Green Bay's glory years under late coach Vince Lombardi.

Keep defense loose

Coach Don Shula's Miami team is reminiscent of the Lombardi steamrollers of the Sixties. With a fine offensive line and backs of Csonka's and Mercury Morris's caliber, Shula uses the pass only as a threat to keep defenses loose, so the battering ram Csonka or the swift as an arrow Morris can get penetration on their runs.

"What do you mean, we don't have finesse," Shula half growled and half smiled in the

dressing room. "It takes finesse to move a team as good as the Raiders out of the way."

Move them out of the way is what the Dolphin offense did with long, time consuming drives for their first two touchdowns.

It was a beautiful day in Miami with slightly soiled cotton puff clouds breaking up the blue sky. It became a perfect day for the 75,105 white handkerchief-waving fans, as the Dolphins hammered their way for a touchdown right from the opening kickoff.

The fans here know their team is nearly unbeatable on the Orange Bowl turf and just about unbeatable, when they get ahead early in the game.

Win refutes statistics

Yesterday's victory was the 24th straight at home, and no matter what the National Football League statistics reveal on the subject of home field advantage, the Dolphins record refutes the "no significant advantage for a home team" contention.

Statistics	Oak.	Mia.
First Down	15	21
Rushes-Yards	26-107	53-266
Passing Yards	129	26
Return Yards	0	79
Passes	15-23-1	3-6-1
Punts	2-51	1-39
Fumbles-Lost	1-0	1-0
Penalties-Yards	3-35	3-26

Oakland	0 0 10	0—10
Miami	7 7 3	10—27

Mia.—Csonka 11 run (Yepremian kick).
Mia.—Csonka 2 run (Yepremian kick).
Oak.—FG Blanda 21
Mia.—FG Yepremian 42.
Oak.—Siani 25 pass from Stabler (Blanda kick).
Mia.—FG Yepremian 26.
Mia.—Csonka 2 run (Yepremian kick).

Individual leaders

RUSHING—Oakland, Hubbard 10—54.
C. Smith 10—35; Miami, Csonka 29—117;
Morris 14—86; Griese 3—39.
RECEIVING—Oakland, C. Smith 5—43.
Siani 3—45; Biletnikoff 2—13. Hubbard 2—11. Moore 2—9; Miami, Warfield 1—27.
Brisco 1—6.
PASSING—Oakland, Stabler 15—23-1,
129 yards; Miami, Griese, 3—6—1, 34.
Attendance—75,105.

Dec. 31

Minnesota outlasts Dallas

NFC

By ALAN GOLDSTEIN
Sun Staff Correspondent

Dallas—The Dallas Cowboy management staged a miniature circus at halftime to entertain the 60,272 fans at Texas Stadium yesterday and both the Cowboys and Minnesota Vikings got caught up in the act in a bizzare, error-plagued second half that resembled basketball more than football.

But the Vikings' opportunistic defense rose to the occasion time and again to thwart the Cowboys' comeback plans and preserve a 27-to-10 victory for the National Football Conference championship and a trip to the Super Bowl in Houston, January 13.

Vikings gamble

The mind-boggling comedy of errors after the intermission came as a complete surprise. The Vikings, under quarterback Fran Tarkenton's flawless direction, had moved to a 10-0 halftime lead on Fred Cox's 44-yard field goal and rookie back Chuck Foreman's 5-yard run, culminating a relentless 86-yard march in the second quarter.

On both these drives, Minnesota elected to gamble on fourth down and short yardage deep in Dallas territory. Both times the Vikings daring paid off, belying Bud Grant's reputation as a conservative coach.

The Vikings appeared in complete control of the situation at the halftime break, but the game suddenly took on a new complexion early in the third quarter when Golden Richards made a spectacular 63-yard punt return to reduce Minnesota's lead to 10-7.

The Vikings struck back with lightening quickness. Only 63 seconds later Tarkenton teamed up with wide receiver John Gilliam on a picture 54-yard touchdown pass play. The speedy Gilliam outran Dallas defenders Cornell Green and Mel Renfro to catch Tarkenton's perfect pass in stride on the 5-yard line and go into the end zone.

Dallas closed to within a touchdown late in the third quarter when a long 71-yard march stalled on the Viking 9 and Toni Fritsch kicked a 17-yard field goal.

Statistics

	Minnesota	Dallas
First downs	20	9
Rushes—yards	47-203	25-90
Passing yards	103	63
Return yards	73	64
Passes	10-21-1	10-21-4
Punts	3-43	4-40
Fumbles—lost	4-3	2-2
Penalties—yards	3-33	2-20

Minnesota	3 7 7	10—27
Dallas	0 0 10	0—10

Minn—FG Cox 44.
Minn—Foreman 5 run (Cox kick).
Dal—Richards 63 punt return (Fritsch kick).
Minn—Gilliam 54 pass from Tarkenton (Cox kick.)
Dal—FG Fritsch 17.
Minn—Bryant 63 interception return (Cox kick).
Minn—FG Cox 34.

Individual leaders

RUSHING—Minnesota, Foreman 19-76;
Reed 18-75; Osborn 4-27; Dallas, Newhouse 14-50; Staubach 5-30; Garrison 5-9.
RECEIVING—Minnesota, Gilliam 2-63;
Foreman 4-28; Voigt 2-23. Dallas, Hayes 2-25; Pearson 2-24; DuPree 1-20.
PASSING—Minnesota, Tarkenton 10-21-1, 133 yards; Staubach 10-21-4, 89.
Attendance—60,272.

But this tense drama soon deteriorated into a slapstick farce as the two teams combined for seven turnovers in the final period.

The Cowboys, time and again, looked the gift horse right in the mouth and proved even more charitable in coughing the ball up four times in the last 15 minutes — twice deep in Viking territory.

The usually pressure - free Roger Staubach proved the most charitable performer on the field. The NFC's No. 1 passer this season had four of his passes picked off and also committed a costly fumble on the Minnesota 45 after Charley Waters had intercepted a Tarkenpass to open the fourth quarter.

Jan. 14

Dolphins Were Super— Game a Drag

Reprinted from
pro football weekly

Vikings accept defeat matter-of-factly

Houston (A)—Wally Hilgenberg calmly stated a fact about the outcome of the Super Bowl.

"They just ran the ball down our throats and we couldn't stop them," the Minnesota Vikings' linebacker said after his team fell, 24-7, to the Miami Dolphins yesterday.

There was virtually no trace of emotion in the cramped Viking dressing room, where the players tried to explain their second Super Bowl loss.

"They not only played as well as they could, they got all of the breaks," said quarterback Fran Tarkenton matter-of-factly. "Just about everything good that could happen to them, happened."

Tarkenton used two plays during action by special teams as examples, and a fumble by Viking Oscar Reed on the Miami 6 just before the end of the first half.

"Jake Scott fumbled our first punt after he was hit by Ron Porter, but the ball bounced right back in his hands and they drove for their second touchdown," said Tarkenton. "Then we get called for clipping after John Gilliam returned the second half kickoff 65 yards."

Viking coach Bud Grant backed up Hilgenberg's observation about Miami's two first-quarter drives, keyed around the rushing of Larry Csonka, that gave the Dolphins a 14-0 lead.

"They took the ball, went down the field and got 14 points the first two times they had the ball," Grant said. "That kind of a lead is hard to overcome against the good teams. We made some errors that prevented us from getting on the scoreboard earlier. There is no secret to this game —you block and tackle. If you don't, you're in trouble."

The Vikings, uncharacteristically, were penalized seven times for 65 yards. Another call was an offsetting penalty.

Grant did not think his players were taking out their frustrations with cheap penalties, such as one called against defensive tackle Alan Page for slamming into Miami quarterback Bob Griese even though he did not have the ball.

"Alan thought Griese had the ball," said Grant. "The quarterback had his back to him."

The Vikings acknowledged the fact that the Dolphins played brilliantly, but refrained from saying Miami would continue to command the National Football League's season-ending extravaganza.

"They outplayed us and got the breaks," said middle linebacker Jeff Siemon. "They have a great team, but I think we can beat them . . . We would need our share of the breaks and we'd have to play without some of the mistakes we made."

Tarkenton was Minnesota's standout with a Super Bowl record of 18 completions which included three outstanding receptions by Stu Voigt.

"Francis faced many difficult situations and under the circumstances, he did very well. When you fall 14 points behind, they know you're going to pass," Grant said.

The Vikings placed regular starting guard Milt Sunde on the reserve squad because of a sore knee. Frank Gallagher, claimed as a free agent from Atlanta in the off-season, started for Sunde.

"That didn't make any difference in the outcome of the game," said Grant, who was hopeful the Vikings would snap back even when down 17-0 at halftime. "It was a decision we made this morning. Early in the week, we were still hopeful Sunde could play."

"We scored 17 points against them in the preseason and beat them," the coach said. "But we had a great kickoff return called back and a penalty cost us on another big play when our fumble recovery was nullified after our touchdown."

The Viking coach also refused to blame last week's practice layoff in Minnesota because of temperatures near or below zero, nor the practice schedules and facilities at a high school stadium after the team arrived in Houston.

Grant could be fined up to $5,000 for criticizing the league about the practice arrangements.

Siemon conveyed the feeling of the players about the facilities: "It got to be a joke by the middle of the week. The practice facility was not very good, but that had no effect whatsoever on the outcome of the game. We were just outplayed."

Statistics

	Minnesota	Mia
First downs	14	
Rushes—yards	24-72	53-196
Passing yards	166	69
Return yards	9	39
Passes	18-28-1	6-7-0
Punts	5-42	3-40
Fumbles—lost	2-1	1-0
Penalties—yards	7-65	0-0

Minnesota	0	0	7	7
Miami	14	3	7	0 — 24

Mia—Csonka 5 run (Yepremian kick).
Mia—Kiick 1 run (Yepremian kick).
Mia—FG Yepremian 28.
Mia—Csonka 2 run (Yepremian kick).
Min—Tarkenton 4 run (Cox kick).
Attendance—68,142

Individual leaders

RUSHING — Minnesota, Reed 11-32, Foreman 7-18, Tarkenton, 4-17; Miami, Csonka 33-145, Morris 11-34, Kiick 7-10.
RECEIVING—Minnesota, Foreman 5-27, Gilliam 4-44, Voigt 3-46, Marinaro 2-39; Miami, Warfield 2-33, Mandich 2-21, Briscoe 2-19.
PASSING—Minnesota, Tarkenton, 18-28-1, 182 yards. Miami, Griese, 6-7-0, 73.

Tired of finesse tag, Dolphins just hit

By a Sun Staff Correspondent

Houston—Coach Howard Schnellenberger of the Colts said during the season that the Miami Dolphin offensive line depended on "finesse. They don't overpower you."

Well, the Dolphin linemen finessed the highly publicized Minnesota Viking defensive four with the subtlety of a steamroller.

"Yep, I've heard we are a finesse team," said All-Pro guard Larry Little. "And it has always made me a little angry. Sure we can finesse, but today we just took it to them. Straight away blocking most of the time.

"What we did was run at their strength, Alan Page. We thought the way to beat him was to run at him. If we couldn't do that we would have had to try something else or been in bad shape.

"But we can come off the ball with the best because we are the best. Finesse, hell."

Little's running mate at guard, Bob Kuechenberg, who played with a broken arm, concurred:

"I don't think anybody can stand up to us. We went out and got the touchdowns and then we got some breaks, but breaks and penalties are deserved.

"On the play they dumped Mercury Morris for a seven-yard loss, I was to lead it and get the cornerback, but Wally Hilgenberg grabbed me by the face mask and I couldn't get out. He was called for the holding penalty and rightly so."

The Dolphins scored shortly thereafter. The touchdown was the one that took the game out of the Vikings' reach.

Page was a frustrated man yesterday. He was straightened up by blocks, knocked down by blocks, screened by blocks and trapped by blocks.

Finally he got a shot at Miami quarterback Bob Griese and clothes lined the passer after Bob had handed off to Larry Csonka.

"I don't think Page did it deliberately," Griese said after the game. "I thought it was a good hit and I told him so. We knew he would be blowing in and that is why we called the play, to take advantage of his rush."

Kuechenberg did not see it that way and took a swing at Page, who received a 15-yard unsportsmanlike conduct penalty.

"I couldn't tell what had happened," said the Dolphin guard. "All I knew was Page hit Bob and Bob didn't have the ball."

Csonka, who carried 35 times for 145 yards, did not come out of the fray unscathed. He had cuts over his eyes, one requiring two stitches, his nose was bent and swollen, his arms skinned and his neck jammed. But he came out joking:

"Coach Shula said we'd have next Wednesday off if we won," said Larry of the incentive for the game. "Seriously, the underlying factor on our team . . . not pep rallies or rah-rah—is that we just have a great coach in Don Shula, and I'm not blowing smoke at him, and 40 great guys."

About the game, Larry said, "The Vikings were very aggressive. They overran the plays. That's why I was able to do so well on the mis-direction plays."

Shula, who has taken the Dolphins to three straight Super Bowls and has been the winning coach the last two years, said:

"In the four years I've been coach, we've gotten a little better each year. The second year we got to the Super Bowl but lost to Dallas. Last year we went undefeated and won the Super Bowl. This year, to do what they did, makes me proudest of all.

"To win back-to-back is something only the old Pack did," Shula said, referring to the Green Bay Packers of 1967-1968, who won the first two Super Bowls.

Reprinted from
The Baltimore Sun

Jan. 14

Super Sundays

I—1967, at Los Angeles
Green Bay 35, Kansas City 10
II—1968, at Miami
Green Bay 33, Oakland 14
III—1969, at Miami
New York Jets 16, Baltimore 7
IV—1970, at New Orleans
Kansas City 23, Minnesota 7
V—1971, at Miami
Baltimore 16, Dallas 13
VI—1972, at New Orleans
Dallas 24, Miami 3
VII—1973, at Los Angeles
Miami 14, Washington 7
VIII—1974, at Houston
Miami 24, Minnesota 7

Reprinted from
pro football weekly

Giants to get Arnsparger, says Shula

Houston (AP)—Coach Don Shula of the Miami Dolphins confirmed yesterday that his top aide, Bill Arnsparger, was going to the New York Giants as that National Football League team's new head coach.

In the victorious Dolphin dressing room following the 24-7 victory over Minnesota in the Super Bowl, Shula presented Arnsparger with one of the two game footballs and wished him best of luck.

"That ends that rumor," Shula said. "The Giants are getting one hell of a coach."

The other game ball went to Larry Csonka, the game's most valuable player.

Arnsparger, 47, replaces Alex Webster, who resigned as coach, effective at the completion of the 1973 NFL season.

Arnsparger, who was given the title of Miami assistant head coach this season to go along with his job as defensive coach, had acknowledged earlier this week that he had met with the Giants' director of operations, Andy Robustelli.

Ten years with Shula

Arnsparger, who has headed the Dolphin defense the past 4 years and has worked with Shula for the past 10 at Baltimore and Miami, turned down an offer as head coach of the Colts last year.

Arnsparger is a native of Paris, Ky., and played tackle at Miami University of Ohio, following service with the United States Marine Corps in World War II.

His first coaching assignment was as offensive coach at his alma mater. He then coached at Ohio State, Kentucky and Tulane. It was at Kentucky where he and Shula began working together as assistant coaches.

Shula threw his arms around Arnsparger as the two approached the tent where interviews were held.

Arnsparger had tears in his eyes.

Meeting due Wednesday

The assistant Miami coach denied he already had accepted the New York job. "It is not definite," he said. "It is something I am considering."

Reports are that he will be in New York Wednesday to close the deal.

"Arnsparger has the job—you can bet on that," a high-ranking official in the Miami organization said. "All Shula did was confirm it."

'Skins' Allen shuns own son

NEW YORK (AP) — Here were the 26 National Football League clubs, staggering their way through the 17th and final round of their marathon two-day draft session. All of the top prospects were long gone and it was the perfect time for a little paternal pride.

But football is a business with no room for family fun for Washington Coach George Allen, who annually shuns draft choices for proven veterans. So instead of indulging himself by picking his quarterback son, George Jr., of Virginia, on the final round, Allen made another draft choice deal, handing off the choice to Baltimore.

In the last round trade, Allen swapped his final 1974 choice and running back George Nock to the Colts for guard Corny Johnson and Baltimore's final choice in the 1975 draft. What Allen wants with that pick wasn't immediately clear.

It was the fourth time in the draft that Allen had traded draft selections for veteran talent. On Tuesday, Washington swapped three picks to San Diego for guard Walt Sweeney. Then Allen struck three times on Wednesday, swapping a ninth-round choice to Los Angeles for wide receiver Joe Sweet, and a 12th-round pick to Baltimore for linebacker Ed Mooney, before completing his final-round swap with the Colts. Allen finished the draft with only 11 picks.

The draft dragged through 22 hours, six minutes with 442 players chosen and was in stark contrast to the crisp six-round draft held in less than two hours by the fledgling World Football League last week.

Three of the players picked in the WFL draft, running backs Kermit Johnson of Southern California and James McAlister of UCLA, and offensive tackle Booker Brown of USC, were signed on the eve of the NFL grab bag by the new league's Southern California club — but that didn't scare off the NFL. McAlister went to Oakland and Brown to Houston on the sixth round and the San Francisco 49ers took Johnson on the seventh round.

Art Johnson, assistant to 49er President Lou Spadia, explained the logic of drafting players already signed by the other league, saying: "we're thinking of the future. There's always an end to a contract."

When the draft was over, 249 offensive players had been chosen compared to 193 defensive players with 77 running backs making that the favorite position in the draft. Only 18 quarterbacks were picked.

There were 47 wide receivers picked including Baltimore's last round choice of Massachusetts' Tim Berra, son of baseball Hall of Famer Yogi Berra.

N.F.L. Draft

FIRST ROUND

Dallas (from Houston)—Ed Jones, Tennessee State de; San Diego— Bo Mathews, Colorado fb, N Y. Giants—John Hicks, Ohio State g; Chicago- Waymond Bryant, Tennessee State lb; Baltimore—John Dutton, Nebraska dt, N.Y. Jets—Carl Barzilauskas, Indiana dt, St. Louis—J. V. Cain, Colorida te; Detroit (from New Orleans)—Ed O'Neil, Penn State lb, San Francisco (from New England)—Wilbur Jackson, Alabama rb; San Francisco—Bill Sandifer, U.C.L.A. dt; Los Angeles (from Philadelphia)—John Cappelletti, Penn State rb; Green Bay— Barty Smith, Richmond rb, New Orleans— Richard Middleton, Ohio State lb; Denver— Randy Gradishar, Ohio State lb; San Diego (from Cleveland)—Don Goode, Kansas lb; Kansas City—Woody Green, Arizona State rb; Minnesota (from Atlanta)- Fred McNeill, U.C.L.A. lb; Buffalo—Reuben Gant, Okla-homa State te; Oakland—Henry Lawrence, Florida A&M ot; Chicago (from Washington through Los Angeles)—Dave Gallagher, Michigan dt; Pittsburgh—Lynn Swann, Southern California wr; Dallas—Charlie Young, North Carolina State rb; Cincinnati—Bill Kollar, Montana State dt; Baltimore (from Los Angeles)—Roger Carr, Louisiana Tech wr; Minnesota—Steve Riley, Southern California ot; Miami—Donald Reese, Jackson State dt.

SECOND ROUND

Buffalo (from Houston)—Doug Allen, Penn State lb; N.Y. Giants—Tom Mullen, SW. Missouri g; Minnesota (from San Diego)— John Holland. Tennessee State wr; New England (from Chicago)—Steve Corbett. Boston College g; N.Y. Jets—Gordon Browne, Boston College ot; Baltimore— Fred Cook, Southern Mississippi lb; St. Louis—Greg Kindle. Tennessee State g; New England—Steve Nilson, North Dakota State lb; San Francisco—Keith Fahnhorst, Minnesota te; New Orleans—Paul Seal, Michigan te; Baltimore (from Philadelphia) —Ed Shuttlesworth, Michigan rb; Miami (from Green Bay)—Andre Tillman, Texas Tech te; Detroit—Billy Howard, Alcorn A&M dt; Cleveland—Billy Corbett, Johnson C. Smith ot; Kansas City—Charles Getty, Penn State ot; Denver—Carl Wafer, Tennessee State dt; San Diego (from Buffalo)—Mark Markovich, Penn State c; Atlanta—Gerald Tinker, Knt Stat wr; Oakland—Dave Casper, Notre Dame te; Pittsburgh—Jack Lambert, Kent State lb; Miami (from Dallas)—Ben Malone, Arizona State rb; Cincinnati—Charlie Davis, Colorado rb; San Francisco (from Washington)—Delvin Williams, Kansas rb; Los Angeles—Bill Simpson, Michigan State db; Minnesota—Matt Blair, Iowa State lb; Miami—Jerís White, Hawaii db.

Feb. 8

Virgil Carter makes first football jump

By The Associated Press

Thursday was pen pal day in much of the National Football League but Virgil Carter used a poison pen and wrote a Dear John letter to the San Diego Chargers.

Four more first-round draft picks signed with the NFL — Colorado fullback Bo Matthews with San Diego, UCLA defensive tackle Bill Sandifer with San Francisco, Michigan defensive tackle Dave Gallagher with Chicago and Southern California offensive tackle Steve Riley with Minnesota.

But the NFL received a blow when Carter, a 28-year-old quarterback who once belonged to the Chicago Bears, Buffalo Bills and Cincinnati Bengals and was traded to San Diego following the 1973 season, became the first player to jump to the fledgling World Football League.

And two other big name NFL draftees — Tennessee State defensive tackle Ed "Too Tall" Jones, the No. 1 pick, and All-American quarterback David Jaynes of Kansas — refused to commit themselves to the established league.

March 14

Pro gridders asking for more...and more

WASHINGTON (AP) — Minimum salaries ranging between $30,000 to $40,000, a Super Bowl winner's check of $25,000, freedom for veteran players to move from team to team and increased pension and insurance benefits.

Those were among the proposals suggested by the National Football League Players Association to its members in a confidential memo sent in preparation for contract negotiations with owners beginning Saturday.

The memo, described as a working paper for internal discussion only, spells out recommendations to be considered for increases in pre-season and post-season games, changes in the standard player contract, increases in meal, moving and travel allowances and improvements in pension, insurance and disability plans.

Ed Garvey, NFLPA executive director who wrote the seven page memo, released a statement through his office in which he said the paper "is not final, in any sense, but will give the public some idea of the demands which are being sought by the Players Association."

The NFL players and owners meet in Washington Saturday to begin negotiations over a new contract, which expired Jan. 31.

In New York, John Thompson, executive director of the NFL Management Council, the counterpart of the players' union, would not have any comment on the Garvey paper except to say, "I have seen the memo, I am aware of it."

The Associated Press obtained a copy of the memorandum Wednesday.

During the past year, Garvey has told news conferences and interviewers that the freedom issues would be a major point in the negotiations and recommendations for discussion are contained in the memo.

They are impartial arbitration, instead of commissioner Pete Rozelle; permitting a veteran to cancel any trade; possible arbitration over salaries; free movement of veteran players from team to team, and allowing a player to negotiate with any club of his choice when released by his own team.

March 26

NFL owners continue talks

WASHINGTON (AP) — National Football League owners and players meet across the contract bargaining table again today as management attempts to obtain a clarification of demands made 11 days ago by the union.

The owners, with the NFL Management Council acting as their bargaining agent, are not expected to respond to the 57 demands made by the NFL Players Association until the next meeting between the two groups, tentatively in New York in early April.

"We are trying to clarify some of the things that turned up at the last meeting," said a council spokesman.

"We've spent the last week going over the proposals, analyzing them and trying to get them in as sharp focus as we can."

The 57 demands include some economic measures but many are aimed at providing greater freedom for the players and a diminishing of the authority now held by NFL Commissioner Pete Rozelle.

Ed Garvey, association executive director, read an opening statement at the first bargaining session in which he charged owners with perpetuating an unjust system of control over athletes, suppressing the constitutional rights of players and with a general disregard of the players' union.

The players have threatened to strike if most of their demands are not met, possibly affecting the start of the pre-season schedule.

The players have demanded, in addition to limiting Rozelle's powers, the elimination of the option clause, waiver system, all fines, reserve lists and training camp curfews.

They also are seeking the right to cancel trades, shorter training camps and a moratorium on further installation of synthetic turf.

March 19

The WFL Draft

First Round
Washington, Charlie Evans, rb, New York Giants. Toronto, Larry Czonka, rb, Miami. Philadelphia, Tim Rosovich, lb, San Diego. Portland, Jim Plunkett, qb, New England. Florida, Virgil Robinson, rb, New Orleans. Detroit, Mike Taylor, lb, New York Jets. Birmingham, Johnny Musso, rb, British Columbia CFL. Southern California, Tom Mack, g, Los Angeles. Chicago, John Brockington, rb, Green Bay. Houston, Pete Beathard, qb, Kansas City. Hawaii, Ted Kwalick, te, San Francisco. New York, Joe Namath, qb, New York Jets.

Second Round
New York, Terry Hanratty, qb, Pittsburgh. Hawaii, Calvin Hill, rb, Dallas. Houston, Pete Lammons, te, New York Jets. Chicago, Don Morrison, g, New Orleans. Southern California, Greg Barton, qb, Toronto CFL. Birmingham, Craig Morton, qb, Dallas. Detroit, Joe O'Donnell, g, Detroit. Florida, Bubba Smith, de, Oakland. Portland, Alan Page, dt, Minnesota. Philadelphia, Dan Yoachim, dt, Montreal CFL. Toronto, Paul Warfield, wr, Miami. Washington, Bill Brundige, dt, Washington.

Third Round
Washington, Terry Hermeling, ot, Washington. Toronto, Jim Kiick, rb, Miami. Philadelphia, Bob Tucker, te, New York Giants. Portland, Rick Eber, wr, Saskatchewan CFL. Florida, Dave Leffers, ot, Oakland. Detroit, Paul Costa, g, Buffalo. Birmingham, Paul Robinson, rb, Houston. Southern California, Ted Hendricks, lb, Baltimore. Chicago, Bill Baker, de, Saskatchewan CFL. Houston, Rick Arrington, qb, Philadelphia. Hawaii, Rocky Freitas, t, Detroit. New York, Dave Williams, wr, Pittsburgh.

Fourth Round
New York, Mike Lahood, g, Los Angeles. Hawaii, Ron East, t, Los Angeles. Houston, Joe Reed, qb, San Francisco. Chicago, Mike McCoy, dt, Green Bay. Southern California, Brian Salter, db, San Diego. Birmingham, Jim Mandich, te, Miami. Detroit, John Henderson, wr, Calgary CFL. Florida, Dave Roller, dt, Toronto CFL. Portland, George Wells, de, Toronto CFL. Philadelphia, Al Atkinson, lb, New York Jets. Toronto, Pete Richardson, db, Buffalo. Washington, Bob Brunet, rb, Washington.

Round Five
Washington, Mike Taliaferro, qb, New England. Toronto, Bruce Bergey, de, Toronto CFL. Philadelphia, Don Strock, qb, Miami. Portland, Ron Curl, dt, Toronto CFL. Florida, Ray Nettles, lb, Vancouver CFL. Detroit, Dale Livingston, k, Detroit. Birmingham, Ron Jessie, wr, Detroit. Southern California, Bill Muson, qb, Detroit. Chicago, Ron Porter, lb, Minnesota. Houston, Daryle Lamonica, qb, Oakland. Hawaii, Bob Grim, wr, New York Giants. New York, Marty Huff, lb, Edmonton CFL.

Round Six
New York, Kent Peterson, te, Cincinnati. Hawaii, Randy Johnson, qb, New York Giants. Houston, Rick Casata, qb, Ottawa CFL. Chicago, Don Talbert, ot, Dallas. Southern California, Willie Buchanon, db, Green Bay. Birmingham, LeVart Carr, g, Houston. Detroit, Cliff Burnett, dt, Edmonton CFL. Florida, Ed George, ot, Montreal CFL. Portland, Ken Matthews, wr, Toronto CFL. Philadelphia, John Babinecz, lb, Dallas. Toronto, Festus Cotton, dt, Cleveland. Washington, Charlie Weaver, lb, Detroit.

Reprinted from
The Washington Star-News

March 31

Dolphins' Csonka, Warfield, Kiick sign with WFL

By The Associated Press

The World Football League attained new stature and prestige when its Toronto team lured Larry Csonka, Paul Warfield and Jim Kiick away from the Super Bowl champion Miami Dolphins and signed them to a collective 3-year, $3 million-plus contract yesterday in Toronto.

The move is effective at the start of the 1975 season — after the three play out the 1974 option on their National Football League contracts.

In Miami, Joseph Robbie, managing general partner of the Dolphins was bitter at the loss. "I am disappointed, shocked, sick, whatever . . ." Robbie said at a news conference.

"I feel Ed Keating [who handled the negotiations for the three] took three of our players to Canada who were in a frame of mind to come back and listen when they left." Robbie added that he thought the three had already signed with Toronto before Keating called him but did not elaborate.

"We were drafted by the Toronto franchise and came up to listen to what they had to say," said Csonka, one of the greatest running backs in the game today.

"I think the general consensus of opinion in the American public was that the World Football League wasn't a serious contender.

"We, however, felt differently and, after coming up here and listening to what they had to say, decided that the financial benefits are considerable."

And he pointed out that, even if the WFL never gets off the ground, they are guaranteed a healthy chunk of money.

Dolphin head coach Don Shula said little at the Miami news conference but remarked that he did not know whether he would play the three next season. "I'll play it by ear," Shula said, "It's never come up before."

Asked how he could replace the three, Shula replied "you don't. ... We were in the unique situation of being able to go after our third Super Bowl in a row next season. Our thought was to do everything possible to get everyone back and go for it."

The signing of Csonka, Kiick and Warfield gives the neophyte WFL instant respectability and a guaranteed gate attraction.

In that respect it was like the Winnipeg Jets' signing of superstar Bobby Hull, which gave the World Hockey Association a vital shot in the arm in its fight against the entrenched National Hockey League.

"Certainly, the financial security is very important to me and to my family," said Warfield, the Dolphins' star wide receiver. "It's almost like saying we're stealing a phrase from a movie of a couple of years ago—they made us an offer we couldn't refuse."

Robbie said Keating asked the Dolphins to match a Toronto offer of $3.5 million, $3 million of which would be deposited in a bank account in advance, and a guaranteed 3-year, no-cut, no-trade contract for the three.

The Miami official said he pressed Keating in the telephone conversation "for time to talk about Toronto's offer." but was told the offer might not exist if they did not accept it today.

"I told him that $3 million wouldn't burn in two days," Robbie said, and asked for further discussion. But, Robbie continued, Keating responded with a "take it or leave it" demand and he refused to negotiate by telephone.

Kiick acknowledged that he signed, in part, because of his dissatisfaction of recent years, when Mercury Morris pushed him out of a starting running back position. "I have a lot of pride and I want to play a lot of football," he said.

"I feel I can contribute to any football team. That is one of the big reasons. Of course, it goes back to financial security. I have a family and I have to worry about them."

All feel the same

Csonka, saying he was speaking for Warfield and Kiick as well, said he was "looking forward to this upcoming season with as much anticipation as any of the years we've played for the Miami Dolphins.

"Nothing would be a greater tribute to the fact that we are leaving than the idea of leaving on a winning note, putting out 100 per cent and possibly having a winning team or even another Super Bowl championship."

Asked whether they were worried that the Miami fans, knowing they would be losing their stars after the season, might turn against them, Kiick said, "I don't think they're that fickle."

They all pointed out that the old American Football League came on the scene in 1960 to challenge the NFL and over a period of years reached parity in playing quality with the established league.

They believe that the WFL, too, will eventually be able to field teams equal to NFL clubs.

"I have a tremendous amount of confidence in the World Football League and I think that, with the idea that we have come over from the NFL, I think a lot of other keynote players within the NFL will play out their option, and come over, too," said Csonka.

"I think perhaps in 2 or 3 years or 4 years, there'll be a leveling off of talent between the two leagues."

Csonka also pointed out that, in the 2½ months since the 1974 Super Bowl, there were no contract negotiations between the players and the Dolphins but that they had been in constant contact with Miami Saturday and yesterday.

"We have a mutual representative in Ed Keating," Csonka said "and he was on the phone two or three or four times with Joe Robbie (managing general partner of the Dolphins) throughout the morning.

April 5

NFL contract talks bitter, unproductive

NEW YORK (AP) — The next step seems to be up to the National Football League Players Association — but it may be a long time in coming following a sometimes bitter and apparently totally unproductive meeting with the NFL Management Council over contract negotiations.

Two weeks ago the players presented their 57 demands, most of them covering either so-called "freedom issues" or financial benefits.

On Thursday, the owners responded to them with what the players association called "no response at all."

And the talks, which were expected to continue next week in Washington, are apparently off for the moment.

The Management Council — the owners' bargaining unit — rejected the two basic issues covering 43 of the demands, contending the players were calling for anarchy rather than freedom and were injecting "double jeopardy" by attempting to have collective bargaining cover issues which will also be open to individual player-club contract talks.

"We gave them the demands and we expected responses," said Ed Garvey, executive director of the NFLPA. "They told us they can't respond. They said they can't get into the economic issues until we've cleared up the freedom issues — and that they can't deal with the freedom issues because there's nothing to deal with, that they'd lead to the destruction of the game . . . They say it's a matter of destruction. We say it's a matter of semantics. They're using the same tactics as they did in 1970."

The problem involving the talks themselves seems to be semantics. The players, who have to send out a call before the next meeting is convened, say they want a written response to the demands and that they haven't gotten one. The owners say they have responded, in writing, and that it's up to the players to make the next move.

That could take a while.

Freedom issues involve, in part, the removal of Commissioner Pete Rozelle from all grievance arbitration and Rozelle's power to discipline a player.

April 10

Sullivan shocked with Patriot dismissal

BOSTON (AP) — Billy Sullivan says his ouster as president and chairman of the board of directors of the New England Patriots he founded is "a shocker," but he's determined to stay on as a director of the National Football League club.

"Now that we're doing well, I get thrown out," Sullivan said Tuesday night after an afternoon announcement by the club that Bob Marr was replacing Sullivan as president of the team.

"But I hung in there before," Sullivan said, "and I'll hang in there now. The Patriots have been my real life's work."

"I'm not a sorehead, but I'm shocked at the way this was done," said Sullivan, who declined to give details of his demise.

"I had been given every indication that I'd be allowed to buy enough stock to own 51 per cent of the club, and had

raised the money to do so. Then everything was turned around and I was voted out. I don't want to say anything in anger that might hurt the club, but my absence from the press conference should speak volumes about how I feel."

Earlier, Sullivan had won an injunction halting the Patriots' board of directors' meeting in an effort to raise money and corner controlling stock. The injunction was later lifted.

April 17

Grid leader seeks to ensure CFL

OTTAWA (AP) — Jake Gaudaur, Canadian Football League Commissioner has appealed to members of Parliament to ensure that the league is not damaged by the intrusion of American interests.

In a letter to all Parliament members dated April 10 and delivered Tuesday night, Gaudaur said that while the CFL is not opposed to World Football League franchise in Toronto, it is concerned about the possible effects on Canadian football.

The appeal came on the eve—likely late today or perhaps Thursday—of debate on a bill that would ban American football from Canada.

The bill is aimed specifically at the WFL's Toronto Northmen owned by John F. Bassett. It was introduced last Wednesday.

Gaudaur said in his letter that the CFL fears that the Northmen, if permitted to play in Toronto, gradually will draw support away from Toronto Argonauts of the CFL.

He said this "most certainly would trigger a chain reaction which would promptly lead to the demise of the Canadian Football League."

June 18

Players charge 'union-busting' try by NFL

Associated Press

ATLANTA — The president of the National Football League Players Assn. charged yesterday that club owners are using "union-busting tactics" and that he sees no alternative to a strike.

Bill Curry of the Houston Oilers, who lives in Atlanta, said, "I see a strike and, yes, the wheels are in motion. The best way to avoid a strike is to be prepared for one."

His comments were in response to an announcement by John Thompson of the NFL Management Council that letters had been sent to rookies asking them not to join the NFLPA until negotiations have been completed.

Bengals Get Writ Halting WFL Raids

CINCINNATI, April 19 (AP) —The Cincinnati Bengals of the National Football League weer granted a temporary restraining order today blocking the new World Football League from raiding the N.F.L. team.

Cincinnati is the first N.F.L. team to sue the rival league. The restraining order was granted by United States District Judge David S. Porter after the Bengals filed suit against the newly formed W.F.L., all its organizations and franchises and Bill Bergey, a linebacker for the Bengals.

Bergey signed Wednesday with the Virginia Ambassadors of the W.F.L. and will begin playing for them in 1976. His contract with the Bengals expires in 1975.

Judge Porter, in a later afternoon hearing, refused to grant a similar order at this time to enjoin Bergey from engaging in activities on behalf of the W.F.L., his attorney, Bart Brown Jr., said.

Brown said, "He wasn't going to do it anyway, and I think we convinced the court of that."

The restraining order ends April 29. Judge Porter will hold a hearing then on the Bengals' request for a preliminary injunction.

In their suit, the Bengals asked the court to rescind Bergey's contract with the W.F.L., prohibit him from promoting the W.F.L. in any way, order him to return any money paid him by the W.F.L., and order him not accept any money until his N.F.L. contract expires.

The suit also asks the court to enjoin permanently the W.F.L. from inducing any player under a Bengal contract to enter into a relationship with the W.F.L. until the player's N.F.L. contract has expired.

Dolphins Sue WFL for 4M

Miami, June 5 (AP)—Larry Csonka, Jim Kiick and Paul Warfield were named as defendants Wednesday in a $4 million suit filed by the Miami Dolphins against the World Football League, its Toronto-Memphis franchise and the players' agent, Ed Keating.

Names of the players were included because the suit alleges they were induced to break their contracts, a Dolphins spokesman said.

The three, represented by Keating, signed a multi-million dollar contract with Toronto, now moved to Memphis, Tenn., to play in the WFL in 1975.

April 26

NFL changes

NEW YORK (AP) — Faced with increasing criticism that its game had become dull, the National Football League has struck back with the the most sweeping set of rule changes for professional football in 40 years.

"It's an exciting package," said Commissioner Pete Rozelle, unveiling the changes that are designed to open up offenses and reduce the ever-increasing roll field goals have played in the pro game recently.

Besides introducing a 15-minute sudden death overtime period to settle ties, the NF moved the goal posts to the end line, meaning that field goal kickers will have to boot those three-pointers 10 yards farther than they have been. Also, missed field goals will return the ball to the line of scrimmage or 20-yard line, whichever is farther from the goal line.

Other changes also were adopted to protect wide receivers from the downfield battering they have been exposed to recently, reducing the penalty for offensive holding, tripping and illegal use of hands from 15 yards to 10 yards, and making illegal the dangerous crack back blocks that have caused many injuries.

Not since 1933 when the league moved to allow forward passing from anywhere behind the line of scrimmage have such widespread alterations been made in the sport. That was the same year the goal posts were moved from the back of the end zone to the goal line to encourage field goal kicking.

April 27

Chargers slapped with fines

SAN DIEGO (AP) — The shell-shocked San Diego Chargers are reeling from yet another blow — discipline from the National Football League for violating its drug policy.

Eight veteran players, General Manager Harland Svare and owner Eugene Klein were fined a total of $40,000 Friday, said NFL Commissioner Pete Rozelle, adding they were also placed on probation.

Rozelle disclosed no details of the violations. But Svare, reached in Clarkfield, Minn., said: "Everybody knows we're talking about marijuana."

It was the first such action since the league announced last June that it was strengthening its anti-drug policy.

Defensive end Deacon Jones and linebacker Tim Rossovich were fined $3,000 each; wide receiver Jerry Levias and defensive linemen Coy Bacon and Dave Costa $2,000 each; and linebacker-coach Rick Redman, running back Bob Thomas and guard Walt Sweeney $1,000 each.

Svare, who coached the Chargers half of last season and then became general manager, was fined $5,000. Klein was fined $20,000.

Drug problems on the Chargers first surfaced when former player Houston Ridge filed suit claiming improperly administered drugs caused an injury that ended his career in 1969.

Ridge settled the suit for $300,000. Sworn statements filed during the case accused the team of passing out as many as 10,000 pills in a year.

The Defectors

Leading players who have signed with WFL clubs:

Charlie Harraway, RB, Redskins to Birmingham, 1974
Paul Robinson, RB, Oilers to Birmingham, 1974
Bill Bergey, LB, Bengals to Norfolk, 1976
Carter Campbell, DE, Giants to N.Y. Stars, 1975
Craig Morton, QB, Cowboys to Houston Texans, 1975
Ron Jessie, WR, Lions to Birmingham, 1975
Calvin Hill, RB, Cowboys to Honolulu, 1975
Randy Johnson, QB, Giants to Honolulu, 1975
Jim Sniadecki, LB, 49ers to Honolulu, 1975
Ted Kwalick, TE, 49ers to Honolulu, 1975
Ken Stabler, QB, Raiders to Birmingham, 1976
Daryle Lamonica, QB, Raiders to So. California, 1975
Larry Csonka, RB, Dolphins to Toronto, 1975
Jim Kiick, RB, Dolphins to Toronto, 1975
Paul Warfield, WR, Dolphins to Toronto, 1975
John Isenbarger, RB, 49ers to Honolulu, 1975
John Douglas, LB, Giants to Honolulu, 1975
Vince Clements, RB, Giants to Honolulu, 1975

Richmond Flowers, DB, Giants to Honolulu, 1975
Edd Hargett, QB, Oilers to Honolulu, 1975
Ron Holliday, WR, Chargers to Philadelphia Bells, 1975
Steve Chomyszak, DT, Bengals to Philadelphia Bells, 1975
Bob Davis, QB, Saints to Washington Ambass., 1975
John Elliott, DT, Jets to N.Y. Stars, 1974
Ron East, DT, Chargers to Honolulu, 1974
Virgil Carter, QB, Bengals to Chicago Fire, 1974
George Sauer, WR, Jets (*) to N.Y. Stars, 1974
Lloyd Voss, DT, Green Bay, etc. (*) to N.Y. Stars, 1974
Gerry Philbin, WR, Eagles (*) to N.Y. Stars, 1974
Don Gault, QB, Jets (**) to N.Y. Stars, 1974
Warren McVea, WR, Chiefs, etc. (**) to Detroit Wheels, 1974
George Mira, QB, 49ers, etc. to Honolulu, 1974
Vernon Vanoy, DT, Giants, etc. to Florida, 1974
Jim Seymour, WR, Bears, etc. (**) to Chicago Fire, 1974
* Denotes had retired.
* Been waived through NFL.

Reprinted from
pro football weekly

June 25

Pessimism marks NFL meetings

By The Associated Press

National Football League owners head back to the bargaining table with the players union today, hoping to do better than they did in court yesterday.

With time running out on the July 1 strike deadline set by the NFL Players Association, both sides concede progress must be made quickly if an agreement is to be reached, but sources in both camps appeared pessimistic.

In Dallas yesterday, State Appeals Judge Harold Bateman dismissed a temporary injunction prohibiting members of the Cowboys from signing with teams of the new World Football League.

The decision, following a case decided in the WFL's favor in Cincinnati, dealt a sharp blow to efforts by the established league to prevent players from jumping to the WFL when their contractual commitments to NFL clubs run out.

Bateman flatly rejected the argument of the Cowboys that recruiting among their players by the WFL constituted illegal meddling with player contracts.

The judge's opinion appeared to reflect much of the position adopted in the case by the NFL players union. "We must consider the freedom of contract of the individual players as well as the rights of the club under its present contracts," he wrote.

"Matter of economics"

"Bargaining for future services is a matter of economics," he added. "The club can assure itself of the continued services and loyalty of its players by offering them long-term contracts and other financial inducements.

"If it chooses not to do so for economic reasons, it has no legal ground to complain if the players look elsewhere for their future careers. . . ."

Tex Schramm, president and general manager of the Cowboys, declined to comment on the decision until team attorneys study it.

Three Cowboy players—Calvin Hill, Craig Morton, and Mike Montgomery—had signed WFL contracts in April before the team obtained a district court injunction against further signings of Cowboy players by the WFL.

July 7

NFL Players' Association Would Prevent Exhibitions

By ASSOCIATED PRESS

Bill Curry, president of the striking pro football players, pledged Saturday his union will do everything legally within its power—including soliciting aid from other unions—to prevent National Football League exhibition games if the strike picket line and then there would be no lights, no one to sell tickets, no ushers, and no concessions," Langer told The Associated Press. "A lot more people are involved in a game than football players."

Langer said the decision to play would have to be made by ing) is a hard thing to swallow."

"I want to play the All-Star game but I do understand the union's point of view," Langer said. "The union is united and behind their cause. They believe if we play the All-Star will loosen the morale around years ago, the union agreed to let the Kansas City Chiefs practice and play in the All-Star game. Many felt the action weakened the union's position. There was no picketing in the 1970 dispute, which ended before the exhibition season began.

July 3

NFL Pickets Make History In San Diego

SAN DIEGO (AP) — Despite the refusal of U. S. International University — site of the San Diego Charger training camp — to permit on-campus protests, the striking National Football League Players Association planned its first picketing for today.

And, even as the NFLPA, striking with the slogan "No Freedom, No Football," readied for the first picket lines in the history of professional sports, a discordant note appeared among the ranks of the union's members.

"We're not going to come out smelling like roses, making ridiculous demands for twice as much money with less work and no discipline," charged center Jim Langer of the world champion Miami Dolphins. He said 80 per cent of his teammates want to play against the College All-Stars on July 25 at Chicago.

Some 50 veteran players were scheduled to throw up a picket line just off the U.S. International University campus at ll a.m., EDT, today in hopes of persuading rookies and free agents not to report.

While the veterans prepared for the walkout, the Los Angeles Times reported that 40 of the 49 rookies under contract to the Chargers were in the training camp before midnight Tuesday.

The Chargers were the first of three NFL teams scheduled to open training camps this week.

An informal survey, however, indicated that many, if not all, of the young players planned to report to the San Diego camp.

And Coach Tommy Prothro said: "All of the rookies we've contacted say they'll come out. We have talked to all but a very few."

NFLPA Executive Director Ed Garvey said the union would abide by the university's decision.

Jesse Freitas, one of the Chargers' two first-round draftees and a quarterback prospect, said he would cross the picket line. "I don't think I should be going on strike for something I really don't belong to."

Rookies are not eligible for NFLPA membership until they make a team and the regular season begins.

July 18   ★ ★ ★

Browns blocked in Beachwood

The Browns veterans who are honoring the strike by the National Football League Players Association are seeking a new practice site after being shut out at Beachwood High School, Tuesday.

After a handful of veterans took the field for a workout, they were asked to leave by a Beachwood school maintenance man.

Robert Holloway, superintendent of Beachwood schools, said he is not in favor of the pro players using his football field for their strike headquarters. In fact, he said, he did not know the Browns players contemplated using his field for practice until he read it in the newspaper.

All-Star game off; meeting set on strike

Aug. 29

Matuszak's Play Stopped

HOUSTON (AP) — Houston quarterback Mike Taliaferro threw two touchdown strikes to lead the Texans to a 14-11 World Football League victory over New York Wednesday night, but defensive tackle John Matuszak lost a round in his team-jumping battle with the Houston Oilers.

Matuszak, pro football's No. 1 choice in the 1973 draft, jumped from the Oilers of the National Football League earlier Wednesday and played for the Texans Wednesday night until he was served with a temporary restraining order on the sidelines to prevent further participation.

Taliaferro, who left the game with a rib injury in the fourth quarter, hit tight end Willie Frazier for a six-yard touchdown in the first quarter and threw 25 yards in the fourth quarter to Rick Eber, who completely fooled the Stars' secondary.

New York, which had a five game winning streak snapped, got on the scoreboard in the second quarter when defensive back Larry Shears intercepted a Taliaferro pass and returned it 43 yards to set up a 34-yard field goal by Moses Lajterman.

The restraining order will keep Matuszak from playing for the Texans pending a Sept. 5 hearing in state district court.

July 11

Bergey traded

Philadelphia .P—The Philadelphia Eagles acquired middle linebacker Bill Bergey from the Cincinnati Bengals yesterday. and immediately signed him to a five-year contract, in exchange for their first-round draft picks in 1977 and 1978 and a second-round choice in 1978.

Bergey, a 6-foot-3, 243-pounder from Arkansas State, was the Bengals' second-round choice in the 1969 National Football League draft.

Bergey, recognized as one of the most aggressive linebackers in the NFL, jumped to the World Football League, effective in 1976, originally signing with the Virginia Ambassadors, who since have become the Florida Blazers.

In Orlando, Bob Deutsch, who is the Blazers' attorney, said Bergey agreed to return an initial contract payment he had received from the team. However, he denied a statement that the Blazers had agreed to release Bergey because they were unable to deliver part of the bonus they owed him.

Deutsch said the team "had a $60,000 check in hand to pay" Bergey, but that Blazers managing partner Ronnie Loudd agreed to release him because of his current uncertain status with the Bengals.

WFL openers attract surprising tournouts

Ever since the World Football League was organized, cynics have wondered if it really would get off the ground. Let it be recorded the new league opened in five cities last night and as first nights go you would have to rate it a resounding success.

The gates, except for 18,625 in Orlando where the Blazers edged Hawaii, were better than even the most wildly optimistic WFL backer was hoping for. People were still coming in midway through the second quarter at Philadelphia as the Bell drew 55,534—45,000 paid—while Birmingham drew 53,231, Chicago 42,000 and Memphis 30,122.

```
SECTION  1
SEC   ROW   SEAT
            449
ADMIT ONE      THIS DATE
JUL  17  1974
DOWNING
STADIUM
RANDALL'S
ISLAND
NEW YORK N.Y.
N.Y. STARS
VS.
BIRMINGHAM
AMERICANS
WED 8:00 PM
NO REFUNDS  PRICE  NO EXCHANGES
COMPLIMENTARY
SEC   ROW   SEAT
            449
ENTR  PRTL  1
```

July 28

Cards whip Bills, 21-13, in Hall of Fame game

By a Sun Staff Correspondent

Canton, Ohio—While the National Football League Players Association picketed in the shadow of the Pro Football Hall of Fame, untried rookies and free agents of the St. Louis Cardinals posted a 21 to 13 victory over untried rookies and free agents of the Buffalo Bills yesterday at Fawcett

Reprinted from
The Baltimore Sun

Stadium in the annual Hall of Fame game.

Four former football greats, who labored under the "bondage and paternalism" against which the modern players' union now protests, were inducted into the shrine in pregame ceremonies while their modern day counterparts manned picket lines.

Tony Canadeo, a halfback for the Green Bay Packers from 1941 to 1952; Bill George, linebacker for the 1952-1965 Chicago Bears and the 1966 Los Angeles Rams; Cleveland Brown offensive tackle and premier placekicker Lou (The Toe) Groza (1946-1967), and Richard (Night Train) Lane, defensive back from 1952 to 1965 with the Rams, Cardinals and Detroit Lions, swelled the ranks of pro football's shrine to 79.

Pickets from the players' union manned every entrance to the small stadium across the street from the Hall of Fame and were supported by strikers from the United Auto Workers.

To all who would listen, the striking players patiently explained their side of the issues in the 4-week-old strike against NFL owners, a strike which already canceled the College All-Star Game, threatened yesterday's Hall of Fame Game and may affect the league's first preseason games this week.

The NFL Alumni Association, a loosely knit association of pre-1958 veterans, counter-picketed to protest their exclusion from the current players' pension program.

The modern players union claim that if pension funds are distributed to the old timers, the average pension would be reduced to too small a sum.

Aug. 13

NFL Arrangement Angers Players

The Associated Press

"It was a long drawn-out strike," said Buffalo guard Reggie McKenzie, "and our side lost."

That was one reaction Monday as National Football League players drifted into training camps across the country under provisions of a 14-day cooling off period decided on by the players association.

Everyone is supposed to report to camp by Wednesday, negotiations with the owners are to resume Thursday and if an agreement isn't reached in two weeks, everyone is supposed to walk out again.

McKenzie wasn't the only one unhappy with the plan which the players say was suggested by chief federal mediator W. J. Usery Jr.

"If I said I was happy about the way we're going in, I'd be lying," said Washington defensive tackle Diron Talbert.

Offensive tackle Dick Himes, Green Bay added, "This could be the worst thing that could happen at a time like this."

Nothing's settled. This could be ruinous to team unity. We're going in without a contract signed and we're no better off than we were a year ago."

Meanwhile, rookies and free agents continued to display their talents in a trio of Monday night games. The Pittsburgh Steelers bombed the Chicago Bears 50-21, the Cleveland Browns edged the San Francisco 49ers 21-20 and the Buffalo Bills beat the Kansas City Chiefs 35-21.

Some veterans were pleased with the plan to return to action.

"I'm not going to waste any time. I've been waiting for a month," said Oakland linebacker Phil Villapiano. "I think it was a great move by the association. I'm very excited."

"This is the only thing we could do at this point, but it's what we wanted to do," added teammate Gene Upshaw, a guard.

Aug. 31

NFLPA Prexy Waived by Oilers

HUNTSVILLE, Tex. (AP) — The Houston Oilers said Friday that Bill Curry, president of the National Football League Players Association, has been waived "by mutual consent."

Curry, a center, left training camp and was not immediately available for comment.

Curry seriously injured his left knee in the fifth game last season and had taken a wait-and-see attitude concerning his future following corrective surgery.

Oiler Coach Sid Gillman, as the team's general manager, made the announcement after meeting with Curry.

"We had three centers and it would take four or five weeks for Bill's leg to get in shape," Gillman said. "We had a long talk and he asked to be waived."

Curry arrived in training camp Aug. 18. He said his reason for reporting was to help the Oilers win if he could make the team.

"That's the same thing I've done for nine years and it's the only reason I'm in camp," the veteran center said at the time.

Aug. 29

Dispute Still Stalemated

NFL Strike Seems Over

CHICAGO (AP) — The National Football League strike appeared ended Wednesday while the dispute that caused it remained stalemated.

The NFL Players Association voted almost unanimously Tuesday night to remain in training camps and open the regular season, if necessary, without a new collective bargaining agreement.

The action, in a 25-1 ballot, came after the latest attempt by federal mediator W.J. Usery to resolve the 59-day labor dispute had to be recessed following 16 hours of fruitless negotiating efforts.

"I don't plan to call both parties into any more negotiations in the near future," said a disappointed Usery. "I encouraged them to play the football season and see where they go from there."

The player union's armed truce action came at the midnight deadline of a 14-day cooling-off period which brought picketing veterans into camp two weeks ago.

Ed Garvey, NFLPA executive director, asserted "this doesn't break the union. The union is stronger than ever and the National Football League never will be the same.

"We'll see how things go for the next couple of weeks and decide whether we should consider affiliation with another union or we should take our case to Congress or should we file grievances with the National Labor Relations Board."

Garvey said he understood the players will be protected by the 1970 collective bargaining agreement which expired last March 1.

John Thompson, executive director of the NFL's Management Council, said it was the players' prerogative whether they wanted to play without a contract.

"Legally, we would not be bound to honor the insurance benefits under the collective bargaining agreement, but of course we will," Thompson said.

An alternative would be for the players to be covered only by the standard player contract and the NFL constitution.

Two of the key conflicts reportedly involve the association's demand for a neutral arbitrator to replace Commissioner Pete Rozelle in all disputes and for a contract lasting a year, two at the most.

The owners insist on a four-year pact, to recoup strike losses and to stave off what Thompson termed a recurrence of "bitterness and fan apathy."

Sept. 4

Allen Reconsiders; Thomas Allowed To Rejoin 'Skins

WASHINGTON (AP) — Duane Thomas has been forgiven his sins and embraced once again as a Washington Redskin.

Coach George Allen had booted Thomas from the National Football League team a week ago for grabbing and threatening an assistant coach who wanted him to stay late after practice to view a game film.

But Allen took Thomas back Tuesday. "He said he was sorry," noted the coach. "He does not want to play for any other team."

Allen, who had agonized for five days over Thomas' plea for reinstatement, said it was his "toughest decision ever as a coach."

Sept. 26

New York Stars Move to Charlotte; WFL Struggling

Sept. 12

Rookies Replacing Vets as NFL Clubs Make Final Release

By The Associated Press

National Football League teams are continuing to give pink slips to large numbers of veteran players as they built much of their squads around rookies and free agents who ignored the pre-season strike.

"I knew it was coming the day I got back to camp," said Charlie Evans, a New York Giants running back who was also his team's player-representative. "I'm convinced it was because of the strike," he said after he was one of eight Giant veterans who were cut.

The Giants now have 18 rookies on their roster of 47, giving them one of the highest concentrations of first-year players in the 26-team league.

Other casualties among the 200 or so players let go early this week were Leroy Kelley, the great Cleveland running back who was let go by Oakland, and Green Bay Packer wide receiver Leland Glass.

Disappearing from many NFL rosters were players who have signed future contracts with the World Football League. The Giants purged themselves of all five players in that category, one of them quarterback Randy Johnson. Wide receiver Fair Hooker, traded by Cleveland when he signed a WFL contract, was let go by New Orleans on Wednesday.

The deadline for cutting rosters to 47 players was Tuesday, but because of technicalities in rules governing the waiver system the final rosters of many of the teams will not be known until Thursday.

It appears that the league may begin the season with the largest number of rookies in years, but the exact won't be known for another day or two.

The Cleveland Browns said they had 13 rookies and free agents on their squad and a team spokesman said counting those persons and veterans picked up in trades this year's team amounts to the "most sweeping change in our roster in one season."

Another team which said it had 13 rookies and free agents was New England, which on Wednesday waived veterans Ron Acks, a linebacker; tackle Rick Cash and punter Dave Lewis.

Oct. 31

Seattle, Tampa in NFL

Associated Press

NEW YORK—Representatives of the 26 NFL teams announced at their annual meeting yesterday that additional franchises will be awarded to Seattle and Tampa, Fla., in 1976.

It also was revealed that two additional franchises will be awarded, and these also could conceivably be in the league by 1976. Sites of these franchises are yet to be determined.

Sept. 23

Steelers 35, Broncos 35

DENVER (P) — "This game was destined to be a tie," Coach John Ralston said in the dressing room after his Denver Broncos played the Pittsburgh Steelers to a 35-35 standoff Sunday in the first regular season National Football League game to require an overtime session.

"**BOTH TEAMS** played their hearts out," Ralston added.

There was no scoring in the 15-minute sudden-death session. Denver's Jim Turner missed a 41-yard field goal attempt that would have won it late in the fifth period.

The Steelers also blew an opportunity to win as time expired in regulation play. Roy Gerela attempted a 25-yard field goal, but Denver's Barney Chavous and Bill Thompson blocked the try.

Brilliant Steeler quarterback Joe Gilliam engineered three scoring drives in the second half as the Steelers rallied from a two-touchdown deficit.

"They got off to a very fast start," said Steeler Coach Chuck Noll. "I was very proud of the way we came back after being down 21-7."

Ralston praised Gilliam, saying, "The way he played he shouldn't have lost it. He was always able to make the big plays. I don't know if I've ever seen better."

Denver's passing game was effective in the first quarter as the Broncos moved out to a 21-7 lead. Pittsburgh put together an 87-yard, 18-play drive in the second quarter, however, and Gilliam scored from the one-yard line to cut the deficit to 21-14 at the half.

The Steelers then turned a pair of interceptions into scores in the second half behind Gilliam's accurate throwing.

	Steelers	Broncos
First downs	33	20
Rushes-yards	40-160	37-156
Passing yards	324	176
Return yards	55	73
Passes	31-50-2	12-27-2
Punts	6-42	7-44
Fumbles-lost	3-2	1-1
Penalties-yards	12-91	7-61

Pittsburgh	7	7 14	7	0—35
Denver	21	0 7	7	0—35

Den—Armstrong 45 pass from Johnson (Turner kick)
Pit—St. Davis 61 pass from Gilliam (Gerela kick)
Den—Moses 7 pass from Johnson (Turner kick)
Den—Keyworth 1 run (Turner kick)
Pit—Gilliam 1 run (Gerela kick)
Pit—St. Davis 1 run (Gerela kick)
Den—Odoms 3 pass from Ramsey (Turner kick)
Pit—St. Davis 1 run (Gerela kick)
Pit—Fuqua 1 run (Gerela kick)
Den—Armstrong 23 pass from Ramsey (Turner kick)
A—51,706

INDIVIDUAL LEADERS
RUSHING—Pittsburgh, Harris 20-70, Pearson 8-47. Denver, Armstrong 19-131, Little 14-21.
RECEIVING—Pittsburgh, Harris 9-84, Lewis 5-65. Denver, Armstrong 5-86, Odoms 3-25.
PASSING—Pittsburgh, Gilliam, 31-50-2, 348 yards. Denver, Johnson 6-15-1, 129; Ramsey 6-12-1, 62.

Oct. 18

Rozelle on Stand In NFL-IRS Battle

ATLANTA, Ga. (AP) — Commissioner Pete Rozelle testified in federal court yesterday that a new National Football League franchise was worth $50,000 in 1966, and not $6.7 million as claimed at the U.S. government.

Rozelle said intense competition for players from the rival American Football League made a new NFL franchise a "high risk investment."

His testimony came on the fourth day of a trial of a suit involving the Atlanta Falcons who paid $8.5 million to join the NFL in 1966.

The Falcons paid the fee over five years and estimated the actual cost of the team at $7.7 million with $800,000 assigned to interest payments.

Of the $7.7 million, they said $50,000 represented the cost of entering the league and the remainder was the price for 42 football players chosen from the rosters of the 14 existing NFL teams.

The Falcons then claimed a $1.47 million deduction in each of their first two years of operation as a depreciation allowance for the wear and tear on their players.

The Internal Revenue Service, however, contended that only $1,050,000 of the original purchase price represented the value of the players and that the rest of the fee represented the charge for joining the NFL.

A minority stockholder filed a suit against the IRS challenging the IRS assessment.

If the IRS wins the case, it could lower the value of professional sports teams by closing a lucrative and frequently used tax shelter. Federal officials said it was the first time this tax shelter had been attacked by the IRS.

N.F.L. in Drug Inquiry

CINCINNATI, Oct. 30 (AP) — A National Football League spokesman said today that a routine league investigation had begun on the arrest of Mike Ernst, Cincinnati Bengals' reserve quarterback, on drug charges.

"It's normal procedure," said Joe Browne of the league office in New York. 'Any violation of law is investigated by our security department."

Ernst, 24 years old, was picked up Sunday night hours after the Bengals' 34-21 los to the Houston Oilers. He was charged with possession of a narcotic. The police said he was arrested after officers had seen him open a vial containing cocaine. The arrest occurred at 3 A.M. in Mount Adams, a popular night-club area.

He was waived by the Bengals on Monday.

The N.F.L. office said a private investigator had been asked for a report on the case.

Last spring the San Diego Charger club was fined $20,000 and eight players were fined $1,000 to $3,000 each for violation of the drug-abuse code.

Oct. 23

QB Trades

By The Associated Press

The National Football League played musical chairs — with quarterbacks.

By the time the game was over, four clubs had new quarterbacks.

The Los Angeles Rams had the biggest surprise Tuesday, final day for interclub trading — and got the biggest reward, five draft choices from the Green Bay Packers for John Hadl.

That's right, the Rams traded away John Hadl, the quarterback who made all pro after leading them to a 12-2 record last year. Hadl couldn't get the Los Angeles offense to move this year.

It meant that James Harris' promotion to starter is permanent. The 27-year-old black quarterback threw three touchdown passes last Sunday and got the Los Angeles offense cracking for the first time in 1974.

In the other deals involving quarterbacks, Craig Morton, the disenchanted Dallas Cowboy backup man, was sent to the New York Giants, who dealt journeyman veteran Norm Snead to the San Francisco 49ers, who then traded Joe Reed to the Detroit Lions.

The Cowboys swapped Morton to the Giants for a No. 1 draft pick in 1975, provided Morton doesn't jump to the World Football League, and Snead was sent from New York to the 49ers for two high draft picks, one in 1975 and the second in 1976.

Morton could play against the Cowboys on Sunday when the Giants entertain Dallas at New Haven, Conn.

Morton, as well as three of the other players involved in Tuesday's trading, has signed with the WFL.

Morton, however, says his contract with the WFL for the 1975 season is void because he had a no-move clause in his deal with the Houston Texans, who have now shifted to Shreveport, La.

The other WFL signees are Matuszak, Culp and Drougas.

Archie Manning, however, stayed with the New Orleans Saints, who apparently couldn't make the right deal for their quarterback by the 4 p.m., EDT, Tuesday trading deadline, even though he was benched last week. Manning had been on the trading block, reliable league sources reported.

In the day's other exchanges, defensive tackle Curley Culp and a 1975 No. 1 draft choice went from the Kansas City Chiefs to the Houston Oilers for defensive tackle John Matuszak and a No. 2 draft pick for 1976. Cornerback Jim Marsalis was dealt by the Chiefs to the Denver Broncos in exchange for tackle Tom Drougas and linebacker Tom Graham.

"John Hadl's experience, ability and leadership qualities should be of great value to the team," said Dan Devine, the Packer coach and general manager. Devine, however, indicated he still plans to start Jack Concannon on Sunday when the Packers play the Lions.

To get Hadl, the Packers agreed to give up their No. 1 and No. 2 draft picks for 1975 and 1976, plus a No. 3 pick for 1975.

Nov. 1

NFL bars signing of WFL stars

Nov. 4

Dallas Deals Cards First Setback, 17-14

DALLAS (AP) — The cliff-hanging odds finally turned on the St. Louis Cardinals Sunday.

St. Louis, owning the National Football League's only unblemished record, tumbled 17-1- to the Dallas Cowboys on Efren Herrera' 20-yard field goal with four seconds left.

The Cardinals had won seven consecutive games—five of them in the final minute— prompting Coach Don Coryell to say "Well, if we're not for real we're damn lucky and I'd rather be lucky than real."

Nov. 17

THOMAS FACES SALARY SUIT

WASHINGTON (AP) — The San Diego Chargers have filed suit against Washington running back Duane Thomas for $12,000 they say he owes them, presumably for salary advances in 1972, the Redskins confirmed yesterday.

The suit, filed in U.S. District Court here Oct. 21, asks that Thomas' salary be attached but, according to Redskins'' comptroller, Chester Minter, nothing has been deducted yet.

"We've got the papers and they're in the lawyers' hands," said George Allen, Redskins coach and general manager. "I don't even know if Duane knows about it. "They've still got to win the case, as far as I know." Allen said.

Van Brocklin Dismissed

ATLANTA, Nov. 5 (AP)— Norm Van Brocklin was dismissed as general manager and coach of the Atlanta Falcons today and replaced as coach by Marion Campbell, the team's defensive coordinator.

The Falcons' owner, Rankin Smith, announced the action in a brief statement.

Van Brocklin was in the midst of one of his most frustrating years since becoming head coach of the Falcons after the third game of the 1968 National Football League season. The team, picked in some preseason estimates as contender for the playoffs, has a won-lost record of 2-6.

Nov. 13

Ewbank to Quit At End of Year

NEW YORK (AP)—Weeb Ewbank, 67, announced his resignation yesterday as vice president and general manager of the National Football League's New York Jets effective at the end of the season.

Ewbank cited family considerations as his reason for leaving the sport.

Ewbank spent 20 seasons as a professional coach and stepped down from that job this year, passing the Jet post off to his son in law, Charley Winner.

As a coach Ewbank won three world championships and four divisional crowns and was the only man to coach championship teams in both the National and American Football Leagues.

Ewbank coached the Baltimore Colts to consecutive NFL titles in 1958 and 1959 and led the Jets to the 1968 Super Bowl championship, upsetting the Colts in the title game.

Nov. 11

Bengals Top Steelers

CINCINNATI (AP) — Ken Anderson completed 20 of 22 passes for 227 yards, then made a game-saving tackle to help the Cincinnati Bengals preserve a 17-10 National Football League victory Sunday that snapped the Pittsburgh Steelers' five-game winning streak.

The nationally televised game ended with the Steelers threatening on the Cincinnati 30-yard line, but Bengal linebacker Ron Pritchard upended quarterback Terry Bradshaw as time ran out.

Anderson completed 15 of his first 17 attempts, setting an NFL consecutive completion record of 16 over two games.

Final WFL Standings

	W	L	T	Pct.	PF	PA
EAST						
Florida	14	6	0	.700	419	280
Charlotte	10	10	0	.500	467	35C
Philadelphia	8	11	0	.421	491	413
x-Jacksonville	4	10	0	.286	258	358
CENTRAL						
v-Memphis	17	3	0	.850	629	36C
Birmingham	15	5	0	.750	500	394
Chicago	7	12	0	.368	446	600
x-Detroit	1	13	0	.071	209	358
WEST						
S. Calif	13	7	0	.650	486	341
Hawaiians	9	11	0	.450	413	422
Portland	7	12	0	.375	264	426
Sheveport	7	12	1	.375	240	415

x-Team disbanded.

Dec. 3

Colts Fly Back Home With Sigh of Relief

BALTIMORE (AP)—The Baltimore Colts, shaken by the fatal crash of a chartered jetliner that was to have picked them up in Buffalo, returned home Monday with a sigh of relief.

Barry Jones, a spokesman for the National Football League club, said the Colts' flight arrived at Baltimore-Washington International Airport shortly after 2 p.m., EST. There were no problems with the plane during the 1½-hour flight from Buffalo, he said.

"Everybody was very tense— there wasn't a sound during either the takeoff or landing," Jones said. "But as soon as we landed and the plane was sliding down the runoff, everybody gave a big cheer."

The Colts had been scheduled to leave Buffalo immediately after their 6-0 loss to the Bills Sunday, but their plane was unable to leave Detroit for Buffalo because of a snow storm.

The players and team officials returned to their motel while arrangements were made to get another plane from New York's Kennedy Airport.

That plane, a Northwest Orient 727, crashed about 20 miles north of Manhattan, killing the three crew members aboard.

Dec. 6

WFL Title

BIRMINGHAM, Ala. (AP) — Veteran George Mira drove Birmingham to three touchdowns in the second and third quarters, and the Americans barely withstood a fourth-quarter Florida rally to escape with a 22-21 victory and the World Football League's first World Bowl.

The margin of victory was a three-yard run by Birmingham rookie quarterback Matthew Reed which produced the game's only point after touchdown.

The WFL, with an uncertain future, attracted 32,376 to Birmingham's 70-000 seat Legion Field for its first championship game. The first championship game of the old American Football League 14 years ago, drew 32,183.

Mira was in complete control throughout the middle of the game, as he alternated four running backs and twice hit tight end Bob Brown with crucial passes in the three Americans' scoring drives.

But it almost faded away in the face of the last-gasp Florida rally.

Trailing 22-0 late in the third quarter, Florida quarterback Bob Davis completed his first pass of the night. It started an 88-yard drive that culminated on the first play of the fourth quarter when he hit Tommy Reamon with a 39-yard scoring strike.

Nov. 22

W.F.L.

MEMPHIS, Nov. 22 (AP)—Christopher B. Hemmeter, a co-owner of the Hawaiians, was named president of the World Football League today as the owners moved to shore up the league's crumbling financial foundation.

Hemmeter, a real estate developer, will administer all financial matters of the league. John Bassett, chairman of the executive committee, said that Hemmeter, with his reputation as a businessman, would give the W.F.L. "credibility in the financial community . . . which we haven't had up until now" and show that "we're responsible people."

Dec. 16

Herron Sets Yardage Mark

MIAMI (AP) — New England's Mack Herron put himself in the National Football League record book Sunday by gaining 185 yards against the Miami Dolphins, but he said "I would rather have had the win.

The Patriots blew a 24-0 lead and lost to the defending Super Bowl champions 34-27.

"This is a team sport. I'm for winning," said Herron, who set a standard for most total yards in a season with 2,444, four more than Chicago's Gale Sayers gained in 1966.

Dec. 25

Packers Name Starr

Dec. 28

Chiefs Fire Hank Stram; 'Fresh Approach' Sought

Dec. 21

NFL Reserve System Ruled Illegal
'Rozelle Rule,' College Draft Also Found in Violation

SAN FRANCISCO (AP) — The National Football League's reserve system, the method which binds a player to one team, was ruled illegal Friday by a federal judge in a decision which could shake the foundations of the sport.

U.S. District Court Judge William T. Sweigert also ruled that a portion of the NFL's college draft, its controversial "Rozelle Rule" and portions of its standard player contract were in violation of the nation's antitrust laws and therefore are illegal.

There was no immediate comment from the NFL, which is certain to appeal the decision that has the affect of making all players free agents one year after they complete their contractual obligation to a team.

The ruling came on a suit brought two years ago by former quarterback Joe Kapp, who quit pro football rather than sign the standard NFL contract which commits a player to the league's reserve system.

This is the system Kapp sought to upset:

A player is bound to his NFL team for the length of his contract and for one year thereafter. If he plays that extra year without signing a new contract, he may negotiate with another team. If he signs with another team, the new club must compensate the old one. If the two teams cannot agree on the compensation, which is usually a player of equal ability, it is decided by NFL Commissioner Pete Rozelle.

Because of this compensation factor, very few players have been able to negotiate contracts with other teams because those teams are leery of who they may have to give up.

Another portion of the reserve clause prohibits a college senior from negotiating with any NFL team except the one which selects him in a draft. Sweigert ruled that the portion of the NFL draft which prohibits a draftee from seeking a better contract than the one offered by the drafting team was illegal.

Sweigert also ruled that the "one man rule" making Rozelle the arbiter in many cases involving interpretation or enforcement of NFL rules "is patently unreasonable."

Vikings Whip Cards, 30-14

BLOOMINGTON, Minn. (AP) — Fran Tarkenton fired two touchdown passes to John Gilliam and cornerback Nate Wright scored with a fumble recovery, leading the Minnesota Vikings to a 30-14 victory over the St. Louis Cardinals in the first round of the National Football League playoffs Saturday.

Minnesota, which captured the National Conference's Central Division title with a 10-4 regular-season record, will host the winner of Sunday's Washington-Los Angeles game Dec. 29 for the NFC championship.

Minnesota scored 10 points in a 64-second span early in the third quarter to take command of the game, which was tied 7-7 at the half.

St. Louis	0 7 0 7—14
Minnesota	0 7 16 7—30

StL—Thomas 13 pass from Hart (Bakken kick)
Minn—Gilliam 16 pass from Tarkenton (Cox kick)
Minn—FG Cox 37
Minn—N. Wright 20 fumble return (Cox kick)
Minn—Gilliam 38 pass from Tarkenton (kick failed)
Minn—Foreman 4 run (Cox kick)
StL—Metcalf 11 run (Bakken kick)
A—44,626

Defense Stymies Redskins

LOS ANGELES (AP) — "George Allen always said that if you can get six turnovers in a game, you'll win it," Los Angeles' Merlin Olsen said of the former Rams' coach, now with the Washington Redskins.

"We got six today," said Olsen after the Rams defeated Allen's Redskins 19-10 to advance to the finals of the National Football League's National Conference. Los Angeles plays the Vikings as Minnesota next Sunday for the NFC crown with the winner earning a trip to New Orleans for Super Bowl IX.

The Rams intercepted three passes and recovered three Washington fumbles in Sunday's playoff game.

SCORING

Washington	3 7 0 0—10
Los Angeles	7 0 3 9—19

LA—Klein 10 pass from Harris (Ray kick)
Wash—FG Bragg 35
Wash—Denson 1 run (Bragg kick)
LA—FG Ray 37
LA—FG Ray 26
LA—Robertson 59 interception return (pass failed)

TD Pass Caps AFC Thriller

OAKLAND (AP) — Clarence Davis outwrestled a crowd of Miami defenders in the end zone and grabbed Ken Stabler's fourth touchdown pass of the game, an eight-yarder with 26 seconds remaining, giving the Oakland Raiders a heart-stopping 28-26 playoff victory that ended the Dolphins' two-year reign as National Football League champions.

The victory sent the Raiders, champions of the American Conference West with a 12-2 record—best in the league—into the Dec. 29 AFC title game here against the winner of Sunday's Buffalo-Pittsburgh game.

Davis' catch, climaxed a frantic 67-yard drive which began with two minutes left, just after rookie Benny Malone's brilliant sideline touchdown run had put Miami in front 26-21.

Scoring

Miami	7 3 6 10—26
Oakland	0 7 7 14—28

Mia—N. Moore 89 kickoff return (Yepremian kick)
Oak—C. Smith 31 pass from Stabler (Blanda kick)
Mia—FG Yepremian 33
Oak—Biletnikoff 13 pass from Stabler (Blanda kick)
Mia—Warfield 16 pass from Griese (kick failed)
Mia—FG Yepremian 46
Oak—Branch 71 pass from Stabler (Blanda kick)
Mia—Malone 22 run (Yepremian kick)
Oak—Davis 8 pass from Stabler (Blanda kick)
A—52,817

26-Point Spurt Ousts Buffalo

PITTSBURGH (AP) — Quarterback Terry Bradshaw, benched, booed and bewildered early this season, led a 26-point second-quarter spurt that enabled the Pittsburgh Steelers to whip the Buffalo Bills 32-14 on Sunday in their National Football League playoff game.

"The best game I've ever had in the pros," Bradshaw said calmly after Pittsburgh moved into next week's American Conference title game in Oakland against the Raiders.

Bradshaw, who charted plays the first six games of the season while Jefferson Street Joe Gilliam quarterbacked Pittsburgh, hit seven of nine passes in the second-quarter burst, which also included three touchdown plunges by Franco Harris.

SCORING

Buffalo	7 0 7 0	—14
Pittsburgh	3 26 0 3	—32

Pitt—FG Gerela 21
Buff—Seymour 22 pass from Ferguson (Leypoldt kick)
Pitt—Bleier 27 pass from Bradshaw (kick failed)
Pitt—Harris 1 run (Gerela kick)
Pitt—Harris 4 run (kick failed)
Pitt—Harris 1 run (Gerela kick)
Buff—Simpson 3 pass from Ferguson (Leypoldt kick)
Pitt—FG Gerela 22
A—48,321

Pittsburgh	0 3 0 21	—24
Oakland	3 0 7 3	—13

Oak—FG Blanda 40
Pitt—FG Gerela 23
Oak—Branch 38 pass from Stabler (Blanda kick)
Pitt—Harris 8 run (Gerela kick)
Pitt—Swann 6 pass from Bradshaw (Gerela kick)
Oak—FG Blanda 24
Pitt—Harris 21 run (Gerela kick)
A—53,515

Steelers' Defense

Steelers

OAKLAND (AP) — Art Rooney, one of the grand old men of pro football, stood in the chilly Oakland Coliseum, as expressionless as ever. After 42 years, he finally had a championship team.

And how did he plan to celebrate?

"The same way as I've celebrated losing," Rooney said with just a hint of a twinkle in his eyes. "In the old days, when we celebrated, we always had big times. But now...well, I took the pledge about 15 years ago."

Rooney, and the entire city of Pittsburgh, have plenty to celebrate. Their Steelers are in their first National Football League championship, an entry in Super Bowl IX following their 24-13 victory Sunday over the favored Oakland Raiders in the American Conference title game. Now, only one more barrier to the ultimate remains— the Minnesota Vikings.

OAKLAND (AP) — The Oakland Raiders' eight-day binge of joy was turned off by the Pittsburgh Steelers' front four.

"They stopped our running plays and that was it. They did what they had to do and we didn't," said Clarence Davis, after Sunday's 24-13 loss to Pittsburgh in the American Football Conference championship game.

"There was a lot of joy and humor in this locker room last week after the Miami game. Look at it now. It's somber, like a tomb," the Raiders' running back added.

Davis was the hero of the dramatic 28-26 National Football League playoff victory here over the defending Super Bowl champion Dolphins Dec. 21, catching a Ken Stabler touchdown pass with 26 seconds to go.

The Raiders, able to gain just 29 net rushing yards against the Steelers, were forced to throw 36 times. Even late in the game, though, they occasionally tried running plays.

Vikings Hold Off L.A.,14-10

BLOOMINGTON, Minn. (AP) — Because Los Angeles marched 98 yards from goal line to goal line without scoring, the Minnesota Vikings are on their way to Super Bowl IX following their 14-10 victory over the Rams in Sunday's National Football Conference championship game.

The victory sends Minnesota into Super Bowl IX at New Orleans Jan. 12 against the Pittsburgh Steelers, who beat the Oakland Raiders 24-13 later Sunday in the American Conference championship game.

A 29-yard touchdown catch by Jim Lash—the first score of his pro career, and a one-yard plunge by Dave Osborn gave the Vikings the points they needed, but it was the LA drive that didn't score that made the difference in this mistake-filled game.

"When they drove 98 yards and came away empty-handed it really made us feel good," said Viking Coach Bud Grant.

The Rams, trailing 7-3, started on their own one-yard line midway through the third period and had advanced to their 25 when James Harris called a pass play in the huddle.

"I saw Roy Winston blitzing," said the young Ram quarterback. "He was right on me, but I just tried the best I good to get away."

Harris slipped Winston's tackle and two others—by Jeff Siemon and Carl Eller—before firing for Harold Jackson.

"He was scrambling around, so I broke my pattern and ran to meet him," said Jackson, who grabbed the ball at midfield and headed for the goal line. He outran Nate Wright, but Jeff Wright caught him at the two.

The Rams had to settle for a 73-yard gain on the broken play. It looked like plenty when they moved the ball inside the one. But then an illegal procedure penalty on Tom Mack pushed them back to the six.

"Our offensive line said there was no movement," said Rams Coach Chuck Knox. "Tom says he did not move."

The official said he did. And it cost the Rams five important yards.

Harris got four of them back on a keeper, giving Los Angeles a third and goal from the two. This time Harris called an option play on which he could either pass or run. He rolled right, looking for Pat Curran.

"I saw Jackie Wallace, but I didn't think he could get turned around and reach the ball," said Harris. Wallace reached it just enough to tip it. When the ball came down, it settled into the arms of linebacker Wally Hilgenberg.

When he grabbed the ball, Hilgenberg dropped to his knees, downing it for a touchback and giving Minnesota the ball at the 20.

Los Angeles	0 3 0 7	—10
Minnesota	0 7 0 7	—14

Min—Lash 29 pass from Tarkenton (Cox kick)
LA—FG Ray 27
Min—Osborn 1 run (Cox kick)
LA—Jackson 44 pass from Harris (Ray kick)
A—47,404

	Steelers	Raiders
First downs	20	15
Rushes-yards	50-224	21-29
Passing yards	81	249
Return yards	101	37
Passes	8-17-1	19-36-
Punts	4-41	5-43
Fumbles-lost	3-2	0-0
Penalties-yards	3-2	5-60

INDIVIDUAL LEADERS

RUSHING—Pittsburgh, Harris 29-111 Bleier 18-98, Bradshaw 3-15. Oakland, C Davis 10-16, Banaszak 3-7, Hubbard 7-7.
RECEIVING—Pittsburgh, L. Brown 2 37, Bleier 2-25, Swann 2-17, Stallworth 2 16. Oakland, Branch, 9-186, Moore 4-32. Biletnikoff 3-45, C. Davis 2-8.
PASSING—Pittsburgh, Bradshaw 8-17-1, 95 yards. Stabler 19-36-3, 271.

	Rams	Vikng:
First Downs	15	18
Rushes-yards	33-121	47-164
Passing yards	219	105
Return yards	76	120
Passes	13-23-2	10-20-1
Punts	5-44	6-39
Fumbles-lost	3-3	5-3
Penalties-yards	7-70	2-20

INDIVIDUAL LEADERS

RUSHING—Los Angles, Bertelsen 15-70. McCutcheon 11-27. Minnesota, Foreman 22-31. Osborn 20-76.
RECEIVING—Los Angeles. Jackson 3-139, Bertelsen 5-53, McCutcheon 2-22. Minnesota, Voigt 4-43. Lash 2-40. Gilliam 2-33.
PASSING—Los Angeles, Harris 13-23-2, 248 yards. Minnesota, Tarkenton, 10-20-1, 123.

Super Bowl IX Steelers Win

Defense Bottles Up Vikings

Super Win Sparks Super Celebration

PITTSBURGH (AP) — Police arrested more than 115 persons as thousands of jubilant fans braved a wet snowfall and subfreezing temperatures Sunday night to throng to downtown Pittsburgh and celebrate the Steelers' first National Football League championship in 42 years.

Police also said a number of persons, including one police officer, were treated at city hospitals, but none was injured seriously. There had been scattered reports of cans, bottles and snowballs being thrown at police.

Police used dogs at one or two particular trouble spots and elsewhere were equipped with hard hats and nightsticks.

The crowd swelled quickly after the Steelers 16-6 victory over the Minnesota Vikings in Super Bowl IX. Pedestrians, dancing in the street and chanting "We're No. 1" or "Deefense, deefense," quickly tied up traffic on the narrow downtown streets.

Most of the arrests were for disorderly conduct and intoxication, police said, and they were held at various city precincts.

Patrolman J.C. Schaff at the downtown precinct said the arrests included one for resisting arrest, one for a drug violation and two for aggravated assault.

Police halted traffic on bridges leading into downtown and began diverting cars away from areas where pedestrians were blocking the streets.

About an hour and a quarter after it all began, a solid line of officers formed in front of a squadron of police vehicles and began sweeping up and down Liberty Avenue, their night-sticks held in front of them, in an attempt to disperse the crowds.

Youngsters poured back into the streets after the officers had passed.

On-street parking was banned in most of the downtown district and city and county police assigned 400 men to keep traffic moving and prevent disturbances.

NEW ORLEANS (AP) — Coach Chuck Noll had a word of encouragement Monday for those National Football League teams which envy his Super Bowl champion Pittsburgh Steelers.

"There isn't a great deal of difference between teams on the bottom and teams on top," said Noll in the wake of his club's 16-6 victory over the Minnesota Vikings. "With us, I think it is desire and the mental aspects of our football team."

Noll said the Steelers had been frustrated with their playoff failures in 1972 and 1973. "They came in this year and they weren't going to be denied. Our team played the best it ever played in the three playoff games against Buffalo, Oakland and Minnesota."

The Steelers did it with defense—a devastating rush led by Mean Joe Greene that held Minnesota to an unbelievable 17 yards rushing. Greene and Ernie Holmes handled the inside rush. On the outside it was L.C. Greenwood, who deflected three passes by Fran Tarkenton, and Dwight White, who spent most of last week in the hospital.

"That Greene," said Noll, obviously marveling over his performance. "To do something like this, you have to have somebody like him. He gets off the ball so quickly. He's moving right with the ball. He doesn't go around people, he goes through people."

Then Noll paused for a moment, reflecting on the devastating rush that Greene led which pressured Tarkenton throughout Super Bowl IX and completely stopped Minnesota's ground game.

"In these playoffs," Noll said, "Joe Greene was the best defensive tackle—no, the best defensive lineman—I ever saw."

Plunkett

SAN JOSE, Calif. (AP) — Quarterback Jim Plunkett said Friday he has undergone knee surgery, the third such operation since he joined the New England Patriots of the National Football League.

Plunkett, 27, said at his home here that the most recent operation involved the removal of cartilage from his right knee.

"The doctor told me the operation was successful," he said. "There wasn't any further damage to the knee.

NLRB rules NFL player fines must be returned

Minneapolis (P)—The National Football League Players Association feels a ruling Monday by the National Labor Relations Board that the NFL must return more than $0,000 in fines to players is a good sign.

The NLRB said the league must reimburse 106 player who were fined $200 each for leaving the bench area during fights on the field. The fines were levied under a rule instituted by the league March 25, 1971.

"This rule and all sorts of other rules that try to regulate player conduct are proper matters for negotiation," said player association executive director Ed Garvey.

"In effect, the NLRB told the owners they have to deal with the union. That's a good sign.

"This is also the first time an unfair labor practice charge has been taken to its conclusion against any professional sport by athletes."

The rule called for an automatic $200 fine for any player leaving the bench area while a fight was in progress on the field.

The 106 fines all stemmed from fights in three games during 1971—Minnesota against San Diego in the preseason, and Atlanta against San Francisco and Chicago against New Orleans in the regular season.

The decision affects only players fined until November 6, 1972, because at that time NFL Commissioner Pete Rozelle instituted another bench fine rule.

The rule is virtually the same as the earlier one, except the 1972 rule was instituted by the commissioner rather than the owners.

The NLRB ruling was limited to the owner instituted regulation.

Weiss said, "We're pleased the board has upheld the commissioner's right to fine, and he will be able to continue to effectively control conduct on the playing field."

Bears draw NFL penalty

Chicago (P) — Commissioner Pete Rozelle of the National Football League has ruled the Chicago Bears must forfeit a sixth-round 1976 draft pick for violation of the league's embargo on attempting to sign World Football League players.

The disclosure yesterday by Jim Finks, general manager of the Bears, followed a published report that new Bear coach Jack Pardee had been reprimanded by Rozelle for purportedly negotiating with six players he coached last season with the WFL's Florida Blazers.

Finks, asserting that he instead of Pardee was involved in the matter, said, "Our anticipation that the embargo would be lifted sooner was incorrect. We were guilty of the violation and agree completely with the commissioner's action.

Palmer invests in WFL Hornets

Charlotte, N.C. (P)—Professional golfer Arnold Palmer has invested a substantial amount into the Charlotte Hornets' franchise of the World Football League, Hornet president Upton Bell announced yesterday.

Bell declined to disclose the exact amount of Palmer's investment at an afternoon news conference, but said it was enough to qualify him for membership in the Hornets' "300 Club."

An investment of $5,000 in stock is required for membership in the 300 club, Bell said.

Seized pacts ruled worthless

Birmingham, Ala. (P) — A judge said yesterday that the contracts of the World Football League Birmingham Americans which the Internal Revenue Service put up for sale this week are worthless.

The IRS, trying to recoup more than $200,000 in federal taxes, seized 59 players' contracts and began advertising them Tuesday.

So far there are no takers.

Alabama circuit court judge William Barber said he certainly would not buy one. He is the judge who ruled that Ken Stabler's contract with Birmingham was void for nonpayment of bonus money.

He said the contracts are personal and cannot be sold or assigned to someone else when they have been broken.

Judge cuts tax writeoff

Falcon-player depreciation held too great

From Wire Services

Atlanta—A federal court judge yesterday ruled that owners of the Atlanta Falcons had claimed more than twice the income tax depreciation allowance than they were entitled to upon purchasing the National Football League franchise for $8.5 million.

Ruling in a case that Rankin Smith, the principal owner of the Falcons acknowledged was "a landmark" for professional sports, Judge Frank Hooper found that the owners were entitled to claim depreciation for tax purposes against the value of the team's players, but he sharply reduced the amount the owners had originally attributed to the players.

The group that bought the Falcon franchise in 1966 had assigned well over $7 million of the original purchase price to players and depreciated that amount over a five-year period, throwing the club into a net loss, meaning they paid no taxes and could claim the loss on their own tax returns.

Judge Hooper ruled yesterday that only $3 million of the value could be assigned to the players, that about $4.3 million of the purchase price was attributable to the value of television rights, which now amount to $2 million annually for each NFL team.

March 24

Players fault NFL owners

Washington (P)—The National Football League Players Association criticized the NFL owners yesterday for refusing to make payments to the players' pension fund this year.

Ed Garvey, the NFLPA's executive director, also said the players are ready to begin negotiations on a new contract immediately, adding there is no need to wait until mid-April, as suggested by the NFL Management Council during the owners' meeting in Honolulu last week.

Garvey, out of town most of last week, made his comments in a statement after reading the comments made by the owners and the Management Council.

He charged that the owners have reneged on their word that the money from the annual Pro Bowl would go into the player pension fund.

"The owners have claimed for years, and again this year, that the Pro Bowl is played for the benefit of the players' pension fund," Garvey said. "The players performed in the 1975 Pro Bowl.

"Then on February 19, during a bargaining session, the Management Council said the proceeds this year will not go to the player pension fund. Last year they cut off all of our health and accident insurance. This year they begin the bargaining process by cutting off future pension, disability and widows' benefits.

"The players performed all year without a contract and we do not think it too much to ask the clubs to continue the pension program which has been in effect since 1963," Garvey said.

The contribution was to be $163,000 a club, or some $4.2 million, Garvey said.

On the final day of their meeting last week, the owners said the payments to the fund, normally made annually on March 31, will not be made this year until agreement is reached in collective bargaining.

The last payment was $4,425,000 on March 31, 1974, but no contract was agreed upon last year when the players went on strike and a stalemate developed in negotiations.

Eventually, a truce was declared and the players reported to their clubs following the second preseason game.

April 17

Reorganized WFL claims it is set to go

New York (P)—Pledging honesty and credibility a new World Football League emerged yesterday to announce it would field at east 10 teams in 1975 and to promise that its past problems would be rectified and never repeated.

League president Chris Hemmeter, admitting the WFL has been the "biggest sports disaster in history," said a new corporation by the same name as last year's collection of broken promises had been formed to play a 20-game schedule this summer and fall.

Hemmeter, who drew up the complicated financing formula under which league teams must place in escrowed bank accounts all anticipated operating expenses, pledged that past and future debts would be paid.

And he said franchises in Honolulu, Anaheim. Calit.; Shreveport, La.; Charlotte, N.C.; San Antonio, Memphis, Chicago, Philadelphia, Birmingham, Ala.; and Jacksonville, Fla., had met all his requirements and would field teams this year.

That gives the league 10 teams, and Hemmeter has given potential franchise holders in Portland, Ore., two weeks to produce enough money to make theirs the 11th WFL team.

When that issue is decided, he league will announce a 22-game schedule—2 of which will be exhibitions. Games will be played on weekends beginning in late July, with the possibility of some television games being played in the middle of the week.

May 29

WFL proposal

Los Angeles (AP)—The World Football League has filed a bankruptcy petition for the purpose of paying off its 1974 creditors, an official of the WFL said yesterday.

Ted Palmquist, the administrative vice president of the WFL last year, disclosed in an interview that league president Chris Hemmeter had made a proposal that was intended to satisfy all creditors. The plan was mailed last week to many persons owed money from the old WFL.

He said creditors are to vote Wednesday on whether to accept the plan.

Technically, the old WFL filed a bankruptcy petition last April 25, changing the name of the company to Football Creditors Payment Plan, Inc. A federal district court spokesman said the Chapter 11 petition was filed for the purpose of arranging payment to creditors.

May 22

Davis signs with WFL Sun

Anaheim (AP) — All-American running back Anthony Davis, the all time rushing leader at the University of Southern California, has signed a $2 million multi-year contract with the World Football League's Southern California Sun, it was announced yesterday.

May 2

Redskins force Jurgensen to retire

Washington (AP)—A reluctant and sometimes bitter Sonny Jurgensen retired from the Washington Redskins yesterday, after 18 years as one of the premier passers in the National Football League.

"It's kind of disappointing to retire this way," said the 40-year-old Jurgensen, who holds a number of NFL passing records. "I feel that I could still make a contribution. I believe I can still help someone win."

Jurgensen claimed coach George Allen said he did not fit into the Washington Redskins' future during a meeting between the two.

"He has to judge what talent the people who play for him have," said Jurgensen at a jam packed news conference in a downtown restaurant. "It's just unfortunate that I'm no longer in the picture at 41. I thought I would make that decision myself."

May 22

Namath declines WFL bid

Calls reasons 'personal and private'

New York (AP)—The Joe Namath-World Football League sweepstakes ended yesterday when Namath turned down a $4 million offer to play with the WFL's Chicago entry.

"After considerable deliberation, and with every wish that the World Football League prove a successful league, Joe Namath respectfully declines the offer from the Chicago Winds football team for reasons which are personal and private," Namath said in a statement.

The statement was released in New York by a spokesman for Jimmy Walsh, Namath's longtime attorney, who was reported to be with Namath in Fort Lauderdale, Fla.

The WFL, believing that Namath would provide it with instant credibility, had put together the $4 million bid to lure him away from the established National Football League.

Broken down, the WFL offer to Namath included a $500,000 signing bonus and a three-year playing contract for $500,000 a year. After that, Namath could retire from the playing field and take down a tidy little pension of $100,000 annually for 20 years. Partial ownership in a future New York WFL franchise also was mentioned. Pullano even hired one of Namath's longtime NFL buddies, Babe Parilli, to coach the team.

June 30

NFL says it will have '75 rosters of 43 men

New York (AP)— The assistant director of the National Football League's Management Council, reacting to NFL Players Association criticism because of the owners' plan to reduce rosters, said yesterday that there will be more players in uniform next season than in any year except 1974.

Terry Bledsoe responded to charges by Ed Garvey, executive director of the players association, and maintained that the 47-man rosters last season was a special response to a special circumstance—the players strike.

In 1973, roster size was 40 players a team, plus 7 taxi-squad members, players who are on the roster but are not activated at game time. In 1974, because of the strike, 47 players were in uniform at game time.

However, the owners announced Friday that the player limit for 1975 would be 43 players and there would be no taxi-squad members.

Bledsoe said the 43 uniformed players represented the second highest total ever, although he admitted there would be fewer total players being paid salaries than previous years.

Bledsoe also denied any illegal action on the part of the owners, as charged by Garvey.

"When the clubs adopted this thing," Bledsoe said, "they clearly made it contingent on bargaining with the union. They specifically instructed contact with the union and satisfaction of all labor laws."

Bledsoe said the management council will formally inform the players association today of the owners' action.

"You can't assume this thing is in its final form," Bledsoe said. "We're going to bargain formally for it."

July 12

Rozelle completes NFL case

Minneapolis (AP)—The future of most teams in the National Football League depends on keeping players tightly knit to their clubs, NFL Commissioner Pete Rozelle indicated in federal court testimony yesterday.

While Rozelle did not concede there is any attempt by owners to boycott players who want to jump to new teams, he said there is a no-tampering "policy" with the Canadian Football League, and said owners in the past felt there was a "taint" in signing a player from another club.

The league rested its case after Rozelle's testimony on the 49th day of the trial, which involves an antitrust suit by 15 players against the Rozelle Rule.

The rule allows the league commissioner to award players or draft choices to a team which loses one of its players to another team. Players theoretically are free to sign after playing an option year beyond their contract, but contend their freedom is curtailed, because compensation must be paid by a club that signs them.

In respect to the Canadian league, Rozelle said: "There is a loose understanding that we will respect each other's contracts."

He called it a "policy" that does not allow NFL teams to bid for players still under contract in Canada.

The Rozelle rule was adopted in 1963, and has been used only four times, he said.

June 10

NFL named in NLRB complaint

New York (AP) — Fifteen charges of unfair labor practices against the National Football League in dealings with its players' union were issued yesterday in a complaint filed by the National Labor Relations Board.

NLRB regional director Sidney Danielson, ruling on 32 charges filed during last summer's strike by the players' union, said 15 of those charges have merit. He ordered a hearing on them before an administrative law judge on July 22 in New York.

Danielson rejected 17 unfair labor practice charges made by the union, the NFL Players' Association. But he found merit in 15 of them. Among them are:

• That the NFL and its clubs instituted a 15-minute overtime period and a change in the punt rule "unilaterally without giving the players' association a chance to bargain about the changes."

• That union officials Bill Curry, Kermit Alexander, Tom Keating and Ken Reaves were cut, waived or traded by their teams because of their union activity.

• That the Miami Dolphins demanded that players Manny Fernandez and Bill Stanfill, "by reason of their participation in the strike ... return to the Dolphins the bonus paid for signing a standard player contract."

• That the Kansas City Chiefs, St. Louis Cardinals and Dallas Cowboys placed meetings between the union and non-striking players under surveillance, that the Chiefs denied the union access to nonstriking players, and that the Houston Oilers threatened its employes with fines and suspensions and other reprisals.

• That the league increased pay for pre-season games for veterans as a means of breaking the strike.

• That the union was denied access to management information on such things as fines, injuries, stadium rent and retired players.

July 24

Tunnell, ex-Giant great, dies

Pleasantville, N.Y. (AP) —Emlen Tunnell, one of the National Football League's all-time great defensive backs and its first black coach, is dead at the age of 50.

Named to pro football's Hall of Fame in 1967, the durable defensive ace, who played 11 years with the New York Giants and three with the Green Bay Packers, was stricken at the Giants' preseason training camp at Pace University. He died in the dormitory shortly before midnight Tuesday.

Tunnell apparently suffered a heart attack. He had had a mild heart attack last October.

Tunnell was one of the scouts attending the workouts. A graduate of the University of Iowa, he had joined the Giants in 1948 to become a member of coach Steve Owen's famed "umbrella defense."

He played with the Giants through 1958, setting all-time league records for pass interceptions and punt returns, and closed out his career under the late Vince Lombardi of the Green Bay Packers in 1959-1961.

He served both the Giants and Packers as a scout, centering his attention principally on the predominantly black colleges in the South, before being named an assistant coach with the Giants in 1963.

At the time, coach Allie Sherman of the Giants said Tunnell's wide experience as a player and his inside knowledge of the pro game were "invaluable."

July 16

Economist says NFL puts profit foremost

Minneapolis (AP)—National Football League club owners place the profit motive ahead of their desire for a winning club, economist Dr. Roger G. Noll testified yesterday.

Noll, a California Institute of Technology professor who has researched sports as a business for several years, took the witness stand for a second day in the Rozelle Rule suit in United States District Court.

Fifteen current or former players seek to eliminate the rule, claiming it infringes on players' freedom to move to other teams in violation of federal antitrust laws.

Under lengthy cross-examination by defense attorney James McKay, Noll was asked, "Do you believe owners seek to maximize the team victories?"

"No, I don't," replied Noll, adding, "I think they attempt to win as many games as they possibly can, provided they've solved their economic problems."

While describing pro football as profit-oriented, the witness conceded that competitive balance touted by club and NFL officials has safeguarded the game from the pitfalls of some pro hockey and basketball teams.

"I have said the revenue-sharing arrangements in the NFL are by far the best of all professional sports, and I think that's a precedent other sports should follow," Noll testified.

He said that without competitive balance, "players' salaries probably would suffer, but a few would benefit."

On direct examination Monday, he told Judge Earl Larson that elimination of the Rozelle Rule would not weaken the NFL, as some defense witnesses warned. But Noll said it probably would free the players to bargain pay hikes of as much as 50 to 100 per cent or more.

The NFL Players Association says a player survey showed base pay of $34,000 last season. Noll testified National Hockey League players' average pay went up from $27,000 to $48,000 the first year the World Hockey Association gave the NHL competition.

July 16

Namath's $5 million Faberge pact

New York (AP)—Joe Namath believes he can have his $5 million for making people want to smell sweet and play football, too.

"I would like to play football two more years," the charismatic 32-year-old quarterback said yesterday after signing a 20-year contract at $250,000 a year with an international fragrance and cosmetics company.

July 24

Owners present proposal

Both sides study offers in NFL talks

Washington (AP)—A proposal and a counter-proposal were made by the National Football League owners and the players' union yesterday during negotiations over a new collective bargaining agreement.

No details were made public for either proposal in the 1½-year dispute which triggered a strike by the players last summer.

The union made its offer late yesterday afternoon after returning to the bargaining table following lunch and a review of the proposal made by the NFL Management Council, the owners' agent, in the first joint session between the two in three months.

"They are now reviewing and studying the offer," said James F. Searce, deputy director of the federal mediation office under whose auspices the negotiations are being held.

The two sides had recessed earlier yesterday after the owners made their offer so that the NFL Players Association could study it.

"I don't know what's in it myself," said Scearce as the two sides broke for lunch. "But we're here to negotiate. We purposely picked the time [Wednesday] to allow the parties as long as possible."

"We are going to press as hard as we can," he said. "We think the timing is right."

Ed Garvey, executive director of the players association, had said before the Wednesday session that if the owners did not place an offer on the table, the meeting would be a short one.

The players' union went on strike for 42 days last year over what they called the "freedom issues" but returned and played the 1974 season without a collective bargaining agreement. The old one expired March 31, 1974.

Aug. 2

Rozelle concedes on Bryant

New York (AP)—Pete Rozelle, the National Football League commissioner, facing another legal battle on NFL policies that bind a player to a single team, announced yesterday that he had canceled the disputed order that had sought to send Cullen Bryant of the Los Angeles Rams to the Detroit Lions.

Bryant, a veteran running back who had won a preliminary restraining order in his attempt to stay with the Rams, was to have gone to Detroit as compensation for the Rams' signing of Ron Jessie, a free agent.

But, yesterday afternoon, Rozelle reversed himself, announcing that the Lions would now receive a first-round choice in the 1976 draft and that Bryant would remain with the Rams.

At issue is the Rozelle Rule, the device that the NFL uses to compensate a team when it loses an athlete who plays out the option on his contract and signs with another club.

Jessie, a wide receiver, played out his option in Detroit and signed with the Rams. When the two clubs were unable to agree on compensation, Rozelle stepped in and announced that Bryant, 24, would go to Detroit.

But Bryant immediately went to court, filing the third current legal challenge to the Rozelle Rule. A federal judge said the rule was illegal, then issued a temporary restraining order and scheduled a hearing for August 12 on a preliminary injunction.

At that time, the NFL said it would fight the case, but Rozelle, in a statement released by his office yesterday, said Detroit no longer wanted Bryant and that the club would instead receive a first-round draft choice.

Rules Changes Slated by NFL In '75 Season

For the record, here are the rules changes and interpretations adopted during the NFL annual meeting in Honolulu this spring:

• Further standardized markings of playing field by requiring that end zone marking and club identification at the 50-yard line must be approved by the commissioner so as not to cause any confusion as to delineation of goal lines, side lines and end lines. In addition, pylons will replace flags for goal line and end line markings, chain crews will be uniformly attired, ball boys will be clearly identifiable, and all clubs must use standard sideline markers.

* Directed officials to interpret current unsportsmanlike language in Rule 12, Section 2, Article 15 (e) as covering any lingering by players leaving the field when being substituted for. Current language reads: "Using entering substitutes, legally returning players, substitutes on sidelines or withdrawn players to confuse opponents."

(Note: This does not represent a change as such, but broadens the interpretation of existing language in the rule book to prohibit the coaching of multiple substitution in a manner designed to deceive.)

• Provides that a team may use a double shift on or inside the opponent's 20-yard-line after it has been shown at least three times previously in the game. In the past, team could not use double shift at or inside 20 unless it was shown at least three times in a quarter.

• Any fourth down pass that is incomplete in or through the end zone when the line of scrimmage is inside the 20 will result in the opponent taking possession at the previous line of scrimmage. In the past, such incomplete pass resulted in a touchback with the opponent taking possession at the 20.

• When there are penalties on each team on the same play and one results in disqualification, the penalties will be offsetting but the disqualification will stand. In the past the penalty involving disqualification took precedence and both 15 yards and disqualification were required while the other team was not penalized.

• Penalty for an ineligible player downfield on a forward pass play reduced from 15 to 10 yards.

• Penalty for offensive pass interference reduced from 15 to 10 yards.

• In the case of defensive holding or illegal use of hands, the penalty will be assessed from the previous line of scrimmage rather than from the spot where the ball is blown dead if that spot is behind the line of scrimmage.

Reprinted from
pro football weekly

Aug. 16

Cowboys' Garrison retires

Dallas (AP)—Walt Garrison, the No. 3 all-time rusher for the Dallas Cowboys, retired from professional football yesterday because of an injury he received in June while pursuing his off-season career as a rodeo cowboy.

Garrison, 31, told Dallas coach Tom Landry Thursday night that he felt it was time to quit. He had torn ligaments in his left knee in Bozeman, Mont., while bulldogging a steer.

"The thing we'll miss most is that Garrison was part of the great tradition of the Cowboys of the last 10 years," said Landry. "A great football player. He did more with limited size, speed and quickness than anybody I've ever seen."

Robert Newhouse, a fourth-year player from the University of Houston, moved into the No. 1 fullback spot for the Cowboys.

The 6-foot, 205-pound Garrison became the second member of the club's 1971 Super Bowl champion team to retire in the past month. Bob Lilly retired because of neck injuries after an All-Pro career at defensive tackle.

Garrison underwent surgery June 21 and it would have been at least three months before he could have played.

The former Oklahoma State University star also was a respected pass receiver, ranking fourth on Dallas's all-time list.

Garrison had considered the retirement decision for weeks before talking to Landry.

"Walt felt it would be best if he bowed out now," said Landry. "He didn't want to hang around unless he could contribute."

Garrison never rushed for a 1,000 yards in a season, but he averaged 4.3 yards a carry and scored 39 touchdowns, including nine on passes. His longest touchdown run was only 41 yards, but it often took several tacklers to bring him down. He also was an accomplished blocker.

Sept. 4

Oakland Raider, Jim Otto, wipes away a tear as he announces his retirement today. The 37-year-old Otto, who has started at center at all 210 regular season games since the formation of the Raiders in 1960, will become business manager of the team.

Sept. 3

World Football League expels Chicago Winds

New York (AP)—The World Football League yesterday revoked the franchise of the Chicago Winds, reducing league membership to 10 teams.

President Chris Hemmeter announced the move at the WFL's offices, saying that commitments by the Chicago investor group concerning minimum capital requirements had not been fulfilled.

Hemmeter said the expulsion move was approved by the WFL's Board of Governors, who rejected a Chicago appeal to continue in the league. The vote was 10-1 with only the Winds voting to remain in the league.

The Chicago players were dispersed through a draft to the remaining teams. Wide receiver John Gilliam, the only Winds' player with a no-trade contract, was moved to the Philadelphia Bell after league officials had consulted with his attorney. The Bell also got quarterback Pete Beathard, an-other of the Winds' no-cut players. Running back Mark Keller and defensive end Larry Jameson, the other no-cuts, were claimed by the San Antonio Wings.

Hemmeter said that all player contracts and other financial responsibilities would be fulfilled. He said the WFL had deposited "about $125,000," in league funds to satisfy refund claims from the 1,600 season ticket holders and any other debts.

The Chicago club's problem was in its basic internal structure, according to Hemmeter. Because of continuing problems in finalizing partnership documents, two of the club's backers turned their investments of $175,000 over to the league to hold pending finalization of the Winds' internal structure.

When there were continued delays in the partnership arrangements, those two investors asked the WFL to return their money and pulled out. The Chicago club then asked for time to find substitute investors but the WFL refused, revoking the franchise instead.

Sept. 11

Players reject NFL bid

Vote against contract offer is 743 to 6

Washington (AP)—By an overwhelming vote, the rank and file of the National Football League Players Association has rejected a management offer for a new contract with the opening of the season less than two weeks away.

Ed Garvey, association executive director, said yesterday that the voting members of the association rejected the collective bargaining agreement proposal by a tally of 743 to 6, with five teams still to be counted.

Garvey declined to speculate on the possibility of a strike by the union, but said the membership would be asked to vote on the issue within a week.

"We will have to see what the players say about it," he said. "The comments insofar as a strike have varied team from team. Some are militant, while others are conservative.

"We hope that this vote will convince all 26 owners to get involved in the bargaining process . . . and give us an offer we can't refuse," he said.

The contract vote was taken during the past weekend in an effort to break the deadlock between the union and management in negotiations that have dragged on for more than a year and led to a 42-day strike during last year's exhibition season. The players returned to camp and played the 1974 season without a collective bargaining agreement.

Sept. 13

WFL lowers minimum

New York (AP)—The World Football League, in an unannounced action taken a month ago, lowered its minimum salary for players from $500 to $250 a game.

The league has also put into force a rule which prohibits any club from signing a player to a fixed salary contract without specific approval of WFL headquarters.

The minimum salary change, decided upon by the WFL on August 14, affects only those players signed after that date. A player signed after August 14 is generally entitled to one per cent of the team's revenues from any single game and will be guaranteed at least $250 if the one per cent does not amount to that much.

Sources confirmed that any player who signed a renegotiated contact after August 14 could have been forced to accept the $250 minimum contract. Players who signed a contract before August 14 and who have not renegotiated it since, still are subject to the $500 minimum salary which the league announced earlier this year

Patriots strike

5 striking teams agree to play in NFL openers

NFL players reject pact offer overwhelmingly

Nov. 1

McKay to coach NFL team

Tampa, Fla. (AP)—John McKay, one of college football's most successful and gregarious coaches for the past 15 years while at the University of Southern California, announced yesterday that he will join the pros next year—the National Football League's new Tampa franchise.

"I'm tickled you picked me," McKay said on a telephone hook-up from Los Angeles to the Tampa Bay Buccaneers owner, Hugh Culverhouse.

Sept. 26

NFL vote team by team

By The Associated Press

A list of the 26 National Football League teams and their votes on the new NFL Management Council contract proposal (exact vote count given where available):

NATIONAL CONFERENCE
Eastern Division
DALLAS: NO VOTE.
N.Y. GIANTS: NO VOTE.
PHILADELPHIA: 24 to 18 to reject.
ST. LOUIS: Majority to reject.
WASHINGTON: 43 to 0 to reject.
Central Division
CHICAGO: 41 to 0 to reject.
DETROIT: 27 to 15 to reject.
GREEN BAY: Nearly unanimous to reject.
MINNESOTA: NO VOTE.
Western Division
ATLANTA: Nearly unanimous to reject.
LOS ANGELES: NO VOTE.
NEW ORLEANS: 43 to 0 to reject.
SAN FRANCISCO: 43 to 0 to reject.
AMERICAN CONFERENCE
Eastern Division
BALTIMORE: NO VOTE.
BUFFALO: 43 to 0 to reject.
MIAMI: 30 to 5 to reject.
NEW ENGLAND: 47 to 0 to reject.
N.Y. JETS: NO VOTE.
Central Division
CINCINNATI: 26 to 13 to accept.
CLEVELAND: 30 to 11 to reject.
HOUSTON: 43 to 0 to reject.
PITTSBURGH: NO VOTE.
Western Division
DENVER: NO VOTE.
KANSAS CITY: 43 to 0 to reject.
OAKLAND: 43 to 0 to reject.
SAN DIEGO: NO VOTE.

Sept. 16

Players warned

Los Angeles (AP)—Owner Carroll Rosenbloom of the Los Angeles Rams said yesterday that if his National Football League club votes to strike, he will call a halt to the Rams' season.

"I believe our club is made up of mature people and would not be a party to such a thing," Rosenbloom said. "If this were not the case, there would be no choice but to folding up for the year."

The New England Patriots went on strike Saturday, bringing a cancellation of their exhibition game against the New York Jets. The Rams are scheduled to open their season Sunday against Dallas.

"I am in favor of the players having a strong association with responsible leadership, but for a team to do what the Patriots did is a disgrace," said Rosenbloom, who controlled the Baltimore Colts before exchanging that franchise to get the Rams.

Sept. 28

Simpson romps, Bills win

Pittsburgh (AP)—O.J. Simpson rushed for 227 yards, including an 88-yard touchdown sprint, and Buffalo's defense turned a bizarre Terry Bradshaw fumble into a touchdown to spark the Bills to a 30-to-21 victory over the Pittsburgh Steelers yesterday in a National Football League game.

The Steelers were bunched at the Bills' 12-yard line in the third quarter when Simpson bounced outside on third-and-1 and easily won a sideline foot race to the end zone to give the Bills a 23-0 lead.

It was the fourth 200-yard game of Simpson's career, tying Jim Brown's NFL record. It was also the most yards anyone ever rushed against a Steeler team. Simpson carried the ball 28 times.

Bradshaw, meanwhile, lost two fumbles and an interception on the first three series of the game by the Super Bowl champion Steelers.

Sept. 27

WFL demands NFL return John Gilliam

New York (AP)—Chris Hemmeter, President of the World Football League, has demanded that the National Football League return wide receiver John Gilliam.

In a letter dated September 25 and obtained yesterday by the Associated Press, Hemmeter told NFL Commissioner Pete Rozelle, "The World Football League demands from the National Football League the immediate return of the services of John Gilliam."

The letter further stated that Gilliam was paid a total of $175,000 by the WFL, in advance, and special bonuses to play for the Hawaiians and the now-defunct Chicago Winds. Gilliam signed originally with the Hawaiians, then was transferred to the Chicago franchise

Oct. 23

Ailing WFL folds

$30 million is lost; NFL can bid for players

New York (AP)—Unable to attract many fans, unable to sign many name players and unable to overcome the bad memories of 1974, the World Football League gave up on its dream of regaining respectability and folded in mid-season yesterday.

In the 12th week of the second year of the most unsuccessful professional sports league ever formed, the WFL left 380 players suddenly without jobs and $30 million lost since the summer of 1974, when Gary Davidson and his supporters were predicting expansion around the world.

Chris Hemmeter, the Hawaiian millionaire who rescued the WFL from almost certain death last winter with a financing formula that tied player salaries to ticket sales, headed back to his island home yesterday after announcing there was no point in the league going on.

As far as is known, Hemmeter's WFL did not lie to the public, did not falsify attendance figures and did not fail to pay its players, all of which were done by some teams in the 1974 league. But the WFL was still unable to attract paying customers, and its owners finally gave up and the league immediately ceased operations.

That action apparently made all its players free agents who can be signed by whatever National Football League team holds their rights.

The NFL ruled a month ago, in the case of John Gilliam, that any player under contract to a team or league which folded could be signed before 4 P.M. October 28, and commissioner Pete Rozelle announced late yesterday that the NFL would stick by that decision.

Nov. 13

NFL old-timers lose suit seeking pensions from league

Providence, R.I. (AP)—After a three-year fight, a federal court judge has ruled in favor of the National Football League and dismissed a class-action suit seeking pensions for more than 1,000 old-time NFL players.

Chief Judge Raymond J. Pettine ruled the NFL had not made any agreement with the former players to extend current pension benefits to the old-timers.

The suit was filed by seven former NFL players from Rhode Island, seeking a pension fund similar to the one in effect for active players as well as death benefits for widows and children.

The NFL, the NFL Players Association and commissioner Pete Rozelle were named as defendants.

The former players claimed in their suit the late NFL commissioner Bert Bell had made an oral promise that as the pension fund increased, benefits would be extended back to include older players.

Pettine said that even if Bell made such a statement, there was no evidence he had authority to bind the league to the promise.

The older players also said in their suit the original NFL Players Association had an obligation to implement pension funds for those who retired before 1959, the cutoff date under the new pension agreement.

The NFL Players Association, a corporation formed in 1967, succeeded the original association.

Nov. 6

Door to NFL is opened

Judge says WFL players can be signed

St. Paul (AP)—A federal judge yesterday opened the way for former World Football League players to go job-hunting in the National Football League, and several contending NFL teams were expected to begin looking for help immediately.

"Professional sports and the public are better served by open, unfettered competition," Judge Edward J Devitt said in United States District Court in issuing a temporary injunction. His order gives all players from the defunct WFL until midnight November 26 to sign with the 26 NFL teams, provided they are not under valid contract to a WFL team or owner.

NFL commissioner Pete Rozelle, who testified during the three-hour hearing, estimated that fewer than 20 WFL players would be signed by NFL teams during the next three weeks.

Nov. 11

Thomas visits 'Skins, says 'they need me'

Washington (AP)—Controversial running back Duane Thomas dropped in unexpectedly on the Washington Redskins yesterday, apparently seeking to regain his job with the injury-battered National Football League team.

Thomas, who played out his option with Washington last spring and later moved to Hawaii of the now-defunct World Football League, met briefly at Redskins Park with Tim Temerario, director of player personnel. He did not meet with coach Geoge Allen.

Before joining Temerario, Thomas was asked by newsmen about his presence in Washington. "I've seen their injury list and they need me," he replied.

After the visit, which the Redskins said was at Thomas's instigation and not theirs, Temerario said Thomas did not ask for a job nor did the Redskins offer him one.

Temerario said the Redskins could not sign Thomas right now, even if they wanted to, because the NFL headquarters had not cleared him and, technically, he should not even have been at Redskins Park.

Nov. 23

Tarkenton sets mark as Vikings triumph

Bloomington, Minn. (AP) —The undefeated Minnesota Vikings whipped San Diego, 28 to 13, in an interdivisional game yesterday.

Fran Tarkenton set a National Football League career record for pass completions, and Chuck Foreman rushed for 3 touchdowns in the game.

Tarkenton, who completed pass No. 2,831 of his career in the second quarter, erased the previous mark set by former Baltimore Colts quarterback John Unitas.

San Diego, now winless in 10 games, moved to the Minnesota 1-yard line in the third quarter, but failed to score in four running plays against the league's top defensive team.

Minnesota finally overcame a stubborn Charger defense and grabbed a 21-7 lead with 9.32 left in the game on a yard run by Foreman. He scored again in the closing minutes on a 9-yard run—boosting his season total to 14.

Foreman rushed for more than 100 yards for the fifth straight week, netting 127 yards in 33 carries. Tarkenton completed 24 of 32 passes for 201 yards.

Dec. 7

Chargers top Chiefs for 1st win of season

Kansas City (AP)—The San Diego Chargers yesterday recorded their first victory of the season, utilizing rookie Rickey Young's 2 touchdowns as the springboard for a 28-to-20 come-from-behind triumph against the Kansas City Chiefs.

The victory enabled San Diego to avoid becoming the first NFL team to ever lose all 14 games in a season.

```
San Diego................ 7  0  7 14—28
Kansas City.............. 3  3 14  0—20
SD—Young 5 run (Wersching Kick).
KC—FG Stenerud 21.
KC—FG Stenerud 22.
SD—Scarber 8 run (Wersching kick).
KC—Green 1 run (Stenerud kick).
KC—Pearson 17 pass from Dawson
   (Stenerud kick).
SD—Young 3 run (Wersching kick).
SD—Fouts 9 run (Werssing kick).
Attendance—46,888
```

	Chargers	Chiefs
First downs	21	17
Rushes-yards	50-47	30-63
Passing yards	165	169
Return yards	131	262
Passes	8-18-3	17-30-0
Punts	4-36	5-38
Fumbles-lost	2-1	6-3
Penalties-yards	8-40	4-30

INDIVIDUAL LEADERS
RUSHING—San Diego: Young 25-124, Bonner 9-32, Scarber 5-44. Kansas City: Green 11-32, Lane 11-24.
RECEIVING—San Diego: Curran 3-95, Garrison 2-41. Kansas City: White 4-53, Pearson 3-61, Masters 3-43.
PASSING—San Diego: Fouts 8-18-3, 168 yards. Kapsas City: Dawson 14-20-0, 154; Adams 3-10-0, 44.

Dec. 10

House panel votes to keep blackout ban

Associated Press

WASHINGTON. — A House Commerce subcommittee voted unanimously yesterday to make permanent a law that allows local television stations to broadcast sports events when the home games are sold out.

The action continued Congress's speedy action on legislation to extend the blackout ban.

The Senate passed by voice vote and without debate Monday a bill to extend for three years the anti-blackout law due to expire Dec. 31.

Dec. 14

Colts defeat Dolphins, 10-7, in sudden death

By CAMERON C. SNYDER

Toni Linhart, the Austrian import, kicked a 31-yard field goal through an eerie, low-lying fog bank with only 2 minutes and 16 seconds left in sudden-death overtime yesterday to give the Colts a 10-to-7 victory over the Miami Dolphins at the Stadium and move the Colts to within one game of gaining the National Football League play-offs.

After the ball penetrated the heavy mist, twisting end over end on its way through the uprights, the screams of 59,398 fans left no doubt of their joy over the Colts having taken another giant step toward ending the Dolphins' strangle-hold on the NFL's American Conference Eastern Division title.

The come-from-behind victory for the Colts, now 9-4 after an horrendous 1-4 start, was one they had to win. Even a tie would have eliminated them from a play-off berth, and the tie was just ticks on the clock from realization.

Miami has the same 9-4 won-loss record, but the Colts have won both head-to-head games, with a 33-to-17 victory in Miami and yesterday's squeaker. The Colts still have to beat New England Sunday to insure a place in the play-offs. A loss coupled with a Miami victory over Denver Saturday in Miami would still deprive the Colts of making the play-offs.

Reprinted from
The Baltimore Sun

Colt statistics

```
Miami.................0 0 7 0 0—7
Baltimore............0 0 0 7 3—10

M—Morris 3 run (Yepremian kick)
B—Mitchell 6 run (Linhart kick)
B—FG Linhart 31
Attendance—59,398
```

	Dolphins	Colts
First downs	15	22
Rushes-yards	43-192	46-146
Passing yards	79	206
Return yards	58	30
Passes	7-18-1	23-39-0
Punts	8-38	8-34
Fumbles-lost	3-1	1-0
Penalties-yards	7-54	6-67

INDIVIDUAL LEADERS
RUSHING—Miami: Morris 21-96, Nottingham 11-37, Strock 3-23, Bulaich 4-18, Malone 2-10, Moore 2-8 Baltimore: Mitchell 30-87, Jones 7-20, Olds 5-17, McCauley 3-17, Doughty 1-5.
RECEIVING—Miami: Moore 4-40, Nottingham 1-18, Solomon 1-17, Seiple 1-15. Baltimore: Chester 5-64, Mitchell 6-53, Carr 4-46, Doughty 3-30, Olds 2-20, McCauley 3-19.
PASSING—Miami: Strock 7-18-1, 90 yards. Baltimore: Jones 23-39-0, 232

Dec. 20

Foreman Scores 4 TDs

Tarkenton, Simpson Set Marks As Vikings Crush Bills by 35-13

BUFFALO (AP) — Minnesota battled not only the Buffalo Bills but also snowballs from fans. The snowballs seem to be more bothersome.

The Vikings, who beat the Bills 35-13 in a National Football League game Saturday, thought Chuck Foreman would have scored more than four touchdowns if it weren't for snowballs.

Foreman said his vision was blurred after being hit in the right eye by a snowball during the second half.

Fran Tarkenton, who threw two touchdown passes that gave him an NFL record of 291 career scoring passes, was particularly upset by the snowball throwing fans.

"I was watching fathers make snowballs for their sons to throw," said Tarkenton. He said he was hit several times during the game, and one snowball caused him to throw an incomplete pass.

"I thought I was being struck on the helmet by a defense end's hand," he said, "It was the worst exhibition I've seen in 19 years of football."

Foreman's four touchdowns gave him 22 for the year, tying Gale Sayers record, which became an old record when O.J. Simpson scored both Bills touchdowns to give him 23 for the season.

Simpson set the record on pass from quarterback Gary Marangi in the third period. Marangi said Simpson suggested the play.

"He was telling the coaches he was open on that particular play the whole game," Marangi said. "When I went out there, I looked for it."

Tarkenton's two scoring passes elipsed John Unitas' record of 290.

Foreman, playing before a nationwide television audience, became the first Viking ever to rush for more than 1,000 yards in a single season.

Foreman carried for two touchdowns, one from four yards out and the other on a one-yard plunge, both in the first half. He caught the TD passes from Tarkenton in the third period, the first on a one-yard play and the other for six yards.

Foreman came close to scoring on another run in the first quarter but fumbled near the goal line and the ball rolled into the end zone where Jim Lash fell on it for a Viking score.

Simpson bolted 24 yards for Buffalo's first touchdown in the second quarter. Gary Marangi, the Bills' backup quarterback behind Joe Ferguson, connected with Simpson on a 64-yard scoring play in the third period. Simpson, all alone on the left sideline caught the pass on the Minnesota 35, eluded one defender and ran in for the score.

Foreman carried 19 times for a total of 85 yards, giving him 1,070 yards rushing for the season.

Minnesota	14 7 14 0—35	
Buffalo	0 7 6 0—13	

Minn—Foreman 4 run (Cox kick)
Minn—Lash recovered Minnesota fumble in end zone (Cox kick)
Buf-Simpson 24 run (Leypoldt kick)
Minn—Foreman 1 run (Cox kick)
Minn—Foreman 1 pass from Tarkenton (Cox kick)
Minn—Foreman 6 pass from Tarkenton (Cox kick)
Buf-Simpson 65 pass from Marangi (Kick failed).

	Vikings	Bills
First downs	28	20
Rushes-yards	41-168	26-120
Passing yards	219	189
return yards	80	49
Passes	27-43-1	16-35-4
Punts	5-40	3-39
Fumbles-lost	5-1	1-1
Penalties-yards	8-44	5-35

INDIVIDUAL LEADERS

RUSHING—Minnesota, Foreman 19-85, McClanahan 12-47. Buffalo, Simpson 12-59, Braxton 7-26.

RECEIVING—Minnesota, Foreman 10-87, Lash 4-61. Buffalo, Simpson 3-66, Chandler 4-33.

PASSING—Minnesota, Tarkenton 25-36-0, 216, Lee 2-7-1, 26. Buffalo, Ferguson 6-16-3, 51, Marangi 10-19-1, 161.

Dec. 23

Eagles Fire Coach

PHILADELPHIA (AP) — Mike McCormack was fired Monday as head coach of the Philadelphia Eagles because he didn t produce a National Football League winner after three years on the job.

Owner Leonard Tose, with general manager Jim Murray at his side, quietly read a brief statement dumping McCormack "with personal regret." Then he swiftly exited, refusing further comment.

"This is an independent judgment made by me on the facts as I know them, and of course in no small way are measured on our won-lost record," Tose said in his statement.

McCormack's Eagles compiled a 16-25-1 record, including this season's dismal 4-10 showing which ended with Sunday's 26-3 upset victory over Washington.

Cleveland tramples error-prone Chiefs

Dec. 14

Cleveland (AP)—the Cleveland Browns scored a 40-to-14 victory against the error-plagued Kansas City Chiefs yesterday.

Elusive Greg Pruitt turned in his best game in three years as a pro by rushing for 214 yards and scoring 3 touchdowns for the Browns.

Pruitt, a 5-foot-10, 195-pound running back from Oklahoma went over the 1,000-yard mark for the season, and three of his 25 carries were scoring bursts of 11, 3 and 14 yards.

The Browns, 3-10, stopped the Chiefs cold in the first three periods, and then allowed 2 touchdowns in the last period. The first K.C. score came with 10.04 left in the game on a yard plunge by Woody Green and the other score came with just 2.06 remaining on a 9-yard pass from Tony Adams to Billy Masters.

Pruitt's 1,030 yards made him the third Cleveland player to break the 1,000-yard barrier in a season and the first since Leroy Kelly in 1968. His best previous game was 110 yards in 1973, also against the Chiefs.

Pruitt also joined Jim Brown and Bobby Mitchell as the only Browns ever to go over 200 yards rushing in one game.

NFL fines officials of four teams for lambasting Dolphins-Bills call

By The Associated Press

Ralph Wilson, owner of the Buffalo Bills, has been fined $5,000 for criticizing National Football League officiating, and Los Angeles Rams' owner Carroll Rosenbloom, Al Davis, who runs the Oakland Raiders, and Minnesota coach Bud Grant have been fined for agreeing with him.

The fines assessed Wednesday by the NFL commissioner Alvin (Pete) Rozelle stemmed from a December 7 game between the Bills and the Miami Dolphins.

Buffalo, trailing 21-0 early in the game, battled back within three points at 24-21 in the fourth quarter. Then, with Miami in possession in its own territory, Mercury Morris of the Dolphins fumbled as he hit the ground.

Buffalo's John Skorupan pounced on the loose ball, but it was ruled no fumble by head linesman Jerry Bergman. And when Bergman was elbowed by Buffalo's Pat Toomay on the play, Buffalo was slapped with a 15-yard unsportsmanlike conduct penalty.

Miami then drove for its final touchdown, won 31 to 21 and knocked the Bills out of the play-offs.

"It was a rotten call that cost our team a chance for the Super Bowl," Wilson said after the game. "I will not again send my team out to play a game that he's working. . . The official who made that call should be barred from football. Anyone that incompetent should not be allowed to officiate."

The next day, Rosenbloom agreed with Wilson and suggested that Wilson should allow him to pay half of whatever fine was assessed. "If he is any kind of man, he's got to give me that privilege," Rosenbloom said.

"When a man gets robbed like that, he must give me part of the action. I know the feeling. I have lost two major play-off games because of bad officiating. I suffered in silence and I wound up with a coronary." On Wednesday, he got a $5,000 fine of his own.

Davis, managing partner of the Raiders, said it had become clear that not all NFL officials were competent. "We have to get rid of the incompetent officials in this league and we will," he said.

And Grant said pretty much the same thing, calling the NFL "a multi-million dollar operation being handled by amateurs on Sunday afternoon," and saying the league should hire full-time officials like baseball, basketball and hockey, rather than using part-time officials.

The amount of the Davis and Grant fines was not known. The league refused comment on the matter.

Dec. 21

Baltimore Trips Patriots, 34-21

BALTIMORE (AP) — "I've always thought of this club as the 1914 Boston Braves of football," said Ted Marchibroda, Baltimore's rookie head coach, comparing the Colts to baseball's "Miracle Braves," who came from last place on July 4 to win a pennant and then the World Series.

The Colts came from behind three times to beat the stubborn New England Patriots 34-21 Sunday, climaxing a season-long struggle to win a National Football League division title.

It was the ninth consecutive victory for the Colts, who finished with a 2-12 record last year and then started this season by losing four of their first five games.

Dec. 17

Joe Namath Fined $500

HEMPSTEAD, N.Y. (AP) — Joe Namath, who earns an estimated $450,000 a year, was fined $500 for breaking curfew Sunday night, Coach Ken Shipp of the New York Jets said Wednesday.

Shipp said the $500 fine is spelled out in the Jets' playbook. A $1,000 fine for curfew violation is assessed if a player makes the bedcheck but is discovered to have later left his room.

The Jets' quarterback broke curfew by 25 minutes and was benched for the first quarter of Monday night's National Football League game at San Diego. The Jets lost 24-16.

Dec. 21

Blanda tops 2,000 as Raiders triumph

Oakland, Calif. (AP)— George Blanda sent Oakland ahead with the 2,000th point of his pro football career—a second-period extra-point conversion—and Pete Banaszak ran for 3 touchdowns in the Raiders' 28-to-20 victory against the Kansas City Chiefs yesterday.

Blanda, who became the National Football League's all-time scoring leader several years ago, reached the 2,000-point level after Banaszak's second touchdown tied the score at 13-13 with 4.06 left in the first half. The 48-year-old placekicker's 4 extra points raised his career scoring total to 2,002.

The victory gave Oakland, which is host to Cincinnati Sunday in the opening round of the NFL play-offs, a regular-season record of 11-3. The Chiefs, 42-10 winners over Oakland in an October game, finished 5-9.

Blanda also made his first appearance of the season at quarterback Sunday for the American Conference West champions and completed the 1,911th pass of his 26-year career in a third-period drive deep into Kansas City territory. But linebacker Willie Lanier intercepted a pass in the end zone, and rookie David Humm finished the game at quarterback for Oakland.

Kansas City	3	10	0	7—20
Oakland	7	14	0	7—28

O—Banaszak 5 run (Blanda kick).
KC—FG Stenerud 35.
KC—FG Stenerud 29.
KC—Pearson 7 pass from Adams (Stenerud kick).
O—Banaszak 3 run (Blanda kick).
O—Bradshaw 16 pass from Stabler (Blanda kick).
KC—Kinney 1 run (Stenerud kick).
O—Banaszak 1 run (Blanda kick).
Attendance—48,604.

	Chiefs	Raiders
First downs	23	24
Rushes-yards	33-117	44-246
Passing yards	229	141
Return yards	12	43
Passes	18-32-3	14-19-1
Punts	3-41	5-42
Fumbles-lost	1-1	1-0
Penalties-yards	3-10	7-71

INDIVIDUAL LEADERS

RUSHING—Kansas City: Green 17-73, Adams 3-26, Kinney 12-24. Oakland: J. Phillips 7-84, Banaszak 17-72, Van Eeghen 8-43.

RECEIVING—Kansas City: Pearson 6-103, White 3-33. Oakland: Moore 3-17, Van Eeghen 3-7, Bradshaw 2-29.

PASSING—Kansas City: Adams 18-31-2, 245 yards; White 0-1-1, 0. Oakland: Stabler 11-12-0, 134; Blanda 1-3-1, 11, Humm 2-4-0, 4.

Pittsburgh Defensive Unit Spearheads 28-10 Triumph

PITTSBURGH (AP) — "We like to think our defense can win a game by itself," linebacker Andy Russell said after the Pittsburgh Steelers survived a rash of turnovers Saturday to beat the Baltimore Colts 28-10 in their National Football League American Conference playoff opener.

"I'm not taking anything away from our offense. They've carried us at times," added Russell, who ran 93 yards with a fumble recovery for an insurance touchdown in the final minutes. "But if our offense isn't functioning, like today, we do whatever we have to do."

The Steelers, who captured the AFC Central crown with a 12-2 record, played like anything but champions on offense for most of the game. Although they moved the ball consistently, powered by Franco Harris' 153 yards on 27 carries, they coughed up three fumbles, two by Harris, and Terry Bradshaw had a pair of passes intercepted.

Russell's touchdown and a pass interception by cornerback Mel Blount provided the spark in a 21-point second-half surge by the defending Super Bowl champions, who host the AFC championship here Jan. 4, facing the winner of today's game between Cincinnati and Oakland.

Baltimore	0	7	3	0—10
Pittsburgh	7	0	7	14—28

Pitt—Harris 8 run (Gerela kick)
Balt—Doughty 5 pass from Domres (Linhart kick)
Balt—FG Linhart 21
Pitt—Bleier 7 run (Gerela kick)
Pitt—Bradshaw 2 run (Gerela kick)
Pitt—Russell 93 fumble return (Gerela kick)
A—49,053

	Colts	Steelers
First downs	10	16
Rushes-yards	41-82	43-211
Passing yards	72	76
Return yards	97	165
Passes	8-22-2	8-13-2
Punts	9-40	4-40
Fumbles-lost	2-1	3-3
Penalties-yards	6-53	5-45

INDIVIDUAL LEADERS
RUSHING—Baltimore, Mitchell 26-63, Olds 5-6, Jones 2-6. Pittsburgh, Harris 27-153, Bleier 12-28, Bradshaw 3-22.
RECEIVING—Baltimore, Mitchell 4-20, Doughty 2-63, McCauley 1-9. Pittsburgh, Lewis 3-65, Swann 2-15, Bleier 2-14.
PASSING—Baltimore, Domres, 2-11-2, 9 yards; Jones 6-11-0, 91. Pittsburgh, Bradshaw 8-13-2, 103.

Dec. 27

Sub Ron Jaworski Guides Ram Win

LOS ANGELES (AP) — Reserve quarterback Ron Jaworski learned just two minutes before the kickoff that he'd be starting for the Los Angeles Rams and then, with the help of a near-perfect defense, led his club to a 35-23 victory over the St. Louis Cardinals Saturday in the opening round of the National Football League's Super Bowl playoffs.

St. Louis	0	9	7	7—23
Los Angeles	14	14	0	7—35

LA—Jaworski 5 run (Dempsey kick)
LA—Jack Youngblood 47 interception return (Dempsey kick)
LA—Simpson 65 interception return (Dempsey kick)
StL—Otis 3 run (kick failed)
LA—H. Jackson 66 pass from Jaworski (Dempsey kick)
StL—FG Bakken 29
StL—Gray 11 pass from Hart (Bakken kick)
LA—Jessie 2 run with fumble (Dempsey kick)
StL—Jones 3 run (Bakken kick)
A—72,65

	Cardinals	Rams
First downs	22	26
Rushes-yards	27-95	50-237
Passing yards	268	203
Return yards	3	137
Passes	22-41-3	12-23-0
Punts	6-43	5-32
Fumbles-lost	3-2	5-3
Penalties-yards	6-70	5-38

INDIVIDUAL LEADERS
RUSHING—St. Louis, Otis 12-38, Jones 6-28, Metcalf 8-27. Los Angeles, McCutcheon 37-202; Scribner 4-16; Bryant 3-12, Jaworski 6-7.
RECEIVING—St. Louis, Metcalf 6-94, Otis 4-52, Gray 3-52. Los Angeles, Jessie 4-52, McCutcheon 3-8, H. Jackson 2-84.
PASSING—St. Louis, Hart 22-41-3, 291 yards. Los Angeles, Jaworski 12-23-0, 203

Dec. 28

NFC

Bloomington, Minn. (AP)—Roger Staubach's 50-yard touchdown pass to Drew Pearson with 24 seconds left to play catapulted the Dallas Cowboys to a 17-to-14 victory over the favored Minnesota Vikings yesterday in their National Football Conference semi-final play-off game.

The touchdown pass, capping an 85-yard drive in eight plays, wiped out a 14-10 Minnesota lead built on Brent McClanahan's 1-yard touchdown run with 5 minutes 11 seconds left in the game.

The Cowboys will play in the NFC championship game Sunday at Los Angeles against the Rams, who beat St. Louis, 35 to 23, Saturday in the conference's other semi-final game.

On the winning drive, Dallas converted on a fourth-and-16 situation from its own 25 when Staubach completed a 25-yard pass to Pearson that put the ball at midfield.

Staubach then overthrew Golden Richards streaking down the left sideline. But on the next play, Staubach faded back to his 40 and unleashed the bomb that Pearson caught at the Minnesota 5-yard line.

The Dallas wide receiver, bracketed by cornerback Nate Wright and free safety Paul Krause, caught the ball between the two defenders and ran into the end zone, then, in jubilation, threw the ball into the stands.

With the Vikings trying desperately to rally in the final seconds, field judge Armen Terzian, the official who had made a controversial call that gave Minnesota its opening touchdown, was hit on the forehead by a liquor bottle thrown from the stands.

He fell to the turf, but was treated and bandaged by Minnesota trainer Fred Zamberletti and was helped off the field.

Tarkenton's father has fatal coronary

Savannah, Ga. (AP)—The Rev. Dallas Tarkenton, Sr., father of Minnesota Vikings' quarterback Fran Tarkenton, suffered a heart attack and died yesterday while watching his son's team play Dallas on television in a National Football League play-off game.

The elder Tarkenton, a Methodist minister, was dead on arrival at Memorial Medical Center at 3.15 P.M. He was 63.

Fran Tarkenton left the stadium in Bloomington, Minn., where the Cowboys defeated the Vikings, 17 to 14, unaware of his father's death. Word reached him soon afterward and family members said he was expected to return to Georgia today with the funeral scheduled tomorrow in Athens, Ga.

A native of Norfolk, Va., Tarkenton served for several years as pastor of a church in Athens, where his son Fran was a football star in high school and later at the University of Georgia, which is located in Athens.

NFC statistics

Dallas	0	0	7	10—17
Minnesota	0	7	0	7—14

Min—Foreman 1 run (Cox kick)
Dal—Dennison 4 run (Fritsch kick)
Dal—FG Fritsch 24
Min—McClanahan 1 run (Cox kick)
Dal—D. Pearson 50 pass from Staubach (Fritsch kick)
Attendance—46,425

	Cowboys	Vikings
First downs	19	12
Rushes-yards	42-131	27-115
Passing yards	225	100
Return yards	18	5
Passes	17-29-0	12-26-1
Punts	6-38	7-40
Fumbles-lost	4-1	2-0
Penalties-yards	4-30	7-60

INDIVIDUAL LEADERS
RUSHING—Dallas: Dennison 11-36, P. Pearson 11-34, Newhouse 12-33. Minnesota: Foreman 18-56, Tarkenton 3-32, McClanahan 4-22.
RECEIVING—Dallas: P. Pearson 5-77, D. Pearson 4-91, Newhouse 2-25, Richards 2-20, Fugett 2-13. Minnesota: Marinaro 5-64, Foreman 4-42, Gilliam 1-15, Lash 1-15.
PASSING—Dallas: Staubach 17-29-0, 246 yards. Minnesota: Tarkenton 12-26-1, 135.

Dec. 28

AFC

Oakland, Calif. (AP)—Oakland quarterback Ken Stabler threw three touchdown passes to seldom-used receivers yesterday and the Raiders survived a pair of fourth-period scoring strikes by Cincinnati's Ken Anderson to hold on for a 31-to-28 National Football League play-off victory over the Bengals.

The triumph again advanced the Raiders to the threshold of the Super Bowl. The Western Division champions earned a berth in the American Conference championship game a third straight year. They will face the defending NFL champion Steelers Sunday in Pittsburgh.

Oakland, since making its only Super Bowl appearance in 1968, has been eliminated five times after making it within one step of the title game.

AFC statistics

```
Cincinnati ..................... 0  7  7 14—28
Oakland ........................ 3 14  7  7—31
```

Oak—FG Blanda 27
Oak—Siani 9 pass from Stabler (Blanda kick)
Cin—Fritts 1 run (Green kick)
Oak—Moore 8 pass from Stabler (Blanda kick)
Oak—Banaszak 6 run (Blanda kick)
Cin—Elliott 6 run (Green kick)
Oak—Casper 2 pass from Stabler (Blanda kick)
Cin—Joiner 25 pass from Anderson (Green kick)
Cin—Curtis 14 pass from Anderson (Green kick)
Attendance—53,039.

	Bengals	Raiders
First downs	17	27
Rushes-yards	25-97	51-173
Passing yards	161	185
Return yards	48	64
Passes	17-27-0	17-23-1
Punts	6-36	1-38
Fumbles-lost	1-0	2-1
Penalties-yards	5-37	7-64

INDIVIDUAL LEADERS

RUSHING—Cincinnati: Clark 8-46, Elliott 4-25, Fritts 6-14. Oakland: Davis 16-63, Banaszak 17-62, Hubbard 12-33.

RECEIVING—Cincinnati: Clark 4-38, Myers 3-67, Joiner 3-60, Curtis 3-20. Oakland: Moore 6-57, Branch 5-89, Siani 3-35.

PASSING—Cincinnati: Anderson, 17-27-0, 201 yards. Oakland: Stabler 17-23-1, 199.

Judge finds NFL's Rozelle Rule to be in violation of antitrust laws

Minneapolis (AP)—The Rozelle Rule, the device used by the National Football League to bind a player to one team, was declared to be in violation of antitrust laws yesterday by a federal judge whose decision could severely affect the sport.

U.S. District Judge Earl R. Larson made the ruling and permanently forbade the NFL and its 26 teams from enforcing the Rozelle Rule. But Judge Larson stayed the ruling and the permanent restraining order pending an appeal from the NFL, an action that is certain to come.

The ruling, coming nearly six months after completion of a trial of a suit brought by the former Baltimore tight end, John Mackey, and 14 other former and present players, strikes hard at the NFL. In effect, it says the league cannot restrict its players from selling their services to the highest bidder.

The Rozelle Rule says that, while a player may become a free agent by playing one year beyond his contract, if the player signs with another team, his old club must be compensated by the new team with players or draft choices, or both.

Judge Larson said such a system held down salaries, kept other clubs from bidding for free agents and combined with such things as the college draft prohibited players from earning their true market value.

The NFL has used the Rozelle Rule to stop a team from buying quality players in an attempt to win a championship. The league argued that the rule was needed to maintain competitive balance, and said its elimination could destroy professional football.

Judge Larson ruled that "elimination of the Rozelle Rule will not spell the end of the National Football League, or even cause a decrease in the number of franchises in the National Football League.

"If the effects of this decision prove to be too damaging to professional football . . . Congress could possibly grant special treatment to the National Football League based on its claimed unique status.

"The Rozelle Rule substantially restricts players' freedom of movements," Judge Larson said. "The existence of the Rozelle Rule substantially decreases players' bargaining power in contract negotiations. As a result, the salaries paid by each club are lower than if competitive bidding were allowed to prevail."

The suit by Mackey, which was tried by the NFL players' union, was viewed as the primary test case to determine if the Rozelle Rule and other restrictions on player movement were legal.

This case only sought to determine the validity of the Rozelle Rule. Other NFL policies, such as the collegiate draft and standard player contract, are being contested in a federal court suit in California brought by Joe Kapp, a former quarterback for the Minnesota Vikings. It is expected to go to trial early next year.

Ultimately, the issues are expected to reach the Supreme Court.

Judge Larson said the Rozelle Rule was "unreasonable in that it is unlimited in duration. It is a perpetual restriction on a player, following him throughout his career. He is at no time truly free to negotiate for his services with any NFL club.

"The rule is unreasonable when viewed in conjunction with the other anticompetitive practices of defendants: the draft; the standard player contract; the option; the tampering rule," Judge Larson said in a part of his decision that heavily criticized the other devices used by the league to bind a player to one team.

Judge Larson said the system under which the Rozelle Rule operates, making a player a free agent on May 1 following the season in which he played out his option, was unreasonable.

"At the end of the option year, which ends on May 1, a player theoretically gains his freedom and may bargain with any club. Such freedom appears to be illusory," he said.

"A club which desires a player who has played out the option and has become a free agent cannot sign that player without an agreement in advance as to what compensation it will pay to the club to which the player was formerly under contract unless it is willing to risk an unknown compensation award by Commissioner Rozelle.

"The fact that unknown compensation would be awarded has acted as an effective deterrent to clubs signing free agents without reaching a prior agreement on compensation with that players' former club . . . ."

And Judge Larson went on to comment on other NFL policies, which he termed "anticompetitive practices." Among those policies and his comments were:

• The college draft, in which a college player must negotiate only with the team drafting him: "If the player does not desire to deal with the defendant club which selected him, or if he is unwilling to accept the terms offered by it, he is effectively boycotted or blacklisted."

• Standard player contract, which ties a player to the team with which he signs: "While minor modifications or departures from the standard player contract are permitted by defendants, no modifications or departures are permitted that would open up a player's services to free competition between the clubs."

• Option clause, in which a player must play one year beyond his contract to become a limited free agent: "The option clause acts to discourage players from playing out the option and becoming free agents . . . During this option year, the player who has not signed a new contract faces possible informal discipline by disapproving coaches and owners. He also risks injury and a poor performance during the option year, facts which would substantially limit his opportunities to go elsewhere if and when he attained free-agent status."

Jan. 4

Dallas Stuns Rams, 37-7

Los Angeles (AP)—Roger Staubach threw four touchdown passes yesterday, three to Preston Pearson, to propel the underdog Dallas Cowboys into the 1976 Super Bowl with a resounding 37-to-7 upset over the mistake-ridden Los Angeles Rams.

The 33-year-old Staubach hit Pearson on scoring plays covering 18, 15 and 19 yards in the National Football League's National Conference title game performance which sends the Cowboys to the Super Bowl for the third time. It is the first time any NFL wild-card team made the championship game.

The Cowboys, who figured to sit out this play-off season because they were rebuilding with 12 rookies on the squad, will oppose the defending champion Pittsburgh Steelers. who defeated Oakland, 16 to 10, in the American Football Conference title game earlier in the day.

Preston Pearson also makes his third Super Bowl appearance, but each time it has been with a different club: 1969 with Baltimore and last year with Pittsburgh, who he now will oppose January 18 in Miami.

Staubach operated the Dallas offense from the T, the I and the shotgun formations, befuddling the Los Angeles defense, which had held foes to just 135 points during the regular season, lowest in the NFL.

And the Rams' offense, operated first by James Harris and then by Ron Jaworski, could do nothing. The Rams were held to an incredibly low 24 yards rushing, and their receivers dropped several crucial passes in the first half when the game was still in doubt. The only Rams score was set up by a pass-interference call.

Staubach scrambled when he could not pass, and twice his runs set up Cowboy scores against a Rams team that went into the NFC championship game favored by 6 points.

Staubach completed 16 of 26 passes for 220 yards and rushed seven times for 54 yards, more than double the Rams' rushing total. Los Angeles did not earn a single first down by rushing against the Cowboys.

Los Angeles had beaten St. Louis, 35 to 23, just a week ago, and the Cardinals had won the Eastern Division of the NFC with Dallas placing second. However, the Cowboys' 10-4 record was the best of any second-place team, and thus they won the right to compete in the play-offs as the so-called wild-card entry.

A week ago, Staubach's 50-yard scoring pass to Drew Pearson beat Minnesota, 17 to 14, with 24 seconds left in their play-off. This time, the Cowboys needed no such heroics.

NFC statistics

Dallas .... 7 14 13 3—37
Los Angeles .... 0 0 0 7— 7

Dal—P.Pearson 18 pass from Staubach (Fritsch kick)
Dal—Richards 4 pass from Staubach (Fritsch kick)
Dal—P.Pearson 15 pass from Staubach (Fritsch kick)
Dal—P.Pearson 19 pass from Staubach (Fritsch kick)
Dal—FG Fritsch 40
Dal—FG Fritsch 26
LA—Cappelletti 1 run (Dempsey kick)
Dal—FG Fritsch 26
Attendance—84,483.

	Cowboys	Rams
First downs	24	9
Rushes-yards	50-195	16-22
Passing yards	246	96
Return yards	69	40
Passes	18-28-1	11-24-3
Punts	4-35	7-35
Fumbles-lost	1-0	1-0
Penalties-yards	5-59	7-35

INDIVIDUAL LEADERS
RUSHING—Dallas. Newhouse 16-64, Staubach 7-54, Dennison 13-35 Los Angeles McCutcheon 11-10, Jaworski 2-12
RECEIVING—Dallas: P Pearson 7-123, D. Pearson 5-46, Richards 2-46 Los Angeles Jessie 4-52, McCutcheon 3-39, T Nelson 3-38
PASSING—Dallas: Staubach 16-26-1, 220 yards, Longley 2-2-0, 26. Los Angeles: Jaworski 11-22-2, 147; Harris 0-2-1, 0.

Jan. 4

Pittsburgh Nips Raiders

By CAMERON C. SNYDER
Sun Staff Correspondent

Pittsburgh—The Pittsburgh Steelers barely outlasted the Oakland Raiders, 16 to 10, for the National Football League's American Conference title yesterday in a game that featured 13 turnovers at frigid Three Rivers Stadium.

Linebacker Jack Lambert of the Steelers set a play-off record with three recoveries of Oakland fumbles as vicious hitting by both defenses plus a wind-chill index of minus 12 degrees (F) made the offenses handle the football like a hot potato.

The victory put the defending Super Bowl champion Steelers into the 1976 Super Bowl game, January 18 at Miami, against the Dallas Cowboys, 37-to-7 conquerors of the Los Angeles Rams in the National Conference title game yesterday.

However, a Steeler team that lost five fumbles and was intercepted three times could not clinch its conference title until the last play of the game, when Oakland ran out of time on the Pittsburgh 15.

The Raiders, who have never won a play-off game in six tries away from their warm-weather sanctuary in Oakland, took a desperate gamble in the last second when on third down and 5 at the Steeler 24, they called on 46-year-old George Blanda to attempt a 41-yard field goal.

He did, and the Raiders trailed by just 6 points with 51 seconds left. It was obvious that the Raiders would try an onside kickoff.

Reprinted from The Baltimore Sun

Ray Guy's squibbler caromed off Reggie Garrett, a ~~wide receiver~~ inserted into the kickoff receiving team's front line for his ability to catch the ball, and Marv Hubbard recovered for the Raiders at the Oakland 45, atoning in part for his fourth-period fumble that led to a Steeler touchdown and a 16-7 lead.

Quarterback Ken Stabler then threw long to Cliff Branch, who was tackled and held in bounds by Mel Blount at the 15 as the final gun went off.

That last-second foray by the Raiders was the most exciting happening on the ice-skating artifical surface at Three Rivers and the most heart-throbbing for the 49,103 fans who braved the arctic conditions to see the game.

AFC statistics

Oakland .... 0 0 0 10—10
Pittsburgh .... 0 3 0 13—16

Pitt—FG Gerela 36
Pitt—Harris 25 run (Gerela kick)
Oak—Siani 14 pass from Stabler (Blanda kick)
Pitt—Stallworth 20 pass from Bradshaw (kick failed)
Oak—FG Blanda 41
Attendance—49,103.

	Raiders	Steelers
First downs	18	16
Rushes-yards	32-93	39-117
Passing yards	228	215
Return yards	11	62
Passes	18-42-2	15-25-3
Punts	8-38	4-38
Fumbles-lost	4-3	5-5
Penalties-yards	4-40	3-32

INDIVIDUAL LEADERS
RUSHING—Oakland: Davis 13-29, Hubbard 10-30, Banazak 8-33 Pittsburgh: Harris 27-79, Bleier 10-16, Bradshaw 2-22
RECEIVING—Oakland: Siani 5-80, Casper 5-67, Branch 2-56 Pittsburgh Harris 5-58, Grossman 4-36, Swann 2-45.
PASSING—Oakland: Stabler 18-42-2, 246 yards. Pittsburgh: Bradshaw, 15-25-3, 215.

Jan. 2

Brown retires as coach

Cincinnati (AP)—Paul Brown, one of pro football's coaching giants, ended a 41-year career in a surprise move yesterday by announcing his retirement and naming long-time Cincinnati assistant Bill Johnson as his successor with the National Football League Bengals.

Brown, 67, and coach of the Bengals since their birth eight years ago, directed his final game last Sunday when the Bengals were knocked out of the NFL play-offs by the Oakland Raiders.

Ted Marchibroda Top NFL Coach

Jan. 6

Steelers made 7-point pick

Las Vegas (AP)—The Pittsburgh Steelers, defending National Football League champions, were made 7-point favorites over the Dallas Cowboys yesterday for the January 18 Super Bowl at Miami.

The Union Plaza Race and Sports Book posted the odds following Pittsburgh's 16-to-10 victory over the Oakland Raiders in Sunday's American Football Conference championship game.

The Cowboys upset the Los Angeles Rams, 37 to 7, in Sunday's National Football Conference title game.

Jan. 15

NFL uncovers bogus tickets

Miami (AP)—Counterfeit tickets are being sold for the Super Bowl between the Pittsburgh Steelers and Dallas Cowboys, a National Football League official said yesterday.

Jim Kensil, executive director of the NFL, said the bogus tickets came to his attention when a resident of Hallandale Fla., a Miami suburb, brought 18 tickets to NFL officials at Super Bowl headquarters, complaining that the seat and row numbers were smudged. The tickets were purchased by the man in "a commercial establishment in Hallandale" for $30 each, Kensil said.

The face value of every Super Bowl ticket is $20.

Kensil said the phony tickets had a white spot in the lower left-hand corner of the picture and the seat and row numbers smudge easily.

Jan. 13

Viking is picked as MVP

Tarkenton also named offensive best

New York (AP)—Quarterback Fran Tarkenton, who has completed his 15th season of professional football, yesterday was named the National Football League's most valuable player and offensive player of the year by the Associated Press.

Tarkenton, record shattering operator of the Minnesota Viking offense, was an easy winner in the balloting by a nationwide panel of sports writers and broadcasters in both the MVP and offensive player polls.

In both votes, he outdistanced running backs O.J. Simpson of Buffalo and Terry Metcalf of St. Louis. Tarkenton's team-mate, running back Chuck Foreman, was fourth in both polls.

Others receiving votes included quarterbacks Billy Kilmer of Washington and Ken Anderson of Cincinnati and running back Lydell Mitchell of Baltimore.

Tarkenton completed his most memorable season in 1975, shattering several of ex-Baltimore star Johnny Unitas's career records. The remarkably durable passer pushed his career attempts total to 5,225 and raised his completion total to 2,931, both figures eclipsing marks that Unitas had set in 18 NFL seasons.

But the most impressive of Unitas's records broken by Tarkenton was the total of 290 touchdown passes. Fran smashed that record on the final Sunday of the regular season, when he hurled a pair against Buffalo, running his career total to 291.

For the season, Tarkenton won his first passing title, completing 273 aerials, the third highest single season figure in NFL history. He threw for 2,994 yards and 25 touchdowns.

Jan. 14

NFL puts off drafts

New teams file suit against players' group

Miami (AP)—The National Football League postponed its scheduled expansion draft to stock the Tampa Bay and Seattle franchises and also its college draft yesterday after the two new franchises had filed a joint legal action against the NFL Players Association.

The expansion draft had been scheduled for January 23-24 and the college draft had been set for February 3-4.

Both were put off following the announcement of the suit filed in federal court in Miami.

Commissioner Pete Rozelle said the delay is necessary in order to permit the court sufficient time to determine the legality of the player allocation, which had been questioned by the NFLPA.

The commissioner said it would be impractical to conduct the college draft with Seattle and Tampa Bay participating, then find that expansion to the two cities had to be postponed or abandoned because of their inability to receive the allocation of veterans.

Named as defendants in the action taken by owners Hugh Culverhouse of Tampa Bay and Herman Sarkowsky of Seattle were the players association, the union's key officials and player representatives of the current 26 NFL teams. The suit asks that an injunction be issued prohibiting the players' union from any unlawful interference in the stocking of the franchises.

This, of course, is not the only case in which the league and union are opposing each other. For instance:

•A National Labor Relations Board judge is considering evidence presented during a three month hearing into 16 charges of unfair labor practices brought against the league by the union. Either side is expected to appeal an adverse ruling.

•Last week, the union filed more charges of unfair labor practices against the league.

•Last month, a federal judge in Minneapolis, acting in a suit argued by the union, ruled that the NFL's Rozelle Rule, which prohibits players from becoming true free agents, was a violation of antitrust laws. The NFL will appeal the case.

On February 23 in San Francisco, trial is scheduled to begin in the Joe Kapp case. In that one, Kapp is challenging all NFL rules which bind a player to one team and is seeking damages on the claim that the league prevented him from earning a living.

While the two sides meet often in court, they do little bargaining. The league and the union have been without a labor contract for two years.

In that period there have been two strikes, but no resolution of the issues. There are reports the league's pension fund could soon be broke because the league has refused to contribute to it in the absence of a contract.

Jan. 17

Over 1,700 Credentials Issued for Super Bowl

MIAMI (AP) — By noon Friday, the National Football League already had broken the record for the number of credentials issued to sports writers covering a Super Bowl game.

The league said 1,735 had been issued by then and that about 50 more would be issued before game time.

Steelers triumph in Super Bowl, 21-17

64-yard TD aerial, Bradshaw to Swann, brings 2d title in row

By CAMERON C. SNYDER
Sun Staff Correspondent

Reprinted from
The Baltimore Sun

Miami—Terry Bradshaw, the last to know that he had connected, hit wide receiver Lynn Swann on a 64-yard pass play for what proved to be the winning points late in the fourth quarter as the Pittsburgh Steelers scored a 21-to-17 Super Bowl defeat of the Dallas Cowboys yesterday in the Orange Bowl.

Bradshaw, who now has guided the Steelers two successive Super Bowl titles—a feat accomplished only by the Green Bay Packers in 1967 and 1968, and the Miami Dolphins in 1973 and 1974 —was rendered hors de combat by blitzing D. D. Lewis after unleashing the TD bomb that traveled nearly 70 yards in the air.

At the other end of the pass, credited as a 64-yard touchdown, was Swann, who had a step or two on Morgan State's Mark Washington. Swann caught the ball on the 8 and nimbly dashed into the end zone.

Bradshaw was helped from the field and into the dressing room after the knockout blow by Lewis, and did not learn of his feat until the cobwebbs cleared five minutes later.

It was a gambling pass, to the 80,192 fans, but Bradshaw had been hurting the Cowboys with long passes most of the afternoon, a perfect one for football at 60 degrees, but unseasonably chilly for Floridians.

By the time Bradshaw's head had cleared, his counterpart, Roger Staubach, had passed the Cowboys to a touchdown, reducing Pittsburgh's mar-

gin to the final 4 points.

With Bradshaw out of action, Terry Hanratty came on and was involved in what could have been the most controversial play of the season—if the Steelers had lost.

After the Steelers fielded the ensuing Cowboys onside kickoff at the Dallas 42, Hanratty came to a fourth-and-9 situation at the Dallas 41.

Everyone was expecting Pittsburgh coach Chuck Noll to send in his punter, Bobby Walden, as Dallas had used up its last time out. Instead, Noll conferred with Hanratty on the sidelines and called for a run by Rocky Bleier.

Bleier gained just 2 yards and with a minute and 22 seconds left to play, Dallas took over on its 39. At this point, the timekeeper took a nap, which added to the tension in the last moments.

The clock was not started for about 10 seconds after the referee had given the signal that time was in. It could have been a serious delay for the Steelers.

However, the Steeler defense, particularly the secondary, was up to the task and with three seconds left, Staubach's desperate aerial into the end zone on third down from the Pittsburgh 33 was intercepted by Glen Edwards.

Pittsburgh's famed steel curtain of defensive linemen, L.C. Greenwood, Joe Greene, Ernie Holmes and Dwight White, although recording seven tackles of Staubach attempting to pass, did not pressure the former United States Naval Academy star as it has other opponents.

Dallas's offensive line controlled the Steeler foursome, but Staubach time after time could not find an open receiver, and finally, after looking and looking, would be dropped for a loss.

If the Steeler kicking game had been adequate, there probably would have been no tingling moments at the end of the game. However, Walden had fumbled the center snap on a punt and Roy Gerela's fan club members must have been ready to turn in their cards after their hero missed field goal efforts of 36 and 37 yards and bounced the extra-point conversion attempt off an upright after Swann's touchdown.

Gerela atoned for his poor place-kicking with two fourth-period field goals of 36 and 18 yards as the Steelers scored in all of the manners that points can be put on the scoreboard —touchdown, conversion, field goal and safety.

Each team scored two touchdowns, with Staubach passing 29 yards to Drew Pearson in the first quarter and to Percy Howard for 34 yards and the last points of the game in the final period.

Bradshaw duplicated Staubach's effort with a 7-yard pass to tight end Randy Grossman and the 64-yarder to Swann.

Toni Fritsch accounted for the Cowboys' other points with a 36-yard field goal that gave Dallas a 10-to-7 lead at halftime, while Reggie Harrison was credited with the safety after blocking a Mitch Hoopes punt, the ball rolling out of the end zone for an automatic safety.

Super Bowl Notes

MIAMI (AP) — Tickets to Super Bowl X were being sold by scalpers for $150 a pair just 15 minutes before the game — and the scalpers were having little trouble finding buyers. National Football League officials said after Pittsburgh's 21-17 victory over Dallas.

Steelers Are 'Super'

Dallas	7 3 0 7–	17
Pittsburgh	7 0 0 14–	21

Dal—D. Pearson 29 pass from Staubach (Fritsch kick)
Pitt—Grossman 7 pass from Bradshaw (Gerela kick)
Dal—FG Fritsch 36
Pitt—safety Harrison, punt blocked through end zone
Pitt—FG Gerela 36
Pitt—FG Gerela 18
Pitt—Swann 64 pass from Bradshaw (kick failed)
Dal—P. Howard 34 pass from Staubach (Fritsch kick)
A—80,187

	Cowboys	Steelers
First downs	14	13
Rushes-yards	31-108	46-149
Passing yards	162	190
Return yards	101	216
Passes	15-24-3	9-19-0
Punts	7-35	4-40
Fumbles-lost	4-0	4-0
Penalties-yards	2-20	0-0

INDIVIDUAL LEADERS

RUSHING—Dallas, Newhouse 16-56, Staubach 5-22, Dennison 5-16, P. Pearson 5-14. Pittsburgh, Harris 27-82, Bleier 15-51, Bradshaw 4-16.

RECEIVING—Dallas, P. Pearson 5-53, Young 3-32, D. Pearson 2-59, Newhouse 2-12, P. Howard 1-34. Pittsburgh, Swann 4-161, Stallworth 2-8, Harris 1-26, Grossman 1-7, L. Brown 1-7.

PASSING—Dallas, Staubach 15-24-3, 204 yards. Pittsburgh, Bradshaw 9-19-0, 209

Jan. 20

5,000 Super Bowl Fans Lose $1.5 Million to 3 Swindlers

FORT LAUDERDALE, Fla. (AP) — Three men may have swindled as many as 5,000 football fans out of $1.5 million by selling Super Bowl tour packages with promises of football game tickets, police said Monday.

Officers said the investigation was continuing but no charges had been filed.

The three men checked out of their hotel Saturday night, the eve of Super Bowl X in the Orange Bowl between the Pittsburgh Steelers and Dallas Cowboys, without producing tickets, police said.

"I will never get involved with something like this un-less I have the tickets in my hand," said James Udichas, manager of a Pittsburgh travel agency which was one of several firms that sold tour packages offered by the trio at between $375 and $800 each.

Udichas said he had arranged a tour for 298 persons on the promise from Super Tours International of Youngstown, Ohio, to deliver the tickets before the game.

He said numerous attempts to get the tickets failed. He added that shortly before gametime, he received a telephone call from someone who said he worked for International Travel Bu-reau, the parent company of Super Tours, saying the tickets could be picked up at the Orange Bowl.

"I went down there in a rush, but nobody at the gate knew anything about them," said Udichas.

At two hotels, angry fans found unsigned notes on bulletin boards or desks which read "Those of you who haven't received your Super Bowl tickets can obtain a $25 refund" from their Pittsburgh travel agents.

"My father paid $65 apiece for two tickets," said Jim Lewis of Pittsburgh. He said others paid as much as $125 for seats

Feb. 9

Vermeil New Coach Of Eagles

PHILADELPHIA (AP) Dick Vermeil, who coached UCLA to an upset victory in the Rose Bowl over Ohio State on New Year's Day, was hired Sunday to coach the Philadelphia Eagles.

The announcement by owner Len Tose of the National Football League team that Vermeil had been given a five-year contract ended a coast-to-coast search for a successor to Mike McCormack, fired after the last day of the 1975 season.

Mar. 17

NFL sets draft dates, rejects bid by Memphis

San Diego (AP)—Dates for the long-delayed National Football League draft were set, New Orleans won the bid for Super Bowl XII in 1978 and Memphis lost its bid for a franchise at the NFL's annual meetings yesterday.

Commissioner Alvin (Pete) Rozelle announced the $173 million Superdome in New Orleans will be the site of the Super Bowl game January 15, 1978. The Rose Bowl in Pasadena, Calif., already had been selected for the 1977 championship battle.

Rozelle said the league owners could not under present conditions go for expansion at this time, which killed the bid by Memphis, where John Bassett has kept more than 30 of his World Football League players under contract.

"The owners reaffirmed their desire to get the league to 30 teams, but felt they should move ahead when they see what the future holds," Rozelle said.

Memphis and Birmingham, of the now-defunct WFL, both have evidenced interest in be-coming members of the NFL. Phoenix was another city mentioned. Bassett and a Memphis booster group were on the scene of this annual meeting, pressing their application.

Rozelle announced the draft of veteran players for the new Tampa Bay and Seattle franchises would be held March 30-31 from the NFL office in New York. The draft of collegians was set for April 8-9.

Mar. 27

Ford, Taylor, Flaherty voted to grid Hall of Fame

Canton, Ohio (AP)—Jim Taylor, Ray Flaherty and the late Len Ford, who helped build dynasties in their respective eras, have been selected for the Pro Football Hall of Fame, the hall announced yesterday.

The threesome, which ties the class of 1973 as the smallest in the shrine's 14-year history, was selected by a 27-man media board.

They will be enshrined in Canton July 24, before the annual Hall of Fame exhibition. The National Football League's Denver Broncos and Detroit Lions will play in this year's contest.

April 4

Calvin Hill Signs On With Over-the-Hill Gang

April 6

Patriots trade Plunkett

April 7

Warfield Returns to Cleveland Browns

April 8

Csonka Signs With Giants

April 9

DRAFT

First Round

1, Tampa Bay, Leroy Selmon, de, Oklahoma. 2, Seattle, Steve Niehaus, dt, Notre Dame. 3, New Orleans, Chuck Muncie, rb, California. 4, San Diego, Joe Washington, rb, Oklahoma. 5, New England, Mike Haynes, db, Arizona State. 6, N. Y. Jets, Richard Todd, qb, Alabama. 7, Cleveland, Mike Pruitt, rb, Purdue. 8, Chicago from Green Bay through Los Angeles and Detroit, Dennis Lick, ot, Wisconsin. 9, Atlanta, Bubba Bean, rb, Texas A&M. 10, Detroit from Chicago, James Hunter, db, Grambling. 11, Cincinnati from Philadelphia, Billy Brooks, wr, Oklahoma. 12, New England from San Francisco, Pete Brock, c, Colorado. 13, N. Y. Giants, Troy Archer, de, Colorado. 14, Kansas City, Rod Walters, ot, Iowa.

15, Denver, Tom Glassic, og, Virginia. 16, Detroit, Lawrence Gaines, rb, Wyoming. 17, Miami from Washington, Larry Gordon, lb, Arizona State. 18, Buffalo, Mario Clark, db, Oregon. 19, Miami, Kim Bokamper, lb, San Jose State. 20, Baltimore, Ken Novak, dt, Purdue. 21, New England from Houston through San Francisco, Tim Fox, db, Ohio State. 22, St. Louis, Mike Dawson, dt, Arizona. 23, Green Bay from Oakland, Mark Koncar, ot, Colorado. 24, Cincinnati, Archie Griffin, rb, Ohio State. 25, Minnesota, James White, dt, Oklahoma State. 26, Los Angeles, Kevin McLain, lb, Colorado State. 27, Dallas, Aaron Kyle, db, Wyoming. 28, Pittsburgh, Bennie Cunningham, te, Clemson.

Second Round

1, Seattle, Sammy Green, lb, Florida. 2, Tampa Bay, Jimmy DuBose, rb, Florida. 3, San Diego, Don Macek, og, Boston College. 4, New Orleans, Tony Galbreath, rb, Missouri. 5, N. Y. Jets, Shafer Suggs, db, Ball State. 6, Oakland from Cleveland, Charles Philyaw, de, Texas Southern. 7, New England, Ike Forte, rb, Arkansas. 8, Atlanta, Sonny Collins, rb, Kentucky. 9, Pittsburgh from Chicago, Ray Pinney, c, Washington. 10, Cincinnati from Philadelphia, Glenn Buinock, og, Texas A&M. 11, Los Angeles from Green Bay, Pat Thomas, db, Texas A&M. 12, Dallas from N. Y. Giants, Jim Jensen, rb, Iowa. 13, Kansas City, Cliff Frazier, dt, UCLA. 14, San Francisco, Randy Cross, c, UCLA. 15, Denver, Kurt Knoff, db, Kansas. 16, Detroit, Ken Long, og, Purdue. 17, Buffalo, Ken Jones, og, Arkansas State. 18, Detroit from Washington through San Francisco, David Hill, te, Texas A&I. 19, Pittsburgh from Baltimore, Mike Kruczek, qb, Boston College. 20, Houston, Mike Barber, te, Louisiana Tech.

21, Miami, Loaird McCreary, te, Tennessee State. 22, Oakland, Jeb Blount, qb, Tulsa. 23, Cincinnati, Chris Bahr, k, Penn State. 24, Buffalo from St. Louis, Joe Devlin, ot, Iowa. 25, Los Angeles, Ron McCartney, lb, Tennessee. 26, Minnesota, Sammie White, wr, Grambling. 27, Dallas, Jim Eidson, og, Mississippi State. 28, Pittsburgh, Jim Files, McNeese State. 29, San Francisco from Tampa Bay, Eddie Lewis, db, Kansas. 30, Seattle, Sherman Smith, wr, Miami, Ohio. 31, Seattle, Steve Raible, wr, Georgia Tech. 32, Tampa Bay, Dewey Selmon, dt, Oklahoma.

April 3

Court Deals Blow to Kapp; Supports NFL

SAN FRANCISCO (AP) — Former quarterback Joe Kapp was dealt a staggering defeat Friday by a U. S. District Court jury which ruled in favor of the National Football League in Kapp's antitrust suit.

Kapp, now 38, contended he was forced out of football five years ago and sought a multimillion dollar settlement from the NFL. A six-person jury took only six hours to decide Kapp had not suffered damages and should receive nothing.

"I'm disappointed, of course, and hope it doesn't hurt the players over-all," said Kapp after the verdict was read.

Judge William T. Sweigert, who presided over the monthlong trial, issued in late 1974 a summary judgement in the case declaring several NFL rules in violation of antitrust laws. Those decisions still stand despite the trial verdict.

Kapp contended he was forced oit of football by an illegal boycott after he refused to sign an NFL standard player contract with the New England Patriots. His attorney and agent, Don Elliott Cook, said the contract was illegal because of certain NFL rules.

Charles Hanger, Kapp's counsel in the trial, said after the verdict came in, "I assume we'll appeal."

Any appeal would have to be based on an error of law by Sweigert during the trial.

Kapp, sitting with his wife and Cook in the courtroom when the verdict was announced, was able to shrug and force a smile. He shook hands with the 77-year-old Cook and said, "You're my man — still."

Cook replied, "Just hang in there, Joe."

Patriots' President Billy Sullivan said, "This is a gratifying experience. I've never had another like it. I feel justice was served."

May 4

Ernie Nevers, 73, Dies Of Kidney Disorder

May 8

Former Cowboy Fugett Signed by Redskins

June 11

'Skins sign ex-Jet Riggins to pact

June 11

Bargaining plan still is NFL players' hope

Las Vegas (AP)—The National Football League Players Association ended its annual convention yesterday still hoping a collective bargaining agreement with NFL owners can be signed before training camps open.

"We're not terribly bad off without an agreement," said the Miami Dolphins' Dick Anderson, association president. "But I think we have a chance to settle. I wouldn't put up with the aggravation of this job if I thought it was all a waste of time, if I didn't think we had a chance."

Whatever happens, in other words, it appears certain there will be no players' strike, and the owners have made a no-lockout promise.

Anderson, NFLPA director Ed Garvey and other union leaders met with a three-man owners committee yesterday afternoon. There was a five-hour meeting Wednesday night.

"These are mostly exploratory sessions," Garvey said, explaining that the owners will be reporting on the situation at the NFL meeting in New York next week.

There has been no collective bargaining agreement enforced since the 1973 season, but since then the NFLPA has won several important court decisions. With the Rozelle Rule stricken down, players have much greater freedom of movement than in the past.

The owners insist they need the Rozelle Rule, or something close to it, to maintain a competitive balance in the league. The players do not buy the argument, and Anderson said, "Before we'd be willing to give up any of our freedom, we'd have to see a lot from the owners at the bargaining table."

Internal problems also were discussed extensively during the five-day convention.

The No. 1 problem is the dropoff in membership, about 60 per cent currently, over the past two years. Anderson said nonmembers must be told, "If you don't like the way things are going, don't just sit back and blame us, come to the meetings and get involved."

The resolution was adopted calling for a change in the traditional team player representative system. The NFLPA, because it was felt the pressure of duties was too much for one man, recommended that each team have a five-man council working with the player representatives.

June 14

Simpson plans to play one more year in West

June 15

Saints Obtain
Joe Gilliam
For Only $100

June 24

Cowboys Sign Johnson

NEW YORK (AP) — Running back Ron Johnson, who played out his option with the New York Giants last year, signed a two-year contract with the Dallas Cowboys, the New York Post reported Wednesday.

June 30

Jets Land Marinaro

The New York Jets signed Ed Marinaro to a one year contract Tuesday. The former Cornell running back played in the shadow of Chuck Foreman in Minnesota last year and complained that he did not get the opportunity to run with the ball often enough. Jets Coach Lou Holtz will use Marinaro in place of departed John Riggins, but says, "We are asking him to be the old Ed Marinaro, not the new Riggins."

June 20

Bills Deny Offer For O.J.

BUFFALO (AP) — Owner Ralph Wilson Jr. of the Buffalo Bills said Tuesday it wasn't true the Los Angeles Rams had made an offer for Bills running back O. J. Simpson. "The only thing which has been decided is that Chuck Knox, coach of the Rams, and Lou Saban, our coach, will talk soon," he said.

In Los Angeles Monday, Rams owner Carroll Rosenbloom said he had made an offer to the Bills for Simpson, that he had met with Simpson Saturday and that he expected a yes or no answer in a week to 10 days.

July 14

Simpson hints Rams
could extend his career

July 17

Saints waive Gilliam
after new violations

Reprinted from
The Hartford Courant

July 9

Bottle incident results in charges

Minneapolis (AP) — A Minnesota man was charged with simple assault and disorderly conduct at a sporting event in connection with a bottle-throwing incident at a Minnesota Vikings football game.

Robert C. Pieper, 21, of Golden Valley, was charged with the two misdemeanors in a complaint filed before Judge Kenneth Gill of Hennepin County Municipal Court.

A National Football League official, Armen Terzian, was struck on the head by a liquor bottle thrown from the stands during the closing minutes of the Dallas-Minnesota play-off game December 28 at Metropolitan Stadium.

Conviction on either of the misdemeanor charges could mean a $300 fine, 90 days in jail or both.

Rain, fans halt
Steelers' 24-0 romp

By DAN ARKUSH

CHICAGO — Unreal. That's the only way to describe last Friday night's College All-Star Game, a sporting event that was easily the strangest this reporter has ever witnessed.

The All-Stars, who were expected by more than a few to have a decent chance of pulling off an upset, were never in the game. The World Champion crew from Pittsburgh methodically took advantage of numerous Collegian miscues and was in complete control — except until 2:25 remained in the third quarter.

That's when the game's real dominating force took charge, Mother Nature.

It was about 10:49 p.m. when the city of Chicago demonstrated to a national television audience why its inhabitants are always bitching about the weather.

WITHIN MOMENTS, massive sheets of rain pelted the Soldier Field Astro-Turf, accompanied by lakefront winds that reached 63 mph at one point.

Customers in the stands headed in one of two directions — toward their cars in the parking lot or on to the field. Most of them chose the latter.

By 10:52 p.m. it looked like a scene out of "Day of the Locusts." The entire playing area was inundated by drenched bodies, romping playfully in makeshift swimming pools. The field had been turned into a gigantic Slip N'

Slide. Scattered scenes left distinct impressions.

One frisky group picked up the cable from an ABC minicam and jubilantly turned it into a jumping rope. On the north end of the field, one youngster was actually floating under water. At the other end, a girl's tight-fitting tank top was just too much for her to tolerate. There are advantages to being a sportswriter.

Three minutes later, both goalposts were ripped from their foundations. At 11:01 p.m. Commissioner Pete Rozelle, after conferring briefly with Chicago Tribune sports editor Cooper Rollow, mercifully called the game with the Steelers ahead, 24-0.

CHICAGO, ILL., JULY 23, 1976

Pittsburgh	3	6	15—24
College All-Stars	0	0	0— 0

SCORING:
Pittsburgh: Gerela, 29-yard field goal 3-0.
Pittsburgh: Gerela, 32-yard field goal 6-0.
Pittsburgh: Gerela, 23-yard field goal 9-0.
Pittsburgh: Safety (Pinney 33-yard center snap into end zone) 11-0.
Pittsburgh: Harris, 21-yard run (Gerela, kick) 18-0.
Pittsburgh: Reamon, 2-yard run (kick failed) 24-0.

Game called off because of rain near end of third quarter.
ATTENDANCE: 52,895.

Reprinted from
Pro Football Weekly

Tokyo Exhibition Won by St. Louis

Aug. 25

Swap Taylor

The Detroit Lions swapped star running back Altie Taylor to the Houston Oilers Tuesday moments after fullback Steve Owens announced his retirement from the National Football League. Taylor, all-time leading ground gainer, had reportedly been unhappy with the team for the past year. The Lions got two undisclosed draft choices for the runner.

Reprinted from
The Hartford Courant

TOKYO, JAPAN, AUG. 16, 1976

St. Louis	3	7	7	3—20
San Diego	0	3	7	0—10

SCORING:

St. Louis: Bakken, 39-yard field goal-3-0.

St. Louis: Tilley, 14-yard pass from Donckers (Bakken, kick)-10-0.

San Diego: Albert, 40-yard field goal-10-13.

San Diego: McDonald, 22-yard pass from Fouts (Albert, kick)-10-10.

St. Louis: Harris, 52-yard pass from Hart (Bakken, kick)-17-10.

St. Louis: Bakken, 21-yard field goal-20-10.

ATTENDANCE: 38,000

TEAM STATISTICS

	S. L.	S. D.
FIRST DOWNS	21	1
Rushing	7	2
Passing	10	8
Penalty	4	1
TOTAL YARDS	324	196
Rushing	138	44
Passing	186	152
PASSES—Attempted	28	30
Completed	19	15
Intercepted By	1	0
Tackled Attempting to Pass	2	2
Yards Lost Attempting to Pass	29	14
PUNTS	7	9
Average	33.4	43.7
Returned (#)	3	4
Yards Returned	14	25
KICKOFFS—Returned (#)	2	5
Yards Returned	45	116
PENALTIES	8	7
Yards Penalized	79	85
RUSHING PLAYS	42	20
Average Gain	3.3	2.2
TOTAL PLAYS (Include plays attempting to pass)	72	52
Average Gain	4.5	3.8
FUMBLES	1	2
Times Ball Was Lost	1	1
FIELD GOALS—Attempted	2	1
Made	2	1

Reprinted from
Pro Football Weekly

Aug. 25

Waived

The Houston Oilers waived defensive end Bubba Smith, receivers Mike Montgomery and Steve Largent and punter Leroy Clark Tuesday, but the Oilers would not confirm the moves until the NFL's waiver process is completed. "I'm going home to Beaumont," said Smith, 31, former allpro who signed with the Oilers to play behind his younger brother Tody. "I don't know what I'm going to do."

Reprinted from
The Hartford Courant

Aug. 25

Traded

The stormy relationship between safety Jake Scott and Miami Dolphins' coach Don Shula came to an end Tuesday when the Dolphins traded Scott and an undisclosed draft choice to the Washington Redskins for Bryant Salter, a defensive back. The Scott-Shula running battle began last year when the two clashed over whether Scott was fit to play in a game. Shula said no, and benched him.

Reprinted from
The Hartford Courant

Aug. 16

Bills turn to Raiders in seeking deal for O.J.

Aug. 25

Mercury Traded

Mercury Morris, who had been placed on waivers Monday by Miami Dolphins' Coach Don Shula, was traded Tuesday to the San Diego Chargers for an undisclosed draft choice. Dolphins' spokesmen would not elaborate on the trade for Morris, second only to Larry Csonka in career rushing for Miami.

Reprinted from
The Hartford Courant

Aug. 28

Judge rejects NFL plea

Delaware grid pool gets green light

Aug. 31

Longley Traded

The Dallas Cowboys traded reserve quarterback Clint Longley to the San Diego Chargers for undisclosed draft choices Monday night. "We felt it was for the best interests of the team as well as Clint that we trade him. It's a good opportunity for him. It's a club that's on the way up and this can be a chance for him to play," said Dallas coach Tom Landry. Longley was suspended by Landry a couple of weeks ago after he punched first-string quarterback Roger Staubach after a training session.

Reprinted from
The Hartford Courant

Bitter Blanda Heading For Hall of Fame

By TOM LaMARRE

OAKLAND — Football has outlasted George Blanda after all.

Blanda, football's Grand Old Man who seemed as if he would play the game forever, is somewhere in Chicago hitting golf balls while the Oakland Raiders and the National Football League go on without him.

The Raiders put Blanda on waivers last Tuesday, and he went unclaimed throughout the league.

But ol' George even got the jump on retirement.

"I don't know if this is it or not," said the soon-to-be 49-year-old as he left the Raiders' training camp in Santa Rosa, Calif., before the end became official.

"I'M GOING home to where I know someone needs me and cares about me," he added with a touch of bitterness. "I've had enough of this bull. I just want to get out of here."

Blanda reported to training camp last month unaware that rookie Fred Steinfort would be given the placekicking job to win or lose during the pre-season. He's won it.

But ol' George wanted to go down fighting.

"I didn't like sitting around as an insurance policy," declared the oldest man ever to play the game. "I enjoyed the sun, the golf and the trip to New York, but the vacation is over.

"They made me feel like I wasn't even a member of the team. I never thought they'd do that to me after all the years I've helped this club. Al Davis has been great to me, but once I leave here I'll never come back even if they somehow need me."

Blanda's 2,002 points rank him 653 ahead of Lou Groza, the former Cleveland placekicking great who is second on the all-time scoring list.

Blanda played 26 years with Chicago, Houston and Oakland. But he will be remembered most for an incredible five week stretch in 1970 when he almost single-handedly gave the Raiders four wins and a tie with some pressure passing and kicking.

"George won a lot of games for us over the years with both his passing and kicking," said Coach John Madden in tribute. "He was the fiercest competitor I ever saw and I'll never forget him."

Reprinted from
Pro Football Weekly

Sept. 2

NFL sets 43-man limit; expansion clubs excepted

New York (AP) — National Football League teams, with the exception of Seattle and Tampa Bay, will be limited to 43 players this season, NFL commissioner Pete Rozelle said last night.

The two expansion teams— the Seattle Seahawks and Tampa Bay Buccaneers—will be allowed to carry 6 additional players for the first two games, then 45 after that. However, the teams may only dress 43 players for any game.

Rozelle said the teams must reach their player limit by Monday at 2 P.M.

NFL Needs Some New Lawyers

By ART ARKUSH

CHICAGO—The NFL was wiped out in the courts again last week. If its teams performed on the gridiron like the league does in court, they would have no wins, no ties—and no fans.

What has become increasingly apparent is that somebody at the top has done some very bad play calling or they are getting some very bad advice. In almost every courtroom tangle with the NFL Players Association, the league has come off second-best. The lone exception was the Joe Kapp case where a last-minute substitute, ex-Mayor Joseph Aliotto, bailed them out.

The latest defeat is undoubtedly the most crushing. When U.S. District Judge William B. Bryant struck down the annual draft of college players on grounds it violated federal anti-trust laws, it knocked the pins out from under the contract negotiations with the players association and set up executive director Ed Garvey in the other alley.

Naturally, Garvey was elated with the verdict. It marked a big win for him and came at a time when the league would have you believe his grasp on the union was slipping. As a matter of fact, worrying about Garvey instead of the more important issues appears to have been one of the league's major mistakes.

THE LEAGUE'S game plan appeared to have been an attempt to sweep Garvey's flank and go around him by reaching an agreement with Dick Anderson, the union's president. The only problem is that they under-estimated Garvey's defenses. His team player reps stood with him and tabled the offer worked out by Anderson and Dan Rooney, representing the owners.

Now Garvey feels the NFLPA has won the one case that must bring his side and the owners together to finally get a contract.

Reprinted from
Pro Football Weekly

Sept. 9

Federal judge rules college draft illegal

Sept. 4

Rift between Thomas, Marchibroda surfaces

Sept. 6

Marchibroda Quits Colts In Dispute With Owner

Sept. 7

Colt Players Meet, Discuss a Boycott

Sept. 9

Marchibroda rehired with 'full control'
Colts extend his contract by a year

All the above reprinted from
The Baltimore Sun

SEATTLE'S FIRST GAME

SEATTLE, SEPT. 12, 1976

St. Louis	3	10	10	7—30
Seattle	3	0	7	14—24

SCORING:
St. Louis: Bakken, 28-yard field goal, 3-0.
Seattle: Bitterlich, 27-yard field goal, 3-3.
St. Louis: Harris, 12-yard pass from Hart, (Bakken, kick) 10-3.
St. Louis: Bakken, 22-yard field goal, 13-3.
St. Louis: Tilley 27-yard pass from Hart (Bakken, kick) 20-3.
St. Louis: Bakken, 26-yard field goal, 23-3.
Seattle: McCullum, 15-yard pass from Zorn (Bitterlich, kick) 23-10.
St. Louis: Otis, 1-yard run, (Bakken, kick) 30-10.
Seattle: McCullum, 72-yard pass from Zorn. (Bitterlich, kick) 30-17.
Seattle: Zorn, 8-yard run (Bitterlich, kick) 30-24.
ATTENDANCE: 58,441

Reprinted from
Pro Football Weekly

TAMPA BAY'S FIRST GAME

HOUSTON, SEPT. 12, 1976

Tampa Bay	0	0	0	0—0
Houston	0	7	3	10—20

SCORING:
Houston: Willis, 13-yard pass from Pastorini. (Butler, kick). 0-7.
Houston: Butler, 33-yard field goal. 0-10.
Houston: Burrough, 44-yard pass from Pastorini (Butler, kick). 0-17.
Houston: Butler, 44-yard field goal. 0-20.
ATTENDANCE: 42,228.

Reprinted from
Pro Football Weekly

Sept. 20

Rams 10, Vikings 10.
A blocked field goal attempt by Minnesota cornerback Nate Allen and end zone interception by Los Angeles linebacker Rick Kay in overtime spoiled scoring chances as the Rams and the Vikings tied. The Rams' Jim Bertelsen plunged a yard for a TD with 1:55 left in regulation to tie the game. Tom Dempsey's 30-yard field goal in overtime was blocked by Allen and Minnesota's shot at a win late in overtime ended when Kay picked off Fran Tarkenton's pass.

O.J. Back to Bills

From THE PFW WIRES

BUFFALO — L. A., Goodbye. The "Juice" will be flowing in Buffalo once again.

O. J. Simpson, the National Football League's premier running back, has reached a "long term understanding" with the Buffalo Bills' owner Ralph C. Wilson, Jr., and has rejoined the team, it was announced last Sunday.

Simpson, who asked the Bills last June to trade him to an NFL club on the West Coast, preferably the Los Angeles Rams, reportedly signed a $2-½ million, three-year contract, plus fringe benefits, following the meeting with Wilson in Los Angeles.

The statement released by the Bills quoted Simpson as saying: "We talked about my association with the Bills, the city of Buffalo . . . and what it would be like to be out of the game. I've thought about those things before, but Mr. Wilson really hit home."

The Rams turned down a deal for Simpson Sept. 6, in which the Bills' offered the former Heisman Trophy winner from Southern California for L. A. defensive end Jack Youngblood, running back Lawrence McCutcheon, reserve defensive tackle Mike Fanning and first round draft choices for 1978 and 1979.

SIMPSON, WHO gained an NFL-record 2,003 yards rushing in 1973, had said earlier that he would retire from football and actively pursue his acting career, if he was not traded to a West Coast team.

"That's all behind us," said Wilson after the signing. "O. J. and the Bills have some great years ahead. We're pleased beyond words that it's been possible to re-unite the 'Juice' with his coaches, his teammates and the loyal fans of Buffalo. We were saddened when O. J. asked to be traded, but because we understood his feelings, we made every effort possible to accommodate him. A trade simply was not possible. The important thing is that O. J. is coming back to Buffalo and will finish his career here."

"I just hope O. J.'s ready to play within a couple of weeks and maybe he'll play some tomorrow (Monday)," said Bills' Head Coach Lou Saban. "From past history, 'Juice' has always been physically sound and physically fit, but it's a little bit different when you're talking about taking those bumps and running into people like you do in football. It's going to take a little while for him to get used to that."

"I never wanted to leave the game," said Simpson, whose wife, Marguerite, was at his side during the meeting with Wilson. "Considering all our conversations . . . Marguerite and I decided it would be best for us to return to Buffalo."

Reprinted from Pro Football Weekly

Editorial...

Commissioner Pete Rozelle needs another problem about as much as O.J. Simpson needs a loan. But because he has fined George Atkinson and Jack Tatum of the Oakland Raiders for "fouls" they committed during the recent Oakland-Pittsburgh game, Rozelle is once more embroiled with the NFL Players' Association.

Gene Upshaw, a vice-president of the NFLPA and a teammate of Atkinson and Tatum, says that Rozelle's $1,500 fine on Atkinson and $750 assessment on Tatum is "outrageous."

"It ticks me off because Rozelle has them tried, convicted and sentenced before they even get a hearing," said Upshaw with more than a little trace of bitterness. He suggested that an abundance of publicity about Atkinson's conduct in nearly decapitating Steeler wide receiver Lynn Swann is what led to the fines.

Well if you checked in at this corner last issue, you know that we were part of that "abundance" and that we felt then Atkinson should have been penalized for the hit. We still do.

In this instance, we believe Rozelle is damned if he does and damned if he doesn't. It appeared to us that there should be a penalty for what Atkinson did to Swann. Rozelle chose to set George back 1,500 bucks and that may or may not be just. There is a hearing on the matter scheduled for Oct. 4, and at that time, all parties will apparently have their say.

One of Upshaw's big beefs is that the hearing should not be held before any punishment is netted out, and that may or may not be. What we hope is that for the immediate future, Rozelle's action may put a damper on the type of hitting that saw Swann decked from behind with a karate-like chop to the head that left the Steeler star with a concussion.

Maybe there is a better way of handling the matter, and it shouldn't be up to the commissioner's total disgression, as Upshaw suggests. But for the moment, it appears that Rozelle was the only one with the authority to act, and he did so promptly and incisively. Let's hope the message the fines are supposed to carry is received loud and clear throughout the league.

And even if it isn't, Rozelle is to be commended for transmitting it.

Reprinted from Pro Football Weekly

Sept. 20

Grogan tosses 3 TD passes, directs Pats to upset of Dolphins, 30-14

Oct. 3

Amazing Patriots Wipe Out Raiders

New England 48, Oakland 17

Oakland	0 10 0 7—17
New Englands	7 14 14 13—48

NE—A Johnson 2 run (Smith kick)
NE—Stingley 21 pass from Grogan (Smith kick)
Oak—Biletnikoff 14 pass from Stabler (Steinfort kick)
NE—Briscoe 16 pass from Grogar (Smith kick)
Oak—Steinfort 44 field goal
NE—Stingley 15 pass from Grogan (Smith kick)
NE—Grogan 2 run (Smith kick)
NE—Grogan 10 run (Smith kick)
NE—Phillips 11 run (kick failed)
Oak—Rae run (Steinfort kick)
Attendance—61,068

	Raiders	Pats
First downs	25	27
Rushes-yards	24-114	52-296
Passing-yards	207	172
Return yards	57	96
Passes	24-44-1	11-17-1
Punts	6-37	4-46
Fumbles-lost	4-3	3-0
Penalties-yards	8-85	10-124

INDIVIDUAL LEADERS
RUSHING—Oakland—van Eeghen 8-34, Davis 6-25 New England—Cunningham 21-101, Johnson 15-67, Grogan 5-56.
RECEIVING—Oakland—Casper 12-136, Davis 4-40. New England—Cunningham 5-94, Stingley 2-36
PASSING—Oakland—Stabler 20-35-1 225, Rae 4-9-0, 21. New England—Grogan 10-14-1, 165, Owen 1-3-0, 7

New England, 30; Miami, 14.

Miami	0 7 0 7—14
New England	0 13 7 10—30

NE—Johnson 15 pass from Grogan (kick failed)
M—Tillman 5 pass from Griese (Yepremian kick)
NE—Grogan 13 run (Smith kick)
NE—Johnson 29 pass from Grogan (Smith kick)
NE—FG Smith 22
M—Bulaich 1 run (Yepremian kick)
NE—Francis 4 pass from Grogan (Smith kick)
Attendance—46,053

	Dolphins	Pats
First downs	17	23
Rushes-yards	22-108	51-278
Passing-yards	146	152
Return yards	21	60
Passes	17-32-3	16-27-0
Punts	6-38	4-46
Fumbles-lost	1-1	3-2
Penalties-yards	7-68	9-70

INDIVIDUAL LEADERS
RUSHING—Miami: Nottingham, 7-10, Malone 7-42, Bulaich 5-9, Griese 2-35. New England: Cunningham 21-106, Johnson 14-35, Grogan 9-76, Calhoun 7-61
RECEIVING—Miami: Moore 3-54, Bulaich 3-16. New England: Johnson 7-93, Francis 3-21, Briscoe 3-27.
PASSING—Miami: Griese 16-26-3, 190; Strock 1-6-0, 8. New England: Grogan 16-27-0, 166.

Oct. 11

Lions stun Patriots, 30 to 10

Detroit 30, New England 10

New England	0 3 7 0—10
Detroit	13 7 0 10—30

DET—Bussey 5 run (kick failed)
DET—D Hill 21 pass from Landry (Mann kick)
DET—C. Sanders 5 pass from Landry (Mann kick)
NE—J. Smith 41 field goal
NE—Vataha 35 pass from Grogan (J. Smith kick)
DET—D. Hill 3 pass from Landry (Mann kick)
DET—Mann 36 field goal
Attendance—60,174

	Pats	Lions
First downs	10	20
Rushes-yards	22-96	48-196
Passing yards	103	133
Return yards	12	126
Passes	11-25-5	15-18-0
Punts	5-42	5-37
Fumbles-lost	0-0	1-0
Penalties-yards	7-52	7-37

Individual leaders
RUSHING—New England—Cunningham 13-50, Johnson 6-35. Detroit—King 32-100, Bussey 12-87.
RECEIVING—New England—Stingley 3-46, Cunningham 3-29, Francis 2-15, Johnson 2-6, Vataha 1-35. Detroit—King 6-45, Hill 4-43, C. Sanders 3-38.
PASSING—New England—Grogan 11-25-5, 131 yards. Detroit—Landry 15-18-0, 146.

Oct. 5

New coach to be named today

Detroit's Forzano quits in wake of another loss

Oct. 6

Back-to-basics Hudspeth is Lions' choice for coach

Oct. 12

Falcons move Peppler into head coach post

Oct. 15

Saban, Bills' Coach, Quits; Ringo, Aide, Named to Post

Winless Giants open smashing new stadium

Dallas 24, N.Y. Giants 14
```
Dallas...................  7 10 0 7—24
N.Y. Giants..............  0  0 7 7—14
```
Dal—Newhouse 8 run (Herrera kick)
Dal—Pearson 40 pass from Staubach (Herrera kick)
Dal—Herrera 24 field goal
NYG—Robinson 30 pass from Morton (Danelo kick)
Dal—Dennison 4 run (Herrera kick)
NYG—Csonka 6 run (Danelo kick)
Attendance—76,042

	Cowboys	Giants
First downs	18	18
Rushes-yards	42-163	33-139
Passing yards	168	153
Return yards	76	94
Passes	13-15-0	12-16-1
Punts	4-37	5-36
Fumbles-lost	1-0	2-0
Penalties-yards	5-55	5-40

Individual leaders
RUSHING—Dallas—Newhouse 16-57, Young 12-43, Dennison 10-42. New York—Kotar 13-59, Csonka 12-53.
RECEIVING—Dallas—Pearson 4-88, Laidlaw 3-29. New York—Tucker 5-74, Robinson 3-67.
PASSING—Dallas—Staubach 13-15-0, 178 yards. New York—Morton 8-12-1, 126; Snead 4-4-0, 64.

NFL rule considered unlawful

U.S. panel upholds antitrust opinion on Rozelle Rule

Seahawks nip Bucs, 13-10, for first NFL victory

SEAHAWKS 13, BUCS 10
```
Seattle..............  0 13 0 0—13
Tampa Bay............  3  0 7 0—10
```
Tam—FG Green 38
Sea—McCullum 15 pass from Zorn (Leyboldt kick)
Sea—FG Leyboldt 25
Sea—FG Leyboldt 39
Tam—Owens 1 pass from Carter (Green kick)
Attendance—43,812

	Sea	Tam
First downs	13	18
Rushes-yards	29-90	33-145
Passing yards	163	140
Return yards	110	123
Passes	12-29-1	19-31-0
Punts	7-39	8-39
Fumbles-lost	1-1	2-1
Penalties-yards	15-120	20-190

INDIVIDUAL LEADERS
RUSHING—Seattle, Smith 10-45, Nelson 4-22. Tampa, Carter 15-66, Johnson 12-54.
RECEIVING—Seattle, McCullum 5-64, Largent 3-49, Howard 2-45. Tampa, Williams 4-42, McKay 4-38, Carter 3-28.
PASSING—Seattle, Zorn 11-29-1, 167 yards. Tampa, Spurrier 18-30-0, 170.

Ho Hum! Tark Completes 3,000th

BLOOMINGTIN, Minn.—The man known as the "Scrambler" completed his 3,000th pass last Sunday—a remarkable feat for a guy who's supposed to be famous for running, not passing.

But Fran Tarkenton, who may never shed his scrambling image no matter how many passes he completes, became the first NFL quarterback to break the 3,000th plateau in leading the Minnesota Vikings to a 24-7 victory over the winless New York Giants.

And in much the same manner he scrambled from oncoming defensive ends for the past 16 years, Tarkenton dodged questions about the record.

"The 3,000 deal has no meaning to me," he said after completing 21 of 30 passes for 228 yards and two touchdowns. "I didn't even know it when it happened."

IT HAPPENED early in the first quarter when Tarkenton hit Chuck Foreman with a seven-yard pass. Foreman caught eight Tarkenton passes in all for 118 yards.

"Jim Marshall (defensive end) came up to me along the sidelines later and asked me, 'how does it feel? I said, 'what are you talking about?' I guess they mentioned it over the public address system but I didn't hear it. I got some of the big records last year (most NFL completions and scoring passes) so this really doesn't mean anything."

The victory lifted Minnesota's record to 5-0-1, while the Giants fell to 0-6.

Arnsparger Dismissed, 0-7 Giants Hire McVay

Arnsparger to Miami

Nov. 1

Dolphins upend Patriots, 10-3

DOLPHINS 10, PATRIOTS 3

New England	0 3 0 0—	3
Miami	0 10 0 0—	10

Mia—Mandich 16 pass from Griese (Yepremian kick)
Mia—FG Yepremian 46
NE—FG Smith 43
Attendance—52,863

	NE	MIA
First downs	11	18
Rushes-yards	27-130	37-157
Passing yards	112	132
Return yards	121	77
Passes	10-31-1	12-22-0
Punts	8-43	7-38
Fumbles-lost	1-0	0-0
Penalties-yards	11-80	5-33

INDIVIDUAL LEADERS
RUSHING—New England, Cunningham 14-79, Grogan 6-15. Miami, Malone 21-119, Nottingham 11-29

RECEIVING—New England, Francis 4-47, Cunningham 3-25, Johnson 2-28. Miami, Mandich 5-51, Tillman 3-32, Soloman 2-38

PASSING—New England, Grogan 10-31-1, 112 yards. Miami, Griese 12-22-0, 132

Nov. 8

Giants Do Everything But Score

EAST RUTHERFORD, N.J. — John McVay failed to pick up in the NFL where he left off in the WFL.

McVay, the most successful coach in the brief history of the defunct World Football League, made his NFL debut as coach of the New York Giants and came away with a 10-0 loss to the Philadelphia Eagles.

It was the first shutout in eight years for the Eagles, and it was the eighth straight defeat for the winless Giants.

McVay, who took over after the firing of Bill Arnsparger, compiled a 25-7 record in 1½ years as coach of the Memphis Southmen of the WFL, including the regular season championship the first year.

BUT LAST Sunday, McVay got his initiation to the NFL. "I feel you have to put three scores on the board to win a professional football game," he said. "If you do that, you figure you'll win 21-14 or 21-10, or 17-14 . . . something like that. This was the exception today. Our defense did a good job and I thought our offense moved the ball pretty good. We just didn't score any points. And that's the name of the game."

Philadelphia quarterback Mike Boryla hit Harold Carmichael with a 13-yard second quarter touchdown pass and Horst Muhlmann added a 29-yard field goal five minutes later to account for all the Eagles' points.

A pair of goalline stands preserved the shutout in the game's final four minutes.

Nov. 8

Raiders Get Help From Ref, Wind

By ED STONE

CHICAGO — Referee Chuck Heberling accidentally blew his whistle and wiped out a legitimate Bear touchdown.

The gusting Soldier Field wind capriciously blew a center snap awry and cost the Bears an extra point.

And Bob Thomas apparently just blew a 31-yard field goal attempt with 20 seconds left as the final twist of fate that salvaged a 28-27 victory for the Oakland Raiders last Sunday.

Despite all that misfortune, the upstart Bears still could have dumped the Raiders with a rousing second-half comeback if cornerback Virgil Livers, trying for an interception, hadn't tipped the ball to Cliff Branch for the winning 49-yard touchdown.

Or if Chicago safety Craig Clemons hadn't dropped a Ken Stabler pass thrown at him three plays before that.

THESE SORT of things left the Bears quietly sullen and frustrated at first. But that mood changed to bitterness and anger when they learned of Heberling's postgame explanation for nullifying defensive end Roger Stillwell's 39-yard scoring romp with a Stabler fumble early in the last period.

"It was an inadvertent whistle," said Heberling, a 12-year NFL official. "I blew it when I shouldn't have, so the only thing I could do was give Chicago the ball, and that's what I did."

Heberling was applying a rule that covers accidental whistles by an official. This one came after Stillwell was already goalward bound, but since play is automatically dead following any whistle, the Raiders didn't chase him.

Although there seemed little chance they could catch him, anyway, it probably would have compounded Heberling's error to allow the touchdown.

But don't try to tell the Bears that. "When they're dreaming up stuff to call on you, then you know you're in trouble," bristled Wally Chambers, who forced the fumble by sacking Stabler. "After Stillwell was gone, I heard a whistle, but not until then."

Nov. 22

Vikings beat Pack, 17-10, for 8th title in 9 years

VIKINGS 17, PACKERS 10

Minnesota	3 7 0 7—	17
Green Bay	3 0 7 0—	10

GB—FG Marcol 22
Min—FG Cox 41
Min—Miller 4 pass from Tarkenton (Cox kick)
GB—Brockington 1 run (Marcol kick)
Min—Rashad 11 pass from Tarkenton (Cox kick)
Attendance—55,963

	MIN	GB
First downs	17	13
Rushes-yards	30-100	38-146
Passing yards	180	100
Return yards	108	77
Passes	23-43-0	12-27-4
Punts	7-39	7-30
Fumbles-lost	4-2	0-0
Penalties-yards	2-25	4-25

INDIVIDUAL LEADERS
RUSHING—Minnesota, Foreman 19-84, Johnson 1-2. Green Bay, Brockington 13-51, Harrell 8-42.

RECEIVING—Minnesota, Miller 9-63, Foreman 5-39. Green Bay, Payne 3-29, O. Smith 2-27.

PASSING—Minnesota, Tarkenton 23-43-0, 180 yards. Green Bay, Brown 11-25-3, 82; Harrell 0-1-1, 0; Beverly 1-1-0, 18.

Nov. 2

Saban accepts position as Cincinnati athletic head

Nov. 20

Saban quits Cincinnati, citing personal reasons

Nov. 15

Cardinals 30, Rams 28

Jim Bakken's field goal with four seconds left provided the winning margin for St. Louis, 8-2, as Lons Angeles, now 6-3-1, failed to pick up any ground on San Francisco in the National Conference West.

NFL standings

American Conference

East

	W	L	T	Pct.	PF	PA
Baltimore	9	2	0	.818	309	186
New England	8	3	0	.727	280	202
Miami	5	6	0	.455	196	191
NY Jets	3	8	0	.273	134	271
Buffalo	2	9	0	.182	183	233

Central

	W	L	T	Pct.	PF	PA
Cincinnati	9	2	0	.818	270	165
Pittsburgh	7	4	0	.636	272	135
Cleveland	7	4	0	.636	223	225
Houston	4	7	0	.364	192	225

West

	W	L	T	Pct.	PF	PA
x-Oakland	10	1	0	.909	242	201
Denver	7	4	0	.636	256	138
San Diego	5	6	0	.455	215	231
Kansas City	3	8	0	.273	212	325
Tampa Bay	0	11	0	.000	95	290

National Conference

East

	W	L	T	Pct.	PF	PA
Dallas	9	2	0	.818	237	146
St. Louis	8	3	0	.727	254	217
Washington	7	4	0	.636	203	187
Philadelphia	3	8	0	.273	131	226
NY Giants	1	10	0	.091	104	207

Central

	W	L	T	Pct.	PF	PA
x-Minnesota	9	1	1	.864	240	140
Detroit	5	6	0	.455	208	162
Chicago	5	6	0	.455	189	171
Green Bay	4	7	0	.364	175	243

West

	W	L	T	Pct.	PF	PA
Los Angeles	7	3	1	.682	239	159
San Francisco	6	5	0	.545	216	154
New Orleans	4	7	0	.364	226	259
Atlanta	4	7	0	.364	138	209
Seattle	2	9	0	.182	196	340

x-Clinched division title

Nov. 15

Giants Finally Win

GIANTS 12, REDSKINS 9

Washington	3	3	3	0— 9
N.Y. Giants	3	3	3	3—12

NY—FG Danelo 30
Wash—FG Moseley 41
Wash—FG Moseley 31
NY—FG Danelo 26
NY—FG Danelo 39
Wash—FG Moseley 32
NY—FG Danelo 50
Attendance—72,975

	WASH	NYG
First downs	20	10
Rushes-yards	36-174	49-144
Passing yards	141	26
Return yards	52	23
Passes	12-30-1	3-14-2

Punts	3-37	4-49
Fumbles-lost	4-3	2-1
Penalties-yards	6-45	5-33

INDIVIDUAL LEADERS

RUSHING—Washington, Thomas 24-106, Riggins 9-48. New York, Csonka 16-55, White 11-48, Kotar 16-45.

RECEIVING—Washington, Jefferson 3-39, Thomas 3-27, Grant 2-12, Fugett 2-31, L. Brown 2-14. New York, Rhodes 1-13, Bell 1-10, Kotar 1-3.

PASSING—Washington, Theismann 12-30-1, 153 yards. New York, Snead 3-14-2, 26.

Nov. 25

Simpson sets one-game rushing mark

By JACK SAYLOR

PONTIAC, Mich.—O.J. Simpson is breaking more records than a deranged disc jockey these days, and now can a 300-yard game for the Buffalo marvel be far behind?

Simpson rambled for 273 yards and two touchdowns before a National TV audience and 66,875 fans in the Pontiac Silverdome on Thanksgiving Day—and he did it at the expense of the Detroit Lions, who at the time were rated as the NFL's No. 1 defense.

The outburst broke his old record of 250 yards (in a 1974 game against the Patriots), and the only thing that kept Orenthal James from gaining 300 in this one was that the selfish old Lions kept the ball for themselves enough of the time to win the game, 27-14.

Nov. 29

Davis Signs With Bucs

By JIM SELMAN

TAMPA—The Tampa Bay Buccaneers obviously need immediate help, but they surely took a big step toward improvement in 1977 when they signed running back Anthony Davis to a multi-year contract last Tuesday.

The Bucs' next goal as far as the '77 season is concerned is to make Southern Cal's Ricky Bell their No. 1 draft choice, if there is a draft.

And if there is not, Bucs operations director Ron Wolf said Tampa Bay will enter a bidding war for Bell.

The prospect of having his two former USC running backs in his backfield has made Bucs coach John McKay very happy.

IN DAVIS, the Bucs have Southern Cal's all-time rushing leader with 3,724 yards and in Bell, they would have a back who was only 280 yards shy of breaking Davis' record before last weekend.

Nov. 29

Steelers Keep Playoff Hope Alive, Beat Bengals, 7-3, in Snow and Ice on Harris Tally

STEELERS 7, BENGALS 3

Pittsburgh	0 0 7 0—7
Cincinnati	3 0 0 0—3

Cin—FG Bahr 40
Pit—Harris 4 run (Gerela kick)
Attendance—55,142

	PITT	CIN
First downs	20	9
Rushes-yards	49-204	30-110
Passing yards	143	115
Return yards	36	54
Passes	10-15-1	10-26-1
Punts	5-39	8-39
Fumbles-lost	3-1	3-1
Penalties-yards	6-40	4-25

INDIVIDUAL LEADERS
RUSHING—Pittsburgh, Bleier 16-97, Harris 26-87. Cincinnati, Clark 14-45, Griffin 8-29, Fritts 4-22.
RECEIVING—Pittsburgh, Swann 5-95, Bleier 2-36, Lewis 2-27. Cincinnati, Curtis 3-86, Trumpy 2-14.
PASSING—Pittsburgh, Kruczek 10-16-1, 163 yards. Cincinnati, Anderson 10-26-1, 145.

Dec. 6

Patriots Triumph, 27-6, And Clinch Playoff Spot

PATRIOTS 27, SAINTS 6

New Orleans	0 3 0 3— 6
New England	0 13 0 14—27

NE—Chandler 12 pass from Grogan (kick failed)
NE—Grogan 11 run (Smith kick)
NO—FG Szaro 50
NO—FG Szaro 29
NE—Grogan 10 run (Smith kick)
NE—Forte 6 pass from Grogan (Smith kick)
Attendance—53,592

	NO	NE
First downs	14	21
Rushes-yards	30-118	42-220
Passing yards	118	108
Return yards	13	46
Passes	18-31-0	9-24-0
Punts	8-32	6-38
Fumbles-lost	2-1	0-0
Penalties-yards	6-55	10-85

INDIVIDUAL LEADERS
RUSHING—New Orleans, Galbreath 13-41, Muncie 12-36, Strachan 4-36. New England, Calhoun 22-113, Johnson 11-73, Grogan 4-27.
RECEIVING—New Orleans, Galbreath 8-58, Muncie 5-35, Herrmann 3-24. New England, Stingley 2-54, Calhoun 2-1.
PASSING—New Orleans, Douglass 10-20-0, 61; Scott 8-11-0, 75. New England, Grogan 9-23-0, 108; Johnson 0-1-0.

Dec. 7

Raiders defeat Bengals

Stabler throws four TD passes in 35-20 victory

Dec. 13

'Skins win wild-card berth by beating Cowboys, 27-14

REDSKINS 27, COWBOYS 14

Washington	0 10 3 14—27
Dallas	0 7 7 0—14

Was—FG Mosely 25
Dal—Dennison 12 run (Herrera kick)
Was—Fugett 6 pass from Kilmer (Moseley kick)
Dal—B. Johnson 43 pass from Staubach (Herrera kick)
Was—FG Moseley 27
Was—Hill 15 run (Moseley kick)
Was—Riggins 3 run (Moseley kick)
Attendance—59,916

	WAS	DALL
First downs	24	10
Rushes-yards	47-184	36-149
Passing yards	174	54
Return yards	47	40
Passes	14-30-2	5-22-2
Punts	6-41	8-37
Fumbles-lost	2-2	2-2
Penalties-yards	7-64	4-25

INDIVIDUAL LEADERS
RUSHING—Washington, Riggins 23-95, Thomas 20-66. Dallas, Dennison 18-76, Staubach 6-32.
RECEIVING—Washington, Thomas 7-89, Fugett 3-43. Dallas, Johnson 2-60, D Pearson 2-19.
PASSING—Washington, Kilmer, 14-32-2, 199 yards. Dallas, Staubach, 5-22-2, 91 yards.

Dec. 10

Lou Holtz quits Jets, admits having interest in U. of Arkansas post

Dec. 15

Grid Giants give coach McVay new two-year contract

NFL standings

American Conference

East

	W	L	T	Pct.	PF	PA
x-Baltimore	11	3	0	.786	417	246
y-New England	11	3	0	.786	376	234
Miami	6	8	0	.429	263	264
NY Jets	3	11	0	.214	169	383
Buffalo	2	12	0	.143	245	363

Central

	W	L	T	Pct.	PF	PA
x-Pittsburgh	10	4	0	.714	342	138
Cincinnati	10	4	0	.714	335	210
Cleveland	9	5	0	.643	267	287
Houston	5	9	0	.357	222	273

West

	W	L	T	Pct.	PF	PA
Oakland	13	1	0	.929	350	237
Denver	9	5	0	.643	315	206
San Diego	6	8	0	.429	248	285
Kansas City	5	9	0	.357	290	376
Tampa Bay	0	14	0	.000	(12)	412

National Conference

East

	W	L	T	Pct.	PF	PA
Dallas	11	3	0	.786	296	194
z-Washington	10	4	0	.714	291	217
St. Louis	10	4	0	.714	309	267
Philadelphia	4	10	0	.286	165	286
NY Giants	3	11	0	.214	170	250

Central

	W	L	T	Pct.	PF	PA
Minnesota	11	2	1	.821	305	176
Chicago	7	7	0	.500	253	216
Detroit	6	8	0	.429	262	220
Green Bay	5	9	0	.357	218	299

West

	W	L	T	Pct.	QF	PA
Los Angeles	10	3	1	.750	351	190
San Francisco	8	6	0	.571	270	190
New Orleans	4	10	0	.286	253	346
Atlanta	4	10	0	.286	172	312
Seattle	2	12	0	.143	229	429

x-Clinched 1st on basis of formula used to break div. ties
y-Clinched playoff spot
z-Clinched playoff spot on basis of formula used to break div. ties

Dec. 13

Pats hand Bucs 14th loss, 31-14

Dec. 19

PLAYOFF GAME

Washington	3	0	3	14—	20
Minnesota	s	14	7	14	0— 35

Minn—Voigt 18 pass from Tarkenton (Cox kick)
Wash—FG Moseley 47
Minn—White 27 pass from Tarkenton (Cox kick)
Minn—Foreman 2 run (Cox kick)
Minn—Foreman 30 run (Cox kick)
Wash—FG Moseley 35
Minn—White 9 pass from Tarkenton (Cox kick)
Wash—Grant 12 pass from Kilmer (Moseley kick)
Wash—Jefferson 3 pass from Kilmer (Moseley kick)
A—48,169

	Wash	Minn
First downs	19	21
Rushes-yards	18—75	46—221
Passing yards	290	163
Return yards	216	53
Passes	26—49—2	12-22—2dPunts
Fumbles-lost	0—0	2—0
Penalties-yards	7—57	5—30

Passing: Washington—Kilmer 26-49-2-298. Minnesota—Tarkenton 12-21-2-170, Lee 0-1-0-0.
Receiving: Washington—Grant 6-70, Fugett 4-61, Jefferson 4-59, Hill 4-31, Riggins 4-29, Thomas 2-18, Smith 1-30, Brown 1-0. Minnesota—White 4-64, Voigt 4-42, McClanahan 3-29, Rashad 1-35.
Rushing: Washington—Thomas 11-45, Riggins 7-30. Minnesota—Foreman 20-105, McClanahan 20-101, Johnson 2-11, Miller 2-1, Tarkenton 1-3, Lee 1-0.

Dec. 19

Bitter Pats Rip Referee

By CARLO IMELIO

OAKLAND — Six years. That's how long Julius Adams has kept quiet.
He's 6-4 and 260 pounds, and a man that size can make a lot of noise if he were so inclined. But angry words? No. Not from Big Julie.

Consider his record broken. For on Saturday last the big defensive end for the New England Patriots let it fly.

"We got screwed," he said. "Screwed."

The Patriots had, only minutes earlier, lost a heartbreaking 24-21 decision to the Oakland Raiders. The Patriots were playing their first playoff game in 13 years. It was the biggest event to hit New England since the tornado leveled half of Worcester.

AT LEAST, it was that big for football fans.

New England has its Red Sox, Bruins and Celtics—and they all have made their marks. But the Patriots were the stepchild, the loser.

Last Saturday the Patriots were primed. They were ready to put it to the Raiders for the second time this season. They were 57 seconds away from advancing to the American Conference final.

Ben Dreith threw his yellow flag. It signalled that Ray Hamilton, the Patriot nosetackle, had roughed Ken Stabler, the Raider quarterback.

So, instead of the Raiders facing a fourth down and 18 at the Patriot 37 the Raiders had themselves a first and 10 at the 13. They won the game moments later when Stabler ran one yard for a touchdown.

The roughing penalty is what frosted Adams' cookies. And the quiet man took off on a tirade that will be heard in New England for a long time to come.

"We took a screwin' out there and I don't care who knows it," Adams barked. "What Ray Hamilton did. . .well, it was a legal hit. I'm not afraid to say it, either. They took the game away from us."

Hamilton blew in on Stabler and croaked him just as he let the ball go.
It fell incomplete, and the Raiders were down to their final shot. Fourth and 18.

OR SO it seemed.

How does a referee toss out a flag on such a crucial play? And particularly that type of call? You'll have to ask Art McNally, head of NFL officials.

Chuck Fairbanks will ask. If he's any kind of football coach he'll ask. And he'll bitch—so maybe next time it'll go his way.

Ray Hamilton swears he tipped the ball. Which means if he did indeed touch the ball, that the play cannot be flagged.

Dec. 20

PLAYOFF GAME

Rams 14, Cowboys 12

Los Angeles	0	7	0	7—14
Dallas	3	7	0	2—12

Dal—FG Herrera 44
LA—Haden 4 run (Dempsey kick)
Dal—Laidlaw 1 run (Herrera kick)
LA—McCutcheon 1 run (Dempsey kick)
Dal—Safety, Rams' R. Jackson ran out of end zone
Attendance—52,436

	LA	DAL
First downs	17	14
Rushes-yards	49–120	28–85
Passing yards	130	126
Return yards	43	73
Passes	15-21-3	15-37-3
Punts	9-28	6-38
Fumbles-lost	0-0	3-1
Penalties-yards	8-94	6-34

INDIVIDUAL LEADERS
RUSHING—Los Angeles, McCutcheon 21-58, Cappelletti 19-54, Haden 8-16. Dallas, P.Pearson 13-43, Newhouse 9-25, Staubach 2-8, Laidlaw 2-2.
RECEIVING—Los Angeles, H. Jackson 6-116, Cappelletti 2-15, Klein 1-12, McCutcheon 1-9 Dallas, P Pearson 6-41, D. Pearson 3-38, DuPree 3-34, Newhouse 2-19, B. Johnson 1-18.
PASSING—Los Angeles, Haden 10-21-3, 152 yards. Dallas, Staubach 15-37-3. 150.

New England	7	0	14	0—21
Oakland	3	7	0	14—24

NE—Johnson 1 run (Smith kick)
Oak—FG Mann 40
Oak—Biletnikoff 31 pass from Stabler (Mann kick)
NE—Francis 26 pass from Grogan (Smith kick)
NE—Phillips 3 run (Smith kick)
Oak—Van Eeghen 1 run (Mann kick)
Oak—Stabler 1 run (Mann kick)
A—53,045

	NE	Oak
First downs	23	20
Rushes-yards	49—164	24—81
Passing yards	167	201
Return yards	13	71
Passes	12—24—2	19-32—0
Punts	3—44.0	5—37.8
Fumbles-lost	1—1	1—1
Penalties-yards	10—83	11—93

Passing: New England—Grogan 12-23-1-167. Francis 0-1-1-0. Oakland—Stabler 19-32-0-223.
Receiving: New England—Francis 4-96, Stingley 2-36, Cunningham 2-14, A. Johnson 2-13, Briscoe 1-7, Chandler 1-1. Oakland—Biletnikoff 9-137, Casper 4-47, Branch 3-32, Van Eeghen 1-8, C. Davis 1-5, Garrett 1-4.
Rushing: New England—Cunningham 20-68, Grogan 7-35, A. Johnson 14-32, Calhoun 5-17, Phillips 3-12 Oakland—Van Eeghen 11-39, C. Davis 7-29, Banaszak 4-8, Garrett 1-4, Stabler 1-1.

Reprinted from
Pro Football Weekly

Vikings, Raiders Gain Super Bowl

Harris, Bleier Not in Game

PLAYOFF GAME

Steelers 40, Colts 14

Pittsburgh	9 17 0 14—40	
Baltimore	7 0 0 7—14	

Pitt—Lewis 76 pass from Bradshaw (kick failed)
Pitt—FG Gerela 45
Balt—Carr 17 pass from Jones (Linhart kick)
Pitt—Harrison 1 run (Gerela kick)
Pitt—Swann 29 pass from Bradshaw (Gerela kick)
Pitt—FG Gerela 25
Pitt—Swann 11 pass from Bradshaw (Gerela kick)
Balt—Leaks 1 run (Linhart kick)
Pitt—Harrison 10 run (Mansfield kick)
Attendance—60,020

	PITT	BALT
First downs	29	16
Rushes-yards	40-225	23-71
Passing yards	301	99
Return yards	50	11
Passes	19-24-0	11-25-2
Punts	1-33	4-40
Fumbles-lost	2-1	0-0
Penalties-yards	12-88	7-59

INDIVIDUAL LEADERS

RUSHING—Pittsburgh, Harris 18-132, Fuqua 11-54, Harrison 10-40. Baltimore, Mitchell 16-55, Leaks 4-12.

RECEIVING—Pittsburgh, Swann 5-77, Harrison 4-37, Harris 3-24, Lewis 2-103, Fuqua 2-34, Bell 2-25. Baltimore, Mitchell 5-42, Chester 3-42, Carr 2-35.

PASSING—Pittsburgh, Bradshaw 14-18-0, 264 yards; Kruczek 5-6-0, 44. Baltimore, Jones 11-25-2, 144.

Vikings 24, Rams 13

Los Angeles	0 0 13 0—13	
Minnesota	7 3 7 7—24	

Minn—Bryant 90 blocked field goal return (Cox kick)
Minn—FG Cox 25
Minn—Foreman 1 run (Cox kick)
LA—McCutcheon 10 run (kick failed)
LA—Jackson 5 pass from Haden (Dempsey kick)
Minn—S. Johnson 12 run (Cox kick)
Attendance—47,191

	LA	MINN
First downs	21	13
Rushes-yards	46-193	29-158
Passing yards	143	109
Return yards	60	128
Passes	9-22-2	12-27-1
Punts	7-29	8-35
Fumbles-lost	4-2	1-1
Penalties-yards	3-33	4-32

INDIVIDUAL LEADERS

RUSHING—Los Angeles, McCutcheon 26-128, Cappelletti 16-59. Minnesota, Foreman 15-118, Miller 10-28.

RECEIVING—Los Angeles, H. Jackson 4-70, Jessie 2-60, McCutcheon 2-18. Minnesota, Foreman 5-81, Rashad 3-28, Miller 3-24.

PASSING—Los Angeles, Haden 9-22-2, 161 yards. Minnesota, Tarkenton 12-27-1, 143.

Raiders 24, Steelers 7

Pittsburgh	0 7 0 0— 7	
Oakland	3 14 7 0—24	

O—FG Mann 39
O—Davis 1 run (Mann kick)
P—Harrison 3 run (Mansfield kick)
O—Bankston 4 pass from Stabler (Mann kick)
O—Banaszak 5 pass from Stabler (Mann kick)
A—53,739

	Pit	Oak
First downs	13	15
Rushes-yards	21-72	51-157
Passing yards	165	71
Return yards	18	44
Passes	14-35-1	10-16-0
Punts	7-37	7-44
Fumbles-lost	1-0	2-0
Penalties-yards	5-29	7-34

INDIVIDUAL LEADERS

RUSHING—Steelers, Harrison 11-44, Fuqua 8-24. Raiders: van Eeghen 22-66, Davis 11-54, Banaszak 15-46.

RECEIVING—Steelers, Cunningham 4-36, Swann 3-58, Fuqua 2-11, Harrison 2-10. Raiders: Branch 3-46, Bankston 2-11, Davis 2-7.

PASSING—Steelers: Bradshaw 14-35, 176 Raiders: Stabler 10-16-0, 88.

Another Jones award

Colt quarterback Bert Jones yesterday was named the National Football League's Most Valuable Player by the Professional Football Writers of America. Earlier, he had been named MVP and offensive player of the year by the Associated Press. Others receiving votes yesterday were Minnesota's Chuck Foreman, Chicago's Walter Payton, O.J. Simpson of Buffalo, Ken Stabler of Oakland and Roger Staubach of Dallas.

Reprinted from
The Baltimore Sun

The New York Jets, admitting errors in the selection of their last two head coaches, elevated WALT MICHAELS from the ranks of their assistants early last week to try and lead the club back from the worst season in its 17-year history.

Michaels, the defensive wizard of the Jets' 1969 Super Bowl triumph over the Baltimore Colts, was passed over for the head coaching job twice by the Jets in the past three years—first when CHARLEY WINNER was selected in 1974 and then last year when LOU HOLTZ was hired.

Michaels and General Manager AL WARD were given three-year contracts, in addition to the club's board of directors appointing LEON HESS as acting president, succeeding PHIL ISELIN who died the week before.

— — —

On the transaction front last week, the big news was made by the San Diego Chargers after signing former Heisman Trophy winner JOHNNY RODGERS to a series of one-year contracts.

The flashy running back-return man who had been dubbed the CFL's "Ordinary Superstar" the last four years, reportedly received the richest financial package the Chargers have awarded since signing JOHN UNITAS in 1973 for an estimated $600,000.

Reprinted from
Pro Football Weekly

Haynes of Patriots, White of Vikings named NFL rookies of the year

Jan. 10

Oakland overwhelms Minnesota, 32 to 14

'Can't win' stigma erased by Raiders in Super Bowl rout

By CAMERON C. SNYDER
Sun Staff Correspondent

Pasadena, Calif.—The Oakland Raiders pasted the scarlet letters of "losers" firmly on the winged helmets of the Minnesota Vikings yesterday with a surprisingly easy, 32-to-14 victory in the National Football League's Super Bowl.

Both teams entered the game in the Rose Bowl carrying the "can't win the big game" stigma, but the Raiders removed theirs for all time, while the Vikings now have lost four straight in the biggest gridiron game of them all.

With a record 100,421 fans in attendance and millions watching on television, the Raiders put the Vikings away in the fourth quarter after an interception by Willie Hall. Oakland quarterback Ken Stabler then threw to Fred Biletnikoff for a first down on the Viking 2, and Pete Banaszak lunged over for the winners' 25th point.

The Raiders' veteran cornerback Willie Brown had no compunction about rubbing it in, however, and later intercepted another Fran Tarkenton pass, returning it 75 yards for a touchdown, the longest in Super Bowl history.

Although Biletnikoff was named the Most Valuable Player in the Super Bowl, the most valuable unit on the field was the apart Minnesota's supposedly stout defense on runs, thereby helping the Stabler-to-Biletnikoff pass combination click.

This line, led by left guard Gene Upshaw and right guard George Buehler, pounded a path over and through All-Pro defensive tackle Alan Page for Raider runners to set a Super Bowl rushing record of 266 yards.

The chief use of this paved highway to the left side of the Raider line was made by a compact two-wheeler named Clarence Davis, who gained 137 yards in 16 carries. Davis, until yesterday, was the 195-pounder who blocked for fullback Mark van Eeghen in the Oakland offensive scheme.

Offensive tackle Art Shell said before the game that the Raider offense had to run at and remove Page, and that is what it did. Shell blocked on Page, who was caught frequently by misdirection plays. Shell completely wrapped up the 17-year veteran end, Jim Marshall, who now says he will retire.

Stabler, Biletnikoff, Davis and the offensive line compiled a Super Bowl record of 429 net yards.

Reprinted from
The Baltimore Sun

FRAN TARKENTON: "I can honestly say they beat us fair and square in every way. Oakland definitely was the better team today, but that doesn't mean they have better individuals or anything like that. Obviously my knee isn't 100 per cent. No, I won't be able to play in the Pro Bowl. They beat us badly but, really, what difference does it make if we lost by a point or by 20."

CARL ELLER: "The Raiders executed real well. We didn't put much pressure on Stabler all day long. They just dictated to us pretty much what they wanted to do all day long."

ART SHELL: "In our system we let you know we're going to come. There's no finessing, no shield blocking. I think New England can beat them. Our job is now complete. When we beat Pittsburgh two weeks ago, we were very happy but we felt we still hadn't accomplished anything. If we came to the Super Bowl and lost, the season wouldn't have been a success. Winning today makes our season complete. Snake (Stabler) called a super game. He was like a computer. He mixed our passes with the run so well the Vikings couldn't handle us. Now we don't have to spend the offseason with the feeling we can't win the big one."

WILLIE BROWN: "When you play 14 years, you anticipate a lot of things. I anticipated a quick out and I was there to get it. Our offense played so well today we got them in a position they had to throw the ball. Anytime you put the ball in the air, our secondary is going to rise to the occasion."

(Regarding charges that Oakland plays dirty football): "We like that. It's to our advantage."

(Regarding first Super Bowl he played in versus Green Bay): "The Packers dominated the game so much we were just happy to be there. I have a pair of sandals I bought in Boca Raton where we practiced. I've kept them ever since, but I promised myself I wouldn't throw them away until we won the Super Bowl."

Reprinted from
Pro Football Weekly

Super Bowl

Scoring

Oakland	0	16	3	13	— 32
Minnesota	0	0	7	7	— 14

Oakland — FG Mann 24
Oakland — Casper 1 pass from Stabler (Mann kick)
Oakland — Banaszak 1 run (kick failed)
Oakland — FG Mann 40
Minnesota — S.White 8 pass from Tarkenton (Cox kick)
Oakland — Banaszak 2 run (Mann kick)
Oakland — Brown 75 interception return (kick failed)
Minnesota — Voigt 13 pass from Lee (Cox kick)
A — 100,421: actual turnstile count. Sellout of 103,424 was announced.

Statistics

	Oak	Minn
First downs	21	20
Rushes-yards	52-266	26-71
Passing yards	163	282
Return yards	134	14
Passes	12-19-0	24-44-2
Punts	5-32.4	7-37.9
Fumbles-lost	0-0	1-1
Penalties-yards	4-30	2-25

Individual leaders

RUSHING — Oakland, Davis 16-137, van Eeghen 18-73, Garrett 4-19, Banaszak 10-19, Ginn 2-9, Rae 2-9. Minnesota, Foreman 17-44, McClanahan 3-3, Miller 2-4, Lee 1-4, S. White 1-7, S. Johnson 2-9.

RECEIVING — Oakland, Casper 4-70, Biletnikoff 4-79, Branch 3-20, Garrett 1-11. Minnesota, Foreman 5-62, Rashad 3-53, Miller 4-19, Voigt 4-49, S. White 5-77, S.Johnson 3-26.

PASSING — Oakland, Stabler 12-19-0, 180 yards; Rae 0-0-0, 0. Minnesota, Tarkenton 17-35-2, 205; Lee 7-9-0, 87.

INTERCEPTIONS — Oakland, W.Hall 1-16, Brown 1-75.

PUNTING — Oakland, Guy 4-162, avg. 40.5 (fifth punt blocked). Minnesota, Clabo, 7-265, avg. 37.9.

PUNT RETURNS — Oakland, Colzie 4-43. Minnesota, Willis 5-14.

KICKOFF RETURNS — Oakland, Garrett 2-47, Siani 1-0. Minnesota, Willis 3-57, S.White 4-79.